D
117
.N48
1995
v.1

S0-AYY-074

DISCARD

The New Cambridge Medieval History

The first volume of *The New Cambridge Medieval History* covers the transitional period between the later Roman world and the early Middle Ages, *c.*500 to *c.*700. This was an era of developing consciousness and profound change in Europe, Byzantium and the Arab world, an era in which the foundations of medieval society were laid and to which many of our modern myths of national and religious identity can be traced. This book offers a comprehensive regional survey of the sixth and seventh centuries, from Ireland in the west to the rise of Islam in the Middle East, and from Scandinavia in the north to the Mediterranean south. It explores the key themes pinning together the history of this period, from kingship, trade and the church, to art, architecture and education. It represents both an invaluable conspectus of current scholarship and an expert introduction to the period.

The New Cambridge Medieval History

EDITORIAL BOARD

David Abulafia Rosamond McKitterick
Martin Brett Edward Powell
Simon Keynes Jonathan Shepard
Peter Linehan Peter Spufford

Volume I *c.*500–*c.*700

Golden Hen and Seven Chicks. Possibly a gift from Pope Gregory the Great to Theudelinda, queen of the Lombards (early seventh century). Cathedral Treasury, Monza

THE NEW CAMBRIDGE MEDIEVAL HISTORY

Volume I c.500–c.700

EDITED BY

PAUL FOURACRE

CAMBRIDGE
UNIVERSITY PRESS

CAMBRIDGE UNIVERSITY PRESS
Cambridge, New York, Melbourne, Madrid, Cape Town, Singapore, São Paulo

Cambridge University Press
The Edinburgh Building, Cambridge CB2 2RU, UK

Published in the United States of America by Cambridge University Press, New York

www.cambridge.org
Information on this title: www.cambridge.org/9780521362917

© Cambridge University Press 2005

This book is in copyright. Subject to statutory exception
and to the provisions of relevant collective licensing agreements,
no reproduction of any part may take place without
the written permission of Cambridge University Press.

First published 2005

Printed in the United Kingdom at the University Press, Cambridge

A catalogue record for this book is available from the British Library

Library of Congress Cataloguing in Publication data

ISBN-13 978-0-521-36291-7 hardback
ISBN-10 0-521-36291-1 hardback

Cambridge University Press has no responsibility for the persistence or accuracy of URLs for external or third-party internet websites referred to in this book, and does not guarantee that any content on such websites is, or will remain, accurate or appropriate.

CONTENTS

PLATES

Frontispiece Golden Hen and Seven Chicks. Possibly a gift from Pope Gregory the Great to Theudelinda, queen of the Lombards (early seventh century). Cathedral Treasury, Monza

MAPS

FIGURES

CONTRIBUTORS

MARK BLACKBURN Keeper of Coins and Medals, The Fitzwilliam Museum, Reader in Numismatics and Monetary History, University of Cambridge, and Fellow of Gonville and Caius College

LESLIE BRUBAKER Reader in Byzantine Studies, University of Birmingham

WENDY DAVIES Professor of History, University College London

JACQUES FONTAINE Académie des Inscriptions et Belles-Lettres, Paris

PAUL FOURACRE Professor of Medieval History, University of Manchester

RICHARD GERBERDING Professor of History, The University of Alabama at Huntsville

GUY HALSALL Reader in History, University of York

HELENA HAMEROW Lecturer in European Archaeology, University of Oxford

LOTTE HEDEAGER Professor of Archaeology, University of Oslo

CAROLE HILLENBRAND Professor of Islamic History, University of Edinburgh

ZBIGNIEW KOBYLINSKI Institute of Archaeology and Ethnology, Warsaw

STÉPHANE LEBECQ Professor of History, University of Lille

MARIA ISABEL LORING Complutense University of Madrid

SIMON LOSEBY Lecturer in History, University of Sheffield

ANDREW LOUTH Professor of Patristics, University of Durham

JOHN MOORHEAD Reader in History, University of Queensland

GEORG SCHEIBELREITER Institut für Österreichische Geschichtsforschung, Vienna

CLARE STANCLIFFE Honorary Reader in Ecclesiastical History, University of Durham

ALAN THACKER Reader in History, Victoria County History, Institute of Historical Research, London

MICHAEL TOCH Professor of Ancient and Medieval History, The Hebrew University, Jerusalem
RAYMOND VAN DAM Professor of History, University of Michigan
IAN WOOD Professor of Early Medieval History, University of Leeds
PATRICK WORMALD† Oxford

PREFACE

It is conventional for an editor to commend the patience of contributors and publisher, as the preparation of a large volume of essays such as this one invariably falls behind schedule. In this case, however, patience has been needed in saintly proportions, for the present volume has been exceptionally long in the making. The original editor of Volume I planned the work in line with the other six volumes of the *New Cambridge Medieval History*, and commissioned all but two of the chapters. Copy began to arrive from 1990 onwards, but then the project seemed to stall. At this point, the present editor then agreed to take on the volume. New chapters were commissioned, on the Slavs, on the Scandinavians, and on money and coinage. New contributors were found to replace those who could no longer participate, and those who had submitted to the original deadline very kindly agreed to revise their chapters. Sadly, Professor Barbero, who had been commissioned to write the chapters on Spain, died before they were drafted. Maria Loring, his widow, agreed to complete the task. The two chapters are listed under their joint authorship, although I have not included Professor Barbero in the list of contributors. In September 2004 Patrick Wormald also sadly died. His chapter on 'Kings and kingship' will be a constant reminder of just how fine a scholar he was.

I am extremely grateful to the original contributors for bearing with the delays with such good grace. Few things in academic life are more irritating than to write a substantial essay to a deadline, only to have it disappear for several years, and then to be asked to rework it. Further delays were inevitable as the whole slowed to the pace of the tardiest contributor. Again, the forbearance of those who did make the effort to submit to deadlines, some at short notice, is much appreciated. One chapter, on Romans and Lombards in Italy in the seventh century, we waited for in vain, and then decided that to find a replacement would delay the volume just too much. There is, therefore, a very unfortunate gap in our history, although several other authors do refer to Italian material. The place of Lombard Italy in European history is briefly discussed in the Introduction. The Introduction also sets out the shape and purpose of the volume.

Thanks are due to a host of people who have helped with this volume. Paul Barford helped to translate chapter 19 into English, and John Hine translated chapter 18. Translation by specialists in the field is very much appreciated. Prudence von Rohrbach put the whole work onto disk and consolidated the primary source bibliography. Her help was crucial in bringing order to a collection of contributions submitted over a decade and in many different forms.

Particular thanks are due to those who agreed at short notice to write chapters, and did so to order and in good time. Guy Halsall responded immediately to a plea to write the survey chapter (chapter 3) on the sources and their interpretation. His excellent discussion draws on his unusual combination of expertise in both history and archaeology, and in both disciplines he is also unusual in that he is literate in both theory and practice. Michael Toch agreed to write his chapter on the Jews in Europe by return of email, and the draft chapter was delivered a fortnight later. It is an astonishing survey that demolishes widely held assumptions about the place of Jews in early medieval history. It was at the late Timothy Reuter's suggestion that Toch was asked to survey the whole period covered by the first three volumes of the *New Cambridge Medieval History*. It was typical of Reuter's care for the series that, having noticed that an important area had not been covered, he made sure that something was done about it. Timothy Reuter greatly encouraged the editing of this work, and he was a great source of advice, typically offered with wry good humour. This volume is dedicated to his memory.

PAUL FOURACRE, MANCHESTER, January 2005

ABBREVIATIONS

AASS	*Acta Sanctorum quotquot toto orbe coluntur*, ed. J. Bollandus *et al.*, Antwerp and Brussels (1634–)
AASS OSB	*Acta Sanctorum Ordinis Sancti Benedicti*, ed. J. Mabillon, 9 vols., Paris (1668–1701)
AfD	*Archiv für Diplomatik*
AHP	*Archivum Historiae Pontificum*
AHR	*American Historical Review*
An. Boll.	*Analecta Bollandiana*
Annales ESC	*Annales: Economies, Sociétés, Civilisations*
ARAM	*ARAM*, Society for Syro-Mesopotamian Studies
ASC	*Anglo-Saxon Chronicle*
ASE	*Anglo-Saxon England*
BAR	British Archaeological Reports
BBCS	*Bulletin of the Board of Celtic Studies*
BEC	*Bibliothèque de l'Ecole des Chartes*
Bede, *HE*	*Historia Ecclesiastica Gentis Anglorum*
BHG	*Bibliotheca Hagiographica Graeca*, ed. F. Halkin, 3rd edn (Subsidia Hagiographica 8a), Brussels (1957) and *Novum Auctarium Bibliotheca Hagiographica Graeca* (Subsidia Hagiographica 65), Brussels (1984)
BHL	*Bibliotheca Hagiographica Latina* (Subsidia Hagiographica 6), Brussels (1898–1901), *Supplementum* (Subsidia Hagiographica 12), Brussels (1911); *Novum Supplementum* (Subsidia Hagiographica 70), Brussels (1986)
BL	*British Library*
BMGS	*Byzantine and Modern Greek Studies*
BS/EB	*Byzantine Studies/Etudes Byzantines*
BSl	*Byzantinoslavica*

BSOAS	*Bulletin of the School of Oriental and African Studies*
Byz.	*Byzantion*
BZ	*Byzantinische Zeitschrift*
CBA	Council for British Archaeology
CC	*Codex Carolinus*
CCCC	Cambridge, Corpus Christi College MS
CCCM	Corpus Christianorum, Continuatio Medievalis, Turnhout (1966–)
CCE	*Cahiers de la Céramique Egyptienne*
CCSG	Corpus Christianorum Series Graeca
CCSL	Corpus Christianorum Series Latina, Turnhout (1952–)
CDL	*Codice Diplomatico Longobardo*
ChLA	*Chartae Latinae Antiquiores*, ed. A. Bruckner, facsimile edition of the Latin charters prior to the ninth century, Olten and Lausanne (1954–)
CIG	*Corpus Inscriptionum Graecarum*
CIL	*Corpus Inscriptionum Latinarum*
CLA	E. A. Lowe, *Codices Latini Antiquiores: A Palaeographical Guide to Latin Manuscripts Prior to the Ninth Century*, I–XI, plus Supplement, Oxford (1935–71)
CMCS	*Cambridge Medieval Celtic Studies*
Cod. Iust.	*Codex Iustinianus*
Cod. Theo.	*Codex Theodosianus*
DA	*Deutsches Archiv für Erforschung des Mittelalters*
DOP	*Dumbarton Oaks Papers*
DR	*Downside Review*
EC	*Etudes Celtiques*
EHD	*English Historical Documents*
EHR	*English Historical Review*
EME	*Early Medieval Europe*
fol.	*folio*
FrSt	*Frühmittelalterliche Studien*
GRBS	*Greek, Roman and Byzantine Studies*
Gregory, *Epp.*	Gregory of Rome, *Registrum Epistolarum*
Gregory, *Hist.*	Gregory of Tours, *Decem Libri Historiarum*
HJb	*Historisches Jahrbuch*
HZ	*Historische Zeitschrift*
JEH	*Journal of Ecclesiastical History*
JESHO	*Journal of the Economic and Social History of the Orient*

JHS	*Journal of Hellenic Studies*
JMH	*Journal of Medieval History*
JRA	*Journal of Roman Archaeology*
JRAS	*Journal of the Royal Asiatic Society*
JRH	*Journal of Religious History*
JRS	*Journal of Roman Studies*
JTS	*Journal of Theological Studies*
LP	*Liber Pontificalis*
LV	*Lex Visigothorum*
MGH	*Monumenta Germaniae Historica*
AA	*Auctores Antiquissimi*, 15 vols., Berlin (1877–1919)
Cap.	*Capitularia, Legum sectio* II, *Capitularia Regum Francorum,* ed. A. Boretius and V. Krause, 2 vols., Hanover (1883–97)
Epp.	*Epistolae Merowingici et Karolini Aevi*, Hanover (1892–1939)
Epp. Sel.	*Epistolae Selectae in Usum Scholarum*, 5 vols., Hanover (1887–91)
Form.	*Formulae Merowingici et Karolini Aevi*, ed. K. Zeumer, *Legum sectio* V, Hanover (1886)
SRG	*Scriptores Rerum Germanicarum in Usum Scholarum Separatim Editi*, 63 vols., Hanover (1871–1987)
SRL	*Scriptores Rerum Langobardicarum et Italicarum sae. VI–IX*, ed. G. Waitz, Hanover (1878)
SRM	*Scriptores Rerum Merovingicarum*, ed. B. Krusch and W. Levison, 7 vols., Hanover (1885–1920)
SS	*Scriptores in folio*, 30 vols., Hanover (1824–1924)
MIÖG	*Mitteilung des Instituts für Österreichische Geschichtsforschung*
MS	Manuscript
NF	Neue Folge
NMS	*Nottingham Medieval Studies*
Paul the Deacon, *HL*	*Historia Langobardorum*
PBA	*Proceedings of the British Academy*
PBSR	*Papers of the British School at Rome*
PG	*Patrologia Cursus Completus, Series Graeca,* ed. J. P. Migne, 161 vols., Paris (1857–66)
PL	*Patrologia Cursus Completus, Series Latina*, ed. J. P. Migne, 221 vols., Paris (1841–64)
PRIA	*Proceedings of the Royal Irish Academy*

RAC	*Reallexicon für Antike und Christentum*
RB	*Revue Bénédictine*
REB	*Revue des Etudes Byzantines*
RHE	*Revue d'Histoire Ecclésiastique*
RHEF	*Revue d'Histoire de l'Eglise de France*
RHM	*Römische Historische Mitteilungen*
RHPhR	*Revue d'Histoire et de Philosophie Religieuses*
RN	*Revue Numismatique*
s.a.	*sub anno*
Settimane	*Settimane di Studio del Centro Italiano di Studi sull'Alto Medioevo*, Spoleto (1954–)
SI	*Studia Islamica*
SM	*Studi Medievali*
TRHS	*Transactions of the Royal Historical Society*
VuF	Vorträge und Forschungen, herausgegeben vom Konstanzer Arbeitskreis für mittelalterliche Geschichte
ZKTh	*Zeitschrift für Katholische Theologie*
ZRG	*Zeitschrift der Savigny-Stiftung für Rechtsgeschichte*
GA	*Germanistiche Abteilung*
KA	*Kanonistische Abteilung*
RA	*Romanistische Abteilung*

INTRODUCTION: THE HISTORY OF EUROPE 500–700

Paul Fouracre

Hegel's notion of a state of transformation, in which the present negates the past in favour of the future, is well suited to this period of European history. At our starting point around the year 500, we may still characterise European culture as 'late antique'; by the year 700 we are firmly in the world of the Middle Ages. A transformation has apparently occurred. The idea that it is developing consciousness that calls changes into being is not far off the mark either, if we think about the triumph of the Christian future over the pagan past and the reconfiguration of culture and institutions around newly hegemonic religious beliefs and practices. This conception of history is avowedly teleological: it is ultimately more interested in what things were becoming than in what they were in their own terms and in their proper context. A survey such as this one, standing at the beginning of a series which looks at history over a 1000 year period, must of course be aware of future development in order to understand the nature and significance of contemporary phenomena. At the same time, however, it must equally be aware that what makes hindsight or overview possible is precisely a detailed knowledge of the past in its own terms. The balance between overview and detail must nevertheless be judicious. The present volume aims for balance in this way. It is organised on a chronological and geographical basis, from which a series of particular histories provide the background to a final section of thematic overviews.

Almost every chapter, whether topical or thematic, situates itself by measuring change from the late Roman period. That the end of Roman power in western Europe should form a common starting point is not meant to underplay the essential continuities between the culture of late antiquity and of the Middle Ages. As Gerberding emphasises, we can already perceive in the Roman world the outlines of much that we would identify as typically 'medieval'. Fontaine, too, explains that the lines of post-classical, Christian education and learning had already been laid down before the mid-fifth century. Nor should beginning with the end of the Roman Empire be taken to suggest that the 'Fall of Rome' was sudden or catastrophic. As Halsall argues, few historians would now think in terms of an empire brought down by the incessant attacks of massed barbarians. He suggests that it is more sensible to think of the 'barbarian invasions' as one effect, rather than the major cause, of Rome's decline. And as Loseby demonstrates, the dislocation of the Mediterranean economic circuits which had lain at the heart of Roman culture was a slow and complex process which cannot be mapped onto a narrative of political and military 'decline'. It is nevertheless true that the often violent ending of Roman imperial rule in Europe did have enormous consequences. Kobyliński's account of the formation of the Slavs in a world made unstable by the disappearance of Roman power firmly brings home the point that those consequences were felt far beyond the borders of the Roman Empire. Hillenbrand and Hedeager investigate the consequences of the end of the Roman cultural and political domination in regions as far apart as Arabia and Scandinavia. In our period, the various governing regimes in France, Italy, Spain and Britain were decidedly 'post-Roman' in the sense that it was the vacuum caused by the disintegration of Roman government which brought them into being. Likewise, changes in education, religion, art and architecture can be described in relation to the failing state of the Roman Empire. And of course, the most dramatic post-Roman movement of all, the rise of Islam, made a clear connection between the failure of Roman power and the need for a new system to replace it.

Although the end of Roman rule did have immediate consequences, the more lasting result was the gradual adaptation of European, Middle Eastern and North African societies to changing economic, political, religious and military realities. The 'Transformation of the Roman World' is the way in which this process is usually described, and the subject of transformation has been a major focus of international scholarship over the past decade. It has taken the form of the European Science Foundation 'Transformation of the Roman World' project which will lead to the publication of no less than eighteen volumes of essays on different aspects of change between 400 and 800. The organisation of this massive multidisciplinary collaboration was thematic. The present volume of just twenty-nine essays, organised on a chronological and regional as well as thematic basis, stands to the 'Transformation of the Roman World' project as a kind of handbook of history. It sets out what is known about the development of each region as concisely as possible on the basis of the available source materials, and in reflection of present scholarly consensus. One cannot read the collection without coming to the conclusion that in our period every region of Europe was in a process of adjusting to the new post-Roman conditions, but 'transformation' itself is not the explicit focus of the volume. To have made it so would have been to anticipate future developments rather too keenly, and organising the volume around the theme of 'transformation' would have imposed too rigid an overview on our material. Each region must speak for itself, through whatever sources have survived. Generally the voices are too close to the memory of Roman culture to express a sense of transformation.

It is striking that the 'Transformation of the Roman World' project followed developments through into the ninth century. The two centuries from 500 AD saw that adjustment to new conditions which would set the agenda for future development, but it is only when one looks back from the ninth century that one can get a clear sense of what it was that the late Roman world had transformed into. It would be in the eighth century that the changes of the earlier period would give birth to new political, social and economic formations. As Lebecq explains, it was in the period 500–700 that the 'North Sea economy' emerged. The simultaneous decline of Mediterranean exchange networks, as described by Loseby, would see a northward shift in the centre of gravity of European culture. This is the context in which we see the consolidation of a dominant power in central and south-eastern England, namely, the kingdom of Mercia. It was likewise in the mid-eighth century that a new dynasty, the Carolingians, emerged in Francia. This was the dynasty which would change the balance of power in continental Europe, extending Frankish power to the Baltic in the north and to the Adriatic in the south. One result of this violent expansion would be the collapse of Avar power in central Europe and in its wake we see the stabilisation of the various Slav cultures whose origins Kobyliński traces so assiduously. The rise of a powerful Bulgarian state would be another consequence of the collapse of Avar power. It was also at this time that the Muslim caliphate shifted to Iraq and into the hands of the 'Abbasid dynasty. The Visigothic civilisation of Spain, the building of which Loring treats in some detail, came to an abrupt end when subjected to the pulse of Islamic conquest. Byzantium's reaction to the loss of its Middle Eastern and North African provinces to the Arabs in the seventh century, a shock dealt with from two different points of view here, by Louth and by Hillenbrand, would be worked out in religious and military terms in the course of the eighth century.

In each of these areas we are dealing with the further consequences of post-Roman development, but by the ninth century we are no longer in a post-Roman world. Now, when people wished to account for their history, culture and institutions, these they traced not to the Roman world, but to themselves. The eighth and ninth centuries boasted many authors who did this. For Bede in England, history effectively began with the coming of the Anglo-Saxons to the island of Britain, and concerned itself with the conversion to Christianity of those incomers, thus focussing on the seventh century. In Italy Paul the Deacon wrote the history of the Lombard people knowing very little of their early history or origins. Like that of Bede, Paul's history had a strongly contemporary message. In Francia, the new dynasty of the Carolingians embarked upon the unique exercise of justifying their assumption of power by denigrating their predecessors, the consequently much maligned Merovingians. They too were in effect writing near contemporary history. So in all three areas a sense of continuity with the Roman past was broken. It is a mark of the distance now felt between the present and that past that the Carolingians began to speak of a 'renewal' of society. They were very impressed by Roman culture, going to great lengths to imitate it, but they thought of themselves as different from, and actually rather superior, to the Romans. When Charlemagne was famously crowned 'Roman emperor' in the year 800, the Franks were clear that his empire was something new and different: it was a Frankish and Christian empire. It is interesting to note that much of the thinking about 'renewing' or 'correcting' society, that is, bringing to it a proper Christian order, originated in England and in Ireland. These were two areas that felt themselves to have little connection with the Roman past, except, of course, in terms of its religious legacy. Here we meet the perfect growing conditions for the developments in Christian education and learning that Fontaine describes.

With the special exception of Justinian's reign, in our period there was not much sense of 'renewal', but there was a sense of progress. Following the lead of Augustine's *De Doctrina Christiana*, learning in the Christian world privileged the religious over the secular: in Fontaine's words, all learned culture became 'a means oriented towards a religious end which surpassed it'. This was progress, because it promised salvation. Wood points out that 'Christianisation' was a far more complex process than the conversion of the heathen. Christian culture, as opposed to the faith of the Gospels, was shot through with pagan or pre-Christian influences and practices. In Rome itself, for instance, Christian festivals held in January of each year involved identifiably pagan elements. The English missionary Boniface complained about this in the mid-eighth century, but the practices continued into the twelfth century. The writers of our period, however, were, like Boniface, perfectly clear in their minds about what was Christian and what was not, and about the differences between the sacred and the profane.

The desire to advance Christian society is what inspired the quartet of historians upon whom we rely for the traditional picture of what happened in the West in our period. These writers, whom Walter Goffart described as the 'narrators of barbarian history', are Jordanes and Gregory of Tours from the sixth century, and from the eighth century Bede and Paul the Deacon, who wrote about earlier times. In the works of Procopius, writing in the East in the sixth century, the Christian agenda is less obvious than conventions of writing history in the classical tradition, although, as Halsall and Louth explain, that tradition would largely disappear after Procopius. There was of course a host of other writers of history in the West – Gildas, John of Biclaro, Isidore of Seville, or the chronicler known as 'Fredegar' to name but a few – but the works of our quartet are essential in providing what seems to be a continuous narrative that gives specific areas a comprehensible history. Halsall demonstrates how these narratives have been reinterpreted by modern historians. Not only have what might be termed 'nationalist' interpretations been challenged, the very sense that history can be reduced to narrative has been questioned. The works of Jordanes, Gregory, Bede and Paul the Deacon are sufficiently long, well provenanced and coherently written to allow analysis in literary critical mode, and this too has undermined confidence in the relevance and objectivity of their narrative. In short, we now understand more about these works as texts rather than as definitive histories.

Despite misgivings about traditional narrative approaches to the history of this period, it is clear that the four great narrative works retain an enormous hold over the imagination. The chapters in this volume refer to our narrative sources, and not just to the four, again and again. Look, for example, at how much of Van Dam on Gaul/Francia in the sixth century is drawn from the works of Gregory of Tours, or at the extent to which Thacker on seventh-century England relies on Bede's *History*. For although we have learned to treat such texts with circumspection, it would be perverse not to make as much use of them as possible, especially as they are often our sole window on events. These works do, after all, allow us to tell a coherent (if sometimes misleading) story about regions that would develop into nations and play a leading role in the formation of Europe. The history of regions for which there is no clear narrative tradition may appear by comparison as impenetrable. This has often been the case with Celtic societies, often regarded as distinctly odd or even exotic. Davies and Stancliffe both show how to approach the history of the Celtic regions, demolishing modern myths and pulling together the disparate evidence to explain how they developed. Likewise Hedeager can discuss the thought world of early Scandinavia without the help of any contemporary writing from the region itself. Kobyliński too must conjure the Slavs out of the writings of other peoples, and in all these cases we see just how much archaeology can be used to fill gaps in our understanding.

Hamerow's chapter on 'The earliest Anglo-Saxon kingdoms' shows that we are almost completely dependent upon the archaeological record for ideas of how lowland Britain became Anglo-Saxon England. Here we find evidence of assimilation and acculturation between natives and newcomers which stands in contrast to the narratives of Anglo-Saxon invasion and conquest which come to us from Gildas and Bede. In fact Hamerow's Anglo-Saxons have much in common with Kobyliński's Slavs, in the way that both groups formed 'new' peoples, the identities of which were expressed through material culture. And in both cases we have narrative material which seems to know nothing of how these peoples were formed, but which treats them as long-established, readily identifiable groups which were well aware of their position in the world. Of course, we cannot expect a Gildas, a Procopius, or even a Bede, to have been able to report on a process of ethnogenesis, nor could they have articulated a notion of acculturation, for both are distinctly modern conceptions. Rather than seeing the formation of new groups, early medieval writers thought in terms of conflict between established peoples. Some of them might have arrived only recently in a given area, but they had come as a discrete 'people'. This is how Gildas described the arrival of the 'Saxons' in England, a picture which Bede elaborated to make three discrete groups of invaders, the Angles, Saxons and Jutes. The archaeological evidence does not support Gildas' picture of the 'fire and sword' conquest of Britain which followed the arrival of the Saxons. One conclusion to draw from this is that Gildas actually knew very little of what happened in Britain in the century before he wrote. Or, at least, that he turned what he did know into a conventional narrative. Bede then added to the story, giving it a chronology and geography, but in reality he knew little more of the 'coming of the Saxons' than Gildas.

The case of Bede and the history of the English reminds us that our major narrative sources are decidedly patchy in their coverage and reliability. It is naturally true that they know most of events close to their own times, and they tend to back-project the conditions with which they were familiar in order to make sense of a confusing past. Thus Bede's division of the fifth century invaders into Angles, Saxons and Jutes was a reflection of the political geography of England in the seventh and early eighth century which Thacker describes. One wonders, similarly, how much Jordanes knew of the early history of the Goths, or how much Gregory of Tours knew about his hero, King Clovis. Perhaps the most unsettling uncertainty of all, and one in which archaeology helps but little, is the history of the Lombards in the seventh century.

As Moorhead demonstrates, one can say quite a lot about later sixth-century Italy by drawing on papal, Byzantine and Frankish sources, but for the history of the Lombards we are dependent upon the account of Paul the Deacon which was written in the later eighth century. For the early history, Paul the Deacon relied upon a now lost source, the history of Secundus of Non, or 'of Trent', as he is sometimes called. Secundus was an adviser at the court of King Agilulf (590–616). He seems to have known much about the early Lombard leaders, but very little about how and where the Lombards were settled in Italy. Paul the Deacon's history is likewise narrowly political and military. It does contain colourful and dramatic anecdotes, but it is a thin narrative which allows us to see little of what went on beyond the confines of the royal courts. The Frankish chronicle known as Fredegar was interested in the contacts between the Lombard and Frankish rulers in the first half of the seventh century, principally because the Lombard king Agilulf took a Frankish bride, Theudelinda, and their daughter Gundeberga would play an important role in Lombard politics. Fouracre discusses Fredegar's treatment of Gundeberga. When the chronicle of Fredegar ends in the 640s, our information on relations between Franks and Lombards stops more or less dead. We can glean a little more from Paul the Deacon, and he also tells us about growing connections between the Agilolfing rulers of Bavaria and the Lombards in the early eighth century. These connections clearly went back a long way, for, as we have seen, one early Lombard king, Agilulf, bore the same name as that of the Bavarian dynasty. The Lombard–Bavarian alliance would eventually spell disaster for both sets of rulers when in the later eighth century Charlemagne felt that it threatened his security. As a result, both Lombard Italy and Bavaria were incorporated into the Frankish empire. Paul the Deacon's history of the Lombards was written in the aftermath of Frankish conquest, and it closed with the reign of King Liutprand (d. 744), when the Lombards were at the height of their powers in Italy. The sequel was possibly too painful or too politically sensitive to write.

Apart from Paul the Deacon, we have a considerable body of law in the so-called *Edict of Rothari* from the mid-seventh century. Wormald discusses this legislation in terms of what it tells us about Lombard kingship. Otherwise, we are nearly in the dark. It is claimed that the 'Three Chapters' dispute, to which both Moorhead and Louth refer, rumbled on until it was finally ended at the Synod of Pavia in 698. Lombard support for schismatic bishops in Milan and Aquileia had been a useful way for the rulers to present themselves as the champions of Italian independence in the face of Byzantine interference. This was especially true in the early Lombard period when memories of the emperor Justinian's intransigence were at their strongest. There is no hagiography from Lombard Italy, and later cults are almost impossible to trace back beyond the eighth century. In fact, so little is known about relations between the Lombards and the native Catholics before the eighth century that historians have found it impossible to agree on what religion the Lombards followed in the late sixth and seventh centuries. Were they stubbornly pagan, or perhaps Arian, or maybe Catholic, or even not particularly interested in religious matters? The latter, at least, seems very unlikely given that religion occupied a central place in the mentality of every other early medieval society we know about.

Muddying the waters still more is a famous passage in Paul the Deacon's history: it says that in the time of King Cleph (572–574) and shortly afterwards the Lombards killed or drove out the more powerful Romans, killed many other Roman nobles and made the rest tributaries. This has been taken to mean that quite literally the Roman elite in the Lombard areas was completely destroyed.

In the eyes of the papacy, the Lombards were 'that most wicked people', their name being almost a synonym for senseless violence. It is, however, possible to come up with a much less pessimistic and far more credible picture of the Lombards' cultural assimilation into Italian society, and it is much to be regretted that this volume was not able to include a planned chapter on 'Romans and Lombards in Italy' that would have explained in some detail how the various scraps of evidence do actually support a more positive view. It must suffice here to note that when we know more about the Lombard areas of Italy from the eighth century onwards, they do not show signs of having suffered chaos, disruption or genocide. Though the papacy continued to hurl insults at the Lombard rulers, at times the popes co-operated with them, and even depended upon their help. When charters begin to survive (from the mid-eighth century onwards) they reveal a society which had preserved much of Roman property law, and the notaries to allow even small transactions to be recorded. It is clear that a degree of functional literacy, and the bureaucracy to go with it, had continued throughout the Lombard period. By the time Paul the Deacon was writing, the Lombard language, dress and even hairstyles had all disappeared. Finally, it is becoming increasingly clear that the Frankish conquest of the Lombard kingdom in 774 was a seminal moment in the cultural revival that took place under Charlemagne. Intellectual capital, as well as the usual forms of treasure, was taken back to Francia. Again, this suggests that the seventh century had been a time of cultural fusion and development rather than of wholesale destruction.

The other area that is not covered in the present volume (although it is featured in subsequent volumes) is the rural economy. In this case, no chapter was ever planned, simply because there is insufficient material to write such a history for the period 500–700. It is only after 700 that we get the kind of detail we need to do this. The detail comes from charters which deal with transactions involving land, and which often name the peasant tenants of a given estate. Then, beginning in the ninth century we have the estate surveys known as polyptychs. Surviving surveys of this type were drawn up for ecclesiastical institutions at the heart of Francia, that is, between the rivers Loire and Rhine. They not only list peasant tenants over wide areas, but also specify what rents and services they owed. From the surveys we can see what was produced, and how institutions could collect a surplus. For evidence for rural markets, where that surplus might be exchanged, we have to wait until the end of the ninth century. Without information on tenants, tenancies, rents, services, land usage, surplus collection and exchange, we are left with some rather formulaic references to land and the people who worked the land in the earliest Frankish charters (from the mid-seventh century). As we have just seen, there are no charters from Italy in this period, and none from Spain either. The few that survive from Anglo-Saxon England pre-700 describe land, but not the people on it. Laws do deal with rural communities, and do refer to activities in the rural economy, such as bee-keeping or cattle-herding, but we can draw from them only the most general statements about rural life. The exception is the laws of Ine, from Wessex in England at the very end of our period, for these do go into much more detail about peasant activities and tenant obligations. We cannot, however, generalise from this unique collection.

Archaeology can tell us about the nature of settlements and their material culture. Hamerow, Kobyliński and Hedeager, as we have seen, make the most of this evidence when faced with the lack of written material. Halsall discusses the changing interpretation of such evidence. But detailed though particular site investigations might be, again we can draw from them only general inferences about the rural economy and social structure. It is clear from a reading of Blackburn, Lebecq and Loseby that more specific conclusions can actually be drawn about long-distance exchange than about rural life. As Loseby explains in some detail, analysis of pottery remains is crucial to understanding the evolution of regional exchange economies in our period. Lebecq can do the same for the North Sea trading network from the evidence of material (above all, metalwork and coinage) found in coastal emporia; Blackburn demonstrates the wealth of information to be gleaned from coinage. The difficulty lies in evaluating this information in the wider social and economic context.

Although we can say relatively little about peasants, it must be assumed that they were the main producers of wealth in our period. Land was the basis of power, and the ways in which land was often held on a temporary basis, could be given as the support for office, and could be divided and inherited in portions, all presume a stable workforce which produced wealth for immediate access by a possible variety of masters. Laws which maintained a fierce division between the free and unfree suggest that the unfree formed a key component of the workforce. It is the unfree who in later charters are named and inventoried as part of the stock on lands which changed hands. The free are prominent in the laws: they are the normative social element. It is, however, impossible to determine the extent of a class of free peasant proprietors, for typically they leave no trace in narrative or early charter sources. It is also impossible to see where a dividing line came between the free and the nobility. Although the latter are the subject of narrative sources, and it is they who figure in land transactions, it is surprisingly hard to see how people were defined as 'noble'. The term 'noble' covers a wide social spectrum. Historians often use the term 'aristocracy' to refer to the more powerful in society, but no early medieval people used the word. They distinguished people in terms of power and wealth, often using comparative adjectives, and they did refer to specific offices which carried with them the highest social status, but overall, terms of social class and distinction remained rather vague. Early medieval Europe was undoubtedly made up of hierarchical societies, but the vagueness of social terminology suggests that elites were not closed in this period. The changing fortunes of families subject to war and facing conditions of fierce competition for limited resources, plus a general tendency to divide inheritances, worked to provide a measure of exchange mobility. Such a generalisation must, of course, be broken down to suit what were very different regions and histories.

One can make a rough distinction here between areas more or less influenced by the culture and practice of Roman government. In the more Romanised areas there was the survival to a significant degree of offices and honorific titles which conveyed high social status. Likewise there survived categories of lesser status, and, as we have seen, unfreedom was widespread. Early medieval social structures in this sense evolved directly from later Roman hierarchies: in southern Europe, at least, in 700 at the top there were *senatores*, and at the bottom *servi*, just as there had been in the year 400. This social continuity is all the more striking when we consider the changing economic, political and military environment. Byzantium is a case in point here. The two centuries of Byzantine history that Louth deals with were a time of enormous change and adjustment. The Byzantine Empire was transformed from a widespread empire of city-based communities, into a much smaller state dominated by one metropolis (Constantinople), with city life fast in decline everywhere else. Armies were pulled back from lost provinces, and the theme system, which subordinated civil to military government, began to form. The Empire's social structure nevertheless retained its late antique form. Even in the tenth century, when government complained about the exploitation of the weak by the powerful, they employed the same rhetorical criticism of the excess of power that we see in the West in the fifth century.

In the West, we have most source material from Gaul/Francia. Van Dam and Fouracre can show how a political economy based on land evolved from the more bureaucratic later Roman government, a government that had been able to rely on considerable taxation. A significant factor in the maintenance of widespread political authority at a time of sharply declining revenues was a high degree of social stability and continuity. *Senatores*, for instance, were still visible in the late seventh-century Auvergne. From Loring's account, Spain too retained a social structure inherited from Roman times. From what little we know, in Visigothic Spain the social hierarchy seems to have been even more conservative, and oppressive, than in Francia. Where Italy is concerned, more guesswork is necessary, but as we have just seen, there is reason to think that there was a great deal of continuity in social structure there too. As Davies and Stancliffe both demonstrate, the Celtic countries of Europe were not quite so exotically different as is often claimed. The term 'Celtic' also covers a wide variety of areas and societies. Generally, however, one can say that continuity in these smaller political units was with a different social past. 'Aristocracies' there certainly were, but not obviously on the later Roman pattern. The greatest contrast comes from areas that lay further away from Roman influence. Hedeager shows how, in Scandinavia, political power was established in a very different social context in which the elite attempted to differentiate themselves by the appropriation of pagan religious ideology and space. Slav cultures, Kobyliński explains, were still emerging in our period, and the Slavs had a social differentiation that was much less marked than in other areas.

Despite regional differences, we can observe common trends. Across Europe rulers were consolidating their position by adding the religious to other forms of legitimation. That Europe should be ruled by kings was not a foregone conclusion in the year 500, but as Wormald puts it, by 700 it was certain that the future would lie in the hands of rulers (kings, emperors and caliphs) who justified their power as God's agents. This is the political dimension of Fontaine's new world of Christian (or Muslim) education and learning. Wood and Brubaker deal with the artistic and architectural dimension. It was of course the church which was the motor force behind the establishment of common practices, and common points of cultural reference. Scheibelreiter's detailed description of church structure is important in reminding us of what having a common institution actually meant in terms of sharing a complex hierarchy and wide range of offices. Structure followed hard on the dissemination of Christian teaching that Wood describes, and it was a structure that acted as a benchmark for all other forms of institutional development.

In setting out what we now know and think about the areas and topics in this volume, time and again it has been necessary to confront old misconceptions and false assumptions. Many of the issues covered remain topical because they relate to modern myths of national and religious identity. This is clearly the case, for instance, in relation to the history of the Celtic regions, or of the Slavs, or of Visigothic Spain. Sometimes debunking has gone too far, as in the case of the insensitive way in which some modern scholars have treated the early history of Islam in order to question the traditional (and sacred) narrative of the religion's beginnings. Hillenbrand's chapter on this subject is a model of how to stand back and let the evidence speak for itself in a truly objective and non-judgemental manner. Toch's chapter on the Jews in Europe challenges head-on the very widely held assumption that anti-Jewish religious sentiment, a commonplace in our period, was a reflection of an active Jewish presence as neighbours and rivals to Christian communities. This is held to be especially true in Spain, for the Visigothic kings promulgated many anti-Semitic laws. An older generation of historians even imagined a 'fifth column' of oppressed Jews aiding the Arabs in their conquest of the peninsula. But Toch is clear:

there is simply no evidence for a substantial Jewish presence in Europe before the tenth century. His careful work reminds us that it is always worth revisiting old orthodoxies in the light of new interpretations, and re-evaluations of the evidence are always in order. This is what the present volume has aimed to do in what one might term the major areas of study in the period 500–700. It is to be hoped that it will then provide a platform for further revisions.

CHAPTER I

THE LATER ROMAN EMPIRE

Richard Gerberding

POLITICAL AND MILITARY DECLINE

Where the Romans came, saw and conquered, they usually stayed a very long time. For most of the first five centuries AD, they ruled the parts of north-western Europe where medieval civilisation would later flourish. This nation of stocky, rather shortish, dark-haired people, although foreigners from the central Mediterranean, none the less profoundly affected north-western Europe's way of life in ways which would linger long after their political system had crumbled into misty and misshapen memories. The Romans gained the time to affect northern Europe more profoundly than any conquerors before or since for two reasons, both, perhaps not surprisingly, military ones.

First, the Romans very early in their history developed their legion and its marvellous system of logistical support. They did this in large part during their wars with the Samnites, at the turn of the fourth to the third century BC. The legion demanded much from its foot soldiers, but it was a fearsome instrument capable of sophisticated tactical versatility. In short, the Romans could usually quite easily conquer any non-civilised people they opposed, and they prevailed over their civilised enemies as well, although with more difficulty. The legion's systems of support also meant it could fight effectively far from home. Under their great general, Julius Caesar, the Romans conquered most of north-western Europe. Caesar did so in a brutally quick seven years.

Second, the Romans knew how to establish and fortify borders. For as far back as historians can see, the sunny and fruitful Mediterranean lands had acted as a magnet to the peoples of the drearier and harsher climes of the north. In two great waves, one in the centuries surrounding 1800 BC and again around 1200 BC, and in many other and lesser movements, peoples from the north migrated southward, many into the Mediterranean basin. But later, wherever the Romans established borders, such movements were largely prevented. The great European borders of the Roman Empire, stretching from the midriff of

Britain to the mouth of the Danube, allowed the peoples within them to enjoy centuries largely free from the unsettling influence of migrating or conquering uncivilised northerners. Thus it was their invincible legions and their well-defended frontiers that allowed the Romans to control north-western Europe for the best part of five centuries and to root their Mediterranean civilisation so deeply into transalpine soil.

To help our understanding of the legacy which the Romans left to the Middle Ages we shall first briefly survey them at home in the heyday of their empire, in the first and second centuries AD; and second, paying attention to those geographical areas which would soon beget medieval civilisation, we shall watch them 'decline and fall' as their political control of the West ends about 500 AD. The fall of the Roman Empire in the West was a process of unparalleled historical moment. It happened very slowly, spanning centuries, and it was largely political. The end of Rome's political control certainly did not mark the end of the Roman era: Roman roots had burrowed too deeply. In almost every other facet of European life – economic, social, intellectual, legal, religious, linguistic and artistic – much of the Roman imprint held firm, sometimes for centuries after the political bonds were loosed.

The system that the *princeps* (or emperor) Augustus (27 BC to 14 AD) established lasted with surprisingly little modification until the death of Commodus in 192. This was the period of the *Pax Romana*, the Golden Age of Rome. Augustus' system, or 'principate', ended the rule of the senatorial oligarchy that had hitherto controlled the Roman state. This process was a slow one, having begun long before Augustus came to power. The principate under Augustus is often called a dyarchy, or joint rule, meaning that he shared real power with the Senate, the political organ of those proud Roman aristocrats. By Augustus' reign, these men, exquisitely educated and unimaginably rich, could boast five centuries of virtual political monopoly, stretching back to the foundation of their Republic and even beyond. The principate may have begun as a joint rule, but in time real power came to rest more and more in the hands of the *princeps* alone. Huge new bureaucracies grew up to serve the *princeps*, helping him to carry out his ever-increasing number of functions. The chiefs of these, the prefects, were usually chosen from the social stratum just below that of the senatorial aristocracy, that is, they were rich and influential people but not members of the traditional oligarchy. The prefects and their minions began to manage some of the most important functions in the Roman state: commanding legions, governing provinces, collecting taxes, supervising public works and controlling the all-important supply of grain. Thus the senators lost their political monopoly in two ways: they lost the power of political decision-making to the *princeps* (emperor), and they now had to share the execution of that political authority with the new prefectures. Consequently the careers of the senators changed. Since they were no longer those who exercised the political authority, they came to serve and advise the one who now had that authority. A cadre of hereditary advisers and courtiers surrounding the ruler may sound very medieval, but it is also very Roman, and we know that it was Roman even at the height of the Empire because people like Seneca and Tacitus so elegantly complain about the new role of the senators. It would change somewhat in the tumult of the third century, but in the fourth, Constantine's family would again surround itself with a hereditary senatorial class.

The principate was a very Italian institution. Even though not all its emperors were born in Italy (some of the most notable came from Spain), none the less it was the Italians who ruled the Roman Empire, and the spoils of imperial rule – military booty, commercial profit and tribute – all poured unfathomable wealth into grasping Italian hands. Under the principate the Romans, that is those from the city of Rome and its immediate environs, lost their monopoly of imperial privilege, but it did not spread far beyond the Italian peninsula. It was Italy that benefited. The boon for the Italians rested, again, largely on their legions. The Italians enjoyed the fruits of Rome's expansion; it was they who controlled the apparatus for protection and rule. But in the centuries after the expansion stopped, Italy slowly began to lose the attendant advantages and was forced to share its privileged position with the rich from the other parts of the Empire. This especially meant sharing with the East, with its rich cities and rich trade routes, heir to millennia of creating and gathering wealth.

This Golden Age of Rome may be called the *Pax Romana*, but the peace of these two glorious centuries had a particularly Roman odour to it: peace was not for everybody. There was war enough, but from the Roman point of view it was war as war should be: far away from the central Mediterranean and providing a glittering source of riches and glory for Rome, her commanders and her legions. As the heartland of the Empire, that is the Mediterranean littoral, basked in the warm confidence that war was something that happened elsewhere, the security brought prosperity. The Mediterranean had never been richer. Its great cities became greater and trade boomed. Splendid evidence of this great Roman peace and prosperity found an incarnation in brick, marble and mortar from Spain to Judaea: monuments, wharfs, warehouses, statues, palaces, governmental buildings, temples, gardens, roads, aqueducts, theatres, shops and fora. The world of thought and letters, too, passed from its Golden to its Silver Age, and like the metals for which these periods are named, literary production passed from relatively few precious nuggets to wider currency. But once again, all these benefits of empire were not for everybody, not even for everybody in the great cities on the coasts of the *mare nostrum.* Amid splendour for the few, most suffered from unimaginable poverty, and even within earshot of the upper classes' elegant Latin, most were painfully illiterate.

The reign of the emperor Commodus (180–192) is taken as the signpost towards the end of Rome's Golden Age. He became deranged and his advisers had him assassinated. Trouble at the top, even mental illness and regicide, did not necessarily spell trouble for the Empire; the Roman government had suffered such things before and had gone on relatively unharmed. But by the turn of the third century, there were forces about which would indeed damage the Roman peace if the central government were not strong. Although the whole Empire suffered, the damage was particularly acute in the West.

First, as power had concentrated more in the hands of the emperor, so too had authority in general come to rest more and more with the central government. This meant that provincial and local governments became less capable of good rule, and so trouble at the top meant more trouble locally than it had in the past. Second, the central government could no longer draw on that vital class of senators in ways it had done in the past. As we have seen, the senatorial class had lost real political power to become a group of officials and functionaries, competent and loyal perhaps, but now equipped with much less experience and ability in real political leadership. Third, border defence, always in need of careful attention, became more demanding as barbarian pressure increased and the Roman military, now without the motivating exhilaration that comes with conquest and expansion, was less competent in its resistance. A telltale effect of the increased trouble at the borders was that it created a greater need for the military, and this in turn meant that the military gained even more political influence. Roman politics had never been a stranger to either pressure from soldiers or control by war heroes, but now increasingly many previously civil functions were assigned to the military: some judicial functions and tax collection, to name just two important ones. Although reliance upon the military may have in some ways helped the government's efficiency, it also brought a dangerous rigidity with it and slowly chiselled away at local political competence all the more. All these developments were long-term ones that would plague the Empire, especially in the West, until its political end.

From 193 to 235 Septimius Severus and his family ruled. Under them the militarisation of the state went on apace. Severus owed his position entirely to the army and he made many concessions to it. In 235 the army murdered the last of the Severans, Severus Alexander (222–235), and it was as if the dam broke. For the next fifty years the army put up twenty-six emperors and then murdered almost all of them. The chaos further weakened the borders and barbarians entered. This 'crisis of the third century' was a low point for the Mediterranean and its peaceful shores. Things would get better again, but not before a good deal of real suffering. Civil wars, foreign wars, loss of territory, brigandage and piracy, and as if these evils were not enough, a plague from the East, all swept across the Empire. The political chaos brought economic hardship, as it almost always does. Agricultural production and manufacturing fell off, hunger deepened, gold and silver went out of circulation, and the penniless government was forced to raise the already stifling taxes. Then, too, Rome's only organised imperial rival, the Persians, enjoyed the beginnings of a sparkling reinvigoration in 227 with the advent of the Sasanian regime. In 260 the Persians actually managed to capture the reigning Roman emperor, Valerian (253–260). The shock was unprecedented; for no mere foreigner had ever captured a Roman emperor.

The crisis of the third century brought the principate to an end in the same way that civil wars of the first century BC had changed the Republic. With the end of its expansion, the Empire was in great need of a fundamental reorganisation; the Italians could no longer claim their previous monopolies of privilege or power. In some ways the crisis of the third century was the resultant violent shudder as the political structure adopted a broader base and the social structure became more rigid to accommodate the changes. These were both long-term developments, but we can see certain striking legislative reflections of them in the third century. Not only were the high positions in the government and army falling more and more to people other than the traditional Italian elite, but the Empire's common people were affected as well. In 212, with a measure now called the Antonine Constitution, the emperor Caracalla (212–217) extended full Roman citizenship to all but the very poorest freemen in the whole Empire. No longer could Romans dangle their citizenship as a juicy carrot of legal and social privilege; it now belonged to everyone. The recruits for the Roman armies, too, were increasingly drawn from the less Romanised provinces. As social and political privilege spread beyond Italy, thus losing its exclusivity based on nationality, it found, in its geographically broader form, new legislative protection. Under Septimius Severus, the upper and lower classes became differentiated legally. The senators, provincial rich, high governmental officials, military officers and the like were termed *honestiores* and given a different status before the law than were the bulk of society, called *humiliores*. The resultant legally privileged status was not all to the advantage of the rich: certain of the *honestiores* were required to take on local governmental offices and bear expenses from their own purse.

In 284 a faction in the army elevated yet another rough-hewn military leader to the purple. This one, an Illyrian known as Diocletian, did not prove to be just another short-lived emperor as had been most of the twenty-six before him; he was to rule for some twenty-one years and, along with his long-reigning successor Constantine (306–337), to institute such sweeping reforms as to be given credit for staving off for well over a hundred years what could have been imminent political collapse. We mention the reforms of these two famous emperors in one breath because the sources often do not allow us to see clearly which one was responsible for a particular measure, and because in both cases it is sensible to view their actions as codifying or reflecting the long-term trends we have been discussing, namely the changes that came about as the Romans (or Italians) were forced to share their empire with the others who lived in it.

Both emperors dealt blows to the political position of the city of Rome. In response to various political exigencies, such as rebellion and the old nemesis of military factions hailing their generals as emperors, Diocletian gave the Empire a radically new four-part structure, now called the tetrarchy. He first recognised Maximian as his colleague in emperorship and then went on to establish four emperors, two seniors, each called augustus, and two juniors, each called caesar. Collegiality is an ancient principle of Roman government, and other emperors before Diocletian had named colleagues to share power and given them the title of augustus or caesar, but Diocletian's tetrarchy was different in two important respects. First, Diocletian tried to regularise the succession. If an augustus died or retired, the caesar was to move up and a new caesar was to be appointed. A grand and very Roman idea, but it worked only as long as Diocletian himself was present to enforce it. Even here in these very Roman years, two centuries before the Empire's 'fall', the force of personal loyalty due to one's commander and his son drew men's allegiance far more than did an abstract loyalty due to the state and its system for succession. There were again civil wars as 'rightful heirs' were passed over in the appointment of new caesars. By 306 there were seven augusti and no caesars. Constantine would wisely, if ruthlessly, return to the principle of hereditary succession.

The second novel feature of Diocletian's tetrarchy was more lasting because it reflected rather than conflicted with long-term developments. Diocletian carved up the whole Roman Empire into four geographical parts, soon to be called prefectures, assigning one to each of the four emperors. The prefectures were subdivided into dioceses and these in turn into provinces. These new provinces were much smaller than the ones they replaced and consequently were both easier to administer internally and less likely to be large enough to be used as a base for rebellion against the central government. Each prefecture had its own army, its own boundaries and its own principal residence for the emperor: Milan for Spain, Italy and Africa; Trier for Gaul and Britain; Sirmium for the Balkans and the Danubian provinces; and Nicomedia for the eastern Mediterranean. Rome was not among them. Diocletian resided at Nicomedia and ruled the eastern prefecture, another situation that reflected the declining importance of Italy and the West.

Although the tetrarchy as such did not survive long after Diocletian's reign, certain features of its geographical division became a part of the history of the medieval West. Obviously the division of the Empire into four parts predicts the more lasting division into two parts, reflecting the growing political divergence of East from West. After the reign of Theodosius (378–395), the Empire would be divided, with one emperor ruling the West from Milan and then Ravenna and the other ruling the East from Constantinople. Furthermore, Diocletian's smaller provincial boundaries in Roman Gaul would enjoy a truly remarkable longevity, becoming, for the most part, the administrative divisions of medieval France (the *civitates*) and remaining so until the French Revolutionary government replaced them with the *Départements.* The Roman Catholic church, no friend of the Revolution, has retained them still further, and they are still today the basis of France's ecclesiastical dioceses. Diocletian had quick and remarkable success. By 298 the Mediterranean was again surrounded by Roman provinces at peace and united, albeit in a new way, under Diocletian as senior augustus. There were still huge and perhaps unsolvable problems facing the Empire.

As we move into the late Empire we can see that the nature of local government was changing significantly. Gone now was the institutionalised corruption that had squeezed the provinces and poured wealth into the coffers of the Roman upper classes. But the regularised and ever-growing imperial bureaucracy, which replaced the senatorial system, brought its own attendant evils. The cities were the points through which the central government governed and taxed locally. Towns and cities of the various legal statuses were usually governed by a town council, or *curia.* Its officials, the *curiales* or *decuriones*, represented the imperial government as well as the locality and knew how to make immense personal fortunes from the taxing of the countryside. Sometimes, however, they had to be forced to serve since they were required to make up certain governmental financial shortfalls from their own funds. This admixture of local urban and central imperial government stifled local initiative in important ways. Localities often took on those projects that had imperial support rather than ones dictated by actual local needs. Officials, too, made their careers by moving up the imperial bureaucratic ladder and their decisions were too often made looking up the line rather than at local requirements. Add to this the obviously cumbersome inefficiency of local policies being formulated and decisions taken by an imperial government far from the locality itself. The result significantly lessened the ability of local communities to cope with their problems, problems which were sometimes those of foreign invasion.

The Empire had experienced foreign invasions in the third century and would do so again in the fifth. But during the fourth century it was much freer from the problem and it was so in large part because of measures instituted by Diocletian and Constantine to improve the border defences. The principal residences of the tetrarchs were all in good strategic locations, close to troublesome borders, and Constantine's New Rome at Constantinople was also far better placed strategically than was old Rome. Diocletian both instituted a mobile striking force some distance back from the border that could be used to reinforce the troops stationed along the border itself whenever they were pressed, and strengthened the borders physically with extensive defence works. The strong leadership exercised by these two emperors also strengthened the morale and effectiveness of the military. Their economic reforms, although substantial, had less enduring effect. They imposed price controls, reformed the coinage and started building programmes. These may have caused some temporary convalescence, but the fundamental economic maladies of labour shortage, declining agricultural production and dwindling trade continued to plague the Empire, especially in the West.

As the size of the imperial government grew, so too did its expense. To meet the constant need for increased revenue, Diocletian instituted a fundamental reorganisation of the tax system. He regularised its two basic components, the *annona*, a type of land tax based on the *jugum*, a measure of its productive value, and the *caput*, a type of poll tax based on a unit of labour, a 'man-day'.[1] The *annona* could be paid in kind, another indication that the moneyed economy was not healthy. This practice had been introduced in the third century because inflation had made the value of payments in money almost negligible.[2] The reforms did increase governmental revenue but they also had a detrimental economic side-effect in that they increased the already growing tendency towards rigidity in the social structure: people were more and more tied to one place and less able to move either socially or geographically. This was not just the usual circumstance in which the small landholders were forced to sell out to the rich and then tied as debt-burdened tenants to the land. Now manufacturers, officials and even merchants suffered regulations which sapped their ability to move freely. The bureaucracy which was needed to implement these new regulations of course grew, increasing an already huge government, which, as we have seen, was increasingly dominated by the army.

The theocratic element in Diocletian's rule was far more prominent than heretofore. There had always been a strong religious element in Roman rule, and it deepened as the Empire aged. Emperor-worship was as old as the principate itself. Although the practice is far more eastern than it is Roman, none the less, statues to the Divine Augustus and even the Divine Julius had been established in the West, especially in Spain. Other emperors had been addressed as 'Lord' (*domine*), one even as 'Lord and God'. But the appeal to divine authority and the use of holy ceremony to the degree that Diocletian used them were new. His edicts became holy, his will an expression of divine will, and even

[1] Contemporary sources do not present a very clear picture of either *jugum* or *caput*. See Goffart (1974), esp. chs. 3–5.

[2] Jones (1975), p. 154.

his chamber was the *sacrum cubiculum.* He was secluded not only from the general population but from dignitaries as well by an elaborate and holy court ceremonial. His public appearances were rare and became occasions for general celebration. Now more than ever, religious dissent approximated political disloyalty, and thus it is perhaps no coincidence that the Great Persecution of the Christians occurred under his rule. Because of the persecution, the Christians of the Middle Ages looked back upon Diocletian as the most evil of all the emperors.

Constantine spent his youth at the court of Diocletian where he learned the lessons and the techniques of theocratic rule. His theocracy, however, had the obvious difference, at least towards the end of this reign, that it was Christian. Since he was the first emperor to embrace Christianity, to the Middle Ages he became the hero *par excellence* among the Roman emperors. To historians, however, he remains an enigma. He was moody, ruthless, and some say of limited intelligence. Despite the fact that the Christians liked him and wrote more about him than about any other late Roman emperor, the nature of his conversion to Christianity is still imperfectly understood. It is clear that after about 313 Constantine's actions began to be of significant benefit to the Christians. Among other things, he all but ended the persecutions, promoted the building of churches, including the first church of Holy Wisdom in his New Rome at Byzantium, made certain tax concessions to the Christian clergy and restored confiscated properties, and he added imperial lustre to the famous ecclesiastical Council of Nicaea in 325 by presiding over the sessions himself. On the other hand, his imperial coinage, long a vehicle for imperial propaganda, continued to display the pagan gods until about 320, and both pagan and Christian officials took part in the dedication ceremonies of his New Rome.

Between 323 and 330 Constantine established a permanent capital for the Roman Empire by expanding the small Greek town of Byzantium on the Bosphorus into his New Rome, which soon became known as the city of Constantine. Although pagans played an important part in the intellectual and court life in Constantine's new capital, it is significant that the city boasted no pagan temples. In every other way, however, he intended his New Rome to equal or surpass the imperial splendour of old Rome, and indeed it did. Its palaces, markets, warehouses, churches and governmental buildings were constructed with the best handiwork and materials the Mediterranean could muster. Grain and circus were even transplanted: Constantinople had its dole and its Hippodrome.

To the people of the medieval West, this magic city on a far-off seacoast, dripping in gold and mosaics, would come to symbolise the mysterious, imperial East. To the historian, Constantine's eastward movement of the capital to the Bosphorus has also come to reflect many of the characteristics and preoccupations of late antique society. The city was beautifully located for defence, sitting between the Empire's two most troublesome borders: the Rhine–Danube in the West and the Persian in the East. Although it was New Rome in name, it was not Roman or even Italian at all, but part of the Greek world and much more oriental in its culture and economy than were both old Rome and all but one of the principal residences of the tetrarchy. And while the ancient pagan gods and their temples still attracted the ruling classes along the Tiber, in New Rome most heads that mattered turned toward the East, to Bethlehem.

The changes instituted by Diocletian and Constantine – the heightened theocracy, the reforms in the military and border defence, the economic measures, the increased social regimentation, the orientalising, and perhaps also the embracing of Christianity – were all meant to preserve the Empire. The fact that both the Empire's borders and its government were more secure in the fourth century than they had been in the third may indeed indicate their success. Not that the fourth century was without serious military disturbance: there were wars among Constantine's heirs until Constantius II (324–361) emerged as sole emperor in 353. But for the coming European Middle Ages the effects of the fourth century's military wars were not nearly as important as the results of its ecclesiastical ones.

The fourth century saw Christianity struggle to mature in several ways. At the century's beginning, under Diocletian, it was a persecuted sect; by its end, under Theodosius, it had become the Empire's official religion, and the once-persecuted Christians began to do the persecuting. Alongside its increasing official status came the increasing need to institutionalise, that is, the increasing need to develop a systematic theology as well as liturgical and institutional structures and procedures for the long duration on earth. This was due not only to the church's increasing size and official status but also to the growing recognition that the *parousia*, Christ's second coming, was not to be as immediate as the early church had assumed. By the time Theodosius made Christianity Rome's official religion, its early, almost informal, congregational organisation under elders and deacons, and its simple forms of worship with readings, psalms and the shared meal seen in the biblical and post-biblical eras, had given way to a hierarchy of clerical statuses and to carefully defined means of formalised liturgical worship[3].

The Roman world would deliver to the European Middle Ages not only Christianity's holy book, its Bible, but also a huge body of systematic theology. The Bible is not systematic; it is a collection of poems, stories, letters and history, all in Christian eyes the inspired word of God, but it does not lay out

[3] For the institutional development of the church, see Scheibelreiter, chapter 25 below.

a systematic view of the divinity and creation, and the relationship between the two, as a philosopher would. Christianity has such a theology, largely the work of Christian theologians living in Alexandria during the late second and early third centuries. The fourth and fifth centuries were the age of the Christological controversies, the age in which the church worked out what would be its accepted view of the nature of Christ. Constantine's great church council held in Nicaea in 325 defined the Orthodox dogma, and although the Nicene teaching has remained official, it did not go uncontested. The contests ranged from learned disputes to actual violence.

The finely honed Nicene view of the nature of God as triune, that is, a one and only God existing in three persons, and the person of God-the-Son, Jesus Christ, having two complete and simultaneous natures, one truly divine and the other truly human, demanded a considerable grounding in Greek metaphysics to be fully understood. Disagreement came from both sides: those who denied the human nature of Christ (the Monophysites) and those who denied that his divine nature was full and complete (the Arians and Nestorians). The Arians were the defeated party at Nicaea but they none the less came to be the dominant influence at the court of Constantius II (337–361). It was largely during the fourth century that the Goths and the other east German tribes also adopted Christianity in its Arian form. Arianism would invade western Europe on a massive scale with the barbarian migrations. Monophysitism on the other hand would remain mainly in the East, capturing large portions of the Egyptian, Ethiopian, Armenian and Syrian churches.

Constantius proved an effective, if ruthless, emperor, largely keeping the internal peace and the borders strong. The succession at his death was again violent until the throne fell to his cousin, Julian (361–363), the last member of Constantine's family to rule. Julian, known as Julian the Apostate, found Christian teaching crude and lacking, and his subtle mind was drawn instead to ancient paganism in its newly resurgent and highly mystical Neoplatonic form. He began to replace Christians with pagans in high governmental and educational positions, so that, for the fortunes of the church, it was providential that his reign was a short one. As medieval Christian authors would look back to Constantine as the great hero among the emperors, they would look back to Julian as a great villain.

The maladies, which the reforms of Diocletian and Constantine seem to have temporarily ameliorated, began to make their return during the last decades of the fourth century. Cooperation between the Eastern and Western imperial governments became increasingly rare as each section began more and more to tread its own path, dealing with its own problems. After Constantine's family left the throne, the two halves would only rarely and briefly unite under one emperor. Internal peace and stability began to wane and barbarians, both inside and outside the frontier, occupied more and more imperial attention. The eastern emperor Valens (364–378) was to lose his life to the barbarians. Unable to deal simultaneously with Persians to the east and Goths to the north, he took the expedient of allowing the Goths to settle on Roman territory in the Balkan provinces. But mistreatment by imperial officials caused them to revolt, and at the famous battle of Adrianople in 378 they slaughtered two thirds of the imperial army along with Valens himself. The defeat left the Balkan provinces defenceless, and the Goths promptly plundered them. The next emperor, Theodosius (378–395), seated the barbarian presence more deeply into Roman soil when he granted the Goths 'federated status'. As *foederati* they were allowed not only to live within the Empire but to do so under their own rulers, not Roman officials. The arrangement obviously provided the Romans with a powerful people having a vested interest in defending their section of the frontier themselves, but it also subjected a large section of Roman territory to a government that was not Roman and to a population not imbued with Roman culture. Although the use of *foederati* would now become a frequent and effective part of Roman policy for defence of the borders, there was little loyalty felt by these peoples for the central imperial state; the interests they served were their own local ones. The practice proved decentralising in the long term, especially for an imperial system finding it increasingly difficult to command the loyalty of even its more Romanised subjects.

Under the western emperor Valentinian II (375–392), barbarian influence manifested itself in another important way: Valentinian was not the real ruler; control lay in the hands of Arbogast, his chief military official, the 'Master of the Soldiers' (*magister militum*) and a Frank by descent, albeit a very Romanised one. It was Arbogast who actually appointed Valentinian's successor as emperor, Eugenius (392–394). Eugenius was not a legitimate ruler: he had no dynastic claim and had not been appointed emperor through legal procedures. He ruled only because Arbogast had placed him on the throne. Illegitimate emperors along with barbarian strongmen did little to maintain the loyalty of Roman citizens. From this point to the end of Roman political rule in the West, the Masters of the Soldiers not only would command the imperial army, itself increasingly made up of barbarian soldiers, but also would control the central government, often for the advantage of their tribe or their own personal ambition.

Theodosius, the eastern emperor, invaded the West in 394, deposed the hapless Eugenius, and for a brief six months united the two parts of the Empire until his death in 395. But this political unity was the Mediterranean's last; increasingly East and West would go their divergent ways. The East, always the richer, was now more Christian, better governed and more stable, and boasted a capital which was splendidly placed both for defence and for commerce. The poorer and more rural West, by contrast, had a far less stable government and was far easier prey to the barbarians. As the two parts diverged politically, the West received less cultural influence, less political direction, and less money from the East; it was forced to rely on its indigenous resources. In a word, it was becoming more European.

Roman imperial politics in the West during the fifth century were not very imperial and hardly Roman. They were mostly conducted through a complicated system of making and remaking confederations with and among the barbarian tribes, largely by means of generous subsidies in gold, by the offer of federated status, or by dangling fancy imperial titles and high office in front of the barbarian leaders. By the time the great Hunnic king, Atilla, died in 454, only Italy and parts of Spain and Gaul were still under direct Roman rule. In addition, the emperors were often children, governed by regents, or were powerless appointees of the barbarian 'Masters of the Soldiers'. The political end came in the famous year 476 when the last reigning western Roman emperor, Romulus Augustulus, was deposed by the German chieftain, Odovacer. Romulus Augustulus was a boy and a usurper, never officially recognised by the government in the East and installed on the throne by his father and his army of barbarians. It was this same army, under the leadership of Odovacer, who later deposed him.

The traditional view of the end of the Western Roman Empire has been one of 'decline and fall', a view due in no small measure to the magnificent work of Edward Gibbon, a book now over two hundred years old but still enlightening.[4] Although it is obvious that there was a huge difference between Roman civilisation and early medieval society, decline and fall is today seen less and less as an apt description of this change, especially when the historian takes a wide view of what is meant by society. Gibbon, and the historians of the nineteenth century who followed him, scholars such as Theodor Mommsen[5] and J. B. Bury,[6] performed monumental tasks in increasing our understanding of the transition from the Roman to the medieval world, at least where the upper levels of society were concerned. Emperors, kings, laws, philosophy, governments, literature, theology, taxes, coins, treaties, wars, constitutions and the like were the objects of their enquiries. But a society is more than its top, and as the historians of the twentieth century such as Mikhail Rostovtzeff,[7] A. H. M. Jones,[8] J. Carcopino[9] and Peter Brown[10] have worked to explain the nature of the lives of the whole society, it has become clearer that for most

[4] Gibbon, ed. Bury (1909–14). [5] Mommsen (1887), (1899), and (1909).
[6] Bury (1923). [7] Rostovtzeff (1957).
[8] Jones (1964) is fundamental. From among his many other studies see Jones (1975).
[9] Carcopino (1940). [10] Brown (1971).

people the change from the late antique to the medieval was a slow one and rarely best described as decline. Even at the top we have seen that the final political fall of the Roman imperial government in the West in 476 to the barbarians was less of a fall and more of stumble since the central imperial government had been in barbarian hands in all but name for over a century. In the more recent broader social view, we find on the one hand that many 'medieval' traits were actually alive and very well during Roman imperial rule, and on the other, that many 'Roman' traits lasted long into the Middle Ages. An increased awareness of geographical diversity also cautions against any idea of ubiquitous decline. The magnificent ruins of the fourth-century Roman villa at Chedworth in the English county of Gloucestershire, with its mosaics, water-borne sanitation and hypocaustic heating, indicated that, at least for the very few, life on the Tiber was transported far beyond the Thames. However, whereas some villa-life in parts of Gaul, Spain and Italy survived the 'barbarian invasions' and even thrived under barbarian rule, at Chedworth it seems to have ceased.[11]

SOCIETY AND CULTURE

Much of what is usually considered medieval actually has a far longer history than the Middle Ages. For instance, there are many ways in which it is correct to view Roman culture as urban and medieval culture as rural. But for all its cities, the late Empire still depended upon its farms. Here, too, was the government's source of income: the commercial taxes of the cities provided only about 5 per cent of its tax income; the rest came mostly from the oppressive land tax, the *annona.* A farmer's rent and taxes could eat up one half of his net production (one fourth to one third of his gross). The taxes kept rural population teetering just this side of deprivation, and any unbalancing event, a bad crop-year, war, drought, a harsh winter, or any factor which raised costs even slightly, caused widespread misery. Tax evasion became a survival technique, and in the fifth century it became so rampant that it was one of the reasons the central government's coffers were constantly empty. Avoidance of the land tax may have hurt the government, but it did not help the late Roman peasant, for as the government became less effective at collecting the taxes, the landlords increased the rents.[12] The collection of a tax on the one hand, or of a rent on the other, was one way in which late antique differed from early medieval society, but both forms of collection existed in both periods, and in the misery

[11] For a careful study of 'medieval' characteristics in Roman villas, see Percival (1969).

[12] Basic to an understanding of late Roman taxation is Jones (1975). See also Wickham (1984) and Goffart (1972).

they caused in the countryside there was little difference. As long as Roman armies fought distant wars and were well supplied, the major economic effect they had upon the rural poor was the heavy taxes needed to support them. But in the late imperial period, huge and badly supplied armies trod the interior of the Empire, feeding themselves by 'requisitioning', that is, by taking what they needed from the local farms. The farmers were entitled to reimbursement by the government, but they rarely received it. No one living along the great military roads was safe. The practice seems to have diminished somewhat in the early Middle Ages when military activity was generally confined much closer to home.

The legal status of the peasantry in the late Empire also endured into the Middle Ages. In the late Empire, the most productive agricultural land formed part of huge estates owned by great landholders, the greatest of whom, by far, was the emperor himself. The majority of farmers were tenants, using the owner's land in return for rent, a share of the produce, labour services or some combination thereof. By the reign of Constantine, huge numbers of peasantry had fallen to a half-free status (*coloni*) and were so bound fiscally and legally that they could not move. These are obviously the antecedents of the medieval serfs, and although the obligations and requirements will take on different forms in the early Middle Ages, the half-free status of most peasants changed very little from the days of the late Roman Empire. In the same regard, the rendering of a service in labour by the poor as opposed to paying a tax in money or in kind is also often hailed as a 'medieval' rather than an 'ancient' practice. Yet we find evidence of the Roman government exacting labour services from those unable to pay in other ways as far back as the late Republic.[13] Poor agricultural technique, heavy taxation, requisitioning by the military, the depletion of nutrients in the soil after centuries of use and misuse, a growing amount of abandoned land and the half-free status of its occupants plagued the rural life of late Empire in the West. From this already sorry state, there was no decline and fall. In fact, in some areas, the disappearance of the Roman military and the Roman tax structure may actually have ameliorated rural conditions somewhat.

In the Roman cities too we find much that was medieval before the Middle Ages began. Although the number and the size of the cities declined from the late Empire to the early Middle Ages, even in the cities' splendid heyday living conditions for all but the rich were anything but splendid; in fact, they evidence many of the characteristics usually considered medieval. In ancient Rome itself, most streets were not paved, and in the city centre only two, the Via Sacra and

[13] The 'Urso Charter', ch. 98, *Fontes Iuris Romani Antejustiniani* (ed. alt.), vol. I, p. 189. See Goffart (1974), p. 92.

the Via Nova, were wide enough for two carts to pass. Very few dwellings had running water, fewer still a connection to the sewers, which were a marvel but inadequate. Even the wonderful public latrines were not often used by the poor. There was a disgusting stench in the streets, which were crowded, noisy, unlit and very dangerous. The rich never ventured into them without the protection of private guards. Most people lived in crowded, stuffy, multistorey apartment blocks called *insulae.* Furniture was sparse: a table, benches, and a pallet for sleeping. Cooking and heating were done with charcoal, and the long flights of stairs to the street dampened enthusiasm for regular emptying of the slop pails.

Medieval towns were small and built within walls for protection, but already in the late Empire the towns were shrinking and building walls. With the crises of the third century and the Empire growing smaller in the fourth and fifth, the cities suffered. Many late antique cities had walled areas of between 10 and 20 hectares, meaning their populations were already probably no more than 5000 people. The great cities of the East, the city of Rome and a few others in the West remained in better physical condition, but for most it was a different fate.

This is not to say that urban building stopped. It certainly did not. Nevertheless after the year 300 private benefaction of public buildings all but ceased, except for churches. The imperial government and its provincial governors continued to provide for the construction of impressive buildings, but in the fourth and fifth centuries these tended to concentrate in the imperial capitals or favoured places of the emperors. Not only the amount of building but the types of buildings constructed saw a decided reduction: town walls, palaces, aqueducts and sometimes baths continued to be repaired or built, but the other splendid monuments of earlier centuries languished. By the late fifth and into the sixth century, construction was more and more limited to building churches. Local aristocrats as well as the central government financed them, and some were architecturally every bit as impressive as the secular buildings of the earlier period.[14] In the late Empire, we notice a change in the sculpture and the decorative arts in a medieval direction as well. Christian subjects, of course, became more common, but even the works treating secular themes became more transcendental and symbolic. The refined techniques of realistic sculpture and painting were replaced by more abstract ones which broke the strictures of the classical rules, employing, among other things, brilliant colour. As the future seemed less and less promising, Roman thoughts withdrew from the here and now, and Roman artists presented even their secular heroes as having contact with the beyond.

[14] Ward-Perkins (1984), pp. 14–84, and for the architecture of this period, Wood, chapter 28a below.

A clear contrast between the ancient and medieval periods is formed by the fact that the powerful in the ancient Mediterranean world lived in the cities, whereas the medieval powerful lived in the countryside. But in this as well it is under the late Empire that a very important group of locally powerful people began to take up permanent residence in the countryside. In the late Republic and early Empire, much of the agricultural land was owned by the rich, living in the cities, who left managers to run their vast estates. Their villas, the country homes, were their temporary escapes from the heat and hassle of the city. In the late Empire, however, many great landholders made the villas their principal residences, abandoning the cities. The phenomenon was not universal; for instance, there does not seem to have been a 'flight from town to country' in fourth-century Britain, whereas there was in Gaul.[15] The villas often became magnificently appointed with splendid mosaics, lavish furniture and spacious apartments. Whereas the towns in the late Empire of the West generally withered, the villas blossomed. Many of them in Britain and Gaul have left archaeological remains of glassworks, forges and workshops, all indicating a much greater amount of rural manufacturing and self-sufficiency than had earlier been the case. They also became more self-contained legally and more self-reliant for protection. Many landlords obtained an exemption from the jurisdiction of the local authorities and began themselves to exercise some jurisdictional functions on their estates. They fortified their residences and provided for their protection. They also managed to escape many of the restricting obligations which the late imperial government laid upon the local urban nobility. Thus the rural estate-owners grew in financial, legal and military importance, and obviously, in many cases, it was they who evolved into the rural elite of the Middle Ages.

A fundamental difference between barbarian and late Roman society shows itself in the nature of ties of loyalty. Concepts of civic loyalty, or allegiance to abstract notions of the state and its institutions, fill much surviving Roman philosophical and historical writing, whereas in the early Middle Ages aristocratic warriors and peasants alike pledged loyalty to the person of their lords by name. In this, the ties of personal rather than abstract institutional loyalty bound society together. But even here, we find the 'medieval' in the 'Roman'. In traditional Roman society, as far back as the Republic and beyond, every male was the client of someone more powerful than he, his patron. Although the tie was personal and not official, it was universal and extremely powerful. The client owed his patron *obsequium*, a term best translated as obedience or respect, and he was reckoned as part of the patron's following. It was normal for him to call his patron *dominus*, master. The patron was obligated to assist

[15] Percival (1976).

his clients with financial help called a *sportula*, often a cash payment, and to represent their interests at law. The personal ties of *obsequium* were of daily importance in the lives of most people, often outweighing the official allegiance owed the state.

Another important matter which remained relatively constant from the late Empire into the early Middle Ages was the position of women. This is because the women's realm was the private not the public life. It is also the reason that they are almost hidden from us; private lives do not generally find their way to the contemporary written sources unless they impinge in some way upon the public sphere. The domain of each sex was so demarcated from the others that when men did cross the gender boundary and partake in activities from the feminine side, they were labelled as soft and degenerate. By the same token, a woman venturing into the male domains of public life would be accused of moral laxity, usually sexual transgression. This is not to say that women were excluded totally from public life, nor men from the private. But acceptable direct female participation beyond the home seems to have been limited largely to public benefaction, mostly funding local buildings, and to religious duties. Both of these were a vital part of late imperial public life. A Roman woman who exercised political control did so through a malleable male member of her family who held office.

Roman men criticised the female's supposed lesser ability in the public sphere. Women were said to be less strong physically, less able to reason and less constant of purpose. In the days of the Republic, when upper-class males were fiercely engaged in public life, women were nearly a legal non-entity, being instead part of the legal personality of their fathers or husbands. Women had very restricted inheritance rights, many could be divorced on the whim of a husband, and they had little or no recourse to legal redress of any grievance. But in the imperial period, as the men found less and less satisfaction in public life with its huge bureaucracy and its increasingly theocratic nature, and as they began to look more and more to matters private for a sense of fulfilment, the condition of those in charge of private life, that is, women, ameliorated significantly. By Hadrian's rule (117–138) women could inherit and pass on land. As the Empire grew older, women came to possess more public dignity and often a legal independence. None the less, despite these significant improvements, the realm of women remained with only rare and magnificent exceptions largely as it had been, the private one. In the late Roman Empire, as in the early Middle Ages, women did not often venture into public life and thus did not come often enough into the light of history.

The fall of the Roman imperial government to the barbarian successor states made little change in the language that most western Europeans spoke. Under the barbarian successors, with the exceptions of those living in one part of the British Isles (roughly modern England) and those in what is now western Germany and modern Belgium, people in every other part of the former Roman Empire in western Europe went on speaking the language they had spoken under Roman rule. For the upper and middle classes this was either some form of Latin (perhaps 'Vulgar Latin'), and for the lower, a similar language heavily influenced by it. So much more lasting is the Romance influence than the barbarian that today one must hunt to find more than a dozen words of Gothic origin in modern Italian or Spanish. In modern French, spoken where the Franks ruled for centuries, only about 300 modern words trace their roots to Frankish. In western Europe where the Romans once ruled, the Romance languages largely still reign.

In some ways the lot of the upper classes, those whom one might think stood to lose the most with the Roman government's collapse, also shows a remarkable continuity. Salvian, a Christian priest from Marseilles, writing in the middle of the fifth century, tells us that some actually welcomed the change to barbarian rule. Many aristocrats carried on their privileged and elegant lives largely as before. The advent of the barbarians could actually enhance the status of the Roman aristocracy. As the late imperial government became less and less able to manage local affairs directly, the responsibility fell more and more on the locals themselves. The Christian bishops often filled the void in secular administration, but the local aristocracy, too, increased its authority as the imperial government retreated. Although many did lose their privileged position to the newly arrived barbarian warrior elite, nevertheless many of these exquisitely educated scions of the late Roman upper class held on locally and even surrounded the thrones of the barbarian kings into the seventh century.

Roman coinage had once been wonderfully stable; but even as early as the mid-third century, the once solid and reliable Roman coins had only a very small percentage of precious metal left in them.[16] As a part of his reforms, in about 309, Constantine issued an *aureus*, the traditional Roman gold coin. It remained relatively unaltered throughout the late Empire and was used on into the early Middle Ages. This is the famous *solidus*, ancestor of the shilling. One good measure of its success is that during the fifth century many taxes formerly demanded in kind were now being reckoned in gold.[17] But gold and silver had never been the money of most people, who, when they did not simply barter, used the various bronze coins. These, however, came to have much more turbulent lives than did the steady *solidus*. The striking of the bronze coins fell under regional and local control and their value changed and sank depending on local conditions. The unstable common coinage did not

[16] See Blackburn, chapter 24 below. [17] Jones (1975), p. 173.

help the lives of the common people, whereas the rich enjoyed the relative fiscal security of 'the solid one'.

Late Roman ideas of law and the ways that it regulates the ownership of property were also passed directly into the early Middle Ages in the West. Law, both in its intellectual conception and in its practical application, is often held up as Rome's finest achievement. The early medieval kings issued compilations of law for the various tribes they ruled. These have come to be known as 'the barbarian codes'. They at first appeared to scholars as 'Germanic' in nature and were thought to codify a very different system of law from the Roman. But work in the mid and late twentieth century has shown that while some parts of them do reflect Germanic custom, there is a great deal about the barbarian codes which bases itself on late Roman provincial or vulgar law.[18] Roman and early medieval law had appeared to differ far more than they actually do because the comparison was made between the barbarian codes and the Roman law of its sophisticated heyday under the late Republic and early Empire. This version of Roman law forms a good part of Justinian's Code, produced in the exuberant 530s when Tribonian's commission recalled and reorganised the many, by then, ancient sources of Roman jurisprudence. But Justinian's Code had not yet been published when the earliest and most influential of the barbarian codes were issued. The type of law then prevalent in the Roman provinces, the law that governed the daily doings of life and property, had grown up since the third century out of a need for simplification and broad application. The splendid jurisprudence of classical times did not fit the needs of the later provinces, which did not at any rate have the cadre of highly trained specialists needed to wield it. In many ways the Theodosian Code, published in 438, that is, before the barbarian codes, reflects these vulgarising tendencies of Roman law.[19] It was this code, rather than the later and more comprehensive one of Justinian, that was influential in the medieval West.

Elementary education in the later Roman Empire had also been vulgarised. For most people it was poor at best and usually did not exist at all. Imperial interest in education was centred upon the senior levels. Diocletian appointed professors in many cities, Julian established a type of university in Constantinople with a permanent staff, and the imperial families and others of the high nobility often sent their sons to Rhodes or to Athens, to the Lyceum and the Academy. Those lucky enough to partake received highly sophisticated training in the classical disciplines of rhetoric and philosophy.[20] But most people

[18] Levy (1951), p. 15. See also Collins (1983), p. 28; Wood (1986), p. 20; (1993), pp. 161–7; (1994), pp. 163–4.

[19] Levy (1951), p. 15. Honoré (1987), p. 135, says, 'That conclusion is premature.' See also Turpin (1985), pp. 339–50.

[20] See Fontaine, chapter 27 below.

never saw any of this. In the high Empire, in the city of Rome, many children from the lower classes did learn some elementary form of halting reading and computation, but they did not progress beyond that. The first years of education were conducted in the home by the parents. Rich Romans often purchased Greek slaves to educate their young children. Schools were private affairs, where the teachers subsisted from the modest fees paid by the pupils' parents. The fees, modest as they were, still prohibited poor children from attending. The instruction was mostly drilling of the three Rs, with frequent application of the cane. There were no school buildings as such, the teacher simply gathered his pupils where he could, usually somewhere in the open in the noisy streets. We have no evidence that the emperors took any interest at all in popular education except to provide certain tax concessions for elementary teachers so that their profession might spread. The late Roman localities, on the other hand, did provide some public elementary instruction and this seems to have lasted in some cities in the more Romanised sections of the Empire well into the sixth century. We have no direct records of secular schools as such under the barbarian kings, but surviving inscriptions, especially on funereal monuments, and a few business records indicate literacy among the urban middle classes. The church did not undertake the elementary education of its clergy or its laity, with the exception of training its monks who had no access to the outside world. It rather assumed the literacy acquired through secular means for its religious purposes. When in the seventh century complaints about illiterate clergy grow louder in the ecclesiastical sources, it is safe to assume that the secular elementary instruction had waned.

For more advanced intellectual activity, the late Roman Empire was the direct antecedent of the early Middle Ages, particularly in that its intellectual climate moulded the Christian thought which it passed on. By the time of the late Empire, the two great Hellenistic philosophies, Stoicism and Epicureanism, had been superseded by a vigorous new interest in Plato, but Plato with an important difference. Plato had called upon the world of forms beyond this one largely in order to create the good citizen; his was a public and political morality. But in the late Empire, the Stoic's call to duty rang increasingly hollow in a world where political freedom had been sapped by huge bureaucracies and far-away imperial powers. Out of the teachings of the Stoics and the Epicureans, and the world-view of the Neopythagorians, a new Plato returned. Neoplatonism taught people not how to be good citizens but how to use their intellect to put themselves in touch with the world beyond. Its approach was contemplative rather than active and its morality private. It is perhaps not at all insignificant that Plotinus, its most influential proponent, studied under Ammonius Saccos, the teacher of none other than Origen, the third century's most important Christian theologian.

GARDNER HARVEY LIBRARY
Miami University-Middletown
Middletown, Ohio 45042

From the time of Constantine onwards we see in the pagan writers a concentration on the values and the ideas of the past. It was these men of late antiquity who put the classical texts into the form in which the early Middle Ages would know them. They were the editors and commentators whom the scholars of the early Middle Ages would study, commentators such as the fourth-century grammarian Donatus (who, incidentally, was a teacher of Jerome) and the Neoplatonist Macrobius. Much, too, of what the early Middle Ages knew about ancient learning came from a fantastic and florid summary written by Martianus Capella, who wrote in the early fifth century. Important as these pagans were, their writings looked backward to the classical past; it was the Christian authors who looked ahead. By far the single biggest bequest the late Roman world made to the medieval was its religion. It is no accident that our words 'culture' and 'cult' share the same root. Late antique intellectual life concentrated more and more in the church and at the imperial court, itself since the days of Constantine an increasingly Christian centre. These were the only institutions which both saw a need for the higher learning and had the resources to support it. It was the Christians who provided answers deemed most useful in solving the problems that troubled intellects in the late Empire, and it was they who wrote the texts that carried those answers into the Middle Ages.

GARDNER HARVEY LIBRARY
Miami University-Middletown
Middletown, Ohio 45042

CHAPTER 2

THE BARBARIAN INVASIONS

Guy Halsall

HISTORIOGRAPHY

The so-called 'barbarian invasions' have a vital role in, and in many respects stand at the beginning of, European history. Almost all national histories in some way or other go back to a group of invading or migrating barbarians: Anglo-Saxons in England, Goths and Lombards in Italy, Franks and Burgundians in France, Visigoths in Spain, or Scots in Scotland. The popularly perceived founders of the national histories of many western countries are those early medieval writers who are deemed to have offered 'national', 'ethnic' histories of these migrating peoples: Bede in England, who wrote an *Ecclesiastical History of the English People* in the 730s, Paul the Deacon in Italy, who wrote his *History of the Lombards* in the 780s, and Isidore of Seville, whose *History of the Goths, Sueves and Vandals* was written in Spain in the early seventh century. Gregory of Tours, author of *Ten Books of Histories* of his own times (the late sixth century), is classed as having written a *History of the Franks.* Although that was in fact the name given to an anonymous seventh-century six-book abbreviation of Gregory's work including only the material to do with Franks, it has nevertheless earned him the title of 'Father of the History of France'.

Most western national consciousness can thus be traced back to notions, however confused, of barbarian invasions or migrations.[1] They are held to have swept away the ancient 'classical' world, the world of Rome, and to have introduced the Dark Ages. This was not always seen as a disaster; far from it, German and English historians in particular have been fond of picturing the barbarians as sweeping away a tired, effete and decadent Mediterranean civilisation and replacing it with a more virile, martial, Nordic one. Even writers who modified the extreme versions of this view still often presented the

[1] For what follows, on the historiography of the barbarian migrations, see the various works of Walter Goffart: (1980), ch. 1; (1989); (1995).

Empire as weak and in decline.[2] French and Italian historians, on the other hand, have tended to see the barbarians as a 'bad thing', destroying a living civilisation, introducing a barbaric Dark Age.[3] Whereas those historians refer to the barbarian invasions in pejorative terms (*les invasions barbares*) German and English historians simply refer to 'migrations', wanderings of peoples, *Völkerwanderungen*. In particular, the Germanic barbarians, who include most of the migrating groups, and are still often seen as unified by some kind of proto-German ethos or nationality, migrate along tortuously winding routes, represented in historical atlases as a spaghetti-like confusion of coloured arrows, to their eventual goals, almost as if these were predestined.

Until recently, historians have agreed on two things: whether they saw them in positive or negative terms, it was the barbarians who put paid to the Roman Empire; and these barbarians were largely 'Germanic'.[4] The fall of the Roman Empire is to be attributed, in however short-term a perspective, to the barbarian invasions (or migrations). This led, in the nineteenth century, to what might be called the 'Germanist' view, which, put bluntly, holds that everything new and different about the fifth, sixth, seventh and later centuries must be attributed to 'Germanic' influence. Consequently, the works of thoroughly Roman writers like Gregory of Tours, Cassiodorus and Venantius Fortunatus were edited in the series of 'Historic Monuments of Germany', *Monumenta Germaniae Historica*.[5] The Germanist view also led to the description of post-Roman law-codes as Germanic law, and, in archaeology, to the new types of rural settlement which replaced the old Roman villas being called 'Germanic', and to new burial forms, like furnished inhumation (with grave-goods), similarly being ascribed to Germanic influence. Changes in urban life, with the shrinking and even abandonment of Roman towns, and the end of classical urbanism were pinned, in a less positive way, on the Germans and either their savage primitive, destructive tendencies, or, alternatively, their noble adherence to more pristine, rural modes of life. The Germans are seen as flooding, or swamping, the provinces in the migrations of whole tribes or nations.[6]

The 'Germanist' view has been countered with the 'Romanist' or 'continuity' view, which holds that the Germanic barbarians created little that was new. In this picture, the migrations are the movements of small warrior elites (and

[2] For example. Delbrück (1980), p. 248. This first appeared in German in 1921. For a recent incarnation of the Germanist view, see Drew (1987).

[3] For an extreme example from just after the First World War, see Boissonade (1927), pp. 14–31. See also Courcelle (1964), who divides his book into parts called 'L'Invasion', 'L'Occupation' and 'La Libération', leaving no doubts as to which then-recent events of French history were conjured up by the study of the invasions of Germanic barbarians.

[4] See, for example, Bury (1926), pp. 2–4. For a more recent example, Heather (1995).

[5] On the *Monumenta*, see Knowles (1962), pp. 63–97.

[6] Settlement forms: Dixon (1982). Burials: Halsall (1995a).

some extreme versions come close to denying that anyone moved at all), and so are unlikely to have been able to bring about such sweeping changes.[7] The administration of the former provinces was essentially that of the Roman Empire, run by Roman provincials for their new barbarian masters;[8] barbarian kingship was largely modelled on imperial Christian Roman ideas;[9] there was continuity of settlement patterns, even if the forms changed; the towns were simply continuing in a process of change which began as early as the third century; and so on. The Romanist argument has even been deployed in Britain, where there is a strongly held common view that the situation was very different from that on the continent.[10]

Although there may be more to be said for the Romanist 'continuity' model than for the Germanist 'catastrophe' view, both models are misleading. There was indeed a great deal of social, economic and political change in the late fourth through to the sixth centuries, but the barbarians cannot be blamed for much of it. As we shall see at the end of this chapter, even controversies over the numbers of the barbarians miss the point of the nature of the changes from Roman provinces to 'barbarian' kingdoms. This chapter will not present a detailed narrative of the barbarian migrations. Instead it offers an overview and interpretation of some of the principal issues which currently engage the attention of historians working on the barbarians and their place in the processes known cumulatively as the 'Fall of Rome'.[11] As such it provides a backdrop against which to set this volume's chapters on the individual 'barbarian' successor states. In particular, it will argue that we should reverse the usual ways of seeing the barbarian migrations and the end of the Roman West. Instead of viewing the end of the Western Roman Empire as the result of the barbarian invasions, we should see the barbarians as being drawn into the politics of an empire already falling apart for quite other reasons; the barbarian migrations were the result of the end of the Western Roman Empire. This chapter will also show that, contrary to commonly held views, Britain cannot be viewed separately from the continent, as something of an aberration or special case: the Anglo-Saxons were no more different from the Franks than the Franks were from the Ostrogoths or the Vandals, and maybe less so.

7 For recent, extremely minimalist views of post-Roman Britain, see Higham (1992); M. E. Jones (1996). For Italy, more sophisticated, but even more minimalist, is Amory (1997).

8 For a study of post-Roman administration emphasising continuity, see Barnwell (1992).

9 The Roman inheritance of post-Roman kingship is best seen in McCormick (1986). See also Wormald, chapter 21 below.

10 Romanist views of Anglo-Saxon England: Barnwell (1997), part IV; Wolfram (1997), ch. 11.

11 For recent works on particular groups of barbarians see, for example, James (1988a); Wolfram (1988); Christie (1994) and Heather (1996). The most recent overview is Wolfram (1997), but see Musset (1975) for a more traditional view. Also Geary (1999); Heather (1999).

WHAT IS A BARBARIAN?

We must, first of all, ask what a barbarian is. The Romans had a reasonably clear answer: in the first instance, it was someone who lived beyond the frontiers of the Empire. There were different kinds of barbarian, based upon the Roman ethnographic tradition and view of geography.[12] To the north, to Roman eyes, were heroic but savage Celts and Germans, living in rural communities and ignorant of urban life; to the south were cunning, slippery Africans or Ethiopians; to the north-east were 'Scythians', nomadic peoples who, as the Romans saw it, lived on horseback; to the east were the Persians, cruel and despotic, but nevertheless with a sort of civilisation (Ammianus Marcellinus, the great fourth-century historian, in fact never refers to the Sasanid Persians as barbarians at all); and finally the Arabs, wild and debauched.

This world-view was bolstered by a sort of geo-biology: in the frozen north, further, as the Romans saw it, from the sun, blood was thicker and was thus drawn down through the body, so Germans were strong and brave, but a bit dim, and with no idea of tactics or strategy; in Africa, closer to the sun, blood was thin and drawn up to the head, so Africans were cowardly but clever and treacherous. Of course, in the middle, the temperate zone, where the Romans were, things were just right, as they were in the socio-political sense too.[13] All Romans, however, were not the same. Roman ethnography included stereotypical views of the regions of the Empire too, so that the Gauls were rather braver than the Italians, and so on, because they lived further north, and were descended from the Celts.[14] This is a point we must come back to, as it raises the issue of what a Roman really was; ethnographic stereotyping was not simply a case of Romans inside the Empire, versus barbarians outside.

Nevertheless, this world-view, in which they put themselves at the centre, surrounded by barbarians with stereotypical attributes, provided the Romans with a ready-made and very varied source of ideas about barbarians, which could then be deployed in rhetoric. This is important. It is often forgotten that when Roman writers talked about barbarians, they were not engaged in a dialogue with the barbarians. It was not a case of saying '*we* are like this, but *you* are like that', nor was Roman ethnography a simple matter of neutral reportage. The Roman idea of the barbarian was essentially a rhetorical device employed against other Romans.[15] The barbarian, by simple virtue of not being Roman,

[12] Balsdon (1979) gives a useful, basic introductory survey.

[13] This Roman idea is found in Vitruvius, *De Architectura* VI.1; Pliny the Elder, *Natural History* II.80.cxc; Vegetius, *Epitoma de Rei Militari* I.2. It differs significantly from the Greek view of these matters, originating with Hippocrates, *Airs, Waters, Places*, 12–24.

[14] For example, Ammianus Marcellinus' comments on the Gauls in *Res Gestae* XV.12.

[15] This interpretation is not yet common in late antique studies, but for similar treatments of earlier Roman and Greek attitudes see Hall (1989) and Dench (1995).

could be deployed in any and all contexts, as an 'other', to make whatever point was at hand. A Roman general could be given extra praise for a victory over the barbarians by stressing the wild, savage bravery of the latter, and their huge numbers – despite, or perhaps because of, the fact that it is extremely unlikely that barbarian armies ever outnumbered Roman ones. On the other hand the Romans could be criticised by deploying the barbarian figure. Tacitus' famous *Germania*, a work of the first century, is in fact a lengthy critique of Roman society. Sometimes Tacitus makes his point by extolling a 'noble savage' view of the German, which is, in a way, a lament for what the Romans had (as Tacitus thought) lost on the road to civilisation. Elsewhere, however, Tacitus portrays the Germans and their behaviour as typically barbaric, warning the Romans to mend their ways lest they acquire these traits or lose their superiority over the barbarians. Despite this, some historians and archaeologists continue to suppose that Tacitus' work is a mine of facts about 'Germanic' society. Positive barbarian imagery continued to be used by late Roman writers. Salvian, the priest of Marseilles in the 440s, could savage Roman society for being less just, less fair, more sinful, even than that of the barbarians. How bad can things be, asked Salvian, when people flee to the barbarians because they can be freer under them than under the Romans. The same point was made by Orosius in his *Seven Books of History against the Pagans*, and St Augustine could say, in *The City of God*, that the barbarians who sacked Rome in 410 were more merciful, less savage, than the Romans had been to their defeated enemies.[16] Classical ethnography provided a wide array of ammunition in the form of stock phrases. One could discuss the good or bad points of urban versus rural life by reference to the stereotypical non-urban 'free' German; the good/bad points of monarchy by reference to the Persians; the good/bad points of settled agricultural life by reference to the Scythians; sexual morality or family life by reference to the Arabs, and so on and so forth. The barbarian is therefore a floating category, difficult, indeed never intended, to be pinned down. This makes it a mistake to try to find out a particular writer's 'view of the barbarians'. The barbarians could be presented in many 'positive' ways without affecting the fact that, as Romans, these writers still viewed the barbarian with a certain terror as a thing untamed. This point is driven home when one considers, as we will below, the use of the word *barbarus* in post-Roman sources, when the barbarians actually controlled the Western Empire.

So what, then, was 'a Roman'? If the barbarian was only really defined by being something that was not Roman, and if Roman writers like Ammianus Marcellinus could hold equally stereotypical views of the inhabitants of

[16] Salvian, *On the Government of God*, Book v, esp. v.5–11; Orosius, *Seven Books of History against the Pagans* vii.41.7 Augustine, *City of God* i, 1–5.

particular imperial provinces, then what was it that made Roman-ness? This is equally difficult to pin down, but by the late Roman period it does not seem to have had very much any more to do with the simple fact of being a Roman citizen, let alone to do with living inside the empire's boundaries. It seems that what Roman-ness meant – the historian's term *Romanitas* is not common in our sources, and may only appear in the third century AD[17] – hinged around an idea of *civilitas*, a certain mode of behaviour, and above all ideas of education, of freedom and of living according to the law. In Roman eyes, barbarians had no law, either that which was imposed from above, or that which they imposed upon themselves from within, in other words, self-restraint. Thus they were doubly unfree, slaves to their rulers, slaves to their passions. Barbarians were simply unruly. That Roman-ness was culturally, rather than linguistically, defined meant that Roman could be as fluid a category as barbarian. Thus a barbarian could behave more like the Romans than the Romans, and Romans could be more barbaric than the barbarians. Hence Salvian's complaint that people think it better to live in freedom under the barbarians than in slavery under the Romans. Roman usurpers or rebels were often classified as barbarians; we find that barbarian ancestry is brought out when someone is opposed to the central, legitimate rule of the emperor.[18]

The other opposite of rule and law was *latrocinium* (banditry), and banditry shaded imperceptibly into barbarism in Roman ideology. Within the Empire, areas which were governed with difficulty, such as the mountainous areas of the Alps, the Pyrenees, the North African Atlas or Isauria in Asia Minor, were all too easily associated with barbarians. One could therefore be labelled as having cast off Roman-ness, not by leaving the Empire, nor by joining barbarian invaders, but by the perceived rejection of certain norms. Theoretically, the Roman Empire could have become barbarised without the barbarians conquering a square metre of imperial territory. This seems to have been what the sixth-century East Roman historian Zosimus thought had happened.[19] People within the Roman Empire could behave in ways which were seen as barbaric; people from outside the Empire, from the *Barbaricum*, as it came to be called in the fourth century, could behave in ways which exemplified the truly Roman. In sum, you did not have to be a barbarian to be barbarian, although no one could deny that it helped.

[17] *Romanitas*: The earliest usage may be Tertullian, *De Pallio* IV. For statements of the barbarians' inability to live according to the law, see Pliny the Elder, *Natural History* II.80.CXC; Orosius, *Against the Pagans* VII.43.4–6.

[18] Compare for example the treatment of the half-Vandal Stilicho before his downfall, in Claudian, *De Bello Gothico*, and after his excution in Orosius, *Against the Pagans* VII.37.1 and Rutilius Namatianus, *On His Return* II, lines 41–60.

[19] Zosimus, *New History* II, 7.

These fluid categories of Roman and barbarian bring us to the subject of ethnic identity. It can be seen that Romanity as an ethnic identity was fluid, and not based upon any inherent, objectively measurable factors; it was a state of mind. A general of 'barbarian' origin could be very consciously brought into the Roman fold, and hailed as a Roman, and Romans could be denied their Roman-ness. Within the Empire, in certain circumstances provincial identities, Gallic or Pannonian for example, could transcend the general Roman identity in dealings with 'Romans' from other areas. Ethnicity is multi-layered, flexible, cognitive (a state of mind) and situational (deployed in situations when it is advantageous).[20] All these points are crucial to understanding how the provinces, and provincials, of the Western Empire became, for instance, Frankish, Gothic or Anglo-Saxon.

THE LATE ROMAN EMPIRE IN THE WEST

The Roman Empire suffered a series of set-backs between 235 and 284, political crises, civil and external wars, and socio-economic disorders which are cumulatively known as the 'third-century crisis', although this crisis appeared at different times with different severity in different regions, and in some not at all.[21] The nature of the 'late' Roman Empire, which emerged from this 'crisis' under the reforming emperors Diocletian and Constantine, is dealt with in the previous chapter of this volume but we need to consider certain aspects of it here, in order to understand fully the nature of the migrations. We shall see that the relationships between local leadership and society and the central government form a complex web in which the Germanic warbands became enmeshed. This is the context for the Germanic barbarians' eventual domination of the West.

The Roman Empire, first, was a big place, extending from Hadrian's Wall to the Sahara, and from the Atlantic to the Euphrates. This huge mass, in crude terms of size, is also hugely diverse, containing desert, pre-desert, mountains, marshlands, forests and so on. Physical geography cuts western Europe into innumerable small regions, whether in mountainous zones, like the Apennines, running down the spine of Italy and cutting the west off from the east, or by high plateaux like the Massif Central in France or the Meseta in Spain, or by major rivers like the Loire or the Rhône, which run across lines of communication as well as forming others. How could a pre-industrial state, with no rapid forms of transport or communication and thus little way of collecting information

[20] On ethnicity, the best recent introduction to the debate is by Eriksen (1993).

[21] Millar (1981), pp. 239–48, gives the best introduction to the 'third-century crisis', but see also Drinkwater (1983), pp. 212–27, and Gerberding, chapter 1 above.

quickly, manage to govern such an enormous and diverse area? How could a huge empire hold together, when the emperor could hardly discover what was happening, and where local communities could deceive him for their own purposes? Gibbon said that the peculiar thing about the Roman Empire was not that it fell but that it lasted so long; as he might be rephrased, it is the early Roman period, not the late, which is unusual and requires explanation. The early Empire held together remarkably well and was run by a minuscule bureaucracy, because, within local communities across the West, competition for local authority was played out by subscribing to Roman culture: by taking part in Roman local government; by competing, within municipalities, in building Roman urban forms; by demonstrating status by building Roman villas; by trying to achieve citizenship. Economically, prestigious goods were made in or near the core of the Empire and travelled out to the provinces; the Empire formed, at least until the mid-second century, a more or less coherent economic system. So the Empire was bound together by the active and eager participation of myriad local communities in its cultural, political and economic life.[22]

After the third century this was no longer the case. The Roman world fragmented economically. Whilst the Mediterranean world still clung together as an economic system, manufacture of most of the artefacts of Romanity passed out into the provinces, creating a series of regional economies.[23] After the third-century economic difficulties and a reversion to frequent barter and to taxation and payment in kind, this was exaggerated. After 212 and Caracalla's granting of universal citizenship, even Roman-ness was no longer something to be fought for. The situation wherein local communities actively wanted to be brought into Rome's orbit, because of the local political and social advantages which that brought, had passed. Historians have long noted the expense of being a late Roman *curialis* (town councillor), the subject of much moaning and wringing of hands by contemporaries. Yet it is unlikely that the burdens of curial office were much greater than before. The key difference was that, earlier, people had been willing to pay the price. Now the rewards were no longer worth it. The physical geographical and regional diversity of the West could begin to rear its head again.[24]

[22] On the early Roman Empire and its administration, Millar (1981); Levick (1985); Wells (1992); Lintott (1993).

[23] See Loseby, chapter 22 below.

[24] On the late Roman Empire the best and most detailed survey remains A. H. M. Jones (1964), which should be updated with Cameron (1993a); (1993b). For regional surveys illustrating the points just made, see Lepelley (1979); Wightman (1985), pp. 219–311; Potter (1987), pp. 192–209; Esmonde Cleary (1988); Keay (1988), pp. 172–217.

Early Roman urban monuments were put up by local municipalities or local magnates, as competitive gestures of good-will and generosity to their community, and so private money went into public buildings. In the later period, however, such building dried up, and that which was done, and it tended to be maintenance rather than new building, was put up not by local officials but by representatives of the imperial bureaucracy, using public money. Private money went into private building, town-houses and rural villas. As is described elsewhere, the late Roman bureaucracy was enormous – 25,000–35,000 people manning a labyrinth of posts each of which brought a social honorific title and certain privileges, and the posts usually held only for a short time.[25] If you waited, your turn would come round. In some parts of the West, the dependence upon imperial office and patronage may have been by far the most important factor in ordering local society, as in northern Gaul and lowland Britain, where there does not seem to be much evidence of huge *latifundia* or aristocratic estates. Elsewhere, in southern Gaul, Italy and Spain, large estates created great wealth and a ruling social stratum less heavily dependent upon participating in imperial government to maintain their position in society. Such people still competed with their equals to order their peer group. This local variety is crucial.

The Empire's difficulties can be summed up by one story. Fourth-century Roman North Africa was a prosperous area of the world, something which often surprises modern students. Here was played out the tale of Count Romanus.[26] The story is unlikely to be as simple as it appears in Ammianus Marcellinus' account, but the outlines of the case are as follows. In 363–364 the inhabitants of Lepcis Magna, in Tripolitania, were harassed by raids by the Austoriani, a local tribe, after one of the latter was burnt to death, apparently for brigandage. The citizens called upon Romanus, the Count of Africa, who came with his troops but demanded large sums in provisions, and 4000 camels. These the locals refused, so Romanus left the area and its citizens to the Austoriani. The Tripolitanians then sent envoys to the emperor Valentinian I to complain. Romanus, however, had a relative at court and tried to have the affair heard by him. As it was, the emperor heard the envoys' complaint and a defence by Romanus' supporters, believed neither and promised a full inquiry. This, however, was delayed, and meanwhile the North Africans were again the victims of serious attacks, which Romanus allegedly did nothing to avert. Valentinian was unhappy when the news of these attacks reached him, and sent a tribune called Palladius to report on the situation, and pay the African army.

[25] See Gerberding, chapter 1 above.

[26] Ammianus Marcellinus, *Res Gestae* XXVII.6; with comment in Matthews (1989), pp. 281–2, 383–7.

Romanus then talked his officers into lodging the bulk of their pay with Palladius. When two local townsmen showed Palladius the damage done and the extent of Romanus' negligence, Romanus threatened to report Palladius to Valentinian as corrupt, and as having pocketed the money entrusted to him. To save himself, Palladius made a pact with Romanus, and both reported to Valentinian that the Tripolitanians had no grounds for complaint. The two townsmen who had notified Palladius were sentenced to having their tongues cut out for lying, but fled. Valentinian, wholly deceived in the affair and not lenient at the best of times, also ordered the execution of the previous ambassadors from the province, and the provincial governor, although, again, one of the accused managed to hide, and disappeared. Eventually a number of the guilty parties (in Ammianus' account) were driven to suicide, and some of Romanus' accomplices were executed by Count Theodosius when he led the military expedition in 373 which finally quelled the unrest of the North African tribes. Romanus, it seems, despite a short spell in prison, got away with it.

It has rightly been said that there is much more to this story than the simple apportioning of blame, and that Romanus' side of the story was probably rather different. The saga, nevertheless, does illustrate graphically the difficulty that emperors had in finding out what was going on 'on the ground' in their huge empire, and how this difficulty could be exploited by local individuals. The story of Romanus, rather than being a simple tale of corruption and deception, is actually a clear illustration of how the late Roman Empire held together. All the local competitors for power strove to share in the imperial administration, to obtain imperial legitimation and backing, so that they could exploit it. They also sought access to the emperor and the power he could bestow, to govern their localities. The late Roman period saw a reversal of the earlier system: in competing for local power one no longer asked 'what can I do for the Empire?' but rather 'what can the Empire do for me?' In the late Empire, the hundreds of local, self-governing cells which made up the Empire no longer clung together; instead they were bound together by an enormous imperial bureaucracy overlying local society, a bureaucracy which was essentially a huge patronage system which needed to be managed effectively or the Empire would no longer be able to do anything for the locals. Otherwise all those local cells would spring apart. Put another way, in the early Empire all roads led *to* Rome; in the late Empire all roads led *from* Rome. Fourth-century western emperors managed this situation very well. As is shown in the previous chapter, they positioned themselves on the frontiers of the Empire, on the Rhine at Trier, or along the Danube, where they could supervise their patronage and actively incorporate the provincials – Pannonians under Valentinian, Gauls under Gratian – in the running of the Empire. Hold the Rhine and you hold

Gaul; hold Gaul and you hold the West. They knew that. But the system was precarious.

BARBARIAN SOCIETY AND POLITICS IN THE FOURTH CENTURY

We often gain the impression of greater pressure on the frontiers in the late Roman period. This pressure has traditionally been explained by supposing an increase in barbarian numbers, through population growth. Sometimes, we are given the impression that the Germanic barbarians were driven by a sort of primeval surge towards the Mediterranean.[27] Another common explanation sees the pressure in terms of a 'domino theory'. In the third quarter of the fourth century, a people known as the Huns are first referred to by Roman writers, and are often thought to have migrated from the Far East.[28] The Huns are thought to have 'pushed' the Goths into the Roman Empire, and to have 'pushed' other Germanic tribes who in turn 'pushed' those in front of them, and so on until the Roman frontier was swamped by fleeing Germanic barbarians.

Instead of these rather dramatic accounts, the impression of increasing pressure on the Roman frontiers is probably best explained by political developments amongst the barbarians themselves. In the third century, as the Roman Empire was undergoing its so-called third-century crisis, changes were under way in *Barbaricum*. In place of, or more probably on top of, the myriad local tribes listed in Tacitus' works, there appeared a series of larger confederacies, which all have classic confederation names: the Alamanni ('All Men') in the south-west of Germany; the Franks ('the Fierce People') along the middle and lower Rhine; the Saxons in the north of Germany; the Picts ('the Painted Men') in the north of Britain; and the Goths ('the Men') in and around the eastern Carpathians and the lower Danube. In North Africa and Arabia other large tribal confederacies appeared. These more powerful confederacies could exert greater pressure upon the Romans.

How had these confederations come into being and how were they ruled? The first question is difficult to answer, but the Romans probably had much to do with it. It has recently been suggested that the Alamanni were a Roman creation, set up to occupy the area between upper Rhine and upper Danube abandoned during the later third-century civil wars.[29] It has been argued, even more radically, that these new 'peoples' were largely talked into existence by Roman writers, puffing up Roman imperial work and presence on the frontiers; inventing the 'barbarian threat' in order to justify the imperial activity which,

[27] Pirenne (1925), pp. 5–8. Goffart (1980), pp. 11–17, discusses this imagery in some detail.

[28] Most famously Ammianus Marcellinus, *Res Gestae* XXXI.2.i–xii.

[29] Nuber (1993).

as intimated earlier, largely held the West together.[30] There may be something in this; the barbarians, even the confederacies, could hardly pose a serious military threat to the existence of the Roman Empire, with an army of, it has been estimated, over 400,000 men. It has also recently been argued that these confederacies hardly existed at all, and that there was little change from the early Roman system.[31] This argument is unconvincing, partly because it leaves us with no option but to explain the fall of the Empire by increased pressure on the frontiers, and it is difficult to see that increased pressure if things were effectively the same as in Tacitus' day. A more convincing treatment of the same evidence shows that the common fragmentation of the confederacies was the result of Roman political hard work beyond the frontier. When the Romans were distracted, usually by civil war, the Franks or the Alamans threw up greater leaders and formed large, effective confederations. Romans had to strive to make sure that this did not usually happen.[32]

How did the barbarians rule their kingdoms? If the emperors had problems, even though they had a taxation system, an army of 400,000 and a 35,000-strong bureaucracy, how much worse were the problems for barbarian kings? There were a number of options. A combination of the war-leader king, with short-lived but widespread powers, paired with the sacral king, with longer-lasting but perhaps more circumscribed areas of authority, is often cited. The evidence for the formal existence of these types of kingship is, however, very insecure. Nevertheless, both forms of rulership seem inherently plausible. The sacral, or religious, king, by controlling certain religious aspects of life, bound local communities to his authority in order to participate in ritual, and oversee the necessities of life. The war-leader would protect or help defend communities in times of warfare. Obviously, the latter type of power existed only with difficulty beyond times of crisis and could be removed if things went badly. The fourth-century Burgundians possibly had a combination of these two types of ruler, though again the evidence is questionable. Another basis for overlordship was arbitration. Local communities might be incorporated into a larger polity by appeal to an outside, higher power who could arbitrate, or adjudicate, in local disputes, with both parties accepting the judgement. Thus, the fourth-century leaders of the Gothic confederation on the lower Danube are referred to by the Romans as 'Judges'. Elsewhere, as in the Frankish and Alamannic confederacies we see many petty kings, ruled occasionally, when the Romans lost their grip, by an over-king.[33]

30 Drinkwater (1996). 31 Elton (1996), pp. 15–44. 32 Heather (1994a).

33 Germanic kingship, Wallace-Hadrill (1971), ch. 1; James (1989) and Wormald, chapter 21 below. Burgundians: Ammianus Marcellinus, *Res Gestae* XXVIII.5.xiv, but for a cautionary note against acceptance of Ammianus' statement at face value, see Wood (1977), p. 27. Goths: Wolfram (1975). Alamans: the *locus classicus* is Ammianus Marcellinus, *Res Gestae* XVI.12.xxiii–xxvi.

What kept these kings in power? One thing was wealth: wealth provided by the Romans. Roman artefacts were much prized in *Barbaricum*, as they had been by Celtic kings on the eve of Roman conquest. If leaders could control the acquisition and distribution of such items, through a system of gift exchange, they had a powerful means of maintaining loyalty throughout scattered communities, especially if they could circulate these goods amongst rival local families and play them off against each other. The Romans could pay out large sums to their friends across the frontier, and these gifts could play a big part in the creation of barbarian political power. This can be detected in what historians and archaeologists call 'Free Germany', north of the Roman frontier on the Rhine, and in north Britain. So, as stated earlier, the Romans may indeed have played a major part in the creation of the new confederacies, in the payment of large tributes to barbarian leaders to keep them quiet in periods of Roman civil war, as was frequent in the third and also the fourth centuries, something which helped barbarian paramount kings to appear when the Romans were distracted.[34] One could also maintain power via trade. Thus, in the late Roman period, we see the creation of trading stations beyond the frontier, as most dramatically at Lundeborg in Fyn, which was paired with a high-status settlement just inland at Gudme. Another such site is known on the other side of the Jutland peninsula at Dankirke.[35]

Such barbarian power could be impressive. Just over the frontier we perceive rulers who were able to control manpower and so construct large-scale defensive sites, bringing together skilled craftsmen to produce their own prestige items and symbols of authority, which could be used to support political power. Interestingly, these items were often based on Roman badges of office; the vocabulary of power was the same on both sides of the frontier. Along the upper Rhine frontier, in the Alamannic region we see a number of *Hohensiedlungen* (high settlements; hill-forts), which reveal high-quality craft-specialisation and manufacture. These may be paralleled in north Britain by sites like Traprain Law. Even in low-lying areas we can find similar prestige sites, such as at Gennep, in the Frankish areas just south of the Rhine. Also in the Frankish lands evidence has come to light of fairly large-scale, organised iron-working.[36]

Around the edges of the Empire larger and potentially powerful kingdoms were being put together. Some depended heavily upon relationships with Rome, but it may be that by the end of the fourth century some rulers just beyond the frontier could maintain quite independent and efficient systems of government. It may be that the Germans further into 'Free Germany' were

[34] Heather (1994a).

[35] Gudme: Nielsen (1994) and Hedeager, chapter 18 below; Dankirke: Hansen (1989).

[36] On *Hohensiedlungen*, see, for example, Steuer (1994); (1997). On Traprain Law, Feachem (1955–56); on Gennep, Heidinga (1994). Iron-working, see Groenewoudt and van Nie (1995).

more dependent upon Roman gifts, paid to help them keep the frontier kings in check. The role of Roman authority in local German society can also be seen in the frequency with which Roman badges of office, like belt-sets, were used in grave-deposits in the large cremation cemeteries of the Saxon homelands, an argument which may very well apply equally to certain brooch-styles.[37] In sum, barbarian politics were played for high stakes, stakes very often raised by the Romans themselves. There were strong barbarian kings on the frontier who could increase their authority over their neighbours, but there was also a considerable extent to which barbarian politics depended upon the continued effective functioning of the Roman Empire, just as provincial Roman society did. What would happen if the Empire ceased to function effectively?

THE COLLAPSE OF THE WESTERN EMPIRE

The key date in understanding the barbarian migrations and the collapse of the Western Empire is not 376, when a large number of Gothic refugees, from the political turmoil in their homeland of which the Huns formed a focus, migrated into the Balkan provinces. Nor is it even 378, when those Goths inflicted a disastrous defeat on the eastern Roman army at the battle of Adrianople. It has recently and persuasively been argued that the significance of Adrianople has been greatly overplayed. By the early 380s the Goths had been contained, defeated and settled within the Balkans, in much the same way as innumerable other peoples had been before.[38]

The decisive date is 388 and the suppression of the 'usurper' emperor Magnus Maximus. After Maximus, no significant western emperor (we may exclude some shadowy and short-lived usurpers) ever went north of Lyons. The defeat of Maximus' western army by the eastern troops of Theodosius I, especially when coupled with the even bloodier slaughter of western regiments, again by Theodosius' men, during the usurpation of Eugenius in 394, was catastrophic for the defence of the region, and it is difficult to see any real imperial activity in northern Gaul or Britain after Maximus' death. Aristocrats fled south; the *Notitia Dignitatum*, the official list of Roman offices, shows that by 418 a number of north Gallic offices had been withdrawn to the south of Gaul; the Gallic capital withdrew from Trier to Arles, probably in 395; a council of Gaul set up in the early fifth century did not represent the north Gallic provinces. The Empire ceased to be able to make itself felt in northern Gaul and Britain, areas where it seems that well-managed imperial patronage was essential for the maintenance of local order, and the results were dramatic.

37 Roman material in cremations in Lower Saxony: Böhme (1974).

38 Burns (1994), pp. 1–91.

Archaeology in these regions reveals the rapid collapse of villa life, of Roman towns and, in Britain, of Roman industries (in Gaul such industries stagnate but do not die out). Cemetery evidence attests to a more insecure command of local authority. North of the Loire, Roman civilisation crashed within the space of two generations.[39]

This affected the barbarians too. On the last day of 406, Gaul was invaded by a huge army of barbarians, not from the frontier kingdoms, whose kings seem in any case to have been further bolstered by the Romans as they withdrew from the Rhine, but from people further inside *Barbaricum*: Vandals, Sueves, Alans, followed by Burgundians. These were probably the groups wherein political power was more heavily dependent upon gifts from the Romans; the end of such gifts, combined perhaps with the appearance of a new source of political power from the east, the Huns, forced some groups out of power and into the Empire, to seek their fortunes.[40] Eventually some of these were to found the Suevic kingdom in north-western Spain, perhaps by treaty with the Romans, and the Vandal kingdom of North Africa, probably the only barbarian kingdom to be created more or less entirely by military conquest from the Roman Empire.

Inside the Empire, the civil wars of the 390s had thrown up another dangerous political grouping based around a band of barbarian descent: the Goths of Alaric. This group, dissatisfied after the suppression of Eugenius, and badly treated by the likes of Stilicho, adviser to Honorius the child emperor, sacked Rome in 410. They were eventually settled by the Romans in Aquitaine, where they established their kingdom. The Gothic settlement in Aquitaine has been the subject of much debate.[41] Why settle the Goths so far inside Gaul? The answer is not so complex. After the early fifth century, the effective frontier of Gaul was not the Rhine, but the Loire, so settlements like that of the Goths, like, *a fortiori*, that of the Burgundians in Savoy, and like that of the Alans in Orléans, can be seen as effectively frontier settlements.[42] Northern Gaul and Britain were left to run themselves.

Here we can return to the differences within provincial Roman society. In Aquitaine, where local society was more easily ordered without Roman patronage, the hand-over to the Goths was managed more or less smoothly, at least before 450. Here the same families stayed in power; and perhaps more

39 On withdrawal to the south: *Notitia Dignitatum* Occ. xii.27. On the Council of the Gauls: Loseby (1997), p. 52. Archaeological evidence of collapse in Britain: Esmonde Cleary (1989), pp. 131–61. On north Gaul: Halsall (1995b), pp. 219–28, 249–51.

40 Heather (1995).

41 Burns (1994), pp. 247–79; Thompson (1956).

42 On the nature of the barbarian settlements, see now the judicious summary and interpretation of Wood (1998).

than anywhere else in the west, Roman society and culture continued.[43] In the north, the collapse of effective imperial rule brought anarchy. There was no neat transfer of power; and there were no independent, local means of establishing anew an effective social-political hierarchy. Into the political vacuum were sucked new authorities. In Gaul the Franks and the Alamans spread their power, often hand-in-hand with local Roman military leaders to whom they gave their support, down to the Loire and the Alps.[44]

In Britain the chieftains, perhaps kings, of the western highland regions had possibly been given authority rather like that of the frontier German kings (certainly their hill-fort power-bases are uncannily similar to Alamannic *Hohensiedlungen*). The distribution of late fourth-century Roman military equipment covers only the lowland provinces, so it is possible that northern and western Britain had been abandoned by the Roman government in the late fourth century, perhaps under Magnus Maximus. If this was the case then local defence may have been given over to local leaders; Maximus certainly features strongly in the origin legends of the Welsh dynasties. It may well have been these upland rulers whose power, less affected by the Roman withdrawal, was sucked out into the lowlands. It is not unlikely that by the later fifth century Frankish power, too, had spread across the Channel into Kent. This is the context for the dimly remembered, semi-legendary Romano-British rulers called Ambrosius Aurelianus and Vortigern, perhaps even Arthur. It is also the context for the account of the invitation of Saxon allies into eastern England, perhaps north of the Thames estuary, rather than in Kent (although it was the kings of Kent who appropriated the story), and for the expansion of Anglo-Saxon, English authority westwards across the lowlands, in competition with that of the west British kings.[45]

In northern Gaul, where things were remarkably similar to those in lowland Britain, by about 500 the stakes were so high that the competitors for power had been reduced by internal violence and external warfare to two major power-blocks: the Franks in the north and south-west, and the Burgundians in the south-east. The same picture is easily as plausible for England as the currently fashionable model of fragmentation of the area into many tiny kingdoms.[46] A third alternative, where local social hierarchies were sufficiently established for the locals to continue to govern themselves even where Roman power just evaporated, as in northern Gaul and Britain, may be demonstrated in Spain.

[43] Stroheker (1948); Mathisen (1993). [44] James (1988a), pp. 67–71; (1988b).

[45] Distribution of late fourth-century Roman military metalwork in Britain: Böhme (1986), p. 492. Magnus Maximus, as 'Macsen Gwledig', in Welsh genealogies and other semi-legendary traditions: Alcock (1971), pp. 96–8. Post-Roman hill-forts: Rahtz (1982–83); Alcock (1988); (1992). Archaeology and the invitation of Saxon allies: Chadwick-Hawkes (1989).

[46] The current model is most clearly expressed by Bassett (1989).

There, the evidence suggests that local aristocrats continued to run their local city-districts themselves, independently of either Roman or barbarian rulers, perhaps until the later sixth century.[47] The processes whereby the western provinces became independent kingdoms were, therefore, not simply the result of large-scale barbarian migrations flooding over the provinces. In some ways we might be better off going back to the term 'invasion', to describe military political take-over by smaller groups of warriors. Sometimes, in some regions, like the Rhineland and eastern England, these warrior-bands were followed by larger numbers of followers, wives and children, but more often the barbarians took power when their leaders became a focus for local provincial society and politics. It is by looking at this that this chapter will end.

LOCAL SOCIETY, ETHNICITY AND THE BARBARIANS

By 500 AD all the Roman provinces of the West had become barbarian kingdoms: the Franks and Burgundians in Gaul, the Ostrogoths in Italy, the Sueves and the Visigoths in Spain, the Vandals in North Africa, the Anglo-Saxons and the Britons in Britain. Ultimately this had stemmed not from huge military attacks and the outright conquest of territory from the Roman Empire, but from a break-down of Roman political structures in the last quarter of the fourth century, which exposed the weakness of Roman rule at the local level.

In areas where everything had hinged upon the presence of the Roman state, there was a dramatic collapse, and people sought new sources of local power. By *c.*500, although many Roman idioms of power persisted, people now also demonstrated their authority with material culture, which directly referred to non-Roman, barbarian sources, and especially to the Danubian Gotho-Hunnic culture of Attila's short-lived empire. The Frankish king Childeric, who died some time around 480, was buried with Roman symbols like his official brooch and seal-ring, but his grave also contained gold-and-garnet ornament of Danubian inspiration.[48] The fourth-century Roman Empire had depended for its further existence upon being able to continue to provide the backing for power at the local level. After 388 it lost, and never thereafter regained, its ability to provide this, so people looked elsewhere. Some barbarian warbands were inside the Empire and could provide alternative foci, especially

[47] Documentary evidence for the military capabilities of Spanish aristocrats: Hydatius, *Chronicle* 81[91], 179[186]; John of Biclaro, *Chronicle* 36, 47; Isidore of Seville, *History of the Kings of the Goths*, 45. For discussion, Collins (1980); (1983), pp. 44–5; Thompson (1976); (1977) and see also Barbero and Loring, chapter 7 below. Archaeologically this seems to be manifest by the continuous occupation of large palatial villas through the fifth and well into the sixth centuries. For a summary, see Keay (1988), pp. 202–17.

[48] Childeric's grave: James (1988a), pp. 58–64, and Halsall (1995a).

when granted the government of particular provinces; other foci were provided by strong barbarian kings on the frontier who had the power to expand into the northern provinces, and could equally provide support for local authority when no alternatives existed.

We must put the provincials back into the history of the end of the Empire and the creation of the barbarian kingdoms. It will no longer do to see them either as passive and helpless or, as A. H. M. Jones, the great historian of the late Roman Empire, thought,[49] as indifferent observers of the changes from Roman to barbarian political authority. Nor will it do to see senatorial aristocrats in southern Gaul, Spain or Italy taking office with the barbarians for the simple purpose of gaining protection. Some Spanish aristocrats tried, and admittedly failed, to hold the Pyrenees against the Vandals in the early 400s, but showed that they could raise armed forces.[50] Southern Gallic aristocrats led military contingents raised from their lands both against the Goths and for them, forming an important component of their armies. In southern Spain, such aristocrats maintained political independence for many decades,[51] so mere protection cannot provide the explanation. In the southern provinces the explanation must be that the new rulers provided what these local aristocrats had had for a long time, and what after 388 they were threatened with losing, that is, access to the centre of political power. The incomers provided the means whereby senatorial aristocrats could maintain their standing *vis-à-vis* their peers, as well as retain their supremacy within their localities. This supremacy was also importantly maintained by the appropriation of ecclesiastical authority, as is well known, but the non-ecclesiastical, military or bureaucratic options were numerically far more significant and have been unduly neglected by historians.[52] In 507 the Franks defeated the Visigoths at the battle of 'Vouille',[53] and within a decade or so had driven them definitively from their Aquitanian kingdom. This led to the southern Gallic aristocrats' removal from the centre of political power, but they soon sought a new one, taking service with northern Frankish kings in order to keep their options open.

In other regions the appeal to barbarian outsiders to maintain power at much more local levels, as in northern Gaul and Britain, was even more necessary. Here, people widely adopted the ethnic identity of the newcomers, as they did, after the political chaos of the mid-sixth century, in the Iberian peninsula.

49 Jones (1964), pp. 1058–64.

50 Aristocrats holding the Pyrenean passes: Orosius, *Against the Pagans* VII.40.5–10.

51 See n. 47, above, and Barbero and Loring, chapter 7 below.

52 Heather (1994b), pp. 177–97.

53 See Gerberding (1987), p. 41, for the suggestion that the battle of *Campus Vogladensis* took place, not at Vouille, as usually proposed, but at Voulon.

By 700, to all intents and purposes, everyone north of the Loire was a Frank, everyone in the south-east was a Burgundian, everyone in Spain was a Goth; everyone in lowland Britain was some sort of Anglo-Saxon; you had to go to Italy to find Romans. Where had the Romans gone? This was a problem even in 700; to explain the Romans' apparent disappearance, Frankish and Anglo-Saxon writers had to invent stories of mass slaughter and expulsion of native Romans, although the problem was doubly serious in Gaul where they had to explain how the Romans had managed to teach the Franks Latin first.[54]

We saw at the beginning of this chapter that the categories of Roman and barbarian were fluid. In the post-Roman centuries this could be graphically illustrated. In Ostrogothic Italy, the Gothic rulers were almost never referred to as barbarians; barbarians were other foreigners, even other Goths! On the other hand, in the Burgundian kingdom, the label barbarian could be actively appropriated by the Burgundians to describe themselves. In Gaul, the Roman/barbarian dichotomy was turned to describe Catholic Christian as opposed to heretics or pagans. By the eighth century a bored Bavarian scribe could even turn the old attitudes on their head and write (in Latin!) 'Romans are stupid; Bavarians are wise.'[55]

The new political identities of the Goths, Franks, Burgundians, Angles or Saxons could hence be adopted without much disgrace. This was particularly so in that it was the military elites of these people, the armed warriors, who called themselves Goths, Saxons or whatever, in the new kingdoms, and who held the military and political power. As further chapters will show, there was frequently a bipartite division of labour: barbarians fought; Romans paid taxes, so becoming a barbarian could bring with it tax exemption. In the post-Roman legal codes the 'barbarian' element of the population was often given legal privilege, another reason to adopt a barbarian ethnic identity. Even Gregory of Tours, a senatorial south Gallic aristocrat, had a maternal great uncle called Gundulf, a barbarian name perhaps associated with the fact that Gundulf had taken service in the Austrasian Frankish court. Returning to local communities, we can see that the adoption of a new ethnic identity could be important in striving for authority and power against rivals, especially in situations where people were looking for new sources of authority.[56]

[54] For example Bede, *HE* I, esp. I, 34. A marginal comment to a ninth-century manuscript of the *Liber Historiae Francorum* adds to its eighth-century account the fact that the Romans were exterminated after teaching the Franks Latin: James (1988a), p. 237.

[55] Gothic attitudes to the term 'barbarian': Amory (1997), pp. 50–85. On Burgundian attitudes to the term 'barbarian': Wood (1990); Amory (1993), pp. 1–28. Bavarian marginalia: Musset (1975), p. 190.

[56] Bipartite divisions: Goffart (1980); (1982); Moorhead (1994), pp. 71–5; Halsall (1995b), pp. 26–32; Amory (1997), pp. 46–85, 91–108. On Gundulf, Gregory of Tours, *Hist.* VI.II.

How did one become a barbarian? Names were one way, as the example of Gundulf shows. We occasionally get references to individuals with two names, one Roman and one barbarian, revealing this process in action. Then there was material culture. In the new, emerging political units of the post-Roman West, dress-style and artefact-forms were important in demonstrating one's political affinity, and this is shown archaeologically in brooch fashions and so on. Other, less archaeologically visible features such as hair-style were also used, as is referred to in a number of sources.[57] However, the effects were not everywhere the same. In Britain, by 700 the language had changed; elsewhere the linguistic input of the barbarians was far less, even if they nevertheless changed people's ethnic affiliation just as dramatically. Why was this? Is it simply a question of the number of barbarians, as is still usually supposed? Is it insignificant? Linguistic changes can be and have been effected by minuscule numbers of immigrants.[58] This is a fair point but cannot stand up to close scrutiny, as it suffers, as do many theories of early Anglo-Saxon history, from its insularity. The Franks, Goths and Burgundians had similar, if not greater, political and military dominance without changing the local language, except along the Rhine. Yet arguments that explain the linguistic change in lowland Britain, and the fact that no such change took place on the continent, by reference to large numbers of incoming Anglo-Saxons are also too crude. We have to consider the other side of the coin; the strength of the provincial identity. In those areas where the transition to barbarian power was smoothest, that is southern Gaul and sixth-century Italy and Spain, Roman identity, especially amongst the aristocracy, was important, a source of pride which could be deployed against the parvenus, the barbarians and their hangers on. It is no surprise that no one changed their language here, although, as we have seen, many changed their names. It took the wars and political disruption of the mid-sixth century and the actual destruction of the old Roman aristocracy to change the situation in Spain and Italy. The situation never really changed in Aquitaine before the eighth century; the Aquitanians never became Franks. Instead, from the seventh century many of them increasingly adopted a Basque, or 'Gascon', identity. The reasons for this ethnic change are probably similar to those discussed above, for Britain and northern Gaul. Removal from, and an inability to participate in, core politics in Gaul meant the end of regularly managed patronage. Disappointed rival competitors for local power sought the backing, and adopted the identity, of a more immediate and militarily effective

57 Names: Amory (1997), pp. 86–91, 97–102, and *passim*. Archaeology: Halsall (1995a), pp. 56–61. On the processes by which the barbarians were integrated into the former provinces of the Empire and created new social and political groupings and identities, see the contributions to Pohl (1997); Pohl and Reimitz (1998); Pohl, Reimitz and Wood (2001).

58 Higham (1992), pp. 189–208; M. E. Jones (1996), p. 39.

power: that of the Basques, who had been attacking southern Gaul since at least the sixth century.[59]

In the north, though, as we have seen, Roman identity counted for much less, and so in northern Gaul change of ethnic identity to the more 'advantageous' Frankish identity was more or less universal by about 600. In lowland Britain, as perhaps along the Rhine, the situation seems to have been even more extreme. It is not unlikely that Latin speech and Roman identity were replaced by both a British political identity, associated with the west British highland rulers, and by the English identity associated with the eastern newcomers. Latin culture rapidly collapsed after 388 and stood no chance. There may very well have been more English migrants than there were Franks in Gaul. On the continent the burial rites of the Germanic barbarians' homelands make little or no appearance in the archaeology of the post-Roman kingdoms, but the cremation rites which the English had employed in northern Germany were adopted in lowland Britain too. It must, nevertheless, be conceded that the adoption of this rite could also be a function of the weakness of local British identity, and it should be noted that many Anglo-Saxons (like their continental counterparts) adopted the common late provincial and post-Roman rite of lavishly furnished inhumation. So we need not invoke huge numbers of barbarian migrants to explain even dramatic culture-change. We must consider the weakness of the indigenous culture as well as the strength of the incoming one.

This chapter has proposed that future work on the barbarians and their role in the changes that took place between the late fourth and seventh centuries should adopt new approaches. We have seen that the barbarian migrations should be understood as the result of the collapse of the Roman Empire, not vice versa; that the formation of the post-Roman kingdoms should be viewed as aspects of provincial history; that the changes of this period, the creation of those kingdoms, and of the new identities, must be understood as the results of active, conscious decisions by many people as part of their struggles and conflicts within their own local societies, because, in this, as in so many other periods of history, we have to put not just the social history back into the political, but the political back into the social, and above all we have to put the people back into their history.

[59] On the Basques and Aquitaine, see James (1977), pp. 3–27; Rouche (1979); Collins (1984); (1986).

CHAPTER 3

THE SOURCES AND THEIR INTERPRETATION

Guy Halsall

The past, as is often said, is made in the present. Today's early Middle Ages are very different from the early Middle Ages of 1911, when the first volume of the first edition of the *Cambridge Medieval History* was published.[1] That difference in appearance stems largely from a difference in the lenses through which the early medieval period is viewed. There are two aspects to these lenses; first, there are the sources of evidence available; and second there are historians' ways of seeing the past. Since the first edition of the *Cambridge Medieval History* both have altered radically. Historical approaches to the written sources have changed in many ways and at several analytical levels.[2] The written record, furthermore, is no longer seen as the only, and in some instances not even as the most eloquent, evidence left of the early medieval past. New evidence – new lenses – have become available. In addition to providing the newcomer to the period with a brief overview of the types of western European sources upon which the other contributions to this volume are based (with some reference to evidential forms further east),[3] this chapter will therefore also present a short survey of the ways in which those forms of evidence are approached and the sorts of questions which they can, and cannot, answer.

ATTITUDES TO HISTORY AND ITS SOURCES[4]

In 1911 approaches to the history of the early Middle Ages were based upon the traditions of positivist empiricism developed in the nineteenth century. In

[1] Linehan (1982) for background. [2] Bentley (1997).

[3] As a survey of written sources for this period, Buchner (1953) and Levison (1952) retain their great value. Van Caenegem (1997) supplies an indispensable research tool, and Buchwald, Hohlweg and Prinz (1991) are similarly useful. See also Dekkers (ed.), *Clavis Patrum Latinorum*; Berlioz *et al.* (1994). Delogu (2002) is excellent and has a very useful bibliography of works in English.

[4] Bentley (1997) gives the most thorough discussion of historiographical development in the twentieth century. For the medieval period see the admirable chapter by Julia Smith (1997).

essence this meant that historians were interested in the recovery of accurate facts, which were then deployed to write narrative political history and the history of institutions. In an atmosphere of rising nationalism, history often became a search for the origins of particular nations and was concerned with identifying their contributions to the political institutions of the day. Attitudes to sources were entirely governed by the use to which they could be put to this end. Sources such as saints' lives were often disregarded as collections of silly tales for the gullible, or dismissed as later fabrications if they did not confirm what was perceived as the correct historical narrative. Some texts were entirely excluded from the canon of early medieval sources on similar grounds. The *Monumenta Germaniae Historica*, the great project set up in the earlier nineteenth century to edit medieval texts,[5] omitted large numbers of lives of ancient martyrs composed in Merovingian Gaul from its seven volumes of *Scriptores Rerum Merovingicarum* ('writers of matters Merovingian'). Such works were simply enough not regarded as having any relevance to the history of early Frankish Gaul because they said nothing (explicitly at least) about the high political events of the time. Early medieval writers were judged according to their perceived reliability: the extent to which they could be trusted to tell things as they really were. Writers of panegyric (praise poetry) like Venantius Fortunatus were dismissed as 'venal flatterers'.[6]

As history developed as an academic discipline, in the early twentieth century, attitudes to history and thus to the sources from which it was written changed. The most notable development was the 'Annales School', pioneered by French historians including Marc Bloch, who worked on the early Middle Ages. In brief, the 'annalistes' wished to move away from political history, famously described by one of the great figures of the movement, Fernand Braudel, as surface disturbances, foam on the crests of the waves of the great tides of history.[7] The 'annalistes' sought instead to uncover the ways in which man interacted with the great forces of climate and the natural environment, seen as forming the essential parameters within which human action could take place. What they proposed was 'total history'. Nothing was to be excluded from the historian's remit. Any and all evidence, written and unwritten (thus archaeological data and the evidence of the landscape), was to be examined for what it could tell the modern scholar about the lives and experiences of past people. In this context, needless to say, attitudes to the sources changed dramatically. Whether or not a source had anything to say about politics was irrelevant. Sources hitherto disregarded as collections of fables were now eagerly explored as valuable ways into the world-views and ways of thinking (the 'mentalités')

[5] Knowles (1963), pp. 65–97 for the history of the *Monumenta*.

[6] Dill (1926). [7] Braudel (1972), p. 21.

of the time. This opened the floodgates for new types of history and for the study of sources never before considered worthy of attention. This development was also bound up with the influence of Marxist thinking upon history, which, because looking for materialist causes for historical change, located in dynamics other than purely political, meant that a wider variety of sources were examined for information on how societies changed.

The interest in 'mentalités' meant that even political history could be looked at anew. Sources were no longer read for facts about high politics or institutions but to shed light upon the *practice* of politics: the rules of the game, so to speak. How did people negotiate power? Institutions ceased to be concrete entities in themselves but came to be seen as much more mutable, constituted by human interaction rather than simply governing the latter. In turn, this also meant that the ways in which the written sources presented the outcomes of political interaction and the development of institutions were of great interest in showing how power was perceived and transmitted. This owed something to the influence of thinkers such as Michel Foucault, who had proposed theories of power and its operation.[8] Further levels of source criticism were thus introduced, in order to examine the ways in which texts functioned as power strategies in their own right. The standard critical questions of why an author was writing, in what circumstances, who for and what for took on new dimensions. What strategies did an author employ to put across his (or occasionally her) point?

The ever increasing concern with the texts in and of themselves, as opposed to their contents, led, from the 1960s, to what has become known as the 'linguistic turn': the influence of critical theorists and philosophers of language upon the study of history.[9] At the risk of oversimplification, what this amounted to was that some writers within the broad theoretical church usually described as post-modernism argued that traditional attempts to uncover the past on the basis of the written sources were ultimately doomed to failure. In this view, the past does not exist as an objective reality separate or separable from its depiction in the written sources. What might appear to be the reality 'described' in texts is mediated through language, shaped by the specific circumstances and background of the author and by the power structures and relationships of the day, as well as by the agenda of the author. Philosophers of language and psychoanalytical theory were therefore also extremely influential in these approaches to texts. Language always has certain deficiencies; it cannot *be* what it describes and thus cannot ever exactly re-create its subject. Therefore, whatever an author may have intended (if that were ever recoverable), a text

8 See, e.g., Mann (1986); Runciman (1989); Foucault (1994).

9 For excellent discussion in relation to early medieval sources see Fouracre (1990); also Pohl (2001).

can always have more than one meaning or reading, to people at the time of its composition and to later readers. Some of these readings, of course, might run entirely contrary to those intended by the initial writer. This could work in two ways: a text's meaning might be 'subverted' by some of its readership, or writings intended to be subversive might nevertheless be made to fit more dominant ways of seeing the world. In this sense, a text and its meaning was as much created by its readers as by its writer. Furthermore, historical research in the present is equally shaped by the background and contemporary interests of the modern historian. Rather than being a matter of testing theories against evidence to further a knowledge of the past, the past only exists in, and is constantly shaped by, modern preconceptions. The texts of the past and the writings of the present become to some extent inextricable. Past reality, which historians seek to describe and more importantly explain, becomes a chimera.

Such theory has had some impact on the history of the early Middle Ages, although many modern historians of the period view it with a certain hostility (usually, it must be admitted, from a position of some ignorance). That said, the theoretical approaches of the 'linguistic turn' are sometimes unhelpful when applied to this period. For one thing, such theories usually begin from a starting point of certainty about the text, which as we shall see is not often available with the sources of the fifth to eighth centuries. Moreover, the dividing lines between more recent theoretical approaches and those of most current historians are in fact far less sharp than one might be led to believe. Modern historians of the early Middle Ages would generally agree that the past only exists as mediated through the texts it has left behind, that the writers of those texts (as we shall see) rarely simply 'told it as it was', and that texts have many layered meanings. Historians of the early Middle Ages have in any case long been used to seeing the early medieval past as constantly mediated and transformed by a whole series of lenses through which it is viewed: both those of the sources themselves and those formed by the constructs of earlier generations of historians. The debate essentially relates to the extent to which it is possible to recover the circumstances in which the people of the past acted. In 2005, most historians of the early Middle Ages would probably argue that it is still possible to use the texts of the period to establish an account of the past. Assuming that authors were agents who acted knowledgeably and intentionally in situations and relationships which had, for them, an objective reality (and taking on board the social theory of writers like Bourdieu and Giddens,[10] who have argued that human actions are not only governed by but constitute the structures of society) we might use their writings, even accepting the points made above, to redescribe those situations and relationships. Early

[10] Bourdieu (1977); Giddens (1984).

medieval texts and their contents exist whether or not we choose to study them. Though the way in which they have been read has, as sketched briefly above, changed very much in line with the concerns and academic discourses of the present, it has still, on the whole, been possible to evaluate the different interpretations of early medieval sources on the basis of the degree to which they find support in those texts. In a historiographical sense, not all readings of texts are equally valid. Nevertheless, so-called post-modernist theory has had a beneficial effect in refining yet further the ways in which texts and their production are viewed, leading to interest in authorial strategies, intertextual cross-referencing, and the possibilities of satire and irony,[11] and also in making modern historians more reflexive about what they do and the ways in which they do it.

THE PRODUCTION, TRANSMISSION, SURVIVAL AND EDITING OF TEXTS

In understanding the textual sources of the early Middle Ages, it is important to repeat the – perhaps obvious – point that writing was not haphazard. It was a costly undertaking. Papyrus was expensive because it had to be imported into western Europe, certainly more difficult after the loss of Egypt to the Arabs in the 640s, although, as has long been known, this was probably not the decisive factor in the replacement of papyrus by parchment (the treated skin of various animals: calves, kids, sheep).[12] Papyrus continued to be used in some parts of the West in any case, but more importantly a cultural shift towards using parchment was well under way by the time of the Arab conquests, a shift which continued in East as well as West. The classical papyrus text was produced as a scroll. This made copying or note-taking while reading very difficult so the scroll was being replaced by the codex (book), which was more easily made from parchment. Four sheets were laterally folded in two and stitched together up the middle (perpendicularly to the fold). The initial fold (along the top edge) was then cut, making a book of sixteen leaves (folios), or a quire. Parchment was also more durable (giving it a further advantage as the importance of retaining legal documents grew during the period) and it could be reused. Writings on parchment could be erased with pumice and written over. Fortunately for the historian the ink of the earlier text tends to rise to the surface and can often still be seen, especially with the aid of various modern technologies. Manuscripts with more than one superimposed text are known as palimpsests. Some important sources, such as the earliest Visigothic laws, are known largely through their survival in palimpsests. Nevertheless,

[11] Goffart (1988); Halsall (2002). [12] Dennett (1948).

parchment was extremely expensive. Herds of animals needed to be slaughtered to make even a fairly small book. The cost of writing had a bearing on what has survived, and considerations of utility could be paramount. Above all else, religious institutions needed biblical and exegetical texts and liturgical sources: prayer books; orders of service. Thus works of possibly more interest to the modern historian than the multiplication of gospels or missals have been lost simply because they were not of sufficient practical worth. On the other hand, from the seventh century onwards it became increasingly necessary to retain charters and other legal deeds to land and privileges, so large numbers of such records survive, of great value to social and economic historians.

If the initial writing of a text had to be a carefully considered undertaking, its copying by later scribes was similarly not a straightforward matter of transcription. Medieval writers took an active role in the transmission of the information contained in their sources. Quite apart from the human errors that can occur in copying an original,[13] they saw nothing wrong in emending or omitting what they (perhaps wrongly) saw as errors or as material unsuitable for their readership, or in adding extra information of their own that they thought would improve the value of a source – usually without making the fact of their interpolation in any way clear. These processes are of double significance to the historian of the early Middle Ages. As the original text of a source very rarely survives, they can make the establishment of what the original writer initially wrote a very complicated and difficult matter. The modern scholar usually works from copies, often of copies of copies. Sometimes the establishment of the earliest version of a text can be relatively straightforward. We have a number of charters from the seventh century and later, which have survived in their original form. What Bede originally wrote in his *Ecclesiastical History* can also be known quite easily as a manuscript survives which, if not Bede's *autograph* (from the Greek for 'written yourself': the copy he actually wrote), seems to be a direct copy of that initial version. We thus seem to be at only one remove at most from the original text. At the other extreme lies the *Pactus Legis Salicae*, the 'Compact of Salic Law', the earliest Frankish law-code. This survives in a plethora of manuscripts, with over eighty significantly different versions, none of which is less than two centuries later than the date of the original promulgation, presumed to have been towards the end of Clovis I's reign (*c.*481–511). As a result the editing of the text was an extraordinarily long and painful process. The generally accepted edition, a considerable achievement in spite of the rather dubious circumstances of its production, can nevertheless not be regarded as anything more than the final editor's best guess at what the

[13] Such as the eye skipping from one occurrence of a word to a later occurrence further down the page, and the omission of the intervening text.

original text may have looked like. The precise details of this are even now a matter of debate.[14]

The quest to establish what an author originally wrote is of course profoundly important for modern scholarship. If, for example, one is interested in the examination of Gregory of Tours' attitude to particular events or aspects of the politics and social structures of his time (the late sixth century) it is essential to work from something very close to his original composition. However, the scholarly editing of medieval works in order to re-create the original texts as far as possible was, to a very large degree, driven by the positivism of nineteenth-century historians, interested mainly, as we have seen, in the recovery of reliable 'facts'. The second issue concerned with the complexities of textual transmission is that focussing on the original versions can lead to the negation, or at least relegation to minor footnotes, of the changes made by later copyists who, as noted, were equally active in the processes of handing information down to later generations. Those copies, though often denigrated as 'corrupt', unreliable or, in polite historian's parlance, 'interpolated', can be of considerable interest in showing the interests and attitudes of writers in later eras. Early in the seventh century, for example, Gregory of Tours' *Ten Books of Histories* were excerpted and compressed into a six-book *History of the Franks*, largely by omitting most of what would today be seen as Gregory's most interesting passages, on holy men, miracles and wonders, and minor local events. Apart from causing confusion by being wrongly seen as Gregory's initial draft, later expanded into a ten-book version,[15] this work deserves far more attention than it has received as a composition in its own right. It is of immense relevance in exploring the historical interests, and through them the political circumstances, of the early seventh century. The six-book version was copied far more often in the Middle Ages than the original ten books, so although his 'remix' of the original went under Gregory's name, this anonymous seventh-century writer might be said to have actually played a greater part than the bishop of Tours in transmitting views of the Frankish past. The idea that there is *a* text of a particular source is, furthermore, a modern notion. If one is interested in the medieval function of a text or in the medieval reception and transmission of the ideas in our sources, one has to abandon the idea of a single authentic text. To be understood in medieval context it must be recognised that a source could exist in a variety of forms, all regarded by contemporaries as authentic.

Some documents purporting to date to our period can also be shown, by various methods – linguistic, diplomatic (the study of the precise formulas used in official documents) or palaeographical (the study of the scripts used[16]) – to be later compositions. Rather than simply dismissing such work as 'forgery',

[14] Callander Murray (1983). [15] Goffart (1987) and (1988). [16] Bischoff (1990).

again a new set of questions arises. Why was this source written at that date, pretending to be something else? Why was such a document perceived to be necessary? Why did an early medieval writer feel the need to disguise his identity beneath that of a well-known author from the past? A significant number of forged charters exists, for example, claiming to be donations to various churches by the Merovingian king Chlothar II (584–628). There are, indeed, far more forged charters of Chlothar II than of Clovis I, the first king of the Merovingian dynasty and seen as founder of the kingdom. Why was Chlothar a more common choice than Clovis, whom one might have expected would be a more obvious candidate as a prestigious king with whom to associate oneself? Answering this question can have important implications.

Writing and copying were thus expensive and deliberate processes. Just as the artistic illumination of early medieval documents can be of breath-taking complexity, so too could the narrative strategies and word-games used by writers. It may be true that there were no great philosophical or theological thinkers in the period between 500 and 700 – Isidore of Seville and Gregory the Great hardly rank alongside Augustine or Aquinas – but this does not mean that sixth- and seventh-century writers were necessarily crude or unsubtle. They enjoyed puns and word-play and could and did make use of complex patterning of words to draw attention to key points. They employed, for example, chiastic patterning, where a passage is structured so that phrases mirror each other about a crux, at which lies the key point or image; such patterning was used in the Bible, obviously one of the prime models for early medieval writing. Authors could adopt complicated and subtle strategies of inter- or intra-textual cross-reference to make their points, and they thought in sophisticated typological fashion. In other words, they used symbols which, in their minds and those of their readers, summoned up biblical images and the exegesis associated with them.

GENRE

That authors could use such imagery and expect its implications to be understood without explication stems from the fact that early medieval writers usually worked within the confines of particular genres, which it is important to understand if one is to make sense of the written sources from the period. Somewhat simplified: to work within a genre is to add to an established body of material rather than to create something entirely original. Writer and audience know what is to be expected, in terms of structure, subject matter and style. Composition takes place within certain rules or guidelines. An author working within a genre can therefore take a number of things for granted and need not explain particular choices or define terms. Cross-references can be made with other works, especially the classic works within the genre, without any need to make clear or explain them: the audience will pick up on them and know the resonance of particular words and phrases. Genres exist in many creative milieux, such as painting, sculpture, fiction writing and classical music, but to explain the concept further we might draw a parallel with modern popular music. An artiste who records within the tradition of, for example, soul music does not aim to create something radically new or different, but to add to a corpus of work with an established canon and an informed audience. Song structure, rhythm and to some extent instrumentation are set out by the norms of genre and so might more subtle aspects. A songwriter may borrow a lyric from a classic song by one of the genre's 'greats' and know that the audience will pick up the reference; a musical phrase may also be so used. None of this, however, means that a work within a genre is necessarily hackneyed or unoriginal. A work may be composed firmly within the guidelines of a particular stylistic form and still be justly praised as great. The existence of accepted norms for works within a genre does not, furthermore, imply either that those norms are immutably fixed or that a work of a particular genre has to possess every defining characteristic of that form. There are probably very few if any such 'ideal types', and genres can shade into each other. Writers can play with the rules of composition as well as within them. An addition to or variation on the norms, regarded as unusual when first made, may simply enter the canon of accepted possibilities. If an audience can be expected to know the accepted norms and their significance, it can also be expected to pick up on deliberate inversion of those rules, and on the point – satirical or ironic for example – of such a strategy. Finally, some writers in the period did invent or rediscover new ways of writing; some, like Gregory of Tours, seem to have started off writing within a particular tradition but then to have abandoned its structures to do something else. Early medieval writers were active agents and not, even in the Byzantine East where, as we shall see, the rules of composition were particularly strict, prisoners of established tradition. This brief discussion of genre allows us to understand why some subjects were written about in the period and others ignored, and why the diverse forms of writing differed from each other and from what one might expect, from a twenty-first-century viewpoint, of historical writing. With this in mind we can now turn to the different genres of early medieval written source.

HISTORICAL WRITING

In the Latin West, the tradition of historical writing in the classical tradition had gone into decline before the start of our period. This tradition, based upon the models provided by Livy, Sallust and Tacitus, focussed upon wars and 'high politics', and, when making use of other sources, even verbatim, did not explicitly acknowledge them except in the most general terms. Although the classics of the genre were still read and had an influence upon historical writing, its last great practitioner in the West (although he was, ironically, an Antiochene Greek) was the late fourth-century author Ammianus Marcellinus,[17] though the work of some apparently early fifth-century writers in this genre has unfortunately been lost. In the West between 500 and 700, possibly the closest work to this form of history is Julian of Toledo's unusual *History of King Wamba*, written in the late seventh century.[18] In the Greek East, however, the tradition did continue through the sixth century and into the seventh, in the histories of Procopius, Agathias and Theophylact Simocatta.[19] The norms of the genre were much the same as in Latin classical narrative history: a concentration upon wars, battles, the diplomacy and other doings of kings, generals and emperors, and some attention to prodigies, astronomy and other things seen as portents. In the early medieval Greek world, however, the classics of the genre – Herodotus, Thucydides and Polybius – were followed to an unusually close degree. Writers in the Byzantine world composed in a form of Greek quite different from the spoken. They were expected to write in the language of the great writers of the past, usually referred to as Attic Greek. Phrases and whole passages could be excerpted from them, and their specific vocabulary was also imported into discussions of the early medieval world. Thus, for example, when writing of peoples, Byzantine writers borrowed fourth-century BC names for generally similar peoples from roughly the same part of the world. Procopius called the Huns Scythians or Massagetae, for example – both names of peoples who lived long before the sixth century. Similarly, other technical terms were borrowed from past writers. Procopius talks about the guards of sixth-century kings and generals as *doryphoroi* and *hypaspistai*, both terms borrowed from Attic Greek models (the *hypaspistai* were the bodyguards of Alexander the Great). When using language not employed by their models, Greek writers were expected to excuse themselves with wordy circumlocutions: 'the *excubatores* (for such the Romans call their guards)'.[20] There were, of course, no bishops, monks or churches in the world of Thucydides, so where archaic words were not used (such as 'temple' for church), again writers had to make a pretence of having to explain this unwanted neologism: 'men who are very exact in their practice of religion, whom we have always been accustomed to call "monks"'.[21] This has sometimes misleadingly given the impression that Procopius was something of a sceptic, or even a pagan. None the less, we should not assume that the works of these authors were simply slavish patchworks of quotes and borrowed

17 Matthews (1989); Drijvers and Hunt (1999).

18 For discussion of which, see, for example Collins (1977).

19 Procopius: Cameron (1985); Agathias: Cameron (1970); Theophylact: Whitby (1988).

20 Procopius, *Wars* IV.12.17.

21 Procopius, *Wars* IV.26.17.

terminology. Again, even these tight structures of composition allowed writers to employ the rules to make their own points.

Historical writing nevertheless continued, taking new forms and developing old ones. Probably the form of written narrative most commonly associated with the period 500–700 is so-called 'national history': Jordanes' *Getica* (mid-sixth century), Gregory of Tours' so-called *History of the Franks*, Isidore of Seville's *History of the Goths, Sueves and Vandals*, of the early seventh century, Bede's early eighth-century *Ecclesiastical History of the English People*, and Paul the Deacon's *History of the Lombards* (late eighth century), to which one should add the anonymous early eighth-century *Liber Historiae Francorum*, the early ninth-century *History of the Britons* attributed to Nennius and the late ninth-century *Anglo-Saxon Chronicle*, and other works. Most of these works were written after the close of the time-span covered by this volume but, as they claim to relate the history of our period, they deserve treatment here. These sources were at first considered to be repositories of the age-old traditions of the different peoples of early medieval Europe. Since, in the nineteenth and earlier twentieth century these peoples were regarded as distinct racial units, in line with the ideas of the nation-state developed at that time, such works were seen to represent the foundations of the histories of modern European nations, their authors portrayed as the founders of national historical traditions.[22] The information they contained was held to be reliable, transmitted down the generations, it was assumed, by oral tradition. As attitudes towards the nature of the barbarian 'peoples' themselves changed, so the ways in which these sources were viewed changed too.[23] Most have been the subject of intense debate. The nature of Jordanes' history has come under close scrutiny,[24] and Gregory of Tours' writing has become the focus of an even larger field of profitable debate, hardly any of which now sees his writings as forming any sort of 'History of the Franks' (as discussed above).[25] Meanwhile, controversy has been provoked by the interesting suggestion that Paul the Deacon's *History of the Lombards* might have been composed for a Frankish audience.[26] The other sources have also attracted debate and revaluation.[27]

Not only are many of these works no longer seen as 'national histories', it is also recognised that they may represent instances of other genres entirely: the *Anglo-Saxon Chronicle*, obviously enough, takes the form of a set of annals

[22] See Halsall, chapter 2 above.

[23] Scharer and Scheibelreiter (1994): *Ethnogenese und Überlieferung*.

[24] Momigliano (1955); O'Donnell (1982); Goffart (1988); Heather (1991); Amory (1997).

[25] Thurlemann (1974); De Nie (1987); Goffart (1988); Breukelaar (1994); Heinzelmann (2001); Mitchell and Wood (2002).

[26] McKitterick (1999).

[27] Nennius: Dumville (1986); *Liber Historiae Francorum*: Gerberding (1987); *Anglo-Saxon Chronicle*: there are numerous studies, but particularly interesting for the period covered by this volume are Sims-Williams (1983) and Yorke (1989).

(Isidore's *History* is also written to an annalistic structure); Bede's is an ecclesiastical history; and so on. Gregory's, as mentioned, was not written as a national history at all, though quite which – if any – genre Gregory was composing in is a matter of debate. At the same time, the purposes to which these sources were put, using the past to serve political needs of later centuries, were also served by works of many other kinds, never viewed as particularly 'nationalistic'.[28] The lesson of the scholarship of recent decades has essentially been that to understand these sources they have to be replaced in the contexts of their composition. The political motives behind their composition make them far more contingent, and concomitantly far less valuable as treasuries of ancient fact, than hitherto believed. At the same time, however, they become very valuable sources for the examination of the political culture and ideology of the times and places where they were written: mid-sixth-century Constantinople; early seventh-century Spain; late ninth-century Wessex, for example. These lessons apply to most other sources written in our period.

The most common form of historical narrative in this period was that based around an annalistic structure: entries, chapters or groups of chapters ordered to deal with particular years. In the late fifth and sixth centuries a large number of so-called *Chronica Minora* ('lesser chronicles') were composed: the so-called 'Gallic Chronicles' of 452 and 507 (named from the year of their last entry); the *Chronicle of Saragossa*; the *Chronicle* of John of Biclar (who may indeed have been the author of the *Chronicle of Saragossa*); the similarly late sixth-century *Chronicle* of Marius of Avenches. Bede began his career as a historian by writing two sets of annals, the *Chronica Minora* and the *Chronica Majora*; and so on. There is reason to suppose that others still must have been lost. In the East this kind of historical writing was represented by works such as the *Chronicon Paschale*, based, as the name suggests, around a series of Easter tables.

The genre of annalistic writing, in general, required the subject matter to be limited to the major events of political history: the occurrence and outcome of wars and battles, the successions of kings and emperors and so on. In the Christian world it was unsurprising that comparable events of ecclesiastical note were soon added to the correct subject matter: the death and succession of bishops; theological controversies; great church councils. Astronomical events (eclipses, meteors) continued to be noted, alongside other possibly portentous events: floods; famines; prodigies. Of course some sets of annals were fleshed out to become very full narratives with only a loose resemblance to the bald lists of years from which they emerged – these are usually called chronicles: the *Chronicle of Fredegar* for example – and the dividing line between them and other forms of historical narrative can be rather blurred. The somewhat terse structure of some sets of annals should not, however, blind the reader to the

[28] See, e.g., Garrison (2000).

potential complexities of their composition. Although some were indeed kept on a year by year basis, others were deliberately composed as unitary pieces of work, but in an annalistic form. This meant that, although these works look like a transparent account of events recorded yearly, the writers could manipulate the story to serve particular agendas. It has been argued that the grouping of particular events in the 'Gallic Chronicles' (including, alas, some of the sparse references to fifth-century Britain) was done artificially to make a certain case.[29] Equally, the entries of the *Anglo-Saxon Chronicle* relating to the fifth and sixth centuries are also complex later compositions making political claims and not, as was once believed, accurate records of the political history of the period derived from now-lost sources.[30]

Another historical genre was that of ecclesiastical history, founded by Eusebius of Caesarea in the early fourth century. Ecclesiastical history, as the name implies, differed from other classical forms of narrative principally by concentrating upon the affairs of the church, although, especially as the church became a significant force in the politics of the Roman Empire, these became interwoven with more secular political events. Another difference from traditional narrative history, however, was the extensive verbatim and acknowledged citation of sources. This aspect of the genre was derived principally from theological exegesis and debate, where a point was supported by quotation of scriptural sources. Islamic historical writing evolved a very similar tradition. Eusebius' *Ecclesiastical History* was translated into Latin and continued by Rufinus of Aquileia in the West, and a series of eastern writers, Sozomen, Socrates, Theodoret and Evagrius, continued the genre through the fifth century in the East. The practitioners of ecclesiastical history between 500 and 700 were rather fewer, however. There are some manuscript indications that Gregory of Tours began his work as an ecclesiastical history, and in the early books of the *Histories* he certainly adhered to some of the rules of the genre, such as the extensive quotation of sources. However, the work turned into something rather different: an extended history of and commentary upon the events of his own times. That apart, probably the most famous ecclesiastical history is Bede's, written just after the close of this period.

HAGIOGRAPHY

The most common form of historical writing, broadly defined, was related to ecclesiastical history: hagiography (writing about the holy).[31] Hagiography is

29 Wood (1987).

30 See, e.g., Sims-Williams (1983); Yorke (1989); for the old view, see Myres (1986).

31 Dubois and Lemaitre (1993) give a useful introduction and bibliography, of use also to the study of the 'religious writings' discussed below.

not technically history at all, though it can be seen to share some features with the latter and can be (and has been) employed to help write narrative political history. A number of different types of source can be gathered under the title of hagiography. There are the lives (*vitae*) of the saints themselves, in the case of martyrs sometimes called accounts of their suffering (*passiones*); collections of post-mortem miracles; collections of short biographies of abbots or bishops; and so on. These types of written source proliferated across Europe and the Mediterranean world throughout the period covered by this volume, from Ireland to Armenia and from the northern reaches of the Frankish world to Africa. Saints' lives tend to be broadly similar in structure and content wherever they were produced, though there are of course regional variations. The point of the saint's life was didactic: to show the wondrous working of God in the world. The miracles which God worked through the saint demonstrated the Lord's continued active presence and interest in the world, and those which took place after the saint's death were the ultimate proof that the holy man had triumphed over death and now resided and could intercede with God. A charlatan, magician or man possessed by the devil could work what looked like miracles during his life, but only the truly saintly had their tombs blessed by the occurrence of cures and other miracles.

The models for saints' lives were, obviously, primarily the Gospels, although Jerome's *Lives of Famous Men* provided another source of inspiration. The *Life of Anthony* (the founding father of monasticism) by Athanasius, and Palladius' *Lausiac History* provided further models, although in the West the most important model was Sulpicius Severus' *Life of Martin* (written, most unusually, before the death of its subject, St Martin of Tours). The extent to which saints' lives followed the normal conventions of biography could vary considerably. Some, Eddius Stephanus' *Life of Wilfrid* for example, were written to a fairly tight chronological structure. With other lives, between the poles of the saint's birth and childhood on the one hand and his or her death on the other, the extent to which the chapters are arranged chronologically or thematically, or based around the model provided by the Gospels, is unclear.

As a body of material, hagiography has probably received more attention from historians since 1911 than any other corpus, and approaches to it have certainly changed the most.[32] As noted, in the nineteenth century attitudes towards saints' lives were governed essentially by the extent to which they were seen as useful for the writing of political/institutional history. Alternatively,

[32] Without doubt, the *œuvre* of P. R. L. Brown has been most influential here: e.g. Brown (1971); (1977); (1978); (1981); (1982a); (1982b); (2000); (2002). For development and response, see, e.g., Van Dam (1985); (1993); Howard-Johnston and Hayward (1999); Lifshitz (1994) has provoked much discussion.

in older editing projects such as those of the Bollandists or the Maurists,[33] carried out by members of religious orders, the study of saints' lives and debate over their authenticity were made to serve ecclesiastical political ends. But no longer are historians only interested in early medieval Lives written about early medieval people; they are also interested in early medieval writing about long-dead (or even fictitious) martyrs and other holy people. Hagiographical works are now seen as invaluable sources for the discussion of social history in the narrow sense (through their discussion of social structures and relationships, the diseases that struck people down and so on), for the history of popular belief and culture,[34] *mentalités* (through discussion of the ways in which healing miracles worked[35]) and the history of ideas as well as religious and political history. In the latter area, though, what constitutes political history has broadened considerably from the simple search to establish and explain a grand narrative. In studies of hagiography throughout the early medieval world, one of the most important features to emerge in recent decades is the extent to which saints' lives were themselves employed politically. The production of miracle collections furthered the reputation of a saint, obviously, perhaps at the expense of other cults, but other political agendas could be served by the writing of hagiography. The production of seventh-century bishops' lives in Francia has been shown to have been driven by the concerns of particular factions, at local and higher levels.[36] Some *Vitae* were written to rehabilitate awkward or even unpopular bishops within local tradition. The writing of saints' lives in early Anglo-Saxon England has also been said to have taken the form of something of a pamphlet war.[37] Some of Gregory of Tours' hagiography was probably written to defend members of his family.[38] Even changes in the type of saint whose cult was promoted or even accepted could be related to high political developments.[39] Our knowledge and understanding of the early medieval holy and their veneration has perhaps been the area of greatest change and expansion during the last hundred years.

LAWS AND LEGAL DOCUMENTS

A common source for post-Roman social history is the series of law-codes issued in the period. Corpora of law exist for this period in the west from Visigothic Spain, Burgundian Gaul, the Frankish kingdoms, Lombard Italy

33 Again, see Knowles (1963) for discussion. 34 Gurevich (1988).

35 See, especially, Brown (1981); Van Dam (1985); (1993).

36 Fouracre (1990). 37 Goffart (1988).

38 The *Life of Nicetius of Lyon* (chapter 8 of Gregory's *Life of the Fathers*), for example, with its extensive discussion of post-mortem miracles.

39 Fouracre (1999).

and Anglo-Saxon England. In addition to the great codification of Roman law ordered by Justinian I at about the same time as the legislation of western rulers, there were also abbreviated codifications of Roman law made in the Visigothic kingdom of Toulouse and in the Burgundian kingdom. Most western law, however, takes the form of collections of short chapters outlining offences and the compensation to be paid by the guilty party to the victims. The clauses relate primarily to crimes against property or the person, though there is also some detailed concern with matters of inheritance. Some law-codes are very lengthy and detailed, most notably the Justinianic code (issued alongside a Digest, an organised compilation of imperial Roman laws still held to be of legal value) in the East and the Visigothic code in the West. Others are rather brief (notably the seventh-century Anglo-Saxon codes) and apparently very selective in coverage, whilst a number of other codes (the Salian and Ripuarian Frankish codes, for example, or the earliest Lombard code, the *Edict of Rothari*) lie somewhere in between.

Historiographically, there have been two main areas of debate: first on the extent to which these laws represent actual legal practice (and, if not, what their purpose actually was),[40] and second the extent to which the post-Roman western laws represent the codification of imported Germanic practice. The two areas of discussion are not entirely unrelated and the debates upon them have not been entirely resolved. It does seem clear, however, that the details recorded in the western law-codes do not represent the totality of legal practice. Law could and did include the customary practice of innumerable local communities. It is, furthermore, very difficult to find evidence, especially in the sixth and seventh centuries, of the written laws being used in practice. For example, the fine for neglecting military service in Frankish Gaul is specified as being 60 *solidi*.[41] However, the only reference to a legal case involving this crime, and the punishment of the guilty, refers to a 600 *solidus* fine.[42]

It is to the seventh century that we can date the beginning of the survival of ever increasing numbers of legal and other administrative documents. Of course, such documents existed in earlier centuries. Because of the hot and dry anaerobic conditions, very many papyrus documents have survived from Egypt and North Africa, dating from the Roman period and before. The written tablets from the Roman fort of Vindolanda in Northumberland,[43] which

40 Mordek (1984).

41 A Roman coin valued at 1/72 of a pound of gold, although it later, as a silver coin, became the precursor of the shilling. Another issue concerning the practicality of the law is how fines and compensation specified in *solidi* could have had any value, as the *solidus* was not in any common use in the West (see below).

42 *Diplomata Regum Francorum*, ed. Kölzer, no. 143.

43 Bowman and Thomas (1984); Bowman (1994).

have survived because of their preservation in quite opposite – waterlogged – anaerobic conditions, are well-known. Fifth- and sixth-century papyri survive from Ravenna,[44] and a fascinating archive known as the Albertini Tablets was discovered in southern Tunisia, shedding invaluable light on everyday life in Vandal Africa.[45] Some documents, called pizarras,[46] were written on slate in Visigothic Spain, and these too are of great interest. However, it cannot be denied that legal documents, for the most part detailing gifts of lands or privileges to churches and monasteries, wills and bequests, sometimes sales, and the results of legal hearings, again most often concerning lands, increase significantly after about 600 and numbers continue to rise exponentially thereafter. Collectively these documents are usually (often technically incorrectly) known as charters and they take several forms depending upon time and place. Needless to say, only a fraction survives as originals, sometimes on papyrus but more usually on parchment, and the authenticity of those charters existing only as copies is a matter of some concern to historians. Because of the legal value of such documents to the ecclesiastical establishments that usually preserved them – they proved their title to lands, revenues and legal privileges – charters could be and frequently were forged. The problems of establishing the authenticity of a document are sometimes easily resolved. In some areas, such as Gaul, charters appear to have been written to fairly standard formulas – indeed we have some formularies (collections of model documents for scribes to copy) from the period. In such areas forgeries tend to stand out quite clearly. In others, however, such as Anglo-Saxon England, where charters took no standard form at all, the authenticity of documents can pose much greater problems. Whether a charter is a faithful copy of a genuine grant, a later fabrication which nevertheless used a genuine document or documents as a core, or an outright fabrication, can therefore be a matter of debate. An extra dimension of the problem arises in cases where a document might clearly in itself be a forgery but where we might suspect that the ecclesiastical institution to which it referred did indeed possess the specified lands and privileges, and might even have been given them in circumstances much as described. 'Forgeries' can furthermore be of considerable interest in showing the historical ideas and interests of the time at which they were composed.

In spite of the many variations in detail, charters tend to share a number of basic features. They begin by specifying the donor, listing his or (occasionally) her titles and honours and the recipient of the gift, following this up with a statement of the motivation behind the donation. Since the gifts were usually made to churches and monasteries, the motivation tended to be religious and

[44] Tjäder, *Papyri*. [45] *Tablettes Albertini*, ed. Courtois, Leschi and Saumagne.
[46] Velázquez (ed.), *Las pizarras Visigodas*.

this passage of a charter is referred to as the *arenga* (which loosely means a sermon; the word is cognate with harangue). There then follows the passage detailing what is to be given. This is known as the dispositive clause. This might include any specified price or exchange (including spiritual services, entry into the monastery's 'book of life', and so on) and is occasionally followed by a clause setting out the punishment (fines or curses) to befall anyone who infringes the terms of the document and, finally, a list of witnesses. Many charters also have a dating clause, either at the beginning or, sometimes, at the end.

Charters, like other types of writing, were first employed in the service of political history. Since many charters, as mentioned, contain dating clauses, and the usual form of dating in this period (AD dating only becoming common from the eighth century) was by the year of a king's reign (the 'regnal year'), dating clauses can provide information for narrative political history. They can, for instance, reveal the day on which a king's regnal year was held to begin or in which areas a king was recognised as ruler. Some issues of the chronology of Merovingian Frankish political history turn on the use of charters.[47] The preambles to royal diplomas also often tell us the titles used by kings, and thus their political ambitions. Witness lists of charters issued at court, or at least in the presence of a king, can indicate who was attending court at particular times, giving us indications not only of who was in – or out of – favour at that point, but also the areas where a king's authority was felt. Charters, however, can tell us much else. They can show us the workings of the law, or of the negotiations of power between magnates, or between church and laity, 'on the ground'. They can give us some indication of the rights and duties involved in landholding. With non-royal charters, the witness lists can provide us with clues to the patterns of family alliances in more local politics. The terms used for settlements and their organisation can also furnish evidence for the rural economy of the period. The potential uses of the charter evidence are great, but, it must be said, most such possibilities do not really begin to present themselves until such evidence begins to exist in greater quantities and in non-royal documents, in the eighth century and later.

LETTERS AND POETRY

Another source of information for the period takes the form of letters. As with other types of written source, this form is not as common as it had been earlier or was to become later, but it still exists. At the beginning of the period, some of the most vital snippets of information about the Frankish political take-over of

47 E.g. Gerberding (1987).

Gaul come from letters: from Remigius of Rheims and Avitus of Vienne to King Clovis of the Franks, and from Clovis himself to the bishops of Aquitaine. As in the late Roman period, letters remained important in maintaining networks of friendship; Bishop Desiderius of Cahors wrote a large number of letters in the earlier seventh century, frequently to men who had served with him at the court of the Frankish kings. Letters also survive from Visigothic Spain, often to and from bishops and arguably for similar purposes. Letters are also valuable because they often give us information on political events, which are otherwise unrecorded. One of the more interesting collections is the *Austrasian Letters* (*Epistulae Austrasiacae*). This probably survives because it was retained as a collection of model documents for use in later letter-writing, a sort of formulary. It contains letters of diverse types, including missives from bishops to kings, a fifth-century verse letter to a count Arbogast of Trier and letters between late sixth-century palatine aristocrats. Most importantly, perhaps, it contains the correspondence between the Austrasian Frankish court and the Byzantine emperor, mostly concerning wars against the Lombards in Italy. Finally, papal letters survive in large numbers, dealing with a wide range of subjects from issues of doctrine, through the management of papal estates, to ecclesiastical and indeed secular politics.

Poetic writing in this period took a number of forms. Some hagiography could be written in verse, such as Venantius Fortunatus' work on the life and miracles of Saint Martin. Venantius frequently wrote letters in the form of poems. He also penned a number of panegyrics – praise poems – one of the more important forms of poetic source for the period. The panegyric continued late antique political traditions, and indeed continued in unbroken lineage in the Byzantine East where, for example, the works of the north African poet Corrippus form an important source. Delivered before an audience of the potentates of the realm, a panegyric could serve several purposes, and represents a somewhat more complex type of evidence than might at first seem to be the case. The standard form of praise poetry inherited from antiquity presented the king or emperor as embodying all the model attributes of the good ruler: justice; piety; generosity; victorious war-leadership. This could indeed be a public display of flattery. However, by publicly holding up this list of ideal virtues, the poet could, in other circumstances, invite the king to meditate on these qualities and to ponder whether he was indeed living up to the ideal. Alternatively again, panegyric could work as – to use today's term – 'spin'. By presenting the king as doing what a model king ought to do, the court could be prepared for changes of policy or new activities which might otherwise seem surprising or unwelcome. It is likely that the late Latin tradition of verse riddles, often playing on ideas of Christian theology, remained popular in the period. However this, and other poetic forms, especially poetry in the vernacular, is again better attested and survives more frequently in the period after 700 than before.

RELIGIOUS WRITINGS

Finally, we should note the proliferation of other religious, especially theological writing in this period. These forms of written evidence are increasingly of interest to historians of the early Middle Ages, certainly far more than was the case a hundred years ago. Sermons and homilies, which exist in considerable numbers in all of the Christian territories covered by this volume, are difficult to use because of the complex rhetorical strategies which permeate them. They are nevertheless important sources for social history as well as for the history of Christianisation, doctrinal development and ideas. Similarly, liturgies from the period have been studied for a number of purposes. As well as being used to examine the possibilities of Christian ideas and doctrines permeating the laity, they can be studied as performances – dramas even – to look at how such rituals functioned in the society of the time.

Monastic rules, which proliferated in East and West during the period 500–700, have also been much studied. The complexities of these texts, which were themselves often composite creations, taking ideas from previous rules and used by individual abbots in a similar 'pick and mix' fashion, have been the subject of much debate. Again, as well as looking at the development of monasticism, something still very much in its infancy in our period, these sources shed light on broader issues, most notably the history of ideas. How was monasticism to be defined? How did it relate to the wider world? How was the office of abbot conceived? What models might it provide for lifestyles outside the monastery?

Amongst this enormous but diverse body of generally 'religious' material, perhaps one of the biggest changes to have taken place since 1911 concerns the attention now devoted by historians to commentaries. This sort of exegetical source, usually taking books of the Bible as the springboard for meditation of the religious life, was, a hundred years ago, rarely looked at outside the confines of theology departments. They are now of great interest to historians for what they can contribute to the history of ideas – and of course the social and political milieux which generate those ideas, for there is much information upon the social conditions of the time contained within these writings. In terms of their numbers, theological sources are probably the largest corpus of evidence for the period between 500 and 700. They may not have interested historians in 1911 very much, but they are of increasingly central concern to scholars in 2005, a fact that again demonstrates how even with a period as remote as the fifth to seventh centuries, history is constantly evolving, with new questions, new answers and new sources.

EARLY MEDIEVAL ARCHAEOLOGY

Without doubt the greatest changes in the evidential base for the study of the early Middle Ages have come about because of the development of archaeology.[48] In 1911 archaeology was very much in its infancy and the sub-discipline of medieval archaeology did not begin to find its feet until well after the Second World War. The adoption of a 'late antique' periodisation in archaeology took place later still, first in mainland Europe,[49] and is only slowly gaining ground in Britain, where the artificial division between Roman and 'Saxon' around 400 still holds sway to a surprising extent.[50] The study of early medieval cemeteries may be traced back to the discovery of the grave of Childeric I in Tournai in the mid-seventeenth century[51] but it was not until the end of the eighteenth and the beginning of the nineteenth century that Anglo-Saxon cemeteries began to be recognised for what they were and studied with some rigour.[52] This was unusually early. In France it was only from the third quarter of the nineteenth century that Merovingian cemeteries began to be identified as such (as opposed to being thought to be the burials of ancient Gauls or Romans) and examined with some care and attention. By the time of the first edition of the *Cambridge Medieval History*, cemetery archaeology was appreciated as a source of information, although as yet (and for long afterwards) simply to illustrate notions derived from the political historical narrative provided by the written sources. The excavation of early medieval rural settlements began to take place in the inter-war years with, for example, the examination of the Anglo-Saxon site at Sutton Courtenay by E. T. Leeds and the excavation of the Merovingian period settlement at Gladbach in Germany. However, early medieval rural settlement archaeology did not become an established branch of the discipline until well after 1945. The same can be said of urban archaeology, although that sub-division of the subject became established more quickly, largely through the opportunities for excavation presented by the pressing need for rebuilding and redevelopment in European cities devastated by the War.[53]

The difference in the dates at which the principal branches of early medieval archaeology became established relates primarily to the technical expertise required for the recognition and excavation of the sites. In many areas, post-Roman burials were easily discovered as they contained large numbers

48 For brief histories of medieval archaeology, see Delogu (2002), pp. 209–13; Van Regteren Altena (1990). For lengthier discussions of the history of early medieval cemetery archaeology, see Périn (1980); Effros (2003).

49 Founding fathers of the archaeology of 'antiquité tardive', which seems to have been pioneered especially in southern France, included P.-A. Février, N. Duval and J.-C. Picard.

50 Its adoption is argued for by Dark (2000).

51 Brulet (1990); (1991); (1997).

52 See above, n. 48, for histories of cemetery archaeology. See also Dickinson (1980) and papers in Southworth (1990).

53 Useful regional accounts of this development are collected in Barley (1977).

of artefacts, eagerly acquired by antiquaries and museums. Some, furthermore, lay underneath distinctive features in the landscape such as barrows or churches and others were fairly elaborately constructed with tiled or stone-walled sides or lay in stone sarcophagi, further facilitating their observation in the course of agricultural activity. On the other hand, early medieval building techniques tended to make use of wood rather than stone, making structural remains, in the forms of holes and slots or isolated pad-stones for timber stakes, posts and beams, more difficult to observe. Furthermore, in the case of western European towns and rural sites on or near Roman villas, early medieval archaeology was lost through the simple fact that its ephemeral traces overlay more easily recognisable Roman structures, stone-built and with tiled or even mosaic floors. Excavation techniques throughout Europe all too often involved the location of stone walls, the recovery of the basic plan of the building through following the lines of these walls, and then digging down in the areas so delineated until a recognisable floor surface was found. These methods, even where, as was not commonly the case, the excavators had any interest in post-Roman archaeology, meant that evidence from the early Middle Ages usually ended up on the spoil heap. Perhaps it is no coincidence, therefore, that some of the first early medieval towns to be studied archaeologically were those without Roman precursors – Dorestadt in the Netherlands, Hamwic in Britain, Hedeby in northern Germany, Helgö and Birka in Sweden, for example. As the twentieth century progressed, however, archaeology became ever more technically sophisticated. Although excavation techniques altered radically, the recovery of data is no longer restricted to 'digging' as field survey methods have developed.[54] The scientific aspect of archaeology has also expanded dramatically so that complex technologies exist not simply for quantifying and dating various materials but also for examining the early medieval natural environment and the states of health, diseases and life expectancy of the people of the early Middle Ages.

Again we are confronted not simply with an array of new data, better recovered and of infinitely greater variety than existed in 1911. The lens through which those data are viewed in order better to understand the early medieval past has also changed radically. When medieval archaeology first emerged it was, as mentioned, used simply as illustrative material and it can be argued that this attitude has never completely disappeared. The theory of archaeology has developed considerably in the last century.[55] Medieval archaeology has also become an academic discipline with an establishment in university

54 The classic introduction to excavation remains Barker (1993), but see now Roskams (2001). For fieldwalking, see Fasham *et al.* (1980), and for 'geophysics', see Clark (1990).

55 For more detailed discussion of theoretical archaeology and its development see Trigger (1989); Dark (1995); Johnson (1999); Preucel and Hodder (1996). Halsall (1997) provides a brief and simplified overview.

departments, research centres and professional archaeological units, although the precise nature of this development has not been the same in all the countries of Europe.[56]

DEVELOPMENTS IN ARCHAEOLOGICAL THEORY

The base line has generally been provided by what is known, at least in British archaeology, as 'Culture History'. At the end of the nineteenth century and the beginning of the twentieth, the development of chronologies came hand-in-hand with an awareness of the fact that certain types of artefact were repeatedly found in conjunction. Associated with them were various forms of settlement, or house type, or style of burial. These associated groups of material cultural features were called cultures and given the name of the site at which they were first or most famously observed (as an example the pre-Viking archaeological period in Sweden and its culture is usually referred to as Vendel, named after a famous elite burial site[57]), or of a characteristic object of that culture (there are no obvious examples from early medieval archaeology for reasons that will become apparent). These cultures were assumed to be coterminous with peoples, in line with nineteenth-century views of the nation-state. In turn peoples were assumed to be discrete biological/genetic groupings. The spread of the traces of cultures was seen as taking place through migration, and the replacement of one culture by another was interpreted as the conquest or subjugation of one people by another. Thus culture history, in prehistoric periods, served to expand a political historical narrative backwards into non-documentary eras. In the medieval period cultures were simply pinned to historically attested (and supposedly racially distinct) peoples. Thus archaeological cultures of the early medieval period have usually been given (on extremely tendentious grounds in many cases) names of the people with whom they are supposedly associated (thus 'Anglian', 'Saxon' and 'Jutish' cultures in post-Roman Britain, or 'Frankish', 'Alamannic' and 'Gallo-Roman' in northern France, the Netherlands, southern Germany and Switzerland).

Archaeologists in Great Britain, the Scandinavian nations and the Netherlands have been at the forefront of theoretical developments moving away from the culture historical paradigm in medieval archaeology.[58] After the Second World War and the disreputable use of culture historical theory to promote the ideologies of Nazi and Stalinist totalitarian regimes, archaeologists studying prehistoric periods turned to approaches owing much to structural

[56] Hodder (1991). [57] Lamm and Nordstrom (1983).

[58] Note that this comment applies only to medieval archaeology. French archaeologists, for example, have played a significant role in theoretical developments in prehistoric archaeology.

functionalist anthropology. Functionalist archaeology itself appears to have had little impact upon the archaeology of the medieval period, largely because functionalists still accorded primacy to oral and written sources where they could be found. The additional techniques which it espoused in its search to recover the whole 'system', of which individual sites and aspects of human activity were considered to be functional elements, were nevertheless readily adopted. These included, for example, environmental archaeology and the study of settlement patterns, especially from the air.

In the 1960s a movement known as the 'New Archaeology' was pioneered, at first in the USA, principally by Lewis Binford, and later in the United Kingdom, where David Clarke played a decisive role. New Archaeologists in essence wished to see archaeology cut its links with history, seen as too particularising, and become more like a natural science. Archaeology, they argued, should seek general, predictive rules or laws of human behaviour, and develop experimental methods through which such proposed laws could be tested. Societies were seen as functioning systems, adapting and changing principally in relation to external stimuli, notably the natural environment (the similarity with some of the agenda of the annaliste movement in history somewhat earlier is obvious, though it was not until the 1980s that archaeologists discovered the Annales school).[59] In this regard, it can be argued that in many ways the New Archaeology did not differ much from functionalist archaeology, but this was largely because it emerged principally in opposition to the Culture History employed by prehistoric archaeologists in North America. In its examination of systems, New Archaeology borrowed models from geography and biology. Because of New Archaeologists' interest in long-term developments or processes, such as the development of social organisation, or the collapse of complex societies, which could be studied in general cross-cultural perspective, their approach has become known as processual archaeology. New (or processual) Archaeology took some time to be adopted in medieval archaeology. It was only in 1982 (twenty years after New Archaeology's first emergence[60]), at the twenty-fifth anniversary conference of the Society for Medieval Archaeology, that Philip Rahtz proposed a 'New Medieval Archaeology'. In the same year, Richard Hodges published a lengthy paper also arguing that the methods and theory of New Archaeology could and should profitably be applied to medieval data.[61] The irony was that by this time, just as New Archaeology began to be discussed in the arena of early medieval studies, it had started to be seriously questioned by British theoretical archaeologists.

59 Hodder (1987); Bintliff (1991). For rather bemused reaction by historians see Delano-Smith (1992); Dyer (1992).

60 Which, for convenience's sake, may be dated to the publication of Binford (1962).

61 Hodges (1982a); Rahtz (1983).

The theoretical approaches that appeared in opposition to the New Archaeology, usually discussed under the umbrella title of post-processualism, did not represent a single, unified 'school'. They simply shared a rejection of the key tenets of processualism – its insistence on cross-cultural laws and long-term process, its usually strictly functional reading of cultural phenomena, the removal of the individual from social change, its often doctrinaire rejection of the value of documentary history, and so on. Post-processualists can be said to hold a few key beliefs in common, principally that material culture is deliberately, actively and meaningfully constituted to create, and not just reflect, the social world of the times. Social change was in turn viewed as dynamic and inevitable. With this in mind the specific context within which the archaeological record was formed became a matter of primary importance. Critical theory also had an effect. As material culture was seen as a means of communicating and representing ideas, means of reading archaeological data were proposed, analogous to the critical methods of studying written texts. Unsurprisingly, therefore, at least some post-processualists (although, ironically, often those not specialising in historical periods) argued that account had to be taken of the information provided by documentary history. Post-processualism took less time than the New Archaeology had done to be taken on board by British medieval archaeologists. This may have been because of the continued development since the 1960s of separate university archaeology departments with component courses on archaeological theory, and the greater provision of medieval archaeology options within degree courses. Currently, theoretical approaches to the archaeology of the early Middle Ages are diverse. Within Britain there are researchers working in Culture Historical, processual, post-processual and Marxist paradigms. In mainland Europe it does not seem unreasonable to state that Culture History, sometimes in more or less modified form, remains the most common framework, although other approaches are also adopted. This does not mean that such work is necessarily of lesser quality; the theoretical developments in British archaeology have not always represented unalloyed blessings. Whereas Culture History can be criticised for its too deferential approach to a framework provided by an often outmoded view of documentary history, processual archaeology and its successors have often adopted a too antagonistic stance towards historians and have taken up often equally deferential attitudes towards other disciplines: critical theory or anthropology, for example. Some work done by avowedly theoretically aware archaeologists can also be, and has been, criticised for its lack of empirical rigour.[62] Although most schools of archaeological thought currently stress the importance of creative links with documentary history (revised processualist

[62] See Dickinson (2002) for such a critique.

thinking also having abandoned its early opposition to history), the creation of a fruitful relationship between the two disciplines, giving due recognition to the equal and independent explanatory voices of each, remains one of the most pressing challenges for early medieval studies as they enter the twenty-first century.[63]

CEMETERIES

The oldest branch of early medieval archaeology is the study of cemeteries, as we have seen.[64] The period covered by this volume was also the hey-day of the custom of furnished burial, where the dead were interred with grave-goods, in much of western Europe. The presence of grave-goods in burials made, as noted above, the discovery of cemeteries easier and provided researchers with a vast body of material, and though these data are of uneven quality even the worst-recorded discoveries are capable of answering some questions. Grave-goods were initially (and in some cases still are) pressed into service to illustrate notions drawn from the written sources: an opposition between Christianity and paganism (grave-goods being an index of paganism), or the movement of Germanic peoples (furnished inhumation being assumed to be a rite imported from the barbarian homelands). Both of these assumptions have been seriously questioned, though, disappointingly, neither has been dispelled. Since the mid-1970s and the publication of Bailey Young's PhD dissertation the idea that grave-goods may be associated with non-Christian religion has been unacceptable.[65] Some more sophisticated uses of furnished burials to study processes of Christianisation have been proposed. Young himself has interestingly suggested looking not at the burial rite but at the potential symbolism of artefacts or designs on them.[66] Carver has proposed that some lavish burials in England, most famously the mound burials at Sutton Hoo in Suffolk, are ostentatiously pagan displays made at a time of conversion.[67] Study of the Merovingian furnished burial rite has proposed means of reading the burials as forms of symbolic communication which, even if incapable of revealing a specific religious doctrine, are best understood through studies of ritual. From that base it has also been suggested that the study of Frankish burials can shed light upon processes of Christianisation.[68]

The ethnic implications of burial with grave-goods are still a matter of debate. Although there is no *a priori* evidence to equate the rite with barbarians from Free Germany, where it was almost unknown in the fourth century

[63] Halsall (1997), for discussion of the problem and some suggestions for how it might be rectified.

[64] Halsall (1995) for brief overview.

[65] Young (1975), partially published as Young (1977). [66] Young (1997).

[67] See, e.g., Carver (1992). [68] Halsall (1998); (2000a).

(the custom emerged inside Roman northern Gaul),[69] it is still customary to equate cemeteries containing furnished burials either with immigrant barbarians or at least with people adopting their rites.[70] Some scholars have rejected the association of grave-goods with incoming barbarians, but they have then sometimes gone on to assume that this means that ethnic identity was unimportant.[71] Other scholars have presented interesting and sophisticated studies arguing for an association of at least certain types of furnished burial with particular social and political identities. This work has still suffered from too rigid an attempt to demonstrate a biological or genetic – even racial – basis for such identity and thus to show that it is evidence of migration, even mass migration.[72] The way forward is surely to realise that, whilst ethnic identities *were* important in the social politics of the early Middle Ages, they were constructs, with no necessary basis in genetics or the geographical origins of one's ancestors. Thus a particular form of ritual, particular artefacts used as symbols within it or dress styles could and probably did signify to an audience a particular social identity based around a claimed ethnicity. A form of brooch may indeed have been viewed as Jutish, for example, or a form of belt-buckle as Gothic, or participation in a form of ritual as signifying Frankish identity, because these objects and rites were what constituted that identity to early medieval people. This did not mean that the wearer or participant was a Jutish, Gothic or Frankish immigrant from outside the Roman Empire, or was descended from such. This form of burial archaeology tells us little about migration itself, but it does shed a great deal of light upon the circumstances in which such barbarian identities came to be of great importance in social politics.

More recent and interesting work has indeed been to look at other forms of social historical information provided by the archaeology of furnished cemeteries. Although customs varied significantly from region to region, within communities the repeated association of particular forms of grave-goods assemblage with particular sexes and ages means that burial archaeology has great potential for the examination of the social construction of age and gender. It can also be used to look at community organisation and the role of the family. Grave-goods cemeteries also permit a way into the examination of social hierarchy. Early efforts to do this were flawed, largely because they saw grave-goods deposition as passively reflecting social structure. Numbers of

69 Halsall (1992); (2000b) for extended critique and references to earlier literature.

70 Anglo-Saxon England: Welch (1992); Frankish Gaul: Périn (1998a); Visigothic Spain: Kazanski (1991); Ripoll (1994); Lombard Italy: Bierbrauer (1992).

71 Lucy (1997).

72 See, e.g., Härke (1989); (1990); (1992a); (1992b). Mass migration is explicitly postulated by Härke's student, N. Stoodley (1999).

grave-goods, or even particular forms or combinations of artefacts, could be read as simply indicating members of specific social classes or ranks, or of particular levels of wealth. These have all been justly critiqued.[73] More interesting ways of using furnished burial ritual to shed light on social organisation come through seeing the rite, and the material culture employed, as representing active strategies, creating as well as signifying social categories. This sort of methodology moves us away from seeing well-furnished burials as simply the graves of 'rich' or 'noble' people. Burial with grave-goods, rather than providing a simple chart from which to identify members of different classes within an established social hierarchy, is in fact a sign of social instability and competition.

Other forms of burial existed in this period. A cremation rite wherein the ashes of the deceased were buried in a vase, sometimes accompanied by some grave-goods, continued to be used in the former Free Germany and Scandinavia and was imported into lowland Britain in the fifth century. This evidence too can be used to study social identities and competition at a local level. In other areas of Europe inhumation with few or no grave-goods was the norm. Burial sometimes took place in elaborate sarcophagi,[74] or simpler stone-lined cists. These burials are more difficult to date and thus, often, to use as sources for information about society.[75] Nevertheless possibilities exist, if more reliant upon good-quality excavation and preservation of bones. Spatial organisation of cemeteries can provide pointers. Were males and females buried separately? Were children buried together in discrete groups? If so, these could suggest community norms or attitudes. Or are groups of both sexes and all ages found together, suggesting family groups? Does study of the bones suggest differences in lifestyle and diet between occupants of different areas of a cemetery? Some work has begun on these sorts of issues. Interesting work has also been carried out upon the siting of burials and the significance of burial monuments in the landscape.[76] The study of early medieval cemeteries still has much to tell us about the early Middle Ages.

RURAL SETTLEMENTS

The archaeology of early medieval rural settlements, as stated, is a much younger branch of the discipline.[77] In the post-Roman period, across the former

[73] See, e.g., Steuer (1982); Samson (1987); James (1989). Périn (1998b) is still rather traditional.

[74] As in southern Gaul: James (1977).

[75] See, e.g., Delestre and Périn (1998).

[76] Williams (1997); (1998).

[77] For recent summaries of developments in north-western Europe, see, e.g., Hamerow (1994); Lorren and Périn (1995); (1997); De Boe and Verhaeghe (eds.) (1997); Van Ossel (1997); Damminger (1998); Périn (2002).

provinces of the Empire, new building styles came into being. In many areas stone was replaced by timber and a similar archaeological repertoire emerged, with large central halls surrounded by ancillary buildings, often with sunken floors or pits beneath a planked floor. Even in areas where stone building remained in use, a similar organisation of dwelling units may be discerned.[78] Early medieval rural settlement archaeology has, as we have seen, often suffered from the crude excavation techniques used to explore Roman sites. This has meant that post-Roman occupation of villas in areas where these sites were not abandoned, notably southern France and Spain, has often been lost, and only recently has the extent of such occupation been realised.[79] Excavation of rural settlements has been increasingly complemented by regional field surveys, wherein a variety of techniques – aerial photography, field-walking and geophysical methods – combine to provide an indication of the broader settlement pattern and changes in it. Examples of such surveys can be found across Europe, North Africa and the eastern Mediterranean. More sophisticated excavation techniques have also allowed the recovery of data about the diet and economy of early medieval settlements. The study of rural settlements provides many ways of examining social structure as well as economy. One might, for example, note whether all buildings or dwelling units are of the same order of size, or whether some (or perhaps just one) seem larger than the others. Do fences surround the different units, suggesting a greater degree of privatisation of property? Is there a hierarchy of settlement types, suggesting the physical separation of different social strata and the exploitation of the surplus of some settlements by others? The fortification of some settlements might also suggest the extraction of surplus in the form of labour services. The layout of individual houses and dwelling units also tells us a great deal about views of the world. Long-houses, incorporating accommodation for animals as well as humans under the same roof, as are found in some areas such as the Netherlands suggest a very different view of cosmology from that expressed in settlements wherein humans and animals lived in different structures. Changes from one form to the other must have been significant. Some possibilities exist for more detailed study of the use of space within settlements or buildings, though these are muddied first by the problems of excavation which, in rural settlements with very shallow stratification, rarely allow absolute certainty that different buildings all existed in exact contemporaneity and, second, by the difficulty of establishing the gender associations of artefacts. While the latter can be identified reasonably clearly in the cemetery evidence, transferring these conclusions to the archaeology of settlements may be difficult. The symbolism

[78] For example the site of Larina (Isère): Porte (1980).

[79] For recent summary see Arce (1988); Chavarría Arnau (2001).

of artefacts in the precise circumstances of funerary ritual may have differed from their use in the more flexible conditions of everyday life. None the less, the archaeology of rural settlements offers considerable scope for advancing the social history of Europe in this period. Some studies, taking account of the charter evidence (see above), have begun to make important contributions in this regard.[80]

TOWNS AND TRADE

At the apex of the early medieval settlement pattern lay the towns. Urban archaeology has been a growth area in early medieval archaeology since the 1940s across Europe and the Mediterranean basin.[81] Even with the problems of recovery, our knowledge of the central places of the early Middle Ages has increased dramatically. In this aspect in particular the early Middle Ages of 2005 differ radically from those of 1911. A general narrative of the fortunes of towns in almost every region of Europe can now be sketched, in the west usually showing stagnation or even accelerated decline from the late Roman situation after 400. In some areas further decline took place from the mid- to late sixth century; in others recovery began in the seventh. As will be discussed in other chapters, the recovery in the north was often focussed upon new types of urban site, the emporia, which were reaching their florescence by the close of the period covered by this volume. The archaeology of post-Roman towns has added greatly to our knowledge of early medieval society, economy and politics. It has done this not simply by adding support to the idea, which could be drawn from the written sources, of a change in the nature of urban settlements from the social and bureaucratic-administrative foci of the late Roman Empire to the much more religious centres of the early Middle Ages. Nor has it simply provided illustrative back-drops to the narratives provided by written sources: Henri Galinié's justly famous work at Tours, for example, does far more than simply set the scene for Bishop Gregory's tales.[82] Close study of the towns allows us to understand more fully their place in early medieval society and politics. That they were clearly not population centres on any great scale nor, most of the time, productive centres permits a rather different understanding of why towns nevertheless remained important foci for society and politics. Understanding the decline of towns from some of their former functions also creates a way into understanding the changing nature of the

80 E.g. Theuws (1991).

81 See, as a sample of collective works since the 1970s: Barley (1977); Hodges and Hobley (1988); Demolon, Galinié and Verhaeghe (1994); Brogiolo and Ward Perkins (1999); Brogiolo, Gauthier and Christie (2000).

82 Galinié (1997); Wood (2002).

state in the early medieval period.[83] Study of urban buildings, most notably churches, can give us a sense of how space was used to transmit ideas and ideology.[84]

All the aspects of early medieval archaeology just surveyed, combined with technological study of the artefacts and the location and techniques of their production, have radically transformed our knowledge of the early medieval economy, as will be discussed in a later chapter.[85] As with the towns, this aspect of the early medieval world has changed dramatically since the beginning of the twentieth century. Then the work of Henri Pirenne was beginning to appear, work that caused controversy and critique. Archaeology has given the debate a new lease of life since the 1980s but at the same time spectacularly changed the outlines of the picture.

NUMISMATICS AND EPIGRAPHY

Lying somewhere between documentary history and archaeology are the disciplines of numismatics – the study of coins – and epigraphy – the study of inscriptions. Both classes of evidence can be viewed as artefacts and thus falling within the remit of material culture studies or archaeology, and both forms are often discovered in the course of archaeological excavation. Yet both are important vehicles of written, textual information, which may bring them within the orbit of history. The period between *c.*500 and *c.*700 can probably not be regarded as a hey-day for either source of data, as we shall see, but numismatics and epigraphy have both played a significant part in understanding the early Middle Ages.

The fact that numismatics is not as important a source for this period as it is for the preceding and succeeding eras is itself a fact of some importance.[86] As the Western Roman Empire imploded in the early fifth century, the western economy underwent something of a recession, and many areas – such as Britain and most of Gaul – became effectively non-monetary. In this case, we can draw important conclusions from the absence of sources! Coinage continued in use further south around the Mediterranean, and further east in the Byzantine Empire, although in the seventh century – though never disappearing as completely as in the north-western provinces of the Western Empire – it went into decline there too.

[83] Haldon (1999). [84] See, e.g., Wharton (1995), pp. 105–47, on Ravenna.

[85] See Loseby, chapter 22 below for extended bibliography. Hodges (1982b) provided an important starting point. See now Hodges and Bowden (1998); Hansen and Wickham (2000).

[86] Delogu (2002), pp. 183–205 provides an excellent introduction, with helpful bibliography of works on English coinage. Grierson (1951) remains a classic. The annotated catalogues of early medieval coins are too numerous to list.

Coins can be important for a number of reasons. They obviously provide a very useful basic chronological index, when found on archaeological sites, though clearly the date at which a coin was minted need not correlate closely at all with the date at which it was lost. They provide only a *terminus post quem* ('point after which'). Coins have a number of economic implications. We need to distinguish between coins which are effectively no more than convenient units of bullion – the late and post-Roman *solidus* for example was always 1/72 of a pound of gold – and coinage in the modern sense, where the intrinsic value of the coin (the cost of the metal which it contains) and its face value are different, the difference between the two being guaranteed by the state minting the coin. The latter form of 'true' coinage existed rarely if at all in this period. However, even where a coin was effectively a simple unit of bullion, its regularity and its acceptance over wide areas can be indices of the complexity of the economy and the state.[87] Related to that issue is the question of the location and number of mints, and of the value of the coinage itself. For example, in much of the sixth-century West, the only coins to circulate were high-value gold *solidi*, either imported from the Byzantine East (perhaps given as political payments) or minted in the West in imitation of them. Such coins were far too valuable to be of any use in most transactions. Though large-scale purchases could have been made with them, it is more likely that their usage was more political than economic (as we shall see). When coinage began to be struck more often again in Gaul, in the late sixth century, it was usually of a lower denomination: the *triens* or *tremissis*. This coin was valued at a third of a *solidus* and so was of rather greater economic use. However, these coins were struck at a large number of mint-sites across Gaul, and although central control is suggested by their uniform weight and gold-content they do not bear a royal name or image but, instead, the name of the moneyer who struck them and that of the place where they were minted. The implication is that coins tended to be accepted only across quite small areas, where a moneyer was known and trusted. As the seventh century wore on and the gold content of these *tremissi* gradually reduced, they were eventually replaced by a silver coin, the *denarius*, of lower value again. This suggests that coinage was used in ever lower levels of transaction. Furthermore, the fact that these coins were minted at fewer locations within the kingdom suggests that they were known and accepted across longer distances. Taken together, the picture is of increasing monetisation and economic growth; a graphic illustration of the eloquent testimony that coins can bear.

However, as intimated above, coins have other than simply economic implications. They were also useful political tools. Some coins, through their

87 Hendy (1988).

inscriptions, could transmit royal or imperial ideology to the political community of the realm. As just noted, the *solidus* was a high-value coin of little economic practicality and so probably circulated only amongst the elite. This made the coin an important vehicle for propaganda. The Visigothic king Leovigild used successive issues of *solidi* to proclaim his reconquest of various cities from his rebellious son Hermenigild.[88] One of the means by which the Frankish king Theudebert proclaimed his equality with the emperor Justinian was by issuing his own *solidi*, bearing his own name. Examples of these coins survive, and we know from Procopius' writing the shock that this flagrant breach of hitherto imperial prerogative caused in the Eastern Roman Empire. Possession of coins like *solidi*, whether imported or locally minted, could, because of their value, be a badge of membership of the political elite. They are to be found in lavishly furnished graves of the period, where they were probably deposited publicly as signs of power and status. The control of the distribution of such coins was therefore an important political mechanism, leading further to royal interest in these issues and giving such coins something of the characteristics of prestige goods.

Like numismatics, epigraphy, staple fare for the classical historian, enters a period of relative decline in this period, and sometimes for similar reasons.[89] The 'epigraphic habit' had begun to slacken off in north-western Europe in the fourth century, though remaining more common further south and east, and in the economic regression of the fifth century died out almost entirely in some areas, such as lowland Britain and much of Gaul. However, post-Roman epigraphy is nevertheless far more common than is often thought, and takes a number of forms.

In the Eastern Empire and in Gaul, Italy and Spain, inscriptions on stone in the classical tradition continued to be employed, for the dedication of buildings, the recording of works of modification or restoration, and, much more commonly, the commemoration of the dead. Under the same heading, an increasingly large corpus of graffiti carved on stone in churches should be included. In North Africa, funerary inscriptions can also take mosaic form. In western Britain, the Roman epigraphic tradition has a clearer legacy than in

88 Hillgarth (1966).

89 There is currently no easily accessible introductory survey of early medieval epigraphy in English. Handley (2003) rectifies this lacuna. See also De Rubeis (2002). An overview with relevant bibliography can also be found in Effros (2002), pp. 79–137, though care is needed with some of the conclusions. Gallic inscriptions were first collected by Le Blant, *Inscriptions chrétiennes*. More recently, see, e.g., Gauthier, *Recueil des Inscriptions chrétiennes de la Gaule*; Descombes, *Recueil des Inscriptions chrétiennes de la Gaule*; Prévot, *Recueil des Inscriptions chrétiennes de la Gaule*. For Spain see Vives, *Inscripciones cristianas de la España romana y visigoda*. For Britain, Ireland and Brittany, see now the Celtic Inscribed Stones Project, whose database is on-line at http://www.ucl.ac.uk/archaeology/cisp/database.

the areas that became Anglo-Saxon. Inscriptions upon stone, commemorating the deceased, are well known in these regions. Names, titles and short texts here are recorded not only in Latin but also in ogham, an alphabet that, though deriving ultimately from the Latin alphabet, takes a quite different form, being read vertically and with the letters denoted by the inscription of straight lines on either side of the vertical edge of the stone or on either side of an inscribed vertical line. This alphabet is usually held to have been developed in Ireland, where ogham stones are most common, although some debate on this issue is possible. Ogham is also quite frequent in South Wales. Inscriptions of the old Latin tradition do re-emerge in Anglo-Saxon by the end of our period. Further north, though usually not employing a recognised alphabet, the Pictish symbol stones of southern Scotland should be included under the heading of epigraphy. Here the stones make use of a selection of recognisable and often repeated symbolic designs. By the end of our period they also use more figurative depictions of people and animals and some have been associated with particular historical events. The Aberlemno stone in Fife, for example, has plausibly been interpreted as commemorating the Pictish defeat of the Northumbrian army at the battle of Nechtansmere in 685.[90] Similar types of stone monument are also found in Scandinavia, sometimes with inscriptions in the runic alphabet and sometimes with no literal inscriptions but with elaborate artistic decoration. To what we might term the 'physical' corpus of inscriptions, we should also add a significant number of inscriptions which now only survive in documentary records. The funerary inscriptions of Venantius Fortunatus are a good example.

As with numismatics, the uses of epigraphy extend much further than simply providing dating evidence and assistance with the narrative of political history, though this source of evidence has been important in both areas. As well as providing evidence for the sponsorship of building work, dedication inscriptions can also reveal information about ideas, such as attitudes to the inheritance of Rome. Funerary inscriptions can permit ways of looking at the family and at family structures. They can give an indication of cultural ideas, for instance through the spread of the fashion for Germanic names through what had been Roman Europe. Many inscriptions record the age of the deceased. This is a particularly interesting source of information. First, close study reveals that the ages inscribed on these memorials were very often rounded to the nearest five or ten years – permitting a priceless insight into attitudes about social age and ageing. Even taking these problems into account, we can still use this evidence to examine issues such as age of betrothal and marriage, and differences between the sexes in this area. Some inscriptions, such as those in Trier, also

90 Hooper (1993); Cruickshank (2000).

record who set up the memorial, as well as the person commemorated, and this too can provide information about family structures and relationships. The relative investment in the memorials of children and women as well as adult male heads of families (which changes significantly from region to region) also sheds light upon issues of social structure.

Some inscribed stone monuments have given rise to debates about the monumentalisation of claims of land-ownership and the desire to make permanent marks upon the landscape, as with the discussion of barrow burials and other such monuments. Most interesting of all, perhaps, has been the study of inscriptions and their measurement of time to examine the expression of local and regional identities. In sixth-century Burgundy, for example, the different cities of Vienne and Lyons chose to measure time as years elapsed since the consulships of two different consuls.[91] Their choice of a 'patron consul' was clearly a means of expressing local identity. Similarly in Spain, the use of the Spanish Era (a chronological system which counted years from the year which we now think of as 38 BC) has been shown to have had a regional and doctrinal association in the sixth century, and then in the seventh to have been employed to enhance Spanish unity.[92]

CONCLUSIONS

The cursory survey above shows that the historian of the period 500–700, even in places such as Britain which are effectively denuded of any written sources for much of this era, is not working in the absence of evidence, as is all too often assumed. In terms of the sources of information available, this is most certainly not a Dark Age. In fact, in terms of the evenness of geographical coverage and the sorts of issues that we can examine on a regional or even local basis, this period is more fully illuminated than the late Roman era. Over the last century, the sources of evidence have increased dramatically, and the remit of the historian (broadly defined as a student of the past) has expanded correspondingly. The biggest challenge facing the early medievalists of the next century will be to develop awareness of all those forms of evidence and the problems and potentials of their use, and to allow all, written, pictorial, archaeological, epigraphic and numismatic, to be able to contribute equally on their own terms. If there is another *New Cambridge Medieval History* in a hundred years' time, the lenses through which we study the early Middle Ages will doubtless have been transformed as much as they were between 1911 and 2005, and with them the early Middle Ages themselves will have changed.

[91] Handley (2000). [92] Handley (1999).

PART I

THE SIXTH CENTURY

CHAPTER 4

THE EASTERN EMPIRE IN THE SIXTH CENTURY

Andrew Louth

The beginning of the century saw Anastasius (491–518) on the imperial throne, ruling an empire that was still thought of as essentially the Roman Empire, coextensive with the world of the Mediterranean, however unrealistic such a view seems to modern historians, who have the benefit of hindsight. Although Anastasius ruled from Constantinople, 'New Rome', over what we call the 'Eastern Empire', the Western Empire having been carved up into the 'barbarian kingdoms', this perspective is ours, not theirs. Through the conferring of titles in the gift of the emperor, and the purchasing of alliances with the wealth of the Empire – wealth that was to dwarf the monetary resources of the West for centuries to come – the barbarian kings could be regarded as client kings, acknowledging the suzerainty of the emperor in New Rome, and indeed the barbarian kings were frequently happy to regard themselves in this light. The discontinuation of the series of emperors in the West, with the deposition of Romulus Augustulus in 476, was regarded by very few contemporaries as a significant event: the notion that East and West should each have its own emperor was barely of a century's standing, and the reality of barbarian military power in the West, manipulated from Constantinople, continued, unaffected by the loss of an 'emperor' based in the West.

The empire that Anastasius ruled was still the Mediterranean world as it had been since classical times in more than just a political sense: namely, in that it consisted of a world, the basic unit of which was the city, which with its hinterland (the country, *chôra*) formed a self-sufficient economic and even cultural unit. Although shorn of the political powers of the old city-state, the notables of the city still exercised considerable political influence and the provincial governors, appointed from the same social class as these notables, frequently found it more effective to recognise local influence than to challenge it. The cities – with fora, theatres, courts and opportunities for education – formed the seedbed for the educated elite who held posts in the imperial administration, and often returned to the cities to enjoy the essentially rural wealth generated by their country estates. All this was to change from the sixth century onwards, though there is a good deal of debate about the rate at which this change took place.

The city was also the basic unit of the Christian church. From the end of the second century, Christianity, which had initially been a predominantly urban phenomenon, had developed an organisation based on the city and its hinterland, which was led by a single officer, called a bishop. With the gradual Christianisation of the Roman Empire from the fourth century onwards, the bishop, who was appointed for life (translation from one city to another was forbidden by canon 15 of the First Ecumenical Synod of Nicaea, though there were rare exceptions), became a considerable figure among the notables of the city. He was sometimes appointed *defensor civitatis*, that is the leader or 'judge' of the city, and he regularly exercised the functions of this post, even when not officially appointed to it. Despite the decline of the city as an economic and cultural entity,[1] the link between the bishop and the city was to continue. Christianity had never been a particularly peaceful religion, and the importance it attached to correctly formulated beliefs, combined with its increasing social influence as fewer and fewer inhabitants of the Empire resisted the pressure to embrace Christianity, meant that well before the sixth century Christian belief had become both a cause of social, political and cultural divisions, and a means of articulating them. Modern historians are shy of regarding religious belief and practice as the reason for social and political divisions, and in general they may well be right, but it is undeniable that in this period division was often expressed and understood in religious terms. As we shall see, issues of religious difference are woven into the narrative of sixth-century history. It is important to understand the basis for these differences before going on to consider other explanations for social, political and cultural divisions that were expressed in these terms. Religious conflict is a theme to which we shall often return.

Anastasius inherited, and promoted, religious divisions that were to cast a long shadow over the Christian Roman (or Byzantine) Empire. These religious divisions derived in the first instance from the Fourth Ecumenical Synod, held in Chalcedon (modern Kadiköy, directly opposite Istanbul (Constantinople) across the Bosphorus). That synod had sought to settle long-standing differences about how godhead and manhood were united in Christ. The pope of the day, Leo I, played an important role through his legates, and the fathers of the synod (almost entirely Greek) eventually agreed on a formula, acceptable to the papal legates, which they regarded as endorsing the teaching of the great

[1] The question of the decline of the late antique city, and how such decline is to be interpreted, really becomes critical in the seventh century: see Louth, chapter 11, below. For two general accounts, see Mango (1980), pp. 60–87, and Liebeschuetz (1992).

patriarch of Alexandria, Cyril (d. 444), who was held in the highest regard by all but a small minority of the Eastern bishops. But a hard-won concession to the papal legates, by which the unity of Christ's person was recognised 'in two natures' (a phrase not found in Cyril, but taken from a papal letter, the so-called 'Tome of Leo', which was received by the synod), spoilt the achievement of Chalcedon: many Christians, especially in Syria and Egypt, felt that the synod had betrayed, rather than endorsed, Cyril. Rejection of the decision of Chalcedon took often violent forms, with Juvenal, bishop of Jerusalem, finding he needed imperial troops to make a safe entry into his episcopal city, and Proterius, appointed to replace Cyril's successor who had been deposed by the synod, being murdered by the mob. The violence that often accompanied these religious differences was regularly fostered by the monks who, increasingly, became a force to be reckoned with in the Christian Roman Empire. After unsuccessful attempts to enforce Chalcedon, in 482 the emperor Zeno issued a statement of belief with the intention of securing unity (called the *Henotikon*), which disowned Chalcedon, though it fell short of condemning the synod. The *Henotikon* was the work of Acacius, patriarch of Constantinople, and Peter Mongos (the 'hoarse'), patriarch of Alexandria. Rome, and the Latin West generally, was not willing to disown what it regarded as the synod of Pope Leo, so the promulgation of the *Henotikon* provoked schism between Rome and Constantinople, known as the 'Acacian schism', after the patriarch of Constantinople, which lasted until the death of Anastasius. For the *Henotikon* remained imperial policy during the reign of Anastasius who, if anything, regarded the edict as too moderate, since he promoted those who rejected the *Henotikon* for not explicitly condemning Chalcedon.

The sources for the sixth century, although on the face of it plentiful, leave much to be desired. Histories on the classical model have survived intact (in contrast to the fragmentary fifth-century histories). Works of this kind are Procopius' *Wars*, and the histories of Agathias and Theophylact Simocatta. Substantial extracts from the history of Menander the Guardsman have also survived. These can be complemented by the new form of history-writing, of Christian inspiration, the chronicle – those by John Malalas (which only survives in an epitomised form) and Marcellinus, as well as the later *Chronicon Paschale* (630) and the chronicle of Theophanes (early ninth century, but incorporating earlier material). Church histories, which evolved from the form of the chronicle, are represented for the sixth century by that composed by the Antiochene lawyer Evagrius. Christian history-writing (including those mentioned) regarded the traditions of saints' Lives as important, and there is a good deal of hagiographical material relating to the sixth century, much of which is valuable for the social, as well as the religious, history of the period, notably the collections by Cyril of Scythopolis and John Moschos, together with the lives of various individual saints (e.g., of the Stylites, or of St Theodore of Sykeon). To these can be added texts that are written, or survive, in Syriac, representing the views of those non-Chalcedonian Christians ('Monophysites') excluded from the imperial church by the drive towards a form of Chalcedonian orthodoxy promoted by Justinian and his successors. These include saints' Lives by Zacharias of Mytilene (originally written in Greek: his *Church History* does not advance into the sixth century), and both a collection of saints' Lives by John of Ephesus (who wrote in Syriac) and his *Church History*, the third part of which survives in a single manuscript, while the first two parts of which survive in fragmentary form incorporated into later Syriac chronicles. There are also an anonymous eighth-century chronicle, attributed to Pseudo-Dionysius of Tell-Mahre, and the twelfth-century chronicle of Michael the Syrian. Traditionally, the tendency has been to take the 'classical' histories at face value as a basic record, to be supplemented, with varying degrees of caution, from the chronicles and ecclesiastical sources.[2] The trend of recent scholarship, however, has been to pay much more attention to the particular intentions and bias of the 'classicising' historians, with the result that we now see in these sources a variety of sharply defined 'perspectives' on the sixth century rather than a straightforward narrative record that can be used as a basic framework.[3] Archaeology is an important resource, not least over major imponderables in this period, such as the decline (or survival) of the city, economic prosperity and climatic change. In addition we can also draw information from epigraphy, coins and seals, and make use of the evidence (traditionally little used) that remains embedded in the conservative, but developing, liturgy of the churches.

Accounts of the second half of Anastasius' reign indicate increasing popular unrest, ostensibly owing to the religious policy of the emperor. Behind this may lie growing economic difficulties and an increasing sense of insecurity in the Empire. At the beginning of the sixth century, the long peace with Persia, the traditional enemy of the Roman Empire, and indeed of its predecessors, came to an end. Refusal by the East Romans to pay tribute, owing to the failure of Persia to restore Nisibis to the Roman Empire in accordance with a treaty made with the emperor Jovian in the fourth century, led the Persians to invade the Roman Empire in 502 and they quickly took a number of frontier towns, including the city of Amida. To begin with, Roman resistance was weakened by a divided command, and it was two years before the Romans recovered Amida in 505. The weakness of the Mesopotamian frontier revealed by this brief war was remedied by the building of the fortress of Dara, close to the

[2] This is Gibbon's method in his *Decline and Fall of the Roman Empire* (1776–88), still used by J. B. Bury (Bury, 1923), and indeed by A. H. M. Jones (1964).

[3] See, notably, Cameron (1985b).

frontier and a few miles from Nisibis, which was called Anastasiopolis after the emperor. In the North too there were threats from invaders in the early sixth century, for there is archaeological evidence that suggests that the fortresses which Procopius says were built along the right bank of the Danube in the reign of Justinian (527–565) were at least begun by Anastasius.[4]

The riots that gave expression to opposition to Anastasius' religious policy were occasioned by a matter of liturgy. From the middle of the fifth century, the chant called the *Trisagion* ('Holy God, Holy Strong, Holy Immortal, have mercy on us') had become a popular part of the liturgy in the East. In Syria this chant was understood to be addressed to God the Son; and to underline the belief of those who rejected Chalcedon's distinction between the two natures in the Incarnate Son, the phrase 'who was crucified for us' was added to the chant, affirming their conviction that in Christ God himself had embraced human suffering (a doctrine called 'theopaschism'). In Constantinople, however, the chant, with its triadic form, was understood to be addressed to the Trinity, so such an addition seemed to imply that the divine nature itself was subject to suffering. Behind the differing texts of the chant, there lay genuine mutual misunderstanding, but that only made the sense of the error of the other side more acute. When Anastasius directed that the 'theopaschite' addition be included in the *Trisagion*, it provoked a riot between non-Chalcedonian monks chanting the amplified form and the clergy and people of Constantinople. This led to popular demands for the deposition of the emperor, demands only quelled by the emperor himself facing the mob, without his diadem, and inspiring an acclamation of loyalty. The next year (513) the emperor faced a further challenge to his authority from Vitalian, a military *comes*, who claimed to represent the reaction of the orthodox to the policies of the emperor. Although unsuccessful in his challenge to the throne, he outlived the emperor.

Anastasius died in 518, having left the question of his succession undetermined. He was succeeded by Justin I, a peasant from Illyria, who had risen through the ranks to become Count of the Excubitors. He was uneducated, perhaps even illiterate, and Procopius wants us to believe that the real power behind the throne was Justin's nephew, Petrus Sabbatius, who took the name of Justinian, whom Justin had earlier brought to the capital and on whom he had lavished an expensive education. How true this is it is hard to say, for there is no independent evidence to support the claim.[5] Justin's first act was to repudiate the attempts of his predecessors to achieve unity among the Christians by ignoring, or even implicitly condemning, the Synod of Chalcedon: the *Henotikon* was revoked and Chalcedonian orthodoxy became imperial policy. The Acacian schism was over, and Pope Hormisdas, to whom Justin announced

[4] Poulter (1983), p. 97, cited by Cameron (1985b), p. 220, n. 90.

[5] Honoré (1978), p. 7.

his election and his religious policy, sent legates to Constantinople, where a synod was held to confirm the ending of the schism, and condemn those who had promoted it, not only Acacius and those successors who had agreed with him, but also – in this exceeding papal demands – the emperors Zeno and Anastasius. Prominent non-Chalcedonian 'Monophysites', including Severus of Antioch and Philoxenos of Mabbug, were deposed and exiled. Reconciliation with Rome only opened once again the wounds that the *Henotikon* had been intended to heal, but very soon a refinement of Chalcedonian orthodoxy was put forward that was to become the focus of Justinian's endeavours to achieve religious unity. A group of monks from Scythia (modern Dobruja, the coastal area of Romania), led by John Maxentius, brought their proposal to Constantinople: it involved supplementing the Chalcedonian definition with the affirmation that 'one of the Trinity suffered in the flesh', an affirmation that would challenge the Monophysites' conviction of the indivisible unity of Christ, which had found expression in the 'theopaschite' addition to the *Trisagion*. Justinian was attracted by this proposal, and sent the monks off to Rome, where they failed to convince Pope Hormisdas, though others, notably Dionysius Exiguus and Boethius, found it acceptable. The proposal remained dormant until the 530s, when Justinian's religious endeavours began in earnest.

In spring 527 Justin fell ill, and Justinian was proclaimed Augustus as his colleague in April. In August Justin died, and Justinian succeeded him. Justinian's reign was a long one, lasting until 565, thirty-eight years in all, or forty-seven if one includes the period as the power behind Justin's throne. Either way, it was an exceptionally long reign, and its duration would be an achievement in itself, apart from anything else. But there was much else: reform of the legal code; reconquest of Roman territories in the West (North Africa, Italy, Spain); grandiose rebuilding projects, notably the rebuilding of the centre of Constantinople, including the Great Church of the Holy Wisdom, Hagia Sophia; the closure of the Platonic Academy in Athens; and a religious policy culminating in the Fifth Ecumenical Synod, held at Constantinople in 553 (or, to adopt a different perspective, in his lapse into heresy in his final months). The temptation to see all these as parts of a jigsaw which, when correctly fitted together, yield some grand design is hard to resist. And then there is glamour in the person of Theodora, the woman he married, circumventing the law forbidding the marriage of senators and actresses, whose beauty even Procopius admits, though he regarded her as a demon incarnate. Procopius wrote a malicious account of Theodora's meddling in the affairs of state in his *Secret History*. He also told of how during the so-called 'Nika riot' in 532, in which Justinian was profoundly frightened by the severe riots against his imperial rule and was contemplating flight, Theodora persuaded him to stay and face either death or victory with the dramatic words, 'the Empire is a fair winding-sheet'.

All this prepares the way for assessments of Theodora that rank her with Byzantine empresses like Eirene, or Zoë, both of whom (unlike Theodora) assumed imperial power in their own right, even if briefly.[6]

The 'grand design' view of Justinian's reign sees all his actions as the deliberate restoration of the ancient Roman Empire, though a Roman Empire raised to new heights of glory as a Christian Empire confessing the Orthodox faith. According to this view, reconquest restored something like the traditional geographical area of the Empire; law reform encapsulated the vision of a Christian Roman Empire, governed by God's vice-gerent, the emperor; the splendid buildings, not least the churches, of the capital celebrated the Christian court of New Rome, with the defensive buildings described by Procopius in the later books of his *Buildings* serving to preserve in perpetuity the newly reconquered Roman world. The defining of Christian orthodoxy, together with the suppression of heterodoxy, whether Christian heresy or pagan philosophy, completes the picture. In discussing Justinian's reign it is therefore difficult to avoid the notion of a 'grand design'. Virtually all our literary sources reflect something of this idea. It is there in Procopius (even the *Secret History* sees Justinian as a grand designer, though a malevolent one), in the legal texts and even in the ecclesiastical texts written by those who experienced persecution at Justinian's hand, for the Monophysites shared with those who embraced imperial Christianity the vision of a Christian empire ruled by a Christian emperor.[7] It is hardly to be denied that there were moments when Justinian fancied that he was fulfilling some such grandiose design. In 536, after the conquest of Sicily, Justinian affirms, 'we have good hope that God will grant us to rule over the rest of what, subject to the ancient Romans to the limits of both seas, they later lost by their easy-going ways' (*Nov.* 30)[8], but whether we should think of Justinian's reign as the fulfilment of a consciously preconceived grand design is another matter altogether. This raises two interrelated questions. First, do all the elements mentioned above fit together to constitute some grand design? And second, even if they do, did Justinian really have access to such power as to bring this grand design to fruition? As we shall see, neither of these questions can be answered in the affirmative without heavy qualifications.

Perhaps the most convincing evidence of such a grand design, at least at the beginning of his reign, is to be found in the revision of Roman law that Justinian set in hand as soon as he was in a position to do so. In this, too, he was fulfilling, in a striking way, one of the recognised tasks of a ruler, that of being ultimate judge and legislator. That was a task especially associated with the emperor of the Romans, for Romans prided themselves on their living under

[6] For a cool appraisal of such accounts, see Cameron (1985b), pp. 67–83.

[7] Fowden (1993). [8] Translation in Honoré (1978), p. 19.

the law (something given signal expression in the historian Priscus' account of the embassy to the court of Attila in the fifth century).[9] Within months of assuming sole rule, Justinian had announced to the Senate in a formal legal enactment (a 'constitution') his intention of having a new law-code prepared, that would bring matters up to date, reconcile contradictions, winnow out irrelevant legislation and introduce clarity. He set up a ten-man commission, led by the quaestor Tribonian, which completed its work in little more than a year. This code no longer survives, but five and a half years later, in 534, it was issued in a revised form, arranged in twelve books and containing constitutions from the intervening period: it is this edition that has survived to exercise such an influence on subsequent European law. By the time of the second edition, there had been a further contribution to the work of legal revision, the publication of the *Digest* or *Pandects*, which reduced to order the legal opinions of centuries of Roman lawyers. This was published in December 533. A further part of the legal reform was the publication of the *Institutes*, a revision of the Commentaries of the second-century jurist Gaius, which was to be the official textbook for students of law at the two official schools of law, in Constantinople and Berytus (modern Beirut). This revision and clarification of Roman law was complemented by the later laws of Justinian, the *Novellae*. Whereas the main body of Tribonian's work was in Latin, most of the *Novellae* are in Greek, for the reign of Justinian marks a watershed between the Roman Empire with Latin as the official language and the so-called 'Byzantine' Empire, in which Greek was the principal, and eventually the sole, language. The purpose of this legal reform is to be seen as twofold. It was practical: the Code and the *Novellae* provided legal norms to be interpreted by judges with the use of the *Digest*. It seems, however, that this function was not to continue much beyond the middle of the next century. But its other purpose was to delineate a world-view, enshrining the inheritance of Roman civilisation, the embrace of Christian orthodoxy, and the paramount position of the emperor. This was an enduring legacy, and at its heart was a vision of the complementarity of empire and priesthood, *basileia* and *hierosynê*, *imperium* and *sacerdotium*. This is expressed nowhere better than in *Novella* 6 (535):

> The greatest of God's gifts to men, given from on high in accordance with his loving-kindness, are priesthood and empire; the one ministers to things divine, the other rules and cares for matters human, both proceed from one and the same source and set in order human life. So nothing is more sought after by kings than the dignity of priests, if they beseech God continually on their behalf. For if the one is always unblemished and has open access to God, while the other rightly and fitly orders the received form of government, then there will be a fair harmony, and everything that is good for the

[9] Priscus, frag. 11; in Blockley (1983), pp. 242–80, esp. 270–2.

human race will be granted. We therefore have the greatest care for the true dogmas of God, as well as for the dignity of the priests, which we believe cares for them, as through it good gifts are given us from God, so that what we have we possess securely, and what we have not yet attained we shall come to acquire. Thus everything will be done rightly and fitly, if the beginning of everything is proper and acceptable to God. We believe that this will be so, if the observance of the holy canons is preserved, which has been handed down by the apostles, who are rightly praised and venerated as eyewitness and ministers of the Word of God, and which has been safeguarded and interpreted by the holy fathers.

Such comprehensive legislative activity can hardly be regarded as other than part of a grand design of imperial rule. The next essential ingredient, the reconquest of lost imperial territory, as we have seen, also inspired in Justinian the conviction that he was the divine agent in reconstituting the Roman Empire in a Christian form. But was this a settled conviction, or a passing hope? The facts about Justinian's reconquest of North Africa, Italy and Spain are not in doubt (though we are poorly informed about the Spanish expedition);[10] their interpretation is, however, much more hazardous. Although Justinian despatched his general Belisarius to North Africa with an impressive force of 10,000 infantry and 5000 cavalry, the reasons for his determination that this enterprise should not fail are perhaps more down-to-earth than the fulfilment of some grand design of imperial restoration. Justinian had only just recovered from the Nika riot, and the emperor Leo's earlier disastrous attempt to dislodge the Vandals (in 468) made it imperative that this expedition be a success if his credibility as emperor were to recover. Even by Procopius' celebratory account, Belisarius' speedy success seems to have been fortuitous. The Italian expedition, which followed up this success, seems to have been a much more modest affair: 7000 troops were involved, which, when compared with the 6000 Justinian sent in the same year with Narses to Alexandria to protect the Monophysite patriarch Theodosius, suggests that at that stage it was little more than a matter of showing the flag, even if the early successes, following so closely on the defeat of the Vandals, conjured up in Justinian's mind ideas of a grand design, as witnessed in the *Novellae* of the period. In reality, the reconquest of Italy proved to be a long-drawn-out affair, in the course of which Italy itself was devastated.[11] By 554, however, when Italy was formally restored to Byzantine rule (by a 'pragmatic sanction'), most of the Mediterranean littoral was once again part of the Roman Empire.

Justinian's rebuilding programmes likewise fit uneasily into the idea of a grand design. Our principal source for Justinian's extensive building activity is Procopius' *Buildings*, which takes the form of a panegyric and consequently presents the fullest and most splendid account, making no distinction

[10] See Barbero and Loring, chapter 7 below. [11] See Moorhead, chapter 5 below.

between new building work, restoration or even routine maintenance. As we saw earlier, the building of fortresses along the frontier, along the Danube and in Mesopotamia, to which Procopius devotes so much space, is not all to be attributed to Justinian himself: as archaeological surveys have shown (and indeed other contemporary historians assert, even Procopius himself in his *Wars*),[12] much of this was begun by his predecessor Anastasius. And the great wonders with which Procopius begins his account, when describing the reconstruction of the centre of Constantinople, were consequent upon the devastation wrought by the Nika riot of 532, which Justinian can hardly have planned. But however fortuitous the occasion, the buildings erected in the wake of the riot are works of enduring magnificence, none more so than the Church of the Holy Wisdom, Hagia Sophia. Contemporary accounts are breathtaking. Procopius says that:

> the church has become a spectacle of marvellous beauty, overwhelming to those who see it, but to those who know it by hearsay altogether incredible. For it soars to a height to match the sky, and as if surging up from amongst the other buildings it stands on high and looks down on the remainder of the city, adorning it, because it is a part of it, but glorying in its own beauty, because, though a part of the city and dominating it, it at the same time towers above it to such a height that the whole city is viewed from there as from a watch-tower.

He speaks, too, 'of the huge spherical dome which makes the structure exceptionally beautiful. Yet it seems not to rest on solid masonry, but to cover the space with its golden dome suspended from Heaven.' Contemporaries were struck by the quality of light in the Great Church: 'it abounds exceedingly in sunlight and in the reflection of the sun's rays from the marble. Indeed one might say that its interior is not illuminated from without by the sun, but that the radiance comes into being within it, such an abundance of light bathes the shrine.'[13] Paul the Silentiary, speaking of the church, restored after the collapse of the dome in 558, says 'even so in the evening men are delighted at the various shafts of light of the radiant, light-bringing house of resplendent choirs. And the calm clear sky of joy lies open to all driving away the dark-veiled mist of the soul. A holy light illuminates all.'[14] This stress on light as an analogy of divinity chimes in well with the vision found in the writings ascribed to Dionysius the Areopagite: a fact surely with bearing on the huge popularity these writings were soon to assume. The novel design of the church, with its dome forming an image of the cosmos, was immensely influential: there are many smaller Byzantine imitations of Hagia Sophia, and the suggestion of the church as a

[12] See Cameron (1985b), pp. 104–10.

[13] Procopius, *Buildings* 1.1.27; 1.1.46; 1.1.29–30, trans. Dewing 7 (1940), pp. 13, 17, 21.

[14] *Ecphrasis* 11.902–6, trans. Trypanis (1971), p. 418.

mimesis of the cosmos influenced later interpretations of the liturgical action that took place within (see the *Mystagogia* of the seventh-century Maximos the Confessor and the commentary on the liturgy ascribed to the eighth-century patriarch of Constantinople, Germanos).[15] But it may not have been novel: recent excavations in Istanbul have revealed the church of St Polyeuktos, built by the noblewoman Anicia Juliana in the late 520s, which seems in many respects to have foreshadowed Justinian's Great Church.[16] Original or not, the Great Church of Hagia Sophia, and the other buildings built by Justinian in the capital, which included more churches, the restored palace (in front of which in a kind of piazza was erected a massive pillar surmounted by a bronze statue of an equestrian Justinian), an orphanage, a home for repentant prostitutes, baths and, finally, a great cistern to secure an adequate water supply in summer, all these created a public space in which to celebrate a world-view in which the emperor ruled the inhabited world (the *oikoumene*), with the support of the court and the prayers of the church, to the acclamation of the people. According to Procopius' description of the mosaic in the great bronze gate (the *Chalke*) that formed the entrance to the palace, there, amid depictions of Justinian's victories achieved by his general Belisarius, stood the emperor Justinian and his empress Theodora, receiving from the Senate 'honours equal to God'.[17]

The world-view that these achievements of Justinian's – with whatever degree of deliberation – were seen to support laid great store by pure prayer being offered by an unblemished priesthood to the true God, the God of the Christians. Unlike other religions of late antiquity, whether the varieties of what Christians called paganism, or Judaism (or even, though it was yet to evolve, Islam), for Christianity 'purity' (or being 'unblemished') embraced not just moral (and especially sexual) purity, but also the correctness of a considerably elaborated system of belief. For most Christians of the sixth century, this system of belief had been defined at synods regarded as universal, or 'ecumenical' (derived from *oikoumene*, a term belonging to imperial ideology), though there were differences, as we have seen, as to whether the Synod of Chalcedon was to be regarded as the fourth universal synod. The emperor Justin's embrace of Chalcedonian orthodoxy had healed the long-standing schism between the East and Rome, but left unresolved the disagreement between those who accepted Chalcedon (with whatever refinements) and those who rejected it as a betrayal of Cyril of Alexandria, the 'seal of the Fathers'.

15 Maximos' *Mystagogia*, in Migne, *PG* 91, cols. 657–717. The text of Germanos' commentary in Migne, *PG* 98, cols. 384–453, is poor. For a critical edition, with English translation, Meyendorff (1989).

16 See Harrison (1989).

17 Procopius, *Buildings* 1.10.15–30. Rousseau detects irony in Procopius' account here: Rousseau (1996), p. 27.

But all Christians, whatever their differences, were opposed to what they had come to call the 'exterior wisdom', the learning of the classical philosophers. As Romanos the Melodist, the Christian poet who spent most of his life in Constantinople during Justinian's reign, put it:

> And why do the fools outside strive for victory?
> Why do the Greeks puff and buzz?
> Why are they deceived by Aratos the thrice accursed? Why err like wandering planets to Plato?
> Why do they love the debilitated Demosthenes?
> Why do they consider Homer a chimera?
> Why do they go on about Pythagoras, who were better muzzled?[18]

This antipathy had been returned in kind, and some adherents of Neoplatonism, as scholars call it, though loftily indifferent to the new-fangled teachings of the 'pale Galilean', developed a world-view that openly ignored Christianity, and religious practices that sought to revive traditional paganism. A notable example of such Neoplatonism was Proclus, a deeply learned philosopher, who lived the life of an ascetic, pagan holy man, with an especial devotion to the sun, and taught for fifty years in Athens until his death in 485 as head (or *diadochos*) of the Academy that had been founded by Plato in the fourth century BC. Part of Justinian's commitment to Christian orthodoxy was expressed in his closing of the Academy in 529. The closure, however, did not take place before much of the 'pagan' language and intellectual structures had found Christian expression in the writings ascribed to St Paul's Athenian disciple, Dionysius the Areopagite, that began to make an impact in the 520s, very shortly, it is thought, after they had been written. In 532, the philosophers, led by Damascius, the last *diadochos*, made their way to Persia, but after a few years returned, Damascius to Emesa, where he seems to have continued to teach.[19] Neoplatonism continued to thrive in Alexandria for another century, where it was not stridently anti-Christian. Indeed most, if not all, of the Alexandrian philosophers were Christian. But the closure of the Academy meant the end of any institutional expression of intellectual opinion.

Alongside the suppression of pagan Neoplatonism, there was suppression of other forms of heterodoxy. In various parts of the Empire we learn of more vigorous attempts to suppress survivals of traditional 'paganism'.[20] In the 540s, the Monophysite bishop John of Ephesus, with imperial support, embarked

[18] Romanos, *Kontakion* 33 on Pentecost, stanza 17: ed. Maas and Trypanis, p. 265 (translation in Lash, p. 215: the Greek original is full of untranslatable puns).

[19] Cameron (1969).

[20] It is probably misleading to regard as paganism the continuation of traditional religious practices by people who thought of themselves as Christians: see Haldon (1997), pp. 327–37, with literature cited.

on a missionary campaign in western Asia Minor, in which he claimed to have converted 70,000 souls, destroyed many temples, and founded ninety-six churches and twelve monasteries. In Egypt, too, we know of the destruction of temples. Other forms of heterodox opinion fared no better: Manichaeism, a dualist doctrine founded by Mani who died in Persia in 276, which had dogged the Christian church through its years of growing success, was an offence punishable by death; the revolt of the Samaritans (who embraced what is perhaps a primitive form of Judaism) against repression was savagely suppressed in 529; ancient Christian heresies like Montanism also suffered repression under Justinian. The Monophysites, who were both more numerous and closer in belief to the imperial church, are a special case to be dealt with presently. The Jews, however, formed a relatively privileged group of second-class citizens. In contrast to heretics and pagans, who had no rights and no civil status, Jews were allowed to exist, and their existence was protected. Jews were allowed to practise circumcision and observe the Sabbath, their synagogues were protected from violence or desecration (not always effectively), they kept their Rabbinic courts of law, and they were not to be molested. But they were to exist as a 'living testimony' to the truth of Christianity, a living testimony to the wretchedness of those who had deliberately rejected their Messiah. So the laws that protected their existence also enshrined the principle that Jews must never enjoy the fruits of office, but only suffer its pains and penalties. They were not to expand, so no new synagogues were to be built, and there were often difficulties made about repairing existing ones. The Jews were to be encouraged to convert, but it was to be from a genuine change of heart: they were not to be coerced. They were thus allowed to exist, with rights and civil status, but in a permanently inferior state.[21]

In the 530s, in parallel with the furthering of legal reform, reconquest and rebuilding, Justinian sought to achieve a reconciliation between orthodox Chalcedonianism and 'Monophysite' anti-Chalcedonianism. The basis for this reconciliation was the doctrine of theopaschism, brought to Justinian's attention by the Scythian monks a decade or so earlier, but which was now part of a wider theological movement, usually known as 'Neo-Chalcedonianism' or (better) Cyrilline Chalcedonianism. This theological movement, which was quite independent of Justinian, seems to have been inspired by attempts to meet the attack by the great non-Chalcedonian theologian Severus, patriarch of Antioch 512–518, on the definition of Chalcedon as incompatible with the teaching of Cyril of Alexandria. Those Eastern Christians (by no means a minority) who had accepted Chalcedon did so believing that it endorsed Cyril's teaching.

[21] Sharf (1971), pp. 19–41. For comparison with the experience of Jews elsewhere in Europe in this period, see Toch, chapter 20 below.

Cyrilline Chalcedonianism sought to interpret Chalcedon in the light of Cyril's teaching, believing (not unreasonably) that this represented the mind of the fathers of the synod. It was based on three clarifications of the definition of the synod: first, that the 'one person' of the Incarnate Christ is the second person of the Trinity; second, consequent acceptance of the theopaschite formula, 'One of the Trinity suffered in the flesh'; and third, agreement that one of Cyril's favourite ways of describing the Incarnate Christ ('one incarnate nature of God the Word') was acceptable and only verbally appeared to contradict the doctrine of one person and two natures (this phrase is the source of the term by which the non-Chalcedonians have come to be called: 'Monophysites', believers in one (only) nature). Notable representatives of Cyrilline Chalcedonianism included John of Caesarea ('the Grammarian') and Leontius of Jerusalem. Justinian was convinced that this provided a way of reconciliation, and at a conference held in Constantinople in 532 a large measure of theological agreement was reached, the failure of the conversations being due to practical considerations (about the terms for the reinstatement of non-Chalcedonian bishops).[22] Thereafter Justinian resorted to persecution, thwarted by the protection given, to the Monophysites in the palace itself, by the Empress Theodora. But he never gave up his attempt to promote Cyrilline Chalcedonianism, which culminated in the synod held in Constantinople in 553, the Fifth Ecumenical Synod.

The Fifth Ecumenical Synod was concerned with two issues: the condemnation of the so-called 'Three Chapters', and the condemnation of Origenism.[23] The condemnation of the Three Chapters was part of Justinian's attempt to achieve reconciliation between the Orthodox and the Monophysites. The 'Three Chapters' were writings by three bishops who were particularly obnoxious to the Monophysites: Theodore of Mopsuestia, Theodoret of Kyrrhos and Ibas of Edessa. Theodore, who died in 428, was regarded as the inspiration behind Nestorius, whose condemnation Cyril had brought about at the Third Ecumenical Synod, held at Ephesus in 431. Theodoret and Ibas had been condemned at the 'Robber synod' of Ephesus of 449, but reinstated two years later by the Synod of Chalcedon. There was considerable resistance to the condemnation of the Three Chapters in the West, where it was regarded as an attempt to interfere with Chalcedon, Pope Leo's synod. Pope Vigilius was forcibly summoned to Constantinople, where he was held under house arrest until he accepted the condemnation of the Three Chapters. His successors

[22] Brock (1980).

[23] Because of the silence of the Western sources (including, crucially, the *Acta*, which only survive in Latin) about the condemnation of Origenism, some scholars still maintain that Origenism was not dealt with at the council. The arguments of Guillaumont (1962), pp. 133–6, however, seem conclusive.

were required to accept his action (though Pope Gregory the Great only ever speaks of 'four synods'). But others in the West were not so pliant: the pope was excommunicated by bishops in North Africa and in northern Italy (the schism between Rome and Aquileia was not healed until 700). The condemnation of Origenism has often been regarded as a counter-balance to the condemnation of the Three Chapters, but there seems no reason at all to believe this, as there was nothing Monophysite about Origenism. It really belongs with Justinian's attack on pagan Neoplatonism, for Origen and the Origenists were regarded as too deeply indebted to Platonism (Origen had been a disciple of Ammonius Saccos, the master of Plotinus), and as such it was an action for which he could count on the applause of most Christians. Such Origenist ideas, however, remained popular among some of the more intellectually inclined monks.

All these attempts to achieve reconciliation amongst the Christians of the Empire achieved nothing, however. Already by the time the synod met, the schism had become irrevocable. In 542 in Constantinople Theodosius, the exiled Monophysite patriarch of Alexandria, had consecrated Jacob Bar 'Addai secretly bishop of Edessa for the Ghassanids, an Arab kingdom allied to the Empire. Once ordained, Jacob set about ordaining bishops for Monophysite congregations throughout the East, thus providing a parallel hierarchy to that of the Orthodox church of the Empire. Imperial attempts to crush this rival church through persecution met with little success.

On the face of it, it looks as if Justinian's religious policies must be accounted a downright failure. That is true, if his endeavours are simply regarded as attempts at healing the schism in the (especially Eastern) church. But these endeavours can be viewed from another perspective: that of leaving the emperor's mark on the Orthodox church of the Empire. From that perspective his success was real. The reception of the Synod of Chalcedon in the sixth century took place along the lines that Justinian promoted: the Christology of the synod was henceforth to be interpreted in the East along the lines of Cyrilline Chalcedonianism, and a theopaschite understanding of the Incarnation became accepted, with implications beyond the narrowly theological. By the ninth century a hymn, 'Only-begotten Son', ascribed to Justinian, formed a regular part of the Eucharistic Liturgy. Whether or not the literary composition was Justinian's, the theopaschite theology of the hymn ('you were crucified, Christ God . . . being One of the Holy Trinity') is certainly his, and such theopaschite devotion, flanked by the development of angelology and Mariology, found expression in the flourishing iconographic tradition of the Eastern church.

The answer to the first question we raised earlier about seeing Justinian's reign in terms of a grand design would seem then to be negative, although in the first decade of his sole rule Justinian may have entertained some such idea. But, to turn to the second question we raised earlier, even if the elements of a grand design to Justinian's reign – legal reform, reconquista, rebuilding, prosecution of orthodoxy – had fitted together as well as it has often been maintained they did, there are other factors in Justinian's reign that would have prevented any such grand design being brought to fruition.

One of these factors was the Persians. They constituted the traditional enemy of the Roman Empire, and after a period of peace in the latter half of the fifth century, war had broken out again, as has been noted above, in the reign of Anastasius, which resulted in the building of the fort at Dara shortly after 505. It was twenty years before war broke out again between the Roman and Persian empires, partly over Justinian's decision to reinforce the fort at Dara. The initial battles took place in Lazica (on the eastern coast of the Black Sea, in modern Georgia), an important buffer zone for the Romans, both against the barbarians north of the Caucasus and against a Persian advance through Iberia. One of the Persian generals on this occasion, Narses, defected to the Romans after having inflicted defeat on them. But the main part of Justinian's first Persian War took place in Mesopotamia, and proved to be the scene of the rise to prominence of another of Justinian's generals, Belisarius. The Romans held their ground, and the war was concluded with a 'Perpetual Peace', negotiated with Chosroes, who had become shah after the death of his aged father on 13 September 531. It was this peace that gave Justinian the resources for the North African and Italian campaigns of the 530s. Chosroes was to reign for nearly fifty years and in Persian historiography is depicted as one of the greatest of the Sasanian shahs,[24] but the 'Perpetual Peace' negotiated at the beginning of his reign was not typical of his relations with his western neighbour. In 540, a territorial dispute between two Christian Arab 'kingdoms', the Nestorian Lakhmids, clients of Persia, and the Monophysite Ghassanids, clients of the Roman Empire, provided an opportunity for Chosroes to respond to pleas from Witigis, the hard-pressed Ostrogothic king of Italy, and from the Armenians, suffering from their incorporation into the Roman Empire as a result of the Perpetual Peace, and invade the Roman Empire. The war was fought on several fronts – in Syria, Mesopotamia and Lazica – and Antioch was seized by the Persians. A truce was called in 545, but there was still fighting in Lazica until 557. In 561 a peace was negotiated, restoring the *status quo*, which was to last for fifty years, during which period the Romans agreed to pay tribute at the rate of 30,000 golden *nomismata* a year.[25] Persia had once again become a force to reckon with, and was to remain so, until it, and a good deal of the Roman Empire itself, succumbed to the Arabs in the seventh century.

[24] See R. N. Frye in the *Cambridge History of Iran*, vol. III (1).
[25] Menander, frag. 6, 1, ed. Blockley.

Persia clearly represents a factor constituting a hindrance to the success of any initiatives undertaken by the emperor Justinian. Another factor restricting his plans, much more difficult to assess, is the effect of natural disasters and changes in climate. The chronicles give a vivid picture of recurrent earthquake, famine and plague, as well as events recorded as harbingers of disaster, such as eclipses and comets. Malalas, for instance, records ten examples of Justinian making grants for the reconstruction of cities devastated by war or natural disaster.[26] Recent studies[27] suggest that the early years of Justinian's reign indeed saw extreme climatic conditions, the causes of which are not yet determined: the years 536–537 saw what is called a 'dust-veil' phenomenon, recorded in the chronicles as a kind of perpetual solar eclipse. One can only speculate about the impact of such phenomena, but it is hard not to think that they led to the disruption of traditional patterns, and a growing sense of insecurity, not to mention the drain on finite resources caused by the need for reconstruction. It is in this context that there occurred the Nika riot of 532, where tension between the circus factions, the Blues and the Greens, erupted in a riot, in which the emperor Justinian was nearly toppled, and much of the palace area, including the churches of Hagia Sophia and Hagia Eirene, was destroyed by fire. Popular anger against resented officials was appeased by the dismissal of the city prefect Eudaemon, the quaestor Tribonian, and the praetorian prefect John of Cappadocia. The riot continued for several days, and was only quelled in the end by the massacre of 30,000 people, trapped in the hippodrome, acclaiming as emperor the unfortunate Hypatios, a general and one of emperor Anastasius' nephews, who was afterwards executed as a usurper.

The reaction of some Christians, at any rate, to the whole sequence of disasters is captured in the *kontakion* Romanos the Melodist composed 'On Earthquakes and Fires' (a *kontakion* is a verse sermon that formed part of the sung vigil, one of the popular services in non-monastic churches). Romanos wrote and performed this *kontakion* one Lent during the period when the Great Church of Hagia Sophia was being rebuilt (i.e., between February 532 and 27 December 537). It is a call to repentance after three disasters that represent three 'blows' by God against sinful humanity: earthquakes (between 526 and 530, several earthquakes are recorded in Constantinople and elsewhere), drought (recorded in Constantinople in September 530), and finally the Nika riot itself in January 532.[28] These repeated blows were necessary because of the heedlessness of the people. Repentance and pleas for mercy began, Romanos makes clear, with the emperor and his consort, Theodora:

[26] Scott (1996), p. 25, n. 37. [27] Farquharson (1996); Koder (1996).

[28] For this analysis see Koder (1996), pp. 275–6.

Those who feared God stretched out their hands to him,
Beseeching him for mercy and the end of disasters,
And along with them, as was fitting, the ruler prayed too,
Looking up to the Creator, and with him his wife,
'Grant to me, Saviour,' he cried, 'as to your David
To conquer Goliath, for I hope in you.
Save your faithful people in your mercy,
And grant to them
Eternal Life.'

When God heard the sound of those who cried out and also of the rulers,
He granted his tender pity to the city . . .[29]

The rebuilt city, and especially the Great Church, is a sign of both the care of the Emperor and the mercy of God:

In a short time they [the rulers] raised up the whole city
So that all the hardships of those who had suffered were forgotten.
The very structure of the church
Was erected with such excellence
As to imitate heaven, the divine throne,
Which indeed offers
Eternal Life.[30]

This confirms the picture of recurrent adversity, found in the chroniclers and (it is argued) supported by astronomical and archaeological evidence. But also it indicates the way in which religion attempted to meet the need of those who suffered – a way that evoked and reinforced the Byzantine world-view of a cosmos ruled by God, and the *oikoumene* ruled, on his behalf, by the emperor. But a study of the *kontakia* of Romanos reveals, too, the convergence of the public (and imperial) apparatus of religion and private recourse to the Incarnate Christ and the Mother of God and the saints, as well as the importance of the relic of the True Cross, and the relics of the saints, as touchstones, as it were, of divine grace. It is in the sixth century, too, that we begin to find increasing evidence of the popularity – at both public and private levels – of devotion to the Mother of God, and of religious art ('icons') as mediating between the divine realm, consisting of God and his court of angels and saints, and the human realm, desperately in need of the grace that flows from that divine realm: icons become both objects of prayer and veneration, and a physical source of healing and reassurance.

[29] Romanos, *Kontakion* 54, stanzas 18–19: ed. Maas and Trypanis, pp. 468ff. Translation, somewhat revised, Carpenter, vol. II, pp. 245ff.

[30] Romanos, *Kontakion* 54, stanza 23: ed. Maas and Trypanis, pp. 470–1. Translation, Carpenter, vol. II, p. 247.

But if the 530s saw widespread alarm caused by natural and human disasters, the 540s saw the beginning of an epidemic of bubonic plague that was to last for somewhat more than two centuries. According to Procopius, it originated in Egypt, but it seems very likely that it travelled from the East along trade routes, perhaps the silk route. It appeared in Constantinople in spring 542, and had reached Antioch and Syria later in the same year. Huge numbers died: in Constantinople it has been calculated that around 250,000 people died, perhaps a little more than half the population. Few who caught the disease survived (this few seems to have included Justinian himself), and those that died did so quickly, within two or three days. Thereafter the plague seems to have declined somewhat in virulence, but according to Evagrius, the church historian, there was severe loss of life in the years 553/4, 568/9 and 583/4. Historians disagree about the probable effect of the plague on the economic life of the Eastern Empire: some[31] take its impact seriously, others, following a similar revision in the estimate of the effects of the Black Death in the fourteenth century,[32] think that the effect of the plague has been exaggerated.[33]

In the final months of his life, Justinian himself fell into heresy, the so-called 'Julianist' heresy of aphthartodocetism, an extreme form of Monophysitism named after Julian, bishop of Halikarnassos (d. *c.*527), which he promulgated by an edict. This is stated by Theophanes and by Eustratios, in his *Life* of Eutychios, the patriarch of Constantinople, who was deposed for refusing to accept Justinian's new-found religious inclination, and is generally accepted by historians. It has, however, been questioned by theologians, who cite evidence for Justinian's continued adherence to a Christology of two natures, together with evidence that he was continuing to seek reconciliation between divided Christians, not only with the 'Julianists' themselves, which might indeed have led to Orthodox suspicion of Julianism on Justinian's part, but also with the so-called Nestorians of Persia. The question is complex, but seems to be open.[34]

Justinian died childless on 14 November 565. The succession had been left open. One of his three nephews, called Justin, who had long occupied the minor post of *cura palatii*, but who was, perhaps more significantly, married to Sophia, one of Theodora's nieces, secured election by the Senate and succeeded his uncle. The only serious contender, a second cousin of Justinian's also called Justin, one of the *magistri militum*, was despatched to Alexandria and murdered, it is said at the instigation of Sophia. Justin II continued (or reinstated) Justinian's policy of religious orthodoxy, though earlier he (or at least his wife, Sophia) had inclined to Monophysitism. In renewing his uncle's religious policy, he restored religious harmony between East and West, and affirmed this shared orthodoxy by the gift of a splendid enamelled crucifix

[31] Patlagean (1977). [32] See, for example, J. Hatcher (1994), pp. 3–35.
[33] Whittow (1996), pp. 66–8. [34] See the discussion in Grillmeier (1995), pp. 467–73.

containing a relic of the True Cross, given to the Frankish queen Radegund, which inspired the greatest Latin hymns in honour of the cross, Venantius Fortunatus' *Pange Lingua* and *Vexilla Regis*. But at the same time he sought reconciliation with the Monophysites. This attempt at reconciliation ended in 572, with the Monophysites' rejection of Justin's so-called 'second *Henotikon*'; this rejection resulted in the persecution of the Monophysites recorded by John of Ephesus in his *Church History*.[35]

But Justin is mainly remembered for his arrogant foreign policy, which, by refusing the maintenance of alliances with barbarian tribes, not least the Avars, and the preservation of peace with Persia, immensely weakened the position of the Empire. Throughout the century, the Romans had been concerned for the security of the Danube frontier. Both Anastasius and Justinian invested a good deal in the building of a line of forts and the fortification of the cities close to the frontier. In addition to this, Justinian established alliances with various of the barbarian groups – with the Antae (nomadic people of unknown origin, who soon vanish from our sources) in around 545, and with the Avars in 558 – and used them to check other barbarian tribes north of the Danube. Another group of barbarians, which proved a constant concern, was the Slavs, who by the middle of the sixth century were established on the north bank of the Danube, from which they made raids across the Danube into Byzantine territory. From around 560 they began to winter on Byzantine territory. Within a few days of Justin's accession, an embassy arrived from the Avars, requesting the tribute they had been accustomed to receive from Justinian in return (as they said) for not invading the Empire and even defending it against other barbarians. Justin haughtily rebuffed them. But as the Avars were more concerned with the Franks at this stage, Justin's action provoked no immediate response from them. Two years later, Justin was able to benefit from war between the barbarians: when the Lombards and the Avars formed an alliance together to crush the Gepids, another barbarian group who occupied Pannonia Secunda and held the city of Sirmium, he was able to seize Sirmium, and held on to it in the war with the Avars that followed. The fall of the Gepids had further consequences for the Empire, for the Lombards, who were occupying the borders of Noricum, now had the Avars as immediate neighbours. To avoid this they migrated south and invaded northern Italy, with which many of them were familiar, having been there as allies of Narses in 552.[36] Under their king, Alboin, they took most of Venetia in 568, and the following year most of Liguria, including Milan. Pavia (Ticinum) offered more resistance, until it too fell to the Lombards in 572.

Elsewhere barbarians made inroads on the Empire. Moorish revolts in North Africa caused the death of a praetorian prefect in 569 and two *magistri militum* in the two following years. In Spain, the Visigoths attacked the Byzantines,

[35] On this see Cameron (1976). [36] Cf. Moorhead, chapter 6 below.

taking Asidona in 571 and Córdoba in 572.[37] The year 572 would not, therefore, have seemed a propitious one to provoke the Persians, but in that year Justin refused the first annual tribute under the Fifty-Year Peace negotiated by Justinian (having evidently paid the three-year tribute due in 568). The Christians of Persian Armenia had risen in revolt against the attempts by Chosroes to impose Zoroastrianism on them and appealed to Justin, who not only refused the tribute due in 572, but also threatened to invade Persia and depose Chosroes if he persisted in his attempts to turn the Armenians from Christianity. The Armenian revolt was successful, and they were joined by the Iberian kingdom. Justin ordered an invasion of Persia. His cousin, Marcian, appointed *magister militum per Orientem*, in 572 attacked Arzanene, on the southern border of Persian Armenia, and the next year attacked Nisibis. Once the Persians had overcome their surprise at the Roman attack, their response was devastating: they invaded Syria and took Apamea, and then went on not only to relieve Nisibis, but to besiege and capture the fortress of Dara. The news of the fall of Dara drove Justin mad, and his consort Sophia took the reins of power. She negotiated a truce of one year with the Persians for which the Romans paid 45,000 *nomismata* (half as much again as had been due); this was later extended to five years, at the old rate of 30,000 *nomismata* a year. But Sophia could not, as a woman, rule as regent herself, and in December 574 she persuaded Justin to make Tiberius, the Count of the Excubitors, Caesar. Although Justin lived until 578, in the interim government was in the hands of Sophia and Tiberius. Sophia is, in fact, a somewhat neglected Byzantine empress. Far less famous than her aunt Theodora, but unlike her aunt she played a direct role in Byzantine politics, securing the succession of her husband, and the succession of Tiberius, whom she vainly hoped to make her second husband. She is the first empress to appear on Byzantine coins together with her husband.[38] Theophanes the Confessor, who clearly disliked women with pretensions to power, paints an ugly picture of Sophia and her meddling in imperial matters, as he did of Eirene, the first Byzantine empress to rule in her own name. It may be significant that he has comparatively little to say about Theodora.

Tiberius became emperor in 578, but by then had already effectively been governing for four years. In many respects he was the reverse of his predecessor: whereas Justin was financially cautious to the point of being regarded as miserly, but militarily ambitious, Tiberius bought popularity by reducing taxes, but in military matters exercised caution. He also called a halt to the persecution of the Monophysites, on which Justin had embarked. Tiberius quickly realized that the Empire did not have the resources to engage with its enemies on all fronts. He thus secured the support of the Avars on the Danube frontier by

[37] Cf. Barbero and Loring, chapter 7 below.

[38] For Sophia, see Cameron (1975).

paying them tribute of 80,000 *nomismata* a year: this secured not just quiet from hostilities, but Avar support against the Slavs, whose homeland on the banks of the Danube was devastated by Avar cavalry, with Byzantine support. This truce with the Avars did not, however, last for long. In 580 they attacked Sirmium, and in 582 after a long siege the city was ceded to the Avars by an agreement in accordance with which the garrison and population were allowed to evacuate to Roman territory in return for a payment of 240,000 *nomismata*, the tribute not paid since the Avar attack. During the siege of Sirmium, many Slavs crossed the Danube and invaded Thrace, Macedonia and Greece: they were eventually to settle throughout the Balkans, though there is no evidence for Slav settlements (called *Sklaviniai* by the Byzantines) until the next century. But the attempt to buy off the Avars and secure peace on the Danube frontier was to enable Tiberius to concentrate on the Persian frontier, where again his aims seem to have been modest: to build up enough strength to secure again the peace that had been broken by Justin. The one-year truce negotiated by Sophia needed to be extended, but the five-year truce that had later been negotiated seemed to Tiberius too long. On his accession as Caesar this truce was set at three years, on the understanding that in the meantime envoys would seek to establish a more enduring peace. At the end of the extended truce, the Byzantine army in the East, led by Maurice, who had succeeded Tiberius as Count of the Excubitors on his becoming Caesar, was now in a position to make inroads on the Persians, and had occupied Arzanene. Negotiations were proceeding for a peace that would restore to the Byzantines the fortress of Dara, but in the course of the negotiations, in 579, Chosroes died. His son Hormisdas, who succeeded him, broke off the negotiations, and war continued. In August 582, Tiberius himself died, having crowned Maurice Augustus the previous day.

Maurice was an effective general, who had already achieved military success under Tiberius before becoming emperor himself. Even if he is not the author of the military treatise called the *Strategikon*, the attribution to him of this treatise is not inappropriate. For it certainly reflects Byzantine military practice of the late sixth century, with its stress on the importance of cavalry in warfare, and it seems to envisage campaigns against Avars and Antae, which again reflects the reality of late sixth-century Byzantine warfare. Like his predecessor, Maurice concentrated his military effort, to begin with, on the Persian front, and sought to deal with the other threats to the Empire by diplomacy and tribute. At the beginning of his reign, he paid the Frankish king Childebert to attack the Lombards in northern Italy, which he did in 584 securing the submission of the Lombard dukes. This was repeated in 588 and 589. On the Danube frontier, Maurice had less success. Two years after his accession, the Avars demanded an increase in their tribute from 80,000 to 100,000 *nomismata*. On Maurice's refusal, they seized Singidunum (modern Belgrade) and attacked other cities in the region around. To recover Singidunum and secure peace, Maurice had to pay the extra 20,000 *nomismata*. But the Avars soon allowed the Slavs to overrun and ravage Thrace; they reached Adrianople and the Long Wall before they were driven back. After that the Avars themselves crossed the Danube and made for Constantinople. They crossed the Haemus mountains, having easily defeated a Byzantine force of 10,000 sent against them, invaded Thrace and besieged Adrianople; they were only defeated by Droctulf, a Lombard duke, who came to the service of the Empire. In the same year (586) Thessalonica was besieged by the Slavs, and was only saved, so the people of Thessalonica believed, by the intercession of their patron saint, Demetrios.[39]

On the Persian front the war dragged on inconclusively. There was a mutiny in the army when Maurice, to alleviate the drain on the treasury, attempted to cut their pay by a quarter. In 590 Martyropolis, in Arzanene, was taken by the Persians. The following year saw a dramatic change of fortune. The Persian shah, Hormisdas, was killed in a rebellion led by one of his satraps, Bahram. His son Chosroes fled to the Byzantines and with their help crushed Bahram's rebellion and secured the Persian throne. In return for the help of the Byzantine emperor, Chosroes gave up his claim to Armenia and Arzanene, and restored Martyropolis and Dara to the Empire. After twenty years, there was again peace between the Byzantine and Persian empires. Maurice now turned his attention to the Danube frontier. In 592 the khagan of the Avars demanded an increase in the tribute paid him, and with the troops transferred from the now quiet eastern front, Maurice responded by confronting the Avars. The siege of Singidunum was relieved; nevertheless the Avars invaded Thrace, but abruptly left under the delusion that their homeland in Pannonia was in danger (Theophylact presents this as a cunning Byzantine ruse, but the twelfth-century Syriac chronicler Michael the Syrian invokes fear of a Turkish threat to their homeland).[40] But the real object of Maurice's military policy seems to have been the Slavs: in the interests both of preserving resources and of effective military strategy, Maurice ordered the Byzantine troops to engage with the Slavs in their settlements north of the Danube. The army, accustomed to rest during winter, threatened to mutiny. The next year another measure, intended both to increase efficiency and to save money, was introduced: instead of receiving cash allowances for their equipment, they were to be issued directly with their military equipment. This was deeply unpopular. The Avars made further attacks, being rebuffed in their attack on Singidunum and Dalmatia

[39] Lemerle (1979, 1981). On the emergence of the Slavs in the Byzantine sources, see Kobyliński, chapter 19 below.

[40] *The History of Theophylact Simocatta*, ed. L. M. Whitby and M. Whitby, p. 166, n. 33.

in 598, and failing to take Tomi on the Scythian coast of the Black Sea in 599. Later they threatened Constantinople itself, but an epidemic of plague in the Avar camp led the khagan to withdraw and agree a treaty in which the Danube was recognised as the frontier. Maurice quickly revoked the treaty and in 600 the Byzantine army defeated the Avars. The next year was quiet, but in 602 the Byzantines made successful attacks on the Slavs north of the Danube. Maurice gave orders that the army should engage in a winter campaign in Slav territory. This time there was open mutiny; the commander of the army fled, and under a new commander called Phokas the troops advanced on Constantinople. Maurice, who had made himself unpopular with his economies, found himself defenceless in the capital. After a bungled attempt to seize his son's father-in-law, Germanus, to whom the troops had offered the crown, Maurice found himself facing a popular riot in which the palace of the Praetorian Prefect of the East was burned down. Maurice fled, and Phokas was proclaimed emperor on 23 November 602. A few days later Maurice was executed, after his sons had been slain before his eyes. The death of Maurice and the accession of the usurper Phokas left the Empire in a fragile state: civil war weakened the Empire within, and external enemies took advantage of the weakness thus revealed. As the seventh century advanced, matters appeared very black indeed.

At the end of the sixth century the Eastern Roman Empire was, as we know with hindsight, on the brink of dramatic transformation: the rise of Arab power would rob it of its eastern and southern provinces; the settlement of the Slavs in the Balkan peninsula would deprive the Eastern Empire of those provinces and isolate New Rome from old Rome; the last vestiges of a traditional city-based society seem to have crumbled in an Empire now barely capable of defending its capital, or regenerating itself after natural disaster or epidemic. It is difficult not to see seeds of all this, as we survey the history of the sixth century. The idea of an Orthodox Christian empire did cause both divisions between Christians in the East, and tensions between the increasingly Greek Christianity of the Empire and the Latin Christianity of Rome and the West; the public spaces of the city ceased to be used, and were left to decay or be encroached on by more private activities. Although all this is true, to think in terms of decline is to look at only part of the picture. The public life of the cities may have declined, but it yielded to the demands of the Christian church for space for its activities: increasingly the urban rituals that expressed what sense of civic identity survived became Christian rituals. The church buildings themselves became increasingly important as public places, and moved from the urban periphery to dominate the centre, while the episcopal offices grew in size, in parallel with the developing role of the bishop. The growth in devotion to icons (for which our evidence increases dramatically in the latter half of the sixth century) has been plausibly attributed to 'the continuing needs of the ancient city'.[41] Such Christianisation is neither a vampirish corollary of 'decline' nor evidence of the success of Christian 'mission': it is rather evidence for change, which needs to be evaluated in its own terms. What was taking place at the level of the city had a parallel in (and may have been inspired by) transformation of imperial ritual. In the latter part of the century, we see a growing tendency to underwrite the imperial structures of authority by appeal to Christian symbols: the court of the emperor is presented as reflecting the heavenly court; Constantine's *labarum* is joined by icons of Christ and his Virgin Mother.[42] If this transformed society was to come close to disaster in the seventh century, it is also true that it contained the seeds of survival and renewal, but what survived was a significantly different society from what the East Roman Empire had been at the beginning of the sixth century.

[41] Brown (1973), p. 21. [42] For this interpretation see Cameron (1979).

CHAPTER 5

THE BYZANTINES IN THE WEST IN THE SIXTH CENTURY

John Moorhead

THE CONTINUING UNITY OF THE POST-ROMAN WORLD

Throughout the political history of western Europe, there have been few periods of such dramatic change as the fifth century. In 400 the borders of the Roman Empire in the West, by then distinct from the Empire in the East which was governed from Constantinople, stood reasonably firm. They encompassed all of Europe south of the Antonine Wall in Britain and the Rhine and the Danube rivers on the continent, extending eastwards of the confluence of the latter river with the Drava, as well as a band of territory along the African coast which extended two thirds of the way from the Straits of Gibraltar to the Nile. But within a hundred years this mighty entity had ceased to east. North Africa had been occupied by groups known as Vandals and Alans, Spain by Visigoths and Sueves, and Gaul by Visigoths, Franks and Burgundians. The Romans had withdrawn from Britain early in the century, leaving it exposed to attacks from the Irish, Picts and Anglo-Saxons, while in Italy the last emperor, Romulus Augustulus, was deposed in 476 by a military commander, Odovacer. The supplanter of Romulus was himself deposed and murdered in 493 by Theoderic the Ostrogoth, who established a powerful kingdom based on Italy. While the Empire had weathered the storms of the fifth century largely unscathed in the East, in the West it had simply ceased to exist. Western Europe, one might be excused for thinking, had moved decisively into a post-Roman period, and the Middle Ages had begun.

However dramatic these events may have been, they did not constitute a definitive parting of the ways between the post-Roman West and what we may now call the Byzantine East. Long-distance trade continued throughout the Mediterranean and beyond, as research on African pots found over a wide area is increasingly making clear.[1] In the year 500, consuls were being appointed

[1] See Loseby, chapter 22 below.

for the West, and when, a few decades later, the western consulship lapsed, there were still people in the West who dated documents with reference to the eastern consuls who continued to be appointed. The Mediterranean was traversed by diplomats, such as a legate of Theoderic who made twenty-five trips from Italy to Spain, Gaul, Africa and Constantinople, and members of the intelligentsia. The West was awash with doctors from the East, among them Anthimus, who lived in Italy and wrote a fascinating book on diet for a Frankish king in which he recommended the use of such foods as leavened bread, beer and mead made with plenty of honey. Another Eastern doctor was Alexander of Tralles, the brother of the well-known architect Anthemius, who practised medicine in Rome and whose *Therapeutica* was translated into Latin in the sixth century.[2] On the other hand Priscian, who was probably an African, was in Constantinople when he wrote what were to become standard works on Latin grammar;[3] we know that Africans in Constantinople were renowned for their Latin accent but reviled for their poor Greek. Latin manuscripts were copied in Constantinople and Greek ones in Ravenna, the Gothic capital in Italy. Furthermore, despite the advent of new holders of power in the West, the new rulers there were keen to represent themselves as in some way subservient to the Roman emperors who still ruled in Constantinople. Theoderic the Ostrogoth wrote to the emperor Anastasius that 'our kingdom is an imitation of yours . . . a copy of the only Empire', and Sigismund the Burgundian informed him that, while he gave the appearance of ruling his people, he believed himself to be merely the soldier of the emperor.[4] In these and many other respects, the post-Roman West remained firmly a part of the Roman world.

THE SUCCESSOR STATES IN THE WEST

Nevertheless, there had been changes, and seen from Constantinople the political situation of the West in 500 cannot have given cause for joy. In the midst of the other problems, both internal and external, with which the emperors of the East had to deal in the fifth century, developments in the West had not passed unnoticed. The last decade of the life of the Western Empire had seen the despatch of new emperors and armies to the West, and the deposition of the last emperor in 476 was recorded by Byzantine authors of the sixth century in terms which suggest they saw it as marking a major change: according to the chronicle of Marcellinus Comes, Rome had been founded 709 years before Octavian Augustus held power, and he had died 522 years before it perished

[2] Alexander of Tralles, *Therapeutica*, ed. T. Puschmann.

[3] Priscian, *Grammatici Latini*, ed. H. Keil.

[4] Theoderic in Cassiodorus, *Variae* I.I.3; Sigismund in Avitus of Vienne, *Ep*. 93.

in 476.[5] Constantinople became a centre for refugees who fled the western kingdoms. African Catholics, such as a widely reported group of people who miraculously found themselves able to speak after King Huneric had ordered that their tongues be cut out, were prominent among these. There were also people from Italy who were said, early in the sixth century, to have received a warm welcome at the court of the emperor Anastasius (491–518), and in one of his works the grammarian Priscian expressed the hope that Rome and Constantinople would both come to be under the emperor.[6] Indeed, emperors who had traditionally had pretensions to rule over the whole known world could not have looked with complaisance on the loss of the western provinces, which constituted the greater part of the territory over which their predecessors had ruled.

When the Byzantines looked towards the West they saw a world dominated by the Mediterranean, and by the year 500 almost all of that part of its coastline which had formerly been within the Western Empire was under the control of three kingdoms. The Vandals had occupied the bulk of the Roman provinces of Africa, and proved stern rulers, whose expropriation of the land-owning class and persecution of Catholics made them unpopular. Making use of their powerful navy they sacked Rome in 455 and they withstood major Byzantine attacks in 460 and 468. They faced two other kingdoms on the opposite shores of the sea. The Visigoths, originally settled as Roman *foederati* around Toulouse, had gradually gained control of most of Gaul south of the Loire and begun moving into Spain, while Italy and some adjacent lands were under the control of the Ostrogoths.[7] They had made their way there in accordance with an agreement concluded with the emperor Zeno, whose successor, Anastasius, in 497, sent back to Italy the ornaments of the palace, which Odovacer had transmitted to Constantinople after deposing Romulus Augustulus. But this degree of recognition does not imply that the Byzantines were happy to accept the Ostrogothic state.

The Vandals, Visigoths and Ostrogoths had far more in common than possessing adjacent kingdoms around the Mediterranean. They were all Arian Christians, adherents of a heresy which denied that the Father and the Son were of one substance as taught by the Council of Nicaea (325), a circumstance which marked them off from both the Byzantines and the great mass of the people amongst whom they settled. The Byzantines, regarding them as speaking the one language and looking the same, saw them, along with the Gepids, as nations that could be distinguished only by their names.[8] They

[5] Marcellinus comes, *Chronicon* s.a. 476, 11. [6] Priscian, *De Laude Anastasii Imperatori*, 242–7, 265.

[7] See on the Vandals, Courtois (1955); on the Goths, Wolfram (1988) and Heather (1991). On the kingdom of Toulouse, Barbero and Loring, chapter 7 below.

[8] Procopius, *Bellum Vandalicum* 1.2.2–5.

were connected by a system of marriage alliances: one of Theoderic's daughters had married the Visigothic king Alaric and his sister married the Vandal king Thrasamund, establishing a web of relationships which may have been anti-Byzantine in purpose.

Of these three states, that of the Ostrogoths was by far the most dangerous. To the east it included Dalmatia, which gave it a border with the Empire hundreds of kilometres long, and even if the sovereign of Italy had no expansionist designs in the East he was well placed to influence developments there in turbulent times. So it was that a Byzantine rebel had sought the help of Odovacer in 486, a circumstance which may have helped prompt the dispatch of the Ostrogoths to Italy shortly afterwards, and when the *magister militum* Vitalian rebelled against Anastasius towards the end of this emperor's reign he was believed to have sought the assistance of Theoderic. Some decades earlier, before he came to Italy, Theoderic had intervened when a rebellion threatened to unseat the emperor Zeno. The grateful emperor subsequently rewarded him with a consulship, and early in the sixth century an Italian author, apparently referring to these events, spoke of Theoderic as having bestowed the diadem on Zeno and compelled his love, with the implication of his being superior to the emperor.[9] It was a perspective unlikely to have been popular in Constantinople. If this were not enough, in 504 one of Theoderic's generals gained control of Sirmium, a city in Pannonia formerly part of the Eastern Empire. The Ostrogoths kept it as their own possession and went so far as to advance further into imperial territory. Following an important defeat the Visigoths suffered at the hands of the Franks in 507, Theoderic ruled their kingdom as well as that of the Ostrogoths. Constantinople had reason to look with fear on the mighty state of the Ostrogoths, in particular, among the states that had emerged around the Mediterranean.

These, however, were not the only successor states to the Empire in the West. To the north were territories that had come under the control of other peoples, in particular Franks and Burgundians, whom the Byzantines distinguished from the Goths by calling them 'Germans', a shorthand way of indicating that they had come from the lands east of the Rhine, which the Romans had failed to conquer. Like the Goths, they had found homes within the borders of the old Empire, and they had been integrated into the system of alliances set up by Theoderic, he himself having married the sister of Clovis, the king of the Franks, and one of his daughters having married Sigismund, the heir to the Burgundian throne. But by the end of the fifth century Clovis had been converted to Catholicism, and whatever his motives may have been in taking

[9] Ennodius, *Panegyricus regi Theodorico*, *Opera* CCLVIII.203–14, at 14, pp. 211–12; on the interpretation, MacCormack (1981), p. 230.

this step it is clear that he saw himself as having come to adhere to the religion of the emperor. Catholic influence was also strong at the Burgundian court, where Sigismund, the heir to the throne, was converted. More importantly, the impact of the Frankish and Burgundian intruders on the Roman world as seen from Constantinople would have seemed less than that of the Goths and Vandals, and their capacity to harm imperial interests was slight. Indeed, with judicious encouragement they could be made to serve imperial policy, and according to a strange story told in a seventh-century text, the Frankish king Childeric (*c.*463–482) had gone to Constantinople and asked the emperor to allow him to go to Gaul as the emperor's servant.[10] Hence it was not surprising that, at the time of conflict between the Franks under Clovis, who enjoyed the support of the Burgundians, and the Visigoths and Ostrogoths, which broke out in 507, the emperor Anastasius intervened on behalf of the Franks. He dispatched a fleet which ravaged part of the coast of Italy and prevented Theoderic from intervening in Gaul as early as he would have wished, and he also made Clovis an honorary consul.

It is therefore clear that Constantinople viewed the West in a differentiated way. The Mediterranean lands were occupied by powers that threatened Byzantine interests, but it was sometimes within the power of the Empire to act so as to destabilise its enemies. The last years of Theoderic were disfigured by charges of treacherous correspondence with the emperor, which were levelled against a group of senators, and what may have been overreaction to reports that Arians were being persecuted in the East. The two issues were recurrent in the history of the Gothic and Vandal states. The Vandal king Huneric had been concerned at the possibility of Catholic clergy sending letters about the succession to the throne overseas, presumably to the Empire, and at one time Theoderic acted to prevent correspondence from Burgundy from reaching the emperor. The Vandals also felt that religious persecution was a tool that could be employed for reasons of diplomacy. The position of the emperor *vis-à-vis* Catholics in the West had been strengthened by the healing in 519 of the Acacian schism, which had divided the churches of Rome and Constantinople since 484.[11] The last years of Theoderic therefore manifested some of the tensions implicit in the relationship between Constantinople and the successor states to the Empire around the western Mediterranean. To the north, on the other hand, were powers from whom good could be expected. It was a basic distinction, and its application became clear during the military ventures of the emperor Justinian (527–565).

[10] Fredegar, *Chronica* III.11, ed. Krusch, pp. 95–7; the story gains in plausibility if we take the name of the emperor which is supplied, Maurice, to have been a slip for Marcian.

[11] See Louth, chapter 4 above.

THE VANDAL WAR

On 19 May 530, the Vandal king Hilderic was deposed by another member of the royal family, Gelimer. Hilderic had enjoyed close relations with Justinian, who was therefore presented with an excellent opportunity to make war on the Vandals. The deposition of his ally was, however, merely a pretext for the emperor's intervention. A later African writer attributed his decision to invade Africa to a vision of a martyred African bishop, while a passage in the *Codex Justinianus* of 534, which may well have been written by the emperor himself and not his chancery, is eloquent as to the persecution of Catholics by the Vandals. It describes the sufferings they endured in language reminiscent of the account written by an African writer, Victor of Vita, in the 480s, and we have no reason to doubt that Justinian's invasion, like so many of his activities early in his reign, was motivated by religion rather than by any ideology of imperial renewal.[12] We are told that the plan to invade Africa was opposed by his advisers, but the imperial will was not to be trifled with, especially when a bishop reported a vision in which success was promised, and in 532 a peace was concluded with Persia that enabled resources to be directed towards the West. Justinian prepared a force which put to sea at about the summer solstice in 533, under the command of Belisarius, a general whose recent activities had included campaigning against the Persians and putting down a rebellion in Constantinople; the religious nature of the enterprise was highlighted as the patriarch prayed over Belisarius' ship and placed on one of the vessels a soldier who had recently been baptised.

We can follow the Vandal war in some detail, the account written by Belisarius' legal assistant, Procopius, being that of an eyewitness. The arrival of the Byzantine forces in Africa occurred in excellent circumstances, for Gelimer, unaware of their approach, had sent part of his forces to Sardinia. The invaders landed unopposed south of Carthage at Caputvada (Ras Kapoudra), whence they proceeded towards the capital, Carthage. They kept close to the shore as far as Grasse, where they turned inland and marched to Decimum, some 15 kilometres outside Carthage. Here Gelimer met them, but after a short encounter he fled, and two days later, on 15 September, the Roman army marched into Carthage. Belisarius dined on food that had been prepared for Gelimer, while his soldiers, behaving with remarkable restraint, are said to have bought food in the market. Gelimer summoned forces from Sardinia, but at the battle of Tricamarium, 30 kilometres outside Carthage, the Vandal army was again turned to flight, and Gelimer took up residence among the Berbers on a mountain where he consoled himself by composing sad verses before surrendering.

12 Visions of martyr: Victor of Tunnuna, *Chronica* s.a. 534, 11. Persecution of Catholics: *Codex Justinianus* 1.27.1. Louth shares the same view of Justinian's motives, chapter 4 above.

Having quickly gained control of Sardinia, Corsica, the Balearic Islands and Septem (Ceuta), a fort adjacent to the Straits of Gibraltar, Belisarius returned to Constantinople with booty which included the treasures of the Jews that Titus had taken from Jerusalem to Rome in the first century and which the Vandals in turn had taken to Africa in 455. The victorious general paraded through the streets of Constantinople in triumph, and both he and Gelimer made proskynesis, a physical act of reverence, before Justinian. The defeated king was provided with estates in Galatia, and Belisarius went on to hold a consulship in 535; the largesse he distributed included spoils won on this campaign. Justinian saw to the making of gold plates that depicted the history of his triumphs and legislated for the return of property the Vandals had taken from its rightful owners. In a matter of months the kingdom of the Vandals that had seemed so strong had collapsed, and Africa found itself governed by a praetorian prefect appointed by the emperor. We have no reason to doubt that its inhabitants approved of these developments.

Nevertheless, there was still fighting to be done. The nomadic Berbers had been pressing increasingly on the Vandal kingdom, and they were to pose a major problem to Byzantine Africa, for their practice of lightly armed and mobile combat made them difficult opponents for the Byzantine cavalry. A series of fortifications was quickly erected to deal with them, of which the impressive ruins at *Thamugadi* (Timgad) still stand, with walls averaging 2.5 metres in thickness and rising to over 15 metres in height. Archaeological and literary evidence both indicate that, contrary to Justinian's expectation, the Byzantines never succeeded in occupying all the territory held in Roman times, but the number and extent of the defences they erected makes it clear they planned to stay in Africa. There were also internal troubles, for many of Belisarius' soldiers had married Vandal women, only to see the property they hoped to gain through their wives threatened by Justinian's legislation for the return of property held by Vandals. They mutinied in 535, and more seriously in 544, after the *magister militum* and praetorian prefect Solomon had been killed fighting the Berbers. But the ringleader of the rebels was murdered in 546 and towards the end of that year a new general, the energetic John Troglytus, arrived. An expedition led by him in the spring of 548 was crowned with success, and Africa knew peace.

THE GOTHIC WAR – EARLY SUCCESSES

Justinian can only have been delighted at Belisarius' triumph in 533, and his thoughts naturally turned to a more ambitious project. Imperial legislation of April 535 referred to the recovery of Africa and the imposition of servitude on the Vandals, but added that the emperor now hoped to receive from God things greater than these.[13] As it happened, it was a propitious time to intervene in Italy. Following the death of Theoderic in 526, his successors had found it hard to step into his shoes, and both his daughter, Amalasuentha, and the man who came to be her rival, Theoderic's nephew Theodahad, entered into negotiations with the emperor. In the spring of 535 Amalasuentha was murdered, so providing a *casus belli*.[14] The reason Justinian gave for intervention in Italy was different from that he had provided for the war in Africa: whereas the Vandals had been attacked for their outrageous treatment of the Catholic provincials, the Ostrogoths were assaulted because of the weakness of their claim to hold Italy. They had done well, it was now asserted, to defeat the tyrant Odovacer, but the proper course would have been for them to have then handed Italy back to the Empire, rather than keep it for themselves. As we have seen, the ending of the line of emperors in the West in 476 had not escaped notice in Constantinople.

The initial attack on Italy took place from two directions.[15] One army occupied Dalmatia, which thereafter remained under almost unbroken imperial control, while Belisarius, at the head of a small force, easily gained control of Sicily in 535. From there he could launch an attack on the Italian mainland which the resources of the Goths, concentrated as they were in the north, were ill equipped to deal with. Theodahad, by then sole ruler, offered to resign his kingdom, a proposal he subsequently retracted, and early in 536 the pope, Agapetus, arrived in Constantinople to hold discussions with Justinian on Theodahad's behalf, but the emperor was in no mood for discussion. A law of 536 refers to the regaining of territory from one ocean to the other, an ambition not hinted at in earlier sources, which indicates that imperial designs had become larger.[16] In the same year Belisarius crossed to the mainland of Italy. The Goths, discontented at Theodahad's failure to lead effectively, raised on their shields Witigis, a man of modest family but proven fighting ability, and Theodahad was murdered. The new king left Rome for Ravenna, taking hostages and an oath of loyalty from Pope Silverius, who had succeeded Agapetus, and on 9 or 10 December Belisarius occupied the eternal city. In the following February a large Gothic force arrived and laid siege to it, cutting the aqueducts which supplied the city with water and ravaging Christian burial grounds outside the walls, but to no avail. In March 538 Witigis withdrew. Fighting spread in the north of Italy, and in 539 the Goths razed the great city of Milan to the ground; we are told that the men were killed and the women

[13] *Novella* VIII.10.2. [14] See Moorhead, chapter 6 below.

[15] The account of Procopius again constitutes a detailed primary source, closely followed in e.g. Bury (1923), see more recently Stein (1949), although the author was probably not in Italy after 540, and as time passed he came to look on the war with less favour: Hannestad (1961).

[16] *Novella* XXX.11.2.

handed over to the Burgundians. The Frankish king Theudebert intervened, seeking to benefit no one but himself, and by the end of 539 the Gothic capital, Ravenna, was besieged by the imperial forces.

In his hour of need Witigis asked Chosroes, the shah of Persia, to break the treaty he had concluded with Justinian in 532 and distract him in the east, a ploy which made the emperor incline towards offering the Goths generous terms.[17] But Belisarius was confident, and when the Goths offered to accept him as 'Emperor of the West', an office which would have prejudiced the position of Justinian, he feigned consent.[18] In May 540 he marched into Ravenna, but refused to honour his agreement with the Goths. Before long he returned to Constantinople, taking with him Witigis and his wife Matasuentha, various Gothic notables and at least part of the Gothic treasure. The reception he received from Justinian was cool, the emperor possibly having been disquieted by the title his general had pretended to be willing to accept. Nevertheless, in 540 the mighty state founded by Theoderic had apparently collapsed.

The Byzantine historian Procopius observed that when Belisarius entered Rome in 536 'Rome became subject to the Romans again after a space of sixty years',[19] and one easily gains the impression of a smooth imposition of Byzantine power. In March 537 Pope Silverius, who had owed his appointment to Theodahad and had subsequently sworn loyalty to Witigis, was deposed by Belisarius and replaced by Vigilius, a protégé of the powerful empress, Theodora. By early 537 Belisarius had appointed one Fidelis praetorian prefect, and by the end of the year a *comes sancti patrimonii per Italiam*, an official with competence in financial matters, seems to have been functioning in the conquered lands. Fidelis' tenure of the prefecture would have overlapped with the end of that of Cassiodorus, who had been appointed to the post by the Goths in 533 and whose last letters on behalf of Witigis were written towards the end of 537. By the end of 539 a scribe at Ravenna employed in a document the formula χμγ, in accordance with Byzantine practice.[20] As early as 535 there had been signs in Rome of discontent with the Gothic government, and the people of Italy, quickly putting aside positive memories they may have had of the reign of Theoderic, happily accepted the advent of imperial power.

In 540 it must have seemed that the Gothic war, like the Vandal war, had come to a wished-for conclusion. In Constantinople, Justinian had a mosaic placed in the ceiling of the Bronze Gate of the palace, showing Belisarius winning victories for him. In the middle of the composition stood Justinian and

17 On Perso-Byzantine relations in the sixth century, Louth, chapter 4 above.

18 Procopius, *Bellum Gothicum* II.29.18. But cf. *Bellum Vandalicum* I.11.20 (misleadingly translated in the Loeb edition).

19 *Bellum Gothicum* I.14.14.

20 It probably stood for Χριστον Μαρία γεννα, 'Mary bore Christ': Tjäder, *Papyri*.

Theodora, the kings of the Vandals and Goths approaching them as prisoners, and around them the members of the Senate who 'rejoice and smile as they bestow on the emperor honours equal to those of God, because of the magnitude of his achievements'.[21] It was the optimism of a golden moment, such as would never again be possible.

THE GOTHIC WAR: THE RESISTANCE OF TOTILA

As it turned out, the war with the Goths was by no means over. Justinian, perhaps afraid of the threat a mighty general could pose, failed to replace Belisarius, and rivalry and corruption became endemic among the Byzantine commanders left in Italy. They showed little inclination to attend to the Gothic resistance that continued north of the Po, and with the coming to power in 541 of King Totila (or Baduila, as his name was spelt on coins) the Goths gained a leader of outstanding calibre. Totila's attitude to Justinian was expressed in his coinage, on which the portrait of the current emperor was replaced by that of Anastasius, who had recognised the kingship of Theoderic in 497: if Justinian challenged the Goths on the basis of legitimacy, Totila was prepared to dispute his claim.

Before long, war was raging again. In the spring of 542 the new Gothic king defeated the imperial army at Faenza and captured its standards, before proceeding to the south where he took Benevento, Cumae and Naples. Belisarius was sent back to Ravenna in 544 to deal with the deteriorating situation, but found himself powerless to stop the Gothic advance. Indeed, his conduct of the war in this period displays an uncharacteristic passivity, which may owe something to the impact on manpower resources of a severe outbreak of the plague, which the Empire was experiencing at the time. In December 545 Totila besieged Rome and twelve months later entered it. He immediately visited St Peter's to pray, an act calculated to suggest continuity with Theoderic, who had himself made devotions at the basilica on his one known visit to Rome, and, beyond him, with the emperors whose conduct Theoderic had imitated. But the act was hollow. There were few people left in the city, and Totila made no secret of his animosity towards the Senate. In fact, he planned to raze the walls of the city, but Belisarius wrote to him warning of the harsh judgement of posterity that would await him if he proceeded in this course. Perhaps he was able to play on the vanity of the Gothic king; in any case, Totila behaved foolishly and abandoned Rome, taking members of the Senate as hostages. For forty days the city was home to neither human nor beast, but by April Belisarius had moved in and commenced work on restoring its defences. During the spring Totila tried to wrest control of the city from him, but failed.

[21] Procopius, *Buildings* 1.10.19.

Nevertheless, the Goths were still masters of much of Italy, to such an extent that Belisarius tended to travel from one place to another by ship rather than overland, and when Justinian recalled his great general to Constantinople a few years later Belisarius must have felt much more subdued than he had on his returns in 534 and 540. In 549 an Ostrogothic fleet ravaged the coast of Campania and Rome was again besieged; in the following January it fell. Totila established a mint in the city, held races and, in the words of a contemporary, lived there 'like a father with his children'.[22] With Ravenna still in Byzantine hands, Rome actually came to hold a political significance to which it had long been unaccustomed. Totila moved to Sicily and ravaged it in 550, whereupon the Franks occupied parts of northern Italy.

A full decade after Belisarius had seemed to have successfully terminated the war, the situation in Italy was not good and Justinian decided to commit resources on a scale he had never provided for Belisarius. An enormous army was placed under the command of the patrician Germanus. He was an impressive figure, for not only was he a cousin of Justinian but he had married Matasuentha, the granddaughter of Theoderic and former wife of Witigis, a circumstance which allowed him to anticipate limited resistance from the Goths in Italy. Indeed, the birth of a baby son to the couple allowed the historian Jordanes to be hopeful of a future union of the families of Germanus and Matasuentha.[23] But Germanus died while preparations for the expedition were still under way, and in 551 the general Narses was appointed to finish the job.

The great army set off overland for Italy in April 552. Franks who had settled in Venetia sought to deny it passage on the grounds that it included a large contingent of Lombards, their traditional enemies, and the Goths tried to make the road impassable, but Narses was able to make his way to Ravenna, which he occupied on 6 June 552. Totila marched out of Rome, and at the end of June or beginning of July the two forces encountered each other at Busta Gallorum, a site in the Apennines.[24] Before the troops of both armies Totila performed a stylish war dance on his charger, but the Goths were heavily outnumbered, and the outcome of the battle was inevitable. The Gothic cavalry could not withstand the enemy archers, and both cavalry and infantry fled, Totila dying of a wound received in flight. Numerous Gothic strongholds surrendered as Narses advanced on Rome, which his enemies were no longer strong enough to defend effectively. The city was easily captured and its keys forwarded to Justinian. In their despair the Goths put to death senators they found and

[22] *LP*, ed. Duchesne, p. 298.

[23] Jordanes, *Getica* 314; Momigliano (1955) provides a rich but inconclusive discussion.

[24] Detailed account in Roisl (1981).

300 children they were holding as hostages, but their cause was now hopeless, and the Franks refused to intervene on their behalf. In October a Gothic force did battle with Narses in the south of Italy at Mons Lactarius, near Nocera, but it was defeated, and Narses gave the surviving Goths permission to return to 'their own land'. Some continued to resist on a local basis until the capture of Verona in 562 or 563, but by the time Narses was recalled, probably not long after the accession of the emperor Justin II in 565, Italy seemed stable. The Gothic war had lasted far longer than the Vandal war, but its outcome was the same.

A puzzling feature of the Gothic war is the failure of the Visigoths to become involved. For much of the war their king was an Ostrogoth, Theudis (531–548), and at one stage his nephew, Ildibad, was prominent in the resistance in Italy, but we have no reason to believe that help from the Visigoths reached Italy. We do know, however, that in about 544 a Visigothic force was defeated at Septem (Ceuta), across the Straits of Gibraltar, which suggests an attempted thrust from Spain into what was by then Byzantine Africa. But in 552 a Byzantine force, purporting to answer an appeal for help from a Visigothic rebel, set out for Spain and succeeded in gaining control of a slice of its south-east coast around Cartagena and Malaga. The area has a mountainous hinterland and looks across the sea to Africa, and the defence of Africa may have been the true reason for Byzantine involvement in Spain.[25] In any case, this modest success in Spain was the culmination of an extraordinary expansion of Byzantine power in the West. Within a few decades Africa and Italy, together with the large islands of the western Mediterranean, Dalmatia and part of Spain had been reintegrated into the Empire, so that the poet Agathias could legitimately claim that a traveller could go as far as the sandy shore of Spain where the Pillars of Hercules lay and still be in imperial territory.[26]

CONSTANTINOPLE AND THE WEST IN THE MID-SIXTH CENTURY

We may take the years on either side of the halfway point of the sixth century as constituting a high-water mark of Byzantine influence in the West. Economic links between East and West were strengthened; the export of African pottery to the East, which had declined during the Vandal period, seems to have grown during the early period of Byzantine rule. Byzantine relations with the West were particularly in evidence in Ravenna, the capital of Italy, where Bishop Maximianus obtained from Justinian the title of archbishop and relics of St Andrew, a saint whose cult could be seen as constituting a possible rival

[25] See also Barbero and Loring, chapter 7 below.

[26] *Anthologia Graeca Carmina Christianorum*, ed. Christ and Paranikas, IV.3.83ff.

to that of St Peter in Rome. It is possible that Maximianus' splendid ivory throne, now to be seen in the Museo Arcivescovile in Ravenna, was made in Constantinople, and it was he who consecrated the church of S. Vitale, with its glowing mosaics of Justinian and Theodora. Justinian failed to visit the West, but no one could doubt that the mosaics of S. Vitale, whatever the precise liturgical significance of the scenes they portray, were powerful statements of imperial power in the conquered territories.

Strange as it may seem, the clearest sign of the centrality of Byzantium in western affairs in the mid-sixth century is to be seen in Constantinople itself and in the variety of westerners, the influential, the ambitious and the captive, who were there. Liberius, whom Theoderic had successively appointed praetorian prefect of Italy and praetorian prefect of Gaul, had defected while on an embassy to Constantinople shortly before the Gothic war. He later participated in Byzantine campaigns in Italy and Spain, and returned to Italy, where he was buried at Rimini. During the war, and in particular after Totila's capture of Rome in 546, many Roman aristocrats made their way to the royal city: Cassiodorus, formerly prominent in Theoderic's administration, and the *caput senatus* Cethegus among them, and in 554 Justinian gave senators permission to live in Constantinople. The Roman deacon Vigilius was on hand in Constantinople in 537, well placed to become pope when Silverius fell out of imperial favour, and when he died in 555 his successor, Pelagius, was similarly conveniently standing in the wings there. From the time of Vigilius, imperial confirmation of the election of a pope was needed before he could be consecrated, which accounts for the long interregna between pontificates that characterised the following period of papal history. Pope Gregory the Great had served as papal *apocrisiarius*, or legate, in Constantinople (*c.*579–585/6) prior to his appointment as pope in 590. His two successors would likewise serve in this position before becoming pope. Clearly, after the conquest of Italy, a period in Constantinople was a valuable item in the *curriculum vitae* of prospective popes. Maximianus was appointed to the see of Ravenna while he was in Constantinople in 546 and was to travel there again, while in 552 the clergy of the province of Milan asked a legate travelling to Constantinople to see what he could do to secure the return of bishop Datius, who had been absent from his see for fifteen or sixteen years, and in the royal city for a good part of that period. One of Gregory the Great's acquaintances while he was in Constantinople, the Milanese deacon Constantius, was appointed bishop of his city in 593, while another, the Spaniard Leander, was to become bishop of Seville. In 551 Reparatus of Carthage and other African bishops were summoned to Constantinople; in the following year Justinian exiled Reparatus and replaced him, against the will of the clergy and people of Carthage, by Primosus, his former *apocrisiarius* in Constantinople. Members of various Germanic royal families, such as the

Ostrogoth Amalasuentha, were also on hand, where an eye could be kept on their activities and they could be called into action as imperial needs required.

No less was the centrality of Constantinople in the intellectual life of the West. A large volume of literature in Latin was produced there during, and immediately after, the reign of Justinian. The Illyrian Marcellinus Comes and the African Victor of Tunnuna wrote their chronicles there, and the Spanish Goth, John of Biclaro, although his chronicle was produced in Spain, wrote it after he had spent some years in Constantinople. It was there that the Goth Jordanes wrote his histories of the Romans and the Goths in 551, that Cassiodorus, to whose lost *Gothic History* Jordanes had access in Constantinople, worked on his *Expositio Psalmorum*, that the African Junilus wrote his introduction to the study of the Bible, that another African, Corippus, witnessed the accession of Justin II, which he described in a panegyric, and from there that various African theologians came to operate. Somewhat later, the future pope Gregory worked on his *Moralia in Job* there. Scholars have sometimes doubted the truth of Gregory's assertion that he did not know Greek, on the basis that it would have been difficult for the representative of the pope to have functioned in Constantinople without knowledge of that language, but given the flourishing and influential community of Latin speakers there, he may not have found a command of Greek necessary.

THE THREE CHAPTERS

But at this very time of the centrality of Constantinople in western affairs, events were under way which threatened its position, and, as often happened in late antiquity, tensions were expressed in disputes over religion. Imperial policy had long sought to bring together adherents of the Council of Chalcedon (451), who believed that Christ had two natures, and their Monophysite opponents, who credited him with only one, and Justinian made an important attempt to bring about unity between the disputing parties.[27] He asked the five patriarchs of the church to anathematise the person and works of bishop Theodore of Mopsuestia, some of the writings of bishop Theodoret of Kyrrhos, and a letter attributed to bishop Ibas of Edessa, which was addressed to one Mari. These three theologians, all long dead, were held to be of Nestorianising tendency, and Justinian believed that their condemnation would be a painless way of conciliating the Monophysites, who held an opinion contrary to that of the Nestorians. But the Council of Chalcedon had accepted the orthodoxy of Theodoret, and the letter of Ibas had been read

[27] For a more detailed discussion of Christological disputes in sixth-century Byzantium, see Louth, chapter 4 above.

out there, so an attack on these thinkers could be construed as an attack on the council. Pope Vigilius refused to accept Justinian's proposal, whereupon, to the astonishment of the populace of Rome, he was arrested in a church in 545 and conveyed to Constantinople. Years of intrigue followed, in which Vigilius was alternately vacillating and resolute. Finally, in 553, the council of Constantinople condemned the Three Chapters, as they came to be called, and Vigilius accepted its decision. In 554 he set out to return to Rome, but died at Siracusa in June 555, a broken man.

As it turned out, Justinian's efforts did nothing to reconcile the Monophysites and the adherents of Chalcedon, but there was an immediate hostile reaction in the West, where it was felt he had acted in a way contrary to the position adopted by the council. So intense were feelings in Italy that it proved difficult to find bishops prepared to consecrate Vigilius' successor, Pelagius, and a schism broke out in northern Italy, which lasted until the end of the seventh century. There was considerable disquiet in Gaul, and throughout the Visigothic period the Spanish church failed to accept the Council of Constantinople. Opposition was, however, strongest in Africa where an episcopate, which had witnessed the end of the persecuting Arian Vandals, was in no mood to be dictated to by a Catholic emperor, and the African church flung itself into the controversy with the learning and vigour which had characterised it for centuries. As early as 550 a synod excommunicated Vigilius, and a series of authors wrote attacking Justinian's position; it was an African chronicler who observed that the Council of Constantinople was followed by an earthquake in that city![28] Small wonder that a bishop from northern Gaul, Nicetius of Trier, wrote a strongly worded but theologically incoherent letter to the emperor in which he informed him that all Italy, the entirety of Africa, Spain and Gaul wept over him: 'O sweet Justinian of ours, who has so deceived you, who has persuaded you to proceed in such a way?'[29]

WESTERN ANTAGONISM TO THE EMPIRE

Early Christian history is full of controversies on issues so apparently abstruse that modern scholars have often felt they were really about subjects far removed from the matters being overtly debated, and the controversy over the Three Chapters in the West may have been one where the real issue was unstated. It is possible to interpret the strong stance the West took against Justinian's line as constituting a response to the impact of his wars of conquest. Doubtless

[28] Victor of Tunnuna, *Chronica* s.a. 553 (*Chronica Minora* II.203).

[29] *Epistolae Austrasiacae*, no. 7. There is a reminiscence here of St Paul (Galatians 3:1). The answer to Nicetius' questions is 'the Devil'.

the heads of churches in Africa and Italy sincerely welcomed the coming of Justinian's armies, but during the period in which they had been governed by Arian regimes they had come to enjoy a *de facto* independence from imperial oversight, which they would not surrender willingly. It is no coincidence that one of the most famous assertions of ecclesiastical power *vis-à-vis* the emperor ever made was that enunciated by Pope Gelasius (492–496) during the period of Ostrogothic power in Italy. The wars created a situation in which an emperor, for the first time in a long while, was able to attempt to impose his will directly on western churches, and some of the opposition to Justinian's policies may have simply been a reaction against the new reality. But it may also have been the case that opposition to the Three Chapters was a vehicle that allowed the expression of hostility towards, or disillusionment with, the outcome of the wars in the West. If we accept this, we will not be surprised to find Cassiodorus, the best-known collaborator with the Goths among the Romans, writing towards the middle of the century in terms which suggest sympathy for the theologians whose condemnation Justinian was seeking. Nor are other indications of western coolness towards Byzantium there lacking in the period after the conquests.

The indigenous inhabitants of Africa and Italy initially welcomed the Byzantine armies. In Italy the Gothic government was worried about the loyalty of the populace even before the war began, and the detailed narrative of Procopius makes it clear that its fears were justified. Yet early in the war a Gothic spokesperson told the people of Rome that the only Greeks who had visited Rome were actors, mimes or thieving soldiers, suggesting that there was already some resentment towards the Byzantines, which the Goths sought to exploit. We are told that during the pontificate of Pope John III (561–574) the inhabitants of the city maliciously told the emperor that 'it would be better to serve the Goths than the Greeks'.[30] The use of the term 'Greeks' is interesting, for in Procopius it is a hostile word placed in the mouths of barbarians, which suggests the possibility that the Romans had come to accept, or at least pretend to accept, such an assessment of the Byzantines. The dire state of the Italian economy after the long war, and the corrupt and grasping nature of the Byzantine administration imposed in both Africa and Italy, made the imperial government unpopular. Further, Italy's integration into the Empire did not imply reversion to the position of independence from the East which it had enjoyed before the advent of Gothic power, nor were its Roman inhabitants able to enjoy the positions of influence they had held under the Goths, for Italy was now a minor part of an Empire governed by a far away *autocrator* who never troubled to visit the West. Power in Africa and Italy passed to Greek-speaking

[30] Gothic spokesperson: Procopius, *Bellum Gothicum* 1.18.40. Message to the emperor: *LP*, p. 305.

incomers, and we have evidence for cults of eastern saints, which they presumably brought with them. Needless to say there were loyalists and careerists who supported the Byzantine regime, such as the African poet Corippus, whose epic *Iohannis* was partly an attempt to justify the imperial cause to his fellow Africans,[31] but they represented minority opinion.

If this were not enough, opposition to Justinian's wars even developed in the East. This can be traced through the works of Procopius, which move from a sunny optimism in describing the Vandal war to the sombre tone which increasingly intrudes in the Gothic war and finally to the animosity towards the emperor displayed in the *Secret History*, but it is possible to deduce from other sources a feeling that resources had been committed in the West to little profit. However impressive their outcome in bringing Africa and Italy back into the Empire, Justinian's wars had in some ways the paradoxical result of driving East and West further apart.

BYZANTINE MILITARY DIFFICULTIES IN THE WEST

Throughout the reign of Justinian, that part of the Empire south of the Danube had been troubled by the incursions of barbarians, in particular a Turkic people known as Bulgars and groups of Slavs whom contemporaries called Antes and Sclaveni. The government dealt with the threat as best it could by building forts and paying subsidies, but following the death of Justinian in 565 the situation rapidly deteriorated. His successor Justin II (565–578) adopted a policy of withholding subsidies, and in particular refused a demand for tribute made by the Avars, a people who had recently made their way into the Danube area. The results were catastrophic. In 567 the Avars joined forces with the Lombards living in Pannonia to crush the Gepids, a victory that signalled the end of the Germanic peoples along the middle Danube. In the following year the Lombards left Pannonia for Italy, whereupon the Avars occupied the lands they had vacated, the plain of modern Hungary, from which they launched attacks deep into imperial territory; the renewal of war with Persia in 572 made the Byzantine response to these developments the less effective. In 581 Slavs invaded the Balkans, and it soon became clear that they were moving in to stay.

These events all occurred in the East, but they had a major impact on the West. The attention of the authorities was now diverted from the newly won provinces, and direct land access to Italy was rendered difficult. Moreover, it may well have been the rise of the Avars that impelled the Lombards to launch their invasion of Italy in 568. This was to have long-term consequences, which

[31] Cameron (1985).

are discussed in the next chapter. Here it will be enough to note that the invaders quickly gained control of the Po Valley and areas of central and southern Italy. The Byzantine administration, under the successor of Narses, the praetorian prefect Longinus, proved embarrassingly ill equipped to cope with them, and a force, which was finally sent from the East under Justin's son-in-law Baduarius, was defeated. In 577 or 578 the Roman patrician Pamphronius, who had gone to Constantinople seeking help, was sent away with the 3000 lb of gold he had brought with him and told to use the money to bribe some Lombards to defect or, failing this, to secure the intervention of the Franks; in 579 a second embassy was fobbed off with a small force and, we are told, an attempt was made to bribe some of the Lombard leaders. Perhaps we are to see here the reflection of a change in imperial policy, for while the emperor Justin had behaved in a miserly fashion, his successor Tiberius (578–582) was inclined to throw money at his problems. Neither strategy succeeded however, and it was all too clear that the situation in Italy was desperate. It was time for Constantinople to play the Frankish card again.

For the greater part of the sixth century the Franks had steadily been becoming more powerful. Their defeat of the Visigoths in 507 was followed by expansion from northern into southern Gaul, while the weakening of the Burgundians and Ostrogoths in the 520s and 530s saw further gains.[32] In the early stages of the Gothic war they were in the happy position of being able to accept the payments that both sides made seeking their assistance, but when King Theudebert marched into Italy in 539, he was acting only in his own interests. He issued gold coins displaying his own portrait rather than that of the emperor and bearing legends generally associated with emperors rather than kings, and responded to an embassy from Justinian in grandiloquent terms, advising him that the territory under his power extended through the Danube and the boundary of Pannonia as far as the ocean shores.[33] Towards the end of his life his forces occupied Venetia and some other areas of Italy, and he inspired fear in Constantinople to such an extent that it was rumoured that he planned to march on the city. The settlement of Lombards in Pannonia by Justinian in about 546 may have represented an attempt to counter the Franks. Following the death of Theudebert in 547, Justinian sent an embassy to his heir Theudebald proposing an offensive alliance against the Goths, but he was turned down, and Frankish intervention in Italy continued to be a problem throughout the Gothic war. The advent of the Lombards, however, meant that the Franks were again located on the far side of an enemy of the Byzantines and could again be looked upon as potential allies. But the attempt made to gain their help occurred against a highly complex political and military background.

[32] See Van Dam, chapter 8 below. [33] *Epistolae Austrasiacae*, no. 20.

It is difficult to reconstruct the web of alliances and animosities that lay behind relations between Constantinople and the disparate parts of the West towards the end of the sixth century. In 579 Hermenigild, the elder son of the Visigothic king Leovigild, revolted against his father, and after the suppression of the rebellion his wife Ingund, a Frankish princess, and son, Athanagild, fled to the Byzantines; the latter was taken to Constantinople, and despite their efforts his Frankish relatives were unable to secure his return to the West. A few years later one Gundovald, who claimed to be the son of a Frankish king, arrived in Marseilles. He had been living in Constantinople, but had been lured back to Francia by a party of aristocrats. The emperor Maurice (582–602) gave him financial backing, and one of those who supported him when he arrived at Marseilles was later accused of wishing to bring the kingdom of the Franks under the sway of the emperor. This was almost certainly an exaggeration, and Gundovald's rebellion came to naught, but again we have evidence of imperial fishing in disturbed western waters.[34] In 584 the Frankish king Childebert, the uncle of Athanagild, having at some time received 50,000 *solidi* from Maurice, sent forces to Italy, but the results were not up to imperial expectations and Maurice asked for his money back. Other expeditions followed, but little was achieved. Finally, in 590 a large Frankish expedition advanced into Italy and made its way beyond Verona, but failed to make contact with the imperial army. This was the last occasion when Constantinople used the Franks in its Italian policy. The fiasco of 590 may be taken as symbolising a relationship which rarely worked to the benefit of the Empire. While it may often be true that the neighbours of one's enemy are one's friends, Byzantine attempts to profit from the Franks had persistently failed.

By the last years of the century the Byzantines were in difficulties everywhere in the West. Most of Italy had come under the control of the Lombards, and severe losses had also been sustained in Africa, although the latter can only dimly be perceived. In 595 the Berbers caused alarm to the people of Carthage itself, until the exarch, as the military governor was known, defeated them by a trick, and a geographical work written by George of Cyprus early in the seventh century indicates that the imperial possessions in Africa were considerably smaller than those which the Vandals had controlled, themselves smaller than those which had been part of the Roman Empire.[35] The establishment of exarchs in Ravenna and Carthage indicates a society that was being forced to become more military in its orientation, and while the Byzantine possessions in Spain are not well documented, it is clear that they tended to diminish rather than grow.

[34] On Gundovald see Gregory, *Hist.* VI.24.291–2; VII.10.332–3; VII.14.334–6; VII.26–38.344–62.

[35] George of Cyprus, *Descriptio Orbis Romani.*

EAST AND WEST: CONTINUING LINKS AND GROWING DIVISIONS

Paradoxically, despite the waning of Byzantine power in the West, the latter continued to be vitally interested in the East. A ready market remained for imported luxury items; goods of Byzantine provenance were included in the early seventh-century ship burial at Sutton Hoo in East Anglia, and Radegund, the founder of a convent at Poitiers, petitioned Justin II and his wife Sophia for a portion of the True Cross, which she duly received in 569. At the end of the century the letters of Pope Gregory the Great reveal a man who saw the Empire as central to his world and had a penchant for wine imported from Egypt, surely one of the few Italians in history of whom this could be said. Byzantine legislation was followed with attention; the Frank Chilperic I did not merely rejoice in the possession of gold medallions that Tiberius II sent him, but an edict he issued shows an apparent dependence on a novel of the same emperor.[36] Eastern liturgical practice was imitated; on the recommendation of the newly converted Visigothic king Reccared, the Third Council of Toledo prescribed in 589 that the Creed was to be sung before the Lord's Prayer and the taking of Communion 'according to the practice of the eastern churches', apparently in imitation of Justin II's requiring, at the beginning of his reign, that the Creed was to be sung before the Lord's Prayer. This is one of a number of indications of the increasingly Byzantine form of the public life of Spain towards the end of the sixth century. The chronicle of Marius of Avenches, written in Burgundy, is dated according to consulships and indictional years, until its termination in 581. Inscriptions in the Rhône Valley were still being dated according to consulships or indictional years in the early seventh century, and coins were being minted in the name of the emperor at Marseilles and Viviers as late as the reign of Heraclius (610–641). Whatever may be the merits of thinking in terms of 'an obscure law of cultural hydraulics', in accordance with which streams of influence were occasionally released from the East to water the lower reaches of the West,[37] there can be no doubt that the West remained open to Byzantine influence, nor that western authors such as Gregory of Tours and Venantius Fortunatus sought to keep abreast of eastern material in a way that few easterners reciprocated.

Emperors moreover gave indications of having continued to regard the West as important. The marriages the emperor Tiberius arranged for his daughters are strong evidence of this, for whereas one of them married Maurice, the successful general who was to succeed Tiberius, another married Germanus, the son of the patrician whom Justinian had nominated to finish the war against the Goths in 550, and of his Gothic wife Matasuentha. Tiberius made each of

36 Stein (1949).

37 See the memorable characterization of this view in Brown (1976), p. 5.

his sons-in-law caesar, and given the strong western associations of Germanus, it is tempting to see the emperor as having thought of a *divisio imperii* into East and West, something that never seems to have crossed Justinian's mind.

If this was Tiberius' plan, nothing came of it, but his successor, Maurice, drew up a will appointing his elder son Theodosius lord of Constantinople with power in the East, and the younger, Tiberius, emperor of old Rome with power in Italy and the islands of the Tyrrhenian Sea. Again, nothing came from this plan, but it was from Carthage that Heraclius, the son of an exarch, launched his successful rebellion against the emperor Phokas in 610. It was later believed that at a difficult point in his reign the emperor Heraclius planned to flee to Africa, only being restrained by an oath the patriarch forced him to take. In the middle of the seventh century Maximus the Confessor, a complex figure who in various ways links East and West, was accused of having had a vision in which he saw angels in heaven on both the East and the West; those on the West exclaimed 'Gregory Augustus, may you conquer!', and their voice was louder than the voices of those on the East.[38] Surely, it appeared, relations between Byzantium and the West remained strong.

But although the West certainly retained a capacity to absorb Byzantine influences and emperors after Justinian continued to think in terms of controlling the West, in other ways the sixth century saw the two parts of the former Empire move further apart. Justinian's wars had overextended the Empire, entailing a major weakening of its position on the northern and eastern frontiers, and as warfare continued against the Slavs, Avars and Persians there were few resources to spare for the West, where the territory controlled by Constantinople shrunk to scattered coastal fringes. By the end of the century there was little trade between Carthage and Constantinople. East and West were drifting apart linguistically: there are no counterparts to a Boethius in the West or a Priscian in the East towards the end of the century. Gregory the Great's diplomacy in Constantinople must have been seriously harmed by his failure to learn Greek, and in his correspondence as pope he complained of the quality of translators out of Latin in Constantinople and Greek in Rome: in both cases they translated word for word without regard for the sense of what they were translating.[39] Byzantine historians rapidly came to display a lack of knowledge of and interest in western affairs. Evagrius, writing towards the end of the sixth century, argued in favour of Christianity by comparing the fates of emperors before and after Constantine, a line of argument that could only be sustained by ignoring the later western emperors.[40] The sources available to

[38] Mansi, *Sacrorum Conciliorum nova et amplissima collectio* XI.3ff. The Gregory referred to was an exarch of Carthage who had rebelled against the emperor Constans II.

[39] Gregory, *Epp.* VII.27, X.39.

[40] Evagrius, *Historia Ecclesiastica* 3.41 ad fin.

Theophanes, when he wrote his chronicle in the early ninth century, allowed him to note the accession of almost every pope from the late third century to Benedict I in 575, but not subsequent ones. Meanwhile Paul the Deacon, writing in the late eighth century, seems to have regarded Maurice as the first Greek among the emperors.[41] One has the feeling that towards the end of the sixth century the West simply became less relevant to easterners.

Meanwhile, the West was going its own way. The discontent, which manifested itself in Africa and Italy over the condemnation of the Three Chapters, may plausibly be seen as reflecting unhappiness at the situation that existed following the wars waged by Justinian. Increasingly, the Italians came to see their interests as not necessarily identical with those of the Empire. In Spain, Justinian's activities left a nasty taste in people's mouths: the learned Isidore of Seville, writing in the early seventh century, denied not only ecumenical status to the council of 551, but also a place among Roman law-givers to Justinian and patriarchal rank to the see of Constantinople. In Africa, the inability of the government to deal with the Berbers prepared the ground for the loss of the province to the Arabs in the following century. It is hard to avoid the conclusion that in the sixth century Byzantium and the West had moved significantly apart; one cannot but see the emperor Justinian as being largely to blame.

41 'Primus ex Grecorum genere in imperio confirmatus est'; Paul the Deacon, *HL* IV.15.123.

CHAPTER 6

OSTROGOTHIC ITALY AND THE LOMBARD INVASIONS

John Moorhead

LATE ANTIQUE ITALY

The situation of Italy during the period now often called 'late antiquity' was not always a happy one. The economy was in transition: the number of occupied rural sites began to fall in the third or even the second century, *agri deserti* were becoming a common feature of the landscape, and towns were losing population.[1] The construction of urban public buildings, one of the distinguishing characteristics of classical civilisation, dried up, and in the early sixth century it was recognised that the population of Rome was much smaller than it had been. As Cassiodorus, a man with long experience in the civil service, wrote: 'The vast numbers of the people of the city of Rome in old times are evidenced by the extensive provinces from which their food supply was drawn, as well as by the wide circuit of their walls, the massive structure of their amphitheatre, the marvellous bigness of their public baths, and the enormous multitude of mills, which could only have been made for use, not for ornament.'[2] The role Italy played in the economic life of the Roman Empire diminished, imported African pottery having come to dominate the Italian market as early as the second century, and its political fortunes were similar. While Rome remained for centuries the capital of a mighty empire, there were very few Italian emperors after the first century, and the advent of Constantinople as the 'second Rome' from the time of Constantine early in the fourth century saw the eastern and wealthier portion of the Empire become independent.

It was against this background that Italy found itself exposed to invasions in the fifth century. Rome itself was sacked by Visigoths (410) and Vandals (455) and threatened by Attila the Hun (452). After the murder in 455 of the last strong emperor, Valentinian III, an event which some were to see as marking the end of the Empire in the West, nine evanescent emperors sat in Ravenna, of

[1] See in general Gïardina ed. (1986). [2] Cassiodorus, *Variae* II.39.1 f (amended trans. Hodgkin).

Map 1 Italy in the sixth century

whom only two died peacefully in office, and effective power was in the hands of a series of non-Roman generals. In 476 one of these, Odovacer, having been proclaimed king by the army, deposed the emperor, the young Romulus Augustulus, whose name implausibly combined the name of the legendary co-founder of Rome and a diminutive of the title 'augustus' given to the first emperor. He was sent to Castellum Lucullanum, a villa near Naples where he may have still been living in the sixth century. So it was that Italy moved into the post-imperial period.[3]

[3] Hodgkin (1896); Hartmann (1897); Wes (1967).

ODOVACER AND THEODERIC

But Odovacer's contemporaries were not disposed to place as much significance on the events of 476 as modern historians have done.[4] In practical terms, little had changed. Political power in Italy continued to be in the hands of a military strongman and, while Odovacer was no longer nominally subordinate to a western emperor, a senatorial embassy to the emperor Zeno in Constantinople had asserted on his behalf that the West had no need of an emperor. Zeno responded by making Odovacer a patrician, and accepted the nomination of a consul, one of the two consuls who continued to be appointed annually, which he made every year. Further, the Catholic church and the senatorial aristocracy, two groups which had been steadily becoming more important in Italian affairs, seem to have lost nothing by the events of 476, and indeed to have looked upon them with equanimity. Their capacity to outlive the empire in the West is a strong indication of the essential continuity of the period. Odovacer, wisely, went out of his way to conciliate the Senate.[5] In 483 the praetorian prefect Basilius, acting on his behalf, was involved in the election of Pope Felix III, a figure unusual among popes of the time in that he was of aristocratic family. It is also likely that Odovacer saw to the refurbishment of the Colosseum, where the front seats were allocated to senators; archaeologists have uncovered the names of senators of the period inscribed into the seats. He also gave the Senate the right to mint bronze coins. Italy continued to be governed, as it had been during the later Empire, from Ravenna, where the high offices of state were maintained, and it is clear that the effective monopoly over some posts which the leading senatorial families had held during the fifth century was allowed to continue. The coming to power of Odovacer made little change to Italy.

His undoing was due to external factors. Early in his reign he had ceded control over Provence to Euric the Visigoth and agreed to pay tribute for Sicily to the Vandals, and towards its end he abandoned Noricum, a province which occupied roughly the territory of modern Austria, thereby completing a process of unravelling which had seen region after region break away from Roman control in the fifth century. But, as we have seen, to the East there hung the cloud of the Empire, whose massive resources were available to back up any claims it might make to territories in the West. Zeno, whose reign was marked by rebellions, lacked the power to move directly against Odovacer even if he possessed the desire, but hit upon the idea of sending against him Theoderic, the king of the Ostrogoths who had been exposed to Byzantine ways during the ten years of his youth he spent as a hostage in Constantinople. This people

[4] Croke (1983). [5] Chastagnol (1966).

had been engaged in intermittent but wearisome activities against the Empire since they had freed themselves from the power of the Huns following the death of Attila in 453, and in 487 Theoderic had gone so far as to lead a force against Constantinople itself. Hence, whatever the outcome of the expedition against Odovacer, Zeno had nothing to lose.

In 488, Theoderic set out from the old military town of Novae, near the modern Svištov in Bulgaria. While those who accompanied him can for convenience be called 'Ostrogoths' it is highly likely that they included members of other peoples, and that the move into Italy was an example of a common tendency for migrating groups to grow like avalanches.[6] Women and children were among the members of what was clearly a migration as much as a military expedition. Theoderic's entry into Italy was challenged by Odovacer at the River Isonzo, but the defenders fled without giving battle, falling back to Verona. After suffering defeat here Odovacer retreated to his capital, Ravenna, to which Theoderic laid siege. Hard pressed, Odovacer entered into negotiations with his assailant in February 493. The antagonists agreed to share the government, but Theoderic lost no time in inviting his colleague to a banquet, where he ran his sword through him. Under such auspices he inaugurated his long reign (493–526).[7]

GOTHS AND ROMANS

Italy was now populated, according to the contemporary formula, by 'Goths and Romans'. It is clear that the Goths, significantly the group named first in this expression, were not always desirable neighbours, for their army was capable of causing havoc in the Italian countryside even during time of peace, and some of the Goths who were assigned to protect individual Romans had no qualms about beating up their charges. In the words which Cassiodorus, the best known of the Romans who made careers in the service of the Goths, put in the mouth of his sovereign, 'To the Goths a hint of war rather than persuasion to the strife is needed, since a warlike race such as ours delights to prove its courage.'[8] Theoderic, who was insistent that the Goths live *civiliter*, in a law-abiding way, had reason to fear for relations between the peoples.

Nevertheless, many Romans could have gone about their daily lives without being affected by the Goths to any great extent. While it is impossible to establish how many people followed Theoderic to Italy, they cannot have

6 Wenskus (1961), pp. 483ff. On the 'ethnogenesis' of the people who came to be called Goths, Wolfram (1988).

7 Discussed in Stein (1949), Ensslin (1947), Moorhead (1992).

8 Cassiodorus, *Variae* 1.24.1 (trans. Hodgkin).

numbered more than a small proportion of the native population, and it is clear from various classes of evidence that they were concentrated in the north of Italy. Even the means by which they were supported allowed them to slip into Italian society unobtrusively, for it seems likely that the *tertiae*, or thirds, which contemporary authors describe as having been assigned to the Goths, were not tracts of land, as has been widely assumed, but units of tax revenue.[9] Hence, the coming of the Goths would have left the economic power of the landowning class unchallenged. The areas in which the newcomers lived were the most sensitive regions militarily, and Goths and Romans could be distinguished with reference to the functions which they fulfilled in society, military and civilian respectively: 'While the army of the Goths makes war, the Roman may live in peace.'[10] But such a division of labour marked no change in Roman practice, for the army had been increasingly made up of non-Romans for centuries, and a cleavage between civil and military careers had become well established in the later Empire. There can have been few Romans who did not regard Italian society as continuing to function as it had during the Empire. A legal code which has been published as the 'Edict of Theoderic', and for which he may well have been responsible, is almost entirely made up of excerpts from late Roman legislation. Like the rise of Odovacer, the coming of the Ostrogoths brought no major change to Italy.

For the Goths, on the other hand, settlement in Italy marked a significant change, and they found it hard to avoid paying attention to the Romans. A minority group, they were isolated from the Romans by their adherence to the Arian form of Christianity, a belief deemed heretical by the people of Italy, and by the convention that they be tried before military courts, a pair of distinguishing characteristics which Theoderic was happy to maintain. But some of the Goths came to convert from Arianism to Catholicism, and as contemporaries regarded Arianism as 'the law of the Goths' and Catholicism as the specifically Roman religion, their conversion meant an abandonment of one of the defining characteristics of the Goths.[11] Some Goths were adopting the language of the Romans; of the eleven Gothic clergy of Ravenna who put their names to a document in 551, seven signed in Latin. These clergy would have conducted baptisms at Ravenna in a baptistery with a mosaic in its cupola, which, imitating as it does an older mosaic in a nearby Catholic baptistery, is further testimony to the susceptibility of the Goths to Roman influences.

9 Goffart (1980); Wolfram and Schwarcz (1988).

10 Cassiodorus, *Variae* XII.5.4 (trans. Hodgkin).

11 Arianism as 'lex Gothorum': Tjäder, *Papyri* pap. 31.1, 7, 8, 10 (vol. II, p. 84ff) pap. 43.108, 122 (vol. II, p. 102); on the interpretation, vol. II, p. 268 n. 3. Arians calling Catholics 'Romani': Gregory of Tours, *Liber in Gloria Martyrum*, ed. Krusch XXIV.52.

Theoderic, who seems to have had a knack for coining memorable phrases, observed that 'the poor Roman imitates the Goth, and the well-to-do Goth the Roman'.[12] The truth of the second part of this statement is confirmed by the circumstance that rich Goths tended to be buried with Roman grave-goods, which implies that wealth and Romanisation went hand in hand. Doubtless there was some move among the Roman lower classes to adopt Gothic mores, and during the 540s the Gothic army was swollen by poor Romans; in the light of the distinction Theoderic drew between civilian and military, this act could be taken to imply not merely support for the Goths but also a measure of identification with them. But in any convergence between the peoples, the Goths were bound to be the losers. Indeed, we know that the two races were coming to intermarry, despite Roman legislation which forbade the marriage of Romans and barbarians, and given the relative size of their populations in Italy this development cannot have boded well for the future of the Goths. The capacity Italy has shown over the centuries to assimilate non-natives was again being displayed.

THE GOVERNMENT OF THEODERIC

For over thirty years Theoderic supplied government of a kind Italy had not known for generations. He strengthened his kingdom in a way Odovacer had failed to, by contracting marriage alliances with all the chief states in the West. His reign was also marked by an unbroken run of military successes won by his generals. In 504 Count Pitzas took Sirmium, a city on the left bank of the River Sava, from the Gepids and shortly afterwards defeated a Byzantine force in the region. The defeat of the Visigoths and killing of their king by the Franks at the battle of Vouillé in 507 cannot have pleased their Ostrogothic kinsfolk, but Theoderic was able to turn the situation to his advantage by moving his frontier forward to the River Durance, a tributary of the Rhône. The administration of the newly won territories was provided for by a praetorian prefect of Gaul, the first to be appointed since the 470s, while Theoderic governed the remaining parts of the Visigothic state in the name of the dead king's heir.[13] In 523, when the Franks attacked Burgundy, Theoderic sent his general Tuluin to intervene, and on this occasion the frontier seems to have been pushed as far north as the River Isère.

A successful foreign policy was not the only achievement of Theoderic. Italy itself benefited from building activity which saw the erection, or at least refurbishment, of palaces, baths, aqueducts, defensive works and an amphitheatre.

[12] *Anonymus Valesianus* 61 (*Chronica Minora* I, p. 322).

[13] For Ostrogothic rule in Spain, see Barbero and Loring, chapter 7 below.

Indeed, apart from his penchant for building churches dedicated to the Arian cult, the king was behaving in a way thoroughly appropriate to a Roman emperor, just as his apparent disinclination to command the army in person after gaining control of Italy is suggestive of the behaviour of an emperor rather than that of a Germanic king. But his conduct was not surprising in one who had spent ten years of his youth as a hostage in Constantinople, an experience from which he may be presumed to have gained a command of Greek far superior to that which most of the Romans around him would have enjoyed. Despite his Arianism he enjoyed good relations with members of the hierarchy of the church, judging a disputed papal election, which had occurred in 498, and being able to impose a candidate on the see of Rome in 526. After the disasters which Italy had suffered in the fifth century, the achievements of the early sixth century seemed remarkable, and Theoderic's subjects compared him to the greatest Roman emperors.

His official title was *rex*, or king. We do not know how his constitutional position was regarded in Constantinople and it is possible that, even after he came to peace with the emperor Anastasius (491–518) in 497, and received back the ornaments of the palace, which Odovacer had sent to Constantinople, his status was not defined. Writing in Theoderic's name to Anastasius, Cassiodorus expressed the relationship between Italy and the Empire in terms designed to flatter the imperial ear: 'Our royalty is an imitation of yours, modelled on your good purpose, a copy of the only empire, and in so far as we follow you we excel all other nations.'[14] The same point was made indirectly by the way Cassiodorus arranged his letters for publication, for the letter to Anastasius is immediately followed in his collected correspondence by one concerning the preparation of purple dye for royal use. In the words of a Byzantine writer, who was enough of a classicist to be able to adapt a phrase of Thecydides, he was 'in name a tyrant but in reality a true emperor'.[15]

So it was that, when Theoderic visited Rome to celebrate his *tricennalia* in 500, the occasion was unambiguously imperial, with ecclesiastical frills of the kind which had become common during late antiquity: a visit to St Peter's basilica, which was made despite Theoderic's not being a Catholic; a reception outside the City from the pope, senate and people; a visit to the senate house; a speech to the people; a triumphal entry to the palace on the Palatine Hill; the holding of circus games and the bestowing of *annonae*. Some years later a senator put up on the Via Appia multiple copies of an inscription describing Theoderic in a term which could only be applied to an emperor, 'ever augustus'.[16] The Empire, it must have seemed, lived on in Italy.

[14] Cassiodorus, *Variae* I.1.3 (trans. Hodgkin).

[15] Procopius, *Bellum Gothicum* I.1.29; cf. Thecydides II.65.9 (on Pericles).

[16] Fiebiger and Schmidt, *Inschriftensammlung* no. 193 (= *CIL* X.6850–52). Cassiodorus, *Variae* II.32ff suggests a date in the period 507–511.

Yet there may have been those who were displeased at the Ostrogothic government. The members of the Senate of Rome regarded themselves as the authentic custodians of tradition and behaved in ways characteristic of their forbears, restoring old buildings, copying ancient texts, writing history, evading taxes and even diverting public water to serve their own ends. If they found themselves more involved than their ancestors had been in ecclesiastical politics, this was simply testimony to their desire to make some of the growing power of the church their own. One of their number, Boethius, the author of books on theology as well as translations of and commentaries on Greek texts, produced works of immense intellectual distinction which were to be influential for centuries; indeed, after the barrenness of secular literary culture in Italy for most of the fifth century, the Ostrogothic period can be seen as marking a distinct revival of letters. As the power of the Roman state had weakened in the fifth century the prestige and influence of the Senate had risen, and Theoderic sought to conciliate its members.[17] His first consular nominee, Albinus, the son and probably the grandson of consuls, was followed in this office by three brothers, and seems to have been a nephew of the man who erected the inscriptions which described Theoderic as 'ever augustus'. Albinus is known to have been involved in administration at Theoderic's court in Ravenna and the life of the circus, to have collaborated with his wife in the building of a church, and to have followed theological affairs with interest. Over the years Theoderic's relations with the old senatorial families varied, but they seem to have improved following the termination of a schism between the churches of Rome and Constantinople in 519. In 522 Boethius' two sons held a joint consulship and their father accepted office as *magister officiorum*, while in the following year an old friend of Boethius, the deacon John, became pope. The ascendancy of the group represented by these men must have seemed assured.

Nevertheless, the reign of the great king was to end with their disgrace.[18] In 523 one of Theoderic's legal officers, Cyprian, charged Albinus with having engaged in treacherous correspondence with the emperor. He denied the charge and was defended by Boethius, but Cyprian then broadened the charge to include his defender as well. In 525 Pope John, accompanied by a group of senators and clerics, was forced to go to Constantinople to intercede for the cause of Arianism. He returned the following year to face a frosty reception, and died shortly afterwards. Boethius and his father-in-law Symmachus were put to death, the former having written in prison his last and best-known book, the *Consolation of Philosophy*. In August Theoderic died in turn, to be buried in the mausoleum still to be seen in Ravenna. It was an inglorious end to a great reign, which led later Catholic writers to put about stories that he had been

[17] Sundwall (1919) remains basic. [18] Moorhead (1992), pp. 212–51.

preparing a general persecution just before he died. The reason for Theoderic striking out in this uncharacteristic way is not clear: his awareness, as he grew old, of the lack of an adult male heir and consequent tensions in Ravenna about the succession, the adoption of pro-Byzantine policies by the Vandals of North Africa, to which he reacted by ordering the rapid construction of a great fleet in 526, and Byzantine intrigue may all have been involved, but perhaps the most important element was the desire of a group of courtiers to undermine the influence of an aristocratic group centred on Boethius whose recent and rapid preferment jeopardised their own position.

THE DEMISE OF THE OSTROGOTHIC STATE

Some three decades before Theoderic died, the deacon Ennodius, an author whose literary output ranged from obscene verse to liturgical prose, wrote a panegyric in which he expressed the hope that the king would be succeeded by a son, but this was not to be the case. Theoderic designated as his heir his grandson Athalaric, but the boy was young and power lay in the hands of his mother, Amalasuentha. Any successor would have found the task of stepping into the shoes of Theoderic difficult; that Amalasuentha was a woman and of intellectual inclinations did not make her task any easier. She began, sensibly, to bid for support. Conciliatory correspondence was dispatched to Constantinople, the estates of Symmachus and Boethius were restored to their heirs, and the pope was given the right of hearing cases involving members of the Roman church in the first instance. The Gothic general Tuluin, who had gained large estates after the war in Burgundy, was elevated to the rank of *patricius praesentalis*.

Despite these gestures, Amalasuentha was unable to prevent an erosion of the government's power. The Franks nibbled at Ostrogothic possessions in Gaul and wiped out the kingdom of the Burgundians, but more alarming were internal developments, known to us from the narrative of the Byzantine historian Procopius. Even Theoderic had found it difficult to dominate the Gothic nobility, and the task was certainly beyond his daughter. Some of the Goths held that, contrary to his mother's wishes, Athalaric should receive his education along Gothic rather than Roman lines, and before long Amalasuentha began to fear for her position. She opened negotiations with the emperor Justinian (527–565) with a view to fleeing Italy, and preparations were made to receive her in imperial territory at Dyrrhachium, but, finding herself able to arrange the murder of some of her enemies, she decided to remain. The death of Athalaric, a victim of youthful excess, in October 534, weakened her position, leading her to adopt the title of *regina* (queen) and take her near relative Theodahad, a wealthy dilettante, as joint ruler. But the ploy backfired, for Theodahad allied himself with her enemies and was able to have the unfortunate Amalasuentha strangled at Lake Bolsena, probably in the spring of 535. Some people felt that her demise was to be attributed to female jealousy, it being suspected that Justinian's wife Theodora was perturbed at the attraction Amalasuentha may have had for her husband. This interpretation of events is an unlikely one, but it has the merit of emphasising how closely Italian affairs had become connected with those of the mighty Empire. Theodahad's decision to free himself of Amalasuentha, who had put herself under the protection of Justinian, was not well advised, for in a brief war in 533 imperial forces had wiped out the Vandal state in Africa, and the speedy success had encouraged Justinian to look across to Italy. War between the Empire and the Ostrogoths broke out in 535. Of its ultimate outcome there could be no doubt: when Amalasuentha planned to flee to the Empire she had 40,000 pounds of gold at her disposal, but when the emperor Anastasius died in 518 he had left eight times this sum in the treasury. The Goths could not match the resources of the Empire.

Nevertheless, the Gothic war lasted longer than Justinian had bargained for. It began well, for his general Belisarius took Rome in 536 and entered Ravenna in 540. Shortly afterwards Belisarius left for Constantinople, taking with him the Gothic king Witigis, a man of military experience whom the Goths had chosen to replace Theodahad. But the heavy-handed Byzantine administrators Belisarius left behind took their obligation to collect taxes all too seriously, and when the Goths gained as their king a vigorous leader, Totila (also known as Baduila), in 541, the stage was set for a conflict which lasted until Justinian sent the general Narses to Italy. Having advanced into Italy from the north, he was able to defeat Totila in 553, although Gothic resistance continued on a local basis until the capture of Verona and Brescia some years later.

THE IMPACT OF THE WAR

The history of the war has been narrated in the previous chapter, and here it will be enough to draw attention to some of its results. The Byzantine historian of Justinian's wars, Procopius, told a story which he professed not to believe, but which he nevertheless thought was worth recounting. At the beginning of the war, we are told, Theodahad asked a Jew what the outcome of the war would be, and was instructed to shut three groups of ten pigs, which he was to call respectively Goths, Romans and imperial soldiers, in pens. On opening the enclosures some days later he found all but two of the pigs representing the Goths dead, and all but a few of those representing the soldiers alive; of those which represented the Romans, about half were alive, although all had lost their hair.[19] This attempt at telling the future was not completely accurate, for we know of many people with Gothic personal names who lived in Italy after the war. But the story is indicative of a perception that the impact on the Romans of the war and, presumably, of the plague which broke out in 543 and continued to recur, had been frightful. When pope Gregory the Great came to write his *Dialogues* during the last decade of the century he gave an account of a discussion which had taken place between bishop Sabinus of Canosa di Puglia and the famous monk St Benedict, probably during 547. After Totila had entered Rome and caused its ruin, the bishop commented that the city would be destroyed by the king and cease to be inhabited. Benedict disagreed: Rome would not be brought to nothing by the barbarians, he said, but, worn out by storms, lightning, various kinds of trouble and the shaking of the earth, it would simply decay.[20]

The two perspectives neatly encapsulate two possible ways of understanding the Gothic war. Given that Rome changed hands five times, that it had once gone unoccupied for forty days, some of the earliest burials within the walls of the city date from the time of the war, and that its senators, who had so recently been proudly celebrating consulships, had been murdered or fled, one might feel inclined to attribute catastrophic significance to the war. Whereas the war between Theoderic and Odovacer had been confined to a small area, the activities of Totila, a man who was remembered towards the end of the century above all for his cruelty, caused more destruction than any war since Hannibal's invasion of Italy in the third century BC, and their impact was heightened by the outbreak of plague. In 557 Pope Pelagius, complaining of great nakedness and want in Rome, tried to have income from the church's estates in Gaul used to buy clothing there which would be sent to Rome for distribution to the poor. Later he wrote to the praetorian prefect of Africa complaining of the poverty of the Roman church. Economic decline was accompanied by a lower level of intellectual life: oddly enough, it seems that more Greek books were produced at Ravenna in the time of the Goths than were during the rest of the sixth century, while the city was part of the Byzantine Empire. Italy also came to know political impotence. Despite its incorporation into the Empire, no sixth-century emperor visited Italy, and yet the independence which it had enjoyed under Odovacer and the Goths vanished. Offices of state such as *quaestor* and *magister officiorum* disappeared from Ravenna, and Italy found itself governed, as did Africa, by appointees from Constantinople; furthermore, the independence of the papacy and other major Italian sees was curtailed.[21] Surely, it could be argued that the impact of the war on Italy was disastrous.

[19] *Bellum Gothicum* I.9.2–7. [20] Gregory of Rome, *Dialogues* II.15.3.

[21] See Moorhead, chapter 5 above.

Yet it would be possible to make too much of the change the war brought about. At Volturno, a hitherto prosperous villa was deserted during the first half of the century, but its abandonment need not have been a result of the war. At Luni, for example, the forum was covered by soil at the beginning of the sixth century, and it is possible to interpret the economic decline which the war brought as simply the temporary speeding-up of a process which, as we have seen, had been going on for centuries. Rome was to experience something of a revival after the war: in 565 Narses erected an inscription which recorded his rebuilding of a bridge over which the Via Salaria passed, destroyed 'by the most wicked tyrant Totila'.[22] Hostility towards Totila is also evident in the Pragmatic Sanction which Justinian issued in 554, in which he sought to regulate the affairs of Italy and, in particular, to re-establish the position of the landowning aristocracy, which had suffered heavy losses in the war.[23] Concessions made by Amalasuentha, Athalaric and Theodahad were confirmed, while those of Totila were declared null and void. The loss of deeds during the war was not to prejudice ownership of property; estates that had been taken during the war from absent or captive people were to be returned, and the rights of slave owners were safeguarded. A desire for continuity is also evident in the provision that the *annonae* which had been given to the Romans, as well as the grammarians, orators, doctors and those learned in the law, were to be paid as they had been. Some of the provisions of the Pragmatic Sanction reflect all too clearly a society undergoing change: senators were to have free access to the emperor in Constantinople, but to be able to go to Italy and remain there to regain their property; provincial governors were to be selected by bishops and magnates, while weights and measures were to be checked in the presence of the pope and the Senate. But even these provisions could be held to reflect nothing more than the increasing pre-eminence of the senatorial and ecclesiastical pillars of Italian society, confirming a tendency that was by no means new. Doubtless the years of Totila had marked an economic regression, but a series of papyri from Ravenna suggest that the land market was brisk in at least that region, and towards the end of Justinian's reign it would have been quite realistic for the inhabitants of Italy to have anticipated a period of healing.

THE LOMBARD INVASION

Such security and prosperity as Italy enjoyed after the Byzantine conquest were destined to be short-lived.[24] From about the time of the death of Theoderic a Germanic people, the Lombards, had been settling south of the Danube in the

[22] *CIL* VI.1199. [23] Archi (1978).
[24] Delogu *et al.* (1980); Wickham (1981); Christie (1995).

old province of Pannonia. They had, in general, been allies of the Byzantines, but had enjoyed less exposure to Roman ways than the Ostrogoths. No king of the Lombards spent a decade in Constantinople as Theoderic had done, and while they included Catholics and Arians most of them seem still to have been non-Christian. In 568, led by their king Alboin, they left Pannonia and moved to Italy.

The reasons prompting their decision to migrate are not clear. According to a story current as early as the seventh century, they had been invited by Narses, Justinian's general who, having remained in Italy after the conquest, was driven to seek revenge for the ill will the Romans displayed towards him by summoning the invaders. While the spite attributed to Narses in this tale is doubtless unhistorical, it has been possible for modern scholars to build up a case that Byzantine officials did invite Alboin to Italy: the Lombards' recent career as allies of the Empire, which had included their sending men to help Narses in his struggle with the Ostrogoths, the failure of the Byzantines to offer serious resistance in the early stages of the invasion, and the continuing threat posed by the Franks to the north of Italy, a circumstance which could have prompted the summoning of potential allies, can all be invoked to support such an interpretation.[25] On the other hand, it is possible that the Lombards came to Italy in response to an appeal for help from the surviving Ostrogoths. But their invasion need not have been in response to any Italian considerations, beyond a feeling that easy pickings were to be had there. In 565 the emperor Justin II, overturning a policy of Justinian, had refused to pay tribute to the Avars, a people who had suddenly come to prominence along the central Danube, and in 567 the Lombards and Avars had joined forces to defeat the Gepids. Alboin himself was said to have killed their king, and went on to marry the dead king's daughter, Rosimund. Doubtless the defeat of a people who had long been their enemies was gratifying to the Lombards, but the rise of the Avars must have made Pannonia a good deal less congenial, and this may be enough to account for their decision to move to Italy. In any case, on 2 April 568 they began their trek, launching an invasion of Italy that was to be more deeply felt and longer lasting in its impact than that of the Ostrogoths.

We have no way of estimating the size of the host Alboin led to Italy. His following included members of peoples other than the Lombards, among whom Saxons were the most prominent; intriguingly, the author of the Old English poem *Widsith* claimed he had been in Italy with Elfpine the son of Eadwine, names suggestive of Alboin, the son of Audoin.[26] Like the earlier invaders Theoderic and Narses, Alboin advanced into Italy by way of Venetia, where he seems to have encountered no opposition. He installed his nephew

[25] See in particular the collected studies of Bognetti (1966–68).

[26] *Widsith*, lines 70–4.

Gisulf as duke of Cividale and the surrounding territory, and gave him various *farae*, an obscure word of Germanic origin which Paul the Deacon, writing in the late eighth century, understood as meaning 'clans or lineages'.[27] The bishop of the nearby town of Aquileia fled to the coastal town of Grado, while in the following year Milan fell to the invaders and its bishop fled to Genoa. At a time impossible to estimate, and for reasons hard to deduce, powerful duchies were established much further to the south by Faroald at Spoleto and Zotto at Benevento. In 572 Alboin entered Pavia, after a siege of three years, and made his way to the palace Theoderic had constructed there.

During their earliest years in Italy some of the characteristics of the Lombard invasion were already apparent: the dislocation they caused society was greater than that occasioned by the Ostrogoths, and they were not as cohesive as their predecessors. Alboin was not to enjoy his success for long, as the year of his entry into Pavia also saw his murder at the instigation of his wife Rosimund. According to Paul the Deacon she came to conceive a hatred for her husband when, at a feast in Verona, he produced a goblet made out of the skull of her father Cunimund and suggested that she have a drink with her father. She took revenge by having Alboin murdered while he slept, but the deed was not popular among the Lombards, and before long she fled to Ravenna, the Byzantine capital in Italy, in the company of other Lombards who took the opportunity to defect. In Ravenna Rosimund was received by the patrician Longinus, who had succeeded Narses as the Byzantine commander, but was to die of poison. The Lombards elected one Cleph to replace Alboin, but after a reign of eighteen months he was murdered by a slave, whereupon the Lombards dispensed with monarchy for a decade (574–584) during which power passed to the dukes, of whom we are told there were thirty-five. The interregnum saw fighting on a wide scale in Italy, and hostilities against the Franks in Gaul. The emperor Justin II (565–578) finally intervened by sending his son-in-law Baduarius to the aid of Italy, but he was defeated and died in about 576. During the pontificate of Pope Benedict (575–579) Justin arranged for ships full of grain to be sent from Egypt to Rome to relieve famine. In 577 or 578, and again in 579, suppliants from Rome arrived in Constantinople. While their trips may have been connected with the accession of a new emperor and a new pope, they certainly sought aid, but little was the satisfaction they received. When Pelagius II became pope in 579, Rome was under siege, and at about the same time Classe, the port of Ravenna, was plundered.

The coming of the Lombards to Italy is not well documented, our main source being Paul the Deacon, who wrote some 200 years after their arrival, although he had access to an important early source no longer extant, a history

[27] Paul the Deacon, *HL* II.9.91 (*generationes vel lineas*).

written by Bishop Secundus of Trent. Many aspects of it remain unclear. For example, we do not know whether the *farae* mentioned by Paul are to be seen as family groupings or wandering military detachments,[28] nor whether the office of duke was primarily a survival from Germanic society or an institution recently developed under late Roman or Byzantine influence. These two issues obviously raise the general question as to the degree to which the Lombards had moved away from their barbarian origins when they came to Italy, and may possibly be connected with a degree of Lombard cooperation with imperial forces in Italy. It has been argued that the men who established the duchies of Spoleto and Benevento, for example, were acting on behalf of the Byzantines.[29] This interpretation seems far-fetched, but there were certainly members of the Lombard forces who acted in the imperial interest. One thinks of the duke Droctulf, who defected to the enemy and was buried before the threshold of the church of S. Vitale in Ravenna, famous for its mosaics of Justinian and Theodora which constitute powerful imperial propaganda.[30] It may not be accidental that archaeology reveals Lombard burials in regions of Italy that remained under imperial control.

Nevertheless, if the Byzantines had seen the Lombards as a way of coping with the Franks, it must have quickly become clear that the experiment of inviting them to Italy had failed disastrously. But as the situation deteriorated there emerged the possibility of doing the reverse, and calling on the Franks to deal with the Lombards, just as had been done during the Gothic war. As early as 580 Pope Pelagius sought their intervention, and a few years later Constantinople sought to use the Franks to solve its problems in Italy. The emperor Maurice conveyed the enormous sum of 50,000 *solidi* to King Childebert, who attacked the Lombards in 584. Details of the Frankish expedition do not emerge clearly from our sources, but it was enough to alarm the Lombards, who in that year elected a new king, Authari, the son of Cleph. It quickly became clear that he was not to be like their earlier kings. The dukes surrendered half their wealth to him, placing the monarchy on a secure economic basis; he adopted the Roman title Flavius; and he forbade Lombard children to be baptised as Catholics, a step indicative of both the authority he felt was his and the non-Roman path

[28] Paul defines *fara* as '*generatio vel linea*' (*HL* II.9), with which compare Marius of Avenches, *Chronica* s.a. 569 (*Chronica Minora* II.238; Alboin with all his followers occupied Italy 'in fara') and *Edictus Rothari* 177 ('si quis liber homo potestatem habeat intra dominium regni nostra cum fara sua megrare ubi voluerit'). The debate is summarised by Harrison (1993), pp. 50ff.

[29] Bognetti (1966–68), vol. III, pp. 456–75.

[30] Paul the Deacon (*HL* III.18) describes Droctulf as being 'descended from the Sueves, that is the Alamanni' who had been brought up among the Lombards. Theophylact Simocatta sees him as a Lombard (*Historiae* II.7), while his epitaph, reproduced by Paul (*HL* III.19) describes him as a Sueve (line 3) yet refers to his long beard (longa . . . barba, line 6)! On S. Vitale and Ravenna, see Moorhead, chapter 5 above.

he saw the Lombards taking. A story told by a Catholic author, Gregory the Great, hints at some of the tensions to which the Lombards were exposed in this period. On one occasion, we learn from one of his letters, a Lombard saw a golden key of St Peter and, wishing to make something else out of it, tried to cut it with his knife. But he drove the knife through his throat and died. King Authari and the other Lombards who were present were struck with terror, and no one dared to touch the key until a Catholic Lombard arrived. Authari had another gold key made and sent them both to the pope.[31] Archaeology gives evidence for Romanisation that is less ambiguous. The earliest burials at Nocera Umbra, a site the Lombards had occupied by 571, contain grave-goods in a style familiar from Lombard burials in Pannonia, but within a few decades, people were being buried there with wares which imitated Roman goods.

In 589 Authari consolidated his position to the north by marrying Theodelinda, the daughter of the Bavarian ruler Garibald. It was a wise move in the light of continuing pressure from the Franks, who had come to control Aosta and Susa, on the Italian side of Alpine passes. In 590 Authari's enemies launched major attacks. The Franks advanced from the west and made their way as far as Verona, while the Byzantines captured numerous towns and welcomed to their side a number of Lombards who defected. But the allies failed to coordinate their activities and were unable to provoke the Lombards, who took shelter in fortresses, to battle, and the Franks withdrew. On 5 September Authari died, of poison it was said. He left no children, and Theodelinda chose as her new husband Agilulf, duke of Turin, a Thuringian who consequently became king. Paul the Deacon tells a story according to which Authari, before he died, rode as far as Reggio, in the far south of the peninsular, and touched a pillar in the sea with the point of his spear, saying 'The territory of the Lombards will extend this far'.[32] Like so many of Paul's stories this is almost certainly apocryphal, and as a piece of prophecy it erred on the side of generosity, but after the collapse of the Frankish and Byzantine operations of 590 it was clear that the Lombards were in Italy to stay.

THE SIGNIFICANCE OF THE LOMBARDS

Early Roman authors who mentioned the Lombards described them as small in number, a remark that the limited size of their burial grounds during the period shortly after their arrival in Italy could be held to confirm. But at one of these sites, Nocera Umbra, over 90 per cent of the males were buried with weapons, and the strategic location of the site, just a few hundred metres from the Via Flaminia, the main road proceeding northwards from Rome across

[31] Gregory of Rome, *Epp.* 7.23. [32] Paul, *HL* III.22.127.

the Apennines, suggests the likely purpose of Lombard settlement there.[33] In Constantinople it was felt that the impact of the Lombards had been dire. Various Italian contemporaries concurred in finding them 'utterly unspeakable' (*nefandissimi*), and Gregory the Great, who succeeded Pope Pelagius II, a victim of plague, two days before the death of Authari, painted a gloomy picture in a sermon he preached early in his pontificate:

> Cities have been destroyed, fields laid waste and the land reduced to a wilderness. There is not a farmer in the fields and scarcely an inhabitant remains in the cities – and yet these small remnants of the human race are still being struck down daily, without pause.[34]

Indeed, the fighting, the concomitant famine and renewed outbreaks of plague led Gregory to believe for some years that biblical predictions concerning the end of the world were about to be fulfilled.

Gregory and his contemporaries contemplated an Italy broadly divided into two fluctuating zones. One of these remained under the control of the Byzantines. To speak in general terms, it included a block of territory extending along the Adriatic seaboard and which penetrated inland to a varying extent; along the Via Aemilia it included Bologna but not Modena. This was connected to another wedge of territory based on Rome, but as the foundation of the duchy of Spoleto had made the Via Flaminia dangerous it had been replaced as the major thoroughfare across the Apennines by a road further to the west that passed through Perugia. The Byzantines also held coastal strips based on Genoa and Naples as well as the heel and toe of Italy. It was an unwieldy agglomeration of territories that owed such geographical unity as it possessed to the undisputed Byzantine control of the sea, which allowed communication to take place easily. Over the remaining and larger part of Italy the invaders held sway, and the Lombards were not averse to making life difficult for those living in the diminished Byzantine portion. Rome and Naples were both harassed in the 590s, and Pope Gregory found it worth his while seeking the help of the duke of Benevento when he arranged to have timber transported from the hinterland of Bruttium to the sea.

Paul the Deacon seems at one point in his narrative to attribute catastrophic significance to the coming of the Lombards. He states that Cleph killed some important Romans and banished others (or 'the others') and that during the interregnum of 574–584 many Roman nobles were killed because of the greed of the Lombards, while the remainder (of the nobles? or of the Italians?) were shared among the Lombards *per hospites* and made tribute payers so that they

[33] Hessen (1983). [34] Gregory of Rome, *Homilae in Hiez.* II.6.22.

gave one third of what their land produced to the Lombards; he writes of churches despoiled, bishops killed, towns overthrown and peoples (perhaps 'populations') being wiped out. In another passage he asserts that under Authari (584–590) the burdened Italians were divided among the Lombards as *hospites* (or 'among the Lombard *hospites*'); however, he believes that this period was a time of remarkable peace within the kingdom of the Lombards.[35]

This author would not be a source to be accepted uncritically even if his language were less opaque, but there is no escaping the initial impact of the Lombards. Some of the traditional functions of the state in Italy lapsed: the land tax, which had provided the greater part of the revenues of preceding governments, was no longer levied, which entailed the Lombard army being supported from the land directly rather than via a tax collected by the state. For the landowners in the territory they overran, so soon after the Gothic war, the advent of the invaders must have been devastating, of much greater moment than the coming of the Goths had been. The impact of the Lombards on church life is suggested not only by their destroying St Benedict's monastery at Monte Cassino, but by the extraordinary fact that within the voluminous correspondence of Gregory the Great all his letters to bishops in the peninsula are directed to those resident in towns controlled by the Byzantines, with the exception of the bishop of Spoleto. Aquileia and Altino may have been among towns that received their *coup de grâce* from the Lombards, while a notable crisis in the urban standard of living is known to have occurred at this time in Brescia. But caution is called for: in many cases towns had been becoming smaller long before the arrival of the Lombards, and any they 'overthrew' may have been fatally weak already; it is difficult to see the Lombards as marking a significant hiatus in the extraordinary continuity of Italian urban life. The claim that the Lombards wiped out peoples is evidently false, but there can be no doubting their malign impact on the landowning class and churches in the areas that they took over.

Nevertheless, those parts of Italy that remained part of the Empire were also affected by the new circumstances, which inevitably led to what we may term a militarisation of society. In 584 there is mention for the first time of the exarch, an official who combined supreme civil and military authority, but who may plausibly be seen as a *magister militum* whose authority had grown so as to encroach on civilian authority. The development was not completely new in Italy, for as early as the Ostrogothic period the *comites Gothorum* had been throwing their weight around against civilians, and at a later date one pope had invoked the aid of *magistri militum* rather than civil authorities

[35] Paul, *HL* II.31–2.108–9, III.16.123.

in dealing with wayward bishops; nor was it unique to Italy, for an identical development occurred in Africa and it can in some respects be seen as analogous to the military 'themes' which were to develop at a later stage in other parts of the Byzantine Empire. Coming as it did just thirty years after the Pragmatic Sanction had sought to reimpose the distinction between civilian and military in Italy, the rise of the exarch was certainly connected with the inadequacy of civilian authority in the conditions of Italy in the late sixth century.

Another response to the enfeeblement of civil authority was the increasingly prominent role played by bishops in society. Our last reference in late antiquity to a *praefectus urbis Romae* occurs in 599. It had been an office to cherish; Cassiodorus mentions its holders being conveyed in a chariot, and judging by the rapid turnover of occupants in the time of the Goths it was a job for which competition was keen. But in the changed world of the late sixth century it was anachronistic: there was no need, for example, for an official to preside over meetings of the senate, for such meetings were no longer held. Within cities a good deal of power passed to the bishop, particularly in cases where, as was true of the bishops of such sees as Rome and Ravenna, he could draw on the resources of estates in Sicily, far from Lombard depredations. The charitable activities Gregory the Great was to engage in, and the negotiations he was to undertake with Lombard leaders, are testimony to the weakness of the state which was met by increased episcopal, as well as specifically papal, authority. If we wish to gain an understanding of the changed circumstances of Italy, however, we could do no better than consider the militarisation of the landscape. Throughout the correspondence of Cassiodorus there are references to military structures (*castra*, *castella*) at only three places, Tortona in Liguria and Verruca on the River Adige, and on the River Durance,[36] all three near or on the frontiers of the Ostrogothic state. The writings of Procopius on the Gothic war, in particular the phase when Totila led the Goths, reveal a landscape where the impact of war was more widely felt; hence, for example, we read of an ὀχύρωμα (fortress) at Centumcellae and a φρούριον (hill-fort) at Nepi.[37] But this does not prepare us for the landscape dotted with *castra* and *castella* revealed in the correspondence of Gregory the Great. Here we find, for example, a *castrum* founded by monks at Squillace in Bruttium, a place concerning which Cassiodorus had commented 'non habet muros', and another at Bagnorea where the people were to join with the *vir gloriosus* Ansfrid, a Lombard to judge by his name, in electing a bishop.[38] The erection of such structures, as well as the fact that the initiative did not always come from the state, is a sign of how Italy had changed as the century wore on.

36 *Variae* I.17, III.48, III.41. 37 *Bellum Gothicum* III.36.11, IV.34.16 (where also a fortress).
38 Gregory of Rome, *Epp.* 8.32 (cf. Cassiodorus, *Variae* XII.15.5), 10.3

THE EXTENT OF CHANGE IN ITALY DURING THE SIXTH CENTURY

The question as to when the ancient world gave way to that of the Middle Ages has produced a disconcerting variety of responses, and it may be a *question mal posée*. Nevertheless, if we are to impose a frontier between two periods termed 'ancient' and 'medieval', there seem to be good reasons for locating it, at least for Italy, during the sixth century.[39] The Senate flourished in the time of Odovacer and the Ostrogoths, but Gregory the Great proclaimed '*senatus deest*':[40] Some of its members had been massacred by the Goths during the war with Justinian, while others fled to Constantinople where some of their descendants were still living at the end of the century, and those who returned to Italy had to face a land ravaged by war. It has been justly pointed out that the destruction of the Senate was the price of the destruction of the Goths,[41] but it was the Byzantines who exacted the price. Indeed, of those who ruled in Italy during the sixth century the Goths were the most effective custodians of classical civilisation. The last games known to have been held in Rome were those presided over by Totila in 549, and a nearly contemporary author, while hostile to this king, echoed language Pliny used of Trajan when he described him as living in Rome like a father with his children.[42] During the period of Ostrogothic power Cassiodorus had penned eloquent words in praise of city life, describing the impeccably classical round of activities a gentleman could expect to enjoy: conversation with his equals, a trip to the forum, inspecting the products of craftspeople, using the laws to promote his affairs, spending time playing draughts, going to the baths with his companions, and providing luncheons.[43] But when he returned to Italy in the 550s after some years in Constantinople, Cassiodorus led a very different life, for he founded a monastery on his family estates in one of the most remote regions of mainland Italy.

Doubtless this was in part symptomatic of a wider trend, the position of the aristocracy having weakened during the sixth century in the East as well as the West. But there was little room after the Byzantine conquest of Italy for a civilian aristocracy of the kind that had flourished during the first third of the century, and the coming of the Lombards made the traditional forms of civilised life still less viable. The contrast between the Goths, for the most part discreetly tucked away in northern Italy, living on tax receipts, tolerant of Catholics and observant of Roman forms, and the Lombards, diffused over most of Italy, living on lands sometimes expropriated, at times enthusiastic persecutors of Catholics, and comparatively heedless of Roman ways, is striking, but no

[39] Stroheker (1965), pp. 305–8, places it immediately after the reign of Justinian; see further the opinions of earlier scholars given on pp. 279, 285ff, 300ff.

[40] Gregory of Rome, *Homilae in Hiez.* II.6.22.

[41] Wes (1967), p. 193.

[42] *LP* (Vigilius); cf. Pliny the Younger, *Panegyricus* 21.4.

[43] *Variae* VIII.31.8.

smaller is the degree of change the latter brought to an aristocracy which had supported itself from its landed estates.

But if the sixth century saw a sad diminution in the fortunes of one of the pillars of Italian society, its ecclesiastical counterpart advanced. While the construction of churches continued apace, a repair to the theatre of Pompey which Symmachus carried out early in the century is the last known example of the private patronage of a traditional secular building.[44] Indeed, secular buildings were alienated for ecclesiastical uses, such as the hall in Rome, probably the audience hall of the city prefect, which was turned into the church of SS Cosmas and Damian during the period 526–530, an act which anticipates the better known transformation of the Pantheon into a church in 609. A parallel clericalisation of intellectual life occurred, for which Cassiodorus again provides an example. As a young man he had come to the notice of Theoderic by delivering a panegyric, and proceeded to be of service to him and later Gothic sovereigns as both a panegyricist and a writer of official letters. The works he wrote as a *vir religiosus* in retirement in Bruttium, on the other hand, were overwhelmingly ecclesiastical in nature, but even so the church history for which he was responsible was too broad minded for the taste of Gregory the Great, and did not enjoy a wide circulation. Horizons, which had been broad enough to accommodate the intellectual work of Boethius and the risqué poems of Ennodius early in the century, had contracted by the time of Gregory, when the bulk of writing was clerical in both authorship and content. The late antique world of the Gothic period was replaced by one dominated by those who fought and those who prayed, its contours distinctively medieval.

While these changes were taking place, the role played by Italy in the wider world was also developing. Denuded of its provinces, Italy may have seemed forlorn when the Ostrogoths occupied it, but the territorial advances they made and the marriage alliances contracted by Theoderic made it central in the Mediterranean region. The success of Justinian's invasion robbed it of this position. Ravenna, which remained its capital, was reduced to the status of a branch office of a corporation controlled in Constantinople, and staffed at the highest levels by non-natives. The environment that was created encouraged the intervention of neighbouring powers. Worse was to follow when the Lombards put an end to its unity and created a divided Italy, a situation that was to last well into modern times. By the end of the century changes which had been going on for centuries had been worked out: politically and economically, Italy was both isolated and divided. Such centrality

[44] Ward-Perkins (1984).

as it had was that possessed by the church of Rome, displayed pre-eminently by the dispatch of missionaries to Kent by Gregory the Great in 596. That the immediate future of the influence of Italy in the wider world was to rest with the authority of the bishop of Rome is a measure of the distance it had traversed in the period since Theoderic celebrated his tricennalia in the City in 500.

CHAPTER 7

THE FORMATION OF THE SUEVE AND VISIGOTHIC KINGDOMS IN SPAIN

A. Barbero and M. I. Loring

The assassination of the emperor Valentinian III, the last representative of the Theodosian dynasty in 455, and the subsequent sack of Rome by the Vandal Genseric, signal the beginning of a profound political crisis in the western provinces of the Roman Empire. The intensification of military activity because of the hostilities of the barbarian *foederati*, and the differing interests of Gaulish and Italo-Roman senatorial aristocracies, led to the triumph of centrifugal tendencies, which would result in the end of the Roman imperial state in the West and its replacement by Romano-Germanic kingdoms.[1] Thus for *Hispania*, as for the rest of the western provinces of the Empire, there began a period of political and military instability, which would eventually distance it from the networks of central power, making way for new regional powers. This process worked not only to the advantage of the Sueves, the only barbarian people who had remained in the Iberian peninsula after the departure of the Vandals for Africa in 429 and who by then were firmly established on its western side, but also to that of the Visigoths. Despite their interests being centred in the south of Gaul in the middle of the fifth century, they soon began to spread out into new bases in Hispania, bases that later would allow them to establish a stable political power there and eventually to annex the Sueve kingdom itself in the second half of the sixth century.

THE END OF THE FIRST SUEVE MONARCHY AND THE SUBMISSION OF THE KINGDOM TO VISIGOTH PROTECTION

At the beginning of the fifth century the Sueves had remained within the western limits of the province of *Gallaecia*, but after the departure of the

[1] The expression 'Romano-Germanic kingdoms', used by Stein, best reflects the character of the first barbarian kingdoms, Stein (1959), I, p. 365. See also Gerberding, chapter 1 above and Halsall, chapter 2 above.

Map 2 Spain under the Visigoths

Vandals they initiated a process of expansion to increase their territory. As a consequence of this, by the middle of the fifth century the Sueves had come to control a wide territory that stretched from *Gallaecia* in the north, as far as Bética in the south, passing through Lusitania, whose capital and the diocesan capital *Emerita Augusta* (Mérida) seems at some time to have played the role of royal seat of the Sueve monarchs. This deployment was initiated during the thirty-year reign of Hermeric, the first Sueve monarch, and continued by his successors, his son Rechila and grandson Rechiarius. The process was marked by several victories of Sueve troops over the Roman generals entrusted with containing their expansion, but finally in 452 the imperial authorities reached an agreement, the exact terms of which are unknown but which at least succeeded in containing the expansion and limiting Sueve influence to the western regions, since by virtue of this accord the Sueves retreated from

Carthaginensis.[2] It must have been difficult for the Sueves to establish effective political control over this broad set of territories, the scene of their advances, but the agreement of 452 left military affairs under the exclusive control of the Sueve monarchs and established the basis upon which the Sueve monarchy could transform itself into a territorial monarchy.

Events following the assassination of Valentinian III, however, interrupted this development. Before the violent death of Valentinian and his replacement by an emperor outside the Theodosian house, the Sueves had considered the pact concluded, but the personal basis upon which the agreement had been negotiated meant that it died along with Valentinian, and that same year, 455, the Sueves renewed hostilities, subjecting the recently restored province of *Carthaginensis* to attacks. The new emperor Avitus (455–456), successor of the epheneral Petronius Maximus, did not hesitate to declare war on the Sueves when diplomacy failed, and he used the Visigoths as his allies. The intervention of the Visigoth Theoderic II was sudden and devastating: the bulk of the Sueve troops were defeated on 5 October 456 in the vicinity of *Asturica Augusta* (Astorga); the city of *Bracara Augusta* (Braga), which was functioning as a capital, was then sacked; the king Rechiarius, who had fled to Porto, was captured and executed; and finally Theoderic entered Lusitania and took Mérida. The campaign, however, was interrupted by the deposition and death of Avitus, the news of which caused Theoderic's immediate withdrawal to Gaul, although as he retreated the troops sacked Astorga and Palencia.

Hydatius' account of the campaign contains information about the sack of Braga and Astorga that is worth noting. The troops, apart from pillaging, also profaned sacred places, massacred part of the population, and took numerous Roman prisoners, including two bishops with all their clergy. This leads us to suppose that, despite Hydatius' representation of the relations between Sueves and provincials as being in a state of permanent conflict, some sectors, including the Catholic clergy, had collaborated with the Sueves, participating in their expansionist projects and breaking with imperial power. This would explain the capture and transport of the two bishops found in Astorga to Gaul. At the same time, the capture and execution of the Sueve king Rechiarius was an event of great significance. Hydatius, after describing these events, affirms 'that the Sueve kingdom was destroyed and came to an end', although a few lines further on he indicates how 'Sueves of the remotest parts of *Gallaecia* took Maldras for their king' and later provides information about other chiefs

[2] The *Chronicon* of the Hispano-Roman Hydatius, who became bishop of Aquae Flaviae in Gallaecia in 427, spans the years 379–469 and is especially useful for pursuing the problem of the formation of the Sueve kingdom, events in which Hydatius was himself involved.

who tried to make themselves kings.[3] These pieces of evidence might appear contradictory, but the death of Rechiarius certainly put an end to the dynasty of Hermeric and brusquely interrupted the formation of a Sueve kingdom, which combined the creation of an institutional monarchy of barbarian origin with the assimilation of late imperial institutional forms.[4]

After the withdrawal of Theoderic, the Sueves achieved a peace with the Gallo-Romans, which at least allowed them to retain a certain control over the province of *Gallaecia*, but they did not manage to recover the stability of the previous period. In the first place, Maldras did not manage to impose his authority on the body of the Sueves, who appear to have been divided and drawn up in opposing factions. In addition Theoderic II continued to intervene actively in Hispania and twice sent troops into Bética, an area over which the Sueves still maintained a certain influence, perhaps owing to Theoderic's prompt withdrawal after the death of Avitus.[5] The Sueves thus remained disunited and this led to the division of the kingdom; the north of Lusitania fell to Maldras and *Gallaecia* to Rechimund. A third pretender, Agiulf, died in Porto in 457 in the midst of struggles to win the kingdom for himself. Finally, relations with the Hispano-Romans seem to have entered a phase of marked deterioration, judging by the evidence in Hydatius of continual plundering campaigns, in Lusitania as much as in *Gallaecia* itself, and even of massacres of the populations.

It is in this context that at the end of 459 a double embassy arrived in *Gallaecia* in the name of the Empire and the Visigoths, informing the Gallaecos about the agreement reached between the new emperor Majorian (457–461) and Theoderic II. This news was related to Majorian's strategy for restoring imperial authority, which had amongst its objectives waging war on the Vandals, whom he was keen to fight from the coasts of *Hispania*. The strategy may have included a fresh offensive against the Sueves. In May 460 Majorian entered Hispania, heading for *Carthaginensis*, while a section of the Visigothic army under the command of the Gothic *comes* Suneric and the *magister militum* Nepotian marched towards *Gallaecia* and sacked the outskirts of Lugo. Nevertheless, according to Hydatius, the Visigothic forces retreated in the face of the intrigues of Gallo-Roman elements favouring the Sueves, but it is possible that they did so because of news of the failure of the Vandal war,

[3] Hydatius, *Chronicon*, 175: 'regnum destructum et finitum est Sueuorum'; 181: 'Sueui, qui remanserant in extrema parte Gallaeciae . . . Maldras sibi regem constituunt'.

[4] Díaz Martínez (1986–87), p. 213.

[5] Hydatius, *Chronicon*, 192, 193, 197. These campaigns were the personal responsibility of Theoderic II; thus Hydatius indicates no intervention of the Roman authorities, and besides they took place in 458 and sometime in 459, but certainly before the Visigoths recognised the authority of Majorian in 459.

which put an end to the programme for imperial restoration undertaken by Majorian. The emperor himself died on his return to Italy in August 461, executed by his most distinguished general, the *magister peditum praesentalis* and patrician Ricimer, a barbarian military chief in the service of Rome, a Sueve in origin and, through his mother, grandson of the Visigothic king Wallia.

Ricimer was also the architect of the succession to the imperial throne, to which he put forward a member of the Italian senatorial class, the senator Libius Severus (461–465), who was to be no more than a puppet in his hands. Outside the Italian provinces, Ricimer could only impose his authority with the support of his Visigothic and Burgundian allies, which in the case of the diocese of *Hispania* and sub-Gaulish provinces meant leaving the key to military affairs in the hands of the Visigoth Theoderic. From then on, Theoderic not only controlled Gothic troops and generals deployed throughout the entire diocese, but also its supreme military command. According to Hydatius, Theoderic himself replaced Nepotian, almost certainly Ricimer's adversary, and appointed the Aquitanian senator Arborius, who bore the title *comes et magister utriusque militia* for *Hispania* and remained at the head of the office until his removal by order of the Visigothic king in 465.

In these conditions of complete autonomy, Theoderic continued intervening in Sueve affairs. The latter remained divided between the partisans of Frumarius, possibly the successor of the recently assassinated Maldras, and of Rechimund, and although there is no evidence of fresh conflicts, there was certainly a constant exchange of embassies throughout 461. The second of these embassies sent by the Visigothic king was led by Remismund and the *dux* Cyrila, who went at the head of a certain number of troops. Remismund returned to Toulouse, but the Gothic general and troops remained. We do not know what happened in the next few years, but Gothic military protection was decisive, since, on the death of Frumarius in 465, Remismund, the one-time ambassador, set himself up as unique monarch of all the Sueves and re-established peace, a little later reaching an accord with the Visigoths, which was ratified with a corresponding matrimonial alliance.

In short, ten years after their initiation, the Sueve wars had resulted in the Sueve kingdom being driven back to its original limits and reduced in its autonomy by the interference, not of the Romano-imperial authorities, but of the Visigoths, who after this established new and powerful interests in *Hispania*. It was also at this time that the conversion of the mass of Sueves took place. As a people they had remained pagan despite the early, and rather unusual, conversion to Nicene Christianity of their king Rechiarius. Hydatius attributes this mass conversion to Ajax, an Arian bishop of Galatian origin, who in his work disseminating Arian doctrine counted on the support of Remismund. He also tells us that this 'pestiferous virus' had been brought from a region of Gaul inhabited by Goths, in 466.[6] Ajax's pastoral work took place in this second phase of the Sueve kingdom, inaugurated by the accession to power of Remismund in 465. On the one hand the divisions, which had been dragging down the Sueves since 456, were overcome at this time, but on the other hand the new kingdom found itself subject to the protection of the Visigothic kingdom of Toulouse, whence the Arian doctrine began to extend over the Sueve Kingdom.

FORMATION OF THE VISIGOTHIC KINGDOM OF TOULOUSE AND THE CONSOLIDATION OF THE VISIGOTHIC PRESENCE IN HISPANIA

The new Visigothic monarch, Euric (466–484), who acceded to the throne having assassinated his brother Theoderic II, has come to be considered the architect of the Visigothic kingdom of Toulouse. During his reign, the *foedus* regulating the relations of the Visigoths with the Empire began to fail definitively and as a result we find the Visigoths more frequently acting according to their own interests (and shaping a new political entity), rather than collaborating with the Empire. This evolution is the logical continuation of the process initiated in the previous period, which had placed all military power in the sub-Gaulish provinces and the Hispanic diocese in the hands of the Visigothic kings. Nevertheless, the break with the Empire was not immediate, and on coming to power Euric sent an embassy to communicate to the emperor his accession to the throne.[7] At the same time, however, other embassies were sent to the Vandal king Genseric, one of the principal enemies of Rome, and to the Sueve Remismund, whose recent alliance was in jeopardy of being compromised as a result of the assassination of Theoderic II.

The advent of Euric was to mark a change in Visigoth–Sueve relations. Remismund, according to Hydatius, despached Gothic legates without delay and sent his own envoys not only to the court of Toulouse, but also to the Vandals and the emperor himself, an initiative which suggests that the king considered Visigothic protection over and that he was trying to reach his own agreements with the Empire. In 468, moreover, Remismund entered Lusitania at the head of an army, sacking the city of *Conimbrica* (Coimbra). Euric's response was swift and in 469 a Visigothic army occupied *Emerita Augusta* (Mérida), making it clear that he was not disposed to allow the Sueves to regain control of Lusitania.

[6] Hydatius, *Chronicon*, 232, 'A Gallicam Gothorum habitatione hoc pestiferum . . . uirus aduentum.'

[7] Hydatius, *Chronicon*, 238. It is possible that this embassy may have presented itself in Constantinople, since in 466 the succession of Libius Severus was unresolved, although Hydatius reports the embassy in the year 468 and by then Leo had already designated Anthemius as his colleague in the West.

This was a significant step, since there is no evidence that before this date the Visigoths had any permanent presence in the peninsula, although one cannot rule out some Visigoth garrisons having remained there on the occasion of previous military campaigns.[8] In any case, the Hispano-Roman population were now forced to recognise their power, for after the taking of Mérida the Roman population of Lisbon, represented by the citizen Lusidius, delivered their city up to the Sueves, provoking a punitive attack from the Visigoths in which neither Sueve nor Roman was spared. That year, 469, the Suevic king reached a peace accord with the *Aunonenses*, a semi-independent people who had been resisting Sueve dominion since 466, and again pillaged in Lusitania. This led to further punitive attacks on the part of the Gothic troops. The Sueve king, Remismund, sent an embassy to the emperor, which included the Roman Lusidius alongside the Sueve legates. The objective could only have been to obtain imperial help. With this information Hydatius' *Chronicon*, and with it to an extent the history of the Sueve kingdom, ends. Later sources maintain a dull silence, which is interrupted only a century later, on the eve of the kingdom's definitive annexation by the Visigoths.[9] It is difficult to know how this fresh war between the Sueves and Visigoths ended, but from the action of the Hispano-Roman Lusidius it is clear that some provincial sectors were more amenable to accepting Sueve rather than Visigothic dominion. This observation allows us in turn to consider the possibility that the incorporation of the north-western regions of Lusitania and interior of *Gallaecia*, corresponding to the *conventus Asturicensis*, took place at this time. For these regions appear fully assimilated into the Sueve kingdom in the second half of the sixth century. This process unfolded in the midst of constant fighting with the Visigoths, who in turn consolidated their presence in the southern and central regions of Lusitania, with Mérida as their principal enclave. A well-known inscription, dated 483, belongs to these last years of Euric's government. It commemorates the restoration of the Roman bridge at Mérida by the *dux* Salla in the times of the *potentis Eruigii regis*, a project that was undertaken once the city walls had been rebuilt and on which the metropolitan Zeno collaborated.[10]

These developments took place on the margins of imperial authority. It is improbable that Anthemius (467–472) had any ability to intervene in the peninsula, since the failure of the expedition that the emperors Leo and

[8] The Hispanic historiographic tradition tends to date the establishment of the first Visigothic settlements in Lusitania to the campaign led by Theoderic II in 456, although for the moment neither documentary information nor archaeological finds allow of support for this thesis.

[9] The *Historia Suevorum* of Isidore of Seville, whose source is Hydatius, is interrupted here and is not resumed until the reign of Theodemir (561–570).

[10] Vives, *Inscripciones Cristianas*, no. 363.

Anthemius jointly sent against the Vandal kingdom in 468 put an end to the restorationist projects of the new emperor of the West, even before they were formulated. This defeat not only strengthened the Vandals, who completed their hold over the western Mediterranean with the occupation of Sicily, but also aided Euric, the Visigothic king, who did not neglect the opportunity to carry through his own expansionist schemes.

In Gaul open war between the Visigoths and the Empire broke out in 469, motivated by the fall of Arvandus, praetorian prefect of Gaul, who was accused before the emperor Anthemius of preparing to partition Gaul between the Visigoths and the Burgundians.[11] Euric, counting on the support of an important sector of the Gallo-Roman aristocracy against Anthemius' centralist policy, won several victories over the Romans and their allies in the following years, which he used to enlarge the territory of his kingdom, fixing its northern borders at the River Loire and approaching the valley of the Rhône in the east. With regard to its southern frontiers, in the summer of 472 his troops conquered *Tarraconensis*. It seems that the Visigothic army divided itself into two bodies; one under the command of the *comes* Gauterit crossed the Pyrenees by Roncesvalles, occupying Pamplona and from there marching into the Ebro valley, where he took *Caesaraugusta* (Saragossa) and other towns in the environs; the other, headed by the *comes* Heldefred and Vincent the *dux Hispaniarum*, traversed the Pyrenees by the eastern passes and after taking Tarragona also took the coastal towns.[12] It is also feasible that the occupation of the interior regions of *Carthaginensis* was initiated at this time, with the object of knitting together previously controlled enclaves in the western parts of the peninsula, especially around Mérida, with others in the Ebro basin.

In this way, part of the Hispanic diocese was thus transformed into an extension of the Visigothic kingdom of Toulouse. The exceptions were the north-western regions under Sueve control and the northern regions inhabited by largely unromanised peoples, like the Cantabrians and Basques. Although *Baetica* and a large part of *Carthaginensis* were cut off from Rome, they continued under the administration of their old provincial establishments.[13] The expansion of the Visigothic dominions during this period of continual war with the Empire developed in a context of collaboration with important sections of the Gallic and Hispano-Roman senatorial class, starting with those of

11 Sidonius, *Epistolae* I.7.5.

12 *Chronica Gallica*, a. DXI, 651–652. Mommsen designates with this name some notes with the character of a chronicle, probably written by a Gaul, which contain extracts from Orosius and Hydatius and which last until 511.

13 Thompson (1976–79), III, pp. 4–9, favours attributing the Visigothic occupation of *Baetica* to the campaigns of 458 and 459, although he admits the lack of evidence.

its members who possessed the most distinguished civil and military offices. This was the case, for instance, in the occupation of *Tarraconensis*, where, alongside Visigothic generals, the *dux Hispaniarum* Vincent, who was the highest Roman military commander in the peninsula, played an important part, although since the fall of Majorian he was, as we have seen, under the control of the Visigoths. This alliance was not exempt from conflicts, as is clear from the tenacious resistance that the senators of the Auvergne displayed to the expansionist designs of the Visigothic king, a resistance made famous by the ferocious criticism and denunciations voiced by their leader, Sidonius Apollinaris. Euric finally imposed himself however, and thus whilst Anthemius had vainly tried to smash the alliance, his successor Julius Nepos would opt to accept it.

When Julius Nepos (473–480) came to power Euric's relations with the Empire were temporarily modified. The new emperor, who in the face of Sidonius' indignation had been named by the eastern emperor in 473, concluded a fresh *foedus* with Euric in 475.[14] This new accord allowed the imperial government to recover the territories in Provence recently occupied by the Visigothic king,[15] who again put his troops at the disposal of the Empire but at the same time sanctioned the Visigothic occupation of all the Gallic provinces south of the Loire and west of the Rhône, which marked the end of the resistance of the *civitas Arverna*. For some authors, this agreement confirmed Euric's full sovereignty over the territories he controlled in Gaul and *Hispania*. However, although Euric's power was no longer merely military, the accord preserved Nepos' sovereignty and even provided for aid from Visigoth troops: conditions at odds with full sovereignty.[16]

The subsequent evolution of events in Italy not only gave further opportunities for the aggrandisement of the kingdom of Toulouse, but also consecrated the *de facto* sovereignty of its kings. Euric was a contemporary of the fall of the Roman Empire in the West in 476, and took advantage of the reigning disorder to occupy in the name of Julius Nepos the last of Gaul dependent on the government of Ravenna, that is to say southern Provence, with the towns of Marseilles and Arles, the latter capital of the praetorian prefecture of Gaul. Odovacer, the barbarian chief who substituted himself in Italy for the last emperor Romulus Augustulus, accepted the final conquests of Euric and

[14] Sidonius, *Epistolae* VII.7.1.

[15] *Chronicorum Caesaraugustanorum Reliquiae* s.a. 473. Mommsen gives this name to the collection of marginalia which appear in the manuscripts in which the chronicles of Victor of Tunnuna and John of Biclaro have been transmitted and which cover events from 450 to 568, with special reference to *Hispania*; it is also known as the *Chronica Caesaraugustana*.

[16] The following support the full sovereignty hypothesis: Demougeot (1979), II, p. 640, and M. Rouche (1979), p. 42; and against it Wolfram (1990), p. 201.

ratified the situation by a treaty with the Visigoths. This agreement, which was apparently ratified by the western emperor Zeno,[17] put an end to the prefecture of Gaul and represented the triumph of the regionalisation of the provinces of the Western Empire. The Visigothic king, Euric, remained the greatest authority in the sub-Gaulish and Hispanic territories of the old prefecture, and although a formal cession of sovereignty never occured, he *de facto* filled the vacuum left by the imperial authorities with his own power, the territories under Visigoth dominion being left outside the sphere of any action by Constantinople.

Euric, in spite of his aggrandisement at the expense of the Empire and the hostility that he manifested towards segments of the Roman population who were not favourable to him, was in a certain way a continuer of the Roman tradition. His role as legislator proves this. This activity developed thanks to the juridical ability of the Roman counsellors with whom he surrounded himself. His work is known as the *Code of Euric* and, in the opinion of one of its last editors, has the character of an *Edictum* of the type promulgated by the praetorian prefects, from which it is clear that with its promulgation the Visigoth king substituted himself in their place in the territories he controlled. Consequently it was not a legal corpus destined exclusively for the Gothic population, but had a territorial value, that is, it was directed at all the inhabitants of his kingdom, whether Goths or Romans, and it is thought that its production was supervised by Leo of Narbonne, one of the principal advisers of the monarch whose legal expertise was extolled by Sidonius Apollinaris.[18] On the other hand, this legislative work confirms the assumption of full power of sovereignty by the Visigoth monarchs.

CONFRONTATION WITH THE FRANKS AND THE END OF THE VISIGOTHIC KINGDOM OF TOULOUSE

Euric died at Arles in 484 and was succeeded without difficulty by his son Alaric II (484–507). His reign coincided with the development in northern Gaul of a new barbarian power, that of the Franks, whose chief Clovis, contemporary and rival of Alaric II, managed to unite all the Franks beneath his royal line and, in 486, finish off the last Roman bastion in the north of Gaul: an enclave between the Loire and the Somme centred on Soissons, which from 465 was ruled by

[17] Stein (1949), II, p. 59; Demougeot (1979), II, p. 612.

[18] D'Ors (1960), pp. 6–7. The territoriality or legal entity of Visigoth legislation continues to be a subject of debate. With regard to Euric's code, García Gallo (1974), p. 435, Collins (1983), p. 29 and Wolfram (1990), p. 211, are supporters of the territorial character hypothesis. Thompson (1969), p. 57, Rouche (1979), p. 37, King (1980), pp. 131–5 and Pérez-Prendes (1991), p. 73, on the other hand favour the hypothesis of its national character.

Syagrius, son of the last great Roman functionary in that area.[19] From then on, the greatest rivals of Frankish expansionism in Gaul were the Visigoths, and confrontation between the two barbarian peoples went against the latter. Alaric sought an alliance with the Ostrogoths, the new masters of Italy, and in 494 he married Thiudigoto, daughter of the Ostrogothic king Theoderic the Great. This failed to avoid the opening of a period of hostility c.494–495, centred in Aquitaine, where in 498 the Franks took Bordeaux. Although it was soon recovered, this was a hard blow to Visigothic interests. This period of wars concluded in 502, the year in which Alaric and Clovis met on an island in the Loire, and the agreement reached re-established the frontier between the two kingdoms on the said river.[20]

During the same period the Visigoths had to crush a rebellion in *Tarraconensis*, led by a certain Burdunellus, who seized power in 496 and was captured a year later and taken to Toulouse, where he was burnt enclosed in a bronze bull.[21] From the nature in which and place where he was presented for execution it is clear that the rebellion was quite widespread, and also that Visigothic dominion in *Tarraconensis* had still not taken sufficient root. Interspersed with this information, the *Chronica Caesaraugustana* indicates that, in 494, 'Gothi in Hispanias ingressi sunt' and also that in 497 'Gothi intra Hispanias sedes acceperunt.' Given that by then the Visigoths had already conquered part of Lusitania and *Tarraconensis*, this has been interpreted as referring to the entry of a significant group of the Gothic population into Spain, not necessarily military, but perhaps émigrés from Gaul in the face of Frankish pressure, who came to establish themselves in the peninsula as colonists, and that the problems generated by their settlement provoked the rebellion of Burdunellus.[22] Recently an identification of these *gothi* with troops sent to reaffirm Visigoth dominion in the peninsula and to this end establish garrisons in the cities has been proposed.[23] In any case, whether they were troops, or groups of Goths not posted to military structures, the reference to the settlements (*sedes acceperunt*) indicates in an express form that during the reign of Alaric II the Visigoth presence in *Hispania* grew. In short, new settlements and a suppression of revolts (there is information about the suppression in 506 of a new focus of rebellion in the city of Tortosa)[24] persuade one that the Visigothic dominions to the south of the Pyrenees were being integrated in a fairly effective way into the Visigothic kingdom of Toulouse in the time of Alaric II.

Clovis and the Frankish nobility, who were still pagan, at an imprecise date between 496 and 506 embraced Catholicism. This fact was very important,

[19] See Van Dam, chapter 8 below. [20] Gregory, *Hist.* II.35.

[21] *Chron. Caesaraugustanorum* s.a. 496 and 497.

[22] Abadal (1960), pp. 45–6; Orlandis (1977), pp. 61–3; Wolfram (1990), p. 206.

[23] García Moreno (1989), p. 80. [24] *Chron. Caesaraugustanorum* s.a. 506.

because until then barbarian peoples on becoming Christian had adopted the Arian creed. By contrast, Alaric at this time was having problems with certain Catholic bishops from the Gallic provinces who were forced into exile. Those repressive measures, however, seem to have derived from political reasons, not from an attitude of religious intolerance towards his Roman Catholic subjects, which would have been at odds with the help which they provided him in his legislative work. Alaric, like his father, was a legislator king. His Code, the *Breviarium Alarici* or *Lex Romana Visigothorum*, promulgated in 506, is a vast juridic compilation, which combines imperial constitutions taken for the most part from the Theodosian Code, with commentaries or *interpretationes*, plus a selection of works by Roman legal advisers. The promulgation of this Code by a barbarian king, preoccupied with disseminating Roman law, updating it and ordering its norms to be legally binding, constituted an event without precedent. The Code's contents show that the work was a collective task by a commission of jurisconsuls presided over by the *comes* Goiaric, and that once finalised it was submitted to the approbation of the bishops and a select group of provincials. Consequently, the promulgation of the Breviary represented a notable effort to make the interests of the Roman population, represented by their leaders in its elaboration, converge with those of the Goths, who also participated in the process and whose interest in being assimilated into the socio-economic order of the late Roman Empire was ever greater.

The Council of *Agatha* (Agde) that Gaulish bishops, some of whom had now returned from banishment, also held in 506 should be read in the same context of assimilation. The acts of this council throw into relief the vitality, as much as the economic importance, attained by the Catholic church. Besides the massive influx – twenty-four bishops and ten priests and deacons representing as many other prelates – the allusion to the king in the provisions, and the importance of the points treated in a total of seventy-one canons, gave this council the character of a national synod. It turns it into the first known church council in a barbarian kingdom and it is good evidence of the integration of the Romano-Christian church into new political realities. Furthermore, at the close of the assembly, the holding of a new council, to be held the following year in Toulouse, was announced. We know from other sources that the bishops of Hispania were also invited. It would thus gather all the bishops of the kingdom together at a fully national synod, to be held in the capital.[25]

All this happened on the eve of the great struggle with the Franks. Following the account of Gregory of Tours, the Visigoths suffered in the conflict from a supposed religious division between the Goths and the Romans, something the events we have just analysed clearly disprove. The Ostrogothic king, Theoderic the Great, who dominated Italy and who to some extent represented imperial

[25] Barbero de Aguilera (1989), pp. 171–3.

power, tried at all costs to avoid war in Gaul, as the correspondence of Cassiodorus shows. However, the complex play of alliances set up revealed their weaknesses once again and in 507 an open confrontation took place between the Franks and the Visigoths in the vicinity of the town of Poitiers.[26] A Burgundian army fought alongside the Franks, while the Visigothic army depended on members of the Roman nobility, such as the son of Sidonius Apollinaris, who without doubt brought with them their retinues and private armies.[27] Theoderic, apparently, attempted to reinforce the Visigothic army with his own troops, but events were rushed and the battle at *Campus Vogladensis* or Vouillé saw a Frankish victory. The Visigoth king Alaric died in the combat. Franks and Burgundians occupied the greater part of the Gallic regions of the Visigothic kingdom, and its capital Toulouse was sacked and stripped of its treasures.

OSTROGOTHIC SUPREMACY AND THE NEW VISIGOTHIC KINGDOM

After the defeat, part of the Visigothic army managed to regroup at Narbonne and chose as king Gesalic, the son of the dead king by a previous marriage. However, this decision did not meet with the acquiescence of Theoderic the Great, who defended the rights of his grandson Amalaric, son of Alaric II and the Ostrogothic princess Thiudigoto, and did not hesitate to intervene to protect him. In the summer of 508 an Ostrogothic army under the *dux* Ibas crossed the Alps and wrested Provence from the Burgundians, after taking Marseilles and raising the siege of Arles, where the Visigothic garrison was still resisting. In the following year the Ostrogothic army took Narbonne, from where Gesalic had been expelled some months earlier by the Burgundians. Meanwhile in Barcelona, where Gesalic had moved, the advance of the Ostrogothic army triggered off a factional struggle, which resulted in the death of the *comes* Goiaric, on Gesalic's orders. From this it is clear that the succession had deeply divided the Visigoths.[28] Confrontation finally took place in the summer of 510 at the gates of Barcelona, and Gesalic was defeated, but managed to flee and seek refuge in the Vandal kingdom. A few months later Gesalic returned to Gaul, where counting on financial aid lent by the Vandals, he did not delay in reuniting his adherents and forming an army, at the head of which he fought the *dux* Ibas near Barcelona. According to Isidore, his luck was out again, and hounded on all sides he was made prisoner and executed.[29]

[26] See Van Dam, chapter 8 below. [27] Gregory, *Hist.* II.37.87.

[28] Fuentes Hinojo (1996), pp. 12–15.

[29] *Historia Gothorum*, 34–7. 281–2. The *Historia Gothorum* by Isidore of Seville is the only continuous source of information on the Visigothic kings, but its value as a historical source is limited, as a consequence of its laudatory function and the practical absence of chronological references, with the exception of the regnal years.

Theoderic the Great, king of the Ostrogoths, thus came to control the sub-Gallic seaboard fringe and the peninsula territories of the old Visigothic kingdom, which he would rule until his death in 526. The historiographic tradition has come to consider the Ostrogothic intervention as preserving the continuity of the Visigothic kingdom, which would otherwise have been submerged beneath the Franco-Burgundian tide. However, it has recently been pointed out that, had it not been for the intervention of the Ostrogoths, the Balt dynasty would have continued reigning. All was not lost when the army of Ibas entered the scenario, and besides, the Franks encountered much resistance to their rule, up to the point that, after the death of Clovis, some cities had to be reoccupied.[30] In the same vein, it is questionable whether Theoderic governed in Narbonne and the Hispanic territories of the old Visigothic kingdom in the capacity of regent for his grandson Amalaric, or whether in fact he held royal power, acquired by the exercise of arms, in his own right, and that he would not have considered Amalaric succeeding him until 522–523.

Numerous events and a lot of evidence support this last interpretation: from the dating of the Hispanic Synodal acts by the years of Theoderic's reign, to the withdrawal of power from Amalaric, who did not occupy the throne until the death of his grandfather, although he had reached majority some time earlier. Most striking is the marriage that Theoderic arranged in 515 between his daughter Amalasuentha and Eutharic, a member of the house of Amal, whose family had lived for generations in the Visigothic kingdom and were related to the Balts, thus linking his family to *Hispania*. This political marriage was destined to facilitate the unification of both kingdoms under one monarch, incarnated in the person of Eutharic and his descendants. The kinship relationships, which united Eutharic with the two royal Gothic lineages, made him the most suitable candidate for the succession. However, his premature death in 522 frustrated Theoderic's ambitious project.[31]

The government of the territories recovered from the ruins of the kingdom of Toulouse was organised by Theoderic on the basis of the late Roman schema, which separated civil and military functions, designating Roman citizens for the former and for the latter members of the Ostrogothic military nobility. Thus, the military headship was entrusted to the Ostrogoth Theudis, who had been sent in 511 as a replacement for Ibas and to whom, according to Jordanes, the Ostrogothic king entrusted the protection of the young Amalaric. Hispanic civil administration's reorganisation is less well documented. There is no information concerning the nomination of any *vicarius Hispaniarum*, although it would be logical in view of the interest Theoderic had in maintaining and

30 Wolfram (1990), pp. 257–8; on Aquitanian resistance to Frankish rule, Rouche (1979), pp. 51ff.

31 For all these questions García Moreno (1989), pp. 89–90; Fuentes Hinojo (1996), pp. 15–17.

even restoring late imperial departments. Other evidence seems to contradict that possibility. The general Theudis, who was married to a rich Hispano-Roman landowner and could dispose of an army of several thousand men, recruited from among the peasants of his lands.[32] He thus achieved a large degree of independence, up to the point of not answering Theoderic's calls for his presence. However, it never came to a break between the two, doubtless because of the fear that the Franks would take advantage of any conflict in order to increase their territories, to the profit too of those Visigoths opposed to Ostrogothic supremacy.

In relation to civil administration, in 510 Theoderic restored the praetorian prefecture of Gaul at whose head he placed an Italo-Roman senator, the patrician Liberius, but there is no information concerning the nomination of any *vicarius Hispaniarum* and it seems the administration of the Hispanic territories remained subject to the directives from Ravenna. This is at least clear from two letters from the Ostrogothic king, dated 523 and 526, addressed to two high-up functionaries of Roman origin, the *comes* and *vir spectabilis* Liviritus, and the *vir illustris* Ampelius.[33] In one of the letters, the king demanded cereals produced in *Hispania* which were to supply the needs of the city of Rome but which had been diverted to Africa. In the other, Theoderic ordered the main defects and abuses of the Hispanic administration to be corrected. He recommended his officials to protect human life and severely punish homicides, to put a stop to fraud and misappropriations in the collection of taxes, and to ensure that the common people's condition was maintained and they were not reduced to servitude.

This direct intervention by Theoderic is noteworthy, given that Liberius, who at least in theory was the intermediary between the court at Ravenna and the governors of Hispania, was still governing in Arles. Some scholars suggest a swift separation of the Hispanic territories from the rest of the prefecture of Gaul with the creation of a separate *praefectus Hispaniarum*, an office which is documented in the reign of his successor Amalaric and which could be that which the *vir illustris* Ampelius held.[34] As Theoderic's letters suggest, the office of the *comes* and *vir illustris* Liviritus, who was the most important person in the management of the royal lands, could well be that identified as *comes patrimonii*, given that Theoderic the Great reorganised the administration of the royal estates, separating them into *res privata* and entrusting their management to a new department called the *patrimonium*.[35]

[32] Procopius, *Wars* v.12.51. [33] Cassiodorus, *Variae* v.35, 39.162–6.

[34] García Moreno (1989), p. 92 and Fuentes Hinojo (1996), pp. 17–18.

[35] For the setting-up of the *patrimonium* in the West, cf. Delmaire (1989), pp. 691–2; on the Visigoth *comes patrimonii* cf. García Moreno (1974a), pp. 35–8, situating the appearance of the office, documented for the first time in the reign of Reccared, to the reign of his father Leovigild.

Together these two letters reflect the adaptation of late Roman institutions to new political and socio-economic realities. Without doubt, the regionalisation of power made the recently restored prefecture of Gaul unviable, and so favoured the creation of a Hispanic prefecture. On the other hand, although from the content of the second letter it can be deduced that although the system of tribute maintained its vitality on the basis of *annonae*, *collatio lustralis* and *telonei*, the corruption of administrators and agents posed problems. The reorganisation of the *res privata* and the new post of *comes patrimonii* suggest that in the financial organisation of the state, income from the royal estates increased its importance. Finally Theoderic's concern that the free population maintain their estate, to this end ordering the abolition of the services demanded of them by the members of the Gothic city garrisons, indicates that the military burdens contributed to the increasing decline of the poorer free into servitude or dependence. It was a situation that led Theoderic to express himself in the following terms: 'in truth, it would not be honourable to try to obtain the servitude of the free, for those we had sent to struggle for freedom'.[36]

THE REIGN OF AMALARIC AND THE END OF THE BALT DYNASTY

On 30 August 526 Theoderic the Great died, and with his death his project for a union of the kingdoms failed and led to the political separation of the Gothic peoples. His grandson Amalaric then came to rule the Visigothic kingdom and reached an agreement with his cousin Athalaric, king of Italy, by which he recognised Ostrogothic dominion in Provence and obtained in exchange the return of Visigothic royal treasure and a renunciation by the Ostrogothic king of supplies from *Hispania*, which were in effect a form of tribute. It was also agreed that Ostrogothic troops stationed in the peninsula and *Narbonensis* might return to Italy, although those Ostrogoths who had married during the preceding period were free to stay or go as they wished. Theudis and other important characters opted to remain in Hispania, where they continued to fill dominant positions in spite of the withdrawal of the Ostrogothic army.[37] The new king Amalaric (526–531) moved his court to Narbonne and in 529, according to the *Chronica Caesaraugustana*, named one Stefanus *praefectus Hispaniarum*. If one accepts that this prefecture had existed since the last years of Theoderic's reign, Stefanus must have replaced the previous *praefectus*, which suggests that both the moving of the court and Stefanus' nomination can be understood as a bid to escape the tutelage of Theudis.

[36] Cassiodorus, *Variae* v.39.166: 'servitia quae Gothis in civitate positis superflue praestabantur, decernimus amoveri. non enim decet ab ingenuis famulatum quaerere, quos missimus pro libertate pugnare'.

[37] Procopius, *Wars* v.13.4–8.

The new king also contracted a marriage with Clothild, a daughter of the Frankish king Clovis, a marriage which had been arranged on the death of this king,[38] when Amalaric was still under the tutelage of Theudis. This matrimonial alliance sought to put an end to Frankish harassment, renouncing in exchange all intent of recovering the old Visigothic dominions in Gaul. None the less, the royal marriage soon itself became a fresh motive for confrontation with the Franks. Gregory of Tours attributed it to the pressure put on the princess Clothild by Amalaric to convert to Arianism. Gregory's reasoning is excessively simplistic. It has been suggested that the king's relations with the Roman Catholic circle of the court at Narbonne were indeed strained, but this was for political rather than religious reasons since this circle continued to be closely connected to Theudis, the true architect of the alliance, who was opposed to Amalaric.[39] On the other hand, the concessions to the Franks may also have been challenged by the new king, whose move to Narbonne revealed an interest in affirming Gothic power in southern Gaul.

In the spring of 531 the Frankish king Childebert entered Narbonnese Gaul, later known as Septimania, at the head of an army and in the neighbourhood of Narbonne confronted Amalaric, whom he defeated. Gregory of Tours gives us details of this triumphant Frankish campaign, recounting how Childebert took with him his sister Clothild, who died on the journey, and also how the Franks obtained an enormous amount of plunder.[40] After his defeat Amalaric took refuge in Barcelona and was assassinated there in unclear circumstances, since the accounts in the sources do not match up, although Isidore suggests that the soldiers from his own army were responsible for the regicide. The circumstances surrounding the death of Amalaric and the deposition in the same year of the prefect Stefanus lead one to suspect the intervention of Theudis, and clarify the words which, according to Isidore of Seville, Theudis pronounced at the moment of his own death, accusing himself of having destroyed his master by means of deception. In conclusion the death of Amalaric, the last representative of the Balt line, is related more to internal conflicts than to problems with the Franks, although undoubtedly his defeat by the army of Childebert served as a spur to his opponents.

THE HISPANISATION OF THE VISIGOTHIC KINGDOM

From 531, with the death of the last descendant of the Visigothic king Theoderic I, the kingdom entered a new phase, in which, the house of Balt having disappeared, the struggles of factions for control of the throne reached even greater

[38] Gregory, *Hist.* III.1.97–8. [39] Fuentes Hinojo (1996), p. 21. [40] Gregory, *Hist.* III.10.106–7.

proportions and had more serious consequences.[41] In the years following their disappearance the Visigoths were ruled by two figures of Ostrogothic origin, Theudis and Theodisclus. The promotion of Theudis to royalty was no more than a logical consequence of the Ostrogothic supremacy of the preceding period. Under his rule the kingdom no longer pursued unification with the Ostrogoths but on the contrary reflected a growing Hispanisation, leaving even *Narbonensis* or Gothic Gaul (Septimania) relegated to the background. Theudis was, as we have seen, a man in the confidence of Theoderic the Great and a military leader whose power was delegated from Theoderic, although he acted in a highly autonomous way. His power and military experience, plus the links that had been established by his marriage with the still powerful senatorial class, made him an ideal candidate to succeed Amalaric, irrespective of whether he achieved the throne by violent means as Jordanes indicated, for Jordanes says that the old tutor *invadit* the kingdom on the death of his charge.[42]

During the reign of Theudis (531–548) and of his successor Theodisclus (548–549) significant progress by Visigothic monarchy is detectable in the territorial control of *Hispania*, especially in the central plateau and southern regions. In 531, still under the government of Amalaric, the second Council of Toledo was held, the acts of which are revealing. They not only show that the relations between the Catholic clergy and the Arian monarchy retained the same fluidity of earlier stages, but also make clear that by then the Visigothic kingdom had fully incorporated into itself central areas of the peninsula. On the occasion of this council, Toledo emerged as a metropolitan see at the head of a new ecclesiastical province called *Carpetana* or *Celtiberia*, which extended its jurisdiction over the two central areas. The new jurisdiction had clearly been separated off from the province of *Carthaginensis* in order to provide a metropolitan see for the Visigothic kingdom, which still did not control the coastal areas of *Carthaginensis*, or its metropolis.[43] The new ecclesiastical province was reflected in the civil administration, and its existence implies that Visigothic dominion now extended without a break from *Narbonensis*, as far as Lusitania. The promotion of Toledo to royal see, an event that has become associated with the reign of Theudis, was a consequence of its excellent location with respect to the ensemble of territories that made up the kingdom.

Other evidence, of a military character, confirms that during the reigns of Theudis and Theodisclus the political centre of gravity seems to have shifted definitively to the Iberian peninsula. Isidore says that during the reign of Theudis several Frankish kings entered *Hispania* and sacked the province of

[41] A reconstruction of the lineage of the Balt from that of *Getica* by Jordanes is in Heather (1991), pp. 28–32.

[42] Jordanes, *Getica*, 302, p. 45.

[43] Barbero de Aguilera (1989), pp. 173–6.

Tarraconensis, laying siege to Saragossa, but that the Goths under the orders of Theodisclus inflicted a crushing defeat on the Frankish army. This incursion, according to the *Chronica Caesaraugustana*, took place in 541, and its failure represents the first victory the Visigoths had obtained since 506, it being also the first time that the conflict was played out south of the Pyrenees. Isidore then relates that, after this happy event, the Visigoths suffered a reverse against the Byzantines, when Gothic troops crossed the Straits and tried to recover the city of *Septem* (Ceuta). This information, at least in the form in which Isidore has transmitted it to us, poses problems, since it is fairly doubtful that the Visigoths would ever have occupied Ceuta. It had fallen into the hands of the Byzantines immediately after the conquest of the Vandal kingdom in 533–534 by Justinian's troops. From a constitution concerned with the city of Ceuta, collected in the Justinian Code of 534, we know that it found itself under the control of a tribune who had at his disposal troops and boats to defend it against Hispania.[44] There is therefore contradictory evidence, although both accounts coincide in stressing that the proximity of the Byzantines to the Iberian peninsula and their stranglehold over the Straits of Gibraltar were motives for the constant tension between them and the Goths.[45]

Information about these conflicts with the Byzantines indicates that during the reign of Theudis the Visigoths had advanced into *Baetica*. It is possible that in the summer of 533 Theudis had set up his court in *Hispalis* (Seville), because the merchants who, after crossing the Straits of Gibraltar, apparently travelled up a river bed in order to get to the royal court, had informed the king of the occupation of Carthage by the forces of General Belisarius.[46] Regions on the coast of *Carthaginensis* also came to form part of the Visigothic kingdom in the time of Theudis, as appears from a council having been held at Valencia in 546, placing it in this king's reign. These territorial successes were without doubt the result of the ability of Theudis to integrate the old Roman provinces, an ability underlined by his marriage, and also by legislative activity. The most striking element of the latter is his law on the costs of procedure, which was incorporated into Alaric's Breviary by express order of the king. In this way for the first time a barbarian king perfected a Roman legal corpus, putting his legislation on the same level as imperial constitutions.

So far we have analysed all the information that refers to the establishment of military or politico-administrative control on the part of the Visigoths in the Iberian peninsula, paying particular attention to the gradual character of this process. Now we will approach the subject of the settlement of the

44 *Cod. Iust.* I.37.

45 Barbero de Aguilera (1987), pp. 137–8. Thompson (1969), p. 15, Orlandis (1977), p. 75, and García Moreno (1989), p. 98, follow Isidore's account here.

46 Procopius, *Wars* III.24.7–18.

Gothic population itself, about which we are less well-informed. The classic thesis began with the studies of Reinhart in 1945 which, basing themselves on the dowries of the necropolis of the northern edge of the *meseta*, proposed a compact settlement of the mass of Goths in the high basins of the Duero and of the Tagus. This thesis found wide acceptance and was fleshed out by Menéndez Pidal and Sánchez Albornoz, who related these settlements to information in the *Chronica Caesaraugustana* about a significant invasion of Gothic groups in 494 and their later settlement in 497.[47] Abadal also gave special relevance to the information in the *Chronica Caesaraugustana*, even though he believed the settlements were located in *Tarraconensis*. In the last few decades more and more scholars have been questioning the possibility of compact settlement on the plateau.[48] This change of perspective is the result of the development of archaeological studies, which have profoundly revised some of the premises from which Reinhart departed. None the less, advances in this field are slow, and one must hope that work in progress will be the object of systematic treatment in order to be able to offer an alternative overview.

In addition it is not easy to know how these settlements took place. One might argue that they were established on *bona vacantia* or *caduca*, or even on the lands of the imperial exchequer, which had now become the patrimony of the Visigothic kings. Alternatively they may have relied upon the system for the distribution of private estates in accordance with the system of *hospitalitas*. The inscription cited above, commemorating the restoration of the bridge of Mérida in 483, indicates that the garrison established there under the leadership of the *dux* Salla received lands for cultivation by order of the king. These lands could have a fiscal origin like the *bona vacantia* of the city, but do not seem to have resulted from the division of private properties. However, it is probable that on other occasions they did turn to such a system, since when in the middle of the seventh century Reccesuinth promulgated a new Code, the *Liber Iudiciorum*, it included two laws, described as *antiquae*, which were supposed to regulate conflicts arising from the lots in the division of estates between Goths and Romans. The two laws were incorporated under the following headings: *De divisione terrarum facta inter Gotum atque Romanum* and *De silvis inter Gotum et Romanum indivisis relictis*.[49] Since they were described as *antiquae* it is thought that they proceeded from the *Codex Revisus* of Leovigild, but Leovigild preserved Eurician precepts on the division of lands. Their later incorporation in the *Liber Iudiciorum* implies that, in some cases at least, the settlements were governed by the system of *hospitalitas*.

47 See above, p. 172. 48 On the state of the question, Olmo Enciso (1992), pp. 185–7.

49 *LV* x.1.8 and 9, pp. 385, 386.

The reign of Theudis ended violently. The monarch was assassinated in 548 and, according to Isidore, the dying king made everyone swear that no one would kill the assassin, because he had received the death he deserved, having destroyed his own master through deception. This seems to allude to the participation of Theudis in the death of his predecessor Amalaric. Theodisclus, the general who had been triumphant over the Franks, succeeded him, but scarcely maintained himself on the throne for a year, since he also was violently assassinated in Seville in 549. Doubtless we should relate these two violent deaths to the delayed reaction of the Visigothic faction, which had fallen from power with the death of Amalaric.

INTERNAL DIVISIONS AND THE ESTABLISHMENT OF THE BYZANTINES

The history of the Visigothic kingdom in subsequent years is characterised by several related events: civil war, the weakness of the Visigothic hold over *Baetica* and the presence of the Byzantines in the south and south-east of the *peninsula*. The most important source for this period continues, in spite of its limitations, to be the *Historia Gothorum* of Isidore of Seville, for it is lamentable that Procopius, whose works constitute a source of exceptional richness, did not concern himself with the Byzantine wars in *Hispania*.

The successor of Theodisclus was Agila (549–554). In the first years of his reign he had to confront a rebellion of the city of Córdoba, in *Baetica*. He was defeated by the Cordobans, losing his son and moneys, and was forced to seek refuge in Mérida in Lusitania. Then a noble Goth, Athanagild, fortified himself in another Baetican city, Seville, and instigated another uprising. He defeated the army sent against him by Agila from Mérida. Isidore placed the disembarcation of Byzantine troops in the peninsula in this context of civil war, that is, they were coming to the aid of Athanagild at his request. The uprising of Athanagild can be seen as a response to the factional struggle unfolding among leading Visigoths for control of the throne since the death of Gesalic. However the defection of the senators of *Baetica* constitutes the actual background of the civil war, and only on the basis of their collaboration could Byzantine troops have transformed their military victories into a stable territorial dominion, although limited to the extreme south-east of the peninsula.

The appearance of the Byzantines may have had as its pretext aid for the rebellion of Athanagild, but it must be placed in the context of Justinian's imperial restoration programme in the old provinces of the Western Empire. In *Hispania*, in contrast to what happened in the north of Africa and Italy, the Byzantines only managed to occupy a small part of the old imperial territory. Byzantine dominions extended along the coast between Cartagena and the outlet of the Guadalete, along with certain pockets in the interior where they controlled Basti (Baza) and Asidona (Medina Sidonia), although their principal centres were the Mediterranean cities of Cartagena and Málaga. Córdoba, contrary to a widely held opinion, did not remain under Byzantine dominion but was controlled by the Roman provincials who managed to maintain their independence until 572, when the city was taken by Leovigild.[50] The territories occupied by the Byzantines were incorporated along with the Balearics into the new province of *Spania*, and subordinated to the praetorian prefecture of Africa created by Justinian in 534, once the conquest of the Vandal kingdom had finished.

The main contingent of troops arrived in the peninsula in 552 under the command of the patrician Liberius, who had been praetorian prefect in Arles in the time of Theoderic the Ostrogoth.[51] The balance of the civil war inclined in favour of Athanagild, and in 555 Agila was killed at Mérida by his adherents, who then joined his rival. Athanagild (555–567) fought against his old allies the Byzantines and tried to re-establish Visigothic authority in *Baetica*, where towards the end of his reign he managed to take Seville, the city which had served as the base for his own rebellion. He also attacked Córdoba on repeated occasions, as the *Chronica Caesaraugustana* notes.[52] Among the main consequences of the civil war was loss of influence in the southern regions of the peninsula, then under the control of Constantinople or of the Hispano-Roman provincials themselves. On the other hand relations with the Franks were peaceful, and Athanagild arranged the marriage of two of his daughters to Merovingian kings: Brunehild to Sigibert I of Metz and Galsuintha to Chilperic of Soissons.[53] Both marriages sought to isolate the Burgundian king, Guntramn, and protect Gothic Gaul/*Narbonensis*. Finally the king died a natural death in Toledo in 567.

THE ERA OF LEOVIGILD

On the death of Athanagild, according to Isidore, the throne remained vacant for five months, until Liuva was elevated to it in 567 at Narbonne. In the second

[50] The geographical limits have been reconstructed by Stroheker (1965), p. 211, and Thompson (1969), pp. 320–3.

[51] The information on Liberius in Jordanes, *Getica*, 303; for the date, Stein (1949), II, pp. 820–1.

[52] *Chronicon Caesaraugustanorum* s.a. 468; the date in the chronicle must be erroneous because other sources and evidence, with the exception of John of Biclaro, agree in dating the death of Athanagild to 567, cf. Grosse, *Fontes Hispaniae Antiquae*, pp. 141–2, this last date being that commonly accepted by scholars.

[53] Gregory, *Hist.* IV.27, 28.106–1, which also informs us of the cruel assassination of Galsuintha by order of Chilperic, whose action was instigated by his lover Fredegund, an assassination which would complicate relations between Visigoths and Franks and worsen still relations between the kingdoms of Soissons and Metz.

year of his reign he nominated his brother Leovigild as co-ruler. Leovigild assumed the government of *Hispania* while Liuva reserved Septimania for himself. In the first year of his reign Leovigild, who already had two sons from a previous marriage, married Gosuintha, the widow of Athanagild, and, according to John of Biclaro, restored the kingdom to its original boundaries, which had been greatly diminished as a result of the various revolts. One has the impression that both circumstances were related and that the marriage to Gosuintha, a woman who was an important political protagonist in the period, contributed to the pacification of the realm, bringing the adhesion of the politico-military clientage of the late monarch.[54] Liuva died shortly afterwards, leaving Leovigild sole monarch from 572.

The era of Leovigild (568–586) marks the apogee of the Visigothic kingdom of Toledo in its Arian phase. For this there is reasonable evidence, since the limitations of the *Historia Gothorum* of Isidore are compensated for by the *Chronicon* of John of Biclaro, a Catholic of Gothic origin who completed his education in Constantinople, where he remained for seventeen years. On his return to *Hispania*, he was exiled by Leovigild to Barcelona because of his faith, and later he founded the monastery of Biclarum.[55] After Leovigild's death, John's career culminated as bishop of Gerona. All these circumstances, plus his erudition and political independence, give John of Biclaro's Chronicle, which covers the period 567–590, an inestimable value.[56]

In the first years of his reign Leovigild focussed his attention on the south of the peninsula, those regions where Visigothic dominion had been endangered as a consequence of the civil war and the Byzantine occupation. According to John of Biclaro, in 570 the Visigothic monarch entered Byzantine territory with an army, devastated the regions of Baza and Málaga, and managed in the following year to recover the city of Asidona in the vicinity of the Straits. In the same period the city of Córdoba rebelled and was occupied by him in 572: an uprising which appears to be an event independent of Byzantine domination and whose antecedents must be sought in earlier rebellions from the time of Agila and Athanagild. The submission of the city of Córdoba was completed with the occupation of the towns and forts in its surroundings, and also with the killing of a large number of *rustici*.

Once his authority had been reasserted in relation to the Byzantines and the Baetican provincials, Leovigild took the war to the northern regions of the peninsula. In 573 the Visigothic king entered Sabaria, fought its inhabitants, the Sappos, and reintegrated the region into his control. The Sappos were a little-Romanised people who retained their ancient tribal name and were

[54] Orlandis (1977), p. 94. [55] Isidore of Seville, *De Viris Illustribus* XXXI.

[56] We follow here the edition of Campos (1960), pp. 77–100.

found in the present-day province of Zamora. In 575, Leovigild entered the *Aragenses* mountains, where he captured Aspidius 'the lord of the area' along with his family, re-establishing his dominion over the territory. The *Aragenses* mountains have been situated in the south of the province of Orense, not far from Sabaria.[57] From their geographical location, these campaigns seem to have been designed to affirm Visigothic dominion in relation to Sueves. In 576 Leovigild took the war to the limits of *Gallaecia* and forced the Sueve king Miro into a peace favourable to his interests.

The expansionist politics of Leovigild ran into difficulties owing to the resistance of two peoples from the north of the peninsula, the Cantabrians and the Basques. Since the last days of the Empire they had managed to turn their precarious assimilation into virtual independence.[58] In 574, Leovigild entered Cantabria, where, as the succinct account of John of Biclaro informs us, he destroyed the invaders (*pervasores*), occupied Amaya and subjected, or perhaps better restored (*revocat*) the region to his authority. The Chronicle goes back to discuss another expedition of Leovigild in the north, this time against the Basques in 581, as a result of which he occupied part of Vasconia and founded the city of *Victoriacum* (Vitoria). The victories of Leovigild did not end the independence of the Cantabrians and Basques, against whom his successors directed fresh and successive campaigns, but Leovigild succeeded in pacifying the territory occupied by these peoples, since both Amaya and *Victoriacum* were fortresses situated in the south of Cantabria and Vasconia. The troops who garrisoned them aimed to guard against incursions, which seems to accord with the term *pervasores* that the chronicler used to describe the Cantabrians.[59]

Among the campaigns of the first years of his reign, John of Biclaro informs us that Leovigild entered Orospeda in 577, occupied fortresses and cities and made the region his. Likewise he adds that a little later there was a revolt of peasants (*rustici rebelantes*), who were punished by the Goths. By this means the Goths came to dominate Orospeda. The conquest of this region, situated in the eastern part of *Baetica*,[60] seems to have been accomplished in two phases: in the first the Goths conquered the towns and fortresses, subjecting dominant social groups; but later, in the second phase, the peasant revolt took place and was suppressed. It is possible that the wars of the Visigoths against local lords temporarily facilitated peasant emancipation. Something similar must have happened when in 572 Leovigild stifled the rebellion of Córdoba, since once quelled, more towns and fortresses in its surroundings also saw

57 The location of Sabaria and the Aragenses mountains is in Campos (1960), pp. 118, 123.

58 Barbero and Vigil (1974), pp. 13–50.

59 Barbero and Vigil (1974), pp. 54–67, 74–80.

60 Campos (1960), p. 126.

themselves obliged to put a multitude of *rustici* to death in order to make their dominance effective.

The evidence from John of Biclaro seems to suggest that up to this point the military campaigns of Leovigild were not so much expansionist, as a drive to re-establish the unity of the kingdom in the face of the Byzantines and Sueves, as well as the local lords who had escaped Visigothic control by taking advantage of the struggles of the previous years. This holds true for the senators of Córdoba (*dominium revocat*), for the inhabitants of Sabaria (*redigit dicionem*), for the mountains of Aragenses (*redigit potestatem*), and even in the case of the Cantabrian *pervasores* (*revocat dicionem*), since all these phrases in the Chronicle seem to refer to a restoration of Visigothic authority, rather than an incorporation *ex novo*. The only exception is the case of the region of Orospeda, which after the submission of its towns and fortresses Leovigild was said to have made *suam provinciam*.[61] This notion is iterated by Biclaro himself, who tells us that in 578 the monarch, once the tyrants were eliminated and the invaders defeated, halted to share his rest with the 'plebe' and founded Celtiberia, a town, to which he gave the name of his son and which was known as Recopolis.

THE REBELLION OF HERMENIGILD

The restoration programme was however threatened by new problems, which broke out the following year in *Baetica* and led to civil war between the king and his son, Hermenigild. In 573 Leovigild had made Hermenigild and Reccared, his sons of his first marriage, *consortes regni*. With them in line to the throne, he was following the example of his brother Liuva and preparing the future succession. According to John of Biclaro, in 579, Hermenigild was put in charge of a province, no doubt *Baetica*, in the capacity of king regent (*ad regnandum*). The same year he married Ingund, a Merovingian princess, who was the daughter of Sigibert of Metz and Brunehild, the latter being the daughter of Athanagild and Gosuintha. Leovigild's grant of royal powers to his son responded as much to the need to control, from close proximity, a region that from 550 had been rocked by continual revolts, as to the pressure of Athanagild's powerful clientage, interested in the proximity of a prince linked by marriage ties to their old master. In the event, if the objective was to strengthen the kingdom, this measure had precisely the opposite effect. Within a short time, the son rebelled against the father and, incited by a faction of the queen Gosuintha (*factione Gosuinthae*), seized power in Seville, including in his rebellion numerous towns

[61] John of Biclaro s.a. 572, 573, 574, 575, 577. We exclude the case of Vasconia, the domination of which came after the outbreak of the revolt of Hermenigild in 579.

and fortresses. Gregory of Tours completes the picture, adding that Hermenigild, inspired by Ingund, abandoned Arianism, taking the name John, and that he sought the help of the Byzantines. The rebellion did not take long to spread, and reached the city of Mérida in Lusitania.

Leovigild did not embark on a military counter-offensive immediately, but for more than two years looked for other remedies, which would allow him to put a peaceful end to the conflict. In 580 he convened a synod of the Arian church in Toledo, where measures were taken to ease the conversion of Catholics, which apparently had certain results. In 581 the campaign against the Basques took place. This coincided with another campaign by the Merovingian king Chilperic of Soissons, with whom Leovigild maintained a close alliance at this time. This had as its objective the neutralisation of possible intervention by the kings of Orléans and Metz, the latter being the brother of Ingund. Finally, in 582, having bought the neutrality of the Byzantines, Leovigild advanced against his son Hermenigild. First he took the city of Mérida in 582, a victory which was commemorated by the minting of coin, and later in 583 he headed for Seville, which was subdued after a prolonged siege. The Sueve king Miro participated and was killed, although it is not easy to determine whose side he was on, whether Leovigild's as John of Biclaro maintains, or Hermenigild's as Gregory of Tours affirms, adding that Leovigild later overcame Miro and forced him to join his camp, imposing on him an oath of fealty. After taking the city in 583, Hermenigild fled, but was eventually captured and executed in Tarragona in 585, while Ingund and their son, Athanagild, remained in the hands of the Byzantines and set off for the East. Ingund died on the voyage and the trail of Athanagild is lost in Constantinople.[62]

The rebellion and death of Hermenigild have been the subject of debate from the time that the events took place until today. For some, like Gregory of Tours and Pope Gregory the Great, the war had a powerful religious motivation and the death of Hermenigild was a sort of martyrdom. On the other hand, Hispanic historians, like John of Biclaro and Isidore of Seville, describe the rebellion as 'tyranny', an illegitimate usurpation of power by force. Today it is believed that distinct factors contributed to the rebellion of Hermenigild and its momentary success, among which it is necessary to emphasise internal dissension, represented by the *factione Gosuinthae reginae*, leader of the house of Athanagild; the hostility of *Baetica* and its great cities to Visigothic dominion; and Byzantine help. To these must be added the religious factor, which, without being as defining as Gregory of Tours pretends, undoubtedly served to lend

[62] The revolt and putting down of Hermenigild were regarded as momentous events in several sources. Here we have largely followed: John of Biclaro s.a. 580–5; Gregory, *Hist.* v.38.243–4, vi.18.287–8, vi.40.310–12; vi.43.314–16, viii.18.384; Isidore, *Historia Gothorum*, 49.

ideological cohesion to the participants in the revolt. We can also state that the end of the civil war marked the end of the traditional revolts of the Baetican cities and signals the beginning of the full integration of its leading groups. It put an end to the centrifugal tendencies of the Baetican senators and halted a process which could have led to a multiplication of Gothic kingdoms, as had happened in Merovingian Gaul.

ANNEXATION OF THE SUEVE KINGDOM

An indirect consequence of Hermenigild's usurpation was the annexation of the Sueve kingdom, without doubt the most significant event from the point of view of territorial expansion in the Visigothic kingdom of Toledo. The history of the Sueve kingdom is unknown for the period that runs from the end of the *Chronicon* of Hydatius, in 469, to the first information provided by Isidore in the *Historia Suevorum*, concerning the reign of Theodemir (561–570). In the second half of the sixth century, the Sueve kingdom, before its incorporation into the Visigothic kingdom, seems to have been a relatively stable monarchy, whose territorial borders continued to be circumscribed by the old Roman province of *Gallaecia* and the north of Lusitania, as outlined in the previous section. In the field of religion, it was immersed in profound change, which caused the conversion of the Sueves to Catholicism and abandonment of Arianism during the reign of Theodemir.[63] This conversion reflects the internal cohesion of the kingdom, since with it a duality of *fides* was ended, making way for the integration of its Sueve and Roman leading minorities. At the beginning of his reign, according to John of Biclaro, Miro, who succeeded Theodemir in 570, undertook a campaign against the 'Runcones' or 'Roccones', a semi-independent and little-known people, who it is assumed were established in the south-east of the Sueve kingdom. This seems to indicate a certain bid for territorial expansion. However a few years later Miro, as we saw, suffered hostilities from Leovigild and was obliged in 576 to agree to a peace favourable to the interests of the Visigoths, that perhaps included military obligations. Hence Miro's presence along with his troops in Seville in aid of Leovigild, as John of Biclaro states, although as already pointed out Gregory of Tours offers a different version of events. Miro died in Baetica during the siege of Seville, and with his death a feud began for the succession, which facilitated the annexation of the Sueve kingdom by the Visigothic monarchy.

The roots of this feud over the succession were the result of the existence of opposed positions over the future of foreign policy towards the Visigothic kingdom. Gregory of Tours states that Leovigild imposed an oath of loyalty

[63] Establishing the specific conditions in which the conversion happened, Thompson (1980), pp. 77–92.

on Miro and that his successor, Eboric, did not come into the possession of his kingdom until after he had tendered his oath of loyalty to Leovigild in his turn.[64] This information indicates a personal dependence of the Sueve kings in their relations with Leovigild. One arrives at the same conclusion if one accepts the version of Biclaro, in which case the military aid lent by Miro points to a similar dependence, although it must have been imposed some time earlier. Perhaps the Sueve kingdom never escaped from a form of effective protection imposed by the Visigothic king Euric in the time of the king Remismund, whose logical conclusion was this process of annexation under Leovigild.

At first Miro's successor was his son Eboric, but Eboric was soon deposed by his brother-in-law Audeca and imprisoned in a monastery with the object of definitively displacing him from the throne. The event served to give Leovigild, in his capacity as patron of the deposed king, an excuse to attack the Sueve kingdom in 585 and depose Audeca. Although the Visigothic king did not reinstate Eboric, according to John of Biclaro, he appropriated his treasure and submitted the 'people' and the *patria* of the Sueves to his power, transforming it into a province of the Visigothic kingdom. Still the Visigothic king had to defeat a certain Malaric who tried to ascend to the throne, before definitively annexing the Sueve kingdom.

During the reign of Leovigild, relations with the various Frankish kingdoms were assiduously maintained, though they were sometimes put under pressure largely because these kingdoms found themselves in conflict with one other. The Visigothic king sought, as his ancestors had done, to make closer links through matrimonial alliances. In this context, the marriage of Hermenigild to Ingund, which meant a rapprochement with the kingdom of Metz, has already been discussed. Afterwards a project existed, ultimately frustrated, to unite Reccared and another Merovingian princess, Rigunth, daughter of Chilperic of Soissons. The proposed match was negotiated through various embassies, as related in detail by Gregory of Tours.[65] Once again, the goal was to neutralise Guntramn of Orléans, who, owing to the proximity of his kingdom, represented a constant threat to *Narbonensis*, and also to avoid the possible intervention of Ingund's brother, the king of Metz, on behalf of Hermenigild.[66] However, at the end of 584 the assassination of Chilperic of Soissons, as his daughter was on her way to Hispania, prevented the wedding, and Rigunth was despoiled of her dowry and imprisoned at Toulouse.

[64] Gregory, *Hist.* VI.43.314–16. [65] Gregory, *Hist.* VI.18.287–8, VI.40.310–12, VI.45.317–19.

[66] It has been suggested that perhaps this matrimonial project was the spark for the revolt of Hermenigild, since Chilperic was responsible for the assassination of the Visigothic princess Galsuintha, sister of Brunehild, mother of Ingund and daughter of the king Athanagild and Gosuintha, the latter being the wife of Leovigild, cf. Isla Frez (1990), pp. 24–5.

In the following year, 585, Guntramn of Burgundy invaded *Narbonensis*. This attack occurred while the Visigothic king was fighting against the Sueves in Gallaecia and it probably answered two objectives: to increase Guntramn's territories at the expense of *Narbonensis* and at the same time to hamper the action of Leovigild against the Sueve kingdom. We learn from Gregory of Tours that beforehand the courts of Soissons and Toledo had exchanged embassies, as Braga and Orléans had also done.[67] Leovigild entrusted the mission of driving back the Frankish troops to his son Reccared. He was victorious and not only expelled the Franks from the territory they had invaded, but also occupied Frankish positions situated beyond the borders of *Narbonensis*. In spite of the interest in neutralising possible Frank offensives, via matrimonial alliances, the Franks did not constitute a serious threat to the Visigoths at this time, largely because of the internecine conflicts that bedevilled the various Merovingian kingdoms.

CONSOLIDATION AND THE REORGANISATION OF THE KINGDOM

The work and personality of Leovigild, as a consolidator and reorganiser of the Visigothic kingdom, and the energy that he displayed in carrying through his objectives and conquering his enemies, did not go unnoticed by his contemporaries. Some years later Isidore of Seville summarised these events as follows:

> He was also pernicious for some of his own, since all those he saw who were very noble and powerful, he had beheaded, or sent them proscribed into exile. He also enriched the treasury, and the exchequer grew with spoils from the citizens and the pillaging of his enemies. He founded likewise, a city in Celtiberia which he named Recopolis, after his son. Besides, in legislative matters he corrected all that which seemed to have been left confused by the establishment of Euric, adding many laws, omitting and removing many superfluous ones.

Isidore also says that: 'He was the first who met his people enthroned, covered in regal clothing; since before him, the dress and seating were communal for the people and the kings.'[68]

[67] Gregory, *Hist.* v.41.248, viii.35.404. Gregory also tells of how Leovigild had plundered Frankish trading boats sailing from Gaul to Galicia.

[68] Isidore, *Historia Gothorum* 51: 'Extitit autem quibusdam suorum perniciosum, nam quoscumque nobilissimos ac potentissimos uidit aut capite truncauit aut prescriptos in exilium egit. Fiscum quoque primus iste locupletauit primusque aerarium de rapinis ciuium hostiumque manubiis auxit. Condidit etiam ciuitatem in Celtiberia, quam ex nomine fili sui Recopolim nominauit. In legibus quoque ea quae Eurico incondite constituta uidebantur correxit, plurimas leges praetermissas adiciens plerasque superfluas auferens . . . primusque inter suos regali ueste opertus solio resedit, nam ante

Isidore's words reflect how the Visigothic state was constituted and what Leovigild did in order to strengthen it. The monarch, who was at the peak of the state, was in principle but one more amongst the most powerful nobles, with both clientages and vast patrimonies in lands and precious metals. Thus, as had frequently happened since the time of Amalaric, whichever of the nobles had the power to challenge the position of the king, and become a pretender and competitor, tended to do so. As a result, Leovigild was not only confronted by enemies outside the kingdom and war against more or less independent peninsula peoples, but, according to Isidore's testimony, he also had to eliminate the most dangerous elements of the nobility, including his own son, whom he killed or sent into exile and whose goods he confiscated. With these confiscations he enriched the treasury that was also fed by means of harsh tributes described as 'spoils from the citizens'. These measures made it possible to mint good quality gold coin again in the form of *trientes* or *tremises* (coins worth a third of a *solidus*), derived from Roman prototypes. These were issued for the first time in the name of the Visigothic monarch, and in this way the previous practice of reproducing the effigy of the emperors was abandoned. It was a bold and politically important initiative, for with it Leovigild gave to understand that the last links that united the Visigothic monarchy with the Roman Empire had been broken. The foundation of Recopolis was the first instance of a barbarian king founding a city, and in doing so Leovigild placed himself on the same level as the emperors who continued to be his institutional models, as is clear from the foundation of the city and the Greek suffix 'polis' chosen for its name. The prestige with which Leovigild wanted to endow the monarchy was also projected on the interior of the kingdom and new visible symbols, such as the throne and royal dress, came to indicate clearly the supremacy of the king over the other nobles.

Isidore also attests to Leovigild's role as legislator, describing how he completed the work of Euric by including a law permitting the intermarriage of Goth and Roman despite the Roman stipulations forbidding unions between Romans and barbarians.[69] This law gave legal status to something which had been happening in practice for a long time and which must have been frequent, although we may only be aware of intermarriage between people of high status, like the Ostrogoth Theudis and the rich landowner he married. Religious unification was another important step in this process of Romano-Gothic identity, therefore it is not surprising that it was a priority in Leovigild's policy. However his aspiration to realise unity by having everyone accept the

eum et habitus et consessus communis ut gentii, ita et regibus erat'; ed. Rodríguez Alonso (1975), pp. 258–9.

69 *LV* III.I.I.

Arian creed warranted serious criticism by Isidore, who accused him of instigating persecution and exiling many of the Catholic clergy, and suppressing the rents and privileges of the church. Catholic clerics of Gothic origin were also among the exiles, like the chronicler John of Biclaro and the bishop Masona of Mérida. Without doubt, Isidore was exaggerating here, and now the tendency is to down-play the extent of this persecution.

Religious differences inside one state always constituted a serious political problem for governments of the day. The Eastern Roman Empire was subject to numerous conflicts because of religious polemics, and the emperors tried to maintain unity, unsuccessfully trying to conciliate the antagonistic positions.[70] On the other hand, the barbarian kingdoms, with the exception of the Franks, also found themselves the subject of tensions as a result of the Arianism of some of their peoples, which was opposed by the Nicene Christianity of the majority of the population. The other barbarian kingdom of the peninsula which had had the same problems, that of the Sueves, had achieved unity in the period immediately preceding Leovigild's assumption of the throne, by abandoning Arianism and adopting the Nicene creed. In his search for religious unity, the Visigothic king tried to attract the Catholic clergy towards Arianism. The most significant step was taken in 580, once the revolt of Hermenigild had erupted, when Leovigild convened an Arian synod in Toledo. At this synod, according to John of Biclaro, measures were taken in order to facilitate the conversion of Catholics to Arianism, it being specified that it was not necessary to be baptised again, but that a simple laying on of hands and recitation of a formula of the faith, *gloria patri per filium in spiritu sancto*, was enough. Toning down some of the old differences between the creeds on the persons of the Trinity, it was a formula for consent. Isidore states that there were numerous conversions to Arianism and alludes to the material advantages gained by the converted, amongst whom he mentions the bishop of Saragossa, Vincent. All in all, this concession made by the Toledan synod and others proposed by the king, and referred to by Gregory of Tours, such as allowing the cult of relics of martyrs in non-Arian churches,[71] were not enough for the drive towards religious unification to succeed. The desired union was not carried into effect until the reign of his son and successor Reccared, already under the sway of a different tendency. The triumph of Catholicism under Reccared would herald the beginning of a new stage in the history of the Visigothic kingdom.

[70] See Louth, chapters 4 above and 11 below.

[71] Gregory, *Hist.* VI.18.287–8.

CHAPTER 8

MEROVINGIAN GAUL AND THE FRANKISH CONQUESTS

Raymond Van Dam

The later Roman Empire provided little indication that the future of early medieval Europe lay with the Franks. From the later third century, Germans whom the literary sources called Franks had joined with other barbarians to challenge Roman rule in Gaul. These Franks included various peoples that had previously settled north and east of the lower Rhine. Although hostilities continued, by the beginning of the fourth century some Franks had been resettled throughout northern Gaul inside the Roman Empire. In particular, by the middle of the century the Salian Franks had settled in Toxandria, a region south of the mouths of the Rhine. In return, the Franks provided recruits, and sometimes entire units, that served in the Roman army throughout the Mediterranean world. Franks also began to serve as officers, and like other Germans some rose to become important generals who influenced imperial politics. The Frank Bonitus, for instance, had supported the emperor Constantine during the civil wars at the beginning of the fourth century, while his son Silvanus learned 'Roman culture', accepted Christianity, and served as a general in Gaul. After being falsely slandered at the court of the emperor Constantius in 355, Silvanus even established himself briefly as a usurping emperor at Cologne – the only Frankish emperor before Charlemagne. The Frank Ricimer became commander-in-chief in the East, and was also a friend of leading aristocrats throughout the Empire; as commander-in-chief in the Western Empire his nephew Arbogast continued to campaign against his fellow Franks along the northern frontier and led the last successful Roman expedition across the Rhine. Arbogast was such an intimidating figure that he drove the young emperor Valentinian II to his death and then promoted Eugenius as a rival emperor to Theodosius, who finally defeated them in 394. Whether as enemies, recruits or mercenaries, from the beginning the Franks appeared in the Roman Empire as warriors: 'even as boys, their love of war was full-grown'.[1]

1 Sidonius, *Carmina* v.249–50. Early Franks: Zöllner (1970), pp. 1–25; Barnes (1994). Franks in Roman service: Stroheker (1955).

Map 3 Gaul/Francia in the sixth and seventh centuries

SAXONS
R. Weser
THURINGIA
R. Unstrut
R. Elbe
R. Saale
SLAVS
(WENDS)
HESSE
Mainz
R. Main
Rhine
Würzburg
Regensburg
R. Danube
R. Danube
ALAMANNIA
Freising
BAVARIA
Salzburg
AVARS
R. Danube
Reichenau
St Gall
RHAETIA
JURA
LOMBARDS

Map 3 (*cont.*)

Military service was not the only connection between Franks and Romans, however. Since the frontiers of the Roman Empire had always been more zones of mutual interaction than impermeable linear barricades, the settlement of the Franks merely extended an ongoing process of barbarianisation into northern and even central Gaul.[2] Despite the presence of an imperial court at Trier during most of the fourth century, northern Gaul had been gradually slipping away from Roman influence. In the early fifth century the Roman administration finally acknowledged these centrifugal cultural and social forces by moving south to Arles. Franks took advantage of the anarchy to expand their ascendancy. Some supported the usurper Jovinus in the Rhineland in 411; others sacked Trier; one obscure Frankish chieftain named Chlogio briefly seized Cambrai and Arras; and in 451 Franks helped the Roman general Aetius defeat Attila and his Hunnic confederation.[3] Without Roman magistrates permanently stationed in northern and central Gaul to provide the semblance of a central authority, Gallic aristocrats and Roman commanders joined barbarian chieftains in asserting their own local influence. During the mid-fifth century Aegidius, a native of Gaul who was also nominally a Roman general, established a renegade principality centred at Soissons, and even some of the Franks in northern Gaul accepted him as their own 'king'; his son Syagrius succeeded him with the wonderfully hybrid title of 'king of the Romans'.[4] At Trier Arbogast (probably a descendant of the general Arbogast) ruled as an apparently autonomous 'count' during the 470s. Although Arbogast was a Frank, one bishop nevertheless complimented him for writing a Latin free of 'barbarisms', and another praised him for having accepted Christianity.[5] Childeric was another prominent chieftain, apparently of the Salian Franks, who had perhaps once been Aegidius' ally against the Visigoths. Through a combination of brief alliances and continuous campaigns he gradually expanded his influence as a warlord in northern Gaul and most likely acquired control over the old Roman province of Second Belgica. His tomb at Tournai pointedly memorialised the dual nature of his prominence, since it contained Frankish weapons as well as Roman coins, the ornaments of a Roman magistrate, and a signet ring depicting him in Roman military attire.[6] Both 'Frankified' Romans and 'Romanised' Franks were the products of the cultural, and now political, assimilation in northern Gaul.

[2] Whittaker (1994). [3] Zöllner (1970), pp. 25–43.

[4] Gregory, *Hist* II.12.61–2, II.27.71; James (1989); Jarnut (1994).

[5] Sidonius, *Epistolae* IV.17; Auspicius of Toul, *Epistolae Austrasicae* XXIII, pp. 132–7; Heinzelmann (1982), p. 558.

[6] Remigius of Rheims, *Epistolae Austrasicae* II, p. 113; Heinzelmann and Poulin (1986), pp. 97–103. Tomb: James (1988), pp. 58–67.

Clovis followed the belligerent example of his father Childeric. His immediate neighbours included the Burgundians, who had established themselves in eastern Gaul, and the Alamans, long settled along the upper Rhine. The Alamans he finally defeated; but with the Burgundians he forged a connection by marrying the princess Clothild. He also began to expand his influence into central Gaul by seizing the 'Roman kingdom' of Syagrius. His new neighbours then were the Visigoths, whom Roman authorities had settled in Aquitaine and who had gradually expanded their kingdom, in particular during the recent reign of King Euric. Initially the Visigoths and the related Ostrogoths in Italy seem to have tried to recruit Clovis into their sphere of political influence; one of his sisters married the Ostrogothic king Theoderic, and another converted to the Arianism of the Goths. But Clovis himself kept his distance from the Visigoths, sometimes fighting, sometimes negotiating, until in 507 he finally defeated them at Vouillé, near Poitiers.[7] While a detachment of Franks and Burgundians besieged Narbonne and Arles, Clovis advanced into southern Gaul, where he spent the winter at Bordeaux, seized the Visigoths' treasure in their former capital of Toulouse, and captured Angoulême. In the military zones of northern Gaul his father Childeric had assumed some of the trappings of a Roman general and the duties of an imperial magistrate. After visiting the more deeply Romanised society of southern Gaul, Clovis returned to Tours in 508, where he not only accepted the codicils of an honorary consulate (and perhaps the title of patrician) from the Byzantine emperor Anastasius, but also donned a purple tunic, a mantle and a crown before processing like an emperor.[8] Then he established his residence at Paris, on the boundary between the Frankish settlements in the north and his newly acquired Roman regions in central Gaul.

Clovis was furthermore consolidating his control over the Franks in typically bloody fashion. Ragnachar, a relative and a king himself at Cambrai, had helped him in his campaign against Syagrius; Clovis later repaid the favour by murdering him and his two brothers. Chararic was another Frankish king

[7] Gerberding (1987), p. 41, now suggests Voulon as the site. Despite the attempt by Gregory, *Hist.* II.35, 37. 84–8, to interpret this battle in terms of a conflict between Catholic Franks and Arian Visigoths, its causes remain obscure: see Cassiodorus, *Variae* III.1–4. 12–13. For Theoderic's attempt to mediate, Avitus of Vienne, *Epistolae* XLVI, pp. 75–6, for a hint of Arian influence on Clovis; *Epistola ad episcopos, MGH Cap.* I, pp. 1–2 for Clovis' instructions to his army. Visigoths and church: Wolfram (1988), pp. 197–202. Franks and Theoderic: Moorhead (1992), pp. 51–4, 175–94. Chronology and politics: Wood (1985), (1994), pp. 41–9; Daly (1994); Spencer (1994). For relations between Franks and Visigoths in general, see Barbero and Loring, chapter 7 above.

[8] In his text Gregory claimed that Clovis was thereafter addressed 'as if consul or Augustus', but his heading to *Hist.* II.38 described Clovis as a patrician: see McCormick (1989). Campaigns in Provence: Klingshirn (1994), pp. 106–12.

who had remained neutral during the war between Clovis and Syagrius, and although Clovis first forced him and his son to become clerics, he eventually murdered them too. Sigibert, another relative and king of the Rhineland Franks at Cologne, helped Clovis against the Alamans, and his son Chloderic helped Clovis against the Visigoths. Clovis later encouraged Chloderic to kill his father, and then avenged Sigibert by having his son murdered. By eliminating his rivals Clovis was able to establish what would be known as the Merovingian dynasty of Frankish kings, and upon his death in 511 only his own sons were left as his heirs.[9] Their inheritance was by now a large kingdom, because by defeating or dominating neighbouring barbarian kingdoms their father had extended his influence throughout much of Gaul. But despite Clovis' efforts to eliminate any relatives who might become rivals, his sons and grandsons continued the family squabbling by feuding among themselves. When Bishop Gregory of Tours began to write his *Histories* towards the end of the sixth century, he noted that Cain had been the first to kill his brother.[10] The early Merovingian kings made sure that he was not the last.

THE MAKING OF THE FRANKISH KINGDOMS

Gregory's extensive writings are by far the most important sources of information about the early Frankish kingdoms, and his *Histories* in particular provides the fundamental narrative tying together the evidence of letters, poems, chronicles, saints' lives, miracle stories, ecclesiastical canons, law-codes, inscriptions, coins and archaeology. Subsequent sections in this chapter acknowledge the importance of his writings in their discussions of the formation of Frankish kingdoms, the working of kingship, the roles of aristocrats and bishops, and the limits of Merovingian rule. Gregory himself, however, was primarily interested in the expansion and success of Christianity in Gaul, and he hence concluded the first book of his *Histories* with the death in 397 of Bishop Martin, the patron saint of his own see who he thought had been responsible for the spread of Christianity into central Gaul. But because Clovis' baptism had seemingly transformed him too into another champion of Catholic Christianity, Gregory concluded the second book with the king's death. Despite Clovis' undeniable ruthlessness, Gregory nevertheless presented him as an Old Testament king who 'walked before God with an upright heart and did what

[9] Although there were still other 'relatives': see Gregory, *Hist.* III.13–14. 109–12, III.16. 116–17, III.23. 122–3; *Vita Patrum* I.2, pp. 262–3. Later traditions described Merovech, the dynasty's eponymous ancestor, as a relative of Chlogio and father of Childeric: see Gregory, *Hist.* II.9.52–8 and, for other legends, Fredegar, *Chron.* II.9.95; *Liber Historiae Francorum* c.5, pp. 245–6.

[10] Gregory, *Hist.* I.2.6. Germanus of Paris, *Epistolae Austrasiacae* IX, pp. 122–4, cited the same example as a warning to queen Brunehild.

was pleasing in His eyes'.[11] This image of the Christian king loomed over Gregory's evaluations of the reigns of Clovis' sons and grandsons; few lived up to expectations.

Theuderic, Clovis' oldest son by a mistress, had already shared in his father's campaigns and also already had a son of his own; yet because there was apparently no expectation of primogeniture and there were few precedents for succession, he ended up sharing Clovis' kingdom with three young half-brothers. By ensuring her own sons' participation, Clothild's influence was decisive both in the immediate division of her husband's legacy and in defining a pattern for subsequent partitions. Theuderic took Rheims; of Clovis' three sons with Clothild, Chlodomer took Orléans, Childebert Paris, and Chlothar Soissons. Each son therefore received a 'capital city' in the heartland of Frankish interests in north-central Gaul; each also possessed a small kingdom that was more a collection of cities than a region coherently defined by geography, ethnography or the boundaries of old Roman provinces.[12] Theuderic's kingdom included cities in north-eastern Gaul, north of the Burgundian kingdom, and was focussed on the Rhineland. Chlothar's kingdom extended north of Soissons towards the mouth of the Rhine and included the region long settled by the Salian Franks. Childebert's kingdom included cities in north-western Gaul. Chlodomer's kingdom in central Gaul was west of the Burgundian kingdom and stretched through northern Aquitaine to the Atlantic Ocean. Even without taking into account the scattered enclaves of cities in central and southern Aquitaine that each king controlled in addition, the establishment of these small kingdoms reinforced the political fragmentation resulting from the collapse of Roman administration.

Nor were the boundaries of these kingdoms stable. Warfare was a major destabilising factor, and if initially the Merovingian kings chose to fight primarily against their immediate barbarian neighbours, intermarriages effectively turned many of these wars into extended family feuds. Clothild encouraged her son Chlodomer to kill her cousin Sigismund, a Burgundian king whose father had killed her father; Godomar, Sigismund's brother, then killed Chlodomer in 524. In contrast, since Theuderic had married Sigismund's daughter, he declined to assist his half-brothers against Godomar; but because his son and successor Theudebert did participate in the final campaign, he shared in the division of the Burgundian kingdom with his uncles in 534. Theudebert received cities in the northern part of the kingdom, Childebert in the central

[11] Gregory, *Hist.* II.40. Historiographical and hagiographical significance of Gregory's writings: Wallace-Hadrill (1962), pp. 49–70; de Nie (1987); Goffart (1988), pp. 112–234; Van Dam (1993); Heinzelmann (1994).

[12] Succession: Wood (1977). Details of this and subsequent divisions: Longnon (1878); Ewig (1953), (1963), pp. 46–53.

part (including Lyons and Vienne), and Chlothar in the south. Theuderic, and eventually Chlothar too, had also begun to meddle in the affairs of the Thuringians, who lived in Germany east of the Rhine, and of those Saxons who had settled further north along the North Sea. At some point the Saxons began to pay tribute to Theuderic and his successors, and along with the Frisians probably helped against raids by Danes. After one battle Chlothar kidnapped the Thuringian princess Radegund, and Theuderic murdered her uncle. Although Chlothar eventually married Radegund, when he finally devastated Thuringia for having assisted a rebellion by the Saxons, he nevertheless killed her brother. So if the acquisition of the Burgundian kingdom extended Frankish control over most of what remained of old Roman Gaul, its partition led to a realignment of the existing Frankish kingdoms; and the campaigns against the Thuringians and the Saxons set a precedent for subsequent Frankish expansion north and east into Germany.[13]

Because of the rather haphazard expansion of their original kingdoms and their scattered interests in Aquitaine, almost all of the Merovingian kings eventually became neighbours of the Visigoths in Spain and southern Gaul, or of the Ostrogoths in Italy and south-eastern Gaul. With the Goths, the Franks combined occasional invasions with diplomacy. Immediately after their succession the four kings had agreed to the marriage of a sister with the Visigothic king Amalaric, but that did not prevent Childebert from eventually attacking his new brother-in-law. Theuderic and Chlothar sent their sons to seize Visigothic possessions in southern Gaul, and about a decade later, in 541, Childebert and Chlothar invaded Spain and besieged Saragossa; after their failure, the Franks were not to invade Spain again for almost a century. All the Merovingian kings had meanwhile threatened king Theodahad of the Ostrogoths for having allowed the murder of Clovis' niece, the daughter of the great Ostrogothic king, Theoderic. Once the emperor Justinian sent his Byzantine armies to reconquer Italy, the Ostrogoths negotiated for Frankish support during the winter of 536–537 and agreed to cede control over Provence and the region around the upper Rhine settled by the Alamans. Theudebert nevertheless eventually led an expedition into northern Italy in 539 and fought against both Ostrogoths and Byzantines; after another invasion a few years later he collected tribute from some of the Alpine regions in north-western Italy; and he was meanwhile extorting subsidies from the Byzantines.[14] At some time the

[13] Burgundy: Marius of Avenches, *Chron.* s.a. 534, p. 235. Saxony: Gregory, *Hist.* IV.10.141. IV.14.145–7; Fredegar, *Chron.* IV.74.158; for the possibility of Frankish claims on southern England, see Wood (1983).

[14] The accounts of Byzantine campaigns against the Ostrogoths by the Greek historians Procopius and Agathias are important sources for Frankish involvement in Italy, often more informative than Gregory's sporadic comments in his *Histories*; Cameron (1968), (1985), pp. 210–13.

Franks also came to dominate the Bavarians north of the Alps.[15] So in the process of gradually consolidating the most geographically coherent kingdom in north-eastern Gaul, Theudebert also expanded his interests into northern Italy and across the Rhine; Chlothar had wider interests in Saxony and Thuringia; and he and Childebert had invaded Spain. Even though the Merovingians were related by marriage with many of their barbarian neighbours, they commonly fought with them too; just as Clovis had established the family dynasty by murdering his Frankish relatives, so his successors often expanded their kingdoms at the expense of their new in-laws. Marriage with a Merovingian was more of a signal for war than an assurance of peace.

But diverging foreign interests were not distracting enough to prevent Clovis' sons and grandsons from feuding among themselves too. In 524 Theuderic devastated the Auvergne for having tried to switch loyalty to Childebert, and he plotted against Chlothar even as they campaigned together in Thuringia. Childebert and Chlothar successfully schemed to seize much of their deceased brother Chlodomer's kingdom by murdering two of his young sons and allowing a third to become a priest. But after they were unsuccessful in preventing their nephew Theudebert from succeeding to his father Theuderic's kingdom in 533, Childebert instead treated Theudebert as his own son and together they marched against Chlothar. Yet a few years later Childebert and Chlothar together besieged Saragossa. In 548 Theudebald succeeded his father Theudebert; but upon his death in 555 Chlothar appropriated both his grand-nephew's kingdom and his wife. Childebert continued to scheme against his brother by allying himself with Chramn, one of Chlothar's sons, and by taking advantage of Chlothar's war with the Saxons to overrun some of his cities. Upon Childebert's death in 558 Chlothar seized his brother's kingdom and sent his wife and daughters into exile. He then defeated his own son Chramn in battle and had him and his family burned to death. The murderous relationships of the Merovingian kings with each other would alone have justified their neighbours' complaints about their savagery and treachery.[16]

Chlothar's behaviour towards his relatives had been no less ruthless than that of Clovis; and like his father he now reunited the Frankish kingdom under his rule. This reunification lasted only until his death in 561, when his four surviving sons initiated again the feuding of the previous generation. In the division of the kingdom they also initially followed their ancestors' lead in designating capital cities. Charibert took Paris, Guntramn Orléans, Chilperic Soissons, and Sigibert Rheims. Their kingdoms largely flared out from their

[15] Gregory, *Hist.* IV.9.140–1, Paul the Deacon, *HL* IV.7, p. 146; Dannheimer and Dopsch (1998).

[16] Disparaging assessments of Frankish character: *Historia Augusta, Firmus* 13.4; Procopius, *Wars* VI.25.2; Isidore of Seville, *Etymologiae* IX.2.10.

capital cities, Charibert to the west and south-west, Chilperic to the north and Sigibert to the north-east, but also included enclaves of cities in Aquitaine. None of the four new kings was content for long. Because Guntramn's kingdom now included the old Burgundian kingdom and most of Provence, it effectively blocked Sigibert from his possessions in southern Gaul. Chilperic immediately took advantage of Sigibert's campaign in Thuringia against the Avars (who controlled the Hungarian plain) and seized Rheims; so Sigibert, upon his return, temporarily captured both Soissons and Chilperic's son Theudebert, who was even compelled to take an oath of loyalty. After Charibert's death in 567, the three surviving brothers divided not only his kingdom, with Chilperic receiving most of its heartland in north-western Gaul, but also Paris, in which each now held a one-third interest.

Since after the partitions of 511 and 561 one of the kings had soon died, there were usually three sub-kingdoms in early Merovingian Gaul. The territorial and cultural identities of the three kingdoms that emerged after Charibert's death proved to have lasting influence. The kingdom in north-eastern Gaul was sometimes known simply as 'Francia'; it also came to be known as Austria or Austrasia (the latter the designation commonly used by modern historians).[17] Although its original capital city had been Rheims, because of their eastern campaigns Sigibert and his successors spent increasingly more time in Metz, as well as in Coblenz and Mainz on the Rhine. With this gradual shift to the east, the core of Austrasia began to approximate the old kingdom of the Rhineland Franks who had accepted Clovis as their king only at the beginning of the sixth century. In fact, the Merovingians made a clear concession to their lingering influence by naming some of their sons Sigibert, after the former king of the Rhineland Franks. Because it included control over the Auvergne, the Austrasian kingdom remained open to the influence of Romans and their classical culture from southern Gaul. But with its interests in regions outside the old Roman Empire such as Saxony, Thuringia and Alamannia the kingdom also became increasingly 'Germanic'; so Sigibert once marched against Chilperic with an army of 'peoples from across the Rhine', and his grandson Theudebert II once raised an army of 'Saxons, Thuringians, and other peoples from across the Rhine'.[18] In contrast, through a constant process of acquisition and attrition the shape of Chilperic's kingdom centred originally on Soissons fluctuated wildly. The remote predecessors to his kingdom included the original settlements of the Salian Franks in northern Gaul, the Roman kingdom of Syagrius, and the cities acquired by Childeric's expansion into north-central Gaul; Chilperic himself always had designs on Paris. But after his death Rouen became the primary royal residence, and by the beginning of

[17] Ewig (1953), pp. 693–4, 710–15.

[18] Gregory, *Hist.* IV.49.185–6; Fredegar, *Chron.* IV.38.139.

the seventh century the kingdom of his son Chlothar II was known as Neustria and was focussed primarily in north-western Gaul, 'located on the edge of Gaul next to the [Atlantic] Ocean'.[19] Once Chlothar II expanded his influence in 613, Paris finally emerged as the capital city of Neustria. The kingdom centred on Orléans had meanwhile changed the most. After 511 Chlodomer's kingdom had extended into western Gaul; but after 561 Guntramn's kingdom stretched east and south of Orléans. It acquired an identity of its own largely because it revived an earlier independent kingdom. Because Guntramn spent increasingly more time in Chalon-sur-Saône, the focus of his kingdom came to resemble the former kingdom of the Burgundians centred around the intersection of the Rhône and the Saône. So although the kings and the royal residences changed, three distinct 'Frankish kingdoms' emerged, Austrasia, Neustria and Burgundy. Aquitaine might have been a fourth, not least because it too had been the basis for another of the barbarian kingdoms that had emerged in Gaul during the later fifth century. After the Visigoths' defeat, Aquitaine initially remained more or less intact, and its linkage with Clovis' interests in north-western Gaul hinted at the possibility of a division between a western Gaul dominated by Clovis and an eastern Gaul dominated, from north to south, by Rhineland Franks, Burgundians and Ostrogoths; so at the council that Clovis convened at Orléans in 511 all of the bishops who attended came either from Aquitaine or from what would later become the kingdom of Neustria. But after Clovis' death the cities in Aquitaine were partitioned among the various Merovingian kings in the north, and unlike the former kingdom of the Burgundians, the former kingdom of the Visigoths had no opportunity to re-emerge as a consolidated Frankish kingdom. Because royal deaths and rapid marriages led to constantly shifting partitions of the cities in Aquitaine, during the twenty years after 567 control over Cahors alone, to mention but one example, bounced among five kings and two queens.[20] During the sixth century the defining characteristic of the region was political fragmentation. Writing at the end of the century Gregory of Tours never mentioned an 'Aquitaine'.

Conflicting interests in Aquitaine led to additional civil wars; so did the isolated location of the kingdom of Neustria. Like his brothers, Chilperic too fought against various northern neighbours such as the Frisians, Saxons and Danes; but because the core of his kingdom was in north-western Gaul, he could expand his resources only by confronting his brothers. After he had his son Theudebert invade the territories of Tours, Poitiers and other cities that belonged to Sigibert, Guntramn tried to serve as a broker, sometimes allied

19 Jonas of Bobbio, *Vita Columbani* 1.24.98, apparently the earliest reference to 'Neustrian Franks'. Soissons: Kaiser (1973).
20 Rouche (1979), pp. 51–85.

with Chilperic, sometimes with Sigibert. By late 575 Sigibert had seized Paris and Theudebert had been killed in battle. At the moment of his triumph, however, Sigibert was murdered by assassins sent by Chilperic's wife Fredegund. Although Sigibert's young son Childebert succeeded him as king in Austrasia, Chilperic's son Merovech presented himself as a rival by marrying Brunehild, his uncle Sigibert's widow. But Chilperic, perhaps at Fredegund's urging, was now the one who felt threatened enough to have his son tonsured in preparation for entering a monastery. Chilperic should not have worried, because the notables of Austrasia soon arranged Merovech's death. Eventually, because illness and intrigues deprived both Guntramn and Chilperic of their sons, each decided to adopt their young nephew Childebert as heir. Childebert's advisers simply took the opportunity to play his two uncles against each other, until Chilperic too was assassinated in 584.

In Gregory's biblical perspective most of these kings had failed to follow Clovis' example; because they 'had not walked rightly before God's sight', He had delivered them 'to the hand of their enemies'. But Gregory did admire Guntramn, who as the only surviving son of Chlothar I now cast himself as guardian for his nephews. He had already adopted Childebert, and once Fredegund asked for his protection, Guntramn eventually supported the rule of her infant son Chlothar II, and finally adopted him too. As 'father' for his two nephews, Guntramn seemed similar to King Chlothar I by holding 'pre-eminence in the kingdom'.[21] So Guntramn quickly tried to expand his own holdings by claiming both Paris and the entire kingdom once held by his brother Charibert and by seizing some of the kingdom of Chlothar II.

As uncle and nephew, as well as father and son by adoption, Guntramn and Childebert were able to reign more or less in tandem. Guntramn warned Childebert of a plot against his life, and in 587 they signed a pact that finally certified the distribution of various contested cities.[22] Their wider interests caused some friction, however, in part because almost any foreign campaign or diplomacy seemed to outflank Guntramn's kingdom of Burgundy at the centre of the Frankish kingdoms. As another aspect of their interests in central Europe the kings of Austrasia had arranged diplomatic ties, and some marriage ties, with the Lombards. But after the Lombards marched into Italy, Childebert used occasional campaigns into northern Italy to extort subsidies and gifts from both them and Byzantines. Guntramn, however, refused to help his nephew, even though marauding Lombards occasionally attacked cities in his kingdom.

[21] Gregory, *Hist.* V.14.212, applying 1 Kings 9:4, 9, to Merovech; VII.13.334, 'regni principatus', with Jussen (1991), pp. 64–97.

[22] Gregory, *Hist.* IX.20.434–9, the so-called 'Treaty of Andelot'.

Instead he launched unsuccessful campaigns against Septimania, the small coastal district in southern Gaul between the River Rhône and the Pyrenees that was still under Visigothic control; but Childebert and Brunehild were meanwhile receptive to envoys from the Visigothic king Reccared.[23] Although Fredegund, still a dominant figure at the court of Chlothar II, also schemed against Guntramn by using her connections with the Visigoths, Guntramn was prepared to preside at Chlothar's baptism at Paris. Childebert's dismay at the time was unnecessary, because upon Guntramn's death he confirmed the alliance between Austrasia and Burgundy by inheriting most of his uncle's kingdom. In 592 only the cousins Childebert and Chlothar II were left as Merovingian kings; but their influence was by now subordinated to the rivalry between their mothers, Brunehild and Fredegund, and to the increasing power of the great aristocrats in their kingdoms.

THE MAKING OF FRANKISH KINGSHIP

Gregory of Tours was duly impressed by one bishop who could recite from memory the complex genealogies in the Old Testament 'that most find difficult to remember';[24] modern readers will probably have a similar bemused reaction to the numbingly intricate intrigues of the early Merovingians. For all their scheming, during the sixth century the Merovingians gradually established over much of Gaul a kingship, or rather several kingships, which combined elements from different traditions. One was Germanic.[25] The Merovingians may have founded and maintained their royal rule by force, but various rituals and symbols then distinguished them from the rest of the population. The usual insignia of royal rule included a throne, a spear and a shield; when Guntramn adopted Childebert, he set him on his own throne and suggested that one shield and one spear defend them both.[26] The most conspicuous distinguishing symbol was the kings' long hair. Despite the obscurity of Gregory of Tours' simplistic explanation for the emergence of 'long-haired kings' from the 'foremost and more noble family' of the Franks, this emblem became the visible badge of royal authority that separated them from their subjects, 'whose hair was clipped all around'. Clovis had used ecclesiastical tonsures as a means of gelding some of his rivals; pretenders to the throne had to wait to grow the required long mane; and the long hair on the head of a decomposed corpse allowed its identification as one of King Chilperic's sons.[27] Queen Clothild

[23] Septimania: James (1980). [24] Gregory, *Hist.* v.42.248–9.

[25] On Germanic kingship, see Wormald, chapter 21 below. [26] Gregory, *Hist.* v.17.214–16.

[27] Gregory, *Hist.* ii.9.52–8, long-haired kings; Agathias, *Hist.* i.3.4, clipped hair. Gregory, *Hist.* ii.41.91–2 for Clovis; v.14.207 for Merovech; vi.24.291–2 for Gundovald; viii.10.376–7 for Guntramn.

knew what long hair meant for the Merovingian family into which she had married: when once confronted with a sword and scissors and forced to decide the fate of some of her grandsons, she conceded that death was preferable to a haircut. During the sixth century the only non-Germanic name that a Merovingian king used for a son was, not surprisingly, Samson.[28] These long-haired kings also retained a value system that, while not uniquely Germanic, certainly betrayed their background in the frontier zones. To preserve their authority the Frankish kings had to demonstrate that they were 'overpowering', especially in protecting their kin and in achieving victories in battles. So although the two had fought in the past, after Chilperic's assassination Guntramn still thought that he had to take revenge: 'If I do not avenge my brother's death this year, I should not be considered a man.' Kings were concerned lest they appear to be 'weak women'; conversely, Queen Brunehild once 'armed herself like a man' in order to stop a war, and Queen Fredegund earned credit for a military victory by suggesting that her troops camouflage themselves as trees.[29] Because an ideology of military success and virile manliness deftly reinforced the warrior symbols of royalty, the Italian poet Fortunatus could ensure his welcome at Frankish courts by shrewdly beginning his first panegyric for a Merovingian king with a coveted title: *Victor*.[30]

A second tradition that influenced the nature of early Frankish kingship was biblical.[31] Although by the fifth century Orthodox Christianity provided a dominant world-view among the Roman population in Gaul, as the Franks expanded into Gaul they nevertheless retained their pagan cults, and even into the sixth century they continued to worship at pagan shrines, especially in northern Gaul. But Clovis had eventually converted to Orthodox Christianity by allowing Bishop Remigius to baptise him at Rheims. In return, Christian clerics would now cast Frankish kings as the equivalents of the kings of the Old Testament. Gregory, as we have seen, often alluded to this biblical model for the Merovingians, and his friend Fortunatus even went so far as to praise King Charibert for displaying the clemency of David and the wisdom of Solomon. Other bishops pointedly addressed the Merovingians as 'Catholic kings', perhaps as a sly admonition of how they were supposed to behave towards the church. Some comments were less subtle forms of intimidation: a bishop in

[28] Gregory, *Hist.* III.18.117–20, Clothild; V.22.122, although Samson, son of Chilperic and Fredegund, died as an infant in 577.

[29] Gregory, *Hist.* VII.8.331, 'de genere nostro robustus'; VIII.5.374, Guntramn; VI.4.268, 'weak women'; IX.19.432–4, Brunehild. Fredegund and camouflage, *Liber Historiae Francorum* c.36, p. 305. On this episode, Gerberding (1987), p. 165, and on Brunehild, Fredegund and female violence, Gradowicz-Pancer (2000).

[30] Fortunatus, *Carmina* 6. la, a panegyric for Sigibert in 566; McCormick (1986), pp. 335–42.

[31] Cf. Wormald, chapter 21 below.

Provence once reminded Theudebert to remember the Final Judgement, when a 'Christian leader' had to render an account to God.[32]

But if this biblical analogy made the Merovingian kings more acceptable for the Roman Christian population, it also posed a dilemma for the kings themselves. In contemporary letters Remigius had suggested that the warrior Clovis should instead look after widows and orphans, and Bishop Avitus of Vienne that the king should exchange his armour for the 'helmet of salvation'; according to a later tradition, Remigius had also praised Clovis' 'meekness'.[33] Gregory constantly reminded the Merovingians that they became 'good kings' only when they demonstrated their charity and kindness, and that what they valued most highly, prowess in battles, was in fact most disruptive in Gallic society. Fortunatus too, who became a priest and eventually bishop at Poitiers, stressed that success presupposed 'ruling without slaughter'.[34] The biblical ideals of these tonsured clerics obviously conflicted with the warrior code of the long-haired kings. So a third tradition influential in the making of early Frankish kingship was the precedent of the Roman or, by now, Byzantine emperors who combined their Christian faith with an ideology of military victory.[35] Constantine had long ago set the example of a triumphant Christian emperor, and at his baptism Clovis was apparently lauded as the 'new Constantine'. After his victory over the Visigoths Clovis had even assumed some of the imperial trappings at Tours where he was hailed as 'Augustus'. Fortunatus supplied additional comparisons between Merovingian kings and Roman emperors. Since he had grown up in a northern Italy that the emperor Justinian's armies had recently reconquered from the Ostrogoths, he was familiar with Byzantine culture and its political theories about emperors. His poems honouring the marriage of Sigibert and Brunehild displayed a mixture of allusions to classical mythology and references to some of the virtues long characteristic of Roman emperors. In a later panegyric he outright attributed to Charibert the piety of Trajan. And in another laudatory poem he compared Childebert with Melchizedek, the Old Testament king and priest who had come to represent the theocratic pretensions of the Byzantine emperors.[36]

For Romans accustomed to emperors and magistrates, and for Franks accustomed to petty chieftains, imagining kings was not an easy process, and

32 Venantius Fortunatus, *Carmina* VI.2.77–80; Gregory, *Hist.* IX.16.505–9, 'sub catholicis regibus'; *Epistolae Austrasicae* X, pp. 124–6.

33 Remigius of Rheims, *Epistolae Austrasicae* II, p. 2; Avitus of Vienne, *Epistolae* 46, pp. 75–6; Gregory, *Hist.* II.31.76–8.

34 Gregory, *Hist.* III.25.123, V. Praef.193–4; Fortunatus, *Carmina* VI.2.38. Views of kingship: Wallace-Hadrill (1968); Reydellet (1981); Brennan (1984); George (1992), pp. 35–61.

35 On the Roman influence on early medieval kingship, Wormald, chapter 21 below.

36 Gregory, *Hist.* II.31.77, 'new Constantine', apparently derived from a *Vita* of Remigius. Fortunatus, *Carmina* VI.1–1a; VI.2.81–2 for Trajan; II.10.21–2 for Melchizedek.

throughout the sixth century this mixture of competing ideas simmered like the discordant babble of languages used to greet kings upon their arrival at Gallic cities.[37] Establishing royal authority in a heterogeneous society presented other, more practical difficulties. Even though Clovis and his successors had eliminated rival Frankish royal dynasties, they were not able to resolve the tensions within their own family. Successive marriages and concubinage produced many brothers, half-brothers and cousins who competed with their fathers, their uncles and each other, and the lingering unresolved implications of the initial division of territories in 511 among all Merovingian sons also challenged the establishment of strong royal authority. The early administration of Clermont and the Auvergne provides one example of this ongoing uncertainty. Upon Clovis' death Theuderic had inherited Clermont as an outlying part of his Austrasian kingdom. But because of the haphazard division of the cities in Aquitaine other kings had interests in the region, and disloyalty was endemic. When it was rumoured that Theuderic had been killed, some local Roman aristocrats offered to betray Clermont to King Childebert. In 524 Theuderic took his revenge. Although he was unable to take Clermont itself, he did turn his army loose to pillage the Auvergne. He then left behind, 'as if for protection', a relative named Sigivald, who now served as a duke. But a few years later Theuderic had Sigivald killed and tried to convince his son Theudebert to kill Sigivald's son too. The promotion of a relative, especially in an outlying city, was perhaps still too much of a challenge to a Merovingian king's authority. In 555 Chlothar inherited Clermont and immediately sent his son Chramn to the Auvergne. Chramn soon began to act like an autonomous king by appointing a new count and terrorising the bishop. But when Chramn seized Poitiers and Limoges 'for his own lordship', his father sent two other sons against him and eventually had him killed.[38] The promotion of a son in an outlying region also raised the possibility of a challenge to a Merovingian king, especially one who reigned too long, and in particular when local aristocrats supported the son in preference to the father. Yet sometimes kings had no choice. When Guntramn remarried, he sent a son by a former mistress to Orléans; and Childebert II later sent an infant son to Soissons and Meaux at the request of local notables. Gregory's comparison of the war between Chlothar and Chramn to the usurpation of Absalom (another long-haired royal son!) neatly encapsulated the dilemma facing the Merovingian kings as they struggled to consolidate their authority.[39] Although the multiplicity of royal courts preserved the rule

37 Fortunatus, *Carmina* VI.2.7–8, Charibert greeted at Paris by 'barbarians' (i.e. Franks) and Romans in their own languages; Gregory, *Hist.* VIII.1.370–1, Guntramn greeted at Orléans by acclamations in 'the languages of Syrians, Latins, and even Jews'.

38 Sigivald: Gregory, *Hist.* III.13.109–10, V.12.201; *Vita Patrum* XII.2.262–3. 'Rex Chramnus': Gregory, *Hist.* IV.13.144.

39 Gregory, *Hist.* IV.20.153, Absalom; IV.25.156, Guntramn; IX.36.457, Childebert.

of the Merovingian family by hampering local aristocrats from establishing themselves as autonomous rulers, it also increased the potential for feuding among the Merovingians themselves.

Each Merovingian king extended his royal authority through the appointment of magistrates, 'counts, domestics, mayors, guardians, and everyone else required for imposing royal control'. Officials serving at the royal courts included mayors of the palace, counts of the palace, counts of the stables and domestics, who might all also function as generals, judges or ambassadors; *referendarii*, secretaries who kept the king's ring, as well as stenographers and clerks; and stewards who administered the royal treasures. Since the Merovingian kings were often leading military campaigns or roving among their various lodges and villas, these court officials were travelling companions as well as royal agents and administrators. Other royal magistrates served outside the courts. Because the Merovingian kingdoms did not respect the boundaries of the old Roman provinces, the largest administrative units that survived from the Roman Empire were the cities, that each usually still included an urban centre and a large surrounding rural hinterland. For many of the cities under their control, kings appointed counts with various responsibilities, including dispensing justice, collecting taxes, and enrolling and often also commanding the local military levies. Kings also appointed dukes, who often commanded armies, sometimes served as ambassadors, but soon became local administrators of larger regions within the kingdoms. During the sixth century the kings of Austrasia appointed dukes for Champagne, for the Touraine and Poitou, for eastern Aquitaine and especially the Auvergne, and for Marseilles and a part of Provence. The kings of Neustria appointed dukes for Soissons and the surrounding area, for the region between the Somme and the Loire, and for Toulouse and a part of Aquitaine that included Bordeaux. The kings of Burgundy appointed dukes for Orléans and the surrounding area, for a collection of cities in Aquitaine, and for Arles and a part of Provence. In Provence the governors were usually known by such Roman titles as rectors, prefects or patricians. Dukes commonly supervised, or at least had higher rank than, the counts within their regions, although there were few counts in most of Austrasia and in Provence. So because these royal administrations combined new and traditional elements, they were certainly neither systematic nor uniform. Shaping and imposing a Merovingian administration in Gaul was an ongoing process throughout the sixth century.[40]

Merovingian authority also rested upon the ability of the kings to accumulate wealth. Rivalries and warfare were two important sources. During their

[40] Gregory, *Hist.* IX.36.457, list; Selle-Hosbach (1974); Weidemann (1982), I, pp. 24–106. Counts: Claude (1964); Murray (1986), (1988). Dukes: Lewis (1976). Provence: Buchner (1933), pp. 15–25, 86–108.

military campaigns kings accumulated much booty, and some neighbours paid tribute after being defeated. Some of their wealth also came from the more or less systematic collection of revenues within Gaul. After taking over the old imperial estates, confiscating the properties of their opponents and rivals, and accepting many gifts, the kings were first of all great landowners who collected payments and services (or consumed the produce) from their own estates. The kings' agents also collected various tolls and fines, as well as the fees required as payments for the arbitration of kings or their representatives in judicial disputes. And finally the kings' agents collected taxes from the lands owned by both individuals and institutions such as churches and cities. In some respects the Merovingians seem to have continued aspects of the old Roman tax system, not least because their agents kept registers and conducted periodic reassessments. But in a larger context of the redefinition of authority the collection of revenues was a precise gauge of the kings' success at extending their influence throughout Gaul. Because during their incessant campaigns throughout Gaul the kings' armies often looted cities, churches and individuals, perhaps it is best to think of these taxes as polite forms of plunder, tokens of intimidation and subordination, rather than as an indication of the imposition of a proper fiscal system for raising revenues. The payment of taxes was the monetary counterpart to the oaths of allegiance that kings expected from the cities under their control. Kings sent counts to cities in order to extract both oaths of loyalty and the taxes; in return, one count once visited Childebert's court in order to present the taxes he had collected as 'the servitude that was owed to the royal treasury'.[41]

For the Merovingian kings sometimes seem to have thought of themselves less as heads of state or chief magistrates in a hierarchy of administrators than as great proprietors who were protecting their interests and their possessions, both personal and public. Justice, for instance, often became a commodity that people purchased rather than the result of the uniform enforcement of a set of values or regulations by kings and their agents; even when kings issued edicts or promulgated law-codes, they seem to have been primarily concerned about imitating Roman emperors and creating a consensus among their subjects.[42] Their kingdoms too were less territorial states than sources of revenue. When Guntramn and Childebert agreed upon the division of various cities, they seemed more interested in the revenues than in the actual territorial boundaries, and their fractional interests in cities represented proportions of the taxes. By defining themselves and their authority in terms of their resources,

[41] Gregory, *Hist.* x.21.519. Royal estates: Ewig (1965), pp. 152–5. Revenues: Goffart (1982); Durliat (1990), pp. 97–121. Coinage: Grierson and Blackburn (1986), pp. 811–54; Hendy (1988), pp. 59–70.

[42] Wormald (1977); Wood (1994), pp. 102–19.

these kings constantly had to negotiate (or fight) with others interested in the same assets. Their policy of granting fiscal immunities was hence a form of diplomacy with other powerful notables and institutions. Churches and shrines requested, and sometimes insisted upon, immunity from taxation for their properties. Theudebert, for instance, demonstrated his royal justice and generosity by remitting the taxes of churches in the Auvergne. Since these churches, like others elsewhere, constantly acquired more properties that were still liable for taxes, at the end of the sixth century Childebert again remitted their taxes. Chlothar II seems finally to have granted to churches and clerics a more extensive privilege that conferred immunity also upon lands acquired in the future.[43] The Franks likewise resisted the imposition of taxation upon their lands, since it could be taken as a sign of subordination and would hence subtly change the relationship between themselves and their kings. They therefore stoned to death one royal official who had inflicted them with taxes; and after one count had forced some Franks to pay the 'public tax', these Franks responded to this affront to their 'freedom' by burning his house.[44] As the notion of 'Frank' hence gradually became associated more with freedom from taxation than with ethnic origins, the acquisition of immunities became one method of assimilation with the Franks.

Having accumulated their wealth the Merovingian kings had to find ways of spending it. Under the Roman Empire the major expense for emperors had been the enormous army, most of whose legions had been camped on various frontiers. But the Merovingian kings kept no large standing army and instead relied on local levies, garrisons and armed retainers for each campaign. By Roman standards their armies were comparatively small, often only a few thousand or a few hundred men; and because their campaigns, whether within Gaul or against neighbours, produced so much booty and so many captives who could be ransomed, the armies were virtually self-supporting. Unlike Roman armies, the armies of the Frankish kings and their magistrates were furthermore not intended to fortify outlying frontiers. Instead, military campaigns were too often simply manifestations of royal (and aristocratic) concerns about manliness and prestige, and the armies of the kings and their magistrates frequently terrorised their own subjects. The devastating impact of one army as it marched through western Gaul was comparable to the destruction caused by a swarm of locusts of biblical proportions. In the evaluation of Gregory of Tours, this army was another 'natural disaster' like frost, storm or drought. In many respects the Merovingians and their armies seem to have treated

43 Gregory, *Hist.* III.25.123, X.7.488; Chlothar II, *Praeceptio*, *MGH Cap.* 1, 8, c.11.19. Immunities: Murray (1994); Fouracre (1995).

44 Gregory, *Hist.* III.36.131–2, VII.15.336–7.

warfare like sport; so when one supporter of Sigibert came upon a son of Chilperic, 'with horns and bugles he pursued him like a fleeing deer'.[45] The Franks and their kings obviously enjoyed the chase, and some of their small-scale military campaigns were similar to hunting expeditions. In fact, after King Chlothar had killed his son Chramn, he requested forgiveness and then went hunting. But Chlothar died from a fever he contracted during this hunt; his nephew Theudebert had been mortally injured in a bizarre accident while hunting, crushed by a tree knocked over by a wild bull; and Chilperic too was assassinated while hunting. During the sixth century the kings who survived royal feuds were more likely to die while hunting than while on military campaigns.

Since the Merovingians therefore had limited military expenses, they used their wealth to bolster their own prestige and authority. The sheer accumulation of valuable objects was a visible manifestation of their standing. Chilperic once tried to impress Bishop Gregory by displaying the gold coins that he had received from the Byzantine emperor; he also showed the bishop an enormous bejewelled gold platter that he had had fashioned 'for the ennoblement of the Frankish people'. Kings, then, dispersed their wealth as gifts that confirmed their relationships with retainers and subjects. In order to acquire or ensure the support of local aristocrats kings distributed estates and treasures; given their mutual interests in warfare and hunting, their gifts often included horses, dogs, hawks, even hunting horns. As the kings appointed many of these same men as court officials, counts and dukes, they clearly relied more on the obligations of these personal ties than on more impersonal notions of bureaucratic authority and efficiency to maintain their magistrates' loyalty. Their wealth was the means for ensuring these personal links and for maintaining royal power, and when one king wanted to appropriate another's kingdom, his first concern was to confiscate his rival's treasury. So upon Chlothar's death in 561 Chilperic seized his father's treasury, sought out the most powerful Franks, and tried to win their allegiance with gifts. The royal treasuries also included the royal archives in which kings kept records of their gifts, not so much to ensure legal title as rather to document the expansion of their influence and the establishment of obligations.[46]

With their wealth, kings could also subsidise some of the trappings of high culture. Although Gregory of Tours may have bemoaned the decline of literary studies, in fact familiarity with classical culture had certainly not disappeared

[45] Gregory, *Hist.* VI.45.319, for locusts; IV.47.183–4, for deer; Bachrach (1972).

[46] Gregory, *Hist.* VI.2.266 and VII.4.328, platter; IV.22.154–5, Chlothar's treasury; X.19.510–13, archives. Expenses: Durliat (1990), pp. 122–30.

in Gaul, either among aristocrats or among churchmen.[47] Many exchanged letters; some, including some bishops, acquired reputations as poets. An illustrious poet such as Fortunatus, who had received a proper classical education in northern Italy, was duly impressed, not least because these aristocrats and bishops also solicited his work. His patrons included the Merovingian kings, some of whom successfully transformed even themselves into learned gentlemen. Clovis had once requested that the Ostrogothic king Theoderic send him a lyre-player; two generations later Chilperic was encouraging education for the boys in his kingdom, ordering old books to be recopied, and even proposing to add letters to the alphabet. He also tried his hand at composing poems, although Gregory, who candidly acknowledged his own difficulty in writing Latin, nevertheless dismissed the king's poems as unmetrical![48]

Another way for the Merovingian kings to display their wealth was by subsidising the construction of buildings and the endowment of institutions in various cities. Chilperic, for instance, built arenas both in his own capital city of Soissons and in Paris. In the latter case, not only was he imitating the behaviour of the Roman emperors who had once presided at circus games, he was also defying the threats of his brother Guntramn and nephew Childebert by staking a claim to the whole of the capital city of his deceased brother Charibert's kingdom.[49] Clovis had set another precedent by supporting saints' cults. He and Queen Clothild had once constructed a church at Paris near the tomb of St Genovefa (St Geneviéve), a contemporary ascetic. Both they and some of their royal descendants were buried in this church, which eventually was also dedicated to the Holy Apostles, perhaps in imitation of the church in which the first Christian emperor Constantine had been buried at Constantinople, and to St Peter, the illustrious patron saint of Rome. So in the process of promoting a local saint's cult Clovis had openly linked himself and his dynasty with the imperial overtones of the great capitals of the Roman Empire. His successors promoted other cults. Also at Paris Childebert constructed a church in honour of St Vincentius, a Spanish martyr whose relics he had acquired apparently during his campaign against the Visigoths. At Soissons Chlothar and his son Sigibert constructed a church in honour of St Medard, the former bishop of Noyon, and Chilperic composed a poem about the saint. At Chalon-sur-Saône Guntramn built, or rebuilt, a church in honour of St Marcellus, an obscure local martyr, and richly endowed both it and a monastery.[50]

47 See Fontaine, chapter 27 below.

48 Clovis: Cassiodorus, *Variae* II.40.70–2. Chilperic: Gregory, *Hist.* V.44.253–4 and VI.46.319–21; for a surviving poem, see *Ymnus in solemnitate S. Medardi*, ed. K. Strecker, *MGH Poetae* IV.2.455–7. The best survey of early medieval education and culture is still by Riché (1962).

49 Gregory, *Hist.* V.17.214–15.

50 Van Dam (1993), pp. 22–8.

ARISTOCRATS AND CHURCHMEN

For all the Merovingians' success in establishing themselves as kings in Gaul, royal authority was still fundamentally fragile. Their relationships with saints' cults provide the first clues. The Merovingians preferred to patronise new cults for new saints, some of whom, such as St Medard certainly and St Genovefa probably, had even had Frankish ancestors. In contrast, they had difficulty ingratiating themselves with established saints' cults. Clovis was thought to have gone into battle against the Visigoths in 507 with the support of St Hilary, the patron saint of Poitiers; but there is no evidence that any of his royal successors during the sixth century subsidised the saint's church at Poitiers or his cult elsewhere in Gaul. After his victory over the Visigoths, Clovis had visited Tours and the church of St Martin, the patron saint of the most prominent cult in late Roman and early Merovingian Gaul. But Clovis soon retired to Paris; according to a later, probably apocryphal, story, after the king had had to pay twice what he intended in order to retrieve his horse from the saint's church, he admitted that St Martin drove a hard bargain for his assistance. His royal successors seem to have agreed tacitly that the price for St Martin's support was too high. When challenged about the taxes they tried to impose on Tours they consistently backed down and conceded exemptions. Chlothar once helped to finance a new tin roof for the church of St Martin after it burned in 559, but during the sixth century he was also the only reigning king to visit Tours and pray at the saint's tomb. Even when other kings wished to consult with St Martin they did not go in person. Chilperic instead sent a letter that was placed on the saint's tomb, along with a blank sheet of paper for the saint's response; significantly, St Martin did not reply. During the sixth century the cult of St Martin was not closely associated with the Frankish kings. In the face of such an influential and long-established cult the Merovingians were duly intimidated, and the patronage of their preferred saints' cults at Paris, Soissons and Chalon-sur-Saône effectively created a buffer of shrines between the centre of St Martin's power at Tours and their own primary interests in northern and eastern Gaul.[51]

This ambivalence about saints' cults reappeared in the uneasy relationship between kings and bishops. Kings often tried to subordinate bishops to their control, in particular by meddling in their selection. Although churchmen and church councils may have repeatedly claimed that the people and clergy should select new bishops, increasingly the kings' preferences became decisive. In 549 a council at Orléans conceded the role of kings by announcing that in the selection of a new bishop no less than 'ancient canons' had sanctioned the

[51] Bargain: *Liber Historiae Francorum* c.17.271. Chlothar: Gregory, *Hist.* IV.20–1.152–4 and VI.9.279; Baudonivia, *Vita Radegundis* cc.6–7, p. 382. Chilperic's letter: Gregory, *Hist.* V.14.211.

importance of the king's wish as well as election by clergy and congregation. As royal appointees some bishops, like the counts and dukes, even took oaths of loyalty to their kings.[52] And just as kings convened their notables for assemblies, so they convened bishops in councils. Already in 511 Clovis had summoned to a council at Orléans many bishops who duly hailed him as the 'son of the Catholic church'. Subsequent kings tried to reinforce (and appropriate) the decisions of councils by issuing their own edicts.[53]

But bishops were not passive in the face of this royal interference in ecclesiastical affairs. First, the support of powerful patron saints transformed bishops too into autonomous, or at least intimidating, figures. Various kings, as we have noted, had often marched against Clermont. Yet in 524, after learning first about the saints' churches that surrounded the city as 'enormous fortifications' and then about the city's bishop, 'who had great influence in the presence of God', King Theuderic quickly retreated. If the Frankish kings were comparable to the kings of Israel, then the bishops were the equivalents of the prophets who advised and admonished them; so Gregory of Tours pointedly noted that Solomon, the wisest of all kings, had nevertheless owed his throne to a prophet's support. When Fortunatus applied Byzantine imperial ideology to Childebert, he too was careful to protect the authority of bishops and clerics by emphasising that the king had performed his 'religious task' (in this case, subsidising the cathedral at Paris) while still a layman. Bishops would not let kings forget that they alone controlled access to the miraculous power of saints. Guntramn was the only Merovingian king credited with performing a miraculous healing; but even then Gregory neatly transformed the significance of the miracle by noting that the king was merely acting 'like a good bishop'.[54]

Second, with the collapse of the Roman administration bishops had become important local leaders, in part because their sees and dioceses coincided with cities and their territories. After the disappearance of the Roman army not only was the church the largest institution in Merovingian Gaul, but its influence obviously transcended the boundaries of kingdoms. Its bishops often met in provincial and regional councils, and its hierarchy included thousands of priests, deacons and lesser clerics. In fact, there were probably as many clerics serving each of the fifteen or so metropolitan bishops and the more than one hundred other bishops as there were functionaries at each of the two or

52 Council of Orléans a. 549, Can. 10, pp. 151–2. Oaths: Gregory, *Hist.* x.9.492; Bertramn of Le Mans, *Testamentum*, ed. Weidemann (1986), p. 15.

53 Council of Orléans a. 511, *Epistola ad Regem* p.4. Royal edict of Guntramn, *MGH Cap.* 1, 5, pp. 11–12; edict of Chlothar II, *MGH Cap.* 1, 9, pp. 20–3.

54 Gregory, *Vita Patrum* IV.2.225, Clermont; *Hist.* I.12.13–14, Solomon; IX.21.441–2, Guntramn Fortunatus, *Carmina* II.10.22, 'conplevit laicus religionis opus'.

three royal courts. And since bishops also administered the often numerous properties and estates that belonged to their churches and shrines, they too could justifiably claim to preside from a 'throne' in their cathedrals. When king Chilperic once surveyed the wealth of churches, he complained, with a hint of resignation, that only bishops 'reigned' in their cities. These enormous resources allowed bishops to assume many social and municipal services. They financed numerous construction projects, including most obviously churches and shrines; they supported hospitals, asylums and almshouses; and they ransomed slaves and prisoners.[55]

Finally, many of the bishops in Gaul were descendants of old Roman aristocratic families that had adopted service in the ecclesiastical hierarchy as yet another strategy for retaining their local influence. Not only did some of them therefore have impressive pedigrees that stretched well back into the Roman period, but many were also members of families that had come to dominate particular sees already since the fifth century. When at the beginning of the sixth century the wife of one Roman aristocrat announced that she was 'pregnant with a bishop', she was candidly articulating the expectations not only of her own family, but of many old Roman aristocratic families. Her prediction was also correct, despite the fluctuations of royal politics; although her husband had declined appointment as bishop of Geneva from the Burgundian king Gundobad, her son succeeded his uncle as bishop of Lyons with the support of the Frankish king Childebert. The emergence of 'family sees' hence imposed a tacit restriction on the power of kings to appoint bishops.[56]

Some bishops had furthermore themselves previously held royal magistracies, and their relatives were still serving the Frankish kings as magistrates, advisers or army commanders. Roman aristocrats had obviously not disappeared. In central and southern Gaul in particular, various families that had come to prominence in the Roman Empire, and then maintained it under Visigothic and Burgundian rule, retained their influence well into the sixth century under the Franks. Not only did few Franks settle south of the Loire, but for these regions the Merovingian kings often appointed Roman aristocrats as counts. Despite the close ties of Clermont with the kingdom of Austrasia, for instance, all but one of the known counts from the sixth century were members of local Roman aristocratic families; at Tours King Chilperic once allowed the people to choose their own count. Even in northern Gaul Roman aristocrats prospered, such as Eleutherius, who was a count before becoming

[55] Bishops' rule: Gregory, *Hist.* VI.46.319–21, *In Gloria Martyrum* c.33, pp. 58–9. Episcopal power: Scheibelreiter (1983); Van Dam (1985); Klingshirn (1985), (1994). Ecclesiastical wealth: Thiele (1969).

[56] Gregory, *Vita Patrum* VIII.1.214, pregnancy; Fortunatus, *Carmina* IV.3.2, 'patriae sedes'. Pedigrees of bishops: Heinzelmann (1976).

bishop of Tournai.[57] Until the early seventh century Roman aristocrats furthermore dominated the great bishoprics at such important northern cities as Trier, Cologne and Mainz. Romans also began to marry Franks, and to adopt their activities and nomenclature. Although leading Franks, including the Merovingians, learned classical culture, after the fourth century they no longer adopted Roman names; in contrast, German names became increasingly common in Roman families. Gregory of Tours, for instance, had a great uncle named Gundulf who was born in the early sixth century. The interests of their new Frankish overlords in hunting and warfare influenced even the Romans who kept Latin or at least Latin-German names; so Lupus ('wolf'), a Roman who served as a duke under Sigibert and Childebert, had a brother name Magnulf ('great wolf') and a son named Romulf ('Roman wolf') who became bishop of Rheims.[58]

In addition to these Roman aristocrats the Merovingians also had to contend with other powerful notables, in northern Gaul in particular, who came from their original Frankish supporters, from other groups of Franks, or from non-Frankish peoples who had only recently been included under Merovingian rule. With the acquisition of land and offices these men too gradually transformed themselves into local aristocrats, 'men distinguished by their birth', 'the foremost men', 'the most noble among their own people', 'those with influence at the king's court'. Although the development of an aristocracy among the Franks remains an obscure process, these descriptions used by Gregory of Tours, admittedly imprecise, already stressed the prerogatives that the members of some families possessed from birth. These Frankish notables also followed the lead of Roman aristocrats in building up their control over and possession of land. Many of their estates and villas they acquired by purchase or confiscation, some as grants from the Merovingians; these lands then passed among family members by inheritances and marriages. Aristocrats accumulated much wealth. Duke Rauching's wife, for instance, paraded through Soissons wearing her jewels and gold ornaments; Rauching himself, to the amazement of King Childebert's retainers, possessed more wealth than the royal treasury. Frankish aristocrats furthermore recruited dependants who supported their lords as armed retainers during feuds and battles. In many respects these new aristocratic families resembled not only old Roman aristocratic families but also the most successful of the Frankish families, the Merovingians, with whom they feasted and hunted and fought and to whom they sometimes provided wives. Kings and aristocrats were locked as partners in a relationship of reciprocal

[57] Gregory, *Hist.* v.47.257, count at Tours; Weidemann (1982), I, pp. 70–3, 77–80. Eleutherius: *Vita Medardi* c.6, p. 68. Survival of Roman aristocracy: Stroheker (1948); Heinzelmann (1975).

[58] Names and ethnicity: Geary (1985), pp. 101–14.

dependence, each propping up the other.[59] Kings needed aristocrats to serve as magistrates, advisers, generals and soldiers, while aristocrats relied upon kings to bestow land, offices and prestige. Yet aristocrats and kings were simultaneously competing for the same limited resources, in particular control over land and subordinates; and bishops too, in their role as administrators of church lands and possessions, were the equivalents of great landowners. Powerful bishops and powerful aristocrats, both Roman and Frankish, hence shared, and sometimes dominated, the political spotlight with the Merovingian kings.

The interaction among kings, aristocrats and bishops was early apparent in Austrasia. Theuderic had inherited the kingdom of Rheims upon Clovis' death, and he soon sent his son Theudebert to campaign in southern Gaul against the Visigoths. Some of the Roman aristocrats Theudebert met there eventually served him as advisers or magistrates after he became king. One was Parthenius, whose ancestors and relatives included a former emperor, a former prefect of Rome and several bishops in central and southern Gaul. He himself had studied in Ravenna before returning to Theudebert's court with the Roman title of patrician. Perhaps because of the influence of these Roman advisers, Theudebert began to develop imperial pretensions. He was the first Frankish king to infringe on an imperial prerogative by minting gold coins bearing his own portrait; he invaded Italy; he politely informed the eastern emperor Justinian that his kingdom also included many of the peoples between the Rhine and the Danube; and he supposedly even contemplated marching across central Europe to attack Constantinople! Theudebert was hence yet another example of a 'Romanised Frank' in northern Gaul; in fact, when he came to the throne in 534 he already had a son with his Roman wife.[60]

But because his uncles plotted against him after his father's death, Theudebert owed his accession primarily to the protection of his *leudes*, his Frankish supporters bound to him by an oath of allegiance. These retainers may well also have been among the Franks who soon compelled Theudebert to abandon his Roman wife in favour of a Lombard princess, and who eventually lynched Parthenius for having imposed taxes on their lands. Theudebert's son and successor Theudebald may have been half-Frank and half-Roman, but initially influential Franks dominated his court too. The bishops of Aquitaine knew

[59] Gregory, *Hist.* IX.9.421–4, Rauching; Fortunatus, *Carmina* VI.1.19, on Sigibert and his dukes: 'culmina tot procerum concurrunt culmen ad unum'. Development of a Frankish aristocracy: Irsigler (1969); Grahn-Hoek (1976); Halsall (1995), pp. 33–9. Archaeology of aristocratic graves: James (1979), (1988), pp. 58–67. One prominent family: Nonn (1975); Weidemann (1986).

[60] Parthenius: Heinzelmann (1982), p. 663. Theudebert: Procopius, *Wars* VII.23.5–6, gold coins; *Epistolae Austrasicae* XX, p. 133, letter to Justinian; Agathias, *Hist.* I.4.1–4, Byzantine suspicions; Collins (1983).

who was in control: when they met in 551 to select a new bishop for Clermont, they were concerned not about the king's preference, but rather that of his 'magnates and chief men', who in fact did impose their own choice.[61] Theudebald was hence an early example of a young king who was effectively powerless in the face of domination by aristocrats.

Not all bishops were so deferential before these great aristocrats, however. One of Theuderic's legacies to his successors was bishop Nicetius of Trier. Nicetius had acquired his see in 525 with the support of Theuderic and other 'men distinguished with great honor at the king's court'. Among his clergy were men from cities in Aquitaine that Theuderic and then his successors controlled; he also corresponded with churchmen in northern Italy and a Lombard queen; and he even wrote an admonitory letter to the emperor Justinian. Much of Nicetius' wider influence and reputation hence mirrored the extensive interests of the Austrasian kings in central Gaul, central Europe and Byzantine Italy. But Nicetius also constructed, on a hill overlooking the Moselle, a large castle that he fortified with saints' relics (and, just in case, a catapult). From this fortress he was powerful enough to challenge a whole succession of Frankish kings and even compel them to become 'more meek'. He threatened Theuderic's supporters for grazing their horses in the fields of the poor; he banned from the Eucharist some of Theudebert's men whom he accused of homicide and sexual misconduct; he often excommunicated Chlothar, who in turn sent him into exile; and he once announced that an angel of the Lord had revealed to him an evaluation of each king's reign. One of his Italian correspondents neatly acknowledged Nicetius' multi-layered influence by requesting his assistance both with King Theudebald and with various saints in heaven. The kings of Austrasia may have had more extensive diplomatic connections than the other Merovingian kings, but not even they could match Nicetius' connections at the court of the King of Heaven. Sigibert finally seems to have understood what he was facing, because upon inheriting the kingdom of Austrasia in 561 he immediately requested Nicetius' blessing.[62]

Competition among factions of powerful aristocrats and bishops became particularly fierce again with the accession of the young Childebert, in particular during arguments over which uncle ought to be his ally. After Sigibert's assassination in 575 Duke Gundovald had immediately had Childebert proclaimed king in Austrasia. Childebert's first *nutricius*, or guardian, was Gogo, another 'Romanised Frank' who was familiar enough with classical culture to

[61] Gregory, *Hist.* IV.6–7.139–40.

[62] Gregory, *Vita Patrum* XVII.277–83, a *Vita* of Nicetius; Fortunatus, *Carmina* III.11–12, castle; *Epistolae Austrasicae* V, VI, XI, XXI, XXIV, pp. 116–18, 126–7, 133–4, 137–8 for letters to Nicetius; VII–VIII, pp. 118–22, for Nicetius' letters to Justinian and a Lombard queen.

write his own letters and poems.[63] Gogo was presumably among the king's 'leading men' who supported an alliance with King Guntramn of Burgundy. But other powerful figures in the kingdom were bishop Egidius of Rheims and Duke Guntramn Boso. Both had been prominent supporters of Sigibert, Egidius by consecrating bishops for cities that the king was trying to control, Guntramn Boso by commanding the army that had killed one of Chilperic's sons; both had also apparently not been among Childebert's early advisers. By 581, however, Egidius had become a dominant figure at Childebert's court and was a member of the embassies of 'leading men' who negotiated a new alliance with Chilperic. With the support of other notables in Childebert's kingdom Duke Guntramn Boso had meanwhile invited Gundovald, who claimed to be another son of Chlothar, back from exile in Constantinople; King Guntramn was particularly annoyed by the challenge this pretender posed. The increasing predominance of Egidius and Guntramn Boso led to the reorientation of Childebert's court away from Guntramn and towards Chilperic. But the influence of both Egidius and Guntramn Boso soon began to fade. In 583 Childebert's army rioted against Egidius for having 'sold' their kingdom; soon thereafter Childebert made another alliance with Guntramn. A year later when Egidius and Guntramn Boso represented Childebert at Guntramn's court, the king became so infuriated that he had the envoys showered with manure and mud; and in the next year he warned Childebert against accepting Egidius' advice. Yet another faction had meanwhile developed around Brunehild, Childebert's mother. During her son's minority her influence had waned. Thus some powerful Franks had forcefully reminded her that Childebert was now under their protection, and Guntramn Boso had repeatedly insulted her. But after Childebert came of age, his mother reasserted her domination and took her revenge. Although Guntramn Boso requested the assistance of important bishops, both Childebert and King Guntramn agreed that he should be executed. Egidius was at first successful in deflecting suspicion from himself by bringing gifts to Childebert, until in 590 he was accused of treason and finally deposed by an ecclesiastical council.

In the kingdom of Austrasia various combinations of Frankish aristocrats, Roman aristocrats and bishops competed for influence at the royal court. For their purposes, rule by a king in his minority was attractive, since it allowed them to pose as his champions. In fact, in 587 some Austrasian aristocrats schemed to kill Childebert, who even though only seventeen years old had nevertheless attained his majority, in order to promote his infant sons as kings under their control. Yet even adult kings were surprised, and irritated, at the

[63] *Epistolae Austrasicae* XIII, XVI, XXII, pp. 128, 130, 134–5, Gogo's letters; XLVIII, pp. 152–3, a letter written in Childebert's name. Fortunatus, *Carmina* VII.2.3, described Gogo as another Cicero.

unruliness and autonomy of their nominally subject aristocrats and bishops. The shifting treaties of the Austrasian kings were indicators not so much of their own considered policies, as of the fluctuating influence of various factions of aristocrats who were in turn allied with other notables elsewhere.

Even if they are not as well documented, similar aristocratic and episcopal factions existed in other Frankish kingdoms, and the kings there likewise needed their support. Immediately upon his father Chlothar's death in 561, Chilperic had tried to win the support of important Franks with gifts. After Sigibert's assassination Chilperic was able to attract into his service Franks who had previously served his brother. When these Franks later abandoned him in favour of Childebert, Ansovald received some of their estates around Soissons. Ansovald was presumably among the 'leading men' who joined bishop Leudovald of Bayeux in confirming Chilperic's alliance with Childebert in 581; three years later he and other notables ensured that the infant Chlothar II became king upon his father Chilperic's assassination. In contrast to the early disdain for Brunehild among the aristocrats of Austrasia, initially these notables seem to have supported Chlothar's mother Fredegund. So when Guntramn quickly tried to minimise Fredegund's influence by banishing her to an estate near Rouen, 'all the men distinguished by birth in king Chilperic's kingdom' accompanied her into exile. But Fredegund's subsequent actions split that consensus. Some Franks, such as Ansovald, continued to support her; but the leading Franks at Rouen became angry at her suspected connivance in the assassination of the city's bishop, and the Franks at Tournai were upset at her lethal interference in a local feud. Since Fredegund nevertheless remained dominant at Chlothar's court, these Franks could only appeal to royal courts elsewhere. In 589, for instance, the 'leading men' at Soissons and Meaux requested Childebert to establish one of his sons as their king to help them resist their enemies (by which they presumably meant Fredegund and her supporters).[64]

As their father by adoption, Guntramn could pose as arbiter for both Childebert II and Chlothar II. Yet he was also a somewhat odd mediator for his nephews and these northern kingdoms with their more extensive settlements of Franks, since with his preference for Chalon-sur-Saône as his residence at the expense of Orléans, he seems also to have turned from Frankish supporters towards other local notables. Unlike the Visigoths who had abandoned Aquitaine after being defeated by Clovis, the Burgundians had remained as a distinct ethnic group in east central Gaul; Guntramn was sensitive enough about their support that he named his first son Gundobad. Guntramn also came to rely upon members of the old Roman families that remained prominent in

[64] Gregory, *Hist.* VII.9.331, support for Fredegund; IX.36.457, request to Childebert.

eastern Gaul. Some served as his high-ranking magistrates, such as Mummolus, who held the offices of count, patrician or duke for over a decade; others served as bishops, such as the ancestors of Gregory of Tours at Langres and Lyons. Even Mummolus' defection to the pretender Gundovald during the early 580s was not enough to upset the king's relationships with these old Roman families. Only after Guntramn's death did Frankish notables begin to claim a dominant position in the kingdom of Burgundy, in part as a reaction to the continued reliance of Brunehild, Sigibert's widow, on Roman aristocrats.[65]

THE LIMITS OF MEROVINGIAN RULE

Surrounding the core of Frankish kingdoms were other regions more or less subservient to the Merovingian kings. In some regions the Merovingians appointed, or perhaps simply acknowledged, various dukes, such as the duke of the Alamans, the duke of the Vascones in the western Pyrenees, and the duke of the Bavarians. Just as some families came to dominate particular episcopal sees or countships within Gaul, so in Bavaria the family of the Agilolfings came to monopolise the office of duke. Since these dukes, unlike those who served at the court of the Merovingians or administered particular regions in the Merovingian kingdoms, ruled over distinct ethnic groups, they had much local support and tended to act independently of the Merovingians, and even to make war on them occasionally.[66] One peripheral region that clearly maintained its local autonomy was Brittany. During the sixth century the four counts who each ruled a small 'kingdom' in Brittany were nominally under Frankish domination, but they also repeatedly attacked neighbouring cities and even provided asylum for men escaping the Merovingians. Although the use of Frankish clothing and weapons spread among the Roman population in the rest of central Gaul, Bretons nevertheless retained a distinctive ethnic hairstyle and costume.[67]

The limits of Merovingian rule were particularly evident in the large region of Aquitaine, which was rarely brought firmly under Frankish control. As we have seen, the early Merovingians had adopted different strategies, such as sending a relative or a son to protect their interests. Clovis' grandsons decided to rely upon local aristocrats and bishops, even when they were uneasy doing so. They clearly did not always trust their own magistrates. When Chilperic appointed Desiderius, a Roman with lands near Albi, as duke over some cities in

[65] Ewig (1953), pp. 703–8.

[66] Alamannia: Keller (1976). Vascones (Basques): Collins (1986), pp. 82–98. Bavaria: Jarnut (1986).

[67] Gregory, *Hist.* IV.4.137–8 and X.9.491–4; Galliou and Jones (1991), pp. 128–47, and Davies, chapter 9 below.

western and southern Aquitaine, he also appointed Franks (or at least men with German names) as counts in some of the same cities. When Guntramn Boso served as duke for the Austrasian cities in eastern Aquitaine, Romans served as counts in some of the same cities. The challenge posed by the rise of the pretender Gundovald is a particularly interesting example of the predictable failure of these attempts at balancing aristocratic interests. Although he claimed to be a son of King Chlothar, for a time Gundovald lived in exile in Constantinople, until in 582 he returned to Gaul at the invitation of Guntramn Boso and other leading notables of the kingdom of Childebert II. Initially, therefore, Gundovald's return seems to have been part of the schemes of Guntramn Boso and his supporters against King Guntramn. But after Chilperic's assassination Gundovald could serve other purposes. When King Guntramn and King Childebert both tried to extend their control into Aquitaine, Mummolus, formerly a magistrate of King Guntramn, and the former Duke Desiderius (who had previously fought against Mummolus) had Gundovald proclaimed king near Limoges. From the cities that had once belonged to Sigibert, Gundovald extracted an oath of allegiance in Childebert's name; from the cities that had belonged to Chilperic or Guntramn, he received an oath in his own name. He also announced a plan to establish his residence at Paris. Gundovald therefore seems to have intended to promote himself as king of Neustria at the expense of the infant Chlothar II, and to revive the alliance between Neustria and Austrasia at the expense of Guntramn. More notables now supported him, among them Waddo, formerly a count of Chilperic, Bladast, formerly a duke of Chilperic, and various bishops, including Bertramn of Bordeaux. In 585 Guntramn finally defeated and killed Gundovald and some of his major supporters.[68]

The attempted usurpation of Gundovald illustrates the tendency for aristocratic interests to take priority over royal concerns; it also demonstrates that the Merovingians could not rely upon the loyalty of bishops either. The bishops of Bordeaux were particularly irrepressible and acquired reputations for reigning like kings in their episcopal sees. Bishop Leontius, for instance, possessed all the right prerequisites for acquiring local authority. He had inherited 'the sort of noble ancestry that the senate at Rome once possessed'; he had fought in one of the Frankish campaigns against the Visigoths; he had married a descendant of a Roman emperor; he owned several lovely villas; and he had hedged his bets by building churches for both St Vincentius, a distinctly royal saint, and St Martin, a distinctly non-royal saint. So when he once announced to Charibert his intention to replace the bishop of Saintes, he had his envoy claim to represent the 'apostolic see' (although this time the king neatly deflated Leontius'

[68] Goffart (1957); Rouche (1979), pp. 70–7.

pretensions by assuming, through a contrived misunderstanding, that the messenger was coming from Rome!).[69] His successor Bertramn was more directly involved in royal politics. In 577 he supported King Chilperic, who was annoyed at Bishop Praetextatus of Rouen for having married Merovech and Brunehild. After Chilperic's assassination Bertramn supported the pretender Gundovald. King Guntramn was particularly upset, not only because of the challenge to his rule but also because, as he later pointedly reminded the bishop, he and Bertramn were related (probably cousins) by marriage. During the sixth century Merovingian kings occasionally allied themselves through marriage with important Frankish aristocratic families; Guntramn himself had once been briefly married to the daughter of a Frankish duke. Guntramn had therefore probably expected more loyalty from Bertramn, one of the first Franks known to serve as a bishop in southern Gaul.[70]

Merovingian kings did not give up on Aquitaine. By the later sixth century they began to invite young aristocratic sons to be educated at their courts, almost as hostages against the good behaviour of their families, before appointing them to various positions. Three brothers from Albi, for instance, grew up at the court of Chlothar II. One became court chaplain and then bishop of Cahors; another became count of Albi and then prefect of Marseilles; the third, Desiderius, was steward of the royal treasury before succeeding one brother as prefect of Marseilles and then the other as bishop of Cahors.[71] For the problem of establishing royal control in Aquitaine was not necessarily a consequence of the survival of ethnic or regional awareness, as rather simply an indication of the difficulty of controlling outlying regions from remote royal courts in northern Gaul. The rise of the Merovingians marked a reversal in political viewpoint rather than a decline in administrative effectiveness. With their Mediterranean perspective Roman emperors had once worried about the creation of an autonomous 'Gallic Empire' in northern Gaul; Merovingian kings still worried about revolts, but now primarily in southern Gaul.[72]

Despite their local connections dukes and counts sometimes fared no better. 'No one fears the king', some dukes once told Guntramn; but in addition, 'no one respects a duke or a count'. In particular, even in cities that were important in Merovingian Gaul, such as Paris and Tours, bishops might become more influential than kings or their magistrates. Already under Clovis Paris had become an important centre of Frankish interests, and it had initially served as the capital of the kingdom of Childebert, who in 556 supported the

[69] Fortunatus, *Carmina* I.6–20, IV.10; Gregory, *Hist.* IV.26.158, 'apostolic see'.

[70] Gregory, *Hist.* IX.33.451–4; Ewig (1974), pp. 52–6.

[71] *Vita Desiderii Cadurcae urbis episcopi* cc.7–15.567–74; Durliat (1979). See also Fouracre, chapter 14 below.

[72] Contrast between northern and southern Gaul: Van Dam (1992).

selection of Germanus as bishop. After Childebert's death, however, subsequent kings could not establish lasting control at Paris, and after Charibert's death in 567 his three brothers had partitioned the city and agreed that none would enter it without the others' permission. Paris may have remained a 'royal city', but in contrast to the fragmented control by various kings only the bishop's power remained constant. Kings therefore competed for Germanus' favour. Chlothar, for instance, once requested Germanus' assistance when suffering from a fever; it vanished after he kissed the bishop's cloak. Chlothar was hence the only Frankish king during the sixth century who indicated his subordination to a bishop by allowing himself to be healed; most kings refused to send even their ill infant sons to saints' shrines for healing. Subsequently Germanus obtained from Chlothar a pardon for some prisoners. Later too, when Sigibert and Chilperic were fighting over control of Paris, Germanus demonstrated his autonomy by going to visit Guntramn instead. In this case his own family and personal connections may have been decisive, since he had previously served as abbot of a monastery dedicated to St Symphorien in his native city of Autun, which was part of Guntramn's kingdom. Guntramn clearly understood the importance of this association, since he now celebrated the saint's festival at Autun.[73] After Germanus' death in 576 Paris remained both attractive and technically off-limits to Frankish kings. Chilperic, for instance, may have wanted Bishop Ragnemod to baptise his son, but he entered Paris only when preceded by saints' relics that he hoped would ward off the curse for breaking the treaty with his brothers. So despite its historical and geographical significance to the Merovingian kings, political feuds and episcopal domination kept Paris peripheral to royal control for decades.

Tours was another city that remained on the edges of royal control throughout the sixth century, in part because it had become a focal point of one family's attempts to maintain its local standing in central Gaul. When Gregory became bishop in 573, he not only succeeded his mother's cousin, he also noted that almost all of his episcopal predecessors there had been his ancestors. Much of this continued influence was of course a consequence of successful marriage strategies; in Gregory's case, his father came from a prominent family in the Auvergne, and his mother from an even more prominent family in Burgundy. These families had been able to protect their local standing despite the transition from Visigoths and Burgundians to Franks by placing family members as bishops at Langres, Lyons and Clermont, as well as at Tours. Thus Chlothar conceded this to be 'one of the foremost distinguished families in the land'; and Guntramn still had dreams about some of Gregory's ancestors who had been

73 Fortunatus, *Vita Germani* cc.68–70, on Chlothar; Gregory, *Hist.* VIII.30.393–7, dukes' comment and Guntramn.

bishops in his kingdom. A second reason Tours remained peripheral to royal control was, again, the feuding among the various Frankish kings. Since Tours was just outside the nexus of capital cities, it usually ended up on the edges of the various kingdoms. During the early years of Gregory's episcopacy feuding among kings caused much misery for both the city and its new bishop. Gregory had in fact become bishop with the support of the Austrasian king Sigibert, who was trying to stake his claim to Tours in the face of Chilperic's opposition. After Sigibert's assassination in 575 Chilperic regained control, and for the next decade his and other royal armies periodically plundered the Touraine. Chilperic was also suspicious enough of Gregory's loyalties to the Austrasian court that in 580 he convened an episcopal council to hear an accusation that Gregory was scheming to return Tours to Childebert. Gregory was in an awkward position. Because the enormous prestige of St Martin, the patron saint of Tours, made kings hesitant to visit the city, Gregory spoke with them only when he visited their royal courts; yet the ceaseless feuding among kings prevented Gregory from visiting often enough to acquire much influence. In 580 the threat to his episcopal authority was so great that even a besotted relic-monger who happened to wander into Tours could threaten him with King Chilperic's vengeance.

But Gregory survived, and after Chilperic's assassination Guntramn soon returned Tours to Childebert. Since these two kings were generally trying to work together, the marginal location of Tours made it possible for Gregory to act as a broker. Gregory's episcopal standing now also intersected with his family's influence, because the maternal side of his family had links in cities such as Lyons and Langres that belonged to Guntramn's kingdom, and the paternal side in the Auvergne that belonged to Childebert's kingdom. Both kings furthermore respected the cult of St Martin. Guntramn once warned an envoy not to desecrate the saint's church at Tours, and Childebert perhaps constructed a church in honour of the saint. So during a visit to Childebert's court Gregory acted as the king's spokesman in responding to envoys from Guntramn. Eventually Gregory seems to have replaced bishop Egidius of Rheims as one of the chief episcopal diplomats for Childebert, who sent him as an envoy to Guntramn.[74] Because of the unique standing of their cities, bishops such as Germanus of Paris and Gregory of Tours were hence well placed to act as mediators among distrustful kings.

In the long run, however, the fates of Paris and Tours went in different directions. Paris was too important a royal city to be ignored, and the burial of deceased kings there led to the reassertion of the city as a prominent royal residence. In contrast, although some Merovingian widows came to live at

[74] Gregory's family and episcopacy: Pietri (1983); Van Dam (1985), pp. 202–29; (1993), pp. 50–81.

Tours, the kings continued to keep their distance from the city of St Martin. Even when they did earn the saint's patronage by acquiring his cape in the later seventh century, they kept the relic not at Tours, but at their own court.[75] The differing destinies of Paris and Tours nevertheless coalesced as indications of an important shift in royal politics. At the end of the sixth century the eminence of Guntramn and his alliance with Childebert II had demonstrated the dominance of Burgundy and Austrasia; but the kings who reasserted the importance of Paris and who acquired St Martin's cape were from Neustria.

ROYAL WOMEN: FREDEGUND AND BRUNEHILD

In the various sub-kingdoms neither the Frankish aristocracy nor the Roman aristocracy nor even the ecclesiastical hierarchy was united in its policies or its interests. Because a king's resources, in comparison to those once at the disposal of a Roman emperor, were quite limited, great aristocrats who accumulated wealth and could raise a band of armed supporters posed genuine challenges. Accumulated wealth could also elevate the power of women, in particular the women who were related to or who married Merovingian kings. Throughout the sixth century Merovingian wives and daughters had acquired 'cities, fields and revenues' as dowries, morning-gifts, ordinary gifts or inheritances. Like wealthy men they then used their resources as benefactions to cities and churches or as rewards for their own supporters. Clovis' widow Clothild, for instance, gave some property to a priest at Clermont and acquired a reputation for her generosity. After she left her husband Chlothar, Radegund used her own resources to found a convent and construct a church dedicated to the Virgin Mary at Poitiers. Clothild hence became powerful enough to influence the selection of some of the bishops at Tours; and Radegund not only remained respected enough in Gaul to appeal to the kings to end their civil wars, she also requested and received relics from the patriarch of Jerusalem and the Byzantine court. In a culture in which the costliness and the magnificence of people's tombs were meant to be eternal validations of their status, Radegund's casket was twice normal size.[76]

As wives these royal women had acquired wealth and influence. Without husbands they were perhaps even more threatening because of their potential for creating rivals to the other kings through their support or even through remarriage. Initially Clothild had remained involved in royal politics, first by

[75] Van Dam (1993), pp. 25–8.

[76] Gregory, *Hist.* IX.20.436, Guntramn's gifts to his daughter; Baudonivia, *Vita Radegundis* cc.14 and 16, pp. 386–9, Fortunatus, *Carmina* Appendix 2, relics; Gregory, *In Gloria Confessorum* 104, pp. 364–6, casket. Women's wealth: Wemple (1981), pp. 44–50; Halsall (1995), pp. 61–73.

encouraging her sons to attack the kingdom of the Burgundians, then by scheming to ensure that her son Chlodomer's young sons would inherit his kingdom. But after Chlothar and Childebert, her other two sons, killed two of these young boys, the dowager queen took the hint and removed herself from royal politics by taking up residence in Tours, a city, as we have seen, that was effectively outside royal jurisdiction. Sometimes kings married royal widows, in part to acquire control over their treasures, in part to ensure that no one else could lay claim to kingship by marrying them. Other royal women, both widows and unmarried daughters, entered convents, either at a king's insistence or by their own choice. Radegund was the only Merovingian queen of the sixth century who voluntarily abandoned her husband in favour of another 'king'. But although she may have offended Chlothar's manliness by preferring instead 'the embraces of the King of Heaven',[77] as a nun she would no longer marry a rival or produce an heir; so she too, despite her lingering influence, was now marginal to royal politics.

In contrast, other royal women such as Brunehild and Fredegund did not accept retirement in a cloister and tried to remain politically active even after their husbands' deaths. During the first half of the sixth century Merovingian kings had often taken wives from neighbouring royal dynasties among the Burgundians, Ostrogoths, Thuringians or Lombards. The kings of Austrasia in particular seem to have been expected to marry foreign princesses, and in 566 Sigibert married the Visigothic princess Brunehild. Not to be outdone, Chilperic then insisted upon marrying Galsuintha, Brunehild's sister. These two marriages were some of the last with foreign princesses; and when Chilperic's marriage soon failed, he had Galsuintha killed and married Fredegund. A later tradition claimed that Fredegund had previously been a royal servant;[78] if so, then she was an example of an increasing Merovingian tendency to limit the use of marriages as diplomatic tools. The early Merovingians had been weak enough to try to enhance their power through marriages with neighbouring royal dynasties, but by the later sixth century the Merovingians were secure enough to select mistresses and low-born wives, especially if an earlier marriage had been childless. Producing sons took priority over diplomatic connections and alliances with aristocrats.

Brunehild and Fredegund therefore represented not only different Merovingian kingdoms but also different marriage strategies. Yet both acquired great wealth, and both also overwhelmed many of their powerful contemporaries, kings, aristocrats and bishops alike. Some aristocrats even conceded that

[77] Baudonivia, *Vita Radegundis* c.4, pp. 308–11; Brennan (1985); Gäbe (1989).

[78] *Liber Historiae Francorum* c.31, p. 292. Royal marriage patterns: Ewig (1974), pp. 38–49; Wemple (1981), pp. 38–43, 56–7.

Brunehild 'controlled her husband's kingdom'. But at the moment of Sigibert's greatest success in expanding his control over Paris, he was killed by assassins sent by Fredegund. Chilperic's first concerns, significantly enough, were about wealth and women: he seized Brunehild's treasures, sent her into exile, and detained her daughters. His attempt to neutralise Brunehild was unsuccessful, however, since she soon married Merovech, one of his own sons by a former wife. So although Brunehild may have temporarily lost influence at the court of her son Childebert II, she was still a nuisance to Chilperic. So was Fredegund. She schemed against her stepsons; she pushed her husband to bring charges against the bishop who had married Brunehild and Merovech; and she was accused of adultery with bishop Bertramn of Bordeaux. The last charge was particularly grave, since it cast doubt on legitimate royal succession. Chilperic was fully aware of the implications: 'an accusation against my wife is a scandal for me'. The rumours about Fredegund lingered. Soon after her husband's assassination she surprised King Guntramn by announcing (falsely, as it turned out) that she was pregnant again, only a few months after the birth of Chlothar II. The next year she had to gather three hundred notables and three bishops to confirm with oaths that Chilperic had been Chlothar's father.[79]

Once Brunehild revived her influence over her son Childebert, her rivalry with Fredegund also reappeared. Childebert once tried to hold Fredegund responsible for the murders of both Sigibert and Chilperic; his aunt responded by sending assassins. Upon Guntramn's death Childebert inherited his kingdom; upon his own death in 595 his older son Theudebert II inherited the kingdom of Austrasia, and his younger son Theuderic II the kingdom of Burgundy. Chlothar II and his mother Fredegund may have seized Paris, but the alliance between Austrasia and Burgundy seemed formidable. Fredegund died in 597. Even more devastating for Chlothar was his defeat by the combined forces of Theudebert and Theuderic, who then reduced their cousin's kingdom to only a few cities. The kingdom of Neustria seemed on the verge of disappearing.

After being expelled from Austrasia, Brunehild was meanwhile trying to stabilise her own influence at Theuderic's court in Burgundy. She encouraged her grandson to be content with his many mistresses rather than to marry; she connived at the deposition of an unfriendly bishop and the promotion of her favourites, in particular aristocrats from Roman families;[80] and she urged Theuderic to attack an army led by Chlothar's son. She and her supporters also urged him to attack his brother Theudebert, in defiance of the wishes of

79 Brunehild: Gregory, *Hist.* VI.4.267–8; Nelson (1978). Fredegund: Gregory, *Hist.* V.49.258–63, accusation, VII.7.329–30, VIII.9.376, rumours.

80 Deposition and assassination of Bishop Desiderius of Vienne: Sisebut, *Vita Desiderii*; Fontaine (1980).

other local notables. Theudebert then contemplated an alliance not only with Chlothar, but also with King Witteric of the Visigoths in Spain and King Agilulf of the Lombards in Italy. The proposed alliance with the Visigoths is another indication of the waning of Brunehild's influence, because although she was related to an earlier Visigothic dynasty and although one of her daughters had once married the son of a Visigothic king, she had nevertheless prevented the consummation of a marriage between Witteric's daughter and Theuderic that aristocrats in Burgundy had arranged. In order to protect her own position with her grandson she had antagonised both the Visigoths and some of the Burgundian nobility. The most vocal opposition to Brunehild's schemes came, however, from Columbanus, an Irish monk who had founded monasteries in eastern Burgundy and who refused to bless Theuderic's bastard sons.[81] After Brunehild finally arranged Columbanus' exile, Theuderic defeated Theudebert in 612 and rejoined Burgundy with Austrasia. As he began to raise an army against Chlothar and his kingdom of Neustria, Theuderic appeared to be the king who would reunite the Frankish kingdoms under his rule.

REUNIFICATION

Theuderic died in 613, and as usual local aristocrats had the last word. In Austrasia an aristocratic faction led by Pippin of Landen and Bishop Arnulf of Metz, both great landowners in the Moselle valley, invited an alliance with Chlothar. Brunehild was meanwhile trying to promote Sigibert II, one of Theuderic's sons, as sole king. Her rejection of the usual Merovingian practice of dividing a kingdom among all surviving sons was presumably an attempt to unite her supporters in both Burgundy and Austrasia. But Warnachar, a Frank serving as mayor of the palace in Burgundy, combined with the notables of Austrasia to betray Brunehild and her great-grandson to Chlothar, who had them executed, but only after first accusing his aunt of the deaths of no fewer than ten Frankish kings. Surprisingly enough, the king of Neustria had reunified the Frankish kingdoms. As one indication of his new prominence, in 614 Chlothar was able to summon almost eighty bishops from Austrasia, Neustria, Burgundy and Aquitaine to a council that met at his capital city of Paris in the Church of St Peter once constructed by King Clovis himself. The chronicler Fredegar supplied a facile comparison: under Chlothar II 'the entire kingdom of the Franks was reunited just as under the rule of Chlothar I'.[82]

Chlothar I had been the sole Frankish king for a mere three years – the only three years after Clovis' death during which there had been one king.

[81] Jonas of Bobbio, *Vita Columbani* I.18–19.86–90; Prinz (1981); Riché (1981).

[82] Fredegar, *Chron.* IV.42.142; Ebling (1974), pp. 235–8.

Regionalism, local autonomy, and the power of great aristocrats and proud bishops had characterised Merovingian Gaul during the sixth century, and remained influential thereafter. Chlothar II therefore had to pay a price for this reunification, first by reappointing Warnachar as mayor in Burgundy and Rado in Austrasia, then a decade later by appointing his son Dagobert I as king in Austrasia, although under the influence of Pippin and Bishop Arnulf.[83] The Merovingians attempted to assert their authority especially in Neustria, in particular by patronising the cult of St Dionysius (St Denis), whose church and monastery outside Paris became a principal site for royal tombs. But aristocrats, Frankish, Roman and Burgundian, also began to use similar methods for promoting their own families. The new style of Irish monasticism introduced by Columbanus and others in eastern and northern Gaul gave them the opportunity to found and endow monasteries in the rural countryside far outside the cities that bishops dominated. Since they remained the seigneurial lords for these new foundations, members of their families became influential abbots and monks, sometimes after having held royal magistracies, sometimes too before going on to become bishops. Eventually some of these men were venerated as saints, whose holiness then validated the prominence of their families too.[84] The 'reunification' of the Frankish possessions hence also marked, not so paradoxically, explicit recognition of the power of local aristocrats and of the distinctive identities of the various sub-kingdoms and other important regions. Chlothar II, Dagobert I and their successors may have preferred comparisons with the paradigm kings from the Old Testament, David and Solomon, but the more appropriate biblical analogy for Merovingian Gaul by the early seventh century would be the situation after Solomon's death, when two kingdoms maintained an uneasy control over the many distinct tribes of Israelites.[85]

83 For a slightly different perspective, see Fouracre, chapter 14 below.

84 St Denis: Semmler (1989); 'self-sanctification': Prinz (1965), pp. 489–503, also Fouracre, chapter 14 below.

85 *Epistolae aevi Merowingici collectae* xv, pp. 457–60, episcopal promotion of David and Solomon in the mid-seventh century; Eddius Stephanus, *Vita Wilfridi* c.33, pp. 68–9, comparison of Dagobert II to King Rehoboam.

CHAPTER 9

THE CELTIC KINGDOMS

Wendy Davies

Ireland, Scotland, the Isle of Man, Wales, south-western Britain (Cornwall and Devon) and Brittany were the principal Celtic countries in the sixth and seventh centuries, although some other parts of western Europe still had a Celtic vernacular language at that time. This was certainly the case in north-west Spain and in parts of England, but may also have been so in central France. These Celtic countries are defined linguistically: they are the areas in which Celtic languages were normally and primarily used. The languages themselves fall into two broad groups, Brittonic (a type of P-Celtic) and Goidelic (Q-Celtic), the language groups of Britain and Ireland respectively. During this period some distinctions between the constituent Brittonic languages developed, but these were relatively slight and did not prevent communication across the group; Primitive Cumbric, therefore, the language of southern Scotland and north-west England, was little different from Primitive Welsh, which was itself little different from Primitive Cornish.[1] Primitive Breton was at this stage indistinguishable from Cornish, although it remains a matter of debate whether Breton was introduced to north-west France by immigrants from Britain or whether some dialects were the natural (or reinforced or brittonised) continuation of the P-Celtic Gaulish that had once been spoken over much of western Europe.[2] The main Pictish language, the language of eastern and northern Scotland, appears to have been a rather different form of P-Celtic (possibly closer to Gaulish) and may or may not have been immediately intelligible to speakers of Cumbric to the south. Though we might expect some regional differences within it, speakers of the Goidelic group were largely confined to Ireland and spoke a single Primitive Irish.[3] However, Irish was also spoken in parts of western Britain: south-west Scotland especially, but also west Wales and west Cornwall.

[1] Jackson (1953), pp. 3–11.
[2] Falc'hun (1963); Jackson (1967), pp. 21–36; Fleuriot (1980), pp. 55–78.
[3] Koch (1995).

Though these areas were all therefore indubitably Celtic, we should no more expect political or cultural homogeneity than we would of Germanic-speaking parts at this time. They did not form a single political unit; there was not even one kingdom per Celtic 'country', but several or many; and some regions did not form a part of any kingdom. In fact, their political structures were in some respects influenced by their experience of the Roman past. Brittany, south-western England and Wales had all been part of the Roman Empire, though the level of participation in Roman material culture and civic life varied enormously across them and though some parts had frequently had a military presence; eastern Brittany and south east Wales had been more affected, and the coasts of Wales, at least, had had forts built and refurbished in the late fourth century. Lowland Scotland, or more precisely the land between Hadrian's Wall and the Antonine Wall, had also at times in the second century been a part of the Roman Empire, and subsequent to that appears to have had a close relationship with imperial governors. Scotland north of the Antonine Wall lay outside the Empire, although Agricola had campaigned in the east in the distant past, and Ireland and the Isle of Man always lay outside it. With such major differences in background, it would be surprising if post-Roman polities had all taken the same shape.[4]

There are also, of course, fundamental differences in geography between Celtic areas, such that one would expect neither economy nor politics and society to be the same all over. Much of Wales is high plateau and much of Scotland is high mountain. Not many people can have lived in these areas and settlement must have concentrated in the coastal lowlands – in the Scottish case in the Western Isles in particular – and in the limited zones of good workable lowland in south-east Wales and eastern Scotland. Ireland and Brittany are quite different; though both have their mountainous parts, they have much less upland than Wales and Scotland, and there is no reason to suppose that the population was anything other than broadly distributed across these regions; both also have substantial areas of high-quality arable land. Cornwall is very similar geographically to western Brittany, while the Isle of Man has a microcosm of Irish landscapes. There are differences, then, both within regions and between them. Accordingly, communication across Wales and Scotland was exceptionally difficult, and communication across Brittany was as difficult as land transport was anywhere in western Europe (although it is likely that the east/west Roman routes were still in operation in the seventh century). In all three, movement by water was far more practicable than over land, and coastal areas therefore have an especial significance. Ireland was a land crossed by major waterways, and dotted with many lakes, and this must have

[4] Cf. Halsall, chapter 2 above.

made communications vastly easier here than was the situation in other Celtic areas.

The very early Middle Ages was a period of climatic deterioration. With a drop in temperature and increase in rainfall since the late Roman period, the highlands would have been even less suitable for cultivation than previously, and marginal lands here and there would have dropped out of use completely – as demonstrated very precisely by excavations at the Roman farm of Cefn Graeanog in north-west Wales, once a cereal-growing area but no more so in the early Middle Ages than it is now.[5] This made the good agricultural lowland even more significant. The other major change in economic determinants in this period was demographic: the sixth and seventh centuries were times of recurrent plague. We know that the plague of the 540s had effects across Wales and Ireland, while that of the 660s is believed to have had major social consequences in Ireland; it certainly reduced recorded activity for a generation.[6] When we remember the fundamental consequences of the plagues of the late Middle Ages, we should be prepared for comparably significant effects at this earlier period.

Despite the geographical differences, the economic base in Celtic areas was one of mixed farming, supplemented by hunting and gathering when appropriate. The balance of the several elements in a mixed farming economy would of course have varied from place to place, and there is reason to suppose that Irish farming put greater emphasis on cattle rearing, while farming in eastern Brittany put more on cereals (and also fostered some specialisation in the cultivation of vines). These were all economies that were characterised by relatively little commercial exchange, and many economic units may well have been for the most part self-sufficient. However, this does not mean that the areas lacked wealth or wealthy people: surplus was generated, and was monopolised by aristocrats here as elsewhere. Some groups or families or some individuals had the capacity, therefore, to patronise the importation of pottery from the continent through the sixth and much of the seventh century.[7] There was certainly some exchange, and this movement of pottery is the most visible expression of it, but everything suggests that its volume, and proportion of total production, was tiny. Not surprisingly, then, these are areas of little or no urbanisation; overwhelmingly rural, in most parts there were no towns at all; Roman Caerwent almost certainly supported a monastery by the late sixth century but no urban life; Roman Exeter and Roman Carlisle probably had much reduced quasi-urban communities; Roman Carmarthen may have had

5 Goodburn, Hassall and Tomlin (1978), p. 406; Weir (1993).

6 *Annales Cambriae* s.a. 547, 682, 683; *Annals of Ulster* s.a. 545, 549, 664, 665, 668; Baillie (1995).

7 Campbell (1984), and comments following his paper; Thomas (1990), Campbell and Lane (1993), Wooding (1996), Hill (1997).

nothing left but dilapidated buildings. It was only in eastern Brittany that towns continued to have some sort of urban character, and Rennes, Nantes and Vannes remained urban centres throughout this period. Ireland completely lacked towns, but it did not lack development. Alone among Celtic areas, there are signs in the seventh century of increasing and increasingly specialised production, particularly in the context of patronage from well-established monastic communities, and this is sufficient to suggest that by 700 Ireland was in the midst of an economically developing trend. The same could be true of eastern Brittany at that time, but we lack the sources to demonstrate it. It does not seem to have been the case in Cornwall, Wales or Scotland.

The structure of Celtic societies in the sixth and seventh centuries is also complicated by the migration factor and its uneven operation, as are societies in so many other parts of western Europe. Some British (and one or two English) went to Ireland, especially in the context of Christian missions, but on the whole Ireland was unaffected by immigration. People had left Ireland, however, both to raid and to settle in western Britain in the fourth and fifth centuries, and that movement continued into the late sixth century. The settlement of Ulster ruling families in south-western Scotland and the Isle of Man in the 560s–580s is of the greatest importance for the future development of those areas, and it is also quite likely that some southern Irish were ruling in parts of west Wales in the early sixth century.[8] Whether or not these leaders were accompanied by sufficient settlers to constitute a mass migration is a contentious issue; the Irish-speaking populations of south-west Scotland and Man may have settled there in the late sixth century, or in the preceding two centuries, or even much earlier; there is, however, absolutely no doubt about the movement of leaders at that time, nor of the fact that the populations of those areas were or became Irish speakers.

There is also good reason to think that there had been some significant movement of British people in the fifth century, and it is likely that some of this continued in the decades after 500. No one believes nowadays that all the British (the indigenous population of Britain) were pushed westwards by the Angle and Saxon settlers, for it is perfectly clear from seventh-century and even some later texts that a Brittonic language was still being spoken in parts of midland and eastern England long after the English settlement. Some British kingdoms also survived in central and northern England until well into the seventh century. However, the early borrowing of Latin words into Welsh

[8] *Annals of Ulster* s.a. 574, 577, 580, 582. Later texts record a very strong tradition that some of the Irish Déisi migrated to Wales round about the fourth century. Several generations from the Irish genealogy also feature in the genealogy of the south-western Welsh kingdom of Dyfed, at a phase which could correspond with the late fifth/early sixth century; Bartrum (1966), p. 4; Thomas (1994), pp. 53–66.

makes it likely that some part of the British people – perhaps the wealthy and aristocratic, perhaps the higher clergy – did indeed move westwards, though we cannot begin to guess at the proportion of the total population.[9] It is also quite clear that some of them went overseas to northern France: by the mid-fifth century there were British on the central Loire and in north-western France; and by the late sixth century there were sufficient numbers settled in the north-west for the peninsula to change its name from Armorica to Britannia Minor – 'Little Britain' or, as we know it, Brittany.[10] We cannot plot this migration precisely, but it seems to have been over by the 560s. Nor do we know much about the circumstances of it, although there is a Welsh tradition that it was plague that sent peoples overseas:[11] we do not know if the several groups of Britons scattered about fifth-century France eventually filtered back into the north-west, or if more and more kept coming from Britain. We also do not know if the British settlement of Armorica was vastly more dense in the west, although seventh-century differentiation between the land of the Britons and that of the Romans may imply that.[12] It is, however, perfectly clear that there were Brittonic speakers in eastern Brittany, for ninth-century personal and topographic nomenclature is overwhelmingly Breton; and although sixth-century Frankish writers saw the River Vilaine as the boundary between Bretons and Franks, Breton-speaking even occurred to the east of that line. It may indeed be that the River Vilaine constituted the boundary between Britannia and Romania; if so, that boundary lies well into the east of the peninsula. How many of the Britons/Bretons of the sixth century and the ancestors of the Breton-speakers of the ninth actually came from Britain and how many were the descendants of the continental Celts of the Roman period is impossible to say. It is a hotly debated issue among Breton scholars and the arguments easily become circular.[13]

The problems surrounding migration issues, whether they relate to Brittany, to England or to Scotland, are severe and most appear incapable of solution. The movements cannot be dated with any precision. We have very little idea of numbers of people involved, either relative or absolute; we have little idea of social composition (did whole communities move, or bands of independent fortune hunters, or aristocrats and would-be rulers, or different combinations in different places?); and we do not know enough about the relationship between linguistic change and settlement. There is no doubt that mass migration can change the language of a region, but we have little idea of the

[9] Jackson (1953), pp. 77–86; Dark (1993), p. 91.

[10] *Concilia Galliae A.314–A.506*, p. 148; *A.511–A.695*, p. 179; Gregory, *Hist.* IV.4.137, V.26.232, X.9.493.

[11] *Book of Llan Dâv*, pp. 107–9. [12] *Concilia Galliae A.511–A.695*, p. 179; *Vita Samsonis* I.61.

[13] Cf. Falc'hun (1970), pp. 43–96; Galliou and Jones (1991), pp. 143–7; Tonnerre (1994), pp. 33–74; Astill and Davies (1997), p. 113 n. 12.

minimum proportions necessary to effect such a change.[14] Place-name evidence can be extremely helpful in suggesting the location of speakers of this or that language/dialect, but even here we have to be careful in our assumptions about who did the coining of names: was it the residents of a place, or their neighbours, or some alien who was making records for fiscal, proprietary or navigational purposes? It is frustrating that we cannot solve these problems, but we should not forget them: migration itself was obviously of enormous political importance at the time and of enormous social consequence subsequently.

SOURCE MATERIAL

The written sources available for considering Celtic areas in the sixth century are exceptionally few and are in some parts little better for the seventh, although by then Irish material is rich and varied. What sources there are can be fragmentary, corrupt and difficult to interpret. We therefore cannot ignore the fact that there are very severe source problems in dealing with Celtic areas in the very early Middle Ages; this means that it is impossible to make a well-evidenced assessment of political history anywhere in the first half of the sixth century, and this remains the case in some parts for most of the seventh. From the middle of the sixth century northern Ireland and western Scotland are reasonably well covered, as increasingly are other parts of Ireland in the seventh century; we can discover this and that about Wales and eastern Scotland, but there is little to flesh out the bare notices of a king here, a death there; what we know of Cornwall and the Isle of Man is fragmentary in the extreme; we get a detailed glimpse of east Breton affairs in the late sixth century but can see virtually nothing for the succeeding century and a half.

In this situation, the evidence from stone inscriptions has a particular importance, for many survive in the original (virtually the only texts to do so) and can be surprisingly detailed, yielding material descriptive of status, character and events as well as names and funerary evocations. Not all inscriptions are precisely dated, but some are, and many can be reasonably dated to within a half-century or so. The Welsh corpus of inscriptions is well studied and especially important, but there are plenty of inscribed stones from Cornwall and Scotland, some from Brittany, and a few of this period from Ireland and the Isle of Man. Most are inscribed in the Latin language, but some use the Irish alphabet ogham, either alone or in association with Latin.[15]

14 See Koch (1997), pp. xlii–xliv, for some thoughtful comments on the process of linguistic change in the early Middle Ages.

15 Macalister (1945–49); Nash-Williams (1950); Bernier (1982); Okasha (1993); Thomas (1994), for easy reference, although there are subsequent discoveries published in many separate journals; see also McManus (1991).

Annals, contemporary notices organised by year, were clearly being maintained in some Celtic religious centres from the late sixth century, although these records are usually brief, sometimes cryptic and often intermittent. At this period they characteristically comprise obits of kings and clerics, and notice of battles, disasters and climatic or astronomical phenomena. The northern Irish series, which lies at the base of the *Annals of Ulster* and is often referred to as the 'Chronicle of Ireland', is important for its coverage of northern Ireland, western Scotland and the Isle of Man, though some of its material also found its way into the Welsh collection, *Annales Cambriae*.[16] It is extremely likely that the monastery of Iona was the initial source of these records, running from shortly after its foundation in 563 until *c.*740, but by the late seventh century records from Irish centres like Armagh and Clonfert survive, some of which came to be incorporated into the *Annals of Ulster* and some in other major collections such as the *Annals of Inisfallen*. A very small number of Welsh annals survives from these centuries, some of Welsh and some of north British origin; and we should not forget that the annals of the English *Anglo-Saxon Chronicle* sometimes refer to Scotland, Wales and the South-West.

A small number of contemporary saints' lives survive from this period and these have a significance for more than purely religious affairs. They are the Lives of Patrick by Muirchú and Tírechán, and the Life of Brigit by Cogitosus, while parts of another Life of Brigit are reconstructable from the so-called *Vita Prima* – all come from Ireland and all from the second half of the seventh century; from Iona we have Adomnán's Life of Columba, written *c.*700, and from Brittany the anonymous Life of Samson, probably written round about the mid-seventh century (though Breton, it is largely about Samson's early life in Wales).[17] A considerable body of ecclesiastical material survives from seventh-century Ireland – penitentials, canons, tracts – but they will not be considered here; and there are also records of sixth-century ecclesiastical councils involving Brittany. There are scholarly works of various kinds, especially from Ireland, dealing with computation, language and grammar, and there are works designed to show off literary skills, like the *Hisperica Famina* and Latin poems and hymns.[18] There are also miscellaneous narratives – tracts and histories – of value to the historian: for western Britain, the tract on the present 'ruin' of Britain by Gildas, written *c.*540 or a little earlier; for Britain and Scotland especially, Bede's *Ecclesiastical History of the English People*, written a

[16] See Hughes (1972), pp. 99–159, and Grabowski and Dumville (1984), for critical assessment.

[17] Lives of Patrick: Bieler (1979), pp. 61–166; Lives of Brigit: *Acta Sanctorum* Feb. 1 (1658), pp. 129–41 and *Vita Brigitae*, ed. Colgan (1647), pp. 527–45 (see McCone 1982); Life of Columba: *Vita Columbae*; Life of Samson: *Vita Samsonis* (see Wood (1988)).

[18] Hughes (1972), pp. 193–216; Ó Cróinín (1995), pp. 197–221; Davies (1982a), pp. 209–14; Herren (1974–87).

couple of centuries later; for Brittany, the *Ten Books of History* by Gregory of Tours (often called *The History of the Franks*), written in the late sixth century, and also the *Chronicle* of Fredegar written in the mid-seventh.[19] The mixture of material put together in north Wales in the early ninth century under the title *Historia Brittonum* contains little that is useful for this period, although it includes some brief notes of north British origin, which are exceptionally important.[20] There are also some Irish tracts of legal and political concern, like the Latin tract on the 'Twelve Abuses' and the vernacular *Audacht Morainn* and *Cáin Adamnáin*.[21] Most of the enormous corpus of vernacular Irish legal material belongs, however, to the eighth century.[22]

There are, finally, large genealogical collections from Ireland and Wales, the latter including genealogies from southern Scotland and the Isle of Man; and a few from Devon and Cornwall, and Brittany. These are potentially relevant to political structures in the seventh century, and even the sixth, but are difficult to use because, like the kinglists of the Picts or the Tara kings, they were mostly drawn up several centuries after this period. They purport to record very long pedigrees of dynasties ruling at the time of each genealogy's compilation; for example, the collection in BL Harleian MS 3859 from mid-tenth-century Wales begins with pedigrees of two principal ruling families of tenth-century Wales, extending back over more than thirty generations; the sections which approximate to the seventh to tenth centuries are at least credible, but some earlier sections are definitely not. In the absence of corroborative evidence it is very difficult to assess the value of the putative sixth- and seventh-century stages of this material; they could as well be wishful thinking, or mistakes, as records. That said, there are genealogies that – terminating well before the tenth century – must derive from much earlier records, like that for the Isle of Man in the Harley collection; they are therefore potentially relevant source material. The English genealogical material and regnal lists incorporated in the *Historia Brittonum* are of comparable value to this latter group.[23]

19 Gildas, *De Excidio*; on Bede, Thacker, chapter 17 below; on the work of Gregory of Tours, Van Dam, chapter 8 above; and on the *Chronicle of Fredegar*, Fouracre, chapter 14 below.

20 *Historia Brittonum* (often known – inaccurately – as 'Nennius'); cf. Dumville (1972–74, 1975–76, 1985); Jackson (1963); Koch (1997).

21 *Audacht Morainn*. Meyer (1965); only a part of this text is of seventh-century date: see Ní Dhonnchadha (1982).

22 Welsh vernacular poems, *Canu Aneirin* and *Canu Taliesin* especially, may have a seventh-century origin, but the redactions we have can be no earlier than the ninth century, and could be from as late as the eleventh century; for a summary of the problems, see Davies (1982a), pp. 209–11; see also Koch (1997). Some Irish vernacular tales could have been written down in the seventh century (Carney (1955), pp. 66–76) but it would be conventional to date these to the eighth or ninth.

23 O'Brien (1962); Bartrum (1966); Ó Riain (1985); Breton genealogies are not collected but most are cited in La Borderie (1896–98). Pictish kinglists: Anderson (1973); Tara – see Byrne (1973), pp. 48–69, and see below, p. 243.

THE IRISH

There are two especial problems conditioning our understanding of the earliest Irish history and both derive from the character of the available written sources. The first concerns the annals: the *Annals of Ulster*, like many of the principal collections, have a series of entries running through the fifth and sixth centuries, and at first glance appear to provide us with very detailed evidence of people, places and events in that early period. This is exceptionally misleading, for most of this material was compiled and inserted by the historians of the late ninth and tenth centuries who created the main collections: they did their best to include the heroes of the past, both ecclesiastical and secular, in a credible chronological framework.[24] What they produced is indeed credible, but its place in the sequence is deduced and its historicity is unverifiable; it does not therefore have the same status as evidence as the material that begins in the late sixth century. The second problem is a related one: such was, and is, the power of legend that it tends to determine the framework of all discussion of these early centuries, whether that discussion took place in the ninth century, or the twelfth, or the twentieth. One story is especially powerful, the story that dominates the Ulster Cycle of tales, whose most famous elements come together in the *Táin Bó Cualnge* (the 'Cattle Raid of Cooley').[25] This is set in a world in which the Ulster people, the Ulaid, politically dominated the whole of northern Ireland, with no hint of the existence of the Uí Néill family (who in fact did dominate northern Ireland for much of the early Middle Ages). The context is seductive and very easily leads us to assume that the Ulaid did indeed 'rule' the north in the late prehistoric period.

Another problem that confronts the ordinary reader is the complexity and unfamiliarity of the political structures that characterised sixth- and seventh-century Ireland. Ireland had many political units at this time, of exceptionally small size – maybe fifty, maybe a hundred, maybe even more of them – and known as *tuatha*. Each *tuath* had its *rí*, its king, who had military and general responsibilities for the polity but who was not – except in special circumstances – a legislator[26]. On top of this base, the political system admitted overlapping structures of overkingship: some kings were also overkings. This meant that they expected military support from their underkings, and tribute too, but it gave them no rights of interference in the *tuatha* of their underkings nor, in practice, any habit of interfering, as far as we can see. Overkingship was not merely a two-way relationship: some overkings were overkings of overkings and correspondingly some were at once overking of one group of kings but underking of another more powerful overking; and so on. To add to the

[24] Hughes (1972), esp. pp. 142–6; Smyth (1972); Grabowski and Dumville (1984), p. 93.
[25] *Táin*; and see comment above, n. 22. [26] See Wormald, chapter 21 below.

complications, at this time overkingship was not institutionalised: overkingships were established here and disappeared there in accordance with the political realities of the moment.

We know vastly more about northern Ireland in this period than about other parts. Its politics, in so far as we can perceive them, were dominated by a complex interplay between the different branches of the Uí Néill family and the rulers of the Ulster people, the Ulaid. By the late sixth century, four major Ulaid *tuatha* occupied the extreme north-east of Ireland (Co. Antrim and Co. Down) and were ruled respectively by the dynasties of Dál Riata, Dál nAraide, Dál Fiatach and Uí Echach Cobo. Usually one of them was also Ulaid overking. The Uí Néill family, that is those families who believed themselves to be descendants of the legendary Niall (pronounced Neil) of the Nine Hostages, had branches based across northern and central Ireland. Of these branches Cenél nEógain, Cenél Conaill and Cenél Cairpri (Co. Donegal) were most prominent in the north, while Cenél Loiguire and Cenél nArdgaile (Co. Meath) were prominent in the midlands; they are known as northern and southern Uí Néill respectively. Their pattern of behaviour suggests that the Uí Néill kings not only sought to make themselves overkings with respect to their own localities but also sought to make themselves overkings with respect to each other. This process only reached its logical conclusion after our period, with the establishment from the 730s of a single Uí Néill overkingship alternating between northern and southern branches. Ulaid and Uí Néill were not the only people of northern and central Ireland, for there were many *tuatha* that the Uí Néill in particular sought to dominate; some of these constituted what look like scattered remnants of earlier 'tribal' groupings – Gailenga, Luigne, Ciannachta, for example – but the most notable were the seven *tuatha* of the central north, known by the historic period as the Airgialla, that is vassal or subject states (see Map 4).

The politics of the century or so after 560 have at first sight a bewildering complexity. Cenél nEógain fought Cenél Conaill; Dál Fiatach fought Dál nAraide; Cenél Conaill fought Diarmait mac Cerbaill of the southern Uí Néill (Ardgal's nephew); Dál nAraide fought Cenél nEógain; Cenél Conaill fought Dál Riata and Dál nAraide; Síl nÁedo Sláine (southern Uí Néill) fought Cenél nEógain, and so on. There is, however, an overall pattern: this is first the simple pattern of increasing Uí Néill success against allcomers, and secondly the pattern of survival of the more successful Uí Néill branches, eventually symbolised by holding the kingship of Tara. The later sixth and early seventh century is a period of frequent and evenly balanced conflict between Uí Néill and Ulaid rulers; now one side is successful, now the other; now one branch tries an alliance, now another; until the 637 battle of Magh Roth. Hence Diarmait mac Cerbaill from the south, king of Tara, was defeated in 561 by

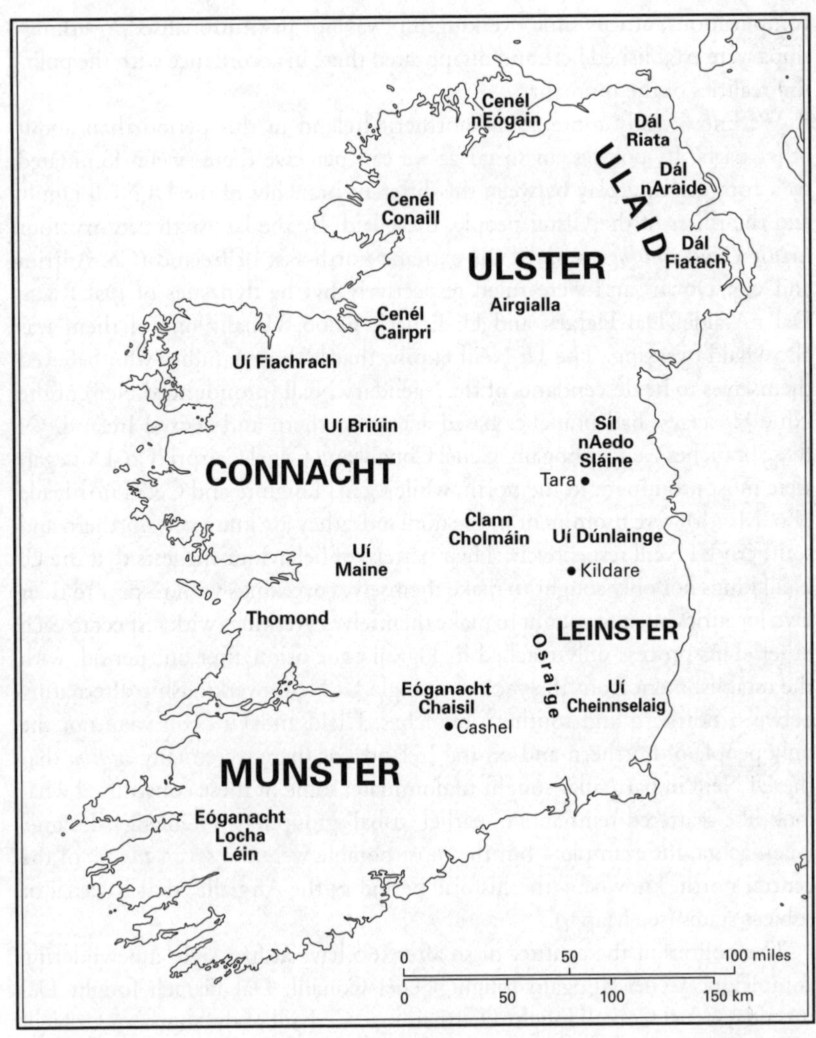

Map 4 Ireland

Ainmere of the Cenél Conaill acting with the Cenél nEógain at the battle of Cuil Dreimne, a conflict instigated – apparently – by St Columba, cousin of Ainmere, whose protection of the Connachta to the west had been violated;[27] Diarmait was finally killed by the Ulaid overking, Aed Dub of the Dál nAraide, in 565. This was the time when Ulaid rulers made expeditions east across the

[27] *Annals of Ulster* s.a. 561; cf. *Vita Columbae* III.3, and pp. 71–4.

sea to Man and south-west Scotland and the battles for the Ulaid overkingship became immensely complicated by the fact of Dál Riata interests (and power) on the British mainland. Ainmere's son Aed opportunely supported Aedán mac Gabráin of Dál Riata at the so-called 'convention' of Druim Cett against the then Ulaid overking, probably Báetán of the Dál Fiatach;[28] the outcome was an agreement that the Scottish Dál Riata should not owe tribute to the Ulaid overking. Battles for the Ulaid overkingship continued on Man in the 570s and 580s, and in Ireland in the 620s, until 637 and Magh Roth; here Aed's son Domnall roundly defeated the Dál Riata, led by Domnall Brecc, both on the Irish mainland, where he had allied with the Dál nAraide overking, and also at sea, where he had allied with the Cenél nEógain. From that time Dál Riata interests focussed much more closely on Scotland, Ulaid overkingship conflicts were less volatile, and the Uí Néill were much more consistently successful. Domnall mac Aedo died peacefully in his bed (and – for his unusual success – was the first to be called 'king of Ireland' by the contemporary annalist).[29]

Though the Uí Néill were more consistently successful, in other words constantly made themselves overkings and overoverkings, until the end of the century they continued to battle with each other for supremacy, that is, to establish overkingships. Although there continued to be conflicts within northern and within southern Uí Néill branches, the most prominent conflicts were between north and south and were increasingly focussed on the kingship of the symbolic site of Tara: he who held Tara might be said to be overking of all Uí Néill overkings. So, Diarmait mac Áedo Sláine of the south shared the Tara kingship with his brother Blathmac and defeated Conall of Cenél Conaill in 654; his successor Finnechta, having killed his first cousin the king, defeated Máel Dúin of Cenél nEógain in 675; but Loingsech mac Oengusso of the northern Cenél Conaill, the second Irish king to be called 'king of Ireland' by a contemporary annalist, took the Tara kingship without opposition and ruled till 703.[30] It is from the late seventh century that the first list of Tara kings survives, the Baile Chuind, and this in itself emphasises the now crucial significance of the Tara kingship in the politics of the north and midlands.[31] During the seventh century the geographical range of the prominent Uí Néill overkings had increased dramatically: originally playing politics within the narrow confines of a few *tuatha*, by 700 they moved over half of Ireland. In the eighth they were to range even wider, as also to establish succession to the Tara kingship, which from 734 alternated between Cenél nEógain of the northern

[28] Traditionally in 575, but perhaps as late as 590, Meckler (1997).

[29] *Annals of Ulster* s.a. 565, 574, 575, 577, 578, 580, 581, 582, 586, 626, 627, 629, 637, 642.

[30] *Annals of Ulster* s.a. 654, 675, 703.

[31] Murphy (1952); Byrne (1973), pp. 91, 104–5, 276–7; Irwin (1998).

Uí Néill and Clann Cholmáin of the southern Uí Néill. By 700 there were still other kings and other overkings – both Ulaid and Airgialla had their own overkings until the ninth century – but it was absolutely clear that the Uí Néill group provided the topmost overkings of the north and midlands.

By this time the Irish were also a significant presence in Scotland. We do not know, as indicated above, when the migration to western Scotland began nor the eventual size of it, but its area seems to have been very confined in the sixth and seventh centuries. Despite this, the rulers of the Dál Riata ranged widely across northern Britain in the late sixth and early seventh centuries, coming at first into conflict with the English as they sought to establish Bernicia (Aedán mac Gabráin was severely defeated by the English at Dawston) and subsequently into conflict with the Picts.[32] The meeting at Druim Cett had been something of a first attempt at loosening the ties with the Irish mainland and stopping the draining of resources to the Ulaid overking; the battles in Man in the 580s were a further manifestation of this dispute. But it was the Magh Roth defeat, in 637, which really concentrated Dál Riata attention on the Scottish mainland. From their political focus at Dunadd – a site that has been well excavated – they went north and east in the seventh century, although there were other forts too, Dunaverty, Tarbert, Dunollie.[33] This threatened the British kingdom of Strathclyde, with its focus at Dumbarton (near Glasgow), and took the Irish over the mountains to the Pictish heartland of Fife. By 700 they were still in the early stages of a development that was to take them in the eighth and ninth centuries to many conflicts in central Scotland and ultimately to the kingship of Scotland.

Even in the seventh century the Uí Néill had sometimes come into contact with the prominent dynasties of southern and western Ireland. The Laigin, the people of the south-east (Leinster), also had claims on the kingship of Tara and they sometimes raided northwards, as they did successfully at Dun Bolg against Aed mac Ainmere in 598, and were themselves raided, as they were by Domnall mac Aedo in 628. Within Leinster two leading dynasties vied for ultimate overkingship, the Uí Dúnlainge in the north and the Uí Cheinnselaig in the south, and though Uí Dúnlainge were often overkings this was by no means invariable. With family connections with the major monastery of Kildare, they sometimes sought alliances with branches of the southern Uí Néill in the midlands (the daughters of Cellach, *c.*700, seem to have taken Uí Néill husbands) and their conflicts extended to the western borders of Leinster, where the unusually large *tuath* of the Osraige sported kings who

[32] Bede, *HE* I.34; see also Thacker, chapter 17 below; *Annals of Ulster* s.a. 681, 683, 694; Koch (1997), pp. xxxv–xli.

[33] Lane (1984); Campbell and Lane (1992); Lane and Campbell (1993).

were extremely resistant to the dominance of overkings, a pattern that was sustained for many centuries after 700. The to-and-fro of battles between Uí Dúnlainge and Uí Cheinnselaig continued past 700 and it was not until the mid-eighth century that the former succeeded in establishing an overkingship of Leinster that then continued until the eleventh century.[34]

The Uí Néill also had close connections in the west, the area from which they were thought to have originated, and one of the several prominent dynasties of the west, the Uí Briúin, had fought with Cenél nEógain and Cenél Conaill against Diarmait at Cuil Dreimne in 561. Later, in 703, it was Cellach of the Uí Briúin who defeated Loingsech, king of Tara. Another dynasty, the Uí Fiachrach, came up against the Cenél Cairpri in 603 in Sligo, at the western extremity of Uí Néill political influence, and against Diarmait mac Áedo Sláine of the south in 649, when he defeated their long-lived king Guaire. Other dynasties vied for overkingships, the Uí Maine and the Uí Ailello especially, although the Uí Fiachrach were most notable through the seventh century and Uí Fiachrach and Uí Briúin were tending to alternate in a principal overkingship of Connacht by 700. But here again it was not until later, in the late eighth century, that control of a consistent overkingship was established by the Uí Briúin.[35]

The south-west, Munster, is the most difficult area to penetrate in the sixth and seventh centuries, for there is little contemporary material in the annals until the eighth. It seems that Thomond (modern Co. Clare) was a region disputed between the overkings of the south-west and those of Connacht to the north. When Guaire of the Uí Fiachrach, together with the Uí Maine, was defeated by Failbe Flann of Munster in 627, this may well have determined that Thomond was to be dominated by Munster kings and detached from Connacht, and the defeat contributed to the weakening of the southern Uí Fiachrach. In Munster itself, Eoganachta kings created overkingships in east and west, but it is too early to discern the pattern of their interrelationships. It is very likely that Cashel, the later symbolic focus of southern overkingship, was already utilised as a strongpoint, but it does not yet appear to have gained the significance that it had by the ninth century. Indeed, it would be straining the evidence to suggest that a single overkingship of the south-west had crystallised by 700. That development was yet to come.[36]

By 700 we can see the shadow of the trend that was to clarify during the eighth century, the establishment of four principal overkingships of roughly equal territorial range, relating to north, west, south-east and south-west (Ulster, Connacht, Leinster, Munster), although the contest for overkingship

34 *Annals of Ulster* s.a. 598, 628, 738. 35 *Annals of Ulster* s.a. 561, 703, 603, 649, 754, 792.
36 *Annals of Ulster* s.a. 627, 721, 737, 793; *Annals of Inisfallen* s.a. 721, 735.

of Munster had yet to start. In 700 the politics of the 'middle' were rather closely associated with the north, although there were forays west and south. In 700 the Dál Riata had a very solid political base in south-west Scotland and an established influence in Scottish politics. These trends are clear, although the framework of the political dynamic can still be puzzling and the observer has to ask why there was so much fighting, whether warfare was endemic and whether early Ireland was in a state of perpetual anarchy. The answers are neither so simple nor so depressing. The record is dominated by fighting because this is what the annalists chose to record. It certainly seems to have been a recurrent activity of a military elite, but this should not make us forget that these were elite rather than common pastimes; fighting did not mean total warfare; production continued (indeed, as I have indicated earlier, everything suggests that it increased in the seventh century); and learning flourished: this is the period when scholars learned to speak and write new languages, grappled with complex computations, and began the high art of ornamental bookmaking.[37] The basis of overkingly power was undoubtedly military; little about it in this period was institutionalised and it had little (perhaps nothing) to do with government; it was largely about the very crude, and unstable, politics of learning how to extract – and keep – surplus. But simple kingship still very much had a function at this time. It was still the king who represented and protected his *tuath*, who dealt with emergencies, who guaranteed prosperity and good fortune, whose wisdom could be evoked to make a judgement, who negotiated with Christian clergy and – increasingly – acquired a foothold of influence in the flourishing religious communities. Even if the course of politics was largely made by overkings, ordinary kings still had local and regional influence. The king of the Osraige, lying between Leinster and Munster, may well have had an unusually large *tuath* but he provides a nice demonstration of what kingship could do, without the complications of overkingship.

> It is through the justice of the ruler that he secures peace, tranquillity, joy, ease, and comfort.
> It is through the justice of the ruler that he dispatches (great) battalions to the borders of hostile neighbours . . .
> It is through the justice of the ruler that there is abundance of every high, tall corn.
> It is through the justice of the ruler that abundance of fish swim in the streams . . .[38]

PICTLAND AND NORTH BRITAIN

Although the Irish were already significant in western Scotland in the sixth and seventh centuries, the major population groups of north Britain were Pictish,

[37] On Christian culture in Ireland, Stancliffe chapter 15 below. [38] *Audacht Morainn*, p. 7.

British and English. The fact that the monastery of Iona was founded off the west coast of Scotland in 563 and the monastery of Jarrow was founded about a century later in the far north of England, and that both were major centres of recording, writing and study, means that we know something about the relationship between these groups at this early period – certainly far more than we know in later centuries.

Though we can learn very little about them before this, by the late sixth century there were a number of British kingdoms in the area which is now the Scottish Lowlands and northern England.[39] British kings fell to the English in the Newcastle–Bamburgh area and beyond in the decades running up to 600 – Morgan, Urien, perhaps Gwallog – but a British king survived in southern Yorkshire until about 617.[40] Despite that survival, this is essentially a story of defeat – of military catastrophe, followed by the loss of political identity and political independence – a tale and a mood encapsulated in the poem known as *The Gododdin* (though more economically, and as powerfully, in the poems of *Canu Taliesin*).

> Warriors went to Catraeth, their host was swift,
> Fresh mead was their feast and it was bitter,
> Three hundred fighting under command,
> And after the cry of jubilation there was silence.
> Though they went to churches to do penance,
> The certain meeting with death came to them.[41]

Warriors assembled from far and wide for the defence of Rheged, a large kingdom that probably spanned the Pennines and may even have extended into Galloway, and they met the English at a decisive battle at Catraeth, probably Catterick, shortly after 600. Thereafter Rheged simply disappeared. Located around the Firth of Forth, the kingdom of the Gododdin itself, whose warriors gave their name to the poem, survived a further generation: its strongpoint at Edinburgh was finally captured by the English in 638 (see Map 5).

The kingdom to the west, Strathclyde, had a far longer life and its kings, who are recorded until 1034, interacted with both the Irish and the Picts over a long period. It lay around the Firth of Clyde, with its political focus at Dumbarton Rock. St Patrick had referred to its king, Ceredig, in the fifth century and Adomnán, writing about 700, knew of a powerful Strathclyde king of the late sixth century who had had dealings with the Irish saint Columba – Rhydderch Hen, Rhydderch the Old.[42] We know very little about the kingdom, beyond the fact that members of its royal family sometimes married into the Pictish

39 Though see below for fifth-century Strathclyde; for all this see Koch (1997).

40 *Historia Brittonum c.*63.

41 Aneirin, *Y Gododdin*, lines 78–84; *Canu Taliesin.*

42 Patrick, 'Epistola' *c.*2; *Vita Columbae* I, *c.*15.

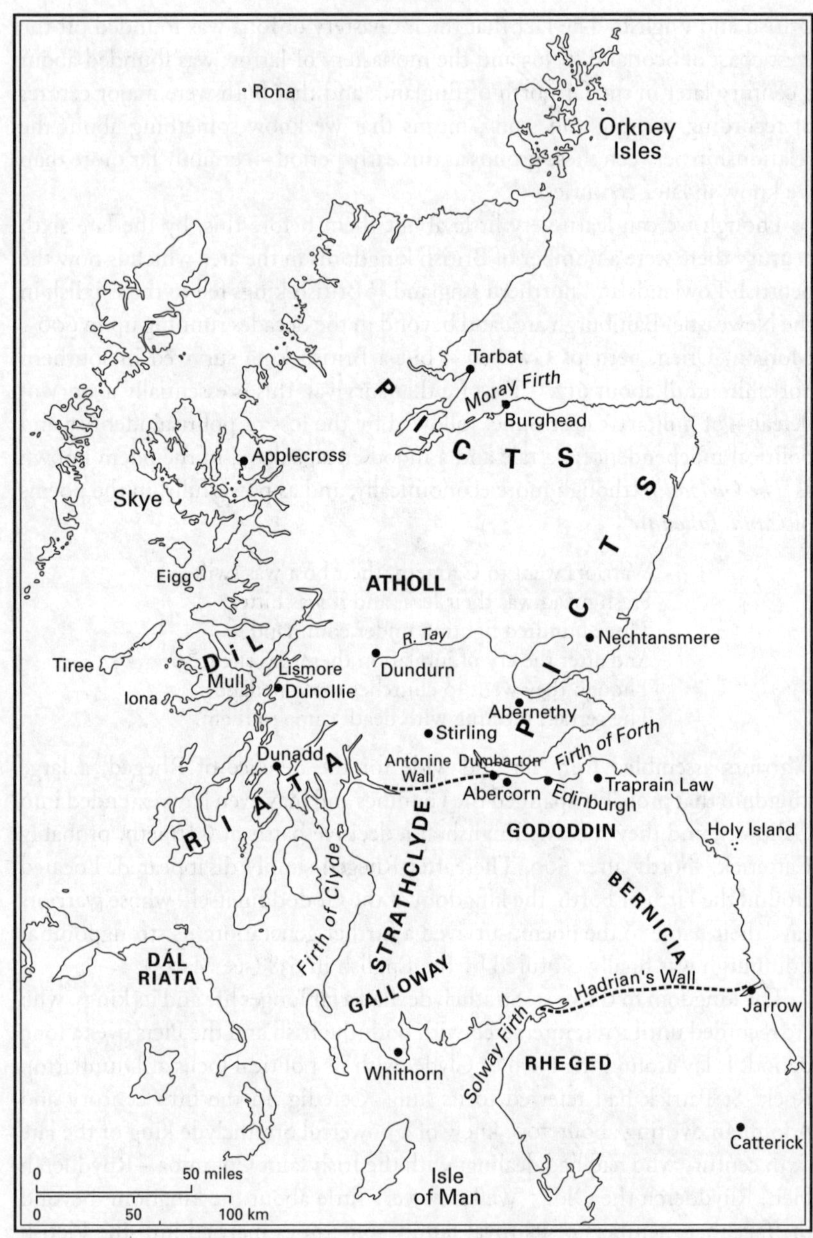

Map 5 Northern Britain

ruling families and that Dumbarton was powerful and symbolic enough in the mid-eighth century to merit attack by Oengus of the Picts and in the late ninth by the Vikings. Though not large, Strathclyde was clearly a consistently significant independent 'enclave', which its more powerful neighbours to west, north and east could not ignore.

We are accustomed, however, to regard the Picts as a problem.[43] There are problems of identity, settlement zone and political structure, to name but the most serious, for the Picts themselves have left no written records beyond the symbol stones, whose reading still poses problems;[44] our knowledge of them derives almost entirely from external observations. Even the name Pict seems to have been devised by writers outside Scotland and probably conceals a range of different tribal identities, for Roman writers in the first and second centuries AD had used tribal names rather than the generic 'Pict'. The Picts of the late and post-Roman period were people who raided the provinces of Roman Britain from their bases in the north, and the name may well have been applied to all the inhabitants of central and northern Scotland beyond the Antonine Wall. This need not imply any single social or political identity of the people so-called, nor even a single language, and it is likely that there were several groups in the fifth and early sixth centuries. The establishment of the Irish in the south-west and the English in the Scottish Lowlands obviously made for change, as did the introduction of Christianity, and though the evidence is far too fragmentary to be satisfactory it is not unreasonable to suggest that by the seventh century – whatever the background and whatever the constituent elements – a single political identity was developing.[45]

The nature of Pictish kingship is a related problem. For reasons of size, space and communications it is extraordinarily unlikely that there was no more than a single Pictish kingship in the fifth and sixth centuries, and as late as 739 we hear of a king of Atholl (in eastern Scotland) who was drowned by the 'king of the Picts'; much later tradition has seven constituent and potentially independent regions (though this could well be a deduction about origins derived from existing administrative divisions).[46] The references are very few but they suggest that until the mid-eighth century there were sometimes (if not always) several kings in Pictland. This seems on the surface to be belied by the Pictish kinglists. A list of Pictish kings was compiled on the assumption that there was a single line of kings, including virtually every Pictish king who is named in any contemporary source. It therefore appears to supply a record of a very long-lived monarchy. It is clearly misleading in its earlier phases, although in the end a single Pictish kingship undoubtedly was established. There is, of

[43] Witness Wainwright (1955, repr. 1980); Small (1987). [44] Forsyth (1997).

[45] Henderson (1967), pp. 15–18, 34–41; (1975).

[46] *Annals of Ulster* 739; *Annals of Tigernach* s.a. 738 (*Revue Celtique* 17: 243).

course, the possibility that the kinglists record not a line of monarchs but a line of Pictish overkings. Although it is true that Adomnán, writing *c.*700, talks of the great king Brude of the late sixth century and a *regulus*, lesser king, of the Orkneys, an overkingship relationship is not made explicit in this reference and there is little else to support it positively. Though possible, it remains to be demonstrated that overkingship was central to Pictish political structures.[47]

Whatever we might think about the background, for much of the seventh century there was a principal king of the Picts, whose focus of royal power lay in the Pictish heartland of eastern Scotland. Although many have disputed the observation, Bede's statement that Pictish royal succession was matrilineally determined makes sense at this period.[48] A king tended to be succeeded by his sister's son, or by his brother, rather than by his own son. The fathers of Pictish kings sometimes have British names, like Beli of Strathclyde, and sometimes have English names, like Eanfrith (of Bernicia), and it is reasonable to suppose that energetic males from neighbouring parts sometimes married eligible Pictish royal females and thereby either acquired kingship for themselves or fathered Pictish kings.[49] The English names are indicative of a sustained interest in Pictland through much of the seventh century. By the late sixth century the English kingdom of Bernicia was well established on the eastern coast of the Scottish Lowlands and its kings campaigned widely; we have already noted that Aedán mac Gabráin was defeated by the English king Æthelfrith in 603. By the second quarter of the seventh century, the English were campaigning northwards, taking the British strongholds of Etin (Edinburgh) and Stirling in 638 and 642, and this brought them into the Pictish heartland.[50] The power of Oswiu, king of Bernicia and Northumbria 643–671 and probably most powerful of all the English kings, seems to have stretched by the 660s to include at least southern Pictland; he and his son Ecgfrith seem to have operated effectively as overlords, with Pictish subordinate kings.[51] Pictland, then, was not only subject to English military campaigning during the seventh century; it was also subject to English political control for about twenty-five years. The control did not go unopposed: the subject king Drost was thrown out, there were rebellions, and ultimately Ecgfrith was defeated and killed at the famous battle of Nechtansmere, Dunnichen, in 685, by the Pictish king Brude, son of the British king of Strathclyde.[52] This was effectively the end of English domination, although there were still some military encounters in 698 and 711 and, for a generation, English officials attempted interference.

47 See Anderson (1973), pp. 77–102; *Vita Columbae* II, *c.*42.

48 Bede, *HE* I.1.

49 Marjorie Anderson's treatment of these problems (1973) remains extremely impressive.

50 *Anglo-Saxon Chronicle* s.a. 603; *Annals of Ulster* s.a. 638; *Historia Brittonum c.*65.

51 See Thacker chapter 17 below.

52 Bede, *HE* IV.26.

We hear of much military activity in the later seventh and early eighth century and of the sieges of military fortresses – Dunnottar on the east coast in 681, Dunadd on the west coast and Dundurn in the midlands in 683, Scone and Moncreiffe a little later. There seem to be at least two elements to the conflict: fighting for supremacy among Picts, perhaps to establish the single kingship, and fighting for control of territory, in particular with respect to the Irish in the west. In the late sixth century, the Picts had been defeated by raiders from Dál Riata; by the mid-eighth they were raiding, and could take Dunadd itself, the Dalriatan centre on the west coast.[53] The period between 685 and *c.*730 seems to be one of clarification and consolidation of the Pictish kingship, of Pictish political identity and of power. Although there were conflicts between Picts, King Nechtan could enter into diplomatic relations with the Northumbrians in the early eighth century and could expel the Columban (i.e. Irish) clergy from the whole of Pictland,[54] while King Oengus in the mid-eighth century could move about central and western Scotland with impressive military capacity. Later material suggests that this Pictish kingship began to develop institutions of government.[55]

WALES

Among the few fragments of contemporary evidence that we have for Wales in the early sixth century, the work of Gildas is exceptionally important for establishing the existence of two major kingdoms, Gwynedd in the north-west and Dyfed in the south-west.[56] He makes it clear that they were not recent creations and that their kings belonged to dynasties with sustained interests in the kingdoms. It is quite possible that one or two of the other kings that he names as his own contemporaries were also Welsh kings, but we do not know where he was writing and we cannot reconstruct with any confidence the local contexts of each man. From the later sixth, and seventh, centuries we have – unusually for Celtic areas – some charter material relating to the south-east, most coming from the Book of Llandaff but with a few charters being attached to the Life of Cadog from Llancarfan.[57] This material has been copied and recopied many times, and 'improved' by a succession of editors, and it cannot be taken at its face value. However, the bare elements that lie behind the surviving charter texts make sense and suggest a coherent and credible pattern of political development for the region.[58]

[53] *Annals of Ulster* s.a. 736. [54] See Stancliffe, chapter 16 below.
[55] Cf. Barrow (1973), pp. 7–68; Davies (1993). [56] Gildas, *De Excidio cc.*31, 33.
[57] *Book of Llan Dâv*, nos. 72a–77, 121–127b, 140–66; *Vita Cadoci cc.*55–68. See Davies (1979a) and (1982b), p. 260, for critical assessment.
[58] See Davies (1978).

The Llandaff material fills out the sixth-century political structure by showing that in the late sixth century there were several very small kingdoms in the south-east; these were Gwent, Ergyng (south-west Herefordshire), an unnamed kingdom near Cardiff and one in Gower. We can also deduce with some certainty, from early seventh-century references in other texts, that another kingdom had its focus in the north-east; whatever it was called then, it was the ancestor of Powys. We therefore have reasonable knowledge that by 600 most parts of Wales were part of some kingdom, although there were considerable differences in the size of these units. (There may of course have been rather more small units, which go unnoticed by our fragmentary source material. We know least about mid-Wales, and about the central eastern borders in particular. It is possible to make a case, for example, for the existence of kingdoms of Rhos (mid-north), Meirionydd and Ceredigion (centre west coast), Builth and Brycheiniog (east, south of centre), and Shropshire/mid-Wales. None of these is evidenced in the sixth century, but Ceredigion, Builth and Brycheiniog – at least – have an eighth-century history and could well have had earlier origins (see Map 6).)[59]

We do not know how the kingdoms arose. Both Dyfed and Ergyng had some relationship with the Roman past, the former taking its name (and basic shape) from the *civitas* of the Demetae, the latter taking its name from the Roman city of Ariconium (Weston-under-Penyard) and perhaps relating to the city's territory. They may, therefore, in some sense be continuities of units of Roman local government, within a different political framework and with a new basis of political power. The Cadelling, the dynasty that came to rule Powys, may well have had a Chester origin. Others could have originated as a result of the settlement of immigrant groups, like the Irish in the west. Later Welsh writers recognised a powerful tradition that some of the Votadini (i.e. Gododdin) had come from northern Britain to settle in the north-west, under a leader called Cunedda.[60] Another tradition about the fifth century had Vortigern's (Gwrtheyrn's) family associated with Roman Gloucester, from which they were displaced to establish the kingdoms of Builth and Gwerthrynion.[61] These are ideas about origins; they suggest models of development; each is possible; they may or may not relate to what actually happened and the real formative processes.[62]

The fifth-century background is exceptionally hazy: we simply cannot perceive the process of devolution from Roman imperial province (or part of one) to complex of kingdoms, although we can see, at a more local (and a more proprietary) level, that in the south-east many late Roman estates continued as

[59] See Davies (1982a), pp. 85–102, for a longer discussion. [60] *Historia Brittonum c.*62.
[61] *Historia Brittonum cc.*47, 48, 49. [62] Cf. Dark (1993), pp. 78–86.

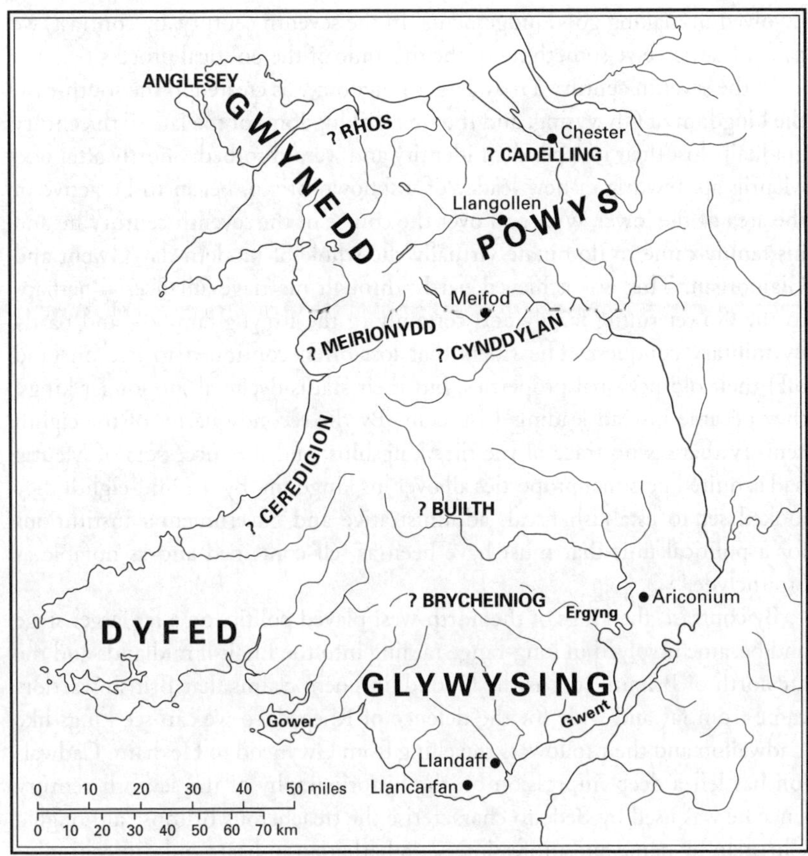

Map 6 Wales

the framework for the exploitation of the land – and the land continued to be exploited (for it was, of course, good arable).[63] The sixth century is still very hazy, although we know that by then a complex of independent kingdoms had been established, that some were very small and some larger, and that some – Gwynedd especially – had kings who were regarded as unusually powerful. We also know that political power was already dynastically transmitted, from father to son through royal families; that the concept of kingdom was strongly territorial: it had borders, physical boundaries, and the land had to be defended; that kings tended to have a military *comitatus*, a warband; and that, though they had little to do with government, they were expected to be just and be

[63] Davies (1978), esp. pp. 24–64, and (1979b).

involved in making good judgements. In the seventh century, by contrast, we can at last perceive something of the dynamic of the political process.

In the seventh century a new, larger kingdom was created in the south-east, the kingdom of Glywysing, and the smaller kingdoms of the late sixth century gradually lost their independent identity and were absorbed. Shortly after 600 Meurig ap Tewdrig, a new leader of unknown origin, began to be active in the area of the lower Wye, and over the course of the seventh century he and his family came to dominate virtually the whole of modern-day Gwent and Glamorgan. This was achieved partly through marriage alliances – perhaps to the Gower ruling family and certainly to the Ergyng family – and partly by military conquest. The rulers that lost often continued to live on (and off) their old personal properties, but their status declined: no longer kings, they became instead leading aristocrats. By the second quarter of the eighth century there is no trace of the tiny kingships, and the successors of Meurig had acquired personal properties all over his kingdom. By the mid-eighth they looked set to establish fiscal, administrative and governmental institutions for a political unit that must have been as self-contained and as notable as Strathclyde.[64]

By contrast, the kings of the north-west played politics on a far larger stage and became involved in long-range raiding into the English midlands and the far north of Britain. Just as the Gododdin poem claims that British warriors came from far and wide for the defence of Rheged, so we can see kings like Cadwallon and their followers travelling from Gwynedd to Hexham. Cadwallon has left a deep impression on the historiography of the seventh century since he was used by Bede to characterise the treacherous Britons: 'although a Christian by name and profession . . . a barbarian in heart and disposition'.[65] He fought with the pagan king of the English midlands, Penda, against the Christian Northumbrian Edwin; after Edwin had raided Anglesey, Cadwallon rushed to midland England and then to northern Northumbria. Although these were hit and run campaigns, they did mean that Gwynedd kings were involved in the politics of the whole island of Britain. Not for nothing was Cadwallon's father, Cadfan, recorded in a seventh-century inscription as being 'the wisest and most renowned of all kings'.[66]

In north-east Wales, and the central marches, the principal trend was one of curtailment and confinement by the English. In 616 Anglian leaders won a major battle at Chester, which gave them control of the city and the Cheshire plain.[67] This may well have displaced the Cadelling and certainly confined

64 Davies (1978), pp. 65–95.

65 Bede, *HE* II.20; *Historia Brittonum* c.64; see also Thacker, chapter 17 below.

66 Nash-Williams (1950), no. 13.

67 *Annales Cambriae* s.a. 613; Bede, *HE* II.2.

the nascent kingdom of Powys to the Welsh hills. Farther south the family of Cynddylan seems to have lost control of Shropshire in the mid- or late seventh century, for the Mercian kings seem to have been running the west midlands by 700. Later poetry regarded this defeat as disastrous for the family: Cynddylan's sister Heledd was left at the Wrekin bewailing the loss of her brothers.[68] So here too, the Welsh were confined to the hills; a ruling family lost its capacity to rule; a kingdom collapsed; and this may well have given the Cadelling the opportunity to become established in the eastern parts of mid-Wales. Meifod and Llangollen became the Powys heartland, rather than Chester. In all this it was contraction and confinement that the English effected, not incursion. In many ways the seventh century is the period of the establishment of the Welsh border, and of the western limits of English political control (although the status of the north and northern border remained uncertain for a couple of centuries more). Despite Edwin's long dart into Anglesey, it is not characteristically a century of English raids into Wales; that was to come, with considerable and repeated force, in the eighth and ninth centuries.

It really is impossible to characterise trends in internal Welsh politics in this period. We can certainly note the English opposition in the seventh century, and the definition of the 'border' (or border area), but we know far too little of the sixth century to say much about it and not enough of the seventh to make much sense of it except in very limited areas. The establishment of Glywysing, and demotion of the petty kings of the south-east, is perfectly clear; so is the range of interests of the Gwynedd kings; and the collapse of the Shropshire kingdom. At best we might say that a number of petty kingships are lost – they just disappear (unlike the Irish situation) – and the process of creating larger, more structured kingships begins, with potential governmental responsibilities and potential administrative frameworks. The possibilities were there but they had not yet been implemented.

CORNWALL AND BRITTANY

Loss of territory to English control is as characteristic of Cornwall and Devon as it is of eastern Wales in the seventh century. In 600 both counties lay within a single kingdom of Dumnonia, a kingdom which probably also initially included western Somerset and Dorset; by 700 that kingdom was confined to present-day Cornwall. In 658 the West Saxon king Cenwalh was fighting on the River Parrett in Somerset; by 690 there was an English monastery in Exeter; and in 710 the West Saxon king Ine was making land grants near the River Tamar,

[68] Davies (1982a), pp. 99–102; see Rowland (1990), pp. 120–41, for a slightly later dating.

the traditional eastern boundary of Cornwall.[69] Thus, quickly and irreversibly, Dumnonia was reduced by more than half its former territory (see Map 7).

As might be expected, we do not know anything about the creation of early medieval Dumnonia, but it was quite clearly in existence – and not new – when Gildas was writing in the mid-sixth century; he referred to its king, Constantine.[70] Like the kingdom of Dyfed in south-west Wales, the name of this unit perpetuated the name of the Roman *civitas*, that of the Dumnonii, and its origin may also have been to do with the continuation of a Roman unit of local government. It is notable that its early sixth-century king bore a very famous Roman imperial name: the rulers of Dumnonia seem to have been influenced by the Roman tradition. Moreover, episcopal properties seem to have continued undisturbed through the late and post-Roman period and this may also have been true of secular landownership. It is likely, however, that there was a little Irish settlement to disturb north Cornwall and south Devon, for there are stones inscribed with the Irish ogham alphabet there.[71]

Everything suggests that this kingdom was a monarchy, and by Celtic standards an unusually large one. There is never anything to suggest that there was other than a single king, and that power was transmitted dynastically; Constantine had two royal males murdered, presumably to reduce the possibility of rival claims for the kingship. St Samson came across a property-owning 'count', who clearly had some influence over the local population; there may have been several such men within the kingdom; we cannot know if they were agents of the king or quasi-independent notables.[72]

There is a suggestion in a ninth-century text, the Breton Life of Paul Aurelian, that at least one king of Dumnonia ruled on both sides of the English Channel: the early sixth-century Conomorus (Cynfawr). It is worth considering this possibility seriously, although there is far too little contemporary material to find sufficient corroboration. It is quite clear from linguistic evidence that people from Cornwall and Brittany were in close contact in the early Middle Ages: the languages were indistinguishable until the tenth or eleventh century, and shared the same sixth-century and later changes. The (admittedly late) genealogy of the Dumnonian kings includes a Kynwawr in the generation before Constantine, a name which is a likely corruption of Cynfawr; and an inscribed stone from Castle Dore in east Cornwall commemorates the burial of one Drustanus, son of Conomorus; so there would appear to have been an early sixth-century Cynfawr in Dumnonia. South of the Channel we have the evidence of the Life of Samson for the appearance of a 'tyrant' Conomorus

[69] See Thacker, chapter 17 below. [70] Gildas, *De Excidio cc.*28–9.

[71] Pearce (1978), pp. 82–92, 165; Okasha (1993), p. 19; Thomas (1994), p. 331.

[72] *Vita Samsonis* I, *c.*48.

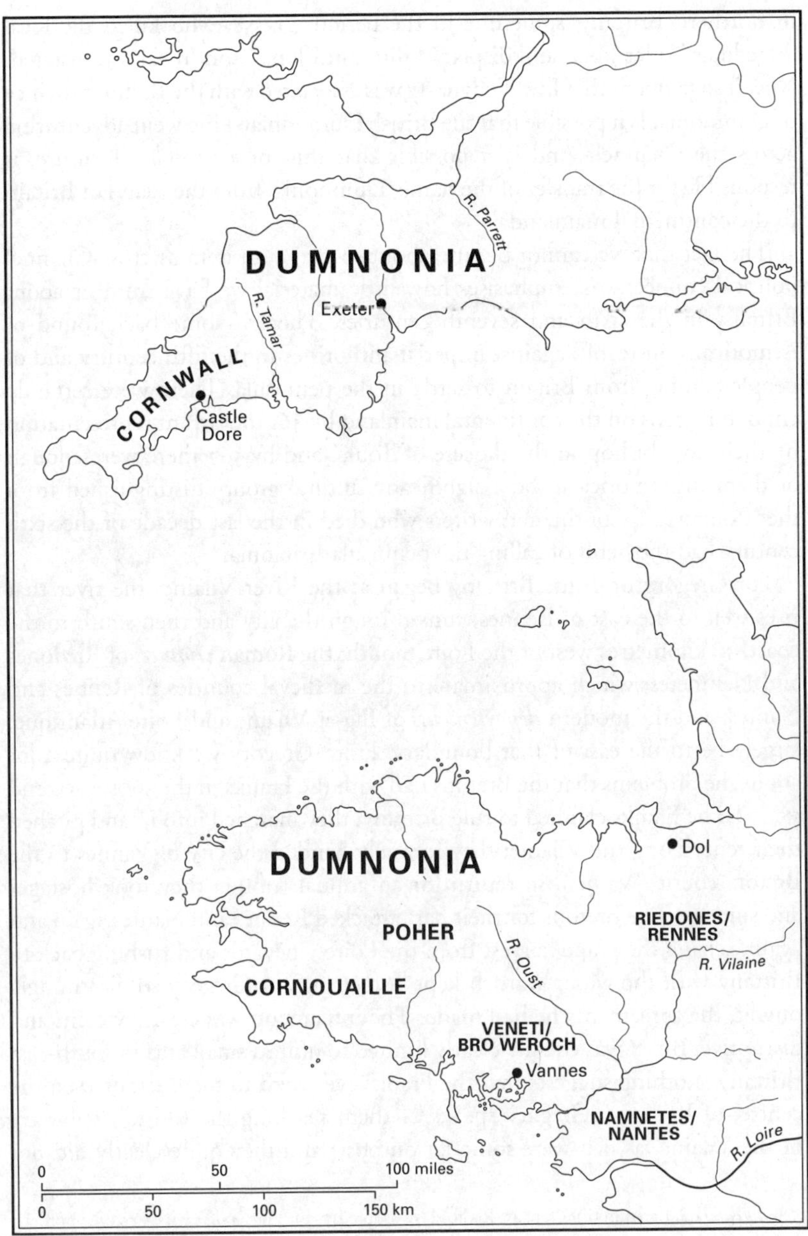

Map 7 Cornwall and Brittany

in northern Brittany, sometime in the period 511–558, who killed the local 'hereditary' ruler Jonas and displaced him until Jonas' son Idwal was instated. Now it so happens that Idwal's dynasty was associated with the Breton province of Dumnonia. Is it possible that the British Dumnonian king went adventuring across the Channel? And is it possible that this, or a similar adventure, is responsible for the transfer of the name 'Dumnonia' from the island of Britain to the continental mainland?[73]

The fact that we cannot be sure about so major an item as cross-Channel political connections emphasises how little material we have from or about Brittany in the sixth and seventh centuries. There is some background of Armoricans 'in revolt' against imperial authorities in the fifth century and of people coming from Britain to settle in the peninsula. There were certainly enough Britons on the continental mainland by 461 to warrant representation by their own bishop in the diocese of Tours; and by 567 there were enough of them in Armorica to be a significant cultural group, distinguished from the 'Romans'.[74] Continental writers who died in the last decade of the sixth century had the habit of calling the peninsula Britannia.

For Gregory of Tours Brittany began at the River Vilaine, the river that rises well to the east of Rennes, runs through the city and then south to the coast, 30 kilometres west of the Loire mouth; the Roman *civitates* of Riedones and Namnetes, which approximate to the medieval counties of Rennes and Nantes, and the modern *départements* of Ille-et-Vilaine and Loire Atlantique, largely lie to the east of that boundary. From Gregory we know quite a lot about the problems that the Bretons had with the Franks in the 560s, 570s and 580s.[75] The Franks claimed to rule Brittany: they marched into it, and pitched their tents along the Vilaine; they formally handed the city of Vannes to the Breton 'count' Waroch, in return for an annual tribute; they took hostages and sureties. The Bretons for their part attacked Rennes and Nantes again and again, seizing the grape harvest from the Loire vineyards and rushing back to Brittany with the wine; Waroch kept 'forgetting', as Gregory so disarmingly puts it, the agreements he had made. The interaction was clearly violent and disruptive. But it was equally clearly limited to quite a small area in south-east Brittany. Nothing suggests that the Franks ever went to the west, or even the centre, of Brittany (Gregory speaks of them reaching the Oust, a tributary of the Vilaine, as if it were some far outpost) and they quite clearly did not

73 *Vita Pauli c.*8; Bartrum (1966), p. 45; Radford (1951), pp. 117–19; *Vita Samsonis* I, *c.*59; cf. La Borderie (1896), I, pp. 459–69. Some of this material is worked into the later medieval story of Tristan; see Pearce (1978), pp. 152–5; Padel (1981), pp. 55, 76–9.

74 See above, pp. 235–6.

75 Gregory, *Hist.* IV.4, 20, pp. 137, 152–4; V.16, 26, 29, 31, pp. 214, 232–6; IX.18, 24, pp. 431–2, 443–4; X.9; pp. 491–4. See also Fouracre, chapter 14 below.

rule the peninsula in practice. Vannes may have been ceremoniously given to Waroch after one expedition that reached it, but by 589 Frankish leaders could only enter it by making an arrangement with the bishop; again and again they had to negotiate with Waroch, even on one occasion sending Bishop Bertram of Le Mans as a member of a deputation pleading for peace. This, then, seems to have been the situation: Frankish kings effectively controlled the counties of Rennes and Nantes, though the Bretons could be disconcertingly disruptive there; they tried hard to get control of Vannes (the *civitas* capital of the Veneti), sometimes succeeding, sometimes not; and they had nothing to do with the rest of the country (see Map 7).

Within Brittany, that is west of the Vilaine, Waroch certainly did not act for the whole region. He was the ruler of the Veneti *civitas*, the modern Morbihan, known as Bro Weroc in the Middle Ages. There were other rulers in other parts, and there were conflicts between them. Waroch's father Macliaw and his brother Iago had been killed by Theuderich son of Budic, a family that may have come from the west (despite Theuderich's Germanic name), while Jonas of the north was killed by the tyrant Conomorus. At this period, the evidence will only permit us to identify two units of rule – Bro Weroc and the northern Dumnonia – and two other rulers, Budic's family and Conomorus. Centuries later we hear of a Cornouaille in the west and Poher west of centre and it is traditional to associate the other rulers with these regions. This is by no means impossible; but it is also possible, as suggested above, that Conomorus was of south-west British origin and attacked from a base north of the Channel. After all, the ruling family of (Breton) Dumnonia was restored in the mid-sixth century and there is nothing to suggest successors to Conomorus ruling on this south side of the Channel.

Whatever the number of political units within Brittany in the sixth century – and all that we can say with confidence is that there were several – what type of political authority did they exercise? Gregory of Tours is very firm in maintaining that the Bretons did not have kings but had counts, and this terminology of political authority is reflected and sustained in contemporary and later saints' lives. Gregory's approach is conditioned, of course, by his desire to present Breton rulers as dependent on the Franks, and even the saints' lives are prone to represent the Frankish king as an ultimate authority; the Life of Samson, written at Dol in north-east Brittany, undoubtedly reflects a Frankish perspective and has Idwal rather mysteriously imprisoned by Childebert and released because of Samson's representations to the Frankish king, allowing him to return to Dumnonia and kill Conomorus.[76] It is reasonable to suppose that literate and political Franks believed this, and the Frankish connection adds a

[76] *Vita Samsonis* I, *cc.*53–9.

dimension to Breton politics that is missing from other Celtic areas, but in practice although the terminology of political authority is largely one of dependence it does not really matter what the rulers were called: they behaved independently and acted like the kings of Strathclyde or Gwynedd or Glywysing. Their power was transmitted dynastically: son followed father (Theuderich – Budic, Idwal – Jonas, Waroch – Macliaw, Canao – Waroch), brother followed brother (Macliaw – Chanao), and even the Life of Samson comments that Idwal stood at the head of a long line that ruled Dumnonia. As for the shape of the political units: the Roman background of *civitas* gave shape to Rennes and Nantes to the east of the Vilaine and Vannes/Bro Weroc to the west, but farther west and north the framework of *civitates* did not hold into the central Middle Ages and it may be that immigration and/or a period of political control from Britain gave shape to these areas.[77]

Although there is some seventh-century archaeological material – metalwork in east and west, coins minted in Rennes and Nantes – there appear to be only two contemporary written references to seventh-century Brittany and they do not allow us to characterise developments with any precision. The Frankish Chronicle of Fredegar relates a tale about the Breton ruler Iudicael: once again (or still) the Bretons had been raiding, and in 635 King Dagobert demanded reparations and threatened to send an army if they did not materialise. Iudicael made the journey to Clichy to discuss the situation and, although he refused to eat at the same table as Dagobert, promised to make good the damage. Unusually for a Frankish source, the Chronicle calls him 'king' and presents him as king of Brittany as a whole.[78] This should not lead us to suppose some movement of Breton unification between 590 and 635: the fuller documentation of the eighth and ninth centuries makes it quite clear that Brittany was politically fragmented until the middle of the ninth century; and, within Brittany, Iudicael and his family were firmly associated with the region of Dumnonia. Ninth-century tradition relates Iudicael to Idwal (of the Samson Life), and Idwal to Riwal (his great-grandfather), the supposed founder of Dumnonia.[79] It therefore seems likely that Frankish rulers had more influence in northern Brittany, and used their contacts there in an attempt to bring pressure on as many Bretons as they could. (This is consistent with the Childebert/Idwal story of the Samson Life and the long conflicts between Dumnonia and the rulers in the Morbihan.) This certainly did not solve Franko-Breton problems for, according to the Prior Annals of Metz, the Austrasian mayor Pippin II defeated

[77] Dumnonia at least in part reflected the territory of the Coriosolites, but may well have extended farther west; see Galliou and Jones (1991), p. 80, for a recent map of *civitates*.

[78] *Chronicle of Fredegar* IV.78.65–7, also Fouracre, chapter 14 below.

[79] La Borderie (1896), I, pp. 350–1.

Bretons among others in 688 and the old-style raiding and border warfare was still continuing in the eighth and even ninth centuries, although in a rather different political context. For the most part we simply do not know what was happening in Brittany in the seventh century.

SOME CONCLUDING THOUGHTS

Despite the unevenness of the available source material there are some genuine comparisons to be made between Celtic areas in the sixth and seventh centuries. There are, of course, some similarities: these are regions which had polities with little or no governmental function, whose rulers had no means of regular communication within and across the polity; they had a tendency to throw up kingdoms, nevertheless; and extraordinarily strong dynastic interests in rulership. It is very striking that ruling families are entrenched all over the Celtic world from the moment that we begin to perceive what was happening; many lasted for generations and some lasted for centuries. But there are differences too between Celtic areas, and these need stressing lest the label 'Celtic' be thought to imply some spurious homogeneity. Kingdoms were common, but although there was nothing of the size of Visigothic Spain or the Byzantine Empire there were considerable variations between them. Most Irish *tuatha* cannot have been much more than 15–20 kilometres across; kingdoms like Strathclyde or Glywysing were more like 80–100 kilometres across, and the Breton polities a little smaller; while early British Dumnonia must have been at least 200 kilometres from end to end. Kingship cannot have been the same sort of experience in all of them. It was overkingship that created the dynamic of politics in Ireland, perhaps assisted by the relative ease of movement across the country and certainly fed by the availability of easily dominated surplus produce. Overkingship may have been a factor in political relationships in early Pictland, but it certainly was not so in Cornwall or Wales nor among the Bretons in Brittany. Perhaps because of this, by 700 the Welsh kingdoms look poised to develop more complex political institutions, as the Pictish kingship did in the eighth century.

Overall, however, the inhabitants of the island of Britain suffered in this period from Irish and English expansion, through both settlement and political conquest. It is difficult to determine how much settlement was still going on in the sixth century, but there was probably some – for example, in south-west Scotland in one case and in the English midlands in another. Conquest and military activity proceeded apace, by the Irish in western Scotland and by the English in eastern Scotland and western Britain. Though their Scottish adventure turned out to be short-term, the confinement of the British by the

English is one of the major political developments of the seventh century. This may seem like an old cliché, but it is still true, whether we are regarding the reduction of Dumnonia or the disappearance of Rheged.

There was, finally, movement between Celtic areas, quite apart from the long-ranging military expeditions of Diarmait mac Cerbaill or Aedán mac Gabráin, Cadwallon ap Cadfan or Waroch son of Macliaw. It is quite possible, as both Welsh and Breton tradition has it, that a significant part of the migration of British to Brittany took place in the mid-sixth century and there was clearly plenty of coming and going between south-west Britain and Brittany for the next 150 years and more. There was also coming and going between northern Ireland and western Scotland in the years before Magh Roth, and even then the traffic did not stop completely, as it tended to do with the coming of the Vikings. Some Celts travelled to England and to the continent beyond Brittany. But these were mostly monks and clerics, and most were Irish. In the end, the most striking migration, and the one that had the greatest consequences for Europe as a whole, was of decidedly religious and not political character.

CHAPTER 10

THE EARLIEST ANGLO-SAXON KINGDOMS

Helena Hamerow

INTRODUCTION

By the time Bede began to write the *Historia Ecclesiastica*, the origins of the earliest Anglo-Saxon kingdoms were believed to lie in the ethnic pedigrees of Germanic invaders, primarily the three tribes named in the *HE*, the Angles, Saxons and Jutes, groups who gave their names to many of the earliest kingdoms.[1] Indeed, the traditional view of kingdom formation takes as its point of departure the accounts of the invasions in the *HE* and the *Anglo-Saxon Chronicle* and sees the distribution of Anglo-Saxon cemeteries and settlements as marking out a process of military conquest and political takeover, in the course of which new kingdoms were carved out.[2] An admirable example of this school of thought is Beck's chapter on 'The Teutonic conquest of Britain', in the first volume of *The Cambridge Medieval History* published in 1911. Modern scholarship has at its disposal a range of data, especially in the form of archaeological remains, unimagined in Beck's day, and the 'conquest model', a central tenet of English history, has crumbled since the 1970s as the origins of the Anglo-Saxon kingdoms have come under renewed scrutiny.

A new understanding, if not exactly a consensus, has emerged which is more complex, though less satisfyingly comprehensive, than Beck's vision. This view of England in the sixth century stems from an ongoing re-evaluation of four related issues: the scale and nature of Germanic immigration and, conversely, of British survival; the formation of 'Anglo-Saxon' social identities; the construction of power; and the formation of new economic structures as reflected in strategies of production and exchange.

The approach taken in this survey recognises, indeed emphasises, regional variability with regard to each of these issues. It has, for example, long been acknowledged that the impact of Germanic immigration varied regionally.

[1] Bede, *HE* 1.15.1. [2] See for example Leeds (1912) and Myres (1954).

Some parts of the country, i.e. much of the south and east, were directly and profoundly affected while in other areas such as the west midlands, Germanic immigration must have had little or no direct impact, although its indirect effects were ultimately no less important. The recognition, furthermore, that early written sources offer little reliable information regarding events, ethnic origins and social identity in sixth-century England[3] means that any overview of sixth-century developments must rely heavily on archaeological evidence which, if it offers few certainties, is at least relatively abundant and steadily increasing.

GERMANIC MIGRATION AND THE FORMATION OF ANGLO-SAXON ENGLAND

The question of continuity: cemeteries and settlements

Central to the re-evaluation of the immigration and its impact on post-Roman Britain is the relationship between Romano-British and Anglo-Saxon cemeteries and settlements. The overwhelming majority of cemeteries founded in the fifth and sixth centuries were *de novo* establishments, even though many lie near Romano-British burial grounds. A prime example is the settlement complex at Mucking, overlooking the Thames estuary in Essex, which contained not only two cemeteries and a sizable settlement, all established during the first half of the fifth century, but also four Romano-British cemeteries. The latest Romano-British burials at Mucking probably post-date AD 350, and some could date to the late fourth, or even fifth century.[4] The period of time which elapsed between the latest burials in the Romano-British cemeteries and the foundation of the 'Anglo-Saxon' cemeteries must therefore have been brief – it is even conceivable that their periods of use could have overlapped – yet the latter were established on new, entirely separate sites. A new settlement and a new burial community were thus defined simultaneously.

We now know, however, that some Romano-British cemeteries remained in use well into the post-Roman period, though how common this was is unclear owing to the difficulty of dating the latest Roman burials. The Romano-British cemetery at Queenford Farm (Oxon.), for instance, lay outside the Roman small town of Dorchester-on-Thames in an area with an early fifth-century Anglo-Saxon presence, yet radiocarbon dates indicate that it continued in use into the sixth century.[5] In such cemeteries may lie many Britons who lived and died in the fifth and sixth centuries, but who are rendered archaeologically invisible by a burial rite which involved no durable, datable grave-goods. Their

[3] See Yorke (1993). [4] Hamerow (1993); C. Going, pers. comm. [5] Chambers (1988).

exact relationship to those buried in nearby 'Anglo-Saxon' cemeteries, and their numbers, remain for the time being moot points.

In the great majority of cases, as at Mucking, communities established new cemeteries in the fifth and sixth centuries, yet a small number of exceptions to this rule are known. At Wasperton, Warwickshire, a cemetery established in the fourth century was still in use in the seventh century, although a radical change in burial rite took place some time in the sixth century.[6] Of the 182 inhumations excavated at Wasperton, thirty-six were characteristically Romano-British and 137 were Anglo-Saxon; nine, it has been suggested, were 'hybrid' burials. It seems likely that Wasperton represents a family cemetery spanning the late Roman and early Anglo-Saxon periods, in which the population remained largely the same even though the burial rite and material culture became 'Anglicised'. The adoption by this community of new and powerful ethnic symbols suggests a profound change, indeed a cultural assimilation of the local population that came to regard itself as 'Anglo-Saxon'.[7]

In light of this kind of evidence, as well as the implausibility of the population of late Roman Britain[8] being numerically dominated or displaced by immigrants crossing the North Sea in small boats, the many thousands of cremations and inhumation burials of the fifth and sixth centuries, where the deceased was buried with continental-style grave-goods and costume, are no longer seen as necessarily those of immigrants, or even the direct descendants of immigrants. Instead, the great increase in the number of sixth-century 'Anglo-Saxon' burials and cemeteries in comparison to those datable to the fifth century must be due in large part to the cultural assimilation of Britons. Much of the fifth-century population would, furthermore, have been rendered archaeologically invisible by the unavailability of durable, mass-produced ceramic, metal, glass and stone goods. Old objects would consequently have been reused, greatly complicating the recognition of fifth-century burials.

Various attempts have been made to identify Britons in 'Anglo-Saxon' cemeteries. It has been argued, for example, that the many burials that contained few or no grave-goods, individuals buried in a crouched position or males buried without weapons may be those of Britons.[9] Yet, whatever it meant exactly to be *wealh* (literally, a foreigner, slave or Briton) in early Anglo-Saxon

6 Esmonde Cleary (1989), p. 201; Wise (1991).

7 The cemetery at Frilford, Berks., incompletely excavated in the nineteenth and early twentieth centuries, is another probable example of the continued use of a Romano-British burial ground into the Anglo-Saxon period. See Meaney (1964), p. 46.

8 This is currently estimated at around three to four million, although it is likely that the later fourth and early fifth centuries saw a substantial decline in population. See Millett (1990), pp. 180ff.

9 See, for example, Faull (1977) and Härke (1992b). A number of post-Roman cemeteries have now been excavated in south-west England that show what British burials actually look like. See Leech (1986), Cox (1989) and Watts and Leech (1996).

England,[10] it was clearly a disadvantage; it may be that many British families sought to conceal their ancestry by adopting an 'orthodox' Anglo-Saxon burial rite in order to improve their social status and economic conditions. In the late seventh-century laws of Ine of Wessex, *weallas* have roughly half the *wergilds* of Englishmen and a number of clauses suggest that most Britons possessed low legal status, despite the fact that the names of several members of the royal dynasty of Wessex contain British elements, itself suggestive of intermarriage.[11] The low social standing which this implies, combined with large-scale assimilation, seems the most likely explanation for the widespread and rapid adoption of Old English and, conversely, the tiny number of British loan-words (only about ten), which survived in English, even in the west of the country.[12] If this conjecture is correct, it would render sixth-century Britons difficult or impossible to identify archaeologically.

Just as new forms of burial rite appeared full-blown in Britain in the fifth and sixth centuries, so too did two new types of building. The first, known variously as sunken huts, sunken-featured buildings (SFBs) or *Grubenhäuser*, are virtually ubiquitous in Migration Period settlements in north-west Europe. They are generally small, with dugout floors, and vary considerably in depth. How they should be reconstructed has generated considerable debate, with some evidence suggesting that they had wooden floors suspended over a kind of cellar, while other buildings have produced evidence of apparent trampling on the base of the hollow. We can be quite sure that they served a variety of functions, although most were probably used for storage and craft-related activities. In any case, their continental pedigree has never been seriously questioned. They are generally found together with another type of timber building about whose origins there is less agreement. These were rectangular, with walls made of timber posts set into postholes, generally with two opposing doorways positioned centrally in the long walls, measuring on average around 10 to 12 metres in length and 5 to 6 metres in width. In at least a quarter of these buildings, a dividing wall in one end formed a small compartment. These buildings were presumably living quarters, although some could represent barns or other special-purpose structures. This 'Anglo-Saxon house' appeared in most regions of England by the sixth century with little regional variation, to the extent that the ground plans of certain buildings in Northumbria, Wessex and Essex correspond almost exactly in terms of dimensions, as well as in the positioning and width of the doorways and internal subdivisions. This type of building did not, however, closely resemble either the traditional long-house found on the

[10] *EHD* 1, p. 402, n. 5.

[11] See, for example, clauses 23.3, 24.2, 32, 33. trans. *EHD* 1, pp. 367–8.

[12] See Hamerow (1991); Higham (1992), pp. 181ff; Charles-Edwards (1995), pp. 729–30, 733; Härke (1997), p. 149; Ward-Perkins (2000).

continent, in which cattle and people lived under one roof, or late Romano-British buildings. The present consensus is that they represent some degree of hybridisation, although the Anglo-Saxon house finds its closest parallels within the building traditions of north-west Europe.[13]

A significant number of early Anglo-Saxon settlements were sited near, or even on the same site as, Romano-British settlements, contrary to the old maxim that the Anglo-Saxons avoided Romano-British settlements. Yet the thorny question of 'continuity' of settlement persists. At Barton Court Farm (Oxon.), for example, timber buildings and burials typical of the early Anglo-Saxon period were erected in the course of the fifth and sixth centuries on the site of a prosperous fourth-century farmstead, where a hoard may have been hidden as late as *c.*430.[14] What, if any, link existed between the people who built these structures and the previous occupants? The layout of the Anglo-Saxon settlement was to some extent conditioned by the Roman boundary ditches, but there is no evidence to suggest that the stone buildings of the Roman period remained occupied; indeed the farmhouse was demolished at the end of the fourth or early fifth century. Yet, despite the lack of any significant break in either time or space between the two communities at Barton Court Farm, their material cultures, in the words of the excavator, 'were poles apart'.[15] The continuity of town life in any meaningful sense into the sixth century also seems highly unlikely.[16] While the *Anglo-Saxon Chronicle* records the capture of a number of Romano-British towns such as Bath, Cirencester and Gloucester by the Anglo-Saxons in the sixth century, implying their survival – at least as defended places – through the fifth century,[17] these are the exceptions which seem to confirm (as does the archaeological evidence) that the majority of Romano-British towns were effectively defunct by the mid-fifth century.

Sixth-century demography and the origins of kingdoms

To Beck in 1911, it seemed 'incredible that . . . the invasion of Britain should have been accomplished without the employment of large and organised forces', though he ventured to suggest that 'many scholars have probably gone too far in supposing that the native population was entirely blotted out'.[18] By the

13 See Hamerow (1999). 14 Miles (1986).

15 Miles (1986), p. 52. Other examples of Anglo-Saxon settlements on the site of Romano-British farms include Orton Hall, near Peterborough, and Rivenhall, Essex. See MacKreth (1996) and Rodwell and Rodwell (1985).

16 See Biddle (1989) and Esmonde Cleary (1989).

17 *ASC* s.a. 577. See Loseby (2000). 18 Beck (1911), p. 388.

1980s and early 1990s, the scholarly pendulum had swung to the opposite extreme, and the early accounts of large-scale migrations were consigned to the realm of mythology. Instead, the transformation from Roman Britain to Anglo-Saxon England was seen as having been carried out by a tiny, military elite aided by the processes of exogamy, assimilation and exchange.[19] Yet the widespread adoption by the mid-sixth century of continental-style dress,[20] itself a powerful symbol of group self-consciousness and common descent, as well as the burial of thousands of individuals in cremation urns which are effectively indistinguishable from Continental examples, cannot be convincingly explained without accepting that immigration, at least viewed cumulatively over a period of some hundred years, took place on a significant scale. Indeed, archaeological and palynological evidence from Schleswig-Holstein appears to support Bede's account of a dramatic depopulation of *Angulus* during the fifth to eighth centuries.[21] There is, furthermore, little sign of socio-economic continuity from the fourth to sixth centuries in lowland Britain. One important exception is land use, as there is increasing evidence, primarily from pollen analysis, which indicates that cleared landscapes were maintained from the Roman to late Saxon periods and that large-scale reafforestation in the fifth and sixth centuries was the exception rather than the rule.[22]

The notion that these immigrants came from ethnically coherent and distinct groups or 'nations', however, is unsupported by the archaeological evidence. Fifth-century Europe clearly did contain groups known, by outsiders at least, as Angles, Saxons and Jutes, as well, of course, as Frisians, Franks and others.[23] The material cultures of the regions they are supposed to have inhabited also display certain distinctive traits, which, for example, distinguish the regions east and west of the Elbe and in northern and southern Jutland. A considerable degree of overlap, however, exists between these supposed 'cultural provinces' and we cannot assume that differences in pottery styles, for example, relate in any direct way to ethnic identity. Ethnic labels such as 'Angles, Saxons and Jutes', at least as they were applied to fifth-century peoples by chroniclers seeking to explain the political situation several centuries later, may reflect groups who originated from the same geographical regions (indeed, Bede defines these *gentes* with reference to geographical territories, not to political or cultural affiliation), but these groups were unstable, mobile tribal confederacies. The cultural unification of the Angles, the Saxons and the

[19] See for example Arnold (1984), Hodges (1989) and Higham (1992).

[20] Particularly in Norfolk and Suffolk, where nearly a hundred early Anglo-Saxon cemeteries are known. See Scull (1993), p. 69.

[21] *HE* I.15. See Müller-Wille *et al.* (1988).

[22] See Murphy (1994) and Tyers *et al.* (1994).

[23] See Hines (1995).

peoples of Kent, which preceded their political unification into kingdoms, was achieved *after* the migrations to Britain.[24]

There is today little doubt that the early accounts of mass invasion and population replacement in fifth-century Britain are in large part 'origin myths' devised to serve the interests of the ruling elites of later periods by offering a unifying, stabilising ideology which would confer political legitimacy.[25] Archaeology nevertheless indicates that immigration did play a critical role in the formation of an Anglo-Saxon identity. Large-scale migration into certain regions and substantial indigenous survival are, however, not mutually exclusive. Yet the complex and absorbing problem of the exact fate of the indigenous population of southern and eastern Britain in the fifth and sixth centuries remains to be resolved. Ethnic identity is of course determined not by biology, but by personal and historical circumstance; under certain conditions, individuals may switch their ethnic affiliation and 'change the label by which they are known . . . according to biographical convenience'.[26] One can only conclude that large numbers of Britons did precisely this and that direct evidence of assimilation and hybridisation will therefore continue to prove elusive. In those areas less directly affected by the collapse of Roman rule and barbarian assaults, for example in the Peak District and the west midlands, very few Anglo-Saxon-style burials of the sixth century have been found and local groups presumably maintained their position; in east Yorkshire, Roman-style burial rites survived well into the post-Roman period.[27] In short, the same demographic model will not do for the whole of Anglo-Saxon England.

While the precise demographic composition of sixth-century England will probably always elude us, we can be sure that the truth was far less clear-cut than Bede's account of the Angles, Saxons and Jutes. By the middle of the sixth century, however, new, relatively coherent regional identities *had* formed, identities that found expression in the archaeological record several generations before the earliest written accounts.

ANGLO-SAXON COMMUNITIES AND THE FORMATION OF IDENTITY

These Anglo-Saxon identities were forged in small, closely spaced communities (see pp. 273–6 below), using a cultural vocabulary derived largely from northwest Europe. The process of 'Anglicisation' itself remains hidden from view, but it is evident that by the middle of the sixth century, many people in southern and eastern England (and some in Northumbria) believed, or at least wanted others

[24] See Hines (1995) and Wood (1997), p. 45. [25] See Pohl (1997), p. 9.
[26] Chapman (1992), p. 22. [27] See Loveluck (1994), p. 140 on cist burials at Elmswell.

to believe, that they were of Germanic descent. The evidence that survives from this period, in particular elements of female costume and the ornamental styles found on pottery and metalwork, suggest that material culture was actively used to signal tribal affiliation. Indeed it was during the sixth century that regional distinctions in material culture, particularly in female costume, were most pronounced. This must have had more to do with the formation of new corporate identities than with any primary ethnic distinctions of the fifth century, since these, as we have seen, were extremely blurred. Thus in East Anglia, for example, 'a new, consistent and distinctive Anglian English culture was rapidly – within a few generations – put together out of a remarkably diverse range of sources';[28] the female costume, with its distinctive Scandinavian-style brooches and wrist clasps (used to fasten the cuffs of a long-sleeved garment), figured prominently as an expression of this new culture. In Kent too, the adoption of Frankish fashions marked out the leading members of communities as distinctively 'Kentish'. These significant regional differences in female dress styles emerged early in the sixth century. They did not arise from fifth-century realities; they had to be formed. Individual communities formed the backdrop to this process of cultural unification and ultimately to kingdom formation, and it is therefore appropriate to review what is known about the internal social organisation of sixth-century communities. Later written sources can be drawn upon to inform the picture, but burials are by far the most abundant source of information for the sixth century, while the growing number of excavated settlements is adding greatly to our understanding of social organisation in important ways.[29]

The burial community

Two main types of burial ground existed in the fifth and sixth centuries. The first of these, the large cremation cemetery, is relatively uncommon and found only in Anglian regions.[30] The best-studied example is Spong Hill in Norfolk, where over 2000 cremation burials are estimated to represent a population of between about 450 and 750 individuals.[31] This number greatly exceeds the size of a single settlement (see below) and indicates that the burial communities represented in such 'urnfields' derive from at least half a dozen large settlements

[28] Hines (1995), p. 81.

[29] It is sobering to realise that, of over 1500 early Anglo-Saxon cemeteries known to date, only fifty or so have been excavated on a scale and to a standard which allow for meaningful statistical analysis (at the time of writing). Only around a dozen have in addition yielded well-preserved skeletal material, essential for the study of age and gender. See Härke (1992a).

[30] On the continent, similar 'urnfields' are found in northern Germany and southern Denmark, especially Schleswig-Holstein and Lower Saxony.

[31] McKinley (1994), p. 70. See also Timby (1994).

and perhaps as many as thirty small settlements. The second, more common type of cemetery contains only inhumations, or a mixture of inhumations and cremations, and is much smaller, ranging from a few dozen to a few hundred burials. These presumably represent single settlements, although the underrepresentation of children in most of these cemeteries begs the question whether all members of the community were in fact buried in such apparently 'communal' cemeteries. Why there were two types of burial community (sometimes even within the same region, for example Caistor-by-Norwich and Morning Thorpe in Norfolk[32]) is far from clear, though they presumably represent two different ways of defining 'the community', perhaps involving different types of clans or moieties.

Where the original extent of the cemetery is known and a substantial percentage has been excavated, the size of the community it represents may be estimated, as at Spong Hill; while such calculations are far from straightforward, they can at least provide a sense of the size of sixth-century communities. At the small, mixed-rite cemetery of Norton, in Cleveland, a population of around twenty-eight has been estimated; at Berinsfield, Oxon., thirty to forty; and at Morning Thorpe, around sixty.[33] As will be seen, these estimates correlate broadly with the size of communities indicated by excavated settlements.

Studies of Anglo-Saxon burials themselves indicate that the internal structure of these sixth-century communities was ranked and differentiated in a way which related to age, gender and kinship, factors which account most obviously for variability in dress style and the kinds of grave-goods buried with the deceased. The existence of age grades is indicated both by archaeological evidence and by written sources, which suggests that rank was in part related to the passing of certain age thresholds. Trends in the number and type of grave-goods with which the deceased were buried appear to mark such thresholds. The quantity and range of grave-goods buried with females, for instance, increased markedly around the age of ten to twelve, while males were buried with more or less the full adult range of weapons from around the age of twelve. An age threshold around ten to twelve years old corresponds well with the evidence from Anglo-Saxon laws.[34]

Gender played a still more pronounced role in determining dress and grave-goods in the sixth century, although much research remains to be done in this area.[35] Children were generally buried in a manner that was 'gender neutral', as were over 40 per cent of adults.[36] Yet certain relatively common items

32 Myres and Green (1973); Green *et al.* (1987).

33 See Sherlock and Welch (1992), p. 107, Scull (1993), p. 72, Boyle *et al.* (1995), p. 116 and Boyle *et al.* (1998).

34 See Härke (1997). See also Stoodley (1998) and Crawford (1999).

35 Stoodley (1999).

36 See Härke (1997), p. 132.

were almost exclusively found with one sex or the other. Thus brooches, necklaces and chatelaines (bunches of metal implements worn at the waist, including real and 'imitation' keys) were buried with females while weapons were buried with males. Different forms of cremation urn also appear to have been deemed appropriate for males and females, the latter tending to be buried in shorter, narrow-mouthed vessels.[37] The cremated remains of animals were sometimes included with the burial, and here too certain correlations with age and gender are apparent; horses, for example, were buried primarily with adult males.[38]

A good illustration of the way in which grave-goods could express social identity is the case of burials with weapons, conventionally known as 'warrior graves'. Around half of adult males were accorded the weapon burial rite in the sixth century. A detailed study of these burials has revealed that the weapons buried were normally not functional sets;[39] in other words, they were not what would have been carried into battle. They were instead carefully selected, and the selection was in part determined by the age of the deceased. Weapon burials also generally contained above-average burial wealth. Yet, some of the males buried with weapons were too young to have wielded them in battle, while others were seriously disabled. This evidence (combined with the distribution of certain epigenetic traits) indicates that burial with weapons did not necessarily denote someone who had been an active warrior, but rather symbolised membership of a certain, apparently ascendant, lineage or clan, and perhaps descent from immigrant groups.

Social rank and identity are thus reflected, at least indirectly, in both inhumations and cremations. The type, quantity and range of grave-goods, the costume worn by the deceased and the burial rite as a whole, co-varied to some degree with age and gender, which were self-evidently among the 'structuring principles of society'.[40] Yet, while the Anglo-Saxon burial rite of the sixth century was clearly influenced by age and gender, invisible aspects of social identity such as kinship, ethnicity and rank, as well as perhaps religion or cult, must also have had a critical bearing on the treatment of the deceased; for this reason, correlations between burial rite, age and gender are rarely absolute and can only provide a small window onto the rich complexity of sixth-century social relations.[41]

37 See Richards (1987), p. 196.

38 See Richards (1992), fig. 22; but see also Hills (1998) for evidence that horses may have been more widely present in East Anglian cremation graves than is usually recognised.

39 See Härke (1992a) and (1992b).

40 Richards (1992), p. 144. It seems unlikely, however, that most grave-goods were intended for use in the afterlife.

41 See Pader (1982); Richards (1987), p. 197, and (1995).

Most sixth-century graves contained grave-goods of some sort and, until the later part of the century, the richest graves arguably represent merely the top end of what was a broad continuum of burial wealth;[42] most attempts to rank graves of this period according to burial wealth have produced spurious results. Where burial plots can be identified, it is unusual to find one which was markedly poorer in burial wealth than other, broadly contemporary plots.[43] If these plots *do* represent households, as seems likely, this suggests that ranking was expressed primarily within households rather than between them, a thesis supported by the evidence from settlements (see below). At the sixth-century cemetery at Norton-on-Tees, for example, the roughly equal numbers of male weapon graves and well-equipped females (approximately a dozen of each) suggest four 'leading' couples over three generations, at the heads of four households, each consisting of nine or ten individuals.[44]

Written sources leave little doubt that kinship played a central role in defining early Anglo-Saxon communities, and suggest that it was essentially bilateral (i.e. no distinction was made between relatives on the mother's and father's side), virilocal and exogamous (i.e. the individual was required to marry outside of his/her own kindred and most females moved to live with their husband's kin).[45] Social and legal status were, in part, determined by one's membership of a particular kin group, which offered protection as well as access to resources.[46] Yet, while it may be possible to identify the heads of households in cemeteries, identifying whole kin groups or households with any certainty is extremely problematic. It nevertheless seems reasonable to suppose that a cluster of graves with a shared orientation or focus (for example around a central burial) are those of individuals who were in some way affiliated in life. At the cemetery of Berinsfield, for example, the distribution of certain epigenetic traits (such as dental anomalies, or the occurrence of sixth lumbar vertebrae), which are probable indicators of genetic links, as well as the distribution of men, women and children, support the theory that the different sectors of the cemetery represent distinct households.[47]

Settlements

Since the 1970s, a few settlements have been excavated on a sufficiently large scale to provide a reasonably clear picture of what a sixth-century village or

42 See Shepherd (1979).

43 See, for example, the cemeteries at Berinsfield, Oxon., Norton, Cleveland, and Apple Down, Sussex. Down and Welch (1990), figs. 2.8 and 2.9; Sherlock and Welch (1992), figs. 21 and 24; Boyle *et al.* (1995), p. 133 and fig. 30; Härke (1997), p. 138.

44 Sherlock and Welch (1992), p. 102.

45 Härke (1997), p. 137.

46 Charles-Edwards (1997).

47 Boyle *et al.* (1995).

hamlet looked like. While their variability in size and layout has made even the use of the term 'village' a contentious matter, most shared certain general characteristics. First, they were relatively small (corresponding in size with the populations indicated in inhumation and mixed-rite cemeteries) and closely spaced. In some regions where intensive archaeological survey and/or excavation have been carried out, such as the terrace gravels of the upper and lower Thames valley, early Anglo-Saxon settlements occur at remarkably close intervals of around 2 to 5 kilometres.[48]

The Anglo-Saxon settlement at Mucking, on a gravel terrace overlooking the Thames estuary in Essex, remains the most extensively excavated Anglo-Saxon settlement published to date.[49] Here, some 14 hectares of land were investigated by archaeologists in the 1960s and 1970s, in the course of which over fifty timber buildings and over 200 sunken huts were uncovered. Not all of these buildings were occupied at the same time, however. The focus of the settlement shifted over nearly a kilometre in the course of some 250–300 years. The very large number of buildings uncovered thus represents on average only around ten household units at any one time, corresponding broadly to the population size indicated by the two contemporary cemeteries excavated at Mucking. There is growing evidence to suggest that such shifting settlement was widespread in the sixth century.[50]

A third characteristic shared by most sixth-century settlements, and exemplified by Mucking as well as West Stow, in Suffolk,[51] is a lack of obvious edges, boundaries or other signs of planning, whether communal or imposed, such as shared trackways, enclosed groups of buildings indicating farmsteads or properties, or an obvious focal or central building or feature. Occasionally traces of fences are found,[52] but virtually none of the more substantial enclosures found so far can be dated earlier than the late sixth or early seventh century. While groupings or clusters of buildings are not uncommon, and most buildings shared a broadly east–west alignment, they do not display a clearly planned arrangement, for example around a courtyard, and one can therefore rarely be certain that they were contemporary.

[48] See Hamerow (1993), fig. 52; Blair (1994), figs. 16 and 24.

[49] See Hamerow (1993). The settlement at West Heslerton in the Vale of Pickering has also been excavated on a large scale and will, when published, contribute greatly to our understanding of settlement in this region. Interim reports suggest that it differed considerably in layout from what we have come to expect from settlements in southern and eastern England. See Powlesland *et al.* (1986) and Powlesland (1997).

[50] See Hamerow (1991) and (1992). [51] See West (1986).

[52] For example at Bishopstone, Sussex, and Mucking, Essex. See Welch (1992), fig. 16 and Hamerow (1993). At Pennyland, near Milton Keynes, and at West Stow, enclosures did not appear until the late sixth century at the earliest. See West (1986) and Williams (1993).

Towards the end of the sixth century, however, a number of settlements appear in the archaeological record with clearly planned layouts and substantial enclosures demarcating properties or households. The earliest dated examples of these characteristics, which became much more marked in the seventh century, are found at the settlements of Yeavering, Northumberland (a royal vill of King Edwin)[53] and Cowdery's Down, Hants. Despite the geographical distance which separates them, these settlements displayed planned layouts containing strikingly similar elements, including alignments of two or more buildings, and rectangular fenced enclosures within which buildings (access to which was thus controlled) were arranged in a perpendicular fashion, with another building adjoining or leading into the enclosure.[54]

The evidence that remains of sixth-century buildings reveals relatively little variation in form or size, although archaeologists are left with little more than ground plans (often incomplete) to ponder; much above-ground variability may of course have existed. A study of these ground plans reveals that standard building 'templates' or modules were used in the construction of at least some of these buildings. This is apparent in the striking correlations that exist in dimensions and layout, even when comparing English and continental buildings, suggesting a widespread and long-lived north-west European timber building tradition.[55]

How the one- or two-roomed Anglo-Saxon house was actually used, however, is far from clear. It may be that functions such as cooking and storage were sited in separate buildings, as was the case by the tenth century to judge from law-codes and other documents.[56] It is, nevertheless, curious that so few examples can be found of hearths in Anglo-Saxon buildings, given their prominence in written sources,[57] though this may be due in many cases to poor conditions of preservation.[58]

Towards the end of the sixth century and the beginning of the seventh century, several architectural innovations were introduced. The first and most common was the use of foundation trenches into which the wall timbers were set, a practice that became widespread in the course of the seventh and eighth centuries.[59] Perhaps the most striking change, however, was the construction of a small number of exceptionally large buildings (i.e. with floor areas greater than 150 square metres) beginning around 600. A few of these larger buildings

[53] *HE* II.14.

[54] See Hope-Taylor (1977), Millett with James (1984) and O'Brien and Miket (1991). It may be that the settlement of Chalton, Hants, which displayed a similar layout, was established in the sixth century, although its date and status are less certain. See Addyman (1972).

[55] See Zimmermann (1988) and Tummuscheit (1995), Abb. 66, 94, 95.

[56] See Dölling (1958), pp. 55ff.

[57] Most famously in Bede, *HE* II.13.

[58] See Hamerow (1999).

[59] See Marshall and Marshall (1994) and Hamerow (1999).

were constructed with annexes at one or both of the gable ends but the 'annexed hall' had largely disappeared by the eighth century.

A period of transition?

The cemeteries and settlements of the sixth century thus indicate that the society within which the Anglo-Saxon identity developed was not rigidly stratified and that high-ranking individuals were integrated within the community, in death as well as in life. Access to power and wealth was not primarily determined by birth, and rank was dependent in large part upon factors such as age, gender, descent and the ability to amass portable wealth, although control over land presumably also played a role (as we shall see later). Certainly, most cemeteries of this period contain burials which are markedly richer in grave-goods than the rest,[60] yet these are most readily interpreted as leading individuals within the local community – heads of households or kin groups, or of some other form of moiety – rather than members of dynasties with supra-local authority.[61] While it is certainly possible that some families managed to maintain pre-eminence over several generations, this would only have been possible through the investment of hard-won portable wealth in expensive displays such as feasting, or burial with ostentatious grave-goods. The fact that the great variability apparent in burial wealth is not obviously reflected in settlements supports the theory that ranking was contained for the most part within, rather than between, households.

Hints of a change to this general pattern began to appear in the later sixth century. The appearance of the first burial mounds, or barrows, is the most striking of these. The first Anglo-Saxon barrows appeared some time in the mid to late sixth century, and occur within flat-grave cemeteries. By the early part of the seventh century, whole cemeteries consisting largely or entirely of barrows were established in some regions, as were a few isolated, exceptionally rich, barrows.[62] Analysis of their contents suggests that their introduction marks the imposition of greater 'constraints . . . on the attainment of positions of rank', although not until the isolated barrows of the seventh century is a pre-eminent group visible, whose status was presumably ascribed rather than achieved.[63] The use, for the first time in the post-Roman period, of a monumental burial

[60] For example Grave 18 at Lechlade, Glos. See Boyle *et al.* (1998), figs. 5.43–7.

[61] Scull (1993), p. 73.

[62] See Shepherd (1979); see also Struth and Eagles (1999).

[63] See Shepherd (1979), p. 70. In the seventh century, weapon burial seems increasingly to denote membership of a narrow, elevated social rank rather than of a broad ethnic group. Thus, while the percentage of the 'top' group (i.e. those buried with a sword, an axe or a seaxe) remained the same at around 6 per cent, the 'intermediate' group dropped from 43 to 17 per cent, while the number of males buried without weapons rose from 52 to 77 per cent. See Härke (1998), p. 45.

rite appears to mark the emergence of a more regulated, closed system of ranking in response to the increased competition for resources and the social instability to which this competition gave rise. Burial mounds would also have been a visible means by which a descent group established ties to its ancestors and staked a claim to territory.[64]

The appearance in some cremation cemeteries of well-furnished inhumations in the mid- to late sixth century may also be significant. The clearest example of this is a group of fifty-seven inhumations at Spong Hill lying at the north-eastern edge of the cremation cemetery.[65] These included a chamber grave and four or five barrows, leading to the suggestion that these burials represent an ascendant group who moved to the area in the sixth century and established a near-separate, elite cemetery.[66] The fact that these inhumations represent only one episode in the use of the cemetery (the latest burials are cremations which post-date the inhumations) indicates that the group's descendants either became assimilated with the rest of the community or, as seems more likely, founded a new burial ground elsewhere.

At the cemetery at Snape in Suffolk, some 18 kilometres from the presumed royal burial ground at Sutton Hoo, a distinctive group of inhumations also appeared in the sixth century. Snape appears to have been established in the fifth or early sixth century essentially as a small cremation cemetery; in the mid to late sixth century, a number of individuals were inhumed (although these were scattered among the cremations and did not form a separate zone as at Spong Hill), some with high-status grave-goods.[67] At least nine were originally buried beneath barrows, one of which was exceptionally rich and buried in a boat. In one of the flat graves, the body was buried in a log-boat and accompanied by a pair of drinking horns, while several others contained what appear to have been parts of real or model boats. The rite of burial in boats is associated with elite groups in Sweden at this period; perhaps these burials mark an ascendant lineage seeking to assert its prestigious Scandinavian connections by adopting a distinctive rite.[68]

The second half of the sixth century also saw the replacement of Salin's Style I, a zoomorphic decoration found widely on ornamental metalwork of the later fifth and first half of the sixth century, with Style II, a more sinuous form of animal interlace which, like Style I, originated in Scandinavia. This

64 See Shepherd (1979), p. 77; also van de Noort (1993). 65 Hills *et al.* (1984).

66 Scull (1993). The distinction between the cremating and inhuming groups at Spong Hill is, however, far from clear-cut. See Hills (1999).

67 Filmer-Sankey (1992), pp. 39–52.

68 Other examples of early cremation cemeteries with later inhumations of the late sixth or seventh centuries include Caistor-by-Norwich and Castle Acre, both in Norfolk. See Myres and Green (1973), pp. 171–2; C. Scull, pers. comm.

may also have a bearing on the question of social change, as Style II was restricted almost exclusively to prestigious metalwork (most famously, a range of gold objects from Sutton Hoo) and manuscripts.[69] A detailed study of Style II motifs and the contexts of Style II objects in Scandinavia suggests that it was introduced in a context of political conflict and was used in public rituals (of which burial was one) as a form of heraldic propaganda by a newly powerful 'class' seeking to establish itself.[70] Regrettably, Style II objects in England are too few and their contexts in many cases too uncertain for this to be anything more than a tantalising possibility here.[71]

Female dress, at least of the elite, was transformed in the seventh century, when the peplos-style dress fastened at the shoulder with large, heavy brooches was replaced by a sewn costume adorned with delicate pins and necklaces in imitation of Mediterranean fashions. This was preceded by the appearance in the late sixth century of brooches, which may reflect a new emphasis on 'badges' of high rank.[72] This is clearest in Anglian regions, with the appearance of larger, highly ornate, so-called 'florid' variants of older forms, notably of cruciform and great square-headed brooches. Furthermore, stylistic analysis suggests some degree of centralised control over the production of these brooches. Square-headed brooches in particular are found in graves of above-average burial wealth and may have served as a means of displaying the status of leading families.[73]

As for settlements, a sufficient number of radiocarbon dates is now available to suggest that the appearance of large buildings, separate, high-status settlements and planned layouts which made use of enclosures and trackways were all introduced in the course of the later sixth and early seventh centuries (see above). The interpretation of these phenomena and how they may have been related is, however, far from clear-cut. The great halls, with their lavish consumption of timber and labour, can be uncontroversially interpreted as the homesteads of 'central people': new landlords who established separate settlements and displayed an ostentatious style of building set within a distinctive layout. But while both Yeavering and Cowdery's Down were founded in the late sixth century, it was not until the seventh century that they took on obviously high-status characteristics, although both made use of alignment and enclosures from the outset. Finally, while in the case of Yeavering and Cowdery's Down their carefully planned layouts and use of enclosures clearly reflect a desire to impress and to restrict access to special buildings and zones,

69 See Speake (1980) and Høilund Nielsen (1997).

70 See Høilund Nielsen (1997) and Hines (1998), p. 309.

71 See Høilund Nielsen (1999).

72 See Hawkes and Meaney (1970).

73 C. Mortimer, pers. comm.; Hines (1984), pp. 30–1 and (1998), p. 34. In the 'Saxon' area of the Upper Thames valley, too, cast saucer brooches, in use since the fifth century, became larger towards the end of the sixth and in the early seventh centuries. See Dickinson (1993), p. 39.

planning need not invariably imply high status. The settlements at Pennyland (Buckinghamshire), Riby Cross-Roads (Lincolnshire), Thirlings (Northumberland) and Catholme (Staffordshire) contained neither large buildings nor exceptionally rich material culture (although none was completely excavated), yet by the late sixth or early seventh century all made use of track- or droveways and fenced enclosures around buildings and paddocks.[74]

The mid to late sixth century also saw the appearance of the first standardised post-Roman pottery to be produced, if not on a large scale at least on a larger scale than early Anglo-Saxon pottery generally. In the fifth and sixth centuries, pottery was hand-made and highly variable, to the extent that it is virtually impossible to find two vessels that are identical in form and decoration, though similar motifs and stamps recur widely. Yet sherds from some 200 vessels (obviously representing only a fraction of the original number of vessels produced) have been found distributed across around a dozen settlements and cemeteries which, though they were hand-made in the same tradition as other pottery of the period, were decorated using a distinctive, standardised range of motifs and stamps.[75] This so-called Illington-Lackford pottery was distributed within a small region (some 900 square kilometres) of East Anglia, bounded by three early medieval linear earthworks. That these vessels derive from a centre of production somewhere in the Little Ouse valley remains no more than a theory, and the mechanism by which they were distributed is unclear. Yet, whether their circulation was governed by gift exchange, trade or redistribution by a local leader, the thesis that they were 'used to maintain relations with neighbouring political units controlling the trade routes along the Icknield Way' is plausible and significant.[76]

Should we see a concatenation in these diverse developments in burial rite, settlements and pottery production? Are they reflections of the same phenomenon and an indication, however oblique, that conditions were right for the emergence of 'a conscious common English identity'?[77] It is important to note at this point that, outside the Anglian regions, the impression of wide-ranging social change is less clear; well-furnished burials, for example, remained relatively common in Kent well into the seventh century, and nowhere outside East Anglia is there an equivalent of Illington-Lackford Ware.[78] Furthermore,

[74] See O'Brien and Miket (1991), Williams (1993), Steedman (1995) and Kinsley (2002).

[75] See Russel (1984), pp. 525ff.

[76] See Russel (1984), p. 528. See also Williams and Vince (1998) regarding pottery, some of which appears to be early, manufactured in the Charnwood Forest region of north Leicestershire and distributed throughout the east and north-east Midlands, and occasionally even further afield.

[77] See Hines (1995), p. 83.

[78] A number of other supposed 'workshops' have been identified, but only Illington-Lackford pottery has been found in sufficient quantity to suggest quasi-'mass' production. See Myres (1977).

because of the crudeness of archaeological dating, what may look like a sudden change in the archaeological record could in reality have spanned several generations. Finally, because of the small number of archaeological examples and the difficulty in dating what are effectively 'prehistoric' developments with the precision demanded of historic periods, it is impossible even to be certain whether these phenomena were contemporary and may therefore be seen as a prelude to the more widespread and obvious changes in burial practices and settlements attributable to the seventh century, such as the appearance of 'princely' graves and royal vills.[79] This alone should warn us against seeking a single, teleological explanation for these changes, and attributing them to a far-reaching, gradual and inevitable process of kingdom formation. Change was surely neither steady nor revolutionary, but rather sporadic and contingent, playing itself out in different ways in different regions, a matter in large part of the timing of particular, mostly unrecorded, events. The concept of 'transitional' periods in history has been challenged, and rightly so,[80] yet there is a consistency to these developments which suggests they are more than an illusion created by the nebulous light cast by seventh-century sources onto the late sixth century.

THE SIXTH CENTURY AND KINGDOM FORMATION

One of the difficulties of dealing with archaeological evidence in the absence of written sources is distinguishing the common causes behind the developments outlined above, in settlement, burial rites and material culture. To do this, the archaeological evidence has to be considered in light of the political and military manoeuvring detailed in later written sources. In addition, having reviewed what is known of social structures within sixth-century communities, it remains to consider the role of relations *between* those communities in kingdom formation, relations seen most clearly in the evidence for trade and exchange.

First, however, it is useful to remind ourselves that in addition to the major kingdoms named in the written sources of the seventh and eighth centuries – Kent, East and Middle Anglia, Lindsey, Deira, Bernicia, Mercia, Sussex, Wessex, Essex – there were several smaller kingdoms (see Map 8).[81] The most widely accepted theory of how these kingdoms came into being has as its central feature territorial conquest. The fluid nature of early Anglo-Saxon social structure provided considerable scope for ambitious individuals to gain rank

79 Some of the most famous of these 'princely' graves are at Sutton Hoo, Suffolk, and Asthall, Oxon. See Carver (1992) and Dickinson and Speake (1992). See also Boddington (1990) and Geake (1997).

80 See Halsall (1995).

81 See Yorke (1990), map 1.

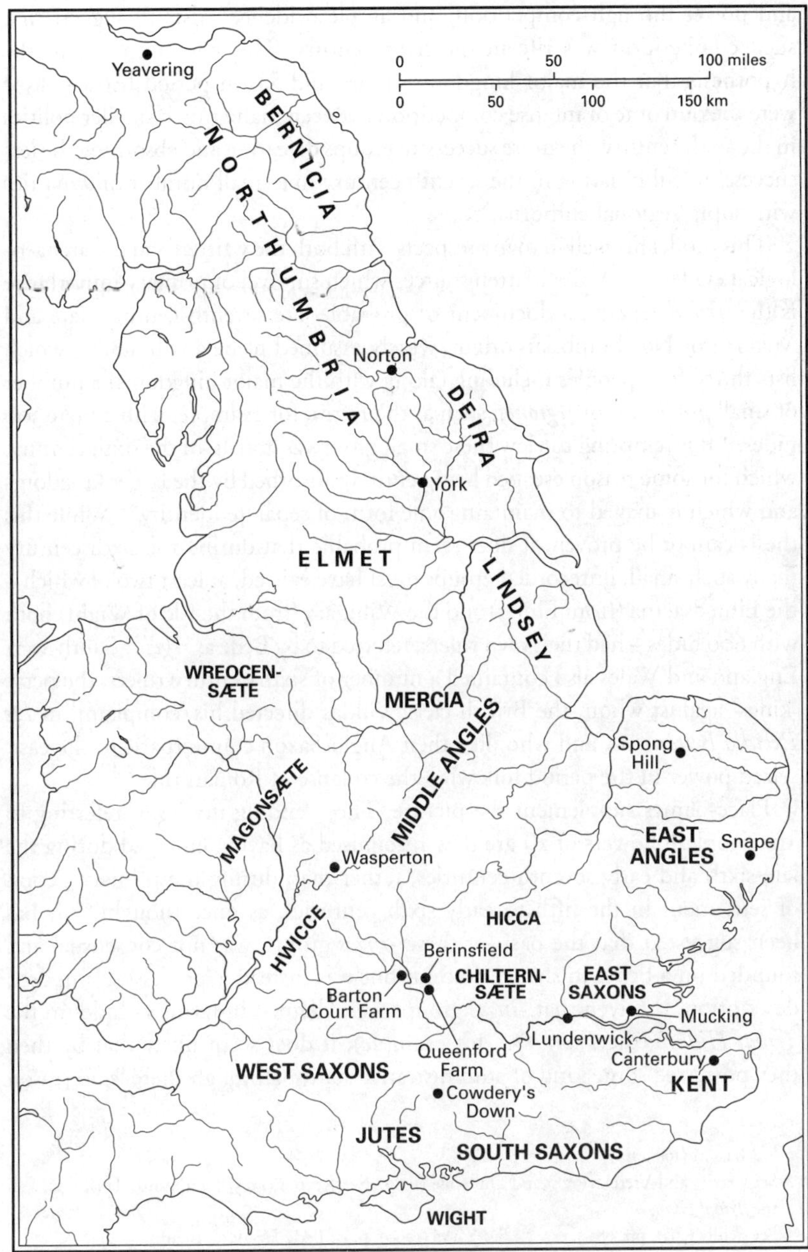

Map 8 The main Anglo-Saxon provinces at the time of the composition of the Tribal Hidage, and principal sites mentioned in chapters 10 and 17 (after Yorke (1990), maps 1 and 2)

and power through competition, and ample evidence exists to suggest that such competition was rife in the sixth century. This has given rise to the hypothesis that the major kingdoms of the mid Saxon period (*c.*650–*c.*850) were the outcome of intense competition between many much smaller polities in the sixth century, the more successful groups defeating and absorbing the less successful, culminating in the seventh century in a small number of dynasties with supra-regional authority.[82]

This model fits well in many respects with both the written and the archaeological evidence. Of the written sources which survive, of primary importance is the *Tribal Hidage*, a document of probable late seventh-century date and Mercian or Northumbrian origin, widely assumed to be a tribute list, which lists thirty-four peoples including (along with the major kingdoms) a number of small *provinciae* or *regiones*, such as the *Hicca*, for example, with a mere 300 hides.[83] It is tempting to view these small groups as 'fossils' of the sixth century, which for some reason escaped being entirely absorbed by the larger kingdoms and which managed to maintain some form of separate identity.[84] While this thesis cannot be proven, it does seem probable that during the sixth century many such small, unrecorded groups must have existed, at least two of which – the Elmedsaetna (from Elmet) and the Wihtgara (from the Isle of Wight) both with 600 hides – had their own rulers, referred to by Bede as *reges*.[85] South-west England and Wales also contained a number of sixth-century rulers, the petty 'kings' against whom the British cleric Gildas directed his 'complaint' in *De Excidio Britanniae*, and who, like their Anglo-Saxon counterparts to the east, seized power in the period following the collapse of Roman rule.[86]

Place-names supplement the picture. Those ending in *-ingas* (referring to 'the people/followers of x') are now recognised as having emerged during the late sixth and early seventh centuries, rather than during the primary period of settlement in the fifth to early sixth centuries, as once thought.[87] It has been suggested that the basis of these *-ingas* groups was not consensual and founded on a belief in shared descent, but was instead a 'possessive, imposed description'.[88] Given that *-ingas* groups were defined in terms of hides in the *Tribal Hidage* (the *Faerpingas* for example), it does seem likely that by then they possessed some kind of administrative status, although there is no reason

[82] See Bassett (1989c).

[83] See Davies and Vierck (1974) and Dumville (1989). See Keynes (1995) for a more sceptical view of the *Tribal Hidage*.

[84] See Scull (1993), pp. 68–9.

[85] See Yorke (1990), p. 11; Bede *HE* IV.16, 19 and 23.

[86] Gildas, *De excidio Brit.*, ed. Winterbottom (text and trans.).

[87] Thus, for example, Hastings derives from *Haestingas*, the people/followers of Haesta. See Dodgson (1966).

[88] See Hines (1995), p. 82.

to assume that they had always done so. Whatever their origins, it is unlikely that these lower-order political entities occupied territories with well-defined boundaries; they may merely have consisted of a group of settlements all of whom paid renders to the same centre through some system of hidation.

Later accounts such as the *Historia Ecclesiastica* and the *Anglo-Saxon Chronicle* describe the origins of kingdoms as the leaders of the day wished them to be seen. This makes them dubious sources for those seeking an accurate account of sixth-century events, yet they make one point abundantly clear: warfare arising from competition for land was rife and territorial expansion was the *sine qua non* of power. The appearance of Woden, god of war, as the progenitor in so many Anglo-Saxon royal genealogies is surely no coincidence.[89] These genealogies themselves indicate a sixth-century origin for the major dynasties, although this requires extrapolating from the dates of historically well-attested rulers the approximate dates of their semi-mythical forebears such as Cerdic of Wessex and Wuffa of East Anglia. Some have argued that these genealogies merely reflect the limits of folk memory at the time when these oral traditions were first written down, extending backwards in time a few generations and no further.[90] Yet when the evidence is taken in its entirety, the conclusion that there were kings in the sixth century seems inescapable, even while the nature and extent of their power remains obscure. Certainly, the laws of King Æthelberht of Kent, dated to the beginning of the seventh century, imply that he, at least, had power and responsibility not only over his immediate followers, but 'over all ranks of society: nobles, freemen (ceorls), unfree peasants and slaves'.[91]

What were the origins of these kings? If there is any truth to Gildas' account of the activities of rebellious Saxon federates in sub-Roman Britain, the possibility exists (on analogy with the Franks, for example) that some rulers of the later sixth century 'evolved' from such opportunistic raiders who began to take control of particular territories which they had been exploiting.[92] Another possible catalyst for kingdom formation in eastern Britain lies in the links between the elites of Kent and East Anglia and the Merovingian courts. Close connections existed between the Kentish and Frankish elites in the later sixth century as evidenced by the marriage of the Frankish princess Bertha to King Æthelberht; a clause concerning escaped slaves in the law-code of the Salian Franks (probably originating at the end of the fifth or early in the sixth century) furthermore suggests reciprocal legal arrangements between Francia and some parts of Britain.[93]

89 See Yorke (1990), p. 16.
90 See Yorke (1990), p. 4 and Scull (1993), p. 68.
91 Trans. *EHD* I. See Yorke (1990), p. 17.
92 I am grateful to Barbara Yorke for this suggestion.
93 See Wood (1997), pp. 47–9.

The changes which took place in the archaeological record of the later sixth century, while they do not provide direct evidence of territorial conquest or warfare, are consistent with the emergence of a new elite and, perhaps, of dominant lineages. These changes, as already noted, are the appearance of the first 'special function' settlements such as Yeavering and Cowdery's Down, which shared a new architectural style and layout, and, as we will see shortly, of the first trading stations; second are the changes in burial rite in which elites are given a new prominence. If ostentatious burial is an attempt by newly pre-eminent families to maintain their standing in unstable times, then the appearance of rich burials suggests intensified competition for local power in these regions.[94] Third is the evidence, not yet considered and notoriously difficult to interpret, for population growth. The number of settlements and cemeteries known from the sixth century is far greater than from the fifth. This must be due in large part, on the one hand, to the difficulty of recognising fifth-century material culture, and, on the other, to the cultural assimilation of indigenous groups who emerged from archaeological invisibility in the sixth century, as we saw earlier in this chapter. Yet, the possibility that even a gradual increase in population during the sixth century could have fuelled competition for land to a significant degree merits serious consideration. Certainly by the seventh century, control over land was essential to maintaining status and power; land was thus not merely an economic resource but a social one,[95] and the imperative for younger sons to obtain land in order to maintain and enhance their power would have fuelled the very competition which ultimately concentrated that power into fewer hands.

If sixth-century England was full of small polities of the kind named in the *Tribal Hidage*, some of which at least can reasonably be called kingdoms, then the administrative infrastructure of late Roman Britain must have disintegrated rapidly into various more or less independent units; the degree to which their territories were conditioned by late Roman administrative organisation, indeed whether they had defined territories, remains a moot point, as we shall see. Given such a scenario, the potential for networks of trade and exchange to provide a framework for later integration would have been considerable.[96]

94 Evidence from the region of Metz during the same period supports this interpretation of rich graves as a sign of competition for local power. Such graves are rare within 20 or 30 kilometres of Metz in the sixth century: 'close to Metz itself, disputes might be resolved by appeal to the king, bishops, dukes and counts in frequent residence there. Further away, this was less easy and so more open displays of access to power and resources were necessary' (Halsall (1995), p. 48).

95 See Charles-Edwards (1972) and Scull (1993), pp. 77ff.

96 Trade has, however, received surprisingly little attention in most current theories of kingdom formation.

When, in the course of the seventh century, a number of royally controlled trading centres or 'emporia' were established along the English coast and major rivers (the major examples being at Southampton, London, York and Ipswich), the extensive, formalised trading networks that sustained them were most likely based on pre-existing axes of exchange.[97] The evidence for fifth- and sixth-century trade routes comes primarily from the appearance of non-local goods in settlements and cemeteries. While such prehistoric exchange networks defy precise definition, the patterns produced by mapping the distribution of obvious imports are revealing. The distribution of Illington-Lackford Ware, for example, traces the outlines of an exchange network centred on the Little Ouse valley and the Icknield Way, as already noted. A much more common artefact, with consequently greater potential for illuminating mechanisms of exchange, is amber beads, which are widely found in female graves of the sixth century. Their distribution (along with that of crystal beads, a less common sixth-century import) clusters at several 'nodal points', such as the cemetery at Sleaford, Lincolnshire, where nearly 1000 amber beads were buried.[98] Around these nodal points lie numerous cemeteries with smaller quantities of amber beads, a pattern best interpreted as reflecting the redistribution of amber by local leaders. Further evidence that access to amber was tightly controlled and preferential is the fact that these cemeteries generally contained one female grave with more than ten times the average number of amber beads. The distribution of other non-local commodities, such as iron in regions without ready sources of ore, would also doubtless repay closer study.[99] Even from such limited evidence, a picture is beginning to emerge of sixth-century exchange networks which were neither market driven nor currency based, and in which the redistribution of many goods, especially luxury items that conferred prestige upon the owner, was controlled by the leading members of local communities.

One hint that the economy was becoming increasingly organised in the later sixth century may be found in the growing number of Merovingian gold coins entering south-east England, some 100 years before the first real Anglo-Saxon currency was minted. A small number of scales and weights (mostly fragmentary) used to assess the bullion value of the coins were deposited in graves; these come mostly from Kent, whose early prosperity derived from its near-monopoly on trade with Francia, and the upper Thames valley, now recognised as the cradle of the kingdom of Wessex.[100]

97 See Scull (1997). 98 See Huggett (1988), p. 89.

99 Recent work on trade patterns in the Upper Thames valley, east Yorkshire and the Peak District suggests differential access to commodities even within a quite limited geographical region. See Loveluck (1994).

100 See Scull (1990) and (1997).

The evidence for exchange should ideally be evaluated alongside the evidence for modes of production. Yet the rapid disintegration of the Romano-British economy led to the collapse of industrial production *c.*400 – the sudden demise of the wheel-thrown pottery industries of Roman Britain has become a virtual cliché – and for the next 200 years, production sites are conspicuous by their absence. Thousands of early Anglo-Saxon brooches have been found, for example, yet the number of surviving examples of the moulds and models used to make them can be counted on the fingers of one hand. In the absence of production sites, the mode of production for early Anglo-Saxon material culture – whether domestic, 'itinerant' or part-time specialist – remains largely a matter for speculation. We can, perhaps, see hints of some limited reorganisation in the later sixth century, for example in Illington-Lackford pottery and possibly in metalwork such as square-headed brooches, but not until the trading centres of the seventh century do we find clear evidence for concentrated industrial activity.

The 'competitive exclusion' model of kingdom formation outlined above is, with its Darwinian overtones, a trifle pat and not without its critics,[101] but it has held the field for some years, with few real contenders. The chief competing thesis (though the two are by no means mutually exclusive) is that the Anglo-Saxon kingdoms largely adopted the political geography of Roman Britain. It has long been recognised that the names of some of the earliest Anglo-Saxon kingdoms derive from Romano-British tribes or districts, such as Cantwarena, Bernicia, Deira and Lindsey. This gave rise to the hypothesis that the earliest kingdoms were based on pre-existing territorial units that were taken over by Anglo-Saxon overlords. A range of evidence exists for the continuity of territories from the Roman (and indeed pre-Roman) to the Saxon periods.[102] Indeed, continuous use of old boundaries and geographical divisions is intrinsically likely; it need not, however, imply that these boundaries were politically maintained. Thus, the seventh-century evidence for the Anglo-Saxon takeover of the west midlands[103] provides an interesting model for what could have happened further east in the sixth century: namely, a considerable degree of territorial continuity as well as reorganisation. Seen archaeologically, however, these regions appear radically different. In short, it remains exceedingly difficult to define

101 See Halsall (1997).

102 See, for example, Balkwill (1993) and Barnwell (1996) on the possible Roman origins of the hide and the hundred.

103 See, for example, Pretty (1989). Bassett, in his consideration of the criteria used in selecting the sites of the first Anglo-Saxon sees, concludes that while 'some weight does seem to have been attached to using places which had had regional importance . . . in the Roman period . . . in most cases it was on account of their again (or still) having an important political role in the seventh century, and sometimes an economic one, not because of their late Roman status *per se*' ((1989b), p. 247).

the limits of a late Romano-British villa or an early Anglo-Saxon royal estate, let alone determine whether they were the same. A frequently cited archaeological example of possible political continuity is the Northumbrian settlement at Yeavering, which was established in the sixth century and was a royal vill by the seventh. Yeavering was certainly the site of a British cult centre and of ritual activity since at least the Bronze Age, but close analysis of the layout of the site suggests that we should not read any meaningful degree of political continuity into the choice of location.[104]

Unlike the other western provinces, Roman Britain did not pass intact into barbarian hands, nor was it conquered rapidly. The old social order, institutions and power structures suffered violent disruption. While the socio-political structure of the earliest Anglo-Saxon kingdoms that replaced them was not entirely new, it does not, in most of southern and eastern England at least, appear to have been constructed using the building blocks of Romano-British political structures.

CONCLUSION

The earliest Anglo-Saxon leaders, unable to tax and coerce followers as successfully as the Roman state had done, instead extracted surplus by raiding and collecting food renders. The portable wealth they amassed in this way was used to maintain followers through conspicuous consumption and ritualised giving of prestigious gifts.[105] The later sixth century saw the beginning of the end of this 'prestige goods' economy, along with the decline of accompanied burial and the appearance of the first princely graves and high-status settlements. By 600, the establishment of the first Anglo-Saxon emporia was in prospect.[106] These centres of trade and production reflect the increased socio-political stratification and wider territorial authority which allowed seventh-century elites to extract and redistribute surpluses with far greater effectiveness than their sixth-century predecessors would have found possible.[107] Anglo-Saxon society, in short, looked very different in AD 600 than it did a hundred years earlier. It would, however, be a mistake to assume that this was the result of a steady evolution or progression. Despite a tendency in current scholarship to seek the origins of the early medieval kingdoms in ever earlier periods,[108] the extent to which the kingdoms of seventh- and eighth-century England were in fact rooted

104 See Bradley (1987). 105 See Scull (1992).

106 It is possible that trading stations had already been established in the course of the sixth century in east Kent, at Dover, Sarre, Fordwich and Sandwich.

107 See Scull (1997), p. 285.

108 See Halsall (1995). This trend is particularly prevalent in Danish archaeology, see for example Axboe (1995).

in the sixth century is debatable. While many of the interpretations offered above are little more than modest speculation, as for an essentially prehistoric period they must be, the combined weight of the written and archaeological evidence indicates that at least some of the earliest Anglo-Saxon kingdoms arose out of a period of intensified conflict and competition during the later sixth century, the outcome of which was far from certain.

ACKNOWLEDGEMENTS

I am very grateful to Dr Tania Dickinson, Dr John Blair, Dr Martin Welch and Dr Barbara Yorke whose comments and suggestions have greatly improved this chapter.

PART II

THE SEVENTH CENTURY

CHAPTER 11

THE BYZANTINE EMPIRE IN THE SEVENTH CENTURY

Andrew Louth

Most centuries can be claimed to have been, in one way or another, a watershed for Byzantium, but the case for the seventh century is particularly strong. At the beginning of the century, the Byzantine Empire was part of a political configuration focussed on the Mediterranean world, that had been familiar for centuries and was characterised by two factors, one external and the other internal. Internally, the basic economic unit of that world was the city and its surrounding territory, which, although it had by now lost much of its political significance, still retained much of its social, economic and cultural position. Externally, however, it was a Mediterranean world: bounded to the east by the Persian Empire, most of the regions that surrounded the Mediterranean formed a single political entity, the Roman (or Byzantine) Empire. At the beginning of the seventh century, this traditional configuration was already being nibbled away: much of Italy was under Lombard rule, Gaul was in Frankish hands, and the coastal regions of Spain, that had been the final acquisition of Justinian's reconquest, were soon to fall to the Visigoths. But by the end of the century, this whole traditional configuration had gone, to be replaced by another, which was to be dominant for centuries and still marks the region today. The boundary that separated the Mediterranean world from the Persian Empire was swept away: after the Arab conquest of the eastern provinces in the 630s and 640s, that boundary – the Tigris–Euphrates valley – became one of the arteries of a new empire, with its capital first in Damascus (660–750) and then in Baghdad (from 750), which by the middle of the eighth century stretched from Spain in the west to the valleys of the Oxus and the Indus in the east. That empire, far larger in extent than Justinian's Byzantine Empire – larger even than the Roman Empire had ever been – and hugely richer than any of its neighbours, caused Europe, East Asia and North Africa to be reconfigured around itself, forcing the Byzantine Empire (and the emerging Frankish Empire) into virtual satellite status. This radical upheaval, together with the persistent aggression of the Arabs on the remaining Byzantine lands, as well as the incursion of Slavs and other tribes from the central Eurasian plain into the Balkans, accelerated the transition of the cities of the eastern Mediterranean world that was already well under way, so that by the end of the century the cities had lost much of their social and cultural significance, and survived as fortified enclaves, and sometimes also as market centres.[1] The only place approximating to the traditional city was Constantinople, and that largely because of the presence of the imperial court; but even Constantinople barely survived, and did so in a much reduced state.[2]

This dramatic transition caused something of a crisis of confidence and even identity for the Byzantine Empire. At least twice the emperor entertained the notion of deserting Constantinople, and re-establishing the capital of the Empire closer to its traditional centre in Rome: in 618 Heraclius thought of moving to Carthage, and in the 660s Constans II settled in Sicily. In both cases we can see how the traditional idea of a Mediterranean empire still haunted the imagination of the Byzantine rulers. In fact, despite the dramatic and permanent changes witnessed by the seventh century, the Byzantine reactions can be seen as attempts to preserve what was perceived as traditional. But, as always with the Byzantines, one must be careful not to be deceived by their rhetoric. This rhetoric – and, as we shall see, administrative changes that were more than rhetorical – spoke in terms of centralisation, an increasing focus on the figure of the emperor and the court, and a growing influence of the patriarch and the clergy of the Great Church of Hagia Sophia in religious matters. In reality, however, events and persons on the periphery were often more important than what was going on at the centre. The transition that took place in the seventh century was not completed in that century: not until the late eighth and ninth centuries, when, with the relocation of the capital of the Arab (Umayyad) Empire eastwards from Damascus to Baghdad, the Arab pressure on the Byzantine Empire relented, did the Byzantine Empire finally complete the transition that began in the seventh. What emerged was an empire and a culture focussed on the emperor and the capital, but much of what the centre by then stood for had, in fact, been worked out, not in Constantinople itself, but at the periphery.

The history of the Byzantine Empire in the seventh century is difficult to reconstruct. Traditional sources are sparse and mostly late.[3] We can draw on Theophylact Simocatta's History and the *Chronicon Paschale*, both of which were probably written at the court of the patriarch Sergius around 630 in the

[1] The pace of this change in the cities, and its interpretation, is the subject of a still continuing debate. See Foss (1975) and (1977), who emphasises the impact of the Persian invasion in the first quarter of the seventh century, and the discussion in Haldon (1997), pp. 92–124, 459–61.

[2] For Constantinople, see Mango (1985).

[3] On the problems of the literary source materials, see Cameron and Conrad (1992).

euphoria caused by Heraclius' triumph over the Persians. The celebrations of Heraclius' Persian victories by George of Pisidia also belong to this period but, after this, history writing in Byzantium stops until the end of the eighth century. For the political history of the seventh century our principal sources are thus two later works: the patriarch Nikephoros' *Brief History*, which was composed in the late eighth century and intended as a continuation of Theophylact Simocatta, and the early ninth-century Chronicle ascribed to Theophanes the Confessor. To some extent the dearth of writing from the period 630 to 790 may be seen to be a consequence of the collapse of much of traditional Mediterranean society at this time. The demise of the ancient city meant the collapse of the traditional base of the educational system: there were fewer and fewer people to write for.[4] There was also less to write about: the details of the collapse of the Byzantine eastern provinces to the Arabs and subsequent defeats and losses would not be welcome material for Byzantine writers, and are either omitted by Nikephoros and Theophanes, or drawn from Syriac or Arab sources. Like these Byzantine historians, we can supplement our sparse resources with oriental historical material. There is an anonymous Armenian history of Heraclius ascribed to the Armenian bishop Sebeos, and dated to the latter half of the seventh century. There is also a world chronicle, written at the end of the century by bishop John of Nikiu in Egypt, which survives, however, only in a mutilated version and in an Ethiopic translation. There are in addition several contemporary and later Syriac chronicles: apart from those that are anonymous, there are those compiled by Elias bar Shinaya, the eleventh-century metropolitan of Nisibis, and Michael the Syrian, the twelfth-century Jacobite patriarch of Antioch, both of whom used earlier sources. Legal sources are sparse for the seventh century, but the *Farmer's Law* probably belongs to the seventh century, as may the *Rhodian Sea Law*. Traditionally, therefore, the seventh and eighth centuries have been regarded as the Byzantine 'Dark Ages', though recently historians have begun to recognise that it is only in respect of traditional historical literary material that one can speak of a paucity of sources for the period. For it was, in fact, an immensely fruitful period for Byzantine theology, dominated by the figure of Maximos the Confessor, perhaps the greatest theologian of the Orthodox East, and certainly the greatest Byzantine theologian. To make full use of these 'untraditional' sources would, however, involve writing a different kind of history, not beginning from the institutional and political, but rather working outwards from the deeply considered world-view to be found in such writings.[5] But it is to be noted that there is a distinct lacuna in the theological sources themselves. They are all from the periphery:

4 See Whitby (1992).

5 For a notable attempt by an historian to use these theological sources see Haldon (1992).

Maximos writing mostly from North Africa, Anastasius and John of the Ladder from Sinai. Elsewhere, Cyprus and Palestine were homes to a good deal of writing, polemical and hagiographical for the most part. We know almost nothing of theology in Constantinople between the middle of the sixth century (such as came from the circle of Justinian, Leontius of Byzantium and Leontius of Jerusalem) and the ninth-century revival of learning (that of the iconodule theologians, Nikephoros and Theodore the Studite, Photios and others). The only exceptions are the metropolitan opponent of Iconoclasm, Germanus, and some traces of the theology of the iconoclasts preserved by their opponents. Virtually all the theology that survives from this period of transition belongs to the periphery.

The method followed in this chapter will be first to give an outline of the political history of the period, and to follow this with some account of the transition that this century witnessed. To do otherwise is nearly impossible, as the elements of the transition – from the transformation of the city, to administrative changes and religious changes – are not easy to date precisely, and consequently would find no natural place in the narrative history.

NARRATIVE HISTORY

The century began with Maurice on the imperial throne, pressing his army to resist the incursion of Slavs across the Danube. Growing discontent culminated in mutiny, when Maurice ordered his army to continue their campaign against the Slavs on the north bank of the Danube into the winter (when the bare trees would provide less cover for the Slavs). Led by Phokas, a relatively minor officer, the army marched on Constantinople, and deposed Maurice, who was executed, along with his sons.[6] Phokas was proclaimed emperor. He was never very secure and faced a number of revolts. More seriously the Persian shah, Chosroes II, used the murder of Maurice, who had protected him in 590 when he fled Persia during a palace revolt, as a pretext to declare war on the Byzantine Empire to avenge his former protector. With the invasion of Syria, there began a war that was to last until 626/627. In 610 Phokas was deposed by Heraclius, the son of the exarch of Carthage, also called Heraclius, who seized the throne, according to Theophanes, at the invitation of the senate in Constantinople. Heraclius' ships displayed reliquaries and icons of the Mother of God on their masts: a sign of the continuing authentication of political authority by supernatural means seen in the later decades of the sixth century. Phokas was swiftly overthrown and executed, and Heraclius acclaimed as emperor and crowned by the patriarch in St Stephen's chapel in the palace.

[6] See Louth, chapter 4 above.

On the same day he married his betrothed, Eudokia, whom he crowned as Augusta.

The situation Heraclius faced was serious. The Persians were now advancing into Asia Minor (in 611 they took Caesarea in Cappadocia), and to the north from across the Danube the Avars were once again a serious menace: in 615 both enemies would make a joint assault on Constantinople. Attempts were made to negotiate a peace treaty with the Persians (according to the eastern sources immediately, but according to the Greek sources in 615, after the Persian forces had advanced as far as Chalcedon), but the peace efforts were repudiated, as the Persians were convinced that the Byzantine Empire was at their mercy. The war took on the character of a holy war between a Christian army, using as banners icons of Christ and the Virgin, and the Zoroastrian army of the Persians. As well as advancing into Asia Minor, the Persians invaded Palestine, taking Jerusalem in early May 614, and then Egypt and Libya. The fall of Jerusalem, by now regarded by Christians as their 'Holy City', was a catastrophe for Byzantium as a Christian empire, and for the emperor as God's vice-gerent on earth; still worse was the seizure of the relic of the True Cross, which was taken back to the Persian capital, Ctesiphon, along with the patriarch of Jerusalem, Zacharias, and the notables among the Christian survivors of the sack of the city (it is reported that tens of thousands were killed).[7]

It was not until Heraclius had managed to negotiate a truce with the Avars that he was able to make a serious attempt to defeat the Persians. From 622 onwards, he conducted a series of campaigns against the Persians. In 626, while Heraclius was on campaign, the Persians joined forces with the Avars to besiege Constantinople. Heraclius himself did not return, but sent a contingent of the field army to reinforce the defenders of the city, who were under the leadership of the two regents, the patriarch Sergius and Bonos, the *magister officiorum*. Constantinople was besieged for ten days by a huge army of various tribes under the command of the khagan of the Avars, while the Persian army under Shahrvaraz held the Asian shore of the Bosphorus. The siege failed when the fleet of Slav boats was destroyed by the Byzantine fleet in the Golden Horn, just across from the Church of the Virgin at Blachernae. The success of the Constantinopolitans' defence of their city was ascribed to the Virgin Mother of God, and it is likely that the famous troparion, 'To you, champion commander', was composed by Patriarch Sergius to celebrate her victory. Heraclius pressed his attack into the heartland of the Sasanian Empire, now disheartened by the failure of the Persian troops under Shahrvaraz to secure Constantinople and smarting under the destruction of another contingent of the army destined for

7 For the most thorough examination of the various sources for the taking of Jerusalem by the Persians, see Flusin (1992).

Constantinople under Sahin at the hands of the emperor's brother Theodore. His successes provoked a palace revolt in which Chosroes was murdered. The Persians sued for peace. All the territory they had taken was restored to the Byzantine Empire, and the Tigris–Euphrates valley became once again the frontier. Heraclius recovered the True Cross, and celebrated his triumph by taking the relic on a tour of the restored Byzantine territories, before restoring it to Jerusalem on 21 March 630.[8]

It was at this stage, it would seem, that Heraclius began to face the religious problems that had plagued the Byzantine Empire since the Synod of Chalcedon in 451.[9] The schism between those who supported Chalcedon and those who repudiated it, whom their enemies called Monophysites, had become institutionalised with a separate Monophysite episcopal hierarchy since the consecration of Jacob Bar 'Addai in 542. The Monophysites had their greatest support in the eastern provinces, especially Syria and Egypt (the Christians in Armenia also refused to acknowledge the Synod of Chalcedon). After his conquest of the eastern provinces, Chosroes had sought to strengthen his hold over his new subjects by exploiting the Christians' schisms. At a meeting held in Ctesiphon, Chosroes met with leaders of the Monophysites, the Armenians and also the Nestorians, the main Christian group established in Persia. These last rejected the condemnation of Nestorius at the Synod of Ephesus in 431, and had fled to Persia to escape persecution in the Byzantine Empire. It was agreed that the Nestorians should retain their position within the traditional Sasanid territories, but that the Persian authorities would support the Monophysites in Armenia and those former Byzantine provinces where the Monophysites were in a majority, that is, Syria and Egypt. The Monophysites welcomed this agreement, the Monophysite patriarch of Antioch, Athanasius (the 'Camel-Driver'), rejoicing at the 'passing of the Chalcedonian night'.

If Heraclius was to be secure in his regained eastern provinces, he needed to gain the support of the Monophysites. The policy he pursued was proposed by his patriarch Sergius, who had foreseen this problem and already begun negotiations with Monophysites, he himself being a Syrian, possibly with a Monophysite background. The proposal was to seek union on the basis of the doctrine of monenergism, i.e. that Christ, while he had two natures, as Chalcedon had affirmed, possessed only a single divine–human activity. This policy achieved some success in Armenia, but the Syrian Monophysites (Jacobites) were not amenable, and required an explicit repudiation of Chalcedon. Monenergism's greatest success was in Egypt, where Kyros of Phasi, appointed patriarch and augustal prefect in 631, reached an

[8] For the date, Flusin (1992), II, pp. 293–309, and the literature cited.

[9] For the earlier religious problems, Meyendorff (1989), pp. 333–73, and Louth, chapter 4 above.

agreement with the main Monophysite group in Egypt (called 'Theodosians', after the sixth-century patriarch of Alexandria, Theodosius). On 3 June 633, a solemn Eucharist celebrated the union with the Theodosians on the basis of a carefully phrased pact of union in nine chapters which placed monenergism in the context of the Cyrilline Chalcedonianism that had been espoused by the emperor Justinian and endorsed at the Fifth Ecumenical Synod in 553.[10]

But it was not only some of the Monophysites who refused to accept monenergism. Present in Alexandria, as Kyros was about to celebrate his triumph of 'ecumenism', was the learned, and highly respected, abbot Sophronius. To him, the Nine Chapters amounted to Monophysitism. He protested to Kyros, to no avail, and took his protest to Sergius in Constantinople. Sergius was sufficiently alarmed by Sophronius' protest as to issue a ruling on the matter (the *Psephos*) in which he forbade any mention of either one or two activities in Christ. But that scarcely satisfied Sophronius, who took his complaint to Pope Honorius in Rome. He seems to have had no success with the pope, and from Rome he made his way to Palestine, where he was elected patriarch of Jerusalem in 634. In his synodical letter, he exposed the heresy of monenergism, without, however, explicitly breaching the terms of the *Psephos*. Before Sophronius' arrival, Sergius had already communicated the success in Alexandria of the policy of monenergism, and in his reply to Sergius Honorius used the phrase that was to lead to the refinement of monenergism, the doctrine of Monothelitism. That phrase was 'one will'. Monothelitism, the doctrine that Christ had only one divine will, was proclaimed as imperial orthodoxy in the *Ekthesis* issued by Heraclius (though doubtless composed by Sergius) in 638.

By this time, the immediate purpose of this religious compromise was being overtaken by events. For Heraclius' triumph over the Persians proved a pyrrhic victory. Even while it was being celebrated, Palestine and Syria began to experience attacks from Arab tribes that within barely more than a decade were to lead to the loss of the eastern provinces of the Byzantine Empire (this time final) and the complete collapse of the Sasanian Empire. In 633 there were attacks on garrisons in Gaza. Soon the Arab armies moved further north. There is considerable confusion in the sources about the sequence of events thereafter.[11] Heraclius mustered an army and sought to defeat the Arabs. The decisive battle took place at the River Yarmuk in 636, at which the much larger Byzantine force was routed. Heraclius abandoned the eastern provinces in despair. The

10 See chapter 4 above.

11 For the traditional account, Donner (1981) and Kaegi (1992), and also Hillenbrand, chapter 12 below. For the difficulties involved in using the Arab sources, see Conrad (1992) and Leder (1992). For a revisionist account of the Arab conquests, see Cook and Crone (1977), and Patricia Crone's later books, Crone (1980) and (1987). For a lucid account of the whole controversy over the value of early Islamic sources, Humphries (1991), pp. 69–103.

year before, Damascus had already fallen (or more probably been surrendered) to the Arabs, and in 638 Jerusalem was surrendered to the Arab caliph Umar by the patriarch Sophronius. Alexandria was taken in 642, and though the Byzantines recaptured it, in 645 it finally fell. By that time Mesopotamia had already fallen to the Arabs, and with it the Sasanian Empire. The speed with which the eastern provinces of the Byzantine Empire succumbed to the Arabs remains to be explained by historians. However, the idea, at first sight attractive, that these provinces, with their attachment to Monophysitism, were already culturally lost to the Empire seems not to be borne out by the evidence we have: on the contrary, there is much evidence for the continuing power of Hellenism in the eastern provinces well into the seventh century, indeed evidence that suggests that Hellenic culture was more potent there than in the capital of the Empire itself.[12]

When Heraclius died in 641, his death precipitated a dynastic struggle. He was succeeded by two of his sons: Constantine, his son by his first marriage to Eudokia, and Heraclius, known as Heracleonas, his son by his second wife, Martina, who was also his niece. Martina herself was given a special role to play as augusta. Heraclius' marriage to his niece after the death of Eudokia had met with opposition at the time, and there was opposition to the association of Martina as empress with the two emperors. Constantine's death (from poisoning, according to a rumour reported by Theophanes) only increased opposition to Martina and Heracleonas, and there were demands that the imperial dignity be shared with Constantine's son, also Constantine, but usually called Constans. As troops from the Anatolian armies appeared at Chalcedon in support of these demands, Heracleonas seems to have acceded to them. Nevertheless, Heracleonas and his mother, together with her other two sons, were deposed and exiled, and Constans II became sole emperor.

Constans inherited the continuing collapse of the eastern provinces to the Arabs. Egypt was slipping away; Arab raids into Armenia began in 642–3. In 647 Muʿawiya led a raiding party into Anatolia and besieged Caesarea, whence they penetrated still more deeply into Anatolia. The Arabs made no attempt to settle there, but huge amounts of booty were taken back to Damascus. Muʿawiya also realised the need for the Arabs to develop sea power, and in 649 he led a naval expedition against Cyprus in which Constantia was taken. In 654 Rhodes was laid waste, Kos taken and Crete pillaged. The following year, in an attempt to destroy the threat to Byzantine control of the sea, the Byzantine fleet, under the command of the emperor Constans himself, engaged with the Arab fleet but was itself defeated, Constans himself barely escaping with his life. The death of the caliph ʿUthman in 656 precipitated civil war

[12] See Cameron (1991).

amongst the Arabs between Muʿawiya, proclaimed caliph in Syria, and ʿAli, the Prophet Muhammad's son-in-law. The civil war ended with the death of ʿAli and the establishment of the Umayyad dynasty under Muʿawiya in 661–2: events that provoked the schism in Islam between Sunni and Shiʿite that still endures. However, those years of civil war provided valuable respite for the Byzantines. Constans was able to turn his attention to the Balkans, where the power of the Avars had waned, and in 658 he led an expedition into the *Sklaviniai*, the regions settled by the Slavs, where, according to Theophanes, he met with considerable success and was able to use Slav prisoners thus taken to repopulate areas in Anatolia that had been devastated or depopulated. This policy of repopulating Anatolian regions by Slavs was to be continued by his successors, Constantine IV and Justinian II.

Constans also inherited the religious policy of his grandfather. By the early 640s, opposition to Monothelitism had developed. Behind this opposition was the monk Maximos, known to later ages as 'the Confessor', formerly a close associate of Sophronius, who had originally stirred up opposition to monenergism. Maximos found support in Palestine and Cyprus, but more importantly in North Africa, where he had been in exile since the late 620s, and Italy. These were areas which, in the sixth century, had protested against Justinian's condemnation of the 'Three Chapters' as compromising the decisions of Chalcedon.[13] In North Africa a number of synods condemned Monothelitism, and Maximos pressed home the attack in a series of skilfully argued tracts and letters. In 645 there arrived in North Africa the former patriarch Pyrrhos, who, as a supporter of the empress Martina, had shared her deposition. In July that year a disputation between the Monothelite former patriarch and Maximos was held in Carthage before the exarch Gregory, in which Pyrrhos admitted defeat and embraced Orthodoxy.[14] It was perhaps the strength of feeling against Monothelitism that led Gregory to allow himself to be declared emperor in opposition to Constans in 646–647, but his rebellion was short-lived, as he died the following year defending his province against Arab raiders. Meanwhile, Pyrrhos had made his way to Rome to declare his new-found Orthodoxy to the pope, followed closely by Maximos. In 648, in a vain attempt to prevent further controversy, the famous *Typos* was issued by the patriarch Paul in the name of the emperor, which forbade discussion of the number of activities or wills in Christ. In Rome, Maximos, together with other Greek monks who had fled west before the Arabs or from the heresy of the Empire, prepared for a synod, finally held in the Lateran Palace in Rome in 649 under the newly elected Pope Martin, at which both the *Ekthesis* and the *Typos* were condemned, together

[13] See chapter 4 above.

[14] The record of the dispute is preserved as Maximos, *Opusc.* 28: *PG* 91, cols. 288–353.

with the patriarchs Sergius, Pyrrhos and Paul (the extent to which this synod was of Greek inspiration has become clear from recent research which has shown that the Greek *Acta* of the synod are the original, the Latin version being a translation).[15] This open defiance of the imperial will could not be ignored. Olympios, the exarch of Ravenna, was ordered to arrest Martin and compel the bishops gathered in Rome to accept the *Typos*. When he arrived in Rome, he discovered that, despite his best efforts, Pope Martin's popularity made it hazardous for him to attempt to arrest him. In defiance of the imperial will, he made his peace with Martin, and departed for Sicily to deal with Arab raiders. There, like the exarch of North Africa, Gregory, he may have been proclaimed emperor. But he died in 652. The following year the new exarch arrived with troops and succeeded in arresting the pope. Martin was brought to Constantinople, tried for treason (Olympios' rebellion being cited as evidence), and condemned to death. The death penalty was commuted to exile, and he was sent to Cherson in the Crimea, where in 655 he died, a sick man who felt he had been abandoned by those who should have supported him (his successor having been elected more than a year before his death). By that time, Maximos had already been arrested and tried (again for treason) and sent into exile in Thrace, where attempts were made to break his opposition to Monothelitism. When that failed, he was brought again to Constantinople for trial, where he was condemned as a heretic, mutilated and exiled to Lazica, where he soon died on 13 August 662.

By the time Maximos had died in exile, the emperor himself was in self-imposed exile from Constantinople. In 662 Constans II and his court moved to Syracuse in Sicily. This attempt to abandon the beleaguered Constantinople and re-establish the court of the Roman Empire closer to the centre of the truncated empire, recalls earlier plans by both Heraclius and Maurice, and reveals that there was no sense that the Byzantine Empire was now confined to the eastern Mediterranean. From his base in Sicily, Constans clearly intended to liberate Italy from the Lombards. Before arriving at Syracuse, he had led a campaign in Italy, which had met with some success, though he had failed to take Benevento and soon retired to Naples, whence he made a ceremonial visit to Rome. But his residence in Sicily was extremely unpopular, imposing as it did an unwelcome financial burden on the island. There was fierce opposition in Constantinople to the loss of the court, and in 668 he was assassinated by a chamberlain.

Constans II was succeeded by his son, Constantine IV. It was during his reign that the Umayyad caliph Mu'awiya made a serious attempt to complete the Arab expansion that had begun in the 630s, to take Constantinople, and

[15] Riedinger (1982).

with it destroy the only serious opposition to Arab rule in the Mediterranean. After his victory over 'Ali in the Arab civil war, Mu'awiya renewed his offensive on the Byzantine Empire. By 670 the islands of Cyprus, Rhodes and Kos, and the town of Kyzikos on the southern coast of the Sea of Marmara had all been occupied by Arab naval forces. In 672 Smyrna was taken, and in 674 the main attack on Constantinople began. A large Arab fleet blockaded the city, and for the next four years the same fleet was to blockade Constantinople, retiring in the winter to shelter off Kyzikos. Each year the defences of Constantinople stood firm, and in the final naval battle the Byzantines secured a major victory. This was achieved by their use of Greek fire, first mentioned in the sources on this occasion. It was a highly inflammable liquid, presumably based on crude oil, that was projected in a stream on to the enemy ships, causing them to burst into flames. At the same time as this naval victory, the Byzantine army was able to surprise and defeat an Arab army contingent in Anatolia. Mu'awiya was forced to break off his attack on Constantinople and sue for peace. This major victory for the Byzantines proved to be a turning point: the Arab threat to Constantinople was withdrawn for the time being, and Byzantium's prestige in the Balkans and the West was enhanced. Embassies from the khagan of the Avars (now restricted mainly to the Hungarian plain) and from the Balkan Slavs arrived in Constantinople, bringing gifts and acknowledging Byzantine supremacy.

The situation in the Balkans was, however, about to change. The Slavs in the Balkans had never formed any coherent political entity, though their presence confined the Byzantines to Thessaloniki, and other coastal settlements. An Asiatic group, the Bulgars, had long been a presence among the nomadic tribes of the Eurasian plain. The Byzantines had had friendly relationships with them, and had supported them against the Avars. With the arrival of another group, the Khazars, the khaganate of the Bulgars, whose homeland was to the north of the Sea of Azov, began to split up, and one group, led by Asparuch, arrived at the Danube delta in 670, intending to settle south of the Danube in traditionally 'Byzantine' territory. The Byzantines saw no threat in the Bulgars, but were unwilling to allow them south of the Danube. In 680, a Byzantine fleet arrived at the mouth of the Danube and Byzantine troops moved up from Thrace, intending to expel the Bulgars. The Bulgars avoided open battle but, as the Byzantine forces withdrew, they took them by surprise and defeated them. Constantine IV concluded a treaty with Asparuch, which granted the Bulgars the territory they already held. As a result of the Bulgar presence, several Slav tribes hitherto loyal to Byzantium recognised the overlordship of the Bulgars. So there began to come into being a Bulgar–Slav country with its capital at Pliska. This independent, and often hostile, presence so close to Constantinople, in principle able to control the route from the Danube delta to Constantinople, was to prove a long-standing threat to the stability of the Empire.

The enforcement of Monothelitism as imperial policy, though it secured papal acquiescence in the years immediately following Martin's arrest and exile, was bound to prove ultimately unacceptable to the West, which saw the Synod of Chalcedon as endorsing the Latin Christology of Pope Leo I. By 680, Constantine came to the conclusion that religious unity with the West was more important than the fragile possibility of union with the Monophysites (now mostly lost to the Umayyad Empire) that Monothelitism had offered. He proposed to Pope Agatho the calling of an Ecumenical Synod to condemn Monothelitism. Agatho enthusiastically concurred, and held synods in Italy and England to prepare for the coming Ecumenical Synod. Armed with these synodical condemnations of Monothelitism, the papal legates arrived in Constantinople. The Sixth Ecumenical Synod met in Constantinople from 3 November 680 until 16 September 681. Monenergism and Monothelitism were condemned, and the patriarchs Sergius, Kyros, Pyrrhos, Paul and Peter anathematised, together with Pope Honorius. There was no word, however, of the defenders of the Orthodoxy vindicated by the synod, Martin and Maximos, who had suffered at the hands of Constans; nor were the emperors Constans and Heraclius mentioned. Constantine IV himself was hailed, at the final session, as a 'new Marcian' and a 'new Justinian'.

The latter part of Constantine's reign saw the Byzantine Empire regain a certain stability. In 684/5 he led a successful military expedition into Cilicia, which forced the caliph 'Abd al-Malik to sue for peace and pay tribute to the Byzantines. Religious reconciliation with Rome led to peace in Italy with the Lombards, brokered by the pope. In North Africa, the Byzantines were able to halt the advance of the Arabs through alliances with Berber tribes, though this only bought time until the Berbers themselves converted to Islam.

Constantine IV died in 685 and was succeeded by his son, Justinian II. It is worth noting that both Constantine IV and Constans II had deposed their brother(s) in the course of their reign – in Constantine's case despite open opposition from the senate and the army – to secure the succession of their eldest son. Justinian sought to build on the relative stability achieved by his father, leading an expedition into the Balkans and reaching Thessalonica. He continued the policy of his father and grandfather of transporting Slavs into Anatolia, and also transported some of the population from Cyprus to Kyzikos, that had been depopulated during the siege of Constantinople, and Mardaites from North Syria and Lebanon to the Peloponnese and elsewhere. His breaking of the truce with 'Abd al-Malik in 692–693 by attacking Arab forces in Iraq turned to disaster when his Slav troops deserted. As a result the Armenian princes once again acknowledged Muslim suzerainty.

In 692 Justinian called a synod, called the Quinisext (Fifth-Sixth), because it supplemented the doctrinal decisions of the fifth and sixth Ecumenical Synods with disciplinary canons covering every aspect of Christian life. In calling such a synod, Justinian was following the example of his father (and perhaps even more of his namesake) and declaring his credentials as emperor and guardian of Orthodoxy, something also manifest in his coinage in which the image of the emperor was displaced from the obverse of the coin to the reverse, and replaced with an image of Christ, the source of his authority as emperor.

In 695, Justinian was overthrown in a palace coup, and replaced by Leontius, the recently appointed general of the *thema* of Hellas. Justinian had his nose slit and was exiled to the Cherson, where his grandfather had earlier exiled Pope Martin. Leontius' reign lasted three years, during which he witnessed the end of Byzantine rule in North Africa. That defeat, and the consequent loss of Carthage, provoked another rebellion in which Leontius was deposed in favour of Apsimar, the *droungarios* of the Kibyrrhaiot fleet, who changed his name to the more imperial-sounding Tiberius. Tiberius Apsimar reigned from 698 to 705, during which time Asia Minor was subject to continual Arab raiding. He was replaced by Justinian, who returned with the support of the Bulgar khan Tervel, making his way into the city through one of the aqueducts. Justinian's final six years – years of terror and vengeance – were brought to an end by a military coup. Thereafter, until the accession of Leo III in 717 (the emperor who a decade or so later was to introduce Iconoclasm), three military leaders succeeded one another for reigns that were short and inglorious.

ADMINISTRATIVE CHANGE

At the beginning of the seventh century the administration of the Byzantine Empire, both civil and military, was essentially what had emerged from the reforms of Diocletian and Constantine in the late third and early fourth centuries. By the end of the eighth century a quite different administrative pattern was in place. There is a fair degree of clarity about the initial state, somewhat less about the final state, but owing to the nature of the evidence, which is both sparse and open to various interpretations, the nature and pace of the transition is still not completely resolved. In general terms the nature of the transition can be stated thus: at the beginning of the seventh century the Empire was divided into provinces that were ruled by civil governors who, though appointed by the emperor, were responsible to the relevant praetorian prefect (the provinces being grouped into four prefectures), the army being organised quite separately; at the end of the eighth century the Empire was divided into districts called themes (*thema*, *themata*), which were governed by a military commander called a *strategos* (general) who was responsible for both the civil and military administration of the province, and directly responsible to the emperor. Let us now look at the changes involved in more detail.[16]

CIVIL ADMINISTRATION

In the civil adminstration inherited from the Diocletianic–Constantinian reforms, alongside the administration of the Empire through the prefectures, there were also departments called *res privata* and *sacrae largitiones*, administered by counts (*comites*), who belonged to the imperial court (the *comitatus*). The *comes rei privatae* was responsible for all land and property belonging to the state (originally he had been concerned with the emperor's private property, as the name suggests, but the distinction between that and state property had long been elided): he was responsible for collecting the rents of all land and house property belonging to the state, and for claiming for the state all property that lapsed to it. The *comes sacrarum largitionum* controlled the mints, the gold (and probably silver) mines and the state factories in which arms and armour were decorated with precious metals. He was also responsible for paying periodical donatives in gold and silver to the troops, and dealt with the collection or production of clothing and its distribution to the court, the army and the civil service. The praetorian prefects were responsible for the fiscal administration of the prefectures, into which the Empire was divided. These prefectures consisted of provinces, governed by governors (with various titles), and were themselves grouped into dioceses, governed by *vicarii*. The praetorian prefects were responsible for the rations, or ration allowances (*annonae*), which formed the bulk of the emoluments of the army and the civil service, and for the fodder, or fodder allowances (*capitus*), of officers and troopers, and of civil servants who held equivalent grades. They had to maintain the public post, and were responsible for public works, roads, bridges, post houses and granaries, which did not come under the care of the urban prefects in Rome and Constantinople or the city authorities in the provinces, or the army on the frontiers. In order to do all this, they had to estimate the annual needs of their prefecture and raise it through a general levy, or tax, called the indiction. The whole operation of raising this tax and servicing the running of the Empire was overseen by the praetorian prefects, who delegated it to their *vicarii* and governors. Only the praetorian prefect in whose prefecture the emperor and his court were located was attached to the court: once the court was permanently settled in Constantinople, this meant the praetorian prefect for the East

[16] What follows is deeply indebted to Haldon's subtle and powerfully argued account of the administrative changes in Haldon (1997), pp. 173–253.

(*Oriens*). Also influential in the *comitatus* were senior officials of the *sacrum cubiculum*, the eunuch chamberlains (*cubicularii*).

By the end of the eighth century, the fiscal administration was organised rather differently. The distinction between the public and the 'sacred' (i.e. pertaining to the person of the emperor) had gone, and instead of the *res privata*, the *sacrae largitiones* and the prefectures, there were several departments, or *sekreta*, of more or less equal status, all subject to the emperor through an official called the *sakellarios*. The heads of these departments consisted of three administrators: the Postal Logothete (*logothetes tou dromou*), who dealt with the post, diplomacy and internal security, the General Logothete, in charge of the *genikon logothesion*, who dealt with finance, and the Military Logothete, in charge of the *stratiotikon logothesion*, who dealt with military pay. There were two treasurers: the *chartoularios* of the *sakellion*, in charge of cash and most charitable institutions, and the *chartoularios* of the *vestiarion*, in charge of the mint and the arsenal. And there were the heads of state establishments: the Special Secretary (*epi tou eidikou*), in charge of factories; the Great Curator (*megas kourator*), in charge of the palaces and imperial estates; and the *orphanotrophos*, in charge of orphanages. In addition there was an official called the *protoasekretis*, in charge of records. Directly responsible to the emperor, and independent of the *sakellarios*, were the principal magistrates, the City Prefect (responsible for Constantinople), the *quaestor* (in charge of the judiciary), and the Minister for Petitions (who dealt with petitions to the emperor). A rather obvious, and superficial change is that of language: whereas the older system used Latin titles, the new system used predominantly Greek titles, bearing witness to the change in the official language of the Empire from Latin, the traditional language of the Roman Empire, to Greek, the language of Constantinople and the Hellenistic East, a change dating from the time of Justinian. More deeply, it can be seen that the change was a reshuffling of tasks, so that they all became subject to a fundamentally civil administration based on the court. The *genikon*, *eidikon* and *stratiotikon* derived from the general, special and military departments of the prefectures (in fact, the prefecture of the East, as we shall see); the *sakellion* from the *sacellum*, the personal treasury of the emperor within the *sacrum cubiculum*; and the *vestiarion* from the department of the *sacrum vestiarium* within the *sacrae largitiones*.

The position of the *sakellarios* perhaps gives a clue to the nature of the changes. In charge of the emperor's personal treasury, this official's rise to pre-eminence was a function of his closeness to the emperor and suggests a change from an essentially public administration, determined in its structure by the need to administer a far-flung empire, to an administration focussed on the court, in which the Empire is almost reduced to the extent of imperial command. The background to this is, of course, the dramatic shrinking of the Empire in the first half of the seventh century: the loss of the eastern provinces, followed by the loss of North Africa, and by the end of the eighth century Italy too, together with the occupation of the Balkans by the Slavs (and the emergence of the Bulgarian Empire south of the Danube), meant that the Byzantine Empire had shrunk to the rumps of two prefectures, of the East and of Illyricum. The reorganisation of the civil administration took place by Constantinople incorporating into a court structure the administrative offices of the Empire. The growing power of the *sakellarios* can be traced back to the time of Justinian; by the middle of the seventh century, as is evident from the role he played in the trial of Maximos the Confessor, he was a powerful courtier who took personal charge of matters of supreme importance to the emperor. Logothetes are also met with in the sources from the early years of the seventh century, but officials bearing traditional titles, such as praetorian prefect, not to mention civil governors of provinces, continue to appear in the sources well into the eighth century. This would suggest that there was a period of overlap, in which the new administration emerged, while the old administration still retained some of its functions. However the whole picture only emerges when we consider the changes in the military administration.

MILITARY ADMINISTRATION

As a result of the Diocletianic–Constantinian reforms the Roman army was separated from the civil administration, so that governors of provinces no longer commanded a provincial army (though they were still responsible for raising funds to support the army). The army was divided into two parts: there were troops protecting the borders, the *limitanei*, under the command of *duces*, and there was a field army, the *comitatenses*, which was mobile, organised in divisions under the command of the *magistri militum*. In addition there were the palace troops, and the imperial bodyguard, whose titles changed throughout the fifth and sixth centuries. By the end of the ninth century, there had emerged a quite different system, with the army divided into divisions called *themata* (or themes), based in provinces also called themes, each under the command of a *strategos*, who was responsible for both the civil and military government of his theme. There is no general agreement about how quickly this change took place, nor why (whether it was the result of some planned reorganisation, or simply a fumbling reaction to the problems of the seventh and eighth centuries). There is, however, general dissent from the theory, which once commanded much support, associated with the name of the great Byzantinist George Ostrogorsky, who saw the thematic army as the result of a deliberate reorganisation of the army and the Empire by the emperor Heraclius. The result, supposedly, was a peasant army, based in the themes, in which land had been allotted to peasant families as smallholdings, in return for each family providing and equipping a soldier.[17] This somewhat romantic idea of the middle Byzantine Empire resting on the popular support of a free peasantry has been generally abandoned. The transition is now thought to have been later than Heraclius' reign, and probably a gradual change. The idea that the soldiers of the themes were supported by their families, who had received grants of land, seems to be a retrojection of the much later notion of *pronoia*, whereby soldiers did receive land in return for military service. But there is no evidence for the system of *pronoia* until the twelfth century, and those who received such grants of *pronoia* then were certainly not peasants.

Part of the problem is terminology. The word *thema* originally meant a military unit, and references to *themata* in the sources in the seventh century may refer to military units, rather than to the land where they were stationed. But even if it seems that the reference is to territory, since our sources are from the ninth century, by which time the thematic system was well established, we cannot be sure that such a reference is not an anachronism. As with the changes in civil adminstration already discussed, it is possible (indeed likely) that the two systems overlapped: for even though there are references to *strategoi* and *themata* in the seventh century, there is still mention of provinces (*eparchiai*) and governors, and use of such titles as *magister militum* well into the eighth century.

The first themes to emerge are the *Opsikion*, the *Anatolikon*, the *Armeniakon* and the *Thrakesion*, together with a fifth division, the fleet of the *Karabisianoi*, which included the islands of the Aegean and part of the south-west coast of Asia Minor. Later these themes were subdivided, but their original boundaries correspond to already existing provincial boundaries. A likely explanation of the origin of these themes, without any close reference to timescale, is as follows. After the defeat of the Byzantine army by the Arabs, the troops retreated over the Taurus Mountains into Anatolia. But the years following the defeat, as recounted above, saw continual raiding by Arab forces into Anatolia, leading finally in the 660s and 670s to a concerted attempt by the caliph Muʿawiya to advance across Asia Minor and take Constantinople. In this situation of prolonged threat, the Byzantine armies were stationed in Asia Minor among the provinces. They would have been provisioned in the traditional way, by a levy raised by the local governors from the civilian population of the provinces. The areas that came to be called the themes of the *Armeniakon* and the *Anatolikon* were the groups of provinces where the armies commanded by the *magistri militum per Armeniam* and *per Orientem* were stationed. The theme of the

[17] Brief account in Ostrogorsky (1969), pp. 96–8. More detail in Ostrogorsky (1958). The romanticism of Ostrogorsky's vision emerges more clearly in Ostrogorsky (1962).

Thrakesion occupied the provinces in western Anatolia where the army of the *magister militum per Thraciam* was established, having been transferred from Thrace to resist the Arabs, perhaps at the same time as the army of the *magister militum per Orientem* withdrew into Asia Minor. The theme of the *Opsikion* were the armies of the *magistri militum praesentales*, some of whom had probably long been established in the area across the Bosphorus from Constantinople. Their name derives from the Latin *obsequium* which formed part of the title of the officer who, during the reign of Heraclius, was appointed to command the praesental armies on the emperor's behalf: he was the commander of the palatine corps of the *domestici*, called the *comes domesticorum*, but also the *comes Obsequii*. The *Karabisianoi*, the fleet, formed part of the old *quaestura exercitus*, probably based at Samos. It seems likely that all of this was established – that is, military units called themes stationed in the provinces of Asia Minor – by some time around about the middle of the seventh century. At what stage, and why, the civil administration declined, to be replaced by the military government of the *strategoi*, is much less clear. But presumably the overriding need to supply a standing army, combined with the final decline of the ancient economy based on the city, meant that the *strategos*, supported by the growing centralised administration emanating from the court, gradually assumed the functions of the old governing elite. The latter had itself lost much of its *raison d'être* because of the increasingly bureaucratic nature of the civil administration.

LEGAL ADMINISTRATION

Given the profound changes in civil and military administration initiated in the seventh century, it is at first sight surprising that there seems to have been so little legislative activity in this century, which has nothing to set beside the major attempts at legislative reform of the fifth and sixth centuries, witnessed in the *Codex Theodosianus* and the *Codex Justinianus*. Apart from the *Farmer's Law*, the date of which is disputed and which anyway is a compilation of Justinianic and pre-Justinianic material, the emperors seem to have initiated very little legislation, and what there was was primarily ecclesiastical in nature (for example, Heraclius' edict of 632 requiring the compulsory conversion of the Jews, his *Ekthesis*, and Constans II's *Typos*). In contrast, the Quinisext Synod, called by the emperor Justinian II, represents a major recapitulation of canonical legislation, which can be compared with the legal *codex* of Justinian II's great predecessor (see below). The explanation for this lack of legislative activity in the secular sphere is probably to be found by recalling the dual nature of Roman legislation: not only a body of rules governing day-to-day behaviour, but more importantly a way of enunciating the world-view and set of values embraced by, in this case, the Roman (or Byzantine) Empire. As John Haldon has put it,

> Seen from this perspective, the legal 'system' became less a practical instrument for intervening in the world of men in order to modify relationships or individual behaviour, but more a set of theories which represented a desired (if recognizably not always attainable) state of affairs. Emperors needed to issue no new legislation, therefore, but rather to establish (or to re-establish) the conditions within which the traditional system would once again conform to actual practice.[18]

RELIGION AND THE CHURCH

It is generally recognised that from the latter part of the sixth century onwards there was an increasing desire to have direct access to the power of the holy. Again, this cannot be demonstrated beyond peradventure, since these means of access – the cult of saints and their relics, and perhaps even the veneration of icons – were already well established by the sixth century. Traditionally imperial authority had been justified by the divinely protected status of the emperor, expressed through an imperial cult. The Christianisation of the imperial cult tended to enhance its authority rather than to diminish it, since the representative of the only God was hardly reduced in status in comparison with a divine emperor holding a relatively lowly position in the divine pantheon. It seems to be demonstrable that this Christian imperial authority and that of the hierarchy of the Christian church, which was closely bound up with it, were strengthened by the authority conceded by holy men and holy images, claiming immediate access to supernatural power. It seems, too, that even traditional imperial authority was increasingly expressed through images that spoke of a more immediate sacred authority. This becomes evident at the beginning of our century in the use of icons of Christian saints, especially of the Mother of God, as military banners, in the way in which Christian armies are seen as fighting for the Virgin, with her protection (and even her assistance), and in the role claimed for the Virgin as protector of the city of Constantinople. A sacralisation of authority is also manifest in the increasing significance granted to coronation by the patriarch in the making of an emperor: it was always conducted in a church from the beginning of the seventh century, and in the Great Church of Hagia Sophia from 641. The institutional church, indeed, may well have felt itself threatened by the proliferation of the holy in the seventh century: the church in the Byzantine East certainly failed to establish the kind of control over the holiness present in saints, their images and relics that the popes and bishops had won in the western church.[19]

[18] Haldon (1997), p. 259. [19] See Brown (1976).

But if there is little evidence of tension between the proliferation of the holy and the hierarchy of the church in the Byzantine East in the seventh century (in the eighth the ready support the Iconoclast emperors seemed to find among the higher clergy may possibly be evidence of a reaction on the part of the hierarchy), there is certainly evidence that there was tension between the centre and the periphery in geographical terms. Despite the wealth of theological literature that survives from the seventh century, we know little about theology at the capital, and that for the simple reason that by the ninth century no one in Constantinople wanted to be reminded of it. Theology in Constantinople was subservient to the emperor, and to the politically inspired doctrines of monenergism, Monothelitism and, in the next century, Iconoclasm. Resistance to all these, a resistance that was finally recognised as 'Orthodoxy', came from the periphery, and in the long term especially from the monks of Palestine, who had long been known for their commitment to Chalcedonian Orthodoxy. This fact had curious long-term consequences for Orthodox Byzantium, and which is worth pursuing briefly here. Resistance to monenergism began with Sophronius, who had been a monk in Palestine, and later became patriarch of Jerusalem; resistance to Monothelitism was led by Sophronius' disciple Maximos, whose impact on the Orthodox in Palestine was such that the Monothelites in Syria and Palestine called them 'Maximians'.[20] In the second half of the seventh century dyothelite ('Orthodox') Christians in Palestine found themselves in a new situation. Previously they had been adherents of an imperial Orthodoxy that had been supported, in the last resort, by persecution. Now they found themselves in a situation where their religious position was opposed by other Christian groups – Monophysite, Monothelite, and even Nestorian – by non-Christians like Jews, Samaritans and Manichees, and eventually by Muslims. They had both to defend what they believed in, and work out exactly what their faith amounted to. To do this they had to pay attention to matters of logic and definition, for the only way to defend and commend their position was by convincing others: they could no longer appeal to the secular arm. One element in this refining of the presentation and understanding of the Christianity of the Ecumenical Synods was dialogue with – or polemic against – the Jews. After a long period when there was scarcely any dialogue with Jews, or even simple refutation of Judaism, the latter half of the seventh century witnessed an extraordinary burgeoning of such works. Most of them came from the provinces seized by the Arabs: Syria, Palestine, the Sinai Peninsula and Cyprus. It is clear from some of these works that Jews themselves took the initiative in the debate, and forced Christians to produce fresh defences of

[20] The view that Maximos was himself a Palestinian, as is maintained in the Syriac life published in 1973 (see Brock (1973) in Brock (1984)), seems to be losing credibility among scholars.

doctrines such as the doctrine of the Trinity, and practices like veneration of the saints, relics and icons.[21] Alongside such doctrinal clarification, there was also, again stemming principally from Palestine, celebration in liturgical poetry of the doctrines of Christianity, which came to form the backbone of monastic worship. This eventually became the worship of the Orthodox church, that is, the Byzantine church, and of churches who learnt their Christianity from Byzantium. The crucial century for this definition, defence and celebration of Orthodoxy was the period from 650 to 750. It is epitomised in the works of John of Damascus, an Umayyad civil servant turned Palestinian monk, who thought of himself as a Byzantine Christian. Its first test was the Iconoclasm of Byzantine Emperors, outwith whose political reach they lived.[22]

As we have seen, this form of Christianity was called 'Maximianism' by its enemies, but it owed more to Maximos than simply its attachment to dyothelite Chalcedonianism, as declared at the Lateran Synod of 649 and vindicated at the Sixth Ecumenical Synod of 680–681. For Maximos' genius as a theologian was to draw together the several strands of Greek theological reflection into an imposing synthesis. One strand in this synthesis was the dogmatic theology of the great patriarchs of Alexandria, Athanasius and Cyril of Alexandria, that formed the basis for the dogmas endorsed by the Ecumenical Synods from the fourth to the sixth centuries. Another strand was the Christian Hellenism of the fourth-century Cappadocian Fathers, Basil of Caesarea, Gregory of Nazianzus and Gregory of Nyssa. A further strand was constituted by the ascetic wisdom of the Desert Fathers of the fourth-century Egyptian desert and their successors in the Judaean desert to the east of Jerusalem, in the coastal desert of Gaza, and in barren mountains of the Sinai Peninsula. These three strands Maximos wove together, the final tapestry being shot through with the Neoplatonic metaphysics of the (probably early sixth-century) Syrian monk who wrote under the name of Dionysius the Areopagite, the convert of St Paul the Apostle. It was this theological vision of St Maximos that inspired the more soberly expressed, even dry doctrinal synthesis that we find in John of Damascus. Maximos' vision, in which humankind, the cosmos and the scriptures themselves were all interrelated, was reflected in the domed interior of the Byzantine church. In that space, as Maximos explained in his reflections on the divine liturgy called the *Mystagogia*, the liturgical ceremonies, involving the clergy and the people, celebrated the whole unfolding of the Christian mystery from creation to the second coming of Christ in a way that probed the depths of the human heart and illuminated the mysteries of the cosmos.[23]

21 See Déroche (1991) and Cameron (1996a).

22 For these developments and John Damascene's part in them, see Louth (1996b).

23 For an introduction to the theology of Maximos, see Louth (1996a).

But to turn from what may seem such giddy heights (though expressed in gesture and movement, melody and colour, that one can well imagine impressed the simplest of Byzantine Christians) we see a more detailed picture of the life of the Byzantine church in the seventh century emerging from the 102 canons of the so-called Quinisext Synod, called by the emperor Justinian II in 692. Like his predecessor, and his namesake, Justinian II wished to mark his reign, and manifest his exercise of imperial power, by calling an Ecumenical Synod. Hitherto, all synods regarded as ecumenical had been called to deal with some pressing doctrinal issue, but with the monenergist/Monothelite controversy now settled, there was no doctrinal issue to provide the occasion for an Ecumenical Synod. However, the previous two Ecumenical Synods, the Second and Third Synods of Constantinople, had issued only doctrinal canons, whereas all the earlier ones had dealt with both doctrinal and disciplinary issues. Thus the synod that Justinian eventually called, which issued only disciplinary canons, was regarded as a completion of the work of the last two synods (the Fifth and the Sixth Ecumenical Synods) and so called the Fifth-Sixth (Quinisext or *Penthekte*) Ecumenical Synod. It is also known as the Synod *in Trullo* (or the Trullan Synod) from the domed chamber (*troullos*) in the palace where the synod took place.

The 102 canons[24] issued by the synod cover many aspects of the life of Christians, including both their religious duties and their behaviour in secular life. The first two canons affirm and define the existing tradition, of which the rest of the canons constitute a kind of completion: canon 1 affirms the unchanging faith defined at the previous six ecumenical synods; canon 2 confirms the body of (disciplinary) canons already accepted by the church.[25] The rest of the canons complete this body of canonical material, and the whole body of legislation constituted by this synod can be compared in some ways to the Justinianic Code in that it is intended as the final statement of an ideal of Christian life, expressed through much quite detailed legislation. It remains the foundation of the canon law of the Orthodox church. In this context it is worth drawing attention to the last canon, which affirms that the administration of penalties in accordance with the canons must take account of the quality of the sin and the disposition of the sinner, for the ultimate purpose of canon law is to heal, not simply to punish. This canon reaffirms a principle already expressed in earlier canons,[26] usually called the principle of 'economy' (Greek:

[24] *Discipline Générale*, ed. Joannou, I.I, pp. 98–241.

[25] For a succinct account of the development of Christian canon law, see Young, Ayres and Louth (2004), chapter 36.

[26] Canons of St Basil 95 (ed. Joannou, II, pp. 193–8), cf. 3 (*ibid.* pp. 100–1); Canons of St Gregory of Nyssa 1 (*ibid.*, pp. 203–9).

oikonomia), which is not unlike the way in which in the seventh century secular law used the code as an ideal which was applied by trying to fit the ideal to the concrete issues, rather than by the issue of new legislation, as we have already seen.

One guiding principle of the canons of the Quinisext Synod was to define the practices of the Byzantine church in conscious opposition to the developing customs of the Latin church. For instance, canon 55, which forbids fasting on Saturdays and Sundays, except for Holy Saturday, is explicitly directed against the practice found in the city of Rome of fasting on Saturdays during Lent. More important are the canons that envisage a married pastoral clergy, though restricted to priests and deacons (married men who become bishops are to separate from their wives, who become nuns: canons 12, 48): again this is in conscious opposition to the Roman canons, though it would be some centuries before a celibate priesthood was strictly enforced in the western church. A similar independence of Rome is manifest in canon 36, which prescribed the order of the patriarchates and, following the canons of the first Ecumenical Synod of Constantinople (canon 3) and the Ecumenical Synod of Chalcedon (canon 28, which had been repudiated by Rome), ranked Constantinople second after Rome, with equal privileges. Although the papal *apocrisiarii* accepted the canons, Pope Sergius refused to sign them, and Justinian's furious attempt to enforce papal consent only exposed the limits of his power in Italy. The introduction of the singing of the *Agnus Dei* into the Mass at Rome by Pope Sergius is perhaps to be seen as a snub to the synod (see canon 82, discussed below).[27] Although Pope John VII seems to have accepted the canons of the synod in 705, when Justinian was restored to the imperial throne, this represented no lasting endorsement of the canons by the western church.

Other canons regulated the life of the local church, still understood as essentially a city church ruled by a bishop, though, as we have seen, the reality of the city was fast vanishing. Provinces, into which city churches were grouped under the leadership of a metropolitan bishop, were to meet once a year (canon 8). Bishops were to live in their sees, and to return to them as soon as possible if they fled during 'barbarian' raids (canon 18). This anxiety that the bishop stick to his city was to ensure partly his continuing pastoral care, but also his control of the church's financial interests, for the local churches were frequently considerable landowners, their estates being administered by the bishop. The requirement that bishops reside in their own sees was taken seriously, as is evident from the more abundant later evidence, especially from the Komnene period, when the

[27] Sergius' introduction of the *Agnus Dei* into the mass is asserted in the *Liber Pontificalis* 86 (Sergius), 14 (ed. Duchesne, I, p. 376).

Empire was even more focussed on Constantinople and provincial sees were regarded as exile by their bishops.[28] There are also canons against purchasing church office, and selling the sacraments: what the West later called simony (canons 22–3). Legislation concerning monasticism, like much earlier legislation, attempted to confine monks to their monasteries, and control the power of holy men (canons 40–9). Legislation concerning the laity forbade various entertainments such as playing dice (canon 50), watching mimes, animal fights or dancing on the stage (canon 51), the observance of civic ceremonies such as the *Kalends*, *Vota* or *Brumalia*, which had pagan associations, as well as female dancing in public, dancing associated with pagan rites, cross-dressing, the use of comic, satyr or tragic masks, and the invocation of Dionysos during the pressing of grapes for wine (canon 62). All of this the church regarded as 'paganising', though such practices should probably not be thought of as the survival of paganism as such, but rather the continuance of traditional liturgical forms that involved the laity.[29] Canons also forbade the confusion of traditional liturgies with the Christian sacraments (for example, canon 57 forbidding the offering of milk and honey on Christian altars), and there were canons that regulated the institution of marriage and the circumstances of divorce (canons 53, 54, 72, 87, 92, 93). Several canons concerned relations between Christians and Jews: canon 11 forbade eating unleavened bread with Jews, making friends with Jews, consulting Jewish doctors, or mixing with them in the baths; canon 33 forbade the 'Jewish' practice of ordaining only those of priestly descent. Both these canons illustrate the way in which Jews were permitted to exist, but separate from the Orthodox society of the Empire. In fact, the seventh century had seen the beginning of a more radical policy towards the Jews: forced baptism on pain of death. In 632 Heraclius had introduced such a policy, to which Maximos the Confessor expressly objected,[30] a policy that was introduced again in the eighth and the tenth centuries, by Leo III and Romanos I Lekapenos respectively. But the more normal Byzantine attitude to the Jews, to be preserved as a standing witness to the truth of Christianity with limited civil rights, is that envisaged by the canons of the Trullan Synod.[31]

Two canons bear witness to the place of religious art in the Byzantine world. Canon 100 forbids pictures that excite immoral pleasure, and makes a point about how easily the bodily senses move the soul. Canon 82 is concerned with religious paintings and forbids the depiction of Christ as a lamb, a popular form of religious art that picked up the words of John the Baptist about Jesus as the 'lamb of God who takes away the sin of the world' (John 1:36). However,

[28] See Angold (1995), pp. 139–262. [29] See Haldon (1997), pp. 327–37.

[30] Devreese (1937). [31] See Louth, chapter 4 above.

the canon argues, such symbolism has been fulfilled since God has come in human form: now the reality of the Incarnation is to be expressed by depicting the Incarnate Word as a man. Such a concern for the content of religious images (icons), expressed in theological terms, prefigures the controversies of the next two centuries caused by Iconoclasm.

The comparatively settled picture of Christian life in the Byzantine Empire presented by the canons of the Quinisext Synod is not, however, the whole story. The latter half of the seventh century saw the production of apocalyptic texts, composed in Syriac. One of these, soon translated into Greek, was ascribed to the early fourth-century bishop Methodios (of Olympus, according to the Syriac original, of Patara, according to the Greek translation).[32] The Pseudo-Methodian Apocalypse responds to the loss of the eastern provinces to the Arabs, or Ishmaelites, 'the wild ass of the desert', by recounting the history of the Middle East since biblical times, and predicting the final overthrow of the Ishmaelites by the king of the 'Greeks' (so the Syriac; 'Romans' in the Greek version) at Jerusalem, whose victory will usher in the end of the world.[33] The emergence of such apocalyptic hopes and fears at the end of the seventh century contrasts sharply with the spirit of the early sixth-century chronicle of John of Malalas, written partly to demonstrate that the world had survived the transition from the sixth to the seventh millennium (*c.* AD 500) without disaster.

The end of the seventh century saw the Byzantine Empire still in a process of transition and redefinition: the Arab threat to Constantinople was to continue well into the eighth century, and Iconoclasm, which is beyond the scope of this chapter, is probably to be seen as a further stage in the Byzantine Empire's search for its identity and ways of expressing this in the aftermath of crisis of the seventh century.[34] But there were scarcely any signs of incipient Iconoclasm at the end of the seventh century: the Quinisext Synod invested a clearly articulated theological significance in religious art, and the process observed since the end of the sixth century of authenticating political authority by imagery invoking the supernatural was, as we have seen, taken a stage further at the end of the century with the appearance of the image of Christ on the obverse of imperial coinage, the imperial image being consigned to the reverse. But the structures of the society that was eventually to emerge from this period of crisis can already be perceived, albeit in inchoate form, as well as some of the limitations of that society, compared with the Roman Empire of Justinian's vision that it claimed to be. Already in the canons of the Quinisext Synod there

32 This confusion as to his see is also found in manuscripts of authentic writings by Methodios.

33 See Alexander (1985), and Brock, *Syriac Chronicles*, trans. Palmer, pp. 222–50.

34 Not all scholars accept that the seventh century is to be regarded as representing a crisis for the Byzantine Empire: see Treadgold (1990) and (1997), pp. xvi and 287–413.

is the sense that Christians legislated for from Constantinople have different customs from those that prevail among those who look to Rome: a difference that will deepen in the eighth century as Rome moves from the sphere of influence of the Byzantine emperor to that of the Franks. The Mediterranean Sea was no longer to unite the territories that bordered it, but would come to separate the several societies that claimed the heritage of that lost unity.

CHAPTER 12

MUHAMMAD AND THE RISE OF ISLAM

Carole Hillenbrand

PRE-ISLAMIC ARABIA

Traditionally, scholars have drawn a firm distinction between south Arabia (especially the south-western corner which corresponds to modern Yemen) and the rest of the peninsula. Although, as we shall see later, it is unhelpful to draw too crude a division between south and north, the dichotomy is essentially dictated by geography: most of Arabia in late antique times consisted predominantly of vast areas of desert, fringed with oases, whilst the southern part of the peninsula, the 'Arabia Felix' of the ancients, was blessed with abundant and regular rainfall and could support a highly developed agriculture, underpinned by extensive and elaborate irrigation systems.

South Arabia was thickly populated, its inhabitants were largely sedentarised and agriculturalist from around the eighth century BC and its towns had provided a milieu conducive to the development of political institutions and material culture. A few kingdoms or city-states, such as Ma'n, Saba', Qataban and Hadramawt, stand out from the blurred outlines of south Arabian history, based as it is on oral tradition. Such states could enjoy brief periods of independent power or could become united for a while, as was the case with the kingdom of Himyar around the beginning of the fourth century AD.[1]

Reliable information about the south Arabian kingdoms is only fragmentary. Classical authors waxed lyrical about the fabled luxury of the Sabaeans (and notably the Queen of Sheba). In spite of the still insecure chronologies of south Arabian rulers, archaeological evidence bears clear witness to a mature urban culture in the area. Indeed, the south Arabians were skilled architects and left behind a vast array of monumental inscriptions, as well as statues inspired by the art of Greece and Rome and the famous irrigation works at Marib, first mentioned in the eighth century BC, which were praised in

[1] For a clear overview of the history of pre-Islamic Arabia, Lammens (1928); Serjeant (1967); Shahid (1970).

antiquity as an engineering wonder. The irrigation provided by the dam in its heyday produced two fertile oases, which may well have comprised *in toto* some 10,000 hectares of arable land and must have supported a substantial population. Recent German archaeological excavations in the Marib area have in fact demonstrated from epigraphic evidence that the dam broke on at least four major occasions (*c*.370, 449, 450 and 542 AD) before its final 'collapse' (or moment when no further repairs were attempted) at some point before the advent of Islam. The inherent flaw in the dam, namely the accumulation of silt, was not understood by those who constructed and repaired it. The dam was not therefore designed to cope with this problem, and the strategies to which the pre-Islamic engineers resorted – namely raising the height of the dam but having to use increasingly thinner courses of masonry to do so – were bound to be merely palliative. Each time the dam broke, widespread economic hardship and population shifts must have occurred. These would have had a disruptive domino effect on adjoining territories, and the shock waves of the disaster would in time have been felt in the far north of Arabia and beyond, notably in the form of successive tribal displacements.[2] The bursting of the Marib dam in Saba is in fact enshrined in Islamic tradition, a moment symbolising the decline of the south Arabian kingdom.

So much for the civilised south-western corner of Arabia. The remainder of the peninsula presented a sharp contrast in many ways. Here, human life was dominated by the desert and the pressing need to adjust to its rigours. The inhabitants of this vast desert, predominantly pastoralists, led a precarious existence based on the domestication of the camel and the cultivation of the date palm. The Bedouin nomads were hardy and resourceful, working as camel-herders deep into the desert or as sheep-rearers closer to the agricultural areas around the oases, such as Yathrib, later to be called Medina, and Khaybar. Here, farmers grew dates and wheat. Camel nomadism had developed in Arabia over many centuries. As the famous fourteenth-century Muslim thinker Ibn Khaldun observed in his well-known analysis of nomad life, camel-herders had greater mobility than sheep-rearers and could cover wider expanses of land between watering holes.[3] The balance of power in the desert areas of the peninsula lay with the camel-herders, whose animals could support more people with meat, milk and hides. They lived in a symbiotic relationship with the semi-sedentarised agriculturalists of the oases, with whom they traded the products of nomad life in exchange for other wares, including weapons. Nevertheless, the camel-herders had the edge militarily, and periodically the farmers would buy protection from them.

[2] Brunner (1982–3), I and II; Glaser (1913).

[3] Ibn Khaldun, *The Muqaddimah*, trans. Rosenthal, p. 92.

The Arabs in north, central and eastern Arabia possessed no centralised government. Such a structure had existed only in peripheral areas, such as the kingdoms of Petra in Jordan and Palmyra in the Syrian desert, which had prospered in Roman times and had been profoundly influenced by classical culture. Bedouin society rejected authoritarian political concepts, being divided instead into egalitarian lineage groups. Such a 'tribal' organisation permeated the life of both pastoralists and farmers. Smaller or larger groups would recognise common ties and unite for economic and defensive reasons. To quote Ibn Khaldun on the Bedouin: 'Their defence and protection are successful only if they are a closely knit group of common descent.'[4] Tribes and clans (the terminology in the Arabic sources is very imprecise) would vary in size, structure and prestige. It is possible that wider tribal affiliations were acknowledged, but everyday life was probably based on smaller pragmatic groupings which shared encampments and watering places. Such groups were not rigidly structured, however, and were flexible enough to allow newcomers in or to reform according to circumstance. Nomadic groups often possessed their own recognised pasturing grounds, but these did not have fixed boundaries.

In principle, Bedouin society was egalitarian, although each tribal unit recognised a chief (*sharif* or *sayyid*) whose own status depended on his personal charisma. Such tribal leaders were both elected and hereditary, for a new chief would be drawn initially from an elite group within the tribe but nevertheless would be chosen outright on merit. His responsibilities included arbitration in disputes, the entertainment of guests, the defence of the tribe and the custody of its sacred symbols. Justice and restraint between tribal groups were achieved by a strict *lex talionis*: the honour of the whole group to which an injured person belonged required that they should exact equivalent retribution from the whole group of which the person who had committed the injury was a member. This process of mutual retaliation, which prevailed not only in the sedentarised areas such as Medina and Mecca but also amongst the desert nomads, could become protracted, until a suitable solution was found. Such a system, which gave each individual membership of a wider group, afforded him personal safety and protection for his dependants and his property.

The Bedouin tribesmen were armed; the exigencies of desert life often necessitated raiding (*ghazw*) the territory of other tribes or of the sedentary peoples. Indeed, this was a militarised society. The rules for *ghazw* had been laid down in ancestral tradition. In their dour desert environment the Bedouin tribesmen had long followed a code of manly virtue (*muruwwa*) in which the qualities of patient endurance (*sabr*), generous hospitality, courage and military prowess

[4] Ibn Khaldun, *The Muqaddimah*, trans. Rosenthal, p. 97.

were especially prized. This code of conduct was probably more important to them than any formal religious observance.

The religious customs of the Arabs in north, central and eastern Arabia are even more difficult to pinpoint with precision than those of the south. The cults of the Bedouin were animistic and varied; they worshipped stones, trees and idols. Muslim tradition speaks of the existence of soothsayers or sorcerers (*kahins*) in the pre-Islamic period; these men or women seem to have resembled the *shamans* of the Turkic world in some of their functions, possessing gifts of foretelling the future, healing and water-divining. They were not associated with specific deities. The Bedouin also acknowledged the sanctity of certain holy enclaves (*haram* or *hawta*).[5] Some of these sanctuaries functioned without guardians; others were organised by a hereditary religious elite. These holy enclaves became places of asylum and were used as a meeting place for the settling of disputes. The sanctuary itself and the area surrounding it were declared inviolable and killing, even fighting, was prohibited. Some sanctuaries acquired as it were tutelary deities. Thus the god Hubal was associated with the Meccan sanctuary, and the triad of goddesses, Allat, al-'Uzza (both normally identified with Venus) and Manat (the goddess of fate) were especially reverenced in the sanctuaries located near Mecca. Annual markets followed by pilgrimage ceremonies, including circumambulation in a ritually pure state, took place at these sites. These last three goddesses were elevated to the title of the 'daughters of Allah', the Creator God, whose importance was widely recognised within the peninsula. These goddesses formed part of the religious milieu of the Prophet's own tribe, the Quraysh, in his lifetime and are attacked in the Qur'an (53/19–23).[6]

It is difficult to evaluate the importance of the religious practices and beliefs of the pre-Islamic Arabs. The Bedouin did not fight in the name of specific deities. Nor did such deities provide them with prophets who propounded ethical codes. Such deities impinged very little on the everyday actions of the Bedouin, or on the rites and feuds of their tribal society. Life had simply to be endured with all its vicissitudes until, after his allotted span, man was struck down according to the inscrutable decrees of Fate.

This pessimistic *Weltanschauung* was common to oasis-dweller and nomad alike. They also shared other cultural norms, which transcended inter-tribal rivalries and fostered sentiments of all-embracing solidarity, unity and pride in being Arab. As already mentioned, during certain months of truce each year, Arabs from different parts of the peninsula would attend fairs before performing

[5] Cf. Serjeant (1981).

[6] 'Have ye thought upon Al-Lât and Al-'Uzzâ and Manât, the third, the other? . . . They are but names which ye have named', *The Quran*, trans. Pickthall, p. 549.

pilgrimage rites together. At such fairs a major attraction would be recitations of poetry, involving panegyric of the bard's own tribe and lampooning of their rivals. This time-honoured oral poetic tradition, retained intact by members of the tribe with prodigious memories, used a high form of Arabic. This was truly a *lingua franca*, which, in spite of numerous dialectal differences between the pre-Islamic Arabs, was understood by all and gave them a sense of shared identity and common heritage. Moreover, no matter how labile and pragmatic the realities of tribal affiliation may have been, it would appear that the pre-Islamic Arabs believed that they shared a common ancestry and, in the fifth and sixth centuries, the elements, at least, of an Arabic high culture in their poetry. Thus, if only in embryonic form, the Arabs possessed the linguistic and ethnic foundations on which Muhammad would be able to build his supra-tribal community. The factor that was to cement the edifice was Islam, the new monotheistic revelation from Arabia itself.

It is appropriate within a discussion of pre-Islamic Arabia to attempt to assess what inroads external religious traditions had made in the peninsula and to look more generally at outside influences on the milieu of Mecca, Muhammad's hometown. Were there special circumstances that led to the genesis of a new religion and a new community? First, it is clear that the Hijaz, the cradle of Islam, was not as isolated as later Muslim tradition would have it; this pious concept of Arabia as an area of ignorance and darkness highlights all the more brightly the glory of the new faith and its cultural manifestations. In fact, in the centuries immediately preceding Islam, the Hijaz was subject to a medley of external cultural and religious traditions and in turn reciprocally exerted its own influence on the adjoining territories.

Despite the geographical contrasts, it is simplistic to divide the Arabian peninsula crudely into the 'civilised' south-west corner and the 'backward' remainder. Too many scholarly hypotheses, even in recent times, have been based on such a dichotomy and have accordingly postulated static models for these pre-modern societies. The balance of power varied, and indeed the actual frontiers between sedentarised and nomadic areas were often shifting. The kingdoms of southern Arabia used the nomads (especially the Kinda tribe) from the central region as mercenaries; periodically the nomads would encroach on the territories of the south. Similarly, population movements northwards from south Arabia that took place as the southern kingdoms declined, must have changed the religious and social configuration of the rest of the peninsula and not merely its demography.

By the end of the sixth century AD, Judaism and Christianity had infiltrated the Arabian peninsula, especially the south-west, and the desert areas that bordered the Byzantine Empire. The conversion of the Negus of Abyssinia in the first half of the fourth century had produced a vigorous Christian state close to south Arabia.[7] There is evidence of Christian communities in Aden in the fourth century. The famous Christians of Najran in fifth-century Hadramawt were in contact with the Monophysite Christians of Syria. Judaism was found in the oases of the Hijaz where its adherents successfully cultivated date-palm plantations. In south Arabia, prominent figures had been converted to Judaism. The king of Himyar, Yusuf As'ar, known in Muslim tradition as Dhu Nuwas, came to power around 510 and proselytised his Jewish faith in his domains; his zeal culminated in the massacre of the Christians of Najran. The Abyssinians, probably with Byzantine encouragement, crossed the Red Sea in 525, destroyed Dhu Nuwas and his kingdom and established a protectorate that lasted for around half a century. Abraha, an Abyssinian adventurer, subsequently took power in south Arabia and, according to Muslim tradition, made an expedition (mentioned obliquely in the Qur'an) as far as Mecca. A second colonising power, Sasanian Persia, also brought its official state religion, Zoroastrianism, to the shores of south Arabia. Around 570 to 575, the Persians occupied Himyar and some Zoroastrian conversions took place.[8]

Thus, the image of a religiously backward Arabia is inappropriate. To be sure, neither Judaism nor Christianity had taken a firm hold of the peninsula. Arabia had its own indigenous religious traditions but it was also subjected to the missionary activities of external colonial powers. The spread of Judaism and Christianity seems to have been piecemeal and uneven. In the Hijaz, the tribes in areas bordering Byzantine Syria had come under the influence of Christianity: some, such as the Ghassanids, had converted to the Monophysite creed, and – at a popular level – many would seek cures from the pillar saints of the Syrian desert. It may also be inferred from the frequent Qur'anic references to prophets common to the Judaeo-Christian tradition, and from the elliptical manner in which they are mentioned there, that the milieux of Mecca and Medina must have been very familiar with this religious background and that those to whom the Qur'anic message was first addressed had no need to be told in detail the stories of, for example, Joseph or Noah.

The Arabian peninsula was also capable of exerting its influence on the Fertile Crescent. Arabs had moved out of Arabia and into Byzantine territory. The power pendulum in Byzantium's eastern provinces as a result swung towards the non-Hellenised elements of the population who were often, moreover, of a different religious persuasion from their Byzantine overlords. Most of the inhabitants of Byzantine Syria and Egypt were Monophysites who used Syriac or Coptic in the liturgy. Their feeling of alienation from the Chalcedonian form of Christianity imposed from Constantinople was enhanced by discrimination and persecution.

[7] Cf. Gibb *et al.* (1960), *Habashat*; see also Glaser (1895). [8] Bosworth (1983), pp. 593–612.

Just before the Arab conquests began, the province of Syria was again under Byzantine control; the campaigns of Heraclius in the 620s (referred to obliquely in the Qur'an) are discussed elsewhere in this volume. These Byzantine military successes could not, however, stem the tide of Syrian urban decline, plague, depopulation and reversion to pastoralism. Heraclius simply did not have sufficient time to reimpose centralised control, to reorganise local defences, before the Arab invasions struck.

What of the other superpower, Sasanian Persia?[9] By the sixth century, the empire of the King of Kings (*Shahanshah*) covered the Iranian highlands and what is now Iraq. Its northern frontier with the lands of the Caucasus was established in the Araxes valley; to the east, the border town was Merv, beyond which lived the Turkic nomads of the steppes. To the south-east the empire stretched to Sistan, corresponding broadly with the frontier between Iran and Pakistan today. The disputed western frontier in eastern Anatolia and northern Syria shifted in accordance with the power struggles with Byzantium. In spite of its Persian origins, the Sasanian dynasty had placed its capital at Ctesiphon on the Tigris, near both ancient Babylon and the future site of Baghdad. Indeed, Iraq was the economic heart of the Sasanian Empire, providing some two-fifths of the imperial revenue. There were signs of tension in the sixth century between the centralised government structure of absolute monarchy, with its official religion, Zoroastrianism, elaborate bureaucracy and hierarchical class structure, on the one hand, and on the other the centrifugal forces of the nobility wishing to keep hold of provincial power. Khusraw I Anushirwan (531–579) brought about wide-ranging reforms designed to strengthen centralised, absolute government. In particular, his fiscal policy produced revenue for a regular army whose strength lay in its heavy cavalry, the cataphracts who had perfected their skills in Central Asia against the Turks. He also recruited nomadic Arabs as mercenaries.

These reforms did not, however, heal deep-rooted divisions and dissatisfactions within the Sasanian Empire and especially in Iraq. The Sasanian aristocracy itself was stratified; its upper echelons could on occasion try to wrest power from the King of Kings himself, whilst the lower gentry, the *dihqan*s, were much less privileged and often liaised between the government and the peasantry. The religious situation in the Sasanian Empire was far from unified. It would appear that by the sixth century the state religion, a Zoroastrianism identified with conservatism, enjoyed only limited popular appeal. This was especially true in Iraq, where Christianity, particularly Nestorianism, had made considerable headway, even with the Persian upper class. Sasanian Iraq was also a dynamic centre of Jewish life in spite of periodic persecutions in the fifth and sixth centuries, and the Jews formed a large part of the population in town and

[9] Cf. Christensen (1944); also Frye (1984), pp. 116–80.

village. Most of the settled people of Iraq spoke Aramaic (the Persians were only a ruling minority there), whilst Arabic was the language of the Jazira and Hira. It can be seen, therefore, that the people of Iraq at least, the first Sasanian province to be subjected to the Arab military onslaught, were estranged religiously and ethnically from their Sasanian masters and that they would not be highly motivated towards defending the *ancien régime* once the Persian armies had been defeated by the incoming Arabs.

The period immediately preceding the Arab invasions had proved as disastrous for the Sasanian Empire as for Byzantium. Khusraw II Parviz (591–628) executed the last of the Arab Lakhmid kings, al-Nuʿman, in 602 and removed this Sasanian-sponsored state that policed the Arab frontier. Probably as a consequence of the resumption of the war against Byzantium under Khusraw II Parviz and Heraclius' highly successful campaigns into Sasanian territory (627–628), the areas east of the Tigris became depopulated. Parts of Iraq were struck by plague, famine, floods and earthquakes. In the period between Khusraw's death in 628 and the eventual accession of Yazdagird III in 632, the year in which Muhammad died, ten claimants tried to seize the imperial throne. The Sasanian Empire was, indeed, seriously vulnerable.

It will be apparent from the preceding discussion that with the generally debilitated state of the two superpowers, the weakness of their frontiers and the internal urban decline of the provinces immediately adjoining Arabia, a power vacuum had developed. It ended with a shift of power towards the Arab nomads. The new conquerors were to come into a world that had undergone considerable changes even before they entered it, and they transformed it further. Within the Arabian peninsula itself too, by the time of the Prophet's career, it would appear that the balance of power lay with the nomads. They already held the ring between the seriously weakened superpowers in the march areas. They infiltrated southern Arabia, exploiting its weakness, already pinpointed by the external intervention of Abyssinia and Persia. Many of the nomads had shown little or no interest in the religions of Byzantium or Persia, possibly because they smacked of identifying with one or other superpower. The influence of Judaism was also probably limited. Islamic tradition often mentions *hanifs*, monotheists in Arabia,[10] who were not associated with Judaism or Christianity but who practised the pure religion of Abraham, the father of the Arabs, who founded the Kaʿba shrine at Mecca. It is debatable whether such a concept is a reflection of historical reality or a retrospective creation portending the forthcoming religion of Islam, which places uncompromising monotheism at its very core. Suffice it to say that the earlier monotheistic revelations of Judaism and Christianity were known widely to the Arabs but had

10 Gibb *et al.* (1960), *hanif*.

not taken root. Arabia now offered fertile ground for a new religion that was to provide the basis of an unprecedented supra-tribal entity that would in turn integrate and channel nomad power. Muhammad came at a hinge of history. The preceding discussion of the historical setting may help our understanding of some of the factors – social, economic, territorial, religious, demographic – which contributed to the success of the Prophet's career and facilitated the spread of the new religious revelation. Nevertheless, the phenomenon of the rise of Islam defies simplistic explanations.

THE PROBLEM OF THE SOURCES

In spite of the vast mass of scholarly writings and the plethora of theories in recent times about the phenomenon of the rise of Islam and the early Muslim empire up to 750 AD, the structure of detailed 'facts' underpinning this phenomenon remains historiographically unsure. The career of the Prophet of Islam soon became the focus of Muslim pious tradition and sacred history: the important stages of his career on earth assumed symbolic significance. It is not 'fiction' or a distortion of historical truth that lies at the heart of the Muslim traditions about the rise of Islam, as some have alleged. It is the exemplary truth of the Prophet's career and the Islamic conquests, which is enshrined in the extant corpus of Muslim historiographical works on which the 'received' version of the rise of Islam is based. In other words, not just the sayings and opinions of Muhammad but also his actions, including the military campaigns, as observed and recorded by his Companions and their successors, became paradigms for the entire Muslim community. In time they were fleshed out with additional anecdotal material and with an apparatus detailing the process of transmission. Thus was fashioned an account of events whose components were, so to speak, interlocking and mutually supportive. The conquests, too, were integrated into this scheme of sacred history, and sacred history is not easily subject to alteration, whether in detail or in its grand sweep. But does this mean that one has to take it or leave it? We shall see that there are indeed some objective controls that can be applied to the information contained in the Muslim literary tradition, and that they tend to substantiate the general accuracy of the grand sweep of that tradition. Perhaps it is the paucity of such controls that has encouraged certain wholesale attacks on the validity of Muslim accounts of the rise of Islam;[11] but one should remember Carl Sagan's dictum that 'absence of evidence is not evidence of absence'. The events of *c.*620–*c.*660 AD, when seen as sacred history in the Muslim tradition, are immutable once they achieved their extant written form. These events, when presented in this way,

[11] Seminal are Crone and Cook (1977) and Wansborough (1978).

do not obey the laws of 'ordinary' history; they operate on a different level altogether. But that they do also enshrine actual historical events need not be doubted – and should not be doubted 'on principle' simply because they are presented in a religious guise.

To the core of sacred history were added (as we shall see) elements from oral tradition, or outright propaganda; these can be identified as extraneous. And of course the more distant events are from the life of the Prophet himself, the more they tend to fall into the category of 'straight' history. But for the study of the earliest decades of Islam the intractable problem remains: sacred history presents the past as a single solid block whose very diverse component parts have been transformed into an integrated whole and which repulses attempts at piecemeal analysis from within. A further dimension of the Islamic tradition needs to be mentioned here. The earliest information about the rise of Islam came from oral tradition. Memory in a tribal society is a finely tuned instrument, with experienced storytellers and poets performing extraordinary feats of narration and oratory. Yet the 'historical' time frame of a society with oral tradition is blurred and usually devoid of precise chronological points. Oral tradition cannot be used to reconstruct the exact sequence of events concerning a historical figure or detailed historical episodes. These remarks are absolutely *not* meant to imply that the corpus of extant Islamic historiographical material (dating mostly from the eighth and ninth centuries) was based on 'fiction'. As already mentioned, sacred history has normative significance, and key events and figures are endowed from an early stage with exemplary value for the faithful. Dating and details become fixed in hallowed tradition.

The received view of the rise of Islam given by the great Muslim historians of the 'Abbasid period (and above all, al-Baladhuri (d. 892) and al-Tabari (d. 923)) springs from the double inspiration of several generations of oral tradition (carefully memorised by the faithful anxious not to forget the contours of the Prophet's career and the glorious victories of the Islamic conquests) and the corpus of material inherited from the first written Islamic historical sources, now no longer extant. In a true sense some of the great 'Abbasid historians were 'compilers'; they were mostly religious scholars meticulously collecting and sifting nuggets of information, however fragmentary or full, left by their predecessors. Such snippets and anecdotes were furnished with an apparatus (the so-called *isnad*s which traced the chain of narrators) intended to demonstrate the authenticity of the data mentioned. It is thus probable that although the first extant Islamic historical sources date from a period much later than many of the events they record, they do contain authentic earlier material. There can be no doubt that many traditionalists, acutely aware of the dangers of transmitting unreliable information, did not simply parrot the material they had inherited or collected, but took inordinate pains to verify it, with the instincts of true historians. It is equally probable, indeed at times proven irrefutably, that the *isnad* apparatus, although interesting in a prosopographical sense, does not guarantee 'reliable' information. Other 'Abbasid historians, such as al-Ya'qubi (d. 897) and al-Mas'udi (d. 956), produced digests which are the result of selecting and interpreting earlier sources now lost. Thus within the Muslim tradition itself there are the makings of internal criticism of historiography, and of the verification of events by means of comparing one source with another.

It is a short step from hallowed reverence of sacred history to the exploiting of it for propagandistic purposes. The phenomenon of the early Islamic conquests lends itself easily to such an approach. The 'Abbasid historians were quick to seize the full propagandistic potential of the Muslim victories – both for the prestige of the 'Abbasid caliphs and for the glory of Islam. Military success was perceived as the manifestation of God's preordained will for man on earth, leading inexorably towards His perfected and final Revelation, Islam. An account of a famous battle often provides little concrete information, but is given layers of symbolic meaning with recognisable *topoi*, including highly stylised exchanges between the protagonists. The description of the battle of Qadisiyya given by al-Baladhuri is a typical example. The 'uncouth' Bedouin al-Mughira b. Sa'd, mounted on an emaciated horse and carrying a broken sword wrapped up in rags, is refused permission by the Sasanian cavalry to sit on the dais beside the 'civilised' Persian commander, Rustam. But the Muslim leader betters Rustam in the ensuing exchange: al-Mughira ignores Rustam's taunt that the Arabs have entered Sasanian territory, driven by economic hardship, and proudly claims that he and his companions have come to call the Persians to embrace Islam.[12] Similarly, accounts of the Muslim capture of individual cities often contain texts purporting to be the actual treaties of capitulation to the Muslims. These ostensibly provide dates, signatories, even the 'precise' amounts of poll-tax payable – but they should not be taken too literally.[13] Rather than being 'accurate' accounts, they seem to be idealised blueprints retrospectively attributed to the individual stages of the Muslim conquests. They reflect the preoccupations of legists in the 'Abbasid period engaged in the codification of the *Shari'a* (the Islamic Revealed Law) who wished to establish models of conduct based on the Qur'an and the *Sunna* (a term which eventually came to mean the idealised conduct of the Prophet).

The Qur'an itself is not easy to use as a historical source, although attempts have been made to extract from it the evolution of the Prophet's life. To be sure,

[12] al-Baladhuri, *Futuh al-buldan*, trans. Hitti and Murgotten, p. 412.

[13] For example the agreement of Khalid b. Walid on the conquest of Damascus in 14 AH recorded in al-Baladhuri, p. 187.

by its condemnation of certain aspects of Arabian life, it sheds light on some of the prevailing social conditions and practices that the Prophet sought to reform, but to try to trace the successive stages of his career through Qur'anic allusions is apt to result in crude and simplistic conclusions. There is even considerable debate about the real chronology of its chapters. The *Hadith*, which incorporate the alleged words or deeds of the Prophet transmitted by his Companions and subsequent generations of early Muslims, have been used by Muslim scholars in conjunction with the Qur'an to clarify and amplify certain elliptical Qur'anic statements. The *Hadith* are, however, also difficult to use as a historical source. Their often fragmentary, parable-like nature makes it impossible to piece them together coherently. They faithfully reflect the fluidity, diversity and evolutionary aspects of early Islamic ritual and law and the efforts of the pious in the first two or three centuries of the Muslim era to establish the path of 'true Islam'. *Hadith* also form the basis for much of the 'received version' of the Prophet's life, the *Sira* (the hallowed biography compiled in the eighth century by Ibn Ishaq (d. 767) and revised by Ibn Hisham (d. 833)). Although it is overlaid with miraculous and legendary elements, it has formed the basis used by modern biographies of the Prophet, including those written by western orientalists. Aware of the historiographical problems associated with the *Sira*, problems that they analyse fully, they resort to its accounts only reluctantly in the virtual absence of any other sources.

Certainly the Muslim historiographical tradition, although difficult to use, should not be dismissed, not least because it is the main corpus of texts available on the rise of Islam and the early Muslim empire. Recently, attempts have been made to step outside the Muslim historiographical tradition and to try to construct the early history of Islam from non-Muslim sources. This approach, although exciting, has proved abortive – Christian and Jewish sources view the rise of Islam through a prism of misunderstanding and prejudice. They span a wide historical time frame too, often suffer from a half-digested understanding of the events mentioned and are as replete with anachronisms and ideological elements as the Muslim writings themselves. Above all, they are not objective enough to constitute a corrective to the Muslim tradition. Certainly, the evidence of seventh- and eighth-century Christian sources needs to be better known, reflecting as they do the context in which Christians were responding to the presence of Islam. However, it is dangerous in attempting to reconstruct the early development of Islam to place credulous reliance on the evidence of non-Muslim sources. Other questions, such as the possible interrelationship between Muslim, Jewish and Christian sources, still need further examination.

To what extent can the contemporary evidence of numismatics, papyri, archaeology and standing monuments shed light on the veracity of the traditional Muslim written accounts? If there is agreement between statements made in the historical sources and the evidence of material culture, then is it not reasonable to adopt a more positive stance towards the value of the information contained in the Islamic historical sources? The evidence of surviving coins, for example, indicates clearly the transition between late antique and early Islamic modes of government.[14] The Arabs did not mint their own coins straightaway. Through an analysis of the evolutionary aspects of early Islamic coinage one may trace the handover of the mint, and all that it implies for government administration, from the Byzantine and Sasanian officials to Muslim ones. There is strong evidence that the existing division between Byzantium and Persia continued to be respected by the Arabs, that Byzantine and Sasanian coins continued in circulation after the Muslim takeover and that certain issues continued to be minted even when they were technically out of date and for use by the Muslims – the disproportionate number of coins in the name of Yazdagird III and Heraclius are revealing in this respect. The bilingual coins of the mid-seventh century, which used Greek or Pahlavi concurrently with Arabic, and the gradual evolution of an Islamic design for coins (removing crosses and fire-altars and substituting religious formulae such as the *Shahada* or the image of the standing caliph) demonstrate the growth of Islamic self-awareness and self-confidence, culminating in the coins of the last decade of the seventh century which bear testimony to the coin reforms and the establishment of Arabic as the official language of the Islamic empire, events recorded in the written histories. Numismatic evidence provides unbroken lists of provincial governors, for example in Iran and Iraq, and confirms textual information about administrative districts.

The surviving papyri are useful mainly for the last decade of the seventh century and the eighth century, although one of them, dated 643, confirms the beginning of the Muslim era as 622.[15] Similarly, a gravestone in Cairo (Museum of Islamic Art, no. 1508/20) in the name of one ʿAbd al-Rahman b. Khayr is dated Jumada II 31/January–February 652.[16] An undated fragment of papyrus, written in Greek and found in the Negev desert by Israeli archaeologists, provides corroborative evidence of another kind. Its authenticity seems to be in no doubt. It mentions names and pay and would appear to be part of an army register (*diwan*); it thus provides documentary proof of an aspect of military administration well attested in the written sources.

As for architectural testimony, the most outstanding monument for the period under discussion is the Dome of the Rock in Jerusalem, with a foundation inscription of 72/692. Orientalist Qur'anic scholars have resolutely turned their faces away from the epigraphy of the Dome of the Rock, with its

[14] See for example Walker (1941a) and (1941b); Grierson (1960); Morony (1984), pp. 38–51.

[15] Grohmann (1952), p. 4. [16] Combe *et al.* (1931), p. 6.

240 metres of Qur'anic inscriptions.[17] Although this evidence was published by van Berchem as early as 1927, few Qur'anic scholars even mention it, let alone draw any conclusions from it. It is an urgent task for future research. So too is the luxury Qur'an recently discovered in the Yemen, now lodged in the House of Manuscripts in Sana'a; a carbon-14 test has yielded, with 95 per cent accuracy, the momentous date of 645–690 AD.[18]

What is the way forward? Those who subscribe to the theory of a historiographical 'black hole' for the early history of Islam express themselves very forcibly on this point and then settle down – evincing remarkably little awareness of the gross inconsistency involved – to reproducing the received Islamic view of the period in all its detailed amplitude. Rather than adopting this schizophrenic approach, one may proceed more cautiously and examine which parts of the Islamic historiographical edifice can be corroborated by external evidence – either from material artefacts or from non-Islamic written sources. When this approach is adopted, certain firm landmarks in the historical picture can be established. Exact dates and sequences for most of the events in the conquests of Islam will never be known, but the relatively early establishment of the new Islamic empire can be confirmed by a whole sequence of Arabo-Byzantine and Arabo-Sasanian coins produced in the early Umayyad period at scores of widely scattered mints. If some of the fixed points in the Islamic tradition can be proven from external evidence, then are there not grounds for a wider acceptance both of the general sweep of events which it records and of some, at least, of their more detailed points of interest?

It has been argued that the best way forward would be to synthesise the results obtained by archaeologists and by historians. This approach sounds very plausible but when it is examined critically it becomes apparent that the two strands do not mesh. Historians and archaeologists talk past each other because each has very different aims. Archaeology yields abundant detail about the kind of pottery people used, the kind of houses they lived in, and settlement patterns, but for the most part written Islamic sources have very little to say about such matters. Archaeology merely proves what common sense would indicate anyway, namely that there was continuity of daily life from late antique to Islamic times. Everything depends on the nature of the questions that are asked of this crucial period. Archaeology says virtually nothing about the microcosmic issues that have traditionally engaged most historians of the early Islamic period. But if the focus is henceforth to shift and to concern itself with macrocosmic issues such as living conditions in the villages and small towns of the Levant in the seventh and eighth centuries or the nature of settlement in steppe/desert areas and of their agricultural exploitation, then

[17] Kessler (1970). [18] Cf. von Botmer (1987), pp. 4–20.

beyond doubt archaeology holds the key. This is especially true of the period 710–750, when most of the Umayyad desert residences were built. But all this has very little to do with the heady controversies of the 1970s. For those who call into question the overall accuracy of the traditional Muslim account of what actually happened between 600 and 650, archaeology provides little help – not least because of the lack of excavation in the key sites of Arabia, notably Mecca and Medina, and disputes about the dates of those early mosques which might reflect the revelation which caused the Prophet to shift the direction of prayer (*qibla*) from Jerusalem to Mecca.

THE CAREER OF MUHAMMAD

The sacred 'bricks' in the traditional edifice of the Prophet's life are immutably fixed in the Muslim consciousness and have been hallowed by generations of piety. In the Muslim view, Muhammad's career is not an appropriate subject for historical enquiry. The historian is nevertheless faced with the phenomenon of a new world religion and empire that emanated directly from Muhammad. Any historical analysis, however tentative, must therefore begin with his life and should attempt at least to discern its major landmarks. The brief account that follows is based on traditional Muslim sources; where appropriate, the testimony of non-Muslim writings will also be mentioned.

The Prophet's birth cannot be securely dated either from Muslim or from external sources, although it was probably in the 570s. He was born in Mecca into a minor branch of the Quraysh tribe, the Banu Hashim, a clan of some prestige but whose wealth and political power had declined after the 570s. Orphaned early (Qur'an 93/6 is clear proof of this),[19] he was raised by his uncle, Abu Talib. As a young adult, Muhammad became involved in commerce, working for a rich widow, Khadija, whom he subsequently married (the Byzantine historian Theophanes writing in the early ninth century mentions both Muhammad's orphanhood and this marriage).[20] The union produced seven children, only one of whom, Fatima, survived into adulthood and was the mother of Muhammad's grandsons – Hasan and the more famous Husayn.

In his middle years (traditionally fixed at around the age of forty) Muhammad began to withdraw from Mecca to meditate for prolonged periods on Mount Hira, where he received his first revelations from God. These overwhelmed him in their impact. After initial self-doubts and with the wholehearted support of Khadija, he became increasingly persuaded of the truth of

[19] 'Did He not find thee an orphan and protect (thee)?', trans. Pickthall, p. 656.

[20] Theophanes, *Chronographia*, trans. Turtledove, p. 34.

his divine call. Around 613 he felt compelled to begin preaching to his fellow Meccans. The initial prophetic message, which forms the earliest Meccan chapters (*suras*) of the Qur'an, stresses the imminence of the Last Day and man's urgent need of repentance. The Qur'anic language is infused with dramatic intensity, gripping those who hear it. Its message, however, fell on deaf ears. Nevertheless, Muhammad was able to gather around himself a small group of enthusiastic converts, who 'surrendered themselves to God' (the meaning of the word *muslim*). The revelations continued. The rift with the polytheistic Meccans intensified, as the uncompromisingly monotheistic emphasis of Islam (evident from the middle Meccan *suras* onwards) became more pronounced. The Muslims were persecuted by the Meccans and some of them, according to Islamic tradition, moved around 615 to Abyssinia, where they were protected by the Negus. At this stage, however, Muhammad still had the support of his clan and its leader, his uncle Abu Talib. A major turning point for Muhammad came in 619 with the deaths of Khadija and Abu Talib; another uncle of his, Abu Lahab, the new leader of the clan, would not tolerate his activities. Bereft of protection, Muhammad was now obliged to seek a different centre in which to propagate Islam.

He was approached around 620 by some inhabitants of Yathrib who invited him to arbitrate in their crippling internal disputes. He eventually accepted their offer and entered the town (soon renamed *Madinat al-nabi* – the city of the Prophet – and known thereafter as Medina) on 24 September 622. Later, when the Muslim calendar was introduced, this date marked the beginning of the Islamic era, commemorating Muhammad's *hijra* ('emigration') from Mecca to Medina. A papyrus from the year 643 and dated 'the year 22' seems to confirm 622 as the beginning of a new era. In Medina the Arabs were divided into two main, mutually hostile tribal groups, the Aws and the Khazraj. Also living there were three principal Jewish clans, the Qurayza, al-Nadir and Qaynuqa. It is difficult to determine either the exact 'ethnic' identity of these 'Jewish' elements (were they Arabic-speaking Jews or Judaicised Arabs?) or what kind of Judaism they practised. What seems certain, however, is that they played an important role in the economic life of Medina and were in touch with Jewish groups in other parts of Arabia. They may well have been responsible for familiarising the Arabs of Medina with monotheistic concepts and biblical stories. The next decade (622–632) in Medina provided the Prophet with an opportunity to preach freely, to worship openly and to create a theocratic Islamic community (*umma*). The newcomers, the Meccan Muslims (the so-called Emigrants – *muhajirun* – a form of this term is used in the earliest Greek and Syriac sources) who had arrived in Medina without resources or support, needed to be integrated into Medinan society. This problem was solved initially by the system of 'brotherhood', established by Muhammad between individual

Emigrants and the Medinan Muslims (the so-called Helpers – *Ansar*). A document known as the Constitution of Medina[21], the authenticity of which seems secure, is preserved in Ibn Ishaq. Dating from the second or third year of the Medinan period, it reveals Muhammad's great skills as an arbitrator and his attempts to weld the heterogeneous elements of Medinan society into a unified community. The text shows that even at this early stage the ethos of the *umma* was clearly Islamic – the highest authority is supra-tribal and belongs to God and His prophet Muhammad – but the Constitution allowed also for the inclusion of Jews and polytheists and suggests that Muhammad was not yet uncontested leader in Medina. However, the pragmatic outlook of this document was soon superseded, as the Prophet's position became strengthened and the need for an exclusively Muslim community became paramount.

As Muhammad laid the foundations of the *umma*, the Qur'anic revelations continued; the Medinan chapters are longer pronouncements on the conduct of the Muslims in every aspect of their personal and communal lives. It is difficult to chart with chronological precision the internal evolution of the Medinan period but it is clear that Muhammad's early attempt to gain acceptance of the Islamic revelation from the Medinan Jews whom he wished to include within the community met with rejection. His familiarity with both Jewish and Christian scriptures is mentioned by Theophanes. However, the Qur'anic message reveals an increasing disenchantment with the Jews and a heightened emphasis on the exclusivity and originality of the new faith, Islam. The Qur'an also speaks of Hypocrites (*munafiqun*), subversive, disloyal elements within the community, who threatened to destroy it.

As well as building a harmonious community from within, Muhammad had to fend off external attacks from the Meccans who threatened the very existence of the *umma*. Islamic tradition records his struggle against the Meccans in a series of battles that have become the prototype of *jihad*, itself defined by Muslims as a defensive struggle against external aggression. His successful struggle against the enemy from without was accompanied by a sharpening of his resolve to remove dangerous elements from within Medina, above all the Jews. The Muslims' first major victory against the Meccans, the battle of Badr in 624, damaged Meccan prestige and provided a vital boost to Muslim morale, a potent proof of the new faith's veracity. Thereafter, Muhammad banished the Jewish clan of Qaynuqa from Medina; their possessions became the property of the *umma*. A year later, although the Meccans defeated the Muslims at the battle of Uhud, they did not succeed in ousting Muhammad. Soon afterwards he moved against the second Jewish group, Nadir, and banished them to Khaybar and other Jewish settlements. In 627 the Meccans' attempt to take Medina by

[21] Cf. Serjeant (1964b), pp. 3–16.

force failed at the so-called Battle of the Ditch. Thereafter, Muhammad dealt with the remaining Jewish group, Qurayza: the men were executed and the women and children enslaved.

Muhammad now established absolute authority within Medina and turned his attention to Mecca. Ideally, he preferred to integrate his home town peacefully into the *umma*, which soon included some of the tribes from the area around Medina; these were won over by astute negotiation and alliances rather than by military force. The foundations for a peaceful entry into Mecca were laid within two years. At the same time the community's horizons widened to include some Arab tribes on the fringes of the Syrian desert whom Muhammad summoned to embrace Islam and submit to the authority of the *umma*. In 628 he announced his wish to perform the pilgrimage to Mecca. In the event he reached al-Hudaybiyya on the outskirts of the Meccan *haram* and concluded a truce with the Meccans, allowing him to enter the city the following year. Shortly afterwards, Muhammad captured the Jewish oasis of Khaybar. The Prophet's conduct on this occasion – he allowed the inhabitants (who were 'People of the Book' with established scriptures) to remain there and to practise their faith on payment of an annual poll-tax (*jizya*) – formed the model for subsequent treatment of conquered peoples. In 629, in accordance with the truce of al-Hudaybiyya, the Meccans vacated their city for three days while the Muslims performed the '*umra* (the lesser pilgrimage). At this stage the Meccans still refused Muhammad's offers of reconciliation. In January 630, Muhammad made a triumphal entry into Mecca, which surrendered peacefully to him. Some weeks later he defeated a large hostile army of central Arabian tribes at al-Hunayn.

The remainder of his life – a mere two years – was spent in Medina, consolidating his policy of securing the northern routes to Syria and expanding the *umma*. Already in 629 he had sent a large force under his adopted son Zayd towards Palestine. This expedition proved abortive. The momentum of expansion was, however, sustained. Muhammad himself took part in a Syrian campaign to Tabuk in 630. In that year numerous tribal delegations came to agreements with the Prophet, probably implying on their part varying degrees of commitment, religious and political, to the *umma*.

In 632 the Prophet performed the Farewell Pilgrimage in Mecca – this time following the full rites of the *hajj*, which became the model for future Islamic practice – and on his return to Medina made preparations for an ambitious expedition across the Jordan, which he himself intended to lead. Shortly before the campaign's departure, he fell unexpectedly and seriously ill. He died on 8 June 632 (Theophanes puts the date a year earlier).[22] By his death most of

[22] Theophanes, trans. Turtledove, p. 34.

Arabia owned his sway. The foundations of the new faith, Islam, had been laid. A dynamic community had been created, which was shortly to burgeon into a vast world empire. This was made possible through the towering figure of the Prophet, through his remarkable qualities of leadership and charisma, the memory of which inspired his followers to carry on the enterprise he had initiated. Whilst noting the exemplary nature of the Prophet's character and career in the religious life of the Muslims, it is important to stress that he viewed himself as only a man and that his contemporaries also viewed him thus. He was the vehicle through which divine revelations came. At the same time he was able to make the revelations the basis of actions and to organise a society capable of perpetuating the new faith.

What were the salient characteristics of 'early Islam', the pristine faith preached and practised by the Prophet? This is not easy to chart from the evidence of the Qur'an, which is a work of revelation and not organised on a thematic basis. It is, however, the most valuable source for determining the evolution of Islam. Revealed as it was in successive stages, it mirrors the internal defining of Islam as an all-embracing faith and way of life and the progression by which Islam distanced itself from Judaism and Christianity, on the one hand, and the pre-Islamic polytheistic milieu on the other. Islam came to emphasise the uncompromising oneness of God, in sharp contrast both to Arab idolatry and to the Christian doctrines of Jesus' divinity and the Trinity. God is transcendent, omnipotent, omniscient, the Supreme judge; yet He is closer to man than his own jugular vein. Early Islam shared features with other Near Eastern monotheistic faiths: in common with Syriac Christianity, the Day of Judgement is terrifyingly imminent, whilst, as in Judaism, Muslims prayed towards a Holy City and emphasised the importance of fasting. But in spite of a common heritage Islam is viewed as the completion and perfection of preceding revelations.

At the outset of his preaching, it would appear that Muhammad saw himself as a prophet, one of a long line of figures shared by the Jews and Christians, who came to 'warn' successive generations that they had strayed from the right path, that God's judgement was imminent and that there was urgent need for repentance. The Qur'an evokes the dire punishments of Hell in memorable imagery. If only man will survey the wondrous signs of God's handiwork, he will surely acknowledge God's omnipotence. The Meccan *suras* also stress the importance of frequent prayer and of charity towards the poor. Gradually the attacks on Meccan polytheism increase; the Ka'ba belongs to Allah, the one true God. When the Meccans refused to heed this message, the Qur'an speaks of the terrible fate that awaited earlier generations who ignored their prophets.

As we have seen, the rift with Judaism became wider in the Medinan period. Initially Muhammad made the 10th of Muharram a day of fasting for the

Muslims (cf. Yom Kippur) and at some point he adopted the practice of turning towards Jerusalem for prayer. Friday became the day for the congregational service, held in the courtyard of Muhammad's house. When the message he preached failed to receive recognition from the Jews of Medina, this crisis led to further redefining of the new faith; the Jews had received only part of the Revelation (Qur'an 4/44). In the second year after the Hijra (623–624) the direction of prayer was changed from Jerusalem to the Ka'ba (Qur'an 2/142–150). The Qur'an also stresses Abraham's role as the Arabs' forefather and as the first Muslim (3/67). The Prophet was to restore the Ka'ba, founded by Abraham (2/125), to its pristine monotheism. In the early Medinan period the rift with Arab polytheism also became sharper. The new faith should replace and transcend both blood loyalty (2/216) and ancient polytheistic rituals, such as the taboo on fighting in the sacred months (2/217).

The role of the pilgrimage as a pillar of Islam was established during the Prophet's lifetime; the Ka'ba became a focal point in the transmuted Muslim *hajj*, through the paradigmatic conduct of the Prophet in his last year. Indeed, by the time of his death, the five pillars of Islam – the profession of faith, fasting, prayer, almsgiving and pilgrimage – were in place. The Qur'anic revelations were being used in early Muslim worship and memorised by the faithful. Like Moses before him, Muhammad, the 'seal of the Prophets', was involved in social action as well as preaching. His message and his activities in Medina emphasised brotherhood and mutual solidarity but the *umma* was a supra-tribal entity based on new Islamic criteria.

For whom did the Prophet intend the message of Islam? The issue continues to be debated. Strong arguments have been made in support of the view that he considered his mission to be for all mankind, not just the Arabs. Conversely, it could be argued from Qur'anic evidence that he was working within his own milieu and that his mission was intended for the Arabs. The authenticity of letters from the Prophet to various potentates of the time, including the Byzantine and Sasanian emperors and the Negus of Abyssinia, inviting them to embrace Islam, has rightly been called into question. It is, however, likely that the Prophet was in regular contact with local rulers whose territories touched Arabia and that he intended to spread Islam to Arabs on the borders or already within Byzantine and Sasanian territories. This is clearly demonstrated by the Muta episode and by his own participation in the Tabuk campaign of 630.

THE CONQUESTS OF ISLAM, 632–711

The formation of the Islamic empire, which followed the death of the Prophet in 632, falls conveniently but not rigidly into two phases. The first was an explosive and surprisingly easy series of conquests of the territories closest to

Arabia, which soon brought Byzantine Syria, Palestine and Egypt as well as Sasanian Iraq into the orbit of government from Medina. The second involved protracted and more difficult conquests that eventually added Sasanian Iran and parts of Central Asia in the east and the North African littoral in the west. The year 711 is a convenient date at which to fix the conquest of both extremities of the Islamic empire, Spain and India; that year established the boundaries of the Islamic polity that were, broadly speaking, to remain unchanged until the eleventh century.[23] By the early eighth century, the Arab Muslim empire had reached the limits of its military and administrative viability and the wave of successful conquests was to subside – a turning point traditionally marked in the West by the battle of Poitiers in 732 or 733, the importance of which has been grossly inflated but which came to symbolise the beginning of a new phase of Muslim territorial withdrawal and consolidation. As a result of Muslim expansion, in the period 632–711, the Sasanian Empire was 'wiped out as if it had never been' (Ibn Khaldun).[24] The Byzantine state, although greatly diminished and stripped of its Levantine possessions, lived on to fight another day, in spite of several determined but abortive Muslim attacks on Constantinople made during the period. Thereafter, the Arabs ceased to have the Byzantine capital as a major focus of their aspirations.

The first external conquests conducted under the banner of Islam were remarkably swift and successful. These took place at the same time as the first caliph, Abu Bakr, was trying to subdue the whole Arabian peninsula. Indeed, these two activities, the beginning of conquest of Byzantine and Sasanian territory and the acquisition of firm control within the peninsula itself, both form part of the first external thrust of the new Islamic polity in Medina, aimed at spreading its faith and hegemony. The reigns of the first two caliphs, Abu Bakr (632–634) and 'Umar (634–644), saw the subjugation of the whole of Arabia, the Levantine provinces of Byzantium and Sasanian Iraq. From the outset, the Medinan leadership seems to have realised the importance of continued military momentum, both for the survival of a unified *umma* and for the extension of its territories. The exact chronology of the first phase of the conquests and the contribution made by individual Muslim leaders are impossible to reconstruct accurately. Even the dates of key battles and of the capitulation of important cities are disputed. Yet the general sweep of Muslim victory is incontestable. Initially, raids were often conducted on two or more fronts simultaneously. They were not always sanctioned or instigated by the caliph at Medina. The problem of communications grew as the distances covered by Muslim armies increased. Certain generals, such as 'Amr b. al-'As

[23] For recent secondary works on the Islamic conquests, Donner (1981); Kaegi (1992).

[24] Ibn Khaldun, *The Muqaddinah*, trans. Rosenthal, p. 1.

and Khalid b. al-Walid, acted on occasion on their own initiative. Even in the earliest phases of Muslim expansion there were temporary setbacks and the Arabs had sometimes to make several attempts to capture individual cities, such as Damascus and Alexandria. Generally, however, the Arabs held on to the territories conquered and began to create a primitive infrastructure for administering the new territories.

Sasanian Iraq proved an easy target for the Muslim armies. According to the traditional Muslim accounts, the chief of the Bakr tribe, Muthanna b. al-Harith, exploited the vulnerable Sasanian frontier, supported by contingents from Medina under the leadership of 'the Sword of Islam', Khalid b. al-Walid. After taking Hira, the Arabs inflicted a heavy defeat on a Sasanian army at the battle of Qadisiyya (636) and built two fortified bases, Basra and Kufa, from which to spearhead conquests further east. With their subsequent capture of the Sasanian capital, Ctesiphon, and a further victory at Nihawand in 642, the Arabs soon became masters of Sasanian Iraq and west and central Iran. The last Sasanian emperor, Yazdagird III, retreated as far as Khurasan where he died in 651.

Like the Arab conquest of Sasanian Iraq, the annexing of Byzantine Palestine and Syria was brought about initially by the actions of those Arab tribes nearest to the frontier, reinforced by contingents sent by the caliph at Medina. The decisive engagements with the Byzantines seem to have been the victory at Ajnadayn in 634, after Khalid had made his fabled crossing of the waterless desert from Iraq to Syria, and the battle of Yarmuk, dated by Theophanes to 23 July 636. Damascus and Jerusalem fell by 638, and with the capture of Caesarea in 640 the conquest of Syria and Palestine was complete. Before 'Umar's death in 644, the Arab armies had penetrated Armenia but had not yet crossed the Taurus mountains into Asia Minor. The conquest of Egypt was achieved by another great Muslim general, 'Amr, who moved into lower Egypt (639), defeated the Byzantine army at Heliopolis (640) and negotiated the capture of Alexandria (by 645). Thus ended the first phase of Muslim expansion. On Christmas Day 634 the patriarch Sophronius, preaching in Jerusalem, had seen the Arabs' taking of Bethlehem as divine punishment for Christian sin and urged repentance in order to defeat the 'Ishmaelites', but such initial optimism on the Byzantine side soon receded. Indeed, in a letter dated between 634 and 640 Maximos the Confessor, the Byzantine theologian, showing greater realism, speaks of 'a barbaric nation from the desert having overrun a land not their own'.[25]

The Arabs' preferred mode of movement was by land, ideally in desert country. But the caliphate of 'Uthman witnessed an important new

[25] On Maximos, see Louth, chapter 11 above.

development – the first Muslim naval expedition led by the Umayyad governor of Syria, the future caliph Muʿawiya. Cyprus was taken in 649, initial raids were conducted against Sicily and in 655 the Arabs won a naval victory over the Byzantine fleet off the Lycian coast (the Battle of the Masts). The second phase of conquest, however, lasted more than sixty years. It might be argued that the initial élan had gone, that the conquerors had much to organise in the new territories and that the progress of further conquests would inevitably be slower than in the decade after Muhammad's death. Other factors contributed to the more protracted struggle to gain control of points west of Egypt and east of Iraq. Internal dissensions at the heart of the new Islamic community preoccupied the caliphs and undermined the triumphal advance of Muslim hegemony. Local conditions also hindered Muslim military leaders. The Arab conquest of Byzantine North Africa, spearheaded from Egypt, was fraught with pitfalls. Even a superficial Arabisation of the coastal strip from Libya westwards to the Atlantic was to take until the end of the seventh century. A natural boundary to the south was provided by the Atlas mountains. Their gradual progress westward arose as a natural extension of the conquest of Egypt. A new factor in North Africa was local resistance, successfully organised by the indigenous Berbers, with or without support of Byzantine military units. Yet, in time the Berbers converted to Islam; indeed, the Muslim army that eventually crossed over the Straits of Gibraltar (in 710–711) was predominantly Berber, with Arab leadership. Berber conversion to Islam was not, however, swift or uniform. The earliest extant Muslim historiography which focusses on the conquest of North Africa comes from the Egyptian historian Ibn ʿAbd al-Hakam (d. 871), who collected tales based largely on oral tradition. His underlying aim was to legitimise the Muslim conquests of Egypt and North Africa. Reference is made to two semi-legendary Berber figures, the warrior Kusayla and the aged queen Kahina, around whom the opposition to the incoming Muslim invaders centred. Although precise chronologies are not available, it appears that as the Arabs moved along the North African littoral the composition of their armies changed to include increasing numbers of Berber contingents attracted to Islam, if not initially by its precepts, at least by the prospect of booty and regular pay. An important new garrison town, Qayrawan (in present-day Tunisia), was built in 670 and became the base for further conquests westwards. The Muslims' conquest of Spain (al-Andalus) followed naturally from their presence in Morocco and was achieved with great ease. By 720 all the major cities of southern Spain, including Granada, Seville and Córdoba, had fallen.

At the other extremity of the Islamic world, the conquest of the Iranian plateau also proved slower. Nevertheless, the easternmost province of the empire, Khurasan, was colonised early by Arab settlers and became a key base for raids into central Asia.[26] In the east, the battle of Talas (751) against the Chinese became identified as the moment at which Arab Muslim territorial expansion halted in the east and consolidation of conquered territory began. From 711 the Arabs had also established a small Muslim presence in Sind in northern India. Thus, within a century after the death of the Prophet, the Arab Muslims ruled a mighty empire into which were integrated vast subject populations that had not yet accepted Islam, but the death knell of Zoroastrianism and North African Christianity had been sounded. Elsewhere in the empire – in Egypt, Syria, Iraq and Spain – Christian and Jewish communities would survive and retain their character and autonomy under Muslim rule.

Much ink has been spilt on the phenomenon of the Islamic conquests, but few firm conclusions can be drawn. Scholars have stressed the weakness of the Byzantine and Sasanian empires and the lack of policing on the borders with Arabia; they have alleged a degree of acquiescence or active complicity on the part of the subject populations of these empires, disaffected with their central governments; and they have adduced various combinations of religious, military, demographic and economic factors which contributed to the Arabs' remarkable success. It seems unlikely that the Arabs possessed military superiority over their opponents. Certainly, they had no secret weapon, no new techniques. Indeed, in some military spheres they were inexperienced; they allegedly learned siege warfare, for example, from the Persians. They were also unfamiliar with how to fight naval engagements. The nomadic Arabs were, however, militarised and hardy as a result of their lifestyle. They could cover enormous distances over difficult terrain, deriving advantage from their great familiarity with the desert and the riding camel. Perhaps above all, the early Muslim armies enjoyed good leadership from seasoned generals.

As already mentioned, profound demographic changes, conveniently focussed on the bursting of the Marib dam, must have occurred, causing populations to spill over into the Byzantine and Sasanian empires from the northern and eastern fringes of the Arabian peninsula. These factors cannot be ignored in the search for explanations but they do not account for the timing of the conquests so soon after Muhammad's death. The conclusion imposes itself that the religious impetus must have played a key role in the early military successes and that it gave the Arabs an ideological edge over their foes. Without this impetus the achievements of the Muslims would have been ephemeral and localised. Initially, those genuinely fired by Islam probably formed a small elite of people who had been privileged to work close to Muhammad. This inner core moulded the religious, political and social framework of the community. Islam provided the *raison d'être* of the embryonic Arab state. Instead

[26] Gibb (1923).

of the time-honoured patterns of Bedouin border raiding followed by a return to Arabia, or of Bedouin integration into frontier localities under the thumb of the Byzantine and Sasanian empires, Muslim rule was now imposed from Medina and the Bedouin settled in custom-built garrison towns in the territory of the former super-powers. It seems unlikely, however, that the rank and file nomads who comprised the earliest Muslim armies were propelled into fighting principally out of religious zeal. Their knowledge of Islam must have been very superficial. Islamic sources themselves stress that inducements of booty and financial remuneration kept the Arab warriors loyal. Gradually, success after success must have engendered greater solidarity and higher morale. Once the Arab tribal contingents were housed in the new garrison towns, it became an important facet of military life to receive instruction in Islam and to 'live' the Muslim life corporately. Quranic recitation and the daily fulfilment of Islamic rituals helped to reinforce the sense of belonging to a movement destined by God to be crowned with success. Islam, conveyed through the unifying power of the Arabic language, enabled the Arabs to establish the most long-lasting of all empires set up by nomads.

Whilst these extraordinary military exploits and territorial gains were taking place in Byzantine and Sasanian lands, the embryonic Islamic state was developing at the heart of the *umma*. Internal disunity soon appeared. Indeed, it could be argued that true harmony existed only in Medina under the charismatic rule of Muhammad himself. His unexpected death in 632 left the community in disarray. Partisan historical sources obscure the true nature of the Prophet's own plans for succession. He left no male heirs and a number of worthy candidates felt they had good right to take on the task. According to the minority Shi'ite sources, Muhammad bequeathed authority to his cousin and son-in-law, 'Ali. The majority of Muslims, the Sunnis, believe that the decision to appoint Abu Bakr, the Prophet's father-in-law and devoted friend, as his successor (*khalifa*, 'caliph') was in accordance with the true wishes of Muhammad and with the consensus of the nascent Muslim community.

Islamic political thinkers have tended to view the period of the four so-called 'Rightly-Guided' caliphs (632–661) as a halcyon era of true theocracy. In reality, the sources reveal a paradox: tremendous vitality and expansion on the one hand and growing internal schism on the other. Three of these first four caliphs were assassinated. The caliphate of Abu Bakr, lasting only two years, was a caretaker government. Islamic sources credit 'Umar, the second caliph, who succeeded Abu Bakr on the latter's death in 634, with the establishment of true Islamic government. Many of the achievements attributed to him may well, however, be retrospective projections: the Islamic state must have acquired its distinctive form over a considerable time. Nevertheless, it is clear that 'Umar held the *umma* together by the force of his iron personality. After his death in

644, cracks in the edifice of the *umma* widened and the impetus of conquest was temporarily halted during the turbulent reigns of the third and fourth caliphs, ʿUthman (644–656) and ʿAli (656–661).

Early Islamic government was at once pragmatic and innovative. At the head of the state was the caliph, who appointed governors over individual provinces. These were usually based on the territorial units already existing under preceding regimes – Sasanian, Byzantine or Visigothic. The Muslims were content to use local administrative institutions (indeed, they were constrained to do so by their own administrative inexperience); this facilitated the gradual transfer of power to the newcomers. Even so, specifically Islamic modes of government probably came into being early. Initially, the empire was ruled from the seat of the caliphate, Medina, and later briefly Kufa, before moving to Damascus with the takeover of power by the Umayyads in 661. Before that date conquest was a fundamental pillar of the *umma*. Its warriors were entitled to a share of the booty; this was divided up on the spot in the case of movable property, one fifth being sent to the caliph to be spent on needy groups within the community and the remainder distributed to those who had participated in the fighting. Islamic tradition also gives ʿUmar credit for the establishment of the *diwan*, the financial system, which paid military stipends and was based on a supra-tribal criterion, namely priority of conversion to Islam.

The 'People of the Book' (Christians, Jews, Sabians, Zoroastrians and, later, Buddhists) were granted the protection of the Islamic state, as well as freedom of worship, in return for payment of the poll-tax (*jizya*), which was collected with the help of the religious leaders of the non-Muslim communities. The early Islamic state demarcated the relationship between the rulers and the ruled. The caliphs derived fiscal benefit from their subject populations; more than this they did not want. Conversion to Islam was not apparently a significant factor. The new faith was for the Arabs at this early stage. The exclusivity of the *umma* was underlined by the physical separateness of their living quarters. The subject populations continued to dwell in long-established urban areas, whilst the conquerors generally lived in the newly constructed garrison towns, strategically sited near the open desert. It was not, however, in the interests of the Muslims to mete out harsh treatment to peoples much more numerous than themselves, peoples who could make valuable contributions to the Islamic state.

The process by which Sasanian Iraq came to terms with the conquerors can be documented in detail from the Islamic sources. The *dihqan* class was quick to negotiate with the Arabs to keep its lands. The chronicler al-Tabari also records that the local population of Iraq built bridges and served as scouts and soldiers for the Arabs. Some contingents of the Sasanian army, notably the group mentioned by al-Tabari as the *Hamra*ʾ, converted to Islam and became integrated into the Muslim army as allies of the Tamim tribe before and after the battle of Qadisiyya. Some *Hamra'* were infantry; they joined the Muslim side and settled in Kufa. Such new non-Arab converts, the *mawali* ('clients', so called because they had to become affiliated to an Arab tribe), made mangonels and helped the Arabs to learn the use of armour and the heavy Persian horse. Thus a picture emerges in which certain elements of the Sasanian population, both those with vested land interests and also military contingents, saw their survival in terms of a quick accommodation with the conquerors.[27]

Can a similar situation be postulated for the Byzantine Empire? Recent research reveals a complex picture and suggests that the population did not welcome the Arabs with open arms. It is certainly too simplistic to argue that local Monophysite Christians supported the Muslim conquerors because of their religious disaffection with Constantinople. There were, however, important individuals who allegedly aided the Muslims; Mansur b. Sarjun, the governor of Damascus, apparently wanted them to capture the city. It was his family that was to provide an array of talented administrators for the Umayyad caliphs. According to Brock, it is possible to gauge some of the attitudes of the Christian population towards the transfer of power to the Muslims.[28] The Syriac writers of the twelfth and thirteenth centuries, relying on much earlier sources, notably Jacob of Edessa (d. 708) and Dionysius of Tell-Mahre (d. 845), reveal a sense of relief at the transition from Byzantine to Muslim rule after the disruptions of the Byzantine/Sasanian wars. Indeed, the Arab invasions are viewed primarily as punishment for the wickedness of Byzantine ecclesiastical policies.[29] An anonymous Nestorian source, dating from between 670 and 680, also shares a positive attitude to the conquerors, claiming that their victory has 'come from God'. How much such statements are attributable to a desire for survival and good relations with the Muslim newcomers it is difficult to say.

No clear-cut principle of succession was established during the reigns of the first four so-called 'Rightly-Guided' (*Rashidun*) caliphs of Islam. 'Umar's assassination in 644 plunged the community into a crisis which was not solved by the eventual emergence of 'Uthman as the compromise choice of the consultative council set up by the dying 'Umar to appoint his successor. With 'Uthman's accession, the Muslim state witnessed the growing dominance of the Meccan elite and, above all, the Umayyad clan, who, with the notable exception of 'Uthman himself, had been the Prophet's main opponents in his attempts to establish the new faith and community. 'Uthman's nepotistic policies, which placed his Umayyad relatives in key administrative posts, proved unpopular. However, not all the blame for internal turbulence can be placed at 'Uthman's door: his caliphate coincided with widespread dissatisfaction and unrest within

[27] Cf. Morony (1984), pp. 181ff. [28] Brock (1982). [29] Brock (1982).

the community. The slowing down of the conquests and concomitant booty, strife in the garrison towns, increasing support for the idea that the caliphate should be in the hands of the Prophet's blood relations (an idea particularly prevalent among the partisans of 'Ali – the so-called *Shi'at 'Ali*, hence the term Shi'ite) culminated in his murder in Medina in 656; the aged caliph was killed whilst reading the Qur'an. 'Uthman's death was a seminal event in the internal development of the community. 'Ali who had been bypassed for the caliphate on three preceding occasions finally took office but was to rule for only two turbulent years before he too was assassinated. 'Ali's impeccable religious credentials and his blood and marriage ties with Muhammad proved powerless to stem centrifugal forces within the community, especially the claims of 'Uthman's Umayyad relatives who demanded vengeance for his murder. The crisis culminated in civil war between 'Ali and the Umayyad faction, led by the talented governor of Syria, Mu'awiya, who had ruled the province since 'Umar's time. Within three decades of Muhammad's death, supreme power in the Islamic empire was now to pass to the Meccan Quraysh elite. The Umayyads ruled the empire from 661 to 750 and brought about substantial changes in Islamic government and society.

It is difficult to give a balanced view of the Umayyad period.[30] There are few extant contemporary sources and the dynasty's achievements have been distorted by the partisan accounts of the chroniclers of the 'Abbasids, their rivals who ousted them in the revolution of 750. Shi'ite groups roundly condemned the Umayyads as political usurpers rather than true theocratic rulers, alleging that they were mere 'kings' who had introduced the principle of hereditary succession into the *umma*. The Umayyads were also opposed by pietistic non-Shi'ite circles. So much can be gleaned from the sources. More recently, a process of re-evaluation has rightly shown the Umayyads to be the true architects of an international empire. The key figures in this process were Mu'awiya (661–680) and 'Abd al-Malik (685–705). During the Umayyad period the embryonic Islamic state was freed from the cultural yoke of the Byzantine and Sasanian empires and came of age: this process can be charted through contemporary numismatic, architectural and epigraphic evidence independently of the written sources which, despite their 'Abbasid bias, also confirm it.

Mu'awiya moved the capital to his power base, Damascus, an important urban centre in late antique times and strategically a more appropriate location from which to administer the enormous Islamic empire. In Damascus, the Arab Muslim governing elite lived close to the conquered Christian population from whose ranks they drew their high-level administrators. A symbiosis was created between Byzantine modes of government and society and new Islamic

[30] For a clear overview, Hawting (1986).

institutions. Muslims and Christians for a while shared the same buildings for religious worship. The caliphal court became the forum for open theological discussion between Christians and Muslims. Each side influenced the other and sharpened their polemical skills in debates before the caliph. By the reign of ʿAbd al-Malik (685–705), self-confidence had grown to such an extent that a programme of religious monuments was initiated. The mosque had developed into a building type easily identifiable with the spread and triumph of Islam. The Umayyad Mosque of Damascus was a tangible sign of the religious prestige of Islam. Even more overt was the propagandistic significance of the Dome of the Rock, erected at the heart of the religious centres of Judaism and Christianity, Jerusalem, and decorated with Quranic inscriptions proclaiming the triumph of Islam. Arabic, the sacred vehicle through which God's final and perfect revelation had come to mankind, became the sole language of government and coinage. The Umayyad caliphs favoured Arab over non-Arab Muslim. Berber and Persian converts to Islam suffered discrimination and their disaffection with the regime grew as the seventh century progressed. The international aspects of the Islamic message, the brotherhood of man mentioned in the Qur'an, came to be emphasised, as the initial 'Arabness' of the revelation receded into the background. Islam was for Berber and Persian as well as Arab. This desire to redefine Islam contributed to the downfall of the Umayyad dynasty in 750.

The preceding pages have shown that, despite the early appearance of debilitating internal disputes about the nature of true succession to the Prophet, disputes which caused civil war and the violent deaths of caliphs, the waves of Islamic territorial conquests which had begun shortly before or after the death of Muhammad in 632 had created by 732 an enormous empire stretching from Spain to India and Central Asia. The Sasanian polity had been wiped out and Byzantium seriously diminished. The reasons for the success of the phenomenon of Arab Islamic expansion remain complex, but the irruption of nomadic forces out of the Arabian peninsula at the same time as the emergence of the Islamic revelation and the career of Muhammad points to the new faith as the mainspring of the inspirational leadership underpinning the military successes. Conquest was followed by consolidation, and in the Umayyad period a series of very gifted caliphs, based on Syria rather than Arabia, elaborated a government system capable of administering this vast empire. Arabic was now its *lingua franca* and Islam, a clearly identifiable new religion, was the faith of its ruling elite.

CHAPTER 13

THE CATHOLIC VISIGOTHIC KINGDOM

A. Barbero and M. I. Loring

With the abandonment of Arianism at the Third Council of Toledo in 589, there began a new phase in the evolution of the Visigothic kingdom. Religious unification facilitated the definitive rapprochement of the Gothic nobility and upper classes of Roman origin, and allowed the Catholic church, the principal repository of the old Roman culture, to acquire a growing prominence in the political life of the kingdom.[1] This active political role was expressed principally through the series of national church councils in Toledo, the regal metropolis, initiated by that of 589. In these the church seemed to play the role of arbiter between the royal power and the high nobility, although a close reading of the conciliar acts reveals its tendency to act in solidarity with the secular nobility. Kings, on the other hand, only exceptionally made use of the councils in order to assert their authority and were generally obliged to negotiate in the face of the powerful secular nobility and church, this being one of the main causes of the weakness of centralised authority. Religious unification also made way for a progressive interpenetration of the spiritual and temporal spheres at every level of Visigothic life and society, in which the former shaped the whole dominant ideological structure.

RELIGIOUS UNIFICATION

In the spring of 586 King Leovigild (568–586) was succeeded by his son Reccared, who had for years been associated with the throne: according to the chronicler John of Biclaro, the succession took place without difficulties.[2] In

[1] For the first steps in this direction, see Barbero and Loring, chapter 7 above.

[2] The early years of Reccared's reign are well known thanks to the *Chronicon* of John of Biclaro, which covers up to 590 and includes the acts of the Third Council of Toledo. Additional sources are Gregory, *Hist.*, which ends in 591, the *Historia Gothorum* of Isidore of Seville, the correspondence of Pope Gregory the Great, and the *Vita Patrum Emáritensium*, a hagiographic work on the bishops of the metropolitan see of Mérida from 500 to 600.

the first year of his reign the new king sought an alliance with Gosuintha, his father's widow, whom he adopted as his mother, and tried to broker a peace with the Frankish king, although Guntramn of Burgundy continued to maintain the bellicose tension along the *Narbonensis* frontier, which had been a feature of Leovigild's reign. Simultaneously, he abandoned Arianism and converted to the Catholic faith, a decision proclaimed before an assembly of Arian clergy whom he urged to follow his example, and which, apart from any personal motives, was intended to complete the political achievements of his father by ensuring the support of the nobility of Roman origin and the Catholic church.

The new religious orientation of the monarch, whilst in pursuit of the same objectives as his father, represented an about-turn in policy from the advocacy of religious union within the Arian creed, and it was not long before it produced conspiracies and revolt: one led by the Arian bishop of Mérida, Sunna, who counted on the support of various notable Visigoths, another, perhaps more serious, headed by the queen Gosuintha and the bishop Uldida, and a third directed by Athalocus, the Arian bishop of Narbonne. To the instability created by these revolts was added a Frankish offensive on Narbonne. After his conversion, Reccared had sent new embassies to the Frankish kings, communicating to them the change. He managed to conclude a treaty with Childebert of Austrasia, which included the marriage of Reccared to Childebert's sister Clodosinda, granddaughter of the queen Gosuintha. However Guntramn of Burgundy refused to seal a peace and invaded Septimania in 589. The attack, which probably coincided with the pro-Arian revolt, was crushingly repelled by the *dux* of Lusitania, Claudius, who had repelled several Frankish incursions over a long period. The proposed marriage of Reccared and Clodosinda never took place since the monarch appears to have been married that same year to Bada, whose name suggests Visigothic origin. It was a marriage that responded to the new play of alliances established with the Gothic nobility and aimed at suffocating the revolts.

Control over the internal situation and containment of the Frankish threat allowed Reccared to conclude his policy of religious unification, to which end he convened a great Synod in Toledo, which began sitting on 8 May 589.[3] According to the acts of the council, sixty-three bishops participated, and an unspecified number of other clergy, abbots and Visigothic nobles. Presiding over the assembly were Leander, bishop of Seville, who had resided at Constantinople and was consequently familiar with the imperial conciliar

[3] The main sources for its study are the acts of the council and information from John of Biclaro. The acts of this and other councils of the Visigothic church are in *Concilios Visigóticos*, ed. Vives (1963); a detailed study of this council in Orlandis and Ramos Lissón (1986), pp. 197–226; and also Orlandis (1991) and Abadal (1962–3).

tradition, and Eutropius, abbot of the monastery of Servitanum. The sessions were opened by Reccared himself, who presented the assembly with a written profession of faith. In it he expounded the orthodox doctrine of the Trinity, condemned and anathematised Arius, and made adherence to the doctrine established by the first four ecumenical Councils of Nicaea, Constantinople, Ephesus and Chalcedon obligatory. It was signed by both himself and Queen Bada.

The royal intervention complete, the assembly rose, acclaiming God and the king. Later, eight bishops and an indeterminate number of clerics and Gothic dignitaries signed another profession of faith, in which Arianism was solemnly abjured. Then the assembly occupied itself with questions of clerical discipline and organisation, which were expressed in twenty-three canons. The acts included the royal edict confirming these regulations and raising them to the status of civil law, the subscriptions of the bishops present headed by that of the monarch himself, and finally a homily by Leander of Seville summarising what had taken place. During the proceedings only eight bishops abjured Arianism. The paucity of this number, together with the feeble showing of pro-Arian revolts put down prior to the council, seems to indicate that many had already followed the example of the king, who was baptised in 587, and that by the opening of the council Catholicism had already made considerable inroads. Although in 590 Reccared had to confront a further revolt led by Argimund, a *dux provinciae* and member of the *cubiculum*, John of Biclaro, who is the source of this information, does not link it to a pro-Arian reaction and in what followed there is nothing to suggest the survival of any Arian groups. The relative ease with which the Nicene creed was accepted is explained as much by the advanced stage of the acculturation between the Gothic nobility and the Roman world as by the strengthening of a monarchy which, despite its differences from Byzantium, represented itself as heir to the Empire.

In this respect it is necessary to point out that when signing the acts of the council, Reccared adopted the name Flavius, the family name of the emperors of the Constantinian dynasty, which all Visigothic kings used from then on. In this way, the monarch presented himself as the political successor to the Roman, and especially to the Christian Roman, emperors. Likewise, John of Biclaro compared the Visigothic king to Constantine and Marcian, at whose instigation the Councils of Nicaea and Chalcedon had been held, and considered the Third Council of Toledo as successor to the grand synods of the Roman Empire. But both John of Biclaro and the acts of the Third Council rejected the canons of the Second Council of Constantinople convoked in 553 by Justinian. This council had taken decisions opposed by most of the western churches, among them those of Hispania, whose ecclesiastics would be some of its fiercest opponents.[4] The independent attitude of Hispanic prelates to the religious policy of the Eastern Empire doubtless facilitated the Visigothic monarch's acceptance of Nicaean Catholicism, his definitive renunciation of Arianism, and the presentation of himself as a champion of orthodoxy.

From the Third Council of Toledo onwards, the state, as much as Visigothic society, existed within parameters characterised by an interpenetration of the spiritual and temporal at all levels of life. Hence Reccared, in one of his addresses to the conciliar assembly, pointed to the obligation of a prince to concern himself not just with temporal matters but also with spiritual ones. In turn, in the *laudes* they addressed to the king, the ecclesiastics extolled Reccared's apostolic labours, indicating that by them he had merited earthly and eternal glory. The canons were consonant with these theoretical principles: they did not regulate solely liturgical and organisational questions, but also matters which were not strictly ecclesiastical. The well-known canon 18 established yearly provincial synods to be convoked by the metropolitans, adapted the old canon law of two annual meetings, and laid down that district governors (*iudices locorum*) and those responsible for tax revenue (*actores fiscalium patrimoniorum*) had to submit themselves to the scrutiny of the bishops, who could deny communion to functionaries who had not acted properly.

The second half of Reccared's reign is not as well documented. Isidore wrote that he fought the Byzantines and Basques, but minimised the importance of these conflicts, comparing them to the games of the arena. The hostile activities of the Basques must have been limited to plundering, but the Byzantine offensives must have been greater in scope. It is possible that they managed to recover some of the territories conquered by Leovigild. We know from an inscription from Cartagena, capital of the Byzantine province, that around 589–590 Byzantines and Visigoths found themselves at war, since it mentions that the patrician Comenciolus, *magister militum Spaniae*, had been sent by Mauricius to struggle against the *hostes barbaros*.[5] Reccared furthermore requested Pope Gregory the Great, with whom both Leander of Seville and the king himself had followed the process of the conversion, to work closely with the Byzantines in order to obtain a copy of the treaty agreed between them and the Visigoths at the time of the conquest. The pope advised Reccared against this, possibly because the Byzantine possessions recorded in the treaty were of greater extent than they were in the time of Reccared.

In contrast to his father Leovigild, Reccared maintained good relations with the nobility, to whom, according to John of Biclaro, at the beginning of his reign

[4] Barbero de Aguilera (1987), pp. 123–44.

[5] The text of the inscription is in Vives (1969), pp. 125–6.

he restored goods that had been confiscated by his predecessors, especially his father. The church also saw itself favoured with the foundation and endowment of churches and monasteries. His policy towards tribute was similar, whether, as Isidore pointed out, by granting exemptions, or by trying to ensure that functionaries did not overstep their duties by unfair impositions. Reccared created the precept for this policy at the Third Council of Toledo, by entrusting the supervision of financial functionaries to the bishops. He also promulgated a law, which reinforced this supervisory role, ordering the bishops to denounce any abuses.[6]

Reccared died in 601, and was succeeded by his son Liuva II, the fourth member of the same family to accede to the throne. After two years he was deposed. The plot which led to the deposition and death of Liuva II was headed by Witteric, a figure from the high nobility who had already participated in the Arian revolt in Mérida against Reccared. Then *comes*, he had managed to save his life by denouncing his accomplices. By deposing Liuva the nobility, which had undoubtedly been strengthened by the policies of Reccared, in effect prevented the establishment of a principle of hereditary royal succession. The tying of the royal dignity to one lineage would have reinforced the institution of kingship and weakened their own position. Once in power Witteric (601–610) did not modify the politics of his predecessors towards the Franks or Byzantines, nor is there evidence that he imposed any change of religious policy. He also died the victim of a plot: the events that had brought him to the throne had repeated themselves.

VISIGOTHIC MONARCHY AND THE END OF BYZANTINE DOMINION IN THE PENINSULA

In the period between the assassination of Witteric in 610 and the dethronement of Svinthila in 631, there were several kings.[7] The most significant accomplishment of their reigns was the destruction of Byzantine power in the Peninsula. These monarchs knew how to capitalise on the crisis in which the Empire found itself as a result of the Persian war, and the Byzantines were finally expelled from Spain.[8] Other constants were the struggles against a people known as the Astures and the Basques. Despite some successes against them, these people

[6] *LV* XIII.1–2.407–8.

[7] For this period we continue to rely on the *Historia Gothorum* of Isidore of Seville, which closes with the reign of Suinthila; this information is complemented by the Frankish *Chronicle of Fredegar*, which contains some evidence about the Visigothic kingdom, and the *Chronicle of 754*, written by a Visigothic cleric under Muslim domination, known as the *Mozarabic Chronicle*. There are also the acts of several provincial synods and letters of the king Sisebut.

[8] On Byzantium in the seventh century, see Louth, chapter 11 above.

were not crushed and they remained the enemies of the Visigoths until the end of the kingdom of Toledo. This period is also marked by struggles for the throne: regicides and dethronements took place with alarming frequency. Although at this time no general synod was held at Toledo, the church continued to intervene in civil life through its provincial synods, and kings continued to act in religious matters.

The most significant example of the latter was the decision, made by King Gundemar (610–612) in common agreement with the bishops of the kingdom, to transfer the regional religious capital of the province *Carthaginensis* to Toledo. In reality, Toledo had come to function as a metropolitan see in relation to the province of Carpetana or Celtiberia, which seems to have broken away from Carthaginensis. Now, Toledo became the ecclesiastical capital of all the churches of Carthaginensis, snatching the primacy from Cartagena that was still under Byzantine control, and it was thus an affirmation of the Visigothic monarchy's authority in relation to the Empire. The metropolitan of Toledo, as bishop of the royal city, was transformed into the foremost ecclesiastic of the Visigothic church and his authority stretched across the whole kingdom. This was established by the sixth canon of the Twelfth Council of Toledo in 681, amongst whose acts Gundemar's decree has been preserved.

On the death of Gundemar, Sisebut (612–621) ascended the throne. He was a prominent man of letters, and some of his letters, poems and a hagiographic work, the *Vita Sancti Desiderii*, have survived. He enjoyed a reputation as a religious man; his correspondence shows him attempting to convert the king of the Lombards to Catholicism. His religious views were manifest above all in his laws against the Jews.[9] Anti-Jewish legislation had ancient roots in Roman law. The regulations collected in canon 14 of the Third Council of Toledo, prohibiting Jews from entering into mixed marriages, purchasing Christian slaves or holding public office, had done no more than reproduce rules contained in the *Codex Theodosianus*, and later adapted for the *Breviarium Alarici*. Reccared had reinforced conciliar regulations with a law that obliged Jews who circumcised Christian slaves to free them without compensation. Sisebut went further, forbidding them ownership of Christian slaves, something Justinian had also done, and obliging them to sell or free them unreservedly, without the recourse to *obsequium*, that is, residual control over them. He also commanded that the donations made by his predecessors be confiscated from the Jews, reiterated the ancient prohibition of mixed marriages, and condemned to death, with consequent confiscation of goods, Hebrews who converted Christians, at the same time punishing Christians who embraced Judaism with various penalties.

[9] *LV* XII.2.13 and 14, pp. 407–8, 418–20.

This anti-Jewish legislation marginalised Hebrews in social, economic and political relations, which must have indirectly provoked numerous conversions. Isidore pointed out, not without criticism, that Sisebut forced many Jews to convert to the Catholic faith, a fact that was the object of condemnation at the Fourth Council of Toledo in 633. Owing to the conflation of religious and political principles, apparent from an analysis of the Third Council of Toledo, Jews outside the *fides* owed to God were excluded from the *fides* owed to the king, and in this sense they constituted not just a religious but also a political problem. Hence the importance that civil legislation, as much as conciliar canons, gave to what was perceived as the Jewish problem, as well as to those who converted from Judaism. The number of these converts continued to grow as a result of the continuing efforts of ecclesiastics and monarchs to eradicate the Jewish religion.

Sisebut was also an outstanding warrior. During his reign several military campaigns were undertaken against the Byzantines and the semi-independent peoples of the peninsula. According to Isidore, Sisebut won victories against the Byzantines, managing to occupy some of their cities, Málaga among them. This we can see from the acts of a provincial council held in Seville in 619. Defeat led the Byzantine governor, the patrician Caesarius, to seek peace. Although Sisebut's correspondence with Caesarius does not give significant details of the treaty that followed, it is believed that Byzantine territories were limited to the city of Cartagena and some other points along the coast. Among the semi-independent peoples against whom Sisebut sent his generals, Isidore mentions the *Roccones*, a people whom the Sueves had already fought and who were now conquered by the *dux* Suinthila, and the Astures, who were overcome by the general Requila after they had risen in revolt.

It seems likely that it was a conspiracy that ended the brilliant reign of Sisebut, for Isidore claimed that the king may have been poisoned. His son and successor, the young prince Reccared II, died a few days after ascending the throne. Finally, Suinthila (621–631) ascended the throne, a seasoned *dux provinciae* and an experienced general. At the beginning of his reign he personally undertook a campaign against the Basques who, according to Isidore, were devastating *Tarraconensis* with their raids. Once defeated, they were made to build the city of *Ologicus* (Olite) for the Goths. Suinthila, like Leovigild before him who founded *Victoriacum* (Vitoria), then ordered the construction of this fortress in Basque territory to limit Basque raids on regions near the Ebro valley. Behind the continual wars against *Astures* and Basques lay differences in social organisation between them and Hispano-Gothic society. The Basques and *Astures* still retained features of their tribal past, and although defeated on occasion by Gothic monarchs, they were never wholly dominated.[10] The

[10] Barbero and Vigil (1974), pp. 51–67.

military successes of Suinthila were even greater against the Byzantines. According to Isidore, Suinthila attained a triumph superior to that of all other kings, since he was the first king to reign over the whole of inter-oceanic Hispania, which suggests that it was he who put an end to the presence of the Byzantines in the Peninsula, an event normally dated to between 623 and 625.[11]

Suinthila associated his son Recimer with the throne, but both father and son were deposed in 631 in a coup mounted by the nobleman Sisenand, with the help of the Frankish king, Dagobert. The Frankish king dispatched an army from Toulouse, which under the command of Abundancio and Venerando reached Saragossa, where Sisenand was proclaimed king by the Goths. Fredegar, who supplies this information, claims Suinthila was an iniquitous king whom the Goths had come to hate. This is in contrast to Isidore's earlier elegies, which described him as receiving the sceptre through divine grace, and attributed to him all the virtues of a good ruler, calling him the 'father of the poor'. The contrast can be explained by a deterioration in Suinthila's relationship with the church and the nobility in the last years of his reign. At the Fourth Council of Toledo in 633, which legitimated Sisenand's seizure of power and whose instigator was Isidore of Seville, Suinthila was accused of all sorts of iniquity. The Council attempted to force him to make a formal renunciation of his power. The deposed king did not lose his life, but he and his family were excommunicated and exiled, and their goods were confiscated. Their property, said the fathers of the council, had been acquired through exactions from the poor. In the seventh century this was equivalent to saying that it had been taken from the church.

THE SACRALISATION OF ROYALTY AND INSTITUTIONAL DEVELOPMENT

It is necessary to place Suinthila's deposition in the context of the tensions between the nobility and the king in defending their respective interests. As has been seen, the system of association with the throne, a formula inspired by late Roman and contemporary Byzantine models, was not enough to put an end to violent deposition. The latter not only undermined royal authority but also endangered the stability of the kingdom, by exposing it to interference from traditionally hostile forces, like those of the Frankish kings. In the reigns that followed the ousting of Suinthila, the political scene was dominated by conciliar activity, which sought a way out of this conflict between nobility and monarchy, by strengthening the institution of monarchy and regulating the process of accession to the throne. The church, far from acting as arbiter, achieved this conjointly with the nobility and through these councils

[11] Vallego Girvés (1993), p. 307.

reinforced its own role as well as that of the nobility in the running of the kingdom.

The first of these councils was convened by Sisenand (631–636), with the object of legitimating his accession to the throne. Isidore of Seville was the key figure at this, the Fourth Council of Toledo held in 633, and the political and religious doctrine developed there can be attributed to him. Despite the fact that one of the objectives of the council was to legitimate Sisenand's seizure of power, it attempted at the same time to avoid further acts of violence, which might endanger the kings and the stability of the Gothic kingdom. Canon 75 began by recalling the sacred character of the oath of loyalty sworn to the king, and that he who broke this accord with the king equally broke faith with God in whose name the promise was made. It decreed that whoever violated their oath would be excommunicated. Likewise, it insisted on the sacred nature of royalty and the divinely elected status of the monarch, in the light of which no one should make an attempt on his life: *nolite tangere Christos meos*, the fathers remembered. It was also prescribed that kings should die peacefully and that their successors should be chosen by the nobility and bishops, an elective principle developed by later councils.

This council had important consequences for the life of the Visigothic church and kingdom, through its institution of national councils. Although the series of general councils was initiated during the Third Council of Toledo, it was the fathers of the Fourth Council who decided that the meetings should be held on a regular basis, differentiating them from the provincial ones and indicating that they would have to meet to consider questions of faith or matters common to all the churches. These councils met on eleven occasions, always convened by the kings, who besides calling upon the bishops to correct abuses in the field of discipline and dogma, also submitted to the deliberation of the assembly, in the so-called *tomus regius*, all those questions considered of significance in the government of the kingdom.[12] The work of these councils was in this sense not limited to ecclesiastical questions, but extended to questions of political interest in conformity with the theoretical principles, which defended a harmonious unity between spiritual and temporal power, already apparent at the Third Council of Toledo.

During the brief reign of Chintila (636–639) two Toledan councils were held, the Fifth and Sixth. At the Fifth Council, held at the beginning of the

[12] The series of Toledan Councils began with III in 589 and terminated with XVIII in 702. However IX and XI had a provincial character and XIV concerned itself solely with theological matters. The acts from XVIII are not extant; the acts of these councils are one of the principal sources of information on the Visigoth kingdom of Toledo. On the Toledan Councils cf. Abadal (1962–3), pp. 69–93, and Orlandis and Ramos-Lissón (1986); acts ed. Vives (1963).

reign in 636, the subjects of public interest tackled at the previous Council were almost the only things dealt with. The canons, on the one hand, insisting on the inviolable character of the person of kings, prohibited attempts on their lives and attacks on their descendants or goods, and on the other hand, with the object of avoiding further conspiracies, proscribed excommunication for those who during the life of a king intrigued concerning the succession. To reinforce this, they declared it obligatory for future councils to read canon 75 of the Fourth Council, which had dealt with these questions for the first time. They also established that kings had to be chosen from the Gothic nobility, and heirs to the throne were not allowed to deprive the *fideles regum* of goods received from princes or acquired justly in recognition of their fidelity.

Two years later, at the Fourth Council of Toledo in 638, these issues were again raised and it was decided that the *fideles regum* could not be dispossessed of public posts and that they not only could keep goods received from princes, but also transmit them to their descendants unless they failed to provide *fidele obsequium et sincerum servitium*, broke their oath of fidelity to the monarch or failed to carry out their functions. The fathers present concluded that it was more just still that the churches of God keep goods conceded by princes to the church permanently in their dominion, since they were the nourishment of the poor. The Synod also insisted again on the inviolable nature of the king, his descendants and goods, setting down that anyone making an attempt on his life ought to be avenged by his successor, who would otherwise be a party to the crime. Finally, in relation to the succession, further restrictions were added to ways in which the throne might be obtained. No one could become king if he had seized the throne by force, had been tonsured in a religious habit or shamefully shaved, or were of servile or foreign origin.

The reigns of Sisenand and Chintila represent a milestone in the institutional political development of the Visigothic kingdom. Subsequent Toledan Councils reinforced the institution of monarchy, through the sacralisation of the royal person: it is probable that the practice of anointing kings was instituted for the first time at the Fourth Council of Toledo. Royal unction was a ritual act, conferring divinely elected status, which, inspired by biblical precedents, the Visigothic ecclesiastics adopted. It also reinforced the cohesion of the kingdom, by sacralising in turn the link which tied subject to king through the oath of fidelity. Possibly of Germanic origin, the oath was seen as a highly important addition to the ancient obligations not to conspire against the king and the patria of the Goths. More positive aspects were developed: i.e. the *fideles regum* were also obliged to defend the life and interests of the king and kingdom.[13]

[13] On the content and scope of the oath of fidelity, Barbero and Vigil (1978), pp. 126–54.

In parallel, these synods gave religious backing to the participation of the nobility and church in the government of the realm and strengthened their fiscal rights. They favoured an elective system, which entrusted the election of the king jointly to the church and nobility, and they confirmed the rights of the *fideles regum* to receive properties and hold offices in recognition of their fidelity. It is important to underline that the *fides* or *fidelitas*, which united subjects and king (including clerics), was an expression of a tie of personal dependency that not only entailed obligations towards the king and the kingdom, but also implied responsibilities on the part of the monarch to the *fideles regum*.

Despite the precautions taken in the previous councils to avoid accession to the throne by force, another, fortunately bloodless, plot soon followed. According to Fredegar, King Chintila proposed his son as his successor before his death. The young Tulga was elected king, but in the third year of his reign he was deposed and tonsured as a cleric, which in accordance with the prescription of the Fourth Council of Toledo disqualified him definitively from kingship. In his place the noble Chindasuinth was promoted to command of the realm by numerous Gothic 'senators' and a large part of the people.

THE REIGNS OF CHINDASUINTH AND RECCESUINTH

The reigns of Chindasuinth and his son Reccesuinth cover a long period (642–672) during which both carried out extensive legislative work culminating in the promulgation of the *Liber Iudiciorum*, a great compilation of law initiated by Chindasuinth and completed by Reccesuinth in 654.[14] The new Code incorporated numerous laws described as *antiquae*. These were mostly revisions from the Code of Leovigild, with some from Reccared and Sisebut. A good number were new laws by Chindasuinth and Reccesuinth, although some of these had been taken with minor modifications from the old laws of the *Breviarium Alarici*.[15] The new Code superseded all earlier law not included in it, especially the Roman laws from the *Breviarium Alarici*. The *Liber Iudiciorum* cannot however be considered a code that was Germanic in character, given that it was conceived within a Roman juridical tradition, and employs the concepts

[14] The *Liber Iudiciorum* was published by Zeumer (1902) together with other Visigothic codes under the title *Lex Visigothorum*. Visigothic legislation has been the subject for a long time of a polemic between the partisans arguing for its territorial character, cf. García Gallo (1942–43) and (1974) and D'Ors (1956), and those distinguishing an earlier phase characterised by the national status of law from a second involving its territorial scope, inaugurated by the *Liber Iudiciorum*, cf. Thompson (1969), pp. 57–8, King (1972), pp. 6–18, and Pérez Prendes (1991), pp. 71–8.

[15] The ninety-nine laws of Chindasuinth and eighty-seven of Reccesuinth constitute one important source of information for these two reigns, to which can be added that provided by the conciliar acts and to a lesser extent by Fredegar and the *Mozarabic Chronicle of 754*.

of Roman law, only exceptionally applying principles from Germanic law.[16] Its promulgation responded to the need to adjust the mass of laws, accumulated over two centuries, to prevailing social conditions. Old laws, which no longer had any social relevance, were changed. Among the laws of Reccesuinth it is worth noting the rigour of those against the Jews, in which the celebration of Passover and other rites such as circumcision were proscribed. In the next reigns new laws were incorporated into the *Liber*, and under Ervig a new revised version was published.

The laws of the *Liber Iudiciorum* reveal that a considerable proportion of the Hispano-Gothic population continued living in slavery, and that freedmen were numerous given the frequency with which they appear, but there is no mention of tenant farmers. This silence, when the existence of *coloni* is attested from a conciliar source of 619, has been linked to a deterioration in the situation of tenant farmers who, besides being tied to the land, were bound to their *dominus* in such a way that legislators ended up disregarding the slight distinction existing between them and slaves, including them all in the category of *servi*.[17] This interpretation is consonant with the evolution of the condition of freedmen, whose dependence in relation to the manumitter saw itself progressively reinforced and was eventually perpetuated beyond the lifetime of the manumitter and freedman, being passed on to their respective descendants. This strengthening of the bonds of dependence also stretched to the free *in patrocinio*, who as freedmen received goods from their *patroni*, over which they had limited powers of disposition, lending services in exchange. Their dependence also tended to be hereditary.[18] From this it emerges that the ties of dependence of persons in slavery or servitude, who for the most part worked on the agrarian estates of their lords, were reinforced to the benefit of a minority of *domini vel patroni*.[19] The pre-eminence of this social group was expressed in the juridical field, Visigothic legislation differentiating between nobles and simple free men when it came to the determination of punishment and monetary compensation, always higher for the *maiores* and capable of resulting in the loss of liberty in the case of the *humiliores*.

The legislation included in the *Liber Iudiciorum* also reflected innovations in the field of territorial administration, characterised by a definitive superseding of the old distinction between military and civil administration, along the same

16 Zeumer (1944), p. 81. 17 King (1972), p. 161.

18 Barbero de Aguilera and Vigil (1978), pp. 22–33.

19 In current historiography, the hypothesis that the regime of slavery was strengthened under the barbarian monarchs, and certainly the slaves did not disappear, has arisen. In our opinion, however, the reduction to servitude of the free peasant population through relations of patronage was more significant, cf. Loring and Fuentes (1998).

lines as was occurring in Byzantium.[20] Thus, by the time of Chindasuinth's reign, the *duces provinciae* had added to their old military powers others of a juridical kind, displacing the old *rectores*, who are no longer mentioned. At a lower level, this evolution had begun earlier. The *comes civitatis* had been assuming military, judicial and financial powers since their appearance at the time of the Visigothic kingdom of Toulouse, powers that had been growing anyway as the old Roman magistracies disappeared, although the *defensor civitatis* is mentioned as late as the reign of Reccesuinth. Subordinate to the *comes* were two other government agents, the *vicarius comitis* and *thiufadus*. The latter was originally the chief of a military unit of a thousand men, and like the *dux* augmented his sphere of action with juridical competencies. It is possible that by this time the *duces* and *thiufadi* also had financial responsibilities, although they are not mentioned until a 683 decree annulling the tributes of Ervig. Some *duces* appear already to have held the office of *comes cubiculariorum* and other court posts, such as *comes scanciarum*, offices related to the private estate of the monarch, no doubt destined to resolve the problem of maintaining an army.[21]

Also innovatory were the important powers dependants or slaves of the king, *servi fiscales*, came to exercise as administrators of the resources of the fisc and royal estates, which even included responsibilities for certain services of the *officium palatinum* (an administrative organ made up of different departments in the service of the king and central administration of the kingdom) at whose head were magnates with the title *comes*. The kings found in this a solution to their need to rely on a loyal bureaucracy with which to balance noble power. The acts of the Thirteenth Council of Toledo of 683, which attempted to put an end to the monopolisation of these functions by slaves and freedmen, testify to this. The solution was very similar to that put into practice in Byzantium, where the *cubiculum* was increasingly powerful at the expense of other services of the central administration, precisely because it was staffed by slaves and eunuchs.

The government of Chindasuinth (642–653) was hard and energetic. According to Fredegar, he suppressed the nobility, ordering the execution of 200 *primates* and 500 *mediocres*, exiling others, and handing over their wives and daughters, together with their patrimony to his *fideles*. Chindasuinth provided himself with legal means to carry out his policies, strengthening royal power and, in the second year of his reign, he promulgated a law against fugitives and those accused of high treason and conspiracy.[22] It made those who took part in attempts against the government of the king and Goth people liable to the

[20] We do not share the opinion of Thompson (1969), p. 216, who considers these innovations the result of political measures to deprive the Hispano-Romans of their political power. Cf. the detailed study of the Visigothic kingdom's administration in García Moreno (1974a).

[21] Barbero and Vigil (1978), pp. 84–5.

[22] *LV* II.1.8, pp. 53–7.

death penalty and confiscation of properties. The rigour of the law was such that, in the case of reprieve, the king could only commute the death penalty to blinding and the restitution of a twentieth part of the confiscated goods. Furthermore, to the end of ensuring greater observance of the law, important dignitaries, lay as well as ecclesiastical, were made to swear a special oath. Two years later in 646, Chindasuinth convened the Seventh Council of Toledo where the seriousness of these actions was discussed and it was set down that clergymen committing such offences would be punished by excommunication and removal from office. The pain of excommunication was similarly extended to include laymen. It also insisted on the obligation of clerics to keep the fidelity owed to the king, reminding them of their obligation to respect the promises sworn and not to break them by consenting to the proclamation of another monarch. Chindasuinth was a king who, because of his rigour, was treated harshly by his contemporaries. Hence, Eugenius of Toledo composed a poem about him, whose epitaph described him as impious, unjust and immoral. However, he had friendships with other prominent clerics, like the Saragossan Braulio, by whom he was advised in political affairs such as that of his son's association with the throne, and who was his collaborator in legislative matters. Besides his legislative work, it is necessary to attribute to this monarch the reorganisation of the exchequer, which no doubt benefited from the confiscations he made from the nobility, and probably from greater efficiency in tax collection. During his reign the law and weight of coinage improved in comparison to earlier times, evidence of this reorganisation.[23]

Chindasuinth, in keeping with his policy of strengthening royal power, associated his son with the throne in 649, yet another attempt to establish a royal dynasty. In fact Reccesuinth did succeed him on his death in 653, although the succession was far from being peaceful. A Visigoth noble, Froya, tried to seize the throne and in alliance with the Basques led an expedition into the Ebro valley, laying siege to Saragossa.[24] The reign of Reccesuinth (653–672) signified a change in the relationship of the nobility and church to royal power. In the first months of his reign, the new king single-handedly convoked the Seventh Council of Toledo, held in December 653, whose principal task was to revise the politics of his father. This council was attended by the majority of the bishops, and next to them, for the first time (if we except the Gothic nobles who abjured Arianism at the Third Council), a group of abbots and lay magnates from the *officium palatinum*. Their presence, habitual thenceforward, was an innovation that gave still greater cohesion to the proceedings of the church and nobility. In accordance with its task of revision, the council discussed the possibility

[23] Grierson (1979), XII, p. 86.

[24] On the succession of Chindasuinth, cf. Orlandis (1977), pp. 168–9.

of reducing the sentences for those accused of high treason according to the law against expatriates and traitors. After long argument mercy prevailed over the inconveniencies of breaches of an oath made in the name of God. Then the conditions, which all good governors must fulfil, were discussed. It was specified that the accession to the throne ought to be elective, and effected by the bishops and court magnates in Toledo, or wherever the king had died. Finally, the conciliar assembly functioned as a high tribunal and issued a decree in which, after voicing strong criticism of the greed of princes, it went on to make a distinction between goods acquired by Chindasuinth after ascending the throne and those which he had possessed before, through inheritance or legitimate acquisition. According to the decision of the assembly, the latter would pass to his descendants, but the former could only be possessed by Reccesuinth as royal patrimony, 'in such a way that everyone may receive that which is justly owed him, and the rest may be employed according to the will of the prince for the relief of his subjects'.[25]

These latter measures were crucial for the interests of the nobility and church, who were concerned as much to put an end to the excessive exaltation of one family and prevent the royal dignity from being perpetuated down one lineage, as to guarantee their own access to the enjoyment of properties from the fisc, which were 'justly owed' to them, and counterbalance the fealty which was established by the fifth and sixth Councils of Toledo. Another law of Reccesuinth's, promulgated at the council, strengthened the regulations of the conciliar assembly, making guarantees so that henceforward nobody could be arbitrarily deprived of their goods by princes, and fixing formulas by which abusive confiscations could be restored. Furthermore, coinciding with the conciliar decree, the law also established that all goods acquired by the king since the reign of Suinthila, if they had not been disposed of by testament, ought to pass into the royal patrimony and be at the disposition of the successors to the throne.

WAMBA, ERVIG AND MILITARY REFORMS

The reign of Wamba (672–680), successor of Reccesuinth, is one of the best known of all the kings of Visigothic Spain, thanks to the *Historia Wambae*, written by the Toledan bishop Julian, who was the king's contemporary. The *Historia* begins with the election of Wamba, which took place on the day of Reccesuinth's death, at Gérticos, a small place about 190 kilometres from the royal city. Wamba did not receive royal unction until nineteen days later in

[25] 'ita ut iuste sibi debita quique percipat, et de reliquis ad remedia subiectorum . . . principis voluntas exerceat', Vives (1963), p. 292.

Toledo. The anointing, the first for which there is evidence, although it can be inferred from the language of Julian that the ritual was already known, was performed by the metropolitan, Quirico.

That year Wamba had to face an uprising in Septimania headed by Ilderic, *comes* of Nîmes. Wamba sent the *dux* Paul to suppress it, but he in turn rebelled, taking with him an important sector of the nobility of *Tarraconensis*. Paul made a pact with Ilderic and his followers, and proclaimed himself king in Narbonne. He was anointed and wrote a letter to Wamba, entitling himself *Flavius Paulus unctus rex orientalis*. He then sought new allies amongst the traditional enemies of the Visigoths, such as the Franks and Basques.[26] At that time Wamba was fighting the Basques, whom he subdued after a rapid campaign, obliging them to accept a peace with a hand-over of hostages and payment of tributes. Later the king made for Gaul and, after subjugating the cities of Barcelona and Gerona in *Tarraconensis*, divided his army into three with the objective of crossing the Pyrenees by three different passes, and occupying the fortresses guarding them. In *Narbonensis*, he reunited the army, took Narbonne and other cities, and finally occupied Nîmes, where Paul had taken refuge, and where he gave himself up. The victorious campaign did not end in the execution of the rebels but, granting the petition of the bishop of Narbonne for clemency for himself and the others implicated, Wamba pardoned them. When the king returned to Toledo and made his triumphal entry, Paul and his accomplices were led into the city in triumph, and paraded through the streets in public ignominy.

As a result of the rebellion, and a little after his victory over Paul, Wamba promulgated a law proposing a reorganisation of the army.[27] Two parts can be distinguished: one treating attacks coming from the outside and the other, internal rebellions. In the first part it was laid down that bishops, clerics of whatever degree, military chiefs, the *dux*, *comes*, *thiufadus*, *uicarius* and *gardingus*, and anyone from the territory where the attack had taken place, or neighbouring territories within a 160 kilometre radius, had to help in the defence of the realm once the *dux*, *comes*, *thiufadus* or *uicarius* had made the danger known.[28] They were all obliged to arrive with all their forces. If they did not fulfil this obligation, and damage was done and captives taken in the provinces in question,

[26] For the Frankish involvement in the revolt, Fouracre, chapter 14 below.

[27] *LV* IX.2.8, pp. 370–3. On this law and the later one of Ervig, cf. Barbero and Vigil (1978), pp. 140–50, and Pérez Sánchez (1989), pp. 155–74.

[28] The *gardingos*, according to Sánchez Albornoz (1974), I, pp. 77–88, were armed clients of the royal retinue derived from the Germanic *comitatus*, similar to the Merovingian *antrustiones*; although here they appear to be endowed with military command. The sources, however, do not allow us to relate them to the rest of those responsible for administration: Wamba's law does not cite them together with the other dignitaries entrusted with the carrying out of the call to arms.

they were to be punished. The bishops and other high-ranking clergy had to pay compensation from their own estates for the damage caused, or be exiled, whilst lower-ranking clergy and laymen of whatever degree lost their capacity to make legal depositions, and were consigned to servitude and left at the mercy of the royal will, their properties being confiscated to compensate those who had lost out. In the second case, of internal rebellion, the penalty was equally harsh for lay people and bishops: confiscation of goods and exile.

The text of this law testifies to a phenomenon of undoubted significance: that the Visigothic army in the last decades of the seventh century had still not completely lost its public character, given that it was regulated by laws determining the authority of military chiefs, in whose hands official announcements lay. It was made up of troops of diverse origin, both public and private. The military chiefs of the Visigothic kingdom could hold permanent troops under orders, and increase their forces with men recruited from the huge estates, which were their personal property or possessed by means of their office. In addition to these armies were the armed retinues of churchmen, recruited in the same way, and those of great landowners who did not hold public office.

The reign of Wamba was brusquely interrupted in October 680 by a plot, which was carried out bloodlessly and by apparently legal means. According to the acts of the Twelfth Council of Toledo celebrated several months later, the king, being seriously ill, had in the presence of important palace dignitaries received absolution and with it the religious habit and tonsure. In accordance with the prescription of the Sixth Council of Toledo this disqualified him from continuing to occupy the throne. Apparently Wamba also signed documents, examined in detail by the conciliar assembly, in which he chose Ervig as his successor and requested the metropolitan of Toledo, Julian, to anoint him without delay. However, an Asturian chronicle from the end of the ninth century relates that Wamba was drugged and the conspirators tonsured him and dressed him in a religious habit, thus leaving him obliged to renounce public life and live as a monk until the end of his days. This version of the deposition of Wamba seems the more plausible, since in its second canon the fathers present at the Twelfth Council of Toledo discussed those who had received penance when unconscious, declaring, in clear allusion to the king Wamba, that 'those who in whatever way they received penance, may never return to put on the military insignia'.[29]

The deposition of Wamba must be related to the serious consequences his law on military obligations had for the church and nobility. His successor Ervig (680–687) set about revising the law at the beginning of his reign, although

[29] 'hos qui qualibet sorte poenitentiam susceperint ne ulterius ad militare cinculum redeant', Vives (1963), p. 389.

the task was complicated and it took two conciliar assemblies before it was effected, beginning with the Twelfth Council of Toledo, held in 681.[30] The conciliar assembly agreed to restore to those who had lost their rights as a consequence of the law discussed above, their ancient dignity and capacity to take out private actions. Likewise it lifted the excommunication of those who had worked against the king or *patria* and had been pardoned by the new monarch. Two years later the Thirteenth Council of Toledo completed these measures and resolved to return, to those who had taken part in the conspiracy of Paul and even those who since the time of the king Chintila had been tainted with this infamy, the right to take out private actions; it was also agreed to return confiscated goods, provided that they had not been granted to someone else, or ceded *causa stipendii*. In the second canon those present, petitioning on behalf of those who had lost dignity because of unjust accusations or confessions elicited under royal pressure, established that from then on ecclesiastics and nobles would enjoy procedural guarantees and could only be tried publicly before tribunals made up of people of the same estate. This canon makes evident the antagonism between the church and nobility on the one side and royal power on the other; it presents kings as the instigators of fraudulent trials and accuses them of using physical violence against nobles and clerics to prove their guilt. It transformed those guilty of acting against the kingdom into innocent victims.

Ervig made further concessions to the church and nobility. The Council's third canon sanctioned a royal decree concerning the remitting of tributes, in which payments from the first year of his reign still owing to the public purse were written off, with the exception of tributes already collected but still not handed over to the fisc by the gatherers. It included the pain of excommunication for whoever contravened the concession. The attention the Council paid to this decree, not only dedicating one of its canons to it but also incorporating it in its acts, seems to indicate that the church and nobility were the main beneficiaries of this fiscal amnesty. The Council in its sixth canon also tried to impose limits to the development of a patrimonial bureaucracy on the part of kings. Henceforth, only freedmen and *servi fiscales* could hold court posts or administer properties of the fisc or the king, and not other slaves and freedmen, with the end of avoiding their becoming lofty, and being transformed in this way into 'the executioners of their masters'.

Ervig not only rectified the policies of Wamba through the Councils, but also used civil legislation to promulgate a new law concerning the army.[31] The legislator complained that those obliged to go to war with their serfs, took

30 The conciliar acts and laws of Ervig are the main sources of evidence for this reign.

31 *LV* IX.2.9, pp. 374–9.

with them not even the twentieth part of them, and established a series of rules which obliged the entire people to answer the royal call, joining the king's army or that of *duces* or *comites* on the day indicated. The law specified that everyone must come, Goths and Romans, free and freedmen, and also the *servi fiscales*, bringing with them a tenth part of their serfs armed at their expense. In the event of non-compliance, a *dux*, *comes* or *gardingus* was to be deprived of his goods and exiled. The *thiufadi* and other lesser functionaries were to be shaved, to be condemned to two hundred lashes, and to pay a quantity of gold, a sanction whose non-completion would lead to perpetual enslavement.

This law has points of contact with that of Wamba, but it tones down the exigencies of the punishments provided for non-completion. Noticeable is the exclusion of ecclesiastics from those who were obliged to go to war. Another innovation was the different punishments laid down, according to whether the person belonged to a higher or lower rank in the administration and army: the only ones now reduced to slavery were those of inferior status and that only in the case of their non-payment of the pecuniary compensation demanded. Finally, whereas in the time of Wamba one had to assist the army with all available forces, the law of Ervig only demanded a tenth part of the serfs. All these modifications did not alter the half-public, half-private character that the army had had at least since the reign of Wamba. It continued to be made up for the most part of private delegations, although the king did not renounce his rights of official notification and direction, whether in person or through his generals.

The legislative work of Ervig was not limited to the promulgation of new laws, for he also undertook a new revised edition of the *Liber Iudiciorum*, which was published on 21 October 681, a year into his reign. Among the laws issued and collected by Ervig in the new Code, those promulgated against the Jews are notable. These laws, which were presented by Ervig at the Twelfth Council of Toledo and approved by the assembly in their eighth canon, were extremely harsh, surpassing even the rigour of previous legislation. In fact Judaism as a religion was prohibited, Jews were given a year to convert, and the prohibition of the Passover and other rites such as circumcision was reiterated. As a result of these measures, although future civil and canon legislation would continue to refer to Jews, it dealt only with those who had converted to Christianity.

EGICA AND THE ATTEMPT TO ESTABLISH DYNASTIC SUCCESSION

Before his death in the middle of November 687, Ervig designated his son-in-law Egica, who was married to his daughter Cixilo, as his successor, thus passing over his own male children. The succession seems to have arisen from an agreement with a powerful noble faction, since six months later, in

May 688, Egica convened the Fifteenth Council of Toledo with the object of freeing him from compromises with the family of his father-in-law, something echoed in Asturian chronicles from the end of the ninth century which links Egica and the family of Wamba. Egica, in the *tomus* which he presented to the Fifteenth Council, stated that he found himself bound to two oaths whose clauses were mutually contradictory. On the occasion of his marriage to Cixilo Ervig had made him swear, by which he was obliged to protect the children of the king, but as a condition of his election as king Ervig had also made him swear to act with justice towards the peoples entrusted to him. According to Egica, Ervig's family had benefited from the abuses and unjust confiscations Ervig had made as king. The assembly believed that it was certainly impossible to complete both promises without committing perjury, so it found that the second oath ought to prevail because its content was fuller, qualifying it by saying that this did not license Egica to leave the royal family unprotected, and protecting them did not prevent him from making legal claims against them. Behind this problem and Egica's fear of violating his oaths, what was really at stake was the destination of properties proceeding from the confiscations made by Ervig, which had passed to his descendants. The new monarch was now trying to take back this property from his in-laws, in order to weaken their position and prevent them from raising themselves as rivals.

In 693, Egica brought together a new Council at Toledo, the Sixteenth, whose acts inform us that a significant rebellion had occurred a little before. It had been led by Bishop Sisbert, who had succeeded Julian as bishop of Toledo, and who, according to the acts, had attempted to deprive Egica of the throne and kill him. The conciliar assembly, acting as a high court, condemned Sisbert and removed him from office. Then those present again took up the doctrine of the inviolability of the royal person, in his quality as the anointed and elect of God, insisting on the obligation to respect the oath of fidelity to the king. They decreed harsh penalties for those accused of high treason, strengthening the rigour of those already prescribed by the old canons. That is to say, removal from office and exile for clerics, and for lay persons, reduction to slavery under the fisc, deprivation from office, and confiscation of property (which was to be taken by the king). Excommunication was an additional punishment.

Two more of Egica's laws can be related to this plot.[32] In one, oaths made to persons other than the king, or those made in the courts, were punishable by the penalties associated with high treason. The other was designed to regulate the way in which the oath of fidelity was taken: the members of the *officium palatinum* were required to take it personally before the king, and other free

[32] *LV* II.5.19, pp. 118–20 and II.1.7, pp. 52ff.

men before functionaries called *discussores iuramenti*, who travelled through the kingdom to this end. Both the members of the *officium palatinum* and other free men who evaded this obligation without justification were to be deprived of their properties, and their persons left to the disposition of the king. These laws confirm that the *fideles regum* were not just a restricted group, commended personally to the king (a deep-rooted interpretation in the historiography of the Visigoths), but included all of his subjects.

In 694, another Council was held in Toledo, the Seventeenth, whose preoccupation was the Jewish question. In the *tomus* he addressed to the council, the king denounced a supposed plot of the Jews, alleging that, in collusion with Hebrews overseas, they were conspiring together against the Christian people. It also affirmed that despite his benevolence towards them, which had led him to restore Christian slaves to those who had been deprived of them (because of their infidelity), the Jews, under cover of their promise of sincere conversion, continued practising their rites and ceremonies. Finally he asked the assembly for a firm decision as to what he should do with their persons and goods. The conciliar assemblies ratified the royal accusations and in the eleventh canon agreed that Jews were to be deprived of all their goods and, together with their women and children, be reduced to slavery, and dispersed throughout all the provinces of *Hispania*, unable to recover their status as free men whilst they persisted in their infidelity. The king could give their Christian slaves letters of freedom and award them part of their former masters' goods. Finally children of seven years and up were to be separated from their parents in order to be educated as Christians. The Jews of Gothic Gaul (*Narbonensis*) were excluded from these measures, owing to the depopulation suffered in the province as a result of the plague, but they did have to assist the *dux* there, with their goods.

The story of the supposed Jewish conspiracy against Christianity in general, and the Gothic kingdom in particular, cannot be accepted as having any historical basis, although the reference to the Hebrews overseas may allude to eastern and northern parts of Africa conquered by the Muslims, where Jews enjoyed greater tolerance. The content of this canon represents the culmination of the comprehensive anti-Jewish legislation of the Visigothic kings. It is worth pointing out that the serious measures decreed at the Seventeenth Council were directed at converts rather than against Jews as such, for the text affirms that 'they had sullied the tunic of the Faith received from the Holy Mother Church at their baptism'.[33] In an epoch when it was difficult to demarcate the boundaries of the religious and the political, where the faith owed to God was conflated with that owed to the king, those who did not participate in the

[33] 'tunicam fidei, qua eos per undam baptismatis induit sancta mater ecclesia maculaverint', Vives (1963), p. 535.

dominant religion began to be marginalised by their religious beliefs and ended up being accused of wanting to seize the throne and kingdom for themselves.

Another matter of interest dealt with by the Seventeenth Council was the protection of the wife and descendants of the king, already tackled at the previous Council where protection and aid had been decreed for the royal family, with the objective of preventing violence against their persons or the seizure of their goods. Forcing them to take the tonsure and religious habit was forbidden, and in addition an obligation to say prayers for the royal family daily, in every church in the kingdom, was imposed. The Seventeenth Council developed these measures, including the queen, Cixilo, in the persons of the royal family who had to be protected, and extending more fully the measures concerning the question of the properties of royal offspring. The children of the king, provided that they were not found guilty in court cases, ought to possess without disturbance that which they had received through hereditary succession, by gift from their fathers or by just acquisition, and should also possess the right to dispose of these goods freely. Finally, if they were left unprotected, the bishops were obliged to offer them help. All these guarantees, made by the Councils in order to protect the descendants of kings, were a new element directed towards strengthening the position of a family at the head of the nobility and also to ensure that the highest dignity, the crown, would not pass outside it. In the reign of Ervig, the Thirteenth Council had been the first to give this kind of guarantee, and although called into question by Egica and in part unfulfilled, this did not stop him from attaining analogous benefits for his own family.

In order to strengthen the dynastic principle, Egica also resorted to the recognised practice of associating a member of the royal family with the throne, in this case his son Witiza, who, as the *Mozarabic Chronicle of 754* relates, reigned alongside him from 698. An entry in the list of kings known as the *Chronica Regum Visigothorum* tells us that in an extension to the previous practices of association, Witiza was also anointed during his father's lifetime at the end of the year 700. Unction made Witiza's association to the throne something more than a co-regency or simple attempt to ensure the son succeeded the father, because it transformed the king into a sacred figure. He was *de facto* a king, chosen by God for the kingdom by means of the ritual act of unction, doubtless carried out by order of his co-regent and predecessor. By this act the *gratia Dei* through which royal power emanated was perpetuated in a hereditary form through the bloodline.

WITIZA, RODERIC AND THE END OF THE VISIGOTH KINGDOM

Information about the reign of Witiza (698/702–710) is scarce and the figure of this monarch is obscured by legendary stories from a later period, which attributed to him a reputation for lechery, through which he corrupted the bishops and the people and provoked the wrath of God. As had become usual amongst the later Visigothic kings, at the beginning of his reign, and on his own initiative, Witiza lifted the condemnations hanging over members of the Gothic nobility persecuted by his predecessor. According to the *Mozarabic Chronicle* he returned to them their dignities and lands. Those pardoned by Witiza and returned to royal favour were those who had participated in the rebellion of Sisbert. The action of Witiza in favour of nobility persecuted by his father probably took place during the Eighteenth Council of Toledo, held at the beginning of his reign, but from which no acts have been conserved.

The *Mozarabic Chronicle of 754* contains an obscure passage in which it says that in the year 701 Egica and Witiza left their palace, moving from place to place in Spain, as a result of a disaster or calamity previously mentioned by the chronicler. This information has been linked with the revolt of a certain Seniofred, who minted coins in Toledo in the last years of the seventh century. It is more likely that Seniofred jointly led the revolt of 693–694 with the bishop Sisbert, since its epicentre was Toledo, and the chronicler refers to the plague, the only general calamity recorded by him during the reign of Egica. According to the acts of the Seventeenth Council of Toledo the epidemic devastated the province of *Narbonensis* around 694 and it is likely that from here it extended south of the Pyrenees and that its devastating effects lasted into 701. A law about fugitive slaves, promulgated by Egica soon before his death at the end of 702, proves that the king had abandoned Toledo, as it is dated in the city of Córdoba.[34] The *Mozarabic Chronicle* gives some information about the brief joint reign of the two princes, that is, between 698 and 702. It narrates that the *comes* Teodemir victoriously repulsed an attack by the Byzantines which had come from the sea, information related to the struggles between Byzantines and Muslims in North Africa which led to the loss of Carthage in 698.

The end of Witiza's reign is not well understood since there is no explicit evidence about his death or about the circumstances that surrounded the succession. Sufficient is known, however, to affirm that it was difficult and not peaceful. The *Mozarabic Chronicle* claims that, while Witiza ascended the throne on the death of his father in conditions of complete tranquillity, Roderic's succession in 711 was accompanied by widespread disorder. We also know from Christian and Muslim sources that Witiza's children attempted to keep the kingdom along with the enormous landed fortune to which they were heirs. On the other hand the *Continuatio Soriensis* of the *Chronica Regum Visigothorum* includes two people following Witiza, Achila and Ardo, the first reigning for three years and the second for seven. Coins from Tarragona and

[34] *LV* IX.I.21.

Narbonne minted in Achila's name have encouraged speculation that he may have been a son of Witiza, but this identification does not fit in with the information that Witiza's family collaborated with the Muslims and readily accepted Islamic dominion. In the light of these indications there can be no doubt that the disappearance of Witiza at the head of the kingdom, presumably owing to natural causes, opened a period of civil war to which the *Mozarabic Chronicle* unequivocally alluded, in its comment about Roderic's tumultuous seizure of the kingdom and also in the comment that at the moment of the Muslim invasion the kingdom was submerged in a civil war, *intestino furore confligetur*.

It was in the context of intervention in this civil war that the Muslim invasion occurred. The intervention of foreign forces in order to support a pretender to the crown had occurred on other occasions, but this time it would have profound consequences for the Visigothic kingdom. The Arabs, who after expelling the Byzantines and conquering the Berber tribes during the last third of the seventh century had established themselves in north-western Africa, saw in the civil war the opportunity to invade the Peninsula. In July 710 a small incursion took place under the command of one Tarif and in the following spring Tariq ibn Ziyad, a freedman Berber client of Musa ibn Nusayr, governor of Ifriqiya, crossed to Spain with a large contingent of troops. The king of Toledo, Roderic, was fighting in the north against the Basques when he was informed of the disembarcation of the Muslim army, which was made up mainly of Berber troops from North Africa, and after reuniting his army he marched south. The definitive encounter took place, according to Muslim sources, in the *Wadi Lakka*, a toponym that has been identified with either the river Guadalete or the Barate, both in the province of Cádiz. There, according to the Mozarabic Chronicle, Roderic was betrayed by his troops who sided with his rival for the throne and the king was defeated and killed in the battle. As we have seen, the Visigothic army was largely composed of private retinues, from which its structural weakness derived, and which was used by the Islamic forces to their own advantage. The latter, according to the *Mozarabic Chronicle*, also killed Roderic's rivals.

Tariq then marched on Toledo, and occupied the royal city with, according to the *Mozarabic Chronicle*, the positive collaboration of the bishop of Seville Oppa, who was Witiza's brother. The role that the Chronicle attributes to Oppa is decisive, in keeping with the narrative's stress on the way in which the civil war had facilitated the Muslim victories. It is also a major argument in favour of showing that Witiza and his family were responsible for the arrival of the invaders, since he appears to have collaborated with them from the first. The rapid intervention against Toledo reveals that from early on, even from their disembarcation, the Muslims were attempting to seize the kingdom. The

Mozarabic Chronicle tells us that some of the nobility of the royal city were executed and that its bishop Sindered abandoned Toledo and the Peninsula, in order to flee to Rome. The execution of *nobiles viros* after the taking of the city, something that did not recur in the conquest of other cities, and the flight or exile of its metropolitan, have been understood as part of a strategy aimed at preventing the election of a new king capable of coordinating organised resistance. In this way the Islamic armies then had only to confront pockets of local resistance.[35]

As a result of the success of Tariq, the governor of Ifriqiya, Musa, arrived personally in the Peninsula with his son 'Abd al-'Aziz at the head of a new Arab and Berber army in the summer of 712. It remained until 714, when Musa and Tariq left the Peninsula and marched to Damascus, where Musa had been recalled by the caliph, leaving 'Abd al-'Aziz in charge of the troops and government of the Peninsula. By then only north-western regions of *Tarraconensis* and *Narbonensis* had escaped Islamic rule, and here Ardo had succeeded Achila, and reigned for seven years. A seven-year reign for Achila corresponds with the information in the Mozarabic Chronicle which says that Valí al-Hurr governed all Spain, both *citerior* and *ulterior,* between 716 and 719. This rapid conquest culminated in the occupation of *Narbonensis* between 721 and 725.

In conclusion, the end of the Visigothic monarchy was a consequence of diverse but related factors. One should cite in the first place the political factors, the most important of which was without doubt the strength of Islamic expansion. But to this must be added the civil war which followed the death of Witiza. The *fideles regum* had a great autonomy of action which belies the apparently centralized structure of the state. This meant that the invaders could reach concrete agreements with the *duces* and *comites* of the different provinces who, doubtless, were more interested in keeping their positions than in fighting for the defence of the kingdom of Toledo. Another factor in the disintegration may be revealed by Egica's law against fugitive slaves, a widespread problem which reflected hostility to the dominant social order and indifference to its political vicissitudes. This was true of slaves and doubtless also of the freedmen and free, especially the large numbers under patronage, whose close links of dependence imply their servility. Finally, the Jewish minority could not but view in a positive light whatever change of dominant politico-religious regime took place.[36]

[35] García Moreno (1989), p. 189.

[36] See Toch, chapter 20 below, for the view that there is no evidence for a large-scale Jewish presence in Spain at any time during the Visigothic period.

CHAPTER 14

FRANCIA IN THE SEVENTH CENTURY

Paul Fouracre

The main focus of the narrative history of Francia in the seventh century is its ruling dynasty, the Merovingians. This is because the precious few Franks who commented upon what was happening around them were primarily interested in a tiny social elite which participated in the exercise of power through the medium of the royal palace. Hardly less for modern commentators, the doings of kings, and of queens, and the arrangement of power in and out of the palace, have become the necessary principles around which we must organise our understanding of events. The very chronology of the period is determined according to which king ruled where, and for how long. The Merovingians themselves have a poor reputation – they are notorious as 'the do-nothing kings' – and given the nature of our sources, this has had the effect of dragging the seventh century down with them. In the most pessimistic view, its main redeeming feature was that it also saw the rise of the family which would form a new ruling dynasty, namely the Carolingians. The 'decline of the Merovingians and the rise of the Carolingians' has thus often been the keynote for studies of seventh-century Francia. But the beginning of the transition from the one dynasty to the other is by no means the most significant feature of seventh-century history. Far more important is that this period saw the maturing of a political culture that would outlast both Merovingians and Carolingians and spread well beyond Francia itself. With a gradual disappearance of direct taxation and with the enlargement of territory under a single ruler, the seventh century saw the development of a regime which was formed out of consensus between the different groups of the powerful in society. It is the power-sharing needed to address a broad coalition of interests which appears from a Carolingian perspective as simply the loss of power by incompetent Merovingians. Two early ninth-century sources in particular, the *Prior Metz Annals* and Einhard's *Life of Charlemagne*, have conditioned our view of the history of this period.[1] Indeed, the durability of that view is lasting tribute to the skill with which the authors of these works justified the Carolingians' seizure of the throne in the year 751. What they described was a Merovingian failure so complete that intervention by the Carolingians was an urgent moral necessity.

Einhard's account of the last Merovingians is compelling, but ultimately misleading. Their energy had gone, he tells us, and they no longer enjoyed the use of their once extensive lands: all that was left to them was a single *villa* and their long hair, the symbol of their former potency. Their eventual successors, the altogether more vigorous ancestors of Charlemagne, treated their nominal overlords the Merovingians with respect and enabled them to carry on with their ceremonial duties which, rather ludicrously, they discharged from an oxcart.[2] No modern historian would seriously dispute that Einhard was highly partisan in his writing, that he displayed ignorance of Merovingian ceremonial and that his account was plainly second- or third-hand. It is nevertheless with his end in sight that many of the truly Merovingian sources have often been read. Superficially, they may seem to confirm Einhard's observations, or, rather, he theirs. At the other end of our period, Gregory of Tours' rather pessimistic view of the progress of the Franks across the sixth century primes us to expect further decline in the seventh.[3] At first sight a comparison between Gregory's fluent history and the guttural and piecemeal narratives of the seventh- and eighth-century chronicles seem to bear out a notion of decline. But we must be careful not to read too much into what is ultimately a literary comparison.

For the basic account of seventh- and early eighth-century history we must rely on the chronicles just alluded to, namely the *Fourth Book of the Chronicle of Fredegar* (referred to simply as *Fredegar*), which takes us up to the year 642 but which was composed or compiled about two decades later, and the *Liber Historiae Francorum* which goes up to 727, when its author signed off.[4] The *Liber Historiae Francorum* was also the basis of Carolingian-inspired *Continuations of Fredegar* which in their first section follow the *Liber* from the mid-seventh into the early eighth century. To supplement the chronicles' rather meagre coverage of events we can also draw upon the numerous saints' Lives written either in the Merovingian period itself or not long after. In fact these Lives are

[1] *Annales Mettenses Priores*, pp. 1–19, first section trans. with commentary, in Fouracre and Gerberding (1996), pp. 330–70; Einhard, *Vita Karoli* 1, c.1, trans. Dutton (1999), pp. 16–17.

[2] Einhard, *Vita Karoli* 1, c.1, Dutton (1999), pp. 16–17.

[3] *Gregorii Episcopi Turonensis, Decem Libri Historiarum*. On Gregory's view of history, Goffart (1988), pp. 112–234, and Heinzelmann (1994), pp. 136–67.

[4] *The Fourth Book of the Chronicle of Fredegar*, cc.20–90, pp. 13–79. On the Chronicle, and its *Continuations*, Collins (1996); *Liber Historiae Francorum*, cc.37–53, pp. 306–28; cc.43–53, trans. with commentary, Fouracre and Gerberding (1996), pp. 79–96. See also Gerberding (1987).

so numerous that they fill no less than five weighty tomes of the *Monumenta Germaniae Historica* series.[5] One collection of letters has also survived, as well as a few other individual letters.[6] Only one piece of secular legislation survives from the seventh century (from the year 614), but there are the records of up to ten church councils.[7] Then there are approximately 200 charters relating to the period, thirty-seven of which have survived as originals.[8] To this list we can add the models of charters provided in the *Formulary of Marculf*[9] and note, finally, the additional information supplied by writers outside Francia: Eddius Stephanus and Bede from England, Julian of Toledo from Spain, and Paul the Deacon from Italy.[10] As we have seen, this corpus of material may be read for signs of progressive Merovingian decline in the light of the dynasty's eventual demise. Alternatively one can steer away from the question of the 'decline of the Merovingians and the rise of the Carolingians' in order to look at the seventh century in its own terms. To do this, let us begin at the start of the seventh century with the unification of Francia under a single ruler, which lengthened the distance between ruler and ruled and made necessary the development of political consensus.

In 613 Theuderic, king of Burgundy, attacked his brother Theudebert, king of Austrasia, in revenge for a raid the latter had made upon Alsace three years earlier. Theuderic defeated Theudebert in a fierce battle at Zülpich and captured his treasure at nearby Cologne. He first imprisoned and then assassinated his defeated brother, killing the latter's young son too. Theuderic then turned on his uncle, Chlothar king of Neustria, but died before an attack could be mounted. Chlothar, taking advantage of the death of his Merovingian rivals, now moved into Burgundy and captured Theuderic's grandmother Brunehild and three of her great-grandsons. Chlothar had Brunehild, with whom he had been in feud all his life, tortured to death and he also killed two of the great-grandsons. The effect of such carnage was to leave Chlothar II king of all the three kingdoms which made up Francia. On the face of it, Chlothar was rather an unlikely winner. Only a few years earlier his very survival as king of Neustria had been in the balance when his nephews Theuderic and Theudebert combined against him. In 613 he was transformed from underdog to overlord more by chance than by conquest, and what allowed chance to work in his favour

[5] *MGH SRM* III–VII. [6] *Epistolae S. Desiderii Cadurcensis.*

[7] *Clotharii II Edictum*, *MGH Cap.* I, pp. 20–3; *Concilia Galliae 511–695*, pp. 273–326.

[8] *ChLA* 13, 14 for the original charters. *Diplomata, chartae, epistolae. Leges, aliaque instrumenta ad res Gallo-Francicas spectantia*, ed. J. Pardessus for all charters. The royal charters are newly edited in *MGH Diplomata Regum Francorum.*

[9] *Marculfi Formularum Libri Duo.*

[10] *The Life of Bishop Wilfrid* by Eddius Stephanus; Bede, *Ecclesiastical History of the English People*; Julian of Toledo, *Historia Wambae*; Paul the Deacon, *Historia Langobardorum.*

like this was the Franks' phenomenal attachment to Merovingian kingship: in Austrasia and Burgundy a Merovingian from Neustria was preferable to no Merovingian at all.

According to the *Chronicle of Fredegar*, Chlothar took control of both Burgundy and Austrasia by agreement with the magnates of each kingdom.[11] This observation has led many historians to judge that Chlothar was as a result dependent upon such men and that it was in return for their help against Brunehild and the sons of Theuderic that in 614 in the *Edict of Paris* he legislated to guarantee their positions, that is, to make them effectively hereditary. The *Edict of Paris* is thus often said to have marked a turning point in the fortunes of the Merovingians: thereafter they would be shackled by a concession which enshrined aristocratic independence. This reading of *Fredegar* and of the *Edict* is not very helpful for it is more concerned with what would eventually become of the Merovingians than with what was actually happening in 613–614. It seems in fact that the invitations to Chlothar to become king of Austrasia and of Burgundy were the product of factional politics, that is, any agreement was between Chlothar and particular magnates opposed to Brunehild rather than between king and aristocracy in general. Secondly, it is clear that the *Edict of Paris* did not actually guarantee the positions of the magnates in the way that it is commonly supposed to have done. The *Edict* contains twenty-four chapters (*capitularia*), but one clause from chapter 12 is usually quoted out of context. It says that counts (*iudices*) should henceforth come from the areas in which they were to hold office.[12] At first sight this statement appears positively to encourage what other states generally tried to prevent: the loss of control over officials who put down roots in the provinces and espoused the interests of the locality rather than of central government. The rest of chapter 12, however, makes it clear that the reason why counts should be local people with hereditary lands in the area of their command was that it would then be possible to control their actions by distraining their property. Far from being a novel concession of principle, this idea harks back to sixth-century legislation which spells out that what was at stake here was the potential for the count to abuse his own powers of distraint by unjustly seizing the property of others. Were he to do this, the remedy was to take his property in return.[13]

The manner of Chlothar II's acquisition of Burgundy and Austrasia, and the legislation he issued shortly afterwards, cannot therefore be taken to show that Merovingian kingship had entered a phase of terminal decline. The Merovingians would survive for another 137 years after the *Edict of Paris*, and

[11] Fredegar, *chron.* IV.40–2, pp. 32–6.

[12] *Chlotharii Edictum* c.12, *MGH Cap.* I, p. 32: 'Ut nullus iudex de aliis provinciis aut regionibus in alia loca ordinetur.'

[13] *Edictus Chilperici* c.8, *MGH Cap.* I, pp. 9–10.

if anything the events of 613–614 help us understand why the dynasty lasted so long, rather than why it eventually came to an end. For they cast light on two essential characteristics of the later Merovingian polity: first, they reveal the way in which rivalry within the aristocracy tended to be expressed through attempts to win influence in the royal palace, and second, they illuminate how the collection of institutions and persons exercising public powers perceived to be derived from royal authority (the 'state', in other words) had a measure of support at local level when and where it was able to guarantee and legitimise property relations. Both of these forces pulled people into political activity around the kings rather more than they pushed people out into defiance and self-help.

Chlothar was descended from the kings of Soissons and all subsequent Merovingians were his direct descendants. The area to the north of Paris towards Soissons thus became the special homeland of the dynasty, and the monastery of St Denis, 12 kilometres to the north of Paris, was built up in the early seventh century as the premier royal monastery. Royal movement outside this area appears to become rare as the seventh century progresses. After 613 Burgundy never again had a king of its own. Austrasia, which *Fredegar* tells us was equal to Neustria-Burgundy in size and population, was ruled by the Neustrian king from 613 to 622, from 628 to 632, possibly from 656 to 662 and from 679 onwards. At other times there was a separate kingdom of Austrasia, but no Austrasian dynasty ever developed beyond two generations. This latter failure is not surprising given the restriction of royalty to the descendants of a single person after 613. For the rest of the seventh century biological accident and three cases of assassination would together make the descendants of Chlothar a very select group. It was only a matter of time, therefore, before the only available Merovingians would be children. What made child kingship possible was the development of government through palaces in fixed centres to which magnates were prepared to travel, even from distant regions. It was in the reigns of Chlothar and of his son Dagobert (d. 638) that leaders from all the regions of Francia became accustomed to attending the Neustrian palace. What would spell trouble for the future was a growing resentment at the privilege which proximity to the king conferred upon the Neustrians and the related tendency of the magnates to feud when they met up at the palace.

Chlothar began by exercising control in Burgundy and Austrasia through the palaces in these kingdoms. The key figures in these now kingless palaces were the 'mayors of the palace', Warnachar in Burgundy and Rado in Austrasia. The 'mayor of the palace' was the most important non-royal leader in the land. His influence came from his position as broker between king and magnates, and his rising power in the seventh century reflects the growing concentration of political activity in the royal palace. In 622, however, Chlothar made his son Dagobert king in Austrasia. If what happened ten years later is anything to go by, it may be that in 622 the Austrasians demanded a king of their own partly to free themselves from dependence on the Neustrians and partly to strengthen their position in the face of pressure from peoples on their eastern border. In 626 Warnachar, mayor of Burgundy, died and according to *Fredegar* the Burgundian leaders asked Chlothar not to appoint a successor, but to deal direct with them. Thereafter the Burgundians attended the Neustrian palace, for example travelling to a meeting which took place at Clichy near Paris the next year. *Fredegar*'s report of this meeting is of great interest.[14] It shows the deliberative nature of the annual assemblies of king and magnates, gatherings which Einhard parodied, but which would be no less important to the Carolingians than they were to the Merovingians. The account also shows how a gathering of leaders, each accompanied by a military following, could erupt into violence, but how the king was able to keep the peace between the different factions of magnates. Successful government meant drawing strength from the dynamic of inter-magnate rivalry without letting the infighting get out of hand.

When Chlothar died in 628, Dagobert his son took his place in Neustria and Burgundy, creating a sub-kingdom south of the Loire for a half-brother, Charibert. But within three years Charibert was dead. Dagobert, it was said, then had Charibert's young son killed, the southern kingdom came to an end, and the Merovingian family was again pruned back to a single stem. Following Chlothar's death Dagobert had visited Burgundy to make his presence as king felt there. He established his authority by doing what early medieval kings did best: by dispensing justice. The next year he made a tour of Austrasia, but after that, as *Fredegar* tells us in a strongly disapproving tone, he set up permanent home in Neustria. Because of this flurry of activity in 628–629, Dagobert has been remembered as a king constantly on the move, a truly vigorous ruler. But once he had taken up residence in Neustria, there is no record of him moving again apart from three forays into Austrasia, two to lead military campaigns against the Wends in 630 and 631, and another to install his son Sigibert as king of Austrasia in 632. Whereas the Burgundians seem to have been content to share a king with the Neustrians, the Austrasians were clearly not happy to do so. According to *Fredegar*, they were demoralised when Dagobert preferred to reside in Neustria rather than Austrasia, and as a result they made a poor showing in standing up to Wendish pressure on their eastern frontier. Once they had again acquired a king of their own they rallied their defences and fought bravely. This suggests that it was necessary to have a king, even an infant king like the two-year-old Sigibert, in order to raise effective armies.

[14] Fredegar, *Chron.* IV.55, p. 46.

Later evidence suggests that the enforcement of military obligations was by royal order. From a reading of *Fredegar* it seems that another important factor was royal largesse. When Dagobert established Sigibert in Austrasia he handed over to him 'the treasure that he needed'.[15] The prospect of reward from this source must have made people keener to fight. Lastly, the setting up of a new palace in Austrasia allowed certain leaders there to maintain their pre-eminence through a palace-based structure of government. Austrasia's military recovery after Sigibert's arrival may thus have been due as much to the reinforcement of a hierarchy amongst the aristocracy of the region as to a general boost in morale.

Amongst those who benefited from the return of a king to Austrasia was Pippin of Landen (also known as Pippin I) who eventually emerged as mayor of the palace to Sigibert, just as he had once been mayor to Dagobert when he had had a palace in Austrasia. A faction led by Pippin and Arnulf bishop of Metz had originally consolidated their predominance in connection with Chlothar's move into Austrasia in 613. Pippin seems to have faced opposition from his fellow Austrasians in the period between Dagobert's departure for Neustria and Sigibert's arrival in Austrasia. Somehow the latter's installation as king allowed Pippin's faction to re-establish their leading position. It is, however, almost impossible to see what was really happening in the internal politics of Austrasia at this time, and it is extremely difficult to gauge the relative importance of Pippin and his family without being affected by the knowledge that that family would eventually replace the Merovingians as rulers of all of Francia.

Under Chlothar and Dagobert Francia remained strong and able to prevent neighbouring peoples encroaching upon its territory. To the east of the Rhine the Franks retained influence over the Saxons, Thuringians, Alamans and Bavarians. The *Liber Historiae Francorum* has a long and dramatic story about Chlothar and Dagobert together fighting the Saxons near the River Weser, but the author seems to have confused the second with the first Chlothar (d. 561) who did fight the Saxons and made them pay tribute, which they did until Dagobert excused them from payment in return for military service.[16] The Thuringians and Alamans were led by Frankish dukes, and Dagobert was able to get the Bavarians to obey his orders. *Fredegar* implies that the lands of all of these peoples were regarded as Frankish territory, at least in relation to the defence of Francia against the Slavonic Wends and the Asiatic Avars.

Throughout the sixth century Slavonic groups had been settling in what is now termed central Europe as far west as the River Elbe in the north and

[15] Fredegar, *Chron.* IV.75, p. 63: 'Tinsaurum quod suffecerit filium tradens.'

[16] *Liber Historiae Francorum* c.41, pp. 311–14.

the confluence of the rivers Ens and Danube in Lower Austria to the south.[17] At the end of the sixth century the Avars, who were a nomadic people from Central Asia, erupted into Pannonia (present-day Hungary) and subjugated all the Slavs around them. The effect of this was to accelerate the coalescence of formerly disparate groups of Slavs into large political and military units, and the first fruit of such development was a revolt against Avar control in the 620s. According to the *Chronicle of Fredegar*, which is the only source for these events, it was actually a Neustrian Frank called Samo who in 623 became leader of a newly formed Slavonic kingdom based probably in Bohemia to the north of the Avars.[18] Under Samo the Slavs, or Wends, raided deep into Frankish territory. How deep it is impossible to tell. Thuringia certainly suffered, and *Fredegar* talks of the Austrasians defending 'their frontier', but when Dagobert attacked the Wends in 630 they took refuge in a place called Wogastisburg which seems to have been well to the east, in Bohemia itself. A fair impression might be therefore of a Slavonic kingdom in Bohemia which on occasion raided deep into Thuringia, but of one which was prevented from actually shifting the Slav–German border further westwards. When the *Chronicle of Fredegar* comes to an end in the mid-seventh century we hear almost nothing more of affairs in this eastern borderland. When we do begin to hear more at the end of the eighth century, the border situation does not seem to have altered very much in the intervening period.

To the south, the Franks' neighbours were the Lombards, the Visigoths and the Basques, and to the west the Bretons. From the time of their establishment in Italy in the late sixth century the Lombards appear to have been tributaries of the Franks, paying them 12,000 *solidi* a year up to 617, when they were released from this burden upon payment of a lump sum. As the payment of tribute suggests, the Lombards acknowledged the superior military power of the Franks, and the latter intervened in Lombard affairs on several occasions in the seventh century. Their particular concern, according to *Fredegar*, was the treatment of Queen Gundeberga, daughter of Theudelinda who had been of Frankish, possibly even Merovingian, stock and had married the Lombard kings Ago and Agilulf.[19] In the next generation and after the death of her brother in 626, Lombard royalty was firmly attached to Gundeberga. Marriage to her provided a route to the throne, and not surprisingly her two royal husbands each tried to dispose of her once they had ascended it. On both occasions (in 629 and in 641) Gundeberga was released from incarceration after strong Frankish protests. It is possible that her vicissitudes also reflect Lombard

[17] For the development of Slav cultures and territories, see Kobyliński, chapter 19 below.

[18] Fredegar, *Chron.* IV.48, pp. 39–40.

[19] Gundeberga is the main subject of three chapters: Fredegar, *Chron.* IV.51, 70, 72, pp. 41–3, 59–60.

attempts to throw off Frankish tutelage in the light of their growing security in Italy. By 663 they were able to defeat the Franks in Provence, although Paul the Deacon's account of this victory suggests that it was won against the odds, through superior guile rather than by the stronger force.[20]

The Visigoths too were wary of the Franks. In this period they managed to hold on to their Gallic enclave of Septimania, but in 630 they were unable to resist an army raised in Burgundy and sent to support Sisenand in his bid for the throne. *Fredegar* says that the Franks intervened in Spain for purely mercenary reasons, Dagobert having been promised a famous golden dish by Sisenand. In the event the Visigoths refused to hand it over and the Franks received the enormous sum of 200,000 gold *solidi* instead.[21] There is some reason to doubt the story about the dish, but for a significant injection of gold into the Frankish economy at this moment there is some numismatic evidence.[22] At the western end of the Pyrenees the Franks faced the Basques. From the later sixth century onwards there are signs of the Basques pressing northward into Francia as well as south into the Ebro valley. Dagobert's half-brother Charibert is said to have subdued them in 631 from his base in Toulouse, which appears to have been the main Frankish stronghold in the area in the seventh century, as it had been since Clovis garrisoned it against the Goths in the early sixth century. In 635, however, the Basques were again raiding into what had been Charibert's kingdom, and so Dagobert raised another Burgundian army which drove them back into the mountains and forced their leaders to agree to present themselves before the Frankish king. But in an episode which prefigures Roland's legendary disaster at Roncesvalles, a part of the returning army was ambushed and destroyed in a Pyrenean valley.

Having mobilised an army to deal with the Basques, Dagobert was able to use the threat of the same force to wring concessions out of the Bretons, forcing them 'to make swift amends for what they had done wrong and to submit to his power'.[23] One can only guess at what lay behind this episode, for we know next to nothing about Frankish–Breton relations in the seventh century, but from *Fredegar's* account it seems to have involved the Bretons not recognising Frankish overlordship and seizing the property of Franks. By analogy with events in the later sixth century, this could have meant Breton raids into the lands around Nantes and Rennes. In contrast with the sixth-century clashes, Breton submission in 636 came before the dispatch of a Frankish army and the Breton leader Judicael came to Clichy to submit to Dagobert. The next year the Basque leaders too came to Clichy and formally submitted.

[20] Paul the Deacon, *HL* v.5, pp. 185–6. [21] Fredegar, *Chron.* IV.73, pp. 61–2. [22] Kent (1972).

[23] Fredegar, *Chron.* IV.78, pp. 65–6: 'Dagobertus ad Clippiaco resedens mittit nuncius in Brittania que Brittones male admiserant veluciter emendarint et dicione suae se traderint.'

From the pages of *Fredegar* it is clear that Dagobert enjoyed an awesome reputation. Historians have generally seen him as the last Merovingian king who was fully in control of Francia, the last to lead from the front, an 'army-king' (*Heerkönig*) who made his kingdom the scourge of its neighbours. But the assumption that Frankish power went into decline after Dagobert requires some qualification. First we must remember that it is overwhelmingly based on a reading of *Fredegar*. The author of this work was very interested not only in the dynastic politics of the Franks' immediate neighbours, but also in Byzantine affairs. 'Foreign relations' thus figure prominently in his narrative. When his coverage ends in 642 we are forced to rely upon the *Liber Historiae Francorum*, a source with much lower horizons, which, for instance, never mentions Italy or Spain. It might be possible to infer from this silence that after the mid-seventh century the influence of the Franks over their neighbours was indeed on the wane, and that control over the borderlands had been lost. Against this, however, we have Paul the Deacon's sense that the Franks were still to be feared in the 660s and we also have a detailed account from the contemporary Julian of Toledo about Frankish intervention in Septimania in 673.[24] As we shall see, at this latter date conflict at the heart of the kingdom makes outward pressure on its borders appear quite surprising. One of the features of Julian's fascinating account might explain that pressure: in a civil war in Visigothic Septimania there were Frankish warriors fighting on both sides, plus the intervention by a Frankish army from across the border. In the later seventh century, it seems, Francia had something of a surplus of warriors and at least in this regard it had not 'declined' since the death of Dagobert. Indeed, taken across the Merovingian period as a whole, Francia's borders and its strength relative to its neighbours changed remarkably little, whatever the fortunes of its kings. We should bear this in mind when evaluating Dagobert's successes. Secondly, we should qualify the image of Dagobert as an 'army-king' by noting that in 630 and in 635 he remained in Neustria whilst armies raised in Burgundy fought on his behalf against the Visigoths and the Basques. Here military organisation reflected the political structure of the kingdom in that leadership was in the hands of dukes and counts who brought their own power to bear on behalf of the state as much as they were serving officers of the crown. On this reading, Dagobert's 'success' lay rather less in constant movement than it did in astute palace-based management. It was the willingness of the magnates to co-operate with the palace which enabled Dagobert in 638 to pass on his kingdoms to two sons aged but about eight and five years old.

The phenomenon of Merovingian child kingship has been often denigrated, but rarely explained. The co-operation between the palace and the wider

[24] *Historia Wambae* cc. 11–29, pp. 510–25.

magnate community which made child kingship possible may perhaps best be understood in sociological terms as a result of the formation of a highly integrated power elite. The palace played a key role in the process of integration, for not only were many magnates educated there from childhood, it also helped form the public identity of those who buttressed their personal power with royal office. The public association of leaders from different regions stimulated the development of a political culture which accommodated a variety of traditions within a fairly elastic notion of custom. What was customary in a legal sense, for instance, included both the use of written law texts of Roman provenance and ritual procedures of more uncertain origin.[25] Such flexibility was necessary to enable negotiation between people from different cultural backgrounds, and what emerged out of it was a common notion of power justified by legal right. Hence the strong emphasis on the judicial process which features in contemporary accounts of political behaviour. Political culture thus had a marked pragmatic element, and being relatively literate, it made extensive use of documents both in government and to protect property. Here again the elite were drawn to the palace which had preserved bureaucratic skills and produced documents which were underpinned by royal authority. Force too played a part in the formation of a single political community, for individual magnates rarely dared stand apart from the collective power which could be mobilised when all of the chief leaders gathered together.

There was an important socio-religious aspect to the process of integration too. The seventh century saw a marked rise in religious activity as Christian culture overflowed from its traditional urban strongholds to penetrate deep into the countryside. The elite shared in this activity by founding monasteries on their lands. At the same time, they came increasingly to occupy leading positions in the ecclesiastical hierarchy. In this way, participation in a common enterprise throughout Francia fostered a religious identity which could override ethnic and regional differences. As royal assent seems to have remained essential to episcopal appointments, and as the Merovingians themselves were leading patrons of the monasteries, the palace provided access to spiritual as well as to earthly prestige, and it thus helped to sanctify, as well as to legitimate, aristocratic power. The key to understanding Merovingian child kingship is the observation that these trends were self-reinforcing. The elite would not easily disintegrate during periods of infant rule. As long as the magnates remained solidly behind the principle of Merovingian authority, upon which their own legitimacy as rulers ultimately depended, regent queens or mayors could govern through the palace in the name of child kings.

25 Cf. Fouracre (1986), pp. 40–3.

The foundation of monasteries is the best-recorded sign of a growing church in the seventh century. Traditionally the upsurge in foundations has been ascribed to the influence of the Irish holy-man Columbanus who founded the monastery of Luxeuil in Burgundy. Expelled from Burgundy in 610 by Brunehild and Theuderic, Columbanus travelled through Neustria and Austrasia before founding the monastery of Bobbio in Italy, where he died in 615. According to one recent writer, 'the list of aristocrats influenced by Columbanus reads like a *Who's Who* of the Frankish aristocracy'.[26] His influence on them was twofold. First he inspired people to found monasteries in areas well away from the traditional centres of monasticism in the Gallo-Roman south, and second he introduced a novel form of monasticism which insisted on the independence of the monastery from the local bishop. Plainly, this double novelty was attractive to the Frankish aristocracy, and from the period from 637 to the late 660s there survives a series of nine charters in which bishops granted independence in Columbanan tradition to monasteries both new and old. Historians have found this Columbanan or 'Iro-Frankish' monastic movement equally attractive.[27] It has been possible to show how the great families of north and east Francia entered into the religious arena and acquired spiritual prestige, for in time monastic founders very often turned into the patron saints of successful establishments. Merovingian political behaviour can also be explained with reference to this new form of monasticism, for rulers used the Columbanan notion of monastic independence to cut the claws of overweening members of the episcopate in what has been termed a veritable *Klosterpolitik* (monastic policy).

The novelty and central importance of Columbanan monasticism has nevertheless been questioned.[28] The notion of a well-defined movement with a common monastic rule now seems to come from the way in which the charters granting monastic privileges established a common terminology rather than from any evidence of actual practice. Columbanus' importance, moreover, appears to have been exaggerated thanks to a persuasive biographer, Jonas of Bobbio. In fact, mid-seventh-century Francia saw other Irishmen who set up monasteries and influenced nobles. There were, in effect, not one but many Iro-Frankish movements. In addition, monasteries claimed to adhere to a bewildering variety of rules, perhaps in effect naming famous abbots (Columbanus amongst them) rather than indicating that they were living according to the rules named after these people. Nor was there a simple opposition between new foundations and old episcopal centres, but a great complexity of relationships

[26] Geary (1988), p. 172.

[27] The seminal work on Frankish monasticism of this period is Prinz (1965).

[28] Wood (1981) sets the parameters for a critique of traditional views of Columbanan monasticism.

which depended upon local circumstances. Audoin, bishop of Rouen 641–684, for instance, secured for his foundation at Rebais the first surviving charter of independence from episcopal control, but in his own work as bishop he seems to have interfered at will in the monasteries of his diocese. Similarly, the founding of new monasteries in the countryside did not mean that the urban and suburban monastic traditions came to an end. These qualifications serve to show that whilst Columbanan monasticism does indeed stand out because it is well documented, it was part of a much wider spread of Christian culture from the town to the countryside to meet the needs of the rural population, beginning with their lords. But at village level the process of Christianisation was slow, for besides continuing complaints about the persistence of pagan customs, the archaeological record suggests that in many rural communities cemeteries were not organised along Christian lines until at least the later seventh century. With Christianisation also came a reorganisation of settlements around a lord's hall and church. Again, in many areas, this pattern was still unfolding in the later seventh century.[29]

The influence of Christian culture on political activity is reflected in the careers of those who in their youth spent time at the royal palace and then in later life became bishops, or founded monasteries or even became monks themselves. In the mid to later seventh century much of Francia was run by people schooled in this fashion through the courts of Chlothar II, Dagobert and his son, Clovis II. The letters and 'Life' of one of them, Desiderius, bishop of Cahors 630–655, gives some insight into the feeling of fellowship amongst this powerful old-boy network. In a well-known letter to Audoin bishop of Rouen, Desiderius recalled his circle of friends at court.[30] The group included Desiderius and his two brothers, Audoin, Eligius who became bishop of Noyon, Paul the later bishop of Verdun, and Sulpicius who became bishop of Bourges. It is striking that this group and the wider circle of Desiderius' correspondents were made up of men of both Gallo-Roman and Frankish stock who occupied important positions in Aquitaine, Neustria and Austrasia. That the court had initially brought them together, and that they kept in contact with one another thereafter, is strong testimony to the integrative force of palace and religion. Here, because we are so much better informed about the church, we must use the bishops to cast light on the magnates in general.

The *Life of Desiderius* shows the bishop controlling Cahors, maintaining both its public services and its defences.[31] Most of the eighteen or so 'Lives' of other seventh-century bishops show them acting in a similarly public manner,

[29] Fouracre (2000), pp. 126–9, for a general discussion of this process; Theuws (1991) for a detailed examination of the effects of Christianisation on the ground.

[30] *Epistolae S. Desiderii Cadurcensis* I, no. II, pp. 30–1.

[31] *Vita Desiderii Cadurcensis* cc.16–17, pp. 574–6.

in effect combining the work of bishop and count. But on whose behalf were these lordly churchmen acting? This important question has been answered in two contrasting ways which express two very different views of seventh-century history. For if it is thought that such bishops were acting independently in what have been termed virtual 'episcopal republics', then the conclusion must be that the Merovingian state had by the mid-seventh century lost control of much of its territory.[32] If, on the other hand, one believes that the bishops were acting on behalf of the state, it is possible to argue that the latter was at this time rather strong.[33] A third more equivocal answer actually makes better sense of the evidence: namely, that bishops, like the counts their secular counterparts, wielded a wide range of powers derived from royal authority, but political considerations at both local and central levels dictated how they should exercise those powers. To be independent, bishops, and other magnates in formal positions of power, had to be free of local rivals who could seek support from the palace and mobilise the collective power of the magnate community against them.[34] As we see it in saints' Lives, such mobilisation might be achieved through a formal judicial process. For this to happen, the palace had to be at the centre of political activity and the magnates willing to back the judicial process. For most of the seventh century in most areas of Francia these conditions prevailed. Lords, both secular and ecclesiastical, usually did have rivals, and as a result the bishops on the whole acted to extend rather than to shorten the range of central authority. The history of Francia from the death of Dagobert to the advent of Charles Martel in the early eighth century is effectively about the political tensions which built up until these conditions were altered and about how the regime attempted to repair itself. It is to this history that we now turn.

Dagobert died on 19 January 638. His son, Sigibert III, aged about eight, continued to rule in Austrasia under the guidance of the mayor of the palace, Pippin, and Chunibert, bishop of Cologne. In Neustria and Burgundy Dagobert was succeeded by his son Clovis, aged about four, with his mother Nantechild and the mayor Aega ruling through the palace. What little we know about Nantechild suggests that she was a powerful ruler, like Brunehild, Balthild and Himnechild, three of the four other seventh-century dowager queen-regents. Their power parallels that of the mayors in that it rested in that influence over the political community which came from management of the palace and from government in the name of the king. Nantechild in addition received as much of Dagobert's treasure as his sons. In 641 she can be seen channelling a feud which broke out at court at Augers, in rather the same way that Chlothar II had

[32] For this view of bishops' rule in the towns, Prinz (1974).

[33] See, for instance, the argument of Durliat (1979).

[34] Cf. Fouracre (1990), pp. 32–3.

contained the infighting at Clichy in 627, and when Aega died, also in 641, her ally Erchinoald became mayor in his place. Nantechild and Erchinoald then resurrected the Burgundian mayoralty, raising one Flaochad to the dignity, and Flaochad married Nantechild's niece. But not long after this Nantechild died and a simmering feud between Flaochad and Willebad the 'patrician' (i.e. ruler) of South Burgundy erupted into fighting between the two factions of magnates. King Clovis II, now about eight years old, could not restrain the violence. Willebad was killed and Flaochad died soon after. What happened next is unknown, for the *Chronicle of Fredegar* ends at this point, but when information starts to flow again about a decade later, it is clear that the magnates from Burgundy and Neustria continued to form a single political community and to attend the same meetings. The 'Flaochad affair' might thus have had few consequences despite the fact that *Fredegar* devoted more space to this than to any other seventh-century event, apart from the story of Columbanus' disagreement with Theuderic and Brunehild.

In Austrasia, Pippin died about a year after Dagobert and was succeeded as mayor of the palace by one Otto, although *Fredegar* makes it clear that Pippin's son Grimoald expected to follow his father and plotted with Chunibert of Cologne to this end. Two years later in 641, Otto was murdered and Grimoald replaced him. Meanwhile, events in Thuringia give a good example of conditions in which a leader did turn his back on the rest of the magnate community, being able to withstand the collective pressure they mounted against him. As a result he took a whole region out of the Merovingian orbit. This was the case of Radulf the duke of Thuringia who in 639 revolted against Sigibert. Radulf had been made duke by Dagobert and did his job of defending Thuringia against the Wends rather well, but this also meant that he acquired the military power to defend himself, which in turn enabled him to reject Sigibert's authority, possibly because of disagreement with another duke, Adalgisel. The Austrasians could now only respond with force and gathered an army to attack Radulf. The latter won the battle which followed, and thereafter he exercised independent authority, securing his position by allying with the Wends. Even so, Radulf did not create a separate kingdom nor, according to *Fredegar*, did he actually deny Merovingian overlordship.[35] This style of secession would be seen many more times in both Merovingian and Carolingian periods as particular leaders or regions went their own way without, it seems, being able to envisage the formation of completely new political entities. Such conservatism, which is another mark of the high degree of integration amongst the elite, goes a long way to explain the long-term territorial stability of Francia.

[35] The Radulf story is related in Fredegar, *Chron.* IV.77, 87, pp. 64–5, 73–4.

On events in the next decade we are singularly ill-informed, though a guess sensible to the hagiography and letter writing which refer to the period would be that it was generally a time of peace. Sigibert came of age in about 645 and Clovis in about 649. Both kings married women who outlived them by more than twenty years and were important as dowagers. Clovis married an Anglo-Saxon, Balthild, who became the subject of a saint's Life.[36] Balthild was said to have been a slave who served in Erchinoald's household, refused the latter's sexual advances and triumphed by marrying the king. Hers may not, however, have been a simple 'rags to riches' story for she may have been of the Anglo-Saxon nobility, or even a princess, rather than a simple slave. Her husband Clovis died in 657, and was the subject of a damning obituary in the *Liber Historiae Francorum* which hinted that he met a violent end.[37] Balthild was left as regent for the eight-year-old Chlothar III, eldest of her three sons. Sigibert married a woman called Himnechild. It seems likely that she was not the mother of Sigibert's son, Dagobert, but she did eventually become regent for her son-in-law, Balthild's third-born, Childeric, who married her daughter Bilichild. The context for the marriage and the insertion of a Neustrian king into Austrasia is what has come to be known as 'the Grimoald coup'. This event has excited a great deal of attention, for it concerns what looks at a glance like an early Carolingian attempt to seize the throne from the Merovingians.[38]

When King Sigibert died he left a young son, Dagobert. But instead of arranging for Dagobert to become king, Grimoald the mayor of the palace seized and tonsured him, handing him over to the bishop of Poitiers who conducted Dagobert into exile in Ireland. Grimoald then elevated his own son to the throne. This king, given the Merovingian name Childebert, and said to have been adopted by Sigibert, ruled for up to five years until there was in turn a coup against Grimoald. What happened to Childebert is unknown, but Grimoald fell into Neustrian hands and suffered a painful death in Paris. In 662 Balthild's youngest son Childeric was betrothed to Bilichild and made king of Austrasia with one Wulfoald as mayor of the palace, and with Himnechild as queen-regent. Behind this apparently straightforward story there are complex chronological problems, not least because the only source to give a coherent narrative, the *Liber Historiae Francorum*, has Clovis II preside over Grimoald's demise, which puts the latter at a date before autumn 657, whereas Childeric's accession in Austrasia cannot have happened before 661.[39] The date traditionally accepted for Sigibert's death, and thus for the beginning of these events,

[36] *Vita Balthildis*, trans. with commentary, Fouracre and Gerberding (1996), pp. 97–132.

[37] *Liber Historiae Francorum* c.44, Fouracre and Gerberding (1996), p. 89.

[38] For different interpretations of these events, Krusch (1910), Levillain (1913) and (1945–6), Ewig (1965), Gerberding (1987), pp. 47–66, Wood (1994), pp. 222–4, and Becher (1994).

[39] *Liber Historiae Francorum* c.43; Fouracre and Gerberding (1996), pp. 87–8.

is 656, a date which again clashes with the *Liber* if we are to fit in a reign for Childebert the adopted. Supporters of the *Liber's* veracity, however, challenge the evidence for Sigibert's survival beyond 651.[40] A further complication has been the suggestion, based upon the confusion of an eighth-century King Dagobert and Mayor Grimoald with their seventh-century namesakes, that Sigibert's son Dagobert ruled for a while before being exiled.

Attempts to interpret these events have been rather less ingenious than the efforts to work out their chronology, for many historians have assumed that a coup against a Merovingian by an ancestor of Charlemagne is self-explanatory, an ill-timed rather than an ill-conceived venture. A variation on this theme which works backwards from the consequences of the coup is that Grimoald was first encouraged and then betrayed by the Neustrians. The chronology must remain a problem, but as one historian has recently shown, it is possible to come up with an interpretation more satisfactory and less anachronistic than one which sees the ancestors of Charlemagne having a trial run at fulfilling their historical destiny.[41] Putting stronger emphasis on the female figures in the historical background, this reinterpretation argues that if Himnechild was not Dagobert's mother, then it is likely that she would have colluded in the latter's exile in order to protect her own position. Some sort of arrangement with Grimoald would have been necessary for her political survival, and from Grimoald's point of view, the marriage of his son to her royal daughter might provide a route to the throne, rather as successive Lombards had become king by marrying Gundeberga. When Grimoald lost support (not surprising in circumstances which may have allowed adherents of his murdered predecessor to seek revenge), Himnechild might then have sought another match for Bilichild, now arranging with Balthild for her to marry Childeric. This argument has the virtue of accounting for Himnechild's continuing influence, hitherto hardly noticed in a coup said simply to have been Grimoald's. All observers none the less agree on one point: that at this stage it was plainly unacceptable for a non-Merovingian to become king.

Of Himnechild's regency we know little, but of Balthild's more because of the information contained in the *Life of Balthild*. She ruled from 657 until her eldest son Chlothar reached the majority age of fifteen in 664. Alongside her in the palace were the bishops of Paris and Rouen, unnamed secular leaders, and the mayor of the palace, first Erchinoald and then Ebroin who took over on the latter's death in 658 or 659. More was written about Ebroin than about any other non-royal secular figure in the seventh century, principally because he appeared as the arch-villain in the widely circulated *Passio Leudegarii*, the story of the martyrdom of his chief political opponent, Leudegar bishop of Autun. Ebroin's

[40] Gerberding (1987), pp. 47–66. [41] Wood (1994), pp. 222–4.

evil deeds subsequently became legendary, and it is hard for us now to put him into neutral historical perspective. It nevertheless seems clear that Ebroin and his supporting faction of Neustrian magnates upset the political balance in Francia by excluding too many others from a share in the fruits of power. This process arguably began with Balthild. Again, all of our information is about the church, but Balthild can be seen pushing her supporters into positions of power throughout the kingdom of Neustria-Burgundy, appointing them, for instance, to the bishoprics of Autun, Lyons and Toulouse. In addition, according to her Life, she forced the 'senior churches', that is, the major cult sites, to take on monastic rules and she made their local bishops grant them independence in Columbanan style, this being her so-called *Klosterpolitik*.[42] An English source, the *Life of St Wilfrid*, tells of how Aunemund bishop of Lyons was executed by Balthild in her attempt to control the church and kingdom and adds that another eight bishops were killed too.[43] For such extensive bloodletting there is no further evidence, but there is another account of how Aunemund met his end, to be replaced by the queen's palace chaplain.[44] This account also serves to warn us against seeing the politics of this period simply in terms of a policy of 'centralisation' directed by the palace against a provincial 'separatism', for it tells of how local people in Lyons combined with the palace to bring down Aunemund. Moreover, despite his princely power in Lyons, Aunemund was an integral member of the wider magnate community, and was even said to have baptised Balthild's son Chlothar.

Soon after Chlothar had officially reached manhood, Balthild was hustled off the political stage into the monastery of Chelles, but Ebroin continued in power. If Bede's story of how in 668 on a journey from Rome to Canterbury, which took them right across Francia, Archbishop Theodore and Abbot Hadrian were monitored all the way by Ebroin's men is indicative of the range and power of the mayor's government, it was effective indeed.[45] But this kind of government, in which the mayor ruled through the king and prevented the other magnates from having access to him, broke with the traditional consensus that was the very cement of the Frankish polity. According to the near contemporary *Passio Leudegarii*, Ebroin became so tyrannical that he banned magnates from Burgundy from coming to the palace unless they had his permission to do so.[46] But then in 673 Chlothar III died, and although he tried to prevent it, Ebroin could not stop the political community assembling to raise

42 *Vita Balthildis* c.9, Fouracre and Gerberding (1996), pp. 125–6.

43 *The Life of St Wilfrid* c.6, pp. 13–15.

44 *Acta S. Aunemundi*, trans. with commentary, Fouracre and Gerberding (1996), pp. 166–92.

45 Bede, *HE* IV.1.

46 *Passio Leudegarii*, trans. with commentary Fouracre and Gerberding (1996), pp. 193–253, here, c.4, pp. 220–1.

the new king to the throne. The assembly then turned on the mayor and he was powerless to resist their collective force. The magnates did this, says the *Passio Leudegarii*, because they feared that Ebroin would control the new king (Balthild's second-born, Theuderic) and if he could act in the king's name without check then he would be able to attack anyone he wished.[47] So Ebroin was driven from power and sent into exile. The Neustrians and Burgundians then called on Childeric king of Austrasia to become their king too, in place of his elder brother Theuderic. But it proved impossible to rebuild consensus because Childeric, naturally, brought members of his Austrasian entourage with him and the palace was now riven by rivalry between the Neustro-Burgundians led by Leudegar of Autun, and the Austrasians, led by the mayor of the palace Wulfoald. Leudegar accused Childeric of going back on guarantees of non-interference in the provinces, and he also, interestingly, tried to separate him from his wife Bilichild. Not surpisingly, Childeric, Wulfoald (and Himnechild) turned on Leudegar and sent him to join the exiled Ebroin. This was at Easter 675. About six months later the Neustrians killed Childeric and Bilichild (who was pregnant) and their infant son Dagobert. They were determined to stamp out the Austrasian branch of the dynasty.

On Childeric's death both Ebroin and Leudegar returned from exile and engaged in a dramatic race to reach the palace and set up a new regime with King Theuderic. Ebroin, realising that he was the weaker party at this stage, turned eastwards to gather forces in western Austrasia. The *Passio Leudegarii* states that in order to do this he had to have a king of his own, so he set up a pretender called Clovis, supposedly a son of Chlothar III. He then attacked the palace in Neustria, captured Theuderic and killed the mayor of the palace, the recently installed Leudesius who was a son of Erchinoald. Ebroin then dispatched an army to Autun against his old enemy Leudegar. Although the bishop was captured, part of the same army failed to take Lyons and Provence. Ebroin next dropped the pretender Clovis, reinstated Theuderic and then, once he had become mayor of the palace again, began to use the judicial process to punish his enemies. Leudegar was finally executed in 677 or 678, having been blinded and mutilated. Ebroin himself met his end in 680, assassinated in a pre-emptive move by another of his intended victims. This, basically, is the narrative of the *Passio Leudegarii*,[48] and though it is plainly tendentious it is essentially corroborated by other early sources.

The *Liber Historiae Francorum* shows that Ebroin had as his ally Audoin of Rouen who was one of the most respected men in all of Francia.[49] The alliance

47 *Passio Leudegarii* c.5, Fouracre and Gerberding (1996), p. 222.

48 *Passio Leudegarii* cc.4–35, Fouracre and Gerberding (1996), pp. 220–48.

49 *Liber Historiae Francorum* c.45, Fouracre and Gerberding (1996), pp. 89–91.

suggests that the mayor was not just a political maverick but represented a faction made up of leading Neustrian families. A certain degree of political disintegration occurred when magnates outside this group understood that they were or would be barred from that access to the king which allowed them to safeguard their positions by participating in the making of decisions. Contemporary sources make it clear that kings or mayors who did not listen to the counsel of their magnates were regarded as intolerably dangerous. The remedy to this injustice, as it was perceived, was to overturn the regime which perpetrated it, and this happened in both 673 and 675. But there were limits to disintegration, for widespread and prolonged disorder was also seen to threaten property and privilege. It is this last perception which may explain how after returning to power Ebroin was able to re-establish some sort of political consensus and to go back to using the judicial process rather than armed conflict to achieve his aims. Significantly, one of the first things he now did was to bring order back to property relations.

Although the upheavals of this period were, as most historians would agree, caused by feuding within the palace-centred political community rather than by attempts by regionally based groups to separate from it, the events did lead to the formation of an independent principality to the south of the River Loire, that is, Aquitaine. In this region, Lupus, the duke based in Toulouse, seems to have joined in the revolt against Ebroin in 673. It was Lupus who at this time led the Frankish intervention into Visigothic Septimania referred to earlier in this chapter. At a church council held in Bordeaux sometime between 673 and 675 he appears as a supporter of King Childeric and although he was said by one source to have been involved in the latter's murder, it is clear that after this event he did not come to terms with Ebroin. So, rather like Radulf earlier in Thuringia, he went his own way, able to secure his position because he had military control of the region. In response, the Neustrian regime confiscated his family lands in the Orléans area, thereby making it unlikely that he would ever return to the fold. Another casualty of the feuding was the hitherto sometimes strained but (since the very early seventh century) peaceful relationship between Neustria and Austrasia.

The murder of Childeric and his family meant that the separate kingdom of Austrasia would come to an end unless the Austrasians could find themselves another Merovingian. This they did. He was Dagobert, the son of Sigibert III who had been exiled to Ireland twenty years earlier. What one thinks happened next depends upon the reading of another chronologically difficult passage in the *Liber Historiae Francorum*. The most recent study of this work argues convincingly for the following sequence:[50] after Childeric's murder Wulfoald

[50] Gerberding (1987), pp. 78–84.

fled back to Austrasia and disappeared from the political scene (as did Himnechild). The leaders of the Austrasian magnates were then one Martin and his probable kinsman Pippin, members of the family to which Grimoald had belonged, known to historians as the 'Pippinids', or 'Arnulfings'. The Pippinids had recovered their fortunes since the demise of Grimoald. It was they who through the agency of the English bishop Wilfrid had Dagobert fetched from Ireland. But Ebroin and the Neustrians did not recognise the latter as king and forced the Austrasians to fight for their independence. The Austrasians mustered a large army around Dagobert and attacked Ebroin's forces. In a great battle in the Ardennes region, Martin and Pippin were beaten, and Martin later killed. When this took place is uncertain, but in December 679 Dagobert was murdered because, according to the *Life of St Wilfrid*, he did not consult his magnates and because he imposed tribute upon his people.[51] Perhaps he had tried to recover his inheritance a little too vigorously. Despite being kingless again, the Austrasians still preserved their independence, possibly because within the year Ebroin too was dead. His successor as mayor, one Waratto, made peace with Pippin.

At this stage opinion in Neustria appears to have been divided between those who, like Waratto and Audoin of Rouen, wanted some sort of agreement with Pippin, and those who, like Waratto's son Ghislemar and his son-in-law Berchar, wanted to attack him. Possibly the last group were still sore from the uncomfortable experience of living with Childeric's Austrasian entourage a decade earlier. From the Austrasian point of view, access to, and influence in, the royal palace was militarily, politically and legally a necessary safeguard to power and privilege. Financially too it was a great attraction. In 684 Audoin of Rouen died, so ending a career which had begun at the court of Chlothar II and continued into his last year with a peace mission to Austrasia where he was venerated as a holy-man. Then in 686 Waratto died and his son-in-law Berchar became mayor, with some dissenting Neustrians crossing over to Pippin in Austrasia. The next year Berchar and King Theuderic III met Pippin in battle near the River Somme. Pippin won. His victory in 687 at this, the famous Battle of Tertry, has often been said to have signified the end of the Merovingian era and the effective beginning of Carolingian rule. This view, first laid out in the early ninth-century *Prior Metz Annals*, does not reflect the seventh-century reality that Pippin and the Austrasians were fighting to be included in the old regime, not to replace it.[52]

Pippin was certainly rich and powerful, with extensive family lands to the east of the River Meuse, but he was not powerful enough to conquer Neustria

[51] *The Life of St Wilfrid* c.33, pp. 66–9.

[52] *Annales Mettenses Priores*, Fouracre and Gerberding (1996), pp. 359–61.

and Burgundy in 687.[53] About a year after Tertry, Berchar was murdered at the instigation of his mother-in-law Ansfled, Waratto's widow. Pippin's son Drogo then married Berchar's widow Anstrude, with Pippin taking over the functions of the mayor of the palace. It was Drogo's match as much as victory at Tertry which gave Pippin access to the Neustrian palace, and this in turn helped him to extend his influence in Austrasia as well as in Neustria. It might therefore be argued that the 'rise of the Carolingians' followed rather than preceded the victory at Tertry, that it came about with Neustrian help, and that it was far from assured by the time of Pippin's death in 714. The sources from which we can reconstruct something of the growth of Pippin's power are, as ever, ecclesiastical in origin and orientation, but they do at least indicate where he had influence. After he had replaced Berchar he can be seen making himself felt in the Rouen area where his daughter-in-law's family was based. Between 689 and 691 he forced Ansbert, Audoin's successor as bishop of Rouen, into exile and replaced him with Gripho, one of his own supporters. Likewise in 701 another of his men became abbot of the nearby monastery of St Wandrille. Elsewhere he appears in the 690s and in the early eighth century with interests in a great arc of monasteries and bishoprics which stretched from the River Sambre through his family lands on the Meuse across to the Rhine and down to the Moselle. The monasteries included Lobbes, Mons, Nivelles, Fosses, Stavelot-Malmedy, Kaiserwerth, St Hubert and Echternach. The bishoprics were Utrecht, Tongres-Maastricht, Cologne, Trier, Metz and Rheims. Impressive though this list is, it is immediately striking that with the exception of Rouen, Pippin's influence over ecclesiastical institutions did not stretch into the Seine-Oise area, the heartlands of the Neustrian regime.

Pippin similarly did not displace the old Neustrian families who clustered around the king, although he was able to make his son Grimoald mayor of the palace in his stead. His eldest son Drogo was given the duchy of the Champagne and did not settle in the Rouen area despite his marriage to Waratto's daughter. Hugo, the son born of this union, was brought up in Rouen, but in the household of Ansfled, Waratto's widow. The documents issued through the palace at this time cast further light on the slow rate at which Pippin's influence in Neustria increased. The nineteen surviving original royal documents issued in Neustria from 691 to 717 have the names of eighty people associated with them.[54] Of these eighty, only nineteen can be connected in any way either with Austrasia or with the family of Pippin, and of the nineteen names, only six can be found amongst the fifty-eight appearing in the witness lists of documents issued by Pippin's family in Austrasia in the period 702–726. In other words,

[53] M. Werner (1982) for a careful investigation of the family and its lands.

[54] *ChLA* 14, documents nos. 572–9, 581, 583–91, 593. See also Fouracre (1984).

Pippin demonstrably did not pack the Neustrian court with his own followers as Childeric had attempted to do two decades earlier. Two of the Neustrian documents are royal judgements and they list all of the magnates present when the cases in question were heard. From these lists it is possible to see that, with the exception of western Aquitaine, magnates from all over the kingdom continued to attend the Neustrian court. If Pippin wanted to validate his own actions by calling on the collective authority assembled at court, it is also clear that he too was bound by that authority. One of these documents and two other judgements demonstrate this nicely, for they record court decisions against Pippin's family, made when the latter tried to get their hands on lands and rights of the premier Neustrian monastery of St Denis. All this is a far cry from the picture the *Prior Metz Annals* and Einhard painted, in which Pippin had full control of the assemblies around the king. Likewise, their insistence that all of the kings of this period were totally insignificant is demonstrably wrong in the case of at least one of them, Childebert III who ruled 695–711.

Childebert's father, Theuderic III, may well have been the puppet of successive magnate factions, as in 673 people had feared he would be. His eldest son, Clovis III (691–695), was a minor at his accession and survived for only three years as an adult king, but his younger brother Childebert ruled for over fifteen years as an adult. Perhaps this was why the author of the *Liber Historiae Francorum* had a special regard for him, calling him 'celebrated', 'famous' and 'just'.[55] It was under Childebert that the three judgements against Pippin's family were made, and under him that we see Antenor the ruler of Provence, a far distant region, attending the Neustrian court. Coins bearing his name were also minted at Marseilles at this time. Childebert may therefore have been politically attractive in his own right. But after his death no more royal coins were minted in Marseilles and it was probably now that Antenor revolted against Pippin. Around this time too, according to a ninth-century source, the ruler of the Alamans and other eastern leaders cut themselves off from the rest of the political community because 'they could no longer serve the Merovingian kings as they had formerly been accustomed to do'.[56] But the success of the regime at the turn of the seventh century, before Childebert's death led to a certain degree of political alienation, may lie in the way in which Childebert and Pippin together made a strong combination. The king could attract the support which allowed the royal court to function effectively as the primary instrument of judicial power, and the fact of Pippin's military superiority discouraged the faction fighting which could disrupt the court's activities. For

[55] *Liber Historiae Francorum* c.49, p. 323, described Childebert upon his accession as 'vir inclytus', and c.50, p. 324 he was remembered as 'bonae memoriae gloriosus domnus Childebertus rex iustus'.

[56] *Erchanberti Breviarum* c.1, p. 328.

Pippin was above all a military leader whose prestige rested in success in battle against the Frisians, and against peoples east of the Rhine, wars which the *Liber Historiae Francorum* placed in the reign of Childebert.

As the behaviour of Antenor and of the Alamans suggests, resentment built up apace with the growing power of Pippin and his family. Then in 714 disaster struck them. Pippin fell ill and his son Grimoald was murdered whilst visiting him. Drogo had died in 707, and the males in the next generation were still young, so Pippin tried to secure his family by making a grandson, Theudoald, mayor of the palace, with his wife Plectrude as a kind of regent. Pippin actually had another wife and another son, Charles, but at this time he was apparently a peripheral member of the family and excluded from its wealth and power.[57] When Pippin died in late 714, the Neustrians drove Theudoald out and then allied with the Frisians to strike at the very heart of the family's power on the River Meuse. It was left to Charles, later to be known as Charles Martel, to rally the family's supporters and its fortunes, beginning his campaign with guerilla actions against the victorious Neustrians and Frisians. The events of 714 thus led to a period of prolonged warfare which finally destroyed the old order of the Merovingian world as the Frankish political community was first broken up and then forcibly reshaped around the person of Charles Martel. Charles as a result, and in contrast to his father, could make Merovingian kingship a mere formality and even rule without a king. He would eventually be buried in the monastery of St Denis, that most exclusive of Neustrian institutions, which earlier had in effect blackballed his family.

We have now followed the basic course of events recorded in the written sources for the history of seventh-century Francia. One of the most prominent features to emerge from these sources is the importance of the royal palace in the political life of Francia. Against this background, political history is revealed as the interaction of kings, queens, mayors and magnates. What shaped that interaction was first the unification of Francia under Chlothar II which led to the formation of a supra-regional political elite, and then a prolonged period of peace. In contrast to the sixth century, in the seventh there was relatively little fighting in Francia itself, and from the time that Dagobert dealt with the Wends, Basques and Bretons until the Frisians began to press down on the north-east at the end of the century, there was also little threat from outside. Peace, however, put the solidarity of the political leaders under pressure as they competed for resources which appeared limited when there was no prospect of the profits which war could bring. Though competition between magnates could be manipulated in the favour of royal government, when rivalry developed into uncontrollable feuding this could paralyse the operation of the

[57] Fouracre (2000), p. 56.

palace, as events in the mid 670s demonstrate. 'Feuding' and 'faction-fighting' are the terms which best describe this behaviour, for they emphasise that strife between *factiones* was within a single political community rather than between different ethnic, social or regional groups. This observation allows us to see that seventh-century Frankish society was at the top level subject to a limited degree of structural instability, but from this it need not follow that it was generally unstable or politically chaotic.

It was in fact the overall stability of the Frankish polity which made child kingship possible. An acceptance of public authority survived the disappearance of direct taxation which had once underpinned it. Royal rights were increasingly exercised locally without the supervision of central government, and by granting immunities to the lands of favoured church institutions the kings actually banned their own officers from exercising those rights in many areas of the kingdom. But a notion of public authority lived on in the hands of those who profited from it, even though they might be beyond the immediate control of central government, or enjoy exemption from dues and services owed to the king, as holders of immunities did. Such people could not deny the authority of the kings without laying open to question the legality of their own power. Even Charles Martel would be thus bound into a notional acceptance of Merovingian authority. In this way public authority was turning from a fiscal into a cultural phenomenon as fiscal rights fell into the hands of magnates, and government was produced through an association of the powerful rather than by bureaucratic direction. It was within these terms that the later Merovingian state evolved, rather than as a result of 'Roman', or centralist, government being overthrown by 'Germanic' or aristocratic systems of rule, which is one way in which the victory of the Austrasians over the Neustrians at Tertry has been interpreted.[58]

The basis of power in society lay, ultimately, in the control of land because this provided access to the only sure source of renewable wealth in the form of what was produced by the workers on the land, both free and unfree. At the same time there was a very strong demand for high-value moveable wealth, 'treasure', which could be acquired in exchange for agrarian products or more spectacularly through warfare or by political means. The writing of this period is saturated with references to treasure. A store of treasure was the precondition for the exercise of power, for it acted as a magnet on people's loyalties, and one of the great attractions of wielding public authority was that it provided access to moveable wealth in the form of judicial fines and what little taxation remained. The granting of immunities to churches, thereby giving them the rights to keep the profits of government, stimulated with cash institutions

[58] K.-F. Werner (1972), pp. 493–4.

which were already well organised large-scale farmers. Whether simply as a result of this, or owing to a more widespread enhancement of landlords' rights, or as a dividend of peace and greater stability, there was in the seventh century the beginnings of an increase in productivity in the countryside. In turn this led to the first signs (albeit faint) of economic growth since antiquity. It is in this context that we see a switch from a gold to a silver coinage in the 670s and the first hints that in some areas the population was beginning to grow. The seventh century therefore saw Francia maturing economically as well as politically and culturally. It had developed into a kingdom which could be massive in size despite its meagre resources and despite the rudimentary nature of its government. This, above all, was what the Merovingians bequeathed to their successors.

CHAPTER 15

RELIGION AND SOCIETY IN IRELAND

Clare Stancliffe

SOCIETY, RELIGION AND THE COMING OF CHRISTIANITY

Christianity had originally spread westwards within the Roman Empire via the mosaic of cities around the Mediterranean; but Ireland lay outside that empire and had an entirely rural society, with no cities or even small towns, no urban lower and middle classes, no coinage, no mass production of goods, and very little trade. The Roman Empire was a hierarchically organised state, with an emperor at the top, and regular subdivisions down the geographical scale to the level of provinces, and within those provinces, the cities with their dependent territories. Ireland, however, was not unified politically; and although the highest-ranking overkings might have their overlordship recognised across an extensive area, this rested on recognition given by the kings of the many individual tribes or *túatha* (singular *túath*).[1] These little *túatha* were the basic political entities, and people had no rights in another *túath* unless (as often happened) there was an agreement between that and their own *túath*.

Although different from the late Roman Empire, however, early Irish society was in many respects comparable with other early medieval societies. The basic unit was not the individual, but the kin group. This would be held responsible for the wrong-doing of one of its members, and for their protection. Besides its peace-keeping role, the kindred was also of fundamental importance in that most agricultural land was 'kin-land': although it could be farmed on an individual basis, it could not be granted away from the kin group, except with its consent.[2] In addition to an individual's blood relations, close bonds were formed through the widespread custom of fosterage.[3] As for the position of women, Irish society was strongly patriarchal: women were generally under the authority of their father, husband or son, and had limited scope for independent action.[4]

[1] Cf. Charles-Edwards (1989), pp. 34–9. See Davies, chapter 9 above.

[2] Kelly (1988), pp. 100–2.

[3] Kelly (1988), pp. 86–90.

[4] Cf. Kelly (1988), pp. 68–79, 104–5.

Irish society was hierarchical, and the law tracts list several different ranks, each with its own honour price. The basic structure was that of kings, lords, and ordinary freemen, all of whom were free and had their own legal independence. Beneath them were the half-free, and, at the very bottom, slaves. In Ireland, however, a distinctive feature was that kings and nobles were not the only privileged groups. There was also an important class of professionals, people who owed their privileged status to their learning or skill. A Munster law tract differentiates between 'noble' and 'dependent' men of skill.[5] It includes brehons (lawyers), physicians, smiths, craftsmen, harpists, charioteers, and jugglers amongst the latter. The poets alone ranked as 'noble' men of skill, and their most accomplished practitioners enjoyed the same honour price as the *túath* king.[6] They also had freedom to travel between the various *túatha* – a privilege which was perhaps shared by the brehons, but which set them apart from ordinary nobles, or even kings.[7] Thanks to this, Ireland enjoyed a high degree of cultural cohesion, and a consciousness of itself as a whole, despite its political fragmentation.

The translation 'poets', for the Irish *filid* (singular *fili*), is misleadingly inadequate. The word *filid* is etymologically linked to words meaning 'seeing' and 'seer', and the *filid* inherited both the status and many of the functions of the pagan druids. Each king had his own court poet to enhance his standing with praise poems and to act as the chief disseminator of propaganda in his favour. The *fili* also knew an impressive number of tales, and was the repository of genealogical lore, historical traditions and place-name stories.[8] Once Christianity had become accepted in society in the sixth century, there was much interaction between the new Latin learning that was introduced in its wake, and the native learning of the *filid* and brehons.[9] This began as early as *c.*600, and produced an extensive quantity of vernacular material of types that are uncommon or unknown elsewhere in western Europe. Most of this belongs after our period; but we should be aware of the important role which the *filid* and brehons played both in early Irish society and equally in their shaping of many of the sources through which we learn about that society.

In the Christian period in which the law texts were written down, the druids were counted at best only amongst the 'dependent' men of skill; but all the indications are that they had once enjoyed the privileged status that later

[5] *Uraicecht Becc* 6, 37, trans. MacNeill (1921–4), pp. 273, 277.

[6] *Uraicecht Becc* 37–8; 16, 20, trans. MacNeill (1921–4), pp. 277, 275; cf. *Bretha Nemed Toísech* 17, trans. Breatnach (1989), pp. 17, 37.

[7] Kelly (1988), pp. 4–5, 46.

[8] Byrne (1973), pp. 13–16; Kelly (1988), pp. 43–9.

[9] Cf. Ó Corráin, Breatnach and Breen (1984); McCone (1990), chs. 1–2, esp. pp. 1, 22–8; Charles-Edwards (1998), esp. pp. 70–5.

belonged to the *filid*.[10] The druids originally formed a pagan priesthood, and although they were too closely linked to pagan rites to retain their high status, they continued to exist right through the period that concerns us. A seventh-century author found it necessary to warn kings against listening to them,[11] and their spells continued to be feared even when Christianity had become dominant. Such fears may have been partially responsible for prompting the Christian *Lorica* or 'Breastplate' prayers as a means of protection.[12]

We can learn about the primal, 'pagan' religion of Ireland only indirectly, but it would appear to have been all-pervasive: there were mountains and rivers which bore the name of a goddess, like the Paps of Anu or the rivers Shannon and Boyne. There were sacred trees and wells.[13] Tribes traced their descent back to Lug or another deity,[14] and kingship was sacral. Kings would regularly summon an assembly (*óenach*) where their people would come together to transact public business, for economic exchange, and for horse racing and other sports. These assemblies, generally held at an ancient burial ground, appear originally to have had a religious as well as a practical significance. Those of the Uí Néill, held at Teltown, and of the Leinstermen, held at Carman, took place at the festival of Lugnasad, which marked the beginning of harvest, and was named after the god Lug. Samain (1 November), Imbolc (1 February), Beltaine (1 May) and Lugnasad (1 August) were the four major festivals of the pagan year.[15] All this means that the 'religious' aspect of pre-Christian Irish society cannot be separated out: the land people lived in, the calendar of the year's cycle, the king who was the focal point of their very existence as a distinct *túath*, and the assemblies where they met – all these had a religious significance. It follows that conversion to another religion would require a complex set of adjustments.

By AD 500, it is likely that Christianity had been preached throughout Ireland,[16] but far from certain that it had yet been embraced by a majority of the population. The first Christian bishop in Ireland was a continental churchman, Palladius, who was sent 'to the Irish believing in Christ' in 431 by Pope Celestine. Christianity had presumably spread to Ireland in casual ways: chiefly, we may surmise, through links with Britain. Palladius' mission, probably to Leinster (then embracing central eastern as well as south-east Ireland), was portrayed as a success in Rome; and Columbanus, a Leinsterman

10 *Uraicecht Becc* 37, trans. MacNeill (1921–4), p. 277; cf. *Bretha Crólige* 51, trans. Binchy (1934), pp. 40–1; Mac Cana (1979), esp. pp. 445–6, 456–60; Stancliffe (1980), pp. 78–83.

11 *De Duodecim Abusivis Saeculi*, p. 51.

12 For example the eighth-century 'Breastplate' ascribed to St Patrick: Greene and O'Connor (1967), pp. 27–32. See also *Hisperica Famina* II, pp. 23–31; Kelly (1988), p. 60.

13 Tírechán, *Collectanea*, *cc.*39 and 51, 1; Low (1996).

14 E. MacNeill (1921, 1981), pp. 46–57.

15 Binchy (1958); M. MacNeill (1982), esp. 1, pp. 1–11, 287–349.

16 Patrick, *Confessio* 34.

writing *c.*600, could still recall that Ireland had received its Christianity from the pope.[17]

The other fifth-century missionary to Ireland who is known by name is the Briton, Patrick. His mission was later than that of Palladius, and was arguably to the northern half of Ireland.[18] Armagh, which later claimed that it was his principal church, was probably just one of his foundations, and one scholar has contested even that.[19] Patrick makes no explicit reference to Palladius, and it is impossible to say whether he had any link with the earlier mission or not. Fortunately two of Patrick's own writings survive, a letter, and his *Confession*. These vividly portray the problems and the dangers of missionary work in fifth-century Ireland. As a foreigner, with no kin at hand to protect him, Patrick found himself despised by the Irish, and compelled to cultivate the goodwill of the powerful in order to remain free to travel and to preach: kings were able to grant protection to outsiders (as were other classes, but only for brief periods). Hence we find Patrick giving gifts to kings and to judges (brehons?); he also paid for a retinue of kings' sons to accompany him. For all that, he was frequently attacked, and in peril of death.[20] Patrick succeeded in converting 'many thousands', including both children of kings and slave women.[21] The conversion of Ireland, however, was a slow process: a missionary would have had to work *túath* by *túath*. He would have gone to the king and to the nobles and privileged classes for support (though Patrick certainly did not restrict his work to these classes); but Irish kings, even if favourable, had no sweeping powers to abolish paganism, while the druids were probably in a position to present a coherent and forceful opposition.[22] In addition, the earliest missionaries do not seem to have been adequately supported from abroad: the papacy seems not to have maintained contact with Palladius' mission, while Patrick was apparently operating in the face of opposition from at least some in Britain – though he also drew some financial support from there.[23] In time, however, Patrick's mission bore fruit: as well as his Irish converts, including native boys whom he trained for the priesthood, he inspired some Britons to follow him. Only one of these, Mauchteus of Louth, is known by name; but extensive British involvement in the fifth- and sixth-century Irish church can be deduced from the fact that the Irish acquired their Latin from British speakers.[24]

17 Charles-Edwards (1993a), pp. 1–10; Columbanus, *Epistulae* v.3.

18 Stancliffe (2004). 19 Doherty (1991), pp. 71–3; cf. Sharpe (1982).

20 Patrick, *Confessio* 21, 35, 37, 51–3, 55; and *Epistola* 1, 10; Charles-Edwards (1976), esp. pp. 54–5.

21 Cf. Mytum (1992), p. 44. 22 Stancliffe (1980), esp. pp. 63–7, 77–92.

23 Patrick, *Confessio* 45–54, and cf. 13 and 26; Stancliffe (2004).

24 Patrick, *Epistola* 3, and *Confessio* 50–1; Sharpe (1990); Greene (1968); McManus (1984); Dumville (1984c), pp. 19–20; Stevenson (1989), pp. 144–7; Dumville *et al.* (1993), pp. 133–45.

In Ireland, paganism was so strongly entrenched that Christianity had to struggle for well over a century before winning formal acceptance. Obviously individual kings and kindreds will have been converted at different rates. But since the privileged classes represented by the druids, *filid* and brehons maintained broadly the same body of teaching and laws throughout Ireland, we may take the inclusion of the Christian church and clergy within their social and legal framework as marking the definitive acceptance of Christianity. The earliest canonical legislation from Ireland, that of the so-called 'First Synod of Patrick', portrays the Christians still as a group within the surrounding pagan society: they are to take disputes to the church, and not to a judge for settlement; they must not, like pagans, swear an oath before a druid (*aruspex*); and the church is prohibited from receiving alms donated by pagan kindreds. The latter may allude to those wishing to keep a foot in both pagan and Christian camps simultaneously;[25] but, given the role played by gift exchange in early Irish society, it implies 'a separation of each *túath* into two societies, one Christian, the other pagan'.[26] Although these canons cannot be accurately dated, the arguments for assigning them to the first half of the sixth century are strong.[27] The continuance of pagan traditions in the sixth century also appears in the annalistic record that the southern Uí Néill overking, Diarmait son of Cerball, celebrated the 'feast of Tara' *c.*560. This was a pagan inauguration rite for the Uí Néill overkings; and although Diarmait was probably not untouched by Christianity, it suggests that it had not yet won a firm hold.[28] In contrast Columba, from the rival, northern branch of the Uí Néill, was founding the monastery of Iona in 563, and late legends portray him as the protector of the *filid.* Although their historicity is unverifiable, the indications are that by his death in 597 the church – or at least, the Ionan church – had come to an understanding with the *filid.* This is implied by the fact that one of their number, by tradition Dallán Forgaill, composed a poetic lament on his death. The text of this poem, in difficult, archaic, Irish, still survives.[29]

Such evidence as we have therefore points to the second half of the sixth century as the time when Christianity won general acceptance as the religion of Ireland. When the law tracts were written in the seventh and eighth centuries, the clergy were included among the privileged classes, alongside the poets.[30]

[25] *First Synod of St Patrick* 21, 14, 13. Cf. the latter with *Apgitir Chrábaid* 19.

[26] Charles-Edwards (1976), p. 56.

[27] Hughes (1966), pp. 44–50, also Dumville *et al.* (1993), pp. 175–8.

[28] *Annals of Ulster* s.a. 558, 560, and cf. 561; Binchy (1958), pp. 132–8; Byrne (1973), pp. 94–104; cf. Charles-Edwards (2000), p. 294.

[29] Most accessibly in Clancy and Márkus (1995), pp. 96–128; also Stokes (1899); note also Adomnán, *Vita Columbae* I.42. See Herbert (1988), pp. 9–12; Sharpe (1995), pp. 89–90, 312–14.

[30] See below, pp. 417–18.

Meanwhile the druids were demoted, although, as we have seen, they did not disappear. Nor, interestingly, did bands of men engaged in *díberg*, which appears to have been a pagan, ritualised practice which involved a group of (typically) nine men taking an oath to kill.[31] Thus active paganism persisted right through the seventh century, though probably as very much a minority affair.

Besides this 'hard' paganism, explicitly opposed to Christianity, several 'soft' pagan figures or practices survived, frequently in Christian guise. Well-known examples are that of Brigit, who appears to have metamorphosed from pagan goddess into Christian saint; of the holy wells, which were now put under the patronage of a saint; and of the celebrations connected with Lugnasad (probably including pilgrimage up Croagh Patrick), where the figure of St Patrick appears to have taken the place of the Celtic god Lug.[32] Alongside these we might note the continuance into modern times of belief in the fairies, who were none other than former pagan deities.[33] Such instances of accommodation were already well under way in the seventh century. Meanwhile the whole question of trying to harmonise biblical teaching and Irish social norms was much discussed in the seventh century. One party, the *Romani* or Roman party, tried to bring Ireland into line with the teaching of the continental church, whereas the Irish party sought – by deft appeal to the Old Testament – to justify the retention of traditional Irish customs such as polygamy and the marriage of first cousins.[34]

THE ESTABLISHMENT OF THE CHURCH AND OF MONASTERIES

We have little evidence for the nature of the church first established in Ireland. Patrick's own writings suggest that he had no fixed see.[35] He was probably the only bishop responsible for scattered congregations in the northern half of Ireland, and travelled between them.[36] He had native Irish clergy, and he fostered the monastic vocation amongst virgins and monks; but the conditions under which he laboured render it highly unlikely that he was in a position to plan an organisation for a church which was only then coming to birth.[37]

Our next evidence is the decrees of the 'First Synod of Patrick', already discussed. These imply that a bishop was in charge of each *plebs*, a Latin

31 Sharpe (1979), esp. pp. 82–92. Was their victim regarded as a sacrifice to the deities? Cf. Ellis Davidson (1988), pp. 58–82.

32 Kenney (1929), pp. 356–8; Ó Catháin (1999); Logan (1980); M. MacNeill (1982).

33 Cf. Tírechán, *Collectanea* 26.3; Danaher (1972), pp. 121–2, 207; Mac Cana (1986), pp. 66–7, 72–4.

34 *Bretha Crólige* 57; Ó Corráin (1984), pp. 157–61. On *Romani* and the Irish party, see below.

35 Patrick, *Epistola* 1.

36 Cf. Patrick, *Confessio* 43, 51; Thompson (1985), pp. 148–9.

37 Sharpe (1984b), pp. 239–42.

word meaning 'people', which here almost certainly denotes the Irish *túath*.[38] Later documentation confirms the norm of each *túath* having its own (chief) bishop.[39] This implies well over a hundred dioceses in Ireland, so by north European standards each Irish bishop ruled a tiny diocese. It has been plausibly argued that a *Domnach Mór* ('Donaghmore') type place-name, followed by the name of a population group, represents the chief or 'mother' church of that people: one that would have had a bishop. The same probably also went for names formed from *cell* plus the name of a population group. What is particularly interesting about the *domnach* names is that because this word for church had fallen out of use by the mid-sixth century, a map of *domnach* place-names (Map 9) records churches probably founded before *c.*550 – albeit with no pretence at completeness.[40] The relatively dense cluster of such names near the centre of the east coast is particularly interesting as it coincides with the area associated with Auxilius, Secundinus and Iserninus, fifth-century missionaries who probably formed part of Palladius' mission.[41]

The role of monasticism in the early Irish church is a question of considerable interest. Patrick had introduced monastic ideals, and his writings show that many individuals became monks and virgins. The latter were drawn from both the highest and the lowest classes in society and endured much persecution. It appears, however, that the virgins were living at home, rather than in separate establishments. Less evidence is available on the monks, but they may have served as celibate clergy, perhaps living in clerical-monastic communities rather than in monasteries that were sharply cut off from ordinary society.[42] In the early stages of conversion there was probably a need for clerical manpower, as also a lack of landed endowments of sufficient size to enable the establishment of separate monasteries.

Those to whom a later age looked back as the founder-saints of the famous monasteries in Ireland generally have obits falling between 537 and 637 in the Irish annals. One might instance Cíarán, founder of Clonmacnois on the Shannon, and Finnian, founder of Clonard, also in the midlands, both recorded as dying (probably prematurely) of plague in 549; Comgall, founder of the austere monastery of Bangor on Belfast Lough, where Columbanus was trained, and Columba (or Colum Cille), the founder of Derry, Durrow (in the

38 *First Synod of St Patrick* 1, 3–5, 23–30; Hughes (1966), pp. 44–51, esp. 50; Charles-Edwards (1993b), pp. 138–9, 143–7.

39 'Rule of Patrick' 1–3, 6; *Críth Gablach* 47, trans. MacNeill (1921–4), p. 306; Charles-Edwards (2000), p. 248. Complications are discussed by Etchingham (1999), pp. 141–8.

40 Flanagan (1984), pp. 25–34, 43–7; Ó Corráin (1981), p. 338; Sharpe (1984b), pp. 256–7; (1992a), pp. 93–5.

41 Dumville *et al.* (1993), pp. 51–3, 89–98; cf. Hughes (1966), p. 68 and map at end.

42 Herren (1989), esp. p. 83; Charles-Edwards (2000), pp. 224–6.

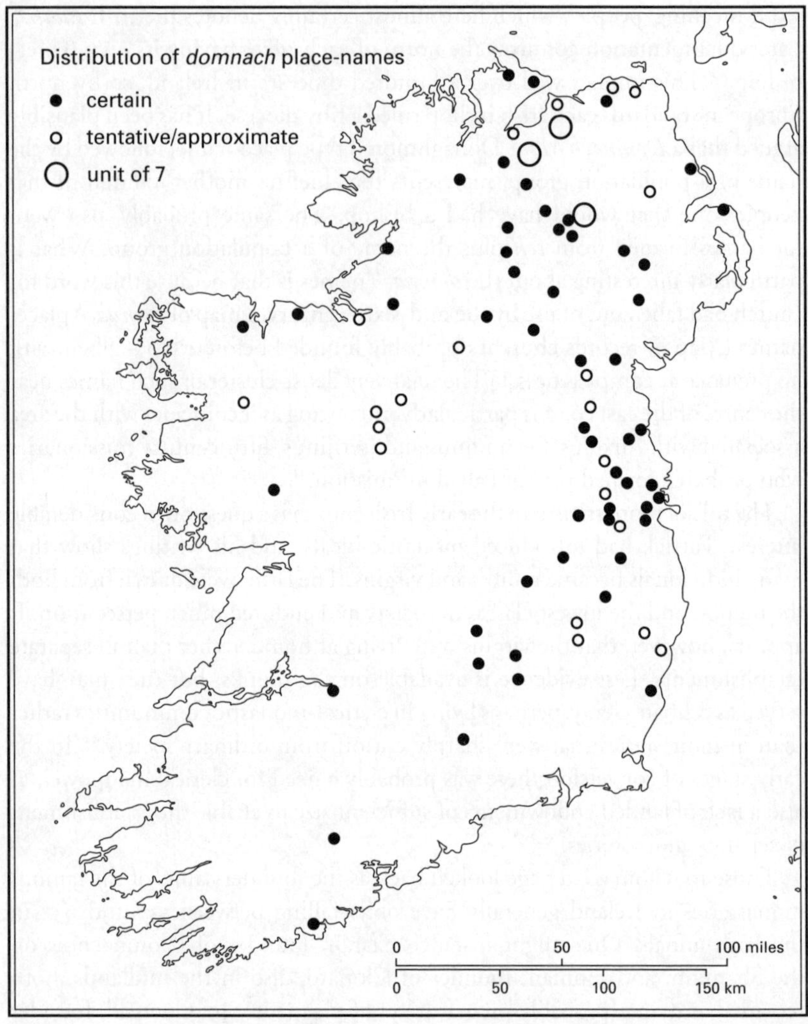

Map 9 Distribution of *domnach* place-names (after Flanagan, in Ní Chatháin and Richter (1984), map 5)

midlands) and Iona (in Scotland); Kevin, the founder of Glendalough in the Wicklow Mountains, and Carthach, founder of Lismore in Munster, just up the Blackwater from the south coast (Map 10); and that is to name just some of the most famous. The implication of this annalistic evidence, that this period saw a current of enthusiasm for the monastic life, is corroborated by Columbanus, writing *c.*600. He mentions the problem of monks who, desiring a stricter life, abandon the places of their original profession, as an issue on which Finnian had questioned Gildas. Moreover much of Gildas' reply survives, albeit in fragmentary form.[43] This evidence implies the existence of established, not too austere, monastic communities, followed by a wave of enthusiasm for a stricter religious life. The latter appears to have developed from *c.*540 in Ireland under the influence of British enthusiasts for the ascetic life.[44] Behind this lay the inspiration of Cassian and other Gallic Christians. The religious ideal that inspired them was to cut themselves free from the pressures of ordinary society and cultivate such virtues as detachment, freedom from egoism, and love, so that they could begin to live as citizens of heaven, in communion with the angels and with God himself. To this end, they adopted the common practices of coenobitic monasticism. Many of them learned Latin in order to read the Bible. This opened up to them the works of the church Fathers and some of the intellectual achievements of the ancient world, while the Irish also made their own contribution to learning and culture in both Latin and Old Irish.[45]

Only a small minority within Ireland will have embraced this religious ideal themselves, but it was still of great importance. The example of its most wholehearted adherents will at least have made people aware of a completely different approach to life. This was particularly so when monasticism was embraced by men like Columba, a prince of the Uí Néill – the most powerful royal dynasty in the northern half of Ireland. Many of the most enthusiastic converts to monasticism left their own *túatha* and travelled elsewhere as religious exiles or *peregrini*. This was an attempt to cut free from their roots, to give up everything for the sake of following Christ, 'poor and humble and ever preaching truth'.[46] Such ascetic renunciation may well have been partly inspired by the immense difficulty of achieving lasting detachment from society while continuing to live in a monastery on home ground where everyone knew one's kin. The *peregrinatio* of Columba from Ireland to Britain in 563 may have occurred for just such reasons.[47] From a historical viewpoint, the practice of religious *peregrinatio* was significant because it led to the displacement of many of the religiously most committed. Some simply withdrew to inaccessible sites, like the rocky islands off the west coast that are scattered with hermitages. But some went elsewhere within mainland Ireland; some sailed to northern Britain, like Columba; and some followed the more austere path of leaving the

[43] Columbanus, *Epistulae* I.7; Sharpe (1984a), esp. pp. 196–9; Gildas, *Fragmenta*. This Finnian may be a separate individual from the founder of Clonard.

[44] See Stancliffe, chapter 16 below, pp. 437, 439–41.

[45] See Fontaine, chapter 27 below; Richter (1999), pp. 137–56.

[46] Columbanus, *Epistulae* II.3; see Charles-Edwards (1976); Hughes (1987), no. XIV.

[47] Cf. Herbert (1988), p. 28; *Vita Sancti Endei c.*6; Stancliffe, chapter 16 below, p. 454 and n. 136.

insular world altogether and emigrating to the continent, like Columbanus, who sailed from Bangor to Francia in 591. Further *peregrini* followed these pioneers, and the whole movement contributed to the Christianisation of northern Britain and to the revival of Christianity in parts of the continent. Columbanus' continental career and his monastic foundations of Luxeuil in Burgundy and Bobbio in Italy were of particular importance since they forged lasting links between Ireland, Francia and Italy, while forcing consideration of how far Irish Christian idiosyncrasies would be tolerated on the continent.[48]

The new monasteries in Ireland itself rapidly attracted both recruits and landed endowments. These institutions helped to secure the future of Christianity in Ireland by becoming thriving educational centres where future monks and priests could be trained, and by producing the biblical and liturgical manuscripts and cultivating the Latin learning which were necessary accessories to Christianity. In theory, the *túath* episcopal churches might have done this. In practice, however, they may well have been on too small a scale; and their worthy, but more mundane objective of giving pastoral care probably did not attract recruits of the calibre of Columbanus, who approvingly quoted Jerome to the effect that whereas bishops should imitate the apostles, monks should 'follow the fathers who were perfect'.[49]

Monasticism will also have influenced lay society because much of the pastoral care was performed by monastically trained clerics, who, as in Gaul, sought to impose ascetic norms on the church as a whole. Whereas the 'First Synod of Patrick' appears to have accepted married priests, the sixth-century ascetics insisted on clerical celibacy, and also sought to impose strict monogamy on lay people, together with long periods of sexual abstinence.[50] Doubtless most lay people took little notice; but tenants of monastic lands were under pressure to conform, and some lay people chose to. They might visit a monastery and stay there for a while, and they might put themselves under the spiritual guidance of a confessor, who would in many cases have been a monk. Regular confession would have allowed much scope for the formation of conscience.[51] The Irish, perhaps following British precedents, were innovating here: they held that even serious sins, such as killing, could be atoned for by repentance, confession and the performance of a penance; and that this could be repeated if need arose. This contrasted with the situation on the continent where the 'public penance' required for serious sins (which included the ubiquitous sin of adultery) was not only public, but also allowed only once in a lifetime. In consequence people were exceedingly reluctant to undertake it before their deathbed – and if they did undertake it, they then had to live the rest of their

48 See Fouracre, chapter 14 above. 49 Columbanus, *Epistulae* II.8.

50 Finnian, *Penitentialis* 46; Hughes (1966), ch. 5, esp. pp. 42–3, 51–5; cf. Markus (1990), pp. 181–211.

51 Adomnán, *Vita Columbae* I.32 (cf. Sharpe (1995), p. 293, n. 144), III.7; Frantzen (1983), pp. 8–12, 30–9; Ó Corráin, Breatnach and Breen (1984), pp. 404–5; Etchingham (1999), pp. 290–318.

lives in a quasi-monastic state, lest they sin again; they were not even allowed to resume conjugal relations with their spouses. In contrast the Irish penitential system, where penance could be repeated whenever necessary, left the person who had successfully completed his penance with freedom to return to ordinary life in society.[52] It is thus likely to have been used more, and Adomnán shows us several penitent sinners seeking out Columba on Iona.[53] In these ways there was considerable scope for ascetics influencing Christian norms within Irish society, although we should not assume that they ever represented the only viewpoint in the Irish church: one eighth-century law text implies that it was perfectly acceptable for bishops or priests to have one wife, though their status was lower than those who remained virgins. Thus married clergy, together with more relaxed views of what should be expected of lay people, may well have existed side by side with ascetic ideals right through our period.[54]

THE CHURCH, THE FAMILY AND LAND

If the church were to thrive, it needed endowments. As elsewhere in early medieval Europe, these consisted primarily of land, although people, animals, jewellery and so on were also donated. Gifts were not given to 'the church', as an impersonal institution, but rather to an individual person, whether alive or dead. One common pattern in these centuries was to donate land to the individual religious or cleric who would found a church on it. The churchman thus became the 'founder-saint' of that church – something that helps to explain the numerous dedications to obscure, local saints in Ireland. If a churchman received land for churches at several sites, the churches he founded would be grouped together as a federation under his rule, even if they were widely scattered across Ireland. After his death they would pass under the rule of his 'heir', who was the head of the federation's principal church: normally, where the founder-saint was buried. Modern historians often dub such federations *paruchiae*. Sometimes, particularly in the case of St Patrick or monastic saints, the donation would be made to a dead saint. In that case, it was in effect made to his heir, and it joined the other churches of that saint's federation. As we shall see below, by the later seventh century these federations were also expanding by taking over previously existing churches.

In Irish society, the hereditary principle was so ubiquitous that it was natural for it to apply within the church as well. It is thus common to find the

[52] Finnian, *Penitentialis* 35; Frantzen (1983), pp. 5–7; O'Loughlin (2000), pp. 49–66. See also Scheibelreiter, chapter 25 below.

[53] Adomnán, *Vita Columbae* I.22 and 30, II.39.

[54] Hughes (1966), p. 135; Etchingham (1999), p. 70; cf. Doherty (1991), p. 65; Cogitosus, *Vita Brigitae* c.32 (*AA SS* edn. c.VIII, 39).

headship of churches being handed down within the family of the founder-saint.[55] This did not necessarily lead to married lay abbots and a worldly church: Iona is the classic case of a monastery which retained its standards, but where the vast majority of its celibate abbots were of the same Uí Néill family as its founder-saint, Columba, with abbatial succession passing to nephews or cousins. In another instance the nobleman called Fith Fio who founded the church of Drumlease specified that its headship should always go to one of his own kindred, provided someone suitable ('good, devout, and conscientious') could be found.[56] Continued family interest in a church might also operate on behalf of the *donor*'s family – as was natural in a society where the norm was reciprocal gift-giving, rather than the impersonal marketplace. Sometimes the donor simply expected the community's prayers, as with the nobleman from whom Colman bought land at Mayo following his withdrawal to Ireland after the Synod of Whitby (664). The donor's family probably gained burial rights as well, but the receiving church could still retain its effective independence, as with Iona.[57] However in some, perhaps many, cases, the donor retained a more extensive interest in the church for his own family. Sometimes, as is said to have happened at Trim, the donor gave land to a close relative, so that the family of both donor and church-founder was the same.[58] In these ways, although the land was donated to the church, it was effectively retained within the family. This was particularly important in Ireland, where normally it was only kings who would have had extensive lands for donating to the church. Irish law forbade the alienation of 'kinland', unless it had the approval of the kin-group as a whole. What is more, the kindred retained the right to reclaim such land for up to fifty years after the donation had been made. A man had more freedom with land that he himself had acquired; but even here, he could only alienate a limited amount.[59] Donations that retained the family's interest in the church would be more likely to win their approval.

The simplest form of endowment can be seen in the case of Iona. Here, King Conall of Dál Riada donated the island to Columba,[60] and Adomnán's narrative shows the monks doing their own farming; perhaps there was no (permanently resident) population on the little island at the time of its donation. Sometimes, however, not just a tract of land but also the people living

[55] Ó Riain (1989), p. 360; Etchingham (1999), pp. 224–8.

[56] *Additamenta* 9; Doherty (1991), pp. 78–9.

[57] Bede, *HE* IV.4; Adomnán, *Vita Columbae* I.8; Macquarrie (1992), pp. 110–14; Sharpe (1995), pp. 16–18, 26–8, 277–8.

[58] *Additamenta* 1–4. Byrne (1984); cf. Etchingham (1999), pp. 227–8.

[59] Charles-Edwards (1993b), pp. 67–70; Mac Niocaill (1984), pp. 153–4; Stevenson (1990), pp. 31–2.

[60] *Annals of Ulster* s.a. 574; cf. Sharpe (1995), pp. 16–18.

and farming it were granted to a church. In this case the population became *manaig* or 'monastic tenants' of that church.[61] *Manaig* (singular, *manach*) is the Old Irish word for 'monks', but *manaig* were like ordinary monks only in the sense that they became members of a church 'family', with the abbot at its head, in lieu of their family head. So, for instance, they could not enter into contracts without his assent. However, they were not subject to his will in the detailed living of their everyday lives, as was normal for ordinary monks. What is more, they continued to live with their wives in their own houses as peasant farmers or warriors much as normal, sometimes at a considerable distance from the church.[62] Their chief characteristics, apart from their recognition of the abbot's authority, were their subjection to a strict sexual regime (monogamy, and no sexual relations at times such as Lent), their obligation to pay the church certain dues, including tithes and burial payments, and a mutual arrangement whereby one son was educated by the church, but was allowed to marry and inherit his share of the property, which he continued to farm as a *manach*. The *manaig* thus represent one of several ways in which monasteries became intimately bound up with Irish society.

One consequence of the wealth accruing to churches through gifts of land is that secular dynasties became interested in controlling them. Members of royal lineages who failed to achieve kingship might seek headship of a church, while a vulnerable *túath* might find its churches' independence threatened by its political enemies. Such intertwining of ecclesiastical and secular interests became widespread in the eighth century, but was already underway in the second half of the seventh.[63]

VARIETY WITHIN THE CHURCH

As the preceding discussion suggests, it is not asceticism but variety that is the keynote of the early Irish church. This can best be appreciated by examining individual churches, beginning with Armagh (Map 10). In the seventh century this claimed that it had been Patrick's principal church. This is unlikely; but it may have been one of a number that owed their foundation to him, and archaeology has confirmed fifth-century activity at the bottom of the hill at 'Na Ferta' ('the gravemounds'), which preceded the church settlement on the hilltop.[64] Armagh's name includes that of the pagan goddess Macha, and its

61 Doherty (1982); Charles-Edwards (1984).

62 There were both 'base' and 'free' *manaig*: cf. Hughes (1966), pp. 136–42; Doherty (1982), pp. 315–18; Charles-Edwards (2000), p. 118.

63 Ó Corráin (1981); Charles-Edwards (1989), p. 36; (1998), pp. 70–4; Doherty (1991), p. 63.

64 *Liber Angeli* I, 7–9, 17; Muirchú, *Vita Patricii* BII.6, and II.4 and 6 (pp. 108–12, 116); Hamlin and Lynn (1988), pp. 57–61; Doherty (1991), esp. pp. 72–3; cf. Sharpe (1982).

Map 10 Location of Irish churches named in the text

site lies just 3 kilometres distant from the Emain Macha of legend, a pre-Christian sacral site. Aerial photography and early maps suggest inner and outer enclosures at Armagh, and the seventh-century *Liber Angeli* reveals that Armagh was then a complex ecclesiastical settlement. It had virgins, penitents and married people, who attended a church in the northern area, while bishops, priests, anchorites and other male religious attended a southern church, which boasted extensive relics. Over all, was the self-styled archbishop. There is also reference to pilgrims, the sick and asylum seekers. Armagh's straitened hilltop site, even with its outlying areas (*suburbana*), was claimed as inadequate for all seeking refuge there.[65] By the late seventh century Armagh was angling for support from the Uí Néill dynasty, while simultaneously cultivating relations with the Dál Fiatach dynasty of Ulster.[66]

Kildare in Leinster presents a similar picture of outer and inner enclosures,[67] of a link with the pagan past, of a large, mixed community looking to the church, and of royal interest – this time from the Uí Dúnlainge. One distinctive feature is that Kildare was a double monastery, reputedly founded by St Brigit, and comprising nuns together with a bishop and his male clerics. It was presided over jointly by the abbess and bishop, and by the later seventh century boasted a large wooden church with internal partitions, which enabled the nuns and clerics, and also lay women and men, to worship simultaneously, but shielded from sight of the opposite sex. St Brigit and her first bishop were enshrined either side of the altar, their tombs embellished 'with pendant gold and silver crowns and various images'. Like Armagh, Kildare was a 'city of refuge' or sanctuary, and was also thronged with people seeking abundant feasts or healing, or bringing gifts, or just gawping at the crowds.[68] The way in which these churches could serve such diverse needs was through internal division of their extensive sites, reserving an inner sanctum just for contemplatives or clerics. A synodical ruling defines the most sacred area as accessible only to clerics (cf. Armagh's southern church); the next area was open to lay people 'not much given to wickedness'; and the outer area was accessible to all, including wrongdoers seeking sanctuary.[69] Sometimes, as at Armagh and Nendrum, internal divisions can still be traced.[70]

At the opposite extreme from the bustling crowds at Kildare are the remote hermitage sites on coastal islands.[71] Most dramatic of all is Skellig Michael, a great pyramid of rock with two peaks, which rises steeply from the Atlantic some 14 kilometres off the Kerry coast. The main monastic site lies underneath the north-east peak, and consists of two small oratories, six beehive huts, a little graveyard with stone crosses and cross-slabs, and a small garden. At most it would have housed an abbot and twelve monks, serving presumably as a communal hermitage. Life there must always have been very harsh; yet Skellig has another, even more ascetic site. Perched high up on the south peak lies a

65 *Liber Angeli* 6, 14–16, 19.

66 Muirchú, *Vita Patricii* I.10–12, II.4–14 (pp. 74–81, 116–23); Moisl (1987).

67 Swan (1985), pp. 84–9, 98.

68 Cogitosus, *Vita Brigitae* c.32 (*AA SS* edn c.VIII, 39). See also Doherty (1985); Ó Corráin (1987), pp. 296–307.

69 *Collectio Canonum Hibernensis* XLIV.5, e; Doherty (1985), esp. pp. 56–9.

70 Herity (1984); Edwards (1990), pp. 105–21.

71 Herity (1989).

tiny hermitage site with its own oratory, hut and water-collecting basins. To get there at all requires rock climbing.[72]

The contemplative function of Skellig is clear: it served as 'a desert in the ocean'.[73] However not all islands were uninhabited, and not all island churches were contemplative hermitages. Just off the mainland opposite Skellig – or rather, in the channel between the mainland and Beginish – lies the tiny Church Island, which originally had a wooden oratory and hut, later rebuilt in stone. This site probably began as a hermitage, but metamorphosed into a small hereditary church.[74] 'The Rule of Patrick' shows that each *túath* might be expected to have not just its principal church but also a number of small churches serving the local *manaig*, and cared for by (at most) a single priest.[75]

As regards the principal churches of the *túatha*, these were headed by a bishop, but may have been multifunctional communities from the outset. Tírechán, writing in the late seventh century, represents the first bishop of Cell Toch in Corcu Teimne (west Connacht) together with his sister as 'monks of Patrick', while the more famous church of Aghagower nearby similarly had a bishop and a nun as its founding figures.[76] During the seventh century these *túath* episcopal churches declined in standing, being overtaken by more recent monastic foundations.[77] Many were subordinated to these monasteries; for instance, Cell Toch was subordinated to Clonmacnois. Sometimes subordination led to loss of their own bishop, as befell Coleraine in the north-east. Often, however, the church continued to function as an episcopal church, with a bishop overseeing the *túath* as before; but it now owed allegiance – and often tribute – to the superior church. Those churches that entered into association with Armagh retained their episcopal status, as did Aghagower.

Let us turn now to the monasteries like Clonmacnois, Bangor and Iona, which were founded primarily as places for living the monastic life on sites with no previous religious history. As such, they may have differed – at least in their early days – both from the *túath* episcopal churches and also from churches like Armagh and Kildare, which had rights of sanctuary (and, perhaps significantly, were on former pagan sites).[78] Iona certainly had a different set of priorities

[72] O'Sullivan and Sheehan (1996), pp. 278–90; Horn, Marshall and Rourke (1990).

[73] Cf. p. 459 below.

[74] Cf. O'Kelly (1958); Ó Corráin (1981), pp. 339–40.

[75] 'Rule of Patrick', 11–16.

[76] Tírechán, *Collectanea*, *cc.*37; 39, 8; 47, 4. These sites lie between Westport Bay and Lough Mask. Herren (1989), p. 83; above, n. 42; Charles-Edwards (2000), pp. 225–6.

[77] Doherty (1991), esp. pp. 60–6, 73–81; Charles-Edwards (2000), pp. 55–60, 251–7; below, pp. 418–200.

[78] Cf. Ó Corráin (1987), pp. 301–3; Clonmacnois and Iona are perhaps examples of those texts' 'apostolic cities'.

from Kildare. It had a guesthouse for visiting pilgrims, but the impression given is that these were people seeking spiritual counsel or wishing to share the religious life for a while, rather than crowds thronging a shrine in expectation of miracles – though this may be due partially to the abbot's perspective, rather than to that of the lay people themselves.[79] Certainly St Columba's remains were not placed in a special shrine to attract pilgrims; and a Columban monk's worry that lay people would crowd to the island for their patron's funeral was divinely answered by a period of stormy weather, which prevented any but the monks themselves being present.[80] Iona's island site thus served its desire to remain a place apart, while yet providing good communications by sea. As well as the main monastery on Iona there were subordinate monasteries on other islands, some of which had specialised functions such as catering for penitents or for anchorites; equally, Iona's foundations in populated areas will have become involved in pastoral ministry, as is attested for the Northumbrian daughter houses of Lindisfarne and Melrose.[81] Thus whereas Armagh catered for everyone from anchorites through clergy and lay people to penitents and sanctuary seekers on the one site, Iona itself remained a monastic community, as we would understand it, though the Columban community as a whole fulfilled most of Armagh's functions.

It is possible, however, that Iona was unusual in maintaining its distance from surrounding society. Sites in mainland Ireland will have needed to provide for their *manaig* and for penitents, at least. A legal text indicates that a church in good standing should have a full complement of clerics to provide baptism, communion, mass, prayer for the dead and preaching; it should give hospitality, and include people living the active life, others living the contemplative life, and also people serving a term of penance attached to it.[82] Another text states succinctly that the three things required of a church are a monk, a student and a penitent.[83] This implies a school. Basic schooling was probably quite widely available, but for more advanced studies it would perhaps be necessary to seek out a renowned master or monastic school, as we see with Columbanus leaving his native Leinster to study with Sinilis of Bangor.[84] Thus by the mid-eighth century most churches of any size in Ireland were probably multifunctional communities; and even those which had started as places for living the monastic life had become so integrated into ordinary secular society that we find them fighting each other, as with Clonmacnois and Durrow in 764.

79 Cf. Adomnán, *Vita Columbae* I.30, 32, 44, with *Amra Choluimb Chille* VI and VII.

80 Adomnán, *Vita Columbae* III.23.

81 Adomnán, *Vita Columbae* I.21 and 30, II.39, III.23; Bede, *Vita Cuthberti* cc.9, 15–16; Thacker (1992).

82 *Bretha Nemed Toísech* 3, 6, 12; cf. *Collectio Canonum Hibernensis* XLII.1.

83 *Collectio Canonum Hibernensis* XLII.15.

84 Charles-Edwards (1998), pp. 66–7, 74; Ó Cróinín (1982), pp. 283–6 and (1995), pp. 174–89.

Early medieval Ireland thus had different types and sizes of church; by no means all of these were 'monasteries', as we would understand the term. Four points are important in bridging the gap between the early medieval reality and popular misconceptions of it. One of these, about the relative importance of bishops and abbots as church leaders, will be discussed later; the remainder will be noted here. First, appearances can be deceptive: several seemingly remote monasteries in fact lay adjacent to medieval thoroughfares, as did Clonmacnois. Skellig and Iona do indeed represent communal hermitage and coenobitic monastery respectively, but neither was necessarily typical. Secondly, there is the problem of change over time. Church Island, for instance, probably began as a hermitage site, but metamorphosed into a family church. Other hermitages may have developed into full monasteries, as perhaps happened with Glendalough in the Wicklow mountains.[85] Most important of all is the intriguing development of such monasteries into multifunctional communities, where those living the religious life might shrink to a tiny proportion of the whole church family. How far this development had gone by 700, it is impossible to know. But it is tempting to suggest that when Cogitosus in the mid or late seventh century described Kildare as 'a monastery city (*monasterii civitatis*) as we call it', justifying the term city (despite Kildare's lack of surrounding walls) on the grounds of the innumerable people flocking thither, he was innovating; and that he was innovating to describe a new development.[86] If so, he was soon followed; and while Adomnán preferred the term *monasterium* (monastery), and early annals kept on Iona used the term *eclesia* (church), by the eighth century the term *civitas* (city) was creeping into the annals, even for Iona itself.[87] This may represent no more than a change of annalists; but it may indicate a change from communities focussed primarily on the religious life to more diverse communities where this concern had become that of a minority.

Thirdly, if terminology can help us in this respect, in others it confuses the modern reader. Thus one crucial question is what is meant by the terms 'monk', 'abbot' and 'monastery'. As the 'Rule of Patrick' shows, even a small church served by (at most) one priest would be supported by *manaig*, 'monks', who in effect were monastic tenant-farmers; the head of the church (either a priest, or a layman who would be responsible for providing a priest) would in legal terms be the 'abbot' of these *manaig*, and the church could thus be described as a 'monastery'. On the other hand, there would, in these very small churches, be

[85] Cf. Oengus, *Félire Oengusso*, prologue 193, 209; *Vita Sancti Coemgeni cc.*6, 16, 24–5; Henry (1964), pp. 50–1.

[86] Cogitosus, *Vita Brigitae c.*32 (*AA SS* edn *c.*VIII, 38).

[87] *Liber Angeli* 17, 21; MacDonald (1982), and cf. *Annals of Ulster* s.a. 555, 558, 635; MacDonald (1984), pp. 273–81; Charles-Edwards (2000), p. 119.

no one living the monastic life as we understand it.[88] Thus to say that virtually every church in seventh-century Ireland was a monastery is technically true; but it masks, rather than reveals, the varied nature of the early Irish church, which contained 'monasteries' as integrated into society as Kildare, as remote from society as Skellig, as straightforward as Iona, and as basic as a tiny church with one priest ministering to the surrounding monastic tenants.

THE EASTER CONTROVERSY

Easter, the most important Christian festival, does not fall on a fixed date, and the difficulties of reconciling lunar and solar prescriptions in the calculation of the date led to the emergence of slightly different rules for determining on which Sunday Easter should fall.[89] In many years, these divergent approaches would still yield the same Sunday; but not always. The British and Irish churches had adopted an eighty-four-year Easter cycle, and assigned Easter to the Sunday that fell between the fourteenth and twentieth days of the relevant lunar month. They apparently based their system on the rules put forward by Anatolius, but as modified by Sulpicius Severus (*c.*400 AD).[90] When Columbanus arrived on the continent in 591, however, he found the Frankish church and the papacy using the tables of Victorius of Aquitaine (457 AD). This was an unsatisfactory adaptation of the Alexandrian nineteen-year cycle. Then, around the 630s, the papacy abandoned that in favour of the true Alexandrian (or 'Dionysiac') system, which was eventually to win the day. Although the Victorian and the Alexandrian approaches differed in several important respects, they generally agreed on which Sunday Easter should be celebrated, whereas the eighty-four-year cycle followed by the Britons and the Irish more often yielded divergent dates.

Columbanus encountered opposition to his divergent Easter dates from early on in his continental career, but he resolutely refused to change to the Victorian system, which he judged flawed. After his death, however, his followers at Luxeuil and Bobbio were forced to adopt it.[91] Pope Honorius' acquaintance with Bobbio alerted him to the fact that Ireland as a whole dated Easter according to different criteria, and *c.*628 he therefore wrote to the Irish on the Easter question, apparently threatening them with excommunication unless they conformed.[92] This prompted Christians in the southern half of Ireland to discuss the matter in a synod, and then to send a fact-finding mission to Rome. When this reported back *c.*632 that all the other nationalities present in Rome

88 Charles-Edwards (1992), p. 67. 89 On all this, see Charles-Edwards (2000), pp. 391–415.
90 McCarthy (1994). 91 Stancliffe (2001), esp. pp. 205–8, 213.
92 Bede, *HE* II.19; Cummian, *De Controversia Paschali*, pp. 90–1.

were celebrating Easter on the same date, whereas the Irish Easter differed that year [631] by a month, this confirmed the southern Irish willingness to adopt the Victorian system. The rest of Ireland, however, did not conform till later in the century – and then to the Alexandrian system, which the papacy had meanwhile adopted. Churches belonging to the Columban (Iona) federation did not conform until 716. Much of the seventh century was therefore marked by the controversy, and separate synods were attended by members of the rival 'Roman' and 'Irish' factions. Their differently shaped tonsures – a way of cutting the hair that served as a badge of clerical and monastic status – were a visible sign of their 'Roman' or 'Irish' allegiance. Further, the two groups probably differed in their exegetical methods and approach.[93]

The Easter controversy was important for its repercussions. The issue is confusing, because sometimes it was treated simply as a case of unfortunate divergence; but sometimes, as in England after Theodore's arrival in 669, adherents of the 'Celtic' Easter found themselves labelled as heretics and schismatics, whose sacraments were denied validity. In an Irish context, the issue was important because it raised the question of how far Ireland needed to conform to continental practices, or alternatively could be allowed to develop its own customs.[94] Although conformity on Easter was eventually achieved, in certain respects the Irish church continued to develop its own synthesis with Irish law,[95] and to evolve rather differently in organisational terms. The controversy also posed the linked questions of how decisions should be reached, and where authority should lie.[96] One can perhaps see amongst the Irish a readiness to seek the answer in scriptural exegesis and in discussion in synods, rather than in decisions reached by those in positions of authority as office-holders, i.e. as bishops or popes.[97] Yet the eighty-four-year-cycle adherents were sometimes as ready to appeal to authorities as the Roman party. It is just that their authorities were highly regarded because of their closeness to God, holiness of life and exegetical skill, rather than because of their office within the church.[98] Thus, what the Easter controversy in Ireland also brings out is their different understanding from the continental church as to where authority within the church lay. This helps to explain why the Irish traditionalists do not seem to have felt the need for an ecclesiastical hierarchy headed by a single leader for the Irish church as a whole. However, the Easter controversy and

93 Ó Néill (1984); cf. Sharpe (1992b), pp. 44–5; Charles-Edwards (2000), ch. 9, esp. pp. 396–405, 411–15.

94 Columbanus, *Epistulae* III.2–3. Cf. Charles-Edwards (2000), p. 391 and n. 1.

95 Cf. Ó Corráin (1984); Mac Niocaill (1984).

96 Cf. Charles-Edwards (2000), pp. 411–15.

97 Columbanus, *Epistulae* II.3–5, 7–8; *Epistulae* V.10–12. Cf. Charles-Edwards (2000), Hughes (1987), no. XV, pp. 6–17; pp. 274–7; Sheehy (1987).

98 Columbanus, *Epistulae* I.5; Bede, *HE* III.25; Stephanus, *Vita Wilfridi* c.10. Cf. Stancliffe (1999), pp. 131–3.

the accompanying links with the continental church introduced such hierarchical concepts to the circles of Irish *Romani*; and the churches of Kildare and then Armagh soon realised that these ideas could be harnessed to their own advantage.

QUESTIONS OF ORGANISATION

The organisation of the early Irish church is a complex, but important topic. It differed in a few, intriguing, respects from the organisation of the church elsewhere at the time – and, indeed, since. Unfortunately, however, the evidence is all too slender, patchy in its incidence, and difficult to interpret, which explains why it has recently aroused scholarly controversy.[99]

One underlying reason was the shifting nature of political power in Ireland, and the lack of a fixed framework and single overarching hierarchy such as the Roman imperial structure had provided on the continent. For instance in seventh-century Leinster the provincial overkingship passed from the Uí Cheinnselaig south of the Wicklow mountains to the Uí Dúnlainge and the Uí Máil, neighbours and rivals to the north-west of the mountains. Such dynastic and geographical shifts occurred frequently at every level of Irish overkingship, and this made it difficult to establish a stable ecclesiastical hierarchy of the type found on the continent, where the bishop of the (fixed) capital city of a province was always the metropolitan bishop. In turn, the overking of Leinster would have seen himself as on the same level as the other provincial overkings. There was thus no agreed leader amongst the provinces, and so no basis for any one church to win recognition as the leading church in Ireland.

When we turn to the structure of society into which churchmen had to be slotted, we discover intriguing differences there also. Society was certainly hierarchical; but parallel to the ordinary lay hierarchy, which ran from the farmer at the bottom up through the grades of nobility to the king at the top, there were also separate hierarchies for men of learning. It looks as though the latter provided the model for accommodating churchmen; and Irish law tracts disclose not a *single* ecclesiastical hierarchy based on clerical orders, but rather *three, parallel* ecclesiastical hierarchies. First, there was a hierarchy of clerical orders running from the lowly doorkeeper up via the exorcist, lector, subdeacon, deacon and priest, to the bishop at the top. Secondly, there was a hierarchy of Christian scholars running from the one who simply knew his psalms up through those who had greater and greater knowledge, which culminated at the top in the master ecclesiastical scholar. Thirdly, there was a hierarchy of

99 Initiated by Sharpe (1984b).

church officers running from the miller or suchlike at the bottom up to the *airchinnech*, the 'erenagh' or church head (Latin *princeps*) at the top.[100] Thus, whereas on the continent the bishop was the single head of the church in his diocese, responsible for teaching and safeguarding the faith and for controlling the church's wealth, in Ireland his functions might be divided. An individual could, of course, be both an ordained bishop and a highly trained scholar, or bishop and church head; but often the roles were separate. In terms of status, it meant that several leaders or experts in their special fields ranked on the same level as the *túath* king and chief poet: bishops, master ecclesiastical scholars, heads of the more important churches,[101] and also the most highly regarded anchorites – though even the lawyers did not construct a sevenfold hierarchy of holiness!

That, at least, is a somewhat schematised portrayal of the status of churchmen as it had evolved by the late seventh century. Let us now go back to the earliest period for which we have evidence. The decrees of the 'First Synod of Patrick' show the church – including its wealth – under the control of bishops; and the individual bishop's sphere of jurisdiction was the *plebs*, 'people', which should almost certainly be equated with the *túath*.[102] We should therefore envisage each *túath* forming a little diocese of its own, with its episcopal mother-church. Within the *túath* there were also small churches, many of them family churches, served by a single priest. In theory, at least, these were supervised by the bishop of the *túath*. By the late seventh century there was a surprisingly dense network of such lesser churches.[103]

At the same time, however, the sixth and seventh centuries saw a wave of ascetic and monastic enthusiasm; and, as we have seen, this resulted in the foundation of several monasteries. We should remember that holy men, rather than bishops, have always tended to attract lay piety. The layman's concern was to engage the intercession of one whose prayers on his behalf would carry weight with God. An ascetic monk like St Cainnech fitted the bill far better than the well-fed head of the local episcopal church, as a story in the *Life of St Cainnech* implies.[104] Further, because such monasteries were sometimes less closely tied to the ruling dynasty of a specific people than was the original episcopal church,

100 Breatnach (1987), pp. 84–5, where minor variations are detailed; cf. Charles-Edwards (2000), pp. 124–36, 264–77, esp. pp. 267–71, 276–7; Picard (2000); see also the following note. Compare the continental organisation, Scheibelreiter, chapter 25 below.

101 See Charles-Edwards (2000), pp. 132–3, 267: by no means every church head attained such high status.

102 *First Synod of St Patrick* 1, 4, 5, 23–7, 30 (for the date, see n. 27 above); cf. Charles-Edwards (2000), pp. 247–50.

103 'Rule of Patrick', esp. 11–16; Ó Corráin (1981), pp. 336–40; Sharpe (1984b), pp. 254–9; (1992a), pp. 86–109.

104 Charles-Edwards (2000), pp. 262–4; cf. Doherty (1991), p. 65.

they might attract support from a greater number of patrons. This applied particularly to churches founded in border 'no man's land' areas, or in an insignificant (and so unthreatening) *túath*. Clonmacnois, in the unimportant kingdom of Delbnae Bethra, is a good example. It lay beside the River Shannon, which marked the boundary between Connacht and the southern Uí Néill spheres of authority, and was able to attract patronage from both.[105] Monasteries could thus be endowed with gifts of land that lay in other *túatha*; and when we also recall that monasteries founded by the same founder-saint could form a federation of churches under the leadership of the church where the founder-saint was buried, we begin to see how they came to eclipse the older, free-standing episcopal churches in power and wealth. Further contributory factors were that the episcopal churches in Ireland had small dioceses, and none of the status and authority that came to bishops on the continent because of political and social circumstances there. The way in which an old episcopal church could in Ireland find itself outclassed by a nearby monastery is illustrated by Tírechán describing the old church of the Corcu Saí as 'Domnach Saírigi, next to Duleek'. Although an ancient church, and originally the chief church of the Corcu Saí, by the late seventh century it was apparently so obscure that its location was described in relation to the more recent and more famous monastery of Duleek.[106]

On the continent, bishops did their utmost to ensure that they retained control over all in their diocese, including hermits and monasteries. Monks were explicitly placed under the jurisdiction of their diocesan bishop at the Council of Chalcedon in 451, and this ruling was re-enacted by synods in Spain and Gaul.[107] However, there is no sign of corresponding canons from Ireland. On the contrary, where a Frankish synod insists that no monk should leave his monastery and found a cell 'without the permission of the bishop and the agreement of his abbot', the same ruling occurs in the Irish collection of canons with a significant difference: the monk now only needs 'the permission of his abbot'.[108] Since both Columbanus and Adomnán's *Life of St Columba* bear out the significance of the abbot's permission, while omitting any reference to the bishop, it looks as though monastic founders in Ireland were never subject to the bishop's authority.[109] It is true that the eighth- or ninth-century 'Rule of Patrick' assigns the bishop the role of acting as spiritual adviser to rulers and erenaghs, and also to clergy in his *túath*; and this has been seen as

[105] Charles-Edwards (2000), p. 26, and cf. p. 257.

[106] Tírechán, *Collectanea* c.27. See Doherty (1991), esp. pp. 54, 60–1, 65–6, 73–5.

[107] Bittermann (1938), esp. p. 200, n. 8; cf. Gregory of Tours, *Hist.* VIII.15.

[108] I Orléans (AD 511), canon 22: ed. Gaudemet and Basdevant I (1989), p. 84; *Collectio Canonum Hibernensis* XXXIX.16.

[109] Columbanus, *Epistulae* I.7; Adomnán, *Vita Columbae* I.6.

indicating the bishop's influence over the monastic church.[110] However, this text probably emanates from Armagh, which was keen to uphold the continuing rights of *túath* episcopal churches.[111] There is no supporting evidence that the heads of important monasteries ever accepted its claims; and the evidence from Columbanus' monasteries on the continent as well as from Bede's account of Iona points rather to the view that the diocesan bishops were not recognised as having rights of supervision and control over Irish monasteries.[112] This is also borne out by Adomnán's story about a Hebridean abbot summoning a bishop and compelling him to ordain an unworthy candidate to the priesthood, in flagrant disregard of the provisions of the 'Rule of Patrick'. We should further note that the abbot was visited by divine punishment, not episcopal correction.[113]

At this point the relevance of our earlier discussion about parallel church hierarchies should be apparent; for alongside the ordinary *túath* bishop, and enjoying the same status, ranked the heads of major churches. So, for instance, the head of the federation of Columban monasteries was the abbot of Iona; and this meant that he ranked on the same level as a *túath* bishop, although in terms of ecclesiastical orders he was only a priest. What is more, we know that the priest-abbot of Iona was responsible for appointing priors to the monasteries under his control in Ireland and Dál Riada, and also for choosing bishops for Northumbria until the Synod of Whitby. The bishops appointed by the abbot were under the abbot's authority; and so, for instance, Aidan, Finan and Colman had to keep to the Easter reckoning in use on Iona; they were not free to adopt the Roman system of reckoning, even if they had wanted to.[114]

As regards the question of how the church was able to reach decisions when authority was dispersed, the answer appears to have been the synod. This enabled representation from all major churches in an area, whether episcopal or monastic in origin; and it also allowed for the coming together of bishops, church heads, ecclesiastical scholars and anchorites.[115] Ideally, issues should be discussed with regard to the principles discernible in Scripture, or failing that, in patristic texts, earlier canons and the examples of the saints; and, ideally, general agreement was reached.[116] Indeed, since synods were church affairs, and their decisions were not enforced by kings,[117] agreement, even if it was only agreement to differ, was the only way forward. In the seventh century,

110 'Rule of Patrick' 1, 6–7. Sharpe (1984b), p. 253; cf. Charles-Edwards (1992), p. 75.

111 Cf. Charles-Edwards (1992), pp. 69–75; Doherty (1991), pp. 61–6, 73–9.

112 Jonas, *Vita Columbani* II.23 and Stancliffe (2001), pp. 201–2, 207–8, 212–16, 219. Bede, *HE* III.4; Stanclifle, below p. 456.

113 Adomnán, *Vita Columbae* I.36; cf. 'Rule of Patrick', 3.

114 Bede, *HE* III.4 and 25.

115 Charles-Edwards (2000), pp. 274–81.

116 Ó Cróinín (1995), pp. 152–3.

117 For the exception to this rule, see Charles-Edwards (2000), pp. 280–1.

however, the repercussions of the Easter controversy led to a division between those who thought that recourse should be had to Rome, if agreement could not be reached within Ireland, and those who continued to favour discussion in Irish synods rather than recourse to such external authority.

Controversy and closer links to the continent provided a forcing ground for the development of ideas of ecclesiastical organisation in Ireland. By the late seventh century we have evidence for three *different* types of organisational structure above the *túath* level. The first type is hierarchical, and is embodied in the claim that one Irish church was the head of all the other churches in Ireland. First Kildare claimed that its jurisdiction (*parroechia*) spread throughout Ireland, 'from sea to sea', although it did not spell out how this would affect other churches.[118] Then, later in the seventh century, Armagh in its turn claimed supremacy throughout Ireland. This may have been in response not just to Kildare but also to Northumbrian pretensions to ecclesiastical overlordship over northern Ireland, with Northumbria opportunistically seizing upon northern Ireland's non-conformity to the Roman Easter.[119] Armagh's claims, made in the *Liber Angeli* ('Book of the Angel'), were coherently expressed and far more concrete than Kildare's. The basis of its claim was that because St Patrick had converted all the Irish, and because Armagh was his special church, therefore God had assigned all the tribes of the Irish to the jurisdiction (*paruchia*) of Patrick/Armagh. Other, independent churches are represented as secondary, and owe their position to Patrick's generosity in sharing all that God has given him. Patrick/Armagh, however, retained various specific rights, including superior status to all other churches within Ireland and appellate jurisdiction, with appeal allowed only to Rome; it also claimed a special relationship with all the original episcopal and *domnach* churches, together with an invitation to all monks to abandon their own monasteries and join Patrick. Here, then, we see a truly hierarchical conception of the Irish church, with the archbishop of Armagh at the apex of that hierarchy, and other churches assigned a lesser status.

The second type of organisational structure is the grouping together of *túatha* into small-scale provinces. In fact, according to one canon attributed to a *Romani* synod, there was quite an ecclesiastical hierarchy: it is implied that not only would there be a metropolitan bishop of the small-scale province, covering perhaps four *túatha*, but that there was also a higher grade of bishop above him, probably at the level of the major overkingdoms (confusingly also known as 'provinces') like Leinster or Munster.[120] The details need not concern

[118] Cogitosus, *Vita Brigitae*, preface. [119] Charles-Edwards (2000), pp. 429–38.

[120] *Collectio Canonum Hibernensis* XX, as interpreted by Charles-Edwards (1992), pp. 65–6, 72 n. 50, and (2000), pp. 126, 423–6.

us; we can content ourselves simply with noting that these canons do seem to imply an ecclesiastical structure similar to that found on the continent, using the political structures of overkingdoms as ecclesiastical provinces. The result would be a small number of over-overbishops of equal status, rather than a single head of the church in Ireland.

The third type of organisational structure implied by our sources is very different: Tírechán shows various major churches competing with each other in an attempt to claim that individual churches should in some sense be subject to them, or federated to them.[121] The basis for this claim was often the accepted principle (operative also in *Liber Angeli*) that all churches established by the same founder-saint or his heir should be grouped together as his *paruchia*, i.e under his jurisdiction. Ambitious monasteries would then claim that a disputed church had really been established by their own founder, or by one of his monks. This was partially, but not entirely, a matter of the more powerful churches forcibly subjugating smaller ones. A more subtle approach was favoured by Armagh, which sought to woo episcopal and *domnach* churches by offering them an honourable relationship and scope to continue to choose their own head, rather than imposing an Armagh nominee.[122] Sometimes, at least, churches felt that it was in their interests to accept Armagh's invitation. A classic case is the decision of the episcopal church of Sletty, the chief church of the Uí Bairrche in southern Leinster – a *túath* of middling importance by the late seventh century – to put itself under Armagh. This is generally interpreted as a pre-emptive move to prevent itself from being forcibly taken over by Kildare.[123] But, however established, the end result was the growth of several federations of churches, or *paruchiae*, the most important being those headed by the greatest churches like Armagh or Clonmacnois. Sometimes, as with Sletty and Armagh, not all members of a *paruchia* belonged to the same province as their head church. One can envisage the mapping of these rival federations as a patchwork quilt, with all the churches marked in one colour belonging (say) to the Columban federation, those in another to (say) Armagh, and so on. Unfortunately, however, any such map would be woefully inadequate owing to gaps in our evidence, and to some churches being disputed between rival claimants.

By this stage, the reader's head will be spinning. How could Kildare and Armagh both claim to be the supreme church in Ireland? How can either of their claims be harmonised with the evidence for Ireland containing a provincial structure where there was no single supreme bishop of all Ireland, but rather

[121] For example, Tírechán, *Collectanea cc.*7, 22, 25, 47.4–48. Cf. Charles-Edwards (1984), pp. 167–9; Doherty (1991), pp. 62–4. Charles-Edwards (2000), pp. 250–7.

[122] *Additamenta* 9; Doherty (1991), pp. 73–81.

[123] *Additamenta* 16; Doherty (1991), pp. 75–8.

one overbishop for each main political overkingdom within Ireland? Further, does not the evidence for individual churches building up federations, which might include churches in a different overkingdom, contradict the provincial model?

Some of these problems can be speedily resolved. First, although both Kildare and Armagh *claimed* to be the supreme church in Ireland, the assertions of Cogitosus and the *Liber Angeli* are evidence of claims made: not of their claims being accepted. On the contrary, *Liber Angeli* is explicit evidence that Armagh refused to accept Kildare's claim; and Tírechán, although writing on behalf of Armagh, openly admits that other churches in Ireland refused to accept its claims.[124] Confirmation that no single church in Ireland was widely recognised as being of superior status can be found in the absence of any citations to that effect in the Irish canonical collection.[125] This, however, does not preclude the likelihood that Armagh was recognised as the first among equals by the late seventh century, even in Munster.[126]

Until recently, the confusing and sometimes contradictory rulings about ecclesiastical provinces in the Irish canonical collection were also dismissed as belonging to the realm of aspiration, not actuality. They are mostly ascribed to synods of the Roman party, and have been seen as reflecting a failed attempt by the *Romani* to impose a continental, hierarchical structure on the Irish church.[127] Recently, however, attention has been drawn to various pieces of evidence which suggest that these canons should be taken seriously. For instance, some Irish texts refer to a 'bishop of bishops', or 'supreme noble bishop', implying that different rankings of bishops did indeed exist.[128] Even more interesting are later annalistic obits recording some individuals who were bishops of an area covering more than one *túath*, sometimes a province. However, the role of 'overbishop' of a province was not tied to a specific church, as on the continent; so, for instance, both Máel-Móedhóc of Killeshin (d. 917) and Anmchad of Kildare (d. 981) are recorded as archbishop or bishop of Leinster.[129] Unfortunately we do not know whether such 'overbishops' had a fixed role in a hierarchical structure, or whether the titles were bestowed on individuals as a personal honour.[130] Such uncertainties make it difficult to know whether a

[124] *Liber Angeli*, esp. 32; Tírechán, *Collectanea* c.18.

[125] I here follow Charles-Edwards (2000), pp. 424–6; for a contrary view, Etchingham (1999), pp. 155, 160–1.

[126] Sharpe (1984c), p. 66; Breatnach (1986), pp. 49–51; Charles-Edwards (2000), p. 426.

[127] Sharpe (1984c), pp. 67–8.

[128] Etchingham (1999), pp. 72, 156, 162; Charles-Edwards (2000), p. 259.

[129] Etchingham (1999), pp. 177–88; Charles-Edwards (2000), pp. 260–1. These show that such titles belonged to individuals, rather than to a fixed church, much as the provincial overkingship could also rotate.

[130] Cf. Davies (1992), p. 14.

coherent system of provincial church organisation, with a hierarchy of levels, did in fact win general acceptance.

As regards the third type of organisational structure, the federations or *paruchiae*, the evidence for these, at least, is convincing. Two further points should be made about the workings of such federations. First, although dependent churches could be affiliated to a church in a different overkingdom, we should not regard this as common. The greatest churches, like Armagh, Kildare and Iona, did indeed have widely scattered churches under them. However, it was commoner for the majority of dependent churches to be in the neighbourhood of the dominant church, as, for instance, with the cluster of churches affiliated to Cork.[131] Often, then, the ties of province and the ties binding together a federation of churches will have reinforced each other. Secondly, we must not assume that whenever a lesser church became in some way linked to a federation headed by a more powerful church it necessarily lost its own identity. It so happens that some of our best evidence for the operation of a federation of churches concerns Iona; and the abbot of Iona did indeed direct the whole as one community (*familia*), appointing priors and transferring monks from one monastery to another.[132] Iona, however, may well have been unusual in this degree of centralisation; and, most of the time, when one church came to 'hold' a lesser church, we should think of the relationship as essentially an economic one. The lesser church would owe some form of tribute, whether this was a symbolic trifle, or an economic burden; but it would generally retain its own status. Thus an episcopal church could become subject to a monastery, but remain the episcopal church for the *túath* it served – though not in every case.[133]

In conclusion, we may say that the Irish church did have a form of episcopal organisation, and of groupings into provinces. Cutting across this structure, however, was the position of the most powerful monasteries, which seem never to have been effectively controlled by bishops; and this, combined with the fact that their heads were of the same status as bishops, had many churches within their *paruchiae* and controlled the resources of those churches,[134] meant that these heads were on a par with the most powerful people in the early Irish church. Thus in 700 Armagh's power in practice rested upon its prestige, lands, the number of churches federated to it and the support it could attract from kings, rather than on the grandiose claims put forward in *Liber Angeli*; and

131 Hurley (1982), pp. 304–5, 321–3.

132 MacDonald (1985), esp. pp. 184–5; Herbert (1988), pp. 31–5.

133 Hurley (1982), pp. 321–4; Sharpe (1984b), pp. 243–7; (1992a), pp. 97–100, 105–6; Charles-Edwards (2000), pp. 251–7; cf. Charles-Edwards (1989), p. 36.

134 Sharpe (1984b), pp. 263–4.

in 700 Adomnán, scholar, head of the Columban federation and – crucially – fourth cousin of the Uí Néill overking, was probably more influential than the bishop who headed the Armagh federation. His achievement at the synod of Birr in 698 testifies to this. Here, he succeeded in promoting a law protecting clerics, women and children from warfare; and this was guaranteed by mustering dozens of kings and high-ranking churchmen to support it, led by the bishop of Armagh.[135] This illustrates the potential scope for a great abbot to provide leadership within the early Irish church.

[135] Ní Dhonnchadha (1995).

CHAPTER 16

CHRISTIANITY AMONGST THE BRITONS, DALRIADAN IRISH AND PICTS

Clare Stancliffe

BRITAIN SOUTH OF THE CLYDE/FORTH AND BRITONS ABROAD

The centuries following the end of Roman rule in Britain were critical for the development of the British church, just as they obviously were for the determination of the political, ethnic and social structure of Britain as a whole. However tricky it may be to piece together the picture from the inadequate and very disparate sources that are available, we must keep in view the major achievements of these centuries. They saw not merely the consolidation of Christianity in those areas that remained free from the control of the incoming pagan Anglo-Saxons, but its spread to areas further north and west. Moreover, this was achieved despite the demise of the Romano-British cities and villas, and the Anglo-Saxon settlement of a great swathe of eastern and southern Britain: precisely those places and areas where the Romano-British church had been most in evidence. Since interpretations of the post-Roman period often depend on those of Christianity's fortunes in Roman Britain, we shall begin with a brief look at the latter.

THE ROMAN PRELUDE

By the time of Constantine I's conversion to Christianity in the early fourth century there were bishops at London, York and (probably) Lincoln.[1] The extent of Christianity's progress by 410 is controversial: we lack written evidence, and the archaeological evidence is open to different interpretations. We cannot reliably distinguish Christian burials from pagan ones unless there is supportive evidence of explicit Christian symbols or inscriptions, as at Poundbury in Dorset. Christians were generally buried in graves oriented west/east, with no grave goods, but so might pagans be; and occasionally there is evidence of

[1] Mann (1961); cf. Toynbee (1953), pp. 1–4.

a Christian burial with grave-goods, or oriented differently.[2] Similar problems can arise with the identification of buildings as Christian churches, as with the so-called 'church' at Silchester.[3] When the more reliable evidence for Christianity is mapped (Map 11), it reveals a significant scatter of evidence down the east side of Britain from York, southwards; and in the south of Britain this evidence extends as far west as Dorset. Contrariwise the western counties, and even parts of the midlands, remain largely blank apart from scattered Christian symbols on building materials and a few portable finds.[4] We must ask, however, whether such maps reflect the *actual* distribution of Christianity in Roman Britain, or simply the recognisable archaeological evidence for it. One warning signal is the correlation between the archaeological evidence for Christianity, and that for 'acculturation' or successful Romanisation.[5] Thus archaeology on its own cannot shed light on whether the population of western Britain was pagan or Christian.

A welcome sidelight is provided here by the writings of Patrick, the British missionary to Ireland. Patrick was probably born at the end of the fourth or in the first half of the fifth century, and Christianity reached back at least two generations in his well-to-do family: his father was a deacon, his grandfather a priest; and since their estate was in an area exposed to Irish raids, it presumably lay somewhere in western Britain within easy reach of the Irish Sea. Although Patrick and the others captured with him 'did not obey our priests', they were all at least nominally Christian.[6] This provides welcome confirmation of the normality of a Christian community in an area where archaeological evidence is sparse.

Archaeology is, however, valuable in showing the type of place and the class of people that had embraced Christianity. A generation ago, Romano-British Christianity was regarded simply as an urban and aristocratic phenomenon. Archaeology confirms this, most strikingly with the discovery of a church actually built in the middle of the forum at Lincoln, and with that of a house-church at Lullingstone villa, Kent.[7] However it also reveals that Christianity had reached the Roman fort at Richborough (Kent), and the small towns, such as Icklingham (Suffolk), Ashton (Northamptonshire) and Wiggonholt (Sussex).[8] This helps us to understand how Christianity could have survived in Britain at a time when the collapse of the money economy

[2] Rahtz (1977), p. 54; Farwell and Molleson (1993), pp. 137, 236; cf. Watts (1991), pp. 38–98.

[3] Toynbee (1953), pp. 6–9; Frere (1976); King (1983).

[4] Thomas (1981), pp. 106–7, 138; Morris (1983), p. 16; Watts (1991), pp. 90, 144; Mawer (1995).

[5] Jones and Mattingly (1990), pp. 151, 299.

[6] Patrick, *Confessio* 1; *Epistola* 10. Dumville *et al.* (1993), pp. 13–18.

[7] Toynbee (1953), pp. 9–12; Meates (1979), esp. pp. 18–19, 40–8, 53–7; Jones (1994).

[8] Brown (1971); West (1976), p. 121; Morris (1983), p. 18.

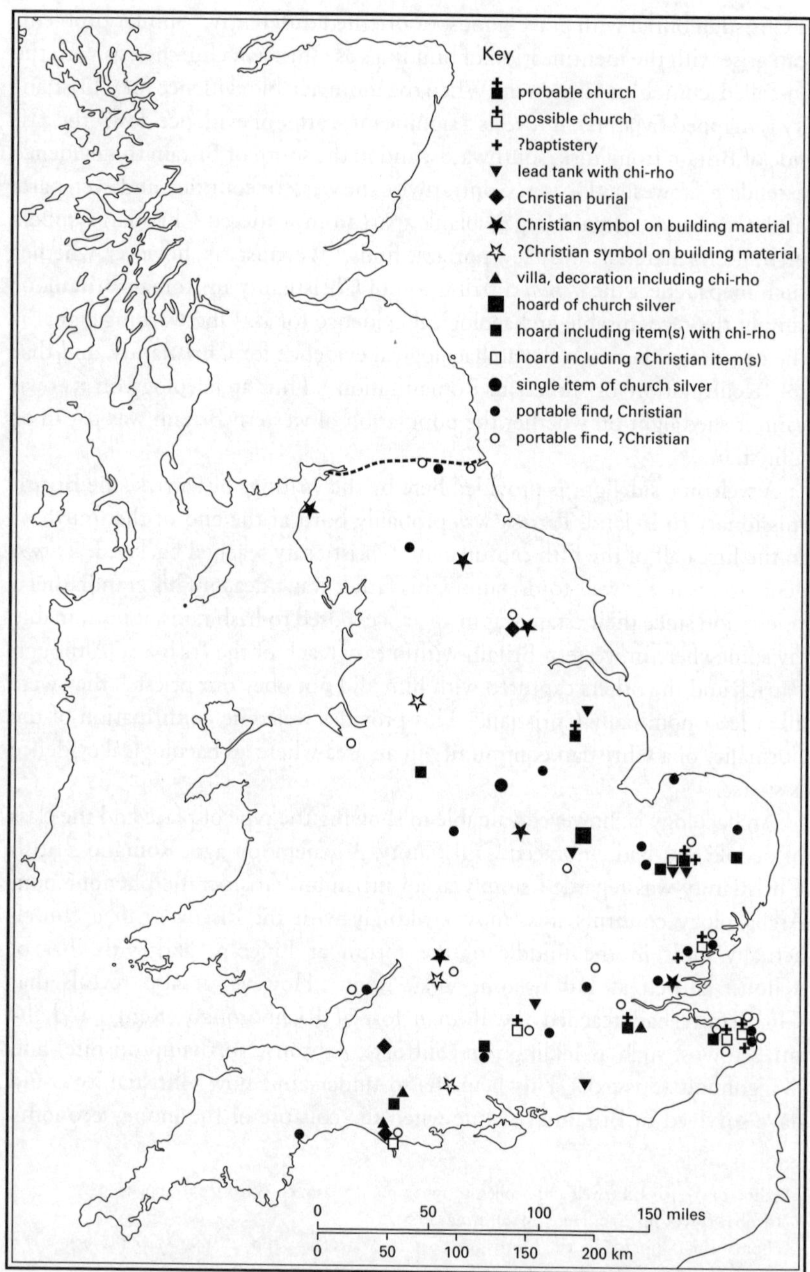

Map 11 Archaeological evidence of Christianity in Roman Britain

and sophisticated distribution systems led to the demise of city life and villa society.

Of course, even where evidence of Christianity is found, it tells us nothing about the proportion of Christians to pagans, and widely different assumptions have been made. The most plausible approach is to look at continental parallels, particularly for the survival of paganism. In Britain, the number of pagan temples in use appears to have peaked in the mid-fourth century, considerably later than on the continent. By the late fourth and early fifth centuries, however, the number of such temples was dropping sharply, albeit not as rapidly as abroad.[9] By the time that Gildas wrote in the first half of the sixth century, the implication is that British society was nominally Christian. Gildas castigates the bishops for failing to denounce sin; but not, we should note, for condoning paganism.[10] This does not preclude the likelihood that pockets of paganism remained in the countryside, out of sight of Gildas and the bishops (as indeed the *Life of St Samson* implies for Cornwall); but it makes 'high-profile' paganism unlikely.[11]

With this background sketched in, we can now turn to a question that has long intrigued the archaeologists. Archaeological evidence for Christianity in the Roman period has a predominantly eastern distribution, as we have seen. However, a totally different distribution appears on a map of the most tangible evidence for Christianity in post-Roman Britain: that is, upright stones bearing what are usually interpreted as memorial inscriptions,[12] many of which are explicitly Christian (Map 12). Most of these date from the fifth to the early seventh centuries, although a considerably longer time span has recently been argued for some of those from Dumnonia (Devon and Cornwall). Approximately 150 occur in Wales and another fifty in Dumnonia, while smaller numbers are found in the Isle of Man and scattered across northern Britain; some also occur in Brittany.[13] What is striking about this distribution is that it lies well away from the evidence of Christianity found on our earlier map, and indeed touches the more Romanised areas only occasionally. Even more interesting is the fact that the Christian formulas used have no ancestry in Britain, but can be paralleled on the continent, where the HIC IACET ('Here lies') type occurs at Trier in the late fourth century and at Lyons *c.*420–450, thereafter giving way to slightly longer formulas such as HIC REQVIESCIT IN PACE ('Here rests in peace').[14]

9 See P. Horne's graphs, *apud* Dark (1994), p. 33. Cf. Salway (1981) and (1984), pp. 734–9.
10 Gildas, *De Excidio*.
11 Cf. *Vita Samsonis* cc.3, 48–50; cf. Olson (1989), p. 16. For Yeavering, see Thacker, chapter 17 below.
12 But see Handley (1998).
13 Morris (1983), pp. 28–33, and cf. 20–3; Nash-Williams (1950); Okasha (1993); Thomas (1991–2); and cf. Thomas (1968); Macalister, *Corpus Inscriptionum* I and II Davies *et al.* (2000).
14 Knight (1981), pp. 57–60, and see now Handley (2001), esp. pp. 186–8; cf. Okasha (1993), pp. 116–21.

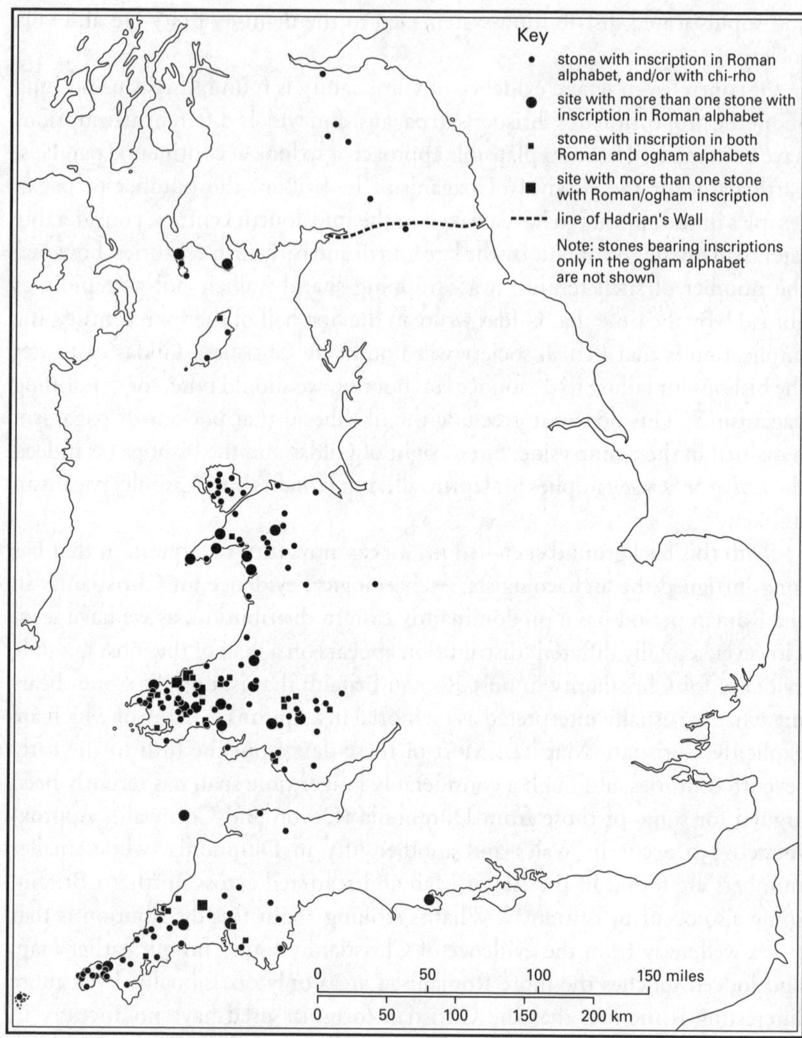

Map 12 Stones with post-Roman inscriptions

How should this disjunction between our two maps be interpreted? A generation ago a distinguished archaeologist surmised that Christianity in Roman Britain had been espoused only by the official and commercial elite; and, having failed to win over the rural population, had died out along with that elite. Britain therefore had to be reconverted by missionaries trained on the continent, who were active up the western seaways – witness the Latin inscriptions – and were credited with introducing monasticism. The suggested prototype of these was Ninian, whose church at Whithorn, dedicated to the Gallic monk-bishop St Martin, was the site of inscribed stones; and whose alleged training at Rome and missionary work among the southern Picts are mentioned – with a precautionary 'it is said' – in Bede's *Ecclesiastical History*, written perhaps three centuries later (731).[15]

The theory that Christianity wholly died out in Britain has since been convincingly rebutted.[16] None the less, the older model still exerts an influence. Thus the fact that Anglo-Saxon Kent was converted to Christianity by missionaries sent from Rome, and not by an indigenous British church, is sometimes attributed to the failure of Christianity to establish itself as strongly in Roman Britain as it did on the continent.[17] Again, the advent of monasticism is still sometimes portrayed as linked to the western seaways and to the distribution of at least some of the inscribed stones, and regarded as the true turning-point between sub-Roman and early medieval Christianity.[18] We will return to the question of the British church's alleged failure to convert the Anglo-Saxons later; in the meantime we shall examine the evidence that prompted the original theory, and reconsider that for Christianity in sub-Roman and early medieval Britain, giving special attention to northern and western Britain.

CHRISTIANITY IN SUB-ROMAN BRITAIN: CONTINUITY OR CULTURAL BREAK?

The contrast between the map of Romano-British Christianity and that of the Latin inscriptions on standing stones is at first striking, but we have already seen that the earlier map represents only evidence for Christianity that is *archaeologically* visible. The map of Latin inscriptions similarly needs to be interpreted aright. The inscriptions are not necessarily all Christian, nor all linked to Gaul. Some of them have closer parallels with Irish ogham stones (which can be pagan or Christian);[19] and a link between the two is supplied by the bilingual (or 'bi-alphabetical') inscriptions in South Wales which are recorded in both the Roman and the ogham alphabets. Where the inscription is recognisably Christian in form, it clearly attests to Christianity; but we must beware of the false assumption that the absence of such inscriptions implies the absence of Christianity. Quite apart from the obvious fact that only the wealthy are likely to have been so commemorated, we must recognise that the erection of such memorials is a cultural phenomenon: people in that society chose to commemorate certain individuals, at least some of them Christian, in that way.

15 Radford (1967) and (1971). 16 Wilson (1966); Thomas (1981), esp. pp. 240–74, 351–2.
17 Frend (1979) and (1992); but see now Stancliffe (1999). 18 Thomas (1981), pp. 347–51.
19 Bullock (1956); Thomas (1994), esp. pp. 67–87; Handley (1998).

A hundred and sixty kilometres further east or south, however, the population might have been equally Christian, but might not have adopted the fashion of commemorative stone inscriptions.

This can be shown to have been the case if we look at a third map, this time illustrating the distribution of Eccles place-names (Map 13). These come from the Vulgar Latin *eclesia* or its Celtic derivatives, all meaning 'church'. Their distribution therefore attests some – though by no means all – of the places which had churches before the Anglo-Saxon occupation of that area.[20] (Wales and Cornwall have deliberately been left blank not because they have no such names, but because such place-names continued to be coined long after the period that concerns us.[21]) This is no place to explore the complexities of why the survival rate of Eccles place-names is so patchy, though we can at least note that apart from three instances in the south-east, which may represent very early borrowings,[22] they occur largely in areas that the Anglo-Saxons conquered only in the seventh century when they themselves were in the process of becoming Christianised. In all events, where such place-names survive, they provide incontrovertible evidence of British Christianity for a period which is approximately that of the inscribed stones. What is interesting is that the Eccles place-names largely bridge the geographical gap between the archaeological evidence for Romano-British Christianity on the one hand, and the Christian inscriptions of the following centuries on the other. Thus where western and northern Britain are concerned, although the idea – and the formulas – of the inscribed stones may have come from overseas, there is no need to think that Christianity itself did. It could more easily have spread from adjacent areas within Britain.

This hypothesis of the transmission of Christianity further north and west within Britain receives confirmation from various sources. Continuity is perhaps clearest in south-east Wales and the adjoining parts of England, with Eccleswell near Ross, and with Gildas' record of the names and burial places (martyrial shrines?) of two citizens of Caerleon (outside Newport), who had been martyred in Roman times and were evidently still honoured at the time of writing (*c.*530).[23] Christianity in the same general area is attested in the *Life of St Samson*, a sixth-century saint from South Wales who ended his days in Brittany, where his Life was written. Its date is much discussed, but a seventh-century origin is the most plausible, and

[20] Jackson (1953), p. 412; Cameron (1968); Gelling (1978), pp. 82–3, 96–9; Barrow (1983). For the addition to the standard corpus of Eccleshalghforth, attested in 1471 as a field name at Warkworth, Northumberland, see Beckensall (n.d.), p. 24.

[21] Cf. Roberts (1992); Padel (1985), p. 91.

[22] Gelling (1978), pp. 82–3.

[23] Cameron (1968), p. 89; Gildas, *De Excidio* x.2; cf. Wendy Davies (1978), pp. 121–59 and (1982), pp. 141–6; Watts (1991), pp. 76, 126–7. Similarly for central Wales, cf. Knight (1999), p. 137.

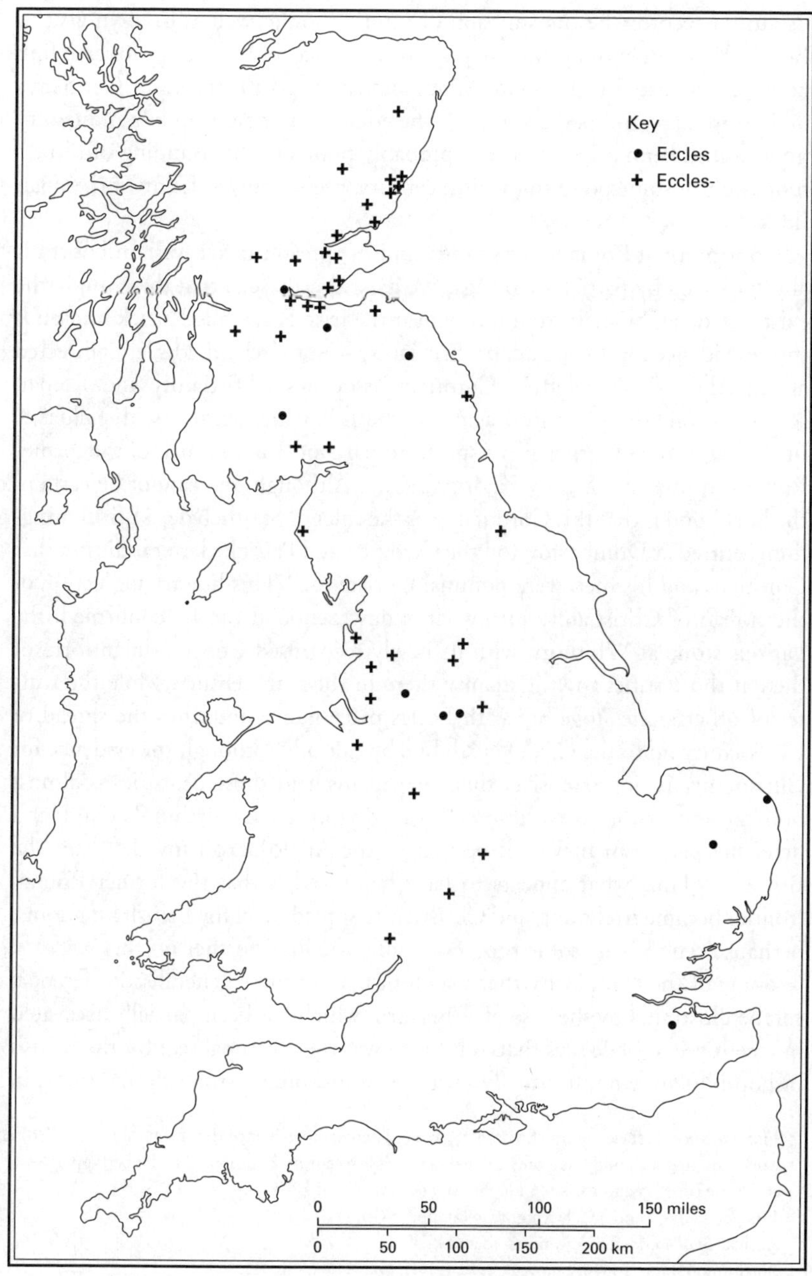

Map 13 Distribution of Eccles place-names

its author records the transmission of information as well as his own visit to Britain.[24] Whether or not we can give any credence to the Life's postulated link between monasticism in South Wales and the visits to Britain of Germanus of Auxerre (429 and perhaps *c*.440), the education of Samson in a monastery under Illtud from a very early age probably points to the founding of Illtud's monastery at some point in the fifth century, presumably at Llantwit (i.e. Llan Ilduti).[25]

Continuity of Roman Christianity and its spread further west and north is also indicated by Patrick's writings. We have already seen that these imply the existence of a Christian community near the Irish Sea, while Patrick himself is prime evidence for the spread of Christianity west to Ireland. His letter directed against the British chieftain Coroticus associates Christianity and Roman society – something we find again in the following century with Gildas;[26] further, it implies Christianity's spread to parts of Britain north of the former Roman frontier marked by Hadrian's Wall. Although one cannot be certain, the likelihood is that this Coroticus was the ruler of Strathclyde, a British kingdom centred at Dumbarton (on the Clyde);[27] and Patrick's letter indicates that Coroticus and his men were nominal Christians.[28] This literary indication of the spread of Christianity into what is now Scotland can be confirmed: the Latinus stone at Whithorn with its newly recognised Constantinian form of the chi-rho testifies to Christianity there in the fifth century, while the scatter of other stones together with Eccles place-names indicates the spread of Christianity up to the Clyde–Forth line by *c*.600.[29] Although the evidence for Christianity is not extensive, that for paganism in those centuries is almost non-existent, with the exception of Yeavering in north Northumberland; and here, the paganism may well be that of the Anglo-Saxon invaders, not the Britons.[30] Thus what appears to have happened is that the former Roman frontier became irrelevant, and Christianity spread to all the British kingdoms, perhaps even making some progress among the Picts further north.

Some of the complexity that may lurk behind these generalised inferences can be illustrated by the case of Whithorn, which has been partially excavated in recent years. Bede says that Whithorn was the episcopal seat for the British bishop Ninian, who, unusually for the Britons, built a stone church there; in

[24] *Vita Samsonis*, Preface 2; and cf. I.52; I.7, 41, 48. There is no evidence that its author knew Bede's works and that it should therefore be dated to the eighth century, as proposed by Flobert, pp. 108–11; cf. Duine (1912–13 and 1914–15); Hughes (1981), p. 4; Wood (1988), pp. 380–4.

[25] *Vita Samsonis* I.7 and 42; cf. Knight (1984), pp. 328–9.

[26] Patrick, *Epistola* 11; cf. below, notes 40 and 43.

[27] Binchy (1962), pp. 106–9; Dumville *et al.* (1993), pp. 107–15, esp. 114.

[28] Patrick, *Epistola* 5, cf. *Epistola* 2.

[29] Craig (1997); Thomas (1991–92); Barrow (1983); cf. Thomas (1968); Alcock (1992).

[30] Cf. Hope-Taylor (1977), esp. pp. 158–61, 244–67, 277–8, 287–9, and Scull (1991).

Bede's day, at least, it was dedicated to St Martin of Tours.[31] The site of the church probably lay on the hilltop where the Latinus inscription was found and the later medieval church built. The recent excavation, however, focussed lower down on the southern slope of the hill, an area that initially lay outside the inner religious precinct. The dig uncovered a complex development beginning with an agricultural phase, then witnessing the import of lime, presumably to make plaster or cement for significant building(s) nearby (on the hilltop?). Next in the area excavated came a number of wattle or stake-walled buildings and evidence of metalworking, together with sherds of amphorae imported from the east Mediterranean between the late fifth and mid-sixth centuries, and also fragments of glass vessels. The amphorae probably contained wine and olive oil, while fine tablewares were also imported from North Africa. Meanwhile at Whithorn the boundary between the inner and the outer enclosures shifted, so that most of the area excavated came to form part of the inner enclosure, and burials began to take place there. The Mediterranean trade ended around the mid-sixth century; but international trade with the continent soon resumed, and flourished throughout the seventh century: imports included some fifty-five glass cone beakers.[32] In some respects the written and archaeological evidence coheres. Clearly, Whithorn was an unusual, high-status site. It had far-flung contacts with the Mediterranean, and then Francia; and the ecclesiastical nature of at least part of the site is borne out by the discovery of some cross-inscribed stones from the excavated area, and also fits with the cemetery established there. But questions remain. For instance, were all the glass vessels imported so that the bishop could feast in style,[33] or could some have been intended for a secular lord based in the immediate vicinity, whose rubbish might have spread over our site?[34] In all events, the implication is that Whithorn belonged to a reasonably civilised world which was 'post-Roman' rather than 'barbarian': a remarkable fact when we recall that in 400 it was outside the frontiers of the Roman Empire.

GILDAS' WITNESS AND THE OUTLINES OF THE BRITISH CHURCH

Our knowledge of Britain in the sixth century depends to a considerable extent upon the writings of a single author, Gildas. His major work, *De Excidio Britonum* (often referred to as *De Excidio Britanniae*, 'The Ruin of Britain'), is a superbly rhetorical denunciation of the failings of those in power, both secular potentates and bishops. Through copious citations from the Bible, Gildas seeks to open their eyes to the yawning gulf between their lip-service to

[31] Bede, *HE* III.4. [32] Hill (1997), esp. chs. 3 and 10. [33] Cf. Gildas' evidence: below, note 44.
[34] Cf. Thomas (1992), pp. 10–13; Hill (1997), pp. 299, 320.

the Christian God, and what that same God requires in practice. There is an urgency to Gildas' appeal: he has imbibed the Old Testament view of a God who would purge a sinful people through visitation of plague or conquest at the hands of foreigners – witness the original Anglo-Saxon conquests.[35] At the time that he was writing, probably the early 530s,[36] Britain was divided into a mosaic of kingdoms or social groupings, British and Germanic, with the latter predominating to the south and east of a line drawn diagonally from Flamborough Head to the Solent. Although peace between the Britons and Anglo-Saxons had prevailed since Gildas' birth some forty-four years previously,[37] his fellow countrymen's behaviour was such as to provoke new disasters, unless they repented.

When due allowance is made for Gildas' slant and rhetoric, much can be learned. First, Gildas had a concept of Britain as a single entity, though subdivided into several kingdoms, and the sweep of the area he addressed ran from Dumnonia in the south-west through Dyfed to Gwynedd in North Wales.[38] Secondly, continuity from Roman Britain is frequently implied by the flow of his historical chapters, which present a seamless account of British Christianity from the days of the martyrs to the present;[39] by his use of the term *cives*, 'citizens', for the British, and designation of Latin as 'our language';[40] and by the very nature of his Latin prose style, which betrays his training in the art of rhetoric, the hallmark of a late Roman education.[41] Throughout his work, the assumption is that the British are all at least nominally Christian: the bishops are castigated for their failure to denounce sin and preach God's word, but not for condoning paganism.[42] Contrariwise, the Saxons are 'hateful to God and man'.[43]

Gildas' work allows one to see a wealthy, established church, with its church buildings and ecclesiastical hierarchy. Power and responsibility fell to the bishops; and so greatly was ecclesiastical status coveted, that men bought the office of both bishop and priest from local kings, or, failing that, travelled overseas to gain it.[44] Clerical marriage was recognised, though continuing sexual relations after ordination as priest were not necessarily allowed.[45] Monasticism was in existence, and its practitioners were then few in number, but highly regarded by the author.[46] In this latter respect, the *De Excidio* differs

35 For example, Gildas, *De Excidio* I.13; XXII–XXIV.

36 Cf. Dumville (1984b); Stancliffe (1997), pp. 177–81.

37 Gildas, *De Excidio* XXVI.1.

38 Gildas, *De Excidio* XXVIII; XXXI; XXXIII.1; cf. Dumville (1984a).

39 Gildas, *De Excidio* IV–XXVI.

40 For example Gildas, *De Excidio* XXVI.1; XXIII.3.

41 Lapidge (1984); Orlandi (1984); Wright (1984); Kerlouégan (1987), pp. 559–64.

42 Gildas, *De Excidio* LXXVI; LXXXIII.1–2; LXXXV.2. But cf. note 11 above.

43 Gildas, *De Excidio* XXIII.1; cf. XCII.3.

44 Gildas, *De Excidio* LXVI–LXVII. W. H. Davies (1968), pp. 140–1.

45 Hughes (1966), pp. 41–3.

46 Herren (1990), pp. 71–6.

from a later work of Gildas, only fragmentarily preserved: a letter replying to a request for advice on various problems, particularly those arising from a clash between relatively comfortable monasteries and individuals seeking a more austere lifestyle.[47] What is interesting is that monasticism seems to have expanded and diversified between the *De Excidio* and the *Fragments*.[48] We will return to this question below; but here, we should note the implication that Gildas' life spanned a crucial period: the *De Excidio* belongs to late antiquity as much as the early Middle Ages, whereas the *Fragments* belong to the phase of monastic expansion and link us with the world of the great Irish ascetic, Columbanus.[49] It has been plausibly argued that what we see here is cause and effect: Gildas' impassioned preaching in the *De Excidio* had perceptible results, inspiring many to embrace the monastic life.[50] *De Excidio*'s impact would have been considerably strengthened if the climatic disturbance around 536 and plague of the 540s followed hard upon its publication, as seems likely.[51]

Other sources corroborate or add to Gildas' evidence. We have what appear to be penalties agreed for various offences at two British synods of approximately sixth-century date. One is headed 'The Synod of North Britain', and provides us with welcome information on an area not covered by Gildas. It has references to the status of bishop, priest, deacon, *doctor* (ecclesiastical scholar), abbot and monk.[52] Nevertheless, our knowledge of the organisational framework of the British church is incomplete because the surviving evidence is patchy. A good case has been made for each cantref of Dyfed having its own bishop, thus suggesting small-scale, territorial dioceses.[53] Dyfed, with its extensive colonisation from Ireland, was not necessarily typical of all areas; but nor was it necessarily untypical. Further to the east the evidence of the Llandaff charters, which survive only in edited form in the twelfth-century *Book of Llandaff*, has been taken to imply a bishopric in Ergyng (south-west Herefordshire) in the sixth century, which would have been comparable in size to the Dyfed dioceses. Later, however, it may have expanded west to cover Gwent also.[54] Evidence pointing in a different direction occurs in the *Life of St Samson*, if we may trust it. Here, Bishop Dubricius of (we may assume) Ergyng is found ordaining Samson at Llantwit monastery, in modern South

47 Gildas, *Fragmenta*; Sharpe (1984a). 48 Herren (1990).

49 Cf. Davies (1968), p. 141; Columbanus, *Epistulae* 1.6. 50 Sharpe (1984a), p. 199.

51 Cf. (with caution) Keys (1999), pp. 109–18.

52 *Sinodus Aquilonalis Britaniae* 1–3. For *doctor*, see Scheibelreiter, chapter 25 below.

53 Charles-Edwards (1970–72).

54 Hughes (1981), esp. pp. 7–8. Cf. Wendy Davies (1978), ch. 8, esp. pp. 144–5, 149–50, 152–9, who thinks the trend was the other way round: that a larger sixth-century diocese later became restricted to Ergyng. Knight (1984), p. 341.

Glamorgan, and even appointing him to monastic office in Piro's monastery on Caldey Island, Dyfed. This cannot have lain within a territorial diocese based on Ergyng; but since Dubricius spent every Lent there, we may be seeing a special relationship between Caldey and Ergyng.[55] A further point is that when Samson was consecrated bishop, there is no indication that this was to any specific see.[56] Perhaps, then, there were some monasteries supervised by a bishop of a more distant diocese than that in which they lay geographically; and some monastic bishops, as well as bishops of territorial dioceses. The latter appear to have retained control over monasteries, unlike their Irish equivalents; but we should not overemphasise the contrast.[57]

As regards the question of where real power and influence lay, we should ponder the implications of Bede's story of the British church's dealings with Augustine. According to Bede, Augustine summoned the bishops and ecclesiastical scholars (*doctores*) of the British to meet him, and after fruitless discussions demonstrated that Roman ways were right through working a miracle. The British delegation was apparently convinced by this, but asked for a second synod with wider representation. Seven British bishops and many most learned men (*doctissimi*), principally from the monastery of Bangor, came to this; and before coming, they sought advice from a holy anchorite. When they had to make a decision, it was the anchorite's advice that they followed.[58] There are two significant points here: first, *doctores*, particularly monastic *doctores*, were involved at both synods alongside bishops. *Doctores* figure in the rulings of the 'Synod of North Britain' as those responsible for assigning penances, even to bishops.[59] Their presence alongside bishops in the synods meeting with Augustine can be paralleled by the presence of similar ecclesiastical scholars, who could equal bishops in status, at seventh-century Irish synods.[60] Thus matters of the greatest significance in the British church would appear to have been the concern not simply of the bishops, but of ecclesiastical scholars also. Secondly, the fact that the anchorite's advice was sought and followed implies that his spiritual wisdom and moral authority were accorded recognition at the highest level. Whether this was a recent result of the ascetic movement we cannot know, though it seems likely. Thus while British bishops continued to be the leaders of the British church, they were not the sole source of authority in the early seventh century, nor is there any mention at this date of an 'overbishop' or metropolitan. Instead, synods were clearly important, and these allowed for the participation of *doctores* alongside bishops in decision-making.

55 *Vita Samsonis* I.13, 15, 33–6; cf. Hughes (1981), p. 15.

56 *Vita Samsonis* I.43–5.

57 See Charles-Edwards (1970–72), esp. p. 260; Sharpe (1984b); Ó Cróinín (1995), p. 162; Mac Shamhráin (1996), ch. 6, esp. pp. 168–72, 206; cf. Hughes (1981).

58 Bede, *HE* II.2; cf. Stancliffe (1999), pp. 124–33.

59 *Sinodus Aquilonalis Britaniae* I.

60 Charles-Edwards (2000), pp. 276–7; Kelly (1988), p. 41.

MONASTICISM

It is highly likely that monasticism reached Britain from Gaul at the end of the fourth or during the fifth century. Gaul was home to two major monastic movements. One derived from the monk-bishop, Martin of Tours (d. 397) via his disciples, and via the hagiographical writings about him of Sulpicius Severus. The other movement derived from twin foci in Provence: the island monastery of Lérins, and the writings of John Cassian, a monk from the east who had visited the Desert Fathers in Egypt, and wrote about them in the early fifth century after settling in Marseilles. Both currents probably affected Britain during the fifth century.

Monasticism in early Britain is a complex subject, partly because there has been much speculation about its origins and achievements, and about its relationship to bishops and territorial dioceses; but equally because there is confusion as to what is meant by 'monasticism' and 'monasteries'. On the one hand, there is a problem as to whether we can always differentiate between monasteries and communities of clerics. In the sixth century at least there probably were some monasteries, as we think of them, consisting of men living in a community in accordance with monastic vows and under the direction of an abbot, with only a minority of them in the orders of deacon or priest.[61] At the same time, given that clergy might legitimately be married and so presumably had their own independent households, and given the distinction implicit in Gildas' *De Excidio* between the responsibilities of clerics as opposed to the withdrawn monks (which implies that the latter bore no responsibility for pastoral care), we may infer that pastoral care was not the concern of monasteries, but rather of separate, secular clergy.[62] However, there may also have been households of clerics living together, as on the continent; and in the course of time the distinction between such clerical communities and monastic communities appears to have become increasingly blurred.[63]

A further confusion arises from the overlap between 'monasticism' and 'asceticism', as illustrated in the *Life of Samson*. Samson was placed in Illtud's monastery (Llantwit) as a young child. When he grew up he desired a stricter, more religious life than Illtud's rather lax establishment afforded, and was able to transfer to the monastery of one Piro, on Caldey Island, which afforded him more scope for extended prayer. When chosen to succeed Piro as abbot – the latter having fallen down a well while inebriated – Samson governed the

[61] *Praefatio Gildae* I–2; *Vita Samsonis* I.13–15, and *passim*.

[62] Hughes (1966), pp. 41–3; Gildas, *De Excidio* LXV; Herren (1990), pp. 74–5; Victory (1977), p. 51. The different inferences drawn by Pryce (1992), pp. 51–2, seem less securely founded on the sixth-century evidence.

[63] Davies (1982), pp. 149–50.

monks in accordance with a Rule, and was personally so abstemious that he was regarded as more of a 'hermit' than a 'cenobite'.[64] After visiting Ireland Samson did not resume his duties as abbot on Caldey, but took three companions and established an eremitic settlement in a fort in a 'desert' near the River Severn. He did not stay with the others, however, but spent most of his time in solitary prayer in a cave, returning to the fort only for mass on Sundays. Summoned from his retreat by a synod and unwillingly put in charge of another monastery, he was soon after consecrated bishop; but then announced that he had been called to live as a *peregrinus*, a stranger or 'pilgrim'.[65] In Celtic countries this developed a specialised sense: renunciation of one's homeland for the sake of Christ, never to return. Samson therefore set out, visiting some of his own family's monasteries in South Wales *en route* for Cornwall. There he preached to pagans and founded a monastery, finally crossing to Brittany where he founded further monasteries, and ended his days.[66] Clearly what we see here is a single monastic vocation which found expression in a variety of forms, as a monk, a hermit and a *peregrinus*, while the family monasteries he visited might have been closer to household asceticism rather than full-blown monasticism; there are plenty of indications that the headship of such monasteries was normally handed down within a kindred. In these circumstances, to attempt a rigid distinction between asceticism and monasticism would be inappropriate.[67]

Samson's desire to exchange a lax community for a more religious one and to devote himself to solitary prayer tallies with the sixth-century evidence of Gildas' *Fragments*. These reveal great diversity of monastic practice. Some established monasteries enjoyed a good diet, including meat and beer, as well as eggs, cheese, milk, vegetables and bread; at others, the food was much less plentiful, while the extreme ascetics used bread and water as their staple. Illtud's monks appear to have supported themselves by farming, and certainly at Bangor-is-Coed all monks undertook manual labour; but in some communities this apparently fell to designated worker monks, rather than being undertaken by all, while at the ascetic extreme, the use of animals even to draw ploughs was rejected, the monks doing all work by hand.[68]

This was the period that later generations regarded as that of the founder-saints of the Welsh church. Reliable evidence is unfortunately lacking on these, though a reading of an inscription at Llandewi-brefi preserved by an antiquarian – the crucial word is now missing – may at least provide

64 *Vita Samsonis* I.6–10, 20–1, 36. 65 *Vita Samsonis* I.40–5.

66 See below, pp. 443–4 and also Davies, chapter 9 above; Olson (1989), pp. 9–20.

67 *Vita Samsonis* I.14, 16, 29–31, 40, 45, 52. Hughes (1966), pp. 76–7. Cf. Markus (1990), pp. 66–8; Stancliffe (1983), pp. 30–8; Knight (1984), pp. 328–9.

68 *Praefatio Gildae* 1, 2, 22, 26, and cf. 7–10; *Vita Samsonis* I.12, and cf. I.35; Gildas, *Fragmenta* 2–4; Bede, *HE* II.2.

seventh-century testimony to St David, patron saint of Wales. His death is recorded in the Welsh annals at 601, and in various Irish annals some twelve years earlier, which suggests a mid to late sixth-century *floruit*. This is plausible, but unverifiable.[69] The account of his community's extremely ascetic lifestyle given in Rhigyfarch's eleventh-century Life does not look like a fabrication of the 1090s, and has interesting parallels in Gildas' *Fragments*; but we do not know what sources lie behind it.[70] Even disregarding such late evidence, however, the sixth century still appears as a time of ascetic fervour on the part of some, which led to new monastic foundations (like those of Samson), and which probably resulted in growing numbers of monks. This is implied by Gildas' *Fragments*, and attested by Bede's account of the monastery of Bangor-is-Coed in the early seventh century, which he records as containing over 2000 monks.[71] This must have been a remarkable community – at least until the Northumbrian slaughter of 1200 of its inmates in 616.

BRITONS ABROAD

In the fifth and sixth centuries the Britons remained within a Roman penumbra, with trading contacts to parts of the former Roman Empire.[72] These were matched by cultural and ecclesiastical links. Gildas still regarded Latin as 'our' language, and some of his fellow countrymen journeyed abroad to receive episcopal consecration, while churchmen with British names turn up as bishop of Senlis in the mid-sixth century (Gonotiernus), or as an abbot in Burgundy in 591 (Carantocus). Thus Britons appear to have preceded as well as accompanied the Irish *peregrinus*, Columbanus, on his continental travels.[73] Most remarkable of all is a record of British churches with a bishop of their own in far-off Galicia in the 560s and 570s.[74]

The most densely colonised area was the western and northern part of the Armorican peninsula, which by the late sixth century had been renamed *Brittania*, Brittany. Officially, this remained part of an ecclesiastical province mirroring the Roman Lugdunensis III, with its metropolis at Tours; and a series of episcopal provincial meetings at Angers (453), Tours (461) and Vannes (462–8) reveal the pre-Breton ecclesiastical structure, with bishops in the *civitates*

69 Gruffydd and Owen (1956–58); cf. Nash-Williams (1950), p. 98, no. 116. See also Davies (1978), p. 132. *Annales Cambriae* s.a. 601; cf. Miller (1977–78), pp. 44–8; Hughes (1980), pp. 67–100, esp. 90–1.

70 Rhigyfarch, *Vita Davidis* cc.21–30.

71 Bede, *HE* II.2; Stancliffe (1999), pp. 124–9; cf. Herren (1990), p. 77.

72 Campbell (1996).

73 Gildas, *De Excidio* XXIII.3; LXVII.5–6. Councils of Orléans V and Paris III, *Concilia Galliae*, ed. Munier and de Clercq in CCSL 148, pp. 160, 210. Jonas, *Vita Columbani* I.7; 13, 15 and 17; Dumville (1984c), pp. 20–1.

74 Thompson (1968).

of Rennes, Nantes and Vannes; and probably also amongst the Coriosolites (perhaps based in the coastal stronghold of Alet), and amongst the Osismii in the west, though here the location of the see is unknown.[75] The first probable evidence of British churchmen in Armorica is the signature of one Mansuetus, 'bishop of the Britons', at the synod of Tours in 461 – though it is just possible that he was a visiting bishop.[76] Certain proof of British churchmen actively ministering to the (British) population comes from a letter written by the bishops of Tours, Rennes and Angers between 509 and 521 to two priests with the Brittonic names of Lovocat and Catihern. The priests had been travelling around with portable altars, celebrating mass in private houses. What angered the bishops was that they were accompanied by women known as *conhospitae*, who administered the chalice.[77] These details are extremely interesting: first, as regards the prominent role played by women, which parallels that of deaconesses in the eastern church, but is scarcely attested in the west. Perhaps the prohibition against ordaining deaconesses at the synods of Epaone (517) and Orléans II (533) should be seen as a reaction against an eastern practice which was spreading in the west, and of which the Breton *conhospitae* provide evidence.[78] A second point is the use of portable altars, illustrating ministry to the population before churches were built in the countryside. Finally, one gets the impression that the priests were operating on their own, with no effective episcopal supervision. For the bishops who write do not address Lovocat and Catihern as though they were ministering within one of their dioceses, and indeed, the priests' probable sphere of operation was in the territory of the Coriosolites; and yet the bishops address them directly, rather than going through their own diocesan bishop. This may hint at the dislocation of diocesan structures as a result of the British influx.[79]

Dislocation of ecclesiastical structures (if they ever fully existed) certainly occurred west of the dioceses of Rennes and Vannes, and is matched by a lacuna in our sources. A synod held at Tours in 567 attempted to outlaw the consecration of anyone as bishop, whether 'Briton or Roman', unless he had the metropolitan's consent.[80] This would surely have been unenforceable in the areas under Breton control. By the mid-ninth century, when evidence becomes available, we find five episcopal centres in Breton hands. The dioceses of Vannes

[75] Pietri and Biarne (1987), pp. 11–16; Duchesne (1910), pp. 245–9; Chédeville and Guillotel (1984), pp. 114–15, 142–3; Tanguy (1984). Some scholars regard the Litard, who signed as bishop 'de Vxuma' at the Synod of Orléans in 511, as from the Osismii: cf. de Clercq in CCSL, p. 13; Gaudemet and Basdevant (1989), pp. 90–1; Duchesne (1910), p. 244, n. 1.

[76] Munier in CCSL, p. 148.

[77] Jülicher (1896), p. 665.

[78] Cf. Daniélou (1961), esp. pp. 22–4; Pontal (1989), p. 67 n. 67, and pp. 264–5.

[79] Cf. Jülicher (1896), p. 671. Tanguy (1984), p. 99, suggests that Languédias (Côtes-du-Nord) takes its name from **Lann-Catihern*.

[80] Council of Tours 567, c. 9: *Concilia Galliae*, ed. de Clercq (1963), p. 179.

and Alet had survived, though the latter's foundation was now attributed to a Welsh ascetic, St Malo, while another bishop was based at nearby Dol, a monastery founded by the Welsh St Samson. In the west, the former territory of the Osismii now had two bishops, at St Pol-de-Léon in the north, and at Quimper in the south.[81] Only in the case of Dol do we have any evidence from a pre-Carolingian source, the *Life of St Samson*. Even this is uninformative about Samson's continental career apart from his visit to King Childebert, discussed below. We can, however, say that Dol was founded as a monastery; that Samson, its founder, was already in episcopal orders when he arrived from Britain; and that Dol seems to have continued to have bishops after Samson's death, since the Life mentions a later bishop, Leucherus, while its dedicatee is Bishop Tigernomaglus.[82] But whether these bishops exercised episcopal oversight over a territorial diocese, as was normal on the continent, or whether they simply had pastoral oversight over Dol's scattered dependent churches, we cannot know. In the case of Paul Aurelian, the reputed founder of St Pol, the Life of the founder-saint appears to give more circumstantial evidence about his career in Brittany, including a local chief's gift of a deserted fort for his episcopal see, and an account of its authorisation by King Childebert. However, although some earlier written material may have been available, the author of this Life wrote only in 884, by which time convincing origin legends were required for propaganda purposes.[83] We therefore cannot trust its details; and the same goes for the other Breton saints' Lives, which are ninth-century or later.

At the local level, there was a generous network of churches by the ninth century: each community, or *plebs* (whence Breton *ploue*), had its own church, staffed by a small group of priests. These *ploue* churches may have formed the basic building blocks of the Breton church, preceding the formation of territorial bishoprics in the ninth century; but we must be wary of too much speculation on this.[84] In addition, Brittany had both hermitages, often on offshore islands,[85] and coenobitic monasteries. St Samson, who founded the monastery of Dol, and indeed 'many monasteries throughout virtually the whole province', is represented as going to King Childebert in Neustria to intercede for the Breton prince, Judwal. He succeeded in this; and, after expelling a dragon (!) he was given land near the Seine mouth to found another monastery, that of Pentale. The dragon story is patently a recurring myth; but the monastery of Pentale was real enough, and an enclave around it remained

81 Smith (1992), pp. 15, 70, 153–6. Cf. Chédeville and Guillotel (1984), pp. 142–4.

82 *Vita Samsonis* Preface 1; and II.1, 2, 15.

83 Merdrignac (1993), pp. 14, 91–2; Jackson (1953), pp. 41–2; cf. Chédeville and Guillotel (1984), pp. 139–40.

84 See Wendy Davies (1983); Chédeville and Guillotel (1984), pp. 126–9.

85 Cf. Chédeville and Guillotel (1984), pp. 121, 125–32; Giot (1982).

in Dol's possession down to the French Revolution.[86] Contact was apparently maintained by sea; and the whole story is important in showing that the Breton church was not wholly cut off from the Frankish mainstream. Confirmation of this also comes from the fact that the synod of Paris, held *c.*562, includes a Samson, probably our Samson, amongst its signatories.[87] Some sixty years later Judwal's grandson, King Judicael of Brittany, was summoned to Dagobert's court. He refused to eat with the king, 'for he was religious and full of the fear of God'; but he did consent to eat with the referendary, Audoenus, who belonged to the circle influenced by Columbanian monasticism. According to late Lives, Judicael eventually retired to the monastery of St Méen, in the middle of the Breton forest, while his young brother travelled north and founded what eventually became the monastery of St Josse-sur-Mer (near Montreuil).[88]

In all this, the limitations of the sources are painfully evident. Looking back from the ninth century, the sixth and early seventh centuries were seen as 'the age of the saints'. These saints were all portrayed as ascetics; and most of them are represented as coming from South Wales, crossing through Cornwall to Brittany, and founding hermitages and monasteries; though Winwaloe, the alleged founder of the monastery of Landévennec, is represented as having been born in Brittany of immigrant British parents.[89] The British origin of most of these 'saints' is attested by their names, while their cults frequently span the English Channel.[90] But how should the late hagiographical evidence about monastic founder-saints be assessed against our sixth-century evidence of the letter to Lovocat and Catihern, and our ninth-century evidence of small communities of clerics? There certainly were some ascetics in sixth-century Brittany: one, called Winnoch, who ate only uncooked herbs, went to Tours in the late sixth century, intending to make a pilgrimage to Jerusalem – though he came to a sorry end in Tours through drink.[91] It could be that Lovocat and Catihern belong to the pre-ascetic period of British Christianity, the church denounced by Gildas in his *De Excidio*; and that the ascetic *peregrini* like Samson form part of the great monastic revival which is deducible from Gildas' *Fragments*.[92] Since *peregrinatio* overseas was seen as an ascetic ideal, it could well be that Brittany did attract a number of ascetics in addition to Samson; and many of their foundations could well have evolved into small groups of priests by the early ninth century. Alternatively, however, the *ploue* churches may represent the successors of churches founded by small groups of secular

86 *Vita Samsonis* I.52–9; cf. Flobert (1997), pp. 12–13; cf. Merdrignac (1993), pp. 95–8.

87 *Concilia Galliae*, ed. de Clercq (1963), p. 210; cf. Pontal (1989), pp. 151–5.

88 Fredegar, *Chronicle* IV.78; Chadwick (1969), pp. 288–9; Merdrignac (1991), p. 129.

89 Wrdisten, *Vita S. Winwaloei* I.1–3.

90 Bowen (1969), pp. 92–8, 160–90.

91 Gregory, *Hist.* V.21 and VIII.34.

92 Sharpe (1984a), pp. 199–202.

priests, like Lovocat and Catihern. It could be, therefore, that the ninth-century Lives give a misleading impression in portraying all founder-saints as ascetics. This could have arisen either because they simply selected and wrote up *vitae* of those saints who were ascetics; or because they wrote up all church founders as ascetics – that being how in the ninth century, influenced by the *Life of St Samson*, they chose to portray them.

Despite all our uncertainties, however, some points do emerge. First, the incoming Britons brought their own Christian traditions with them, rather than being absorbed by those that they found in Armorica. They appear to have brought or evolved the *ploue* churches, the monastery bishops, and a tradition of insular hermitage sites such as we find in western Britain and Ireland, while continued close contact with the Insular world is apparent in the script and content of manuscripts.[93] Secondly, continental Britons were involved in Columbanus' mission, and Irish/Breton contacts were maintained: a disciple of Columbanus founded a monastery at Coutances in an area of strong Breton influence just outside what later came to be regarded as Brittany;[94] and the monastery of Landévennec in western Brittany still retained its Irish tonsure and rule in 818, when Louis the Pious ordered it to conform to the Rule of St Benedict.[95] Third: despite this, there is no evidence that the Breton church was viewed as schismatic in our period. Gregory of Tours had no qualms about ordaining a devout Breton pilgrim, and bishops were regularly used as emissaries between the Bretons and the Franks.[96] Around 600, the Bretons presumably kept the 'Celtic' Easter, rather than that of Victorius of Aquitaine; but there was still some divergence within Francia, and since the Bretons lived in their own discrete area, it may not have caused much trouble. We may assume that they had conformed well before 818 – perhaps in the years following Luxeuil's conformity at the synod of Mâcon (626/7). Despite some such idiosyncracies, we should not view the Breton church as having been wholly isolated from the Frankish church. Although it was not under the effective control of the metropolitan bishop of Tours, links were forged by monks with a reputation for sanctity: Samson of Dol and Pentale, and St Josse, Breton founder of the hermitage which later took his name; meanwhile Carantocus in Burgundy and Gonotiernus at Senlis were either Britons or Bretons – the distinction cannot be made at this period. Thus, our final point is that British churchmen were not confined to Brittany in these centuries, but settled sporadically elsewhere on the continent as well, though these have tended to be forgotten in comparison to the better-known Irish *peregrini*.

93 Smith (1992), pp. 167–77.
94 Jonas, *Vita Columbani* I.21; cf. Fleuriot (1980), p. 151.
95 Wrdisten, *Vita S. Winwaloei* II.12–13.
96 Gregory, *Hist.* V.21; V.26; IX.18.

THE BRITISH CHURCH, THE ANGLO-SAXONS, AND THE ROMAN MISSION

Major changes befell the Britons after the mid-sixth century, perhaps following on from climatic disturbance and plague. The expansion of the Anglo-Saxons restricted the areas they controlled to the less Romanised, less fertile lands of Dumnonia, Wales and the kingdom of Strathclyde, while in 597 the arrival of Augustine to convert the Anglo-Saxons threatened them with ecclesiastical subordination. Augustine's mission marks the beginning of historical records for the Anglo-Saxons. At the same time, one result of the dislocation and defeat experienced by the Britons is that almost nothing survives from their side. The effect of this is to make us view the confrontation of the two Christian traditions through the eyes of the Romans and Anglo-Saxons, and, in particular, through the eyes of the Northumbrian historian Bede. Bede takes over Gildas' portrayal of the Britons as sinners, but adds an additional charge: that they never preached to the Anglo-Saxons. He portrays the Britons as an introverted group, who, when challenged by Augustine to drop their idiosyncrasies, accept his leadership and join his mission, spurned him. In effect, they preferred their own customs to those of the universal church; and so un-Christian were they that even when the Anglo-Saxons received Christianity from others, they failed to respect this. Indeed, they carried on refusing to be in communion with the Anglo-Saxons.[97]

Bede's interpretation has been enormously influential, but it is flawed. His accusation that the Britons never preached to the Anglo-Saxons probably rests upon his misunderstanding of a text; and his other criticisms arise from a readiness to generalise, misleadingly, from individual cases.[98] In reality, the Britons' missionary record was creditable by the standards of the day.[99] As regards their refusal to join Augustine, the prior issue here is why Pope Gregory ignored the existence of the British church when he first sent Augustine, and why he provocatively laid down that the British bishops should be treated as Augustine's inferiors, not colleagues. He appears to have thought in terms of integrating the British church into the new church he was establishing among the English, rather than vice versa.[100] Thus, while it is true that the Britons did refuse to give up their traditional calculations for the date of Easter and join Augustine's mission, the real obstacles to agreement were the fact that Augustine demanded unequivocal submission to his authority, while simultaneously coming as the bishop of an Anglo-Saxon king, and offering no safeguards for the British. The latter would understandably have feared that

97 Bede, *HE* I.14, 22; II.2, 20; V.22.

98 Stancliffe (1999), pp. 108–10.

99 Above, pp. 400, 432–5; Davies, chapter 9 above, and Thacker, chapter 17 below. Thompson (1963).

100 Bede, *HE* I.27.vii and 29; Stancliffe (1999).

ecclesiastical subordination to a bishop based in Canterbury would jeopardise their future independence from the Anglo-Saxons.

Although the Britons did not join Augustine's mission, it is likely that they did in fact play some part in converting the Anglo-Saxons. This has been suggested for the Hwicce and the Magonsætan, peoples settled around the lower Severn between (approximately) Bath and Much Wenlock. Bede has no conversion narrative for them, but the Hwicce in particular appear in his text as a Christian people of many years' standing, and burial evidence implies that they were Christian throughout the seventh century. In addition, a strong case has been made for seeing St Helen's, Worcester, as a British church in origin that pre-dates the Anglo-Saxon cathedral of *c.*680, and the same may well go for other churches in the area.[101] A similar pattern of unobtrusive conversion by the British population together with Anglo-Saxon takeover of pre-existing British churches has been argued for western parts of Wessex, and the origins of such churches as Wells and Sherborne, while a British contribution to the church of Northumbria can also be postulated for some areas north of the Tweed and west of the Pennines.[102] Whether anything similar occurred further east is much less likely, though continuity of cult site can be argued for St Albans and perhaps St-Paul-in-the-Bail, Lincoln.[103] Our only explicit written reference to Britons converting Anglo-Saxons is a riddling claim that a Briton, Rhun, baptised Edwin of Northumbria and his people. The source is late, and appears to be contradicted by Bede's earlier account; but this section of the source draws on earlier material and contains some accurate information, which is not in Bede, so we should not dismiss out of hand the idea that Rhun may have had something to do with Edwin's conversion.[104]

Collaboration is likely to have occurred at least in some areas and some circumstances. In part this will have arisen out of the complexity and untidiness of the situation, which would have made total separation between 'Celt' and 'Roman' difficult – particularly in the mission-field. One reason for the complexity is that alongside the Britons and the Roman mission, a third party was also involved as major players: the Irish mission to Northumbria led by Aidan, a monk from the monastery of Iona in Irish-colonised Dál Riada (Argyll). At this date there was no significant difference between the Christian practices of Iona and those of the British church; and yet, Bede himself tells us that Aidan

[101] Bede, *HE* IV.13; Sims-Williams (1990), pp. 54–91, esp. 75–9, 83–6; Bassett (1992), esp. pp. 15–26.

[102] Yorke (1995), pp. 177–81; Loyn (1984), pp. 13–15; Stancliffe (1995), pp. 76–80; cf. Barrow (1973), pp. 7–68, esp. 26–7, 64–5 and Gelling (1978), pp. 96–8.

[103] Morris (1989), pp. 35–9; Jones (1994); cf. also Stancliffe (1999), pp. 121–2.

[104] *Historia Brittonum* c.63; cf. Chadwick (1964); Jackson (1964).

was respected by bishops of the Roman party, despite his Easter allegiance.[105] Equally, there must in practice have been recognition of the other's Christian allegiance between the Iona-converted Northumbrian king, Oswiu, and his Roman-converted wife from Kent. All this implies mutual recognition between the Ionan Irish missionaries and the Roman party prior to the Synod of Whitby in 664; and since the former held to the same practices as the Britons, there was scope for considerable co-operation between them in the areas they evangelised, primarily Northumbria and Mercia. Confirmation that such co-operation did sometimes occur can be found in the fact that *c.*665 two British bishops collaborated with an Anglo-Saxon bishop to consecrate Chad.[106]

While a first reason for the complexity of the situation arises from the fact that the Irish were involved as well as Britons and the Roman party, a second reason is that whereas in 600 all the British and Irish churches were at one in the customs that marked them off from continental Christians (such as how to calculate the date of Easter), different areas conformed to the Roman Easter at different times: the southern Irish, *c.*632; much of midland Ireland between 640 and 690; Anglo-Saxon areas evangelised by the Irish, in 664; many Dumnonian Britons, *c.*675; other Britons (perhaps those of Strathclyde), together with the rest of Ireland apart from the churches of the Columban federation, *c.*700; the Picts and the Columban federation headed by Iona, *c.*716; and the Welsh in 768. On top of this, the continental traditions and practices brought by various missionaries to the Anglo-Saxons were themselves not uniform: in addition to missionaries from the papacy, there were others from elsewhere in Italy and also from Burgundy, who probably came from Irish circles on the continent; and there was more than one continental system of calculating the date of Easter.[107] Thus, while none of the continental missionaries was still using the 'Celtic' reckoning of Easter, some of them may well have felt more sympathetic to it than was Augustine – or Bede; and the same was probably true of those Irish who had already conformed to the Roman Easter.

The foregoing paragraphs will not have made easy reading; but they should have conveyed a sense of the complex cross-currents involved in the Easter controversy in Britain before 664. These will have made it as impossible for them as it should be for us to see all this in terms of a simple polarisation between 'Roman' and 'Celt'. In the 660s, however, three events occurred; between them, these were to lead to just such a polarisation. The first was the Synod of Whitby in 664, at which the Northumbrian king decided to accept the Roman Easter and to eject those who refused to conform. The second was the appointment of the Romanising Wilfrid as Northumbrian bishop; and the third, the arrival

105 Bede, *HE* III.25 (p. 296). 106 Bede, *HE* III.28.

107 Campbell (1986), pp. 57–9; Charles-Edwards (2000), pp. 405–11.

in Canterbury of the papally appointed Theodore as 'Archbishop of the island of Britain'[108] in 669. As a result, an attempt was made to enforce the view that British and Irish adherents of their traditional Easter calculations and tonsure were heretics, whose orders were invalid. However devout their ascetics might be, they were not to be honoured as saints: rather, their relics should be burnt.[109] Much bitterness and mutual antagonism resulted from this, and still affected Bede's view of the British in 731, although in practice it is likely that relations varied according to the personalities holding power. For instance, Eata and Cuthbert took a more conciliatory view than Wilfrid, as bishops; and Aldfrith differed from his predecessor, Ecgfrith, as king of Northumbria.[110] On the British side, also, there were varying attitudes to Anglo-Saxon Christians. Most extreme were those of the clergy of Dyfed. According to Aldhelm's letter to the king of Dumnonia, written *c.*675, they compelled visiting Anglo-Saxons to spend forty days in penance before admitting them to communion. On the other hand, the implication is that the British clergy in Dumnonia did not go to these lengths.[111]

CONCLUSION

Given the scarcity of our sources, it is difficult to paint an accurate picture of the British church in this period. Perhaps the most fundamental point to bear in mind is that that church varied enormously. In the first half of the sixth century, it belonged to a sub-Roman world in contact with the continent; but by 700 it had been restricted to the least Romanised parts of Britain, while its refusal to participate in the Augustinian mission to the Anglo-Saxons had had the effect of distancing it from the mainstream church.[112] The British church also contained much variety within itself at one time. Thus the worldly clergy attacked by Gildas co-existed with the ascetic minority, who pioneered a spiritual revival. We should therefore beware of fastening simultaneously upon the corruption of the clergy at the time of the *De Excidio*, and the rigorist, stand-offish approach of the Dyfed clergy in Aldhelm's time, as though the same group was involved both times. Instead we should realise that the latter was an extreme development out of the ascetic revival, which itself arose in reaction to the clerical corruption attacked by Gildas; and also that its extremes had been criticised by none other than Gildas himself.[113]

108 Bede, *HE* IV.17, and see also Thacker, chapter 17 below.

109 Bede, *HE* III.25; III.28–IV.2. *Penitential of Theodore* I.v and II.ix; Stephanus, *Vita Wilfridi*, chs. 10, 12, 14–15; Aldhelm, *Epistulae* IV.

110 Cf. Kirby (1995).

111 Aldhelm, *Epistulae* IV; cf. trans. Lapidge and Herren (1979), pp. 140–3, 155–60.

112 Cf. Campbell (1996), esp. pp. 94–6.

113 Gildas, *Fragments* 3; Stancliffe (1999), p. 110.

The criticisms of Gildas and Bede are well known. They should be offset against some of the positive achievements of the British church that are often associated not with it but with the Irish, Welsh or 'Celtic' churches; their roots, however, lie in the British church of our period. Of prime importance was the sixth-century ascetic revival, for this underlined many of the most significant developments of the Celtic churches.[114] One can instance the high value set on holiness of life, seen from an ascetic perspective; this gave God-centred ascetics equal authority with those holding the highest ecclesiastical office, and led to interesting ways of combining the two callings.[115] A second development was the *peregrinatio* tradition, which may have been as responsible for the journeying overseas of the Britons who established a community in Galicia as it was for the pilgrimages of Samson, Columbanus and many others.[116] Thirdly, the British appear to have been at the root of the development of 'private', repeatable penance, which did much to develop a Christian conscience and render people's Christianity something that was lived, rather than seeing it simply as adherence to a set of rules; Uinniaus, the author of the earliest penitential, was probably a sixth-century Briton.[117]

In all of this the British church appears innovative, rather than conservative. Similarly there is good evidence that at least some in the British church had a concept of mission, and felt called to bring the Gospel to other peoples, rather than turning their backs on their neighbours in the way that Bede portrays it. The prime example here is Patrick's mission to the Irish; and although Patrick was criticised by the conservative church establishment of fifth-century Britain, in the longer term his vision inspired other British missionaries to follow him. We seldom know their names, but the linguistic evidence unambiguously points to Britain as the chief source of Ireland's conversion.[118] Similarly in northern Britain, the Britons appear to have spread Christianity not simply to their fellow Britons, but to the southern Picts as well.[119] All this means that we should not assume that the British church was, from the start, too xenophobic ever to have considered joining Augustine's mission to the Anglo-Saxons, if only it had been set up in a way that did not appear to threaten them with subordination to their political rivals.[120]

As well as its spiritual vitality, the British church may also have had greater cultural achievements to its credit than we customarily assume: Gildas used a

114 Cf. Sharpe (1984a), esp. pp. 199–202.

115 Bede, *HE* II.2; Stancliffe (1999), pp. 131–3; Cogitosus, *Vita S. Brigitae*, preface; Charles-Edwards (2000), pp. 264–81; Stancliffe (1989), pp. 39–40.

116 Charles-Edwards (1976); cf. Stancliffe, chapter 15 above, pp. 405–6.

117 Frantzen (1983), pp. 4–60; Dumville (1984c).

118 Stancliffe (2004); Greene (1968), pp. 78–85; Sharpe (1990), esp. pp. 92–3; Dumville *et al.* (1993), pp. 139–45.

119 See Stancliffe below, pp. 451–4.

120 See further Stancliffe (1999).

colourful rhetorical style for his *De Excidio*, and the same correct, but flowing and expressive style was later used by Columbanus; presumably the Irish learnt it from the Britons.[121] At least one memorial inscription from South Wales is in hexameter verse.[122] The British may well have written letters, history, possibly even saints' Lives, which have not come down to us.[123] On the artistic side, arguments have recently been put forward for seeing a late antique illuminated manuscript, the Roman Vergil, as a product of sub-Roman Britain.[124] Perhaps we should also learn to look at some of the British hanging bowls as artistic achievements, rather than just archaeological objects. All this should make us view this 'dark age' of British history with new eyes.

NORTHERN BRITAIN (INCLUDING MODERN SCOTLAND)

Northern Britain, with its upland expanses and mountain ranges impeding communication between east and west, had a character of its own long before the emergence of Scotland and England as coherent political entities. The reason for preferring the term 'northern Britain' to 'Scotland', however, is not simply to avoid anachronistic nomenclature: it is not just that Scotland was then inhabited by Britons, Dalriadan Irish (*Scoti* in Latin, whence Scots), Picts and – as our period progresses – Anglo-Saxons, each with their own language and political and cultural identity (see map 5). A more subtle point is that northern Britain is an elastic term which can be stretched to include everything north of the Humber, contracted somewhat to focus on the area north of Hadrian's Wall along the Tyne/Solway line, or contracted again to focus more precisely on the area north of the short-lived Antonine Wall along the Forth/Clyde line. This elasticity is helpful, for the Anglo-Saxons and the Britons between the Humber and the Forth/Clyde line faced both south and north simultaneously, and thus played a key role in transmitting religious and cultural influences between the north and the south of Britain.

NORTHERN BRITONS AND SOUTHERN PICTS

In the fifth and sixth centuries, as we have seen, Christianity spread north from the Roman-ruled area to the British peoples living between the two walls: this is implied by Patrick's letter against Coroticus, by the distribution of Eccles place-names, and by the scatter of Christian Latin inscriptions from Whithorn and Chesterholm as far north as the Catstane, which stood in a

[121] Cf. Winterbottom (1976); Wright (1984) and (1997), pp. 82–7; Kerlouégan (1987).

[122] Nash-Williams (1950), p. 77, no. 62; cf. also no. 139.

[123] Cf. Jackson (1964); Hughes (1980), pp. 68–73, 88–94; Sims-Williams (1998); Stancliffe (1999), pp. 124–9.

[124] Dark (1994), pp. 184–91.

fifth- to seventh-century long-cist cemetery near Edinburgh.[125] Some 50 kilometres east of the latter lies Traprain Law, an important stronghold of the (British) Votadini (or Gododdin); and here excavations have revealed the foundations of a building which has been plausibly identified as a church.[126] A Brittonic poem, *The Gododdin*, portrays the Votadini warriors attacking the Anglo-Saxons as Christians (though it must be recognised that the poem reached its written form some centuries later, and details could thus have been altered).[127]

What, however, of the peoples of northern Britain taken in its narrowest sense, the Picts and the Dalriadan Irish north of the Forth/Clyde isthmus? Unfortunately, very little literary evidence survives from the Picts themselves; we therefore have to fall back on information gleaned from their Anglo-Saxon and Dalriadan neighbours (both of whom sought to dominate the Pictish church at different stages of its development), together with archaeology and place-name evidence. First, Bede's account:

> In the year of our Lord 565 . . . there came from Ireland to Britain a priest and abbot named Columba . . . to preach the word of God to the kingdoms of the northern Picts . . . The southern Picts who live on this side of the mountains had, so it is said, long ago given up the errors of idolatry and received the true faith through the preaching of the Word by that reverend and holy man Bishop Ninian, a Briton who had received orthodox instruction at Rome in the faith and the mysteries of the truth. His episcopal see . . . is commonly called Whithorn.[128]

Thus according to Bede, the Picts were converted in two stages: the southern Picts (i.e. those between the Forth and the Grampians) by the Roman-trained British bishop, Ninian; and the northern Picts by the Irish monk, Columba. It can be inferred that Bede was here drawing on a Pictish, not a Columban source of information;[129] and Bede will also have derived information on Ninian from Whithorn.

Bede's account, written long after the events he was describing, arouses various misgivings. First, the picture seems too tidy, with two separate missions to two separate political groupings amongst the Picts. Historical reality was probably more complex: for instance, an early source alludes to Columba preaching to the tribes of the Tay, i.e. the *southern* Picts.[130] Secondly, Bede misrepresents Columba as coming to Britain specifically as a missionary: Adomnán's *Life of St Columba* shows that although he did preach to particular Pictish households, this was not his sole concern. Perhaps Bede has distorted the career of Ninian, for whom our sources are poor, in much the same way: his evangelisation of

[125] Thomas (1991–2), p. 4; Dalland (1992), pp. 203–4. Cf. pp. 429–35 above.
[126] Smith (1996), pp. 25–6. [127] Wendy Davies, chapter 9 above. [128] Bede, *HE* III.4.
[129] Cf. Kirby (1973), pp. 21–4; Duncan (1981). [130] See p. 458 below.

the Picts figures little in the (historically inadequate) Lives of Ninian. Thirdly, there is surely a deliberate agenda in Bede's portrayal of these two contrasting missions. His stress on Ninian as a *bishop* trained *at Rome*, who preceded Columba, cannot but remind one of the fact that *c.*710–715 the Pictish king turned to Bede's own monastery of Jarrow for information about the Roman Easter, and shortly after expelled the Columban clergy, who followed the rival usage, from Pictland. It would have been very convenient for the king to claim that his church had an earlier, unimpeachably Roman origin, in contrast to the Columban church of Iona, where bishops came under the authority of the priest abbot.

Unfortunately, our sources for Ninian are too poor to enable us to penetrate behind Bede's account. Some modern scholars doubt whether he ever visited the Picts, while others would accept his mission, but not take his training at Rome in a literal sense. However, Bede seems to have been accurate in portraying the southern Pictish area as deriving its Christianity in the first instance from the post-Roman British church to its south (though this should not exclude an Irish contribution also). The evidence for this is threefold: the literary evidence about Ninian, just mentioned; that of Eccles place-names; and, in a subsidiary role, the archaeological evidence of long-cist cemeteries. The significance of the Eccles place-names is that whereas, for the British, this word denoted a church, such a usage was not typical either of Gaelic-speaking *Scoti* or of English speakers, both of whom left their mark on south-eastern Scotland. This enables us to identify a British contribution with some confidence, although we must recognise that not all Eccles churches will belong to the pre-Columban period; such names might still have been coined up to *c.*800. With this qualification, however, the Eccles names provide valuable evidence for the British contribution to the Christianity of the southern Picts. They also confirm the accuracy of Bede's differentiation between the church's origins amongst the southern and the northern Picts: there are fifteen Eccles names between the Forth and the Grampians, with only one outlier further north.[131]

The cemetery evidence tallies with that of the Eccles place-names: the area containing long-cist cemeteries, with bodies being oriented west/east in stone-lined graves, spans the area south and north of the Forth.[132] It would be rash to interpret the long-cist cemeteries as necessarily Christian, rather than representing a burial rite that began before Christianity, and was compatible with it.[133] None the less, the distribution of such cemeteries does testify to

[131] Barrow (1983); map 13, p. 433 above.

[132] Alcock (1992); Foster (1996), p. 79; Smith (1996), pp. 27–9.

[133] See Alcock (1992), p. 127; Proudfoot (1996), pp. 440–4; Burt (1997); Yeoman (1998), p. 83.

common cultural features south and north of the Forth, and thus provides a context that makes the spread of Christianity from the former to the latter plausible. Such contact also appears in the *Gododdin*'s representation of a Pict amongst the Christian British warriors who were feasted at Edinburgh before attacking the Anglo-Saxons.[134] We will return to the Picts shortly. First, however, we need to focus on the work of Bede's second missionary, Columba.

IONA AND ITS OUTREACH

While in the east Christianity was spreading up from the Britons between the Walls to the Picts north of the Forth, in the west the Irish colony of Dál Riada was gaining a major Christian focus with the foundation of the monastery of Iona. The indications are that Dál Riada was largely Christian already – albeit with some notable exceptions.[135] Then in 563 Columba, of the royal Uí Néill dynasty, left Ireland, ostensibly as a *peregrinus* ('pilgrim'), perhaps because in Ireland he was unable entirely to distance himself from the power struggles of his royal kinsmen.[136] Columba founded the monastery of Iona on the little island of that name, which lies off the western tip of Mull; and although he was to return to Ireland on various occasions, it was on Iona that he was to be based for the rest of his life. Iona thus became the chief monastery of a federation of Columban churches that spanned Argyll and mainland Ireland, and it retained its position after Columba's death in 597.

Our earliest source for Columba is a panegyrical lament composed in Irish shortly after his death. It is the work of a professional poet, written in an extremely obscure style; but it is valuable both for being so close to Columba in time, and also for giving us a lay perspective on the saint.[137] In this it differs from the *Life of St Columba*, which was written about a century after his death by Adomnán, abbot of Iona from 679 to 704. Adomnán was able to draw on material that had been continuously handed on within the community, as well as on an earlier written Life, which does not survive, and his work contains much of historical value.[138] This makes Iona the best-recorded Irish monastery from our period.

The surviving evidence of literary works, manuscripts and stone carving reveals Iona as one of the major literary and artistic centres of the early Middle

[134] Hughes (1970), p. 13.

[135] Cf. Adomnán, *Vita Columbae* II.22 and 24; Sharpe (1979) and (1995), pp. 327–8, n. 258; Dumville *et al.* (1993), pp. 188–9.

[136] Cf. Adomnán, *Vita Columbae*, Second preface (at 4a); *Annals of Ulster* s.a. 561; Byrne (1973), p. 95; Herbert (1988), pp. 27–8. See also Stancliffe, chapter 15, p. 405 above. The date of his crossing to Iona is given as 563 in *Annals of Ulster*, but 565 by Bede, *HE* III.4: see Duncan (1981), pp. 4–7 and 10.

[137] Clancy and Márkus (1995), pp. 96–128.

[138] Herbert (1988), pp. 12–26, 134–48.

Ages. The historical notes kept there from its foundation lie at the basis of the Irish annal collections that have come down to us,[139] while by the seventh century Columban monks were producing poetry in Latin and Irish, saints' Lives, an account of the Holy Land, and legal texts. It is also likely that Adomnán was responsible for putting together a commentary on Vergil's *Georgics* and *Bucolics*, suggesting that at least some classical poetry was studied there.[140] On the artistic side, Iona and its dependent houses appear to have been at the heart of the development of insular illuminated manuscripts which begins, in a simple way, with the 'Cathach' (a psalter) and the fragmentary Gospel-book or New Testament now preserved in Durham, and reaches its first flowering with the Book of Durrow, which probably belongs to the second half of the seventh century. This is a magnificent Gospel-book where the groundwork of Celtic scrolls and spirals is joined on one page by interlaced animal ornament, betokening a Germanic contribution, and elsewhere by influences from both the Mediterranean and the Pictish worlds. The chief developments in stone carving occur after our period, but crosses (probably of wood) were already being erected, and simple crosses were incised on stones.[141]

Underpinning these achievements were impressive leadership, a coherent organisation, and royal and noble patronage. Columba appears in Adomnán's work as a true man of God, who experienced mystical revelations and enjoyed prophetic foresight, while governing his monastery with discernment and humanity. He also engaged with kings on matters of political moment. Indeed, Columba may have been the moving spirit in building an alliance between Dál Riada and his northern Uí Néill kinsmen in Ireland. The Dalriadan king donated Iona for his monastic foundation, and his successor was rewarded with Columba's prayers – even when he entered battle as the aggressor.[142] Adomnán further depicts Columba 'ordaining' him king of Dál Riada, although this can more plausibly be interpreted as reflecting the concerns of Adomnán than of Columba himself.[143] Columba's royal connections, coupled with his religious stature, account for the donation of land for church foundations in southern and northern Uí Néill areas of Ireland (Durrow and Derry) and in Scottish Dál Riada, where there were subordinate houses on Tiree and other islands, as well as at Cell Diúin on Loch Awe on the Scottish mainland. Columba himself

139 Smyth (1972); Bannerman (1974), pp. 9–26.

140 Kenney (1929), no. 113, pp. 286–7; Lapidge and Sharpe (1985), no. 1235, p. 327; Stancliffe (1997), p. 169, n. 371.

141 Adomnán, *Vita Columbae* I.45; *Argyll* IV, pp. 180–92.

142 *Annals of Ulster* s.a. 574 and 575; Adomnán, *Vita Columbae* I.7–8; Herbert (1988), pp. 28–9. On Bede's claim that the Pictish king donated Iona (*HE* III.4) see Bullough (1982), pp. 82–3.

143 Adomnán, *Vita Columbae* III.5, and the note by Sharpe (1995), pp. 355–6; cf. also Adomnán, *Vita Columbae* I.9.

appointed the heads of all these subordinate houses, normally nominating a monk of his own family.[144] This family connection continued after his death in typical Irish style, with six out of eight abbatial successors coming from the Uí Néill in the course of the seventh century. This, however, did not impair the quality of abbots selected, who were all celibate monks.[145]

Bede's description of the governmental structure of the Iona federation is important:

> From both [Iona and Durrow] sprang very many monasteries . . . in Britain and Ireland, over all of which the island monastery in which his body lies held pre-eminence. This island always has an abbot-priest for its ruler, to whose authority the whole *provincia*, including even bishops, are subject, according to an unusual arrangement.[146]

Thus the abbot of Iona, albeit in consultation with his senior monks, exercised overall control; on the Northumbrian evidence this included nominating bishops and laying down the line on major issues, such as the Easter controversy.[147] This would not necessarily prevent bishops exercising effective day-to-day pastoral oversight over their dioceses; but it did place the abbot in a position of authority, which elsewhere in the church belonged to the bishop. How far this pattern was normal in the early Irish church, and quite what its implications were for the relative positions of bishop and abbot, is currently the subject of scholarly debate.[148]

Comment is also needed on the geographical extent of Iona's rule, which did not cover all of Scottish Dál Riada. Some churches were founded quite independently of Iona, often by monks connected with the Dál nAraide, the neighbouring – and rival – tribe to the Dál Riada in north-east Ireland. The island of Tiree contained both Columban and non-Columban monasteries.[149] The island of Lismore, strategically sited east of Mull in the mouth of the sea loch leading up to the Great Glen, had an important church founded by Mo Luag (or Lugaid: d. 592). On the island of Eigg, a monk named Donnán was martyred with his companions in 617, while further north still, opposite Skye, Mael Ruba founded the monastery of Applecross in 673 (Map 5). This was linked to Bangor on the Irish mainland.[150] These foundations, and others

[144] MacDonald (1985); Herbert (1988), pp. 34–5. [145] Herbert (1988), p. 310, and cf. pp. 36–56.

[146] Bede, *HE* III.4. On *omnis provincia*, Wallace-Hadrill (1988), pp. 93–4.

[147] Cf. Bede, *HE* III.5 and 25; V.15 (at pp. 228, 294, 296, 506); but on V.25 see Picard (1984); Charles-Edwards (1992), pp. 72–3.

[148] Cf. Charles-Edwards' succinct note on Bede, *HE* III.4, Wallace-Hadrill (1988), p. 230. Sharpe (1984b) and (1992a), pp. 97–109, and Etchingham (1994) stress the continuing importance of bishops in Irish prescriptive texts, but do not adequately discuss the Bedan passage nor Adomnán, *Vita Columbae* I.36. See further Stancliffe, chapter 15 above.

[149] Adomnán, *Vita Columbae* I.36 and III.8; cf. Sharpe (1995), notes 107, 182, pp. 279–80, 303.

[150] *Annals of Ulster* s.a. 592, 617, 673; Anderson (1965), esp. pp. 29–30, 32; MacDonald (1974); Mac Lean (1997), pp. 173–6.

which are not reliably recorded, would have lain outside Iona's jurisdiction.[151] On the other hand, to the south-east Iona's jurisdiction expanded dramatically, though not permanently, in the course of the seventh century.

The decisive step here occurred in 634 when King Oswald of Northumbria turned to Iona for missionaries to convert his newly won kingdom – Oswald having previously been baptised on Iona while in exile. From Oswald's initiative stemmed the mission of Aidan, a monk from Iona who was consecrated bishop for the Northumbrians, and established his monastery on Holy Island (Lindisfarne). With the active support of King Oswald, Aidan and his companions were able to establish Christianity in Northumbria, and indeed Ionan monks were also instrumental in converting Mercia further south. Up to the Synod of Whitby in 664, this extensive mission-field formed part of the area under the abbot of Iona.[152] Something similar may also have occurred amongst the Picts; but here, the picture is more uncertain, and requires separate consideration.

CHRISTIANITY AND THE PICTS

Written sources for the Picts are so poor that one scholar, Kathleen Hughes, concluded that Christianity, with its close association with literacy, can have made but slow headway there during the seventh century, and did not win full royal support until the early eighth.[153] Her handling of the evidence has, however, been criticised.[154] In reaching her conclusions she was influenced by the fact that seventh-century incised symbol stones from Pictland, depicting Pictish symbols like the crescent and V rod or the 'Pictish elephant', show no sign of accommodation with Christianity ('Class I' stones). In the eighth century, however, we see finely executed cross-slabs carved on dressed stone; these have a cross on one side, and on the other secular scenes such as hunts and battles, together with Pictish symbols ('Class II' stones). Certainly, the Class II stones do show an accommodation between Christianity and a warrior aristocracy. We should, however, be wary of concluding that the absence of the cross from Class I stones shows these to have been pagan, rather than secular. Indeed, it has been pointed out that the superb Class II stones stem from a deeply Christianised milieu which cannot have sprung up overnight; the implication is, therefore, that Christianity was already becoming well established in Pictish society in the seventh century. The upshot of this is that we cannot use the distribution of Class I and Class II stones to map Pictish conversion.

Archaeology is unfortunately of limited value for illuminating the conversion of the Picts. We cannot use the evidence of burial rites in any but a subordinate

151 Cf. below, p. 459 and note 163. 152 Bede, *HE* III; Thacker, chapter 17 below.

153 Hughes (1970). 154 Henderson (1987), esp. p. 48; Forsyth (1998), pp. 39–42.

capacity;[155] and although we may hazard the view that both Burghead in the north-east and Abernethy in the south were pagan sites before becoming Christian ones, we lack any means of dating the changeover (Map 5).[156] We are therefore forced to rely on the distribution of Eccles place-names and on such literary evidence as we have. We saw above that the southern Pictish area appears to have derived its Christianity from the Britons to its south, presumably in the fifth and/or sixth centuries. In addition, we have strictly contemporary evidence for Columba converting some of 'the tribes of the Tay' in the late sixth century.[157] By the early seventh century we have evidence that Christianity was well established in the upper echelons of Pictish (or at least, southern Pictish) society, for Bede implies that a Northumbrian prince could be converted to Christianity in the 620s when staying amongst the Picts as well as amongst the Dalriadan Irish.[158] Further, Northumbria's dealings with southern Pictland later in the seventh century presuppose that it was already Christian.[159]

Northern Pictland, focussed around the Moray Firth, presents a different picture. Adomnán shows Columba operating in a pagan society in this area. When he visited the Pictish king Bridei at his fortress in the vicinity of Inverness, he was opposed by the king's foster-father, a pagan priest (*magus*); and although Columba's miraculous powers reputedly won him the king's respect, there is no reference to Bridei accepting Christianity.[160] We do not know which Pictish king was the first to be baptised, but Northumbrian sources would probably have remarked on Pictish paganism if it had still persisted at the highest level of society in the second half of the seventh century. Columba did convert some individual Pictish nobles and their households on Skye and around Inverness, and a monastery may have been founded at Deer (west of Peterhead) by the early seventh century.[161] It is likely that Columban monks carried on this work in the course of the seventh century: referring to the plague years in the 660s and 680s, Adomnán comments that the Irish living in Britain and the Picts were the only two peoples to be spared – an escape he attributed to St Columba, whose monasteries, 'placed within the boundaries of both peoples, are down to the present time held in great honour by both'.[162] Alongside this passage we may set Bede's reference to Iona as 'for a long time chief amongst almost all the

155 Contra Smith (1996), pp. 27–9; cf. note 133 above.
156 Ritchie (1989), pp. 12–16; Proudfoot (1997), esp. pp. 58, 61.
157 *Amra* I and VIII: Clancy and Márkus (1995), pp. 104–5, 112–13, and cf. 118–19.
158 Bede *HE* III.1; and, for Eanfrith's Pictish links, Kirby (1976), p. 289; Miller (1978), p. 47.
159 Bede *HE* III.25; IV.3; Kirby (1973), pp. 10–11.
160 Adomnán, *Vita Columbae* II.33–5 (and I.37). Cf. Anderson (1973), p. 100 and n. 95, and p. 248; Bede, *HE* III.4; Duncan (1981), pp. 7–10, 27.
161 Adomnán, *Vita Columbae* I.33; II.32; III.14. O'Rahilly (1946), p. 373.
162 Adomnán, *Vita Columbae* II.46.

monasteries of the northern Irish and of all the Picts, ruling over both peoples'. The precision of Bede's language here implies that, regardless of their seemingly diverse Christian origins, by *c.*700 Iona was regarded as the head church for all the Picts.[163] A major Pictish monastery has recently been identified at Tarbat (Portmahomack), on the south side of the Dornoch Firth, and is currently under excavation.[164]

In addition to preaching to individual households and engaging with kings, Irish monks are also likely to have spread Christianity through their custom of *peregrinatio*, ascetic exile. Adomnán tells of monks setting out in boats 'to seek a desert in the ocean'; and Columba enlisted King Bridei's influence over a sub-king of the Orkneys to obtain protection for such ascetics if any should land on Orkney, which they duly did.[165] Hermitages are found on remote islands like Rona, 70 kilometres north-east of the Butt of Lewis, or the less isolated Eileach an Naoimh, south of Mull.[166] Other ascetics voyaged as far afield as the Faroes and Iceland in the pre-Viking period.[167] The latter were uninhabited, but Orkney was not, and its inhabitants may well have first encountered Christianity through such voyagers. It is therefore important for us to realise that the distinction between a withdrawn monk and a pastor engaging with society was less clear in the early Middle Ages than it seems today: well-documented Irish *peregrini* were frequently both,[168] and hermitages could evolve into major monasteries.[169] In addition to the archaeological evidence of ruined chapels and early cross-slabs, the distribution of Papar place-names indicates pre-Scandinavian church sites, whether of hermitages (cf. Farne Island) or of monasteries (cf. Lindisfarne). There are twenty-seven Papar names in Scotland, predominantly in the Hebrides, Orkneys and Shetlands.[170]

NORTHUMBRIA, THE PICTS AND IONA AFTER THE SYNOD OF WHITBY (664)

At the Synod of Whitby in 664, King Oswiu of Northumbria decided to adopt the Roman Easter and tonsure in place of those favoured by Iona. This was a highly political act: he was simultaneously aligning himself with

163 Bede, *HE* III.3; Henderson (1967), p. 79.
164 Harden (1995); Carver (1999); cf. Higgitt (1982).
165 Adomnán, *Vita Columbae* II.42; see also I.6 and 20.
166 Nisbet and Gailey (1960); *Argyll* V, pp. 170–82; cf. also Lamb (1974) and (1975–6).
167 Radford (1983), pp. 14–21.
168 E.g. Columbanus and Fursey: Stancliffe (1989), pp. 39–40; cf. Charles-Edwards (1976), pp. 54–8. See also Stancliffe, chapter 15 above, pp. 405–7.
169 E.g. Jonas, *Vita Columbani* I.6 and 10.
170 MacDonald (1977); Crawford (1987), pp. 164–7; Pringle (1994), p. 21.

the Christian tradition of southern England which he sought to dominate, seizing back the initiative from his son, the sub-king of Deira, and declaring effective independence from the Columban church. Equally important, he was also embracing a Christian tradition that assigned the ruler an important place in the church, after the manner of the emperor Constantine. Hitherto, Northumbria's bishops had been Irish monks, sent from Iona; now they were to be Anglo-Saxons, nominated by the king. A remarkable letter from the pope urged the king to play an active role in dedicating 'the whole of your island to Christ', and Oswiu responded.[171] Northumbrian overlordship was extended over the Britons, Picts and Dál Riada in the north, and this was accompanied by ecclesiastical overlordship.[172] A short-lived bishopric for the Picts was set up at Abercorn, on the south side of the Firth of Forth, and Cuthbert visited the church further north while prior of Melrose.[173]

Northumbria's military superiority in northern Britain was overthrown by the Picts in 685, and this ended its attempt to dominate the Pictish church; the bishopric of Abercorn collapsed. Close relationships between the different peoples continued, however, though now on a more equal footing. The new Northumbrian king, Aldfrith, was half-Irish, had studied on Iona, and probably owed his successful bid for the Northumbrian throne to the Pictish/Irish alliance which had overthrown his predecessor.[174] He was a friend of Adomnán, abbot of Iona 679–704, and the political stability of his reign enabled contacts to flow in all directions between the churches of Iona, Pictland and Northumbria. Disagreement over the correct system of calculating the date of Easter still existed, but it ceased to be a matter of national antagonism: Adomnán himself adopted the Roman system, and persuaded many to do likewise – though not his own community on Iona.[175] His *Life of Columba* has been seen amongst other things as a tribute demonstrating that a pro-Roman position on the Easter question did not preclude a glowing regard for Columba as a man of God, comparable to the greatest followers of Christ – not excluding Saints Peter and Paul – wherever in the church they might be found.[176] Under Adomnán Iona was at its height, a position symbolised by his success in persuading some forty churchmen and fifty kings to subscribe to a law exempting churchmen, women and clerics from the violence of warfare (697). The signatories, headed

[171] Bede, *HE* III.29 (pp. 320–1).

[172] Bede, *HE* IV.3; Stephanus, *Life of Wilfrid*, cc.21 and 53; Kirby (1976), pp. 289–91; Moisl (1983), pp. 117–20; Charles-Edwards (1992), p. 66, n. 19.

[173] Bede, *HE* IV.26; Bede, *Vita Cuthberti*, ch. 11; Kirby (1973), pp. 9–12.

[174] Moisl (1983), pp. 120–4.

[175] Bede, *HE* V.15; Picard (1984), pp. 60–70; Herbert (1988), pp. 48–50; Charles-Edwards (1992), pp. 72–3.

[176] Adomnán, *Vita Columbae* II.32; Herbert (1988), pp. 142–4.

by the bishop of Armagh, were mostly Irish, but also included the king of the Picts and their bishop, Curetán.[177]

The second decade of the eighth century saw significant changes. First, Bede tells us that Nechtan, king of the Picts, resolved to follow Roman usage as regards Easter and the tonsure, and applied to Bede's own abbot at Wearmouth/Jarrow for information to confute the traditionalists, as also for architects to build him a stone church to be dedicated to St Peter.[178] Secondly, the Irish annals record that in 716 Iona adopted the Roman Easter, that in 717 King Nechtan expelled Columban monks and clerics, and that in 718 Iona adopted the Roman tonsure. They also reveal some confusion over the succession of abbots on Iona.[179] The traditional interpretation of this evidence would see Nechtan between 710 and 715 acting in a way comparable to Oswiu in 664: he was in all likelihood won over to Roman customs both by the teaching of a Northumbrian *peregrinus* called Ecgberht and also by the opportunity which this gave him to take control of the Pictish church himself, rather than remain beholden to the abbot of Iona. Hereafter the king and his nobles would exercise effective patronage and influence on the Pictish church.[180] This interpretation has recently been challenged by scholars who emphasise that Nechtan was probably acting in accordance with the more progressive elements among the Iona community, who, like Adomnán, favoured the Roman Easter. On this view, Nechtan's expulsion of a rump of non-conforming Columban clerics was a minor, short-lived affair, which did not break the substantial continuity of Columban influence within Pictland, while the approach to Jarrow/Wearmouth was made primarily for political reasons: the Picts had been defeated by the Northumbrians in 711, and so sought allies within the Northumbrian church.[181] We may adopt the latter view as regards Nechtan's need to secure Northumbrian allies and to end those ecclesiastical practices that might offer a pretext for Northumbrian intervention, and also recognise that the progressives within the Iona community might well have prepared the ground. But the reality of a shift from Iona's control to an independent Pictish church under the king, in accordance with the traditional interpretation, is borne out by close examination of another passage of Bede, where he uses the past tense when describing Iona's role as head of the Pictish church.[182] This implies that at the time of writing in 731, Iona no longer held that position. King Nechtan was thus not the first Pictish king to support the church, but rather the first to assert royal control over the church.

177 Ní Dhonnchadha (1982), esp. pp. 191, 214.
178 Bede, *HE* v.21.
179 *Annals of Ulster*, s.a. 716, 717; *Annals of Tigernach* i, pp. 185–6; Herbert (1988), pp. 57–62.
180 Henderson (1967), pp. 82–4; Kirby (1973), pp. 19–20; Foster (1996), p. 90; for Ecgberht's role, Duncan (1981), pp. 20–3, 26–7, 34–5.
181 Veitch (1997), pp. 635–42; cf. also Smyth (1984), pp. 137–9.
182 Bede, *HE* iii.3.

CHAPTER 17

ENGLAND IN THE SEVENTH CENTURY

Alan Thacker

INTRODUCTION: THE INFLUENCE OF BEDE

Our picture of England in the seventh century is inescapably dominated by a single source: Bede's *Ecclesiastical History of the English People*, completed in 734. That at once lends it vividness and makes it problematic. For Bede was a very skilful and intelligent writer with his own agendas; we know only what he chose to tell us and we have few other written records against which to assess his interpretation of events. Bede's narrative focusses on what was for him the only significant issue: the progress of Christianity among the English. He constructed it from a very distinctive perspective: to show that his people, the English, the *gens Anglorum*, and above all his own particular branch of that people, the Northumbrians, had been called by God to a special role in the history of salvation. They were a new Israel, charged with mission – to spread true faith and observance among their insular and continental neighbours. In Bede's view, in his own day they had fallen away from that vocation and had to be recalled to the right path. The *Ecclesiastical History* was overwhelmingly coloured by these concerns. It avoided difficult contemporary events and focussed on the glorious and exemplary recent past – the seventh-century past – of the English (and especially the Northumbrians), showing how they received and spread the Christian faith under the leadership of kings and pastors who lived up to their high calling.[1]

Although politically aware, Bede was thus not primarily interested in political or material culture. He simply sets his Christian narrative in a political context as far as is necessary and as far as he could reconstruct it from his mainly ecclesiastical sources. Inevitably, therefore, he was much better informed about long-Christian Kent than late-converted Mercia. Bede's concern with the church, moreover, gave him a distinctive ethnic perspective. For him, the

[1] Thacker (1983); Wormald (1983); Campbell (1986), pp. 1–48.

Germanic peoples inhabiting the various English kingdoms had acquired a unified identity through their submission to a united church. They could all be included under the single designation English, *Angli*. They were, moreover, set in contrast to the British, whom Bede treated with active hostility, alleging that they had failed in their Christian duty to bring the faith to the pagan English.[2] Except as external enemies, the British are largely invisible in the *Ecclesiastical History*.

The very few narrative sources, apart from Bede, are all quite brief and all Lives of saints. In one instance only, Stephen of Ripon's remarkable account of the Northumbrian bishop Wilfrid, do they enable us to check up on the *History*. The result is disturbing. It reveals that Bede's treatment of a difficult figure, controversial and yet crucial to his conversion story, was highly selective and discreet.[3] Other written sources – the laws, the few administrative documents, the ecclesiastical penitentials – by their nature cannot provide a narrative and have to be read in the light of the all-encompassing vision of Bede. Much the same is also true of the material evidence provided by the surviving buildings and by archaeology. Bede, then, is the lens through which we view seventh-century England. And, to say the least, that lens is highly idiosyncratic.

THE POLITICAL LANDSCAPE IN THE SEVENTH CENTURY

Some dozen or so political units are named in Bede, the charters, and other, later, sources, as ruled by English kings during the seventh century. The most enduring units, those which survived throughout this period, each with their own bishop or bishops, included in the north Bernicia and Deira (for much of the century uneasily united as Northumbria), and in the midlands and the south Wessex, Mercia, Kent, East Anglia, Essex and Sussex. From time to time we read also of kings of the Hwicce, Lindsey, the Isle of Wight, Middle Anglia, and, more dubiously, the Magonsæte and Surrey; among the South Gywre we hear of a *princeps*.[4] (See above, map 8.) Embedded within this political landscape, especially in the west, were the contemporary British kingdoms, under increasing pressure as the century wore on. In Wales the kingdoms of Gwynedd, Powys, Gwent or Glywysing, and Dyfed largely retained their independence, despite victories in the north, which in the period up to 633 brought Northumbrian kings temporary sway as far as the isles of Anglesey and Man.[5] In the south-west, the kingdom of Dumnonia, largest of British kingdoms, was in the process of being absorbed into Wessex.[6] In the south Pennines we

[2] Charles-Edwards (1983); Thacker (1996). [3] *Vita Wilfridi*.

[4] Bassett (1989a); Yorke (1990); Kirby (1991); *HE* IV.19.

[5] Davies (1982), 90–102; *HE* II.5. [6] Yorke (1995).

hear of a British kingdom, Elmet, conquered by Northumbria before the mid-seventh century. In north-west England and south-west Scotland lay Rheged, probably brought under Northumbrian lordship in the later part of the century. In Scotland too in the late seventh century Northumbria extended its rule over territories hitherto held by the Picts and the Scots of Dál Riada (see map 5, above). At its apogee, therefore, in the third quarter of the century, Northumbria, then the most powerful political entity, occupied vast territories extending in the east from the Humber to the Firth of Forth and in the west from Lancashire to beyond the Solway Firth.[7] The centre of gravity of the English world lay then in York, Bamburgh and great monasteries between Tyne and Wear, in a kind of middle kingdom, almost as much in later Scotland as in England.[8]

Bede tells us that in the seventh century the English kingdoms south of the Humber (except, initially, Kent) acknowledged an overlord, in Old English the *bretwalda*, ruler of Britain.[9] What, if any, authority resided in this title is unknown. Almost certainly, it was of a personal nature and depended on the resources and personality of the holder. There is evidence that most, if not all, of those so named by Bede had influence outside the confines of their own territories, even though they can in no sense be said to have ruled the whole of southern England. At most the *bretwalda* may be interpreted as a kind of high king, levying tribute on (temporarily) subordinated kingdoms.[10] After the brief sway of the rulers of the south-eastern kingdoms of Kent and East Anglia in the early decades, the high politics of the seventh century, south of the Humber, were dominated by the struggles between Northumbria and Mercia for supremacy. As David Rollason has recently emphasised, the stakes could hardly have been higher. For much of his reign the pagan Mercian king Penda (626 × 633–655) was a threat to the very existence of Northumbria, responsible for the deaths of two of its most successful rulers and capable of mounting an assault which enabled him to besiege the royal seat of Bamburgh itself. By the same token, when he in turn met defeat and death at Northumbrian hands, for a while Mercia itself ceased to exist as a politcal entity.[11]

Political narrative

The extreme and varying fortunes of the main kingdoms in seventh-century England illustrate the instability and fragility of political authority during

[7] See now Rollason (2003). [8] Campbell (1982). [9] *HE* II.5; *Anglo-Saxon Chronicle* s.a. 827.

[10] John (1966), pp. 1–63; Stenton (1970), pp. 48–66; Yorke (1981), pp. 171–200; Wormald (1983); Fanning (1991); Rollason (2003), ch. 2; *HE* II.5; *Vita Wilfridi* c.20.

[11] Rollason (2003), ch. 2; *HE* II.20; III.9, 16–17, 24.

this period.[12] At the opening of the century the main focus of English power lay in the south-east. The acknowledged overlord of southern England was Æthelberht, ruler of the rich kingdom of Kent (d. 616), who introduced Christianity to his people. Kent, however, suffered in the political and religious divisions which followed Æthelberht's death, and by the 620s the overlordship had passed to Rædwald, king of the East Angles (d. 616 × 627), who maintained altars to both the old gods and the new.[13] The wealth and power of the East Anglian political establishment is reflected in the royal tombs at the burial ground of Sutton Hoo, above all in the celebrated finds from the ship burial in Mound One.[14] Even so, the East Anglians' hold on political power proved only brief, and after Rædwald's death the overlordship passed to the recently united Northumbria of King Edwin (616–633), a former refugee at Rædwald's court.[15]

The bringing together of the two major English kingdoms north of the Humber, Bernicia and Deira, was a gradual process, accomplished initially by the Bernician king, the pagan Æthelfrith (d. 616) and continued by his conqueror and successor, the Christian convert and Deiran Edwin. When, some time after his defeat of the Bernicians at the battle of Idle in 616, Edwin assumed the southern overlordship, he could be patriotically credited by the Northumbrian Bede with rule over all four of the peoples of seventh-century Britain – the English, British, Picts and Irish. Only Kent lay outside his power. Under Edwin, in the mid-620s, the Roman missionary Paulinus set up new Christian institutions in Northumbria, but this initiative foundered with Edwin's defeat and death in 633 at the hands of the British (and Christian) king Cadwallon of Gwynedd, and his pagan ally, the Mercian king Penda.[16] As elsewhere, Edwin's defeat inaugurated a pagan reaction, and for a year the new Northumbrian kingdom dissolved into its constituent parts under his apostate successors. By 634, however, the union had been restored under a new Bernician overlord, King Oswald (d. 642), characterised by Bede as *christianissimus rex* and one of the heroes of his *History*. Oswald defeated his British enemies at the battle of Heavenfield (*Hefenfelth*) far in the north near Hadrian's Wall. He re-established the Northumbrian supremacy in the south and maintained Northumbrian overlordship of the British, Picts and Irish in the north. But his achievements also collapsed with his defeat and death in 642 at the hands of Penda and his allies at the battle of *Maserfelth*, usually said to be Oswestry in Shropshire.[17]

After a period of more than usual confusion, the Northumbrian supremacy was reasserted under Oswald's successor Oswiu (642–670). With the defeat and

[12] Best discussion, Campbell (1982). [13] *HE* II.15; Yorke (2003), pp. 243–57, esp. 244–5.
[14] Bruce-Mitford (1975–83); Carver (1992) and (1998). [15] *HE* II.9.12.
[16] *HE* II.5, 9–20. [17] *HE* II.5; III.1, 6, 9; Stancliffe and Cambridge (1995).

death of the Northumbrians' longstanding political rival, Penda of Mercia, at the battle of the *Winwaed* (near Leeds) in 655, Oswiu took much of the Mercians' territory under his direct rule and set up Penda's son the Christian Peada as his under-king in south Mercia. In 658, however, the Mercians expelled the Northumbrians from their heartlands and established a new regime under Penda's son, the Christian Wulfhere (d. 674).[18] Even so, for a while they apparently continued to render tribute.[19] Similar claims were made for Oswiu's supremacy over the Irish and Picts as for his two great predecessors.[20] Under Oswiu's son and successor, Ecgfrith (670–685) the Northumbrians retained a degree of political dominance in the south until they were defeated by Æthelred at the battle of the Trent in 679.[21] That battle finally settled the issue of the control of the province and former kingdom of Lindsey (in modern Lincolnshire), long disputed between the Deirans, Northumbrians and Mercians; henceforth it lay firmly within the Mercian sphere of influence.[22]

Ecgfrith's reign initially saw the confirmation of Northumbria's continued dominance in the north. In the early 670s he brutally crushed a Pictish revolt,[23] and in 684 launched an ambitious military expedition against the Scots in northern Ireland. A further campaign against the Picts ended in his defeat and death in 685, and thereafter, as Bede noted, the power of the Northumbrian kingdom began to 'ebb and fall away'. The Picts regained the land they had lost, while the Scots in the mainland kingdom of Dál Riada and some at least of the conquered Britons recovered their independence.[24] The defeat of Ecgfrith marked the end not only of Northumbrian expansion in the north but of any further pretensions to overlordship of England south of the Humber. Henceforth King Æthelred of Mercia was the dominant figure in the south.

Mercia, the midland kingdom, whose heartlands lay around Lichfield, Tamworth and Repton in Staffordshire and Derbyshire, was late in emerging as an effective political unit and late in adopting Christianity.[25] Although the pagan Penda had acquiesced in the conversion of his son Peada upon his marriage to Oswiu's daughter, the first bishop was only established by the conquering Oswiu himself in the mid-650s. Temporarily halted during its subjugation in the mid-650s, Mercian expansion resumed after it regained its independence in 658. Penda's work was consolidated and continued by his sons Wulfhere (658–675) and Æthelred (675–704), and after the Mercians' decisive victory in 679 most of the kingdoms and provinces of southern England were brought under their supremacy. When the *Ecclesiastical History* was being

[18] *HE* III.24. [19] *Vita Wilfridi* c.20. [20] *HE* II.5. [21] *HE* IV.21–2.
[22] Eagles (1989); Vince (1993). [23] *Vita Wilfridi* c.19. [24] *HE* IV.26.
[25] Dornier (1977); Brown (2001).

finished in 731 the Mercian king Æthelbald (716–757) was overlord of the southern kingdoms 'right up to the Humber', in effect *bretwalda*, although he is not so named by Bede.[26]

By the late seventh century the most powerful kingdom apart from Northumbria and Mercia was Wessex. Although it was named as one of the tributary kingdoms in the document known as the *Tribal Hidage* (discussed below), its enormous notional assessment, 100,000 hides – more than three times any of the others – is sufficient indication of its importance. Its rivalry with Mercia was already evident by 628, when its kings fought with, and were defeated by, Penda at Cirencester; King Cynegils' adoption of Christianity under the sponsorship of Oswald of Northumbria was probably part of a search for new and powerful allies in response to this. While its expansion eastwards was blocked by Mercia, it seems to have been growing westwards at the expense of the British throughout the seventh century.[27] In the 680s King Cædwalla achieved the brutal conquest of the still pagan Isle of Wight, suppressing the kingdom and eliminating the royal family. Before he became king he had also slain Æthelwealh, king of Sussex, an ally of Mercia, and after 685 for about twenty years that kingdom was subject in ecclesiastical matters to the West Saxon bishops of Winchester.[28]

The dynamics of political development

It is now widely assumed that most if not all of the English kingdoms came into being in the late sixth century. Their emergence has been seen as the product of a competitive process in which the successful groupings absorbed or subjugated formerly independent tribal units represented by the *regiones* or *provinciae* of the Latin sources or by place-names in *-ingas*, a continuing dynamic which dominated the politics of the seventh century.[29] There are, however, difficulties with this tidy model.[30]

In the first place, despite the varying fortunes of its components, the English political framework in the seventh century could be regarded as relatively stable. A considerable number of the kingdoms known to have had an independent existence in the early seventh century stayed the course. The major loss was Deira, subsumed into Northumbria, its kings after 634 being usually drawn from the ruling Bernician dynasty. It is also possible, though by no means proven, that the kingdom of Wight, suppressed in the 680s, was a

[26] *HE* III.24, 30; IV.12; V.23; *Vita Wilfridi* c.20. [27] *HE* III.7; Yorke (1995), pp. 57–60.

[28] *HE* IV.15–16. [29] See esp. Bassett (1989b).

[30] I am much indebted to Dr G. Halsall for discussion of what follows and for generously making available a copy of his unpublished paper, 'The origins of the Anglo-Saxon kingdoms: a Merovingianist speaks out', delivered at the Institute of Historical Research in 1997.

well-established independent political entity.[31] On the other hand, there were also new kingdoms. Some of these were of a temporary nature – fleeting *ad hominem* creations for members of existing royal lines. The kingdoms of the Middle Angles and of south Mercia created for Peada by Penda and Oswiu in the 650s and the kingdom of Surrey created for Frithuwold in the 670s are notable examples.[32] Other longer-lasting units, such as the kingdoms of the Hwicce and the Magonsæte, may actually have been late seventh-century creations (like their bishoprics). The existence of the kingdom of Lindsey is perhaps the most difficult to explain. Although its royal genealogy suggests that at some stage it may have been independent, there is no evidence that in the seventh century it ever was so. It seems always to have been ruled by Mercia or Northumbria, through men whom they termed officials (*ealdormen* or *praefecti*) but who in the province itself may have been regarded as kings.[33] In Wessex there were multiple kings throughout the seventh century. In some instances close relatives shared the kingship, usually brothers inheriting from their fathers. But there were also numerous under-kings. While these may be interpreted as descendants of the ruling families of subordinated provinces or kingdoms, they are just as likely to represent collateral lines of the royal house. There is no reason to assume that Wessex expanded through an aggregation of pre-existing smaller kingdoms. The subkingships may have been new creations within annexed territory, assigned to members of the royal clan.[34]

A key document for considering these issues is the *Tribal Hidage*, generally regarded as a tribute list of dues payable to a Mercian or perhaps Northumbrian *bretwalda* and probably dating from the seventh century.[35] It omits Northumbria but ascribes assessments in terms of hides to a wide range of other political units beginning with the Mercian heartlands (assessed at 30,000 hides) and concluding with East Anglia (30,000), Essex (7000), Kent (15,000), Sussex (7000) and Wessex (100,000). In between are twenty-eight other units assessed at hideages ranging from 7000 (Lindsey, the Hwicce, the Magonsæte, and the Wreocensæte) to a mere 300. The political situation implied by this is complex and will never be fully known. Suffice it to say here that the entities listed after Mercia itself have often been taken to be its subkingdoms and dependencies. Even if this is allowed to be the case, there is, however, no reason to suppose that all or even most of these units were ever independent entities. Even the largest of these presumed dependencies, which have assessments equal to lesser kingdoms known at some stage to have been independent, may always have been subordinate units of a greater power. Indeed, it is not even necessary to

[31] Yorke (1989). [32] Blair (1989) and (1991); Dumville (1989); Sims-Williams (1992), pp. 16–53.

[33] Thacker (1981); Vince (1993). [34] Yorke (1995), pp. 79–84.

[35] For text and important analyses see Davies and Vierck (1974); Brooks (1989); Dumville (1989); Higham (1995).

suppose that all these groupings were tribal; some at least of the smaller units may have been primarily administrative – governmental areas, created by their overlord in an area where there had long been confusion and instability.[36]

A further factor in the politics of the seventh century was the shift in political dominance away from the kingdoms of the south-east to the midlands and the north, away from Kent and East Anglia to Northumbria and Mercia. One explanation of this shift is that the latter (together with Wessex, also by the late seventh century a rising power) all had a frontier with the British, offering them greater opportunity to expand. Such expansion, with the concomitant fighting and looting, provided the kings who conducted it with the prestige and the wherewithal, in the form of treasure and land, to attract the personal followings upon which political power was primarily based. Since there is plenty of evidence that the English were prepared to fight one another, this change in the balance of power presupposes that the British kingdoms in the west were in some way a softer target. For reasons probably both political and economic they appear to have been in decline during this period.

Ethnic identities

Consideration of the role of the British requires us to assess the nature of ethnic identities within the British Isles in this period.[37] It is clear that the ruling elites of the English kingdoms, whatever their early origins, no longer distinguished themselves (if they ever had) on the basis of ethnic and political identities determined on the continent.[38] Although some kingdoms incorporated the words Angle and Saxon into their nomenclature, it is difficult to discern any thoroughgoing consistency in the use of the terms. Indeed, it has recently been argued that in the seventh century, if they thought of themselves generically, even those eventually labelled *Angli*, such as the Northumbrians, regarded themselves as Saxons, the ethnic nomenclature they had preferred since late Roman times.[39] That usage finds its parallel among the British who, Bede tells us, also had a word for the English as a single grouping: 'Germans', *Garmani*.[40]

The existence of such collective designations raises the whole issue of the degree to which the English elites identified themselves as members of a single English people, those who in the eighth century came to be known as the *gens Anglorum*. Bede, of course, is the most famous exponent of this emerging Englishness, and as Patrick Wormald has argued, it is essentially the view of a churchman, who lived in Northumbria but whose world was also focussed on an archbishop based in Canterbury.[41] In his *History* Bede was keen to

[36] Cf. Campbell (1982). [37] For recent discussion see Frazer and Tyrrell (2000).
[38] See Hamerow, chapter 10 above. [39] Brooks (1999). [40] *HE* v.9. [41] Wormald (1983).

stress the common culture of the English, their shared language and their religious unity. He was not, however, the first to express such sentiments. As Nicholas Brooks has argued, the story of Gregory the Great's punning allusions to the *Angli*, pagan captives in Rome whose people were to be delivered from God's wrath (*de ira Dei*), related around 700 by a Deiran text, clearly indicates that educated clerical Deirans could think of themselves as part of a larger people.[42] In so doing, like Bede himself, they were following an agenda probably set by Canterbury. In particular, the promotion of the designation *Angli*, which superseded the earlier collective 'Saxons', probably reflected a Canterbury preference based on the usage of Pope Gregory himself.

How far such sentiments ever translated into political action is, of course, quite difficult to determine. As Barbara Yorke has pointed out, Bede himself neither believed in nor sought to promote a concomitant political unity.[43] As opportunity offered, the English kingdoms made ruthless war upon one another, and it is clear, for example, from the case of Penda that they did not scruple to ally with the British in such encounters.[44] In any case, new and more focussed identities were being forged in Britain itself, as the ruling dynasties of the newly established kingdoms constructed their own past through genealogies and origin myths. In some cases at least, such as Kent, the construction of such myths, including the link with southern Scandinavia, goes back at least to the sixth century, even if it achieved renewed and revised expression in the eighth.[45] In East Anglia a new political culture had developed by the later sixth century, focussed upon a kingship with strong links with Scandinavia.[46] These relatively new groupings clearly commanded important loyalties. Bede's story of the treatment of the Northumbrian King Oswald's remains by the monks of Bardney is revealing here: because he 'had sprung from another province and had taken possession of the kingship over them, they pursued him even when dead with their former hatred'.[47]

Bardney lay in the disputed province of Lindsey, immediately south of the Humber, an area where there is reason to think that ethnic loyalties may have been particularly complex. The anonymous *Life of Pope Gregory*, to which we have already referred, tells of the translation of the Northumbrian king Edwin's body from Hatfield Chase in Lindsey, where he was killed, to the royal monastery of Whitby, ruled by women of his kin. The transaction involved a royal monastery lying well to the north of the Humber, a priest in a monastery of the 'southern English', and a ceorl (*maritus*) living near Hatfield Chase. Significantly the Whitby author alludes to Edwin as 'the king of our people,

42 Brooks (1999), p. 19. 43 Yorke (2000), pp. 71–6. 44 *HE* II.20; III.1.

45 Behr (2000). 46 J. Hine, in Carver (1992), pp. 315–29; Yorke (1990), p. 61.

47 'quia de alia provincia ortus fuerat et super eos regnum acceperat, veteranis eum odiis etiam mortuum insequebantur': *HE* III.11.

known as the Humbrians' (*gens nostra quae dicitur Humbrensium*); in so doing he seems to be thinking of the inhabitants of an interlinked world on either side of the Humber. A river like the Humber was not necessarily a source of division; it may have connected. When the monks of Bardney rejected Oswald they may have done so not as a Northumbrian *tout court*, but as a Bernician, a member of the dynasty which had destroyed Edwin, who had commanded trans-Humbrian loyalty – in their province as in his own Deiran kingdom.[48]

The story of Imma, a young Northumbrian nobleman (*iuvenis de militia regis*) captured by a Mercian *gesith*, after the Mercians' victory at the battle of Trent (679), suggests that, as we might expect, these new identities were strongest among the ruling elites.[49] Bede makes it plain that Imma is afraid to disclose his noble status lest he be put to death in compensation for the deaths of his captor's kinsmen. To escape his fate he asserts that he was a poor peasant (*rusticus pauper*) who had brought food to the noble *milites* of the Northumbrian army. As such, he could be spared the ultimate penalty. The implication is an obvious one: the dependent peasant was less identified with the *gens* than a noble warrior. The killing of a Northumbrian *rusticus* was no satisfaction for deaths of the kinsmen of a Mercian noble.[50] The difficulty is where we draw the line. The story of the recovery of Edwin's body suggests that a non-noble but free husbandman might feel a sense of involvement with the *gens*; that of Imma suggests that the more subordinated peasantry might not.

Alongside these emerging English identities, focussed on new kingships and aristocracies, we have to set those who identified themselves as British or Irish. For Bede the British lay outside the English kingdoms. They were defined as for the most part opposing the English through native hatred (*odium domesticum*), and were said to be partly their own masters and partly under English rule.[51] Are we to assume, then, that in general in the English kingdoms (with the exception, as we have seen, of Wessex) there were few if any who thought of themselves as British? Bede's viewpoint is to a degree confirmed by the archaeological and linguistic invisibility of the British within those kingdoms. One plausible explanation is that we are looking primarily at the disappearance of an elite, and that those of modest status who remained had never identified very closely with that elite and adapted without difficulty to the world of their new rulers.

48 *Earliest Life of Gregory*, cc.12–19. 49 *HE* IV.22.

50 Cf. Higham (1995), pp. 225–6; Moreland (2000), pp. 47–8.

51 *HE* V.23. Particularly interesting is Bede's treatment of the apparently mixed visiting of Oswald's death site at *Maserfelth*, which included one whom he identifies as a Briton. The location of the site has not been certainly established; probably it was in a liminal, marcher area, where there could be such a mixing of residents. In any case the Briton was described as a traveller (*HE* III.10).

It has recently been argued, however, that in Northumbria at least we may construct a different scenario and that Bede's hatred of the British may reflect an outlook which is specifically Northumbrian. There is considerable evidence not just of Northumbrian military activity against the British but of unusually bitter hostility between the two peoples. An ingrained hatred seems to lie at the root of Bede's gloating account of the Northumbrian Æthelfrith's slaughter of hundreds of British monks at Bangor on Dee in 616, or his intemperate denunciation of Cadwallon of Gwynedd as a savage tyrant and infamous ruler.[52] The English conquest of what was to become Northumbria may have entailed particular violence, involving a ruthless destruction, degradation or driving out of the resident British. In this scenario, the place-name and other linguistic evidence could be interpreted as suggesting that it was more than simply an elite among their seventh-century successors who regarded themselves as English.[53]

The relations between the English and the Irish are much less problematic. In the seventh century the Irish had their own language and some at least had distinctive religious customs, including the way they were tonsured and the calculation of the date of Easter. They were clearly present in considerable numbers in the Anglo-Saxon kingdoms and did not pose a problem. Bede clearly generally regarded the Irish with affection; for him they were 'a harmless people (*gens innoxia*) always most friendly towards the English nation (*natio Anglorum*)'. Although he disapproved of Iona's idiosyncratic traditions, he revered the community as the Northumbrians' mother church and the community's conversion to the orthodox Easter is a high-point in his *History*.[54] He rarely fails to give the Irish their due. A notable exception, his deprecation of the Irish community at Bosham in Sussex as 'a very little monastery' (*monasteriolum permodicum*) which made no impact on the pagan South Saxons, is perhaps dictated by a desire to emphasise the Northumbrian contribution to the conversion of that kingdom.

The English and the Franks

The nearest continental neighbour of the English, Merovingian France, enjoyed especially close relations with the kingdoms of the south-east in the earlier seventh century. Before 580 King Æthelberht of Kent had married Bertha, the daughter of Charibert I, king of Paris (d. 567), who brought with her a Frankish entourage.[55] The marriage provides secure evidence that Franks were a highly visible and accepted element within the highest levels of Kentish society, and

[52] *HE* I.34; II.20; III.I. [53] Rollason (2003), ch. 3.
[54] Thacker (1996). [55] Wood (1999), pp. 70–4.

it has even been suggested that it was an expression of Merovingian overlordship.[56] Æthelberht's son Eadbald also married a Frank, Emma, plausibly identified in a late source as the daughter of the princely family of Erchinoald, mayor of the palace of the kings of Neustria. Thereafter several members of the Kentish royal family bore names closely related to or the same as their Neustrian cousins, including Eadbald's son King Earconberht (640–664), and his granddaughter, Earcongota, who died in a Frankish nunnery.[57]

By the mid-seventh century East Anglia, under King Anna, whose daughter had married Earconberht, was also included in this web of relationships. Erchinoald not only patronised Irishmen coming from East Anglia, he was probably also instrumental in bringing his half Kentish, half East Anglian kinswoman Earcongota and her East Anglian relatives to the important Neustrian monastery of Faremoutier-en-Brie. In this he was apparently aided by his former slave, the Neustrian queen Balthild, probably herself of East Anglian origin.[58]

Anglo-Frankish links went far beyond these princely interchanges. Frankish coins and items of dress and ornament are to be found at many high-status sites in Kent and elsewhere in the south-east. We know too that in the middle and later seventh century high-ranking Northumbrian ecclesiastics including Benedict Biscop and Wilfrid went first to Kent and thence to Francia and Rome to seek builders, books and the necessities of Christian worship.[59] The Northumbrian bishop Wilfrid sought consecration in France and modelled his episcopal style on that of Frankish peers.[60] Despite problems of communication, Frankish bishops officiated in Wessex and played a leading role in the Northumbrian synod which ruled definitively on matters of ecclesiastical discipline in 664.[61] In the 630s East Anglia, whose king Sigiberht had been in exile in Gaul during Redwald's reign, received the Christian faith through the ministry of a Burgundian, Felix, founding bishop of the see of Dunwich.[62]

At these high levels, then, England, Ireland and France formed in many ways an interconnected world. Bishop Agilbert, for example, arrived in Wessex in the mid-seventh century after a long period of study in Ireland. Wilfrid was especially well connected. In the 650s he was allegedly offered the see of Lyons and in 676 he brokered the return of the exiled Dagobert II from Ireland to the Frankish kingdom of Austrasia, a role apparently of sufficient prominence to earn him the homicidal enmity of the king's opponent, the Neustrian *maior* Ebroin.[63] There was much coming and going at a high level between all these

[56] I. Wood, in Carver (1998), pp. 235–41. [57] Wood (1994), p. 177.

[58] Fouracre and Gerberding (1996), pp. 97–114; Thacker (2002), pp. 58–9.

[59] Bede, *Opera Historica* I, ed. Plummer, pp. 364–404. [60] *Vita Wilfridi* c.12.; *HE* III.28.

[61] *HE* III.7, 18. [62] *HE* III.15; Campbell (1986), pp. 49–84.

[63] *Vita Wilfridi* c.28; Wood (1994), pp. 231–2.

societies, and in the church at least foreign origin and speech were clearly no bar to the highest office.

KINGS AND KINGSHIP

Kingship was the key institution in sixth- and seventh-century English politics: 'Peoples did not produce kings', as Edward James has remarked, 'kings produced peoples'.[64] Anglo-Saxon kingship in its seventh-century form was probably quite a recent development. The dominant royal families seem largely to have emerged in the later sixth century. It is then, for example, that a rich and distinctive ruling class is first evident in East Anglia, buried under the opulently furnished barrows of which the most celebrated example was the early seventh-century mound at Sutton Hoo in Suffolk, with its outstanding jewellery, silver, armour and weapons.[65] It is the early seventh century too that sees the building of the great wooden complex at Yeavering in Northumbria with its succession of enormous halls, the greatest able to accommodate over 300 people, and its strange rostrum, like the segment of an amphitheatre, probably designed for public assemblies.[66] Such discoveries indicate rulers with considerable wealth and aspiration and with international contacts. Sutton Hoo in particular suggests a figure who could stand comparison with his Merovingian contemporaries, possessed of highly sophisticated gold and garnet buckles, clasps and purse-mounts, an exotic ceremonial whetstone or sceptre, a splendid helmet modelled on Roman parade armour, silver from the Roman East and gold coins from Francia. Inevitably these indications of grandeur have been read in the light of Bede's narrative, and associated with the *bretwaldas* Edwin and Rædwald. At the very least, such evidence shows that seventh-century England contained rulers who sought to appropriate elements of *Romanitas* and whose lives had a public dimension 'that was to a degree ceremonious'.[67]

Although by the later eighth century English kings were laying claim to genealogies which established them as continental god-descended royalty, those descents cannot be shown to contain historical figures before the sixth.[68] The written record was presumably the final stage in a process of constructing origin myths that began in the later sixth or early seventh century. Despite the inclusion of Woden and other heathen gods in the genealogies, it is now generally thought that they were the fabrications of Christian authors, using the pagan past to confer prestige on their by then Christian royal patrons.[69] Recently,

[64] James (1989), p. 47. For Anglo-Saxon kingship in the wider context, see Wormald, chapter 21 below.

[65] Bruce-Mitford (1975–83). [66] Hope-Taylor (1977).

[67] Campbell (1982), p. 58; Filmer-Sankey (1996).

[68] Dumville (1976); Sisam (1953). [69] See now esp. North (1997), pp. 111–17.

however, Charlotte Behr has argued that this may be too narrow and sceptical a view. Using place-name evidence and the iconography of gold bracteates or pendants discovered in a number of high-status, mainly female, graves in Kent she has established that there was a cult of Woden in sixth-century England. The occurrence of graves containing these bracteates at significant, probably royal, estate centres has analogies in southern Scandinavia and, she suggests, indicates that 'the kings of the migration period attempted to connect their ideals with the gods, especially the king of the gods, Woden, and to claim divine descent'.[70] Kingship in seventh-century England was a fluid institution, and kings were perhaps evolving new claims to special status, in contributing to which pagan and Christian ideologies could interact.[71]

A key problem is the matter of royal status. It is possible that, like Ireland, England was full of kings, that every tribal grouping had its own native ruling dynasty with attributes of regality. In the seventh century sources, however, royal status is ascribed to a relatively restricted and interrelated group of families, equipped with a genealogy of the kind that has just been described, such as the Woden-descended Oiscingas of Kent or the Wuffingas of East Anglia.[72] Clearly, however, there were many families of lesser standing – those, for example, whose members appear in the sources as *reguli, duces regii* or *principes* – who were in some sense royal.[73] There are indications that some at least of these lesser royal figures either descended from or claimed to descend from one of the principal royal houses. The kings of Wight, for example, may have been related to the kings of Kent;[74] the names of the kings of the Hwicce suggest that they may have derived from members of the Northumbrian royal house established there by Oswiu in the 650s after his temporary conquest of Mercia.[75]

It is clear that there were ambiguities in royal status, degrees of kingship. One explanation, already discussed, might be that dynasties formerly independent had been degraded but still retained pretensions to regality. Another, more evident in the sources, is that, as with the Merovingians, kingliness inhered in all male members of a royal clan.[76] That would explain the instances of multiple kingship in Wessex and Essex already discussed.[77] In such circumstances one ruler might, so to speak, be the 'main' king, other members of his family holding specially created subkingdoms or high-ranking official positions by virtue of their kingliness. Although Penda made his son Peada king of the Middle Angles, Bede could still also allude to the latter as *princeps*.[78] In Wessex

70 Behr (2000). 71 See further on the church and the role of kings, pp. 484–5.
72 Dumville (1976). 73 Campbell (1979); Thacker (1981). 74 Yorke (1989).
75 Finberg (1972); Pretty (1989), p. 176. But cf. Bassett (1989b), p. 6; Sims-Williams (1990), pp. 16–53.
76 Halsall, unpublished paper, 1997.
77 Wood (1977), pp. 17–23; Yorke (1990), pp. 52–7, 142–6, and (1995), pp. 79–84.
78 Campbell (1979).

the ealdormen of King Ine's laws, who in some sense were clearly officials, are probably to be equated with *reges* or *subreguli* of the royal clan.

Royal government

What did seventh-century English kings do and what was the nature of their power? Above all they were war-leaders. On their charisma and personal prowess depended the survival of the newly constructed *gentes* that they embodied. Bede himself, ever prone to emphasise the virtues of the monastery, was well aware of this. The Northumbrian Oswald (634–642), his ideal king, is admired for his war-like virtue, his pugnacity in defending his people from attack and indeed in extending their power. A monk-king like Sigiberht of East Anglia (630/1–early 640s?) is extolled for his personal piety, but is not held up by Bede as a model of specifically kingly virtue.[79] The dynamics of power in this world, as James Campbell has persuasively argued, are well illustrated by the celebrated poem *Beowulf*, even though the date of the poem remains uncertain. The king lives surrounded by his company of personal retainers, who are expected to be ready to die for him and whose loyalty is ensured and enriched by gifts of treasure in the form of gold and fine weapons. It is an unstable world that can only end in defeat and death, since the seizure of treasure, essential to success, is bound to build up enemies driven by the ideals of the bloodfeud.[80]

All this, as Campbell eloquently points out, finds its echoes in the treasure of Sutton Hoo, the great halls of Yeavering and the violent deaths of so many successful seventh-century English kings. There was, however, another and more public side to this highly personalised world. While military activity probably depended in the first instance on royal companions (*comites*, *gesithas*), who, if young, lived in the king's presence at court, it undoubtedly also involved older more settled men who might be summoned to serve from their estates. Beyond this lay a wider obligation on the part of the free to obey the summons to fight beside the king. In the laws of Ine, for example, heavy penalties were laid down for neglect of military service by the noble (*gesithcund man*) holding land, by the unlanded noble and by the non-noble free man, the *ceorl*.[81] This ruling must relate to the celebrated threefold obligations referred to in the early charters, of military service, fortification and bridge-building, which presumably provided the means to realise the large-scale frontier earthworks dating from this period, such as the East Wansdyke.[82]

The king also had a public role at the apex of quite complex governmental institutions. He was expected to consult his ealdormen and 'other distinguished

[79] *HE* III.18; Wallace-Hadrill (1971), esp. pp. 72–97. [80] Campbell (1982), pp. 53–6.
[81] *Laws of Ine* 51. [82] Cunliffe (1993).

councillors' (*gethundene witan*).[83] His territory was organised into administrative units, such as the Kentish lathe or the West Saxon shire (*scir*), governed by an official, an ealdorman, who might well be a relative but whose appointment was revocable, not hereditary. Such units have been characterised as 'small regions' and are perhaps exemplified by some of the lesser units of the *Tribal Hidage* as well as by the early shires mentioned in the West Saxon laws.[84] Through them the king could operate an elaborately organised and standardised system of assessment, valued in hides (a unit representing sufficient land to support a single free household), arrangements which can be regarded as 'landscapes of obligation rather than ownership'.[85] The royal administration was focussed on centres, often at or near important Roman and pre-Roman sites, at which recognised authorities received tribute in the form of rent or goods and services and where the disputes were settled and social or religious events involving the whole area took place.[86]

The economic foundation of royal authority in seventh-century England was the king's ability to exact tribute in the form of a food render (*feorm*) from all those holding or working the land within his kingdom. Some indication of the substantial and highly organised nature of these dues is obtained from the laws of the seventh-century West Saxon king, Ine (688–726): every ten hides of land owed annually ten vats of honey, three hundred loaves, twelve ambers of Welsh ale, thirty ambers of clear ale, two full-grown cows or ten wethers, ten geese, twenty hens, ten cheeses, a full amber of butter, five salmon, twenty pounds (in weight) of fodder and a hundred eels.[87] Such renders were collected at royal estate centres, around which the king journeyed with his retinue, either consuming the royal dues in kind or receiving their equivalents in commuted form. Seventh-century English kings were thus generally peripatetic.[88] Although a powerful king such as Edwin of Northumbria might establish grand structures such as his great wooden complex at Yeavering, in general rulers did not have a single capital. Even a complex as palatial as Yeavering seems to have had a relatively short life, and with the death of Edwin to have been abandoned for a nearby site after no more than perhaps fifty years.[89]

Lawmaking and the administration of justice

Kings played an important role in the administration of justice and in dispute settlement. They were, for example, undoubtedly involved in the making of

[83] *Laws of Ine* 6.2. Cf. the *ieldestan witan* of the preface. On consent see Wood (1977), pp. 4–29.

[84] E.g. *Laws of Ine* 36.

[85] Faith (1997), p. 10, quoting J. Bossy.

[86] For a recent assessment of the subject see Faith (1997), esp. pp. 8–11.

[87] *Laws of Ine* 70.1.

[88] Stenton (1971), pp. 286–9; Charles-Edwards (1976); Campbell (1979); Yorke (1990), pp. 162–7.

[89] *HE* II.14; Hope-Taylor (1977).

law. In a famous passage Bede records that after his adoption of the Christian faith, King Æthelberht of Kent (d. 616) 'thoughtfully established . . . enacted judgements' for his people.[90] These dooms (*domas*) that Æthelberht put in writing for the first time were almost certainly not innovatory but derived from established custom (*þæw*), to the determination of which (as Bede makes clear) Æthelberht's advisers, his *sapientes*, also contributed.[91] Æthelberht's pioneering code was followed in Kent by those of his immediate successor Hlothere (673–685) and of Wihtred (690–725), the prefaces to which make it plain that they were an extension of customary law. The nature of the process is defined especially clearly in Wihtred's code, in which the king is characterised as adding to the legal usages of the people of Kent decrees that had been drawn up by the notables (*eadigan*) with the consent of all.[92]

The purpose of these early laws has been much discussed. If they are important indicators of *Romanitas*, why are they written in English? What is the basis of the selection of what can only have been a representative sample of the customary judgements and penalties? Clearly they may have been intended to amend existing law; the church in particular had an obvious interest in ensuring that its newly won position was properly enshrined in the native law and custom. Æthelberht's code is well organised. It opens – significantly – with rulings protecting the church, and then moves on to similar groupings relating to kings, earls, ceorls, enclosures, injury, women and slaves.[93] It is highly unlikely that all this matter represented amendment or innovation. Patrick Wormald has recently and convincingly suggested that these subjects were selected primarily because they were subjects upon which Frankish legislators had pronounced. In other words, the committing of laws to writing was a function of kingship and good government as displayed in Kent's nearest and most powerful Christian neighbour, and the subject matter was configured accordingly.[94]

By the late seventh century the Kentish example had been followed in at least one other kingdom, the Wessex of Ine (688–726).[95] Ine's law-code is less well organised than those of his Kentish predecessors and does not look so preplanned. As Wormald points out, his rulings often give the impression that they are responses to individual cases. The code consists of an original core added to successively, perhaps over many years. Presumably, therefore, making law and causing it to be written down had by then become 'part of the king's job'.[96] Although Ine acknowledges the role of his advisers, his ealdormen, and makes explicit the contribution of the church in the persons of his bishops

[90] *HE* II.5, as translated by Wormald (1999), p. 29. [91] Wormald (1999), pp. 94–6.

[92] *Laws of Wihtred*, preface. [93] *Laws of Wihtred*; Wormald (1999), p. 96.

[94] Wormald (1999), pp. 100–1; also Wormald, chapter 21 below.

[95] *Laws of Ine*; Wormald (1999), pp. 103–6. [96] Wormald (1999), pp. 104–5.

Hædde (of Winchester) and Earconwald (of London, d. 694), there are signs that the royal grip over law-making had intensified.[97] By contrast with the Kentish kings, Ine issued his laws as his personal commands, expressly to ensure that no official or subject should pervert them. His preface assumes that all law – both existing and newly codified – was his business.[98] This had important practical effects. Above all, for many offences those responsible were obliged to pay a fine (*wite*) to the king.[99] The ultimate sanction to exact recompense for wrongdoing was of course the feud, which rested with the kin. The tariffs of blood-prices, laid down by the laws, were intended as a substitute to guide the parties to settlement. They do not envisage that royal officers will intervene in such transactions. Nevertheless, the king still had a major role. Besides cases involving men in his service, to him fell the 'marginal cases', those involving the kinless or the foreigner or the merchant. Although it is clear that private individuals also had a financial interest in justice, the lion's share of the profit went to the king. By the late seventh century English rulers had learned from Roman example to generate income as well as to derive status from their role in making law.[100]

THE IMPACT OF THE CHURCH

Introduction: narrative of events

There were already Christians at the court of King Æthelberht when in the 590s, after his encounter with Anglian slave boys in Rome, Pope Gregory the Great conceived his project for the conversion of England. Æthelberht had married Bertha, daughter of the Merovingian king Charibert, who had brought with her from Tours a bishop, Liudhard, and established Christian worship in Æthelberht's capital, Canterbury, in a British church dedicated to St Martin, the celebrated confessor-bishop of Tours.[101] The Italian monk Augustine and an initial band of missionaries were sent from Rome in 596 and the Gallic bishops of Arles, Tours and Marseilles were asked to assist them *en route* with necessaries, including interpreters.[102] The missionaries arrived at Thanet in eastern Kent in 597, preached before Æthelberht and his *gesiths* and were invited to establish themselves in Canterbury. By 598 the pope could claim that 10,000 English had been converted. Whether at that stage the king himself was included in their number is uncertain, but he had certainly been baptised before his death in 616. In 597 or 598 Augustine was consecrated bishop, probably by the

97 *Laws of the Earliest English Kings*, p. 36; Wormald (1999), p. 104.

98 *Laws of the Earliest English Kings*, p. 36.

99 E.g. *Laws of Ine* 3.1–2, 6.2–5, 7, 9, 10, 13, 14, etc.

100 *Laws of Ine* 23, 50; Campbell (1982), pp. 98–9; Wormald (1999), p. 105.

101 Wood (1999).

102 *HE* 1.23–33; Mayr-Harting (1991).

Gaulish metropolitan, the bishop of Arles.[103] A second band of missionaries, led by the monks and priests Mellitus, Justus and Paulinus, was sent out from Rome in 601, with all that was necessary for the ministry of the new church, including liturgical vessels and and relics. At the same time Gregory announced his plan for its organisation. Augustine was to receive the pallium as a sign of his authority as metropolitan. He was to set up his see in London and to consecrate twelve suffragan bishops for the south. A second metropolitical see, to be fully independent of London after Augustine's death and with another twelve suffragans, was to be established for the north, in York.[104] Although this plan was never fully implemented and indeed was probably never practical, in the short term the mission achieved some striking successes. Following the example of Rome itself, Augustine founded a cathedral church in Canterbury, dedicated to the Holy Saviour, and an extramural burial church, dedicated to Saints Peter and Paul. He consecrated Mellitus and Justus as his first suffragan bishops, the former for the East Saxons, the latter for western Kent. The East Saxon king, Æthelberht's nephew, quickly followed the example of his overlord, and in 604 Æthelberht established a see at London.

After the death of their protector, Æthelberht, in 616 and of his nephew Sæberht of Essex shortly afterwards, there was a reaction against the new religion. Æthelberht and Saeberht's successors were pagans and Mellitus and Justus fled from their sees to Gaul. In Kent the reaction was short-lived, but Essex was to remain without a bishop until the 650s.[105] Meanwhile, the missionaries had scored a notable success, in the conversion of the *bretwalda*, Edwin of Northumbria, after his marriage to Æthelberht's daughter Æthelburh in 625. Bede depicts the king as taking this decisive step after consultation with his chief councillors and ealdormen, and gives a dramatic account of the apostasy of the pagan priest Coifi, who personally profaned and burned the precinct and idols of the important shrine of Goodmanham. In 627 the king was baptised at York with his sons, his nobles and many of the common people. Further mass conversions took place in Bernicia while the king was residing at his palace of Yeavering, and in Lindsey at Lincoln. Paulinus himself was consecrated bishop of York by Augustine's third successor, Justus. These successes were short-lived. With Edwin's destruction at Hatfield in 633, the Northumbrian kingdom fell apart and its rulers apostasised. When their successor, the Christian Oswald, re-established the church in Northumbria, he looked not to Canterbury, but to the Dalriadic Irish monastery of Iona where he had himself been a refugee during the reign of Edwin.[106]

103 It is uncertain whether he was consecrated on his initial journey through Gaul, as Bede thought, or on a later visit (*HE* I.27).

104 *HE* I.29.

105 *HE* II.2–8.

106 *HE* II.9–20; III.I–3.

The collapse of the Roman mission in Northumbria concludes the first phase of the English conversion. In the middle decades of the century the initiative lay with the Ionan monks. That mission, led by the Irishman Aidan, established itself not in Deiran York but in Bernician Lindisfarne and is the subject of some of the most famous chapters in Bede's *History*.[107] Bede idealised the community of Lindisfarne, depicting it as a model monastery along the lines recommended by Gregory the Great. Its priests and clergy, he asserted, lived and dressed simply and, fired with evangelical zeal, travelled out into the surrounding country to preach the word to the common people.[108] Under Aidan and his successors, a strongly monastically based Christianity was firmly established in Northumbria and with the aid of the Northumbrian *bretwaldas* was also introduced into Wessex in the 640s and Mercia and Essex in the 650s. When the great plague swept through England in the 660s, taking with it bishops Deusdedit of Canterbury and Tuda of Northumbria, the effective jurisdiction of the former was probably largely confined to Kent.[109]

The fracture in missionary activity introduced by Paulinus' expulsion from Northumbria brought with it problems of church discipline and observance. The Ionan missionaries followed distinctive Irish customs in certain matters of appearance, such as the form of tonsure, and, most importantly, in the calculation of the date of Easter. As a consequence, they did not necessarily celebrate the principal feast of the church at the same time as the heirs of the Roman mission in Kent, a particular problem for the Northumbrian court, which during the reign of Oswiu (655–670) had a Kentish queen who followed Roman custom. These issues, of importance to contemporaries, but of especial significance for Bede as an accomplished computist and exegete,[110] were settled in 664 at the Synod of Whitby. At that famous meeting, convened and presided over by King Oswiu, Bishop Agilbert and his protégé Wilfrid represented the pro-Roman party and Bishop Colman of Lindisfarne and Abbess Hild of Whitby spoke for the Ionan observance. Oswiu gave his support to the Roman party, and the defeated Colman left Northumbria with the dissentients among his monks. The victor, the pugnaciously pro-Roman Wilfrid, gained the Northumbrian see, after the death of Tuda, Colman's successor, in the same year. His appointment, however, was controversial, and during his prolonged absence in Gaul, whither he had gone to seek consecration, Ceadda (Chad), who had been trained at Lindisfarne but accepted the ruling of Whitby, was intruded into the see. After Wilfrid's return *c*.665, the situation remained unresolved for several years.

107 *HE* III.3, 5–7, 14–17.

108 *HE* III.26. Cf. Bede, *Vita Cuthberti*.

109 *HE* III.21–4, 27; IV.1.

110 Bede, *Opera de Temporibus*, ed. Wallis (1999).

A third phase in the spread of Christianity among the English was inaugurated in 669, when, after the death in Rome of the English bishop-elect of Canterbury, the pope nominated an elderly Greek-speaking monk, Theodore of Tarsus, as his successor. The unlikely appointment was a notable success. Theodore energised the failing church of Canterbury, and reshaped its metropolitical status along the lines of his native church. By 679 he no longer styled himself metropolitan bishop of Canterbury, but adopted instead the title archbishop of Britain. At the same time, he promoted the cult of Gregory the Great as apostle of the English, in conjunction with the monastery of Whitby, burial place of Paulinus' patron Edwin. Paradoxically, therefore, Theodore enlisted Gregory's prestige to subvert the pope's plan for two independent metropolitans in favour of, so to speak, an autocephalous church of the *gens Anglorum* as a whole, under a single head. He used his authority to introduce another major change: he sought to divide up the very large English sees, hitherto organised on the principle of one, or at most two, bishops for each major kingdom or province. This policy was facilitated by the fact that after the plague there were only two bishops with unimpeachable credentials in all the English kingdoms.[111] It brought Theodore, however, into conflict with Wilfrid, whose appointment to the great Northumbrian see he had confirmed on his arrival in England.

Wilfrid, apart from Theodore himself, was the most influential churchman of his day. Patron of the arts, friend of kings, founder of a family of monasteries spreading from Bernicia in the north to Mercia (and ultimately to Sussex) in the south, he was wedded to notions of episcopal grandeur formed from his early visits to Gaul. As bishop of York, which he made the seat of the Northumbrian diocese, in the 670s he was at the apogee of his career, the friend of Ecgfrith's queen Æthelthryth with whose support he established the great monastery of Hexham. In 678, however, after quarrelling with Ecgfrith, he was expelled from Northumbria, and Theodore seized the opportunity to divide his diocese into three. Wilfrid forcefully resisted the move, and journeyed in person to Rome to seek papal support in overturning it. On his return, after a brief period of imprisonment, he went south to work on the conversion of the still pagan kingdoms of Sussex and the Isle of Wight, where he became involved in the West Saxon Cædwalla's violent conquest. With the death of Ecgfrith Theodore determined to make peace, invoking the aid of the Mercian King Æthelred and Ecgfrith's sister Ælfflæd of Whitby. Accommodation was finally reached with Ecgfrith's successor Aldfrith in 686 and Wilfrid was restored to a curtailed see of York. He continued, nevertheless, to work for the restoration of his see, and in 690 was again expelled from Northumbria, taking refuge with Æthelred of

111 *HE* IV, *cc.*1–2, 5–6, 17; Thacker (1998).

Mercia. His long and stormy career, which included a second appeal to Rome in 703, ended with his death as bishop of his church of Hexham in 710.[112]

Theodore himself died in 690, leaving the English church in a very different position from that in which he had found it in 669. He had expanded the number of bishops and brought them together in council. He had founded a remarkable school at his episcopal see, especially learned in eastern, Antiochene theology, and a nursery of bishops whose most notable pupils held sees in Wessex, Northumbria and among the Hwicce.[113] He had developed the discipline of the laity through a series of rulings embodied in his penitential. Above all, he had established a single archbishopric with undisputed authority over the whole English church, with Gregory the Great as its patron. In so doing, he had transformed the fortunes of the Roman mission and the see of Canterbury, whose pre-eminence remained largely unchallenged even after a metropolitan see was finally established at York in 735.

In Northumbria, the settlement achieved after the angry disputes at Whitby is best exemplified by the episcopate and subsequent cult of Cuthbert, bishop of Lindisfarne, 685–687. An ascetic, trained in the Ionan tradition, Cuthbert conformed to the Roman Easter and after his death was held up by Lindisfarne and by Bede as a model Hiberno-Gregorian monastic pastor. His splendid burial deposit, including silk vestments, a gold and garnet pectoral cross, an ivory comb, a small gospel book and a silver-plated portable reliquary, suggests that, while not perhaps of Wilfridian magnificence, his was an opulent milieu. In 698 the translation of his imperishable remains followed ceremonial recently developed in Gaul and set the seal on the new synthesis.[114]

The impact of the conversion

At the beginning of the seventh century the English elite was mostly pagan. We will probably never know much about the nature of their beliefs, because Bede has chosen to tell us so little. He does, however, make it clear that by the early seventh century in Northumbria at least there was a priestly cadre, headed by a 'high priest' (*primus pontificium*), who was not allowed to carry arms or ride upon a male horse. By then worship was coming to be focussed upon sanctuaries, probably square ditched enclosures, which might be equipped with images and sacrificial altars.[115] While we cannot know how far these features are evidence of a well-defined hierarchy or a systematic theology, it seems

[112] *HE* IV.13; V.19; *Vita Wilfridi*.

[113] Bischoff and Lapidge (1994); Lapidge (1995); Stevenson (1995).

[114] *Two Lives of St Cuthbert*, ed. Colgrave; Bonner, Rollason and Stancliffe (1989).

[115] *HE* II.13; Blair (1995b); North (1997).

likely that seventh-century English paganism was pervasive – tied into social activities and attitudes – and, in particular, shaped attitudes to the role of the supernatural in daily life.

We should probably not think of late Anglo-Saxon paganism and Christianity as two opposed and mutually impermeable systems; attitudes to religion among the newly emerging elite of the later sixth century may have been evolving through contact with the church. At least one English ruler seems to have tried to bring the two faiths within some sort of loose continuum: notoriously, the powerful East Anglian king Rædwald (d. 616 × 627) set up a sanctuary containing altars both to his pagan gods and to Christ.[116] The East Anglian royal house has sometimes been regarded as a bastion of traditional paganism, expressed in the richly furnished ship burials beneath the barrows of Sutton Hoo. But there is no need to interpret Sutton Hoo in such terms. Undeniably the East Anglian kings' great funerary mounds stand in marked contrast to the cement-shrouded tombs of Æthelberht and his spouse in their burial church in Canterbury; and it may well be that their burial rites included sacrificial rituals involving horses and even men. Nevertheless, a magnificent barrow-burial like that in Mound One at Sutton Hoo is likely to have been as much about secular display as religious belief.[117]

In the last resort, the primary impact of the English conversion was upon the belief systems of an elite. The dynamics are clear. The key figures, as Gregory himself and those whom he sent patently realised, were the kings, who in accepting Christianity imitated their barbarian neighbours in adopting the most potent of all signifiers of *Romanitas*. Their companions and nobles generally followed their lead. Powerful kings moreover influenced subordinate rulers. Æthelberht 's own conversion undoubtedly owed much to the example of his powerful neighbours, the Merovingian kings, into whose family he had married. He in turn brought with him his nephew in Essex. A similar pattern can be detected among the Northumbrian *bretwaldas*. Oswald, for example, exacted baptism with himself as sponsor from the West Saxon Cynegils as the price of a marriage alliance, just as Peada converted when he married Oswiu's daughter.

Christianity had much to offer kings. As Bede observed, their intensified participation in *Romanitas* brought with it a new role in the making of law.[118] Æthelberht's law code opens by expressly noting that it was written down in the lifetime of his bishop, Augustine.[119] Later codes such as those of Wihtred and Ine also record the participation of bishops, and the church's primary involvement in the process is evident from the prominence with which the laws

[116] *HE* II.15; Yorke (2003). [117] Cf. Halsall (1995), esp. pp. 61–3.

[118] *HE* II.5. [119] *Laws of the Earliest English Kings*, pp. 4–17, at p. 4.

enshrine its rights and privileges.[120] Alongside written law came the charter, the solemn and grand uncials of which linked it in appearance with the holiest of the church's texts, its great Gospel-books. Borrowing formulas from the diplomata of Gregory the Great, such instruments offered the king a new flexibility in the disposal of property, of which in the seventh century the church and more particularly the royal monastery was the main beneficiary. Although, as Patrick Wormald has argued, they were idiosyncratic documents with diverse origins, the church, in the person of Augustine or Theodore, had a primary role in their introduction.[121]

Above all, the church offered a vital new means of conferring prestige on the experimental English kingships. Dynastic saints put kings in touch with the supernatural. They could make royal descent special and royal residences a centre of cult. As Janet Nelson has pointed out, a Christian saint differs from a sacral person in that the saint is dead and has acquired recognition through a process of external recognition quite unlike the inherent quality of sacrality.[122] Undeniably, however, the saint-king posthumously acquired some sacral characteristics.[123] If churchmen as a result remained very cautious in their treatment and recognition of such figures, they also found them useful. Concerned as they were with what kings might offer the church, they could employ the royal saint, and especially the holy king, as a role model.[124] From the works of Bede, for example, we can distil a notion of an exemplary king, whose personal virtues 'corresponded to the requirements of the church' – who could offer 'protection, endowment, largesse, the prosecution of Christian warfare, and, above all, obedience to its [the church's] teaching'.[125]

That conversion made a difference to kings and their followers is clear. What is much less clear is how far down the social scale its impact was felt. Bede is explicit that in Northumbria at least there were mass conversions. He expressly states that many of the common people (*plebs perplurima*) followed the lead of King Edwin.[126] The most obvious ways in which the new religion could have made an impression would have been through relocated cult sites and a revised cultic calendar. Here, however, there may well have been continuities. The progenitor of the Roman mission, Pope Gregory himself, envisaged his envoys taking over pagan cult sites and structures and dedicating them to Christian worship. Although Gregory probably knew little of the situation in England around 600, there is some evidence that in late pagan Kent there existed links between royal estate centres and cult sites similar to those which

120 *Laws of the Earliest English Kings*, pp. 24, 36. 121 Wormald (1984).
122 Nelson (1986), pp. 69–74. 123 Thacker (1995), pp. 98–104; Cubitt (2000).
124 Nelson (1986), pp. 69–74. Cf. Wallace-Hadrill (1971), pp. 47–97.
125 Wallace-Hadrill (1971), p. 86. 126 *HE* II.14.

can be discerned after the conversion.[127] If the pattern remained unchanged, so perhaps did the sites themselves. It has recently been suggested that the medieval parish church of Goodmanham stands on the site of Edwin's shrine.[128] Other continuities are also suggested by the English name for the greatest of Christian feasts, that of the Saviour's resurrection. According to Bede, in his great work on time, *De Temporum Ratione*, the word Easter derives from the Anglian goddess Eostre, traditionally worshipped in April, the paschal month.[129]

One major discontinuity has been detected, which has been thought to stem from the influence of Christianity. The change in burial custom reflected in the disappearance of grave-goods has been regarded as an index of the progress of the church.[130] That, however, is almost certainly too simple a model. There is nothing specifically Christian or pagan about burial goods: a holy bishop saint could as easily be buried with the emblems of his vocation as a pagan warrior noble. It was to be a long while before the church insisted on distinctive sites or rituals for the burial of the dead.[131]

We may distinguish between the precisely locatable moment when Christianity was officially accepted by a ruling elite and the much longer and less clearly defined process of Christianisation. There has been much debate about the part played in this by the Christian culture of those British who survived in the early English kingdoms (if such there were).[132] Here the prejudices of Bede are particularly significant. His famed dislike of the British has led to the suspicion that he wrote them out of his history. While Bede accused the British of failing in their duty to convert the pagan English, he clearly assumed that there had been external contact with the Christian inhabitants of British kingdoms. That is certainly suggested, for example, by his treatment of Augustine's meeting with the British church in the conference at Augustine's Oak held on the borders of the kingdoms of the West Saxons and the Hwicce.[133]

Bede, however, has nothing to say of the survival of Christianity among those former Romano-Britons who became subject to the English elite. There are a few indications that this may have been more important than his silence suggests. In particular, in the south-east the burial place of the British protomartyr, Alban, seems to have remained an active cult site. In Kent, too, Augustine seems also to have encountered another British martyr, Sixtus, whose cult he

127 Behr (2000). 128 Blair (1995b).

129 North (1997), pp. 178, 227–8; Bede, *De Tempore Ratione* c.15.

130 E.g. Campbell (1982), pp. 48–9, 51.

131 Bullough (1983). On the gradual process of Christianisation, see also Wood, chapter 26 below.

132 See Rollason (1989), pp. 3–20; Sims-Williams (1990), esp. pp. 54–85; Stancliffe (1997), and Stancliffe, chapter 16 above.

133 *HE* II.2.

effectively suppressed by replacing it with that of his namesake, the papal martyr of 258.[134] The survival of such cults, however, does not prove institutional survival in any meaningful sense. Even the cults themselves could have been episodic.

There are hints of contact elsewhere. In Wessex, which in the west had an exceptionally large and well-organised British population, the English bishop Wini consecrated Chad to the see of Northumbria with the assistance of two British bishops in 664.[135] The British probably also had a hand in the conversion of the English in the western kingdoms of the Hwicce and the Magonsæte,[136] while in Mercia itself a case has been made for identifying the episcopal see of Lichfield as a British ecclesiastical site.[137] On the other hand, there is little indication of contact with British Christians in East Anglia and the east Midlands, and if anything, the evidence, such as it is, suggests mutual hostility.[138] In the north, in Bede's own homeland of Northumbria, the evidence is equally dubious. There is evidence that, at the height of his power as bishop, Wilfrid of York appropriated vacant British ecclesiastical sites, perhaps west of the Pennines.[139] Bede tells of a Briton who benefited from the curative powers of the site (perhaps at Oswestry in Shropshire) where Oswald, the Northumbrian *rex christianissimus*, met his death in battle against the pagan Penda.[140] But on the whole, if he and the author of Wilfrid's biography are to be believed, the British made little contribution to the development of Christianity in English Northumbria.

Nature and organisation of early English Christianity

In seventh-century England dioceses were large and there were few bishops. English bishops, while undoubtedly of high social status, and in a few cases (such as that of Bishop Wilfrid) heavily involved in politics, were less powerful than their Frankish or Italian counterparts. Probably too there were few priests and deacons. Such as there were, were mostly concentrated in the lavishly endowed religious communities established on royal estates, already mentioned. There has been much debate on the nature of these communities. Were they strict monasteries, essentially inward looking, concerned with their own discipline and with the spiritual and moral welfare both in life and in death of the royal and aristocratic patrons? Or were they constituent members of an ordered network of pastorally active centres, each with its own large 'parish' (*parochia*), established at or near royal estate centres to minister to everyone on those estates? The truth probably lies somewhere between these two

[134] Sharpe (2002), pp. 124–5; Brooks (1984), p. 20.
[135] Bede, *HE* III.28; Yorke (1995), pp. 43–51, 66–72.
[136] Sims-Williams (1990), pp. 55–86.
[137] Gould (1973).
[138] E.g. Felix, *Vita Guthlaci*.
[139] *Vita Wilfridi* c.17.
[140] Bede, *HE* III.10.

positions. It seems clear that the religion of a seventh-century English king was not purely a private affair but mattered to his followers; that explains the Roman missionaries' concentration on kings, and the mass conversions such as those effected by Paulinus under King Edwin. On the other hand, contemporaries appear to have made some distinction between clergy who functioned in churches and monks based in monasteries. Moreover, the distribution of these early communities is such that their establishment cannot have been entirely systematic and may well reflect differences in function. Whether, in this early phase, all communities, whether of *clerici* or *monachi*, had pastoral functions must remain a moot point. It seems certain, however, that many did, or at least were intended to have them.[141]

The cult of the saints, as we have already seen, played an important role in making Christianity attractive to kings. It also offered an important means by which it could reach the common people; the tombs and relics of saints were regarded as the principal means by which men could engage with supernatural power and manipulate it for their benefit. When the missionaries arrived, the English had no saints of their own and the relics which they brought (almost certainly from Rome) had immense prestige.[142] By the mid-seventh century, however, influenced by their Merovingian neighbours, the English were establishing their own saints in their see churches and most notably in their royal monasteries. A process had been initiated which was to gather momentum in the eighth century and see most minster churches endowed with their own local saint.[143]

A key institution in these developments is the family monastery, the resting place of the dynastic saint, and repository of the traditions and treasures of a specific royal lineage. Such institutions were generally presided over by a royal abbess. They have been misleadingly called 'double monasteries', but essentially they were royal nunneries served by communities of male chaplains. The great Northumbrian monastery of Whitby and the Kentish foundations of Sheppey and Minster in Thanet are leading seventh-century examples. Like the royal nunneries of Ottonian Germany, they formed a stable focus for the accretion of family lands and wealth in an unstable world in which male members of the kin were frequently killed, taking with them the fragile personal loyalties on which their power depended.[144] These female communities may have developed out of an older pre-Christian pattern. As Charlotte Behr has convincingly suggested, the opulent royal jewellery, enriched with images of the Woden cult, apparently worn predominantly by women in late pagan Kent,

[141] Blair and Sharpe (1992), esp. the contributions of Blair, Cubitt, Foot and Thacker; Cambridge and Rollason (1995); Blair (1995a).

[142] Thacker (2000). [143] Blair (2002).

[144] Thacker (1992), pp. 142–5; Foot (2000), pp. 35–61.

suggests that high-status women already had a significant involvement in the transmission of their families' religious and political role.[145]

ECONOMIC AND SOCIAL ORGANISATION

Territorial organisation

Seventh-century England was overwhelmingly rural. In general, the principal settlements were estate centres where there was a royal hall or an important church. Landholding, it is currently thought, was organised through large units termed 'multiple estates'.[146] Such units enabled a minority to control and exploit the people and resources of a wide and, to a degree, dispersed territory. The multiple estate was composed of 'hierarchies of settlements'. Its essential features comprised a central place, where the lord had his hall and probably his principal church, associated with which was 'inland' settled by dependent tenants and, almost certainly, slaves. Beyond lay groupings of outer settlements bound to supply their lord with rent, food renders and a variety of services, including perhaps various labour services to assist the lord in exploiting the land directly in his hands. In some instances at least such units may have been, as Jones believed, simply the early shire or small provinces in another guise. Recently, however, Rosamond Faith has argued that the estate developed from the early shire as 'rule and control over people gradually evolved into ownership of land'.[147]

Within these estates lay many settlements. 'A kin-based group living in a nucleated settlement surrounded by its own land has long been taken as a primary type of northern European settlement',[148] and it has often been assumed that it was widespread in England. Much about the early period, however, remains unresolved. Although in some places we may detect what have been termed stable 'pre-village nuclei', perhaps in origin early farmsteads supporting a single family, in others settlements seem to have moved, although the estate boundaries within which they were situated remain stable.[149] The physical nature of such settlements is very difficult to establish. They were no doubt, however, comprised of groups of wooden structures, presumably farmhouses and associated outbuildings.

Social organisation

The laws are our best source for the social structure of the early English kingdoms. The classic view of early English society, drawn from a reading of those

145 Behr (2000).

146 The classic statement is Jones (1976), pp. 15–40. For recent discussion see Faith (1997), pp. 11–14.

147 Faith (1997), p. 11.

148 Faith (1997), p. 129.

149 Taylor (1984); Hamerow (2002), esp. pp. 93–9, 120–4.

laws, has been that its bedrock was the thriving free peasant, the ceorl, who worked land sufficient to support his household and some dependants and owed only modest services to his lord, if he had one. His primary support system was his kindred, who were entitled to compensation for offences against his person and his household, and who might enforce such compensation, if all else failed, by the feud. But, although they take the freeborn man as the basic element within society, the laws also assume a high degree of social differentiation and allude to complex hierarchies of rank. The great variation in wergilds, the compensation due to a family for the killing of one of its members, suggests that there were very considerable inequalities in early English society. That picture is confirmed by the existence of extremely rich and well-furnished burials in the earlier seventh century. It is also clear that for many the bonds of kin did not provide sufficient sustenance and protection. For that, most men depended upon a lord. The existence of lords (*hlafordas*, *dryhten*) is taken for granted in the early laws and the effects of lordship are all-pervasive. The laws of Wihtred, for example, contain clauses which enforce penalties on the servile (*esnas*) for offences against their lords or provide for lords clearing those who serve them.[150] Those of Ine show that freemen and even noble (*gesithcund*) men could have lords.[151] They also make provision as a matter of course for the rights of lords and not only are full of the penalties payable for offences against them, but make explicit their legal responsibilities for the doings of their slaves (*theowas*) or servants (*geneatas*).[152]

That the nobles formed a class is evident from references in the early laws to the *eorlcund* or *gesithcund* – those born into the noble rank of eorl or royal companion. In the laws, the killing of such men and peace within their households were protected by especially high penalties, which might be double those for the non-noble free man. The king drew his companions and councillors, his ealdormen and bishops, and his warriors from the ranks of the noble. Status clearly mattered and was evident in behaviour and speech. When the captive Imma claimed to be a poor peasant, his appearance, bearing and speech betrayed that he was not a peasant but *de nobilibus*. His fate was that appropriate to the humble: he was sold to a Frisian slave merchant in London. Similarly he owed the fact that he was eventually spared to his noble connections, for he was ransomed by King Hlothere, nephew of his former mistress, Queen Æthelthryth.[153]

This noble class clearly owned and could grant land. The laws of Ine envisage a *gesithcund* man who might hold an estate assessed at as much as twenty or as little as three hides and head a household which might include a reeve, a

150 E.g. *Laws of Wihtred* 9–10, 23–4.

151 E.g. *Laws of Ine* 50, 70.

152 E.g. *Laws of Ine* 3.1–2, 22.

153 *HE* IV.22.

smith and a nurse for his children. They also envisage him moving willingly from this land or being evicted. Nobles, it appears, could have tenants owing both service and rent and probably holding on fixed leases. They themselves, it has been suggested, may also have taken fixed period tenancies.[154] There has been much debate over whether or not such land was held by revocable royal grant or inalienable family right. Ine's laws suggest that some estates at least were held on a temporary basis. But it seems likely that there was also inalienable family land. The way in which such land was passed on is unknown. The analogy of kingship would suggest that there may have been some form of shared inheritance. This could easily lead to the fragmentation of inheritance. The 'booking' of land to the church by charter offered a means of circumventing this, and it led in the first instance to the establishment of the family monasteries of which Bede so disapproved. It was only later, after 700, that the secular application of bookland made such monasteries unnecessary.[155]

Below the noble in rank lay the thriving free ceorl, traditionally regarded as the mainstay of early English society. His status is quite difficult to define. 'Peasant' carries the wrong connotations; in many ways his property and his privileges before the law placed him closer to the noble than the poor and economically dependent tenants and labourers. The *ceorl*, assigned by Ine a wergild of 200 shillings (one-sixth of that of the landed royal companion), held sufficient land to support a single household, himself, his family, his servants, unfree tenants and slaves. This is the hide, the English unit of assessment (not a measurement of acreage), which Bede termed the *familia*, and it was crucial to the status of the ceorl, his qualification for the rights and obligations of the free.[156] The ceorl's 'enclosed farmsteads and personal property rights',[157] protected by the laws, comprised the one-hide family farms which Rosamond Faith has traced in many parts of England. Such holdings were probably heritable and in some way partible, in some instances the land being physically divided while in others it was farmed jointly.[158]

Below the ceorl lay a variety of smallholders, living on the margin with insufficient land to support themselves and usually owing heavy dues to their lord. They were probably very numerous in seventh-century England. Three classes of semi-free *laets* occur in the laws of Æthelberht, while in those of Ine the less free include the *gafolgelda*, who held land from a lord in return for rent, and the *gebur*, who received land and stock from his lord in return for agricultural and other services.[159]

[154] *Laws of Ine* 44.1, 51, 63–8; Charles-Edwards (1976). [155] Faith (1997); Brooks (1971).
[156] E.g. *HE* I.25; II.9; III.4, 24; IV.13; 19; Charles-Edwards (1972). [157] Faith (1997), p. 116.
[158] Faith (1997), pp. 126–40. [159] *Laws of Æthelberht* 26; *Laws of Ine* 6.3; Chadwick (1905).

At the very bottom of the social order lay the slave. The famous story of Pope Gregory the Great's encounter with the Anglian slave boys in the market at Rome is one among several which show that in the late sixth and seventh century England was known, indeed probably well known, as a source of slaves.[160] Slaves could be obtained in a variety of ways. Most obviously, perhaps, they were taken in warfare or carried off in raids, as Bede's account of the fate of Imma makes plain. But slaves could also be created through judicial process, as a penalty for severe or uncompounded crimes, and they could even be the result of voluntary action. And, of course, numbers were increased through the reproduction of those who were already slaves.[161] The laws of Ine treat penal enslavement for both his English and his British subjects as a matter of course; they even envisage whole families being enslaved.[162] For many offences, they impose very high fines payable to the king for which the alternative was presumably slavery.[163] It would seem then that enslavement was a common event in seventh-century England. That slaves were numerous is confirmed by the frequency with which the sources refer to their existence. Some indication of this is provided by Bede's account of Wilfrid in the 680s freeing 250 slaves on the eighty-seven hide estate granted him by King Æthelwealh of Sussex.[164]

Ine's laws also include a further category absent from the other early codes: the Welsh (*Wealas*). They suffered legal discrimination: the penalties for offending against them were generally half those for their English counterparts.[165] Nevertheless, they comprised a particularly complex grouping. Provision is made for the landless, for men holding from a half to five hides of land, for the Welsh *gafolgelda*, and for Welsh horsemen in the king's service.[166]

Towns and trade

There were very few towns in seventh-century England. One or two Roman towns, such as Canterbury and perhaps York, had remained to some degree inhabited centres of power, or perhaps been revived at an early period. London still remained of sufficient importance for the Roman missionaries to establish an episcopal see there in 604 and to be the home of a mint by the 630s. By the late seventh century a number of maritime trading centres, known to historians as *wics* or 'emporia', had emerged in the south-east, most notably at Southampton (*Hamwih*), Ipswich and Aldwich (*Lundenwic*), outside the

160 *Earliest Life of Gregory the Great* cc.9–10; *HE* II.I.
161 Cf. McCormick (2002), p. 744.
162 E.g. *Laws of Ine* 3.1–2, 24, 48, 54.2.
163 E.g. *Laws of Ine* 3.2.
164 *HE* IV.13; Pelteret (1995), p. 137.
165 *Laws of Ine* 23.3, etc.
166 *Laws of Ine* 23.3, 24.2, 32–3.

Roman *civitas* of London.[167] By then the kings of Kent had a royal reeve in *Lundenwic* in whose hall disputes about property involving their people were settled.[168]

We are not well informed about the nature of the trade carried on at these centres. The merchants at the *wics* were almost certainly involved in importing the rich and exotic luxury objects upon the possession and distribution of which royal and elite status depended. There is ample archaeological evidence that such objects were brought into England in the seventh century. In return, they seem to have exported animals, or animal products such as hides: the large quantity of animal bones found at *Hamwih* suggest the slaughter of herds acquired through the collection of tribute or as booty.[169] Despite the prohibition (in Wessex at least) of the sale of a member of one's people overseas, slaves, acquired as war captives or through voluntary or penal action, were almost certainly another valuable export. The story of Imma shows that London was the basis of an international trade in such captives.[170]

All this suggests that the motive force of trade in seventh-century England lay in the exaction of tribute and the exercise of power rather than the operation of a free market. The degree to which coin was involved is uncertain. We do, however, know that by the 630s English kings in the south-east had mints which produced gold coins known as *thrymsas* (probably the *shillings* of the early Laws). Such coins, progressively debased, continued to be produced until the late seventh century when they were replaced by the silver coins known to numismatists as *sceattas*. They too circulated mainly in the south-east, except for those bearing the name of the Northumbrian king Aldfrith.[171] The distribution of the major English *wics* indicates that by the late seventh century England was part of the network of North Sea trading sites. By then the main focus of trade had settled firmly in the English kingdoms of the south and east, and away from the British kingdoms in the west.

CONCLUSION: AN ENGLISH GOLDEN AGE?

By the close of the seventh century the new Christian culture of the English had entered what has often been regarded as a golden age. It was a period of remarkable literary achievement. The writings in Old English are impressive enough: the law-codes, the first in Europe to be recorded in the vernacular,

167 For most recent discussion and bibliography see Hill and Cowie (2001). See also Lebecq, chapter 23 below.

168 *Laws of Hlothere and Eadric* 16.

169 Campbell (1982); Hill and Cowie (2001), pp. 89–92.

170 *Laws of Ine* 11; *HE* IV.22. Cf. McCormick (2002), pp. 737–8.

171 Campbell (1982), pp. 62–3; Gannon (2003), pp. 7–13.

reached a new flowering with those of Ine (d. 725) which deal with a particularly wide range of complex issues; and there was almost certainly poetry of considerable sophistication. More remarkable still was the Latin culture of the new monasteries. In Northumbria, a small group of saints' Lives produced in the early eighth century are striking for their vigour and individuality. In Wessex, Aldhelm was producing texts which if less attractive to modern eyes are nevertheless characterised by great learning and complexity.[172] Above all there is the colossal figure of Bede: historian, hagiographer, exegete, computist, scientist, poet and grammarian, his achievements dominate our picture of the age. And while he is the most remarkable, he is not alone; the letter of his pupil Cuthbert on the death of his master shows that others at Wearmouth and Jarrow could deploy a Latin of equal limpid purity.[173]

In the visual arts, a fusion of English, Irish and more exotic influences produced a succession of great manuscripts, mostly of Gospel texts, adorned with remarkable illuminations and exquisite Insular script, beginning with Durrow and culminating in the Lindisfarne Gospels, the Biblical pandects of Wearmouth-Jarrow, and the purple-stained pages of the lost books of Wilfrid.[174] In architecture, new stone churches had been put up, including the lost basilicas of Wilfrid with their complex arrangements of arcades and galleries and their wonderful crypts which still evoke so vividly the catacombs of Rome. In sculpture, the plastic fullness of the figures on the Ruthwell cross and its contemporaries represents a unique classicising renaissance.

By the early eighth century, the rich monasteries of England and especially of Northumbria, although located on the edge of Christendom, were in no sense remote provincial outposts. They were in touch with major cultural centres in Francia and southern Gaul. Above all they were in close contact with Rome, itself energetically developing liturgy, chant and papal ceremonial.[175] The double monastery of Wearmouth-Jarrow, in particular, had introduced a specialist in Roman liturgy and chant attached to St Peter's itself and was actively engaged in the study of biblical text. That one of Ceolfrith's three great pandects of the entire text of the Bible was designed as a gift was wholly appropriate: the project to take it to Rome at once demonstrated the achievements of one of the richest and most advanced monasteries in the Latin West and reciprocated the gifts which it had itself received from the eternal city.

These, of course, were the achievements of an elite. Monasteries such as Wearmouth and Jarrow with their buildings in the Roman style, adorned with

[172] Aldhelm, *Prose Works*, ed. Lapidge and Herren; *Poetic Works*, trans. Lapidge and Rosier; Orchard (1994).

[173] Bede, *Opera Historica* 1, pp. lxxii–lxxv, clx–clxiv.

[174] *Vita Wilfridi* c.17; Alexander (1978). Further on the art and architecture, Wood, chapter 28a below.

[175] See esp. McKinnon (2000).

glass windows and floored with the artificial stone known as *opus signinum*, were very grand indeed. And they were very rich. They were the focal points of great estates together assessed at 110 hides, over a third of the size, on the evidence of the *Tribal Hidage*, of a small province or kingdom.[176] They were in no way remote. According to a late source, Jarrow was known as *portus Ecgfridi*, and we may suspect that its founder intended it to be developed as a major commercial and perhaps military and administrative centre.[177] An army of dependants, probably of slaves, toiled to support the outstanding cultural activities of the privileged community of ecclesiastics which lay at its heart. Christianisation reinforced a social structure, already by 600 marked by growing differentiation. In every sense, then, the seventh century represents the point at which England became fully a part of Christian Europe.

176 Bede, *Opera Historica* I, pp. 367–8, 370–1.

177 Symeon of Durham, *Libellus de Exordio* II.5. I am grateful to Ian Wood for drawing my attention to this reference.

CHAPTER 18

SCANDINAVIA

Lotte Hedeager

Our image of the societies of Scandinavia (present-day Denmark, Sweden and Norway) in the late Iron Age has been based predominantly on their economic character, involving aspects such as agriculture and settlement, economy and society, trade and urbanisation. Combined with studies of burial evidence, these topics have been the starting point for models of the social and political situation, including the earliest form of state-formation in Scandinavia.[1] In more recent years, however, ideological aspects of late pre-Christian society have also started to come into focus.[2] A number of new excavations have contributed to a keener interest in 'cult sites', while major new finds of gold hoards have encouraged interpretations using terms such as 'ideology', 'kings', 'aristocracy' and the like.[3] This has provided a concrete counterpart to Old Norse literature, new directions in research into the history of religion, and in place-name studies. A new, interdisciplinary research movement is developing around these issues where religious, judicial and political conditions are seen as closely interwoven and where an alternative understanding of the connection between political authority, myths and memory, cult activity, skilled craft production and exercise of power has emerged.[4] In the following outline, I have decided to concentrate mainly on this new approach. First, however, special attention will be paid to Scandinavia as part of early medieval Europe.

[1] Mortensen and Rasmussen (1988) and (1991); Fabech and Ringtved (1991); Hedeager (1992a).

[2] Myhre (2003) gives the most recent summary.

[3] Amongst the most important sites in this respect are Gudme/Lundeborg on Fyn: Nielsen, Randsborg and Thrane (1994); Hedeager (2001); Sorte Muld on Bornholm: Watt (1992); Uppåkra in Scania: Larsson and Hårdh (1998), and recently Hårdh (2003); Borg in Lofoten: Munch, Johansen and Roesdahl (1988), Munch (2003).

[4] In addition to my own works from 1992 onwards, there is a range of substantial studies by Scandinavian scholars: e.g. Herschend (1993), (1994), (1996) and (1998); Kristoffersen (1995) and (2000a); Johansen (1997); Skre (1998); Jakobsson (2003).

THE HISTORICAL SETTING OF LATE IRON AGE SCANDINAVIA

What are known as the Middle Ages in Scandinavia begin around the year 1000, half a millennium later than for the rest of western and central Europe. Only from this date onwards did Scandinavia consist of unified kingdoms and was Christianity established as a serious force in pagan Scandinavia. It is consequently only from this date onwards that Scandinavia has its own written history. By this date Iceland had been added to the Scandinavian lands, and much of what was written about Scandinavian history actually comes from Iceland.

Sure enough, Scandinavia had not been totally illiterate in the preceding centuries. The runic script was used for magical purposes, as well as for messages, for protective charms, for memorials and so on, primarily on wood but also on bone, metal and stone. There were, however, no extended literary texts in this form. The runic script was not especially Scandinavian: early runes are known from many Germanic peoples in fifth- and sixth-century Europe, in England, the Netherlands, Germany and central Europe.[5] In those areas, however, the roman script was adopted at an early date, and only in Scandinavia did the runic script develop further during the Viking period. This is the reason why the runic script is so well known from this area, although it also explains why we have to wait until as late as the twelfth century for Scandinavia to get a written history of its own. This does not, however, mean that the people of Scandinavia were without history, or without any knowledge of ancient events. Quite the opposite, in fact, but their historical tradition was oral, transmitted from generation to generation within the constraints of rules and traditions of composition and performance.

The research tradition in Scandinavian Iron Age archaeology from the 1990s and onward has been juxtaposed with the Old Norse sources (which include a great deal of material from Iceland) from the twelfth to the fourteenth century. This is due to a new approach in archaeology, focussing on cognitive structures, mentality, cosmology and systems of belief. However, the use of the Old Norse sources from the thirteenth century as an explanatory framework for the late Iron Age (from the sixth to the eleventh century) involves obvious reservations. These sources originate from early Christian times and are therefore not to be treated as a reflection of 'genuine paganism'. Despite this, it would be going too far to discard all written texts as useless to our endeavour and so leave archaeologists without any relevant written evidence from the North. If used carefully, the Old Norse texts yield valuable information. In addition, an anthropological approach based on non-western, pre-industrial

[5] Düwel (1978).

societies furnishes archaeologists with a general theoretical framework, enabling them to get beyond the archaeological and textual evidence. Lacking the modern separation of economic, political and religious institutions, pre-Christian Scandinavia can be compared to traditional communities; in both cases the world-view of a given society tends to fuse these separate domains into a coherent whole. Since much cosmological information is thought to be contained in myths,[6] special attention is paid to the myths of Old Norse literature, primarily incorporated in the *Poetic Edda* and in the *Edda* of the Icelander Snorri Sturluson (a kind of textbook for poets who wished to praise kings). These high-medieval texts do not of course necessarily fit the material evidence from the late Iron Age, but they may create a plausible setting. Central myths representing the wisdom and knowledge of the pre-Christian world may contain core elements that remain in place through time, although encrusted in new layers of meaning, and adapted to new contexts. As an example, an extensive pagan wisdom still existed in pre-Reformation Icelandic society, in the guise of traditional esoteric knowledge, which then was transformed into Satan-worship and witchcraft in the seventeenth century.[7] *Galdur* (galdring), *galdraastafir* (magic staves), *runs* (secret or occult), *skaldskapur* (poetry) and *hamrammr* (a person who could change shape at will) were too much rooted in everyday life and thought to lose their role as meaningful concepts. The runic staves from Bryggen in Bergen also indicate that the Eddic poems were still well known in Norway in the late Middle Ages. From another perspective it has convincingly been argued that mythological texts such as the *Poetic Edda*, some scaldic verses and Snorri's *Edda* incorporate myths that explain fundamental ideas with regard to life and death in Nordic societies. These ideas retained their relevance when the majority of the population on Iceland had become Christian.[8]

Snorri's role in writing the *Edda* has been a matter of debate for a long time. Some scholars have seen him as a creative literary artist, others as a far more reliable communicator of pre-Christian mythology[9] who had no obvious reason to disparage the faith of his ancestors, although he probably did not share it himself.[10] Although Snorri's work has been influenced by Christianity – as he wrote in a Christian society – one may well wonder whether he could manipulate old and familiar myths to the extent of giving a false image of the pre-Christian cosmology still known to his audience. Within a Christianised society, pre-Christian traditions were still kept alive, possibly perceived through a Christian perspective, and therefore distorted. Also, we should not discount

[6] E.g. Weiner (1999). [7] Hastrup (1990), p. 401. [8] Clunies Ross (1994).

[9] In general modern scholars represent the 'positive' opinion, among others Holtsmark (1964); De Vries (1970); Turville-Petre (1975).

[10] Hultgård (1999).

the possibility of some 'invention of tradition', and of authors like Snorri being eager to incorporate traditional myths within a new framework, stressing the continuity between 'old times' and the new world they inhabited. Incidentally, Snorri's narratives correspond in many details to other early medieval texts from different parts of Scandinavia. In spite of all these problems, we cannot afford to disregard Snorri's information and the information given in the *Poetic Edda*. We are dealing with fundamental myths and systems of beliefs, which should not be regarded as the mere product of the late pre-Christian era in Scandinavia. On the contrary, their roots must be deeply anchored in the traditional pagan universe,[11] i.e. the late Iron Age, and must as such be treated as a valuable source for archaeologists studying these centuries.

The great literature of early Scandinavia, written in the Old Norse language but in the roman script, includes other works of Snorri Sturluson, such as *Heimskringla*, composed about 1230 with the encouragement of the king of Norway with the purpose of picturing a coherent narrative of the Norwegian kings and their descent from the legendary Ynglinga kings of Sweden (*Ynglinga saga*). In Denmark, around 1200, Saxo Grammaticus wrote his Latin *Gesta Danorum*: the history of the Danish people from prehistory to the present, again with the encouragement of the Danish king. Even though these historical accounts reach far back in time and tell of kings, heroes and events which may – and may not – have some distant connection with historical reality, they are not historical sources which can simply be used to gain an insight into the history of Scandinavia in the fifth, sixth and seventh centuries. The only possibility for this lies in whatever information about Scandinavia other early medieval European texts contain.

SCANDINAVIA IN EUROPEAN HISTORIOGRAPHY

'From the mouth of the Rhine my fleet sailed over the sea in the direction of the rising sun to the land of the Cimbri [presumably Jutland], whither no Roman had ever gone before, either by land or by sea.' Thus wrote the emperor Augustus around the time of the birth of Christ in *Monumentum Ancyranum*, an extract from his now lost autobiography reproduced on a temple wall in Ancyra (now Ankara) in Asia Minor. At that time Scandinavia was beginning to take its admittedly remote place in the Roman world-view. Even though we find scattered 'information' in the early Greek sources and the Roman historian Pliny the Elder (d. 79 AD), it is in the Roman historian Tacitus' work *Germania* of the end of the first century AD that we can first talk about a real description of the northern neighbours of the Roman Empire, the Germanic areas (i.e.

[11] Meulengracht Sørensen (1991).

Europe north of the Roman frontier along the Rhine and the Danube, and west of the Vistula). The composition of the *Germania* should probably be seen as a logical consequence of Augustus' information about the Cimbric land in far, unknown parts, in other words in military terms. Tacitus was describing those areas which were beyond the border but within the Roman sphere of interest, and his *Germania* distinguishes between parts of Germanic territory and different Germanic peoples, many of which, such as the Goths, the Svear, the Langobards, the Suebi (Sueves), the Heruli and more, reappear as tribal names in the early Middle Ages. A number of the factual, ethnographic details given by Tacitus are also found practically unchanged in Langobardic tradition five or six centuries later.[12]

A more substantial geographical description of Scandinavia comes from the middle of the second century in the work of the Greek geographer, astronomer and mathematician Ptolemy, who lived in Alexandria from *c.*90 to 160 AD. As a geographer he sought to map and measure the then known world, which included the north-west of Europe. His world map is much closer to geographical actuality than that of the later Middle Ages, which is an ingenious composition with Jerusalem at the centre. In his *Geographica* ('Guide to Geography'), which consists of eight books, Ptolemy states that there were four islands east of the Cimbric peninsula, 'Insulae Alociae' (northern Jutland) and Insulae Saxonis (west and south of Jutland). These are known as *Skandiai*, three small ones and one very large one which was that furthest east and lay opposite the mouth of the Vistula, the latter being the true *Skandia*. He also gives the names of several different peoples (*Geographica* 2.11).

Ptolemy's information was repeated around 550 AD by the Ostrogothic historian Jordanes, who wrote his *Getica* (*De Origine Actibusque Getarum* (the history of the Gothic people)) in Constantinople. The *Getica* is part based on the now lost work on Gothic history by the Roman senator Cassiodorus, Chancellor at the Ostrogothic court in Ravenna, Italy, in the first half of the sixth century.

Jordanes began his account with a geographical introduction in which *Scandza* (Scandinavia) was described quite thoroughly. This not only refers to Ptolemy but also includes a surprisingly comprehensive account of a large number of named tribal areas, beginning with the northernmost, the *Adogitti*. Jordanes gives a careful account of the extraordinary circumstances in which they lived, in an area where there was unbroken sunlight for fourteen days in the summer, while there were forty days with no real daylight during the winter. This is because, he explains, the sun can be seen throughout its course during the summer while in the winter it does not rise up above the horizon

[12] Ausenda (1995), pp. 32–3.

(*Getica* III.19–20). However strange this must have seemed to someone residing in Constantinople or Ravenna, it is a reasonably correct account of the situation in the north of Scandinavia.

Amongst the many tribal groups Jordanes named are the Finns, the Lapps, the Svear, the East Goths, the Gaut-Goths, the Swedes, the Danes and the Heruli. They are all names which are well known in early medieval Europe in other contexts. This detailed description may be attributable to the King Rodulf Jordanes refers to: he had left his kingdom, that of the Ranii, possibly Romsdal in southern Norway, to seek sanctuary with the Ostrogothic king Theoderic.[13] It could have been him (or, indeed, some of his subjects) who provided Cassiodorus with information about the Scandinavian peoples at the beginning of the sixth century. Even though several of the groups concerned can apparently be located on the map, approximately at least, using either linguistic or archaeological evidence,[14] Jordanes' text is anything but an uncomplicated one, and its value as a source is much debated.[15] What it does demonstrate, however, is the existence of tribal groupings as the basis of the geographical subdivision of Scandinavia, while the account of Rodulf indicates that the king was the political linchpin of the tribe.

This perception is supported by, *inter alia*, Gregory of Tours' description of what seems to be a real historical event. In his history of the Franks, the *Historiae*, from the end of the sixth century, reference is made to a Danish king Chlochilaic (Hygelac) who, around 515, brought a fleet to raid the Frisian coast but was slain by King Theuderic's son Theudebert who had been dispatched to the area with a large army (*Historiae* III:3). The account of this episode contains several interesting points.[16]

First and foremost, the event itself must have been something quite special, simply because Gregory, who otherwise wrote very little about Scandinavia and the north-eastern regions, actually recorded it. Secondly, it is worthy of note that Gregory uses the term *rex* for the Danish king. Gregory was very careful in his use of royal terminology, and he always used the term *dux* for kings of peripheral areas or areas which were subject to Frankish overlordship such as the Bretons, the Frisians, the continental Saxons, the Thuringians, the Alamanni and the Bavarians. When, therefore, he refers to Chlochilaic as *rex* he concurrently recognises that the leader of the Danish fleet was effectively independent of the Frankish king. And it is finally noteworthy that the Danes are not mentioned at all after 515, either by Gregory or in other Frankish sources. The explanation may be that the victory over Chlochilaic was such a serious defeat for the Danes that their raids and attempts to dominate the

[13] See Skre (1998), ch. 5.1.2. [14] Callmer (1991).
[15] See in particular Svennung (1967) and (1972) and references. [16] As pointed out by Wood (1983).

Frankish-controlled Frisian littoral ceased throughout the following centuries. The popularity of this story in the Germanic epic tradition, in, for instance, the much later Old English poem *Beowulf*,[17] helps to underline the importance attached to the event. Southern Scandinavia never fell under Frankish hegemony as it was too far away, but after 515 the Danes kept away from Frankish territory and consequently stayed comprehensively out of European history for several centuries to come.

'SCANDZA' – A EUROPEAN ORIGIN MYTH

In the sixth and seventh centuries Scandinavia nevertheless held quite a special position in the minds of the Migration-period Germanic peoples in Europe as the place from which many of them, or at least the royal families, claimed their origin. Between the early medieval peoples on the continent and in England there were three alternative origin myths: looking back to Troy and the Trojan heroes (like the Roman origin myth), to Palestine and the biblical people, or to *Scandza*, Scandinavia.[18] The former two are explicable in terms of the Greco-Roman and Christian influence from late antiquity; the earliest of these, and the one which is not immediately explicable from this perspective, is the third.

In his *Getica*, Jordanes placed his description of Scandinavia in the introduction, and it is followed by an account of the long history of the migration of the Goths which began there. Jordanes himself declares that his knowledge derives from Ablabius (*Getica* IV.28), who had written the history of the Goths in the middle of the fifth century. This may have been incorporated by Cassiodorus, who in turn passed it on to Jordanes, who completed his *Getica* in 551. But this does not explain why this migration history recurs in the majority of the early national/royal origin myths, such as those of the Langobards, the Burgundians, the Anglo-Saxon peoples, the Heruli and more besides.

Since Cassiodorus wrote his Gothic history in order to make the Ostrogoths and their royal family, the Amali, equal in birth to the Romans (who came from Troy), it is all the more remarkable that he 'adopted' and developed Ablabius' account of their origins in Scandinavia. But this was not all. Cassiodorus also copied the Roman royal genealogy, in which there were seventeen generations between Aeneas and Romulus, by linking Theoderic's grandson Athalaric to the first king of the Goths, Gaut/Gapt, through seventeen generations of Gothic Amal kings, and Gautr is the name Odin gave himself.[19]

[17] E.g. Storm (1970). [18] Hachmann (1970), pp. 109ff.

[19] In *Grimnismal* (54). Parts, perhaps all, of this poem were composed in Norway in the late ninth or tenth century. The Old Norse form corresponding to Gapt is *Gautr*, one of Odin's names (North (1997)). Whatever identity one finally attributes to Gautr, the connection with the Scandinavian pagan pantheon seems to be clear. See also De Vries (1956), p. 41.

Both Cassiodorus and Jordanes thus allowed the Christian Ostrogoths and their powerful kings in Italy to trace their descent from Scandinavia and a pagan god; and this they did two centuries after this people had converted to Christianity. In this, however, the Ostrogoths did not differ essentially from other Germanic peoples such as, for instance, the Langobards in Italy in the seventh century[20] or the Anglo-Saxons in England,[21] where *Christian* authors legitimise their *Christian* people and *Christian* kings in a *pagan* prehistory.

The Scandinavian origin myth maintained by the Germanic peoples of early medieval Europe was more than just a series of authors copying one another. Myths played a vital role in the creation of a political mentality amongst the new Germanic warlords and kings in Europe.[22] And this myth takes a special turn when the example of the Heruli is taken into consideration.

The Heruli were one of the many Germanic peoples who are alleged to have come from Scandinavia. Their own tribal history was never written – or at least has not survived – so we know of them only from other sources. On the other hand, this is one of the Germanic peoples whose fate is relatively well recorded and whose connection with Scandinavia appears to be real. From as early as the third century, after they had left their original homeland in Scandinavia, they are referred to in written sources as auxiliary troops for the Romans both in Europe and in Asia Minor, and on a raiding expedition through the Balkans, along with the Goths amongst others, in 267.

Procopius, the Greco-Byzantine historian who lived *c.*490–555 AD and thus was a contemporary of Jordanes, wrote profusely about the Heruli. After their defeat by the Langobards in 512 they obtained the permission of the emperor Justinian to settle in Illyria (in modern times the former Yugoslavia) although many of them, in these circumstances, preferred to migrate northwards, back to their original homeland. This led to a split, with one group remaining in the Danube area while the other moved north. This migration is described in some detail by Procopius (*Wars* VI.14, VIII.36, XV.1–4). It is stated, for instance, that 'they reached the land of the Varnii [the Schleswig area], and then moved rapidly through the land of the Danes to the sea and crossed over to Thule [the Scandinavian peninsula], where they were received by the Gauts, who were one of the largest groups there'.

Subsequently Procopius' account traces how the southern group of Heruli lacked a royal dynasty as the royal clan did not have many suitable members (*Wars* VI.15, 27–33). A deputation was sent to the Scandinavian group to fetch

[20] The history of the Langobards was first written down in 643 when they ruled Italy. The story of the Langobards and King Rothari's genealogy form part of the legal text *Edictus Rothari* written about thirty years later. See further Gasparri (1983) and (2000).

[21] According to Bede's *Ecclesiastical History of the English People* (completed in 731), I.15.

[22] Hedeager (1997), (1998) and (2000); Geary (2003); Hill (2003).

a suitable candidate. When, however, the chosen one died, the deputation had to set off once again, and then came back with Datius and his personal retinue of about 200 young warriors. In the meantime the southern Heruli had given up waiting, and had asked the emperor Justinian to choose a king from amongst themselves. Justinian selected Suartus, and when the deputation with Datius and his retinue arrived from Scandinavia it caused yet another split as some pledged loyalty to the one and some to the other of the two kings. When Justinian gave his support to Datius, the Scandinavian king Suartus and his supporters left Roman territory and became allies of the Gepids in Hungary.[23]

The historical tradition concerning the Scandinavian origin of the Heruli appears, in other words, to reflect a definite piece of historical reality. The question naturally is whether the same can be the case with the many other Germanic peoples who claimed descent from Scandza. Naturally, the factual element within these early European migration myths is much disputed.[24] What is crucial, however, is not to what extent these people once emigrated in small groups from Scandinavia, but that their royal identity was linked to Scandinavia and that their kings were divine because they descended from Gautr or Odin/Wotan, with this figure's clear association with the German pagan religion and, maybe, the Scandinavian pantheon.

The much later Old English epic poem *Beowulf* may well also draw on traditions that have roots in the fifth and sixth centuries. Here there are possibly ties between the ruling families of the Wylfingas, etymologically identical to the Wuffingas, the East Anglian royal family, and the Wulfings who are thought to have lived in what is now south-western Sweden and south-eastern Norway during the late fifth and sixth centuries. Furthermore, there are archaeological indications of kindred relations between the royal families of East Anglia and Scandinavia in the sixth and seventh centuries, not least the connection revealed between the Sutton Hoo ship burial and the ship burials from Vendel and Valdgärde in the mid-Swedish Mälar area.[25]

SCANDINAVIAN ANIMAL ART

From the sparse written but rich archaeological material it is evident that close contacts existed between the royal families of southern Scandinavia and

[23] Heather (1998).

[24] E.g. philologically and historically: Weibull (1958); Svennung (1967) and (1972); Wagner (1967); Hachmann (1970); Goffart (1980) and (1988); Gasparri (1983) and (2000); Heather (1989), (1993), (1994), (1995) and (1998); Wolfram (1990) and (1994); Pohl (1994); North (1997); Hedeager (2000); Archaeologically: Hachmann (1970); Svennung (1972); Hines (1984), (1992), (1993), (1994) and (1995); Menghin (1985); Busch (1988); Näsman (1988); Heather and Matthews (1991) with refs.; Kazanski (1991); Godlowski (1992); Härke (1992a) and (1992b); Hedeager (1992b), (1993), (1998) and (2000); Christie (1995); Bierbrauer (1994).

[25] Bruce-Mitford (1979); Lamm and Nordström (1983); Newton (1993), p. 117.

those of the continent during the fifth, sixth and seventh centuries. The Scandinavian origin myth among the Germanic royal families/peoples, expressed in contemporaneous written sources, is supported by the archeological evidence, notably weapons, jewellery and not least the iconography.[26] All over Migration-period Europe, in Scandinavia, on the continent and in England, a new iconographical style appeared in the middle of the fifth century. The development of the earliest animal style was closely connected with southern Scandinavia.[27] A remarkably rich variety of figurative and geometric figures, often with human features (masks) as part of the whole,[28] developed in this area during the first half of the fifth century, known as the Nydam style and Style I[29] (see Fig. 1). Finds on the continent and in England are well represented from the latter half of the fifth century up to the end of the sixth,[30] when a new style, Style II, emerges, homogeneous from Italy to the Nordic countries.[31] Style II is, like the first one, remarkably uniform, and both styles are found on jewellery and weapons from most parts of Europe[32] (see Fig. 2).

From about the beginning of the fifth century up until the seventh, the Nordic figurative world was used as a symbolically significant style amongst the migrating Germanic peoples. It was imitated and elaborated, becoming an impressive elite art style.[33] Style II continued into the late seventh century, and from then on it is no longer possible to define a common Germanic animal style. Once Catholic Christianity had put down firm roots a new iconographic style developed: one that blended insular with Frankish elements, and was closely connected to the Irish/Anglo-Saxon mission which began in Friesland in 678/9 and reached central and south Germany during the first half of the eighth century.[34]

While this style was so indisputably linked with missionary activity, and can be found on a lengthy series of different ecclesiastical objects, it is not restricted to 'church art' alone. A wide variety of secular objects of precisely the same kind as earlier were now decorated with this new Christian style: dress accessories, riding equipment, stirrups, spurs, bracelets and so on, thus signalled a new form of ideological legitimisation for their owners. Southern Scandinavia, in particular, was not uninfluenced by the ideological attachment to Latin Christianity of the European warrior elite and their powerful rulers. Though Nordic animal style continued independently, with the disintegrated animal figures being to some extent recreated to recover their zoomorphic

26 Hedeager (1998). 27 Roth (1979); Haseloff (1981) and (1984).

28 Haseloff (1986). 29 Salin (1904).

30 Roth (1979); Haseloff (1981); Hines (1984); Näsman (1984), map 10 and (1991), fig. 8.

31 Salin (1904); see also Lund Hansen (1992), p. 187 with literature.

32 Karlsson (1983). 33 Speake (1980); Høilund Nielsen (1997). 34 Roth (1979), p. 86.

Figure 1. Silver brooch with early animal style from Sealand, Denmark (after Åberg (1925), fig. 161)

character, the new style from the eighth century onwards absorbed some insular elements, such as decorative plant motifs, but this was only briefly.[35]

In Scandinavia, where a pagan warrior elite and a fragmented state structure persisted during the Viking Age, pagan myths and iconographic symbols – the animal style – therefore continued to play an organising role in the cosmology of this warrior society up to the end of this period. Although still in

[35] Karlsson (1983); Hedeager (1999a).

Figure 2. Silver brooch with style II from Hordaland, Norway (after Åberg (1925), fig. 169)

use, the Nordic animal style ceased to develop from around 1100.[36] On this premise, elements of style, not least iconographic ones, are presumed to have

[36] It did not survive the meeting with a new belief system and the political and social implications that this entailed. This can of course be explained through the idea that people – especially the elite – had acquired different tastes and therefore preferred a new style around 1200 under the influence of the church. More convincingly, however, it can be argued that the lack of potential for survival and renewal of the animal styles in a Christian context had to do with its anchoring in a quite different system of belief (Hedeager (2003)).

been selected with a great deal of care, just as objects are very carefully selected for use in ceremonies because they are embedded with special qualities and are the bearers of important messages, communicating, for example, social relationships, group membership and ethnic identity.[37] Style, then, must also be seen as involved in the creation and maintenance of the socio-cosmological order and as such participates in the legitimisation of power. Upholding style can be regarded as a part of the elite's strategy in the same way as the maintenance of ritual functions, myths, legends and symbolic objects – in short, all that embodies the group's identity. Seen in this light, Germanic animal styles acquire a new, more significant function.

Even though there can therefore be little doubt about the signifying function of animal ornament or its elite character, this does not explain what the animals symbolise or why it was animal ornament in particular which took on such great importance. However, the role of animal style as an inseparable part of the pre-Christian material culture implies that the animals also had an indisputably significant position in the pre-Christian perception of the world.[38] If this is the case then it might just be possible to come closer to some central, cognitive structures in sixth- and seventh-century Scandinavia by focussing on these animals and the iconographic depictions as such.

CENTRAL COGNITIVE STRUCTURES IN SCANDINAVIAN SOCIETIES

It is hardly surprising that the perception of the Scandinavian world underwent changes during a period of 800 years, from the fourth to the eleventh century. That the animal ornamentation did the same thing is a logical consequence. But in spite of any stylistic variations and new elements, there is one fundamental element that connects all the styles together, namely the *animal*. From being a simple classificatory element, suitable for chronological and stylistic classifications in traditional cultural-historical archaeology, the enquiry shifts from investigating animal representation in this art and becomes a topic with complex implications for cognitive archaeology. Representation is always more than a matter of whether the animal's naturalistic form is reproduced, and animal representation cannot only be explained in terms of artistic expression. Representation operates within a particular set of cultural codes, and the animal representations therefore become part of the cognitive structures. And as such, the styles are not just 'art for art's sake', but also must be seen as a form of

[37] Earle (1990), p. 73; DeMarrais, Castillo and Earle (1996).

[38] Kristoffersen (1995) and (2000b); Glosecki (1989); Hedeager (1997), (1998), (2003) and (2004); Gaimster (1998); Andrén (2000); Lindstrøm and Kristoffersen (2001); Magnus (2001); Jakobsson (2003).

cultural knowledge, settled into the constitutional context of society. Animal representations must then be an expression for the way animals were perceived and the significance they were given.[39]

The Nordic animal ornamentation does not merely incorporate animals, it *is* animals, that is to say, it is entirely a paraphrasing of a many-faceted complex of animal motifs. Whole and half animals, small and large animals, animal fragments and anatomically complete animals, along with animal heads without bodies and animal bodies without heads. This complex representation, far removed from naturalistic animal depictions, reveals that the styles do not attempt to mirror the animals themselves. Complex composed animals may express a reality that is more precise, more revealing and more ambiguous, than the naturalistic representation ever could. Here species are created that cut across all categories by transgressing the boundaries of what is considered 'natural'.[40] This ambiguity, where a figure on closer inspection is shown to represent something else entirely, reflects hidden meaning, where one level, so to say, hides the other and makes the styles more powerful than otherwise would be possible to achieve through the written or spoken word. Their complexity suggests that these styles, structurally speaking, incorporate an overriding abstract principle, reflecting social order and – perhaps subconsciously – also the physical order of the universe.[41]

Another characteristic of mainly the sixth- and seventh-century styles is the representation of animal heads inside each other, as part of each other, and to this complexity human representations are attached. Human bodies are also reproduced cut into pieces, and human faces ('masks') are included in the animal representations, e.g. bodies with human heads and human faces as part – normally the thigh – of the animal or the bird. Thus, the renderings cross not only the boundaries between various animal species but also the boundaries between animals and humans.

It can be argued that the animal styles – consciously or unconsciously – reflect cognitive structures in sixth- and seventh-century pre-Christian societies. Even when the structural levels in the styles include abstract and often unconscious principles that reflect social and universal order, they are hardly a conscious representation of the myth. The mythical level, on the other hand, is represented through the obvious visual message, with the iconography and oral rendering referring to the same 'story'. This level can, however, be reflected in the naturalistic and therefore immediately more accessible iconographic art from these centuries. Two examples are to be mentioned.

39 Morphy (1989), p. 2.

40 Morphy (1989), p. 5; Ingold (2000), p. 130; Kristoffersen (2000b), p. 265; Lindstrøm and Kristoffersen (2001); Jakobsson (2003); Hedeager (2004).

41 Roe (1995), p. 58.

Figure 3. Gold bracteate from Lilla Jored, Sweden (after Hauck (1985–89), no. 107)

First, special attention may be paid to the gold bracteates. Although their motifs and designs are unmistakably Nordic, the bracteates have their origin in late antique art and Byzantine emperors' medallions[42] (see Fig. 3). Several of the depicted scenes appear to be an illustration of central myths in Nordic mythology,[43] for example Balder's death[44] (see Fig. 4) and Tyr, who, in order to save the world, offered his right hand in the mouth of the Fenris wolf (*Snorra Edda*, chs. 24 and 33)[45] (see Fig. 5). Both appear to belong to the central myths of the fifth and sixth centuries.[46] The majority of the bracteates, however, reflect what has been interpreted as Odin at the height of his power, i.e. on his journey to the Other World in disguise as a bird (see Fig. 6). A large animal, a hybrid between a horse, a moose and a goat, escorts him. From its mouth it is not uncommon to see the sign of a breath. That is to

42 Hauck (1985–89). 43 Hauck (1986).

44 Ellmers (1970), p. 210; Hauck (1978), p. 210 and (1994).

45 Oxenstierna (1956), p. 36; Ellmers (1970), pp. 202, 220; Hauck (1978), p. 210.

46 Hedeager (1997).

Figure 4. Gold bracteate from Fakse, Denmark (after Hauck (1985–89), no. 51)

say, the animal is animate. Birds and snakes often follow on the journey. The shape-shifting ('shamanistic')[47] element in this rendering seems convincing: a 'human' in bird disguise and animal followers (the snake, the bird and the big four-legged animal) are fundamental components in the iconographic universe of the bracteates.[48] That the origin of the bracteates stems from the late Roman emperors' medallions only confirms the strong symbolic importance which resides in comparing the Roman emperors to the Asir kings.[49] Everywhere in the Old Norse texts Odin appears in the guise of others; he crosses the boundary between human and animal, between male and female. He is in control of the specific magical power called seiðr, i.e. shape-shifting, and this specific skill is what makes him king of the Asir.[50]

47 Price (2002) has examined the ritual practices of the north in relation to the 'shamanistic' culture of the Sámi people with whom they shared much of the Scandinavian peninsula.

48 Hedeager (1997), (2003) and (2004).

49 Axboe (1991); Andrén (1991).

50 E.g. Hedeager (1999a); Price (2002); Solli (2002). The indisputable nexus between seiðr, ecstasy and soul-journey is identical to the religious complex known as 'shamanism': Strömbäck (1935),

Figure 5. Gold bracteate from Trollhättan, Sweden (after Hauck (1985–89), no. 190)

Second, from the Migration period to the Viking Age depictions of humans in animal form can be found, primarily attached to the rich warrior equipment from the sixth and seventh centuries, e.g. Vendel and Valsgärde in the mid-Swedish Mälar area and Sutton Hoo in East Anglia. Most commonly portrayed is the so-called wolf warrior,[51] but the warrior in a wild boar skin or disguise can also be found.[52] And the helmets have a complete animal symbolism in themselves, with either a boar or an eagle on the crest, or as part of the helmet's composition.[53] These splendid helmets consist then of three animals,

(1970); Ohlmarks (1939); Brøgger (1951); Buchholz (1971); Ellis Davidson (1988); Eliade (1989), etc.; cf. also Polomé (1992), who argues against such an interpretation. See the comprehensive studies by Karl Hauck, where the motifs on the A- and C-bracteates (Mackeprang (1952)) have been interpreted as representing one and the same person, most probably Odin (Hauck (1974); for an extensive bibliography see Hauck (1985–89)). Odin is depicted as magician and shaman (Hauck (1978), p. 211).

[51] Høilund Nielsen (1999), p. 332. [52] Hedeager (2004), fig. 16.

[53] Bruce-Mitford (1979), p. 35; Glosecki (1989); Hedeager (2004), fig. 22.

Figure 6. Gold bracteate from Skydstrup, Denmark (after Hauck (1985–89), no. 166)

all significant in the 'shamanistic' system of belief: the snake that collects knowledge from the underworld, the bird that flies to all corners of the world to get information, and the large animal, protecting the journey to the other world.

As a recurrent theme in the Old Norse texts we find this dualist relationship between man and animal. It is expressed in the words 'hugr', 'fylgja' and 'hamr'. 'Hugr' means 'spirit' or 'soul' that can leave the body in the guise of animal or human;[54] 'fylgja' means a sort of doppelgänger or alter-ego[55] or eventually 'skin', 'cloak' or 'animal clothing'.[56] It represents the protective spirits which attach themselves to individuals, often at birth, and remain with them right through to death, when they transfer their powers to another member of the family. 'Fylgja' often appears as an animal (or a woman) and it is usually visible

[54] Ellis Davidson (1978). [55] Simek (1996), p. 96. [56] Glosecki (1989), p. 186.

only at times of crisis, either in waking or in dreams. It is an externalised 'soul' but also an embodiment of personal luck and destiny and the concept has much in common with the less attested 'hamr'.[57]

Thus the figurative art, the animal ornamentation and the Old Norse texts show the same transcendental perception of metamorphosis between man and animal. In the sixth and seventh centuries especially, wolf, wild boar, eagle and snake are organising elements in the ornamentation's metamorphic representation of humans and animals. The animals could do what man was not capable of doing, namely cross the threshold to the Other World. Only in the guise of an animal could man transcend the boundaries between life and death. Acknowledging that contact with the Other World passed through the animals and that the 'fylgja' was the embodiment of personal destiny also helps us understand how animal ornamentation could sustain an organising role in Scandinavian – and Germanic – society up until the introduction/consolidation of Christianity.[58] Last but not least, it makes sense of why wild and dangerous animals were so important as artistic expression to the pre-Christian warrior elite of Scandinavia, on the continent and among the Anglo-Saxons.

GIFT-GIVING AND POLITICAL AUTHORITY

Although most Germanic peoples had a king or kings, powerful central rulers were lacking. The tribes consisted of a large number of relatively independent and autonomous elements based on kinship and residence in the same geographical area. A tribe was composed of several sub-tribes, who in turn included separate entities eventually with their own king. The tribe not only was an entity in a political sense, but also constituted a cult community and the kings were descended from the gods. Although the kings were members of long-distance networks of marriage and gift exchange, they did not uphold a political monopoly within the tribe. The warrior elite played an important role because, like the king, they possessed their own armed retinue. Relationships between king and noble, between king or noble and the warrior-followers ('hird'), etc. were, like the relationship between kings, reciprocal, although by nature more or less asymmetrical.[59]

The written sources, whether Old Norse or from early medieval Europe, give the impression of gift-giving as the decisive instrument in creating and upholding these political alliances, between lord and warrior-follower and within the warrior elite itself. Whether characterised as inalienable or alienable objects,[60]

[57] Orchard (2002); Raudvere (2001), pp. 102ff., and (2003), p. 71.

[58] Hedeager (2003) and (2004).

[59] Bazelmans (1999), pp. 3ff.

[60] Cf. Parry and Bloch (1993), p. 8.

moveable wealth of specific symbolic value circulated as rewards from the fifth century onwards.[61] No doubt gift-giving was an important political instrument all through the second half of the first millennium, but the Migration period not only created special opportunities for access to gold but at the same time claimed extraordinary investments in these values too. Gold – and silver – could play an important role in political strategies because – first of all – they were to a great extent accessible from outside the local system.

The idea of bestowing honorific gifts was embedded in the cosmological world and the system of cultural values and as such highly ritualised, and gold and silver, often lavishly ornamented, played an important role for ritual and ceremonial use in the social reproduction of late Iron Age societies. Even if gift-giving was highly ritualised throughout the late Iron Age, the intense competitive display in the fifth and sixth centuries (and in the Viking Age) must have been outstanding.

Strictly speaking, the 'golden age' of Scandinavia is the Migration period. Immense numbers of gold hoards were deposited during a few generations in the fifth and sixth centuries. These gold depositions fascinate and challenge the academic world of archaeologists and historians of religion because they signal 'wealth' and 'power', keywords in the modern world. From the point of view of profit and economic strength it is easy to explain our 'rational' approach towards the gold depositions, although no consensus exists as to the meaning of these hoards. They have, broadly speaking, been explained as treasures, that is 'economic' depositions meant to go back into circulation – or as tactical gifts, that is ritual sacrifices, meant for the supernatural world and a way of creating alliances with the gods. Recently the latter explanation has been the dominant approach.[62]

The Migration-period hoards consist of a wide variety of precious objects: bracteates, finger-, neck- and arm rings, so-called payment rings, and relief brooches, often highly decorated with animal ornamentation. If metal objects such as these were circulated as gifts, there may be no evidence at all in the archaeological record. If the strategy of gift-giving included an element of competitive display, however, gift-giving would be drawn more centrally into the process of the political strategy and we should expect to find some evidence of the ritualised consumption of these artefacts in hoards and in graves.[63] This

[61] Bazelmans (1992), (1999) and (2000).

[62] For discussion see in particular Geisslinger (1967); Herschend (1978–79); Fonnesbech-Sandberg (1985); Hines (1989); Hedeager (1991), (1992a) and (1999b); Fabech (1994a), (1994b) and (1997); Wiker (1999).

[63] Barrett, Bradley and Green (1999), p. 240.

is obvious in the case of the Migration period, where the gold hoards reflect a short 'horizon of investment'.[64]

Although many of the gold hoards are found in areas which, from a modern and rational economic point of view, are marginal, in an overall perspective they are connected to fertile agricultural areas. This is particularly clear in Sweden where a majority of the gold finds come from the most fertile Swedish provinces of Scania and Västergötland (approx. 22 kg, i.e. more than half of the gold from mainland Sweden in this period).[65] The hoards have been found in central settlement areas, in or very close to houses, and they have been found in marginal areas. The hoards are linked to a particular kind of marginal area, namely bogs, streams, coasts, etc. as a kind of border zone to areas in agricultural use. They must reflect some kind of past ritual practice since they obviously were deposited in deliberately chosen localities in the landscape.

The fact that physical boundaries such as rivers, streams, bogs, etc. were in use for depositions of wealth during the Migration period indicates that these areas played an important role in people's perception of the landscape. This period was characterised by extensive changes in settlement structure and land use. When old boundaries were changed and new land was taken into agricultural use, the cultural landscape – as well as the cognitive – must have been dramatically reorganised. The landscape had to be domesticated and given a new place in the discursive knowledge and the cosmology for people living – or going to live – there. The hoards were deliberately placed on boundaries between cultivated/domesticated land and wilderness,[66] often in the transitional zone between land and sea, earth and water, where a majority of sacral place-names, i.e. names with Odin, Tyr, Freyr and God, are also located.[67] The transitional zones between land and water appear to uphold a special position in the perception of the cultural landscape as places for negotiation with the Other World. Once deposited, the hoards for generations shaped the landscape by creating a sacred topography in people's mind. They represented the link between past and present, between this world and the Other World, and as such they gave legitimacy to the land by becoming part of the discursive knowledge of the people who lived in these areas. Although hidden, these hoards remained 'visible' for generations, continuing to play an active role in people's negotiation with the past.[68]

The gold hoards were deposited in a period with great social stress and radical changes in the organisation of the settled land during the Migration period

64 Comparable to the Viking period hoards (Hedeager (1999b)).

65 Hedeager (1999b), p. 246. The total amount of gold in Denmark is about 50 kg; in Norway it is much less (estimated one third or less) (Hedeager (1999b)).

66 See also Johansen (1996), p. 97.

67 Jakobsson (1997), p. 91; Andersen (1998), p. 26.

68 Hedeager (1999a).

all over the fertile part of Scandinavia. They may have played a special role as an important mediator in resource-consuming political alliances and long-distance networks as well as perhaps serving as an instrument in organising – or reorganising – the cultural landscape according to the cosmological world in a slightly more hierarchical political structure.

HIERARCHICAL SETTLEMENT PATTERN

The settlement structure in late Iron Age Scandinavia clearly developed hierarchically with respect to size and function. The concept of 'central places' has been developed in Scandinavian archaeology since the 1970s to classify specific rich settlement sites from these centuries, often with great quantities of metal finds indicating extended casting activity.[69] For the Nordic realm before 800, where there is no textual evidence of any specific locations of religious or political power, the archaeological sources and the toponymic evidence provide the only basis for analysing the hierarchical structure in this settlement structure.

However, Old Norse literature does throw some light on certain essential components of 'powerful' places in Scandinavia. For example, the hall assumes great importance in the ideological universe represented in these texts.[70] Given the prominent role of the hall in Old Norse literature, it is remarkable that the word 'hall' hardly ever turns up in Scandinavian place-names. The reason may be that the Scandinavian language of the time used another word, such as *sal*, as in Uppsala, Onsala, Odensala or just Sal(a): the god whose name is compounded with *sal* is always Odin, the king of the gods.[71] The word *sal* is sometimes linked with *zulr* (thyle), the term for a particular type of leader or priest. The 'thyle' is regarded as a poet, a skald or storyteller: in other words the person who preserves the treasure hoard of mystical and magical knowledge that was necessary to understand the *Edda* poetry and fundamental to upholding political authority. He was the cult leader who understood the cult activities and uttered the proper magical words. His primary function was to speak, whether this was to recite the verses and sacred stories, to know and to declare the laws, or to function as the spokesman of a king or earl during a feast, a cult festival or a legal moot.[72] In other words he was one of the specialists who controlled the society's esoteric knowledge on the king's behalf.

Apparently 'sal' means the king's and earls' assembly hall, cult hall or moot hall: the place in which the functions of 'theatre, court, and church' were united.[73] The 'sal' or the hall was the centre of the human microcosmos, the

[69] Larsson and Hårdh (1998); Hedeager (2001); Hårdh and Larsson (2002); Jørgensen (2003).

[70] Enright (1996); Herschend (1997a), (1997b), (1998) and (1999), p. 414.

[71] Brink (1996). [72] Brink (1996), pp. 256–7.

[73] See the comprehensive account in Herschend (1998).

Figure 7. 'Guldgubbe' from Lundeborg, Funen, Denmark (drawing: Eva Koch)

symbol of stability and good leadership. The hall was also the location where communal drinking took place, which had the purpose of creating bonds of loyalty and fictive kinship; liquor was the medium through which one achieved ecstasy, and thus communion with the supernatural.[74] The high seat, that is, the seat with the high-seat posts, served as the channel of communication with the supernatural world. Since the hall with the high seat served as the geographical and ideological centre of leadership, it is understandable why the earls and kings, as the literature tells us, could suppress and ruin each other by simply destroying their opponent's hall.[75]

There is a group of finds which may reflect a ritual practice associated with lordly power, namely the gold foil plaques, 'guldgubber': small (max. 1 cm) pieces of thin gold foil, often depicting a man and a woman although both men and women also occur as single motifs, as also animals. The pair motif always shows a loving pair standing in profile, facing one another, finely dressed and often provided with jewellery and other requisites such as a staff, beakers, etc. (see Fig. 7).

Such gold foil plaques occur all over Scandinavia, in several cases in direct association with places with religious names such as the Danish localities Gudme on Funen and Gudhjem, Bornholm (home of the gods), and can be dated from the beginning of the sixth century into the tenth century.[76] The find circumstances indicate that the foils with the pair motif are associated

[74] Enright (1996), p. 7. [75] Herschend (1995), p. 221 and (1997b). [76] Watt (1992).

with a particularly special building in the Scandinavian Iron Age and Viking period: the longhouse comprising just one large chamber, the hall. Gold foil figures have been found at the foot of the central, roof-bearing posts with striking frequency: in other words by the posts of the high seats, as at Slöinge in south-western Sweden, Helgö and possibly Svintuna in the mid-Swedish Mälar region, as well as the Norwegian Borre, Mære and Borg in Lofoten.[77] In all, 2600 gold foil figures are so far known from thirty-one localities all over Scandinavia. About 2300 of these are found at Sorte Muld near Gudhjem on Bornholm, and nearly all depict a single figure,[78] while 224 plaques depicting two figures are known.[79]

According to *Skirnismal* in the Edda Poetry, the context of the marriage between Freyr and Gerr is specified as the god having taken his place on the high seat. This mythical scene can be understood as an initiation ritual, the role of which was to mark the status and power of the new lord.[80] The foil figures with the pair motif are regarded as ritually connected with the high-seat posts in a similar manner as the *hieros gamos* in 'Skirnismal' is interpreted as being mythologically linked to the high seat. The deposition of gold foil figures by the high-seat post was very probably part of the initiation of a new king or earl: the symbolic appropriation of the high seat.[81]

Historical and archaeological sources are mutually corroborative of the interpretation of the high seat as the absolute centre of the exercise of special leadership functions, and of the high-seat posts themselves as sacred.[82] This phenomenon is known from a considerable number of traditional cultures, where posts or stakes in particular are attributed with divine functions.[83] This is linked to an understanding of the cosmic order, in which the significance and content of 'distance' are crucial.[84] The cosmic order was physically grounded in the high-seat posts.

The multifunctional role of the hall thus extended beyond the site itself. The hall was at the centre of a group of principal farmsteads; it was the heart of the central places from the later part of the Iron Age.[85] That such places existed all over Scandinavia is now increasingly recognised, for example Gudme/Lundeborg, Sorte Muld, Lejre, Tissø, Toftegård, Boeslunde, Jørlunde, Kalmargård, Nørre Snede, Stentinget, Drengsted and Ribe in Denmark; Trondheim, Kaupang, Hamar and Borg in Norway; Slöinge, Helgö, Birka,

77 Nordén (1938); Lidén (1969); Munch, Roland and Johansen (1988); Myhre (1992); Herschend (1995); Lundqvist *et al.* (1996); Munch, Johansen and Roesdahl (2003).

78 Watt (1992). 79 Andréasson (1995). 80 Steinsland (1994), p. 627.

81 Steinsland (1991) and (1994), p. 630.

82 See, *inter alia*, Herschend (1994), (1997a), (1997b), (1998) and (1999).

83 Eliade (1989). 84 Helms (1988) and (1993).

85 A possible ranking of these places can be found in Näsman (1999), p. 1; Jørgensen (2003).

Uppåkra, Vä, Gamla Uppsala, Högum, Vendel and Valsgärde in Sweden.[86] Characteristically, many of these sites are located a few kilometres inland, relying on one or more landing places or ports situated on the coast.[87] Although this is still a matter of debate, such central places may have served as a basis for some form of political or religious control exercised over a larger area; the radius of their influence went well beyond the site itself. Furthermore, on several of these places a special building seems to have served cultic functions as a pagan 'vi', e.g. Tissø on Sealand, which actually means 'Tir's/Tyr's Lake'.[88]

On the basis of toponymic evidence from Sweden and Norway, it has been argued that rather than being a precisely defined site, such central places should be understood as a somewhat smaller or larger area encompassing a number of different but equally important functions and activities.[89] Both toponymic evidence and archaeological finds suggest that this was a recurrent pattern. This means that it is inadequate to refer to these sites as 'trading sites', 'cult sites', 'meeting or thing places', emphasising only one of their many functions. Instead, these locations should be perceived as multifunctional and composite sites. In addition to their 'official' function as trading and market sites, and as centres where laws were made and cults were established, the central places were probably also associated with special functions such as the skilled crafting of jewellery, weapons and clothing,[90] and furthermore with special cultic activities performed by religious specialists. These places were also the residences of particularly privileged warriors or housecarls. Some of the central places go back to the fourth century (e.g. Gudme/Lundeborg), but the majority did not come into being until after 400. Many of these sites remained centres of power and of economic activity far into the Middle Ages.

SCANDINAVIA AD 500–700: EMERGING KINGDOMS AND ROYAL CENTRES

In the aftermath of the West Roman Empire, the Merovingians and subsequently the Carolingians gained supremacy over neighbouring kingdoms by military conquest and networks of long-distance alliances and gift-giving. Their form of political and economic organisation, with centrally positioned

[86] Munch *et al.* (1988) and (2003); Duczko (1993); Jørgensen (1995) and (2003); Brink (1996); Callmer (1997); Larsson and Hårdh (1998); Hedeager (2001); Hårdh and Larsson (2002); Skre (2004).

[87] Fabech (1999).

[88] Tir/Tyr was the war god in the Asir pantheon (Jørgensen (2003)).

[89] Brink (1996). In several articles Fabech has developed this model in archaeological case studies; most recently Fabech (1998). However, the model of ritual depositions in the cultural landscape, which plays an important part in this general model, has been the subject of debate: see Hedeager (1999b).

[90] Jakobsson (2003).

production sites, markets and emporia, is reflected among the petty kingdoms of Scandinavia. Kings and nobles developed a great need for luxury goods to fulfil the social and ritual obligations necessary to remain in power. The metal items, primarily weapons, jewellery and drinking equipment, are well known in the archaeological record, while carved wood items, luxurious dress and fur, food, alcoholic drinks and the like are less well preserved and therefore less recognised. The need for exotic raw material was the background for the increasingly intensive exploitation of resources in northern Scandinavia[91] and for closer contact with the Sámi population of the North. Both are manifested through the impact on the Norse religion in the late Iron Age.[92] The emerging Scandinavian warrior society with its dynamic and changing political configurations based on alliances and military power demanded extensive agricultural resources for its social institutions as well. The reorganisation of arable land, intensification in the production process, expansive resource utilisation, a hierarchical settlement structure, etc. responded to this need. Manors with high density of buildings and evidence of extensive resource consumption, including highly skilled metalworking and imported luxury goods, were developing during these centuries.

Against this background, however, the burial evidence is remarkably low key. Generally speaking, during the late Iron Age, cremation graves dominated and usually the grave-goods are therefore so heavily damaged that only small fragments have been preserved. However, they confirm the impression of the rich material culture that existed among the Scandinavian elite. Some impressive grave monuments were constructed during this period, mainly on the Scandinavia peninsula. They are found in the inner part of south-eastern Norway, generally in the best agricultural districts, close to rivers and important land routes, and at strategic places along the coast. A remarkable site is Borre in Vestfold, with an impressive burial ground with a number of large mounds; the earliest were built in about AD 600 and the others in the following centuries up to about 900. Borre is mentioned in the skaldic poem *Ynglingatal*, as the burial place for the royal dynasty of the Ynglingas who, the poem claims, reigned in Vestfold during the seventh to ninth centuries.[93] During the same period comparable mounds were erected in Götaland, Svealand and Medelpad in Sweden. They too were situated in the most fertile areas of the cultivated landscape. Close to the old church of Old [Gamla] Uppsala, three of the largest mounds in Scandinavia are to be found. They were all cremation graves from around 500 and the early sixth century and the quality of the fragmented

91 Myhre (2003); p. 91. 92 Price (2002); Solli (2002).

93 Myhre (1992) and (2003). *Ynglingatal* is first mentioned by Snorri Sturluson in 1230, but is probably from the ninth century (Myhre (1992), p. 301).

grave-goods confirms the status of the deceased. Old Uppsala, which is known as the religious and political centre of the Svea kings in the Viking Age, had probably been so since the Migration period. Close to Old Uppsala two special burial grounds, at Vendel and Valsgärde, contain burial mounds with unburned boat graves and grave-goods comparable with those of Sutton Hoo, East Anglia.[94] The cemeteries are dated from around 500 to 800.[95]

In Denmark, the rich archaeological material comes from Migration-period hoards and from the sixth-, seventh- and eighth-century rich settlements, while grave finds from this period are sparse. No doubt the cremation burial practice was absolute during these centuries, except in Bornholm, where well-equipped inhumation graves still survive.[96] The only impressive burial mound from Denmark is located in Old Lejre on Sealand, dated to the sixth century. Old Lejre is mentioned *inter alia* in the *Beowulf* poem and in *Gesta Danorum* by Saxo Grammaticus from around 1200 as the royal centre of the Skjoldungs, the dynasty of the Danish kings during the Migration period. A newly excavated manorial site of extensive size supports Lejre's special position as royal centre in early Danish history. At present traces of about fifty houses have been excavated, dated between the seventh and the tenth centuries. During this period four large halls (some 50 × 11.5 m) and four smaller ones (some 40 × 6 m) existed. Approximately 4000 small finds have been recovered. Tools and implements can be added to a substantial quantity of high-quality objects such as imported jewellery, coins, weights, bars of silver and bronze mountings and glass of Carolingian and Anglo-Saxon origin.[97]

Lejre illustrates the kingly organisation in the late Iron Age. The presumed royal seat was established and consolidated during the formative period of the sixth, seventh and eighth centuries, as were the royal centres at Borre and Old Uppsala. Whether the written evidence contains a core of historical reality or not, the archaeological evidence points to the establishment of a new political structure all over Scandinavia around AD 500. At the same time, origin myths, royal genealogies, mythical tales and legends, together with the symbolic language of animal style, ought to be perceived as the ideological articulation of this new warrior elite, and the prerequisite for the emergence of Germanic royalty. In their own way, they played an organisational role in the establishment of these new kingdoms and served to demonstrate common cultural codes.

Whilst the myths were the warrior-elites' political ideology and a type of legitimisation performed on special occasions, the iconography of animal style

94 Lamm and Nordström (1983). 95 Arrhenius (1983), p. 44.

96 Jørgensen (1990); Jørgensen and Nørgård Jørgensen (1997).

97 Christensen (1991); Jørgensen (2003).

functioned in an overt context, depicting a pre-Christian symbolic universe and a shared Germanic identity among the elite. The fifth, sixth and seventh centuries were to a great extent characterised by contact between the various parts of Europe, from Italy in the south to Norway in the north. A universe of shared experience was created, in sharp contrast to the segmented and divided Europe that some researchers have wanted to identify from the historical sources.

CHAPTER 19

THE SLAVS

Zbigniew Kobyliński

In his *Secret History*, the Byzantine historian Procopius of Caesarea states that after Justinian (527–565) had come to the throne, the Huns and Slavs (Sclavenoi and Antes) had attacked Illyria and the whole of Thrace on an almost annual basis, hitting everything from the Ionian Gulf nearly to the gates of Byzantium itself. Greece and Chersones (in Thrace) were badly affected, and the invaders were oppressing the inhabitants of these territories.[1] Who were these mysterious Slavic people who had arrived so suddenly on the scene, and created a threat to the Byzantine Empire, breaking through the Danubian frontiers, and in a relatively short time settling half of Europe from the lower reaches of the Elbe and the Baltic in the north, down as far as the Adriatic in the south? The earliest description of the Slavs comes from *De Bellis*, another work of Procopius, which was written just before the middle of the sixth century. He portrays them as unusually tall and strong, of dark skin and reddish hair, leading a rugged and primitive style of life and constantly covered in dirt, living in squalid huts which were isolated from one another, and often changing their place of abode.[2] According to Procopius, the Slavs were not ruled by a single man, but for a long time they had lived in a democracy. They believed in one god, the creator of lightning, who was the only ruler of everything, and they made sacrifices to him of oxen and other animals. They went into battle on foot, straight at the enemy, and in their hands they had small shields and spears, but they did not wear armour. The information which Procopius gives us is supplemented somewhat later (at the end of the sixth or beginning of the seventh century) by the writer known as Pseudo-Maurice who in his work *Strategikon* describes the Slavs, again calling them Sclavenoi and Antes, as a very numerous people but one that lived in a disorganised, undisciplined and leaderless manner, not allowing themselves to be enslaved or conquered. The Slavs were resistant to hardship, able to bear both heat and cold, and rain,

[1] Procopius, *Secret History (Historia arcana)* XVIII.20.

[2] Procopius, *Wars* VII.14, 22–30.

Map 14 The Slavs: geographical context

lacking clothing and other necessities of life. They had their homes in the forests, by rivers, swamps and wetlands which could be penetrated only with difficulty.[3]

Where was the homeland of the Slavs, where their ethnogenesis took place and whence they set out on their migration? This problem remains the subject of discussion among historians and archaeologists, despite intensive study of the subject since at least the first half of the nineteenth century. Various arguments (linguistic, historical, archaeological and ethnographical) have been used in

[3] *Strategikon* IX.3.1; XI.4.1–45.

this discussion and the origin of the Slavs has been placed by different authors in different regions of Europe, from areas on the Elbe in the west to the Ural Mountains in the east, and from the source of the Dnepr in the north to the Danube and the Balkans in the south.

The problem of the location of the so-called 'homeland' of the Slavs has evoked (and still evokes) heated scientific discussions, which are reflected in the vast literature on the subject. Disagreement results not just from the different types of information utilised by different scholars or from the different ways of thinking about the issues involved, but also from the strong political influences which, until recently, determined how the problem of the origin of the Slavs was seen. History and archaeology were often used in central Europe in arguments justifying modern political frontiers or the need to change them by territorial annexation. Autochthonous theories on the local origin of the Slavs appeared in several regions in different periods, most often as a reaction against conquest, or loss of independence, for example in the nineteenth century in the Balkans as a reaction against Ottoman rule, or in Bohemia as a reaction against the Austro-Hungarian hegemony. The strongest reaction arose in the period after the Second World War as the natural result of Nazi Pangermanism. At the beginning of the twenty-first century in a period of European unification when historical arguments have ceased to have meaning for the justification of frontiers, which are now disappearing, we can perhaps see the problem of the origin of the Slavs more objectively and without emotion.

Up to now, discussion on the origin of the Slavs has given great weight to linguistic arguments. The basic hypothesis of the linguists is the existence of a common Proto-Slavic language, which later, in the period of the Slavic migrations, became differentiated into discrete languages and dialects. The appearance of the Proto-Slavic language was supposed to have been preceded by the existence of a Balto-Slavic linguistic community. Linguists seeking the original homeland of the Slavs have attempted to define the chronology of these processes on the basis of philological arguments, and to identify the place of origin of the Proto-Slavic language. While unusually strong relationships between the Slavic and Baltic languages seem clear, for some this seems to mean the existence of a Balto-Slavic linguistic community as early as the second millennium BC. Others see the relationship between the two languages as evidence for the territorial proximity of the two peoples and argue for the late disintegration of that linguistic community, which only just preceded the migrations of the Slavs. Linguists have been unable to agree, even approximately, on the region within which the Proto-Slavic language was thought to have arisen. This is despite the repeated attempts that have been made to resolve the question on the basis of place-names, and the names of rivers over wide areas of Europe, as well as to define the homeland on the basis of the names of plants, animals and geographical terms known to them.

The name 'Slav' does not appear in antique written sources before the period of their migrations and thus the analysis of the historical texts does not have much to add to this discussion. Even so, attempts have been made to identify as Slavs the ethnonyms known from the works of Pliny the Elder, Ptolemy or Tacitus. Special attention has been paid here to identifying the place of settlement of the Venedi/Venethi, who have been associated with the Slavs. In analysing the information on these people transmitted to us by Pliny the Elder from the end of the first century AD and by Ptolemy of Alexandria of the second century AD, it has been suggested that the Venedi inhabited huge areas of central Europe to the east of the Oder and south of the Baltic. Other scholars, however, have tried to show that these ancient authors in fact speak of two different peoples: the Venedi living in a small region on the Baltic coast and the Venethi, who occupied great areas of central and eastern Europe. In turn Tacitus, writing at the end of the first century, located the Venethi somewhere in the wooded steppe and forest zones of eastern Europe, east of the Suebi (Sueves), between the Peucini (who should be located on the Black Sea steppe) and the Fenni, occupying the north-eastern borders of Europe. Tacitus' Venethi occupied the same territory that the Stavanoi did in Ptolemy's text, the latter being identified with the Slavs. The neighbours of the Stavanoi were the Sarmatian Alans, located on the Black Sea steppe, and the Galindians and Sudovians (Baltic tribes on the Baltic sea coast). There they occupied great areas of the central European lowlands.

Referring to a much later period (the first half of the sixth century AD), Jordanes in his *Getica* located the Venethi (divided into the Sclaveni and Antes) in the region north of the Carpathian Mountains, between the upper Vistula and the middle Dnepr and the upper Danube.[4] Such a location of the Venethi (identified with the Slavs) is not in disagreement with Tacitus' information on the Venethi and that of Ptolemy on the Stavanoi, but it requires the acceptance of the thesis that the Venethi and Venedi were indeed two different peoples. The seventh-century work known as the *Ravenna Cosmography* localises the original homeland of the Slavs in the land of Scythia, suggesting by this the steppe-lands of eastern Europe. This information, while not very accurate, nevertheless agrees with what the sources say about the homelands of the Venethi and Stavanoi, suggesting the origin of the Slavs in the region of the Ukraine. These scraps of information given by the written sources are, however, far too enigmatic to form the basis for the proposition of unequivocal conclusions.

4 Jordanes, *Getica* IV.34–6.

In the face of such uncertainty archaeology seems to offer the best chance of locating the original homelands of the Slavs, although the relationships between the archaeologically investigated remains of material culture and ethnicity are still unclear. It is easy mistakenly to associate so-called archaeological cultures (and thus the area in which there appears a specific type, or definable group of types, of artefacts) with the tribal territories of peoples known from later written sources. In the archaeological literature attempts have been made to assign a Slavic or Proto-Slavic ethnicity to different archaeological cultures from quite different periods. For a long time such an ethnicity was assigned to the Late Bronze Age and Early Iron Age Lusatian Culture occurring in the area of modern Poland and to all successive archaeological cultures in the same area of central Europe. Since the 1980s increasing popularity has been gained by an opposing theory, which suggests that we should assign the settlement of the territories of modern Poland, Bohemia, Slovakia and Ukraine to Germanic rather than Slavic tribes, at the end of the so-called period of Roman influences (mid-fifth century AD).

It has been shown by archaeologists that at the close of the first half of the first millennium AD, and across the territory of a large part of central and eastern Europe, there occurred the widespread breakdown and disappearance of the cultural and settlement systems which had, over the preceding few centuries, formed a specific cultural province. The latter had included the whole of *Barbaricum* from the territories of the Goths on the Black Sea and Sea of Azov to the settlement areas of various tribes in the Elbe valley. The collapse and disappearance of the existing structures affected successive territories from the Ukraine and Moldavia in the east where it happened first (at the turn of the fourth and fifth centuries), through south-east, southern and into western Poland (during the first half of the fifth century), central Poland (end of the fifth century or beginning of the sixth century), Polish Pomerania (in the first quarter of the sixth century), and last, up to the line of the Elbe and Saale (end of the sixth century). In these areas we see the gradual appearance of more or less numerous cultural assemblages, which represent a completely new cultural model. Extensive settlements with post-built ground-level wooden buildings, with separate craft areas and radial organisation around an empty space, and with differentiated structures of presumably ritual function, all of which was typical for the previous period, disappear. The huge manufacturing centres of iron and ceramics cease functioning. The large cemeteries containing rich graves furnished with weapons and ornaments also disappear. In their place appears a simple egalitarian material culture with small square sunken-floored wooden buildings, with hand-made ceramics and devoid of ornamental metalwork. These phenomena may be explained, in the opinion of the majority of investigators, by the replacement of previously existing populations by the Slavs.

If we agree with such an interpretation of the archaeological sources, in searching for the original homelands of the Slavs we should first of all turn to the western Ukraine. Here in the valleys of the upper Boh, Dnestr and Prut rivers the first square sunken-floored huts with stone corner-ovens appear at the beginning of the fifth century, or maybe even at the end of the fourth century. Their fills contain pieces of simple hand-made egg-shaped pottery vessels. These finds form the indicators of the so-called Prague Culture, associated with the Slavs and later spreading to the north-west and south-west. An intriguing phenomenon is the fact that the oldest Slavic cultural elements appear within the area of the so-called Chernyakhov Culture, which most archaeologists agree was a material culture which reflected the existence of a multi-ethnic Gothic state on the Black Sea. What is more, these Slavic traits appear in their classic form, which is later duplicated over large areas of central, eastern and southern Europe. This means that the creation of the Slavic cultural model and the development of the elements of material culture which later formed the ethnic identification features thus occurred within a foreign, multiethnic cultural environment, no doubt as a result of the need for self-identification in order to manifest their differentiation from other groups.

Whence and why did the Slavs come to the territories along the Dnestr and Prut? It is most probable that the Slavs or their predecessors lived at the end of antiquity in the forest zone on the upper and middle Dnepr, at this point not yet having an express awareness of their ethnic differentiation. Here, they were represented to the second century AD, by the Zarubintsy Culture and later (from the third to the fifth centuries) by the Kiev Culture. At the end of the fourth and beginning of the fifth centuries these stagnating cultures underwent poorly understood cultural changes which led to their greater cultural unification and pressure on their southern neighbours on the Black Sea steppe, undergoing political stimulation from the stormy events surrounding the fall of the state of Ermanric after the Hun attack of 375 AD. It may be assumed that in the process of the ethnogenesis of the branch of the Slavs emerging against this background in the basins of the Dnestr and Prut, other ethnic groups (Germanic and Sarmatian) which inhabited these territories also took part.

Taking advantage of the weakening of the Gothic state as a result of the Hun invasions, another branch of the Proto-Slavic population of the upper and middle Dnepr moved down that river to the south and south-east. Interaction with the existing populations represented by the Chernyakhov Culture gave rise to the Penkovka Culture related to the Prague Culture and represented by the appearance in the fifth century of square huts with stone ovens in the corner.

The historical reflection of these movements may be Jordanes' reference to the armed struggles between Vinitharius and the Antes.[5] The latter, to judge by the naming of their leader Boz as 'king', would seem to have attempted to form their own 'state' organisation on the fringes of or even within the boundaries of the Gothic state. Proto-Slav groups remaining in their original homelands in the valleys of the upper and middle Dnepr were represented by material culture assemblages described by archaeologists as the Kolochin Culture, which was a transformation of the old Kiev Culture. Thus three archaeological cultures, the Penkovka, Prague and Kolochin Cultures, occupied an extensive area from the Dnepr valley in the east to the eastern Carpathians in the west, denoting the area occupied by the Slavic ethnic group in the fifth and at the beginning of the sixth centuries. It is not out of the question that the Sclavinoi and Antes, the Slav tribes named by Jordanes and Procopius, may be related to the Prague and Penkovka archaeological cultures respectively. It was from these territories that during the sixth century the Slav migrations set out in two major directions, along the eastern arc of the Carpathians, to the north-west and south-west. There may also have been a westward migration of the Kolochin Culture into eastern and central Poland, though this is as yet poorly documented archaeologically.

The question of rapid population growth among the Slavs is often discussed in the literature. These people, starting from the Ukraine, were in a relatively short time able to colonise huge areas of Europe, but without causing clear signs of a depopulation of their homelands. The fertility of the Black Soils of the Ukraine in conjunction with the assimilation of members of other ethnic groups caused a population explosion, which allowed them to settle a series of territories in succession. Pseudo-Maurice in his *Strategikon* notes that it was with ease that the Slavs accepted into their ranks prisoners from other tribes.[6] Here it should be noted that the apparently poor and rather unimpressive cultural model of the Slavs, based on home-grown produce and domestic-scale crafts, could have had a magnetic attraction for various groups of people disorientated by the collapse of the great political organisations on the fringes of the Roman Empire. While the Germans had formed 'client states', to a large extent dependent on exchange with the Roman Empire or military service in the imperial army, the Slavs were totally independent of Rome, and when they crossed the frontiers, unlike the Germans, they did not wish to become part of its political and economic structures. They did not wish to exploit the inhabitants in the same way as the nomads, but sought lands for settlement useful for the development of agriculture. In this manner they undoubtedly absorbed the local inhabitants who underwent Slavicisation. It is

[5] Jordanes, *Getica* XLVIII.246–8. [6] *Strategikon* XI.4.4–5.

in this process that we should seek the explanation of the phenomenon of the rapid growth of the Slav population.

Slavic expansion to the north-west passed along the eastern edge of the Carpathians through southern Poland towards the Vistula valley, along which they moved further to the west, at the beginning of the sixth century reaching the vicinity of modern Cracow. They penetrated as far as the source of the Vistula, according to Jordanes, and likewise in the sixth century they moved to the north in the direction of the fertile soils in central Poland (the region of Kuyavia), which they could also reach along the Bug river. Nevertheless, at the beginning of the sixth century the whole area of Silesia and central and western Poland remained outside the area of settlement of the Slavs. This seems to be indicated by Procopius when he writes of the migration of the Heruli who, after being defeated by the Lombards in 509, probably in 512 passed through all the tribes of the Sclavenoi and then, after passing through a considerable area of empty countryside, reached the lands of the Warni (in the middle reaches of the Elbe), and thence to Denmark where they boarded boats to Thule (Scandinavia).[7] The empty countryside must have been Silesia. This region must have still been deserted in 566–567 when, as Gregory of Tours tells us, the Avar expedition against the Franks, which passed through the southern territories of Poland, suffered from a lack of supplies, which seems to suggest that they travelled through deserted territories.[8]

Already in the sixth century, however, typical Slav settlements with square sunken-floored huts with corner-ovens appear on the middle Oder and Neisse, and at the beginning of the seventh century (or perhaps, according to the latest dendrochronological dates, by the middle of the century at the latest) we find them on the middle Elbe. The settlement of Slavs in these territories was made possible by their desertion by Germanic tribes. In 531 the kingdom of the Thuringians was conquered by a coalition of Franks and Saxons; in 568 groups of Thuringians and Saxons joined the Lombards venturing on the conquest of Italy; and in 595 the Merovingians destroyed the state of the Warni on the Saale, the last independent Germanic state in this area of Europe. By this means by the second half of the sixth century a political and perhaps settlement vacuum had formed in the valleys of the Elbe and Saale, which could be filled by the Slavs. Archaeological evidence of the contacts between the Slavs and the Germans suggests a direct relationship between the abandonment of their settlements by the Germans and the arrival of the Slavs at the end of the sixth century and the assimilation of the remaining indigenous inhabitants. The presence of the Slavs on the Baltic by the end of the sixth century is attested by the

[7] Procopius, *Wars* VI.15.1–4. On this episode, see also Hedeager, chapter 18 above.

[8] Gregory, *Hist.* IV.29.

History of Theophylact Simocatta, who mentions two prisoners captured by the Byzantine army about 591 who were supposed to have come from the coast of the 'Western Sea'.[9] From the chronicle of Fredegar we learn that the Serbs (*Surbii*) under the leadership of Dervan joined the tribal union known in the literature as the 'state of Samo' in 632/3, although they had for long been part of the Frankish hegemony. After 632 the Slavs, known as Wends, says Fredegar, took part in armed attacks on the territory of the Merovingians west of the Saale and probably annexed part of these regions for some time.[10] It is unclear whether the oldest phase of Slavic settlement in the Elbe region spread from the north flanks of the Carpathians and Sudeten Mountains (i.e. through southern Poland), or from the south, through Bohemia, where one may suspect their settlement already by the mid-sixth century. Here also, as on the Elbe, there was direct contact and cohabitation of the Slavs with the remaining German population. By the middle of the sixth century a few groups of Slavs penetrated southwards from Bohemia into the area of modern northern Austria.

A specific phenomenon associated with the penetration of the Slavs is the appearance at the beginning of the seventh century of the first defended settlements (strongholds), the oldest example of which known from the written sources may be the Wogastisburg, which Samo defended against the Franks. Apart from their military role, these sites probably fulfilled a ceremonial and cult function. Their genesis should probably be sought in the stronghold-temples dated to the fourth and fifth centuries in the region of the upper Dnepr. In a later period the construction of strongholds by the Slavs in the regions of modern Poland, eastern Germany and Bohemia became a typical form of settlement. They probably formed the centres (or marked borders) of so-called 'small tribes' ruled by leaders who are referred to in the written sources as *archontes*, *hegemones* or *etnarchai*. Such 'small tribes' continued to exist separately until the tenth century, when the first stable Slavic state organisms in this zone emerged. According to recent theories the mechanism of this process was military conquest, and the role of the princely retinue in the rise of state organisations in this region seems to be crucial.

The second main direction of expansion of the Slavs, which brought them into the orbit of the Byzantine Empire, probably came from the region of the oldest Slav settlement in western Ukraine. They moved through Moldavia along the eastern arc of the Carpathians to the lower Danube in the south, and then west along the north bank of that river. According to Procopius,[11] the first Slav attack on Byzantium took place in the time of Justin I, most probably in

[9] Theophylact Simocatta, *Historiae* VI.2.10–16.

[10] Fredegar, *Chron.* IV.68. On the situation in eastern Austrasia see also Fouracre, chapter 14 above.

[11] Procopius, *Wars* VII.40.

523 (though according to some authors as early as 518). The ethnic picture of the Danubian territories and the Balkan peninsula at the end of antiquity was very complicated. The indigenous peoples of these areas, apart from Greeks and Macedonians, were Thracian tribes, Geto-Dacians, Illyrians and Celts who had come under Roman cultural influence long before their political conquest, leading to their gradual Romanisation. At the end of the fourth century the population of the northern and western provinces – Noricum, Pannonia, Dalmatia and Moesia – to a large degree spoke Latin and had accepted many technical aspects of Roman civilisation and the Roman way of life, including belief systems. Larger communities of unromanised Thracians and Illyrians could survive only in the inaccessible mountainous interiors of the Balkans. In the south-eastern parts of the peninsula to the south of the Balkan mountains and especially on the coasts of the Black Sea and in many towns of Thrace and Macedonia, the influences of Greek culture were very strong, and despite losing political control to the Slavs, the urban centres retained their Greek character.

At the end of the fourth century and in the fifth century these provinces were troubled by various barbarian tribes, especially the Huns. Destruction in wars and the ceaseless attacks led in particular to significant depopulation of the northern provinces (along the Danube). Here were the most numerous settlements of barbarian *foederati*. Here could be met different groups of Sarmatians, Alans, Goths and Huns, which dominated the local rural population. In this zone, only the towns were still bastions of Romanisation. In the 430s the Huns took over the Danubian area and, after conquering the people living there, created a powerful but short-lived empire centred on the Tisza river. After the death of Attila in 453 and the destruction of the Hun empire by the Gepids and their allies in the battle of Nedao, political supremacy in the Danube basin was achieved by Germanic tribes, especially the Gepids centred on the old Roman province of Dacia and also the peoples settled in former Pannonia, above all the Ostrogoths, but also for a time the Quadi, Heruli and Vandals on the fringe of the weakening Western Roman Empire. In 474 the Ostrogoths migrated from Pannonia to Lower Moesia, and at the end of 489 under the leadership of Theoderic they entered Italy.[12] After overcoming Odovacer they became rulers of Italy and the territories forming what was left of the Western Empire (Noricum, Dalmatia and part of Pannonia). The rule of the Ostrogoths lasted until the middle of the sixth century, when they were overcome by the Byzantines and Dalmatia became part of the Byzantine Empire. Pannonia was taken over by the Lombards and Noricum was annexed by the Franks, who were forced out by the eastern emperors. Little Scythia

[12] See Moorhead, chapter 6 above.

(in the region of the Danube delta), occupied since the end of the fourth century by the Huns, was settled by the related Bulgars.

The Slavic tribes were to penetrate this ethnically, socio-economically and culturally varied area. The appearance of Slavic settlement on the Danube seems to have had its beginnings already by the first half of the sixth century. After the collapse of the Hun empire in the middle of the fifth century, and after the stormy events which followed, conditions were right for the effective expansion of the Slavs to the south. The first stage of this expansion was into the territory on the lower and middle Danube. About the middle of the sixth century, Slavic settlement in this area had become established. According to Jordanes, the 'Sklavenoi inhabit the territory from the town of Noviedunum and the Mursian lake to the Dnestr'.[13] The use of this record to determine the territory of the Slavs comes up against a number of difficulties. The town of Noviedunum is usually located at the mouth of the Danube, and the Mursian lake identified with Lake Balaton, or with the muddy confluence of the Tisza and the Danube, or with the region lying further to the west at the mouth of the Oltul river. Even if at the beginning of the sixth century Slavic settlement did not extend very far to the west, in the middle of that century the Slavs reached as far west along the Danube as the Iron Gates and the Banat. The information from Jordanes is supplemented by Procopius, who writes: 'the Sclavinoi and Antes . . . have their homelands on the Danube not far from its northern bank'.[14] In another place the same writer said that 'on the other side of the Danube . . . mainly they [Sclavinoi and Antes] live'.[15] Less certain are the sources for Slav settlement on the middle Danube. Only the information of Procopius on the contacts of the Lombard prince Hildigis with the Slavs[16] allows the detection of their presence shortly before 539 close to the territory ruled by the Lombards, most probably in the Moravian-Slovak area where their presence is archaeologically attested by the discovery of settlements and cemeteries of the Prague Culture in the valleys of the Váh and Morava to the middle Danube. From this region the Slavs spread further to Bohemia, from whence they could expand into the Elbe region.

The information, from the written sources on the subject of Slavic settlement north of the Danube, is confirmed by the archaeological evidence. In the zone of direct contact between the South Slavs and the Byzantine Empire, to the north of the lower Danube, in Wallachia and Moldavia, between the eastern Carpathians and the Prut, archaeological remains dating to the sixth and seventh centuries are similar to the Prague and Penkovka cultures. These cultures are a specific mixture of different elements: Slavic, Daco-Getic,

[13] Jordanes, *Getica* V.35. [14] Procopius, *Wars* VII.14.30.

[15] Procopius, *Wars* V.27.2. [16] Procopius, *Wars* VII.35.13–22.

Daco-Roman and Byzantine. The earliest of these are groups of the first half of the sixth century of Costişa-Botoşana type found in Moldavia. This reflects the intermarriage of Slavic and autochthonous cultures, and is evidence of the settlement of the Slavs along the eastern flanks of the Carpathians. Groups of the second half of the sixth century of the Ipoteşti-Ciurel-Cîndeşti Culture in Romania north of the Danube contain ceramics of Slavic type of the second half of the sixth century, which is in accord with the information from the written sources on the presence here of the Slavs.

In these mixed cultures which penetrated the Carpathian passes into south-east Transylvania the elements connected with the presence of the Slavs are primarily pottery vessels, among them those of Prague type or the related Korchak type, but we can also detect building types known previously from the Ukraine (among them square sunken-floored buildings with corner-ovens) and burial rites involving cremation. The Daco-Roman elements are represented by some types of hand-made ceramic vessels related to the former Dacian culture, certain building types (such as sunken-floored buildings with free-standing fireplaces), but especially the frequent occurrence of wheel-made vessels, the form of which recalls provincial Roman ones. The third element in these cultures is represented by Byzantine influences in the form of some wheel-made ceramic vessels and the character of some ornaments (fibulae, earrings) and coins. The mixed ethnic makeup of the Ipoteşti-Cîndeşti-Ciurel-Costişa Culture is generally accepted, but the most dynamic component of the sixth-century population north of the lower Danube was formed by the Slavs. The written sources also allow us to see another component – prisoners taken from the Balkan areas, deported in huge numbers from the middle of the sixth century, many of whom seem to have stayed in the territories north of the Danube and did not return home. The relative stability and peace lasting in the Slavic territories on the Danube through several decades of the sixth century which is suggested by the written sources, and the peaceful mode of their expansion into that area, encouraged close contact between the new peoples and the local population, who either entered the area willingly or were led there by force. This hastened the processes of acculturation of the new arrivals, as well as the assimilation and Slavicisation of part of the foreign population.

The Suchava-Şipot Culture in Moldavia, dated to the late sixth or early seventh century, represents a second wave of Slav settlement. This has a different character, for most of its elements are linked to Slavic material culture. Above all the influence of the Penkovka Culture, often connected with the Antes, is strongly represented. The ornaments occurring in the same groups are considered as belonging to the Martynovka type, with close North Pontic connections. This may be evidence of contacts with Alan tribes and possibly other nomad peoples of this zone. From the moment of the strengthening of Slavic settlement on the Danube, the second stage of expansion of the Slavs to the south began. The first signs of this can be observed in the middle of the sixth century. Settlement increases in intensity at the end of the century and ends about the middle of the seventh century, when considerable areas of the Balkans were already occupied by the Slavs. The colonisation was preceded in the first decades of the sixth century and maybe even at the end of the fifth century by raids by Slavs from beyond the Danube, organised either by the Slavs themselves, or with the help of other peoples, mainly Bulgars from Little Scythia (*Scythia Minor*) in the region of the delta of the Danube.

The Slavic raids of the first half of the sixth century had a destructive character, being carried out mainly for the purposes of looting. They increased in the reign of Justinian (527–565), when the Byzantine armies were involved in long campaigns to restore the frontiers of the Roman Empire.[17] Justinian attempted to strengthen the north-eastern frontiers, rebuilding many destroyed Danubian fortresses, and also refortifying existing and building new forts in the interior of the Balkan peninsula, for example near important passes through the Balkan mountains. The fortresses themselves could not hold back the tide of northern barbarians, and from the time of that emperor come frequent (annual, according to Procopius) attacks of the Sclavenoi and Antes who spread destruction and desertion in the whole of Thrace and Illyria, taking loot and herds of cattle, seizing numerous prisoners, taking fortresses and being faced with only weak resistance from the imperial armies. In the years 545–551, especially, the presence of the Sclavenoi was known even in the furthest Balkan provinces. In 550 a large group of Sclavenoi were preparing for an expedition to Thessalonica, but with the news of the approach of a great Byzantine army they abandoned this expedition, and moving instead from the area of Naissus (Niš), 'crossing all the mountains of Illyria', found themselves in Dalmatia.[18] It is also to this period that we should date the sporadic settlements of small groups of Slavs in the deserted areas of Moesia Superior and Inferior. We should note too the presence of certain groups of Slavs in the Byzantine Empire as soldiers.[19]

The appearance of the Avars in this area of Europe additionally complicated and hastened further developments. This nomadic people arrived about 558 on the Black Sea steppes, fleeing from central Asia before the Turks and becoming involved in political struggles between Byzantium, the steppe peoples of the Black and Azov Sea coasts, and Persia. In defiance of Byzantium they attacked the Utrigurs and Sabiri and defeated the Antes between the Dnepr and Dnestr. They then turned their attention to the west, to the Franks, with whom they

[17] On the reign of Justinian, see Louth, chapter 4 above.

[18] Procopius, *Wars* VII.40.7. [19] Procopius, *Wars* V.27.1–2.

fought twice (561/2 and 566/7). They then got involved in a Lombard–Gepid conflict, and after overcoming the latter occupied their territory in the Tisza valley. The Avars next in 568 took the Lombard territories in Pannonia, the Lombards leaving for northern Italy.[20] In this manner the Avars very quickly took over a large area of central Europe from the eastern Carpathians to the eastern Alps. They conquered all the peoples living in this area, above all the Gepids, the remains of the autochthonous population, and the Slavs. Besides the Avars themselves, their kingdom was inhabited by other tribes with whom they were allied, especially the Bulgars. The written sources tell us about the presence of Slavs in the Avar realms, including information that Slavic masses took part in various military expeditions under Avar leadership, especially in the Balkans.

At least to the end of the sixth century the Wallachian Slavs probably did not come under Avar domination, but they did take part in joint military action. The Byzantines tried to prevent this by encouraging conflicts between these Slavs and Avars. For instance, in 578 Byzantium encouraged the Avars to attack the Wallachian Slavs with the aim of preventing them attacking the Balkans. The Avar envoys informed the emperor that the Avar khagan 'wished to crush the Sclavinoi, common enemies of himself and the Romans'.[21] Other groups of Slavs living in the Danube valley came under Avar rule, and suffered oppression. According to the chronicler Fredegar, writing some time between 640 and 660, the Slavs took part in military expeditions, doing the bulk of the fighting for little reward, paid tributes, and suffered many other burdens under their rule.[22] The character of the relationship between Slavs and Avars may nevertheless be interpreted somewhat differently in the light of the archaeological evidence. In Moravia and Slovakia there appears in the seventh century a mixed Slavic–Avar material culture, interpreted as an expression of peaceful and harmonious relationships between Avar warriors and Slavic peasants. It is also thought that at least some of the leaders of Slav tribes could have become part of the Avar aristocracy. It is with this period of the Avar rule of the Danube basin that the expansion of the areas settled by the Slavs in the middle Danubian regions and eastern Alps is associated. The area of former Pannonia, especially its north-western part and the north-eastern part of Noricum Ripensis, had already been penetrated by Slavic settlers from the north or north-east by the middle of the sixth century, and we may observe the settlement in this period of the Danubian areas in the region of modern north-east Austria by the Slavs. Mixed assemblages of Slavic and German finds from this area suggest the peaceful nature of the settlement processes taking place here.

[20] On the Lombards' move into Italy, see Moorhead, chapter 6 above.

[21] Menander Protector, *Historia* II.30.

[22] Fredegar, *Chron.* IV.48.

The second wave of colonisation penetrated from the east by the main river valleys and was connected with the political expansion of the Avars to the west, enabled by the movement of the Lombards to northern Italy (568). By about 580, it seems, Slavic settlement in the northern direction had enveloped the Mur valley and eastern Carantania. By 587/8, penetrating up the Sava valley, they reached the region of today's Ljubljana. Before 591 they had reached the upper Drava (Drau), and before 600 the valleys of the Soča (Isonzo) and Vipava. We have clear information on the progress of the Avar–Slavic military expeditions, and the progress of colonisation which followed them, from the data on the destruction of the most important towns of Noricum and Pannonia. Before 579 the towns of Poetovio (today Ptuj) and Virnum (near Klagenfurt) were destroyed; before 588 Celeia (today Celje) and Emona (Ljubljana) in the Sava valley both fell; and some time before 591 so too did Teurnia (St Peter im Holz) and Aguntum (near Lienz) in the upper Drava valley. In 592 and 595 we hear of the conflict between Slavs and the Bavarians on the upper Drava. The archaeological confirmation of these events lies in traces of the destruction of certain Lombard–Roman settlements. For example, in Kranj a settlement of this type was destroyed around 580–590, and the Lombard fort at Meclariae located in the lower Ziller valley was destroyed shortly after 585. The east Alpine area, especially western Carantania, was not thickly or evenly settled because of the mountainous terrain. We should expect a significant proportion of the autochthonous population to have survived here, as well as perhaps the residue of a German population. This is expressed in the character of the oldest cultural group defined in this territory, the so-called Carantanian Group dated to the seventh and eighth centuries, in the inventory of which we can find material with many connections to the material culture of late antiquity and also analogies with the contemporary Germanic culture.

The last decades of the sixth and beginning of the seventh century are a period of increase in the military activity of the Avars against the Eastern Empire. Many times negotiations took place, high tributes were paid, and attempts were made to turn Avar attention to the east, but this did not suffice to defend the Balkan provinces of the Empire from destructive attacks, in which masses of Slavs also took part – both those under Avar rule and allied tribes. In this period more and more frequently Slavic groups settled in the Balkans. About 581, many Slavic tribes settled in the region of Thessalonica, creating there a 'Macedonian Sclavinia'. As John of Ephesus (also known as John of Amida) tells us in 581:

> The accursed nation known as the Slavs wandered across the whole of Greece, the lands of the Thessalonians and the whole of Thrace, taking many towns and forts, which they destroyed and burnt, enslaving the people, and making themselves rulers

of the whole country. They settled by force and behaved just as if they were in their homelands, and even today [i.e., in 584] they still live there and lead a peaceful life in Roman territory, free of anxiety and fear. They take prisoners, murdering people and burning houses.

It is suspected that after the great siege of Thessalonica, about 586, part of the Slavic tribes together with the Avars reached the Peloponnese, annexing fertile lands in the western part of the peninsula and provoking the escape of the Greek population to Sicily and other islands. The so-called *Monemvasia Chronicle* states that in the years 587–588:

The Avars and their Slav allies took all of Thessalonica and Greece, Old Epirus, Attica, and Eubea, they attacked the Peloponnese and took it by force. They settled here, driving out and destroying the local Hellenic peoples. Those who could escape from their murderous hands scattered here and there, thus the inhabitants of Patras moved to the region of Reggio in Calabria, the inhabitants of Argos on the island known as Orobos, the Orynt inhabitants to the island of Aegina . . . only the east part of the Peloponnese, from Corinth to the Cape of Maleas, remains untouched by the Slavs because it is mountainous and inaccessible.

The taking of Sirmium by the Slavs in 582 weakened the defences of the northern frontier, allowing the barbarians access to the Balkans. At this time many Danubian towns, such as Castra Martis, Ratiaria, Oescus and Acra, disappear from the pages of history, and after the sixth century there is no further mention of them. The looting expeditions of the Avars and Slavs reached the shores of the Black Sea and the Adriatic. Many Dalmatian towns fell victim to them. In 592 Byzantium attempted for the last time to halt the barbarians on the line of the lower Danube. The end of the wars with the Persians allowed the emperor Maurice (582–602) to transfer the army to the northern frontier. Wars with the Avars and Slavs continued mainly in the Danubian area with varying fortunes until 602 when, as a result of a military revolt, Maurice was deposed and killed. From that time the Danubian frontier is considered to have ceased to be defensible and the Balkans were open to barbarian settlement. Only a few Danubian forts and towns lasted through the first decades of the seventh century. The beginning of the seventh century also sees the attack of the Avars on the Antes (602), who were allied with Byzantium.[23] This is the last mention of the Antes in the written sources, and some scholars believe that this attack was the cause of the end of that tribal union. Archaeological support for such a thesis is the disappearance of the Penkovka Culture at this time. The areas occupied by this cultural group were not, however, depopulated, which is suggested by the numerous finds of objects belonging to the Luka Rajkovetska Culture, genetically related to the Korchak material.

[23] Theophylact Simocatta, *Historiae* VIII.5.13.

In the first decades of the seventh century Byzantium found itself in an extremely critical position. Threatened by Persia in the east, it had no possibility of opposing the settlement of Slavs on the frontiers of its Balkan possessions. Both Phokas (602–610) and his successor Heraclius (610–641) attempted to buy off the Avar attackers with high tributes.[24] However these did not prevent the Avars from looting raids. In the years 612–614 Dalmatia especially suffered on this account. Salona, the capital of the province, fell. A series of towns on the Adriatic coast and islands escaped destruction, and in them the inhabitants of other regions of Dalmatia defended themselves. In 626 there was a joint Avar–Persian military expedition as a result of which Constantinople itself was besieged by land and sea by the Persians and Avars, who brought with them large numbers of Slavs. Constantinople was able to defend itself owing to naval supremacy (using Greek Fire among other tactics), and the defeat which the Avars suffered broke their power and brought an end to their military supremacy in the Balkans.

At the same time the supremacy of the Avars was challenged on the north-west and north-east fringes of their state. A revolt against Avar rule broke out among the peripheral Slavic tribes, as a result of which arose the ephemeral structure known in the literature as the 'state of Samo'.[25] The existence of this political organism is known from the chronicle of Fredegar.[26] According to Fredegar, the Frankish merchant Samo came to the Slavic territories in the reign of Chlothar II about 623–625, at a time when the Slavs were revolting from Avar rule. He joined them in this fight, and soon became their leader. The rise of a Slavic tribal union under Samo was disturbing to the Franks, and so in 631 King Dagobert led an expedition against Samo, but was defeated at Wogastisburg, the Slavic stronghold at an unidentified location which we have already mentioned.[27] The state of Samo, the first state organisation of the Slavs to be historically confirmed, lasted until sometime between 658 and 669 and fell apart after Samo's death. The slight information contained in Fredegar's chronicle does not allow the frontiers of the state to be defined with any certainty, but it has often been suggested that its centre lay in Moravia. It would have had the character of a federation of many Slavic tribes, amongst whom would be found the Czechs, Sorbs living on the Elbe river, and probably the Carantanian Slavs. At this time Dalmatia too was probably freed from the domination of the Avars. There were disturbances on the Black Sea and Caspian steppes and internal troubles in the Avar state. As a result of these events the Avar state became a political organism the influence of which did not extend beyond the Danubian area.

24 See also Louth, chapter 11 above. 25 See above, p. 532.
26 Fredegar, *Chron.* IV.48, 68. 27 See above, p. 532.

The settlement by the Slavs of new lands in the Balkan peninsula was a long-term process, taking place over many decades. It should not be thought that the Slavic settlement took the form of a powerful wave of people who flooded into the deserted areas of the former Balkan provinces. The results of anthropological investigations, as well as an analysis of the material culture of the South Slavs, clearly demonstrate the significant biological and cultural contribution of the previous populations of these territories in the formation of the South Slavs. It should be observed, however, that the Slavs clearly represented a group of considerable demographic potential, which was able to assimilate the remains of the earlier populations. The beginnings of the process can be seen in the Danubian phase of Slavic expansion, an indirect indicator of assimilation being the character of the material culture of this phase found in Wallachia, Moldavia and south-east Transylvania. The rise of cultures composed of material from various groups is also found in the material culture from the seventh and eighth centuries on the north-western edge of southern Slavic territory, in the so-called Carantanian Group, and in Istria.

The first attempts at Slav settlement in the Balkans, which one may presume took place in the middle of the sixth century, had little influence on ethnic and settlement patterns, but in the later sixth century the central part of the Balkans along the communication route from Pannonia to the Aegean Sea was permanently occupied. It is to this period that we should assign the colonisation of large parts of Greece, a time which probably also saw the beginnings of Slavic settlement in the areas between the Danube and the Stara Planina mountains in Bulgaria, although there are only a few archaeological traces from the late sixth century in the Balkan peninsula. The oldest Slavic sites in northern Bulgaria are likewise dated to the sixth century. On sites such as Popina I, and others of its type, there are links to the Hlinca I Culture in the form of the vessels appearing in Moldavia from the middle of the seventh century and regarded as the indicator of a new wave of colonisation of settlers from East Slavic territory. There are no signs of the cohabitation of populations that left the material culture of Popina I type, which can be explained by the different political and settlement conditions north and south of the Danube. The sixth and seventh centuries, a period of unceasing barbarian attacks on the Balkan provinces, connected with the looting and cruelty so evocatively described in the written sources, did not create the right conditions for closer relationships between the attackers and the local populations, which generally fled to defensible places. This is also why, one may suspect, many earlier Slavic settlements south of the Danube have material of relatively 'pure' type. The influences of more advanced cultures and other groups of Slavs in closer contact with the Roman and Romanised populations are nevertheless visible in the rapid and significant advances in the development of these Slavic cultures, and the rapidity with which they accepted the trappings of civilisation. The manifestations of Slavic culture from other areas of the Balkan peninsula which can be linked with the early phase of colonisation are still poorly known. An important discovery is the find in Olympia in the western Peloponnese of a sixth- or seventh-century Slavic cremation cemetery with urns of a type closely allied to Prague-type pottery. Radiate fibulae from Greece and Macedonia are also linked with Slavic occupation. The pattern of disappearance of monetary finds may likewise serve as an indirect indicator of Slav settlement: in Macedonia the youngest coins are of Justin II (565–578), and on the Peloponnese they are coins of Constans II (641–668).

The younger phase of colonisation falls in the first half of the seventh century. This is a period of the arrival of new tribes to the Balkans, as well as so-called 'internal colonisation', the movements within the area of tribes already settled there. Among the new arrivals are usually counted the Serbs and Croats. According to the tenth-century account of Constantine Porphyrogenitus, the Serbs and Croats arrived in the area from the north from beyond the Carpathians in the reign of the emperor Heraclius. They were supposed to have freed Dalmatia from the Avars and settled there themselves. According to the written evidence, the whole of Dalmatia was said to have been overrun by the Slavs about 641/2. It was at this time that Abbot Martin was sent by Pope John IV to pay ransoms for prisoners and relics captured by the Slavs. The process of the settlement of the Dalmatian coast and islands was to last for another century. In the same period Istria was settled by the Slavs, spreading first from the east Alpine area, but from the beginning of the seventh century Slavs from Dalmatia too began to penetrate the area. Despite the destruction, which the larger centres in this area were not able to escape, the main towns survived, among them Tergeste (Trieste), deserted by the Lombards but rebuilt by the Byzantines, and which retained rule over the Istrian peninsula. A significant number of the Romanised population also survived. There was a long-term process of Slavic–Roman symbiosis in this area, which had to a greater extent than in any other Slavic territory considerable effect on the Istrian Slavic culture, leading to the acceptance of a series of traits derived from late Roman culture. At the beginning of the seventh century other parts of the Balkans also became settled by the Slavs. In this period Slavic settlement penetrated Thrace. In the seventh century we also observe the extension of Slavic colonisation of Transylvania from various directions.

Byzantium did not prevent Slavic settlement in the Balkans. The colonisation by the new agricultural populations of territories which were on the whole devastated and depopulated would have been advantageous for the rulers of the Eastern Empire, on condition that it would have been able to make these new populations their subjects, paying their taxes to the central power. At first the Slavic tribes in the Balkans retained independence and their own political structures. The term 'Sclavinia' is often met in Byzantine sources, and means, most probably, a Slavic tribal territory independent of imperial rule. Quite early on, moves were made to change this state of affairs. The politics of Byzantium concerning the Balkan Slavs were varied. Already by the second half of the seventh century attempts were being made to absorb the tribes living closer to the capital into the socio-economic system of the metropolitan state. This was partly successful in Thrace: the Thracian theme which had originally included only the early provinces of Europa and Adrianopolis was organised in 680–687 and represented the return of imperial power over these territories. It is likely, however, that some of the Slavic tribes living there retained their autonomy. It was more difficult to subdue the Macedonian and Greek Slavs by force. Military expeditions were organised against them (by Constans II in 656, and Justinian II in 686). Great numbers of Slavs taken prisoner in these expeditions were resettled in Asia Minor. The tribes that came under Byzantine rule were obliged to pay tribute, supplying military aid and fulfilling other obligations. More than once it was necessary to renew military action against mutinous Slavic tribes. In other territories they retained relative independence. The Helladian theme organised in 695 included Attica, Boeotia and several islands, but without those areas of Greece that had been settled by Slavic tribes.

In the peripheral areas, far from the main centres of the Empire, the power of the Byzantine state was more nominal. Relatively early we see signs of socio-economic changes leading to transformation of Slavic tribal organisations into separate states, albeit ones with fairly weak political institutions. Sometimes an important role in this process was fulfilled by foreign elements, as occurred for example in the north-eastern part of the Balkan peninsula, where at the end of the seventh century the core of the Bulgar state appeared. This was organised by the so-called Proto-Bulgars, a nomadic tribe of Turkic origin. At the end of the seventh century, after the collapse of Great Bulgaria, this people had arrived in 'Little Scythia' by the Danube delta. Under the leadership of the khagan Asparuch they had come from the Azov and Black Sea steppes along the traditional routes of the peoples of the steppes. Byzantium, perceiving the danger posed by the Bulgars, sent an expedition against them, which ended in defeat for the imperial army. The Proto-Bulgars moved to the territory of Lower Moesia, and in 678–680, according to the early ninth-century account of Theophanes Homologetos, subdued the Seven Clans and Severs (*Siewierzanie*), the Slavic tribes already living there, and resettled them on the periphery of the territory which they occupied, that is, on the frontier between the Avars and the Bulgars, and in the Balkan foothills. The Bulgars thus strengthened their hold over the territory between the Danube, the Balkans and the Black Sea, and began to threaten the Byzantine possessions in Thrace. This forced the Byzantines to sign a 'dishonourable' treaty with them in 680/1 by which they were allowed the rights to inhabit the territory that they held but which obliged them to pay a tribute. The Slavic tribes, which found themselves under the political and economic domination of the nomadic Proto-Bulgars, none the less retained their ethnic and organisational differentiation and their own tribal leaders.

In the north-west fringes of southern Slavic territory, among the Alpine Slavs, a proto-state political organisation was also forming. At the end of the sixth and beginning of the seventh century the Carantanian Slavs were dependent on the Avars, but this dependence was weaker than that of the tribes inhabiting the Carpathian basin. In the period of the crisis of the Avar state in the 630s, Carantania became independent of the Avars. From this time come references to the rule of a Prince Valluk over the 'Vinedian March' (identified with Carantania). The relationship of Carantania with the state of Samo is debated, but it cannot be discounted that there was some co-operation in the interests of fighting a common enemy. After the collapse of Samo's state, and once most of its territory had been retaken by the Avars, Carantania proper in the valleys of the Drava (Drau) and Mur rivers retained its independence and for some time defended itself effectively against the Lombards and Bavarians to the west and the Avars to the east. It was in this period that a process of internal consolidation and socio-economic change took place, which was to lead to the creation in Carantania of an early form of state.

We have now seen how by the year 700 the Slavs had colonised the eastern half of Europe and stabilised the western border of their settlement from the rivers Elbe and Saale in the north, and southwards almost in a straight line down to the Istrian peninsula on the Adriatic Sea.

PART III

THEMES AND PROBLEMS

CHAPTER 20

THE JEWS IN EUROPE 500–1050

Michael Toch

INTRODUCTION AND SOURCES

The early Middle Ages saw the establishment of Jewish life in major parts of Europe. In this period the Mediterranean–Hellenistic Jewry of antiquity separated and developed into Byzantine–southern Italian, Roman, Catalan–southern French and Arabic–Sicilian branches. During the later part of the period *Ashkenazic* (north-western and northern European) and *Sephardic* (Iberian) Jewry came into being as distinctive entities very different from earlier patterns. There were (probably) also some Jews in eastern Europe, of which almost nothing is known but a vague association with Byzantium. Jews held to a common creed yet differed in language, religious custom and ritual, social organisation, occupations and legal standing, a fact that militates against easy historical inferences from an ostensibly fixed character. At different times and to differing degrees, they were under the influence of the centres of gravity – demographic, religious, intellectual – of Jewish life in the Middle East, especially Palestine and Babylonia. Compared to these, throughout most of the period under consideration, European Jews in numbers or intellectual creativity were yet barely remarkable. None the less, modern historians have usually accorded them a significance out of proportion. In this they faithfully followed medieval churchmen, to whom Jews presented a challenge far in excess of their actual presence and impact.

It is thus not by accident that our view is further hampered by an ambiguous and severely unbalanced source tradition. For the greater part of Europe there exists a considerable body of texts of ecclesiastical provenance – the Lives and miracles of saints, chronicles and histories, epistles, form letters, the decisions of synods, canonical collections, theological treatises – complemented by law-codes, imperial or royal legislation and charters. However, in the light of recent studies into hagiography and religious polemics, many of these sources should be handled with great circumspection, cautioning us from naïvely quarrying them for straightforward data. Clerics all over Europe employed Judaism and Jews to drive home moral and theological messages destined for internal Christian consumption. Not every metaphorical reference – for instance the denunciations of a seventh- or eighth-century canonical collection from Ireland, to cite an extreme case – speaks of actually living Jews.[1]

For a long stretch, information provided by Jews themselves, funeral epigraphy and a family history in Hebrew, come solely from the Mediterranean south.[2] So do the first literary works produced by Jews in Europe: religious Hebrew poetry written in southern Italy from the ninth century onwards.[3] Somewhat later *Responsa* literature sets in, first in Arab Spain and then in Germany and France. These deliberations and decisions of the rabbis, drafted in response to litigation and requests for religious-legal advice, constitute the main medieval corpus of information on internal Jewish life.[4] Some data can be culled from the writings of the Babylonian heads of Talmudic academies, even though their contacts were mainly restricted to Jews in Muslim Spain and Byzantium.[5] By the end of the tenth century the immense wealth of the Cairo *Genizah* begins to shed light on Jews in the Muslim world including Arab Sicily and, to a much lesser degree, in Muslim Spain and Byzantium.[6] The fact that almost none of the many thousand documents of the *Genizah* bears on Latin Europe is an incisive comment on the widely held notion of a Jewish mobility (and solidarity) straddling continents.[7] Indeed, the order of magnitude of Jewish life in northern and western Europe is strongly indicated by the veritable absence of a written record produced by Jews, as compared to Italy, the Middle East and North Africa. By the same token, its emergence between the late ninth and the eleventh century speaks of a decisive change in the presence of Jews. Fittingly, by then something of the daily stuff of life too, property and landed possessions, comes to light in Latin cartularies and Hebrew deeds from France, Italy, Spain and Germany.

POPULATION

In the course of Roman antiquity Jews came to be a significant ingredient of some town populations of the Empire. In Byzantine parts, mainly in Asia

[1] Linder (1997), pp. 593–5. See the debate between Lotter (2001) and Toch (2001a) and (2001b).

[2] Noy (1993) and (1995); Klar (1944/74), pp. 11–41 = Salzman (1924).

[3] Klar (1944/74), pp. 55–108, cf. Schirmann (1966). The tenth-century Book of Yosippon, an ancient history of Israel, was also written in Italy, cf. Bowman (1993).

[4] Bar-Ilan University (2002). For translations see Agus (1965), Mutius (1984–90); for orientation Grabois (1987/93).

[5] Mann (1973); cf. Brody (1998), pp. 19–34.

[6] Mann (1931), pp. 3–59; Ashtor (1964); Goitein (1968); Ben-Sasson (1991); De Lange (1996); Gil (1997); Simonsohn (1997).

[7] Toch (2001c).

Minor and to a lesser degree in Greece (Thessalonica) and on the isles (Cyprus, Crete and Rhodes), the foundation of Jewish communities goes back to the pre-Christian era, and that of Constantinople to the period of Theodosius II, if not earlier.[8] In later times various places are mentioned in the sources, mostly in Asia Minor,[9] but the fragmentary state of the documentation makes it impossible to retrace local developments. For example, the author of a tenth-century religious poem called himself 'Menahem the Small, son of R. Mordecai Corizzi from the community of Otranto'. His family had probably moved to Italy from Koritsa, nowadays Albania, and this is the only indication that there were Jews there. Menahem's cultural background was surely a Byzantine one, as evident from his frequent use of Greek terms.[10] The list of places of settlement grows significantly once the Karaite nuclei and the later evidence of Benjamin of Tudela (*c.*1160) are taken into account.[11] With great caution one can assume renewed growth beginning in or after the mid-tenth century, parallel to and possibly caused by Byzantine reconstruction in the east and in the Mediterranean. It is safe to state that two phenomena mark Byzantine Jewry. Even with the basically hostile attitude of government there was a continuity of the Jewish presence in the Eastern Empire. Secondly, there was a geographical dissemination and migratory flow throughout the Byzantine space, including the Middle East with Palestine, Egypt and North Africa (three areas not treated in the following), as well as southern Italy. The former regions remained in some contact with Jewish Byzantium even after the Arab conquest. Although there are no direct indicators except cultural affinities, Byzantine Jewry appears to have been the medieval foster mother, via Italy, for much of European Jewry.[12]

In Italy epigraphy and textual sources single out Rome as the oldest community, going back to Republican times and continuously inhabited by Jews.[13] North of Rome, Jews organised in proper communities are still mentioned in the early sixth century in Genoa and Milan. They then disappear from the record, to resurface, haltingly and only as individuals, in the eighth century (Pavia, Asti) and in greater numbers and detail from the tenth century onwards (Ravenna, Verona, Pavia, Treviso, Lucca, Rimini, Ancona).[14] The main body of Jews outside Rome lived in the south, on the mainland and in Sicily, in areas mainly under Byzantine rule or influence until the coming of the Arabs and the Normans. In late antique Apulia and Calabria they must have made up a significant ingredient of urban population. Emperor Honorius in 398 saw the

[8] Jacoby (1993), esp. pp. 126–7, and (1995).

[9] Adrianople, Corinth, Sparta, Chios, Pylae, Ephesus, Mastaura, Attaleia, Synnada, Nicaea, Cotyaeum, Amorium, Khonai, Strobilos (?), Seleucia: Starr (1939), *passim*; Ankori (1959), pp. 113–19.

[10] Roth (1966b), p. 257.

[11] Ankori (1959), *passim*; Adler (1907).

[12] Zimmels (1966). A case study: Ta-Shma (2001).

[13] Toaff (1996).

[14] Colorni (1980).

very functioning of town governments threatened by their claim to exemption from service in the *curiae*.[15] This southern centre of gravity, including Sicily, remains prominent in the sources of the sixth century, funeral epigraphy and the extensive correspondence of Pope Gregory I, as well as in the poorly documented seventh century.[16] Jews are mentioned in southern Lazio (Terracina), in Campania (Venafro, Naples, Nola), in Apulia (Taranto, Oria), in Venosa at the northern border of the province of Basilicata, in Sicily (Palermo, Agrigent, Syracuse), in Sardinia (Cagliari), and without exact location in the papal patrimonies of Campania and Sicily. Afterwards it is difficult to decide whether there was serious disruption, slow decline or hidden continuity, except for Venosa, where there is an almost unbroken epigraphic record as well as written evidence to Jewish settlement, including in villages around the town.[17] Definitely by the early tenth century Jewish life had picked up again, on the mainland in places like Gaeta, Benevento, Capua, Naples, Salerno, Siponto, Lavello (?), Trani, Taranto, Oria, Bari and Otranto, and in abundance in Arab Sicily. The latter, superbly documented by the Cairo *Genizah*, saw a considerable influx from North Africa and Egypt.[18] By then the contours of Jewish culture in southern Italy, as compared to late antiquity, had decisively changed. Funerary conventions demonstrate that up to the sixth century Italian Jews articulated their identity in the idiom of their surroundings, especially by the use of Greek, which connected them to the Hellenistic–Byzantine diaspora. Now they did so exclusively in Hebrew, employing the rabbinical vocabulary and mind-set of the Mesopotamian houses of Talmudic learning, as well as developing a rich religious poetry drawing from Palestinian sources.[19] Myths of origin too point to the re-establishment of intellectual ties between southern European Jewry and the centres of religious learning and law in the Middle East.[20]

Visigothic Spain (not including Septimania, which is treated below with Gaul) confronts us with an enigma. From the fifth and sixth centuries there is a small number of epigraphs, four or five altogether from Tarragona and Tortosa on the eastern coast, as well as some legislation.[21] At most this hints at modest Jewish life in a few places. In stark contrast, there is a spate of documentation setting in immediately with the Visigoths' conversion to Catholicism (589) and running up to the Arab conquest of 711. This derives almost entirely

[15] *Codex Theodosianus* XII.I.158 = Linder (1987), no. 29.
[16] Noy (1993), *passim*; Linder (1997), pp. 417–43; Colafemmina (1980).
[17] Leon (1953/54); Klar (1944/74), p. 16 = Salzman (1924), p. 68. [18] Above, note 7.
[19] Simonsohn (1974); Zimmels (1966); Klar (1944/74), pp. 55–108; cf. Schirmann (1966).
[20] In southern Italy: Klar (1944/74), pp. 12–16 = Salzman (1924), pp. 62–7; cf. Bonfil (1983). In Spain: Cohen (1960–61). In Narbonne: Régné (1912/81), pp. 13–30, cf. Grabois (1997).
[21] Noy (1993), pp. 247–61; Linder (1997), pp. 217–33 (*Lex Visigothorum* or *Breviarum*).

from ecclesiastical and royal legislation, with one clearly influencing the other in a rising spiral of missionary zeal.[22] In the same polemical vein run theological and historical treatises, by Isidore of Seville, Julian of Toledo and some lesser authors.[23] The sheer bulk and fervour of these writings are unlike anything else encountered in early medieval Europe. Scholarship has usually understood this as a response to a tangible challenge, of proselytising, economic or social domination, or other manifestations of Jewish expansionism. Only a substantial Iberian Jewry, a force to be reckoned with, could have been capable of generating such a threat. From there a Jewish aristocracy of landholders, international merchants and slave traders has been postulated.[24] However, outside legal and theological polemics there is no evidence for this assumption and the inferences drawn from it. The incongruity makes sense if understood as representing separate phenomena: on one hand, for political and religious purposes not yet clear, an escalating obsession with Judaism as declared enemy to be eradicated; on the other hand rather few genuine Jews, who in the course of the seventh century were apparently forced to convert, become crypto-Jews or emigrate. The collaboration of Iberian Jews with the Arab invaders of 711 has been adduced as support for the traditional view. Examination of the sources, however, has found this 'fifth column' to be a myth.[25] It belongs to the highly popular topic of 'Jewish treason', whose literary history can be traced back to the hagiographic account of the siege of Visigothic Arles in 508.[26] Developed in Visigothic Spain and Septimania and also by expatriate Spaniards, it is a literary invention serving polemical purposes. Real Jews in Visigothic Spain thus appear to have been less than a significant entity, even though as an idea they loomed very large in the minds of rulers and churchmen.

Some hundred years after the conquest of Andalusia sources in three languages start speaking of Jews.[27] They bear Arab names, speak and write Arabic and appear thoroughly adjusted to the North African–Oriental Jewry to which the Cairo *Genizah* bears such eloquent testimony. Thus it stands to reason that after 711 a sizeable immigration from North Africa took place, which established *Sepharad*, a new Iberian Jewry with a different cultural profile and an order of magnitude unlike any Jewish population outside the Middle East. Only there could be found a 'Jewish town where there are no Gentiles', Lucena

22 Linder (1997), pp. 484–538 (Toledo III–XVIII), 257–332 (LV). On this legislation, see also Barbero and Loring, chapter 7 above.

23 Albert (1990); Cohen (1999), pp. 95–122; González-Salinero (1999).

24 Thus the thesis of Bachrach (1977) and Lotter (1999).

25 Roth (1976); Toch (2001b), pp. 474–7; see also Katz (1937), pp. 114–17. On the events leading up to the Arab conquest of Spain, see Barbero and Loring, chapter 13 above.

26 Cyprianus, *Vita S. Caesarii*, *MGH SRM* III, p. 468.

27 Mann (1973), pp. 485–7; Ashtor (1964); Baer (1929). Cf. Beinart (1992), pp. 14–20; Roth (1994), pp. 73–112.

south of Córdoba. The Babylonian sage writing this in the mid-ninth century exaggerated only slightly, as borne out by slightly later Arabic sources.[28] Jews lived in nearly all major towns and apparently also in many more small ones, as well as in villages. They are explicitly mentioned in Córdoba, Seville, Calsena, Lucena, Granada, Illiberi, Badjana, Jaén, Toledo, Calatayud and Saragossa. In this climate flourished personalities like Hasdai ibn Shaprut (*c.*915–*c.*970/5), physician and senior diplomat to emir 'Abd al-Rahman III of Córdoba, prolific letter-writer, tireless defender of Jews abroad, and patron to a circle of Hebrew-Arabic poets as well as to Rabbinical learning.[29] As in the Italian case sketched above, the Jewish culture emerging in Spain drew from the centres of learning and law in the Middle East to develop within a short time a distinctive profile of its own, in which Arab influences were a major component. These were indeed the beginnings of a Sephardic 'golden age' of medieval Jewish life.[30] The demographic upswing so noticeable in al-Andalus appears to have carried Jewish life also into Christian lands. From the ninth century onwards Jews, some of them called by Arabic names, appear sparsely in the north-east in places like Gerona, Barcelona, Tarragona and Tortosa, as well as in the countryside; in the north in Puento Castro, Castrojeriz near Burgos, León, Sahagún and Belorado; in the west in Coimbra, Corunna, Mérida and Béja.[31] Despite occasional manifestations of religious zeal, the exigencies of border warfare and colonisation appear to have led rulers of the Christian principalities to adopt a more tolerant attitude than their Visigothic ancestors.

In Roman Gaul Jews had left only some fleeting traces, probably of itinerant merchants.[32] The epigraphic record is limited, late and confined to the south: four inscriptions between the seventh and the tenth centuries from Narbonne, Auch, Arles and Vienne.[33] Against such scantiness, for two hundred years (449–647/53) there is quite a profusion of literary and legal sources: letters of Sidonius Apollinaris and Pope Gregory I, hagiography by Gregory of Tours and others, Gregory's *Histories* of course, and the councils of the Septimanian and the Frankish church, altogether thirteen between 465 (Vannes) and 647/53 (Chalon-sur-Saône). This richness has uniformly been viewed as confirmation for a substantial Jewry established all over Gaul. However, a closer look at the sources, both as literary genres and by themselves, raises some questions.

[28] Mann (1973), p. 487; Máillo Salgado (1993). Bachrach (1977), pp. 69–70, by mistaking this Andalusian town for Ausona (Vich) in Catalonia, argues for the systematic employment of Jewish fighters, settlers and officials in the establishment of the Spanish March.

[29] Ashtor (1973), pp. 155–227; but cf. Roth (1994), pp. 79–86; Cohen (1960/61), pp. 115–19.

[30] Cohen (1960/61), pp. 94, 113–23; Ashtor (1973), pp. 228–63, 382–402; the articles in Beinart (1992); Assis (1995). For a cautionary note, cf. Cohen (1994).

[31] Cantera Burgos (1966); Ashtor (1973), p. 116; Romano (1991).

[32] Thus my reading of the evidence adduced by Blumenkranz (1969) and (1974).

[33] Noy (1993), pp. 263–70, 281–3.

Among the stock miracles performed by holy bishops we find the conversion to Christianity of the Jews of their town.[34] Given the widespread Augustinian notion of the Jews as the proverbial unbelievers but eventual witnesses to Christian truth,[35] making them see the light is indeed a feat worthy of a holy bishop and clear proof for his saintliness. In addition, such performance heals dissent and re-establishes harmony within the city, yet another rhetorical task of hagiography pointed out by recent scholarship. This double purpose also animates the hagiographic accounts of Jews lamenting the dead bishop of their town.[36] In a similar vein, they are made advocates for the saint's power, for example when one Jew's sarcasm sets in profile a healing miracle performed by St Martin at Bordeaux.[37] On the strength of these texts the existence of organised communities has been asserted for a number of places – Tournai, Paris, Nantes, Tours, Orléans, Bourges, Bordeaux, Uzès. Unconfirmed by other evidence, such literary devices are hard to accept as speaking of actually existing Jews. In consequence, the notion of an early medieval settlement by Jews of central, western and northern Gaul is untenable, with the possible exception of Clermont. This does not rule out occasional appearances of individuals in these regions. Settled communities, apparently reaching back to Roman times, did however exist in Narbonne, Arles and Marseilles. They should be seen as part of the littoral Mediterranean pattern characteristic of late antiquity and the very early medieval period.

Between the mid-seventh and the mid-eighth centuries no sources mention Jews in Frankish lands. Of the time of Charlemagne there is some anecdotal and legislative evidence for Jews in the emperor's entourage and, slightly, elsewhere.[38] The references do imply the existence of roving merchants, in one case of a physician, but not yet of settled communities, as has been asserted for instance in Aachen. First indications for change emerge during and after Louis the Pious' reign. Hinting at a likely source for growth, there is at least one documented and one more possible case of immigration from Spain.[39] Additional evidence from the eighth and ninth centuries points to sizeable, probably growing numbers of Jews in the south.[40] From there settlement spread out along the Rhône river to the centre of France, to Vienne, Lyons,

34 Twice in Bourges: *MGH AA* IV.2, p. 24; *MGH SRM* IV, pp. 374–5. In Clermont: Gregory, *Hist.* V.11, ed. Buchner, I, p. 298; Venantius Fortunatus, *Carmina* V.5, *MGH AA* IV.1, pp. 107–12. In Uzès: Aronius (1902), p. 12.

35 Blumenkranz (1949); Cohen (1999), pp. 23–71.

36 Toch (2001b), pp. 469–74, with references.

37 Gregory, *Libri Quattuor de Virtutibus S. Martini*, III.50, *MGH SRM* I.2, p. 644; similar in Gregory, *Hist.* V.6; IV.5, ed. Buchner, I, p. 292; II, p. 8.

38 Aronius (1902), nos. 68, 71–5, 80.

39 Linder (1997), pp. 341–2, 367.

40 Noy (1993), pp. 281–3; Linder (1997), pp. 443–4, 368–74; Dhuoda, *Liber Manualis*, *PL* 106, col. 117. For legends tied to Narbonne see Grabois (1997).

Mâcon and Châlons.[41] Slowly in the course of the tenth and definitely by the early eleventh century, proper communities become visible in Maine-Anjou, Bourgogne, Champagne, Lorraine and Normandy.[42] Such growth is clearly confirmed by the onset of intellectual production of French Ashkenazic scholars, especially their religious-legal deliberations, which now attest to community institutions and a settled way of life. Their writings become distinctive enough to reconstruct biographies of some sages. By the eleventh century this body of learning and law-finding became independent enough to dissociate itself from the tutelage of the Babylonian sages.[43]

The growth of the northern French community is tied to the parallel development, chronologically and in terms of cultural affinity, of German Jewry.[44] Here too no continuity can be assumed from the Jews apparent in late antique centres like Cologne and Trier.[45] Here too in the ninth and early tenth centuries some brief hints attest to itinerant merchants. In the course of the next century some more must have arrived, from Italy as well as from France.[46] Their first places of residence, at the end of the ninth century, were Metz and slightly later Mainz. Only during the second half of the tenth century is there sparse evidence from Hebrew sources for some elements of organised structures. By the late eleventh century these had expanded to populous and thriving communities at Trier, Cologne, Mainz, Speyer, Worms, Regensburg and Prague, and probably also at Magdeburg. Ashkenazic Jewry in both its northern French and its German branches began to expand geographically at the very end of our period. In England the arrival of Jews, from Normandy, is clearly tied to the Conquest. The few Jews making an appearance in eleventh-century eastern Europe apparently came from Byzantium as well as from Germany.[47] In both peripheries, more substantial settlement only took place after *c.*1100.

The early settlement history of Jews in Europe should then distinguish between two spheres, south and north, and two periods, from late antiquity to *c.*800, and afterwards until *c.*1050/1100. Continuity from classical times in probably declining numbers is found only around the Mediterranean seaboard: in Byzantium, in Italy from Rome southwards, and in a few places in southern

[41] Linder (1997), pp. 333–8, 341–3, 368–9; *Agobardi Opera, Epist.* 11, 14, pp. 195, 231.

[42] For the Latin sources see Devroey (2000), pp. 347–53, for the Hebrew ones Gross (1897/1969), *passim.*

[43] Agus (1966); Grossman (1995).

[44] Toch (1998a), pp. 5–6, 80–2.

[45] For Cologne such continuity has been postulated by arbitrary archaeological interpretation, cf. Toch (2001a), pp. 12–13, note 26. For the archaeological record see Lapp (1993).

[46] Grossman (1975) and (1982). Cf. Schwarzfuchs (1980) for an alternative view, by which the communities of northern France derived from immigrants from Germany.

[47] Mann (1920), II, p. 192; Starr (1939), pp. 183, 192–3; Agus (1965), nos. XIX, XXI, LXV. For the imponderables of the Chazars' kingdom, Kievan Russia and Hungary see Dunlop, Ettinger and Scheiber in Roth (1966).

France and eastern Spain. By the end of the ninth century new growth, slow at first and then accelerating, becomes visible everywhere. In Spain (and possibly also in Sicily) this is clearly tied to the more favourable Arab regime, to immigration from North Africa and to new links forged with the Oriental centres of Jewish learning. In Italy and southern France the sources for expansion are still obscure, but trends are similar. In central and northern Gaul and western Germany, called in Hebrew *Ashkenaz* or *Lothir*, Jewish presence was a new phenomenon wholly dependent on immigration from the south. From there it drew demographic and cultural resources, to be transmitted and transformed with a time lag to the north. By the eleventh century both northern and southern Jewries had come of age: part of the European landscape, strong enough to claim their intellectual independence from the centres of religious authority in the Middle East.

OCCUPATIONS

One view has hitherto dominated the understanding of Jewish livelihoods in the early Middle Ages: privileged and protected by rulers, uniquely equipped by their Talmudic law, community organisation and family ties, as well as by inbred inclination and/or the Diaspora experience, Jews were the proverbial long-distance traders connecting Europe with the Middle East and Muslim Spain. In the earlier period they are thought to have done so along with other Orientals; from the Carolingian period and into the eleventh century on their own. For many scholars they even possessed a veritable monopoly over commerce, particularly in the slave trade.[48] This notion has to be discarded. It is clearly tied to contemporary (nineteenth- and twentieth-century) polemics and apologetics. It assumes a system and purpose where none existed. Its documentary basis is exceedingly thin and lends itself to a more convincing, even though less glamorous interpretation.

At the beginning of our period Pope Gregory I in his letters affords a reasonably comprehensive gaze over parts of the Mediterranean scene. His evidence matches the information provided by late antique epigraphy from the city of Rome, indicating a pattern of varied occupations. Jews appear in substantial numbers as *coloni* on papal estates in Sicily, but also as possessors of estates worked by Christian *coloni* and *originarii* in Etruria; as a buyer of precious metal and plate; as a ship owner heavily in debt and deprived of his vessel in Palermo; moving between Marseilles and Rome on their business, probably as merchants; and settled in Naples, as purveyors of slaves from Gaul for

48 For the extensive historiography see Devroey (2000) and Toch (1998a and b, 1999, 2000a and b, 2001a and b).

officials in their town.[49] In other sources Jewish owners sail their ship along the Provençal coast, while at Naples Jews take upon themselves to provide the besieged city with food.[50] Some merchants appear in the Byzantine space of the sixth and seventh centuries.[51] In Constantinople there is a glass worker, admittedly suspect: his trade conveniently supplies the stage and means for a miracle, the furnace in which his boy, converted to Christianity, miraculously survives.[52] At Tours there arrived a Jew in order to realise a debt owed him in lieu of public taxes, promptly to be murdered by a converted Jew. Some merchants in *species* (spices?), indeed *magna species*, are active in Clermont, and so is one at King Chilperic's court, 'who served him as a buyer of spices'.[53] It is difficult to decide whether a Jewish physician at Bourges was real or a literary invention designed to highlight a healing miracle.[54] Given the chronology of settlement outlined above, the few Jews roaming the Merovingian realm most probably were visitors from the south.

Later data augment the range of Mediterranean livelihoods and point to a quickening economic pulse. In northern Italy a Jew formerly associated with Charlemagne's court was held to be an expert in precious metalwork. In mainland Italy there were additional practitioners of this craft, and considerably more merchants and craftsmen.[55] In Byzantium, Muslim Spain and Sicily, one finds yet more merchants, and, significantly, craftsmen and entrepreneurs in textiles, tanning and, to judge from slightly later evidence, silk working.[56] For the eleventh century the Cairo *Genizah* evinces an intensive trade by Jews between Egypt, the Maghreb, Muslim Spain and Arab Sicily, in which Jews

49 Gregory, *Registrum Epistularum* II.38, V.7, VIII.23, IV.21, I.45, VI.29, IX.105 (see Linder (1997), pp. 423, 428–9, 432, 426–7, 418, 431, 436); *Epistulae* IX.40, *MGH Epp.* II, p. 68. A reference to Jewish coloni in Clermont (Venantius Fortunatus, *Carmina* V.5, *MGH AA* IV, p. 110) is probably nothing more than literary allegory, cf. Goffart (1985), pp. 486–7.

50 Gregory of Tours, *Liber In Gloria Confessorum*, c.95, *MGH SRM* I.2, p. 809; Procopius, *Gothic War* I.8, p. 85.

51 *Doctrina Jacobi*, pp. 214–19; Nelson and Starr (1939).

52 Evagrius, *Ecclesiastical History* IV.36, p. 241; Gregory of Tours, *Glory of the Martyrs*, c.9, trans. Van Dam (1988), p. 29; *Georgii Syncelli Ecloga Chronographica* II, p. 654. But cf. Benjamin of Tudela and the Cairo *Genizah* on later glassmakers: Adler (1907), pp. 26, 30; Goitein (1967), index. In early modern Germany this was a Jewish craft.

53 Gregory of Tours, *Hist.* VI.5; VII.23, ed. Buchner, II, pp. 8, 118.

54 Gregory of Tours, *Hist.* V.6, ed. Buchner, I, p. 292.

55 *MGH SRL*, p. 372; Linder (1997), pp. 349–50, 159, 375–6, 384–5; Starr (1939), pp. 124, 161, 169; Mann (1931), p. 24; Milano (1954), *passim*; Colorni (1980), p. 260.

56 Merchants: Mann (1920), I, pp. 87–93, 204–5; II, pp. 87–92, 214, 344, 364; Starr (1939), pp. 121, 191, 214; De Lange (1996), pp. 21–7; Linder (1997), pp. 151–2, 159. Crafts: Starr (1939), pp. 137, 148, 167–9; Goitein (1967), p. 50; Bresc (1998); Jacoby (2001), esp. p. 12; Ashtor (1973), pp. 271–5; Cohen (1960/61), pp. 66–7.

of Christian Europe however did not take part.[57] Physicians remain a frequent feature, some of them metaphorical but others true historical figures, such as Shabbetai Donnolo from tenth-century Oria, the earliest medieval medical writer and a distinguished philosopher, or his contemporary, the already mentioned Hasdai ibn Shaprut in Spain.[58] Even Pope Gregory's I Jewish *coloni* of Sicily may have had eleventh-century heirs on the island of Chios, although their serfdom was probably of more of a legal than an economic nature.[59]

The ownership of agricultural land by Jews is definitely demonstrated by Latin charters of the ninth to eleventh centuries in Italy, Christian Spain, and southern and east-central France.[60] It must surely have been more widespread than is indicated by the chance survival in ecclesiastical charters. Ownership, transmission and mortgage of landed property come up many times in *Responsa* arising from actual litigation.[61] They dominate the formula books for Hebrew deeds extant from Muslim Spain and southern France.[62] Apparently non-Jews worked such lands, more often vineyards than fields, for their Jewish proprietors, sometimes in partnership arrangements suggestive of sharecropping. Significantly, of all the Mediterranean regions only Byzantium is absent from the record of Jewish landholding, perhaps because of the sorry state of the evidence. However it seems more likely that here the tight control of an inherently hostile state apparatus as well as the high degree of urbanisation indeed prevented Jewish ownership. If this was the case, the Empire's sway did not extend to southern Italy, where ownership of agricultural land is well attested.

Sparse references to landholding in northern France and Germany cannot compare to the extent of findings from the south.[63] The contrast reflects an important difference. In the north, Latin writers, when not engaged in religious

57 Ben-Sasson (1991); Simonsohn (1997); Goitein (1968), p. 211; Gil (1997), I, pp. 559–70; cf. Citarella (1971); Toch (2001c).

58 *MGH Form.*, p. 448; *Annals of St Bertin* s.a. 877; *Gesta Episcoporum Leodiensium*, c.44, *MGH SS* VII, p. 216; *Life of St Nilos*; Starr (1939), p. 162. On Donnolo see Sharf (1976).

59 Linder (1997), pp. 160–3; cf. Argenti (1966).

60 Italy: Colorni (1980), pp. 247, 248, 257; Starr (1939), p. 141, 257; *MGH Diplomata Regum et Imperatorum Germaniae* II.2, p. 520. Spain: Romano (1991), pp. 328–31; Linder (1997), p. 559; Baer (1929), p. 2; Blumenkranz (1960), p. 23, nn. 132–5. France: Linder (1997), pp. 443–4, 365–75; Latouche (1966); Blumenkranz (1960), pp. 24–30, and (1989).

61 Work in progress by the author. 62 Rivlin (1994); Mutius (1994), (1996) and (1997).

63 Metz before 945: Blumenkranz (1960), p. 29, n. 195; near Orléans before 972: Halphen and Lot (1908), p. 82; eleventh-century Normandy: Golb (1998), pp. 552–3; tenth-century Regensburg: *MGH Diplomata Regum et Imperatorum Germaniae* II.1, p. 279. This does not yet include the Hebrew record, see note 61.

polemics, perceived Jews only as merchants and physicians.[64] They were not wrong in this observation. In the Hebrew record, from the second half of the tenth century onwards, commerce is the patent mainstay of livelihood in central and northern France as well as in western Germany. This was succinctly stated by Gershom ben Jehuda 'Light of the Exile' of Mainz, the foremost Ashkenazic religious authority of his time (*c.*960–1028): 'Their [the Jews'] livelihood depends on their commerce/merchandise.'[65] The Hebrew record also allows corrections to some inflated inferences drawn from Latin sources. Movement of merchants was plentiful but took place mostly along local circuits and well-known itineraries between inland markets, at times also abroad, to and from Hungary, Poland, possibly also Russia. There is very little of the treasures of intercontinental commerce, nothing at all of the slave trade. A blend of staple goods and more costly merchandise was bought, transported and sold: salt, wine, dyes, medicine, salted fish, cattle, hides and pelts, ready-made garments and textiles, also silk, gilded and copper vessels, and some precious metals. The customers were bishops and priests, in one case the treasurer of a bishop, affluent ladies including a queen of Hungary (the only royalty mentioned in the sources), magnates and counts, in short the upper classes. A foremost issue in the discussions of the rabbis is the deplorable fact that Jews borrowed money from Jews, by direct interest-bearing loan in the north and by mortgaging landed property in the south. Creating capital for commercial ventures was thus a problem at this early stage, and so was competition in a constricted and highly personalised market. When rivalry got out of hand, hatred, murder and the instigation of Christian authorities against the Jews could follow.[66] Among the earliest community legislation two ordinances were designed to curb such anarchy: *Herem ha-yishuv*, which gave the community the right to veto the settlement of newcomers; and *Maarufiya* (a term of Arabic derivation), by which the community assigned a potential customer to a single merchant.[67] Money changing and bullion transactions were part of the merchant's activities, important enough to be regulated by religious authority so as to avoid the taking of interest between Jews. In this time of monetary dearth merchants certainly made some funds available as loans, especially to their privileged customers, with and without interest. However, most of the references adduced for early

[64] Notker, *Gesta Karoli* I.16; II.14, *MGH SRG* XII, pp. 19–20, 77; Linder (1997), pp. 348, 344, 333, 336, 341, 351, 349, 377–8, 380, 382; *MGH Leges* I, p. 363, cap. 19.

[65] Mutius (1984), I, p. 58. Further references in Toch (1998b) and (2000b). See also Brody (1998), p. 134, for merchants visiting a fair, possibly St Denis in the mid-ninth century.

[66] See the Hebrew horror tale, embellished as an instance of religious persecution, placed in late tenth-century France: Habermann, *Book of Persecutions*, p. 12, cf. Chazan (1970). Incidentally, it uncannily parallels Gregory of Tours: Gregory, *Hist.* VI.17, ed. Buchner, II, pp. 34–6.

[67] Rabinowitz (1945); Eidelberg (1953).

money lending are better understood as debts arising from the provision of goods.[68] Despite the clear preponderance of trade as livelihood, not each and every Jew was a merchant. There were lowly craftsmen as well as Jews and Jewesses of the serving classes, even slaves. Clearly, these people had no legal or economic footing of their own and must have existed as part of the households of affluent merchant families.

During the whole period under consideration, such households also included non-Jewish slaves, a fact that gave rise to great ecclesiastical agitation. Much of this is yet more religious polemic, making use of the metaphors of slavery and enslavement in order to point out the scandalous corruption of order: Jews are on top rather than at the bottom, where they belong according to Augustinian theology. Modern historians have usually taken this barrage of indignation as evidence for a slave trade dominated by Jews from Merovingian times and into the eleventh century. Amongst others they point to an infrastructure of Jewish 'colonies' spread over the entire European-Asiatic continent, which must have served as a relay system of slave transport. But most of these entrepôts, for instance the much-quoted Verdun, had yet no Jewish population at all. Our recent re-evaluation of the Latin, Hebrew and Arabic sources has found unambiguous references to only two European Jews actually dealing in slaves, one in the sixth and the other in the ninth century. In addition, one of the numerous synodal exhortations might possibly relate to actual slave trade (by Christians and Jews). All other texts speak of slaves employed in households, possibly also by merchants as transport personnel. Given even some additional unrecorded slave traders, this is still a far cry from a network conveying many thousands of European slaves, indeed a whole army of *Sakaliba*, from the eastern fringes of Europe to the realm of Iberian as well as oriental Islam.[69]

Did early medieval Jews wield a mercantile hegemony or even monopoly? For a number of considerations, the answer must be no. To begin with, one must beware of exaggeration. For example, one scholar who sought to highlight the influence of the Jews in early medieval Europe described a certain Priscus as 'a wealthy Jewish merchant and government official who dealt with kings and controlled the mint at Chalon-sur-Saône'.[70] If we are to believe Gregory

[68] For instance Dhuoda, note 40 above; or archbishop Anno of Cologne, *Vita Annonis* III.11; *MGH SS* XI, p. 502.

[69] Gregory I, *Epistulae* VI.29; IX.105, Linder (1997), pp. 429–30, 436; *Agobardi Opera*, p. 195; Meaux–Paris 845–6, can. 76: Linder (1997), p. 548. For the sources as well as for scholarly flights of fancy, most notably by Charles Verlinden, see Toch (1998b), (1999) and (2000a). The most recent analysis of the slave trade by McCormick (2002), pp. 733–77, interprets some sources differently. Slave trading by Jews in the Muslim world still awaits elucidation, but see the negative assessment of Goitein (1968), p. 140, and Roth (1994), pp. 153–62.

[70] Bachrach (1977), p. 56. The source (note 54 above): 'Iudaeus quidam Priscus nomine, qui ei ad species quoemendas familiaris erat'.

of Tours in this case, Priscus was indeed Jewish, probably a merchant, and dealt with King Chilperic. The rest of the statement is simply not justified by the source in question. Scholars have frequently been led astray by the phrase *Judei et ceteri mercatores* ('Jews and other merchants'), which appears a number of times in slight variations.[71] Rather than read this as Jews the proverbial merchants, with the 'other merchants' added just as an afterthought, it is better understood as a simple distinction by the main trait apparent to the writers of these texts: Jews by their religious adherence, Christians by occupation, thus 'merchants, Jews and others'. The very phrase constitutes irrefutable proof, backed up by the whole range of modern research, for the existence of merchant groups other than Jews in Carolingian and later times.[72] Ibn Khordadbeh's mid-ninth-century account on the *Radhanites*, hitherto a crown witness for European Jews trading from Spain to India and back again, has definitely been proven to relate to oriental Jews.[73] Their economic contacts followed a very different pattern and cast no light on the position of European Jews in international commerce, as amply confirmed by the Cairo *Genizah*. Established substantially by *c.*1000, written in a period of commercial expansion in the Mediterranean and by merchants who were intimately informed of the affairs of their business partners, this huge repository of business information mentions numerous merchants from Europe, but hardly any European Jews. The ones noted, from Byzantium, came to attention only when they were taken by Arab pirates in the Mediterranean and carried to Alexandria for ransom.[74] Consequently, if a trade system existed, Jews of Europe and of the Muslim world did not operate it in tandem.[75] *Responsa* literature mentions frequent exchanges between scholars, sages and students, but almost no commercial contacts even within Europe, between *Ashkenaz* and *Sepharad*. Once the evidence misread for slave trading has been discounted, as it must be, the whole intercontinental trade system is reduced to the humbler proportions indicated above. Such proportions agree with population numbers, which during most of the period were yet slight (in the south) or non-existent (in the north). When numbers began to grow in the eleventh century, powers much more significant than the Jews were already dominating the trade of Europe.

In the south, Jews found livelihood in varied occupations, including crafts, trade and the working of landed property. In the north, they were indeed mainly

[71] Linder (1997), pp. 344, 349, 377, 380, 382, 384, 389; *MGH SS* III, p. 758.

[72] For instance Verhulst (1970) and (1995); Devroey (2000); McCormick (2002).

[73] Gil (1974). For the source, Pellat (1993).

[74] Above, note 56, the references by Mann (1920) and Starr (1939), cf. Goitein, p. 211. One possible exception, though not datable, is a Byzantine Jew in Egypt (?) in contact with Crete: De Lange (1996), pp. 21–7.

[75] Cf. Toch (2001c).

engaged in commerce, and their arrival from the later Carolingian period onwards is one indicator for the renewal of commercial activity. However, at no point did Jewish trade constitute the critical mass needed to provide the bridge between Occident and Orient. Thus three interrelated myths should be laid to rest: of Jewish ubiquity, of commercial hegemony and of the slave trade.

JEWS IN CHRISTIAN SOCIETY

For the attitudes of Jews towards their host society there exists one primary source, extant in a number of variants, the acerbic Hebrew travesty of the Christian Gospel known as *Toldot Yeshu* (The Life of Jesus). This source is almost impossible to place in time and may well stem from outside Europe, even though Christians had known of its existence since Agobard of Lyons.[76] *Toldot Yeshu* and other indications in liturgy and religious poetry point to a 'polemical imperative' in early medieval Jewish culture that is almost the matching image of the Christian approach to Judaism. Sources extant from the twelfth century onwards indicate a complex mixture of hesitant attraction and belligerent repulsion, acculturation and at the same time self-imposed as well as enforced separation.[77] Modifying the traditional picture of isolation and segregation, a recent re-examination of the religious polemics of medieval Christians and Jews thus sees an ongoing two-way traffic, in which each side sought to appropriate the other's symbols of God's love, holiness and purity.[78]

Of Christian attitudes towards Jews we know more than of any other aspect. To judge from the main extant body of sources, the writings of churchmen, the basic attitude towards Jews and Judaism was a mixture of confrontation, agitation, and frustration at the negligible concrete results. Attempts at explanation have usually viewed early medieval Judaism as a single entity endowed with remarkable resources and posing a tangible threat. According to this view, it must have been allied at different points to secular, typically royal interests, in order to have been able to defeat much of the ecclesiastical interference. This in turn has been expanded to constitute a 'Jewish policy' of kings, favourable to an important constituency of Jews and at variance with a supposedly uniform ecclesiastical line. In this view ecclesiastics reacted to a real challenge and to concrete issues.

An alternative approach takes as point of departure the existence in Christianity of a 'polemical imperative', which employed Judaism as a body of beliefs

[76] Krauss (1902); cf. Bonfil (1994b).
[77] Sapir Abulafia (1985); Marcus (1996); Toch (1998a), pp. 120–42.
[78] Yuval (1999) and (2000).

and behaviour in direct denial of Christian truth.[79] In this discourse the Jew's function was one of illustration, of personifying such attitudes. However, for theological reasons succinctly argued by Augustine, rejection was to be balanced by a modicum of toleration of the Jews as bookkeepers of and eventual witnesses to Christian truth. Both principles were laid down in an extensive and much copied body of imperial constitutions, especially the *Codex Theodosianus*, and in numerous writings of the Patristic period.[80] They permeated also the genres of history, hagiography and ecclesiastical law-making. Playing out the principle of rejection, theological treatises, polemical tracts and synodal legislation re-enacted the stubborn wickedness attributed to Jews in the Christian exegesis of the Old and New Testaments. In hagiography and historiography, Jews were assigned the complementary role implicit in the principle of toleration, of mouthpieces of denial eventually swayed to testify to Christian truth and sanctity. By the onset of the Middle Ages the vocabulary, grammar and syntax of this ambiguous discourse were already in place. For internal ecclesiastical developments only recently explored, the later Carolingian period saw a new surge of theological anti-Judaism.[81] Thus, 'constructions of Jews and Judaism, embedded in the dictates of Christian theology and hermeneutics, continued to enjoy a life of their own'.[82]

The writings thus produced make up the vast majority of sources at our disposal. They dwell upon a small number of concrete issues – the scandal of slaves in Jewish hands, of Jews tempting or forcing Christians into proselytism, of Jews lording it over Christians. Jewish proselytising appears as the most important bone of contention, if one were to judge by the frequency with which it was addressed in writing. The literary setting is usually the same, positioning wily Jews bent on seduction against simple Christian folk incapable of protecting their own faith.[83] Scholarship has by and large accepted such texts as evidence for a genuine and successful Jewish drive to win converts. The mere logic of slavery was thought to provide proof, since slaves are by definition helpless objects for the designs of their masters. Jewish slave dealers too have been pressed into service: they buy up slaves in order to swell the flock of Israel.[84] The converts of late antiquity and the early Middle Ages were thought to be numerous enough to produce the substantial Jewish population of central and northern France emerging in the eleventh century.[85] There is

[79] Cohen (1999), pp. 5–65, the quotation on p. 39.

[80] Linder (1978), pp. 400–13. For the texts and authors see Linder (1987); Blumenkranz (1963); Schreckenberg (1995).

[81] Albert (1996); Heil (1998a and b). [82] Cohen (1999), p. 94.

[83] For instance Amulo, *PL* 116, cols. 170D–171A.

[84] For instance Blumenkranz (1960), p. 160. Cf. Toch (2000a), for more examples of dubious source readings.

[85] Bautier (1991).

little probability or evidence to support such claims. It is hard to see slave traders, largely imagined as argued above, endangering their stock by circumcision. They also present us with a strange breed of dealers ready to abstain from profit for religious merit: devout Jews would have to abide by the Talmudic precept forbidding to sell a slave, once made Jewish, to a Gentile. What evidence there is for proselytising makes sense solely in regard to house-slaves, not at all to slaves as merchandise, nor to slaves of (again, imagined) *latifundia* work gangs. Even if each and every Jewish family did take part in the drive for converts, the limited Jewish population argued above could not but produce a limited number of converts. The results are indeed not impressive. A very small number of epitaphs from Rome do mention proselytes, and so does a single one from outside the city, all pre-medieval.[86] From the period 500–1050 we know of just six certain proselytes in all of Europe. They came from respected families; and were mostly churchmen who arrived at their decision after much soul-searching.[87] In the rich Hebrew material from Germany of the end of the eleventh century there are three to four proselytes out of the over 1200 Jews and Jewesses known by name and murdered in 1096 in Mainz, Worms and Cologne.[88] Thus throughout our period proselytism, while existing, can hardly be called substantial and appears to have been mostly a preoccupation of panicky churchmen. Consequently, the topic of a 'missionary contest' between Judaism and Christianity must be relegated to the realm of literary discourse.[89]

On the other hand, there is a much better case for Jews turning to Christianity. Discounting miraculous conversions by holy bishops and some dubious indications of forced baptism,[90] there is enough evidence to conclude that throughout our period individuals did indeed give in to religious doubt, enticement or pressure.[91] In Byzantium periodically, and in Spain for almost a century before the Arab conquest, the forced conversion of Jews as a collective

86 In Rome seven out of 595 identifiable persons: Noy (1995), nos. 62, 218, 224, 392(?), 489, 491, 57; outside Rome one person out of 298: Noy (1993), no. 52.

87 Blumenkranz (1960), pp. 161–2, 166–7; Golb (1987), pp. 2–15, 21–31. A Christian lady, converted and married to a Jew in Narbonne, probably belongs in the thirteenth rather than in the eleventh century: Mann (1931), pp. 31–3.

88 Neubauer and Stern (1892), pp. 10/103 = pp. 56/184, 22/126; Salfeld (1898), p. 110.

89 Contra Blumenkranz (1961) and (1960), pp. 159–211. On the misuse of legislative and literary evidence for late antique proselytising, cf. Rutgers (1995b); Goodman (1994).

90 Above, note 34; Stemberger (1993).

91 Sidonius Apollinaris, *Epistolae* VIII.13, *MGH AA* VIII, p. 144; Gregory, *Hist.* VI.17, ed. Buchner, II, pp. 34–6; Gregory, *Registrum Epistularum* I.70, PL 77, col. 526B; Gregory, *Registrum Epistularum* I.45, I.69, II.38, IV.31; V.7; VIII.23, see Linder (1997), pp. 418, 420–1, 423, 427–9, 432; *Doctrina Jacobi*; Starr (1939), p. 137; Amulo, *PL* 116, col. 170D; *MGH Epp.* V, p. 239; Aronius, *Regesten*, p. 51; Halphen and Lot (1908), p. 82; Salzman (1924), p. 80; Baer (1929), p. 2; Cantera Burgos (1966), p. 361 and note 11; Linder (1997), p. 438; De Lange (1996), p. 22/3; Habermann, *Book of Persecutions*, p. 11.

became government policy and must surely have had some results. In France and Germany of the tenth and eleventh centuries, sources tell of instances of baptism forced on whole communities.[92] Some of these are clearly made-up literary exercises in Christian holiness. Others were contemplated and some actually attempted, even though their impact was yet far removed from the ferocity of compulsory conversion in 1096. Conversion was serious enough a problem to trouble the most important sages of eleventh-century *Ashkenaz*. Out of this tension they eventually developed the religious-legal principle that apostasy does not remove Jewishness: 'Even Though He Sinned He Remains an Israelite.'[93] In the period 500–700 Jews also had to cope with mob attacks on their synagogues, usually fanned by zealous bishops.[94] This urban agitation looks very much a continuation of the eastern Mediterranean pattern of taking religious arguments to the street, and disappears in the following period.

In contrast to such instances of confrontation, there is also evidence for more relaxed relations. In sixth-century Naples and Arles as well as in tenth-century Oria, three places with considerable Jewish populations, Jews defended their town alongside Christians.[95] Throughout the entire period church synods produced prohibitions against clerics and plain Christians marrying, drinking, eating, bathing, celebrating, lodging and even praying with Jews.[96] Though copied from one council to the other and thus possibly yet more rhetoric, such exhortations may be an indication of a daily life different from the fury of religious polemics. Even allowing for lots of hyperbole, a sense of close cohabitation pervades Agobard of Lyons' epistles of the earlier ninth century against the Jews of his town.[97] An approximation of normality and tension dwelling together can be gained from the letters of Pope Gregory I.[98] For Gregory, Jews should be converted if possible, without however using force and committing excessive church resources. Extreme and unlawful hostility

92 Linder (1997), pp. 622–33, Aronius, *Regesten*, nos. 123, 124, 125, 142, 144, 160; Habermann, *Book of Persecutions*, pp. 19–21. Cf. Dagron and Déroche (1998), pp. 28–38, 43–5; Chazan (1970/1); Linder (1997), pp. 414–20.

93 Grossman (1988a), pp. 122–7, 163–4, and (1995), pp. 152–5; Katz (1958).

94 Rome 508–512, Milan 523–526: Linder (1997), pp. 203–5. Ravenna 509–526: *Anonymus Valesianus*, cap. 81. Clermont 576: Venantius Fortunatus, *Carmina* 5.5, *MGH AA* IV, pp. 107–12, Gregory, *Hist.* V.11, ed. Buchner, I, p. 296, cf. Goffart (1985). Orléans before 585 (?): Gregory, *Hist.* VIII.1, ed. Buchner, II, p. 160. Terracina 591, Palermo 598, Cagliari 599, Naples 602: Gregory, *Epistulae*, Linder (1997), pp. 417, 421–2, 433–5, 438–9, 442. For the Eastern Empire, cf. Dagron and Déroche (1998), pp. 18–22.

95 Procopius, *Gothic War* I.10.90; *Vita Caesarii*, *MGH SRM* III, pp. 467–9; Italy, Roth (1966), p. 107.

96 Linder (1997), subject index, Prohibitions on Christians; *Vita Beati Ferreoli*, p. 101. Cf. Blumenkranz (1965).

97 *Agobardi Opera*, pp. 115–17, 191–5, 199–221, and esp. 231–4; cf. Cohen (1999), pp. 123–45.

98 Linder (1997), pp. 417–43. On the theological aspects of Gregory's writings see Cohen, J. (1999), pp. 73–94.

and mob violence towards them needed to be curbed. They should be defended if need be, yet not beyond the clear limits set by (Christian) Roman law. Their slaves should be encouraged to progress towards Christianity, but cautiously so as not to appear to attack private property rights. Gregory's is a single voice of realism in a world of high-tempered literary shadowboxing, yet he too was bound by the precepts laid down by the church Fathers and his own beliefs, as well as by the tensions besetting majority and minority.

What can be found of legal principles or practice does not allow for consistent Jewish status in the whole of Europe. Only in Byzantium did Jews constitute a distinctive minority group, tolerated and at the same time despised and discriminated against by Justinian law. Strongly coloured by the religious convictions of the Byzantine state, such legal standing translated into inferior social status, low-prestige occupations and residential segregation in a Jewish quarter as documented for Constantinople.[99] For other Mediterranean regions scholars have asserted undisturbed Roman citizenship and the high social status of Jews, to continue unabated until the end of our period, or alternatively to be eventually eroded by Byzantine and/or ecclesiastical influence. Roman citizenship of Jews does indeed appear in the *Breviarum*, but so do other legal principles of old. It is also mentioned as a matter of fact by Pope Gregory I.[100] Even so, it was more breached than honoured. As noted above, Gregory himself was frequently called upon to resolve clashes between legal principle and Christian zeal in regard to forced conversions and the destruction of synagogues. Besides Roman citizenship, the possession of slaves and landed property, the holding of governmental positions, and honorary titles on funeral inscriptions are seen to prove elevated social status. As already argued, the mere existence of slaves in Jewish hands does not necessarily translate into possession of large estates and thus into high social status. Jews as judges, toll officials and tax collectors are indeed mentioned in the complaints aired at ecclesiastical councils.[101] Similar to the equally frequent complaints about Jewish ownership of slaves, such texts suggest yet more of the well-known metaphor for a world in disarray: Jews lording it over Christians. Independent evidence for such offices and functions is nowhere available.[102] The epigraphic record belongs entirely to late antiquity rather than to the Middle Ages and, though not unequivocal, holds more evidence for the low social status of Jews, especially in the city

99 Jacoby (1993), pp. 129–32. See also Louth, chapter 4 above.

100 *Breviarum* II.1.10; Gregory, *Registrum Epistularum* II.6; see Linder (1997), pp. 218–19, 422.

101 Clermont 535, Macon 581/3, Paris 614, Clichy 626–627, Toledo III 589, Toledo IV 633, LV XII.3.19; Meaux-Paris 845/6, Pavia 850, Benevento (?) and Siponto *c.*900, Rome 1078: Linder (1997), pp. 320, 470, 474, 478, 479, 484, 490, 540, 541, 548, 549, 551, 559; Amulo, *PL* 116, col. 170D.

102 The Parisian toll official and minter Salomon, placed by the ninth-century *Gesta Dagoberti* in the seventh century (*MGH SRM* II, p. 413), was certainly not a Jew, if he existed at all.

of Rome, than for the opposite.[103] Given these imponderables, nothing more than the obvious can be stated. In Mediterranean regions there were some Jews of considerable social status, as indicated by landed possession, and others of a low one, as indicated by occupation, with the greater numbers probably in-between as befitting an urban population. Individual Jewish status might mesh with general status: in the late fifth century there was the Jewish client of a Christian magnate of Narbonne, one century later a Jew who had both Christian and Jewish clients.[104] By the end of our period Hebrew sources of the south of Italy and France envisage communities stratified according to intellectual distinction, ancient family lineage, and a hierarchy in which uncouth 'villagers' are at the bottom of society.[105]

In the north, Jewish status was determined by royal privilege. For over two centuries all we know comes from a small number of charters. Of these, emperor Louis the Pious granted three between 822 and 827, and Henry IV of Germany one in 1090.[106] The recipients were: 'David, grandfather of David, and Joseph and . . . (lacuna) with their spouses, living in the city of Lyons; Donatus rabbi and Samuel, his grandson'; 'Abraham, inhabitant of the city of Saragossa'. In Speyer they were 'Iudas son of Kalonymus, David son of Massulam, Moses son of Guthiel, with their associates . . . children and all those who are seen by law to depend on them'. It is abundantly clear that these privileges do not constitute a general 'Jewry law' of Carolingian to Salian times. The three ninth-century charters were nevertheless considered typical enough to be incorporated in a collection of imperial form letters. In phrases reminiscent of the language of vassalage, the persons named were received into the ruler's defence: *sub mundeburdo et defensione nostra*. This extended to freedom of property, movement and action. Specifically permitted were the acquisition and sale within the empire of non-Christian slaves and the employment of Christian servants. The beneficiaries were exempted from tolls, road dues and proof by ordeal. Living by their own law, in cases of legal deadlock in their places of residence they could appeal to the emperor. One charter illustrates the system in action: Gaudiocus appeared in 839 with his two sons before emperor Louis at Frankfurt, to have his property rights in the south of France restored to him in the face of local 'animosities, nay, depredations'.[107] Yet another Jew enjoying the status of royal *fidelis noster* served as messenger between the inhabitants of Barcelona and Charles the Bald, conveying in 876

103 Solin (1983), p. 715; Rutgers (1995a), p. 186.

104 Sidonius Apollinaris, *Epistolae* III.4, *MGH AA* VIII, p. 90; Gregory, *Hist.* VII.23, ed. Buchner, II, pp. 118–20.

105 Klar (1944/74) = Salzman (1924), cf. Bonfil (1983); Grabois (1997).

106 Linder (1997), pp. 333–8, 341–3, 391–6; cf. Patschovsky (1993), pp. 333–6.

107 Linder (1997), pp. 365–7.

news of their fealty and, in return, a pious donation of ten pounds of silver to be handed over to the bishop of the city.[108] The privileged position thus created is appropriate to the type of merchant active in the later Carolingian period. Indeed, the Carolingian charters are formally and in content very similar to privileges granted to Christian merchants. In exchange, both were expected to deliver: 'to serve our palace faithfully'. By the eleventh century rulers had no more need for merchants directly accredited to the palace, a telling indication for the growth of a market economy. However, they reserved the right to regulate and tax such merchants, Jewish and non-Jewish. This source of income comes into view when given as gift to deserving trustees, for instance the churches of Treviso, Magdeburg and Merseburg in the tenth century, those of Rimini or Gerona in the eleventh.[109]

The founding fathers' migration, settlement and dependence on rulers later found their way into legend, embellished so as to serve as emblems of social status. An anonymous Hebrew tale set in 1007 portrays Jacob ben Yekutiel, a rich and pious Jew of Rouen, who saved the Jews of the kingdom from forced conversion by personally intervening with the pope in Rome. After this accomplishment he was solemnly invited by Count Baldwin of Flanders to make his home, along with thirty fellow-Jews, in Arras.[110] In the twelfth and thirteenth centuries German Jews held that an emperor Charles had invited the ancestor of the eminent Kalonymus clan to move his residence from Lucca to Mainz.[111] In Narbonne Jews rendered the ancestor of the leading family as descendant of the Davidic dynasty from Babylonia, who had been bidden by King Pippin or Charlemagne to rule the Jews and a third of the town.[112] This tale even found its way into early French romance and was recently expanded to prove the existence of a 'Jewish princedom in feudal France'.[113] Fantasy this may be, but high social prestige was no mere wishful thinking. It is indeed indicated by the lifestyle of the Jewish upper class in eleventh-century Germany: Jewish and non-Jewish household servants and slaves, expensive garments, remarkable figures given for dowries and bequests, the expensive ornaments of women made of gold and silver. But this elite had little of the status symbol of the Mediterranean south: landed property.[114] High status is still

[108] Linder (1997), p. 367.

[109] Linder (1997), pp. 375–80, 382, 384–5; Thietmar of Merseburg, *Chronicon*, *MGH SRG* III, p. 758; Colorni (1980), p. 257; Baer (1929), p. 2.

[110] Habermann, *Book of Persecutions*, pp. 20–1, cf. Chazan (1970/1); Stow (1984).

[111] Grossman (1975).

[112] Régné (1912/81), pp. 13–30, cf. Grabois (1997). For further aspects of such legends see Bonfil (1983); Marcus (1993).

[113] Zuckerman (1972).

[114] Agus (1965), index: clothing, dowry, wedding gift, employee, inheritance, jewellery, wills and testaments. Cf. Grossman (1988b).

evident under the terribly strained circumstances of the First Crusade, when Hebrew sources speak in terms of social equality between prominent Jews (and Jewesses) and their peers amongst the Christian town burghers and episcopal *ministeriales*.[115] That all Jews could not equally acquire social prominence or riches is clearly indicated by the early emergence of organised charity, indeed at the very moment that communal institutions come into view.[116]

In conclusion, the high social rank of some Jews does not derive from ancient lineage as claimed by medieval Jewish legend, or from late antique landed property as asserted by some modern scholars.[117] Rather, it was a new phenomenon clearly dependent on and at the same time illustrative of a new set of circumstances: the immigration and settlement of family groups of merchants, their integration (along with other groups) into late Carolingian and post-Carolingian economies, the ensuing close relationship with the powers that be, and the existence of a lower layer of Jewish population dependent for their livelihood on serving an elite of merchants and notables.

CONCLUSIONS

By the end of our period, the different Jewries of Europe exhibited a new face, first of all in their cultural profile. In a long process they had become acculturated to the rabbinical Judaism radiating from early medieval Babylonia by means of emissaries, the circulation of manuscripts, and the exchange of questions and *Responsa*. Channelled through Muslim Spain, Byzantium and Italy, procedures and institutions of Talmudic learning as well as liturgy were diffused.[118] This process also implied the adoption of a social profile that put a primary value on intellectual and religious distinction.[119] It was a strained one, involving first the replacement of adherence to Palestinian cultural modes by Babylonian ones, and then, towards the end of our period, the emancipation from the authority of Babylonian religious leadership. Such tension can be gauged in the myths of origins and legends of descent created in eleventh- and twelfth-century Italy and Spain.[120] One consequence of these cultural changes needs to be especially noted. Jews in the Muslim world, including Spain, remained linguistically open to their surroundings. Jews in southern Italy and elsewhere in the Mediterranean, however, stopped using Greek and Latin as a means of articulating their identity. Instead of an idiom that had become the

115 Agus (1965), no. LXXVI; Neubauer and Stern (1892), pp. 86, 101, 116ff, 126, 128, 143, 160, 164, 171, 176.

116 Agus (1965), index: charity, social stratification.

117 Agus (1969), esp. p. 168; Golb (1998), pp. 33–135.

118 Simonsohn (1974); Bonfil (1983), pp. 152–5; Gil (1993); Brody (1998), pp. 100–34.

119 Grossman (1980).

120 Bonfil (1983) and (1994a); Cohen (1960/61).

domain of Christian clerics, they readopted their own priestly Hebrew, thus erecting a linguistic barrier towards their neighbouring world.[121]

Jews did so at a time when they had become more urbanized, populous and prosperous, and thus decidedly more visible. Even though still resident in only a few towns, in some places they came to constitute a considerable part of the urban population, for example up to one tenth or more in eleventh-century Mainz and comparable numbers in some other German or Iberian towns. This was to have important implications in the following period, as Jewish social structure expanded to include a sizeable middle class. Internally, this led to changes in a bifurcated community structure hitherto dominated by the economic and cultural elite. The rapid growth of community institutions and legislation during the twelfth and thirteenth centuries is a clear indication of this development. As sedentary merchants and by the twelfth century also as moneylenders, they came in contact with growing numbers of members of the host society. This also holds true for the south, where the twelfth and thirteenth centuries saw the final dismantling of significant landed property held by Jews.[122] There, as in the north, the main thrust of economic development was to be towards credit and money lending.

Thus, from the eleventh century onwards, Jews left the shelter characteristic of their existence both in the south and in the north of Europe during the early Middle Ages: small numbers, close ties of an even smaller elite to the powers that be, and, in the south, occupations and cultural modes little different from those of the host society. The eleventh century also marked the beginning of a long process that eventually marginalised Jews in Europe. Under the new circumstances and tensions of a changing society, Jews were less and less perceived as the biblical counterfoil, for good or bad, to Christian belief. Adding to earlier polemical anti-Judaism a perception, albeit twisted, of real Jews, the style and content of this discourse began to enter both government policies and popular attitude. From this period onwards Jews were assigned the images and functions characteristic of an exposed minority group, with all the accompanying dangers inherent in such a role.

These processes paralleled and depended on developments in larger society: urbanisation and economic growth; religious elaboration, centralisation and unification; and the growth of an increasingly monolithic society. Thus the Jewish case appears, chronologically and substantially, as a variation on an all-European experience: a long drawn-out late antique phase centred in Byzantium and southern Europe in the period 400–800, followed by a period

[121] Bonfil (1996), pp. 3–63, esp. pp. 24–5; personal communication by I. Yuval. On other contrasts between Jews under Muslim and Christian rule see Cohen (1994).

[122] Régné (1912/81), pp. 164–84, for Narbonne.

of incipient growth from the late eighth to the eleventh centuries, especially to the north of the Alps and in Iberia. This in turn led to the full bloom of Jewish life in Europe of the central Middle Ages and, for reasons implicit in this very growth, to marginalisation. In both the internal and external senses, the eleventh century was to be the beginning of an entirely new era for European Jews.[123]

[123] I thank my friends Israel Yuval, of the Hebrew University of Jerusalem, and Alexander Patschovsky, of the University of Constance, who consented, at impossibly short notice, to cast a critical eye on this chapter.

CHAPTER 21

KINGS AND KINGSHIP

Patrick Wormald

INTRODUCTORY: A WORLD OF KINGS

Throughout the first millennium AD, much of the known world was ruled by monarchies. A good part of it has been for most of the second. In the first millennium BC, a number of the most self-confident societies were not. The records of the Jewish, Greek and Roman cultures that underpin European civilisation are laden with suspicion of individualistic authority. Nothing can be less readily assumed than that kings or emperors are the natural order of things.

Discussion of early medieval monarchy ought therefore to begin with a glance at the *anti*-monarchical traditions of the cultures most admired in the early Middle Ages. The Old Testament provided early medieval rulers with one of their main role models, and the Books of Kings would have been familiar for anyone exposed to basic Judaeo-Christian teaching. This was not a good advertisement for royal rule. Samuel prophesied that a king would make God's people his slaves, when the Israelites insisted that he provide them with one.[1] What followed was a catalogue of deviants and backsliders. Sixth- and seventh-century Europeans with only marginal education could also have known of the fall of the kings of Rome. Isidore of Seville, in the period's most influential epitome of kingship, derived *rex* from *regere*, in the sense not only of 'ruling' but also of 'doing right' (*recte facere*) and 'putting right' (*corrigere*). 'Hence the ancient proverb', he wrote, 'you will be king if you do right; if you do not, you will not.' For when the Romans could not tolerate the proud domination of kings, they organised annual governments and a pair of consuls; for the marks of kingship were not benevolence in counsel but pride in dominance.[2]

[1] 1 Samuel 8:4–17.

[2] Isidore of Seville, *Etymologiae* IX.iii.4–6; Isidore was probably drawing upon Orosius, *Historia adversus Paganos* II.iv.13–15, the early medieval West's equivalent to J. R. Green's *Short History of the English People*.

The lesson of ancient wisdom was that kingship was an admirable method of rule in ideal circumstances. However, it was subject to the most absolute of corruptions and especially if exercised absolutely.

These paradigms are a reminder that some societies at the same sort of stage of development as the early medieval West have opted against monarchy. Yet in 700 AD a governmental gazetteer of what had once been the Roman Empire would consist almost wholly of monarchs. Moving from south-east to north-west, it would begin with beyond doubt the mightiest, 'Abd al-Malik, caliph of Islam, based at Damascus.[3] He was the only ruler west of China whose power approximated in scope and intensity to what Roman emperors had enjoyed. By then, the Roman Empire itself, that is the throne of Constantinople, was in dispute (as was not infrequently the case). The legitimate emperor, Justinian II, was the last of the dynasty of Heraclius, which takes the credit for saving the Eastern Roman Empire from complete extinction. But the territory it now ruled was an impoverished fragment of what it had inherited.[4] Only Asia Minor was in any way secure. The Balkans were largely in the hands of rulers whose names are seldom known, and the extent of whose authority is often debatable. We know that the Avars, whose great days were long past by 700, were subject to a khagan, because a Frankish source was under the impression that such was the ruler's name. Asparuch, ruler of the Bulgars, another Turkic people that had established itself south of the Danube by 700, must also have been a 'khan', to judge by inscriptions of his successors.[5] Avars and Bulgars claimed, and up to a point exercised, lordship over various Slav groups. However, much of the Balkans was peopled by Slavs owing merely nominal allegiance, or none, to other powers.[6] So far as the Byzantines were concerned, they were indeed devoid of monarchy. Like most imperialists, Constantinople liked to deal with single rulers, and was hard put to find Slavs who fitted this bill.

In Italy in 700, the Byzantine outpost at Ravenna had fifty years of constricted life left, though in the south, especially Sicily, emperors were able to exert more authority.[7] The main ruler in northern Italy had some pretensions to be an heir of Rome. King Cunipert of the Lombards had a title that included the Constantinian *praenomen* Flavius, and was the first Lombard ruler to issue a gold coinage in the Byzantine idiom.[8] But his kingship also shared the instability besetting the imperial throne. Like his father, he was under pressure from the normally semi-detached Duke of Benevento. Liutpert, his young heir, would meet the very Roman fate of murder in his bath. Meanwhile, the last Byzantine outpost in Spain had been overrun at the same time as the Near

[3] See Hillenbrand, chapter 12 above. [4] See Louth, chapter 11 above.

[5] On the Avars, Fredegar, *Chronicon* IV.48. On the origin of the titles of early Bulgars, Stepanov (2001).

[6] See Kobyliński, chapter 19 above. [7] Brown (1984).

[8] Grierson and Blackburn (1986), pp. 56–66.

East.[9] The Spanish regime of the Visigoths had much in common with the Lombard, including the Flavian *nomen* and problems in reconciling a dynastic principle with a military aristocracy's wish to be given (or provide) strong leadership. The usual solution was that an emergent successor married into his predecessor's family: King Egica was son-in-law to Ervig (680–687). But such a system was inevitably attended by palace intrigue. Egica's son was succeeded by a grandson of a mid-seventh-century king, and his rule was in turn disputed by rebels who may or may not have had their own dynastic claims.[10] Controverted succession was a luxury no medieval kingdom could afford. Within two decades of Egica's death, Visigothic Spain was engulfed by Islam.

North of the Alps and the Pyrenees, where by 700 AD there had long since ceased to be any question of Roman rule, the political scene was ostensibly very different. The only king in Frankish Gaul was Childebert III. He had come to the throne as a boy like several later Merovingians, but lasted, unlike most, well into adulthood. Child kings reflected the *strictly* hereditary nature of kingship in this part of the West. But this also meant that actual power was often in the hands of regents, the 'Mayors of the Palace'.[11] The strongest of these in 700 was the Austrasian, Pippin II. It was his descendants who would halt the Muslim advance into Gaul and finally take control of both Frankish and Lombard kingdoms. Unlike the Romans, the Franks laid claim to the lands across the Rhine. They met with only mixed success. Their sources call Radbod of the Frisians a 'duke', where Anglo-Saxons with no political axe to grind regarded him as a 'king'. The Alamans and Bavarians were ruled by 'dukes', who were already *de facto* self-governing and would soon aspire to formal independence, though the mounting power of Pippin's dynasty did not allow them to enjoy it for long. References by the biographer of the Anglo-Saxon missionary Boniface to 'tyrannous dukes' of the Thuringians may mean that they were similarly placed.[12] Among the Saxons to the north, constitutional arrangements were not even formally kingly in the eyes of the Anglo-Saxon historian Bede writing in 731, nor was there as yet any question of Frankish overlordship. To their north, however, some Danes at least were ruled by a king, Ongendus: nothing is known of either him, his antecedents or his posterity, except that, though 'crueller than a beast and harder than a stone', he treated the visiting St Willibrord with studied courtesy.[13] It was presumably his style of authority that enabled someone in Jutland not long afterwards to erect the complex of frontier defences known as the *Danevirke*.

9 See Barbero and Loring, chapter 13 above.

10 Claude (1971), pp. 195–8; Collins (1983a), pp. 112–16, 120.

11 See Fouracre, chapter 14 above.

12 Wallace-Hadrill (1971), p. 19 (n. 65); Werner (1972), pp. 503–14; Willibald, *Vita Bonifatii c.*6; Mordek (1994); Wood (1994), p. 163.

13 Alcuin, *Vita Willibrordi, c.*9.

The British Isles was less ambiguously a world of kings, whether in the Germanic parts where Rome had held sway, or in the Celtic areas where on the whole it had not. Kings in the Anglo-Saxon lowlands seem *less* numerous and correspondingly more powerful the further west and north one looks.[14] In the small south-eastern realms of Kent, Essex and Sussex, kingship was often shared, though Wihtred of Kent had shaken off his partners to reign with some effect. To the south-west, Ine of Wessex controlled a territory that now stretched to the River Tamar, though he had apparently shared power with his father for a while. North of the Thames, the East Angles were a distinct kingdom under Aldwulf, but the rest of the midlands as far as the Welsh border made up Æthelred's Mercia; by 700 or soon after, the dependent rulers of the principalities either side of the Severn could no longer call themselves kings. Aldfrith's Northumbria was bigger yet. Its extent, to the Forth and beyond the Solway, may partly explain a level of Northumbrian political instability, which was already as notorious in the later eighth century, as it has become for historians. British Britain constituted a similar political patchwork, though its kings are incomparably more obscure. Of the rulers of the four main political quarters of Wales, Morgan ap Athrwys can be named, because charters of his south-eastern area survive. That Idwal, Gwalluc and Cadwgan were kings of Gwynedd, Powys and Dyfed has to be guessed from their place in the genealogies of later rulers.[15] Outside Wales proper, Beli of Strathclyde and Geraint of Dumnonia are historically identifiable, but Geraint is the only king from the sixth century to the ninth-century extinction of Cornish independence of whom this is true. The Irish record, by contrast, is rich enough to reveal a plethora of kings. No less than forty-four men listed as guarantors of the 'law' protecting clerics from the hazards of warfare which Abbot Adomnán of Iona issued in 697 could be called kings.[16] They ranged from Loingsech, the Uí Néill over-king, down to the regal midgets who were still kings in Irish eyes, however petty their status. Other royal guarantors were the supremos of Munster, Ulster and Leinster and the heir to that of Connacht. They were accompanied by Eochu, king of Dál Riada, the Irish (or, as Romans and some Irishmen preferred, Scottish) offshoot in the Isles and Argyll, whose expansion would one day recast the politics of north Britain. And, also on the list, was the ruler of the most obscure, Slavs apart, of Europe's polities, the Picts of north-eastern Britain. They too may have been a people of many kings, but only one royal line was preserved for posterity. Its representative in 697 was Bridei son of Derilei: and intriguingly, his affiliation

[14] See Thacker, chapter 17 above.

[15] Davies (1978), pp. 68, 79, 88–9, and see Davies, chapter 9 above.

[16] Ní Dhonnchadha (1982): a prosopographical *tour de force* facilitated by the unparalleled detail of Irish annals and genealogies.

has been taken to mean that what had qualified him for office was his mother's identity.[17]

Nearly all these men had titles reasonably translated as 'king'. Even 'Abd al-Malik's name is Arabic for 'son of a king', while the title 'khagan' is Turco-Mongol equivalent to Persian *Shahanshah* (i.e. king of kings).[18] This single political label obviously covers a multitude of very different jobs. A kingly title was perhaps about all that rulers on the Bosphorus and on Loch Tay had in common. Monarchy was none the less the norm. This chapter is mainly concerned to ask why. No early medieval regime, not even 'Abd al-Malik's, had the resources in men or money of their earlier or later equivalents. Royal behaviour was therefore more completely dependent on at least passive assent from those who could otherwise have resisted it. The enquiry is thus a study in what can loosely be called the political culture of early medieval communities: the theories of the articulate but also the assumptions of the elite as a whole. What are kings said to be *for*? What did kings *do*, as a matter of course? It is fundamental that these were still open questions in post-Roman Europe. Because they were open, their answers might vary from one context to the next. This in turn means that they are answerable only by attention to the specifics of each regime. Above all, it must never be forgotten that there was nothing foregone about the pattern that emerged from events.

IMPERIAL RULE

The main reason why almost the whole of the area covered by this chapter was a mosaic of monarchies in the year 700 is transparent. Over the previous seven centuries, it had all been affected directly or indirectly by experience of Rome. The Roman Empire was in fact an autocratic monarchy, whatever the constitutional niceties. The story of post-Roman kingship thus begins with 'New Rome' on the Bosphorus. When writing to the senate, Roman emperors used a formula which pithily expresses their relationship with the state: 'If you are well, it is well. I and the army are well.'[19] The primary, perhaps always the fundamental, sense of *imperator* was 'commander-in-chief'. It was command of the army that made Rome once again a monarchy, against its basic principles. Triumphs for emperors – and none but emperors – in full military rig

[17] Anderson (1973), pp. 175–6. The possibility of multiple kings of the Picts is explored in unpublished work by A. A. M. Duncan.

[18] Kollautz (1954), pp. 136–7, though cf. Pohl (1988), p. 396, n. 15.

[19] The formula finds its clearest Latin form (ironically) in Cicero, *Ad Familiares* XV.I.2: S.V.V.B.E.E.E.Q.V.: *si vos valetis bene est ego exercitusque valeo*. The Greek version, already normal for Julius Caesar and Augustus, is reported as habitual by Dio, *Roman History* LXIX.xiv.3: see Millar (1992), p. 353.

highlighted their image as bringers of victory.[20] Coins whose obverses almost always carried an imperial portrait had reverses which, in at least one issue for nearly every emperor, harked on military themes: victory itself; avenging Mars; a captive or otherwise humiliated barbarian; a loyal soldiery attending its commander's speech or receiving his bounty.[21] Yet it is possible to overstress the military essence of imperial rule. Emperors were pre-eminently members of a cultivated upper class. The Roman military aristocracy had a thick civilian patina from its earliest recorded days. The acceptable face of imperial rule was perforce civil even as its sinews were military.[22] Emperors were rarely if ever in the front line. For two centuries after the 390s, they ceased to go on campaign altogether, while offering their subjects the doubtful reassurance of an enhanced martial image on their coins; both developments may be attributed to the deterioration of the real military situation.[23] Generalship seldom led directly to the throne between 306 and 602.[24] Only in the Western Empire's last two decades did commanders make and unmake emperors at will: a process that reached a logical *dénouement* when barbarian soldiers opted for rule by a barbarian king.

So it was that Justinian, self-styled victor over so many barbarians, was rarely seen outside his palace complex. And when the emperor Maurice was minded to take the field in 590, he was successively discouraged by senatorial advice, an eclipse of the sun, assault by a wild boar, a horribly deformed birth, and, finally, the arrival of an embassy from Persia.[25] It took the post-610 revival of the Persian threat, in a more explicit form than had been known since Xerxes' day, to induce an emperor to revive the role of Alexander and to better effect than had been managed by almost a millennium of imitators.[26] George of Pisidia made a point of Heraclius' exchange of an emperor's red buskins for the black boots of a soldier. But the inspiration by then transcended even Alexander. Heraclius aimed to retake Jerusalem and to recover the True Cross. His was in a real sense the first of the crusades. A famous set of silver plate depicting the Life of David was almost certainly made with him in mind.[27]

[20] Campbell (1984), pp. 133–42; McCormick (1986), pp. 112–15. Much that follows is indebted to these two notable studies.

[21] Campbell (1984), pp. 142–6, 182–4. See, for example, Kent (1978), nos. 168, 178, 204–5, 213–14, 235, 238, 244, 252, 263–4, 294–6, 312, 318, 341–2, 347, 349–50, 356.

[22] Cf. Millar (1992), pp. 63–6, on the emperor's military ambience.

[23] McCormick (1986), pp. 41–4, 47, 78. Kent (1978), nos. 695, 702–3, 705–6, 711, 726, 729, 731, 738–40, 743, 745–6, 752.

[24] Jones (1964), pp. 322–5.

[25] Theophylact, *Historiae* V.xvi.2–6; VI.i.58, VI.iii. 5; cf. Mi. Whitby (1988), p. 156.

[26] On the lure of Alexander and its generally unfortunate effects, see Campbell (1984), pp. 391–3, and Matthews (1989), pp. 137–8.

[27] Ma. Whitby (1994, and cf. 1995); Mango (1994), pp. 122–31.

Militant Old Testament heroes provided imperial rule with a new inspiration. Even so, Heraclian coinage remained strikingly civilian: the helmet, dropped by Justinian I, made a brief comeback only under Constantine IV, as the Arabs invested the city itself.[28] Thereafter, Byzantine emperors often led armies on campaign but rarely in battle. Too military an image was a solecism that could be as lethal as enemy action. One of the few emperors who died sword in hand was the last.

Emperors were generals by definition. Most Romans, like most Roman historians, probably saw their ruler as above all a military man. But it is as judge that he appears in the many thousand transactions of emperor and subject recorded by subjects themselves on inscriptions or papyrus, or else in the great codes of Theodosius II and Justinian. The words with which Justinian launched his *Institutes* would ring down the centuries: 'Imperial Majesty should not only be distinguished by arms but also armed by laws . . . so that the Roman emperor . . . should appear as devout in justice as triumphant over defeated enemies.'[29]

We tend to think of the Roman Empire as a galvanic force imposing its will on a huge swathe of humanity until finally overwhelmed by forces beyond even its control. But emperors in a legal role were more often passive than active parties. The main influence on the development of imperial jurisdiction was the expectation that imperial power evoked in Hellenistic cities whose political culture predisposed them to seek monarchical patronage. Emperors were from the outset deluged by petitions, legal grievances prominent amongst them.[30] The urge that promoted an 'appeal to Caesar' predictably made the most of the reply ('rescript'), regardless of its formal status; and the fact that most rescripts owe their survival to incorporation in Justinian's code shows that they certainly came to be seen as law. Constantine's reign appears to mark a change because the *Theodosian Code* (438) took its starting point from 311, and was meant to include only laws with 'sacred generality'. Yet what had really changed was not the pressure of petitions but the tone of response. Under Constantine the 'Quaestor of the Sacred Palace' became the imperial spokesman. To judge from the job-description given by Cassiodorus, who held it under the Ostrogoths (506–512), legal expertise was relevant, but rhetorical technique more so.[31] Petitions to the emperor had always needed to be couched in the stylised rhetoric that was an educated Greco-Roman's hallmark. The

[28] Breckenridge (1959); Whitting (1973), pp. 33–9, 133–52, 154–8.

[29] *Corpus Iuris Civilis* XVI.I.xxiii. On what follows, see especially Millar (1992), chs. V–VIII and 'Afterword'; Honoré (1978), chs. 1–4, 8–9; (1981), chs. 1–2; (1982), chs. 1, B-9; (1986).

[30] See the example discussed by Halsall, chapter 2 above.

[31] Cassiodorus, *Variae* VI.5, cf. X.6. See Honoré (1986) (especially pp. 147–50 on Ausonius' contribution) and (1993).

skills, which had earlier won the emperor's favour, now took control of his pronouncements.[32] The tendency of later emperors to meet specific grievances with general fulminations, that were then collected into huge codes in their name, made them look more and more like makers of law.

Such was the context of the supreme legislative achievement of this or any age, Justinian's *Corpus Iuris Civilis*.[33] Even here, the all-encompassing imperial initiative is in part illusory. The constitutions introducing the various stages of the project were written by the Quaestor, Tribonian; his were the priorities that have seemed typically Justinianic. Eastern intellectuals had always seen law as the one area where Latin culture measured up to Greek philosophy. Since the third century they had thronged the Beirut law-school whose professors were among Tribonian's colleagues.[34] Justinian's temple to the 'public reason of the Romans' (in Gibbon's phrase) can thus be seen as a crucial stage in the recasting of imperial rule by a Hellenistic intelligentsia. Two otherwise puzzling facts then come into focus. The first is that Justinian's great project was of course in Latin, but his *Novels* over the last thirty years of his reign were overwhelmingly in Greek. Had Latin been relevant in legal practice, it should not have given way so soon. Secondly, there was marked decline in the number of laws Justinian made in either language after 539. For all that it is a monument to the human intellect of measureless importance, the artificiality of the *Corpus Iuris* in its own time is exposed by its lack of immediate resonance. Justinian's successors down to Heraclius issued few laws. Heraclius seemingly made none, except when trying to crystallise doctrinal orthodoxy.[35] Leo III's *Ecloga* (741) has a pertinent prologue: 'knowing that the laws enacted by previous emperors have been written in many books and . . . that the sense is difficult . . . we considered that the decisions . . . should be repeated more lucidly'.[36] The eighteen succinct Greek chapters that follow are perhaps the nearest to a real 'Digest' of law for routine use that any early medieval ruler managed. In addition, in twice citing 'the wise Solomon', the prologue chose a model who would have more influence on western royal law-makers in the coming centuries than any Roman.

One of the nostrums of Roman history is that an 'imperator', with his austere if informal 'senatorial' style, made way for a 'basileus', a title that had once symbolised the difference between Greek freedom and enslavement to a Persian autocrat. Much discussion has attended the formal adoption of this title by Heraclius in 629.[37] Greek speakers had in fact been using the word

[32] See Wieacker (1963), but also Voss (1982). [33] See Louth, chapter 4 above.

[34] Collinet (1925). See also Honoré (1962), pp. 85–96.

[35] *Ius Greco-Romanum* I.i.xxv, ed. Zepos; Cf. Haldon (1990), pp. 254–64.

[36] Burgmann, Das Gesetzbuch: trans. Freshfield, *Ecloga*, pp. 67–9.

[37] *Ius Greco-Romanum* I.i.xxv, ed. Zepos; cf. Bréhier (1906); Rösch (1978), pp. 37, 106–7, 170; Chrysos (1978).

of emperors for centuries. Its 'official' appearance (if that is what happened in 629) merely set a seal on the Hellenistic influences to which Roman rule had so long been exposed.[38] The educated easterners who pressed hardest on an emperor's business came eventually to dictate his patterns of behaviour.

This sea-change is most vividly reflected in the new significance of the palace. The word derives from the fact that the first imperial headquarters was an admittedly unusually opulent private house on the Palatine. No one could mistake Constantinople's sacred palace for an aristocratic residence. Already by the fifth century it covered quarter of a million square metres.[39] For imperial rule, the late Roman rebirth of a 'palace culture', such as had not been seen west of the Levant since Mycenae, meant two things above all. First, it both symptomised and facilitated the emergence of a bureaucracy. The total staff actually present under the palace roofs may have run to four figures, as against an attendance on early emperors of under two hundred.[40] This burgeoning government machine was what gave educated provincials their new access to the levers of power. To emperors it brought a more systematic approach to the raising of revenue and the keeping of archives than was ever possible on the Palatine.[41] Second, the rise of the palace entailed the elaboration of the court ritual for which 'Byzantine' is a byword. It is hard to say how much of the ceremonial codified by Constantine VII in the tenth century goes back to the sixth or seventh. But appendices to Book I of Constantine's collection include excerpts from Peter the Patrician's sixth-century *De Magistro Officiorum*, which show that emperors were by then crowned in the Byzantine tradition: senior or solo emperor by the patriarch, associate by senior emperor, with no unction of any sort involved.[42] Already in evidence too are the elaborate diplomatic protocols which would before long be ridiculed and resented in the West. The Persian embassies at whom they were mainly aimed may have been more impressed.[43] But the most illuminating aspect of court ceremonial was perhaps that centring on the Hippodrome, an extension of the palace complex. It had always been in the circus or amphitheatre that emperors staged their dialogue with the Roman people. At Constantinople, however, the circus factions of the

[38] This is perhaps the central motif of Millar (1992) (e.g. pp. 613–15); it is already foreshadowed in Millar *et al.* (1967).

[39] Mango (1986), p. 28; cf. the plans at the end of *Constantin VII*, ed. Vogt (1935–40), I. Finsen (1962) shows the (increasingly large) first-century palaces on the Palatine.

[40] Heather (1994a).

[41] Jones (1964), pp. 412–62, 572–92; Kelly (1994), pp. 161–7: cf. Sirks (1993), pp. 49–56.

[42] *De Ceremoniis* I.91–5, which can be compared with the tenth-century ceremony at I.38. See discussion by Av. Cameron (1976), pp. 154–79, of Justin II's coronation, and cf. Theophylact, *Historiae* I.i.123, I.x.19 for that of Maurice; also Gregory of Tours, *Hist.* V.30 on Tiberius.

[43] *De Ceremoniis* I.87–90; Al. Cameron (1976), p. 257; for Carolingian opinion, see the splendid story in Notker, *Gesta Karoli Magni* II.6, with comment by Leyser (1988), pp. 134–42.

Blues and Greens were no longer mouthpieces of public opinion; their role was ever more tightly circumscribed by the orchestration of imperial acclamations. It is typical that a *Book of Ceremonies* provides most of the evidence of what went on at the races.[44]

An obsession with ceremony was one of the few brickbats that Procopius did not throw at Justinian, preferring to stress his lack of dignity. But few of his images are as unforgettable as that of an emperor pacing the corridors of his own labyrinth by night, scorning sleep and snatching odd bites off the imperial table as he passed.[45] One way towards a more sympathetic view of Justinian is to appreciate that in the professionalism that so enraged Procopius lay the way ahead. Palace officers after the 630s had little time for history, panegyric or even invective, which is why this is Byzantium's Dark Age. The East Roman aristocracy was no longer an elite for whom service to the state was a function of its culture, but a service elite proper, its literary culture less a qualification than an option, and its education dedicated to the very survival of the world it knew.[46]

Within a year of founding his city, Constantine was ensconced at Nicaea among the bishops of his empire, debating the structure of the Trinity. It was an image the Byzantine Empire never forgot. His burial twelve years later in his new Church of the Twelve Apostles was profoundly symbolic. He was 'the equal of the apostles', *isapostolos*. His heirs would stand as guardians not just of the church's interests but also of its teaching. Byzantine emperors were the first to act on the principle espoused by European monarchs until the Enlightenment: rulers answer to God for their people's observance of the Faith.[47] It is reasonable to see the emperor's prominence in church affairs as one more aspect of the acceptability of the imperial destiny to those with a background in Hellenistic notions.[48] Emperors seemed to give a spiritual lead. It was because the patriarch Acacius' *Henoticon* formula (482) had been promulgated in the emperor Zeno's name that Pope Gelasius rebuffed it as he did in a fateful letter.[49] Emperors chaired sixth- and seventh-century ecumenical councils, which got under way with chanting of the imperial *laudes*.[50] The 'Quinisext' Council of 691–692 bears several marks of Justinian II's personal initiative and set about the detailed ordering of a Christian society in ways that foreshadow Carolingian approaches.[51] As thus implied, however, one can draw too sharp a line between eastern and western ecclesiologies. Justinian I's doctrinal expositions were his own work (which is how we know that the constitutions introducing the *Corpus*

[44] Al. Cameron (1976). [45] Procopius, *Anecdota*, 12.
[46] Whitby (1988), pp. 347–57; Haldon (1990), pp. 388–99, 426, etc.
[47] Ensslin (1967), pp. 7–13; Lane Fox (1986), pp. 643–62.
[48] Sansterre (1972). [49] See Louth, chapter 11 above. [50] Chrysos (1979).
[51] Herrin (1987), pp. 284–6 (and for the more general point, pp. 116–18).

Iuris were not).[52] Emperors were not otherwise authors of doctrine. Heraclius was said to have disavowed his *Ecthesis* as the work of the patriarch Sergius.[53] What embroiled emperors in ecclesiastical dispute was their duty as much to preserve peace as to formulate orthodoxy. Conversely, the easterner Maximos the Confessor was as ready to anathematise imperial intervention as any pope, so inaugurating an illustrious Byzantine tradition.[54]

Imperial apostleship was articulated in quite another way by care for the poor. There is a difference between the provision for fellow-citizens that pagan emperors channelled through recognised corporations with some of the status of trade unions, and the targeting of the destitute as a religious duty that was tirelessly reiterated by Old and New Testaments.[55] Procopius' account of the hospices for the incurably ill and *xenodochia* for the merely itinerant built by Justinian in the capital and elsewhere is circumstantial.[56] It is revealing that the stuff of panegyric, which had always covered an honorand's constructions, should now extend to foundations like these. The work of Justinian and Theodora for repentant prostitutes even attracted the notice of the faraway Monophysite chronicler John of Nikiu.[57] It was an item to this otherwise 'unorthodox' emperor's credit.

The Empire's traumatic seventh-century experience of loss, recovery and loss again lent imperial religious leadership new urgency.[58] Heraclius' 'David plates' show enhanced sensitivity to the Old Testament model of a people embattled but beloved. The critical point about Heraclius' new title was that it was '*pistos basileus*', or, as Latins would have it in similar contexts, '*rex fidelis* (faithful king)'.[59] When Justinian II relegated his own image to the reverse of his coins, and replaced it on the obverse with that of Christ, the ideal of Byzantium as a new Holy Society reached an apogee. Emperors would soon seek to enforce God's Law against idolatry. Meanwhile, a sinister side-effect of this heightened consciousness was increased pressure on the original people of God. Heraclius had introduced a programme of forced baptism for Jews by

52 Honoré (1975). 53 Léthel (1979), pp. 48–9, 104.

54 Herrin (1987), pp. 206–19, 252–9, gives a particularly telling evocation of this and other themes in the so-called 'Monothelite' controversy.

55 On this see Brown (1993), pp. 78–103, 15–27. I am also much indebted for what follows to unpublished work by Peregrine Hordern.

56 Procopius, *Buildings* I.ii.14–17; I.ix.1–10, 12–13; I.xi.23–7; II.x.25; IV.x.21; V.iv.17; V.vi.25; V.ix.4, 22, 27, 34–5, 38, etc.

57 *The Chronicle of John of Nikiu*, pp. 139, 143.

58 Av. Cameron (1979); Haldon (1986); cf. Haldon (1990), pp. 281–375.

59 Some of the endless Hippodrome rehearsal of the 'Orthodox emperor' theme, *De Ceremoniis* I.69, may go back to this period: as it stands, the ceremony of the presentation of flowered crosses clearly relates to the defeat of more 'recent infidels' (*Constantin* VII, ed. Vogt, II, pp. 137–9); but it would not have been out of place in the fevered context of Heraclius' defeat of the Persians.

the 630s.[60] In the world of the new Israel, there was less and less room for the old.

Damascus

Islam and Central Asia have their own *Cambridge Histories*. But each spawned models of imperial rule at least as conspicuous as New Rome's in the sixth and seventh century. These alternative models can serve to offset post-Roman regimes elsewhere. Given that the Arab conquerors of the civilised world came from one where leadership was ostensibly limited to that of the '*shaikh* (old man)', it seems unlikely that the structure of authority in Islam's new empire would owe much to models imported by its makers, and the sheer speed of the conquest left much of the machinery of power in the Fertile Crescent intact. Middle-Easterners could and did expect to serve and exploit the new rulers as they had the old.[61] The profile of khalifal rule thus in many ways resembled that of Roman and Persian hegemonies. They were more rarely seen on campaign even than fifth- and sixth-century emperors. Caliphs too were creatures of the palace. The Baghdad extravagances immortalised in the *Thousand-and-One Nights* were previewed in Umayyad desert lodges (*qu'sur*).[62] Justinian II is known to have sent men and materials to assist 'Abd al-Malik's mosque-building programme.[63] More fundamentally, a judgemental role for God's caliph was implied in what the *Qu'ran* itself had to say of David and Solomon. The Umayyads are found issuing edicts in imperial style: it could be claimed, perhaps with some exaggeration, that '[no] governor nor judge would ever give judgement without referring it to the caliph in Syria'.[64] It is hard to resist the impression that a caliph's legislative activity arose more from the pressure of his new subjects, with the expectations they were bound to have of rulers, than from those who saw him as super-shaikh or successor to the prophet.

All of that said, it is hardly probable that an Arab regime would have been entirely unmarked by ancestral political culture, least of all when it was now suffused by a gleaming religious ideology. It was a criticism of Mu'awiya, founder of the Umayyad dynasty, that he was '*hiraqliyya*' ('like Heraclius').[65] Caliphal authority was inspired by the sense that God must retain a deputy on

60 Sharf (1971), pp. 43–7; cf. Haldon (1990), pp. 345–8.

61 Nasrullah (1950), pp. 154–7. For the ex-Sasanian *dihqan* who set the tone at Baghdad, cf. Kennedy (1981), pp. 101–2, and (1986), p. 11, etc.

62 Hillenbrand (1982); see note 58.

63 Theophanes, *Chronographia* AM 6183; Gibb (1958).

64 Crone and Hinds (1986), pp. 44–8; cf. Gibb (1955).

65 Crone and Hinds (1986), p. 115. Another term of abuse was '*kisra l'arab*' after the great Shah Khusro I.

earth after Muhammad's departure, albeit his revelation was less privileged.[66] Hence, if Byzantine emperors were political leaders who had acquired quasi-religious authority, a caliph was the reverse: a religious authority who by that token wielded political power. When 'Abd al-Malik got a khalifal currency going, it was adjusted to Arabic standards, and it was not his (or of course any) image that was on it, but texts from the *Qu'ran*.[67] In the *qu'sur* on the Umayyad empire's desert fringe, enthusiasm for Romano-Persian models was not entirely untrammelled.[68] The walls of Qusayr 'Arnra were decorated with a fresco of kings of the earth (among them the captive Roderic of the Visigoths) come to do homage to their lord, in an unmistakable echo of the scene envisaged in the one-time throne-room of Ctesiphon.[69] But at Khirbat al-Mafjar, the ceremonial of the Sasanian court seems to have been deliberately 'sent up'.[70] The conquerors were not so smitten with the new world at their feet that they could not laugh at it.

The Balkans

The political culture of Byzantium's northern enemies has left no memorials of its own. But there is a good chance that the down-to-earth prose of the so-called '*Strategicon* of the emperor Maurice' lacks ancient ethnography's obsession with barbarian eccentricity. 'Scythians', it says (meaning Avars and Turks), 'have a monarchical form of government.'[71] It was surely right. Just as the Avars fade from the pages of history, Frankish sources deck them out with a bewildering array of titles (largely again mistaken as personal names). Every one is part of the governmental vocabulary of other Steppe empires.[72] No matter what their functions under the Avars, they are incontrovertible evidence that the khanate was conceived like a steppe power. The same goes *mutatis mutandis* for the Bulgars. Khans certainly led armies in person.[73] They were in some sense law-givers.[74] Above all, they had the ideology that enabled steppe hegemonies to

66 Crone and Hinds (1986), p. 105 and *passim*.

67 Grierson (1960), but note that 'Abd al-Malik's very first issue in his series was iconic: his own image, or even the Prophet's?

68 For instructive debate on these, see Hillenbrand (1982); MacAdam (1986); Helms (1990); I owe guidance on the matter to Dr Jeremy Johns.

69 Grabar (1954): Almagro *et al.* (1975).

70 Hamilton (1959): but I owe this insight to Dr Julian Raby.

71 Maurice, *Strategicon* XI.2 (pp. 360–1); trans. Dennis (1984), p. 116.

72 Pohl (1988), pp. 292–306: see above, p. 572 and note 5.

73 Pohl (1988), p. 177; though cf. Menander, *Fragment* 12 (5) (pp. 136–7). *Miracles de Saint Démétrius* I.13 (II, p. 46), and Fredegar, *Chronicle* IV.48, for the khagan's preference to be served by those 'whose destruction will cause me no pain'.

74 Browning (1975), pp. 124–5.

deal with Romans on terms of equality, as few other barbarians could. When the Avar khan claimed in true steppe style that 'there existed no one, even as far as the sun extended its gaze, who would be able to confront him', a diplomat treated him to the story of the Egyptian tyrant Sesostris, just as another had done for the Shahanshah's ambassador a few decades before.[75] Nomads faced Rome for the first time with polities that needed handling as Persia always had been: like a partner in an armoured diplomatic minuet. They acquired their style not from Rome itself nor only from Persia, but in all probability also from China.

The *Strategicon*'s Slavs are in strong contrast. 'They absolutely refuse to be enslaved or governed . . . There are many kings (*rhegon*) among them, always at odds with one another.'[76] Slavs have rulers, but so many and disparate that they defy treatment as an organised polity. This assessment too can be confirmed. Slav chieftains played mostly bit-parts in the drama of Thessalonica's many sieges.[77] Some are called *rhex*, but Byzantines were habituated to this term by knowledge of Latino-Germanic monarchy.[78] The Slavs' own word may have been '*knez*', their basic noun for '(local) lord'.[79] They could form warbands, but seemingly without the potential to snowball into kingdoms like those of Germans.[80] The *Strategicon* ascribes this plausibly if predictably to backward military technique. At any rate, Slav culture *was* somehow antipathetic to political coagulation. The Wends made Samo, a trader from a Frankish background, their 'king' after he helped their revolt against Avar taskmasters; he ruled for thirty-five years, but set up no dynasty (for all his twelve wives and twenty-two sons), nor any other apparatus of a monarchical system.[81] Aversion to state-formation is no longer so unfashionable as Slav nationalists once found it. Slav society may have looked acephalous because their settlements, as in parts of pre-colonial Africa, were governed by their own headmen. Kingship as understood by the other cultures covered in this chapter was something Slavs were by and large able to do without.

75 Theophylact, *History* VI.xi.8–15; *Menander* VI.1, pp. 64–7 (cf. V.1, XV.3, pp. 48–9, 150–1).

76 *Strategicon* xi.4 (pp. 370–3, 380–1), trans. Dennis (1984), pp. 120, 123.

77 Menander, *Fragment* 21, pp. 194–5; *Miracles de Saint Démétrius* i.13, ii.1, 2, 4 (II, pp. 46–7, 87, 95, 112, 122–4). The exception, 'Kouber', ii.5, was almost certainly a Bulgar in charge of ex-Romans (II, pp. 38–50); and the relatively active Mauros had been in Roman service, ii.5 (II, pp. 151–8).

78 Theophylact, *History* I.vii.5, VI.vii.1–5, and especially VI.ix.1; cf. Procopius, *Wars* V.1.26, and M. Whitby (1982), pp. 426–7.

79 Kahl (1960), pp. 178–9: certainly it cannot have been *król* (etc.), a word derived, doubtless along with loftier kingly conceptions, from Charlemagne: cf. Wolfram (1970), p. 7.

80 Pohl (1988), pp. 97–8, 126–7.

81 Fredegar, *Chronicle* IV.48, 68 and for comment, Pohl (1988), pp. 256–61. Cf., however, *Gesta Archiepiscoporum Salisburgensium*, pp. 7–15, where Samo heads the list of Carinthian rulers. See also Fouracre, chapter 14 above and Kobyliński, chapter 19 above.

BARBARIAN KINGSHIP: CELTS

The rest of this chapter will show that sub-Roman monarchy in the West derives substantially from the Roman imperial model. The question is whether it does so exclusively. Did anything in their own traditions anticipate the experience of kingship among Europe's post-Roman masters? The best place to begin answering this question is with the Celtic-speaking peoples of the far north-west. Rome had not overrun Ireland or Scotland, so there is a chance that their kingships were essentially native organisms. Celtic evidence has often been read as a reflection of ancient indigenous arrangements.[82]

The first thing to be said is that 'Celtic' for present purposes must mean 'Irish'. There is a rich body of material from seventh- and eighth-century Ireland. The comparable Welsh evidence is very largely high medieval in date and relates only problematically to an earlier period. There is almost nothing comparable from Scotland.[83] Incidental references occasionally serve to align (or contrast) the Irish world with that of Briton or Pict. Only for Ireland itself can any coherent picture be drawn. A second and seminal point is that the chief determinant of the texts on Irish secular culture is that they were produced and preserved by men who made a fetish of the past. The *filid* were in recognisable line of descent from the druids of pre-Roman Gaul and Britain. The label 'druid' had been dropped along with the priestly functions of paganism. But *filid* was the same sort of privileged class, membership of which came partly by birth and partly from exhaustive training in its own schools. Their speciality too was recording of all varieties of tradition, from genealogy and saga, through praise of rulers (and their rebuke in satire or curses which *filid* prestige had a way of bringing to fruition), to the preserving and expounding of law, the province of the distinct 'brehon' branch of the learned orders.[84] Much that we know about the theory of early Irish kingship, and quite a lot about the practice, was transmitted by men with a professional archaising bias.

It is no longer fashionable to stress pre-Christian strands in this tradition as much as 'nativist' scholars used to. The new view is that, whatever its position in prehistoric society, the *filid* class was in effect coterminous with the monastic clergy when it began to put its traditions into historical form. As soon as such traditions appeared in writing, they were deeply marked by

82 What follows draws on Wormald (1986a), but reconsideration has been prompted by important work since this was written (in 1983). Lack of space precludes discussion of succession and inauguration. For which cf. O'Corráin (1971), with Dumville (1977), pp. 85–8, Wormald (1986a), pp. 158–60, and (for Scotland) Wormald (1996), pp. 134–7 with n. 5.

83 For what can be said about the development of the 'Celtic Countries' in this period, see Davies, chapter 9 above and Stancliffe, chapters 15 and 16 above.

84 See, for example, Dillon (1946), pp. 259–63; Kenney (1968), pp. 19–26, 34–46; Byrne (1973), pp. 13–16, and (1974): Mac Cana (1979).

Romano-Christian influences.[85] The fact remains that what we have is a blend, and one that derived more of its flavour from unquestionably pre-Christian ingredients than did other 'barbarian' political cultures. But the extent to which this put a brake on historical development in fact as well as image can be ascertained only by testing the *filid* model against the known performance of Irish potentates.

Ri, the Irish word for king, is cognate with its Latin and Sanskrit equivalents *rex* and *raj*. A series of echoes suggests that the office designated by this word may itself have taken a similarly quasi-religious form in each of these three cultures. It is thus that early Irish kingship can be described as 'sacral'.[86] Yet the Irish tradition had been thoroughly Christianised by the seventh century, as appears from the tract *On the Twelve Abuses of the World*. The misfortunes attendant on the 'abuse' of an 'unjust king' mirror the blessings of 'true' kingship promised in the supposedly pre-Christian *Testament of Morann*: 'the fruits . . . of the earth are diminished . . . hurricanes and stormy winters forbid the earth's fertility and the sea's good gifts', and so on.[87] Had this tract seemed in any way 'pagan' to contemporaries, it would hardly have become the formative text it was for early medieval authorities on kingship. Its definition of justice entails defence of strangers, wards and widows, punishment of thieves and adulterers, protection of the church, sustenance of the poor. As for the unjust king, 'as many as are the sinners that he hath had beneath him in the present, he shall have over him by way of torment in future'. It was the Old Testament that taught the Irish, as it did the Byzantines and would the Carolingians, their standards of what kings should and should not do. Special consideration was to be visited on the indigent, and fierce reprisals on offenders against God and His churchmen. An Irish canon, ascribed to Jerome but certainly a native composition, says that 'the word of a king is a sword for beheading, a rope for hanging, it casts into prison, it condemns to exile'. Those who shed the blood of a bishop, abbot or scribe were to be 'crucified' (with the alternative of paying seven 'slave-girls' in the native currency). Men are in fact on record as being executed in 746 for 'violation of St Patrick's sanctuary'.[88]

If the past had an enduring effect on post-conversion kingship, it may have lain not in voluntary pagan impulses but in the way that traditional *filid* defiance of kings was given new legitimacy by Old Testament prophets like Elijah. Irishmen were not the only saints to follow St Martin in this mode of behaviour, but they were perhaps particularly susceptible to it. Columbanus' notorious abuse of Frankish kings was not an isolated phenomenon: Columba

[85] Above all, McCone (1990), pp. 22–7. [86] Binchy (1970), pp. 1–12.

[87] *De Duodecim Abusivis*, ed. Hellmann, pp. 52–3, trans. Laistner (1957), p. 145.

[88] O'Corráin, Breatnach and Breen (1984), pp. 390–1.

correctly forecast the death of kings.[89] Two other details may be pertinent. Irish kings were more prone than their Germanic colleagues to resign the throne altogether and take up life as a monk.[90] Second, Irish church councils never had royal chairmen. There were many kings at the 697 Synod of Birr, but its president was Abbot Admonán. Conceivably, enough of a pre-baptismal aura lingered over Irish royalty to foster reserve about outright ecclesiastical leadership by kings.

For all its image of priestly inaction, Irish kingship yielded a richer crop of rulers killed in battle than anywhere else in the West. From when they become contemporary (which for these purposes is *c.*600) until 707, the *Annals of Ulster* list at least fifty kings as casualties.[91] It seems that armed conflict could be expected to result in deaths at the highest level.[92] In accounting for so much kingly fatality, can we go beyond the expectation that kings would lead their peoples in war, as in many of the world's chieftaincy systems? The first explanation is simply that, as the gazetteer of European monarchs in 700 showed, there were so many Irish kings. The number of kingdoms (*tuatha*, literally 'tribes') has been variously reckoned between 80 and 185.[93] The reason why they were so many and so small was that the force of Irish tradition, whether or not bolstered by a lingering sense of royal blood's mystique, did not allow the elimination of subordinate kingships. Dignitaries hung on to the title of king when elsewhere in Europe they would have become *subreguli* or *praefecti* (if surviving at all).[94] The numerous obscure kings from midland dynasties recorded as falling in Uí Néill battles might therefore have gone down in most European chronicles as victims of aristocratic feud. A further point is that this multitude of royalty was marshalled in an elaborate hierarchy whereby any *ri* was subject to a *riuri* ('great king') and he to a *ri riuirech* ('king of great

89 Adomnán, *Life of Columba* I.36: in this instance the prophecy was of something remarkably like the 'threefold death' of Irish saga (see below). For the overall problem, Wood (1989).

90 Stancliffe (1983): for Anglo-Saxon cases, see below, pp. 596, 604.

91 Calculations are confined to *The Annals of Ulster* as the only set of annals to give a generally contemporary picture for the seventh century; on the date from which they *can* be considered contemporary, compare Hughes (1972), pp. 115–19, with Smyth (1972): a debate best resolved by accepting that entries were made from the late sixth century, but go into detail only from the mid-seventh.

92 The figure of fifty omits all those identifiable as members of royal families who are not known to have reached the throne.

93 O'Corráin (1978), pp. 10–11.

94 Charles-Edwards (1989), pp. 34–8, though cf. O'Corráin (1978), pp. 9–10. Wormald (1986a), p. 165, needs qualification to this extent. Davies (1993), pp. 105–10, sketches a contrast in number and size of kingdoms between Ireland and other 'Celtic' areas, notably Scotland; but it may not be sound to base conclusions about the extent of Pictish royal power on the survival of a single king-list: Adomnán, *Life of Columba* XI.42, describes a '*regulus*' of the Orkneys at King Bridei's court, such as to imply a relationship of Irish hierarchical type.

kings') who might also be a *ri cóicod* ('king of a fifth', meaning one of the five provinces of Ulster, Leinster, Munster, Connacht and Meath). As elsewhere, an overlord's prerogatives included command of a subordinate's military service.[95] The roll-calls of royal dead in Uí Néill battles show that this right was more than a legalistic abstraction.

Another royal entitlement was to tribute, which, as so often in early medieval Europe, was in food-renders. Kings could travel around their own people consuming its renders as hospitality, but it was safer to take the tribute of the subjugated in the form of herds on the hoof.[96] The distinction between tribute-levies in live cattle and cattle-raiding may not have been too clear.[97] Furthermore, one reason why legends have so many kings meeting their fate in a house rather than on the field may be that dependence was marked by the ritual of entering a lord's home or entertaining him at table. The risk of erupted tension on such occasions was real enough. Thus, while the preponderant evidence from early Christian Ireland breathes the spirit not of warrior culture but of traditional learning, there was ample scope for royal aggression. What set the pattern were the multiplicity of kings and the mechanisms of regnal hierarchy – each themselves functions of Irish tradition.

The key texts for the domestic context where Irish kings so often appear are law-tracts and quasi-legal statements of royal dues and duties. The fullest of these date to the twelfth century and may reflect later intensification of royal power.[98] The outlines of such a schema are, however, visible in *Críth Gablach*, a tract of probably the early eighth century that draws on earlier material.[99] Basically a disquisition on status, from the lowest ranks of the peasantry up to the afore-mentioned kingly pyramid, it defines ranks in terms of their accoutrements. For a king as for peasants, this involves an account of household organisation. Listed rights and obligations include not just food-supply and military service but summons of the assembly (*oenach*) that was the main point of contact between king and people. Attendants range from those hostages to which overlordship entitled him, to musicians and jugglers. Prescribed royal activities, each assigned its weekday, are drinking, judgement,

[95] Binchy (1970), p. 31. Cf. Charles-Edwards (1989), p. 38, for the military obligations of the Airgialla to the Uí Néill, and Byrne (1973), pp. 196–9, for those of Munster kings to Cashel: the comparison is worked out by P. Irvin in an unpublished paper that he kindly showed me.

[96] Charles-Edwards (1989), pp. 28–33, gives a pellucid account of the logic of this process.

[97] In saga form, the struggle of the Uí Néill to enforce their lordship over Leinster is represented as a series of attempts to collect vast herds of livestock allegedly owed for a Leinster king's dishonouring of a king of Tara's daughters: Dillon (1946), pp. 103–14.

[98] *Lebor na Cert. The Book of Rights*, ed. Dillon; Byrne (1973), pp. 43–7; cf. also O'Corráin (1978), pp. 26–30.

[99] *Críth Gablach*, ed. Binchy; Mac Neill (1923); Charles-Edwards (1986).

the board-game *fidchell*, hunting, sexual relations, horse-racing and judgement again. The point is to fit the pattern of kingly existence into the frame of the seven-day Romano-Christian week: sex is on Thursday because an Irish synod had prohibited it on Sundays and the fast-days of Wednesday and Friday.[100] What emerges through these stylised obscurities is that the military and legal activity common to mainline European kingship accompanies the same social priorities of drinking and hunting.

A similar programme of royal deportment can be glimpsed between the lines of sources whose main concern is with other matters. One of his late-seventh-century Lives sets St Patrick in confrontation with a whole court full of 'kings, satraps, dukes, princes and magnates' around the malignant King Laogaire at Tara, which is called a *palatium* with a *cenaculum* ('dining-room'). It would be a fair deduction that royal residences of the historical period, like nearby Lagore or Knowth, could be described in similar terms.[101] Like many another early medieval king, Laogaire felt constrained to consult an assembly of 'elders and all his senate' before committing himself to the new faith.[102] Much the same impression of the Pictish court is given by Adomnán.[103] However strange the things that foreign visitors to an Irish royal court might have been *told* about the way kings behaved, the evidence before their eyes would have been reassuringly familiar, its minuscule scale excepted.

A law-tract, *The false judgements of Caratnia*, tells how cases submitted to a legendary king would be referred by him to his judge, Caratnia. In all fifty-one suits, the king declares that Caratnia's judgement is false. Each time Caratnia can show that it is correct. An Irish king could apparently come under the same sort of petitioner pressure as a Roman emperor, but it is brehons that are credited with reliable response.[104] There is no extant legal statement by an early Irish king. Irish – and Welsh – law consists overwhelmingly of tracts transmitted by the professional elite who produced them. Yet 'good judgement' was clearly a prime requisite of ideal kings. Apart from allotting two weekdays to judgement, *Críth Gablach* envisages (usually emergency) conditions in which kings might issue decrees. It also avers that 'he is not a king . . . to whom no fines for breach of promulgated law are paid'.[105] A text laying out the arrangement of

100 *The Irish Penitentials*, ed. Bieler, pp. 116, 265; Charles-Edwards (forthcoming).

101 Muirchu, *Life of Patrick cc.*15, 19. Cf. Eogan and Byrne (1968); and, on the realities of historical Tara and other alleged royal centres, Wailes (1982).

102 Muirchu, *Life of Patrick c.*21.

103 Adomnán, *Life of Columba* II.32–5; cf. *Annals of Ulster* 729, and Alcock (1988).

104 Kelly (1988), Appendix 1, no. 5: this appendix is an invaluable 'layman's guide' to the range of extant Irish legal materials. Cf. *ibid.* p. 24, and Kelly (1986), p. 80.

105 Kelly (1988), pp. 19–24; Charles-Edwards (forthcoming). Cf. Binchy (1971); O'Corráin *et al.* (1984), pp. 386–7 and notes; Gerriets (1988); McCone (1990), pp. 9, 24.

law-courts puts a king in what looks like a presiding, if not directive, position.[106] The 'Instructions' of Cormac mac Airt, a legendary Irish king, expect much of royal justice.[107] He has been compared with Numa Pompilius, second king of Rome; the parallel shows how jurist law might find ideal royal prototypes. An Irish king could no more pronounce law without attendant experts than Justinian, Edward I or Napoleon. He might lack the resources or the special duty to implement law that these rulers had. He still stands for the law, as they did.

There is no reason to doubt that Irish kings had less dominant roles in the societies they ruled than their counterparts. Nor can it be doubted that this relative reticence was linked with the ascendancy of learned orders. Kings in Ireland had less power than elsewhere; lawyers, poets and prophets had more. But it was not that the strength of the professions caused the weakness of kings. Rather, the degree to which Irish kingship remained small-scale gave the professions their scope.[108] Whether their tradition could have retained its hold had kings commanded the sort of resources they did in the rest of the West is a quite different question. By the High Middle Ages, Irish, Welsh and Scots had constructed quite elaborate structures of ruler power. There is no longer any question about a hierarchy of officials, nor of the taxation and services they could enforce. The moral here is important. Traditional Celtic learning was no more proof against escalating royal power than against the appeal of Christianity. The problem that remains is how far such developments were already under way in the period when law-tracts and sagas were first committed to writing. The likelihood is that, if they were in train by 700, the evidence would have hidden this from us. In any event, Irish society was not necessarily stuck in the time-warp that has distorted the vision of contemporary commentators, and of some of their latter-day avatars.

BARBARIAN KINGSHIP: GERMANS

For the purposes of this chapter, 'Germanic' kings are defined as those whose own names and/or that of the people they professed to rule derived from languages philologists call Germanic. This section thus covers the kings who governed the one-time dioceses of Italy, Spain, Gaul and Britannia in the post-Roman era. The definition is somewhat hesitant because many modern scholars are far from sure that either societies or their rulers are helpfully described as 'Germanic'.[109]

[106] Kelly (1986) and (1988), Appendix 1, no. 71.

[107] *The Instructions of King Cormac mac Airt*, ed. Meyer; cf. O'Cathasaigh (1977), pp. 10–11, 59–65, 105.

[108] Davies (1993), especially pp. 122–3.

[109] Cf. Halsall, chapter 2 above.

The conundrum has a twofold root. In the first place, a cardinal fact of early German history is that we never meet persons or classes whose position approaches that of Celtic *filid*. The Germanic past had no guarantors. Almost all we know of the Germans' history before, during and after the era of the invasions comes from pens which, whether or not wielded by those of Roman origin, were steeped in Roman values.[110] Secondly, the Germans were affected by Rome long before the invasions, in ways and to extents which those Celts who withstood Roman conquest were not.[111] Well-known 'barbarian' royal mannerisms such as the giving of gold rings or military gear to followers, or fixing an enemy's head on a stake, were anticipated by victorious emperors.[112] Yet to say that is clearly not to say enough. Those mannerisms became firmly embedded in a barbarian idiom. The Roman legacy was so thoroughly mediatised that scholars have barely recognised it, and contemporaries could never have done. Germanic *rex* and Byzantine *basileus* may have a common ancestry, but they are no more the same animal than gorilla and chimpanzee. So it is still necessary to explore the accessible past of 'Germanic' kingship: and, whether or not this is meaningfully called 'Germanic', it remains convenient to do so – without inverted commas.

Proto-kings

Two considerations suggest that Germanic kingship was already ancient before the barbarian invasions, but each also implies that its powers and responsibilities were then very different from what they became. In the first place, the earliest monument of a Germanic vernacular, Ulfila's fourth-century translation of the Bible into Gothic, exploits quite a rich vocabulary of rule. Especially striking is *reiks*, meaning a ruler of the synagogue like Nicodemus, but also the chief Pharisees, and indeed the 'Prince of Devils'.[113] Though confined as a noun to Gothic, other derivatives recur widely: we need look no further than *Reich*. The first of two important things here is that its near-universal stem strongly suggests that the word was borrowed from Celtic, and so dates back to the distant

[110] The central contention and principal foundation of the important recent studies by Goffart (1980), ch. 1, and (1988).

[111] Thompson (1965), especially chs. 2–3; Hedeager (1988); Todd (1992), especially chs. 3, 5–6: Heather (1994c).

[112] For example *Inscriptiones Latinae Selectae* no. 2313 for a legionary receiving gold collars and armlets at the behest of Hadrian; *L'Année Epigraphique* (1956), p. 124 for a soldier being given a horse and weapons by Marcus Aurelius; cf. generally Campbell (1984), pp. 198–203. For heads on stakes, see McCormick (1986), pp. 18, 36, 40–1, etc., and fig. 6. One might ponder in the same spirit the obsequies of Beowulf (lines 3169–82); for Augustus, Dio, *Histories*, LVI.42, and Attila, Jordanes, *Getica* XLIX.256–8.

[113] Wolfram (1970), pp. 3–6; Heather and Matthews (1991), pp. 190–5.

time when Celts and Germans were in close contact. Secondly, Procopius says that *rhex* was the title used of no less formidable a suzerain than Theoderic the Ostrogoth, and 'was what barbarians were wont to call their leaders'; the appearance of *rix* on Ostrogothic coinage is supporting evidence.[114] One implication is that the *reiks* of Ulfila's day had grown very substantially in power by Theoderic's. Another is that the terminology of early Germanic kingship was not only diverse but also fluid. The same point is made by the word, which had the greatest future in this respect, though conspicuously absent from Ulfila's 'wordhoard', *kuningaz*. It was well enough established in West Germanic to be borrowed by Finnish and Slavonic; the distinctly underpowered chieftaincy represented by Slavonic *knez* may be the clue to the term's lack of resonance for Ulfila.[115] There is no reason why a word meaning merely 'member of a kin' should come to designate anything special, *unless* the 'kin' represented were the 'tribe' or people: that is, a ruler so described was a focus and symbol of ethnic identity.[116] If that were its basic meaning, we might very well expect it to acquire new significance in an age of new ethnic formations.

The other evidence on early Germanic kingship is of course that of Roman writers, and their lessons are ultimately the same as that of vocabulary. That Tacitus should have thought that Germans had kings when Caesar did not is best explained if they were generally too marginal to attract Caesar's notice. Tacitus' famous formula, 'reges ex nobilitate, duces ex virtute sumunt' (literally translated 'they take kings for their high-birth, war-leaders for their courage'), appears to mean that kings were not war-leaders, nor, apparently, did they have much influence in the judicial or religious spheres.[117] Yet Caesar and Tacitus both knew of figures altogether more formidable than such royal wraiths.[118] Moreover both writers say enough about early Germanic society to suggest what worked the transformation. Each implies that a chieftain might attract followings of warriors in return for hospitality, and a share of the loot in treasure and particularly weapons that their service had secured. Hence, whatever the notional position of kings, the initiative in the conditions of more widespread warfare from the late second century onwards lay with anyone offering the prospect of the glory and plunder that was war's reward. A *dux ex virtute* appointed in an emergency might thus acquire the permanence of a *rex* for himself and his family; a *rex* might indeed achieve the role of a *dux*. Warband

114 Procopius, *Wars* v.i.26: De Vries (1956), pp. 303–5; Wolfram (1967), pp. 41–2.

115 De Vries (1956), pp. 291–2; Kahl (1960), pp. 178–84, 238–9 (n. 212); above, p. 572. On the problem of the North Germanic forms of the word, see Kahl (1960), pp. 198–204; also Green (1965), p. 347.

116 Green (1965), p. 317, n. 4; Wallace-Hadrill (1971), p. 13.

117 Caesar, *Gallic War* vi.21–3; Tacitus, *Germania* x–xii.

118 Caesar, *Gallic War* i.31–53: Tacitus, *Annals* i.55–68, ii.9–17, 26, 44–6, 62–3, 88. On all this, see Schlesinger (1956), pp. 116–21; Wallace-Hadrill (1971), pp. 5–7.

activity would meanwhile fracture tribal structures into a flotsam which new leadership could reconstitute as new peoples. This would in turn explain the emergence of a royal terminology whose point is precisely that a ruler embodies his people's entity.[119]

Such a model does make sense of some of the evidence from late antiquity and even the time when Germanic kings already controlled much of the West.[120] Ammianus Marcellinus is one of a set of fourth-century authors who call Athanaric, ruler of the Goths, *iudex*, not *rex*. Athanaric was certainly a war-leader and a member of a dynasty. He was also, if the Roman label has any meaning, responsible for law, and perhaps in a sense for religion. However, he was not what Goths gave Romans to understand that they meant by 'king'.[121] Procopius has a remarkable story about the Heruli. They decided to dispense with their *rhex* whom they anyway treated with little respect. Second thoughts persuaded them that they were badly off 'without ruler or general', so they sent a deputation all the way to 'Thule' (apparently Scandinavia) to find a replacement among those with 'royal blood', of whom there turned out to be a handsome number. Like any good ancient historian, Procopius was an *afficionado* of the tall tale where barbarians were concerned. But this story may serve to confirm that royal *nobilitas* was something Germans took seriously, even if not quite sure why.[122] Finally, Bede says that the eighth-century Old Saxons 'have no *rex* but only a number of satraps . . . and when . . . war is about to break out, they cast lots . . . and all . . . obey the one on whom the lot falls for the duration of the war'.[123] This is like the system among Germans of the first centuries BC and AD, which was yet compatible with *reges* distinguished by *nobilitas*. It is a fair guess that, like Caesar, Bede just could not recognise kings who did not square with his own experience. His 'satraps' were quite probably what other sources called *regales*; and his temporary Saxon *duces* were what could develop into the sort of *rex* he did understand. How much of this model of emerging Germanic kingship is really valid can never be known. Monarchy would be recast all over again on Roman soil. What seems safe to say is that kingship was hardly less native to Germans than to Celts. That, in

[119] For fuller statements of this (hypothetical) schema, see Wormald (1982), pp. 145–6, and (1986a), pp. 163–4.

[120] For what follows, cf. Wallace-Hadrill (1971), pp. 8–20, and the especially penetrating survey by James (1989).

[121] Thompson (1966), pp. 44–6; Wolfram (1975); but for the true meaning of Themistius' much-quoted passage, see Heather and Matthews (1991), pp. 42–3, n. 91; also Heather (1991), pp. 98–107, 120–1.

[122] Procopius, *Wars* VI.14–15; cf. Av. Cameron (1985), p. 219. On this episode, see also Hedeager, chapter 18 above.

[123] Bede, *HE* V.10. Bede also supplies dispassionate evidence that Anglo-Saxon kings were descended from Woden, I.15; for the genealogical *corpus*, see Sisam (1953); Dumville (1976).

the last resort, must be why it was *king*ship, not emperorship, that was the West's central political institution for the next millennium and more.

Kings in power[124]

In working the transformation of *rex* into *rex/dux*, Roman example as well as Roman money and Roman policy was surely decisive. It was in battle that barbarians most often met an emperor. As time went on they were also likely to be found in the ranks of his army. Imperial victory, humbled barbarians, generosity to troops, were constant iconographical motifs, sounded not only by dozens of triumphal arches all over the provinces, but also by coins and medals circulating beyond as well as within the Empire's borders.[125] For that vast majority on either side of the frontier whose experience of emperors remained exclusively pictorial, the image of ruler as generalissimo must have been almost subliminal. A strong case can be made that the Anglo-Saxon potentate honoured at Sutton Hoo was meant to represent a Roman emperor, from gorgeous parade-ground armour to rod of consular office.[126] Yet Sutton Hoo gives notice that however necessary is Roman example in explaining the styles assumed by post-Roman rulers, it is not in itself sufficient. Two similar military artefacts make the point. In the helmet-plate showing the Lombard King Agilulf enthroned between winged victories and suppliants emerging from towered cities, there is much beyond crude workmanship to announce a *post*-Roman world. Agilulf has flowing hair and beard and carries a sword, as emperors are rarely if ever seen to do. Yet this is still a Roman victory ritual.[127] The Sutton Hoo helmet also has ancient-world prototypes, but its closest analogues lie in headgear from similar burials in sixth- or seventh-century Sweden. The late antique echoes here hardly have the resonance they had for Agilulf's smith.[128] Whatever its Roman roots, the warrior ethic had been thoroughly assimilated.

Sutton Hoo Mound One contains treasures, weapons, and weapons that are themselves treasures: it is demonstrably a warlord's monument, testimony to a more specifically military power than that of emperors. However, it is not demonstrably a *king's* monument. Sutton Hoo could be the cemetery of

[124] Succession to kingship is overlooked here, as for the Irish. The important discussion of the Merovingian position by Wood (1994), pp. 58–60, 91–101, 123–36, 234–8, may well hold good, *mutatis mutandis*, for Visigothic, Lombard and perhaps even West Saxon monarchies.

[125] Campbell (1984), pp. 35–6, 72–85, 142–8, 182–4; McCormick (1986), pp. 24–8, 32–4, 57–8; and, for more on penetration of the Germanic hinterland by these images, Hedeager (1978).

[126] W. Filmer-Sankey (1996).

[127] Illustration, analysis and bibliography in McCormick (1986), pp. 289–93.

[128] Bruce Mitford *et al.* (1975–83), II, pp. 186–97, 205–25; Campbell (1992), pp. 92–3: Sasanian prefigurations do not exclude the dance's connection with the cult of Woden: Ellis Davidson (1988), pp. 88–9.

a dynasty of *duces* on its way to what would later be recognised as *regalitas*.[129] However, a grave of a century and a half earlier, which heralds military power as lustily as Sutton Hoo, was that of the known Frankish king Childeric I, and its contents included his seal-ring. The worlds of barbarian warlord and sub-Roman official had met when Clovis' father was buried at Tournai in 481.[130] Tournai and Sutton Hoo are merely the most spectacular specimens of warrior burials distributed throughout sixth- and seventh-century Europe (except in Gothic areas).[131] One reason why late Roman emperors were decreasingly military in style and record was probably the resolutely civilian timbre of upper-class life. The elite of the sub-Roman West looked more unambiguously for leadership in battle.

It is most unlikely that all those buried as warriors belonged ethnically to the Germanic-speaking peoples who had crossed the Roman frontier.[132] But the personal names that aristocrats were beginning to give themselves point to a more specifically Germanic legacy. As soon as they occur in significant quantity, one or other of the two elements making up Germanic names is likely to have warlike overtones:

Ag(il/n)/Ecg:	(sword) blade	(C)Hild:	battle
Ang:	(spear) point	Gais, Gar:	spear
Asc/Æsc:	spear	Grim:	mask, helmet
B(e)adu:	fight	Gunt/Gu/yth:	fight
Brand:	sword	Hath/Head:	battle
Brunn:	breastplate	Sige:	victory
(C)Hari/Here:	army	Vig:	war, warrior

Other name-elements have equally pertinent connotations. 'Wulf (Wolf)' and '(C)hramn (raven)' are the battlefield beasts of prey in heroic saga.[133] Evidence of this sort of course needs careful handling. But there are cases of sixth- and seventh-century individuals thinking about their names' military meaning.[134] Another important etymological point is that a word for king used in Germanic languages by the sixth century was in Anglo-Saxon form *dryhten*, meaning

[129] This point, originally argued by Wallace-Hadrill (1960), and later abandoned by him ((1971), pp. 69–71, and (1975), pp. 53–6), has recently been restated by Campbell (1992). Even if this was the graveyard of those who led the East Anglians in battle, one might still argue that Bede's *HE* II.12, III.18 read back the vocabulary of his own day into the early seventh century, much as he may have seen Old Saxon conditions in the light of his own experience (above, p. 593).

[130] Description: James (1988), pp. 58–67; and further discussion, James (1992).

[131] See the map in Engel (1970), p. 64; and for the Goths, cf. James (1980b), pp. 23–37.

[132] James (1978). [133] Förstemann (1900).

[134] Venantius Fortunatus, *Ad Chilpericum Regem*, lines 27–8 (a partly false etymology, however!); Felix, *Life of Guthlac* c.10.

'warband-leader'.[135] Its use is not confined to the literature of war. Its semantic core contributes to the formation of a term for the king's picked followers, *antrustiones*, in Frankish law-codes.[136] The relevance of warrior society's staccato rhythms to the hectic geopolitics of the 'Heroic Age' is clear enough, whatever the date assigned to heroic poetry like *Beowulf*. Clovis for one did not doubt it: when Ragnachar's followers complained that he had won them to his side with arm-rings of false gold, he observed that as betrayers of their lord they deserved no better.[137]

Again, however, battlefield experience is what says most about the war-leadership of Germanic rulers and its attendant risks. Of eight Northumbrian kings down to 685, only Oswiu died in his bed. The East Anglians had four kings killed in battle. The case of Sigeberht is instructive. He had taken monastic retirement, and on his refusal to emerge in face of Mercian attack, the East Anglians 'dragged him to the fight . . . in the hope that soldiers would be less . . . ready to flee if they had . . . one who was once their most vigorous . . . leader. But remembering his profession . . . he refused to carry anything but a rod . . . He was killed.'[138] It is no surprise that those who erected Sutton Hoo Mound One should believe in a king's effect on a battle regardless of his will to participate. Sigibert's Frankish contemporary and namesake, by contrast, did not doubt his duty to take the field against Thuringian rebels even though he was a mere child. But Sigibert III's army was slaughtered; he was left 'seated on his horse weeping unrestrainedly for those he had lost'.[139] This was arguably the beginning of the end for Merovingian kingship in Austrasia. Military leadership increasingly passed to mayors of the palace, whose warrior record finally bore fruit in the decision that those who held real power should also be called kings.

Early Germanic kings were no more makers of law than their Irish equivalents. Royal law-giving in the sub-Roman West arose, as in the early Roman Empire, from subjects' expectations.[140] The *Variae* of Cassiodorus are *belles-lettres* by an Italian aristocrat who, as Quaestor and Praetorian Prefect for the Ostrogothic kings of Italy, continued a family office-holding tradition

135 Green (1965), part II.

136 *Lex Salica* XLII.1–2; LXX–LXXI, LXXIII; cf. *Pactus pro Tenore Pacis* LXXXIV, XCI. Cf. also Wood (1994) on the Frankish king's '*leudes*'. Both *dryhten* and *leudis* appear in royal contexts in the seventh-century Kentish laws: Laws of Æthelberht 2; Laws of Wihtred 5, 9–10, ed. Liebermann.

137 Gregory, *Hist.* II.42; Campbell (1982), pp. 53–5.

138 Bede, *HE* III.18; Campbell (1982), p. 56.

139 Fredegar, *Chronicle* IV.87. See Fouracre, chapter 14 above.

140 What follows takes much the same line as Wormald (1977), but aims to amplify and clarify what was not then adequately brought out, and these objectives are further pursued in Wormald (1998), ch. 2, and (1999).

stretching at least two generations back to imperial times.[141] The *Variae* are not laws, but many are (suitably florid) replies to legal grievances. Topics on which Italy's new masters were invited to pronounce were, to use Cassiodorus' word, breaches of *civilitas*: judicial sharp practice; crimes, and escape of slaves; sexual misdemeanours, sorcery and homicide; property rights in long-established tenure; and not least, use of Gothic military leverage both by territorially acquisitive Goths and by Romans in search of powerful patrons.[142] The letters and poems of Sidonius suggest that Gallic counterparts to Cassiodorus actively encouraged their Visigothic and Burgundian rulers to accept similar responsibilities.[143] Barbarian kings were being kitted out to take on the legal role of emperors and praetorian prefects.[144] That they should go on to issue codes like their major legislative model, the *Theodosian Code* (438), was the next logical step. Isidore wrote that under King Euric the Goths began to have 'institutes of law in writing, for before they were governed by tradition and custom alone'.[145] He did not say that Euric legislated for Goths only. Nor need Alaric II's issue of a *Breviarium* of Roman law imply that his father was unconcerned with Romans.[146] Cassiodorus' formula for a *comes Gothorum* distinguished suits between Goths, 'terminated according to our edicts', from those of Goth and Roman, 'decided by fair reason in association with a Roman juris-consult', and those of Romans, 'whose decision rests with Roman examiners'. Goths came under the remit of 'civilised' written law. Romans were by and large left to their own legal devices. But Cassiodorus' whole output shows that this was far from a bipartite legal regime.[147] The new kingdoms were governed by the king's written pronouncements as necessary, by written Roman or unwritten barbarian custom as otherwise appropriate.

141 Cassiodorus, *Variae* I.3–4: his *encomia* in the king's name on his father's and grandfather's records: for his own, see *Variae* IX.24–5.

142 See especially *Variae* IX.18–20 (the Edict of Theoderic's grandson, Athalaric); and, for Romano-Gothic relations, I.18; II.16–17; III.13; IV.28; VII.39, 42; VIII.28 (on which Boethius, *Consolation* I.4).

143 Sidonius, *Poems* VII.311–13; V.562; XXIII.447–9; *Letters* II.3.3; V.5.3; VIII.4.3. Cf. also Gregory, *Hist.* II.33.

144 So cogently Collins (1983a), pp. 27–9.

145 Isidore, *Historia Gothorum* XXXV. For a different view of this endlessly masticated problem, see Wolfram (1988), pp. 194–7 and notes.

146 Arguments for the 'personality' of Euric's code tend to be (good) arguments against the 'territoriality' of Alaric's: King (1980). The *Breviary* is as likely to reflect the support of Romans who themselves feared the Franks (Gregory, *Hist.* II.36–7), as a concession from a government haunted by Catholic fifth columns.

147 *Variae* VII.3. The much-debated 'Edict of Theoderic' was, as Dr Sam Barnish persuades me, the work of Theoderic the Ostrogoth, though not without Cassiodoran ornament; it is a code for Goths and Romans, even though *Anonymus Valesianus* II.12.60 might be read as evidence of Theoderic legislating for Goths exclusively.

The crucial point is that Germanic kings replaced emperors as makers of new law.

The main statement of Visigothic law was issued by Chindasuinth and Reccesuinth in the mid-seventh century. This was the purest post-Roman manifestation of Roman legislative priorities. Arranged in twelve books like the Twelve Tables, it was meant to supplant *all* previous legislation. It did.[148] This most Romanised of early medieval law books was, logically enough, the only one to abolish Roman law, but Roman inspiration was no longer all that was at work. Councils of the whole Spanish church at Toledo published both Reccesuinth's code and Ervig's revision. Reccesuinth was lectured on a law-giver's business. Ervig invited the assembled fathers to vet his decrees.[149] The code's first book draws on the theories of Isidore. Law is 'the soul of the whole body politic'. As that body's head, the king is source of its guiding principles, but head and body follow the one programme.[150] In their close association of church and king, Visigothic law-makers not only echoed Theodosius but also anticipated Charlemagne.

The Lombard *Edict of Rothari* was issued at much the same time as the Visigothic Code. In contrast to Visigothic legislation, it explicitly claims to state 'the ancient law of the Lombards'. There is quite enough in it that can hardly be Roman, notably laws about feud, for this claim to be taken seriously.[151] Yet if Rothari was codifying Lombard law for Lombards, he was committing to writing what the 'leading judges' and 'most happy army' invoked in his epilogue should already have known. It is hard to resist the conclusion that his code is first and foremost a symbol of his people's new place in a civilised world. At the same time, there is much that is 'civilised' about it. Marks of Roman influence shared with the Visigoths are scale and comprehensiveness. It is authenticated and dated, as Roman law should be. For all its 'barbarism', it is conceivable only in terms of the extensive survival of Roman legal culture in Italy.[152] The best proof of this is that it would ultimately be cited in court proceedings more often than any post-Roman laws bar the Visigothic.

Something comparable, but in important ways distinct, happened in northern Europe. *Lex Salica*, the primary law of the Franks, was later ascribed to Clovis, almost certainly correctly.[153] But its earliest prologue attributes it to

[148] *LV* II.1.10; for the viability of Visigothic legislation in an age when there is evidence to check it, see Nehlsen (1977), pp. 483–502, and Collins (1985).

[149] *Council of Toledo* VIII, X, p. 265, XII, p. 383. On all this see King (1972), pp. 23–39, but also Collins (1983a), pp. 115–29, for political considerations that weighed as heavily as ideological.

[150] *LV* I.2.2, II.1.4. For a good case that the author (or at least editor) of the code was Isidore's pupil, Bishop Braulio of Saragossa, see Lynch (1938), pp. 137–40.

[151] *Edictum Rothari*, 386. [152] Bognetti (1939); Wickham (1981), pp. 36–9, 69–70.

[153] Wood (1994), pp. 108–13 – a notably hard-headed analysis.

four otherwise unknown men 'from beyond the Rhine', so presumably from the pre-invasion past.[154] Royal sponsors are also lacking in its seventh-century sister code, *Lex Ribuaria*, and in the first English code.[155] This confirms that Germanic political culture was initially as hesitant as Celtic about royal law-giving. Kings as explicit legislators are one more symptom of Romanisation. But Clovis' successors and Anglo-Saxon kings after Æthelberht were increasingly preoccupied with the concerns of the church and with law and order as such. The Frankish Childebert II and Ine of Wessex punished Sunday work. The former even forbade taking of revenge.[156] Frankish kings made subject peoples 'civilised' by giving them written law.[157] As kings came to seem wardens of social peace, earlier kings were retrospectively credited with a legislative role they perhaps could not claim at first. Romanisation never went so far in northern as in southern Europe. References to 'lex' in law suits often have no basis in written law, since by no means all law had been written down.[158] Yet Germanic kings became law-makers under the sort of pressure from their new subjects that Hellenistic cities had exerted on Roman emperors. Even where written law remained more an object of aspiration than an accomplished fact, there was intensification of the idea, perhaps already residual in Germanic as in Celtic society, that kings stood for justice. It was an idea that would achieve enhanced intensity under the Carolingians.

Early medieval western kings inherited what was, by the standards of the time when Germans first became familiar with Rome, a massive palace mechanism. Among the themes of their rule was its scaling down until it again resembled what had been at Augustus' disposal. The charters whereby Merovingian and Lombard kings gave judgement represent them formulaically as 'residing at their palace' amidst an array of court personnel.[159] The protocol of Toledo Councils was attested by 'comites' from the *officium palatinum*,[160] but the reality of the position is well conveyed by the word *gardingus* also used for these counts. Of Gothic origin, it means 'house-man' (compare Anglo-Norse *garth*),

[154] *Lex Salica* (*65 tit.*), Prologue. The 'Epilogue', *Lex Salica* (*65 tit.*), p. 253, a later Merovingian text of questionable authority, ascribes the code only to 'primus rex francorum'. But if the early Carolingian 'Longer Prologue', *Lex Salica* (*100 tit.*), Prologue, understood Clovis to be meant, we need not hesitate to do the same.

[155] Bede was the first to say that Æthelberht issued the code that has come to stand in his name, *HE* II.5; the introductory clause printed in *Gesetze* I, p. 3 is a manuscript rubric: Wormald (1995), p. 983.

[156] *Decretio Childerberti* III.7, II.3; Laws of Ine 3–3.2 (and Laws of Wihtred 9, 11); cf. Wormald (1995), pp. 977–87. For the development of Frankish royal measures against theft, see Murray (1988).

[157] *Pact, Lex Alamannorum* Prologue; *Lex Baiwariorum*, Prologue. Cf. Wood (1994), pp. 115–17.

[158] Nehlsen (1977), pp. 453–83; Fouracre (1986), pp. 29–37; Wormald (1986b), pp. 152–7.

[159] *Diplomata Regum Francorum*, nos. 48–9, 60, 64, 66, etc.; *Codice Diplomatico Longobardo* III (1), 12, 14–15, etc. The documentary evidence is assessed by Brühl (1968).

[160] *Council of Toledo* VIII, p. 289; IX, p. 307; XII, pp. 402–3; XIII, pp. 434–5; XVI, p. 521.

and is the strict equivalent of the Merovingian *domesticus*.[161] A western king's home in this era and for long afterwards was his 'hall'. Anglo-Saxon historians have become familiar with the diptych of Sutton Hoo and Yeavering. The one testifies to the technology with and for which warriors fought and died; the other to the environment where they sang and drank and had their being.[162] Again, then, it is no matter if *Beowulf*'s vivid festivities in the royal hall of Heorot are not contemporary evidence. Yeavering's hall, which measured 25 by 12 metres, is eloquent enough of the early medieval royal lifestyle.

It is not that Byzantine models struck no echoes in the West. The Visigothic and Lombard monarchies had what they clearly considered capitals at Toledo and Pavia.[163] The Visigoth Leovigild (568–586) was said by Isidore to have been 'first to sit openly in royal garb upon a throne', when 'before . . . both costume and seat were the same for people and king alike'. This probably involved wearing a crown; votive crowns of Visigothic kings survive.[164] He was certainly the first Visigothic king to issue gold coins in his own name and image, and in evident imitation of Byzantine models.[165] When a Frankish king did this, Procopius thought it a blatant trespass on an imperial preserve.[166] A fascinating and near-ubiquitous echo is of Hippodrome ritual. Agilulf proclaimed his son's succession in the Milan theatre. King Chilperic of the Franks built amphitheatres at Soissons and Paris, and his cousin staged chariot-races at Arles.[167] It has been shown that the street-plan of Canterbury was modified so that all roads led to the theatre. And one of the most striking Yeavering structures is a building of theatrical design.[168] In the end, though, so much aping of Byzantine styles does no more than offset the irreducible East–West contrast.

Sub-Roman government of course had officials; and not only in Germanic-speaking England but also in Francia, Italy and Spain some of these officials had Germanic titles.[169] The point is that the apparatus of government was now quite different, in spirit as much as size. Cassiodorus' *Variae* show that Theoderic's regime made a systematic attempt to prolong late Roman palace government, in the interests of the senatorial class that had found a new elixir

[161] Claude (1971), p. 15. [162] Hope Taylor (1977). [163] Ewig (1963).

[164] Isidore, *Historia Gothorum* LI; Talbot Rice (1966), pp. 180–1. Julian's *Historia Wambae* c.26 seems to describe the rebellious Count Paul using one of these to crown himself, which would tell us that kings normally wore something of the sort.

[165] Grierson and Blackburn (1986), pp. 49–51.

[166] Procopius, *Wars* VII.33.2–6; cf. Collins (1983b), pp. 27–30.

[167] Paul, *HL* IV.30; Gregory, *Hist.* V.17; Procopius, *Wars* VII.33.5. Cf. McCormick (1986), pp. 312–14, for a ruthlessly theatrical Visigothic evocation of Roman triumphalism.

[168] Brooks (1984), pp. 24–5; Hope Taylor (1977), pp. 119–22.

[169] Most obviously the Frankish *graphio* (cf. Anglo-Saxon *gerefa* = reeve), the counterpart to the *comes civitatis*: see Murray (1986).

from participating in it. Theoderic still had palaces to accommodate it.[170] But most post-Roman governments, like that of early emperors, were regularly on the move, and mobility is not conducive to heavy government machinery.[171] The roll-call of Visigothic, Lombard or Frankish officialdom is attenuated almost beyond recognition. There is a bleak discrepancy between the luxuriant lists of office-holders in the *Prosopography of the Later Roman Empire* and those of its successor states.[172] For all the Roman relics in the Frankish government system, the impression that lingers is of a barely differentiated personnel.[173] A 'provost of the sacred bedchamber' was replaced by a 'mayor of the palace': no eunuch, but an aristocrat of military background and increasingly military function. Society was returning to the days when a ruler's chief assistant was his second-in-command. A significant twist was also affecting the terminology of service. The future great title of 'seneschal' is a Germanic word whose suffix (as in 'marshal') has menial connotations. Young nobles served apprenticeships in the king's entourage, specifically at table or in his stable, before moving (it may be) to more responsible posts in local government.[174] Attendance in the privacy of a ruler's bedroom had made way for servicing his wholly public feasts and hunts. However else it is described, post-Roman government cannot be called bureaucratic. Hence, kings were no longer equipped to tax as emperors had, and were beholden to an aristocracy whose idea of patronage was not office but land.[175]

A crucial difference between post-Roman regimes that foundered like the Ostrogothic, and those that ultimately flourished, above all the Frankish, was not that the one was heretically Arian and the other orthodox, but something crystallised by the religious difference: the maintenance of a gulf between barbarian and Roman in the name of the basic late antique divorce of military and civilian. The kingdoms that prospered were those that integrated their elite. The price of integration was the ascendancy of military values that had little use for governmental hierarchies and that made the hospitality of a lord's hall the fulcrum of upper-class solidarity.[176]

As rulers who with few exceptions absorbed Christianity as part of the imperial legacy, barbarian kings were bound to aspire to Constantinian status.

170 Cassiodorus, *Variae* VII; cf. Barnwell (1992), part III: Ward-Perkins (1984), pp. 158–66; Johnson (1988).

171 Cf. Millar (1992), pp. 28–53, 203–72.

172 Jones, Martindale and Morris (1971–92); Jarnut (1972); Ebling (1974); García Moreno (1974).

173 Ganz (1983); Barnwell (1992), pp. 101–8; Wood (1994), pp. 262–3.

174 Cf. Claude (1971), p. 208, on the destiny of Visigoth *gardingi*. The Visigothic *comes scanciarum* in *officium palatinum* lists appears to be an official charged with dispensation of liquid refreshment.

175 This ever-controversial issue cannot be debated here. But I find unanswerable the case put by Wickham (1984) and (1993) (rebutting the most ambitious attempt to give Roman taxation prolonged afterlife).

176 See now Heather (1994b), especially pp. 192–7.

It is no accident that Clovis' first foundation was a Church of the Holy Apostles at Paris, or that he was buried there; nor indeed that this was where his great-grandson, Chlothar II, held the greatest of Merovingian church councils in 614.[177] The western scene was complicated by ideological cross-currents. The Latin church learned from Augustine, its one great theoretician, to look more askance than easterners at secular power's spiritual role. Germanic kings joined the church when emperors were Arian, and several dynasties stayed that way for much longer. In Augustine's North Africa, Vandal kings evoked memories of a Diocletianic persecutor, not a thirteenth apostle.[178] None the less, kings furnished the post-Roman West with its best-known martyrs. The cult of the Burgundian king Sigismund, killed in 523 by the Franks, looks like the kind of devotion that clustered around the victims of medieval politics until the days of Simon de Montfort and beyond.[179] However, the sanctification of Oswald was another matter. Oswald could be seen, however dubiously, as a king who had died for Christ in battle with a pagan enemy. As a martyr, he was a hero of Christian warfare. His fame thus deserved, as Bede stressed, to eclipse that of any of his race's other martial heroes.[180] It may not be too much to see here a conscious counterpart to the heroic fame which the *Beowulf* poet thought the sole reward for a life of spectacular endeavour.

Germanic kings were in general ready to give their churches a lead. The evidence is uneven, but it can be argued that the councils of the Merovingian church should be seen in the same light as the more familiar assemblies of church and state under Visigothic kings.[181] A curious poem implies that Cunipert should be credited for the synod that ended the 'Aquileian' schism in Italy.[182] Oswiu of Northumbria, not the assembled ecclesiastics, took the crucial decision at the Synod of Whitby.[183] But the Visigothic kings remain the best exemplifications of the Constantinian role, here again anticipating the Carolingians. From the moment when a newly converted Reccared was hailed by the third Toledo Council (589) as 'a new Constantine, a new Marcian', Visigothic kingship was set firmly into a Byzantine mould. That may be one thing that turned them almost at once into persecutors of the Jews. Another, already implied, was that rising Christian interest in Old Testament example might well, as Isidore argued, be at the expense of the ex-beneficiaries of God's special relationship.[184] Spaniards were ahead of all Westerners in seeing that

177 Périn (1992); Wood (1994), p. 154.

178 Moorhead (1992); but compare the realities as reflected in Clover (1986).

179 Wood (1994), p. 52; the cult of later episcopal casualties of Merovingian politics provides a parallel: pp. 142, 230.

180 Bede, *HE* III.9–13.

181 Wood (1994), pp. 105–6.

182 *Carmen de Synodo Ticinensi*, pp. 189–91.

183 Bede, *HE* III.25.

184 Collins (1983a), pp. 129–42. Note that the *Carmen* of the Pavia Synod (n. 171) says that Perctarit had forced baptism on the Jews.

the Old Testament offered the best ideological underpinning for an integration of Christian principles with martial priorities. Their kings were the first to be anointed when inaugurated, perhaps already in 631, certainly by 672.[185] Especially notable was the Church's liturgical commitment to Visigothic royal victory. Carl Erdmann found Spain 'out of line' with the rest of Europe in its precocious development of the crusading ideal.[186]

As at Byzantium, a biblical model had more attractive facets. It was presumably its harping on the duty to provide for the down-trodden that induced King Oswald to break up the silver dish from which he had been consuming his Easter banquet to supply largesse for beggars. Frankish contemporaries of Justinian built *xenodochia*.[187] St Denis was already the 'special patron' of the Merovingian dynasty, and kings were mainly buried in his abbey. But Clovis II was said to have scandalised his monks by stripping silver from the apse of the church so as to benefit the poor.[188] A paradox of late Roman rule thus recurred in the sub-Roman West: kings whose power increasingly distanced them from the run of their people (not that they were so far removed as in Constantinople's palace) were brought closer in principle to their least privileged subjects.

CONCLUSION: DOLITTLE KINGSHIP

In the winter of 749–750, the pope was visited by the abbot of St Denis and an English bishop from the Bonifatian circle. They had been sent by an unidentified but hardly mysterious authority to ask whether it was a good thing that Frankish kings should not have 'kingly power'? One of history's most famous leading questions duly produced the right answer: 'Pope Zacharias instructed Pippin that it was better to call him king that had power than him who remained without royal power.' Pippin was accordingly 'elected king according to Frankish custom, anointed by the hand of Archbishop Boniface . . . and elevated by the Franks to the kingdom . . . while Childeric, who was falsely called king, was tonsured and sent to a monastery'.[189]

Zacharias' answer has ever since seemed the only one possible. But this was because it led to the masterful rule of the Carolingians, and still more pertinently to Einhard's *Life of Charlemagne*, where the last Merovingians were unforgettably reduced to laughing-stocks. The circumstances have ensured that the pre-750 period's best-remembered legacy was not the formidable force

[185] King (1972), pp. 48–9 (n. 5).

[186] Erdmann (1935/1977), pp. 6, 22, 30, 39, 43, 82 (which made it a backwater to his Francocentric view); contrast the powerful discussion by McCormick (1986), pp. 304–12.

[187] Bede, *HE* III.6: Wood (1994), p. 184.

[188] Wood (1994), p. 157: for 'peculiaris patronus noster' and the more normal Merovingian reciprocation of his favours, see *Diplomata Regum Francorum* 48, 51, 61, 64, etc.

[189] *Annales Regni Francorum*, s.a. 749–50, pp. 8, 10.

Germanic kingship had become, but the notion of a 'shadow-king', a *roi fainéant*, kingship in decline. Yet at least one Frankish aristocrat might not have agreed with the pope.[190] The author of the *Liber Historiae Francorum*, writing in the 720s, gloried in past Frankish triumphs. He was not hostile to Carolingian military achievement, nor was he contemptuous of the position the Merovingians by then occupied. So far as he was concerned, at least one recent king, Childebert III, had done a good job. The job was to 'do justice', which apparently meant to mediate in the feuds of his greater nobles without excess commitment to any one faction, and to dispense what was left of his patronage to its most deserving (i.e. already privileged) recipients. There is not the least hint that kingship in this style was set upon the path to its own destruction. Further afield, the papal view would not have been the one taken by the *Liber* author's Old Saxon contemporaries. The fierce resistance they put up to Charlemagne's campaign of Christian conquest is partly explained by attachment to a system where rulers took 'kingly power' temporarily and by casting lots.[191] Even Bede, another contemporary, who deplored the dissipation of his native Northumbria's royal resources as forcefully as any Einhard, had learned from Augustine and (it may be) from the Irish that the *summum bonum* was not the rule in this world. He could not withhold his admiration for strong kings like Ine who forsook all to seek St Peter's threshold.[192] In 700, European kingship was still hedged about with the ambiguities bequeathed by its Hebrew and Roman models, and perhaps by abiding barbarian traditions, both Celtic and Germanic.

But it was the sort of answer to be expected of a Greek-speaking inhabitant of Byzantine Calabria like Zacharias, and one whose office embodied the 'Ghost of the old Roman Empire, sitting crowned upon the ruins thereof' (in Hobbes' classic phrase). It was the answer expected not only by the Frankish nobles whose support the Carolingians had assiduously cultivated but also by Boniface, a regular correspondent of Zacharias, who went on to play Samuel to Pippin's Saul. He had recently welcomed the kingly power of his fellow-Englishman, Æthelbald of Mercia, while earnestly threatening him (the fate of Islam's Spanish victims on his mind) with what would come of failing to exercise it in accordance with God's law.[193] The western European future did now lie with kings who, like *basileis* in Constantinople and *khalifah* in Baghdad, were God's agents on earth.

190 For what follows, see Gerberding (1987). 191 Cf. Mayr-Harting (1996).

192 Bede, *Epistola ad Ecgbertum Episcopum* 10–13, pp. 413–17; *HE* v.7.19. Cf. Stancliffe (1983); Thacker (1983).

193 *Bonifatii Epistolae*, no. 73.

CHAPTER 22

THE MEDITERRANEAN ECONOMY

S. T. Loseby

CONTEXTS: EVIDENCE AND ANTECEDENTS

Two issues that shape any general interpretation of the Mediterranean economy of the sixth and seventh centuries are the problems of the available evidence and the question of the nature of the ancient economy that preceded it. The limitations of the written sources are well known. In particular, no documentary data survive of a type that permits any serious attempt at quantitative analysis. Instead of the records which are the stuff of economic history, we usually have only stories. There are a handful of short texts that are wholly or partly concerned with economic matters. For the most part, however, we depend upon anecdotal indications afforded by a host of authors united by little more than their indifference to economic affairs, in whose writings the fleeting appearances of merchants or traded goods are almost invariably tangential. Gregory of Tours, for example, reports how a ship from Spain put in at Marseilles in 588, carrying the 'usual cargo'. He tells us this to provide the context for an outbreak of the plague, disseminated through the port via the purchase of this merchandise, but in the absence of any other direct references to Mediterranean exchange between Spain and Francia in this period, its nature remains a matter for speculation.[1] Even Leontius of Naples' *Life of St John the Almsgiver*, which offers an exceptional series of insights into the commercial relationships of the church of Alexandria in the early seventh century, does so less from any sense of their intrinsic importance than because of their value as illustrations of the charitable behaviour of its main protagonist.[2]

The economic history of this period has necessarily been constructed through the prising of such jewels of information from their various settings, but also their intricate rearrangement in the service of more ornate general arguments. The classic and most ambitious example is the thesis of Henri Pirenne,

[1] Gregory, *Hist.* IX.22. [2] Leontius, *Life of St John the Almsgiver*.

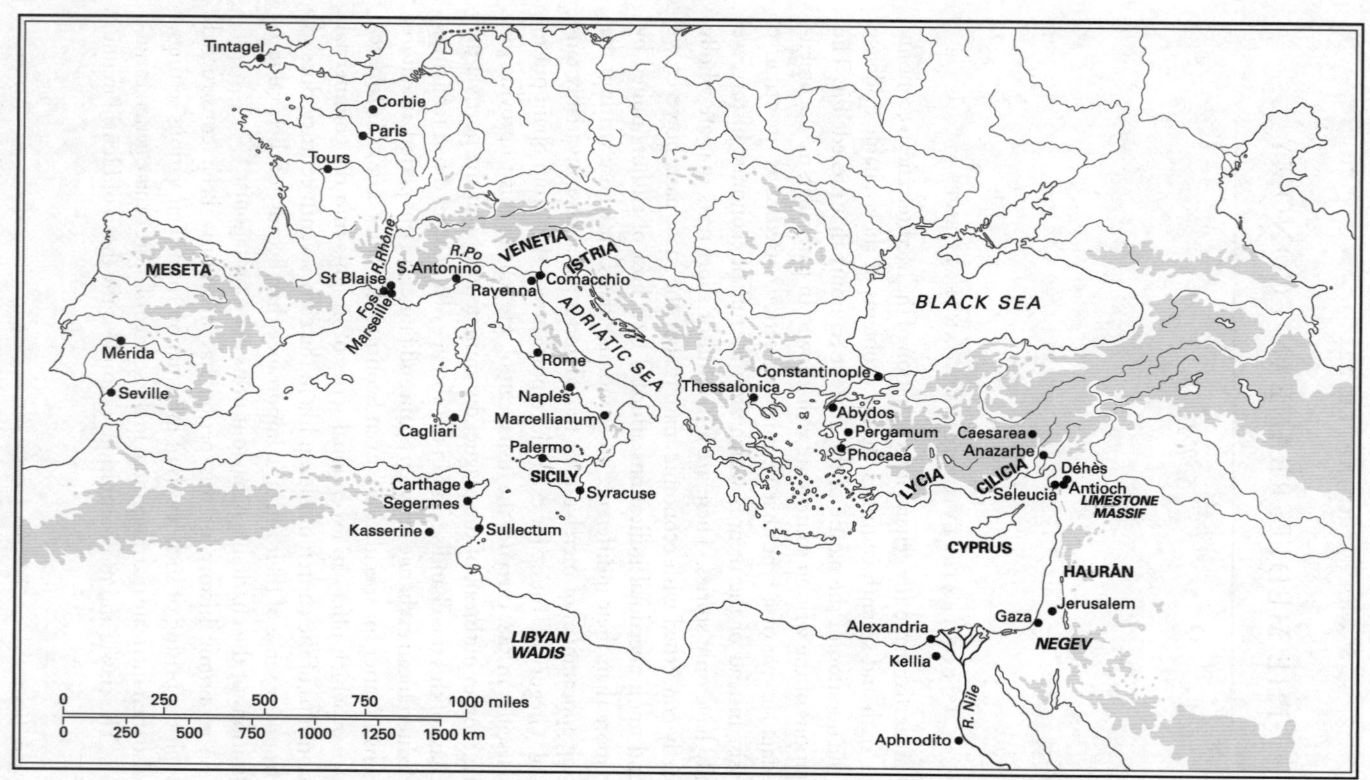

Map 15 The Mediterranean economy: sites and regions mentioned in the text

whose shadow has loomed large over the subject ever since the posthumous publication of his provocative work *Mahomet et Charlemagne*. There he argued that the ancient economy survived the barbarian invasions of the fifth century unscathed, but was destroyed by the rise of Islam in the seventh, which ruptured the unity of the Mediterranean. This established the framework of the historiographical debate about the post-Roman Mediterranean economy for decades, even as his numerous critics demonstrated the fragility of many of Pirenne's assertions.[3] A less impressionistic approach has been to organise the fragmented data thematically in the hope of identifying general patterns, a method which reached its apogee in the compendium of references to western Mediterranean trade in the early Middle Ages assembled by Dietrich Claude; this has the twofold merit of being both more comprehensive, and more cautious in its conclusions, than many of its predecessors.[4] Works such as this provide an invaluable (and virtually fixed) canon of the available evidence, but cannot alter the fact that its deficiencies remain considerable, and in some cases frankly insurmountable. In part this is a function of familiar imbalances in the early medieval documentary tradition; we have far more data from some regions than from others. More generally, the limited quantity and relentlessly anecdotal nature of the evidence that does survive makes it decidedly hazardous to elucidate general economic circumstances from the specifics of any given story. Our knowledge of the whys and wherefores of early medieval exchange is a composite, pieced together from assorted snippets of information, which are neither necessarily typical nor readily comparable, and virtually never comprehensive.

To take just one example, a Jewish merchant named Jacob set off from Constantinople in around 632 on a commission from a distinguished inhabitant of the city to sell illicitly textiles worth two pounds of gold, receiving an annual retainer of around 10 per cent of the value of the goods for his pains.[5] Jacob had considered the possibility of finding buyers in Africa or Gaul, but eventually managed to dispose of all his stock on the quiet to customers in Carthage. Shorn of the many complications involving Jacob's conversion from Judaism to Christianity (the latter being the main point of this probably fictional narrative), the commercial *mise en scène* seems highly plausible, but many of its details remain exceptional or enigmatic.[6] It is, for example, the only recorded instance from our period of a Mediterranean merchant working on commission for a member of the secular elite, and the only explicit statement of a

[3] Pirenne (1939). The critiques and sequels Pirenne inspired are too many to list, but see especially Riising (1952), and Hodges and Whitehouse (1983).

[4] Claude (1985).

[5] *Doctrina Jacobi* v.20, with the commentary in Dagron and Déroche (1991).

[6] Other data on the activities of merchants in this period are collected in Claude (1985), pp. 167–244.

conscious awareness of alternative markets. It is left unstated whether Jacob was acting solely on behalf of his patron, whether he was paid in cash or kind, and whether he might also have intended to exploit the possibilities of the voyage on his own account, for example by bringing back a cargo for sale in Constantinople. Fascinating though Jacob's story is, without comparable information its value as evidence of normal commercial practice is extremely difficult to assess. The necessity of accumulating such anecdotes from different times and places, with their diverse emphases and omissions, encourages the plugging of the gaps in one singular story with equally unique details from another. The written sources enable us to see what was possible; the idea of Jacob undertaking such a voyage early in the 630s is in itself intriguing. But the information they provide is too meagre to show what was typical.

The somewhat sterile debate about the nature of the early medieval Mediterranean economy, long structured around an inadequate corpus of documentary evidence and a conceptual framework bequeathed by Pirenne, has since the 1970s been reinvigorated by continuous transfusions of new archaeological data. Changing patterns of urban and rural settlement offer numerous insights into economic relationships, whether through case-studies of particular sites, or by the exploration of more extensive areas via field-survey and even, in privileged areas such as the limestone massif of northern Syria, examination of standing structures.[7] The analysis of archaeological finds yields more explicit information concerning the production and distribution of certain manufactured goods. In particular, the recovery of thousands upon thousands of sherds of pottery (useless to its owners once broken, but invaluable to archaeologists because it is virtually indestructible in the ground) allows the detailed study both of pottery as a traded commodity in its own right, and also of the exchange of those foodstuffs which in antiquity were routinely transported in ceramic amphorae, including such Mediterranean dietary staples as olive oil, wine and fish-sauce. Much painstaking research now makes it possible to assign a lot of this ceramic material to a specific region of production, and to classify and date the most common and widely exchanged ceramic types with ever-increasing precision.[8] Ceramic assemblages can then be analysed in various ways, for example to show the patterns of consumption implicit in the range of amphorae recovered from a given site (Map 16), or the distribution of a certain form of pottery (Maps 17A and 17B). All this offers the mass of serial data and the possibilities for statistical analysis conspicuous only by their absence from the written record. Ceramic distributions can be used to reveal

7 For an overview, Ward-Perkins (2000a).

8 Among a vast literature one should single out the pioneering work of John Hayes (1972) and (1980) on African Red Slip ware, and the widely used classifications of the most common amphora types established by Riley (1979) and Keay (1984).

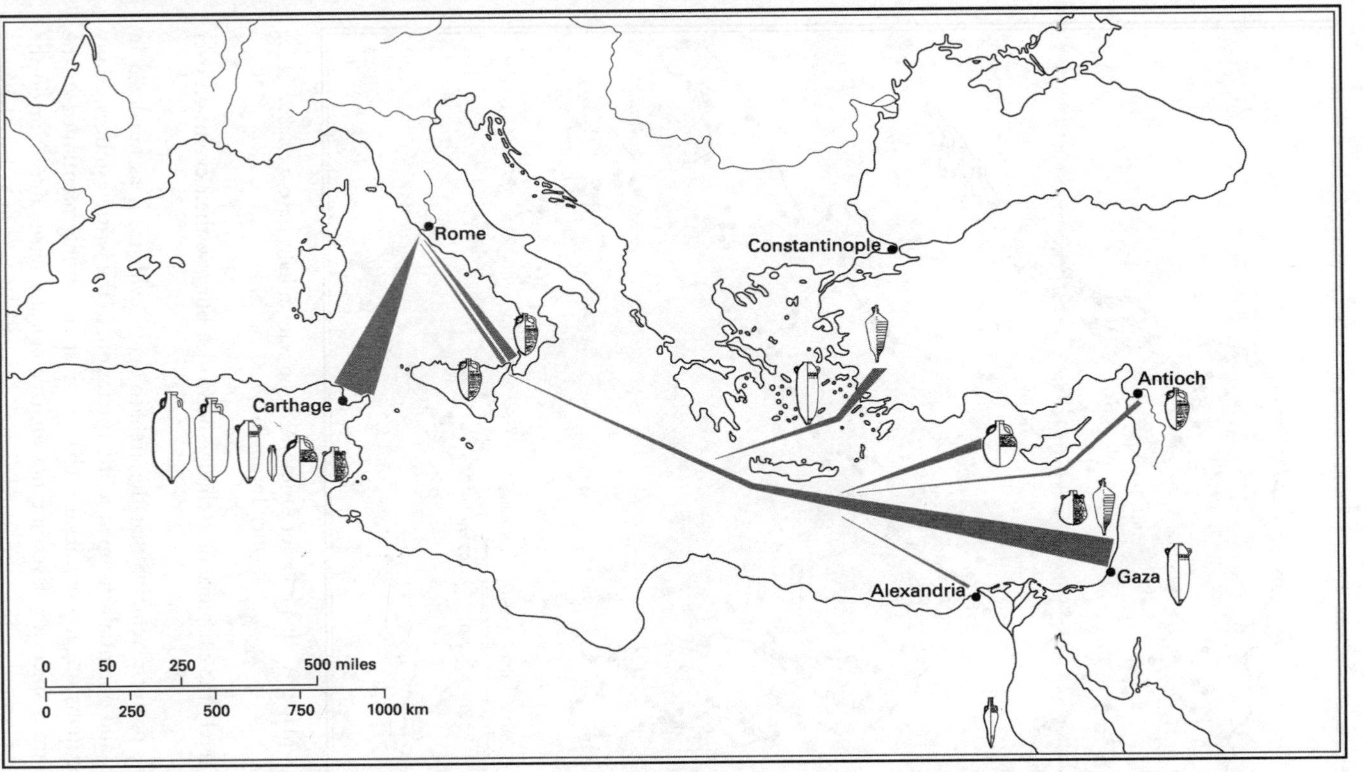

Map 16 Imported amphorae (see Figure 8) in a late seventh-century deposit at the Crypta Balbi, Rome; the arrows represent import volumes calculated on the basis of amphorae capacities (after Panella and Saguì (2000), fig. 4)

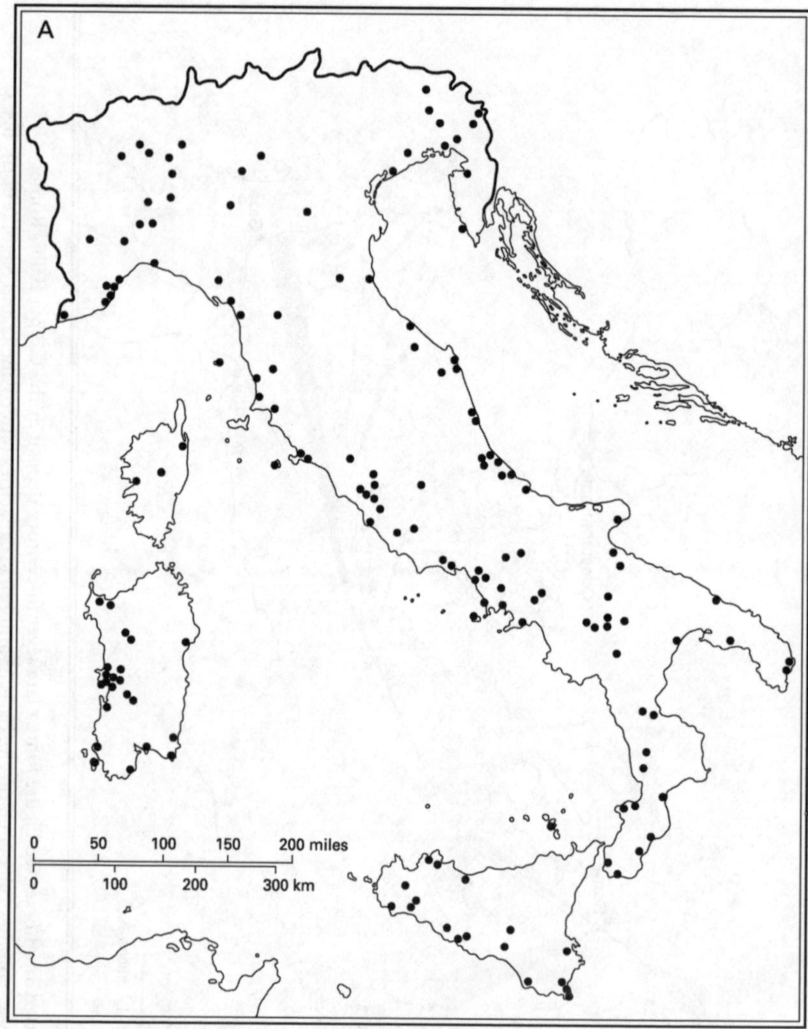

Map 17A Findspots of African Red Slip ware in Italy: *c.*450–570/580 (after Tortorella (1998), fig. 7)

not merely the existence of exchange networks, but also their evolution over time.

The problem remains that the archaeological evidence is as restricted in scope, and potentially as open to interpretation, as the written sources. Many of the items of early medieval exchange most commonly mentioned in the texts, from spices to slaves, are not archaeologically retrievable. Nor do the types of container that circulated alongside amphorae, such as barrels, sacks and skins, normally survive in the ground. Closer analysis of the production

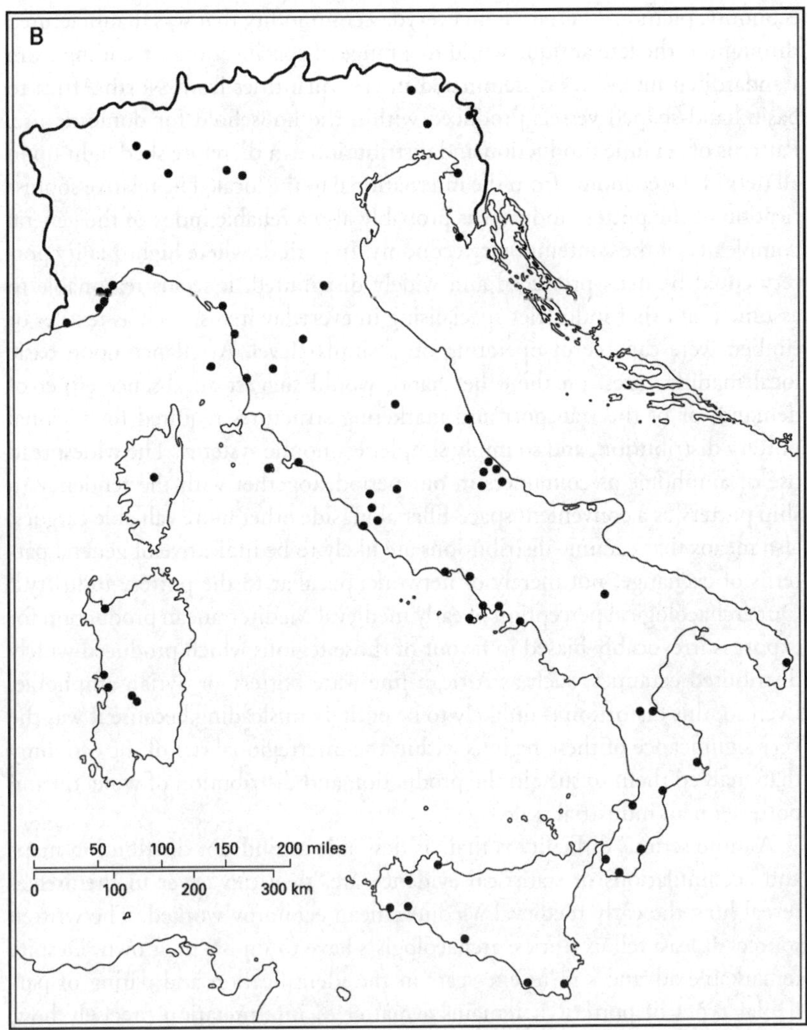

Map 17B Findspots of Red Slip ware in Italy: *c.*550–seventh century (after Tortorella (1998), fig. 8)

and distribution of other materials which can be recovered, such as glass, or building-stone, may in time prove possible, but our archaeological perception of the post-Roman Mediterranean economy will remain overwhelmingly dominated by the ceramic evidence.[9] This is far from ideal, but the impression it gives is nevertheless likely to be broadly representative of the wider

[9] Such analysis is currently only possible for the production and distribution of one easily distinguishable, but particularly valuable and so atypical building-stone, marble: see e.g. Sodini (1989).

economic picture.[10] Pottery is an everyday commodity that was manufactured throughout the late antique world to a range of specifications extending from standardised fine wares disseminated in vast quantities from North Africa to basic hand-shaped vessels produced within the household for domestic use. Patterns of ceramic production and distribution can therefore shed light upon all tiers of the economy from the international to the local. The relative sophistication of the pottery industry is probably also a reliable index of the general complexity of the contemporary economy. In periods where high-quality pottery could be mass-produced and widely distributed, it seems reasonable to assume that other industries specialising in everyday items, such as textiles or timber, were capable of operating on a similar level. A reliance upon basic local manufactures, on the other hand, would suggest an absence either of demand, or of the transport and marketing structures required for regional pottery distribution, and so imply simpler economic systems. The widespread use of amphorae as containers in our period, together with the tendency to ship pottery as a convenient space-filler alongside other more valuable cargoes, also means that ceramic distributions are likely to be indicative of general patterns of exchange, not merely of networks peculiar to the pottery industry.[11] Our archaeological perception of early medieval Mediterranean production for export is irrevocably biased in favour of those regions which produced widely distributed ceramics, such as African fine-ware pottery or Syrian amphorae. Even so, this distortion is unlikely to be entirely misleading because it was the very significance of these regions within the interregional tier of the economy that enabled them to sustain the production and distribution of wine, oil and pottery on an industrial scale.

A more serious difficulty is that, as desirable as findspot distribution maps and accumulations of statistical evidence are, they can never in themselves reveal how the early medieval Mediterranean economy worked. The written sources at least tell us stories; archaeologists have to supply their own. Despite remarkable advances in recent years in the identification and dating of particular types of pottery, it remains a matter of interpretation precisely how, why and for whose benefit such items were transported around the Mediterranean. Excavations have shown, for example, that the inhabitants of St Blaise, a Provençal hillfort reoccupied in late antiquity, were able to acquire imports from distant regions of the Mediterranean until at least the late sixth century.[12] They drank Gaza wine, one of the *grands crus* of the day, shipped in distinctive elongated chestnut-coloured amphorae known to specialists as Late Roman Amphora (LRA) type 4 (Map 16 and Fig. 8). They ate from fine bowls and

[10] Peacock (1982). [11] Peacock and Williams (1986).
[12] Démians d'Archimbaud *et al.* (1994).

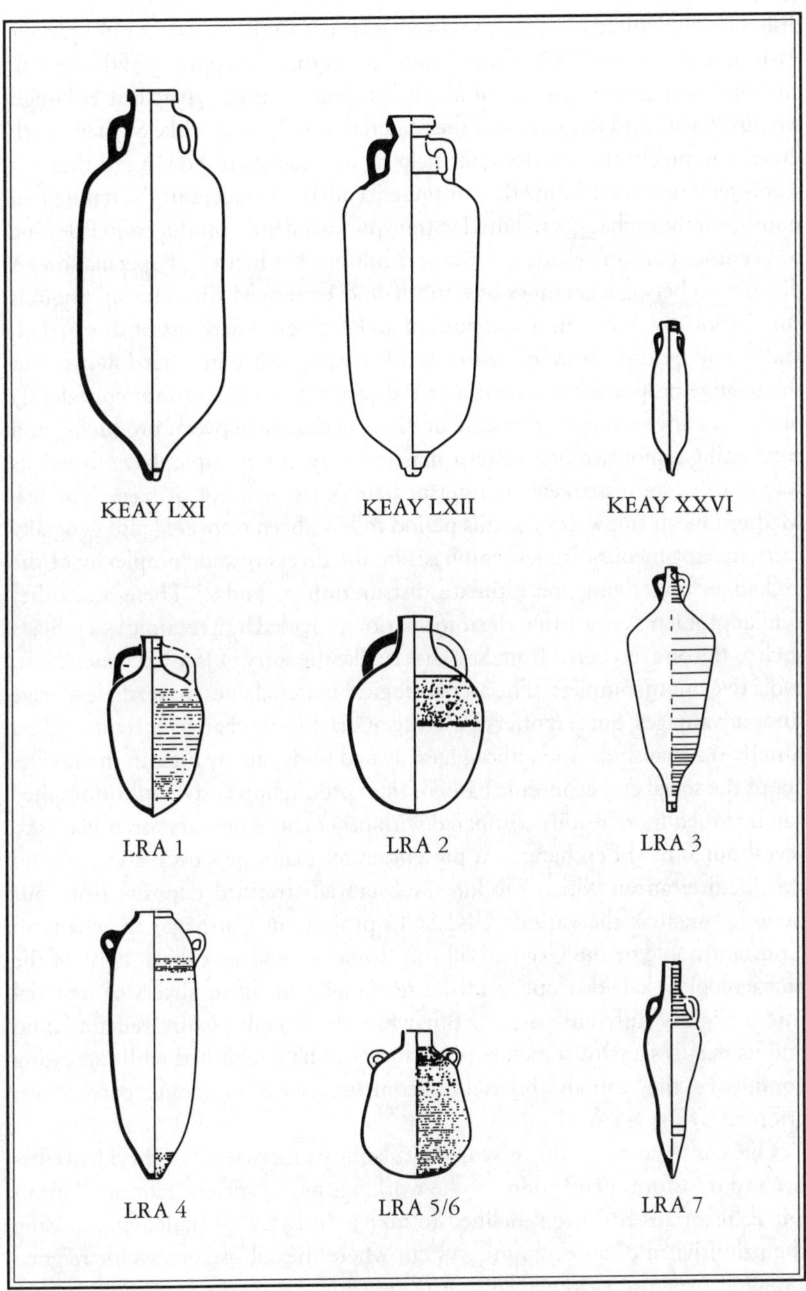

Figure 8. Some of the principal classifications of African and eastern Mediterranean amphorae in interregional circulation in the sixth and seventh centuries (African: Keay XXVI (spatheion); Keay LXI; Keay LXII. Eastern Mediterranean: LRA 1–7)

dishes manufactured in workshops in what is now Tunisia; this is the ubiquitous African Red Slip ware (ARS), the dominant international pottery of the period, and the most closely studied of all late antique ceramic types. But although we can classify and date some of the material found on sites like St Blaise with increasing precision, this does not help us to understand how it got there. It seems reasonable to assume that its presence involves trade, but the nature and number of the exchanges required to transport wine from producers in Palestine to eventual consumers on a Provençal hilltop is a matter of speculation. A distinction between ceramics of 'African' and 'eastern Mediterranean' origin is conventionally drawn in discussions of archaeological deposits of this period, and it will be used *faute de mieux* as a heuristic device in what follows. But the relative proportions of such material at any given site cannot confidently be used as a reflection of the scale of direct exchange between producing and consuming regions; much eastern material may, for example, have found its way onto western markets via intermediate ports such as Carthage. The few Mediterranean shipwrecks of this period to have been recovered also generally carry heterogeneous cargoes, emphasising the diversity and complexity of the exchanges underlying the ultimate distribution of finds.[13] These and other similar problems ensure that the information provided by a ceramic assemblage such as the one recovered from St Blaise is, like the story of Jacob the merchant, evocative but incomplete. The archaeological material does, nevertheless, have some advantages. Since it offers a picture of diachronic change, it is more like a film than a snapshot. And although excavated finds can say little in themselves about the social and economic bases of their production and distribution, they can be much more readily compared with other contemporary assemblages to reveal outcomes of exchange. At present, every major new excavation around the Mediterranean which produces substantial stratified deposits from our period – such as the various UNESCO projects in Carthage, Saraçhane in Constantinople or the Crypta Balbi in Rome – involves a sharp twist of the archaeological kaleidoscope, and the rearrangement of its slivers of material into a slightly different pattern. But while the overall picture remains fluid and its details sketchy, some broad outlines can be established with increasing confidence; they can also be usefully compared with the variant perspectives afforded by the texts.

One consequence of the increased availability of archaeological evidence has been to transform perceptions of the workings of the ancient economy. Influential historians had been inclined to take a dim view of trade, emphasising the primitivism of an economic system where the subsistence sector reigned supreme over the commercial.[14] Any role for the market economy within

[13] Parker (1992). [14] See esp. Jones (1964), pp. 824–58 and (1974); Finley (1985).

this minimalist perspective was strictly local. Widespread poverty restricted demand, while on the supply-side a lack of specialisation, investment and innovation, prohibitive transport-costs, and the attitudes of an elite who prized landownership and conspicuous consumption over the maximising of production and profit, were all deemed to have conspired to stifle trade. Only the state, faced with the necessity of supplying its vast personnel and the inflated populations of its capitals, engaged in the circulation of foodstuffs over long distances, but as far as possible this was achieved via the *annona*, in essence a compulsory purchase and distribution system.[15] Much of the exchange which did take place within the ancient world and on into our period was therefore seen not in commercial terms, but as the redistribution of resources by the state, elites, and latterly other wealthy institutions such as the church, without recourse to a market economy.[16]

This interpretation is text-based, but the archaeological evidence, by revealing the myriad outcomes of exchange, exposes both the limitations of our sources and the excessively bleak assumptions of the minimalist viewpoint. The vast quantities of ARS found on sites all around the Mediterranean in late antiquity, even in relatively humble rural contexts, are indicative of the large-scale manufacture of a high-quality product which was sufficiently affordable to make its overseas distribution viable even where it had to compete with local fine-ware production. The circulation of commodities such as ARS was almost certainly influenced by the currents of exchange generated by the state, but it can hardly have been dictated by them. Similarly, although the state sector was directly responsible for a significant proportion of interregional traffic in foodstuffs, the range of amphora manufactures and the fiendish complexity of their distributions suggests that at least some of this traffic was responding to commercial imperatives. Since the activities of these pottery industries have largely escaped the notice of the written sources, it follows that the exchange of other manufactured goods on a substantial scale, such as textiles, is equally possible, even if it cannot be so readily confirmed archaeologically.[17] Some archaeologists have explicitly offered more commercially driven interpretations of the ancient economy; others have been content to do so implicitly by routinely describing the distributions of excavated material in terms of trade.[18]

None of this is to deny, of course, that imperial interests were crucial to the evolution and nature of interregional exchange within the ancient economy. Even if the archaeological evidence strongly suggests that the importance

15 Durliat (1990). 16 Whittaker (1983).

17 The surviving documentary evidence from Egypt is the exception: see e.g. Johnson and West (1949), and Wipszycka (1965) and van Minnen (1986) for textiles.

18 Carandini (1981) and (1986), with the helpful historiographical commentary in Wickham (1988); Panella (1993), the finest analysis of the archaeological evidence; Reynolds (1995).

of the commercial sector has been underestimated, the requirements of the Roman state did significantly distort the currents of such traffic. The foundation of a new imperial capital at Constantinople in the fourth century had, for example, generated new flows of exchange that bear some responsibility for the unprecedented intensity of rural settlement and agricultural production in several regions of the eastern Mediterranean in late antiquity.[19] In the West, meanwhile, it has been plausibly argued that a crucial factor which underpinned the international distribution of ARS was the dominance of Africa within the state sector of the economy. More generally, the Roman state had indirectly stimulated commercial exchange in various ways. The taxes, which it demanded from the peasantry, required them to commoditise their surplus to turn it into coin. Those coins, minted primarily for fiscal purposes, offered an empire-wide medium of exchange in the form of a single currency. The infrastructural and financial underpinning of the *annona* system may have been in the public interest, but, as we shall see, it also greased the wheels of the private enterprise carried on alongside it.[20]

In the eastern basin of the Mediterranean, the intertwining of the state and commercial sectors of the economy created complex networks of interregional exchange, which would persist for much of our period, until they were eventually dislocated by the near-collapse of the Byzantine Empire.[21] In the West, however, the disintegration of the imperial fiscal and military machine in the fifth century perpetuated an existing pattern of decline which the reincorporation of some regions of the western Mediterranean – notably Africa – into the eastern system as a result of Justinian's reconquests would do little to arrest. Here the sixth and seventh centuries are marked not by any radical break with the past, but by the relentless contraction of the economic networks inherited from antiquity. On the one hand, this supports the view that the commercial sector of the Mediterranean economy had always been important, and, as such, could continue with or without an empire; the hegemony of African ceramics on overseas markets, for example, survived both the supposed disruption of the Vandal conquest and the restoration of imperial authority from the east.[22] On the other hand, it is striking that no wholly new networks of interregional exchange emerge from the wreckage of the Western Empire. As a result, the grand narrative of the sixth- and seventh-century Mediterranean economy, in so far as such a thing exists, is about the impact which the disintegration of

19 Abadie-Reynal (1989).

20 Hopkins (1980) and (1983); Mattingly (1988); Wickham (1988); McCormick (1998).

21 Kingsley and Decker (2001).

22 Panella (1993), esp. pp. 641–54. Various efforts have been made to interpret the ceramic evidence in the specific light of these political changes (e.g. Fulford (1980) and (1983)), but these are not compelling (Tortorella 1986).

the military, political and (not least) cultural authority of the Roman Empire, gradual in the West and more dramatic in the East, had upon the continued functioning of the ancient exchange-system. But the Mediterranean is a complex of seas, and as such has always nurtured a complex of economies.[23] So before embarking upon that grand narrative, some attention must first be paid to the local and regional orbits of exchange which lurk beneath the surface of the pan-Mediterranean economy, and to the commodities which were circulating within these subsidiary systems.

CONTENTS: ORBITS AND OBJECTS

One of the defining characteristics of pre-industrial economics is the considerable differential in the respective costs of land- and water-transport. Although precise information from the Roman period is in short supply, it is compatible with the better data which survive from later centuries in suggesting that transport overland was about five times more expensive than by river, and well over twenty times more expensive than by sea. Jones put this briskly into perspective by using the authorised carriage-tariffs in Diocletian's price edict to show how it was cheaper to ship grain from Syria to Spain than to cart it just 120 kilometres.[24] In normal circumstances it made no commercial sense to transport overland low-value or bulk items such as grain; the state would do so to secure essential supplies, but here the inflated expense was not the main concern. Moreover, transport by sea was much quicker, given a fair wind, although the Mediterranean was considered too hazardous for sailing for almost half the year, and the dangers involved are frequently highlighted by the written sources.[25] During the patriarchate of John the Almsgiver, for example, at least thirteen vessels belonging to the church of Alexandria were hit by a storm in the Adriatic and forced to jettison their entire cargoes; the Alexandrine sea-captains who were in the habit of sprinkling their ships with holy water from the River Jordan before setting out were taking a reasonable precaution.[26] The risks, however, were well worthwhile, since the Mediterranean opened up commercial possibilities for coastal centres, or those with access to a navigable waterway, which were denied to communities inland. In recounting the problems in times of famine of a landlocked city like Caesarea in Cappadocia, set amid the mountains some 200 kilometres from the coast, Gregory of Nazianzus offered a succinct summary of the structural constraints

[23] Braudel (1972), p. 17.

[24] Jones (1964), pp. 841–2; cf. Durliat (1998), pp. 92–3. For a not altogether convincing attempt to play down this differential, see Horden and Purcell (2000), p. 377.

[25] Claude (1985), pp. 31–2.

[26] Leontius, *Life of St John the Almsgiver* c.28; *Antonini Placentini Itinerarium* 11.

which continued to apply throughout our period: 'coastal cities support such shortages without difficulty, as they can dispose of their own products and receive supplies by sea; but for us inland our surpluses are unprofitable and our scarcities irresolvable, because we have no means of disposing of what we have nor of importing what we lack'.[27] The relative ease of water-transport was not only vital in a crisis; potentially, it also afforded regular access to a wider market for the disposal of surplus production.

This ready maritime 'connectivity' was the essential precondition for the existence of a Mediterranean economy.[28] In practice, however, the similar ecological resources of its shores, where differences tend to exist within rather than between regions, might have been expected to reduce the commercial possibilities. Most importantly, all of them are capable of sustaining the production of the trinity of sixth-century Mediterranean staples: grain, oil and wine.[29] The interregional shipment of foodstuffs was not generally necessary for subsistence purposes, except to supply the imperial capitals. When poor harvests and crop failures inevitably did occur, neither the bad news nor the necessary relief could usually arrive fast enough to permit the opportunistic exploitation of short-term crises by distant producers and suppliers.[30] In normal circumstances, meanwhile, goods transported hundreds of kilometres by ship could perhaps compete in price with equivalent items conveyed relatively short distances overland, but scarcely with the local grape harvest or pressing of olive oil. John the Almsgiver admired the heady bouquet of the expensive Palestinian wine he was offered in the church of St Menas in Alexandria, but, with characteristic abstemiousness, he spurned it in favour of the local vintage from Lake Mareotis; its taste was nothing special, but the price was low.[31]

In the sixth and seventh centuries, as throughout the Roman and medieval periods, transport costs combined with the relative poverty of the population to ensure that the most significant tier of the exchange-network for producers and consumers alike was the local one. The vast majority of people were directly engaged in labour-intensive agricultural production. Their primary aim was to grow enough food for their dependants and themselves to survive the year (and the risk of starvation was real), whilst meeting the demands for tax or rent from the state and from landlords; when these demands were expressed in cash rather

[27] Gregory of Nazianzus, *Orations* XLIII.34. [28] 'Connectivity': Horden and Purcell (2000), ch. 5.

[29] Cassiodorus, *Variae* XII.22.1 for wine, grain and oil as the three 'excellent fruits' of agriculture. Justinian, *Institutiones* IV.6.33 cites the same trilogy of goods as selling at different prices in different places.

[30] Cassiodorus, *Variae* IV.5, with Ruggini (1961), pp. 262–76, and *Miracula Sancti Demetrii* I.9.76, for King Theoderic's and St Demetrius' exceptional attempts to use their respective powers to get round this problem.

[31] Anon., *Life of John the Almsgiver*, c.10.

than in kind, their participation in the market economy was essential to convert their produce into coin. If they managed to produce a surplus after this, they are most likely to have exchanged it locally for other foodstuffs or manufactured goods. This level of exchange usually takes place beneath the notice of the written sources, although the occasional anecdote confirms its existence. After invading Vandal Africa, for example, the Byzantines gained entry to Sullectum by the simple expedient of attaching themselves to the peasants entering the city at first light with their carts, clearly an everyday occurrence.[32] A fragmentary inscription from Cagliari in Sardinia sets out the customs dues levied in kind by the civic administration in the reign of Maurice (582–602) on goods entering the territory of the city on pack-animals, small boats or, easiest of all, on the hoof. In describing the convergence of a range of basic commodities upon a local market by land and sea, it offers an unusual glimpse of what must have been the normal relationship between peasant producers and neighbouring communities.[33] In return, of course, these communities afforded access to expertise as well as agricultural produce. In the time of Justinian, the vibrant Egyptian village of Aphrodito supported at least sixty shopkeepers, artisans and professional men divided between nineteen specified occupations, including a potter of some substance.[34] Exchange at this local level is now becoming more perceptible through patterns of pottery production and distribution. Even so, the study of the common wares of this period is in its infancy, and the unchanging nature and household manufacture of many of these items means that progress is slow. Although archaeology can also tell us a great deal about the provisioning of specific sites through, for example, analysis of pollen grains and, perhaps most promisingly, animal bones, at present it remains easier to assert the fundamental importance of exchange at the local level – and of myriad micro-economies within the Mediterranean economy – than it is to subject the operation of these networks to meaningful comparative analysis.[35]

The same is no longer true of the regional networks, which make up the intermediate tier of Mediterranean exchange. The ever-expanding number of sixth- and seventh-century pottery assemblages and the growing sophistication with which these can be analysed make these systems increasingly distinguishable as specific entities. Many regions of the Mediterranean sustained

32 Procopius, *Wars* III.16.10.

33 Durliat (1982). Cf. the fifth/sixth-century customs tariff from Anazarbe in Cilicia: Dagron and Feissel (1987), pp. 170–85 (no. 108).

34 *Catalogue général d'antiquités égyptiennes*, ed. Maspero, III.67283, 67288; Jones (1964), pp. 847–8; Keenan (1984). The exceptional survival of data from Aphrodito should not blind us to the fact that, as a demoted metropolis beside the Nile, it was not an average village.

35 For various studies of common wares, especially in Italy, see Saguì (1998).

fine-ware pottery production in late antiquity; these industries often operated from a number of regional centres and sometimes exported beyond their immediate localities, but without ever achieving the Mediterranean-wide distribution of the ARS ware which in some cases they consciously strove to imitate. In southern Gaul, for example, widespread production of a category of fine-ware pottery known by a variety of unprepossessing names, including *dérivées des sigillées paléochrétiennes* (DSP) or orange/grey stamped ware, began late in the fourth century and, in places, continued on into the seventh. These wares were not greatly exported overseas, unless to the adjacent Mediterranean coasts of Catalonia and Liguria; even within Gaul their distribution falls into distinct sub-groups, such that the orange DSP manufactured in Languedoc is rare in Provence, and vice versa for the grey Provençal variety.[36] Similarly, in the eastern Mediterranean, a growing number of fine wares can be identified which tended to circulate within particular regions, such as the metallescent ware from Pergamum in Asia Minor, Egyptian versions of Red Slip Ware, or the Glazed White Ware which emerges at Constantinople and would continue to dominate the market there for centuries.[37] These regional types were very occasionally disseminated more widely, but in the East only the Red Slip Ware produced at Phocaea on the west coast of Asia Minor achieved an international distribution remotely comparable to that of ARS.[38]

Although this tripartite ranking of pottery types – local, regional, international – is somewhat crude, the ceramic evidence provides a useful illustration of the enduring complexities of the economy at the intermediate level, especially since it is not easy to identify such networks of exchange in the written sources. Here the distinction between local and regional markets is rarely drawn as nicely as in Cassiodorus' description of the commercial connotations of the feast-day of St Cyprian at a sacred spring near Marcellianum, in Lucania in southern Italy: 'all the notable exports of industrious Campania, or opulent Bruttium, or cattle-rich Calabria, or prosperous Apulia, with the products of Lucania itself, are on display to the glory of most admirable commerce, such that you would be right to think that such a mass of goods had been gathered from many regions'.[39] Such fairs also presumably encouraged the circulation – and celebratory consumption – of the wine carried in the amphora type known as Keay LII, now known to have been produced in southern Italy and Sicily.[40]

36 Reynolds (1995), pp. 36–7; Rigoir (1998). The distribution patterns of contemporary southern Italian red-painted wares are similar: Arthur and Patterson (1994).

37 Hayes (1992), pp. 12–34; Panella (1993), pp. 657–61, 673–7; Sodini (1993), pp. 173–4. For Egypt see Bailey (1998), esp. pp. 8–58.

38 Phocaean Red Slip: Martin (1998). In the East PRS is rare only in Egypt. It also reaches the West, though never in quantities equivalent to those of ARS in the East: Reynolds (1995), pp. 34–6, 132–5.

39 Cassiodorus, *Variae* VIII.33.

40 Arthur (1989); Pacetti (1998).

Only reports of the muggings of visiting merchants by the rascally local peasantry spoil the festive scene. Another staple, which may well have circulated commercially hereabouts, was grain. Pope Gregory I, for example, was perennially anxious to secure grain-supplies for Rome from Sicily, usually through imperial functionaries or from the extensive papal estates, but he also resorted to purchasing it on the open market, in 591 spending fifty pounds of gold on buying up additional supplies from the island for storage in response to a poor Roman harvest.[41] Across the Apennines, meanwhile, the inhabitants of Venetia and Istria at the head of the Adriatic were dealing in wine, fish-sauce, oil and salt, as well as grain; some of these goods were intended for Ravenna, but they were also traded on the open market.[42] Two centuries later the merchants of Comacchio at the head of the Po would secure from the Lombards an agreement granting them trading rights along the river in exchange for tolls in kind, among which salt again figures prominently.[43] Salt is precisely the sort of commodity that one might expect to circulate over some distance – everybody needs salt, as Cassiodorus observed – but not too far. Its extraction is widely possible around the Mediterranean, transporting it over long distances by sea ran the risk of ruining it, and, unlike wine, specific types of salt are not known to have carried any premium. Its presence in these texts is one indication that the exchange they describe is regional in nature.

The early medieval Mediterranean thus sustained a series of regional economies, some of which appear to have been more developed, or more dynamic, than others. The variable experiences of Italy's regions, in particular, already suggest that generalised explanations of economic change, such as the impact of warfare or of environmental crisis, are insufficient.[44] The extension of such studies offers our best hope of developing comparative perspectives and achieving a deeper understanding of early medieval exchange in all its complexity. But for the Mediterranean economy writ large, we must return to the exchange which continued to unite those who lived around Rome's Internal Sea (and even some out in the Ocean) long after the political fragmentation of its shores. The term 'long-distance trade' conventionally used to describe this type of traffic is not entirely helpful, because, as we have seen, it is not distance but access to the sea or to navigable waterways that really matters. In this sense, the inhabitants of the Spanish coast were 'closer' to Carthage or

41 Gregory I, *Reg.* I.70; Arnaldi (1986). Gregory's anticipation of crisis seems to have been exceptional: cf. note 30 above.

42 Cassiodorus, *Variae* XII.22, 24, the latter showing how the inhabitants of Venetia directly exchanged cylinders of salt for foodstuffs.

43 Hartmann (1904), pp. 123–4, for the text of the early eighth-century Comacchio 'capitulary', translated and discussed in Balzaretti (1996).

44 Wickham (1994), pp. 752–6, Marazzi (1998b), and for the ceramics Saguì (1998).

Rome than to the high plateaux of the adjacent Meseta; for the same reason, if we venture out momentarily beyond the Straits of Gibraltar, scattered finds of Mediterranean ceramics seem more common in sub-Roman western Britain than in northern Francia. The famous story of how an Alexandrine sea-captain sailed, however inadvertently, from Egypt to Britain may well be apocryphal, but the sixth-century ARS and eastern amphorae which link the monastic site of Kellia in Lower Egypt and Tintagel in Cornwall in a maritime community of taste are not.[45] Nor should the notion of a voyage from Egypt to Britain conceal the likelihood that most 'long-distance' exchange was carried out in sundry short hops, either along the coast from port to port, or across the open sea, exploiting the convenient island stepping-stones across the Mediterranean pond.[46]

The 'long-distance' tier of the exchange-system has often been dismissed as epiphenomenal: luxury in nature, trivial in scale, marginal in importance. One type of foodstuffs which may fall into this category are the exotic fruits, nuts and especially spices shipped from the eastern Mediterranean, Arabia and India to western consumers throughout our period, whether to meet the enthusiasm of individual hermits for an authentic taste of Egyptian asceticism, or to cater for the more substantial demands of institutions, most obviously monastic communities.[47] The Frankish king Chlothar III (657–673) authorised the agents of his newly founded monastery at Corbie to collect annually a cornucopia of imports – *selon arrivage* – from a royal warehouse in the Provençal port of Fos.[48] Alongside olive oil, fish-sauce, Spanish animal skins and Egyptian papyrus, their shopping-list featured more than a dozen different eastern fruits, herbs and spices, totalling 825 pounds in weight. This may appear trivial when set alongside the 10,000 pounds of oil which heads the list, but it is worth remembering that this supposedly represents the annual consumption of a single community. And although the ultimate recipients of such 'luxuries' were often institutions, there is little doubt that much exchange of this type was commercial; Isidore of Seville warned against unscrupulous merchants who adulterated pepper with shavings of lead or silver to make it more valuable, simply by weight alone, or because fresh pepper was known to be heavier.[49]

45 Leontius, *Life of John the Almsgiver* c.8. Kellia: Egloff (1977); Ballet and Picon (1987). Tintagel: Thomas (1981), with the papers in Dark (1995).

46 Documented routes: Rougé (1966), pt 1; Claude (1985), pp. 131–66, with Reynolds (1995), pp. 126–36, for a stimulating attempt to deduce them from ceramic assemblages, alleging more direct traffic. Pond: Socrates, in Plato, *Phaedo*, 109B: 'we inhabit a small portion of the earth . . . living about the sea like frogs and ants around a pond'.

47 Hermits: Gregory, *Hist.* VI.6. Monasteries: Lebecq (2000), and also chapter 23 below.

48 Levillain (1902), no. 15, pp. 236–7. Recent discussions (with anterior references): Loseby (2000), pp. 176–89 and (more optimistically) Horden and Purcell (2000), pp. 163–6.

49 Isidore, *Etymologiae* XVII.8.8.

Whilst only a lucky few presumably needed to heed the warning against eating too many dates offered to a sixth-century Frankish king, neither the extent of such traffic nor its economic importance should be unduly minimised.[50]

The quantity of oil stipulated in the Corbie diploma nevertheless suggests that the real weight of interregional Mediterranean exchange lay elsewhere, and involved the shipment of staple commodities. The scale of this traffic is now abundantly confirmed by the masses of excavated fragments of the amphorae in which oil, wine, fish-sauce and other items were transported. Much research remains to be done, for example in further refining the classifications of better-known amphora types to tie them more closely to particular regions of production or to specific periods, or in identifying the significant proportion of 'unknowns' present in some sixth- and seventh-century assemblages.[51] However, the continuing accumulation of amphora data already gives crucial new insights into the range and complexity of the networks by which foodstuffs were distributed around the early medieval Mediterranean, and some broad trends emerge with growing clarity. Like pottery, some types of amphorae appear to have circulated primarily within local or regional orbits, but others achieved Mediterranean-wide distributions in the sixth and seventh centuries. Significantly, these were exported either from Africa, or from the coasts of the eastern Mediterranean, in an arc circling from the Aegean (LRA 2 and 3) round Asia Minor (LRA 1), Syria and Palestine (LRA 4, 5 and 6) to Egypt (LRA 7) (Map 16 and Fig. 8).[52] The evidence of these containers is thus broadly consistent with that of fine-ware pottery in emphasising the dominance of African and eastern Mediterranean production within the interregional tier of the exchange-system.

In the case of Africa this hegemony goes back at least to the third century, but the rise of eastern exports is more recent; amphorae from this area begin to reach the western Mediterranean in quantity only from the later fifth century.[53] As such, the sixth- and seventh-century pattern represents what would turn out to be the final phase in a sequence which dates back to the days of the Roman republic, and which had seen different regions – Italy, south/central Gaul, Spain, Africa, the Near East – supersede each other as the dominant force within the wider Mediterranean economy. In this respect, as in others,

[50] Dangers of dates: Anthimus, *c*.92. Documentary references to fruits, nuts and spices: Claude (1985), pp. 81–4, and, more widely for the spice trade, Miller (1969).

[51] For the high proportions of 'unknowns', Arthur (1986), pp. 655–6, Panella (1993), pp. 662–3, with Arthur (1998) for some of the general problems and possibilities of amphora data.

[52] Among sundry studies, see e.g., Keay (1984) and (1998) for African amphorae; Empereur and Picon (1989); Panella (1993), pp. 662–72. For eastern Mediterranean amphorae, Reynolds (1995), pp. 38–85, gives an overview of the data.

[53] Panella (1993), pp. 625–48.

our period is more redolent of the last hurrah of the ancient economic system than the dawning of a new era. The extraordinary vitality of the countryside in the late antique Near East was first emphasised by Georges Tchalenko in his pioneering survey of the stunningly well-preserved villages of the Syrian limestone massif.[54] Similar evidence of a burgeoning rural economy has since been emerging from the rugged coast of Lycia and neighbouring Cilicia on the southern shores of Asia Minor, from the basalt outcrops of the Haur south of Syria, and from the wadis of the Negev in southern Palestine.[55] Most of these areas are agriculturally marginal in one way or another, and could have been cultivated only with considerable determination and investment. But by the start of our period they were supporting settlement unprecedented in extent, intensity and prosperity, which in some cases has never been repeated, helping to explain why the evidence is relatively well preserved.

It is tempting to think that it was the integration of their surplus production into the Mediterranean economic-system via centres such as Antioch and its outport at Seleuceia (for the limestone massif), or Gaza (for the Negev), which made exploitation of these marginal lands not just viable, but positively profitable. The coincidence between the escalating prosperity of these rural areas and the appearance on overseas markets of LRA type 1, emanating from workshops in the north-eastern corner of the Mediterranean around Antioch, Cilicia and Cyprus, and LRA 4, predominantly from the vicinity of Gaza, is striking. LRA 1 is the most commonly found, and widely distributed, of all late antique eastern amphorae, and was probably used to transport both oil and wine.[56] LRA 4 is plausibly associated with a specific item periodically highlighted in the texts: Gaza wine. The widespread presence of these amphorae in western Mediterranean deposits confirms that references to this commodity in the works of Gregory of Tours, Isidore of Seville and others represent more than literary conceit or poetic licence.[57] This evidence is wholly consistent with the earlier Roman pattern, whereby growth in rural settlement and investment within a region is paralleled by evidence of significant exports from that region to other areas of the Mediterranean.[58]

[54] Tchalenko (1953–58), with the important reconsiderations of Tate (1992), and Sodini *et al.* (1980) for the specific case of Déhès.

[55] Overviews: Sodini (1993); Foss (1995) and (1997). Lycia: Foss (1994); Cilicia: Eyice (1988); Hauran: Dentzer (1985) and Sartre (1985); Negev: Shereshevski (1991), with comments in Foss (1995).

[56] Van Alfen (1996); Decker (2001).

[57] Gregory, *Hist.* VII.29, Gregory, *Glory of the Confessors*, 64, trans. Van Dam, pp. 70–1; Isidore, *Etymologiae* XX.3. Bonifay and Villedieu (1989) for eastern amphorae in Gaul, Gutiérrez-Lloret (1998a), pp. 165–7 for Spain, Arthur (1998) for Italy. Mayerson (1985) and Gatier (1988), for the texts, with Kieslinger (1999) on the wine-trade in general.

[58] E.g. North Africa: Mattingly (1988), with Vera (1983) on investment strategies.

There are several aspects of this phenomenon that are likely to remain mysterious. Much interregional exchange was probably not strictly necessary. Archaeology cannot tell us why Antiochene oil, Gaza wine or, for that matter, ARS should have been more prized than the pressings, vintages or wares which must normally have been readily available to eager Mediterranean consumers from producers closer to home (and which, in the case of ARS, local potters specifically sought to imitate). Texts of our period only offer fleeting hints of qualitative distinctions. Gregory of Tours describes the wines of Gaza as *potentiora* ('more powerful'), seemingly by comparison with local vintages, possibly in reference to their body or flavour, perhaps even suggesting that, then as now, alcohol could be sold on the basis of strength as well as refinement.[59] But what our sources never mention, sadly, is just how big a premium these products carried. Some mark-up must have been essential to reflect transport costs and, presumably, scarcity value, but was it sufficient to take them beyond the reach of all but the elite? The exceptional market penetration of ARS, although declining by the sixth century, suggests that some of this interregional trade had once catered for a less exclusive clientele, but its real volume remains frustratingly elusive. Ceramic assemblages can reveal the evolution over time of the relative proportions of imports from different regions, but it is extremely difficult to use them to assess changes in absolute quantities of interregional exchange within our period.[60] Even so, rural survey data and ceramic distributions combine to suggest that participation in the interregional tier of the economy, so far from being epiphenomenal, is closely associated with mass specialist production, staple items and regional prosperity. They also show that the shores of the Mediterranean remained integrated into an overarching economic system for much of our period. What drove this economy, and for how long did it continue to exist?

MEANS AND ENDS: THE FATE OF THE INTERREGIONAL MEDITERRANEAN EXCHANGE-NETWORK

The biggest player in the sixth- and seventh-century Mediterranean economy was obviously the Byzantine Empire, which alone maintained the means and the motive routinely to encourage the bulk transportation of staple items between regions. Part of the agricultural surplus from the wealthiest of all the lands around the Mediterranean, Egypt, had long been diverted to assure

[59] Gregory, *Hist.* VII.29.

[60] Fentress and Perkins (1987) for an innovative attempt to do this for ARS, suggesting a steady decline setting in from the early fifth century and reaching oblivion in the mid-seventh; the approach has to date been pursued only by Zanini (1996).

supplies of grain for the imperial capital at Constantinople. A proportion of African production was also clawed back into the state sector after the Justinianic reconquest of 533, establishing a regular trading axis between Carthage and Constantinople.[61] Across the East more generally, the needs of the imperial military and administrative apparatus continued to drive the fiscal cycle of coin circulation, tax-collection and expenditure, which, as we have seen, was an important incentive to production and distribution. In the interior of Asia Minor, for example, Justinian's scaling-down of the imperial transport-system along the main road from Constantinople to the eastern front and his withdrawal of military units is said to have brought ruin to neighbouring landowners by depriving them of the opportunity both to pay their taxes in kind, and of consumers who might enable them to turn their surplus into cash.[62] The anecdote neatly illustrates how the state stimulated economic activity, but it also confirms the continuing advantages of access to the Mediterranean. Like Gregory of Nazianzus before him, John Lydos makes this point clear: 'the taxpayer was ruined . . . since he could not sell his crops, living far from the sea'. Further south in coastal Lycia and Cilicia settlement was, as previously noted, still flourishing in this period. The Mediterranean afforded wider opportunities for coastal producers to market their surplus, whether in dealings with the state or independently of it.

In the western Mediterranean, however, the state sector of the economy had collapsed in the fifth century, for good in some regions, temporarily in others; some of its fiscal and physical infrastructure may have survived, but in an ever-disintegrating state of repair.[63] Much interregional exchange here must have been commercial in nature. The secular elite had engaged in so-called 'tied trade', the shuttling of their own resources between regions or the sharing of them with others on a non-commercial basis, but this must also have greatly diminished as a result of the political fragmentation of the West and the demise of that class of super-rich aristocrats with lands in several provinces.[64] Major churches, however, continued to be blessed with extensive landed resources and regular international contacts. Gregory the Great's correspondence shows how the papacy was extremely active in Mediterranean exchange at the end of the sixth century, not only in soliciting imperial food-supplies for the Roman poor (or, increasingly, replacing the state as the main organiser of those supplies),

[61] Panella (1993), pp. 655–7. Textual confirmation is scant, but see Theophanes, AM 6100, I.296, 2–3, for the failure of the grain-ships to set out from Africa as a result of the revolt against Phokas.

[62] John Lydus, *De Magistratibus* III.61; Procopius, *Secret History* 30, 1–11 (with slight differences of emphasis, but similar hostility to Justinian). Discussion in Hendy (1985), pp. 295–6.

[63] See e.g. Hendy (1988) and (1993), for western coinages, and Blackburn, chapter 24 below.

[64] Whittaker (1983) for the importance of 'tied trade' in the later empire (in my view exaggerated).

but also in redistributing the produce of its own extensive landed patrimony.[65] It was potentially convenient for churches to exchange these resources on a non-commercial basis, though in practice this was not always as easy as it sounds. Gregory spent eight summers struggling to arrange the shipment of shipbuilding timber from southern Italy to Egypt in response to a request from Eulogius, patriarch of Alexandria; we never find out if he eventually succeeded.[66]

All 'tied trade' was presumably not as entangled as this, but exchange of this nature seems likely in any case to account for only a fraction of ecclesiastical involvement in the interregional tier of the Mediterranean economy. In one of his letters to Eulogius, Gregory wryly quotes the phrase 'trade till I come' from Christ's parable about making the most of one's talents;[67] the church of Alexandria was certainly an especially active participant in overseas exchange, as the traditions surrounding St John the Almsgiver, who became patriarch in 611, four years after Eulogius' death, make abundantly clear. Its direct interests were ensured through the maintenance of a substantial seagoing fleet, but equally significant was its role as a silent partner, underwriting with cash, cargoes and even ships the trading ventures of the city's merchants, whose recurrent misfortunes were often set right by displays of divine power. Presumably these favours, human and providential, came at the price of a share of the profits, though this is a subject upon which our sources choose not to dwell. It is evident, however, that these church-backed merchants also enjoyed considerable discretion in how they went about their business. Some specialised in interregional trade, to judge from the story of how 'one of the so-called *Gallodromoi*', men whose enterprises were presumably concerned primarily with Gaul, refused to repay his loan.[68] Other tales of John's charity evoke connections with Palestine, the Adriatic, Sicily, Africa and even Britain.[69] One simple reminder of how these traders will have dealt in a variety of commodities (and that not all of them made it home again) is provided by the epitaph of one Peter, a linen-merchant of Alexandria, who died at Palermo in 602.[70]

65 Marazzi (1998a). 66 Gregory I, *Registrum* VI.58, VII.37, VIII.28, IX.176, X.21, XIII.43 (596–603).

67 Luke 19.13. Gregory I, *Registrum* VII.37. Gregory notes that he cannot trade (presumably in reference to the political situation), but that he rejoices in Eulogius' successes.

68 Leontius, *Life of John the Almsgiver* c.36. The association of the term with underhand dealings later became proverbial: Claude (1985), 185, n.137. There were also *Spanodromoi* at Alexandria in the fifth century: Palladius, *Lausiac Hist.* 14.

69 Leontius, *Life of St John the Almsgiver* c.18 (Palestine; cf. Anon., *Life of St John the Almsgiver* c.9); c.28 (Adriatic), c.11 (Sicily), c.25 (Africa) (cf. John Moschus, *Pratum Spirituale*, 76), c.8 (Britain). Discussion: Hollerich (1982) and, more generally, Wipszycka (1972).

70 *CIL* X.2.7330.

Few hagiographers were as prepared to associate their heroes with merchants as those who celebrated the virtues of John the Almsgiver, and nor were many cities as ideally situated for trade as Alexandria, the port where the Mediterranean and Indian/Arabian exchange-networks naturally overlapped.[71] It can only be wondered, therefore, how far eastern churches of similar wealth and standing, such as Antioch and Constantinople, may have supported interregional exchange to a similar degree. Pope Gregory I certainly had regular dealings with merchants on behalf of the Roman church, though it is doubtful whether the papacy ran its own fleet, and some of Gregory's problems were forced upon him by the contemporary political situation and the particular history of Rome's institutionalised food-supply.[72] Other western churches – and rulers – seem to have been more inclined to deal with individual merchants on an *ad hoc* basis. Quite a number of merchants are incidentally mentioned in sixth- and seventh-century western sources, several of whom are said to be of eastern origin. There were many eastern merchants in Carthage, for example, even before the Byzantine reconquest, and others in sixth-century Italy and Sicily.[73] Greek merchants arriving in Spain from the East journeyed upriver to Mérida and 'according to custom' presented themselves to the bishop, another easterner named Paul.[74] In Paris, the Syrian merchant Eusebius beat the priestly brother of the former incumbent to episcopal office (by bribery, sneers Gregory of Tours), and promptly staffed his household with fellow-Syrians.[75]

The rise of the likes of Eusebius to prestigious positions is intriguing, as is the coincidence between the heyday of eastern exports to the western Mediterranean in the archaeological record and the cameo appearances of easterners, some of whom are identified as merchants, in western sources of fifth- to early seventh-century date. But the temptation to infer too much from the chequered careers of a handful of individuals should be resisted.[76] Our documentary information is too meagre and nebulous to tell us about the precise origins of many of those who engaged in overseas trade in this period, or to enable us to build up a picture of their activities which could convince as typical rather than particular. It seems clear (albeit not very surprising) that some individuals did specialise in interregional trade, especially from the eastern

[71] Mundell Mango (1996). [72] E.g. Gregory I, *Reg.* I.70, IV.43, IX.10, IX.40.

[73] Procopius, *Wars* III.20.5 (Carthage). For Italy and Sicily, cf. *ibid.* IV.14.7 (Syracuse); V.8.21 (Naples); Gregory I, *Reg.* IV.43 (Sicily); note 69 above.

[74] *Vita Patrum Emeretensium* IV.3. Paul had previously been a doctor, a useful reminder that not all Syrians or Greeks mentioned in western sources (still less Jews) should be automatically identified as traders; cf. Ruggini (1959).

[75] Gregory, *Hist.* X.26. Eusebius and his cronies may not have come from Syria itself; *Syrus* and, less often, *Graecus* seem to be used generically by western writers for all easterners.

[76] Evidence: Claude (1985), pp. 167–200. Devroey (1995) for a critique of exaggerations by Pirenne and others of the number and potential significance of foreign merchants in Francia.

Mediterranean to the west. Jacob, whom we met earlier, is one of them. But their mercantile strategies seem to have been as varied as their relationships with lay and ecclesiastical patrons. In our period, the majority were probably tied neither to the service of the state nor to a specific church or monastery, but nor could they be entirely independent. At the simplest level, members of these wealthy institutions were the merchants' likeliest customers; the customary visit of the Greek merchants to the bishop on arrival in Mérida was a matter of common-sense as well as courtesy. More fundamentally, mercantile ventures involved substantial risk; all but the richest merchants needed backers with capital, commodities and ships (or at least cargo-space) to spare, or who might bail them out when things went wrong.[77]

In the eastern Mediterranean, meanwhile, by far the most significant source of this financial backing remained the Byzantine Empire. The *annona* system may have tied shippers into the regular transport of Egyptian grain to the imperial capital, but not so tightly as to preclude them from the simultaneous pursuit of private profit.[78] To compensate them for supplying the state at a loss, it appears that these *navicularii* enjoyed a series of fiscal advantages. Some of these privileges offered highly desirable exemptions from common burdens such as the land-tax and service on town-councils, but others conferred more immediate commercial advantages, including the offlaying of much of the cost of building ships, and the transference of the risk of loss to the state (with all the concomitant opportunities for fraud). Most importantly, as long as they fulfilled their obligations to the state, *navicularii* were allowed, subject to certain restrictions, to conduct their own business on the side, free from the assorted customs-dues for which merchants were ordinarily liable. The massed Egyptian *annona* fleet in full sail made the Mediterranean look like dry land and, once it had reached Constantinople, its captains could stock up with cargoes on their own account, their return voyages effectively subsidised by the state.[79]

One of these return cargoes must have been the variant of Red Slip ware manufactured at Phocaea, in the immediate vicinity of the imperial capital, and widely distributed around the eastern Mediterranean and, to a lesser extent, across to the west.[80] The restoration of imperial control over Africa in 533 was probably also instrumental in a renewed flow of ARS into the eastern

[77] Justinian's attempt to fix the maximum interest rate on nautical loans at 12% per annum seems to have been unpopular precisely because the risk of loss was greater: Jones (1964), pp. 868–9.

[78] McCormick (1998), esp. pp. 65–93, for a fine analysis of the benefits to trade of the *annona*, fleshing out the suggestions of Wickham (1988). Durliat (1990) takes a more pessimistic view.

[79] For the scale of the fleet, Theophylact Simocatta, *History* II.14.7 (of the late 580s); for return cargoes, Procopius, *Buildings* V.I.II.

[80] Abadie-Reynal (1989), esp. pp. 150–7, with the works cited at n. 38 above.

Mediterranean.[81] In both cases these pottery exports will have travelled as secondary cargoes alongside other goods, and so indicate general currents of exchange, but the ceramic evidence suggests that the impact of state interests on distribution is hardly consistent in its effects. In the West, it seems to have encouraged exports from the main *annona*-supplying region, Africa; but there is no comparable overseas dissemination of local amphorae or fine-ware pottery from Egypt, the eastern equivalent, nor the significant imports of PRS, which one might expect to find there if traffic between Egypt and Constantinople was simply reciprocal in nature.[82] While the flows of traffic generated around Constantinople, and probably other major centres such as Antioch and Alexandria, certainly helped to structure the interregional tier of the economy in the eastern Mediterranean, the relative importance of state and commercial shipping within these exchange-networks is extremely difficult to assess.[83] Two fragmentary inscriptions recording the fees payable by vessels entering the ports of Abydos, controlling the Hellespont outside Constantinople, and Seleucia, serving Antioch, offer rare textual confirmation of the varied provenances of shipping and the assortment of goods drawn towards major centres, but there is nothing to show whether these concern state or private traffic.[84] State interests alone seem insufficient in any case to account for all the manifold ramifications of interregional exchange suggested by the archaeological evidence, which shows how all the coastal regions of the eastern Mediterranean continued to trade foodstuffs in amphorae not only with each other, implying the existence of several interlocking regional systems, but also across to the West. Here the rising proportions of eastern amphorae present in some fifth- and sixth-century assemblages can only stem from commercial exchange, and probably represent the discovery of new and lucrative markets by private shippers.[85] The same surely goes for much interregional exchange within the more dynamic eastern economy, especially given the scope for private enterprise and the commercial advantages enjoyed by those involved in the *annona*. The classification of exchange as 'state' or 'tied' (and so non-commercial) on the one hand, or 'private' (commercial) on the other, is too inflexible; it neglects the extent to which these various types of transaction were interdependent.

81 Panella (1993), pp. 658–61.

82 Abadie-Reynal (1989) for the likely difference in eastern and western distribution-systems. Local and Cypriot fine wares seem far more common in Egypt than PRS: Ballet and Picon (1987), pp. 26–8.

83 Besides Constantinople, there is limited evidence for state-supply systems at Alexandria and Antioch, esp. Justinian, *Novels* VII.8, but their existence elsewhere is conjectural: see Carrié (1975) and Durliat (1990).

84 Abydos (of *c.*492): Durliat and Guillou (1984); Dagron (1985), pp. 451–5. Seleucia (probably dating from early in Justinian's reign): Dagron (1985), pp. 435–51.

85 Eastern circuits: Abadie-Reynal (1989); Panella (1993), pp. 657–73; Kingsley and Decker (2001). Eastern exports to the West: Reynolds (1995), pp. 70–83.

The entwining of public and private interests means that the patterns of sixth- and seventh-century interregional Mediterranean exchange defy easy synthesis.[86] But a basic distinction must be drawn between the eastern Mediterranean, where, as we have seen, all the evidence points to a widespread late antique boom in the rural economy, closely associated with exports to overseas markets, and the western Mediterranean, where interregional exchange had been declining in volume and complexity for some time, and was dominated by African goods. If producers in Spain, Gaul or Italy regularly marketed their surplus overseas, they rarely did so by transporting their agricultural surplus in amphorae or shipping fine-ware pottery alongside it, and although African ceramics continued to be distributed widely around the Mediterranean through the sixth century and on into the seventh, even here there are signs of a simplification of production before the end of the fifth century.[87] Of the three main categories of ARS only one, the D ware produced in northern Tunisia, was still manufactured by *c.*550, and the number of forms of this ware in circulation diminished considerably over the next century.[88] Late antique African amphorae cannot yet be classified and dated with similar precision, but the evidence implies a similar contraction in variety and complexity of production. The data from African field-surveys around Segermes and Kasserine and in the Libyan valleys further suggest that rural settlement was already past its peak by our period, but that this decline began to accelerate from perhaps the mid-sixth century.[89]

In the eastern Mediterranean, by contrast, patterns of production and overseas exchange remained far more diverse and polycentric, and the late antique settlement boom was probably sustained throughout the sixth century. The preceding period of dramatic expansion and investment may have been over in some regions, such as the Syrian limestone massif, but this is perhaps better seen in terms of consolidation rather than stagnation, especially since similar areas, such as the interior of Palestine, exhibit continuing prosperity. In any event, there is little sign of any widespread crisis of production or distribution in the eastern Mediterranean before 600.[90] The scale of production and the

86 Best for the archaeology is Panella (1993), but the characterisation of the seventh century is now too pessimistic. For a wider overview of fifth- and sixth-century exchange, see Ward-Perkins (2000b).

87 Precisely when this begins, however, is a moot point; its origins may precede the Vandal conquest: Panella (1993), pp. 641–5.

88 Reynolds (1995), pp. 12–14, 28–34, citing a fall from fifteen forms in 533 to only three a century later. This may be too precise, but the trend is clear. Cf. Mackensen (1998) for seventh-century ARS production.

89 Helpful overview (and further references) in Mattingly and Hitchner (1995), esp. pp. 189–96, 209–13.

90 For 'stagnation' in the limestone massif *c.*550–610, Tate (1992), pp. 335–42, in my view overstated; cf. Orssaud (1992) for ceramic continuity. The lively debate about the general state of Syria and Palestine in the later sixth century lies outside the scope of this chapter. For overviews see Foss (1995); Kennedy (2000), and also Louth, chapter 4 above.

complexity of exchange-networks here is especially evident in the bewildering range of eastern amphora manufactures and the heterogeneity of their distributions. Although many of these amphorae fall into broad categories which can be associated with particular regions of production, these major classifications conceal a plethora of sub-groups, and a significant proportion of types are as yet not closely provenanced; all of this implies the existence of a host of independent producers and distributors involved in overseas exchange.

The overlapping distribution-networks of African and eastern ceramics confirm that the economic interdependence of the Mediterranean lasted well into the seventh century. Beneath this veneer of a shared material culture, however, the cracks were beginning to appear. The signs are most obvious in the slow but inexorable retreat of ARS, the epitome of late antique interregional exchange, first from inland sites, then from some coastal areas of the Mediterranean[91] (see Maps 17A and 17B). This development should not be viewed from the wrong end of the telescope; the economic integration implicit in the availability of ARS to peasants in the Italian Apennines or on the Arabian desert margins is more remarkable than its eventual disappearance. But this era was drawing to an end. In Italy, for example, where the evidence is both relatively abundant and well studied, ceramic assemblages recovered from inland rural sites remain similar to those found in cities until the early sixth century; imports then progressively disappear from all but urban or coastal centres. In some Italian regions, this is but one aspect of a more radical transformation in material culture manifested in very basic forms of pottery production and even the use of wooden dishes, implying not merely the decline of overseas exchange but the disintegration of regional production- and distribution-systems. Elsewhere in Italy, the manufacture and distribution of fine-ware pottery suggests that economic involution was less drastic, but here too imports become increasingly rare.[92] In general terms the pattern is similar in other western regions. In Mediterranean Spain and Francia the ceramic evidence increasingly permits the identification of local or regional exchange-networks of variable extent and sophistication, but by the seventh century these regions show increasingly sporadic integration with the wider Mediterranean economy.[93]

Although the diminishing reach of ARS is a particularly valuable indicator of the steady contraction of interregional exchange, recent excavations suggest that the final crisis came only in the seventh century. The prolonged political turmoil which engulfed the territories of the Byzantine Empire as a result of

[91] Overviews in Panella (1993), pp. 673–80; Reynolds (1995), pp. 31–4. Regional updates: Tortorella (1998) (Italy); Gutiérrez-Lloret (1998b) (Spain); Bonifay *et al.* (1998), esp. pp. 361–5 (southern Gaul).

[92] Arthur and Patterson (1994), esp. pp. 425–9, and Fontana (1998) with other papers in Saguì (1998b) and review by Wickham (2000b) for regional variation in Italy.

[93] See note 91 above, with CATHMA (1993) for Languedoc, Pelletier (1997) for Provence.

civil war, the mutually destructive conflict with Persia, and the Arab conquests, brought in its train a profound restructuring of the eastern Mediterranean economy.[94] Its most significant effect was to impose the regionalisation of exchange that was already characteristic of the West. In Byzantine-held territories this seems to have coincided with widespread and relatively radical changes in the organisation of production and perhaps also in the tastes of consumers. The manufacture of PRS, for example, came to an abrupt end around the mid-seventh century, superseded around Constantinople by Glazed White Wares; these belong to a different ceramic tradition, and they initially enjoyed a more limited distribution.[95] In the territories conquered by the Arabs, however, there was no dramatic transformation of ceramic styles; in Palestine and Jordan, for example, production of existing regional fine wares continued, and if anything their quality improved. Indeed, the archaeological evidence for settlement and production suggests that catastrophist interpretations of the Arab impact are seriously misplaced.[96] As in the case of Vandal Africa in the fifth century, there is no neat coincidence here between political and economic change, and no necessary cessation of traffic between conquered and imperially held territory. In his eye-witness account of his visit to the holy places in the 680s, the pilgrim Arculf mentions an annual fair in Jerusalem attended by 'a throng beyond number of all races from almost everywhere'.[97] Even so, the various regional varieties of Red Slip did eventually go out of production, and while amphorae from these regions were still manufactured, they ceased to be widely distributed overseas, and were very slowly superseded by alternative types of container. Only in Egypt would the late antique ceramic tradition represented by local Red Slip wares and late Roman amphora types persist for centuries to come.[98] By the eighth century the polyfocal exchange-system of the eastern Mediterranean had disintegrated, leaving in its wake the series of regional economies which had always existed. Some of these were well developed, especially those of Syria and Egypt, but there seems to have been much less overlap between them than before, and they were no longer oriented towards the Mediterranean.

In the western Mediterranean, meanwhile, there was no such radical seventh-century interruption to existing trends. The interregional tier of the economy continued to dwindle away, and no new networks of overseas exchange were yet emerging to replace it. But recent excavations have implied that its twilight lingered far longer than had previously been thought. In Africa production

94 Haldon (1990) and (2000). 95 Hayes (1992), pp. 12–34.

96 Sodini and Villeneuve (1992); Watson (1992); Schick (1998); Walmsley (1996) and (2000).

97 Adomnán, *De Locis Sanctis* I.7; cf. Arthur and Oren (1998) for the persistence of imports from Africa and other eastern regions to Egypt through the seventh century, long after the Arab conquest.

98 Walmsley (2000), pp. 317–31, for slow change in Syria; Bailey (1998), pp. 8–58 for Egypt.

of an attenuated range of pottery, lamps and amphorae continued up to and beyond the Arab conquest.[99] Meanwhile, a select but increasing number of western Mediterranean sites are now known to have gone on receiving imports from both Africa and the East, in some cases throughout the seventh century. In the south of France, for example, Marseilles had from the sixth century resumed its pre-Roman role as an emporium mediating Mediterranean exchange with north-western Europe. Although the port was clearly in decline by the late seventh century, an assortment of African ceramics and a few eastern amphorae of various types were still arriving, showing not only that the interregional circulation of pottery and foodstuffs persisted, but also that it was by no means confined to the remaining western outposts of imperial authority.[100]

At Rome, two substantial and closely dated ceramic assemblages from the Crypta Balbi, a site plausibly associated in this period with the monastery of S. Lorenzo in Pallacinis, seem to mark the final eclipse of the ancient Mediterranean economic system.[101] In the first, dating from *c.*690, ARS was almost the only fine ware present, but the common wares, though mostly local, also included a scatter of African and eastern imports.[102] The amphora assemblage was also dominated by African models, but it also included a wide variety of eastern imports, containers from southern Italy, and a significant number and proportion of unknown types, which, whatever their origin, can only imply greater diversity and complexity of exchange (Map 16). The second deposit from the same site, dating from perhaps *c.*720, offers an immediate and startling point of comparison. It contains neither ARS nor any of the standard African or eastern late antique amphora types. Instead, all the identifiable amphorae were manufactured in southern and central Italy. Indeed, the overall proportion of amphora sherds in the ceramic assemblage falls from 46 per cent to 25 per cent, perhaps reflecting this decline in imports, or more likely increasing resort to other forms of container.[103] Whereas around 80 per cent of the ceramics in the late seventh-century deposit were imported from outside Italy, hardly any of the pottery in the later assemblage came from further afield than Sicily. It appears that while Rome still needed imports, it was acquiring them

99 Mackensen (1993), esp. pp. 493–4; Reynolds (1995), pp. 31–4, 57–60; Ben Abed *et al.* (1997).

100 Bonifay and Pieri (1995); Bonifay *et al.* (1998), esp. pp. 357–8; Loseby (1998) and (2000). Cf. Mannoni, Murialdo *et al.* (2001), for later seventh-century material at S. Antonino di Perti in Liguria.

101 Saguì, Ricci and Romei (1997); Saguì (1998a); Bacchelli and Pasqualucci (1998); Ricci (1998).

102 For the low-level circulation of common wares around the Mediterranean in our period, a further marker of economic integration, see e.g. Reynolds (1995), pp. 86–105.

103 Arthur (1989) and (1993) for observations on the decline of the amphora in Italy; Hayes (1992), pp. 61–79, for later medieval amphora series at Constantinople.

closer to home, and stimulating the regional economy into new and diverse forms of production in the process.[104]

It is obviously simplistic to place too much emphasis on a single site, or, more generally, to suggest that the ramifications of the Mediterranean economy can be entirely deduced from ceramic distributions. But the archaeological evidence from the Crypta Balbi, and from the small but increasing number of other sites where seventh-century deposits have been recovered, is increasingly consistent with the conclusions about the timing of the end of the ancient exchange-system drawn by some scholars from the more impressionistic, but also more multifaceted indications of the written sources. Most famously, as we saw at the beginning of this chapter, Henri Pirenne had argued that it was not the barbarian invasions of the fifth century, but the Arab conquests of the seventh which had destroyed the Roman economic legacy.[105] His use of evidence was selective, and his reasoning seriously flawed, but his chronology deserves to be taken seriously. Indeed, in his much more thorough analysis of the documentary evidence for western Mediterranean trade in the early Middle Ages, Dietrich Claude inclined cautiously towards a similar date for the nadir of Mediterranean trade, in the period between the late seventh and the middle of the eighth century.[106] But Pirenne's monocausal explanation of this phenomenon in terms of the rise of Islam will not do. It had certainly not been business as usual in the West until the later seventh century. In the East, meanwhile, the Arab conquests are but one element in a radical transformation of the internal structures of the Byzantine Empire, now greatly diminished in extent, and, with the loss of its richest provinces, even more so in resources. The grip of the state on remaining surplus production was tightened as a result and, once its links with Carthage were definitively broken, Constantinople fell back upon the Black Sea and the northern Aegean for supplies.[107] In the areas newly conquered by the Arabs, in contrast, change was more evolutionary in character. Even so, evidence for the participation of these regions in Mediterranean exchange does gradually diminish, whether because of the nature of the Umayyad state, devolving power and taxation to the regional level, or perhaps because of the reorientation of the main flows of exchange eastwards towards Mesopotomia and the Indian Ocean.[108] The Mediterranean never became a barrier, as Pirenne had claimed, but no longer did it serve as the primary focus of interregional exchange for the Byzantine or the Arab lands around it.

104 Marazzi (1998a). 105 Pirenne (1939).

106 Claude (1985), p. 303. 107 Haldon (2000), esp. pp. 255–60.

108 See note 96, above, with Kennedy (1995) for the Umayyad state.

Back in the western Mediterranean, the contrast in the two assemblages from the Crypta Balbi offers an unusually stark and late illustration of the breakdown in the late antique exchange-network, which had progressively affected all communities around its shores from the fifth century onwards. Within our period the imported ceramics which represent our clearest markers of engagement with interregional exchange had receded first from the hinterlands of the Mediterranean, then from some coastal regions, and ultimately even from Rome itself. The reasons for this contraction are many and varied, but its gradual nature, the absence of any clear indications of generalised technological or environmental change, and the telling failure of any new networks of interregional exchange to emerge over the period all suggest that the explanation is essentially structural. In the third century, rural Italian peasants could both afford and acquire ARS; in the seventh they could not. On the supply side, the absolute quantities of ARS in circulation were almost certainly declining, political disaggregation had ended or restricted the underpinning of distribution networks by the state, and the integration of the regional market economy which permitted the circulation inland of imported goods had in places been undermined by protracted periods of warfare, most obviously in Italy. On the demand side, it is likely that the needs of the state were greatly reduced, and that many private consumers were increasingly impoverished, in some regions to such an extent that even regional economic systems were undermined, and exchange contracted to a rudimentary level.[109] The basic tax-and-spend dynamic of the Roman state was primarily concerned with ensuring its own survival, but it had incidentally provided mechanisms which both enabled and encouraged peasants to convert tiny agricultural surpluses into profit, purchasing-power and material wealth. The Roman economy was nowhere near as state-directed as has sometimes been supposed, but in some important respects it was state-inspired. This meant that the collapse of imperial control in the West could not destroy the economy, but it could gradually undermine it. The combination of reduced production, an increase in the cost or difficulty of distribution, and declining demand was corrosive; as consumers became poorer, so imports became scarcer and more expensive. A mass-produced, widely diffused commodity like ARS was progressively transformed into a luxury item.

Although the interregional tier of the exchange-network survived in some form in the western Mediterranean until the end of our period, therefore, it had become more of a cultural than an economic phenomenon. The reduction in the range of available manufactures of African goods suggests that production was in decline, but the distribution pattern confirms that they were still notionally available around the Mediterranean well into the seventh century.

109 Wickham (1998) offers an alternative hierarchy of explanation, emphasising demand.

The problem was that they were no longer so readily affordable. The reach of the Mediterranean economy recedes, not just geographically, but also socially, and perhaps politically. The Crypta Balbi excavations show that as long as interregional exchange continued to exist, some people in Rome were served by it. Their privileged access to imports is perhaps the result of state-directed exchange, but the continuing availability of a wide range of overseas goods in the Provençal ports shows that such traffic was also commercial, and not confined to Byzantine-held regions. Indeed, the determination of Merovingian kings to organise the redistribution of the remarkable range of Mediterranean imports mentioned in the Corbie diploma to their chosen beneficiaries, the expense of inland transport notwithstanding, shows how the elites of the northern world had remained almost touchingly devoted to certain deeply ingrained habits derived from antiquity: churches illuminated by oil lamps rather than wax candles, charters written on Egyptian papyrus rather than parchment, food flavoured with exotic spices, and perhaps still washed down by the occasional beaker of powerful Gaza wine. All this forms the material equivalent of, for example, respect for Roman administrative practices, and illustrates the enduring appreciation of late antique and Byzantine cultural norms among western elites. In Francia all this was a matter of choice, not of economic necessity, and it continued until the supply of such imports finally dried up.[110] In Rome, any crisis the end of African and eastern imports caused was soon met by a rapid restructuring of the economy to establish regular regional networks of supply. But nowhere in the West was demand sufficient to necessitate interregional exchange. Only the Roman world-system had made a Mediterranean economy essential, and only a community of taste had sustained it through to the end of our period as a cultural phenomenon.[111]

At privileged western sites like Rome and Marseilles, or Carthage and Naples, the archaeological evidence suggests that the late antique exchange-network persisted in an etiolated form through to the close of the seventh century. Until then, indeed, many of the essential features of the Mediterranean economy – the main exporting regions, the types of pottery and amphorae in overseas circulation, some of the major flows of exchange – were still recognisably those of 500. But over the intervening period the whole system had relentlessly declined in the West, such that participation in interregional exchange gradually became the exception rather than the norm. In the East, the collapse of this tier of the economy was both more sudden and more complex, but the outcome was similar. Some trading-ships continued to ply the Mediterranean in the eighth century, and some regional economies around its shores were thriving, although

110 Loseby (2000), pp. 189–93. For lighting practices, Fouracre (1995), pp. 68–78.

111 For the Roman Empire as world-system, Woolf (1990).

others, for example those of southern Francia, parts of northern Italy and probably north Africa, were sunk deep in recession.[112] However, the interregional Mediterranean economy described in this chapter ceased to exist in around 700, and the break was both real and profound. To this limited extent, Henri Pirenne's instincts were right. When an integrated, complex Mediterranean economy (as opposed to a series of incidental exchanges) began slowly to re-emerge in the Middle Ages, its organisation, its poles of activity and its currents would be substantially different from those of antiquity.[113]

[112] Horden and Purcell (2000), pp. 153–72, for a recent assertion of continuing Mediterranean exchange, but one which in my view goes too far in denying early medieval change. McCormick (2001) takes an even more optimistic view of the ensuing period, not yet supported by the archaeological evidence. For regional variety, Wickham (1998) and (2000a).

[113] I am extremely grateful to Ruth Featherstone, Paul Fouracre, Brigitte Resl, Bryan Ward-Perkins and Chris Wickham for comments on drafts of this chapter, and to all the members of the 'Production, Distribution and Demand' working group of the ESF-funded Transformation of the Roman World project, from whom I learnt a great deal.

CHAPTER 23

THE NORTHERN SEAS (FIFTH TO EIGHTH CENTURIES)

Stéphane Lebecq

It is a well-known fact these days that the seas of northern Europe – from the Atlantic to the Baltic, by way of the Channel and the North Sea – are amongst the busiest and most used in the world. But at what point did they begin to play a significant role in Europe's system of communications and trade? Despite the numerous claims handed down to us by Pytheas, Caesar, Strabo, Pliny, Tacitus, Ptolemy and others in their travel memoirs or in their geographies, it is clear that, in ancient times, northern Europe was a distant horizon. It was almost the furthermost, just like certain of its inhabitants, such as the Morins of the Pas-de-Calais, whom Virgil described as *extremi hominum*.[1] At that time, the Mediterranean was the chief axis for trade and exchanges, not only between East and West, but also between South and North. The Northern Seas were then simply a distant destination in a communications system in which – to take a single example – traffic between Roman Britain and the continent was justified chiefly by the military requirements of the Empire and by its need for supplies of metal. It is clear from studying written sources and archaeological and numismatic artefacts that it was during the early Middle Ages that the Northern Seas started to play an essential role in the communications system and economy of the Western world.

Henri Pirenne, the founding father of the economic history of medieval Europe, was the first to declare that it was in the eighth century that the Western world's political and economic centre of gravity moved away from the South towards the North. This was when Islam's lightning conquest had succeeded in tying up a large section of the Mediterranean coasts and coastal lands. It was then that the Northern Seas began to play an active role in the European system of communications – even if only at a modest level until the beginning of the eleventh century.[2] The most recent research, in which archaeology and numismatics have, to some extent, begun to fill in the gaps in

[1] *Aeneid* VIII.727. [2] Pirenne (1939), *passim.*

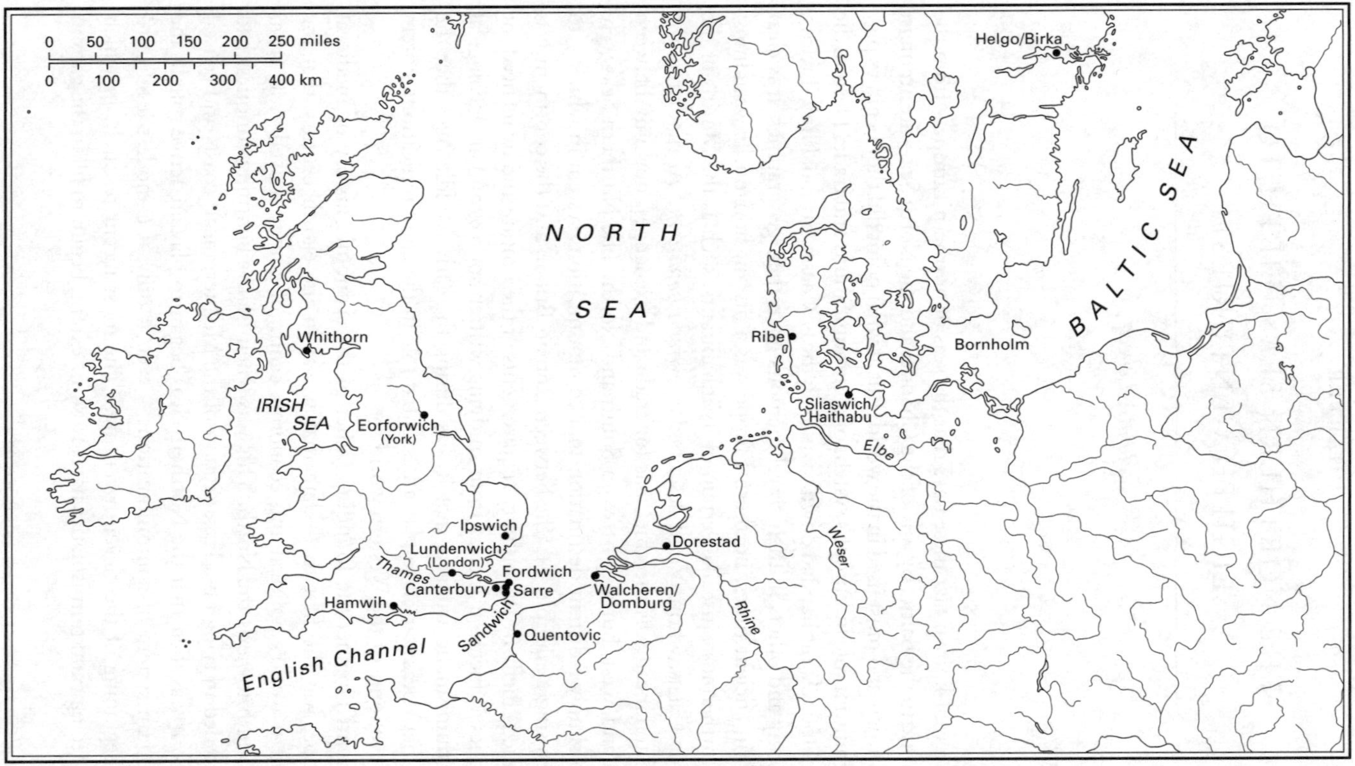

Map 18 North Sea emporia

the rather fragmentary written evidence, has largely confirmed Henri Pirenne's overall chronology, but has challenged his explanations.[3] In fact, it appears, first, that it was between the end of the sixth century (when the major Celtic and Germanic migrations in the Northern Seas basin came to an end) and the course of the ninth century (when increasing Viking piracy began to disrupt Western communications) that a real maritime economy developed in northern Europe for the very first time. Secondly, this phenomenon cannot be explained as a result of the transformation of the Mediterranean world. Thirdly, it can be explained by reasons peculiar to the coastal lands of the Northern Seas, and in particular to changes in their ethnic, political and social environment and to their own economic development. But before discussing the emergence of this new maritime economy, it is appropriate to recall just what was happening in the Northern Seas at the end of the sixth century.

THE LEGACY OF LATE ANTIQUITY

Since the end of the third century, communications in the northern seaways, especially between the British Isles and the continent, had been interrupted by maritime migrations and concomitant piracy. This was to be rampant for two or three centuries, even though an important part of these movements had been undertaken and controlled by the Roman Empire itself for the purpose of its coastal defence.[4] However, the movements of Celtic peoples in the western seas (from Ireland to western Britain; from Scotland to southern Britain; from south-western Britain to Brittany) began to slow down during the second half of the sixth century.[5] And in the East, after two centuries of a so-called 'Saxon' migration and piracy (where, in fact, Saxons were accompanied, or followed, by Jutes from northern Denmark, Angles from Schleswig-Holstein, Frisians from the Netherlands, and even Franks from the Rhine and Meuse delta area),[6] the raid of *Danus rex Chlochilaichus* (probably the *Hygelac* of the poem *Beowulf*) around 525 to the northern shores of Gaul was the last maritime movement of a Germanic people to be explicitly recorded in written sources.[7]

Of course, insecurity made peaceful communications along the northern and western seaways more difficult, but not necessarily impossible, and some ancient shipping routes remained busy. For instance, we know that, during the period 450–650, there was a relatively important connection from the eastern Mediterranean to far north-western Europe, which passed along the Spanish and Gaulish coasts. The *Life of John the Almsgiver* (a patriarch of Alexandria, who died in 619) tells us of a merchant ship which sailed from Alexandria to

[3] Hodges and Whitehouse (1983). [4] Higham (1992); Jones (1996); James (2001).
[5] Thomas (1986); McGrail (1990). [6] Myres (1989); Jones (1996). [7] Gregory, *Hist.* III.3.

'the Isles of Britain' (i.e. probably the islands known during antiquity as the Cassiterides – the Isles of Scilly and the south-western British mainland) in twenty days and nights with a cargo of corn, and returned with a cargo of gold and tin.[8] So long after the collapse of the Roman Empire and the end of the *pax Romana*, the reader might easily dismiss this account as a fable. However, the discovery of a significant quantity of fifth- and sixth-century jars, bowls and amphorae (the so-called 'A' and 'B' wares of the archaeologists) from the eastern, central and western Mediterranean in several aristocratic and/or princely sites in Ireland (Garranes and Clogher) and the British far west (Tintagel in Cornwall, Dinas Powys in Wales) and north (Dumbarton Rock) proves that such connections lasted during the Dark Ages.[9]

But such a well-documented (in a manner of speaking) example is rare, because usually the written sources are very sketchy. Except for a few rare, late and sometimes doubtful allusions in some Irish saints' Lives to the relations between Atlantic Gaul and the distant Celtic countries of north-western Europe,[10] the sources of the sixth century tell us nothing about any commercial traffic between the continent and the British Isles. The most important Roman ports (like Gesoriacum-Bononia (Boulogne) on the continent, or like Dubris (Dover) or Rutupiae (Richborough) in Britain) are no longer mentioned. These were military ports connected, during a first period (the first to third centuries), with the *Classis Britannica*, the fleet which controlled imperial relations with the province of Brittania, and, later (the fourth to fifth centuries), with the defensive coastal system of the *Litus saxonicum*.[11] And if the names of ancient cities like Rotomagus (Rouen), Namnetas (Nantes), Londinium (London) or Eboracum (York) still appear in sources, they are no longer referred to as ports.

Of course, this does not mean that all types of relations ceased to exist between the Isles and the continent – far from it, because the migrations resulted in the settlement of actively maritime peoples in all the coastal areas of north-western Europe. Henceforth (say from the middle of the sixth century), there was an almost continuous Celtic settlement along the western seaways. There were more and more Scotti (Irish) from Hibernia (Ireland) in Caledonia (Scotland) – particularly in Dál Riada (the south-west of Scotland) – and in Cambria (Wales) – especially in Dyfed;[12] more and more Brittones from Cambria and Dumnonia (Cornwall and the south-western peninsula) were to be found in ancient Armorica, which began to be called Brittania (Brittany) in the second half of the sixth century.[13] As for the maritime Germans, they settled not only in the east and south of Britain where, in spite of recent arguments to

[8] Leontius of Naples, *Life of John the Almsgiver*, ed. Festugière, pp. 353–4 and 452–3.

[9] Thomas (1988) and (1993), pp. 93–6; Fulford (1989).

[10] James (1982), pp. 375–8; Johanek (1985), pp. 227–8. [11] Johnson (1976) and (1977).

[12] Thomas (1986). [13] Fleuriot (1980); Cassard (1998), pp. 15–57.

the contrary,[14] we must reckon that the presence of the Anglo-Saxons was dense and numerous along the coasts.[15] It was also significant on some continental shores, especially in the Boulonnais, the Bessin (around Bayeux) and the lower valley of the Loire, where Saxon settlement has long been identified from written and place-name evidence. It is evident too in the Ponthieu (a coastal area in northern Picardy, between the rivers Canche and Somme) and the Caen area, where a Saxon presence has recently come to light in cemetery excavations, especially at Vron and Nouvion (in Ponthieu), or at Frénouville, Hérouvillette, Giberville and St Martin-de-Fontenay (in Normandy).[16]

A relative cultural and linguistic homogeneity (Celtic in the western areas; Germanic, or, as current linguistics call it, *Nordseegermanisch*, in the central and eastern areas) resulted from these movements and coastal settlements. In fact, the existence of such widespread linguistic communities facilitated the contacts between the different shores of north-western Europe, and certainly helps to explain the archaeological distribution of some specific items, like the 'D ware' (bowls and plates) and the 'E ware' (wheel-thrown pots and jars), originating from western Gaul, which were found in many sixth-century sites in Ireland, Scotland, south-west Britain and the Scilly Isles;[17] similarly, some kinds of the so-called 'Anglo-Saxon' brooches (disc brooches or button brooches) which have been found not only in the south of England (in the cemeteries of Kent, Sussex and the Isle of Wight), but also in all the cemeteries which have been excavated in the Ponthieu and Caen areas.[18]

If such exchanges took place, this would imply the existence of some sort of transport system, with men, ships, landing places, perhaps some trade instruments. But supporting archaeological evidence is rather scarce – just a few weighing scales have been found in English and continental graves,[19] and written evidence says little more, except perhaps about the ships. For instance, in his *De Excidio et Conquestu Brittaniae*, Gildas speaks of the Celtic *currucae* (the famous curaghs) and about the coming of the Saxons in 'tribus ut lingua eius Saxonum exprimitur cyulis, nostra longis navibus' ('three *cyuls*, as Saxons call in their language what we term in ours "long boats"').[20] So, according to Gildas, the sixth-century Britons or Romano-Britons knew of two kinds of boats. The curaghs or hide boats were described by Caesar in the first century BC and by Adomnán of Iona in the eighth century. Curaghs could be propelled by oars and by sail, and probably looked like the first-century BC gold model found in Broighter (Co. Derry, Ireland), or like the ship carved on the Kilnaruane pillar (Co. Cork, Ireland). Secondly there were the *longae naves*, probably

14 Higham (1992). 15 Myres (1989); Jones (1996). 16 Lebecq (1989); Welch (1991).
17 Thomas (1990). 18 Welch (1991). 19 Steuer (1987).
20 *De Excidio et Conquestu Brittaniae*, *cc.*19 and 23, ed. Winterbottom, pp. 94 and 97.

planked boats that were propelled by sail, as suggested by the coins issued by Cunobelin in the first century AD, or by the St Peter Port (Guernsey) wreck from the third century.[21] The Anglo-Saxons, as we have just seen, had long ships that they called *cyul(i)* (OE *ceol*, modern English *keel*), a word which probably refers to ships such as the famous fourth-century Nydam boat, found in Schleswig-Holstein, i.e. approximately the ancient *Angulus* or *Angeln*, the land from which, according to Bede, the *Angli* came. These were long clinker-built wooden ships, which, during the Migration period, were more probably propelled by oars than by sail, as we can see from writings of Sidonius (fifth century) and Procopius (sixth century).[22] From stem to stern, all these ships had a symmetrical profile and a relatively flat bottom, and so they could be landed almost anywhere.

Landing places must, therefore, have been numerous, particularly on the sandy shores of the southern coasts of the Northern Seas. Moreover, traffic must have been so scattered that it is difficult to identify real trading ports between the end of the third century, when Roman ports started to decline, and the beginning of the seventh, when a real revival of port activity took place. But, here and there, it is not impossible to find the remains of beach markets or trading posts, probably connected with high-status settlements or centres of local power, as in the Danish prototype of Gudme/Lundeborg, excavated on the Baltic isle of Funen, and where a lot of rich, especially gold, material from the third to sixth centuries has been found.[23] This was perhaps the case of the fort of Dalkey Island, on the southern end of Dublin Bay, where fifth- and sixth-century imported material from the Mediterranean and from Aquitaine has been found.[24] Other cases could be Benouville (on the Orne estuary, near Caen), where archaeologists have found items which may be related to the material found in the nearby hinterland cemeteries; Sarre, on the bank of the Wantsum Channel in Kent, where a large cemetery from the sixth century has been excavated, with a variety of material including scales;[25] or the *terp* (i.e. the artificial mound on the maritime plain) of Wijnaldum in Frisia, where very rich material from the sixth and seventh centuries was imported and/or transformed.[26]

None of the newly settled populations in the maritime countries minted coins, however. If they did need currency, they still used the late Roman, then Byzantine coins, such as the *solidi*, or the thirds of *solidi* called *trientes* or *tremisses*, which were reproduced by the Frankish mintmasters in Gaul. It is not, however, certain that they needed currency, except for its metal weight (which

21 McGrail (1987) and (1990). 22 Ellmers (1972); McGrail (1990).

23 Thrane (1987); Clarke and Ambrosiani (1995). 24 Hodges (1982), p. 67; Edwards (1990), pp. 41–3.

25 Hodges (1982), p. 69 and (1989), pp. 55 and 92–3.

26 Heidinga (1997); Besteman *et al.*, forthcoming.

could explain the use of scales, like those found in some Kentish cemeteries). According to an anthropological perception of the early history of barbarian societies, exchanges between the peoples of northern Europe during the Dark Ages consisted mainly of scattered or occasional contacts, barter, reciprocal gift-exchange – all practices which were part of diplomatic, matrimonial or social customs and rituals.[27] So the few continental coins that arrived in the British Isles during the fifth and sixth centuries seem mainly to have been used as ornaments.

Such was probably the social background in which an East Anglian prince (perhaps King Redwald) was buried in Sutton Hoo around 625–630, and which accounts for the heterogeneous quality of the objects found in his grave, the famous ship-burial Number One.[28] Besides the material of Eastern, Scandinavian and Rhenish origin which was found in the grave, a hoard of thirty-seven *trientes* from thirty-seven different Frankish mints was found. This shows the artificiality of such a collection, possibly a diplomatic gift (why not the dowry given to the deceased by a Frankish wife?). This collection, to which were added three coin blanks and two little ingots, was perhaps put together, as Philip Grierson has suggested,[29] to pay the forty oarsmen and ferrymen of the soul of the dead man to another world. This treasure seems to make Sutton Hoo the best example of this period of peaceful but not yet commercial exchanges between the Isles and the continent. But it is also one of the last archaeological examples of such exchanges; for, from the beginning of the seventh century, things began to change.

THE DEVELOPMENT OF A MARITIME ECONOMY

Towards the year 600, in fact, trading in the Northern Seas began to take on a better-defined structure. Written sources, which had been almost silent on the subject since the migratory period, started to make mention again of independent, professional merchants. These sources refer to the commercial rebirth of ancient maritime cities and of port activity unknown until that moment, but the existence and spread of which are often confirmed by archaeology. Finally, one sees the continental Frisians and insular Anglo-Saxons, chief instigators of this rebirth, beginning to mint coins, copying the model of the Frankish mints that had themselves imitated the late Roman and Byzantine models.

In order to explain this rebirth, one has to invoke the end of the maritime migratory movement and the stabilisation of peoples sharing the same cultural horizons along the North Sea coasts, for it is obvious that an ethnic explanation is not sufficient. A noticeable improvement in climate reached north-west

[27] Grierson (1959) and (1961). [28] Evans (1986); Carver (1998). [29] Grierson (1970).

Europe, which was soon to be free of the last great epidemic threat from antiquity (this was the plague, sometimes known as 'Justinianic' because it came from the East, and which was far more lethal in southern Europe than in the north). The area benefited from the beginnings of a demographic and economic growth such as had not been seen since the third century.[30] Everywhere around the Northern Seas one witnesses the rise of ever more powerful aristocracies and monarchies. These (for example, the Franks in southern England) were looking to exercise a certain overseas supremacy, through diplomatic or matrimonial channels.[31] Above all, however, they wanted to stimulate, support and influence activities of production and trade, and thereby to direct future surpluses towards external markets by developing port activity in places that would henceforth be better controlled.

Thus, at the turn of the sixth and seventh centuries, the whole of the Northern Seas basin, from the Atlantic coasts of Europe as far as the great delta of the Meuse and the Rhine, in the heart of what is now the Netherlands, seems to have been affected by this revival of commercial activity. One only has to refer to Adomnán of Iona who, in his *Life of St Columba*, mentions those 'Gallici nautae de Galliarum provinciis' who, at the end of the sixth century frequented Hebridean waters;[32] or to Jonas of Bobbio who, in his *Life of Columbanus*, refers to the presence in Nantes, on the Loire estuary, of those 'naves quae Scottorum commercia vexerant', which were preparing to set sail with a cargo of wine.[33] Bede himself, in his *Ecclesiastical History of the English People*, turns the London of *c.*604 into an *emporium* frequented by 'multi populi terra marique venientes', amongst whom, some tens of years later, he would distinguish a Frisian slave trader.[34] Archaeologists have uncovered, from the beginning of the seventh century, the first harbour development of sites such as Domburg (formerly Walacras, Walcheren, in Dutch Zeeland)[35] or Ipswich (formerly Gipeswic, in Suffolk).[36] Finally, numismatists see an increase in the minting of coins around 600, not only in ancient sites such as Rouen, at the head of the Seine estuary, but also amongst those new populations – Frisian, Anglo-Saxon – who had not previously minted coins at all.[37]

Initially, this was the case amongst the Frisians of the Low Countries who, having imitated the gold *trientes* struck by the Franks at Maastricht, launched themselves into minting more original coins. Numismatists describe these as being of the 'Dronrijp type', after the Dutch site where an important hoard was found. Then it was the turn of the Anglo-Saxons to mint coins, first of all in Kent (probably in Canterbury), then in London. The minting of

30 Lebecq (1997). 31 Wood (1983).

32 Adomnán, *Vita Sancti Columbae* I.28; Thomas (1990).

33 Jonas, *Vita Columbani* I.23. 34 *Bede, HE* II.3, and IV.22. 35 Lebecq (1995).

36 Wade (1988); Hodges (1989), pp. 97–101. 37 Grierson and Blackburn (1986).

these *thrymsas* – it is appropriate to call them this after the Old English word meaning *tremisses* – was at first sporadic. However, it increased during the course of the seventh century, perhaps under the impetus of those kings whose names feature on certain coins, such as Eadbald, successor to Æthelbhert of Kent in 616.[38] The coincidence between these first mintings by Frisians and by Anglo-Saxons is disquieting. If one can continue to explain the development of their production and circulation by the claiming of power and of prestige by the issuing authorities, it is likely that the simultaneity of the phenomenon can be explained by the requirements of trade, especially between south-east England and the mouths of the Meuse and the Rhine. Proof is there in the fact that workshops were often set up in port sites, and that it is at these same sites that the most important coin finds have been made.

The beginning of the seventh century saw an increase in port activity that affected not only the old cities already mentioned, such as Nantes, London or Rouen, but above all the new sites, and which generally promised a great future. The first generation of these ports flourished mainly in the area found between south-east England and the great delta of the Meuse and the Rhine.[39] In the texts they are called *portus*, *emporia* or, most often, *vici* – from the Latin word *vicus* in its Germanic form *wik* which would occur in so many place-names ending in -vic, -wich, -wijk, -wig. The chief ports were as follows:

Quentovic (the *wik* of the river *Cuenta* or *Quantia*, the Canche) was situated in Ponthieu, twenty or so kilometres to the south of Boulogne. The first written references appear in English sources at the end of the seventh century. However, the name of *Quantia* on one of the coins of the Sutton Hoo treasure and that of *Wic in Pontio* (Wic in Ponthieu) on one of the coins of the Crondall hoard (*c*.640) suggest a history reaching back to the first half of the seventh century. The names of the first mintmasters who produced the Quentovic coins – *Dagulfus, Dutta, Anglus, Donna, Ela* – suggest an Anglo-Saxon origin, which underlines the links existing between the south of England and what was to become the important port of Merovingian Neustria. According to Eddius Stephanus (Stephen of Ripon) in his *Vita Wilfridi*, the *via rectissima*, which allowed his fellow countrymen to make their way to Rome, passed through here.[40]

Walcheren/Domburg lay on an island in Dutch Zeeland, where, according to a very empirical archaeology, a new port began to be developed towards 600. This was near to an ancient sanctuary devastated by a great flood at the

[38] Grierson and Blackburn (1986).

[39] Hodges (1982), pp. 47–65; Clarke and Ambrosiani (1995), pp. 5–45; Verhulst (1999), pp. 44–7.

[40] Lebecq (1993); Zedelius (1991).

end of the second century and where numerous seventh- and eighth-century coins from all over northern Gaul and England have been discovered.[41]

Dorestad was situated on one of the starting points of the Rhine delta near a Roman fort, at the very place where the river's main current turned north (i.e. towards Scandinavia) and where the Lek took on a westerly direction (i.e. towards Britain). Like that of Quentovic,[42] the name Dorestad only features in texts from the end of the seventh century, but it appears on coins struck by the mintmasters Madelinus and Rimoaldus from about 630–640. Although the port's origin was certainly Frisian, it was to develop much more after the end of the seventh century, when the site, together with the whole of Rhenish Frisia, would fall to the power of the Franks. Archaeological excavation has revealed that Dorestad benefited from a large port complex, consisting of a huge system of wharves/landing stages deployed along the banks of the Rhine.[43] As such, it was to become the main turn-table for trade between the Rhineland, eastern England and Scandinavia. In the ninth century its reputation would become such that Dorestad was described in written sources as *vicus famosus*, or even as *vicus nominatissimus*.[44]

Lundenwich, a suburb of London, was thus renamed by eighth-century sources inspired by the new toponymic fashion. If one can believe the numerous discoveries of Saxon material made during the last thirty years, it seems to have been situated between the Thames and the Strand, and thus only a little upstream from the ancient city.[45]

Ipswich, already mentioned, like Dorestad, has been subjected to systematic diggings. These have revealed a site occupied since the beginning of the seventh century, and rich in a considerable quantity of pottery, mainly East Anglian in origin, but also from the Rhineland, the Meuse basin and Flanders.[46]

The Kentish ports developed around Canterbury: Fordwich, mentioned in a deed of 675; Sandwich, considered to be the *portus salutis* in Stephen's *Vita Wilfridi*; Sarre, whose activity, mentioned as early as the sixth century, seems to have continued at least until the eighth century, if one believes the exemptions from transport taxes granted at that time to churches in the region; and not forgetting the *suburbium* to the north-east of Canterbury, where a *vicus* on the banks of the Stour has recently been identified.[47]

Later in the seventh and during the eighth century, the circle of this maritime activity widened to take in more distant lands, as suggested by the accounts of

41 Lebecq (1995). 42 Lebecq (1991).

43 Van Es and Verwers (1980); Van Es and Hessing (1994).

44 Lebecq (1983), vol I, pp. 149–50 (from the *Vita Gregorii Traijectensis* by Liudger, and the *Annales Xantenses* s.a. 834).

45 Vince (1990). 46 Wade (1988); Hodges (1989), pp. 97–101.

47 Hodges (1989), pp. 92–4; Lebecq (1999).

the *Life of Willibrord* left to us by Bede and Alcuin.[48] The Anglo-Saxon monk first of all left Northumbria for Ireland, where he went on retreat with some compatriots in the monastery of Rath Melsigi (i.e. Cluain Melsige, nowadays Clonmelsh, Co. Carlow, in the south-west of Ireland). From there, in about 690, he set off for Frisia, which he traversed in all directions. He went to Walcheren to fight paganism and to Utrecht to found his cathedral there. From this region – that of the Rhine delta – central to the communications system of the time and consequently the subject of dispute between the independent Frisians and the conquering Franks, Willibrord went not only to the south, going up the Rhine and the Moselle to found his monastic refuge of Echternach (nowadays in Luxembourg), but also to the distant north-east where a boat eventually set him down in Denmark where he tried to convert the king Ongendus (*Angantyr*?). The long *peregrinatio*, which led Willibrord from one end of the northern European seas to the other, can only be explained by the expansion of the horizon mapped out by the merchants/navigators of the time who guaranteed a transport system. This widening of mercantile horizons was marked by a development in the port activity of sites which the missionary possibly visited during his journey. This development was twofold: the revitalisation of ancient sites sluggish since antiquity, such as the former Eboracum, and the creation of new ports such as Hamwih, Ribe or, a little later, Sliaswich-Haithabu.

Eboracum, or rather one of its trading suburbs, in conformity with the new toponymic usage (just like Lundenwich), was renamed Eoforwich. In due course the Vikings made this into Jorvik, i.e. York. No doubt this *vicus* was to be found to the south of the Roman wall, in the Fishergate area, at the confluence of the rivers Ouse and Foss. Here, archaeologists have found not only many artisan constructions of the seventh to ninth centuries, but also much imported material originating in particular in the Rhineland. This suggests that it was here, in the second half of the eighth century, that the Frisian merchants mentioned in Altfrid's *Vita Liudgeri* set up their community.[49]

Hamwih, on the site of the future Southampton, is mentioned in written sources as the key to communications between Wessex and the Seine in around 720. However, excavations have revealed the presence of a port settlement planned (laid out?) in around 700, in close contact with the continent (the lower Seine valley, the Paris region and, to a lesser degree, the Rhineland), and above all with its nearby hinterland, especially the royal site at Winchester. This is why we have been able to attribute Hamwih's origins to the initiative of Ine, king of Wessex from 688 to 726.[50]

48 Bede, *HE* III.27; and Alcuin, *Vita Willibrordi*.

49 Hall (1978) and (1988).

50 Hodges (1980) and (1989), pp. 80–92.

Ribe, on a small river flowing out into the North Sea at the foot of western Jutland, was founded most probably at the beginning of the eighth century. It is less likely to have been established by the Frisians, as suggested by earlier hypotheses, but more probably by an emerging Danish monarchy. (Why not at the time of King Ongendus whom Willibrord met?) The settlement does not seem to have had long to wait for visits from western merchants and their money, found in such abundance that one might almost think it had been minted there.[51]

Sliaswich, the *wik* of the Schlei, was the first trading post set up towards the middle of the eighth century by westerners on the Baltic, or more exactly at the end of a fjord in Schleswig-Holstein. The settlement (the *Südsiedlung* of archaeologists), where basalt from the Eifel and amber from the Baltic were transformed, scratched a modest living until the beginning of the ninth century. It then was systematically rebuilt by the Danish king, Godfred, a few hundred metres to the north (*Siedlung* A). Scandinavian sources and posterity mean that this site would be known by its Scandinavian name of Haithabu.[52] It would command a new navigational route towards the eastern Baltic, particularly Lake Malar in the heart of Sweden, where the new *emporia* of Helgo (from the middle of the eighth century) and Birka (which took over at the beginning of the ninth century) would, in turn, be developed.[53]

This 'gazetteer of emporia', to quote Richard Hodges,[54] could be expanded almost to infinity. If archaeology indicates trade movements, texts, particularly hagiography, show clearly how missionaries, monks or bishops used navigation routes, which seemed to be getting more and more regular.[55] For example, the *Vita Columbani* reveals the role of Alet (nowadays St Malo) and of Nantes in communications with Ireland around 600; the *Vita Wilfridi* by Stephen of Ripon shows the links between Sandwich, Quentovic and Frisia (possibly Dorestad) at the end of the seventh century; Willibald's *Vita Bonifatii* shows the links between Lundenwich, Quentovic and Dorestad at the beginning of the eighth century; the nun Hugeberc's *Vita Willibaldi* shows the links between Hamwih and Rouen in around 720; the *Vita Anskarii* shows the importance of the Dorestad–Sliaswich/Haithabu–Birka route in the first half of the ninth century. One can thus fairly easily sketch out the chief lines of the maritime communications network in seventh- and eighth-century northern Europe: from the coasts of Ireland and western Britain towards the ports of Brittany (chiefly Nantes) and Atlantic Gaul; from the Wessex coast (Hamwih in particular) towards the Seine valley and the Paris basin; from the ports of south-eastern England (London and the Canterbury satellites) towards Quentovic,

[51] Bencard (1981); Jensen (1991). [52] Jankuhn (1986).
[53] Clarke and Ambrosiani (1995), pp. 68–76. [54] Hodges (1982), pp. 66ff. [55] Lebecq (1999).

the true gateway to northern Gaul and Neustria; from eastern and south-eastern England (London again, Ipswich, Eboracum) towards the great delta of the Meuse and the Rhine (Walcheren/Domburg and especially Dorestad, gateway to Frisia, to Austrasia and to the Rhineland); from the Rhine delta, from Dorestad in particular, towards Denmark and then across to Scandinavia and the Baltic.[56]

Not only did maritime links multiply in all the northern European seas, but shipping technology changed during the seventh and eighth centuries. From this time on, continental, British and Scandinavian boats were increasingly equipped with a sail. This was not yet, perhaps, the case of the ship in tomb Number One at Sutton Hoo, which was in the nautical tradition of the Nydam boat; nevertheless its length/breadth ratio suggests the presence of a rudimentary sail.[57] This was certainly true of the ships represented on the stelae carved on the island of Gotland in the eighth century, and on the coins struck in Quentovic and Dorestad at the end of the eighth and the beginning of the ninth centuries. The first of these coins, dating from the reign of Charlemagne, perhaps remain influenced by ancient coins as regards the type of ship. The next ones, dating from the reign of Louis the Pious, show in great detail what the ninth-century North Sea boats had become, though they were still clinker built, following traditional construction methods of the ancient Germans. This construction guaranteed suppleness and elasticity, but the rigging for sails demanded an increase in the breadth relative to length. Above, such vessels now had a low profile in the water, such as one finds in the two great models that were to dominate the waters of northern Europe over a long period. These were the flat-bottomed boat of the East Frisians, the forerunner of the *kogge*, and the round-bottomed boat of the sailors of the Rhine delta and of southern England, perhaps the forerunner of the *hulk*.[58] One can surmise that, beginning in the great delta, the use of sail spread initially towards English waters, then, keeping pace with the expansion of westerners towards the east, moved towards Scandinavian and Baltic waters. Whatever the details, its spread had important economic consequences: it allowed a reduction in the number of crewmen needed (henceforth reduced to four or five men on ships which were about 20 metres in length and which carried 10–20 tons of freight); it enabled more cargo and more passengers to be taken on board; it made the crossing easier, quicker and, above all, cheaper.

This transport system allowed the diffusion of the various products discovered by archaeologists along and at the end of the routes frequented by the merchants/navigators of the seventh to ninth centuries. For example, there are the ceramics of La Londe, whose centre of production has recently been

[56] Johanek (1985). [57] Evans (1986). [58] Ellmers (1972); McGrail (1987) and (1990).

identified in the vicinity of Rouen. These ceramics are the principal imports discovered in the Hamwih site, justifying the allusions in the *Vita Willibaldi* to the importance of the links between the lower valley of the Seine and the Wessex coast.[59] Or there are the products of the Rhineland: so-called 'Badorf' or 'Tating' ceramics, manufactured near Cologne and Coblenz respectively; mill stones made from Eifel basalt; glassware; arms. Their discovery seems to mark out the routes of the 'great Frisian trade', a trade that in fact became Franco-Frisian after the conquest of the Rhine delta by the Franks.[60] These products went to Dorestad, naturally, the unrivalled turn-table, but also to London, to Ipswich, to Hamwih, to York, to the Irish *crannog* of Lagore, to the new Danish port sites of Ribe and of Sliaswich-Haithabu, and even, a little later, to those of central Sweden, namely Helgo and Birka.[61] There is the diffusion of the new silver coins introduced by the Frisians and the Anglo-Saxons which shows, perhaps better than all the rest, the intensity of maritime trade at the end of the seventh and during the eighth centuries.

It was at this moment that a veritable revolution took place in the history of western money.[62] Up until about 670–680, the whole of the West had remained faithful to the ancient or Byzantine standard, and to the minting of *trientes*, *tremisses* or other *thrymsas*. These were supposedly of gold but, because of an increasing lack of the yellow metal, silver was playing an ever more important part in their manufacture. At this time the workshops of south-eastern England and of Frisia began to put out pure silver coins. They were not much lighter, initially, than the first *tremisses*, but they were, by all accounts, better adapted to the necessities of the market (the precious metal production market, of course, but also the distribution market which coped badly with coins whose buying power was totally overvalued). The first specimens, although often without any inscription, were inspired by pre-existing models, but with a stylised engraving which perhaps linked up with the Celtic or more generally protohistoric tradition. These are the coins which, because of a misinterpretation of ancient Anglo-Saxon laws, have been called *sceattas* since the end of the seventeenth century. In fact, for their Anglo-Saxon contemporaries they were 'pennies', and for their continental contemporaries 'deniers'.

No doubt it was in Kent that these first so-called *sceattas*, which really should be called *proto-pennies* or *proto-deniers*, were struck. But production was taken up almost immediately by all the workshops in the south of England and in Northumbria, as well as by those in Frisia and the Rhine delta (especially Dorestad) which were in the process of coming under Frankish rule. This indicates to what extent these regions were economically interdependent.

59 Hodges (1980) and (1991). 60 Lebecq (1986). 61 Lebecq (1983), I.
62 Hill and Metcalf (1984); Grierson and Blackburn (1986).

The multiplicity of finds, as hoards (which allows a relative chronology to be established) and as isolated coins, suggests that the use of *sceattas* became widespread almost immediately. Above all, they could be used for small transactions. Starting in the central part of the North Sea basin, the new money reached the whole of the West between the end of the seventh and the middle of the eighth centuries. The first types of *proto-pennies* (struck before 700) have been found mainly in hoards in Kent and Essex. Later ones have turned up in Frisia and the rest of Europe, and the last ones have been discovered in a noticeably extended radius, from Scandinavia to the whole of Gaul, even southern Gaul. It is true that some mints had been created far from the first centres of production, for example in the lower Loire valley.[63] Following the example of their English and Frisian counterparts, the Frankish kings and mints were soon to abandon gold coin altogether and mint only silver 'deniers'. Once measures for the standardisation and conformity of Charlemagne's coins had been taken (at the very end of the eighth century) that was the end of gold coin and of the ancient, Mediterranean monetary standard in almost all of the West, until the thirteenth century.

The success of this money can be explained by the way in which the new coins met the needs and reflected the economic realities of the time. A further explanation is the influence henceforward exerted over the whole of the continent by the seafarers and merchants from the north. Their activity, starting from bases which the new *wiks* and revitalised old cities provided for them, came to compensate for the slow decline of the southern routes and the progressive loss of the Mediterranean as an intermediary for trade.

THE NORTHERN SEAS AND THEIR HINTERLAND

The whirlwind activity which reached the Northern Seas from around 600 had such an influence on the whole of the West because, throughout the seventh and eighth centuries, there was a progressive integration of the coastal area with its more distant hinterland. This was due, on the one hand, to the attraction exerted by the coastal area on the social and economic elite of the hinterland, and, on the other hand, to the progressive penetration of interior markets by the maritime population.

To begin with, one must mention the fascination that, from earliest days, the coastal area exerted on the monastic movement, especially that of Ireland. This latter developed an original form of littoral or insular monasticism, the pure product of the attraction/repulsion dialectic exerted by the sea. Its rigours (those of solitude, wind and water) encouraged the most heroic forms

[63] Hill and Metcalf (1984). For more detail see also Blackburn, chapter 24 below.

of asceticism and of mortification. A good example is that of the monastery of Skellig Michael, probably founded in the seventh century, on an isolated rock in the sea off the coast of Kerry.[64] Since the Irish monks were followers of the *peregrinatio pro Deo* they carried this original conception of monasticism with them, first into the Scottish islands (Iona in 563), then into England (Lindisfarne in 635), and finally to the continent. This monasticism did its best to reconcile the contradictory virtues of cenobitism and eremitism, of asceticism and a social life, in a specifically marine environment. Even when Benedictine spirituality had become the dominant force in western monasticism, the attraction of coastal sites remained very strong. The adhesion of Frankish and Anglo-Saxon elites to this new model of religious life and the deliberate support of the monarchies, often owners of the coastal *saltus*, resulted, during the seventh century, in the multiplication of monastic foundations on off-shore islands, on continental shores, at the end of, or very near to, estuaries, or even on the low rivers which flowed into them. Among the most famous were Whitby, Wearmouth, Jarrow and Crossland in England; Noirmoutier, Fontenelle/St Wandrille, Jumièges, Centula/St Riquier, St Bertin and St Pierre et St Bavon of Ghent on the continent.[65] Moreover, each time, the foundation accounts delighted in praising the advantages of a position on waters frequented by merchant shipping and open to the world, as well as of the isolation necessary to asceticism. This was why these institutions became poles of economic development, endowed with port infrastructures and a good communications system with their hinterland. Not only the network of allied families but also the lands which they had been granted and which would one day become refuges could all be found there.

It was at this time too that the monarchies of the interior sought to lay their hands on the *wiks* whose development, often originally spontaneous, had escaped them until then, or else kings sought to create new *wiks* more or less *ex nihilo*.[66] At all events, for the rulers, it was a question of controlling the navigation routes which the *wiks* commanded, of supporting and developing a policy of overseas contact and future expansion, of facilitating the export of the surpluses of their own estates, and of retaining for themselves part of the profits generated by the *wiks*. We have glimpses of the kings of Wessex and of Denmark founding Hamwih and Ribe respectively at the beginning of the eighth century, or refounding Sliaswich-Haithabu at the beginning of the ninth century. Yet we can see little of the efforts of the Frankish kings (particularly in Dagobert's time), or of the later mayors of the palace, to lay their hands on the *wiks* of Quentovic and of Dorestad. These were the maritime

[64] Edwards (1990), pp. 116–20. [65] Lebecq (1989) and (2000). [66] Sawyer (1977).

outlets of a huge, rich hinterland where they had much fiscal and patrimonial wealth.[67]

Thus, as soon as Frankish rulers had taken full control of them, around the end of the seventh century, they endowed both Quentovic and Dorestad with customs and monetary systems. These were entrusted to important officials to whom Charlemagne later granted full authority over all the customs dues and all the monies under their respective jurisdiction. The areas of jurisdiction most likely included the whole of the Neustrian shores for Quentovic, and the whole of the Austrasian and Frisian shores for Dorestad.[68] Just like the *wic-gerefan* ('provosts of the *wik*'), mentioned in the laws of Hlothere of Kent at the end of the seventh century,[69] the Frankish monarchy had at its disposal in its offices in Quentovic and Dorestad *ministeriales* controlled by a *procurator* or *praefectus*. They were charged not only with ensuring the policing of the area and the legality of transactions, but also with collecting landing dues (*ripaticum*) from passing ships and customs dues (most probably a *decima*, going by ninth-century sources) on unloaded goods.[70]

Kings and princes, and with them the magnates of their kingdoms, were not the only ones to be attracted by this port and shoreline activity. Anxious to ensure their salvation in the next world, they wanted to let the churches profit from it too. Thus, from the beginning of the eighth century, Frankish rulers offered a tenth of all the revenue they drew from trade from the port of Dorestad to the cathedral of Utrecht. Almost immediately the cathedral created an important parish and baptismal church on the spot, corresponding perhaps to the *Upkirika*, the 'high church' mentioned in later sources.[71] In Quentovic there is greater evidence of this, since one can see a number of religious settlements endowing themselves with a veritable 'window to the sea', open to all sorts of trade. Not only had the great neighbouring abbeys, such as St Vaast, St Bertin and Centula/St Riquier, acquired riches in the *wik* itself, in the form of parcels of land known as *mansi* or *setici*, or in the immediate localities (as at Tubersent or at Campigneulles), but some more distant abbeys were also drawn there by royal concessions. For example there was Ferrières-en-Gâtinais, to which Charlemagne gave the neighbouring *cella* of St Josse. There was Fontenelle/St Wandrille, which, not content to benefit from its own *portus* in the lower Seine valley, received several *mansi* which were *in portu Wiscus*, erecting on one of them perhaps the church of St Peter *quae vicina est emporio Quentovico*. In the ninth century this would become one of the refuges for monks fleeing Norman aggression. One can therefore understand

67 Lebecq (1986). 68 Lebecq (1991).

69 Trans. Whitelock, *English Historical Documents*, I, p. 395. See Sawyer (1977).

70 Lebecq (1983). 71 Lebecq (1983); Van Es and Hessing (1994).

why at the end of the eighth century the *procurator* nominated to represent Charlemagne at Quentovic, to supervise all the customs activity of the area, and even to negotiate with Anglo-Saxon kings, especially Offa of Mercia, was a man of the highest status, Geroald, abbot of St Wandrille.[72]

Even a monastery such as St Germain-des-Prés, already master of a *villa supra mare* (probably Quillebeuf, in the lower Seine valley), received no part of the actual income from either Quentovic or Dorestad. And so it was careful, in 779 at the latest,[73] to get exemption from all transport tax there – as well as in Rouen, Amiens and Maastricht, that is, in all the main ports of northern Gaul open to maritime trade. Clearly the Parisian monastery wanted to profit from this privilege. If one accepts the current interpretation[74] of certain passages in the polyptych of Irminon, dated around 820, the monastery ordered its men from Villemeult (in Beauce) and from Combs-la-Ville (in Brie) to undertake regular transport services as far as Quentovic.[75] One can easily imagine that these carts transported the estate surpluses as far as the port – for example wines which were in demand by the people of the north. One can just as easily think that these carts did not come back empty, and that it was in Quentovic's market that the monks of St Germain-des-Prés found a return cargo. This could well have consisted of those basic materials, for example minerals or textiles, whose British origin is freely underlined in our sources, or in those liturgical books upon which the reputation of the insular *scriptoria* was founded.

But while the overlords and the institutions of the hinterland were installing themselves on the shorelines and in port sites, the merchants/navigators, who had initiated the commercial rebirth of the northern seas, going up river with the help of those boats which they could beach anywhere, began to prospect the continental markets. This was the case in particular of the Saxons in the Seine basin, and of the Frisians in the Rhine basin. One imagines that what attracted the men from Wessex into the Seine basin, and more especially into the Paris region, was wine rather than the ceramics from La Londe discovered in great quantities in the Hamwih excavations. In a privilege granted in 634–635, the Frankish king Dagobert had authorised the monks of St Denis to hold an annual fair on their patron saint's day, 9 October, in other words around the time of the launch of the new wines. Purely a local fair in the beginning, it is possible that it became the great wine fair for the whole of the Paris region. At all events, the monks of Saint-Denis drew great advantage from it because, under the terms of the royal privilege, they were the sole beneficiaries of its *teloneum* ('toll') for the duration of the fair.[76] Wine was sadly lacking in

[72] Lebecq (1989) and (1993).

[73] *Chartae Latinae Antiquiores* XVI, ed. Atsma and Vezin, no. 625, pp. 38–41.

[74] Devroey (1984).

[75] *Das Polyptychon von Saint-Germain-des-Prés*, ed. Hägerman, pp. 58 and 139.

[76] Lebecq (1989) and (2000).

northern countries, and so one is not surprised that a diploma of 709 mentions the Saxons (West Saxons probably), the only foreigners referred to, as being amongst the most assiduous customers at the St Denis fair.[77] A diploma of 753 adds the name of Frisians to these customers, in a position that one imagines to be subordinate.[78]

It was mainly in their immediate hinterland, that is, in the Rhineland, that the Frisians made a habit of going to seek out the wine, which was so lacking in the maritime plain. In addition they got wood, corn and local Rhineland products – the ceramics, glassware or arms that have been found in abundance at Dorestad and in all the major sites of northern Europe. This is why we catch glimpses of Frisians at Trier on the Moselle, in an eighth-century source, then at Xanten, Duisburg, Cologne, Mainz, Worms, Strasbourg and other Rhine sites, in ninth-century sources. In several of these towns, they created significant settlements often connected to great religious institutions. At Trier, for example, a Frisian gave himself with *sua substantia* (a fortune which certainly included boats and slaves) to the monastery of St Maximin, in order to do for the church's sake what he had until then done for his own sake, namely travel overseas. At Cologne, the Frisian settlement grew in the shadow of the suburban church of St Géréon, and was no doubt dependent upon and under its protection. At Duisburg, the Frisians worked in the service of the abbey of Prum, that had a landing stage at the confluence of the Ruhr and the Rhine. At Worms, the Frisians appear as the only foreign merchants running a market overlooked by the cathedral church.[79] Given these conditions, one can believe that the complaint formulated towards 826 by Ermold the Black against the *Frisionibus atque marinis* ('the Frisians and the seafaring people') who came right into the upper valley of the Rhine to carry off everything that Alsace and the Vosges produced – in particular wine, corn and wood – was not mere rhetoric.[80]

In all these cases, the presence and demands of the merchants/navigators from the north could only have stimulated the activity of these old cities, of their suburban churches and of their riverside port sites, which they frequented in great numbers. This happened to such an extent that, from the seventh century, the whole of the hinterland of the northern seas enjoyed a tangible improvement in the conditions for trade and enjoyed the benefits of a relative peace. Above all it benefited from the progressive integration of pockets of production into organised estates, upon which the dependent peasants and the small peasant farmers, granted real freedom of management, were judged to be economically more productive than the prebendary slaves who

77 *Chartae Latinae Antiquiores* XIV, ed. Atsma and Vezin, no. 586, pp. 49–54.

78 *Chartae Latinae Antiquiores* XV, ed. Atsma and Vezin, no. 598, pp. 15–21.

79 Lebecq (1983). 80 Ermoldus Nigellus, *Première épître au roi Pépin*, lines 97–120.

had worked the old *latifundia*. It is clear that each one of the two economic agents (the producer in the hinterland and the merchant from the sea) exercised a decisive influence on the activities and performance of the other. In particular – to take only the best-documented example from our sources – that the merchant/navigator stimulated the productivity of the wine-producer, and the wine-producer encouraged the merchant/navigator to improve his transport system.

CONCLUSION

The seas of northern Europe formed a single economic basin at the turn of the eighth and ninth centuries. It was brought to life by the merchants/navigators who went from port to port and who did not hesitate to go up river to reach the very heart of the hinterland's production area. From the continent, heading north, went corn, wood and above all wine from the basins of the Loire, the Seine and the Rhine; manufactured or half-worked products from the workshops of Aquitaine, the Parisian basin and the Rhine valley; linen from Frisia and elsewhere; not to mention the silver coins, now being minted under the control of the Carolingian monarchy, at the palace, in Dorestad, in Quentovic and in many other workshops. From the north came slaves, metals, skins and furs, oil from sea mammals, ivory from walruses, amber from the Baltic, and all those other products that have left scarcely any archaeological trace. This multifarious trade was not without its chaos, and the kings, not content with ensuring the policing of the ports, were led to legislate and even take measures to defend their nationals against the least scrupulous merchants. The correspondence exchanged on this subject between Charlemagne and Offa of Mercia resulted, in 796, in what Frank Stenton called 'the first commercial treaty in English history'.[81]

How far we have come from the first stumbling attempts at trading activity in the Northern Seas of the sixth century. In the final analysis, the development of a true maritime economy in northern Europe from the seventh century onwards was the result, not of the closure of the Mediterranean by Islam (this not being achieved until later), but of the combination of three factors. First we must recognise the vitality of the hinterland, stimulated by an agricultural growth such as had not been seen since the third century, organised by ever more powerful aristocracies and religious institutions, and benefiting from a relative peace, the *pax Carolina* of early Carolingian times. Second, there was the vitality of the maritime milieu, starting from the central regions of the Northern Seas between south-eastern Britain and the mouth of the Rhine and

[81] Stenton (1971), p. 221.

which then extended to new horizons, from Ireland as far as Scandinavia. This milieu benefited from technical innovations in the art of sailing, and spread in all directions the use of silver coin, much better adapted to the volume and the value of the trade. Finally we have the coming together of these two dynamic forces in the median places of trade: the great coastal monasteries, the markets, the fairs, the riverside cities with their *suburbia* and their churches, the river ports and especially the sea ports.

All that remains of Henri Pirenne's theory is that the centre of gravity in the west shifted well and truly from the south towards the north, and that the role played by the Mediterranean in the sixth century was then taken up by the seas of northern Europe. These latter, in the seventh and eighth centuries, became the principal axis for long-distance trade, an axis extended after the eighth century as far as the Baltic, and as a result, ready to link up with the Near East and Far East by the Russian river routes. The increase in traffic over this new trade route, which for several centuries was to take over from the old Mediterranean route, perhaps finds its best expression in an archaeological discovery: in the heart of Sweden, a few metres away from each other on the Helgo site but at the same eighth-century level, lay a crozier of Irish origin and a statuette of Buddha originating from Kashmir.[82]

But, by penetrating Scandinavian waters with these formidable 'calling cards' of wine, arms and silver, the merchants/navigators of the west did more than introduce the Vikings to the use of sail, for they also attracted the greedy eyes of the latter to their ships, their navigation routes, their ports, their churches and, finally, their lands. The first attacks by these northern pirates on the coast of Northumberland (Lindisfarne, 793) and on the coasts of Frisia (810) undoubtedly marked the start of another era. It was only after two centuries of disruption to the maritime links by these predators from the north that a new trade atlas would be sketched out, round about the year 1000. Its horizons would be extended to match the Viking voyages of discovery (from Newfoundland to the White Sea and to the rivers of Russia). There would be a new distribution of ports, with the old ones, too exposed and too fragile, giving way to new sites, better rooted in their environment and better protected, and there would be a new generation of *animateurs*. The Frisians, Anglo-Saxons, Franks and Celts would give way to Iro-Scandinavians, to Anglo-Danes, to Flemings, to those from the Meuse and, later, to those from the Hanseatic lands.

[82] Hodges and Whitehouse (1983).

CHAPTER 24

MONEY AND COINAGE

Mark Blackburn

Coinage in the Roman world in the early fifth century consisted of a multi-denominational system in gold, silver and bronze.[1] By the eighth century the coinage of western Europe was entirely of silver essentially in one denomination, the thin broad Carolingian penny. The change from a classical to a medieval coinage was radical, but the way in which it came about was neither sudden nor dramatic. It was a gradual process of transformation and evolution. This chapter will trace those developments from the earliest Germanic coinages of the fifth century to the introduction of the silver penny in the late seventh century, at which point the story is picked up in the second volume of the *New Cambridge Medieval History*.

The late fourth and fifth centuries saw the movement and resettlement of the peoples of central and eastern Europe on a scale that is unprecedented in historical times. Most of the tribes that settled within the former Roman Empire and established new Germanic states had at some stage acted as mercenaries for or concluded treaties with the emperor, which instilled in them a degree of respect for imperial authority, albeit a precarious one. They would have obtained substantial amounts of coin, mainly gold, as mercenaries, in tribute and as plunder, which gave them experience in dealing with money, even if they had not struck coins of their own before moving into the Empire. This was, no doubt, a factor in encouraging the continuity of circulation and minting that we find in most of the newly established Germanic kingdoms. Only in England and the northern fringes of Gaul did the circulation of coinage cease for a while after the collapse of the Roman administration. There the use of money had to be relearnt a century or more later from their Germanic neighbours.

The coinages of most of the new states passed through two phases: a 'pseudo-imperial' phase in which the coins purported to be issued with the authority

[1] For surveys of late Roman coinage see Grierson and Mays (1992) and Kent (1994); for early medieval European coinages other than Byzantine see Grierson and Blackburn (1986); and for Byzantine coinage see Grierson (1982), Hendy (1985) and Hahn (2000).

of the current or some former emperor, and a 'national' phase in which the inscriptions and designs deliberately reflected the state's independence. For each kingdom this change came at different times and was expressed in different ways. The first to suppress all reference to the empire on their silver and bronze coins in the late fifth century were Odovacar in Italy (briefly) and the Vandals in North Africa. The Visigoths and Franks both transformed their coinages in the later sixth century, the first adopting an overtly regal currency and the second choosing to permit a variety of semi-private issues. A century later the Lombards in Italy were the last to relinquish the imperial tradition by adopting a combination of regal and municipal coinages. Of course, official Byzantine issues continued in their remaining possessions in central Italy, Sicily and parts of the Balkans.

Although there are few written texts that shed light on the nature of money in the early Middle Ages, the coins themselves have survived in substantial quantity, and by studying their inscriptions, designs, dies, weights, metallic compositions and find contexts we can achieve some understanding of the monetary systems in which they were used. In the late Roman Empire coin production had been concentrated in a small number of mints, amounting in the west to four in Italy (Rome, Ravenna, Milan and Aquileia) and three in Gaul (Arles, Lyons and Trier); the London mint, having closed in 325, was perhaps revived during the 380s and Barcelona had operated briefly under the usurper Maximus (410–411). By the seventh century there were still only a handful of mints in Italy, but several hundreds in Gaul, perhaps fifty in Spain and a few in England. Coin production thus remained essentially within the bounds of the old Roman Empire, but, as one might expect, with a much greater degree of local minting.

In the fourth century an elaborate range of denominations had been issued by the Romans in three metals – gold, silver and bronze – but in the early fifth century production in silver and bronze was severely reduced. In Gaul and Britain the silver coins in circulation were clipped down to reduce their weight and the few new ones struck in Gaul were produced to a much reduced weight standard. Bronze was limited to the smallest denomination, the *nummus*. Only the gold coinage was produced on a moderate scale, and came to dominate the currency. Of the three denominations in gold – the *solidus*, its half the *semissis* and its third the *tremissis* – the largest and smallest formed the basis of most coinages in western Europe in the succeeding two centuries. Thus the dominance of gold, which is so striking a feature of early medieval coinage of the sixth and seventh centuries, was already established under the later western emperors.

Gold had a special status that went beyond its high intrinsic value, for it was regarded as an imperial metal that should always carry an emperor's name – if the current emperor was politically unacceptable, then an earlier one would suffice. Lesser rulers put their own names on their gold coinage at their peril, as with the Frankish king Theodebert (534–548) who was severely criticised by Procopius for having the impertinence to do so: 'it is not considered right . . . for any . . . sovereign in the whole barbarian world to imprint his own likeness on a gold stater'.[2] Silver and bronze were quite a different matter, and rulers were more confident in recording their names on these, with or without that of the emperor. It was this convention, the emperor's prerogative in respect of gold, that perpetuated the pseudo-imperial phase.

The coinages of the Visigoths, Sueves, Franks, Burgundians, Anglo-Saxons and Lombards were essentially mono-metallic in gold, with some very limited and local issues of small silver and bronze coins. Even in the Byzantine Empire silver had fallen out of use save for ceremonial purposes, and there was nothing to bridge the very high-value gold denominations and the small bronze *minimi*. However, in the late fifth century Odovacar and then the Ostrogoths succeeded in re-establishing in Italy an impressive range of denominations in all three metals, providing an adequate currency for all types of transactions. Likewise in North Africa the Vandals re-established a range of silver and bronze denominations, but unusually without any gold coins. In both regions after the reconquests of the 530s and 540s, Justinian maintained the production of silver and bronze. By the third quarter of the sixth century, however, the minting of silver coins in Europe was confined essentially to Ravenna, and its economic impact was minimal.

Precious metals were more valuable in the early Middle Ages than they are today, and the standard gold coins were, therefore, very high denominations. A *solidus*, for example, bought 90 kg of butchered pork in Rome in 452, so it was hardly suitable for domestic transactions.[3] The *nummus*, by contrast, was a very low-value coin, fluctuating between 7200 and 12,000 *nummi* to the *solidus* in the fifth and sixth centuries. A building-labourer in the early sixth century could earn 200 *nummi* a day.

ITALY AND NORTH AFRICA

It is not surprising that Italy, which saw the strongest survival of Roman culture and institutions, should show not merely continuity in its coinage but development influenced by traditional Roman practice. Odovacar (476–493), a high-ranking army officer of mixed Germanic/Hunnish origin, ruled Italy not as a usurper but on behalf of the last western emperor, Julius Nepos, from

[2] Procopius, *Bell. Goth.* II.33.5–6. [3] Spufford (1988), p. 8.

477 to 480, and the eastern emperor Zeno during 476–477 and 480–491, and hence most of his coins carry their names. The same is true of the Ostrogothic kings from Theoderic (490–526) onwards, who similarly ruled on behalf of the eastern emperors, at least until Justinian launched his campaign to oust them in 535.

The coinage from Odovacar's period of rule is remarkable in three respects. He revived the production of silver, in Zeno's name, on a substantial scale at three mints, Milan, Ravenna and Rome, a feature that would be maintained through the Ostrogothic period. Secondly, although bronze coin production had virtually ceased, an issue of large bronze 40 *nummus* pieces was instituted at Rome in Zeno's name. What is remarkable is that they appear to have anticipated or even inspired the major monetary reform that Anastasius implemented at Constantinople in 498, providing a range of bronze denominations headed by a *follis* of 40 *nummi*. The portrait on the Zeno issue is quite different from the stylised imperial busts current in the fourth and fifth centuries, for it has a naturalistic, rather rugged image that seems to strive for a true likeness of the emperor. This concept, like other features of the design and inscriptions, including the use of 'SC' (*Senatus consulta*), deliberately harks back to the coinage of the early Empire. The dating of this issue is unclear – it may even have been produced not by Odovacar but by the Ostrogothic leader Theoderic while controlling Rome in 490–491.[4] It was succeeded by a series of large anonymous bronzes, generally termed 'municipal' or 'senatorial' issues of Rome, which continue through much of the Ostrogothic period.

The third feature of Odovacar's rule is the issue of silver and bronze coins carrying his own name (FL ODOVAC) or monogram and again a naturalistic portrait. This is certainly the earliest, and virtually the only contemporary portrait of one of the barbarian leaders – the bronze coins of the Lombard king Aistulf (749–754) are another notable exception. Odovacar is shown bareheaded with a bushy moustache and without regalia, emphasising his non-imperial status. These coins, struck at Ravenna, belong either to the period in 477 before he recognised Julius Nepos as emperor, or more likely to the latter part of his reign when Odovacar was at war with the Ostrogoths and was from 490 effectively confined to Ravenna.[5] They provided a precedent for Theoderic to place his own name or monogram on the gold and silver and may have inspired Gunthamund (484–496) to initiate a regal coinage for the Vandals at Carthage.

4 Grierson and Mays (1992), pp. 186–7, dating it to 477; Kent (1994), pp. 218–19, dating it 490–491 under Theoderic.

5 Grierson and Blackburn (1986), p. 28; Kent (1994), pp. 213–14.

In many respects, then, Odovacar's coinage set the pattern for the large and impressive coinage of the Ostrogoths. Under them gold continued to be issued at Rome, Ravenna, Milan and, after the loss of Ravenna in 540, Pavia (*Ticinium*), always in the name of the reigning emperor except under Baduila (541–552) who, while resisting the conquest of Justinian, preferred to acknowledge the long-deceased Anastasius on his coins. The other notable exception is a magnificent triple *solidus*, a medallic piece, which has Theoderic's name and titles (REX THEODERICVS PIVS PRINCIS) around his facing bust. Although it was clearly issued to celebrate an important event (which one is still hotly disputed),[6] because of its medallic character it should not be seen as breaching the convention that gold coinage should bear the name of the emperor.

Theoderic built on Odovacar's initiative of issuing a silver half-*siliqua* by adding a smaller denomination, the quarter-*siliqua*. However, unlike Odovacar's coins, which were either in the name of the emperor, Zeno, or that of Odovacar himself, the Ostrogothic coins normally carry both the name of the emperor around the imperial portrait, and on the reverse the name or monogram of the king. Thus it is an overtly regal coinage issued under the auspices of the emperor. Although all three mints initially participated in striking silver, under Theoderic's successors its production was concentrated at Ravenna until 540 and then at Pavia. Ostrogothic bronze followed a rather different pattern, for the bulk of it was issued at Rome in at least five different denominations, and without any reference to either the emperor or the king because the Senate was formally responsible for authorising its issue. A notable exception is the *follis* of Theodahad (534–536), which has a very imposing bust of the king, who we know intended this image to perpetuate his memory for centuries.[7]

Interesting parallels are to be found in the coinage of the Vandals of North Africa. The Vandals do not appear to have minted coins while in Spain (409–429), but from their North African kingdom, based at Carthage (439–533), there is a substantial and innovative coinage. They were probably responsible for two series of pseudo-imperial silver coins in the name of Honorius (395–423),[8] and for some of the many varieties of bronze *minimi* current in North Africa in the fifth century. This pseudo-imperial phase was short-lived, for by the end of the century Gunthamund (484–496) had initiated a regal coinage, which, like Odavacar's independent issue, made no reference to the emperor.

6 Arslan (1989) argues it marked the final conquest of Italy in 493; Alföldi (1978) and (1988) the thirtieth anniversary of Theoderic's reign over the Ostrogoths in 500; and Grierson (1985) his conquest over the Franks and Burgundians in 508/9.

7 Cassiodorus, *Variae* I.6.7.

8 Although Kent (1994), pp. 232–3, proposes a pre-Vandal origin for one of them.

A sequence of 100, 50 and 25 *denarius* pieces in silver and 1 *nummus* bronze coins were issued, and broadly maintained by succeeding kings down to the Byzantine reconquest. In parallel with this was an anonymous civic coinage of 42, 21, 12 and 4 *nummus* bronze coins apparently modelled on the civic issues of Rome, even if the denominational system was different. These were issued in two series, the earlier depicting the deity Carthego holding ears of corn, and the later one combining a standing soldier and the head of a Punic horse with the legend KARTHAGO.

A curious subsidiary coinage supplemented these large bronze issues and provides further evidence for links between Italy and North Africa. This consists of a substantial number of old, worn bronze coins mainly of the first century AD which have been incised with a mark of value – LXXXIII (83) on *sestertii* and XLII (42) on *asses* and *dupondii*. They evidently belong to the fifth or sixth century, but their origin is uncertain,[9] for while their denominations conform to the Carthaginian system and a few specimens have been found in North Africa, many more have been found in Italy.

With Justinian's success in partially rebuilding the Empire, he had to decide whether to impose a uniform monetary system on all the reconquered territories. As already indicated, silver currency was not used elsewhere in the Empire, so in continuing their production at Carthage and in Italy the local denominations and weight standards were adopted. The copper coinage was a different matter, for a range of denominations based on the *follis* of 40 *nummi* had been produced in Constantinople since Anastasius' reform of 498, and Justinian himself revised their weights and designs several times to accommodate changes in the relative value of gold to copper. For bronze, then, the systems implemented in Africa and Italy were essentially those of Constantinople. In both regions, production of silver and bronze was highest during the decade following their reconquest as the Vandal and Ostrogothic coins were reminted into Byzantine ones. Gold *solidi* and *tremisses* were struck at Rome and later Ravenna with some continuity of Ostrogothic practices. It is now evident that a third mint, in Sicily, was opened soon after the reconquest of 535,[10] and this was later to grow into one of the Empire's most productive mints in the seventh and eighth centuries. At Carthage, where no gold had been struck under the Vandals, Justinian initially sent gold coins from Constantinople to pay the troops, but from 537 until the Arab conquest of the city in 698 it produced a distinctive gold coinage comprising almost exclusively *solidi*.[11] The conquest of a strip of south-eastern Spain in 553, a Byzantine toe-hold which was maintained

9 Morrisson (1983) argues for a North African origin; Grierson and Blackburn (1986), pp. 28–31, for an Italian one.

10 Hahn (2000), pp. 47–8.

11 Morrisson (1988).

until 624, led to a mint being established probably in Carthagena, the administrative centre. For much of the period of Byzantine rule it produced a modest number of gold *tremisses*, the main denomination of Visigothic Spain, and one that could not be supplied from Carthage.[12] In the Balkans, the Ostrogothic colony at Sirmium, which Theoderic had captured from the Gepids in 504, was also a victim of the war in Italy, and control reverted to the Gepids in 540. A series of locally minted silver half *siliquae*, which began with ones in the name of Theoderic, of Italian type, continued under the Gepids until their defeat by the Avars in the 580s.[13]

The Indian summer of Byzantine rule in Italy lasted barely two decades before the Lombards invaded in 568/9 and established their own kingdom, initially in the north, in Lombardy, but subsequently extending to Tuscany and to a vast tract of central and southern Italy, governed from Benevento and Spoleto. Three distinct strands of coinage developed in upper Italy, Tuscany and Benevento; Spoleto did not strike its own coins. The earliest was in the north and consisted of imitations of *tremisses* of Ravenna of the emperors Justinian I (d. 565), Justin II (565–578) and Maurice (582–602), coins that would have been circulating in the region during the period of their campaigns. These imitations were initially of reasonably good style and of similar fabric to the originals, but the Maurice copies continued to be issued for almost a century, gradually becoming more stylised, with meaningless inscriptions, and developing a very distinctive broad thin fabric with a saucer-shaped profile. In Tuscany a very different coinage was produced, based on *tremisses* of Heraclius (610–641) and Constans II (641–668) with a cross potent reverse design. They also developed an unusual fabric, but rather than growing wider, as in Lombardy, they became smaller and thicker, though also with a dished profile. By the second half of the seventh century the inscription had become merely a series of alternating 'V's and 'I's. Both series of coins had become so characteristic of their regions that they were in effect anonymous 'national' coinages, but the transition to overtly Lombard issues came at the end of the seventh century, and again the two regions followed very different paths. In Lombardy a royal coinage was established by Cunipert (688–700), which retained the previous broad fabric and subtly exchanged the image of the king for the imperial bust, and the winged figure of St Michael for the winged Victory. The Tuscan coinage, by contrast, became a series of municipal issues, with the monogram or name of the city: Pisa, Lucca, Pistoria and possibly Chiusi. The third series mentioned above, the coinage of the Duchy of Benevento, only started at the end of the seventh century, with pseudo-imperial

[12] Grierson (1982), p. 56.

[13] Metlich (2004), pp. 43–4 suggesting the 'Theoderic' pieces are later Gepid copies of Ostrogothic coins.

solidi and *tremisses* attributed to Gisulf I (689–706), and although the Beneventan coinage flourished for almost two centuries, it falls effectively outside the scope of this survey.

GAUL AND IBERIA, PSEUDO-IMPERIAL COINAGES

The monetary circulation was quite different in Gaul and the Iberian Peninsula, where from the early fifth century there was already a shortage of silver and bronze coins. Here during the fifth and sixth centuries the Visigoths, Sueves, Burgundians and Franks produced coinages predominantly in gold and imitating imperial designs and legends. In addition there were occasional small issues in silver or bronze. This pseudo-imperial phase lasted until the 580s, when distinctive 'national' coinages developed.

The Visigoths were the first to issue coins of their own. The series could be seen as being led by issues of Priscus Attalus, the Prefect of Rome whom Alaric I (395–410) had proclaimed emperor after the siege of 410. Rare coins were struck in his name at Rome in that year, and he accompanied the Visigoths when they crossed the Alps into Gaul in 412. Two years later he was again proclaimed emperor by the Goths, and a few *solidi* and *siliquae* were struck by him at Narbonne in 414–415.[14] These apart, the Visigothic coinage consisted entirely of anonymous pseudo-imperial issues throughout their main Gallic phase based at Toulouse (418–507) and for the first seventy-five years of their kingdom in Spain (507–711). These appear to have begun before 421, and may well have been produced with the consent of Honorius, whose name they bear and who had approved the settlement as *feoderati* in south-west Gaul. It is notable from the succession of emperors named on Visigothic coins that those absent are the ones who failed to make peace with the Visigoths and whose imperial authority they seem to have been unwilling to acknowledge on the coinage.[15] As with the Ostrogoths in the sixth century, the names of deceased emperors may have been used instead. The series comprises mainly *solidi* and *tremisses*, without any indication of mint-place, though for the majority of fifth-century issues Toulouse, as the capital, is the most likely. Some rare silver issues in the names of Honorius and Valentinian III are also attributed to the Visigoths. There is a clear break in the coinage coinciding with the expulsion of the Visigoths from Gaul after their defeat at Vouillé in 507, for the Iberian series, recognised by its distinctive style and local find distribution, starts with copies of Anastasius' new *solidus* introduced at Constantinople in 507. The *tremisses* are of an Ostrogothic type, used only by Theoderic, who in 508 intervened on behalf of the Visigoths against the Franks and became regent to the young

[14] Kent (1994), pp. 138–42. [15] Kent (1994), pp. 220–1.

king, his grandson, Amalaric (507–531). Although subsequently the emperor's name was changed, the original type, with a Victory running to the right with a palm and wreath, was used until the end of the Visigothic pseudo-imperial series and became a distinctive Gothic design. Already there are signs of a consistent monetary policy and of careful management of the coinage, which are features that are less evident under the Franks.

The Sueves were also among the earliest to issue their own coins, starting in the 430s or 440s with *solidi* copied from ones of Honorius (393–423) and *tremisses* from ones of Valentinian III (425–455). Honorius' name may have been used because he was ruling in 411 when the Sueves were first allowed to settle as *foederati* in the western half of Gallaecia (north-western Spain). Their subsequent expansion under King Rechiarius (438–455) south and east as far as Mérida and Seville, in the wake of the Vandal passage into Africa, marked the watershed of their political fortunes. Rechiarius is one of only two Suevic kings to be named on the coinage – on an extremely rare silver *siliqua* copied from one of Honorius, but with the reverse inscription IVSSV RICHIARI REGES and the letters BR (for *Bracara*, their capital Braga in northern Portugal). The Sueves did not change their coinage to acknowledge the current emperor, but continued to produce the same types of *solidi* and *tremisses* intermittently for 150 years, until their conquest by Leovigild and incorporation into the Visigothic state in 585. In the final years of the coinage there are signs of a transition to a 'national' series, as the names or initials of several mints appear in the inscriptions, and one unique piece has ODIACCA REIGES, interpreted as the name of the last Suevic king Audeca (584–585).

The Burgundians, whose kingdom was short-lived, being conquered by the Franks in 534, left a small but highly accomplished coinage. Only coins of the last three kings – Gundobad (*c.*473–516), Sigismund (516–524) and Gundomar II (524–532) – can be identified today by the monograms of their names included in the design. These comprise *solidi* and *tremisses* in the names of the current emperor, starting with Anastasius (so after 491), together with rare silver issues of Gundobad and Sigismund, and bronze *nummi* of Gundobad with the mint abbreviation LD for *Lugdunum* (Lyons), where the other coins may also have been struck. It is likely that these were preceded by an anonymous series of coins that today cannot be distinguished from other Gallic issues attributed to the Visigoths.

In contrast to most of the other Germanic kingdoms, the Franks were slow to produce their own coinage. Their gold coinage does not begin until the early sixth century, perhaps after their conquest of the Visigothic kingdom of Toulouse in 507. In the mid-fifth century, when they occupied northern Gaul and western Germany, they seem to have produced a variety of very thin light silver coins, some in imitation of issues of Valentinian III of Trier, and others in the names of Majorian (457–461) and Anthemius (467–472).[16] However, it is difficult to determine the status of each issue, whether Frankish or perhaps quasi-Roman, produced by Aegidius, Majorian's loyal *magister militum* in Gaul, or his son Syagrius. These fragile coins have mostly been found as offerings in graves, but their original purpose was presumably for monetary circulation.

The Frankish gold of the sixth century is readily distinguished from the Visigothic issues by its designs and find distribution. It consists of *solidi* in the names of Anastasius and Justin I and *tremisses* naming all the emperors from Anastasius down to Justin II (565–578), indicating the period over which they were struck. Within them there is a variety of styles and designs, particularly among the *tremisses* of the mid-sixth century, and it is evident that a number of mints were operating. In addition to these pseudo-imperial issues, there are two royal ones. One consists of small silver and copper denominations with the names or monograms of Childebert I (511–558) and his successors. These were produced in Burgundy and Provence, principally at Lyons and Marseilles, in continuation of the small change that had been issued by the Burgundians and Ostrogoths. The second series has already been alluded to – *solidi* and *tremisses* of Theodebert of Metz (534–548) struck in celebration of his successful campaign in Italy in 539–540, annexing much of the north. The coins have such legends as DN THEODEBERTVS VICTOR, around the king's helmeted bust, and it must be these to which Procopius was referring when he commented that Germanic peoples now occupied all the west, including Provence, where their kings could preside over chariot races at Arles and did not even scruple to strike gold coins bearing their own effigy and name.[17] Imperial pressure prevailed, and Theodebert's initiative was not followed by his contemporaries or immediate successors. Yet a precedent had been set, and a generation later the Visigoths and Franks were moving towards establishing their own distinctive 'national' coinages.

ESTABLISHMENT OF 'NATIONAL' COINAGES

The simpler and more orderly of the two coinages is that of the Visigoths.[18] By the third quarter of the sixth century the pseudo-imperial *tremisses* had a design that was effectively Visigothic, rendered in a characteristic and highly stylised way, while the emperor's name had become barely legible. The weight standard had been adjusted to align with that of the Frankish *tremissis*, and it is evident from the variety of styles that there were already a number of mints operating even though these were not named. Hence, this was already a very distinctive

[16] Lafaurie (1987); Kent (1994), pp. 171–2, 187, 198. [17] Procopius, *Bell. Goth.* III.33.5–6.

[18] Miles (1952); Grierson and Blackburn (1986), pp. 49–54.

Visigothic coinage, but its transition into an overtly regal one was prompted by political events. Leovigild (568–586), who had been active throughout the 570s campaigning against the Byzantines and the Sueves, became engaged in a civil war with his usurping son Hermenigild (579–584), who had established an independent kingdom in the south based on Seville.[19] It is not clear whether Leovigild had already begun issuing coins in his own name,[20] or Hermenigild took the initiative in order to assert his own regal authority,[21] but it is clear that both rivals used the coinage for propaganda purposes. Hermenigild's coins are of the usual Visigothic type but bearing his name, ERMENIGILD, qualified by *rex inclitus* ('illustrious king') or *regi a Deo vita* ('life to the king from God'). Leovigild's of similar type use either the *rex inclitus* title or a version of *Dominus nostra Livvigildus rex*. In a further development Leovigild changed the reverse design to a cross-on-steps and added the name of the mint with appropriate epithets for those that had been recaptured from Hermenigild or taken from the Sueves, e.g. *Emerita victoria* ('Mérida conquered'), *Cum Deo Ispali adquisita* ('Seville acquired through God').

Finally, as the civil war ended in 584, Leovigild made a still more radical reform of the coinage, placing his own facing bust on both sides of the coin and returning the weight to the Roman standard, but reducing the fineness of the gold to about 75 per cent. Coins of the new type at Córdoba have the inscription *Córdoba bis optinuit* ('Córdoba twice obtained'), referring to the fact that Leovigild had taken the city first from Byzantium in 572 and then, in 584, from Hermenigild. Immediately one sees that at least twenty mints were then operating, and the number rises to thirty-five or more in some subsequent reigns. More than eighty mints in total are named on the Visigothic coinage, but many of them were small unidentified places that either did not survive the period of Arab rule or lost their identity. More than 60 per cent of the coins were struck at four principal mints (Mérida, Toledo, Seville and Córdoba) in southern and central Spain, while moderately productive mints include Barbi, *Eliberri* (near Granada) and Tucci in the south and Tarragona, Barcelona, Gerona and Narbonne in the north-east.[22] In the former Sueve territory in northern Portugal and Galicia there was a proliferation of small mints, suggesting a different administrative arrangement there.

Leovigild's last coinage established a system that survived with little change until the end of the Visigothic era. The uniformity of design, with the king's facing bust on both sides, was of necessity broken during the joint reign of Chindasuinth and Reccesuinth (649–653), when in order to accommodate

[19] For the details of Leovigild's reign, see Barbero and Loring, chapter 7 above.
[20] Gomes, Peixoto and Rodrigues (1985), p. 28.
[21] Grierson and Blackburn (1986), pp. 49–51. [22] Metcalf (1986).

both names the mint had to be represented as a monogram in the centre of the reverse. Thereafter there was more variation in the types, with either a monogram or cross-on-steps reverse and facing or profile busts on the obverse. An exceptional design from the reign of Ervig (680–687) shows the facing head of Christ superimposed on a small cross-on-steps, which significantly pre-dates Justinian II's 'Bust of Christ' coin type, also backed by a cross, introduced at Constantinople in about 692. Both seem to reflect a current theological debate as to how Christ should be represented in art.[23] The fineness of the gold was maintained at Leovigild's standard of about 75 per cent until the early seventh century, after which it fluctuated between 50 and 70 per cent until the end of the century, slipping to about 35 per cent in the last decade before the Arab conquest of 711.

It had been thought that the Visigoths issued only high-value gold coins, until the recent recognition of a series of small bronze coins.[24] There are at least four distinct types, which are attributed to Seville, Mérida and possibly Córdoba and Toledo. Although difficult to date, they appear to belong to the eighth century. They have been found on sites in southern and central Spain, together with earlier North African bronze *minimi* and later Arab *fels*.

The Merovingian 'national' coinage developed at much the same time as the Visigothic one, but the form it took was quite different. The first signs of the transition came in the third quarter of the sixth century, when occasionally a place-name or personal name – that of a mint or a moneyer – can be discerned within the normally corrupt pseudo-imperial inscriptions. Only rarely can the name of a king be found on *tremisses*, the earliest in this phase being that of Sigibert I of Austrasia (561–575). A more distinct change took place probably in the 580s with the wide-spread adoption of new designs, usually combining a bust on the obverse with a cross design on the reverse, and inscriptions giving the names of the mint and moneyer. By the end of the sixth century a pattern was established that would persist until the end of the Merovingian era in 751.

In contrast to the well-managed centrally controlled Visigothic coinage, the Frankish system appears quite chaotic. Only a tiny proportion of the coins carry the name of a king, though others indicate that they were issued from the palace (*In palacio fitur*, *Palati moneta*, *Racio domini*, etc.). Some are clearly ecclesiastical issues (*Racio ecclesiae* or *Racio* followed by a saint's name), but most have merely the name of the place at which they were struck, often with that of the moneyer who was responsible for them. This has been interpreted as a quasi-private coinage, with the moneyers acting either for the town or on their own account to exchange old and foreign coin and bullion for acceptable new money. Yet there must have been a degree of administrative control over

[23] Grierson and Blackburn (1986), pp. 51–2. [24] Crusafont i Sabater (1994).

minting to maintain standards of weight and fineness and some standardisation in design found among the coins of particular regions.

The coinage of Provence under the Franks is a notable exception to this diverse pattern, revealing its distinctive Ostrogothic heritage and system of government under the Patricians of Provence. Highly literate pseudo-imperial issues continued down to the reign of Heraclius (610–641), and were succeeded by royal ones from Chlothar II (613–629) to Dagobert II (restored 676–679).[25] There was considerable uniformity of design – an imperial or royal bust and a cross-on-step or globule, often flanked by the initials of the mint name (Marseilles, Arles, Uzès or Viviers); there were no mint/moneyer issues. *Solidi*, as well as *tremisses*, continued to be struck in considerable numbers. Interestingly, when production of silver deniers replaced that of the gold coins in the 670s the king's name was no longer put on the coins, but rather that of the patrician, indicating a survival of the belief that gold was the most noble metal, appropriate for an emperor or king.

The Merovingian gold coinage was a large one. It survives today in thousands of specimens struck at several hundred mints, many of them no longer identifiable because the place-name is a common one or has changed. The most productive mints were in major centres, such as Chalon-sur-Saône, Paris, Le Mans, Rouen, Quentovic, Dorestad, Mainz, Trier, etc., but many must have been in small settlements or on individual estates. A significant proportion of the coins has occurred as stray finds, arguably representing accidental losses from circulation. Such high-value coins as these are not readily abandoned without a search, which makes the find record still more impressive and suggests that they represent a very substantial and active currency. The currency may well have been expanding during the seventh century, but if so it was against a background of a limited or even contracting volume of gold available for monetary purposes. From the beginning of the seventh century the fineness of the Merovingian *tremissis* started to decline from a level of around 90 per cent. Evidence drawn from a series of coin hoards of different dates and from the fineness of the royal coins that can be accurately dated suggests that there was a broad and progressive decline in the proportion of gold to around 70 per cent by *c.*630, 50 per cent by *c.*650 and 30 per cent by 670, though these figures should only be taken as marking a general trend, for there could be considerable variation between coins of similar date.[26] In the early 670s the production of base gold *tremisses* was superseded by that of new deniers of fine silver.[27] Another stage had been reached on the journey from an antique to a medieval coinage.

[25] Rigold (1954). [26] Kent (1975); Brown (1981); Stahl and Oddy (1992). [27] Blackburn (1995).

Britain had lost the use of money soon after the Roman army and administration left in 410, as the importation of coins all but ceased. The Anglo-Saxons did not establish their own mints for a further two hundred years, so that they skipped the pseudo-imperial phase of coinage in the West. Roman bronze coins, rediscovered by Anglo-Saxons, and contemporary gold coins imported from the continent were occasionally used in the fifth to seventh centuries as personal ornaments or as grave offerings. The earliest known Anglo-Saxon 'coin' – the magnificent gold piece with the name of Bishop Liudhard, Queen Bertha's chaplain at Canterbury in the late sixth century – was intended as a medallion. Gradually, during the sixth century, imported gold coins came to be used as money as well. By about 620, when the grave-goods for the Sutton Hoo ship burial were being assembled, the forty gold coins, all continental, could well have been taken from local circulation.[28] The first concerted production of Anglo-Saxon coins began in south-east England *c.*630, probably motivated by the need to remint older Merovingian *tremisses* into coins matching the current reduced levels of fineness. Production was small but so was the currency, so that by about 645 these new Anglo-Saxon issues accounted for two-thirds of the hundred coins deposited in the Crondall (Hants) hoard.

This Anglo-Saxon gold coinage was modelled on that of the Franks, comprising mainly *tremisses* (probably the shillings, OE *scillingas*, of the law-codes). Only one rare issue carries the name of a king – Eadbald of Kent (616–640) – while others more commonly have the name of a mint (London) or a moneyer (Witmen, Pada, etc.).[29] Some of the designs copy those of late Roman coins, indicating the esteem in which these were held by the Anglo-Saxons. By the third quarter of the seventh century the scale of production had increased and minting had spread out from the south-east to East Anglia and York. However, as in the Frankish kingdoms, the metal content was becoming progressively based, and in the 670s the pale gold shillings were replaced by new coins of fine silver, the first English pennies.

CONCLUSIONS

In the two or three centuries since the break-up of the Roman Empire in the West money had evolved significantly and would have hardly been recognised by someone who lived in the fifth century. By the year 700 each of the constituent states had its own distinctive monetary system, and its coins had become a useful national emblem signifying its independence and, one hopes, its sound financial condition. The process by which this had been achieved

[28] Stahl (1992), arguing against the previous view that the coins were collected in Francia.

[29] Metcalf (1993–4), I, pp. 29–62.

sheds some light on the evolution of the states themselves. The pseudo-imperial phase of coinage is particularly difficult to interpret. The copying of imperial coinages may have been motivated in part by economic factors – when establishing a new currency, countries often emulate the successful coinages that are circulating in the region. But as the comments of Procopius and the pattern of coin inscriptions show, the imperial prerogative to strike gold coins was also a powerful force, and the emperors appear to have maintained sufficient influence over the new Germanic states to enforce it during the fifth and much of the sixth centuries. Most of the states appear to have sought legitimacy for their coinages by implying that it was authorised by the emperor, whether through an ancient agreement as perhaps with the Sueves and Vandals, or through the continuing consent of the current emperor in the East, as not only the Ostrogoths but also the Visigoths and the Franks appear to have done. Yet the apparent dullness of these anonymous imitative coinages can easily mask signs of fundamental developments taking place in the organisation of minting and regulation of the monetary system. With the transition to so-called 'national' coinages, when the names of mints and/or moneyers are displayed and there is freedom to adopt new coin designs, we get a much clearer insight into the organisation that lay behind it.[30] Then one can see just how far the states had already come in the development of their own monetary systems.

[30] Hendy (1988).

CHAPTER 25

CHURCH STRUCTURE AND ORGANISATION

Georg Scheibelreiter

INTRODUCTION

By the later third century, when it began to be widely persecuted, the Christian community of believers had already created within the Roman Empire the basic forms of church organisation. In the first decade of the third century we see in the work of Tertullian the first signs of a link between Christianity and the Roman legal system, along with an attempt at co-ordination between Christian belief and contemporary philosophy in the writings of Clemens of Alexandria and Origen. But serious disputes with the state over both the separation and the self-government of the church took place during the Constantinian period. At this time the structure of the newly liberated church was clearly in place but the lead that the church in the Eastern Roman Empire had acquired, could not be ignored. There, Christianity could be constructed using the economic and administrative prerequisites of older cultures and therefore it soon reached a high level of organisation. In the West conditions were less favourable. Civilisation was not so far advanced and was at first partly threatened by paganism and barbarianism, which it overcame only slowly. Mediterranean urban culture was not as strong in the West and because of this the church lacked a basis on which to form a full infrastructure. Until the sixth century the church in the West was occupied with solving elementary problems. This task was hindered by the collapse of the unified Western Empire into separate barbarian regimes whose leaders initially had to be converted to Catholicism. This lengthened the transitional phase of the church's development from an only partly effective, troubled religious sect into an institution with many branches. This phase lasted until the end of the seventh century, during which time the African church, which had been highly developed and influential, was lost and west European Christianity had in practice to make some concessions to Celtic and Germanic mentalities.

The development of the papacy between 500 and 700 demonstrates the problems: continuing quarrels within the municipality of Rome, disputes with the Ostrogoths and Lombards, and an often humiliating dependence on the emperor in Constantinople which put the papacy in a defensive position. Although the new churches in the barbarian kingdoms developed under the aegis of Rome's control, they were orientated more towards their own kings. Rome only became more influential from the time of Pope Gregory the Great (590–604) onwards, a development which would continue throughout the seventh century.

The constitution of the church drew upon a secular model but it was not brought into force everywhere or equally. Social and political changes demanded adaptation of the church's officials. Great faults became evident in the organisation of the church and these prompted the introduction of priests who, in some areas of Europe, only began to be effective in the eighth century. The big councils, which were used as arenas for opinions and as a stage for the development of the church, were all held in the Greek East and only superficially concerned themselves with the modest Christianity of the West. In the latter, the life of the church was organised along the lines of the individual kingdoms within which the only controversial issues concerned the ordination of unsuitable people. In the sixth century the bishops came to have secular careers and they increasingly became the officials of the barbarian kings and exponents of local rule by the nobility. The issue of celibacy proved intractable in the face of demands for radical change and casual contemporary practices, and it revealed the first fundamental conflict with the attitudes of the East. This was all that had remained of the influence of the clergy on the law because they had not been able to protect their late antique privileges. With the help of the regional rule-making assemblies (synods), however, the clergy created a special status for themselves, which was not always easy to put into practice.

The economic organisation of the church developed from initiatives begun in late antiquity: in the East it grew into a coherent and competent system of support, whilst in the West economic support was much patchier. In the sixth century, instead of voluntary contributions, obligatory Sunday offerings were introduced and the upkeep of the clergy was funded by the church. In the seventh century the so-called 'private churches' (*Eigenkirche*) appeared and remained a typical phenomenon of western Christianity until the Gregorian reforms of the eleventh century.

The liturgy had its first flowering in the period 500–700 and it grew out of the variety of prayer and church services which had evolved under Byzantine influence and which were consolidated in the first big liturgical collections. Spiritual welfare, which was then beginning to be established, was at first the preserve of rhetorically expressed preaching. But this soon gave way to a simpler transmission of God's word in a more topical mode. Basic missionary practices were introduced with this. In the sixth and seventh centuries baptism and penance took on a modern form, that is, the baptism of children, and the introduction of individual penance and private confessions.

With the introduction of monasticism in the sixth century an important part of the Christian way of life became an institution in the West. The dispute between continental (Benedictine) and Irish traditions over the setting up of monasteries in association with the diocese became a major problem of the time. With this, certain difficulties became evident which the institution of the church in the Middle Ages had to deal with.

These are the general lines along which the church developed in our period. In what follows each major element of church structure and organisation will be examined in more detail in order to give the general picture greater depth.

THE PAPACY

The Acacian and Henotikon schisms were a legacy of the fifth century, in which the papacy was embroiled up to the end of the century. These disputes led to a declaration by Pope Gelasius (492–496) in which he clarified his position within the church and also his stance towards worldly power. The differences between his view of episcopal *auctoritas* and imperial *potestas* brought about the determined opposition of the emperor Anastasius I (491–518). However, this did not put Gelasius at a political disadvantage because he was supported by King Theoderic who, as an Arian, took no interest in the matter. The situation worsened in 498 because of a disputed papal election (the Laurentian schism). The two candidates acted in a politically ruthless manner and greatly harmed the reputation of the papacy. After the death of Laurentius in 506, Pope Symmachus was forced to look for greater support in the West because of the hostile attitude of the emperor, but he took no part in the conversion of the Franks and the Burgundians. These would be of great significance for the future.

Pope Hormisdas (514–523) brought about a reconciliation with Constantinople in 519, thus ending the Acacian schism, but he also established a strong connection with the Spanish and Gallic churches. The political and theological struggles of the following decades nevertheless threw the papacy into great confusion during which much was lost. A low point was reached in 553 with the arrest of Pope Vigilius in the course of the 'Three Chapters' dispute. In addition, the invasion of Italy by the Lombards created a political problem that brought the papacy to the brink of disaster.

Gregory the Great (590–604) became pope at this time. As a representative of a new outward-looking papacy he recognised the emperor as the leader chosen by God, but his concept of Christian power went further than this. He believed that when new nations were converted they had also to be politically pacified. Complete pastoral effectiveness now became a concern of the papacy: to achieve this a reorganisation of the patrimony of the church of Rome was necessary, followed by certain social reforms (prevention of the exploitation of tenants, supervision of officials and the provision of social help). An attempt was also made to improve the level of education of the clerics through practical teaching, conveyed through his *Regula Pastoralis*. Gregory linked the promotion of monasticism with his plan for missionaries and he made piety an intelligible and praiseworthy attribute in all circles of society. This thinking informed his view of hierarchy, as when he peacefully opposed the title 'Ecumenical Patriarch' with which the bishop of Constantinople questioned the precedence of Rome, styling himself *servus servorum Dei*.[1]

Gregory had won back for the papacy in Italy prestige that could never again be completely destroyed. But in the seventh century the popes became strongly dependent on the emperor. Clashes over Monothelitism led to intervention by the emperor, which culminated in Pope Martin I being forcefully exiled in 653. Tension remained after the condemnation of Monothelitism by the Council of Constantinople (680–681) and this tension led to a new crisis under Pope Sergius I (687–701). The so-called 'Trullanum Council', convened by the emperor Justinian II in 692, amounted to a declaration of war on the western church led by the pope, but the arrest of the pope failed this time, owing to the anti-Byzantine stance of the army in Italy. This event symbolised the beginning of the papacy's break from the Byzantine Empire and its turning towards the young church in the West.

The churches in the West were self-assured in their Christian belief and respected Rome as the city of the apostle. But the churches in Spain and Gaul (Francia) were not otherwise orientated towards Rome. After 587 Toledo became the autocratic centre of the Spanish church and its links with Rome weakened in the seventh century. In Lyons the metropolitan threatened to create a leadership completely independent from Rome as part of an independent Frankish church. The expansion of the Arabs into Spain, and the rise of the Carolingians in Francia would eliminate these threats to the unity of the church in the West, and for the first time papal centralism could be developed.

A requirement for the latter was a functioning church bureaucracy. This came about because of the practical needs of pastoral care as well as the administration of the Roman diocese. *Notarii* had existed even in the period of persecution; in the sixth century they were brought together to form the *schola*

[1] Markus (1997), pp. 94–5.

notariorum whose leader was the *primicerius*.[2] Under him was the *secundicerius*. The *notarii* investigated civil and criminal matters but were also used as ambass-sadors. The *primicerius* played an important role when the throne of St Peter was vacant or during the papal election.

Another category of papal officials were the *defensores*: mostly laymen and lawyers, they appeared in the fourth century as protectors of the poor. Since the time of Gregory the Great they had formed a working party (*collegium*) of seven men of which the leader, the *primicerius defensorum*, led the administration of justice in the church of Rome and was its general advocate. Since the end of the sixth century notaries and *defensores* had been taken from the ranks of the lower clergy. More important than both groups of officials were the seven deacons of the city of Rome. They also formed a *collegium* with the priests of the so-called title church. Because they were at the *cardo* (the hub) of the life of the church they became known as *cardinales* (*diaconi* from around 500, and *presbyteri* after around 700). Moreover participating bishops of neighbouring Roman dioceses were added to the liturgy of the pope as *cardinales episcopi*.

In the fifth century a single papal *scrinium* was created, whose job was the management of the possessions and the income of the church in Rome, and which soon became the heart of papal bureaucracy. *Scriniarii* and *chartularii* had been referred to since the time of Gelasius I. Since the sixth century payments had been made for the management of papal property: first the posts of *acarius* (head of financial management) and *sacellarius* (job co-ordinator) appeared. The model for these posts was the imperial chancellery in Constantinople; the posts of *vestiarius* and *nomenculator*, which dealt with petitions, were also taken from the imperial chancellory.[3]

The apokrisiar (*responsalis*) also attained great importance and from the fifth century worked as the papal ambassador in Ravenna and Constantinople. This became a standing arrangement in the imperial capital after 500. The presence, or long absence, of the apokrisiar at the court was soon interpreted as indicators of the state of relations between the pope and the emperor.

Gregory the Great appointed a vice dominus as his deputy next to the archdeacon and furthermore relied on people like the *cubicularii* from his immediate surroundings. For the first time monks were also brought in to help with the government's business, admittedly working only as *consiliarii* in matters of a topical nature.

As far as the papal election was concerned, Pope Symmachus (498–514) had already issued an election decree, which stipulated the designation of his successors and excluded the rest of the community from involvement. A century later

[2] The name originally meant 'he who signed the wax tablets (*cerae*) first'.

[3] Plöchl (1953), pp. 128–31; Angenendt (1990), p. 244.

these rules were finally abolished but the ordinary people remained limited in their involvement in the acclamation of a new pope. Overall the papal election was impressively organised in both legal and liturgical terms. The election and enthronement took place in the Lateran church and were followed by the claiming of the Lateran palace, through which the taking over of the administration was symbolised. The consecration and taking possession of the Petrine throne in the church of St Peter completed the ceremony. Through this, a change in the view of the importance of the papal office became evident: the elevation of the bishops of Rome became an indication of the universality of the pope.[4]

METROPOLITAN AND DIOCESAN CONSTITUTION

Signs of subdivisions in the united church had been evident since the third century. The regulations for consecration made by the Council of Nicaea in 325 (c. 4) presupposed the existence of the church provinces. It is accepted that the dioceses were structured around a secular model. The boundaries of bishoprics regularly corresponded to those of civil administration, although this was not a definite rule. Some bishoprics were centred upon settlements that were not towns and they could also extend over several towns. But the dioceses were mainly dependent on the big urban settlements.

The metropolitan was the head of an ecclesiastical province and he ruled from the civil capital of the province. His job involved leadership of the provincial synod and issuing *litterae formatae* which served the bishops as a means of control. However this metropolitan arrangement was not practised everywhere. In North Africa the primate took on the role of the metropolitan. The primate was the bishop of the province who had been ordained for the longest time, so the post was not connected to any specific metropolis. An exception to this was the position of the bishop of Carthage who, along with the primate of the African province, held the title of *Primus totius Africae*. As such he was in charge of summoning and leading the plenary African council.

In Italy there were special arrangements. Milan became the metropolitan see for several civil provinces, as did Aquileia. In these provinces (Venetia, Rhaetia, Istria and Noricum) there were relatively few towns, and so Milan merited its special position because of its status as an imperial residence and also because of its demographic situation. However both metropolitan sees were surpassed by Rome whose apostolic tradition meant that it was accorded pre-eminence. The bishop of the ancient capital of the Empire had control of ten provinces as well as the islands of Sicily and Corsica, which tallied with the number of civil administrative provinces in suburbicarian Italy.

[4] Angenendt (1990), pp. 43–4.

In Gaul too, the alignment of the organisation of the church with that of civil administration is clearly visible. The transfer of the Gallican prefecture to Arles in 392 was followed by the rise in importance of the church of Arles, at the expense of that of Narbonne. The orderly development of metropolitan sees in Gaul collapsed because of the political division of the country in the sixth century.[5] Caesarius of Arles claimed, with papal authority, the highest position in the church in Gaul, but as a member first of the Visigothic and then of the Ostrogothic kingdoms he could attend neither the Burgundian Synod of Epaon in 517 nor the Frankish councils.

In Spain the bishop who had been ordained for the longest time held the position of *prima cathedra episcopatus.* Until the sixth century this was certainly without metropolitan authority. After the conversion of the Visigoths to Catholicism, Toledo became the ecclesiastical as well as the political capital of the kingdom, a double role that previously only Constantinople had enjoyed. The bishop of Toledo, who had until then been subordinate to the metropolitan bishop of Cartagena, became the primate in 589. The remaining bishops were committed to appear once a year *ad limina*: they could also be appointed from Toledo, being approved or dismissed from post by the primate at the behest of the king. After 656 the bishop of the capital also became the senior figure in the council of the kingdom, an honour which had previously been bestowed upon those who had been ordained for the longest time and who were deemed worthy. This unusually powerful position of the primate actually undermined the metropolitan structure and his strong connection with the king encouraged a secular element.

In England, because of the relapse of the mission from Rome, it was difficult to maintain the new metropolitan administration based on Canterbury. Here the archbishop developed a position which did not arise from the co-operation of *comprovinciales* but became effective through direct papal authority. The pope sent the archbishop the *pallium*, which signified his legitimisation by Rome. This new arrangement, having resulted in the novel title of 'archbishop', then came to the continent with English missionaries in the eighth century and there helped to revive the declining metropolitan administration. The archbishopric signified the unification of several smaller dioceses, and encouraged the formation of a hierarchy which was enclosed within the church but which had a strong link to Rome.

In the East the metropolitan administration was destroyed not only by the incredible rise of the patriarchs of Constantinople but also by the emergence of so-called autocephalous archbishoprics. The life of the imperial church was gradually concentrated solely on Constantinople, as the patriarch soon

[5] Heuclin (1998), pp. 69–70.

acquired the right of consecration, as well as authority over offices and teaching. Autocephalous archbishoprics were simple dioceses. They did not have any suffragans and often owed their existence to political or personal rivalries. These circumstances led to the fixing of the status of individual churches, as we see for Constantinople in the *Notitia Episcopatum* under Justinian I,[6] or in the *Notitia Antiochena* in the second half of the sixth century.

According to the laws of the church, bishops were inaugurated on the basis of election by both the clergy and the people. More and more frequently in the East this was contrary to imperial legislation and the decisions of the council. In practice it was the will of the emperor that was the deciding factor. The minimum age of 35, the obligatory residence and the prohibition of long absences from the diocese played a part in the decision, which in reality was hardly according to the rules. The obligation to pay a fixed tariff when appointed, in order to pre-empt a possible charge of simony, was also a dubious regulation.[7]

In the church in the West the right of appointment was likewise the prerogative of the king. Under the Visigoths this remained an unchallenged process, whereas the Franks continually protested against it. Even the recognition of the rights and regulations of the church by King Chlothar II in 614 did not really change anything in practice.[8] The position of the bishops in Francia could not be freely determined within the categories of the church alone. With the taking over of the office of *defensor*, the bishop acquired a position of public responsibility. In the seventh century these responsibilities grew to include the gathering of taxes, which bound the bishop and the property of the church even closer to the king. So an episcopal *dominium*, or lordship, gradually developed, and this made it even more necessary for the king to have influence over who occupied the bishoprics.[9] On the other hand in Gaul, from the middle of the fifth century, the office of bishop gave the senatorial class their only opportunity to exercise public influence and consequently this soon led to the office of bishop becoming strongly hereditary. The collapse of the metropolitan synods in the second half of the seventh century also furthered the autonomy of the episcopal position in ecclesiastical terms: the bishop now ruled his diocese almost unhindered.

Amongst the diocesan officers, the highest post was that of archdeacon. The archdeacon was entitled to stand in for the bishop at the councils and his

[6] After that thirty-three metropolitan and thirty-six autocephalous archbishoprics belonged to the patriarch of Constantinople.

[7] L. Bréhier in Fliche and Martin (1948), p. 538.

[8] *Concilium Parisiense a.614 cc.*2, 3. However it was already limited in the same year according to *Clotharii II. Edictum, c.*1: 'certe *si de palatio eligitur, per meritum personae et doctrinae ordinetur*'. Pontal (1986), pp. 225–34; Heuclin (1998), p. 190.

[9] Heinzelmann (1976), *passim*; Kaiser (1981), pp. 55–74; Scheibelreiter (1983), pp. 172–201.

job included the management of the episcopal residence as well as the other residences of the diocese. Further responsibilities which the archdeacon held were that of an appointed judge, leadership of care for the poor, the education of young clerics, supervision of moral and spiritual discipline amongst the clergy, and the management of the diocese during any episcopal vacancy. His power was completely bound to the authority and directive of the bishop, who chose his representative from the circle of deacons.[10] Tenure of this highly responsible post was often the prerequisite for the attainment of the office of bishop itself. In Gaul/Francia the archdeacons often became dangerous enemies of the bishops within the church. The bishops therefore tried to get rid of troublesome archdeacons by ordaining them as priests.[11]

The archpresbyter was originally the oldest priest amongst the clergy of the cathedral, who had priority in liturgical functions. In the hierarchy of ordination he was above the archdeacon but as an officer he was well below him. He was the bishop's appointed representative in his sacred occupation and was appointed by him with the agreement of all the priests. Repeated attempts to replace the archdeacon with the archpresbyter failed.

The *oeconomus* had an essential function in the financial administration of the diocese. First he represented the church's property before the court, he supervised the setting up and the maintenance of churches and he allocated the clergy their keep. Apart from this he also supervised the serfs who worked with the church's goods and managed them at times of episcopal vacancy. The *oeconomus* was generally a deacon. In the Frankish kingdom a *vicedominus* did the job of the *oeconomus* from the end of the sixth century. As well as responsibility for economic administration he also had responsibilities in the bishop's household.

All over the West institutions developed which created dangers that threatened vacant dioceses from within.[12] In the fifth century the post of *interventor* or *intercessor* had already been invented in Africa and can be seen to have been that of an administrator of the diocese. In Italy and Gaul the *visitator* appeared a little later and he was entrusted with the same responsibilities as the *interventor* by the relevant metropolitan or provincial synod. Reasons for his appointment were the death, serious illness or dismissal of the bishop. Legally this official was treated in the same way as a deputising bishop. His job consisted primarily of taking in hand pressing business and making a detailed inventory of property. He was also supposed to organise the election of a new bishop. The post of *commentator*, which existed in Spain in the sixth century, was similar: a bishop from a neighbouring diocese was usually appointed to this position. All of these arrangements showed the weaknesses that existed

[10] Plöchl (1953), p. 154. [11] Scheibelreiter (1983), p. 103. [12] Plöchl (1953), pp. 162–3.

in the management of property when episcopal power was lost. Nevertheless these officials disappeared in the seventh century because they could not fulfil their functions of control and order.

The organisation of sees developed rather differently in England. There the ecclesiastical officials were supposed to be monks. In the diocesan centres cathedral monasteries were set up and genuine monastic characters arose who should not be confused with the collegiate clergy of cathedral churches elsewhere. In contrast with Ireland, this monasticism did not have a destructive effect but rather incorporated a peculiar organisational form of spiritual life into the constitution of the diocese.

THE PAPAL VICARIATE

As *vicarius papae in Hispania*, Bishop Zeno of Seville (472–486) was said to have taken care of maintaining ecclesiastical regulations.[13] The papacy had thereby introduced a special arrangement to control a self-contained church that was outside of the hierarchy. Pope Hormisdas (514–523) thus limited the authority that the bishop of Seville had had over the provinces of Baetica and Lusitania. At the same time it was made clear that the privileges of the metropolitans were not allowed to be encroached upon, even if synods were summoned by the papal vicar. Because, in 517, Bishop John of Elche was also entrusted with the preservation of conciliar canons, the papal decrees and the conveyance of *causae ecclesiasticae* to Rome, one should doubt whether the institution of the papal vicariate in Seville was a lasting creation; rather, individual special authorities seem to have been called into being by particular popes. With the conversion of the Visigoths to Catholicism after 587, the supposed vicariate ended along with papal influence in Spain. The conferment of the *pallium* on Bishop Leander of Seville (579–600) was a personal honour that was part of Seville's traditions; it did not, however, signify a revival of the vicariate.

In Arles a papal vicariate is documented for 417–418, and in the second half of the fifth century reports about ecclesiastical circumstances and problems there were expected in Rome. The bishop of Arles was supposed to summon synods and issue recommended writings for Gallic clerics. Nevertheless in 500 rivalry existed between Arles and Vienne whose renowned bishop, Avitus, extended his power of consecration to the territory of Arles with the agreement of the pope. Out of this a conflict developed, which was ended in 514 by the conferment of the *pallium* on Caesarius of Arles. Through this the latter became a sort of super metropolitan for all the provinces of Gaul and Spain, which were ruled by King Theoderic. Despite his ecclesiastical pre-eminence Caesarius

[13] The authority which was granted by the pope Simplicius (468–483) was removed by Felix II.

behaved with great caution towards Rome: he had the decisions of the Gaulish synod confirmed there and entrusted himself with the supervision of vacant sees only on an *ad hoc* basis. Such behaviour was not necessary for a papal vicar. It obviously stemmed not from a structural arrangement, but rather from occasional orders *ad nutum pontificis*.

Pope Vigilius (537–555) wanted to revive the vicariate in Arles in accordance with the wishes of the emperor Justinian I. Pope Pelagius I (556–561), on the other hand, acknowledged the bishop of Arles as the primate of Gaul and the representative of the apostolic see, but the bishop of the time must have requested the conferment of the vicariate. From the letters of Pope Gregory the Great it becomes clear that at the beginning of the seventh century the metropolitan of Arles was regarded as a special intermediary of the pope in Gaul.[14] Along with general administrative tasks on Rome's behalf, the bishop was supposed to function as the pope's representative in the kingdom of King Childebert II (575–596). Only he could issue permits for other bishops to travel. A new task assigned to him was the chairmanship of a group of twelve concerned with matters of belief.[15] Although the pope requested the support of the king in this institution, the vicariate had no future in Francia and it is questionable whether the bishop of Arles became at all active in this sense. In the seventh century Lyons was to become the leading ecclesiastical authority in Gaul. For geographical reasons Arles could not maintain a central role in a Frankish kingdom, which was expanding northwards and eastwards.

With the extensions of the authority of the patriarch of Constantinople over Illyricum after the Council of Chalcedon,[16] the vicariate, which had been created in Thessalonica, fell into oblivion at the end of the fourth century. When in 535 (or 545) the emperor Justinian I raised the town of his birth, *Justiniana prima*, to the status of metropolitan capital, it obtained jurisdiction over provinces that had previously belonged to Thessalonica as a papal vicariate. Forced to agree, Pope Vigilius now gave *Justiniana prima* this position, but its status was raised only at imperial request, and amounted to no more than a change in terminology. Of a papal appointment to the vicariate here, one hears nothing. Nor did anything change when Pope Gregory the Great recognised the new vicariate by the sending of a *pallium*. The pope increased his influence in the Balkans by having his administrative officials intervene in synods there. In the seventh century Thessalonica was again twice referred to as a papal vicariate (in 649/53 and 681); but this seems to have been an empty tradition, which reflected the interlude with *Justiniana prima*.

[14] Gregory, *Papae Registrum Epistolarum* I.6.53. [15] Gregory, *Papae Registrum Epistolarum* I.5.58–60.

[16] The Council of Chalcedon, *c.*28, made it clear that the dioceses of Asia, Pontus and Thracia now belonged to the patriarch.

The chequered history of the vicariate shows the attempts of the papacy to assert claims in areas that were self-contained or open to other influences. It had not been preserved in this form in the West and with the collapse of the metropolitan constitution and the holding of synods it no longer had a workable basis. In the East, political and religious growth continued their separate development, so the papal vicariate had only a temporary influence and did not become a permanent structural element in the organisation of the church.

PARISH ORGANISATION

The term *parochia* originally meant the town community led by the bishop. The rural communities were at first called *diocesis*: they were units of administration for local episcopal churches. Since the end of the fifth century both terms had been used interchangeably.[17] *Parochia* has been used in its modern meaning since the sixth century. In the seventh century *diocesis* meant bishop's parish. This conceptual change indicates that religious life in the parishes changed. For the individual communities the bishop was no longer an immediate authority.

In the fourth century the lines of future parish organisation were already visible in the great metropolitan sees of late antiquity (Rome, Alexandria and Carthage). Around 400 in Spain, churches in *castella*, *vici* or *villae* were not unusual. These were not exactly parish churches, but those that offered more or less regular services without having a resident clergy permanently there to perform religious duties. Occasionally in the sixth century they were made into parish churches.

In southern Gaul churches were established in what had been pagan religious centres. In later centuries the parish system was linked to the continuing process of conversion, although around 600, a regular subdivision of dioceses into parishes still did not exist.

In England in the seventh century local churches could be found scattered across the whole country, but without local resident priests. Instead they were more like *oratoria*, and were comparable to the great crosses that were erected in prominent places in order to maintain prayer and private worship in rural areas. The 'minster' was of great importance to religious communities, which were sometimes subordinate to the big monasteries such as Whitby, Barking and Wearmouth. They often took over the pastoral duties in rural areas.[18]

[17] Vogt in Jedin (1975), p. 226.

[18] Mayr-Harting (1977), pp. 246–7. On the question of whether in the seventh century a parish organisation led by a bishop, or the pastoral activities of monasteries and similar communities, was predominant there is no agreement. On the so-called minster debate, see Foot (1989), pp. 43–54, (1992a), pp. 185–92, and (1992b), pp. 212–25, and Thacker (1992), pp. 140–51. See also below,

In the seventh century the network of country parishes became stronger. The organisation progressed slowly from the south to the north. England and the area on the right bank of the Rhine both received their first proper parish organisation in the eighth century.[19] The central figure in this development appears to have been Caesarius of Arles. He strengthened the financial position of churches in the country that were only allowed to enlist the help of the episcopal churches in cases of dire emergency. He also granted the right to preach to the clergy in the country and encouraged the setting up of local schools to educate young people in the ways of the clergy.

The increase in the number of rural churches led, in the sixth century, to a definition of the priest's role and to a fixing of his prerogatives. In 506 the Visigothic council in Agde stressed that weddings should only be performed in cathedral or parish churches. In the first half of the sixth century the Frankish councils indirectly reflected an increase in the number of parish churches. They were to enjoy the same rights as the episcopal churches, which involved them taking part in the most important liturgical celebrations.[20] Later, regulations of this kind were no longer made, so that one can conclude that a sufficient number of clergy were now to be found in the rural communities. In Spain, however, there seems to have been an insufficiency. There many priests had to look after several churches on Sundays because they did not have their own permanent clergy.

COUNCILS AND SYNODS

At Nicaea in 325 it had been stipulated that every province should hold a synod twice a year, which all the bishops should attend.[21] The metropolitan was the chairman and the synod was supposed to handle such matters as the questions of discipline and liturgy, the legality of election to bishoprics and the general establishment or division of dioceses.

In the East the provincial synod was completely effective. In the West, where the metropolitan constitution was not so well developed, it did not achieve the same level of importance, and in Italy it appears not to have taken place at all. Whether this lowest level of church assembly was derived from a secular model is questionable, but there are signs of parallels in the way in which its business was organised. The most developed form of synod, involving several provinces, was the so-called plenary council of the North African church. This

p. 708, note 53. The Arian church in Vandal Africa probably had rural parishes around the year 500, according to the *Vita Fulgentii cc.*6, 7.

19 In Italy too *pieve* are first mentioned in the eighth century.

20 The councils of Orléans (511), *c.*25, Clermont (535), *c.*15.

21 Note that the pre-Constantinian church gatherings were already called *concilium* or *synodus*.

was held once a year, every province sending three representatives who were chosen at the provincial synods. Carthage held the chair and the council dealt with matters throughout Africa.

The synod in Rome had a special position because it brought together all the bishops in suburbicarian Italy. At this synod the strong position and the far-reaching authority of the bishop of Rome were obvious, but the synod also dealt with matters which affected other primary areas of ecclesiastical jurisdiction. The decisions that were made here were often of import for the whole church. The important provinces of Milan, Aquileia and Ravenna also held joint synods for several provinces and this later became the normal form for church assemblies.

In Gaul no single pre-eminent ecclesiastical site for the holding of synods could be established. Because the concept of power above metropolitan level had in reality collapsed (despite papal support), the church assemblies of the early sixth century had a somewhat 'national' character: thus Agde for the Gothic enclave in the south, Epaon for the Burgundians and Orléans for the Franks. Later, in Francia there was no single council for all the Frankish lands, but rather synods for each of the Frankish kingdoms (*Teilreiche*), and it was upon these that the awareness or horizons of the church were based.[22] A strong relationship with Rome was not developed, the pope was not remembered at assemblies, no concern for the problems faced by the Visigothic or the Anglo-Saxon church was noted and somehow the rich legislative tradition of the Spanish councils remained quite unknown in Francia. In the Frankish synods the matter of religious practices was constantly discussed because this had not been fully determined and caused social and disciplinary problems.

In England Theodore of Canterbury initiated a period of intense synodal activity, beginning with the Council of Hertford in 673. Theodore's aim was to build up the fundamental structure of the English church. The subjects discussed were the lifestyle and the spiritual welfare of the clergy, the powers of the office of bishop, the nature of monasteries and the problems of marriage, but above all the difficult question of the borders of the dioceses. A big problem for the 'national' councils was the influence and participation of secular powers. Since Hertford the synods in England had been 'king free': the archbishop was the chairman. Considering the power that the kings possessed this appeared to be the best way of avoiding political agitation.[23] At the same time it is accepted by historians that whatever powers any Anglo-Saxon overlords (*bretwalda*) might have wielded, they did not include the power to summon, lead or chair councils for the whole of England.

[22] Pontal (1986), pp. 113–68.

[23] For the same reason the Anglo-Saxon synods were dated after the *incarnatio verbi*.

In late antiquity the imperial church council was summoned at the will of the sovereign and this had implications for its content and form.[24] Clovis, king of the Franks (481–511), exercised this imperial right in his kingdom. When he called a council to Orléans in 511 this way of proceeding was perfectly in order from the church's point of view. The *mens sacerdotalis* of the king was acknowledged, and he also announced the *tituli* (items on the agenda) of the assembly. Through this the king became a sacred person and a holder of ecclesiastical rights. With the decline of Merovingian power in the later seventh century, Frankish synodal activity came to an end because only the king could organise it.

The position of the king in the Spanish church had been even stronger since the Council of Toledo in 589. Summoning councils, deciding the subjects to be discussed and giving legal force to the resolutions of the councils were all the rights and duties of the king. The councils in Spain thus became more and more like the old imperial assemblies. They secured the king's leadership through the construction of a legal order of succession. The Visigothic king was not only made the guarantor of a Christian way of life, he was also bound to the Christian ethos when exercising his power. These were elements of the Spanish synods in the seventh century and in this respect they were the most advanced church assemblies in the West.

THE CLERGY

Since the fourth century the conviction had existed in the church that a single clerical rank containing different steps was necessary. This stated the conditions for admission and created levels of competence. In the fifth century a differentiation was already being made between *clerici superioris* and *inferioris ordinis*. Bishops, priests and deacons belonged to the first category and were exclusively consecrated by the bishop. Their special status was recognised by the state. The positions of the lower clerics were not so clearly fixed. The most frequently mentioned are the subdeacon, acolyte, exorcist, ostiarius and lector. These ranks did not exist all the time or everywhere; neither was it necessary to progress through all the ranks. The spiritual nature of some of the posts was even disputed.

The post of lector was regarded as the first step in a clerical career and was often occupied by boys. It involved reading and singing psalms at services. In Rome the lectors formed the choir at Mass, whereas in the East singers and

[24] The pope was mostly represented by legates, the results of the negotiations being communicated to him. After Leo the Great (440–461), however, the popes repeatedly tried to check the council's decisions.

lectors were separated. The *psalmista* mentioned in the *Statuta Ecclesiae Antiqua* occupied a lower rank and was subordinate to the lector. A lector needed to have a good education because this was often a requirement for entry into higher orders.

The authority of the ostiarius is not easy to decipher. In late antiquity this was a clerical grade but in the sixth century it was not occupied by a cleric. After the Trullanum council (692) it was no longer mentioned. The ostiarius' job was to supervise the congregation during the liturgy, and during ordinations the key of the church was ceremoniously handed to him.

The exorcist held a clerical position without receiving the required ordination. Charisma conferred from God was necessary for his job. He looked after the catechumens and *energumeni* (epileptics). However this job was not one of great importance. It was already rare in the sixth century and seems to have disappeared shortly afterwards.

Despite its Greek title the acolyte was hardly mentioned in the East. In the West he carried out charitable works and performed sacramental services (bearing the host, helping with confirmation). In Rome there were forty-two Acolytes so probably six worked with each deacon. They are documented in Gaul from the time of Caesarius of Arles.

The post of subdeacon had been separated from that of deacon in the fourth century. The function of the subdeacon is not clearly discernible everywhere. In Rome they appear to have been helpers of the seven deacons but to have gradually withdrawn from participation in services and sacraments in favour of responsibilities in the management of the church's property.

It is often difficult to distinguish between the functions of the deacon and the priest. The deacon appears often to have been a direct employee of the bishop, sometimes even his representative in secular affairs. His responsibilities included the management of the church's property and also the choosing of candidates for ordination. His standing was quite often greater than that of the priest. In Rome since the end of the sixth century the deacons formed a group of seven men at whose head the archdeacon stood. These men became the most important clerics in the diocese after the bishop.

In the East deaconesses had a certain significance. They had to be at least 40 years old and virgins or once widowed. They were admitted by the laying on of hands and through prayer. The area of the sacrament was not accessible to them; but they prepared women for baptism, cared for people in times of illness and maintained contact with the clergy.

Since the fourth century there had been disputes over the differences between the priest and the bishop. At first this lay expressly in the power of ordination. In the early seventh century Isidore of Seville maintained that as *sacerdotes*, priests and bishops were indistinguishable, but already in the fifth century priests were often described and acknowledged as *secundi sacerdotes*. Only when the priest had been allocated his own church did he have the authority to perform baptisms and celebrate the eucharist; but he was not always allowed to preach.

In Gaul the post of archipresbyter (arch-priest) was created, which presupposed that several priests were active within one church.[25] The archipresbyter was only responsible for the spiritual welfare of the parish, above all for the supervision of the way of life of the other parish clergy. In the seventh century the post was often occupied by laymen, as is shown by the resolutions that the synods issued to ban this. The usefulness of powerful laymen representing clerics in court must have played some part in making lay people seem suitable for this role. But these lay archipresbyteri disappeared again in the eighth century, which was perhaps a preliminary stage in the development of the church advocate, again a layman who was the legal representative of a church.

In Spain each episcopal church had an archipresbyter whose job it was to administer one third of the church's income for religious purposes. In the seventh century he was granted the right to represent the bishop at councils, which in general meant that he had priority over the archdeacon.

In England the tendency to recruit the cathedral clergy from monasteries continued. Therefore most of the clergymen came from cathedral monasteries. The idea prevailed that only those who themselves lived in the highest possible degree of renunciation and purity could deliver salvation.

Originally, a cleric was supposed to prove himself in the first grade of ordination, before he went any further. However Pope Gelasius I urged flexibility where festivals and ember days were concerned, in order to facilitate preaching. The age of ordination was not definitely standardised, but there was a minimum age.[26] The qualifications for a post inside the church were firstly dependent on physical integrity. Therefore those with externally visible defects were usually excluded from ordination along with the mentally ill and epileptics. A moral lifestyle and proof of faith were required. New converts or lapsed Christians were not ordained. Those repenting, profiteers or troublemakers were also considered to be unsuitable for a post within the church. But these standards were often ignored, as complaints about the ordination of *indigni* prove. The admission of slaves, dependent peasants or freedmen was also problematic because of their social inferiority in the late antique and early medieval periods. Reservations against people who had previously held secular office and who could be accused of bloodshed or participation in pagan festivals died out

[25] The Council of Tours (567), *c.*20, speaks of *Archipresbyteri vicani.*

[26] Thus acolytes and subdeacons were not supposed to be younger than 21. Deacons were supposed to be 25 at the youngest, priests more than 30, bishops 45–50.

in the fifth and sixth centuries, as to move into the higher ranks of the clergy meant rejecting a secular career.

The appointment to a post in the church in principle came about through election by the clergy and the people. However at the election of the bishop all that remained to the people was the right of acclamation, whilst the influence of the leading lay men increased. Neighbouring bishops and metropolitans often made the final decision. The Germanic ruler had very great influence upon the outcome because the bishop, as a ruler himself, had a series of responsibilities to the king. Apart from designation by predecessors (who were often relatives), dishonest aiding and abetting and simony all had to be reckoned with. Elections and ordinations were also sometimes carried out through conspiracies and surprise attacks in which the principle *vox populi* equals *vox Dei* was followed. The ordination always took place during the celebration of the eucharist. Bishops had to be consecrated on Sundays, priests and deacons on Ember Saturday or on the Saturday before Passion Sunday.

A theological pastoral knowledge was called for as a spiritual requirement for a post in the church. At first training was in the classical and secular mode, for proper theological education was lacking. The *Statuta Ecclesiae Antiqua* stated that a candidate for the post of bishop should be experienced in the interpretation of the Holy Scriptures and be level headed, that he should know the ecclesiastical rules and agree with the fundamental truths of faith. These requirements became obsolete in the sixth century: training was mainly poor; the Frankish synods say little about it. In general the principle was upheld that laymen who wished to become priests and bishops had to spend at least a year studying the discipline of the church. Caesarius of Arles demanded that every deacon should have read the Bible four times; bishop Magnerich of Trier was happy with it being read once. Council regulations in the sixth century were satisfied with the art of reading and writing. Uneducated deacons and priests were urged to overcome their faults.

Theological disputes were not possible in the West for a long time. Even with the completion of the orderly ecclesiastical career ladder, theological knowledge remained modest.[27] In order to be prepared to some extent, schools for the clergy began to be established in the sixth century, although they can hardly be described as institutions. It was therefore ruled by the Visigothic synods that young lectors should be introduced to a knowledge of ecclesiastical principles in the bishop's household. In Gaul Caesarius of Arles made a similar proposal for rural priests in order to advance local young people. Bishops with a literary education existed only in Spain in the sixth and seventh centuries. They were brought up in monastery schools where the individual priests received a *libellus*

[27] Scheibelreiter (1983), pp. 100–1.

officialis (a sacramentary) from the bishop. But clerics were not supposed to limit themselves to books: they also had to know the psalter, hymns, cantica and baptism rituals by heart.

Special regulations were supposed to ensure the moral character of clergymen. Therefore they were prohibited from certain professions, such as the management of goods and property, pleading at law, money lending and public office. They were not allowed to be active as *theatricus* or to practise astrology or magic. That this detachment from the social environment was very difficult is indicated by further prohibitions in the sixth and seventh centuries: on gambling, the carrying of weapons, the ownership of hawks and hunting dogs, visiting public houses or going around in splendid clothes.[28] A sure *stabilitas loci* was also demanded. Priests and deacons were only allowed to go on journeys with an episcopal pass (*litterae formatae*). Living with lay people was also only allowed with episcopal permission.[29]

The legislation of the councils was dominated by the problem of celibacy. High clergy had not been allowed to marry since the fourth century. Pope Leo the Great demanded celibacy from all ordained ranks above subdeacon. Celibacy was the safest guarantee of the officials having no heirs, for the latter could be dangerous for the church's property. Under Gregory the Great married men who became high clergy did not have to divorce their wives, but they did have to live in complete chastity. In Francia the vow of complete chastity extended to acolytes and exorcists and their wives were obliged to follow it too. As widows they could not marry again![30] Nevertheless it appears that until the sixth century an unmarried bishop was very rare. The wife of a bishop was called an *episcopa* and often undertook an important role in the management of the diocese. She was mainly in charge of charitable works but was also engaged in the dignified decoration of the bishop's church. The Council of Tours (567) said that a bishop without a wife had to be served by clerics. The same council also referred to *presbytera*, *diaconissa* and *subdiaconissa*.[31] All these married women were recognised by society but they were not allowed to live in matrimony with their husbands.

The conversion of Arian clergy to Catholicism created fresh problems with regard to celibacy. These clergymen wanted to continue undisturbed with their full marriages in the new hierarchy. The Council of Toledo in 589 decided that such clerics should be demoted to lectors.[32] In the seventh century the subdeacons in Spain demanded the right to marry for a second time. They

[28] Riché (1962), pp. 324–35; Scheibelreiter (1983), pp. 76–91.

[29] Riché (1962), pp. 336–50; Scheibelreiter (1983), pp. 91–8; Heuclin (1998), pp. 190–5.

[30] II Mâcon (585), *c.*16. This extreme chastity was derived from the word of St Paul (1 Corinthians 6:5). There, however, it is meant only to be temporary: Heuclin (1998), pp. 112–14.

[31] II Mâcon, *cc.*14 and 20. [32] III Toledo (589), *c.*3.

argued that they had not received the *benedictio* at their ordination. This is why the latter had to be introduced into the ordination ceremony. Concubinage was punished severely; in 589 it was decided that guilty clerics should be removed from office and sent to a monastery whilst the concubine could be sold into slavery. Around the middle of the seventh century an attempt was made to stem the lack of restraint with which children were born to clerics (from subdeacon upwards) after they had been ordained, and to exclude them from inheritance. At the same time they were supposed to remain slaves of the church forever. How far all this was from the church in the East is shown by the Trullanum legislation of 692 in which priests were given the right to marry.

THE RIGHTS OF THE CHURCH

As early as the fourth century the special position that the clergy held within the church was recognised by the state. This must have had an effect on ecclesiastical jurisdiction. Nevertheless, for a long time, the efforts that the clergy made to achieve a *privilegium fori* had little success. Eventually Justinian's legislation in the Novels strengthened the powers of the ecclesiastical court, and in the East after 629 the ecclesiastical court of jurisdiction for clergy was obligatory.

The Germanic *leges* differed from each other with regard to ecclesiastical jurisdiction. With the Visigoths the provincial synods competed in matters of civil law with the secular courts. The latter had in any case been given the right to operate by the bishop. The Fourth Council of Toledo in 633 established that criminal matters concerning bishops were the Council's concern,[33] a principle that was however often broken in practice. In Francia the royal court also had jurisdiction over the clergy, but in the Edict of Paris in 614 civil jurisdiction over *homines ecclesiastici* was granted to the church. Clerics' *causae minores* were also assigned to the bishop's court. With the Lombards, on the other hand, the settling of disputes by the church was the exception. In internal matters too the clergy was subject to the king's court. Even when a bishop was the chairman the case went before a secular court.

Criminal proceedings against a bishop were at first organised according to Roman law. With priests and deacons co-operation already existed between secular and ecclesiastical authorities. The lower clergy had to answer to a secular court if they were caught red handed or produced a confession. As confused as the situation may have been, Germanic law showed an improved representation of the clergy in the secular court through the increased protection of the person (through the *wergild*) and the special protection of the church's possessions.

[33] This corresponds to the regulation in which a bishop of the patriarchate of Constantinople had to answer before the *Sinodus Endemousa*.

The organisation of the ecclesiastical courts was not uniform: a clear allocation of responsibilities was lacking. The most important court in the diocese was the episcopal court, of which the archdeacon was more and more frequently the chairman. The official channel of appeal was to the provincial synod. In Africa it was to the primate. The proceedings were a simplified form of the Roman process of accusation. As well as this model, Germanic law had also been an influence since the time of Gregory the Great. The punishments the church courts could give out were not yet conclusively defined but the principles, which were developed later, were recognisable. The people who were entitled to give out punishments were the bishop, the councils and the pope, but there were still conflicts over the competence of each authority.

Depositio (dismissal) meant complete loss of ecclesiastical position and dignity, along with all its rights and income and, in addition, it meant exclusion from the ranks of the clergy and a permanent ban on re-entry (*depositio perfecta*). Ordination remained unaffected but the disgraced cleric was not allowed to make use of it. External consequences were the removal of religious garments and signs of status. A milder form was partial deposition. This meant a lowering of rank but not total exclusion from ecclesiastical status.

Excommunication meant the loss of the right of membership of the church. It was mainly a punishment for laymen, which was imposed upon clerics in especially serious cases. Complete excommunication meant total exclusion from the life of the religious community, but partial excommunication only meant exclusion from communion services. Excommunication could be permanent or limited to a certain period and it could be simply or ceremoniously pronounced (the anathema).

Suspension was a temporary punishment, which was handed out to clergymen mainly to deprive them of practising their ecclesiastical ceremonies or rights. It concerned either the power of ordination and that of office, or just the latter. Interdict, as an effective local and personal punishment for laymen, does not, in the sixth and seventh centuries, yet appear to have much importance. Less severe punishments were: expulsion from the parish, a transfer, withdrawal or reduction of income, confinement to a monastery, or chastisement. Furthermore they could also be publicly pronounced.

The spreading and strengthening of the church as an organisation led to an expansion and consolidation of ecclesiastical law-making. Laws were introduced by the emperors, kings, popes and councils. In this the church in the East had a clear lead. However, its unity began to weaken during the Acacian schism (484–519). The several Christological disputes in the East became indissolubly mixed with politics, so it became apparent that there was a growing need to obtain standardisation through a codification of the laws.

The West was at first dependent on the systematic collections of the East. As part of this came papal decrees and records in which both source collections were mixed. The reception of the Oriental collections did not signify a legal acceptance of everything that they contained. They were made up partly from private works, which were accepted as legally valid. This was regarded as heretical in the West, and casts light on the flawed spiritual assimilation of these borrowings. Obviously here much remains unknown and we must manage with reconstructions and hypotheses.[34]

The oldest collection in the West was the so-called *Vetus Romana* (between 350 and 410), which recorded the canons of Nicaea and Sardica. To the first half of the fifth century belongs the *Versio Isidoriana* (or *Hispana*), which had originated in Africa or Italy. Younger but more significant was the *Prisca* (or *Itala*) which was put together in Rome around 500. Between the pontificates of Gelasius I (492–496) and Hormisdas (514–523), collections were started in Rome, which strove for standardisation and the removal of particularist law and uncanonical texts, as well as giving a special emphasis to the papal decretal right. These collections achieved far-reaching recognition, which came from the inclusion of established and tried canons from the African councils. In Gaul the well-known *Statuta Ecclesiae Antiqua* attracted the most attention. It was put together in Arles in about 450 and made use of the acts of Gaulish and eastern synods and papal laws. Later works in the sixth century were limited to Francia but they offer valuable insight into the development of laws in the ecclesiastical West. The *Capitula Martini* (also: *Collectio Martini Bracarensis*) was another of the most important collections of the sixth century. It had been started around 540 in the circle of the great religious leader Martin of Braga. He strove specifically to give the clergy and the lay people better knowledge of the sources conciliar and papal, a goal that appears to have been particularly important to him, like an inner mission.

THE ECONOMY OF THE CHURCH

Until the sixth century the church's property and income were handled according to the principles of Roman law. With the setting up of the Germanic kingdoms this standardisation was lost in favour of corresponding measures in the various *Leges*. In Merovingian Francia the clergy was gradually freed from the poll tax whilst the property tax was maintained, but numerous privileges existed. There was the principle that the church's fortune belonged to it as an institution and not to the clerics working in separate churches. The rule was that, with the exception of an individual's inheritance, everything given

[34] The detail in Plöchl (1953), pp. 251–9 is most useful.

to a cleric after his ordination belonged to the church and not to him personally. But the numerous complaints made by councils, against clerics using the church's wealth for their own or their relatives' purposes, show that here no clear legal separation existed. Bishops were in charge of making inventories in which the different categories of the wealth were supposed to be stated.

According to the *Lex Romana Visigothorum* the church's property was *res divina*. How far this concept was followed can be seen by the fact that the leasing out of church property for money by managers could be regarded as simony. Every church owned the wealth that was given to it when it was founded, and to safeguard this an episcopal confirmation was required. In a *petitorium* the founder was bound to these provisions and had to relinquish all his rights over his church. Only then could the church be consecrated. This sort of church foundation was so common in papal Italy, Spain and Francia, that the model of the private church (*Eigenkirche*) eventually declined in the face of it. The dispute over the origins of the *Eigenkirche* has produced different theories, which cannot be expanded on here.[35] Even at the beginning, in the pre-Constantinian period, private church services took place. The development of estates owned by landlords, with its implications for the law of property, also affected the situation: everything that belonged to a church went to the site of the altar. Thus much of the explanation for the creation of *Eigenkirche* lies in the social structure of the time. It was not only the founders of the churches who claimed their property and acted in a high-handed manner, but also those who were protecting the *clerici* of the church from episcopal discipline. It is clear that everywhere where authority was publicly and legally exercised over the land and people, rule was also acquired over the church. So the phenomenon of the private church corresponded to the contemporary conception of power and rights. We cannot go further into the religious mentality that gained further expression through the formation of private monasteries (*Eigenklöster*) here.

At first the church survived on voluntary contributions. Under Pope Damasus I (366–384) the particular principle of an ecclesiastical tax on profits was established. Supported by numerous councils it was introduced generally in the sixth century. An obligatory tax, which the separate churches paid to the bishop, was the so-called *cathedraticum*. Whether or not it was a general arrangement is unclear: it was first mentioned at the Third Council of Braga in 572, and in the seventh century met with repeated opposition at Visigothic councils. The offerings, which the faithful brought to the church, had been used by the priests themselves since the sixth century. Now an offering at the altar was stipulated as an obligation for lay people on Sundays.

[35] Feine (1950), pp. 195–208.

The person in charge of the church's wealth was the bishop: without his agreement no decisions or changes could be made. In the East, Justinian's laws established a hierarchy of personnel to manage the wealth. There were *defensores* (to protect the rights of the wealth), *dioketai* (to manage the landed property) and *custodes* (to manage the moveable goods), and there were also secondary assistants. They all had to report to the bishop once a year. In the West there was not such a variety of management personnel. One person who is referred to is the *oeconomus*. King Chlothar II stipulated in the Edict of Paris (614) that the church's economic officials should be taken from the inhabitants of the *pagi*, in which the goods concerned lay. Episcopal influence may have declined because of increasing specialisation in management of the diocese, but the pope generally became more active in management matters. This activity intensified when Gregory the Great came to power. As an experienced and practical man he undertook the reorganisation of the *patrimonium Petri* and of the economic management of the church in general.

The church's wealth was in principle used for services, for charitable concerns and for the upkeep of the clergy. Pope Simplicius passed a law in 475 that divided the wealth into four parts, which as well as for the aforementioned needs, also provided for the bishop. But in the sixth century there was a return to division into thirds, in which the services were no longer referred to. In the sixth century a clergyman no longer received his upkeep from his community but received instead a wage from the collective wealth. It had to be ensured that he could live in a manner befitting his rank on this wage. For this reason precise regulations were made concerning the number of clergy at each church.

Numerous limitations were placed on the alienation of the church's wealth. Thus abbots and priests needed episcopal agreement to dispose of it. In Italy in 483 the *praefectus praetorio* Basilius issued a ban on the alienation of the church's income. This was, however, lifted by a provincial council in 507 because it had been made without the pope and clergy. At the same time a decision was made in response that publicly declared that lay people had no right to make such rules. Nevertheless, King Theoderic passed another law to protect the church's property. Pope Symmachus (514–523) differentiated between permanent estrangement and *usus fructus* (temporary enjoyment of income) but at the same time he issued a ban on its disposal. The church's property could only be used, in *usu fructu*, for life by clerics, monks, the poor and foreigners.[36]

The danger of alienation existed because of the frequent loan of the church's property to lay people, which was initially in the interest of the church. In

[36] For detail on relationships in Gaul, Lesne (1910), pp. 143–94. On the general relationship between power and possession of property in the church, Ganz (1995).

Francia the instrument of *precaria verbo regis* (lease of church land to laymen at the king's command) did not exist in pre-Carolingian times, although compulsory leasing could occur at the request (*petitio*) of the king or mayor of the palace. Constant uncertainty surrounded the law of inheritance concerning clerics: it was limited in favour of the church, which was the natural heir, but there was hardly a clear division between the church's goods and personal property. The church had suffered greatly in disputes over wills, arbitrary gifts and ruling decisions.[37] A bishop's estate, which was often claimed by his wife in an arbitrary manner, was subjugated to particularly strict regulation.[38] Non-Christian relatives were, under these circumstances, completely cut out from inheritance.

THE LITURGY

In the period between Leo the Great (440–461) and Gregory II (715–731) the Roman liturgy was fully developed. The oldest collections of prayers for mass (*sacramentaria*) can be traced to popes Leo I, Gelasius I and Gregory I. The prayers, which were newly formulated by different popes, had been written down by priests and kept in the Lateran archives.

The *Sacramentarium Leonianum* (or *Veronense*) represents the joining together of separate mass *libelli*, giving different forms for the same mass, or other services. The beginning has been lost, the contents only covering the months April to December. The author was probably a compiler who strove to include everything that he knew, and because of this he sometimes made mistakes in the order. The *Sacramentarium Gelasianum* is a reproduction of Roman liturgical material, as it was taken up in Francia. The oldest specimen there comes from the seventh century. For the *Sacramentarium Gregorianum* there are two traditions. First there was the so-called *Hadrianum*, which was sent to Charlemagne by Pope Hadrian I (772–795) and was added to in Francia because it missed out the Sunday mass. The other version was the *Paduense* (named after the home of the manuscript). This mass formulary was linked to Gregory the Great because it is the work of a man who possessed clarity, understanding and openness, and this pope was regarded as an ecclesiastical organiser. However, because it already included a Gregorian festival on 12 March it probably took on its final form in the time of Gregory II. The first redaction was still used in the time of Honorius I (625–638), and since it also cites the stations of the Roman church it was probably created for papal worship.

37 Plöchl (1953), p. 245.

38 Gregory of Tours offers a characteristic example from Le Mans: *Hist.* VIII.39.

The *Gelasianum*, on the other hand, only cited the mass times and appears therefore to have been a priest's mass book. It is probably not a genuine Roman work, for it recognises many Campanian saints and mixes their festivals with those more generally established in ecclesiastical tradition. On the whole it was concerned with the patron saints of the church who had been established in the sixth century. Bishop Maximin of Ravenna (546–556) could have been the author of the *Gelasianum*, and in any case it is older than the *Gregorianum*. It can have reached Francia no earlier than 628 because it already contained the festival of the Raising of the Cross (14 September), which had been introduced by the emperor Heraclius on the occasion of the winning back of Jerusalem.

The sacramentaries give insight into the form of the mass, but they contain no liturgical directions. For these one must fall back on the *Ordines Romani*. These are *libelli* in which rites, ceremonies and liturgical prayers for different sacramental occasions and holy services (ordination of the clergy, the eucharist and the liturgy for the holy week) were recorded. *Ordo* I, for instance, which appeared at the end of the seventh century, described the external order of events in a papal mass in a very exact sequence. A Byzantine influence is to be assumed here. Perhaps the *ordo* was put together in the time of Pope Vitalian (657–672) who had also introduced new hymns to the Lateran in the *schola cantorum* (the *Vitaliani*). It was a period of new development in rites and hymns, which differed from the old Roman models owing to Byzantine influence. Benedict Biscop strove to bring this new Roman liturgy to England. In 680 he persuaded Abbot John of St Martin's in Rome, who was the *archicantor* of St Peter's, to go with him to educate the English clerics in this matter and to write liturgical books.

The availability of sacramentaries and *ordines* should not lead one to conclude that prayer and song were subject to strict validation. Prayer material was still freely changeable and bishops were in a position to be creative themselves.[39] A unified Gallican liturgy did not yet exist, rather there were characteristic common features of the local forms. Likewise the numerous benediction formulas suggest a strongly pastorally organised liturgy.[40] In Rome on the other hand, the Byzantine style of the seventh century turned the participants in the services into mere listeners and spectators. Gaul and Spain did not succumb to this from a pastoral point of view, as long as the people there could still understand the language of the liturgy. England followed the direction of Rome. The

39 So in Gaul and Spain before the middle of the sixth century Gospel readings and sermons came first after the preparation for the offering and the *missa catechuminum*. In 538 Pope Vigilius sent an *ordo precum* to Braga which recognised the great flexibility of liturgical possibilities: Heuclin (1998), pp. 201–5.

40 In Rome the benediction before the communion was replaced by an *oratio ad populum* in the sixth century: Heuclin (1998), pp. 205–10.

Gelasianum and *Gregorianum* were used next to one another and they were often combined 'to the taste of the individual cathedrals and monasteries'.[41]

Prayers at certain times throughout the day were also a part of the regular liturgy. This custom was introduced to the clergy in cathedrals through monasticism and spread from there to the people. Caesarius of Arles got the clergy and people to pray throughout the daily offices. Participation in hourly prayers was obligatory during the period of fasting, this being regarded as a pointed sign of piety. In Spain the people did not take part in this, but in rural churches, as well as in other places, psalms were sung as morning and evening prayers. The order of reading depended on the beginning of the church year: in Rome this was a week before the Lenten fasting in spring, whilst in Francia, Advent marked the beginning. Although the *Gelasianum* and *Gregorianum* had the church year beginning at Christmas, it was said to have started on 1 March by analogy with the pagan Roman calendar. In Spain, 17 November was chosen because it was regarded as the beginning of the long preparation for Christmas.

A separate liturgical garment, which was different from everyday robes, was evident in the seventh century (in contrast to the usual clerical vestments.) The deacon wore the *dalmatica*; all other clergy from the acolyte to the bishop wore the so-called *planeta*, a very wide, fine, long robe. It enabled the mass book or holy equipment to be held with covered hands.

PASTORAL CARE

The sermon was the main instrument of pastoral care in the sixth century. It was also indirectly a missionary device, for it was thought that pagans came to services out of curiosity and were converted by the preaching, the worth of which was highly estimated. Caesarius of Arles believed that the word of God (along with its interpretation by the preachers) was no less important than the body of Christ. It is evident that this opinion owed much to the highly valued rhetorical tradition in Gaul but it also indicates a lack of interest among the people. Already the *Statuta Ecclesiae Antiqua* had threatened people who left the service during the sermon with excommunication. Caesarius of Arles forced people to stay by closing the church doors and only opening them after the benediction. However, signs of participation in the sermon are also attested to, such as applause or grumbles of disapproval. Moral warnings, which were purposefully made, occasionally produced unpleasant reactions. Most sermons lasted only half an hour, and their contents were simple because of the low level of education among the priests since the sixth century. Nevertheless, in

41 Mayr-Harting (1977), pp. 272–5.

a period of declining education, a certain degree of understanding could still be achieved. Caesarius asked all his colleagues to preach on every Sunday and holiday and even twice a day during Lent. The bishop of Arles himself could adapt to different levels of understanding. He therefore put his model sermons at the disposal of his colleagues and sent them out as the first ever collection of sermons.

In general, preaching was tailored to the different festivals of the church year. But the sermons were used above all to tackle current issues that needed Christian comment. An essential aim of the sermon was to tear people away from everyday materialism. People were supposed to think about the next world and eternity and not to live carefree lives. Gregory the Great demanded cheering contents, to put new heart into the people who were exhausted by the misery of daily life. Next, the sermon was supposed to encourage the listeners to lead actively Christian lives, at the heart of which were appropriate virtues, social relationships and the promotion of the church. The necessity of keeping Sunday as a day of rest was also impressed upon the people; this concerned agricultural work above all and was directed against an exaggeration of the Jewish sabbath. In missionary areas, respecting Sunday as the day of rest was seen as a sign of Christianity, because previously Thursday, as the day of Jupiter, had been the day of rest.

Baptism, as the initiation ritual into Christianity, was correspondingly given lots of attention. Therefore in Gaul in the sixth century more and more babies and children were baptised, often in parish churches. Our knowledge of this is based, however, almost exclusively on Caesarius of Arles. The date for baptisms was originally Easter night, later, Christmas or festivals of known saints. In the case of infant baptisms, the long preparation for baptism, which was carried out during the period of fasting, was shortened. First infants were given the *competentes* (laying on of hands and anointing on the forehead with oil). After this, in Rome, the *scrutinia* followed. Strict checks of the beliefs and lifestyle of the candidate (for adults) were made. Earlier, in Africa and Gaul, exorcism was performed. The godparents made a commitment to give the baptised child a minimum amount of religious knowledge (the creed, the Lord's prayer). At other times in the church year the preparations were shorter and requests for immediate baptism were not denied. Following the baptism came the *consignatio*, the marking with the cross. After the celebratory rejection of the Devil, a declaration of faith was called for. In Gaul this was followed by the newly baptised having their feet washed. Unusual features of baptism in Spain were the strict dates for learning the creed. It was ceremoniously handed out on Palm Sunday and had to be recited on Maundy Thursday. In contrast to Gaul, baptism in Spain was performed predominantly on adults.

Penance and reconciliation were, in general, matters for the bishop; only in Rome were they part of the priest's responsibilities. On Maundy Thursday the penitents were received into the community again. Repentance began with the laying on of hands and the presentation of the *Cilicium*. The penitent had to put on special clothes and have his hair cropped. Penitents had to live withdrawn from public life and they were supposed to secure their penance through vehement praying and fasting, through many acts of compassion and also through essential helpful services such as cleaning the church. A lasting consequence of penance was the need for chastity in marriage and exclusion from the clergy. Rigour in these matters made penance problematic, especially as repentance made on the death-bed had the same consequences for those who recovered. Eminent bishops such as Avitus of Vienne or Fulgentius of Ruspe could also only offer emergency solutions, such as easing the effects of death without repentance by getting the spouse to agree to take on the penance. In seventh-century Spain, numerous sinners were reported to have committed suicide to free themselves from the burden of penance. The dilemma was inescapable. Therefore the concept of penance was not only reduced to absurdity but it was clear that the collapse of public penance was inevitable. The time was ripe for private penance. This was particularly propagated by Irish monks, although it began on the continent. At the end of the sixth century the rehabilitation of a penitent cleric was possible. He had to spend his period of penance in a monastery and abstain from the ceremony of the eucharist. This was public to an extent, but did not hinder his return to office. Caesarius of Arles also encouraged a form of private penance in self-punishment and examination of one's conscience. In the year 570 Bishop Philip of Vienne appointed the priest Theudarius as penitentiary for the diocese. Many people came to him and confessed their transgressions in private. With this the door to confidential confessions was opened. Gregory the Great recognised that the prayers of known sinners were a means of repenting and so in the seventh century penance was no longer linked to the public status of penitent.

The anointing of the sick is also already attested in the seventh century. In Spain the oil was consecrated during the festival of Cosmas and Damian (27 September) in which a prayer for health in soul and body was linked to the sufferings of Christ. In Gaul lay people also used oil for secular healing of the sick or for driving out demons, which even Caesarius of Arles encouraged. But it was better still for the sick to come to the church to receive communion and to be anointed.

MONASTICISM

Whilst during the fifth century in the East the number of monasteries was already increasing at a tremendous rate, the West was just seeing the beginning of its own monasticism. Its exemplary value as a highly respected ideal was strengthened during the period of mass migration. But if monasticism in the

East was more of a movement than an institution, in the West it had already become stronger from an organisational point of view. This was because of the characteristically pragmatic way of life of the Latin monks, who did not blindly copy the Orientals, but adapted themselves to reality. This was already obvious in the early rules (those of John Cassian, Macarius and the *Regula Quattuor Patrum*). In southern Gaul, which became the centre of early western monasticism, there were already gatherings of abbots who made agreements about the inner structure of monasticism.

Monasticism became a very significant factor of religious life in the West, but only in the sixth century, during which the great western rules were created. Now the interest of the bishops began to stir. They wanted to have the monasteries under their jurisdiction and thereby have the power to add to the regulations of the Council of Chalcedon.[42] In the case of Italy, it can be seen how varied in reality was the effectiveness of episcopal control over the monasteries. In the Byzantine influenced south, the bishop had pastoral care over the monks, whereas in the Gothic–Lombard areas, the monasteries were much more independent. First Gregory the Great placed the monasteries under general episcopal supervision, which was already the case in Spain and Gaul. The main focus of this right was the exertion of influence in the election or approval of the abbot, as well as control over the management of wealth. But in the seventh century this system began to relax: under Irish influence the ties to the bishop were lifted through privileges and exemptions.

In Italy the eastern model dominated.[43] The Egyptian style of anchorism was maintained in the sixth century through the translation to Italy of the *Apophthegmata Patrum* (or *Verba Seniorum*). In coenobitic monasticism too the situation was the same, as seen in the *Regula Orientalis* of *c.*500. Laurentius, the founder of the monastery of Farfa (in around 500), came from Syria.[44] At the same time African influences from refugees from the Vandal kingdom came to southern Italy where a community of monks also existed at the grave of St Severinus in Castellum Lucullanum.

It is against this monastic background that we see the emergence of the two definitive rules, the so-called *Regula Magistri* and the *Regula Benedicti*.[45] A strong and formal relationship exists between these two works. Today it is believed that the anonymous, essentially more extensive *Regula Magistri* is the older work (created between 500 and 530). It is based on a less-developed coenobitic monasticism and uses more apocryphal literature. It was probably written in Rome: Eugippius (d. 530) knew of it, as perhaps did Benedict. But for his Rule, the latter drew upon a wider range of monastic writings such as

42 Baus, in Jedin (1975), p. 267. 43 Jenal (1995), pp. 131–41. 44 Penco (1959), pp. 22–3.
45 Jaspert (1971) offers a bibliography of research.

the *Vitae Patrum*, the rules of Basil and Pachomius, and Augustine's *Historia Monachorum*, which he mixed with his own experiences to create a form of rule based on practical realities. The fundamental thought behind his rules was a concentration on Christ, which monks should express in everything that they did. The work is a strongly composed synthesis which would have a widespread distribution in the future.

In the second half of the sixth century Cassiodorus made an attempt to form an intellectual elite of monks, which was unique at the time. In his Calabrian monastery, Vivarium, he organised a programme of study, which went a lot further than the usual *lectio divina*. A library of the Holy Scriptures and secular works, and a scriptorium, were required for the intellectual activity of the monks to whom he gave guidance in his institution. After Cassiodorus' death in 583 this activity declined, but his emphasis on the importance of study would become an enduring feature of monasticism in the Middle Ages.[46]

Under Augustine's patronage the monasteries in Africa flourished in the early fifth century. However the Vandal invasion soon caused a decline. Many monks and nuns converted to Arianism. The tradition of the rules remained, but it is questionable whether Augustine's basic principles were contained in them. After 534 Africa became the goal for religious refugees who did not agree with Justinian I's religious policy. In the seventh century Byzantine monasteries also existed in Africa. An important representative of this type of monasticism was Maximos the Confessor (d. 662), the courageous opponent of Monotheletism in the disputes at Carthage in 645. All this came to an end with the Arab conquest of North Africa.

In Spain in the sixth century the tradition of hermits still dominated in Galicia, Asturia and the Balearics.[47] From the middle of the century more monasteries began to be founded. Martin of Braga began with the monastery of Dumio, the rule of which showed Egyptian influence. In 570 the African refugee Donatus founded the monastery of Servitanum with the help of numerous immigrant monks. Beside this stood the practical and theoretical effectiveness of the brothers Leander and Isidore of Seville, authors of the *De Institutione Virginum et Contemptu Mundi*, and the *Regula Monachorum*. Each of the great religious leaders of the seventh century (John of Biclaro, Braulio

[46] This has recently been called into question. Cassiodorus may have consulted classical texts only to aid a deeper understanding of the Bible. An 'intellectualisation' of monasticism was far from his mind. *Vivarium* was thus only 'a variant of the many forms that early monasticism took': Jenal (1995), pp. 660–1. But this does not alter the fact that Cassiodorus pushed his monks in the direction of intellectual activity and that he was uncomfortable with contemplation and rough manual labour. See further Fontaine, chapter 27 below.

[47] Díaz y Díaz (1970), pp. 49–62; Linage Conde (1973), pp. 244–50.

of Saragossa and Fructuosus of Braga) had a strong and supportive relationship with coenobitic monasticism. Different sets of regulations which have been partly lost, but whose contents are open to deduction, reflect the spiritual open-mindedness of Visigothic monasticism. Comprehensive knowledge of writing, including secular literature, was encouraged and the production of manuscripts was an important activity.[48] The monastic ideas were those of Augustine, Jerome and John Cassian. The religious terms in which monasticism saw itself were fairly conservative. Particularly appropriate here was the late antique *Pactum* of the *Regula Monachorum* (ch.22), in which every new monk had to proclaim the voluntary nature of his decision and his duty to fulfil the monastic statutes.

Monasticism in Ireland was one of the most influential religious phenomena of the early Middle Ages although details of its development are unknown.[49] In no other western church did such a transformation of monasticism take place. Here we can recognise the work of the great abbots of the sixth century such as Finian, Comgall, Brendan and Columcille (Columba). The foundations made by these men became the central point of Irish Christianity. Their monasteries at Clonard, Bangor, Clonmacnoise, Clonfert, Lismore, Moville and Kildare were supported by princes and kings. A monastery consisted of a group of separate buildings, which were surrounded by a wall. Links with the outside world were made by the abbot as the representative of the founding family. Each of these abbeys soon developed into a *paruchia*, a centre of pastoral care, which disrupted the structure of the diocese. The bishoprics thus had to adapt to monastic organisation and eventually became subordinate to it. The abbot became the leader of the *paruchia*, and one of the monks held the office of bishop. This splitting of jurisdiction and office was contrary to the traditional Christian order and remained an Irish peculiarity that must have been regarded as an anomaly on the continent.

Big monasteries with several daughter houses were at the centre of widespread associations, which in the church hierarchy corresponded to the metropolitan province. Kildare became the *urbs metropolitana* of Leinster, Armagh that of Ulster. The abbot was the *archiepiscopus*. Forming convents was difficult because of strong family ties, which often forced women to marry. So the model of double monasteries was developed in which the monks carried out the hard physical work and performed the holy services.[50] Rules did not play a major role in Irish monasticism. It was based mainly on the tradition of John Cassian, with greater emphasis on moral-ascetic instruction. More importance

48 Riché (1962), pp. 342–50. Orlandis (1991).

49 Hughes (1966), *passim*; Mayr-Harting (1977), pp. 78–85. See also Stancliffe, chapter 15 above.

50 Ewig in Jedin (1975), pp. 100–2; Angenendt (1990), pp. 205–8.

was placed on the effect of a living example. Boys lived with older monks in the same cell; they awoke, kept vigils and sang together. 'In such a way boys were initiated into the spiritual life.'[51] The *lectio divina* actually avoided pagan classics but the monks learnt the important elements of exegesis, grammar and *computus* (chronological calculation).

Early church history in England was also extensively influenced by monasticism.[52] The Irish influence predominated as it came to fruition through the political dominance of Christian Northumbria. Columcille (Columba), who had been a missionary among the Picts, became the father of monasticism in northern England with the foundation of his second monastery, Iona. From Iona a monastery was established on the North Sea island of Lindisfarne, which became a very important Irish-type monastery bishopric.

In the middle of the seventh century, under influence from Francia and Rome, an independent Anglo-Saxon monasticism began to develop which was particularly associated with Wilfrid of York and Benedict Biscop. At the Synod of Whitby in 664 Wilfrid overcame Irish monastic supremacy. The monasteries in Ripon and Hexham along with the new metropolitan see of York now replaced the old monastery on Lindisfarne as the centre of Roman observance. Lindisfarne itself became a Roman monastery. That this change did not affect the substance of Christianity, or rather of monasticism, is proven by the life of the celebrated monk Cuthbert (d. 687), who lived as an ascetic in the Irish fashion in the monasteries of Melrose and Ripon, and who then converted to the Roman movement without changing his attitudes or behaviour. At the same time the school in Canterbury was revived by the African abbot Hadrian and Theodore of Tarsus, who had been sent to England as archbishop by the pope. However the most important figure in English monasticism at this time was Benedict Biscop. This man, who had been educated at Lérins and who had travelled to Rome six times, in 674 founded the model monasteries of Monkwearmouth and Jarrow, which formed a joint community. The founder had drawn up a monastic order after visiting numerous continental monasteries. The library in his establishment was one of the most remarkable of the time, into which numerous literary treasures from Italy found their way. The possibilities such a place offered for monastic culture are shown by Bede's magnificent work. Another piece of evidence for the upturn of the English monastery schools in the late seventh century is the work of the monk and bishop Aldhelm (d. 709), who worked in the south. English monasteries became places of education much more than Irish ones did because, in contrast to the latter, they were not under the strain of the responsibility of pastoral care. Current research, however, makes it clear that they were not completely

[51] Mayr-Harting (1977), pp. 159–60. [52] See Thacker, chapter 17 above.

free from this. Smaller communities were able to take on pastoral duties more easily because they were hardly ever involved in cultural activity.[53]

A special development occurred in the Anglo-Saxon double monasteries which were mostly governed by abbesses.[54] Pure convents do not appear to have existed. The abbesses decided on the rules, the discipline in the monastery, prayer and work and eventually consecration and penance. In these organisations men and women could live together in a single monastic community or there could be two separate monasteries for men and women. Abbess Tetta of Wimbourne gave 'her commands to the monks through a window'[55] and did not let any men, neither cleric nor layman (on one occasion, not even a bishop), over the threshold. The most famous monastery of this type was Whitby (Streaneshalch), founded and governed by Hild (d. 680), a descendant of King Edwin of Northumbria and also related to the royal house of Kent.

The main areas of early monasticism in Gaul were the Rhône valley and Aquitaine.[56] The island monastery of Lérins remained prestigious in the sixth century because it had Caesarius of Arles as a pupil and promoter who, through his rules for nuns and monks, had an effect far to the north. The Frankish queens Radegund and Brunehild used these rules for their establishments in Poitiers and Autun. In his regulations Caesarius had linked traditions from Lérins with the principles of Augustine whom he respected highly. Besides those of Caesarius, other rules were introduced in the sixth and seventh centuries, such as the *Regula Tarnatensis* and the *Regula Fereoli* which were partly mixed with the rules of both Benedict and Columbanus (for instance in the Rule of Donatus of Besançon). In the centre and west of Gaul the Martinian tradition remained strong. This was eremitical in character and rejected rules of *stabilitas loci*. There were many random establishments that soon collapsed. A lack of discipline and organisational ability existed throughout the sixth century, and even the councils here looked for help. Under Frankish influence the monasteries were regarded more as 'professional communities of prayer', which were in many cases treated as places of family remembrance by their founders.[57]

A deciding factor in further development was the appearance in Francia of the Irishman Columbanus (d. 615) with his twelve companions in 590.[58] He linked a strict coenobitic monasticism with work for spiritual welfare. This combination compelled him to become part of the church in Francia, but on the other hand he remained within the Irish monastic tradition. For his

[53] Blair (1995), pp. 193–212; Cambridge and Rollason (1995), pp. 87–104.

[54] Hilpisch (1928), *passim*; Prinz (1988), pp. 658–83.

[55] Mayr-Harting (1977), pp. 151–2.

[56] Prinz (1988), pp. 19–117. On the situation before the baptism of Clovis, cf. Biarne (1997), pp. 115–26.

[57] Wallace-Hadrill (1983), pp. 60–1.

[58] Riché and Prinz in Clarke and Brennan (1981), pp. 59–87; Wallace-Hadrill (1983), pp. 63–74; Prinz (1988), pp. 121–51.

establishments in Burgundy (Annegray, Luxeuil and Fontaine), Columbanus wrote two sets of rules: the *Regula Monachorum* (a laying down of the basic principles of asceticism) and the *Regula Coenobialis* (an order for penance for transgressions in monastic life, in notebook form). Both works reflect the theory and practices of his home monastery in Bangor. Through the rather accidental link between asceticism and social impact, Columbanus introduced a new religious aspect into what was a rather materialistic Gallic Christianity. Columbanan monasticism had a great significance for the whole of Francia and no doubt Europe in the seventh century. Numerous foundations of the lay nobility modelled themselves on the example of Luxeuil in Burgundy. A novel element was the freedom that these monasteries had from episcopal control. Many bishops who came from the Columbanan school granted their own establishments this 'great freedom'. With this the bishop lost the right to correct the monastery's discipline, to appoint the abbots and of consecration. But neither monastic anarchy nor a change in the hierarchical structure came about as it had done in Ireland; rather the privileged abbey became subordinate to the pope. This peculiarity in Columbanan monasticism was respected in the Lombard kingdom, as can be seen from the privilege granted the monastery of Bobbio, and extended to Byzantine Italy.

CHAPTER 26

CHRISTIANISATION AND THE DISSEMINATION OF CHRISTIAN TEACHING

Ian Wood

The three centuries that followed the fall of the Western Roman Empire were in many respects seminal for the emergence of western Europe. In no area was this more true than in that of religion. By the early fifth century the Empire was theoretically Christian. That is not to deny the existence of pagans within its boundaries: there were many, and they were to be found at all levels of society. There were still pagan intellectuals among the upper classes, and there were also plenty of more ordinary folk – especially among the lower classes of the countryside, but also among those who lived in the cities, including Rome itself – who continued to perform rituals which were condemned as idolatrous by the church. Nevertheless, from the fourth century onwards Christianity was the religion of the emperor and of the state, and the church was well established. It had numerous places of worship, especially in the towns; it was endowed with vast estates and a considerable amount of revenue, and it had a hierarchy of officials. Its leading clergy legislated on doctrine and on Christian behaviour in numerous councils, and they were among the most influential figures within the Empire.

The barbarian invasions upset, but did not destroy, this state of affairs. In some peripheral areas the church suffered considerably. In Britain, after the Saxon invasions, its survival was confined largely to the west, although there were Christian communities further east, whose existence is chiefly attested by place-names, but can also be inferred from the survival of such cults as those of Alban and Sixtus.[1] In the provinces of Germania and Belgica some dioceses experienced considerable disruption: in one or two instances episcopal appointments appear not to have been kept up, and some ecclesiastical organisation may consequently have collapsed, only to be restored one or two centuries later in a period of growing pastoral enthusiasm. For the most part, however, the church survived, despite some loss of buildings and estates. Indeed

[1] Wood (2000).

the church and churchmen played a major role in the construction of the post-Roman world, helping to negotiate terms with the barbarians, and to preserve and transmit much of the administration and culture of the Empire to the so-called successor states.

Although the post-Roman period witnessed the expansion of Christianity in those rural communities which had remained pagan in imperial times, or which had drifted back into paganism following the barbarian settlements, it was above all the newcomers to what had been imperial territory who were subjected to the processes of Christianisation in the centuries which followed the fall of Rome. This is not to say that there was no spread of Christianity in this early period among barbarian peoples who did not cross into what had once been the Empire. Indeed the history of Christianity among the barbarians began long before there was any significant migration across the imperial frontiers. Most significantly there is evidence for Christian communities among the Tervingi, or Visigoths as they are known to most historians, who lived to the north of the Danube.[2] In all probability, Christianity was introduced to these people by captives taken during raids on Cappadocia in the 250s. In *c.*340 a party of Christian Goths visited Constantinople, where one of their number, Ulfila, was consecrated bishop by Eusebius of Nicomedia, politically the most influential cleric of his day. One result of this consecration was Ulfila's association with the doctrine traditionally labelled 'Arian', but more correctly called 'Homoean', which was favoured by Eusebius and by the then emperor, Constantius II. It was a doctrine which rejected the notion that the three persons in the Christian Trinity were 'of one substance' and, as propounded by the followers of Ulfila, emphasised the distinctions between Father, Son and Holy Ghost. Ulfila returned to the land of his birth, where he worked for seven years until persecution drove him to take refuge within the Empire, probably in 347/8. In addition to working as bishop among the Goths he embarked on the translation of the Bible, with the exception of the excessively warlike *Books of Kings*, into Gothic. In all likelihood this undertaking occupied him and others after his retreat to the Balkans. Christianity, meanwhile, survived among the Tervingi despite the persecution of the late 340s and another in 369/70, instigated by the Tervingian leader Athanaric.

In 376, six years after this second persecution, outside circumstances radically altered the position of Christianity in Gothic society. As a result of Hunnic attacks a group of the Tervingi, led by Fritigern, petitioned the emperor Valens to allow them to seek refuge within the Empire. It is probable that one condition put on them was the acceptance of Christianity, in its Homoean, or as its

[2] Heather and Matthews (1991).

detractors would have said 'Arian', form.[3] Ulfila himself may have been involved in the negotiations, but in any case the emperor Valens, like Constantius II before him, subscribed to Homoean doctrine. That Fritigern and his followers accepted a version of Christianity which was at loggerheads with what came to be established as Orthodoxy was a matter of great importance, for the Visigoths seem to have influenced other barbarian peoples in their choice of Christian doctrine.

The entry of the Visigoths into the Roman Empire in 376 and their defeat of the emperor Valens in 378 marked the beginning of a century of barbarian invasion and settlement. In 406 the Vandals, Alans and Sueves crossed the Rhine. By 411 the Burgundians under the leadership of Guntiarius were active in Gaul. During the following decade the Visigoths entered Spain. In the second half of the century the Ostrogoths moved into the Balkans, and then in 489, led by Theoderic the Great, they entered Italy. Eighty years later they were to be followed by the Lombards, the last of the great Germanic tribes to enter what had been the Empire. In time all these peoples came to be labelled as 'Arian'. Moreover, historians, ancient and modern, have ascribed their Arianism to Visigothic influence. Jordanes claimed that the Ostrogoths and the Gepids had been Christianised by their Visigothic neighbours.[4] Furthermore, Nicetius of Trier seems to have associated Lombard Arianism with Gothic influence.[5] On the other hand, it is by no means clear who converted the Vandals to Christianity;[6] indeed, influences other than Visigothic were noted even by contemporaries. Hydatius identified the Galatian bishop Ajax as an Arian missionary to the Sueves.[7] In fact the routes by which these peoples became Arians were widely divergent, and there is a danger of assigning too much importance directly to Visigothic influence.

There is even a danger of overemphasising the Arianism of these peoples. Writing in 417, or thereabouts, Orosius thought that the Burgundians were subject to Catholic, Roman, clergy. In viewing the Burgundians as Catholic, at least in the first half of the fifth century, Orosius also has the support of the Greek historian Socrates.[8] In the late sixth century, by contrast, Gregory of Tours regarded the Christian Burgundians as having been Arian until 516.[9] Certainly King Gundobad and some of his followers were Arian in the last decades of the fifth and first decade and a half of the sixth century. At the same time it is important to recognise the presence of Catholics within the Gibichung family and among its Burgundian supporters. In fact it is possible to accept

[3] Heather (1986). [4] Jordanes, *De Origine Actibusque Getarum*, 133.

[5] *Epistulae Austrasicae* 8, 11–14.

[6] Courtois (1955), p. 36, offers two possibilities; Thompson (1982), p. 157, merely identifies a period.

[7] Hydatius, *Chronicle*, 228, s.a. 465–6. [8] Wood (1990), pp. 58–61. [9] Gregory, *Hist.* II.9.

Orosius' claim that the Burgundians were first converted to Catholicism, and to see Gundobad as their one and only Arian ruler. His religious stance may well have been influenced by that of his Arian mentor and relative by marriage, Ricimer.

Just as Gregory's view of the Burgundians as Arians may be misleading, so too may be his insistence that the Franks moved directly from paganism to Catholic Christianity. The Franks first appear in our sources in the third century, by which time they were already settled in the region of the lower Rhine as immediate neighbours of the Romans. In the fourth century, as a people they provided a constant (but probably slight) threat to the Empire, while at the same time individual Franks served loyally in the imperial army. When the frontiers were breached in 406 the Franks were not among the invaders. Their move into what had been Roman territory was relatively slow and unadventurous. Under their king Clovis (481–511), however, they established a kingdom which ran from the Rhineland to Brittany, and which was soon to expand south into Aquitaine and then into Burgundy and Provence. It was Clovis also who led his people to Christianity. According to Gregory, the king's Burgundian wife, Chlothild, tried to convert him without success. A crisis in battle, however, led him to call on her God, and thereafter to discuss Christianity with the bishop of Rheims, before securing the approval of his people, and converting to Catholicism. The date, again according to Gregory, was 496.[10]

There may well be something in Gregory's emphasis on the part played by Chlothild, and in the notion of a wartime conversion. In other respects Gregory is arguably either wrong or misleading. A more plausible date for Clovis' decision to convert to Catholicism is 507, during a war against the Arian Visigoths, when he may well have been looking for support from the Catholic clergy of Gaul and from the emperor in Byzantium, whom he probably assumed – wrongly as it happens – to have been Orthodox. His baptism may well have followed a year later.[11] More important than the question of the date, however, is the evidence that the Frankish leadership did not pass directly from paganism to Catholicism. Although Clovis had been subjected to the advice of Catholic bishops from the start of his reign,[12] a letter written at the time of his baptism is explicit in saying that he had long been influenced by heretics,[13] and his sister Lenteildis is known to have converted to Arianism in the first instance.[14] Clearly Arians had been influential at the Frankish court, and the standard image of the Franks as the one people uncontaminated by heresy

[10] Gregory, *Hist.* II.29–31. [11] Shanzer (1998).

[12] *Epistulae Austrasacae* 2: Wallace-Hadrill (1962), pp. 166–7.

[13] Avitus of Vienne, *Epistola* 46: Shanzer (1998), pp. 31–7. [14] Gregory, *Hist.* II.31.

in their move to Christianity emerges as nothing more than sixth-century propaganda.

Nor are the Burgundians and the Franks the only peoples for whom Christianisation entailed hesitation between Arianism and Catholicism. The same is true of the Sueves in Spain, who switched from Catholic to Arian belief in the course of the fifth century, probably under pressure from their Visigothic neighbours.[15] The Lombards changed doctrine yet more often and for a longer period of time than any other people.[16] Identified as Catholic in 548,[17] they were certainly Arian two decades later. Although Arian himself, King Agilulf (590–616) had a Catholic wife and son Adaloald (616–626), who was deposed in favour of the Arian Arioald (626–636). Such variation continued for much of the seventh century. These shifts between Arianism and Catholicism at court do not seem to indicate extreme hostility between the adherents of the two doctrines, despite the deposition of Adaloald. According to the Catholic Paul the Deacon, John the Baptist himself warned a thief against stealing from the tomb of Rothari (636–652), even though the king had been an Arian.[18] The doctrinal choices of the Lombards may have been influenced less by religious commitment than by political factors, in particular relations with Rome and the threat posed at any given moment by the Byzantines in Italy.

By the end of the sixth century the majority of those barbarian tribes which had established themselves in the territories of the Roman Empire had accepted Christianity: most, indeed, had become Catholic. Even the Visigoths had abandoned Arianism in 589.[19] Some tribes who had remained on or beyond the borders of the old Empire had also been Christianised. The *Rugi* of the Austrian Waldviertel north of the Danube were certainly Arian before the end of the fifth century.[20] Further to the north the Thuringian royal family may have become Catholic as early as the Merovingians. The Thuringian princess Radegund, who was to become a monastic founder and a saint in the Frankish kingdom, is not said to have had to convert from paganism or from Arianism to Catholicism.[21] Christianity, even Catholic Christianity, may therefore have spread across the Rhine by the time of the Frankish conquest of Thuringia in 531.

The one group of peoples who did not accept Christianity shortly after, or even before, entering what had once been imperial territory were the Anglo-Saxons. Nevertheless, by the 590s missionaries were being sought from neighbouring Christian peoples by someone within the kingdom of Kent. Requests

[15] On Suevic Chistianity, Thompson (1982), pp. 196–7, 203–6, and see also Barbero and Loring, chapter 7 above.

[16] Christie (1995), pp. 183–90.

[17] Procopius, *Wars* VII.34.24.

[18] Paul the Deacon, *HL* IV.47.

[19] Collins (1983), pp. 53–8.

[20] Eugippius, *Vita Severini* V.I.

[21] For her *Vitae*, ed. B. Krusch, *MGH SRM* II (Hanover, 1888).

for religious help seem to have elicited no response from either the British or the Franks, but news of the Kentish appeal reached Gregory the Great.[22] Who was behind this local desire to Christianise the people of Kent is nowhere stated, although one may suspect the involvement of members of the court of king Æthelberht, who may only have come to the throne after 590. During his father's reign Æthelberht had married a Christian Frankish princess, Bertha, and she had come over with a Christian entourage, which included a bishop, Liudhard.[23] It is likely that the queen and her household had some impact on Æthelberht and his court, although Bede does not say so, and despite a letter of Gregory which may imply that Bertha could have done more to promote the faith.[24] It is even possible that Æthelberht himself was converted to his wife's religion before any Christian mission arrived in his country, again despite the main thrust of Bede's narrative.[25] What is certain is that Gregory the Great responded to the news that missionaries were needed. Mission to the heathen was a cause that was very dear to him, and he consequently sent Augustine, together with a number of monks, to supervise the Christianisation of Kent.[26] In addition Gregory and Augustine between them galvanised the Franks into supporting the mission: Merovingian kings and clergy were to continue to show an interest in the Christianisation of the English for some decades. The British, by contrast, were to remain aloof from missionary activity, at least in the south-east of Britain, despite the fact that they appear to have been in close contact with Augustine.[27] Further west, however, they may have been more active.[28]

Augustine's mission to Kent was a success, and Æthelberht's prestige in England meant that Essex and East Anglia also accepted Christianity. Politics would play a major role in the ensuing Christianisation of the English, with powerful rulers putting pressure on their weaker neighbours, sponsoring them in baptism, and supporting missions to their kingdoms.[29] In many respects the Christianisation of the English, at least as presented by Bede, is a classic example of Christianisation from the top down. This association of religion with a monarch, however, had its drawbacks. On Æthelberht's death there was a temporary pagan reaction in Kent and a longer-lasting one in Essex.[30] In East Anglia the court seems to have indulged in a period of religious syncretism under King Redwald. Nevertheless Edwin, a protégé of Redwald, by whom he had been assisted to the throne of the Northumbrian kingdom, promoted Christianity in the north following his marriage to a Christian daughter of Æthelberht. Again, however, the fate of Christianity was linked to that of

22 Wood (1994b). 23 Bede, *HE* I.24. 24 Gregory the Great, *Register* XI.35.
25 Wood (1994b), pp. 10–11. 26 Markus (1997), pp. 177–87.
27 This, at least, is the implication of Meens (1994). 28 Sims-Williams (1990), pp. 78–84.
29 Angenendt (1986). See also Thacker, chapter 17 above. 30 Bede, *HE* II.5.

the king, and the death of Edwin in battle in 633 was followed by a pagan reaction, which was only reversed with the establishment of a new Christian king, Oswald, who had been converted by the Irish while in exile. As a result, in addition to Romans and Franks being involved in the Christianisation of the English, the Irish came to play a part as well.

Although Ireland had never been part of the Roman Empire, Christianity spread across the Irish Sea at a surprisingly early date. Already in 431 Pope Celestine had sent Palladius as bishop to the Irish 'believing in Christ'.[31] The establishment of Christianity amongst the Irish before Palladius' arrival was probably dependent on trading contacts. There were also Christians, like Patrick, who had been taken as slaves from Britain. The duration and impact of Palladius' mission cannot be assessed because of a lack of evidence. Patrick's work as an evangelist is much better attested, but the only reliable accounts are those of Patrick's own writings.[32] Here we learn of his capture by Irish raiders while he was yet a boy, his enslavement and escape, and his subsequent return to Ireland to work as a missionary. His dealings with Irish kings, with a hostile clergy back in Britain, and with a British pirate who killed and captured some of his converts, are also touched on, albeit less clearly than modern historians would have wished. Patrick himself provides no dates and no unambiguous indication of the geography of his mission. He was almost certainly active in the second half of the fifth century, and in the north-east of Ireland. There seems good reason for thinking that he was buried at Downpatrick.[33] It is, however, impossible to correlate Patrick's own writings with the propaganda put out by the clergy of Armagh from the seventh century onwards. Indeed, it is difficult to see how the early work of Palladius and Patrick developed into the churches that were well established in Ireland by the mid-sixth century. By that time a major monastic tradition had been established. One of its leading figures was Columba, who founded the island monastery of Iona, off the Scottish coast, in 563,[34] and it was to this monastery that Oswald turned for help in the reinstitution of Christianity in Northumbria in *c.*636.[35]

It was not only among the Anglo-Saxons that the Irish were active. In the early 590s the monk Columbanus left Ireland for the Frankish kingdom, where he established several monasteries, of which the most notable was Luxeuil. Driven out of Burgundy in 610 he made his way first to Bregenz and then to Bobbio, in Italy.[36] Although Columbanus' own contribution to the history of mission is easily exaggerated, the same is not true of that of his pupils. Among his direct disciples, Eustasius, his successor as abbot of Luxeuil, was responsible

31 Prosper, *Chronicle* s.a. 431: Charles-Edwards (1993). On the Christianisation of Ireland, see further Stancliffe, chapter 15 above.

32 Ed. Howlett (1994).

33 Dumville (1993), pp. 184–5.

34 *Annals of Ulster* s.a. 563 (4).

35 Bede, *HE* III.3.

36 For the chronology, Wood (1998), p. 105.

for undertaking and organising missions to the Bavarians.[37] Equally important were a number of leading clerics who were influenced by Luxeuil in the days of Eustasius and his successor Waldebert. Among these were bishops, including Eligius of Noyon, active in the restoration of the church in the north-east of the Frankish kingdom. There were others who involved themselves in the missions in Anglo-Saxon England.[38] Above all there was Amandus, who played a major pastoral role in promoting Christianity in what is now Belgium, but who also worked among the Basques and the Slavs. Influenced by the traditions of Luxeuil, and also, it seems, by the ideas of Gregory the Great, Amandus was perhaps the first missionary in the West to formulate a notion of universal mission.[39]

As a result of the work carried out by those influenced by Luxeuil, the north-east of the Merovingian kingdom was evangelised in greater depth than had earlier been the case, and the territories east of the Rhine were also subject to a considerable degree of Christian influence. Christianity seems to have survived since Roman times in Augsburg.[40] Yet in other parts of Bavaria the evidence for a Christian church is poor – and the references to Eustasius' missions are sadly imprecise. By the end of the seventh century, however, Emmeram, who had intended to work among the Slavs, had established a church at Regensburg. Nor does he appear to have been the first to do so.[41] Further north Kilian was active at Würzburg before 689, when he was martyred as a result of a conflict over marital practices within the local ruling family.[42] Some degree of evangelisation, therefore, had been achieved in Bavaria, as in Thuringia, before the end of the seventh century. To judge by the linguistic evidence, it had been effected largely by Franks.[43]

Work had also begun in Frisia. Here it was the Anglo-Saxons who seem to have led the way. The Northumbrian bishop Wilfrid spent some time preaching there in 678.[44] In the following decades other Anglo-Saxons also worked as missionaries in the region of the lower Rhine. Some of these were the pupils of the Northumbrian Ecgberht, who was himself ensconced in Ireland.[45] The most important of Ecgberht's pupils was Willibrord.[46] He too came from Northumbria. Indeed, before joining Ecgberht he had been a monk of Wilfrid's monastery of Ripon. He arrived in Frisia in 690, and was established, with backing from the Arnulfing leader Pippin II, in Utrecht in 696. He continued

[37] Jonas of Bobbio, *Vita Columbani* II.8.
[38] Campbell (1986), pp. 49–67; Wood (1991a), pp. 8–9.
[39] Fritze (1969), pp. 78–130; Wallace-Hadrill (1983), pp. 72–3.
[40] Wolfram (1987), pp. 115–16. [41] Arbeo of Freising, *Vita Haimhrammi.*
[42] *Passio Sanctorum Martyrum Kiliani et Sociorum Eius.*
[43] Green (1998a), pp. 325–40, and (1998b), pp. 343–61.
[44] Eddius Stephanus, *Vita Wilfridi* c.26. [45] Bede, *HE* v.9. [46] Bede, *HE* v.10–11.

to work among the Frisians until his death in 739, although his mission was interrupted by periods of war between the Franks and the Frisians, when he had to retire to his monastery of Echternach on a tributary of the River Moselle. In 716 he was joined by Wynfrith. The time, however, was one of war, and Wynfrith returned to Wessex. Three years later he went to Rome, where he received the name Boniface. Charged by Pope Gregory II with reporting on religion in Germany, he returned to help Willibrord, which he did until 722, after which he turned to work in Hesse, Thuringia and even Bavaria. It was not until 754 that he moved back to Frisia, only to be martyred at Dokkum.[47] The further reaches of the region were still pagan.

Boniface's avowed intention was to evangelise *Germani*, most particularly the continental Saxons. In fact this was not to be his achievement. Despite a brief flurry of expectation after Charles Martel defeated the Saxons in 738, no Saxon mission materialised in the first half of the century. Work among the pagans in Frisia took scarcely four years of Boniface's long continental career. Certainly there were pagans in Hesse and Thuringia: notably those for whom the oak at Geismar was a sacred object.[48] Nevertheless Boniface's energies were devoted more to stamping on some bizarre forms of Christianity that had developed in the aftermath of earlier missionary work, to establishing a system of ecclesiastical organisation and to promoting monasticism east of the Rhine. The greatest of his monastic foundations, Fulda, was to receive his body after his martyrdom. Like other monastic houses, such as Luxeuil, Echternach and Corvey, it was at times a point of departure for mission, and a place of rest for missionaries. It was also, and perhaps rather more significantly, to be one of the major centres of learning in the ninth century.

The earliest *Life of Boniface* was probably written at Mainz, where the saint had been bishop. Mainz and Fulda were central in the propagation of the cult of Boniface, but they were not alone. A second Life of the saint was written at Utrecht, possibly in the early ninth century.[49] Boniface also plays a central role in the *Life of Gregory of Utrecht*, written by Liudger, probably between 800 and 809.[50] This text portrays the Anglo-Saxon, inaccurately, as a great missionary saint who spent over eleven years in Frisia. It also presents Gregory as one of the dearest of Boniface's pupils: not an impression to be gleaned from Boniface's own letters. However close Gregory and Boniface may or may not have been, the former does seem to have been a significant patron of missionaries working in Frisia and northern Germany. Gregory's biographer and pupil, Liudger, was active in Frisia and also in the region around Münster, where he established a

[47] Willibald, *Vita Bonifatii c.*8. [48] Willibald, *Vita Bonifatii c.*6.
[49] *Vita (Altera) Bonifatii.* [50] Liudger, *Vita Gregorii.*

see.[51] At much the same time the Northumbrian Willehad undertook missionary work, first in Frisia, and subsequently in the district around Bremen, where he too founded a diocese.[52] Another of Gregory's pupils, Lebuin, preached in Saxony.[53] His attempts to spread Christianity by peaceful means were ultimately overtaken by forcible Christianisation, which went hand in hand with Charlemagne's conquest of the area.

The eighth and early ninth centuries, therefore, saw the creation of a church organisation in northern Germany. In the ninth century the missionary field was extended to Scandinavia. Willibrord had already visited Denmark,[54] and Liudger had wanted to do so, but had been prevented by Charlemagne.[55] In the 820s a Scandinavian mission was set up within the context of the diplomatic involvement of Louis the Pious in the kingdom of Denmark. Ebbo, bishop of Rheims, initiated the work of evangelisation, which was continued, and extended to Sweden, by Anskar.[56] The latter achieved considerable, temporary, success among both the Danes and the Swedes, despite occasional setbacks, like the destruction of his German base of Hamburg by Vikings in 845. Rimbert, his successor in the combined diocese of Hamburg-Bremen, initially continued his work, but the escalation of Viking activity brought the Scandinavian mission to a halt. The work of Anskar and Rimbert was a natural development of the evangelisation of northern Germany. Anskar himself may well have been the author of an account of the miracles of Willehad.[57] The collapse of the Scandinavian mission, therefore, marked the end of a continuous history of evangelisation, which stretched back into the seventh century and beyond.

Despite the continuity within the process of evangelisation, its history has to be reconstructed from a variety of sources. Of these, few are concerned to present a historical account of mission. The Lives of saints provide invaluable evidence on the activities of specific individuals, but they are, nevertheless, works of hagiography with particular spiritual, pastoral and devotional concerns. They rarely have any interest in setting the careers of their subjects within a wider history of evangelisation. Here the Lives of Gregory of Utrecht, Liudger and Lebuin are exceptional. Unique is the sustained account of the Christianisation of Anglo-Saxons to be found in Bede's *Ecclesiastical History*. No other historian of the early Middle Ages concerned himself so directly with the evangelisation of a whole people, not even Gregory of Tours, despite the importance of Clovis' conversion to his interpretation of the rise of the Merovingians. In some ways as remarkable as Bede's work, however, is the *Conversio Bagoariorum et Carantanorum*, a relatively short, but invaluable, account of the establishment

[51] Altfrid, *Vita Liudgeri*. [52] *Vita Willehadi*. [53] *Vita Lebuini Antiqua*.
[54] Alcuin, *Vita Willibrordi c.9*. [55] Altfrid, *Vita Liudgeri* 1.30.
[56] Rimbert, *Vita Anskarii*. [57] Anskar, *Miracula Willehadi*.

of the church in Bavaria and Carinthia, written at Salzburg in 871.[58] The next work to rival Bede's would be the late eleventh-century *History of the Bishops of Hamburg*, by Adam of Bremen.

The various sources for the early Middle Ages do allow the construction of a narrative of the Christianisation of the barbarians,[59] but as the above cases suggest, it is nevertheless important to recognise their differing and, sometimes, conflicting aims. For instance, Orosius' reference to the churches of East and West being filled with Huns, Sueves, Vandals and Burgundians may provide an indication of the spread of Orthodox Christianity among those peoples before 417, but it may equally be no more than an over-optimistic assertion made by the author in support of his theme, that times were not as bad as the pagan Romans were insisting. Equally, Gregory of Tours' accounts of Visigothic and Burgundian Arianism and of Frankish Catholicism are almost certainly determined by his view of the Franks as a 'chosen people', whose success was related to their orthodoxy and God's favour. So too Bede's emphasis on the Augustinian mission, and the absence of any comment on the involvement of Bertha and Liudhard, may reflect a concern to associate the origins of the Kentish church exclusively with the papacy.

Such bias is also present in the saints' Lives.[60] Sometimes they lead to totally fraudulent assertions. Thus, the Life of the seventh-century saint Wulfram of Sens made him the leading figure in the evangelisation of Frisia during the lifetime of the pagan ruler Radbod.[61] Unfortunately the account presented is chronologically impossible. In all probability the author, although writing about a bishop who really did undertake mission,[62] altered events in an attempt to challenge the reputation of Willibrord, whose Life Alcuin had written only a short time before.[63] Equally impossible is Liudger's account of Boniface's mission to Frisia, which is extended from three to thirteen years in the *Life of Gregory of Utrecht*. Here the author seems to have been intent on providing Bonifacian origins for churches at Woerden, Achttienhoven and Velzen, and on creating a model for missionary activity sanctioned by its association with Boniface.

Other, more political bias may be involved elsewhere. In his account of Boniface's work in Thuringia, Willibald attributes the poor state of the church there to Theobald and Heden, whose unpopular rule had led many to become subject to the Saxons, while enthusiasm for Christianity had waned and heresy had flourished.[64] On the other hand, Heden is also known as one of the benefactors of Willibrord's monastery of Echternach,[65] which suggests that

58 *Conversio Bagoariorum et Carantanorum.*

59 For detailed accounts, Brown (1996); Fletcher (1997).

60 Wood (1999a). 61 *Vita Vulframni.* 62 Lebecq (1994). 63 Wood (1991b), pp. 12–14.

64 Willibald, *Vita Bonifatii* c.6. 65 Wampach (1930), nn. 8, 26.

there is something odd about Willibald's insinuations against him. These may be explained by the fact that Heden rebelled against the Carolingians and was consequently driven out of Thuringia.[66] Both secular and religious politics may have weighed upon Willibald. As a result his account of Boniface's activity east of the Rhine may have led to an underestimation of the achievements of earlier generations of missionaries, achievements that are only attested in the linguistic evidence.[67]

More complex issues seem to underlie other problems presented by Willibald's narrative. For instance the *Life of Boniface* depicts its subject as the founder of four dioceses in Bavaria, but he names only three, Salzburg, Freising and Regensburg.[68] The fourth diocese, Passau, he could not name because its bishop, Vivilo, had already been appointed by Pope Gregory III. Moreover, of the three that he does name, not one was actually founded by Boniface. There had been a bishop of Salzburg in the late seventh century,[69] as there had been of Regensburg, and of Freising, where Corbinian had been established a generation earlier.[70] The evidence for Regensburg and Freising is contained in two *Lives* written by Arbeo; those of Emmeram and Corbinian. Both date to the period shortly after Willibald's composition of the *Life of Boniface*. They suggest that claims and counterclaims over the church in Bavaria were being made by different ecclesiastical groups. Despite the high regard in which Willibald's work is held, indications that the cults of Emmeram and Corbinian were established before 739 suggest that the general tenor, if not the detail, of Arbeo's account of the Bavarian church has much to commend it.[71]

Other sources present similar problems. All hagiographical texts were composed for specific reasons. Some were written to promote the cult of the saint, others to set out particular jurisdictional claims, or to propagate a specific monastic ideology or theological position.[72] Alcuin's *Life of Willibrord* is, in many respects, disappointing as a narrative, because it is constructed not to recount history, but in order to present a precisely balanced model of a missionary saint as both evangelist and wonderworker. It is only rarely that the aims of the hagiographer and the requirements of the student of Christianisation exactly coincide. The narrative evidence for the history of mission, therefore, needs to be treated with considerable caution.

Despite all the caveats, the basic narrative of the history of Christianisation in the early Middle Ages is clear enough,[73] although it should be recognised that concern for the narrative tends to emphasise top-down patterns

66 *Passio Kiliani* c.14. 67 Green (1998a), pp. 325–40, and (1998b).

68 Willibald, *Vita Bonifatii* c.7. 69 *Vita Hrodberti*: Wolfram (1987), pp. 118–24.

70 Arbeo of Freising, *Vita Corbiniani*; Wolfram (1987), p. 125.

71 Wood (1994a), pp. 307–9. 72 Wood (1999b). 73 See Brown (1996); Fletcher (1997).

of evangelisation, since it is kings and dukes who most attract the attention of our written sources. The less dramatic work of minor missionaries usually goes unrecorded – although the outcome of such work, at least, is detectable east of the Rhine and in western England. It is almost as difficult to establish what people were converting from, what they were being converted to, and how this was being achieved. Nevertheless these are all questions that deserve consideration.

There were probably distinctions between the paganism that continued to exist among the indigenous population of the Roman Empire, and that followed by the barbarians, but there may also have been similarities. There were certainly features common to paganism and the semi-Christian and heretical practices which were also the target of some missionaries. Indeed, there is considerable difficulty in differentiating between the religious practices of various pagan groups and semi-Christians.[74] Evidence for the worship of gods of the Germanic pantheon in the late and post-Roman period is slight. In a letter to Boniface, Daniel bishop of Winchester talks of gods and goddesses, without naming them.[75] Thor (Donar), Woden and Saxnot are denounced specifically in *formulae* for the renunciation of paganism,[76] and later Woden appears in Old English charms.[77] There are also denunciations of Jupiter, who was equated with Thor, Mars equated with Saxnot and Mercury with Woden.[78] The oak at Geismar in Hesse, which was cut down by Boniface, is said to have been known as the oak of Jupiter;[79] in other words it was probably dedicated to Thor. Further indications of pagan Germanic cults can be found in the association of individual gods with specific days of the week: Tiw with Tuesday, Woden with Wednesday, Thor with Thursday and Frija with Friday[80] – the equivalent days in the Roman calendar were associated with Luna, Mercury, Jupiter and Venus. Place-names also sometimes indicate a site associated with a particular Germanic god and there are artefacts which may carry iconography alluding to individual deities. It has been suggested that the so-called bracteates, which are found in some quantities in north Germany, may be connected with the cult of Woden.[81] When all is said and done, however, such interpretations are no more than hypotheses, and in any case the evidence cannot be taken as proof that devotion to these particular deities dominated the religion of those tribes

[74] *Indiculus Superstitionum et Paganiarum.* [75] Boniface, *Ep.* 23.

[76] Ed. Boretius (1883), p. 222. [77] Mayr-Harting (1972), pp. 26–7.

[78] E.g. *Indiculus Superstitionum et Paganiarum*, ed. Boretius, pp. 222–3. On the *interpretatio Romana*, see Wood (1995), p. 54. But see Wallace-Hadrill (1983), pp. 18–19, for the possibility that some Franks may have worshipped Roman gods.

[79] Willibald, *Vita Bonifatii, c.6.* [80] E.g. Mayr-Harting (1972), p. 25.

[81] Hauck (1957), pp. 361–401. See also the comments of Axboe (1995), pp. 231–2.

which entered the Roman Empire in the fourth, fifth and sixth centuries, or of all those which remained in Germany.

There are numerous references to shrines or idols that are not explicitly linked to the gods of the Germanic pantheon.[82] Bede does not name the devils to whom Redwald supposedly offered sacrifice,[83] nor the gods culted at the temple at Goodmanham which was desecrated by its own priest, Coifi.[84] References to the idol and sanctuary of the Irminsul, destroyed by Charlemagne in 772, do not specify which god was worshipped there.[85] Idols and shrines seem to have been common in Frisia, although the details of which cult was involved are rarely provided by hagiographers: at times one may suspect that of Nehalennia, which is attested in the Roman period. The sacred place most fully described in an eighth-century source is the island dedicated to the god Fosite, probably Heligoland.[86] According to Alcuin, no pagan dared to touch the animals on the island or to drink from the spring. Willibrord, by contrast, used the spring to perform baptisms.[87] The same site was later visited by Liudger, who also baptised there. His biographer adds to Alcuin's description of the island a temple, which was destroyed by the saint.[88] The impression is one of a cult site devoted to a god of localised importance, Fosite, but located on a major seaway. Whether or not the shrine had a priest, like Coifi at Goodmanham, or even a group of priests is nowhere stated – though outside England there is little evidence for Germanic priests.[89] Down the coast at Walcheren, Alcuin does record the existence of the guardian of an idol[90] who tried, unsuccessfully, to kill Willibrord.

On the whole it is not the cults of major gods, their shrines or their acolytes which constitute the paganism denounced in contemporary sources. They existed, but they do not appear to have been the chief problem facing the missionaries of the early Middle Ages. Commitment to them was apparently limited, perhaps to certain groups or classes, and they could be abandoned with relative ease. Much more prominent in the sources, and probably more tenacious, is the threat of superstition or magic.[91] Describing this there are a number of works, in particular the *De Correctione Rusticorum*, written by Martin of Braga in the north-west of the Iberian peninsula shortly after 572,[92] two sermons attributed to the seventh-century bishop Eligius of Noyon,[93] and the *Scarapsus de Libris Singulis Canonicis*, compiled by Pirmin, a monastic founder and reformer in the Luxeuil tradition, active in southern Germany

82 Wood (1995), pp. 255–7. 83 Bede, *HE* II.15. 84 Bede, *HE* II.13.
85 Wood (1995), pp. 255–7. 86 Wood (1995), pp. 255–60. 87 Alcuin, *Vita Willibrordi*, 10.
88 Altfrid, *Vita Liudgeri* I.19, 22. 89 Wood (1995), pp. 257–9. 90 Alcuin, *Vita Willibrordi* c.14.
91 Flint (1991). 92 Martin of Braga, *De Correctione Rusticorum*.
93 *Praedicatio Sancti Eligii*; see also the comments of Hen (1995), p. 197.

during the first half of the eighth century.[94] Despite their importance, these three works present the historian with problems of interpretation. The Eligius sermons and the *Scarapsus* of Pirmin both draw heavily on the work of Martin of Braga, which in turn is heavily indebted to Augustine of Hippo and Caesarius of Arles, whose writings also had a direct influence on the seventh-century sermons.[95] Thus condemnations of paganism in fifth-century North Africa and sixth-century Provence, both heavily Romanised areas, are reused in sixth-century rural Galicia and seventh-century north-eastern Gaul, both of which had been within the Roman Empire, but which had been less influenced by Roman culture and had been settled by barbarian invaders. These same condemnations are also reused in eighth-century Alamania. There is an acute difficulty in determining how far there were superstitions common to all these areas, and how far the content of these works was determined merely by literary tradition. The dependence of Martin of Braga, the Eligius sermons and Pirmin on earlier authors is unquestionable – and the problem of mistaking a literary borrowing for a description of current practices is, therefore, considerable. At the same time, there is enough evidence, both written and archaeological, to show that the sorts of practices they name, even if not the specific ones originally condemned by Augustine and Caesarius, were common across western Europe in the early Middle Ages.

One of the fullest lists of superstitions compiled in the early medieval period is the *Indiculus Superstitionum et Paganiarum*. It was apparently prepared in 743/4. In these years Boniface called three church councils, one known as the *Concilium Germanicum* (743), the others held at Estinnes (744) and Soissons (744) respectively.[96] The clear parallels between the canons of the *Concilium Germanicum* and the *Indiculus* suggest that the latter was drawn up as part of this conciliar activity. Unfortunately the *Indiculus* is cursory in the extreme, providing no more than a list of superstitions, without any attempt to describe them. Most of them, however, can be identified with practices known from other sources. Only one, the *cursus* called *yrias*, is otherwise unattested, while only one other, *de petendo* (or possibly *petenstro*) *quod boni vocant Sanctae Mariae*, has proved impossible to interpret with any degree of certainty.

Two of the thirty entries in the *Indiculus* indicate the cult of Mercury and Jupiter, presumably Woden and Thor, and their feast days. Others refer to idols made of dough and rags, and idols carried through fields. Sanctuaries and holy places including springs as well as rites performed in woods are listed, as are wooden hands and feet used in pagan rites. The celebration of the *spurcalia* in February is mentioned, and so too are actions performed on stones. *Nodfyr*, or

94 Pirmin, *Dicta de Singulis Libris Canonicis* (*Scarapsus*). On Pirmin see Angenendt (1972).

95 Boudriot (1928). 96 Ed. Werminghoff (1906–8).

fire produced by rubbing sticks together, appears, as do incantations. All these may suggest formal cults of one sort or another and there were clearly also rituals associated with the dead. The first two titles are directed at sacrilege committed at the graveside whilst other headings deal with everyday superstition. Amulets are on the list, as are furrows dug around *villae*, presumably to ward off evil. The moon is twice a matter of concern, in eclipse and because some thought that women could eat it, as they could the hearts of men. An entry on storms, horns and snails also suggests superstition. Auguries are the subject of four titles, including one relating to the brains of animals and another to the inspection of the fire on the hearth. The remaining three entries refer to practices that are semi-Christian: sacrilege in church, sacrifice offered to saints and the belief that all the dead were saints.

Despite the references to Woden and Thor, the weight of the document is concerned with natural religion, with auguries, with superstition and with the dead. This natural religion is equally apparent from the archaeological record. Offerings at springs are known. There is evidence for funerary banquets in cemeteries, and some graves include the bones of birds associated with divination.[97] It seems to have been practices by which man defined his relations with nature and with the dead that formed the bulk of the superstitions, and not the organised cult of gods of the Germanic pantheon, which confronted the missionary in the sixth, seventh and eighth centuries.[98] Superstitions of this type may well have been common across much of western Europe, both within and without what had once been the territory of the Roman Empire. It is also clear that some of these practices were still observed by Christian communities. The need to enforce higher standards on the church east and west of the Rhine, which was the dominant feature of Boniface's career however much he wished to follow a life of mission to the pagans, is apparent from the *Indiculus*, which, so far as can be ascertained, is a description of religion to be found within a Christian state.

For the paganism beyond the immediate confines of the Merovingian and early Carolingian state, it is the evidence for Frisia that is most illuminating. The *Life of Liudger* provides information on the workings of pagan society in addition to that on the island of Fosite. Much of this is admittedly very generalised: the comment on the temple of Fosite apart, references to shrines are only made in passing. The work begins, however, with a long and detailed account of Liudger's family.[99] The saint's grandmother was a formidable pagan: when her daughter-in-law gave birth only to daughters, the old lady ordered that the infant Liafburg should be drowned. The child was saved only because it survived for long enough to be given honey by compassionate neighbours.

97 Salin (1959), pp. 35–9. 98 Wood (1995). 99 Altfrid, *Vita Liudgeri* 1.1–7.

It was not legal to kill a child that had tasted food. Although this story is not, technically, concerned with sacrifice, but rather with child-exposure, the social traditions involved overlap with descriptions of sacrificial practices in Frisia. In particular the *Life of Wulfram of Sens* refers to drowning as a standard method of sacrifice,[100] suggesting that water played a very prominent role in Frisian religion, which is not surprising given the geography of the region.

The *Life of Wulfram* is potentially as important a text as that of Liudger in providing evidence on Frisian paganism. It is, however, a forgery from *c.*800. Not only is it a forgery in the sense that it claims to have been written shortly after the saint's death, which occurred in the 690s; it is also suspect in that much of its narrative is palpably untrue.[101] On the other hand Wulfram was, unquestionably, a missionary bishop, and it is likely that the author of his *Life* worked from genuine information about him.[102] Moreover, the monks of St Wandrille, where the *Life* was composed, could have had other sources of information about Frisian paganism. Abbot Wando had been in exile in Maastricht between 719 and 747.[103] He could well have been in contact with Willibrord, and may have brought information on the Frisian mission back to his own monastery. Thus, although its narrative is a farrago of lies, the *Life of Wulfram* may on occasion present an accurate picture of pagan practice. Where the picture that it presents overlaps with that to be found in other sources, they may be used in conjunction.

Victims condemned to death by ritual drowning in the *Life of Wulfram* had been chosen by lot.[104] The casting of lots seems to have been integral to Frisian paganism. According to Alcuin, when Willibrord desecrated the island of Fosite, the king, presumably Radbod, cast lots to determine what punishment, if any, should be meted out. As a result one of Willibrord's companions was martyred.[105] The importance of the casting of lots within Frisian society is further confirmed by its survival into the Christian period. In the *Lex Frisionum* of the early ninth century a Christianised version of the casting of lots is used in the identification of murderers.[106] Lot casting was not confined to Frisia: it seems to have been common in parts of western Europe and in Scandinavia, where it is attested in the ninth century.[107] It apparently played a significant part in Frisian religious practice.

The *Life of Wulfram* is otherwise most interesting where it is most suspect: in the saint's dealings with Radbod. Since Wulfram died long before Radbod, the stories relating to the attempts to convert the king and to save him from damnation cannot be accepted at face value.[108] Even so there are elements in

100 *Vita Vulframni cc.*6–8. 101 Wood (1991b), pp. 12–14. 102 Lebecq (1994).
103 Wood (1991b), pp. 12–14. 104 *Vita Vulframni cc.*6–8. 105 Alcuin, *Vita Willibrordi, c.*11.
106 *Lex Frisionum* 14. 107 Rimbert, *Vita Anskarii cc.*18, 19, 24, 26, 27, 30; Wood (1995), p. 260.
108 But see Lebecq (1994).

the stories which tally with other information. Thus, according to the *Life of Wulfram*, Radbod was so nearly baptised that he actually had one foot in the font, but he withdrew when he learnt that by receiving baptism he would be separating himself from his unbaptised forebears, who would remain in hell while he was in heaven.[109] Concern for one's ancestors may not be stated so explicitly elsewhere, but Avitus of Vienne, in his letter congratulating Clovis on his baptism, made much of the king's breach with his forebears.[110] The issue may well have been one of substance for the potential convert.

Having withdrawn from the font, Radbod, according to the *Life of Wulfram*, was visited by the Devil, who urged him to return to the cult of the gods, promising him a heavenly mansion. A beautiful house appeared in due course, only to vanish at the sign of the cross, but Radbod himself had been tricked, and died a pagan.[111] The story of Radbod's death, as presented by the hagiographer, is certainly a work of fiction, but it may contain a reference to a pagan tradition of an afterlife. Norse mythology obviously provides an analogue with Valhalla, and the presence of grave-goods in cemeteries may suggest that the afterlife was a matter of concern to pagans.

Paganism encompassed a multitude of beliefs. Christianity, although more precisely defined, was not monolithic: it was made up of 'micro-Christendoms'.[112] Yet for most Christians there was a commonly accepted core: belief in the Bible; the performance of certain rituals and the rejection of others. In his *De Correctione Rusticorum* Martin of Braga begins his attack on superstition with an account of the Creation, the fall of Satan, Adam and Eve and the Flood. Having provided a biblical context in which the origins of paganism could be placed, he described how the Devil and his demons began to deceive men, persuading them to offer sacrifice on high mountains and in woods, and calling themselves by the names of pagan gods. From this developed the use of temples, the worship of idols, and the veneration of mice, worms and locusts as gods. The use of divination and augury also flourished. Against this Martin asserts God's Creation and the Incarnation, before warning that those who lapsed into idolatry, homicide and perjury after baptism were damned. He emphasises the importance of baptismal vows, and then defines Christianity in terms of renunciation of the Devil and all his works. Worship of stones, trees, springs, cults at crossroads and the ritual burning of corn he condemns as idolatry. Divinations, auguries and the dedication of certain days to idols are described as the cult of the devil, as are celebration of the *Vulcanalia* and the Kalends, and such rituals as the decoration of tables. For a woman to call on Minerva and Venus on her wedding day was to invoke the demonic,

109 *Vita Vulframni* c.9.
110 Avitus, *Ep.* 46.
111 *Vita Vulframni* c.10.
112 Brown (1996), pp. 216–32.

as was the use of herbs and incantations. In place of all should be the sign of the cross, the Lord's Prayer, penitence, good works, belief in the Resurrection, Sunday observance and prayer.

Martin's work thus defined not only paganism, but also the Christian life. In this Pirmin followed him. The opening of the *Scarapsus* is heavily indebted to Martin's work, although Pirmin follows his own account of the origins of idolatry with a brief narrative of the Incarnation, the Passion, the harrowing of Hell, the Ascension, Pentecost, the dispersal of the Apostles and the institution of the church. Thereafter he provides a rather more extensive list of pagan practices to be abjured, defining a Christian as one who does not perform pagan actions. The work concludes with a fuller list of Christian duties than that provided by Martin. Tithes are now required, as is confession; the education of children in religion is specified, as are the duties of godparents. The church's idea of what constituted Christianity had developed between the late sixth and the early eighth century.

The Eligius sermons, like the *Scarapsus* of Pirmin, echo the emphasis on the importance of Christian doctrine and condemnation of pagan practice to be found in the *De Correctione Rusticorum*, while Daniel of Winchester, in his letter of advice sent to Boniface in the early 720s, also emphasised the importance of belief.[113] Christianisation, therefore, involved the dissemination of biblical teaching, the condemnation of superstition and the development of a Christian lifestyle, which included the performance of specified rituals and duties. To supervise all of this an organised church was necessary.

At one level church organisation was a matter of buildings and priests. It is possible to chart the Christianisation of the Touraine in the late fourth and early fifth centuries by noting the foundation of churches by St Martin and his followers.[114] Churches, as opposed to oratories, would be staffed by a priest or priests who could ensure the regular and frequent provision of Christian cult. The importance of church-foundation is most apparent in the *Conversio Bagoariorum et Carantanorum*, which describes the Christianisation of Bavaria and Carinthia largely in terms of the foundation of churches. Churches and their priests provided the basis on which a parish system would in time be built. The establishment of bishops and dioceses to supervise churches at a local level and to provide such necessary functions as baptism and ordination took place sometimes after, sometimes alongside and sometimes before the creation of local churches.

The creation of a diocese, however necessary to the dissemination of Christian teaching, did not always command general agreement even within the church. The allocation of land to a new bishopric might be thought of as

113 Boniface, *Epistola* 23. 114 Stancliffe (1979).

undermining the claims of an established see. In the eighth century Cologne was hostile to the existence of a diocese at Utrecht,[115] and in the ninth century its bishop opposed the amalgamation of Hamburg and Bremen.[116] Boniface was faced with opposition of a rather different type when Pope Zacharias questioned the suitability of Würzburg, Buraburg and Erfurt as diocesan centres, on the grounds that such centres should not be established on estates or in small towns for fear of undermining episcopal prestige.[117] Although such a ruling may have made sense in those areas where the effects of Roman civilisation had included urbanisation, in a free Germany it was unworkable.

Supervision was certainly needed if the church was to maintain a single orthodox tradition. What confronted Boniface in Bavaria, Thuringia and Hesse was not so much paganism as a level of superstitious survival which he found unacceptable within the Christian church. Similar problems could be found further west in Francia. The two heretics Adalbert and Clemens were both clerics, however bizarre and indeed idolatrous their actual beliefs may have been.[118] Adalbert promoted himself as a saint, consecrating chapels to himself and setting up crosses and shrines at springs and in fields. He also distributed his hair and fingernails as relics. Clemens rejected the teachings of the Fathers, and asserted that Christ had delivered idolators as well as Christians from hell. That these two clerics were heretical was clear enough to Boniface and to the papacy. In other cases, however, there was room for disagreement. While Boniface thought that a priest who had performed the baptismal rite ungrammatically was acting heretically, Pope Zacharias, by contrast, insisted that the baptism was valid, and that for Boniface to rebaptise was heretical.[119]

Despite the common emphases of works like the *De Correctione Rusticorum* and the *Scarapsus* of Pirmin, there was a wide variety of opinion on what was acceptable within Christianity and the Christian life. Boniface took a more puritanical stance than the papacy over the question of baptism, but on other matters he was more pragmatic. Unlike Pope Zacharias he was aware that the tradition of establishing diocesan centres in cities was unworkable in a free Germany. Similarly, he was aware of the difficulty of enforcing the increasingly harsh definition of the prohibited degrees of marriage, which had been extended from the third or fourth to the sixth degree since the early seventh century.[120] Indeed Boniface was so alarmed by the current papal ruling that he asked the archbishop of Canterbury, Nothelm, to check the *Responsiones* of Gregory the Great over the issue.[121]

115 Boniface, *Epistola* 109. 116 Rimbert, *Vita Anskarii* c.23. 117 Boniface, *Epistola* 51.
118 Boniface, *Epistolae* 59, 60, 62, 77; Council of Soissons (744), *cc.*2, 7, ed. Werminghoff; Willibald, *Vita Bonifatii*, c.7.
119 Boniface, *Epistola* 68. 120 Goody (1983), pp. 134–44. 121 Boniface, *Epistola* 33.

It is in the letters of Gregory the Great more than in any other surviving block of pre-Carolingian evidence that an awareness of the difficulties of prescribing what was and what was not acceptable within Christianity is most readily apparent.[122] In June 601 Gregory responded to Augustine's request for helpers by sending a second party of missionaries to Kent, led by Mellitus, who carried with him a letter from the pope to Æthelberht, telling the king to destroy idols and shrines. Meanwhile Gregory must have continued to ponder what he had learned about the progress of the mission, for in July of the same year he sent a letter to Mellitus ordering him to advise Augustine not to destroy pagan shrines, but to asperge them with holy water and to set relics and altars in them. He also instructed Mellitus to tell Augustine to make use of the pagan practice of sacrificing cattle to devils, by encouraging the people to slaughter the animals on the festivals of the martyrs, and to celebrate them with feasting. Gregory clearly came to appreciate that the survival of certain elements of pagan practice could usefully be preserved within Christianity. He, or the author of the *Libellus Responsionum*, attributed to him by Bede among others, also saw the advantage of dealing sympathetically with established social practices.[123] Thus marriages between first cousins, and between a man and his brother's widow were to be frowned upon, but those contracted by parties while they were still pagan were to be dealt with gently. Gregory's final position on Christianisation did not require an absolute break with the social traditions of the pagan past.

Gregory's correspondence sheds some light on the pagan practices encountered by Augustine, and on the Christianity which was to replace them. It also provides an insight into one method of evangelisation. There were others. To a large extent the possible forms of mission were determined by circumstances. The opportunities for mission within an officially Christian state differed from those within a pagan state where the ruler was tolerant towards missionaries, and they differed yet again from those where the governing classes were divided in their attitudes. Missionaries were sensitive to such circumstances: not surprisingly they tended – at least in those narratives which have come down to us – to prefer to work with royal support, or at least permission, something which gave them at least a modicum of physical security. Within the Frankish kingdom a bishop like Eligius acted as an official of the established church. In Kent Augustine had the approval of a king who may have accepted Christianity even before the bishop's arrival. Both in Merovingian Francia and in Augustine's Kent missionaries could work from ecclesiastical communities, from episcopal households or from monasteries. Elsewhere such bases and retreats were not available. Nevertheless pagan kings were prepared to allow

[122] Gregory, *Register* XI.37, 56: Markus (1970), pp. 29–38. [123] Bede, *HE* I.27.

missionaries to preach. Penda in Mercia[124] and Radbod in Frisia[125] were both tolerant in this respect. In Saxony, however, Lebuin at best had the support of some members of the aristocracy, but he was certainly opposed by others.

Despite the variety of circumstance, in all these cases preaching was at the heart of missionary work. Sometimes it required translators. The Northumbrian king Oswald initially acted as an interpreter for the Irish missionary Aidan.[126] In some instances the question of language involved forethought. Augustine took Frankish interpreters to Kent.[127] Sometimes slaves were purchased and trained to act as missionaries to their homelands. This was a policy used by Anskar in the ninth century,[128] but it may have been developed earlier by Willibrord, who took thirty Danes back to Francia with him.[129] Earlier missionaries, including Aidan and Amandus, also bought slaves and trained them as clerics,[130] while Gregory the Great had already instructed his agent Candidus to do something similar.[131] These freedmen may have gone on to help in missionary work, even when the sources do not say as much.

The message of the missionaries seems largely to have been a statement of the Christian faith, together with a condemnation of idolatry. The sermons ascribed to Eligius and the letter of Daniel of Winchester to Boniface suggest that what was preached in the field during the seventh and eighth centuries differed little from the content of the *De Correctione Rusticorum* of Martin of Braga and the *Scarapsus* of Pirmin. Daniel does, however, suggest an additional line of approach. He points out that the gods fail to take revenge on the Christians who destroy their idols, and also that the Christians possess the most fertile lands.[132] Lebuin is said to have drawn the attention of his Saxon hearers to the threat posed to them by the Christian empire of the Franks on their doorstep.[133] The hagiographer says that Lebuin's words fell on deaf ears. Although the speech given to him is a literary invention, perhaps of the late ninth century, some pagans may well have found comparison with the greater power, wealth and achievement of the Christian Franks' telling. The Hewalds who followed Willibrord from Ireland to the continent, and who worked among the Old Saxons, were killed by barbarians who were afraid that the message of the two Christians might prove attractive to the local 'satrap'.[134] He in turn ordered the destruction of the murderers and their village. Some

124 Bede, *HE* III.21.

125 Despite the hostility of the hagiographers it is clear from the narratives of Alcuin's *Vita Willibrordi*, the *Vita Vulframni* and Altfrid's *Vita Liudgeri* that Christianisation was carried out at various times during Radbod's reign.

126 Bede, *HE* III.3.

127 Bede, *HE* I.25.

128 Rimbert, *Vita Anskarii* c.15.

129 Alcuin, *Vita Willibrordi* c.9.

130 Bede, *HE* III.5; *Vita Amandi* c.9.

131 Gregory, *Register* VI.10; see Markus (1997), pp. 177–8, for a discussion.

132 Boniface, *Epistola* 23.

133 *Vita Lebuini Antiqua* c.6.

134 Bede, *HE* V.10.

were clearly willing to listen to and be convinced by the arguments which the missionaries put before them.

The reaction of the 'satrap' to the martyrdom of the Hewalds is an indication that even in pagan areas Christians could expect a hearing. Indeed there is little evidence for outright hostility to missionaries when they first arrived in their chosen field of work. According to Alcuin, Willibrord was well received by Radbod and by the Danish king Ongendus, who was supposed to be more cruel than any wild beast and harder than any stone.[135] Although he achieved nothing in Denmark Willibrord apparently met no difficulty in approaching the king. It may be that traditions of hospitality among the Germanic peoples here facilitated the work of a missionary.[136]

At the same time the clearly distinctive features of a missionary's lifestyle, those points which distinguished him as 'other', could cause problems. Bede, in his account of the martyrdom of the Hewalds, stresses that it was their habit of reciting the psalms, of saying prayers and of celebrating mass which identified them as Christians, and which first made them suspect to their killers.[137] Clearly this is a reconstruction of events on Bede's part, but it is one which fits well with other evidence. Boniface, for instance, was martyred on a day which he had set aside for the confirmation of Christian neophytes.[138] Later, in the last decade of the tenth century, Adalbert of Prague seems to have recognised the gulf caused by the practice of Christian rituals and a Christian style of life, or so his hagiographer, Bruno of Querfurt, who was himself a missionary, claimed.[139] Doubtless the performance of Christian rituals was comforting to the individual missionaries, but at times it seems to have made them too ostentatiously different from those they wished to evangelise. Christian rites could provide the flashpoints which led to martyrdom.

By comparison the aggressive tactics adopted by some missionaries could be less hazardous than the simple singing of psalms, saying of prayers and celebration of mass. Certainly missionaries did come close to being lynched when they attacked pagan shrines and other objects of devotion. Even inside the Roman Empire, Martin of Tours was attacked by incensed pagans on more than one occasion,[140] and in the Merovingian period, Gallus of Clermont narrowly avoided martyrdom when he desecrated a temple in the Trier region.[141] Willibrord was physically attacked when he destroyed an idol on Walcheren.[142] When, however, he broke the taboos at the shrine of Fosite the pagans only took action after they had consulted the *sortes*: as a result one, but only one,

135 Alcuin, *Vita Willibrordi* c.9.

136 Wood (1987), pp. 349–51.

137 Bede, *HE* v.10.

138 Willibald, *Vita Bonifatii* c.8.

139 Bruno of Querfurt, *Vita Adalberti* c.26; Wood (1987), pp. 358–9.

140 Sulpicius Severus, *Vita Martini* c.15.

141 Gregory of Tours, *Vitae Patrum* vi.2.

142 Alcuin, *Vita Willibrordi* c.14.

of Willibrord's companions was killed.[143] Willehad was also spared by the *sortes*, even though some pagans thought that he deserved to die because of his preaching against idolatory.[144] On the other hand he and his companions risked death when one of them destroyed a shrine at Drenthe.[145] When Boniface cut down the oak at Geismar, he is said to have met with no opposition from the pagan crowd which had gathered.[146] Geismar, though, was within the Frankish sphere of influence and it may be that Boniface could in this instance rely on the support of the mayors of the palace.

Missionaries may at times have had the backing of secular forces in their acts of desecration. Certainly they worked together with the secular arm when force was employed as a means of Christianisation. Amandus was so appalled by the prevalence of apostasy in the region of Ghent that he persuaded Bishop Aicharius of Noyon to obtain letters from King Dagobert, authorising forcible conversion.[147] The chief example of the use of force in evangelisation during the early Middle Ages, however, is the Christianisation of the Saxons, which came to be intimately related to their conquest during the reign of Charlemagne. From 772, when he attacked Saxony and destroyed the Irminsul, until 804, when he resorted to mass deportation in order to solve the Saxon problem, Christianisation was central to Charlemagne's policy.[148] In 776 the Saxons promised to become Christians as part of their submission to the Frankish king. In 778 and 782 they rebelled under the pagan leadership of Widukind against Carolingian rule and perhaps particularly against the strident Christianity of Charlemagne's first Saxon capitulary.[149] In 785 Widukind accepted terms and baptism, but there was still pagan reaction to come between 792 and 804.

The Saxon revolts are an indication of the weakness of force as a method of effecting religious change. Ultimately the Saxons did accept Christianity, although even in the late ninth century there was still fear of violence at the hands of pagan robbers.[150] It is doubtful whether the Christianisation of Saxony really was achieved by force rather than by a longer-term transformation of beliefs, taboos and social norms. What ultimately caused such a transformation is impossible to determine. Preaching may have had some effect, though the message propagated by the missionaries, to judge by the writings of Martin of Braga and Pirmin, is not self-evidently attractive to pagans whose cosmology or view of religion was very different. At times a missionary may have found a way of presenting the Christian message so as to challenge common assumptions and prompt conversion. In the late eighth century the Bavarian priest Ingo shocked pagan aristocrats by treating their Christian servants with greater

143 Alcuin, *Vita Willibrordi* cc.10–11. 144 *Vita Willehadi* c.3. 145 *Vita Willehadi* c.4.
146 Willibald, *Vita Bonifatii* c.6. 147 *Vita Amandi* c.13. 148 Büttner (1965), pp. 454–87.
149 *Capitulatio de Partibus Saxoniae*. 150 *Vita Liutbirgae* c.12.

respect than he treated them.[151] The servants he entertained to food and to wine served in golden goblets, while he left the masters outside to be fed like dogs. On other occasions more may have been achieved through Gregory the Great's policy of assimilating as much pagan tradition as possible into new Christian celebrations. In the long run, however, most was probably achieved through the steady influence and example of the more impressive clergy. Augustine, Fursey, Boniface, Gregory of Utrecht and Anskar are all said to have won converts by their style of life. At this level Christianisation, which in many respects was a formal and outward process, could develop into conversion, that is into a much deeper transformation within the life of an individual. Such conversions, however, take us beyond the history of the Christianisation of western Europe, into the history of piety and monasticism.

[151] *Conversio Bagoariorum et Carantanorum* c.7.

CHAPTER 27

EDUCATION AND LEARNING

Jacques Fontaine

In 476 the overthrow of the last emperor of the West symbolised the discrete disappearance of Rome. But during the following two centuries, this political break-up affected the economic and social structures of the Roman world only partially, and even less those of its education and culture. In fact, huge changes in these latter, compared to the Hellenistic civilisation of the *paideia*, had already taken place between the third and fifth centuries, during the period which we now call later antiquity. But it was only after the end of the fifth century that the last ancient schools were to disappear one by one. At least, that was true in what had been the Western Empire. For in the East, it was only in the seventh century, following attacks from Persians, Avars, Slavs and Arabs, that the transmission of antique culture and the exercise of literary creation was to suffer a true eclipse. There would eventually be a complete break in linguistic communication between the Latin world and a Greek empire in which the abandonment of bilingualism and total Hellenisation would form part of a strategy for survival.

Research over the last century has destroyed the traditional view that the political and military collapse of Rome led to the 'barbarisation' of a western world overwhelmed by 'massive invasions'. What followed the collapse of Rome, 'the Middle Ages', was famously denigrated by Gibbon as 'the triumph of barbarism and religion',[1] and that late eighteenth-century view remained largely unchallenged until the publication of a work by Pierre Riché in 1962.[2] Riché's *Education et culture dans l'Occident barbare* was more closely related to historical reality, taking up the challenge issued by Gibbon. It found support in works which pleaded the cause of important political, social, institutional and even fiscal continuities between the civilisation of late antiquity and that

[1] Gibbon (1839), 12 cap. 71, 2, p. 392.

[2] Riché (1972) and the other works of this author: bibliography in Sot (1990), pp. 15–22; but also Illmer (1971); *Settimane* of 1971 focussed on the school in the early Middle Ages: *La Scuola* (1972); and *La Cultura* (1981).

of the so-called 'Germanic' kingdoms which in the fifth century shared out amongst themselves the lands of the Roman West.[3]

One must, therefore, keep the following two points in mind, balancing one against the other: on the one hand, the material destruction brought about after 406 by civil war and invasions, the growing paralysis of public scholastic institutions, and the scarcely intellectual forms of education and way of life of the Germanic invaders, caused serious damage to the vitality of antique culture and even to the civilisation of the written word in the West. On the other hand, this written civilisation nevertheless survived, by keeping alive the ideals of later Roman culture among a traditionally educated elite, and then by developing new forms of education.[4] It was the Christian church that had earlier begun to put these new forms in place in order to provide training for future clerics and monks, and even for all those who were baptised. Whilst amongst the Roman nobility of the towns and the provinces family education was retaining or resuming its ancient place, the bishoprics and the monasteries were gradually taking over the public schools of the late Empire.[5]

Cultural continuity was aided by the delayed effects of the shocks to the political and military establishments. In towns and on large estates – spared, restored and even shared out by the new masters – cultural activity was pursued with pride as a fundamental component of Roman identity. People there continued to read and write, to copy and correct the manuscripts of ancient works; they still composed inscriptions in prose and in verse; they educated children by the acquisition of a traditional Latin, and more rarely, Greek, culture. Elsewhere, the first courts of the Germanic kings willingly welcomed Roman writing specialists whom these princes needed to manage their new states, and to draw up the respective rights of their Germanic and Roman subjects. The demographic and cultural superiority of these latter in the majority of the 'occupied' regions tilted the gathering process of cross-cultural fertilisation towards Romanisation, and thus towards Latin culture. This process was particularly rapid amongst those peoples who, like the Goths, had for some time already been in continuous contact, if not cultural osmosis, with the civilisation of *Romania*.

[3] In particular the works of Werner (1989) and (1992), pp. 173–211 (both works have full bibliographies). For the thesis of fiscal continuity, Durliat (1990).

[4] A useful essay on cultural definition and periodisation is Martin (1976). See also the posthumous work of Marrou (1977).

[5] Sidonius Apollinaris read and commented on Terence and Menander with his son: *Epistolae* 12, 1–2; and Paulinus of Pella evoked his own family education in Gaul: *Eucharisticos* 60–7. This pedagogical function of the family had existed from the time of the oldest Roman education: see the *Libri ad Marcum Filium* of Cicero; and Marrou (1950), pp. 316–18.

Continuity was even more solidly manifested in ecclesiastical society. The principles and the programmes of a new Christian culture, *propaideia*, which integrated into that culture a good proportion of the ancient *paideia*, had been laid down by St Augustine between 397 and 421, in his treatise *De Doctrina Christiana*. This blueprint for preaching in fact traced the programme of a new culture, closely linked to a teaching which was essentially religious, and which aimed at proclaiming and communicating the contents of Christian doctrine.[6] Beyond an intellectual *cultura animi* of which Cicero had defended the end and the classical means, it proposed what some years previously Paulinus of Nola had already called a *cultura cordis* – in the biblical, and therefore Augustinian sense of the word *cor*.[7] The classical exercising of intelligence found itself directed towards a spiritual decision of an existential nature. All culture, understood in the ancient and therefore Ciceronian sense, thus becomes a means oriented towards a religious end which surpasses it: the personal encounter with God in the Holy Scripture, which preserves his presence via his Word, and in the *vita communis* of a monastic or clerical community. All cultural activity – writing or reading, spoken or written, heard or read exegesis, the spiritual discourse of the *confabulatio* or of the more widely collective *collatio*, right up to the conceptual systematisation of a 'theological' discussion on God – is thus integrated into a specifically religious activity.[8] Integrating profane authors by recognising in them a value for training in the foundations of culture, this radical co-option of ancient culture can also be viewed as the cultural conversion of Christianity.[9] It founded a new civilisation: that of a *paideia* of which Christ alone was the 'pedagogue', as Clement of Alexandria wrote back in the third century. Christ was 'the interior master' who, as Augustine later wrote in his *De Magistro*, taught the faithful to 'become like little children' and to allow themselves to be instructed by him, in the Pauline sense of the edification of the inner man.[10]

[6] See the introduction and notes to Combes and Farges (eds.), *Œuvres* de St Augustin, and especially the new edition by Moreau, Bochet and Madec (1997); classic commentary by Marrou (1958), pp. 329–540; cf. also Duane and Bright (1995).

[7] Cicero, *Tusculanes* II.13: 'ut ager . . . sine cultura fructuosus esse non potest, sic sine doctrina animus . . . Cultura autem animi philosophia est'; and Paulinus of Nola, *Epistolae* 39, 3: 'qualem agri tui speciem fieri a uilico tuo postulas, talem Deo Domino cordis tui redde culturam'. Paulinus' use of the term *cor* goes back to the biblical, even psalmist sense in Latin translations of the Bible: Bauer and Felber (1988). Compare the Augustinian uses, for example, in Maxsein (1954), pp. 357–71; for Paulinus: Fontaine (1972), pp. 585–6.

[8] Marrou (1937), pp. 209–86.

[9] This is drawing on Brown's playful but apposite formula 'The conversion of Christianity' which forms the title of Brown (1971), ch. 7 (p. 82).

[10] Luke 18:16 and Matthew 18:3. On this evangelical and Christic basis of all Christian education, see for example Fontaine (1992a), pp. 6–10. The semantic values of *rabbi* and *didaskalos* converged in the evangelical designation of Christ as *magister*.

In these last centuries of later antiquity, the continuity of ancient forms was therefore accompanied by a progressive conversion of the content and meaning of *cultura*, in a slow process that took no account of the violence of a break. From this double perspective during the sixth and seventh centuries, the history of culture and of education appeared to be that of the slow assimilation of the problems and solutions proposed in the *De Doctrina Christiana*. This new *De Oratore* was then read, copied and applied by the great Christian writers who would both reflect and quite clearly inform the culture and the education of their own time.[11] For this slow metamorphosis was far from being homogeneous: it differentiated itself in time and space, in the uneven rhythms of a *Romania* in the process of regionalisation since the fourth century, but also of new Christianities in the Celtic and Germanic countries of the north. These rhythms were subject to the pulsations of a political history, which could oppose or favour the reorganisation of education, and the flowering or the overthrow of cultural activity. What a contrast, at the end of the sixth century, between the ruins of Italy and the rebuilding of Spain!

The end of the sixth century, and the decades which followed it, saw an increase in speed in the changes in the political and religious field: the decline of Byzantium between the end of the long reign of Justinian (565) and the assault by the Persians and Slavs against the Empire (between 622 and 630), the disappearance of the Burgundian and Ostrogothic Arian kingdoms, and the conversion of the Visigoths of Spain to Nicaean Catholicism (589). This was truly the period when the debate between the antique past and new future of Christian Europe was at its most lively. Great writers – and men of action[12] – then began to intervene in this cultural debate, by producing the works upon which rests their reputation as 'the founders of the Middle Ages'.[13] These writers were Cassiodorus in Italy, Gregory of Tours in Gaul/Francia, Pope Gregory the Great, and in Spain, Isidore. Were they still 'ancient' or were they already 'medieval'? It is significant that a recent essay on periodisation should have dismissed this alternative as too simplistic and that it should have called some authors 'rather ancient' and others 'rather medieval'.[14]

Just as much as the differences between these intellectual giants, the common features of their contributions clarified the evolution of culture. For cultural

[11] See for example the debt of Gregory the Great's *Regula Pastoralis* to the Augustinian treatise: *Règle pastorale*, ed. Judic *et al.*, pp. 39ff; and in the case of Isidore: Fontaine (1983a), II, pp. 794ff and 933 (list of references). More widely, Opelt (1974).

[12] Gregory of Tours, Gregory the Great and Isidore of Seville were bishops charged with heavy pastoral and administrative responsibilities. The laymen Cassiodorus and Boethius assumed high office in the Ostrogothic state.

[13] Rand (1928).

[14] Banniard (1980), pp. 113–14, declared Fortunatus and Isidore to be 'rather ancient', but Gregory of Tours and Gregory the Great 'rather medieval'. See also Fontaine (1983a), II, pp. 807–30, for Isidore.

differentiation did not disintegrate in a flash. In all four, in fact, in explicit theory or in tacit practice, one can see the same concerns: to preserve elementary grammatical training without which the Christian message cannot be correctly transmitted in Latin by either spoken or written word; to ensure the correct delivery of this message to every single member of the Christian people, whatever their background, their state of life, their level of culture, or their linguistic ability; to reveal, to practise, to teach to this end an attitude of true balance between a faith more or less strictly adhering to the heritage of later antique culture – profane and Christian – and the necessary adaptations which would allow it to be received by an elite. In order to do this Cassiodorus and Isidore put the accent on faith, if not on restoration, particularly by producing encyclopaedic works. The two Gregories were more aware of the urgent need to adapt to all audiences – even illiterate ones (which does not mean to say that they were uncivilised) – and each in his own way boldly set an example by using literary styles appropriate to uneducated audiences, or at least to those with little education in the traditional sense of the word.

In the seventh century the influence of these four authors was to make itself felt in a western Europe where, geographically, culture was in full transformation. The most active centres were beginning to shift from the Mediterranean towards the west, the north and the north-west, and new partners were increasingly coming into this 'incubation of European culture'.[15] The growing stagnation of Byzantine Africa even before its conquest by Islam, the distress of an Italy still ruined by the Byzantines and then by the Lombards, the deterioration of the Merovingian kingdoms, frequently split up and paralysed by impotence, all created in the south and in the centre of the former Roman West what could be called 'depressed areas'. Culture, and in particular literary culture, went into a sort of stagnant period there. The more innovative centres were to appear elsewhere: in northern Italy, in the abbeys in the north of France, in the north-west of Spain with its monastic school and writers from Bierzo; even, on the wider scale of new European regions, in the wake of the 'Isidorian renaissance', in Betica, then in Toledo, in Galicia, and even in Ireland.

But it was the British Isles that were, for two centuries, going to pick up and assume the leadership of the new culture.[16] The Celts in Ireland, who from the fifth century had received both Christianity and Latin at the same time, would develop and export to England, and then to the continent, to Gaul and Germany, their ideal of a monastic lifestyle, pure and firm, but attentive to an intellectual and even literary education. Christianised in their turn from the end of the sixth century, the Anglo-Saxons would bring about the rebirth in

[15] Curtius (1938), p. 130. For other designations, Fontaine (1983a), II, p. 826.
[16] On development of Christian culture in Ireland and Britain, see Stancliffe, chapters 15 and 16 above.

southern England and the birth in Northumbria of a new Latinity, the result of a beneficial encounter between the cultural influxes from Ireland, Gaul and Rome. This Latinity would have as its greatest representative a learned, lettered, artistic monk, the Venerable Bede (d. 735), rightly considered as the last of the 'great founders of the Middles Ages' and the immediate precursor of the Carolingian *reformatio*. One can see that the seventh century scarcely deserves its reputation as the nadir of European culture.

For better or worse the long reign of the emperor Justinian (527–565) dominates the historical imagination of the sixth century. The attempts by this emperor to reconquer the former western part of the Empire and thus to bring about the unification of the imperial lands which bordered the Roman Mediterranean ended in failure.[17] From the point of view of culture, and of the ancient institutions that had ensured its transmission, this interference by Byzantium in the West produced contradictory effects, but all three of which had an effect upon the change that was in progress. Indeed, depending on the place and the time, this change could be seen as a restoration or a challenge but also as acting as a brake.

In truth, Justinian's restoration of public scholastic institutions in the ancient mould produced lasting effects only in the capitals of the West (Carthage, Rome and Ravenna) where they had deservedly succeeded in surviving until then. At the request of Pope Vigilius, Justinian promulgated in 554 the Pragmatic Sanction which, amongst other things, re-established the official salaries traditionally paid 'to grammarians, orators, doctors and lawyers, in order that in our republic there should flourish young men instructed in liberal studies'.[18] But the difficulties of the Byzantine reconquest in Italy did not allow Justinian either the time or the necessary resources to put this fine decision into effect. In Africa, reconquered as early as 533, the restoration of imperial power nevertheless favoured the resumption of a scholarly and literary life which, for a long time, had been thwarted by the hostility of the Vandals to the Catholic Romans. In about 550 the grammarian Flavius Cresconius Corippus praised in Virgilian hexameters the Byzantine victories of General John Troglytus over the Berber invaders, in the last Roman epic on a war theme: the *Johannide*. After that, towards 566, he would compose panegyrics in Latin verse about the emperor Justinian and the quaestor Anastasius.

Southern Spain, where from 554 to 624 the soldiers of the *basileus* only occupied a coastal strip of varying width, was far from enjoying the same cultural vigour. There is scarcely any comparison between the long African

[17] On Justinian's aims and strategies, see Louth, chapter 4 above.

[18] Justinian, *Novella, pro petitione Vigilii, Novellae* 7, 22: 'annonas quae grammaticis uel oratoribus uel etiam medicis uel iurisperitis antea dari solitum erat . . . erogari praecipimus, quatenus iuuenes liberalibus studiis eruditi per nostram rem publicam floreant'.

Johannide and the nine emphatic verses, which in 589 or 590 the Byzantine patrician Commentiolus had engraved on the walls of his capital Cartagena, which he had restored.[19] But a recent identification attributes to Bishop Severus of Málaga several cantos of a biblical epic that follows the ancient tradition of the *Evangeliorum Libri* of Juvencus. Such a discovery illustrates the fact that the Hispano-Romans of Betica as 'frontiersmen' were aware of this foreign presence of Greeks who had come from a different political and cultural world: the most educated ended up by seeing in this a sort of challenge hurled at their own creativity. The chronological coincidence between the last decades of Byzantine occupation and the appearance, in Seville, of the literary works of Isidore makes one think even more about this point. Certainly, some Hispano-Romans of the south had gone to be educated in the East, such as John of Biclaro did towards 558; and in the 580s Leander, the older brother of Isidore, had not thought it wrong to go to seek the support of the Byzantines against the still Arian Visigoths.

But the conversion of the latter to Catholicism changed the balance of power between the Visigothic kingdoms and the Empire of the East, and consequently, the attitude of the inhabitants of Betica towards the Greeks who were firmly established in the south of their province. Isidore, the younger brother of Leander and his successor as bishop of Seville, never knew very much Greek. His clear-cut choice was for the Goths and not the Byzantines, and in 624 he would celebrate the expulsion of these last soldiers of the *basileus* from a land that was rediscovering peninsular unity.[20] Isidore's distrust of oriental Christianity was in accord with his 'national' political stances: at the Council of Seville in 619 he had a Syrian bishop condemned as guilty of 'acephalous' heresy.[21] Conversely, in the inscriptions that decorated his library, he still manifested a warm liking for the great Christian doctor of the third century, the Greek, Origen, condemned in 552 by a Council of the East that Justinian had summoned.[22] One has to put oneself in this double perspective in order to understand the meaning of the work of Isidore. Even if it were possible that Isidore could have used technical manuals and theological *florilegia* translated from the Greek, it remains true that his grammatical, encyclopaedic, historical and religious works were inspired by Latin sources. For his purpose, Hispanic culture had

19 Vives (1969), inscr. 364, p. 127. The bishops Licinianus of Carthagena and Severus of Málaga were Hispano-Romans who wrote in Latin: see Isidore, *De Viris Illustribus* 42–3; and especially the edition of Severus, bishop of Malaga?, *In Evangelia*, ed. Herzog et al.

20 See the last chapter of the second edition of his *Historia Gothorum*; and Teillet (1986).

21 Council of Seville II, canon 12: *De quodam Acefalorum episcopo*. The Monophysites who, refusing the Henotikon of the emperor Zeno, broke communion with the five patriarchs of the East were called 'acephalous' (literally: 'without a leader').

22 On these passages see Fontaine (1983a), II, p. 756; and for commentaries, pp. 757 and 851–2.

to be capable of rivalling the literary productions of Justinian's century, as well as responding to the proper needs of the church and kingdom of Spain.

Nothing of this sort happened in Gaul/Francia, where the soldiers of the East never set foot. But an isolated case shows indirectly the beneficial influence there of the Latin schools re-established in the capital of the future Byzantine exarchate of northern Italy. It was indeed in Ravenna that the Cisalpine Venantius Fortunatus undertook the excellent studies which enabled him to display later, in the service of the Frankish courts of Thuringia and northern Gaul, the refined talent of an ancient poet: *rara avis* in the northern Gaul of the end of the sixth century.

But the military impact of the Byzantine reconquest did not exert purely positive influences, favourable to the renewal of western culture. It also plunged Italy into the anguish of an interminable war (536–555); it ruined the Ostrogothic kingdom and at the same time destroyed an already fruitful co-operation between Italians and Goths, which held out hope for a process of assimilation comparable to that which, half a century later, Hispano-Romans and Visigoths of Spain would bring to a successful conclusion.[23] This all too brief a flowering was illustrated, at the beginning of the sixth century, by two senators from Italy. These were Boethius and Cassiodorus, both of whom were still receptive to Greek language and culture. Connected to the illustrious Roman *gentes* of the Anicii and the Symmachi, the philosopher Anicius Manlius Torquatus Severinus Boethius left a work that made a threefold contribution to medieval culture. He devoted four treatises to the four mathematical arts and designated them for the first time by the term *quadrivium*. He undertook the translation of the work of Aristotle, but his execution in 525 brutally interrupted this work, although fortunately he had already managed to translate the Stagirite's works of logic. The result of this was that Aristotelian logic dominated western thought for half a millennium, whilst the other works of Aristotle would only be known in the West from the twelfth century onwards, via Arab translations. The Byzantine reconquest thus slowed down, if not seriously mutilated, the thought of a West which, with some rare and brilliant exceptions, would no longer read Greek. The third cultural contribution of Boethius was, paradoxically, the result of his dramatic end. Condemned to death, he composed in his prison the last ancient *chef d'œuvre* of philosophical prose and poetry, the *prosimetrum* entitled *The Consolation of Philosophy*. This rational and fervent meditation on the blessings of good fortune, and on evil, on true good and happiness, and on Providence and Free Will, can be read, as it were, as the spiritual testament of ancient wisdom.[24]

[23] On the Byzantines in Italy, see Moorhead, chapter 5 above.

[24] On Boethius, see the studies published for the fifteenth centenary of his birth (480–1980), especially Gibson (1981). On the *Consolatio*, O'Daly (1991) and Courcelle (1967).

Around the time of the death of Boethius, in Italy there were two others who retreated from the world. Each one is significant for the future of culture, particularly monastic culture. As early as 496, Benedict of Nursia retreated to Subiaco, and in 537 Cassiodorus retreated to Vivarium. Having come to Rome to pursue his studies, Benedict abandoned them in order to seek God in the 'desert': 'Seeing many men run to the precipices of vices, he drew back, as it were, the foot which he had stretched forward to enter the world, fearing that, if he so much as brushed against the knowledge of this world, he himself would lose himself in this monstrous gulf.'[25] Beneath the rhetoric of this narration, the idea is clear: profane studies of the traditional type seemed to Benedict unsuitable for satisfying his aspiration to the perfect life, and he abandoned them without regret for hermetic, and then coenobitic, asceticism.

Starting with the disciples of Jerome in the fourth century, the life of the Christian ascetics was based entirely around intelligence and the prayerful meditation of the Bible, in readings which were sometimes collective, sometimes personal: in liturgical celebrations and in the solitude of the *lectio divina*.[26] It was therefore logical that the Rule, drawn up by Benedict for his monks at Monte Cassino in the middle of the sixth century, gave a primordial place to this reading in the monastic timetable: that is, collective reading in the eight offices of the *opus divinum* which put rhythm into the daily prayer of the community. But he also stipulated private reading throughout all the time reserved for the monk's individual activities. The last chapter of the Rule enumerates the authors whom Benedict put on the reading list: not only the Old and New Testaments but 'the works of the Holy Catholic Fathers' (or patristic literature, as we would say), 'the Conferences of the Fathers, their Institutions' (i.e. probably the two major works of John Cassian), 'and their Lives' (doubtless the Lives of the Fathers of the desert), and finally 'the Rule of our Father St Basil' (certainly in one of its Latin translations).[27]

Curiously, the Rule of Benedict made no reference to any school or to any elementary intellectual training; but amongst the monks' equipment it

[25] Gregory the Great, *Dialogues* 2, prologue: 'Sed cum in eis multos ire per abrupta vitiorum cerneret, eum, quem quasi in ingressum mundi posuerat, retraxit pedem, ne, si quid de scientia eius adtingeret, ipse quoque postmodum in inmane praecipitium totus iret.'

[26] On the *lectio divina*, see *Dictionnaire de spiritualité*, Paris (1976), IX, cols. 470–87. The exercise was described as early as the third century in a famous text by Cyprian, *Epist.* I.15: 'Sit tibi vel oratio adsidua vel lectio: nunc cum Deo loquere, nunc Deus tecum.' It held a very important place in the monk's activities: *Regula Benedicti* 48, ed. de Vogüé (1977), VII, pp. 338–49 for commentary.

[27] *Reg. Ben.* 73, 3s.: 'sermo divinae auctoritatis Veteris ac Novi Testamenti . . . liber sanctorum catholicorum Patrum . . . Collationes Patrum et Instituta et Vitas eorum, sed et Regula sancti Patris nostri Basilii'. All this made up the *doctrinae sanctorum Patrum*: to be understood, according to de Vogüé, *La Règle* IV, p. 110, in the sense of 'the whole of the writings of the Fathers, ecclesiastical as well as monastic'.

mentions a pen and some writing blocks.[28] The prologue to the Rule does designate the community as the *schola* in the service of the Lord, but the meaning of the term *schola* seems to be an elite group schooled for spiritual warfare through the *vita communis* of the monastery.[29] The monastic way of life was about 'putting oneself in the school' of Christ, the Magister; and if in this continual conversion, intellectual culture always remained necessary, it stayed tightly linked to spiritual progress, that is to say, to an interior quest for God.

One can see that, for its part, the secular church felt very early on the necessity of organising the intellectual and religious education of those clerics called to proclaim and explain the word of God, but education was also necessary for the church to carry out its administrative duties, especially in the cathedral cities. It was at this training of the teachers that the *De Doctrina Christiana* aimed first of all. In the second quarter of the sixth century, three texts in succession prescribed, or projected, the establishment of new institutions, intended to train future clerics. They appeared respectively in southern Gaul, in Spain and in Rome. In 529 a council meeting in Provence, at Vaison-la-Romaine, stipulated that the 'priests installed in a parish' should follow the customs, already old, of Italy, and to 'bring up religiously, as good fathers, the young readers' by teaching them the psalmody, the reading of the sacred texts, and the Law of the Lord, 'in order thus to ensure the emergence of worthy successors'.[30] Two years later in 531, the Second Council of Toledo ordained that children destined for the church 'should be taught in the house of the Church in the presence of the Bishop, by a person appointed to that post' until the age of 18, when they would choose between the church and the worldly life.[31] Finally, in Rome, in 535, Cassiodorus planned to set up next to the library of Pope Agapitus a sort of Christian university, on the model 'of what had been done formerly in Alexandria and of what was being done now in the Syrian town of Nisibis', that is to say of the Didascaleion of Alexandria at the time of

[28] *Reg. Ben.* 55, 18–19: 'quae sunt necessaria . . . grafium . . . tabulas'.

[29] *Reg. Ben.* prologue, 45: 'Constituenda est ergo nobis dominici scola servitii.' De Vogüé, *La Règle*, IV, p. 63, admits that in this text 'the scope of scola . . . perhaps goes beyond our notion of school', meaning that it should have a multiple interpretation: cf. also Illmer (1971), p. 193. The context invites both the military metaphor (*militanda*) and that of teaching (*magisterio . . . doctrinam*).

[30] *Concilium Vasense* c.1: 'Placuit ut omnes presbyteri, qui sunt in parrociis constituti, secundum consuetudinem quam per totam Italiam satis salubriter teneri cognovimus, iuniores lectores . . . secum in domo . . . recipiant, et eos quomodo boni patres spiritaliter nutrientes psalmis parare, divis lectionibus insistere et in lege Domini erudire contendant, ut et sibi dignos successores provideant.'

[31] Toletana Synodus II (Second Council of Toledo), 1: 'ut mox cum detonsi vel ministerio electorum contraditi fuerint, in domo ecclesiae sub episcopali praesentia a praeposito sibi debeant erudiri'. The reading *electorum* (Mansi, followed by Vives) should perhaps be corrected to *lectorum* (reading in the manuscript in the *collection conciliaire* of Novara).

Origen, and of the school of exegesis and theology of Nisibis in Asia Minor.[32] The failure of this plan combined with the desire to carry it through were to encourage Cassiodorus, in retreat from the world, to bring it about in another form a few decades later in the lands of Calabria, in the monasteries which he founded at Vivarium.

New episcopal and parochial institutions came into existence as a result of the pastoral cares of the bishops: it was in the canons of provincial synods that they appeared first of all.[33] The church's awareness of its cultural responsibilities could already be seen quite clearly at the beginning of the sixth century in the life of one bishop from Provence: a century after Augustine, Caesarius, bishop of Arles from 503 to 542, played a decisive role in the adaptation of preaching to the Christian people. Like many bishops of preceding centuries, he led a communal life with his clerics, he had them celebrate the three daily offices in his presence, he instructed them, made them read and questioned them on their readings. At the same time, he addressed to his lay listeners, country folk in the main, a preaching adapted to their level of language, in order to ensure a good reception. And he justified this use of a down-to-earth language (*sermo humilis*) as a reflection of Christ's own humility.[34] This ideal of clerical life and of clerical training, and the practice of a language intelligently appropriate to the new conditions of the exercise of preaching, were to exert a lasting influence on the culture of the clergy, and on the oral teaching dispensed to Christian people by sermons and by the private reading of the Bible. The historical and ethnic duality of the Roman civilisation, between 'hairy Gaul' and the 'Province', was intensifying during the late Empire, at which time Gaul was divided into two civil dioceses.[35] The density of the Frankish occupation in the north of the former 'hairy Gaul' had only accentuated the opposition between the south, more deeply Romanised, and the north where a better-balanced, mutual cross-culturalisation between Franks and Gallo-Romans was developing. Germanic education, essentially oral, physical and military, came into contact there with the Roman traditions of a written culture, which was indispensable to the good administration of the kingdoms. In this new education, given and received in the Germanic courts, the theoretical knowledge of the 'seven arts' gave way to the acquisition of empirical and utilitarian

32 Cassiodorus, *Institutiones*, praef.: 'ut, sicut apud Alexandriam multo tempore fuisse traditur institutum, nunc etiam in Nisibi civitate. Syrorum Hebreis sedulo fertur exponi'.

33 For the details, see Scheibelreiter, chapter 25 above.

34 On Caesarius' pastoral letter, and his desire to instruct the people and even to make them read the Scriptures, see Delage (1971), pp. 143ff. On his theory and practice of the *sermo humilis*, Auerbach (1958), pp. 25–53.

35 This can be seen at the beginning of the fifth century in Sulpicius Severus, *Dialogues* I.27 and II.I. On this text, Fontaine (1983b), pp. 189–91 and (1994), pp. 17–32.

techniques: surveying and architecture, medicine and law. But if one could consider the court as a 'management school'[36] one must observe that this metaphor could already have been applied, as early as the end of the third century, to the 'Menian schools' of Autun, restored by the emperors of the Tetrarchy with a view to training the managers whose number the new regime had multiplied.[37]

Whilst northern Gaul in the sixth century enjoyed a certain artistic and cultural awakening, a Christian Latinity and culture of another style were developing in the insular lands of the north-west. It was between 525 and 540 that the monk Gildas probably wrote in southern England his curious work *On the Ruin of Britain*. As the first literary witness to an insular Latin culture, which was still (or already) most estimable, this book linked 'lofty (affected) vigour and baroque elegance'.[38] This strange mixture heralded the originality of the insular Latin culture that would develop over the next century.

The stagnation or the flowering of culture, in the different areas of *Romania* which were engaged in distinct political evolutions, were accentuated in the course of the decades which preceded and followed the year 600. It was during this half-century (575–626), after the death of Justinian in 565, that the decline of the Empire in the East grew worse, sorely tried by successive assaults that came from the east and the north. Byzantine Africa withered into a growing insecurity in the face of attacks from the Berbers in the interior. Italy was colonised by the Lombards, whose invasion, starting in 568, plunged it yet again, and for decades to come, into disorder and insecurity. In 590, when the future Gregory the Great acceded to the pontificate, Rome was prey to the ravages of flooding, plague and famine.

In Gaul, in spite of political instability and civil wars caused by the dividing up of kingdoms and the bloody rivalry of the magnates, written culture spread amongst the Frankish nobility; it even attracted literate princes such as Chilperic; and above all, it held together and developed in the 200 or so monasteries which covered the Merovingian lands. At the same time a determined desire to reform (itself) was manifest in the whole church. This we see through the Acts, written in a still worthy Latin, of almost thirty Councils held in Gaul between 560 and 637.[39] Then, in a few years, Spain brought about a political, religious and cultural recovery, which was unique in the West of that time. Between 567 and 586 the peninsula was almost totally reunified by

36 Riché's formula (1962), p. 284.

37 *Panegyrici Latini* 5 (= 9): 'Eumenis pro instaurandis scholis oratio'; and more precisely ch. 5, which evokes the future careers in high administration which await students from these schools.

38 Kerlouégan's phrase (1993), p. 9.

39 Edition, with an excellent French translation, by Gaudemet and Basdevant (1989). Study: Pontal (1989).

the Arian king of Toledo, Leovigild, and the authorisation of mixed marriages agreed to by this king hastened the Romanisation of the Visigoths and thus the formation of a Hispano-Gothic nation.[40] Religious unification then followed, thanks to the conversion of his son and heir Reccared in 587, then of all the Visigoths in Spain at the Council of Toledo in 589. The conditions necessary for a restoration of culture and its transmission were present even before the end of the sixth century. During a good third of the next century, until his death in 636, Isidore, bishop of Seville, would devote his pen and his action to these, both through the church and alongside literate monarchs such as King Sisebut.

It is a sign of Italy's distress in the middle of the sixth century that the most innovative cultural effort took refuge in the shelter of a large estate, behind the walls of two private monasteries, almost at the southern tip of the peninsula. This was Vivarium, near what is now Squillace (Calabria), the family property of Flavius Magnus Aurelius Cassiodorus Senator, to which he finally withdrew towards 550. There he brought to fruition his project of 535, but in another form, more appropriate to the misfortunes of the times. In fact he organised a monastic community there and set up a library, with a scriptorium where Greek works were also translated; and he made it an intellectual and editorial centre that was exceptionally active. From Vivarium the instruments of a culture which was both ancient and Christian would be transmitted across Europe. In the open spirit of the Augustinian tradition, Cassiodorus thus taught to western monasticism the art of reconciling the love of letters and the desire for God.[41] His two books of *Institutions* bear a title inherited from Quintilian, from Lactantius and from Roman legal literature, and whose meaning is clearly pedagogical. The first book, the *Divine Institutions*, is devoted to sacred reading and to the logical sequence of the different books of the Bible; the second, the *Human Institutions*, to profane culture, that is, in the main, to an abridged version of the seven liberal arts which fourth-century Neoplatonism had organised into an introduction to philosophy.[42]

The pedagogical interest in this double *aide-mémoire* is considerable, because of its influence on the future of culture rather than its already considerably reduced content. The collected presentation of each piece of knowledge is in fact accompanied by a methodical bibliography and commentary, which leads one to suppose that there was an exceptional concentration of

40 See further Barbero and Loring, chapters 7 and 13 above.

41 On Cassiodorus, O'Donnell (1979), and the Colloquium published by Leanza (1986).

42 In a philosophical education, this function was devolved into the seven arts by Porphyrius (234–304?), as Hadot has shown (1984). This study plan was then Christianised by Augustine, who gave a place to these arts in the initial programme of a Christian culture arranged around the understanding of the Bible.

manuscripts – biblical, patristic, 'technical', Latin and Greek – in the library at Vivarium. The later diffusion of these, and also copies of translations by Cassiodorus which got as far as Northumbria and the court of Charlemagne, bears material witness to the profound impact that the work of Cassiodorus was to leave on medieval culture.[43] Isidore was to reproduce (without saying so) a large part of Book II of Cassiodorus' *Institutions* at the beginning of his *Etymologies*, but he would do it in a spirit of direct and global return to the past, whereas Cassiodorus made much clearer reference to the intermediary authority of Augustine and of the *De Doctrina Christiana*.[44] The most modest but perhaps most effective aspect of Cassiodorus' teaching concerns the works of his copyists. He saw to their material needs as well as to all the intellectual and religious aspects of their work, and it was for them that he composed, at the age of 90, a treatise *On Orthography*, which was a sort of Appendix to his *Institutions*.[45] Retaining the taste that literate men of late antiquity had for the copying and correction of manuscripts, Cassiodorus thus laid the foundations for the practice and theory of the medieval monks. Their respect for the nobility of the *ars antiquaria*, of all the monastic works, resulted from the understanding of preaching and of spiritual combat, which Cassiodorus gave explicitly to that activity.[46]

Having become pope in 590, some fifteen years after the death of Cassiodorus, Gregory displayed many points in common with him. He too came from a great family, and he too had received an antique-style education; he had also had a worldly career that had taken him as far as the Prefecture of the City before he entered the Roman monastery of St Andrews. But his profound monastic vocation inspired in him a more distant attitude towards profane culture. As the biographer of St Benedict in the second book of his *Dialogues*, Gregory was aware of and retained a longing for the contemplative life of the cloisters. However, having become 'God's Consul', he managed the Roman papacy efficiently in a dramatic conjuncture of cultures. It was in his commentaries on the Books of Kings that he defined, in an expressive metaphor, his considered and strongly Augustinian position with regard to profane culture: one must cross the plain of liberal arts

43 See Courcelle (1948), pp. 342–88; and Holtz in Leanza (1986), pp. 281–301.

44 In *Institutiones* I.16.41, Cassiodorus recommended in a warm and explicit manner the reading of the *De Doctrina Christiana*. But Isidore presented the content of these borrowings from Cassiodorus without any reference, thus giving the reader the illusion of a direct access to the ancient wisdoms, which he was offering. See Fontaine, in Leanza (1986), pp. 72–91.

45 See also *Institutiones* I.30, *De arte antiquaria et de commemoratione orthographiae*.

46 The copying of scriptural texts was for the monk a sort of 'manual' for preaching: 'manu hominibus praedicare, digitis linguas aperire', and a fight against Satan: 'tot enim vulnera Satanas excipit, quot antiquarius Domini verba describit'.

before climbing the mountain in order to raise oneself to the contemplative life.[47]

The quality of his language and of his style demonstrated that Gregory the Great had used his time well whilst crossing this plain during his adolescence. With a finely tuned awareness of the diversity of his public, their needs and their levels of culture, Gregory never ceased to vary his precepts to preachers. Attention to the diversity of listeners, of their status in life and of their capacity to listen is a primordial theme of the advice that his *Pastoral Care* proposed. He even gave some moderated examples of the *stilus humilis* in the *Dialogues* where he dared to address himself to very different audiences, educated as well as illiterate.[48] From a documentary point of view, these *Lives of the Fathers of Italy* offer, as it were, an instructive slice through the different levels of culture of urban and rural populations of the beginning of the seventh century. The letters and the sermons of Gregory attest not only to his literary talents, but also to the still-living use of Latin in the Italy of his time. This purified culture, which was still faithful to the ancient and patristic lessons, this language which still knew how, with skill, to 'make itself everything to everyone in order to save them all' (1 Corinthians 9:22) would not cease to bear fruit amongst Gregory's readers, particularly amongst the shepherds of souls for whom he would remain a model, including his severe but balanced attitude towards the culture which was necessary and sufficient for the Christian preacher.

Within the framework of a provincial bishopric, but also of a famous centre for pilgrimages to the tomb of St Martin, Gregory, bishop of Tours from 572 to 594 (and thus scarcely any older than his contemporary Gregory the Great), was a good example of the evolution of culture in south-central Gaul at the end of the sixth century. He too was the son of a 'senator'; he had received an education, which was both familial and clerical, in the *domus ecclesiae* of his uncle Gallus, bishop of Clermont-Ferrand. Having become Bishop of Tours, he wrote the ten books of his *History* (for a long time known as the *History of the Franks*). His initial résumé of universal history is less original than his portrayal, in Books VI–X, of the often violent vicissitudes of Merovingian society between 580 and 591. In the preface of his *History* Gregory of Tours deplored the decline of Gallo-Roman culture in severe terms; one would be wrong to see in that only a form of *locus humilitatis propriae*, recommended by the ancient rhetoricians and becoming a ritual cliché in the prefaces of late antiquity. This sense of deterioration, which his sometimes laborious, but so picturesque and personal Latin communicates to the reader, comes from a still

47 Gregory, *In Reges* V.30: 'Hanc quippe saecularem scientiam omnipotens Deus in plano anteposuit, ut nobis ascendendi gradum faceret, qui nos ad divinae Scripturae altitudinem levare debuisset.' Commentaries: Riché (1972), pp. 197–200, and Dagens (1977), pp. 37ff.

48 Cf. Banniard (1992a), pp. 112–27.

lucid knowledge of what must have been a more correct language and thus from a fairly ample and direct reading of ancient and patristic literary works.[49] His numerous hagiographical works, on the lives and miracles of Martin of Tours and Julian of Brioude, of the Desert Fathers, of confessors and martyrs of yesteryear, answered an increasing demand from uneducated listeners. Such works bore witness to the increasing place which the production and the more or less liturgical reading of these hagiographical texts was taking and would take in the seventh century in the living culture of Christianity among the Gauls. Gaul/Francia would produce more hagiographical texts than any other area of *Romania*.

In the first third of the seventh century, the sixteen still extant works of Isidore of Seville, reorganiser of the church in Spain and friend of the princes of Toledo, gave full expression to a rebirth of the Hispanic Latin culture which had been heralded in the sixth century by the phenomena of peripheral cultural revivals, from Justus of Urgel to Apringius of Béja. Such had been above all the reforming action and the rich and varied literary works of Martin of Braga, in a Galicia which was still under Sueve rule.[50]

The Isidorian renaissance was the result of an exceptional historical conjuncture: the unification of the kingdom, the conversion of the Visigoths, and the birth of a Hispano-Gothic ideology. The craftsmen of this religious, social and, in the widest sense, cultural change were Leander, the elder brother of Isidore, the instigator of the Third Council of Toledo in 589, then Isidore himself, organiser in 633 of the Fourth Council of Toledo, in respect of which it has been possible to talk of a 'constituent work'.[51] Both wrote in order to support and develop their action: Leander by polemicising against Arianism, Isidore by dedicating to different members of the new society which had sprung from these changes – princes, bishops and clerics, monks and laity, Goths and Romans – works that transmitted a new culture which was intellectual, moral, historical and religious.

It is within the breadth of such a project that one must situate, without isolating it, Isidore's encyclopaedia of *Etymologies* 'on the origin of certain things'. This sort of 'data bank' in twenty books held in stock knowledge borrowed

49 On the last page of his *Historiae*, he insisted upon excusing himself for the 'rusticity' of his style. These declarations should not be taken literally nor considered as purely conventional protestations: the truth no doubt lies somewhere between the two. See Heinzelmann (1994), especially pp. 7–10.

50 Martin, abbot then bishop of Braga from 561 to 580, extended his pastoral care from the still half-pagan Galician peasants to the Sueve princes, for whom he wrote small manuals of practical morals/ethics inspired by the works of Seneca. Other Hispanic writers of the second half of the sixth century made the Mediterranean regions and the south-west of the peninsula illustrious: see Fontaine (1997), VII, pp. 774ff.

51 Orlandis and Ramos Lissón (1986), ch. 4, p. 261: *La obra constituyente del IV Concilio de Toledo.*

from ancient and patristic sources. The work took the form of entries of etymologies and synonyms, but also of 'differences' and of simple glosses. But this manual of education of erudite reference was also a dictionary which fixed the meaning of words, thus contributing to the defence and propagation of a correct use of Latin vocabulary, and of a grammatical knowledge whose categories of thought and methods of work went back to Hellenistic culture.[52] The *Etymologies* served, in short, as a cultural memory bank to which westernised Latin intelligence and language would come constantly to stock up. Proof of this lies in a diffusion of a work which was as exceptional by its rapidity and its duration, as by its geographical spread and the number of its manuscript copies.[53] Isidore joined to this manuals of sacred exegesis, historical works, disciplinary and moral treatises for use by clerics and laity and even a monastic Rule.

He was very careful to endow the new Hispanic nation, the beneficiary of both Rome and the Gothic people, with a sort of historical and spiritual charter. This ideology inspired the imagery of the *Praise of Spain*, a work in a lyrical tone which acts as a prologue to his *History of the Goths*: having espoused Rome, Spain had just celebrated her second wedding with the people of the Goths who had 'seized' her.[54] His new vision of Hispanic history, however, did not make Isidore in any way neglect universal history, literary history or that of the institutions and rites of the church.[55] The rebuilding of Spain and of her new culture culminated in a sort of manifesto for a new Christian society, contemporary with and complementary to the provisions of the Fourth Council of Toledo: that is, the three books of *Sentences* in which are formulated the doctrine, spirituality and morality which should guide those responsible for the new society.[56] But none is prophet in his own country: in the seventh century Visigothic Spain would barely keep the promises of this great Isidorian plan. Its realisation was to come up against the egoisms of a nobility incapable of a new civic order, against the anarchy of a frustrated society, and against the disorders sparked off by an ever more ferocious intolerance towards the Jews. It was later, outside of Spain, that the ideas and the culture of Isidore would

[52] Comprehensive study by Fontaine (1983a), including an important bibliography in the 2nd edition, vol. III. See also Fontaine (1996), and Díaz y Díaz (1982).

[53] A fundamental, comprehensive view, starting from codicological data, by Bischoff (1960).

[54] *De laude Spaniae* (end): 'Et licet te sibimet eadem Romulea virtus primum victrix desponderit, denuo tamen Gothorum florentissima gens post multiplices in orbe victorias certatim rapuit et amavit.' On this text and on the Isidorian exaltation of the *regnum Gothorum*, see Teillet (1986), pp. 463–502, and especially pp. 498ff.

[55] *Chronicon*; *De Viris Illustribus*; *De Origine Officiorum* (in two books). See *Clavis Patrum Latinorum* (1995), nos. 1190–1215.

[56] See the convincing studies by Cazier (1986), pp. 373–86, and (1994).

find their most effective application in the *reformatio* of church and culture, which we call the Carolingian renaissance.[57]

There are good reasons why it would be the island races that became the most effective diffusers of the Isidorian culture and of its ideal on the continent. In the most ancient Irish and Anglo-Saxon Latin writing, the emphasis on erudition and on grammatical thought was a response to the primordial needs of these young Christianities, which had barely emerged from their pagan cultures and from their native tongues. The double flame of island culture, especially from the second half of the sixth century onwards, would owe its influence not only to the dynamism of the wandering apostolics of the Irish monks in Great Britain and on the continent (the *peregrinatio Scottorum*) but primarily to the upsurge of Latin culture in the islands: it was in 597 that the monk and missionary Augustine, sent by Gregory the Great, became archbishop of Canterbury. A little before this date, Columbanus had left Bangor to go from Ireland to the continent. He and his disciples went there to create new monasteries, from Burgundy, via Switzerland, as far as Cisalpina where Bobbio was founded in 614. In Great Britain and in Ireland, the turn of the sixth century thus also seemed to be a period of intense change.

By their action, their thought and their literary legacy, the great 'founders of the Middle Ages' gave a fresh face to the culture of the seventh century. They made use of the legacy of antique education and the new demands of a Christian education in a pastoral impulse which differentiated between clerics, monks and laity. Adapting it to the different conditions of their responsibilities and of their respective commitments to religious life, they gave a positive impulse to the diversified cultural activity of that century. It was an activity which was to spread with particular vitality in the north and north-west, in regions where the ecclesiastical and therefore cultural *reformatio* of the Carolingian age would start to build up.

Spain lived on the crest of the Isidorian age, but without the remainder of the century seeing any minds which were as original and creative as that of Isidore. The royal city of Toledo, capital of the kingdom, was the centre of cultural activity. Many sons and daughters of the Gothic nobility came there to receive an education. The monastery of Agali at the gates of the city educated monks and clerics, but also lay people. Even at court, certain educated princes followed the tradition founded by king Sisebut, the friend of Isidore, exercising a sort of patronage and frequenting the archbishops of Toledo, of whom several left grammatical, poetical, historical and theological works. The most talented was Julian, bishop of the capital from 679 to 690. Theologian

[57] On the Carolingian reception of Isidore, Fontaine (1992b). See also *La Scuola*, in *Settimane* (1972).

and exegete, poet and liturgical writer, he was also the author of a grammar, and the chronicler of the *Rebellion of Paul against Wamba*, the only work of the Visigothic age whose very lively tales were comparable to those of Gregory of Tours. At the same time, a very different literary activity was developing in the north-west of the peninsula, in the mountainous solitudes of Bierzo. The works of the monks Fructuosus and Valerius expressed the narrowly ascetic ideal of an austere and rural Christian culture, quite removed from the Isidorian tradition and more analogous to that of the insular monks. During this time the Latin culturalisation of the Lombards was much slower in Italy, even if the arrival of a Catholic dynasty in Pavia hastened this process there after 650; but literary production only became perceptible again there from the next century onwards.

Despite a certain atony in seventh-century continental Europe, including among the Gauls/Franks who were scarcely distinguished by the mediocre works of the chronicler known as Fredegar, of a Defensor of Ligugé or of a Theofrid of Corbie, the resumption of cultural activity can be measured in quasi-material fashion, particularly in the second part of the century, through the copying and the circulation of manuscripts. In this field the progress made, during the last half century, by codicological science nowadays provides the means of following with a certain precision the circulation of books as well as their carriers, from Spain to Ireland and to Germany, and from Rome as far as the British Isles. This we can illustrate with a single example, the research on the most ancient manuscript tradition of Isidore's *Treaty on Nature*, which has allowed us to see its diffusion in Europe and its successive editions in the courts of the seventh and eighth centuries.[58] The stemma of these ancient manuscripts, established by the traditional philological method of classification according to common faults, has been able to be projected into time and space, thanks to the codicological analyses now available in the collection of the *Codices Latini Antiquiores*. It has thus been possible to write a few novel pages of cultural history on 'the diffusion of *De natura rerum* in Europe from Sisebut to Charlemagne' and to show the routes taken in the seventh century by the ancestors of the three groups of manuscripts – Hispanic, Gallic then Italic, insular then Germanic – which transmitted the text to us.[59] It has even been possible to determine that it was in the islands, and most probably in Ireland, that the text was glossed and augmented by one chapter. Of course, we must have as much critical apparatus as possible at our disposal in order to supply the materials for a later study of the spelling and the quality of the Latin of the

[58] Fontaine (1960).

[59] *Ibid.*, pp. 69–84, and the classic stemma of witnesses of the seventh and eighth centuries (facing p. 70), projected on to a map (facing p. 84).

copyists in a given scriptorium. Thus one can get an idea of the possibilities offered by codicology, in tracing a concrete history of the living culture and a mapped geography of the circulation of manuscripts: the philological task of the textual editor has thus become inseparable from that of the historian, and helps to open up new perspectives.

The journeys of the *Scotti* and their ideal of missionary *peregrinatio* contributed in no small way to expediting the circulation of manuscripts between the islands and the continent.[60] The movements of the Irishman Columbanus are a classic example. At the beginning of the century he went from Burgundy across the Alps, and new monastic foundations marked out his routes: from Annegray and Luxeuil to St Gall, Bregenz and Bobbio. One other example is notable: that of the Northumbrian abbot Benedict Biscop, who accomplished no fewer than six journeys to Rome between 653 and 668.[61] Not only did his toughness allow him to bring back to the north of England quantities of precious manuscripts, some of which even went back to copies from Vivarium.[62] Biscop also succeeded in bringing back to Northumbria the archichanter of St Peter's at Rome, in order to have him teach Latin chant directly to the Northumbrian monks.

Such achievements were not isolated. They explain the rapid development of Latin culture amongst the islanders and the quality of their knowledge and of their Latin. The early arrival in Ireland of several works by Isidore of Seville in the middle of the century illustrates the diversity of the sources of this enrichment. In this island, which Rome had never conquered, the Christianisation and the development of monastic life (so pre-eminent that the bishops were abbots[63]), together with the adoption of Latin as a written cultural language, rapidly brought about the appearance of a new literary production. The latter co-existed, if not interacted, with Celtic literary traditions, as one can see in the oldest Irish Christian hagiography.[64] One can see it too in the singular poems of 'hisperic' Latinity, these strange *Hisperica Famina* (Irish or perhaps Gallic?) whose title alone testifies to an extreme research in lexical hermetism.[65] The taste for rare words (sometimes borrowings from Greek and Hebrew), intertwining constructions and rhythmic lines all make up a refined and artistic language whose obscurity is sometimes compensated for

[60] Starting with the classic works by Levison (1946) and Laistner (1957). On Colombanus, see the papers in Clarke and Brennan (1981), also the bibliography by de Prisco in Polara (1987), p. 278. On the Irish and the continent, Löwe (1982) and Picard (1991).

[61] On Benedict Biscop and his travels Hunter Blair (1970), pp. 155–83.

[62] Courcelle (1948), pp. 356ff and 374ff.

[63] On the issue of Irish abbot-bishops, see Stancliffe, chapter 15 above.

[64] For a subtle interpretation of these developments, see the exemplary study by Stancliffe (1992).

[65] Starting from the annotated edition by Herren (1974) and (1987). Both have a detailed bibliography.

by a freshness of inspiration, which is not without taste. From the memories of these 'wandering scholars', descriptions of inland and coastal landscapes deliver up the poetic keys of an original world, far removed from that of the classical Mediterranean.

The influence of Celtic-Roman culture crossed, in England, with that of the new missionaries who came from Rome to Canterbury in 669: the African abbot Hadrian who had been bishop of Naples, and the eastern monk Theodore of Tarsus.[66] The synthesis of these Roman, Gallo-Roman and Irish currents was to find its highest expression in the monasteries of Northumberland. The literary and spiritual genius of the Anglo-Saxon monk the Venerable Bede made him the last and not the least of the founders of the Middle Ages.[67] In his *Ecclesiastical History of the English People* Bede rightly paid homage to the cultural work of the two Roman missionaries: 'Both being abundantly educated in sacred as well as secular letters, never surely was there a happier time since the Angles conquered Britain.'[68] It was only in the middle of the century that this Roman influence had begun to penetrate the Northumbrian foundations of Lindisfarne (established in 635 by Aidan of Iona) and of Whitby.[69] It could be seen clearly in the monastic education dispensed by the twin monasteries of Wearmouth and Jarrow, founded in 674 and 685 respectively.

In the course of the half century which he spent in Jarrow (between 685 and 735), Bede acquired his immense knowledge and rediscovered the secret of a pure Latinity, linking Roman gravity to a classical fluidity. He described his serene and hardworking life, divided between intellectual and spiritual joys: 'Living since then all the time of my life in this same monastery, I devoted all my cares to meditating upon the Scriptures, and whilst observing the regular discipline and the practice of singing each day in church, I always found it sweet to learn, to teach or to write.'[70] Is there a finer expression of the monastic alliance between the love of letters and the desire for God? Still, one must note the way in which Bede is no longer Isidore. Like Aldhelm of Malmesbury in the south of England, Bede distrusted rhetoric and dialectic and also ancient cosmology (it is a pity that it had not been Christianised by Isidore), and he

[66] Cf. Bischoff and Lapidge (1995). For England in the seventh century, see also Thacker, chapter 17 above.

[67] In addition to Hunter Blair (1970), see Bonner (1976) and King and Stevens (1979). Also Diesner (1981).

[68] Bede, *HE* IV.2: 'et quia litteris sacris simul et saecularibus . . . abundanter ambo erant instructi . . . neque umquam prorsus ex quo Brittaniam petierunt Angli, feliciora fuere tempora'.

[69] On Iona and its influence, Stancliffe, chapters 15 and 16 above, and on the Northumbrian monasteries, Thacker, chapter 17 above.

[70] Bede, *HE* I.5, 24: 'cunctumque ex eo tempus vitae in eiusdem monasterii habitatione peragens, omnem meditandis scripturis operam dedi; atque inter observantiam disciplinae regularis, et cotidianam cantandi in ecclesia curam, semper aut discere aut docere aut scribere dulce habui.'

turned most frequently to the sole authority of the Bible. Amongst profane wisdom he tolerated only a grammar purged of all allusion to antique paganism, and the techniques which made possible the calculating of periods in monastic life: cosmography, astronomy and calendar computation. Despite his praise of the profane and sacred knowledge of Theodore and of Hadrian, he well and truly renounced ancient culture as such, at least in theory.

Insular culture was to work wonders on the continent, in the restoration there of the observance of the precepts which ruled monastic life and also in the correct application of the Latin language, indispensable to the elementary culture of the monks and the good keeping of the services. Faithfulness to the old and new rules, which resulted from this contribution, was expressed by the diffusion of the so-called 'mixed' Rule of Benedict and Columbanus in the continental monasteries of the seventh and eighth centuries.[71] Moreover, the pure insular Latin of which Bede was to leave the most polished literary models struggled effectively here against the graphical, if not already grammatical, corruption of the Latin which many continentals practised, even the *litterati*. It was because, despite their bilingualism, Celts and Saxons who had thus become Latinophones, spoke and wrote an acquired Latin language without any connection with their maternal language, Celtic or Germanic, that this rather stiff language was paradoxically more correct than that of what would become the Romance-speaking lands, where the language was bastardised by the accelerated evolution of a spoken Latin from the old Roman stock. Later on, this reimportation of a sort of colonial Latin from Ireland and Britain slowed down the divergence between written and spoken Latin, and it helped to consolidate the positions of Latin culture on the continent. A little later, however, the refound awareness of classical correction would only increase the feeling of distance, henceforward insurmountable, between the written and spoken languages. The emergence of the continental romance languages would follow.

A new cultural species was in the process of being born from these contacts. In Frankish Gaul, as in Spain, whilst some classical traits flourished in the Latin texts edited by hardly literate scribes, such as in the *Formulary* of Marculf and the *Chronicle* of Fredegar, or on the inscribed slates of the Visigoths,[72] it was the reading of ancient and patristic works, including those of the great writers of the beginning of the century, that supported the effort to restore a Latin which was faithful to the norms of the traditional school. But this effort came up against the lowering of the level of teaching then being given in the bishoprics

[71] This mixed form spread particularly in the foundations of Queen Balthild from 650 onwards. One can find it in the eighth century in the abbey of St Wandrille: see Fontaine (1982). On Balthild, Fouracre, chapter 14 above.

[72] Editions of the slates by Velazquez (1989) and (1991). But this is still Latin, in the judgement of Díaz y Díaz (1992).

and the monasteries. The hagiographers nevertheless allow us to glimpse the variable modalities of the scholars' training of the seventh century when they sketch the infancy and youth of future saints.[73] Besides the education given in the bishoprics and monasteries, one can see from these texts that a certain intellectual and/or spiritual initiation remained guaranteed in several places. First of all in the family, which sometimes entrusted the child to a preceptor; then in the public schools, for which the bishops continued to assume the patronage in certain towns; lastly in the princely courts, where the adolescent was often taken in charge by a nutritor who guaranteed that he had some sort of material, moral, intellectual and even religious tutelage. Except for the child's initial education in the family, there was scarcely any canonic order in the subsequent attendance at these different places by adolescents; for this order varied at random in the individual biographies. The methods and the content were different depending on whether it was a monk, a cleric or a layman who was being educated, even if many examples showed a great variety of movement or crossings between these three ways. One can also distinguish geographical divergences: the south remained more faithful to the antique legacy, the north was more a tributary of Celtic and Germanic customs. The diversity of methods and objectives thus reflected, in theory and practice, the differentiation of the new societies in the making. But these latter all took pains to maintain the practice of writing, indispensable to administration as well as to religious life, even when faced with popular cultures whose oral traditions were strengthened and renewed by the constant practice of Christian liturgy, through listening to readings, homilies and prayers, and the singing of psalms and hymns.[74]

The tension between the spoken and the written language had not yet reached breaking point. The precepts and diversified linguistic practice of a Gregory the Great remained a model for the preachers who tried very hard to lower the stylistic level of their Latin in order to be understood by all their listeners. In northern Gaul, the *Life of St Eligius*, composed shortly after his death in 660 by his friend Bishop Audoin of Rouen, shows that at the end of the seventh century communication in the Latin language between a priest and his listeners was still acceptable on condition that the speaker forced himself to 'give his pronunciation as rustic an inflection as his style'. The fragments of the sermons of Eligius, which were transcribed in this Life, bear witness to this effort at simplification, even if it remains 'highly likely that part of the message escaped its listeners'.[75]

The cultural divergence between East and West thus reached a critical degree at the end of the seventh century. It had been accentuated by the mutual distrust engendered by the military adventures of Justinian in the western

[73] Heinzelmann (1990). [74] Van Uytfanghe (1974) and, for the oral culture, Richter (1994).

[75] This is the clear and nuanced conclusion of Banniard (1992b).

Mediterranean, and no less by the theological positions he adopted. It had been aggravated by the increasing ignorance of Greek in the West, and of Latin in the East where, under Heraclius, it ceased to be the official language of the Empire.[76] In the West, in the course of these two centuries, the Greek language and Greek culture ended up by retaining no more than a few bridgeheads in certain privileged centres. In the time of Bishop Martin, Braga, for example, had a school of monastic translators, and for a few decades Canterbury saw the spreading influence of the twin Greek and Roman culture of Theodore of Tarsus, but neither the Byzantine officials of Ravenna nor the refugees from the East in Rome seem to have contributed towards any local restoration of Greek language or culture. Only Sicily remained the foyer of a Hellenism sufficiently vibrant for the emperor Constans II in 660 to have thought of transferring his capital there when the Empire was nearly overwhelmed by Islam and by Slavs; but this Hellenism remained insular and, as such, isolated. Byzantine Africa itself fell into the hands of the Arabs who seized Carthage in 695 before occupying the greater part of Spain from 711 onwards: Byzantium then lost its last positions in the western Mediterranean, with the exception of the exarchate of Ravenna.

All these Arab conquests of lands which were formerly Roman, were to bring in their wake a long exodus of educated men, and thus of manuscripts, towards the Christian territories situated to the north-west of the Mediterranean, a factor which was most important in preparing the way for the Carolingian renaissance. This latter was an indirect consequence of the political change which one can see beginning at the battle of Tertry in 687. The victor at Tertry was Pippin of Herstal, 'mayor of the palace' of Austrasia, and victory heralded the eventual transfer of sovereign power from the Merovingians to the Pippinid family.[77] Educated in St Denis, the Pippinids (or, later, 'Carolingians') were to concentrate on the abbeys in the north and the east of Gaul, especially those of their own region, between the rivers Scheldt and Meuse. They were to value monastic education so much that they had it given to their children. In the same département (nowadays the Somme), where the battle of Tertry was to be fought, the Irish founded a monastery in the second half of the seventh century at *Peronna Scottorum* (on the site of the future town of Péronne) near the tomb of their compatriot St Fursey who died about 650. This monastic establishment was to become one of the most active missionary bases of their religious and cultural influence on the continent, on both sides of the Rhine. It was also at the end of the seventh century that Latin culture began once again to be the object of official recognition in northern Italy. Byzantines and Lombards

[76] See Berschin (1968) and (1980); also Herren (1988).

[77] For a different view of the Battle of Tertry and its consequences, Fouracre, chapter 14 above.

signed a peace treaty there in 680; and a few years later King Cunipert solemnly welcomed a Latin grammarian to his court at Pavia, whilst a literary creation worthy of this name was reborn: in prose, with the writing of the *Origo Gentis Langobardorum* towards 671; in poetry with the composition of the *Rythmus de Concilio Ticinensi* in 698.

Whilst signs of such a renewal were multiplying across the Christian West, the Islamic grip was tightening its hold on all the Byzantine East – with the exception of Asia Minor – and Constantinople was besieged five times by Arab troops between 673 and 677. The inevitable decline of cities, and the destruction and massacres provoked by these invasions dealt blows to ancient and Christian Hellenism which could scarcely be put right again, and to scholastic institutions which had hardly changed their programmes or their methods since the separation of the two *partes imperii* in 395. These disasters brought about a veritable rupture of cultural traditions in the thus reduced Empire.[78] Hence the production in Byzantium of florilegia and of apocalypses, but also of the historical fiction of the 'patriographers' who imaginatively tried to rewrite the past in order to compensate for the present-day reality of despair. In a sort of examination of conscience, the men of these generations tried to redefine their knowledge and to 'reach a safety and permanence in the midst of uncertainty'. Thus, in an as yet obscure way, they prepared for a profound change in Byzantine culture, and thus for the painful birth of another Middle Ages.[79]

[78] On this late continuity and its violent break, see Lemerle (1971), although this excellent work unfortunately separates Christian culture and production. See also Kazhdan (1983) and Wilson (1983).

[79] The exploration of the crisis of conscience and of the slow changes that affected Byzantine culture in the seventh century has been undertaken in particular by Cameron (1992), from whom this final paragraph takes its inspiration.

CHAPTER 28A

ART AND ARCHITECTURE OF WESTERN EUROPE

Ian Wood

The end of the West Roman Empire led to the fracturing of western Europe into a host of sub-Roman states. The new masters of what had been the west Roman provinces were for the most part Germanic war-leaders, although in the western parts of Britain there was a resurgence of Celtic power, while Ireland and much of Scotland had never been subject to Rome. The emergence of Germanic, and the development of Celtic kingdoms introduced or at least gave greater prominence to non-Roman artistic traditions, especially in metalwork and subsequently in manuscript illumination. At the same time Roman cultural traditions did continue, and indeed develop, and not only in those parts of the West which were reconquered by the Byzantines, like Ostrogothic Italy. The barbarian kingdoms of the West modelled themselves in many respects on the Roman Empire, and this modelling included the acquisition of Roman objects and the commissioning of objects in Roman style. Yet the desire to ape Rome was not strong enough to create anything like a unified artistic culture.

Neither did the growing uniformity of religious belief create such a culture, even though Christianity gave the West a single religion, a common set of religious practices (for instance in the liturgy and pilgrimage), and, perhaps, a more unified exegetical position for understanding art.[1] Individual scenes from the Bible were depicted time and again. Furthermore, the leading saints of the church were provided with a recognisable iconography, making them an identifiable presence in much of the post-Roman West.[2] Despite all this, the dominant feature of western art and architecture in the centuries following the demise of the West Roman Empire was the absence of any single defining style.[3] As a corollary, however, sheer variety and experiment is in itself a distinguishing mark of the period.

[1] Elsner (1995).

[2] On the change within artistic representation, see Brown (1999) and Wood (1999).

[3] Nees (1997), p. 966.

ARCHITECTURE

In many respects architecture was the least innovative area of western art in the early Middle Ages. Unlike Byzantium, western Europe did not witness anything as striking as the developments which culminated in the building of the dome of Hagia Sophia. Certainly there were centrally planned buildings, most notably baptisteries, but also churches such as S. Vitale in Byzantine Ravenna. For the baptismal liturgy a square, circular or octagonal building was functional, and also ideologically appropriate, since such shapes had been associated with the architecture of tombs: and what was baptism but the death of the Old Adam and the birth of the New?[4] Most western church architecture, however, derived in one way or another from the rectangular basilica, whose form was well suited to the requirements of the liturgy of the mass.

Yet there were other pressures which determined the shape of early medieval churches. Even in Rome buildings were reused, either in their entirety or as *spolia*. Several of the most important papal churches of the sixth and seventh centuries were adapted from previous buildings: SS. Cosmas and Damian (*c.*530) was created out of two imperial buildings, S. Maria ad Martyres (609) was created out of the Pantheon, and S. Adriano (*c.*630) had been the senate house itself.[5] The first and last of these were rectangular in plan. In all three cases the take-over of a previous building must also have signalled something of the papacy's relation to the past: to the old administrative structures of imperial or senatorial Rome or to the failed religion of the pagans. The papacy was heir to one and victor over the other.

There were, however, some major churches which were 'built from the ground up': including Pope Pelagius' S. Lorenzo (*c.*580) and Pope Honorius' S. Agnese (*c.*630), both of them, significantly, overlying catacombs outside the walls of the city.[6] One of their functions must have been to cope with pilgrims in search of the shrines of the martyrs. The most influential piece of Roman architecture to be erected in this period was, however, not a complete church, but rather the new annular crypt created by Gregory the Great (590–604), built, like the shrines of Laurence and Agnes, to cope with the crowds of pilgrims: in this case for those visiting the chief shrine of Rome, that of St Peter.[7]

New building was more obviously in evidence in Ravenna, the administrative capital of Byzantine Italy. The city had seen a building boom throughout the fifth century, having become the favoured city of the last western rulers of the Theodosian dynasty. There the empress Galla Placidia (d. 450) built a palace chapel, the basilican church of S. Giovanni Evangelista (post-425), and a complex dedicated to the Holy Cross, which included a shrine to

[4] Krautheimer (1942). [5] Krautheimer (1980), pp. 71, 72.
[6] Krautheimer (1980), pp. 83–5. [7] Krautheimer (1980), p. 86.

St Lawrence, now known (wrongly) as the Mausoleum of Galla Placidia. At the same time the bishops of Ravenna were involved in building the city's cathedral and its baptistery. This monumental tradition continued under the rule of the Ostrogothic king Theoderic (493–526), who was himself buried just outside Ravenna, in a remarkable two-storied mausoleum, whose only unquestionably Germanic feature is a thin ornamental frieze which recalls barbarian metalwork. (Plate 1).[8] The majority of the buildings surviving from Theoderic's reign, however, are churches, notably those constructed for the king's Arian followers, among them the basilican court chapel, now known as S. Apollinare Nuovo, and the Arian baptistery. The greatest of Ravenna's surviving Catholic churches, S. Vitale and S. Apollinare in Classe, were also planned in the period of Ostrogothic rule. They were, however, completed after the Byzantine reconquest of Ravenna in 540,[9] when they probably benefited from imperial largesse: certainly the church of S. Vitale boasts capitals supplied from the imperial quarries of Proconnesos in the Sea of Marmara.[10]

Ravenna was not the only Adriatic city to gain a fine new church in the mid-sixth century. Scarcely less impressive than the great Ravenna churches is the surviving episcopal complex of basilica, atrium and baptistery, built by Bishop Euphrasius in the Istrian town of Porec.[11] The Euphrasiana also seems to have benefited from Justinian's support, boasting marble capitals from Byzantium. Elsewhere, in the West, however, the history of architecture is difficult to follow. Few standing buildings of the Germanic successor states of western Europe can be attributed with certainty to the sixth and seventh centuries. In Visigothic Spain there is a handful of possible examples, among them the crypt of the cathedral at Palencia, and the churches of San Juan de Baños (Plate 2), Quintanilla de las Viñas and San Pedro de la Nave.[12] This last church was moved wholesale from its original site, and the authenticity of parts of its reconstruction is questionable. In any case its original date of construction is unclear. So too the building of Quintanilla de las Viñas presents a considerable chronological problem, though an inscription recording the restoration of the church in 879 provides a clear *terminus ante quem* for the first phase of the monument, which seems to be Visigothic. Another inscription, of the year 661, provides a more firm date for the building of Reccesuinth's aisled church of San Juan de Baños, though it is known from excavation that the east end of the church, which was originally trident shaped, has been radically altered. Despite the problems of dating these buildings and establishing their original form, it is certain that stone buildings, some of them aisled, were erected in

[8] Deichmann (1974), p. 221. [9] Deichmann (1976), pp. 48–9, 234–5.

[10] Deichmann (1976), pp. 96–105.

[11] Prelog (1994). [12] Fontaine (1973), pp. 173–7, 195–209.

the Visigothic kingdom, and that among the patrons of surviving buildings were the Visigothic kings themselves. Royal patronage is even more clearly demonstrated in the decision of the sixth-century king Leovigild (568–586) to build a new city, Reccopolis, named after his son Reccared.[13]

The Frankish kingdom, whose kings arguably had greater resources and more power than those of Spain, presents yet more problems for the architectural historian. No royal building from the Merovingian period survives. The date of the most imposing building that may come from this period, the baptistery at Poitiers, is hotly debated.[14] There is more general agreement about the chronology of two semi-subterranean buildings: the crypt of the seventh-century monastery at Jouarre,[15] and the late seventh- or early eighth-century mausoleum at Poitiers, known as the Hypogée des Dunes.[16] In terms of remnants of greater buildings there are, at best, the plans uncovered by archaeological excavation, notably from the sixth-century phases at Paris,[17] and from later Merovingian Nivelles.[18] Even church descriptions are few and far between,[19] although Gregory of Tours' description of the church of St Martin at Tours gives an indication of the opulence of a major sixth-century shrine, while the texts of inscriptions from the church show how a pilgrim was supposed to be spiritually affected as he or she progressed towards that shrine.[20] For the seventh century there is a tantalising description of an apparently complex monastic church at Manglieu.[21]

In fact there seems to be more surviving work of seventh-century Gallic stonemasons in England than in the territories of the Merovingians themselves. Benedict Biscop was provided with Gallic stonemasons by an otherwise unknown Frankish abbot, Torhthelm,[22] and he likewise turned to Francia for glaziers.[23] Wearmouth (founded 674), whose west front survives,[24] and Jarrow (founded 682), whose present choir was a complete Anglo-Saxon church,[25] thus provide our largest identified sample of Merovingian building techniques. Further, since Biscop had royal support,[26] it is likely that his builders were the best available. Whether such high, aisle-less buildings were the norm for seventh-century Francia, it is impossible to say. Jarrow also boasts the best evidence for the art of the Frankish glazier, notably in a window with a representation of a human figure.[27] To the examples of Wearmouth and Jarrow may

13 Heather (1996), pp. 293–5. See also Barbero and Loring, chapter 13 above.

14 Duval (1996), pp. 290–301.

15 De Maillé (1971); Duval (1998), pp. 188–97.

16 Duval (1996), pp. 302–9.

17 Duval (1998), pp. 151–83.

18 Mertens (1979).

19 See, however, the collection of material in Knögel-Anrich (1936). For building in the sixth-century kingdom of the Burgundians, see Wood (1986).

20 Van Dam (1985), pp. 230–55, and (1993), pp. 308–17.

21 *Vita Boniti* c.16.

22 *Vita Ceolfridi* c.7.

23 Bede, *Historia Abbatum* c.5.

24 Taylor and Taylor (1965), pp. 432–46.

25 Taylor and Taylor (1965), pp. 338–49.

26 Wood (1996), pp. 1–3.

27 Webster and Backhouse (1991), pp. 138–9.

be added the evidence of the crypts of Wilfrid's foundations of Ripon (*c.*671) and Hexham (*c.*672),[28] with their reused Roman masonry, although here the model may be Italian rather than Frankish.

The Anglo-Saxon evidence is not just important for revealing the skills of Frankish masons and glaziers. It is also important because the surviving material remains and the literary evidence, when taken together, allow some insights into the meanings of buildings. Some were intended to evoke Rome, being built of Roman stone, even though in scale and style they could in no way compare with any major imperial or papal building. In Britain traditions of stone-building seem to have failed in the course of the fifth century, and thereafter both Britons and incoming Irishmen built in timber.[29] The Germanic incomers too were used to traditions of timber-building. To build in stone, therefore, was a deliberate act, and it was one which involved the reuse of material from Roman buildings. Stone buildings in seventh-century England thus came to imply an adherence to Rome, or to the Roman church: Benedict Biscop's buildings at Wearmouth and Jarrow, built of Roman stone, signalled the patron's ideological connections.[30] Wilfrid's buildings may have had more specific resonances: the church at Hexham, with its catacomb-like crypt and with its galleries, may have been conceived as a copy of a Roman pilgrim church such as S. Agnese, which would still have been new at the time of Wilfrid's first visit to Rome.[31] Rather than the catacombs, however, Wilfrid's crypts seem to have been intended to bring to mind the Holy Sepulchre in Jerusalem.[32] Jerusalem, like Rome, may also have been represented by Benedict Biscop's buildings at Wearmouth and Jarrow, although here the intention seems to have been to recreate Solomon's Temple.[33]

SCULPTURE

Whilst Rome and Ravenna could outshine Francia and Britain in terms of the scale and technique of their buildings, Italy boasts little by way of known architectural sculpture from the sixth and seventh centuries. Even new column capitals from this period are rare, leaving aside those from the Proconnesian quarries. The systematic exploitation of the various styles of capital, Ionic, Corinthian and composite, which had had a new lease of life in the Christian Empire of the fourth and fifth centuries, also seems to have come to an end in this period.[34] Furthermore, although there was to be a significant school of Lombard carving, particularly in Cividale, this only comes

[28] Taylor and Taylor (1965), pp. 297–312, 516–18. [29] Bede, *HE* III.25.
[30] Bede, *Historia Abbatum* c.5. [31] See the description in Stephanus, *Vita Wilfridi* c.22.
[32] Bailey (1991), pp. 20–2. [33] Wood (1996), pp. 15–16. [34] Onians (1988), pp. 59–73.

into the limelight in the mid-eighth century, in the time of Ratchis (744–749, 756–757).[35]

In Spain the largest expanses of architectural carving which may plausibly be dated to the period are the great friezes, including one of inhabited vinescroll, from Quintanilla de las Viñas, which run round much of the exterior of the building.[36] More problematic is the date of the figured capitals of San Pedro de la Nave – art-historically the most intriguing aspect of the building.[37] Despite the lack of any clear analogues, they may be of the Visigothic period, since a Merovingian source seems to talk of figured capitals.[38]

No certain figured capitals of Merovingian date survive, although some of the capitals from the crypt at Jouarre do appear to be Merovingian, while others are Roman *spolia*, and yet others are nineteenth-century substitutes.[39] There is, however, other figure sculpture at Jouarre. Notably, there is a panel with a carving of a pair of figures, one of whom is censing, which appears to have been part of some architectural decoration. Better known are the sarcophagi of the crypt, notably those of Abbess Theudechildis and Bishop Agilbert (d. 680/90). Although the date of these pieces is disputed, and although the Theudechildis sarcophagus, with its fine run of scallop shells, may be Carolingian, there is a strong case for seeing the Agilbert sarcophagus, with its apparent depiction of a resurrection scene on the side and its image of Christ with the symbols of the evangelists on the end, as belonging to the Merovingian period (Plate 3).[40] Nor does Jouarre boast the only figure sculpture known from Merovingian Francia. Less fine, but nevertheless of extreme interest, is the early eighth-century depiction of Abbess Chrodoara from the lid of her sarcophagus at Amay.[41]

Moreover, like the crypt at Jouarre, the Hypogée des Dunes at Poitiers boasts considerable amounts of sculpture, though in the latter case the surviving sculpture is almost entirely architectural. The entrance passage down to the Hypogeum is lavishly decorated with various geometric and animal ornament, some of which has been seen as having a magical function, intended to guard the monument.[42] Once again there is figure sculpture: rows of incised angels, of dubious orthodoxy, and what seem to be representations of the two thieves from the Crucifixion, probably remnants of a Calvary scene. There may be an implication that the Hypogeum, like the crypts at Hexham and Ripon, was intended to call the Holy Sepulchre to mind.

35 Christie (1995), pp. 199–203.
36 Fontaine (1973), pp. 206–7.
37 Fontaine (1973), pp. 203–4.
38 *Vita Boniti* c.16.
39 De Maillé (1971), pp. 145–50; Duval (1998), p. 193. On the declining production of capitals from the Aquitanian quarries, Cabanot (1993), pp. 111–19.
40 De Maillé (1971), pp. 195–216; Duval (1998), pp. 193–5.
41 Gaillard (1996), p. 453.
42 Duval (1996), pp. 302–9; Kitzinger (1993), pp. 4–6.

The identified remains of architectural sculpture are perhaps more extensive in England than in Spain or France. At Wearmouth the western porticus and tower boasts two pairs of intertwined serpents, again perhaps apotropaic, on its lowest level, and there are remains of a figure higher up.[43] At Ledsham, the doorway into the tower, with its vegetal ornament, appears to be pre-Viking in concept, even if most of the stone has been renewed at some point.[44] So too Ledsham boasts a string-course of marigolds, similar to those at San Juan de Baños, on either side of the chancel arch. The majority of other pieces of architectural sculpture which survive unfortunately have no clear architectural context. Thus there are numerous baluster shafts from Wearmouth and Jarrow, which may have been intended to turn the churches into representations of the Temple of Solomon.[45] Both sites also boast fragments of what may have been liturgical furniture. Hexham retains an early Saxon frith-stool, as well as numerous sculptured fragments, some of which appear to have come from an early frieze.[46] What all these fragments demonstrate is that the overall effect of a major Anglo-Saxon church must have been very much richer than the austere walls at Jarrow and Escomb suggest.

Architectural sculpture is currently placed at the head of the development of Anglo-Saxon stone sculpture. The more famous pre-Viking crosses of Anglo-Saxon England are now seen as being secondary developments, and none of them can be placed before 700.[47] The earliest Irish stone crosses are dated even later, to the late eighth century at the earliest.[48] Crosses are also known from literary sources to have been erected in the Merovingian kingdom,[49] though what they were made of, and whether they were decorated, is unclear.

Uncertainty also surrounds the origins of the insular crosses. One source of inspiration is probably to be found in crosses which had been set up in the Holy Land, for instance on Golgotha and by the Jordan. Fanciful representations of these existed in the West, the former being portrayed in the apse-mosaic of S. Pudenziana in Rome,[50] the latter, possibly, on the dome mosaic in the Orthodox baptistery in Ravenna. In Northumbria King Oswald erected a wooden cross, before the battle of Heavenfield.[51] At some point, probably in the early eighth century, such influences were absorbed into a sculptural tradition which had already encompassed architectural decoration and liturgical furnishings. It may be significant that the most studied of surviving Anglo-Saxon crosses, that at Ruthwell, seems to have begun as a pillar, and only had a cross-head added in a second phase.[52] The cross on Golgotha was covered with jewels, and it is

[43] Cramp (1984), pp. 125–6; Kitzinger (1993), p. 4. [44] Taylor and Taylor (1965), pp. 380–2.
[45] Cramp (1984), pp. 118–21, 128–9; Wood (1996), p. 15.
[46] Cramp (1984), pp. 174–93. [47] Bailey (1996), p. 42. [48] Harbison (1998), pp. 151–3.
[49] Wood (1987), pp. 26–9. [50] Bailey (1996), p. 47. [51] Bede, *HE* III.2.
[52] Orton (1998), pp. 65–106.

likely that some Anglo-Saxon crosses were similarly decorated:[53] certainly the Anglo-Saxon poem the *Dream of the Rood* conjures up an image of a jewelled cross.[54] Yet the surviving stone crosses suggest that the Anglo-Saxons tended to deploy sculptural decoration where their Middle Eastern models had used precious stones.

MOSAIC DECORATION AND PAINTING

What Italy lacks in terms of architectural stone sculpture from the period, it makes up for in terms of its mosaic decoration. Ravenna in particular boasts a number of major schemes of mosaic decoration dating from the late fifth and sixth centuries, with two important panels from the seventh.[55]

Much has been made of the stylistic shifts evident within the art of Ravenna, from the Hellenistic mosaics commissioned by Galla Placidia, to the more iconic images of the reigns of Theoderic (493–526) and Justinian (527–565).[56] A simple comparison may be made between the cupola mosaics of the Orthodox (*c.*450) and Arian (*c.*500) baptisteries. Both monuments have a central roundel with a representation of the baptism of Christ, surrounded by a procession of Apostles. The figures in the earlier cupola, however, appear less stolid: and they are set against a blue background, rather than the otherworldly gold of the later image.

There are further contrasts to be drawn between the mosaics of Theoderic's reign and those of Justinian. Only part of the original scheme of the court chapel of Theoderic, now S. Apollinare Nuovo, survives, notably a remarkable New Testament sequence, in which Christ's miracles and passion are treated separately, with Christ himself appearing as a clean-shaven youth in the former cycle and as a bearded adult in the latter. Strangely the cycle forms the uppermost level of the decoration and can never have been easy to read: it should perhaps be seen primarily as marking out sacred space.[57] The lowest register of decoration at the west end of the church contains representations of the palace at Ravenna and of the port of Classe. Originally there were figures, presumably the king and courtiers, in the buildings, but in the Byzantine period these were removed, as was whatever lay between these architectural landscapes and the images of Christ and of the Virgin and Child which dominate the east end of the frieze. Instead, processions of virgins and martyrs, in style not unlike

[53] Bailey (1996), pp. 7–11; Hawkes (1999), p. 213. [54] Ed. Swanton (1970).

[55] There is a complete pictorial record in Deichmann (1958), and full commentary in Deichmann (1974) and (1976).

[56] See, for example, Kitzinger (1977), pp. 60–1. For a consideration of changing perception rather than style, Kitzinger (1993).

[57] Wood (1999), p. 36.

the apostles of the Arian baptistery, were inserted after the Byzantine conquest. These focus attention on Christ and the Virgin,[58] while at the same time the leading figures of each procession, Martin and Euphemia, emphasise the Orthodoxy of the new decoration: the bishop of Tours was known for his anti-Arianism, while Euphemia was the patron saint of the church in which the great Council of Chalcedon had been held in 451. Doctrine was of concern for Bishop Agnellus (556–569) when he ordered the redecoration of Theoderic's church. So too was a *damnatio memoriae* of the Gothic court, though one image of Theoderic seems to have survived in S. Apollinare Nuovo, albeit out of context, and relabelled as Justinian.[59]

The original inspiration for Theoderic's portrait may have been a group of imperial images which Galla Placidia had commissioned for her court church of S. Giovanni Evangelista.[60] Justinian's portrait more famously adorns the sanctuary wall at S. Vitale, where the emperor, offering the patten at the mass, looks across to a representation of his wife, Theodora, bearing the chalice. The eucharistic motif is continued on neighbouring panels, with representations of the sacrifices of Abel and Melchisadek on one wall, and that of Abraham, together with the same patriarch's entertainment of the three angels, on the other.[61] The portrayal of Melchisadek, priest and king, may have been intended to refer to Justinian. Further, Moses appears three times in the decoration, as he does in Justinian's church of St Catherine's on Mount Sinai,[62] and this may suggest an additional allusion to Justinian, as lawgiver. Despite this, and despite the column capitals from the imperial quarries of Proconnesos, the church of S. Vitale is not an imperial church. It was begun by Bishop Ecclesius, completed by Bishop Maximian, and funded by the banker Julianus Argentarius. Small points of detail, like the three Magi on the gown of Theodora which are reminiscent of the Magi in S. Apollinare Nuovo, suggest that this is also the work, somewhat self-referential, of a Ravennate workshop.

Local ideology is even more apparent in the decoration of S. Apollinare in Classe. Here Apollinaris himself stands, wearing his *pallium*: above him is a massive cross in a circular mandorla, at either side of which appear Moses and Elias, while three sheep look on (Plate 4).[63] This highly complex scene is at one level a representation of the Transfiguration, with Christ represented by the cross, and Peter, James and John by the trio of sheep. The image contrasts sharply with the less symbolic representation of the same scene in St Catherine's, Sinai. The Ravenna image also alludes to the celebration of the mass, for that was the moment when it was appropriate to wear the *pallium*.[64] In this

[58] Elsner (1995), pp. 222–39. [59] Deichmann (1974), pp. 151–2.
[60] Davis-Weyer (1971), pp. 16–17. [61] MacCormack (1981), pp. 259–66.
[62] See, for instance, Galey (1980), ill. 119. [63] Von Simson (1948), pp. 40–58.
[64] Markus (1981), p. 575.

particular instance, however, the bishop's vestments have a special significance, for it was only in 546 that Maximian was granted the *pallium*.[65] The iconography has further resonances: the saints of Ravenna reflect the increasing status of the city – Vitalis, supposedly the father of the Milanese martyrs Gervasius and Protasius, indicates Ravenna's growing independence from imperial Milan, while Apollinaris, supposedly a disciple of Peter, was particularly appropriate for a city whose bishops tried to elevate their status as close as possible to that of the popes.[66] For a brief moment they were to achieve near-parity, when in 666 they received from the emperor Constantine IV a grant of autocephaly, which was commemorated in a mosaic panel inserted into the decoration of the sanctuary of S. Apollinare in Classe.[67] Significantly the artists of this later panel modelled the composition on the image of Justinian in S. Vitale, showing a self-conscious continuance of Ravennate artistic culture.

The nearest surviving parallel to the mosaic schemes of Ravenna is that of the basilica of Bishop Euphrasius in Porec. Here, however, the iconography is Marian, with images of the Annunciation and Visitation.[68] Although the church may have benefited from Justinian's patronage there is no imperial iconography. Such imagery is equally absent from the mosaic cycles surviving from Rome in the sixth and seventh centuries. By far the most influential papal mosaic of this period is that set up by Pope Felix IV in the apse of SS Cosmas and Damian between 526 and 530.[69] Here Christ appears, clutching a scroll with seven seals, against a dark sky, standing on apocalyptic clouds, while saints Peter and Paul usher the martyrs Cosmas and Damian into his presence, with St Theodore and Pope Felix flanking the central composition. If the building had previously been the audience hall of the city prefect, as used to be argued, the portrayal of an apocalyptic Christ in the apse, above where the prefect would once have delivered legal judgements, would have been loaded with significance for those who first saw the mosaic. The image, moreover, retained its power, being recycled by Pope Paschal (817–824) in the ninth century, in the apses of his churches of St. Prassede and St. Cecilia.[70]

A rather softer image is to be found in the apse of S. Agnese, built by Pope Honorius (625–638), where the saint, herself almost incorporeal in golds and browns, appears against a golden background, with the slightest touches of red under her feet to signify her death by fire, while the popes Honorius and Symmachus stand at a distance on either side.[71] The incorporeality of the figure suggests that the viewer was being offered a glimpse of the heavenly

[65] Markus (1979), pp. 292–9.

[66] Von Simson (1948), pp. 5, 13–18, 50–8: but note the caution of Pizarro (1995), p. 12, n. 8.

[67] Deichmann (1976), pp. 273–9; von Simson (1948), pp. 59–60.

[68] Prelog (1994), p. 75, ills. xxxvii, xxxviii, li.

[69] Oakeshott (1967), pp. 90–4.

[70] Oakeshott (1967), pp. 204–13.

[71] Oakeshott (1967), p. 148.

world, which the martyr, buried in the catacomb below, had already entered. Although its restrained form appears not to have had the same artistic impact as the Christ of SS Cosmas and Damian, its colour scheme was to be copied by Pope Paschal's successor-but-one, Gregory IV (827–844), in the apse-mosaic of S. Marco, where the design of the SS Cosmas and Damian mosaic was again repeated, but in the colours of the S. Agnese mosaic, and, to tighten the connection, Agnes herself appears, similar in form to her image in her own extra-mural church.[72]

Although the apse mosaics of SS Cosmas and Damian and S. Agnese are the best known of the mosaics to have been set up by the papacy before the Carolingian period, mosaic work continued under papal patronage through the seventh century, for instance in the oratory of S. Venanzio in the Lateran, built by Pope John IV (640–642), in the mosaics set up by Pope Theodore (642–649) in S. Stefano Rotondo, and in those, known only from fragments, commissioned for Old St Peter's by Pope John VII (705–707).[73]

Running parallel to this history of mosaic is a history of fresco painting, though here the evidence comes largely from a single Roman site, S. Maria Antiqua. In origin this building seems to have been a vestibule for the palaces on the Palatine. It was converted into a church, probably around the year 500, and between then and 847, when the site was sealed off by an earthquake, its walls were redecorated on a number of occasions, most notably during the pontificates of Martin I (649–655) and John VII (705–707). In places strata of decoration lie one over the other, particularly on the 'Palimpsest' wall, so-called because it holds the remains of at least six phases of decoration. Although this makes identification of complete iconographic programmes difficult, it has ensured that S. Maria Antiqua is a touchstone for examining and dating changes in the style of painting from the sixth to the eighth centuries.[74]

Outside Rome, Ravenna and Porec there is a dearth of mosaic and fresco work, apart from a number of mosaic pavements from Italy and Istria which record the names of donors.[75] Mosaics and frescoes have not survived from Spain, France or England, although it is clear from comments in Gregory of Tours' writings that there were pictorial decorations in such churches as that of St Martin at Tours, and that these decorations belonged to complex artistic schemes.[76] The evidence for England is somewhat scantier, perhaps reflecting an absence of wall-painting, though Wearmouth is known to have been decorated with panel-paintings brought back by Benedict Biscop from

[72] Oakeshott (1967), pp. 213–16.
[73] Oakeshott (1967), pp. 150–8.
[74] Nordhagen (1990), pp. 150–317.
[75] Caillet (1993), pp. 447–8: Prelog (1994), pp. 16–18.
[76] Van Dam (1985), pp. 230–55, and (1993), pp. 308–17. The Gallic evidence is surveyed by Markus (1978), pp. 151–7.

the continent.[77] Bede records paintings of the Virgin and the twelve apostles, hung on what seems to have been something like a screen, as well as cycles of images from the Gospels and the Book of Revelation. The description brings to mind that of the seventh-century church at Kildare in Cogitosus' *Life of Brigid*, which records a building partititioned into northern and southern halves, and with something like an iconostasis cutting off the east end.[78] In describing the images at Wearmouth, Bede explains that they were intended to make the onlookers, literate and illiterate alike, contemplate the figures of Christ and the saints, and thus examine themselves.

There is clearer evidence for panel-paintings outside England and Ireland. Some actually survive in Rome,[79] and others are recorded in Francia. Gregory the Great's correspondence reveals that images were causing excitement in late sixth-century Marseilles, where some were destroyed by Bishop Serenus because he objected to his congregation adoring them.[80] Popular veneration of images, however, seems not to have caught on in the West, where Gregory the Great's notion that icons were 'not for adoration, but for the instruction of ignorant minds'[81] seems to have been common from the sixth century onwards.[82]

MANUSCRIPT ILLUMINATION

Some illuminated manuscripts from the late antique West still survive, notably the *Vergilius Vaticanus* and the *Vergilius Romanus*. Others, like the Vatican Terence, as well as the Calendar of Filocalus and the *Notitia Dignitatum*, are known from later copies. From the post-Roman West there is, likewise, a handful of illuminated manuscripts, though, unlike their predecessors, they are almost always Bibles or biblical books. But while the range of books comes to be limited, the style of illumination becomes more varied.

Italian Bibles of the sixth century are represented by the remaining pages of the Corpus Christi Gospels, which were arguably brought to Canterbury by Augustine in the Gregorian mission of 597.[83] Only one evangelist portrait, that of Luke, survives in the manuscript. It is a standard late Roman author-portrait of a type that would be used again and again in the early Middle Ages. Surrounding Luke, however, are scenes from the Gospel. Meanwhile on a separate folio is part of a New Testament cycle, running from Palm Sunday to Christ's journey to Golgotha.

[77] Bede, *Historia Abbatum* c.6; on the question of Bede's meaning, Kitzinger (1993), pp. 6–7.
[78] Kitzinger (1993), p. 6. [79] E.g. Beckwith (1979), pp. 88–96.
[80] Gregory I, *Register* IX.208; Markus (1978), pp. 151–7.
[81] Gregory I, *Ep.* XI.10. On Gregory's meaning, Chazelle (1990), pp. 138–53.
[82] Brown (1999). For a detailed discussion of the transmission of Gregory's ideas, Chazelle (1995).
[83] De Hamel (1986), pp. 11–12; Weitzmann (1977), pp. 112–15.

Such intensive illustration of narrative is, however, rare in the pre-Carolingian West. The provenance of one major exception, the Ashburnham Pentateuch, which is dated to the seventh century, has still to be determined: it may be either Visigothic or North African.[84] The other major sixth-century Italian Bible whose decoration can be reconstructed with some probability, the *Codex Grandior* of Cassiodorus, apparently eschewed narrative illustration.[85]

Although the *Codex Grandior* no longer survives, it is thought to have provided the model for the *Codex Amiatinus*, one of three copies of the Bible produced at Wearmouth/Jarrow before the year 716. Certainly the palaeography of the Northumbrian manuscript is so exact a copy of that of an Italian codex of the sixth century that its provenance was not properly identified until modern times.[86] *The Codex Amiatinus* contains an image of the prophet Ezra, as reviser of the Old Testament, which is certainly derived from a late antique author-portrait.[87] The manuscript boasts only one other major figurative image, a rather less successful *Maiestas*, as a frontispiece to the New Testament. Otherwise illustration is confined to various diagrams of the books of the Bible, the Tabernacle and the canon tables. The *Codex Grandior* had an additional plan of the Temple.[88]

Through the model behind the *Codex Amiatinus* late antique illumination also influenced the Lindisfarne Gospels of *c.*698, where the author-portrait which underpins the depiction of Ezra was again used, this time as a model for St Matthew.[89] So too must late antique models lie behind the other evangelist portraits of the Lindisfarne Gospels. Yet these only account for one of the influences on the scribe-artist of the Gospels, who drew on insular as much as Mediterranean tradition.

The origins of insular manuscript illumination are hotly debated, but the earliest major Gospel-book to survive from the British Isles more or less in its entirety is agreed to be the Book of Durrow, which was produced in the second half of the seventh century, apparently at an Irish centre associated with the monastic *paruchia* of St Columba, probably at Iona.[90] Like other insular Gospel-books, Durrow portrays evangelists by their symbols, Man, Eagle, Calf and Lion: the representations are anything but lifelike, revealing instead the influence of metalwork[91] – while in their turn these manuscripts may have had an impact on stone-carving.[92] Yet more striking than the evangelist symbols are the carpet pages which accompany them, where again the inspiration seems to come from Celtic and Germanic metalwork (Plate 5).[93] The carpet pages

[84] Weitzmann (1977), pp. 22–4, 118–25. [85] Meyvaert (1996).
[86] Bruce-Mitford (1967), pp. 2–9. [87] Meyvaert (1996), pp. 870–82.
[88] Meyvaert (1996), p. 853, [89] Wilson (1984), pp. 40, 49.
[90] Henderson (1987), pp. 19–55. [91] E.g. Henderson (1987), pp. 48, 52.
[92] Stevenson (1993), pp. 19–20. [93] E.g. Wilson (1984), p. 34; Henderson (1987), p. 32.

may have been intended to encourage contemplation.[94] This was probably one purpose of the *incipit* pages, where the opening words of each Gospel are transformed into complex patterns, which have to be studied with care to reveal the words underlying them. It is as if the insular artist was intent on showing how the Word of Christ could be made flesh, to paraphrase St John's Gospel.

Through their carpet and *incipit* pages the insular Gospel-books came to be more than simple transcriptions of holy text. They may have been regarded as icons or relics from the moment of their creation, and, even if they were not, it is clear that some were special productions for specific cult centres: thus the Lindisfarne Gospels were produced for the burial-place of Cuthbert, and it is likely that the Books of Durrow and Kells were intended for Columban shrines.[95]

Debate has raged over the extent to which the great insular Gospel-books are of Irish rather than Northumbrian inspiration and manufacture. The solutions propounded relate as much to national pride as to any irrefutable evidence.[96] Certainly there were production centres both in the Irish world (including Iona) and in Northumbria, and indeed the centres influenced one another. Lindisfarne itself began as a member of the Columban *paruchia*, although it was to break ties with Iona in 664. In addition, insular figures took their traditions of book production to the continent. Willibrord, who was born in Northumbria (*c.*658) but who trained in Ireland, founded the monastery of Echternach, where Irish, Anglo-Saxon and continental styles of book production and illustration blended, as can clearly be seen in the case of the Trier Gospels.[97]

METALWORK AND THE MINOR ARTS

Much of the inspiration for the carpet pages of the insular Gospel-books comes from metalwork, whether Celtic or Germanic. Parallels can be found on brooches or other items of polychrome jewellery and on such objects as hanging bowls, examples of all of which can be seen in the treasure found at Sutton Hoo.[98] The amount of high-quality metalwork produced was considerable, and the producers were men of great skill. In Germanic tradition smiths, like Wayland, could be hero-figures.

For the barbarians jewellery helped identify status. A king gave out gold rings and other tokens of esteem, and they were worn with pride.[99] Yet it was not only the Germanic and Celtic peoples who placed so much weight on the distribution and display of gold and silver. The nomadic peoples of the

94 Wood (1999), pp. 42–3.
95 Henderson (1987), pp. 54–5, 179–98.
96 Mostert (1995), pp. 92–115.
97 Netzer (1994).
98 Bruce-Mitford (1975–83).
99 Wood (1997), pp. 118–19.

Asian steppes, who periodically threatened the balance of western Europe, had a similar attitude to display, to judge by such finds as those of Pietroassa. The Romans too, particularly the Roman military, had long placed great emphasis on display. Buckles and brooches signified status. One type of brooch, the so-called *Kaiserfibel*, seems to have been associated with the emperor himself. When such brooches are found outside the boundaries of the Roman Empire, as at Pietroassa, the student is forced to ask whether this was a Roman gift or an imitation of a Roman object, and if the latter, whether the intention was merely to imitate the emperor or, more assertively, to emulate him.[100]

Some Roman objects became transformed out of all recognition at the hands of Germanic craftmen: thus, beyond the frontiers, Roman coins or medals became the models for types of medallions known as bracteates. The imperial inspiration of some of these objects is plain, though others are less derivative. Further, as their form changed, so too, it seems, did their function, for the contexts in which bracteates are found suggest that they, like the relief brooches of southern Scandinavia, were, or at least could be, the property of women who had a role to play in pagan cult.[101]

It was, however, not just jewellery that the Roman emperor distributed to those he wished to honour. The distribution of silver and gold plate was an imperial act.[102] Pieces given to barbarian rulers were much treasured: thus a *missorium* given by Aetius (d. 454) to Thorismund was jealously kept in the Visigothic treasury.[103] Some *missoria* with imperial images have survived. Other pieces of silverware, like the Anastasius dish from Sutton Hoo, might have reached a western treasury through the process of diplomacy. Some western kings, in their turn, attempted to emulate the Byzantine emperor in commissioning plate. Chilperic I (561–584), who received various pieces of treasure from Byzantium, had a dish and medallions made to his own glory and that of the Franks.[104]

Largesse in gold, silver and jewels was not just confined to the lay world. Bishop Eligius of Noyon (d. 660) transformed gifts of gold and jewellery to adorn Frankish shrines, and a fragment of a polychrome cross made by him for the church of St Denis survives.[105] Most of the treasure heaped up in early medieval churches has, however, long disappeared, recycled from the Viking Age onwards. A rare survival in the West is the Visigothic treasure from Guarrazar. Probably part of a church treasure from the royal city of Toledo, it was discovered in 1859. Among the pieces that remain is a magnificent gold

[100] Schmauder (1998), pp. 281–97.

[101] Magnus (1997), pp. 194–207. On the bracteates and Scandinavian influence, Hedeager, chapter 18 above.

[102] MacMullen (1962); Delmaire (1989).

[103] Fredegar, *Chron.* IV.73.

[104] Gregory, *Hist.* VI.I.

[105] *Naissance des arts chrétiens* (1991), pp. 311, 314.

votive crown, whose donor, King Reccesuinth (649–672), is named in letters hanging down as pendants (Plate 6).[106] Votive crowns in a Christian context are known from the time of the emperor Constantine onwards: they are attested in numerous records, and depictions of them occur in Carolingian ivories, but the treasure of Guarrazar is a rare indication of the bejewelled decoration possible on such a crown.

Gold, silver and precious stones were not the only valuable objects distributed in this period. In the later Roman Empire consuls sent out invitations to their ceremonial games on diptychs of ivory, a number of which have survived.[107] Some were preserved in cathedral treasuries, others were at least accessible to royalty. The famous Barberini diptych, representing a Byzantine emperor on horseback, appears to have been in the hands of the Frankish queen Brunehild (d. 613), or one of her supporters, since names of members of her family were scratched on to the back of it.[108] The fact that the door jambs of the ninth-century church of San Miguel de Lillo, built by King Ramiro I (842–850) on Monte Naranco outside Oviedo, are modelled on a games scene from an ivory diptych shows that the model was accessible to the ninth-century Asturian court.[109]

By contrast with the Carolingian period, that of the successor states boasts little fine elephant- or walrus-ivory carving, although there are numerous minor pieces such as combs. One eighth-century object, however, deserves mention. The Franks Casket is a whalebone box, apparently produced in Northumbria. On its front are two scenes: Wayland makes a goblet out of the skull of the son of King Nithud, before raping the king's daughter, Beaduheard, who would bear a demi-god son, Widia, as a result: alongside, the Magi approach Christ, the True God, who is held by the Virgin (Plate 7). The sides of the casket boast Romulus and Remus and a panel whose meaning is disputed: on the back there is a representation of the Sack of the Temple in Jerusalem by the emperor Titus, while the lid shows a legendary hero under siege. The scenes are identified by inscriptions, mainly runic, in Old English, although there are some Latin words and letters. The front has a riddle, whose answer is the whale from which the casket was made.[110] With its iconographic and stylistic references to Jerusalem and Rome, to Germanic legend and paganism, and to Christianity, the Franks Casket holds in balance many, though not all, of the strands which made up early medieval art and architecture. Although western art of the period boasts no dominant style, it has recurrent concerns – with status; with the past, Roman and, less often, Germanic; and with Christianity.

[106] Fontaine (1973), pp. 242–9. [107] Delbrück (1929). [108] Wood (1994), p. 135.
[109] Wood (1997), p. 124. [110] Wilson (1984), pp. 85–6.

CHAPTER 28B

ART AND ARCHITECTURE: THE EAST

Leslie Brubaker

The two centuries covered by this volume saw profound changes in material culture, though these changes were configured somewhat differently in the western and eastern halves of the old Roman empire. In both, however, the late antique city and its hegemonic culture increasingly gave way before new urban ideals and new social constructions that affected all aspects of the material world. Established media were given new uses: mosaics, for example, spread from floors to walls and ceilings, and in these cases came to be made predominantly of glass cubes, which allowed a greater range of colours than had the stone cubes suitable for flooring. Relatively new media, such as texts in the form of codices rather than scrolls – a format that became dominant only *c*.400 – expanded in importance and became a significant marker of church status. Other changes were more geographically constrained. In the eastern half of the Empire, for example, the dome, once restricted to centrally planned structures, joined longitudinal plans by the sixth century. Architectural sculpture continued across the old Empire, but monumental free-standing sculpture was rarely produced; and the bronze doors of Hagia Sophia in Constantinople demonstrate that while the technical skills required to cast large-scale bronze forms persisted in the East, they temporarily atrophied in the West. Meanwhile other techniques, and the motifs that they conveyed, moved in: what used to be called the 'arts of the migrations' – primarily metalwork and primarily non-figural – became entrenched in the areas west of the Balkans.

THE EASTERN MEDITERRANEAN

By 500, the split between the eastern and western halves of the old Roman Empire was irrevocable. The eastern half of the Empire is now usually called Byzantium, a name that originally designated the Roman settlement on the site of the capital city Constantinople established in the fourth century and which was used in the medieval period only as the familiar name of that city. The people we call Byzantines called themselves Romans, and the art and architecture of Byzantium between *c.*500 and *c.*700 developed from traditions established under the Roman Empire, with regional variations.

ARCHITECTURE AND ARCHITECTURAL DECORATION

Domestic architecture in the eastern Mediterranean between *c.*500 and *c.*700 is primarily represented by the so-called 'dead villages' of northern Syria. Over 800 settlements, which range from small clusters of well-cut masonry buildings to extensive communities, are spread between Antioch and Aleppo. Many of them are remarkably well preserved; they incorporate a variety of domestic plans, some developed over three storeys, from rooms over shops to modified forms of the old Roman atrium house.[1] A considerable number of fortified sites – often composed of a barracks, one or two churches and an administrative centre of some sort – also survive from the period.[2] Many of these were commissioned by the emperor Justinian to secure the frontiers of the Empire, a project described by Procopius in his *Buildings*,[3] among them the fortified monastery at Mount Sinai built around 540, which retains its original walls and central church, a flat-ceilinged basilica probably built by local masons. The mosaics at the eastern end represent the major biblical events that took place near the site (the Transfiguration, Moses Receiving the Laws, and Moses and the Burning Bush) along with medallion portraits; these are thought to have been produced by artisans from Gaza or Constantinople.[4] Existing religious centres in strategic locations, such as Sergiopolis (R'safah) in northern Syria, received fortified walls and, in this case, major urban improvements including a new tetraconch church, dated to the mid-sixth century.[5] Such programmes of fortification and, sometimes, consolidation were not restricted to Justinian's reign but occurred throughout our period from Gortyna on Crete to Nikopolis in modern Bulgaria. While in part a response to the insecurity of Byzantine borders, the reconfiguration of towns and villages (now often called *kastra*, after the Latin *castrum* or fort) also corresponds with a changed attitude

[1] Tchalenko (1953–58); Tate (1992).

[2] E.g. Haldra in modern Tunisia, Caricin Grad in the Balkans, Qasr Ibn Warden in Syria, with an inscription of 564: Krautheimer (1986), pp. 247–9, and more generally pp. 258–62.

[3] Ed. H. B. Dewing with G. Downey (Loeb) VII, rev. edn (1954).

[4] Forsyth and Weitzmann (1973); Krautheimer (1986), pp. 259–60, 276–7; on the site as a pilgrimage centre, see Coleman and Elsner (1994).

[5] Krautheimer (1986), pp. 261–2, with bibliography.

towards urbanism.[6] Archaeology has, however, as yet revealed little about the way people lived in these settlements. But while the interior features of the non-religious buildings have largely disappeared, extensive segments of a mid-sixth century mosaic floor from the imperial palace at Constantinople preserve at least the deluxe extreme of secular architectural decoration: here, landscape and urban motifs mingle with people and animals on a white ground set in a scallop pattern.[7]

Considerable quantities of urban ecclesiastical architecture survive from the sixth and seventh centuries.[8] In Constantinople alone, four major churches stand at least in part. The earliest is the large and elaborately decorated Hagios Polyeuktos, completed between 524 and 527 by the *patrikia* Anicia Juliana, which was perhaps a domed basilica.[9] The smaller SS Sergius and Bacchus (now a mosque), once adjacent to the Great Palace, is an irregular centrally planned church focussed on a pumpkin-shell dome that was completed between 527 and 536, perhaps for the Monophysite community favoured by the empress Theodora.[10] The churches of Hagia Eirene and Hagia Sophia, in the heart of the Palace and hippodrome area of the city, were destroyed by the civic riot of 532 and rebuilt on the emperor Justinian's orders soon thereafter. The former was again rebuilt in the mid-eighth century, but the building apparently retains some sixth-century masonry in its lower walls.[11] The Great Church (Hagia Sophia), designed by Anthemius of Tralles and Isidorus of Miletos and completed by 537, was the largest in the world until the sixteenth century (Plate 8). It consists of a huge dome supported on four massive piers, with half-domes extending the longitudinal east–west axis and helping to counter the thrust of the main dome (despite which, the original dome collapsed in 588 and had to be rebuilt); aisles surmounted by galleries run along the north and south sides, and a double narthex provides the western entrance. The original (fixed) decoration consisted of deeply carved 'basket' capitals, carefully matched marble revetments on the walls, most of which remain, and gold mosaic, sometimes with crosses or with geometric or vegetal motifs, traces of which survive on the vaults and soffits.[12] The oldest preserved figural religious mosaic from Constantinople, a panel showing the Presentation in the

6 See esp. Brogiolo and Ward-Perkins (1999) and Lavan (2001); also Ruggieri (1991), pp. 264–6; Dunn (1994); Poulter (1995); Christie and Loseby (1996); Haldon (1997), pp. 92–124, 459–61; Liebeschuetz (2000).

7 Brett (1947); Talbot Rice (1958). The final report of the Austrian-Turkish excavations of 1983–97 has not yet appeared; for an interim report, with bibliography, see Jobst *et al.* (1997).

8 For surveys: Krautheimer (1986); Mango (1975); Ruggieri (1991).

9 Harrison (1986) and (1989).

10 Mango (1972b) and (1975); Krautheimer (1986), pp. 222–6.

11 George (1912); Peschlow (1977) and (1996). See also Louth, chapter 4 above.

12 Mainstone (1988); Mark and Çakmak (1992), both with bibliography.

Temple that was found during excavations at the Kalenderhane Camii, also probably dates to the sixth century.[13]

The martyrium church of St John the Evangelist at Ephesus in Anatolia was also rebuilt under Justinian. Begun before Theodora's death in 548 (her monogram appears on some capitals), the structure was completed in 565.[14] The five-domed cruciform plan, with elongated nave, is thought to have been inspired by the church dedicated to the Holy Apostles in the capital, with which it is specifically compared by Procopius in his work on Justinian's building programmes.[15] Churches in the Holy Land were also rebuilt in the sixth and seventh centuries: the fourth-century Church of the Nativity of Bethlehem, for example, was apparently replaced between 560 and 603/4 by a basilica with a trefoil-shaped eastern end.[16]

As these examples suggest, the standardised basilican form of the late Roman period, with its flat or coltered wood ceiling and strong longitudinal axis, was becoming outmoded. Domed or vaulted ceilings and a more centralised focus were increasingly common. These were, however, often imposed on a basic basilican plan, as may be exemplified by Basilica B at Philippi in Greece of *c.*540, where a dome sits over the crossing, a single massive groin vault covers the nave and barrel vaults top the transept arms.[17] Architectural variations become even more pronounced along the edges of the Empire – in Armenia, eastern Turkey, the coast of North Africa – where, apart from fortified imperial commissions that were presumably inspired at least in part by ideas from the capital, church architecture is often only tangentially allied with that of the Byzantine heartlands. Strong regional traditions developed in, for example, the Tur Abdin (the 'mountain of the servants' [of God], a collection of monasteries and churches in Mesopotamia) and in Armenia, both of which flourished and produced an extraordinary number and variety of churches in the late sixth and especially the seventh century.[18]

In short, despite the appellation 'Dark Ages' that is sometimes applied to this period, with its implications of stagnation, the scale of building in the eastern Mediterranean seems not to have contracted significantly, and the formal vocabulary was far from static. The focus, however, seems to have gradually shifted: like the traditional form of the basilica, the old shape of the *polis*, with its broad colonnaded streets and regular grid plan clustered around a monumental core, increasingly fell out of favour and was replaced by walled, compact settlements with ecclesiastic rather than civic structures at their heart.

13 Striker and Dogan Kuban (1997), pp. 121–4.
14 Krautheimer (1986), pp. 242–4 with bibliography.
15 *Buildings* v.1.4–6, ed. Dewing, VII, pp. 316–19.
16 Krautheimer (1986), pp. 266–7 with bibliography. 17 Lemerle (1945).
18 See e.g. Der Nersessian (1978); Bell and Mundell Mango (1982); Krautheimer (1986), pp. 321–7.

ICONS

The role of holy portraits (icons) in Orthodox theology developed over the course of the sixth and seventh centuries.[19] Holy portraits were known earlier, and were accorded respect, but it was only in the third quarter of the sixth century, when *acheiropoeita* (images not made by human hands) are more or less simultaneously attested in Edessa, Kamoulianai and Memphis, that such portraits began to acquire miraculous properties.[20] By *c.*590, the Edessa *acheiropoeiton* image of Christ was credited with saving the city from Persian attack, and soon Constantinople too had a sacred portrait as an urban palladium: in 626 an image of Christ repulsed an Avar attack.[21] However, there is little evidence for what is sometimes called the 'cult' of images until the end of the seventh century, at which point sacred portraits seem to have been absorbed into the cult of relics and to have become conduits to the saint represented;[22] the theology of icons, implicit in the 82nd canon of the Quinisext Council of 692, was fully developed only during Iconoclasm.[23] Until the very end of the period covered by this volume, holy portraits are best seen as commemorative or *ex voto* images rather than as intermediaries between the viewer and the person represented. There is no evidence that icons played any liturgical role in Byzantium before the ninth century.[24]

Over thirty icons, mostly preserved at the monastery on Mount Sinai, have been attributed to the sixth or seventh century.[25] Most are panel paintings on wood, in encaustic (pigment suspended in wax) or tempera (pigment suspended in egg yolk), though sacred portraits were also worked in tapestry (as in a sixth-century Virgin and Child now in Cleveland, Ohio) and ivory (as in a sixth-century archangel now in the British Museum) (Plate 9); there were also mural portraits, such as the seventh-century medallion and *ex voto* portraits at Hagios Demetrios in Thessalonica.[26] Single figures or linked groups such as the Virgin and Child with saints, or saints Sergius and Bacchus, predominate; narrative compositions, which will become increasingly common after Iconoclasm, appear rarely, an example being an Ascension panel at Mount Sinai.[27]

[19] For general surveys, see e.g. Weitzmann (1978); Maguire (1996). See also Louth chapter 11 above.

[20] See Kitzinger (1954); Cameron (1983).

[21] Cameron (1979) and (1983), pp. 84–5; Pentcheva (2002).

[22] Auzépy (1987) and (1995); Brubaker (1998).

[23] Kitzinger (1954), p. 121; Auzépy (1987); Sansterre (1994), pp. 208–9; Brubaker (1998). For the canon, Mansi XI, 977–80; trans. Mango (1972a), pp. 139–40.

[24] Ševčenko (1991).

[25] See Weitzmann (1976), pp. 12–61.

[26] Cormack (1969), pls 3–4, 7–8; Weitzmann (1978), pl. 4; Buckton (1994), pp. 73–4.

[27] Sinai B.10: Weitzmann (1976), pp. 31–2. Hendy (1989), pp. 13–18; Grierson (1992).

SILVER AND METALWORK

Little silver coinage was minted between 395 and 615, leaving the silver supply available for plate; hence, a high proportion of preserved Byzantine silver dates from the fourth to the seventh century.[28] Decorated silver plate, usually hammered rather than cast, is well attested for private domestic use and for imperial commemorative gifts;[29] for example, the so-called David plates – nine silver plates in three standardised sizes decorated with scenes from the life of David and dated by their stamps (see below) to 613–630 – were presumably made either for display in the imperial palace or as an impressive presentation group.[30] Another well-documented group of objects came from churches, which continued the Roman 'banking' tradition of storing precious metals: twelve of the forty or so known hoards of silver represent ecclesiastic treasures, and silver (along with textiles, manuscripts and other metals) also appears in some thirty preserved church inventories from our period.[31] Ecclesiastical silver was predominantly used for furniture revetments, liturgical vessels (often inscribed), *ex voto* panels, and sometimes lighting fixtures, though lamps are most commonly made of bronze or clay; churches also kept secular silver that had been donated for its monetary value.[32] The more valuable gold is attested mainly in urban sites, where it was apparently mostly used to gild ceilings or was sandwiched into mosaic cubes that were applied to wall or ceiling surfaces.[33]

About 10 per cent of all known pieces of early Byzantine silver are marked with control stamps, with a five-stamp system introduced under Anastasius I (491–518) and continued through the reign of Constans II (641–668).[34] The stamps are not confirmations of metallic purity – all Byzantine silver, stamped or not, is 92–98 per cent pure – but may indicate imperial control of production in Constantinople and perhaps in imperial mints or *thesauri* (treasuries) elsewhere in the empire.[35]

Other metals, notably bronze, were used for a variety of domestic items, often decorated.[36] Silver, lead, clay and other materials were formed into pilgrimage *ampullae* (small flasks to contain blessed oil) or tokens, decorated with scenes

28 Hendy (1989), pp. 13–18; Grierson (1992).

29 See Kent and Painter (1977); Dauterman Maguire *et al.* (1989), pp. 152–3, 163, 172, 194.

30 H. L. Kessler in Weitzmann (1979), pp. 475–83; Mundell Mango (1992b), p. 212.

31 See Mundell Mango (1986); Boyd and Mundell Mango (1992), here esp. pp. 123–4.

32 Mundell Mango (1992a); for non-silver lamps, see e.g. Dauterman Maguire *et al.* (1989), pp. 64–81.

33 Mundell Mango (1992a), pp. 125–6.

34 Dodd (1961) and (1992); Mundell Mango (1992b).

35 See Hendy (1989); Dodd (1992); Mundell Mango (1992b).

36 In addition to the lamps noted above, see e.g. Dauterman Maguire *et al.* (1989), pp. 50, 173–6, 189, 195.

relevant to the sites visited;[37] the same media, along with various stones and semi-precious gems, were also formed into amulets decorated and inscribed to protect from a variety of fates.[38]

ILLUMINATED MANUSCRIPTS (GREEK AND SYRIAC)

Fewer than a dozen books written in Greek or Syriac with representational miniatures survive from the period.[39] One, the Syriac Rabbula Gospels (Florence, Laur. plut. l. 56), is dated to 586 in a colophon that also identifies the scribe Rabbula and apparently the illuminators John of Larbik and John of Ainatha, all of whom came from Beth Mar John at Beth Zagba near Apamea.[40] The illuminations are collected together in the first fourteen folios of the Gospel-book; most (fols. 3v–12v) consist of decorated canon tables flanked by marginal images of prophets, scenes from Christ's life, animals and plants. Larger compositions at the beginning and end of the canon tables present portraits and additional scenes from Christ's life, notably the crucifixion, ascension and pentecost. Several other sixth- and seventh-century Syriac Gospel-books with ornamented canon tables survive,[41] but only one – Paris, syr. 33, at one time in a monastic library near Mardin in Mesopotamia and perhaps from there[42] – includes figures. Portraits or scenes also introduce each (preserved) book of a Syriac Bible (Paris, syr. 341) dated to *c.*600.[43]

Greek religious manuscripts with figural imagery are limited to the fragmentary Cotton Genesis (London, BL Cotton Otho B.VI),[44] the Vienna Genesis (Vienna, Nationalbibliothek, theol. gr. 31), with large purple-stained pages each containing a half-page miniature and a condensed version of Genesis written in gold and silver script,[45] and two Gospel-books. The Rossano Gospels (Diocesan Museum) retains an evangelist portrait and a series of introductory miniatures, most of which show Old Testament figures holding scrolls inscribed with passages related to the New Testament scenes above them;[46] the Sinope Gospels (Paris, suppl. gr. 1286) is related.[47]

Non-ecclesiastical books with miniatures include the Vienna Dioskourides (Vienna, Nationalbibliothek, med. gr. 1), a medical handbook with

37 Grabar (1958); Vikan (1982); Dauterman Maguire *et al.* (1989), pp. 207–10; and the essays collected in Ousterhout (1990).

38 Vikan (1984); Dauterman Maguire *et al.* (1989), pp. 210–17.

39 For a general survey, see Weitzmann (1977).

40 Cecchelli *et al.* (1959); Leroy (1964), pp. 139–97; Wright (1973); Mundell Mango (1983), pp. 428–9 for the colophon.

41 E.g. London, BL Add. 14450 and 11213; Berlin, Phillipps 1388: see Leroy (1964), pp. 128–30.

42 Leroy (1964), pp. 198–206.

43 Omont (1909); Leroy (1964), pp. 208–19.

44 Weitzmann and Kessler (1986).

45 Gerstinger (1931); cf. Lowden (1992).

46 Cavallo *et al.* (1987).

47 Grabar (1948).

introductory portraits, images of healing plants and of animals, and a few initials with scribal decoration commissioned *c.*512 for Anicia Juliana, the Constantinopolitan aristocrat mentioned earlier,[48] and the papyrus Alexandrian World Chronicle (Moscow, Pushkin Museum) of 675–700.[49]

Sometime during the eighth century, the majuscule script used for all earlier Greek manuscripts was supplanted by a new minuscule script, that was faster to write. Eventually, the Byzantines found it hard to read majuscule (the Vienna Dioskourides, for example, has middle Byzantine minuscule 'translations' of its sixth-century text in some of its margins) (Plate 10). Many early texts were recopied, especially in the tenth century, and the old versions are lost. It is thus particularly hard to estimate the number of books produced between 500 and 700, and impossible to know what percentage of them were illustrated, though it seems reasonable to suppose that the material value of illustrated books resulted in extra security and hence that a disproportionately high number of books with pictures have been preserved. The most secure location for holding books was in church treasuries, where religious books were more likely to be stored than secular ones; for this reason, it is possible that more non-religious books were illustrated than the surviving evidence would indicate.

TEXTILES

Silk apparently began being produced in Byzantium in the sixth century and during our period was predominantly twin with a single main warp.[50] Examples assigned to the sixth and seventh centuries incorporate religious subject matter (e.g. Joseph, Daniel, the Virgin Mary), continue older motifs such as Nilotic scenes or dancers, or display overall patterns of animals, birds, plants or non-representative geometrical ornament.[51] Linen and wool were also decorated, often with panels woven separately that could be moved to another garment; the decorative motifs were sometimes protective.[52]

IVORY AND BONE

Objects carved of ivory (dentine) and the less expensive bone survive in considerable quantities from the sixth century; none, however, can be firmly attributed to the seventh, perhaps because ivory imports were affected by the Arab conquest of North Africa, home of the elephants from which most of the tusks carved in Byzantium originated.[53] Consular diptychs, issued yearly (probably

48 Gerstinger (1931); Brubaker (2002).
49 Bauer and Strzygowski (1906); Kurz (1972).
50 Muthesius (1997), esp. pp. 145–7.
51 See Muthesius (1997), pp. 80–4.
52 Dauterman Maguire *et al.* (1989), pp. 138–52; Maguire (1995).
53 See Volbach (1976); Cutler (1985) and (1994).

from Rome and Constantinople) by consuls on their accession for distribution to supporters, continued until 541; most portray the consul presiding over the games in the hippodrome that were the most costly responsibility of his rank.[54] Other diptychs, such as the archangel plaque in the British Museum, showed religious subjects.[55] Similarly, the 'five-part diptychs', with a central panel framed by four smaller plaques, present state and church themes: the Barberini panel portrays an emperor (probably Justinian) on horseback receiving homage, while on a panel now in Ravenna that may have been intended as a book cover, the central image of Christ and apostles is surrounded by biblical scenes.[56] The lavish use of ivory during the sixth century exemplified by the large size of many plaques, the extensive areas covered by multiple panels on objects such as the throne of Maximianus,[57] and the frequency of so-called pyxides – round boxes formed from complete sections of tusk – have suggested to some scholars that the cost of ivory was less high than in later periods.[58] Ivory or more commonly bone was also used for a range of domestic objects such as spoons, hairpins, musical instruments and toiletry boxes, which were sometimes decorated with small-scale motifs.[59]

The primary distinctions that can be made between the material culture of *c.*500 and *c.*700 are, then, that the concept of urbanism seems to have been moving away from the ideal of the antique *polis*; that the old basilica was increasingly augmented by domes and/or vaults or was replaced by a centralised church plan; and that holy portraits ceased to be simply commemorative and became transparent conduits to divine presence. These changes are significant, but compared to the material culture of western Europe in these same centuries, that of Byzantium remained remarkably coherent, stable and anchored to the Roman past.

54 Delbrück (1929).
55 Volbach (1976), no. 109; Buckton (1994), pp. 73–4.
56 Volbach (1976), nos. 48, 125.
57 Volbach (1976), no. 140.
58 See Cutler (1985), pp. 20–37.
59 See e.g. Dauterman Maguire *et al.* (1989), pp. 157, 190, 193, 225–7.

PRIMARY SOURCES

Acta S. Aunemundi alias Dalfini episcopi, ed. P. Perrier, *AASS*, Sept VII, Antwerp (1760), pp. 744–6

English trans. P. Fouracre and R. Gerberding, *Late Merovingian France*, Manchester (1996), pp. 166–92

Acta Conciliorum Œcumenicorum, series II, vol. I, ed. R. Riedinger, Berlin (1984); series II, vol. II in 3 parts, ed. R. Riedinger, Berlin (1990–5)

Acta Conciliorum Œcumenicorum, vol. III, ed. E. Schwartz, Berlin (1940) (Origenist Controversy and Synods of Constantinople and Jerusalem 536), tomus 4, vol. I, ed. J. Straub, Berlin (1971) (Fifth Ecumenical, Constantinople II, 553)

English trans. (of canons of Œcumenical Councils, as recognised in the West): N. P. Tanner (ed.), *Decrees of the Ecumenical Councils*, 2 vols., London and Washington, DC (1990)

Additamenta, ed. and trans. L. Bieler, *The Patrician Texts in the Book of Armagh*, Dublin (1979), pp. 166–79

Adler, M. N., *The Itinerary of Benjamin of Tudela*, London (1907)

Adomnán, *Cáin Adamnáin*, ed. K. Meyer, Oxford (1905)

[Adomnán] Adamnan, *De Locis Sanctis*, ed. and trans. D. Meehan, Dublin (1983) (and see Adomnán below)

Adomnán, *Vita Sancti Columbae*, ed. and trans. A. O. Anderson and M. O. Anderson, *Adomnán's Life of Columba* (Oxford Medieval Texts), 2nd edn, Oxford (1991)

Agathias, *Historiae*, ed. R. Keydell, *Agathiae Myrinaei Historiarum Libri Quinque* (Corpus Fontium Historiae Byzantinae, Series Berolinensis 2), Berlin (1967)

English trans. J. D. Frendo, *Agathias, The Histories* (Corpus Fontium Historiae Byzantinae, Series Berolinensis 2A), Berlin (1975)

Agobardi Lugdunensis Opera Omnia, ed. L. van Acker (CCCM 5, 2), Turnhout (1981)

Agus, I., *Urban Civilization in Pre-Crusade Europe*, 2 vols., New York (1965)

Alcuin, *Vita Sancti Willibrordi*, ed. W. Levison, *MGH SRM* VII, Hanover (1920), pp. 81–141

Alcuin, *Vita Willibrordi*, ed. and German trans. H.-J. Reischmann, *Willibrord – Apostel der Friesen*, Sigmaringendorf (1989)

Aldhelm, *Epistulae*, ed. R. Ehwald, *Aldhelmi Opera*, *MGH AA* XV, ii, Berlin (1914)

Aldhelm, *Letters*, trans. M. Lapidge and M. Herren, *Aldhelm: The Prose Works*, Ipswich (1979)
Aldhelm, *The Poetic Works*, trans. M. Lapidge and J. Rosier, Cambridge (1985)
Alexander of Tralles, *Therapeutica*, ed. T. Puschmann, Vienna (1878–9), reprinted with addenda, Amsterdam (1963)
Altfrid, *Vita Liudgeri*, ed. W. Diekamp, *Die Vitae Sancti Liudgeri*, Münster (1881)
Ammianus Marcellinus, *Res Gestae. Ammiani Marcellini Rerum Gestarum libri qui supersunt*, ed. W. Seyfarth, Leipzig (1978)
English trans. Walter Hamilton, *The Later Roman Empire (A.D. 354–378)*, Harmondsworth (1986)
Ammianus Marcellinus, *Res Gestae: Ammianus Marcellinus*, ed. and trans. J. C. Rolfe, 3 vols., London (1935–39)
Amra Choluimb Chille, ed. and trans. W. Stokes, 'The Bodleian Amra Coluimb Chille', *Revue Celtique* 20 (1899): 30–55, 132–83, 248–89 and 400–37
Ed. and English trans. T. O. Clancy and G. Márkus, *Iona: The Earliest Poetry of a Celtic Monastery*, Edinburgh (1995), pp. 96–128
Aneirin, *Y Gododdin*, ed. and trans. A. O. H. Jarman, Llandysul (1988)
Angiolini Martinelli, P. *et al.*, '*Corpus' della scultura paleocristina, byzantina et altomedioevale di Ravenna, diretto da Guiseppe Bovini*, 3 vols., Rome (1968–69)
Anglo-Saxon Chronicle, ed. B. Thorpe, Rolls Series, London (1861)
English trans. G. N. Garmonsway, *The Anglo-Saxon Chronicle*, London (1953)
Annales Cambriae, ed. E. Phillimore, 'The *Annales Cambriae* and Old Welsh genealogies', *Y Cymmrodor* 9 (1888): 152–69
Annales Mettenses Priores, ed. B. von Simson *MGH SRG* x, Hanover and Leipzig (1905)
English trans. (chs. 43–53), P. Fouracre and R. Gerberding, *Late Merovingian France*, Manchester (1996), pp. 330–70
Annales Regni Francorum, ed. F. Kurze, *MGH SRG* vi, Hanover (1895)
Annales Xantenses, ed. B. von Simson, *MGH SRG*, Hanover (1909)
Annals of St Bertin, trans. J. Nelson, Manchester (1991)
Annals of Inisfallen, ed. S. Mac Airt, Dublin (1951)
Annals of Tigernach, ed. and trans. Whitley Stokes (1895, 1896, 1897), *Revue Celtique* 16, pp. 374–419; 17, pp. 6–33, 119–263, 337–420; 18, pp. 9–59, 150–97, 267–303; reprinted as 2 vols, Felinfach (1993)
Annals of Ulster (to A.D. 1131), ed. and trans. S. Mac Airt and G. Mac Niocaill, Dublin (1983)
L'Année Epigraphique, Paris (1956)
Anonymous, *Life of St John the Almsgiver*: 'Une vie inédite de Saint Jean l'Aumônier', ed. H. Delehaye, *An. Boll*. 45 (1927), pp. 5–74.
Anonymus Valesianus, ed. I. König, *Aus der Zeit Theoderichs des Grossen: Einleitung, Text, Übersetzung und Kommentar einer anonymen Quelle*, Darmstadt (1997)
Anonymus Valesianus, ed. and trans. J. C. Rolfe, *Ammianus Marcellinus*, iii (Loeb Classical Library), Cambridge, MA (1939), pp. 506–69
Anselm, *Gesta Episcoporum Tungrensium, Traiectensium et Leodiensium*, ed. R. Koepke, *MGH SS* vii, Hanover (1846), pp. 191–238
Anskar, *Miracula Willehadi*, ed. A. Poncelet, *AASS*, November iii, pp. 847–91

Anthimus, *De Observatione Ciborum ad Theodoricum Regem Francorum Epistola*, ed. E. Lichtenau (Corpus Medicorum Latinarum 8.1), Berlin (1963)

Anthologia Graeca Carmina Christianorum, ed. W. Christ and M. Paranikas, Leipzig (1871)

Antonini iter Britanniarum, ed. R. Gale, London (1709)

Antonini Placentini Itinerarium, ed. C. Milani, *Itinerarium Antonini Placentini: un viaggio in Terra Santa del 560–570* (Scienze filologiche e letteratura 7), Milan (1977)

Apgitir Chrábaid, ed. and trans. V. Hull, '*Apgitir Chrábaid*: the Alphabet of Piety', *Celtica* 8 (1968): 44–89

Arbeo of Freising, *Vita Corbiniani*, ed. B. Krusch, *MGH SRG* XIII, Hanover (1920)

Arbeo of Freising, *Vita Haimhrammi*, ed. B. Krusch, *MGH SRG* XIII, Hanover (1920)

Argyll IV: *An Inventory of the Monuments*, IV: *Iona* (The Royal Commission on the Ancient and Historical Monuments of Scotland), Edinburgh (1982)

Argyll V: *An Inventory of the Monuments*, V: *Islay, Jura, Colonsay and Oronsay* (The Royal Commission on the Ancient and Historical Monuments of Scotland), Edinburgh (1984)

Aronius, J., *Regesten zur Geschichte der Juden im fränkischen und deutschen Reich bis zum Jahre 1273*, Berlin (1902)

Ashtor, E., 'Documentos españoles de la Genizah', *Sefarad* 24 (1964): 41–80

Audacht Morainn, ed. F. Kelly, Dublin (1976)

Augustine of Hippo, *De Doctrina Christiana*, ed. P. Tombeur, Turnhout (1982)
English trans. R. P. H. Green, Oxford (1995)

Augustine of Hippo, *The City of God*, trans. H. Bettenson, Harmondsworth (1979)

Augustine of Hippo, *The City of God*, ed. and trans. W. M. Green *et al.*, 7 vols., London (1957–72)

Augustine of Hippo, *Œuvres de St Augustin*, XI: *Le magistère chrétien*, ed. G. Combes and J. Farges (Collection Bibliothèque Augustinienne), Paris (1949); new edn, ed. G. Madec, Paris (1996)

Avitus of Vienne, *Epistolae*, ed. R. Peiper, *MGH AA* VI.2, Berlin (1883), pp. 29–103

Baer, F., *Die Juden im christlichen Spanien. Erster Teil. Urkunden und Regesten*, Berlin (1929)

al-Baladhuri, *Ansab al-ashraf*, I, ed. M. Hamidullah, Cairo (1959); IV, ed. I. Abbas, Wiesbaden (1979); IV/2, ed. M. Schloessinger and M. J. Kister, Jerusalem (1971); V, ed. S. D. Goitein, Jerusalem (1936).

al-Baladhuri, *Futuh al-buldan*, ed. M. J. de Goeje, Leiden (1866)
English trans. P. Hitti and F. C. Murgotten, *The Origins of the Islamic State*, Beirut (1966).

Bar-Ilan University, *The Responsa Project*. Version 10+, CD-Rom, Ramat Gan (2002)

Baudonivia, *Vita Radegundis*, ed. B. Krusch, *MGH SRM* II, Hanover (1888), pp. 377–95
English trans. in J. A. McNamara, J. E. Halborg and E. G. Whatley, *Sainted Women of the Dark Ages*, Durham, NC and London (1992), pp. 86–105

Bede, *Historia Ecclesiastica*, ed. C. Plummer, *Venerabilis Baedae Opera Historica*, Oxford (1896), pp. 5–360

Bede, *Ecclesiastical History of the English People*, trans. L. Sherley-Price, revised by R. E. Latham; new introduction and notes by D. H. Farmer, Harmondsworth (1990)

Bede, *Ecclesiastical History of the English People*, ed. and trans. B. Colgrave and R. A. B. Mynors (Oxford Medieval Texts), Oxford (1969)

Bede, *Epistola ad Ecgbertum Episcopum*, ed. C. Plummer, *Venerabilis Baedae Opera Historica*, Oxford (1896), pp. 405–23

Bede, *Historia Abbatum*, ed. C. Plummer, *Venerabilis Baedae Opera Historica*, Oxford (1896), pp. 364–87.

Bede, *Opera de Temporibus*, ed. C. W. Jones (Medieval Academy of America 41), Cambridge, MA (1943); trans. F. Walls, *Bede, The Reckoning of Time* (Translated Texts for Historians), Liverpool (1999)

Bede, *Vita Sancti Cuthberti*, ed. and trans. B. Colgrave, *Two Lives of Saint Cuthbert*, Cambridge (1940)

Benedict, Abbot of Monte Cassino, *Regula*, ed. R. Hanslik, 2nd emended edition (Corpus Scriptorum Ecclesiasticorum Latinorum 75), Vindobonae (1977)

Benedict, *Regula Benedicti*, ed. A. de Vogüé, *La Règle de St Benoît*, 7 vols. (Sources Chrétiennes 181–6, 260), Paris (1971–2, 1977)

Ben-Sasson, M., *The Jews of Sicily 825–1068: Documents and Sources*, Jerusalem (1991) (Hebrew)

Bertramn of Le Mans, *Testamentum*, ed. G. Busson and A. Ledru, *Actus Pontificum Cenomannis in Urbe Degentium* (Archives Historiques du Maine 2), Le Mans (1901), pp. 102–41

Ed. and German trans. Weidemann, M., *Das Testament des Bischofs Berthramn von Le Mans vom 27. März 616. Untersuchungen zu Besitz und Geschichte einer fränkischen Familie im 6. und 7. Jahrhundert* (Römisch-Germanisches Zentralmuseum, Forschungsinstitut für Vor- und Frühgeschichte, Monographien, Band 9), Mainz (1986), pp. 7–49

Bieler, L. (ed. and trans.), *The Irish Penitentials* (Scriptores Latini Hiberniae 5), Dublin (1963)

Bieler, L. (ed.) *The Patrician Text in the Book of Armagh*, Dublin (1979)

Boethius, *Consolation of Philosophy*, ed. and trans. H. F. Stewart *et al.* (Loeb Classical Library), Cambridge, MA (1918)

Boniface, *Epistolae*, ed. M. Tangl, *Die Briefe des Heiligen Bonifatius und Lullus, MGH, Epp. Sel.* 1, Berlin (1916)

Braulio Caesaraugustanus, *Epistolae*, ed. and Spanish trans. L. Riesco Terrero, *Epistolario de San Braulio: introducción, edición crítica y traducción*, Seville (1975)

Braulio Caesaraugustanus, *Vita Sancti Aemiliani*, ed. J. Oroz, 'Vita Sancti Aemiliani, Hymnus in testo Sancti Aemiliani abbatis', *Perficit* 9 (1978): 119–20, 165–227

Braulio Caesaraugustanus, *Vita S. Aemiliani*, ed. L. Vázquez de Parga, Madrid (1943)

Braulio Caesaraugustanus, *Works*, trans. C. W. Barlow, *The Iberian Fathers* (The Fathers of the Church 63: 2), Washington, DC (1969)

Bretha Crólige, ed. and trans. D. A. Binchy, '*Bretha Crólige*', *Eriu* 12 (1934): 1–77

Bretha Nemed Toísech, ed. and trans. L. Breatnach, 'The first third of *Bretha Nemed Toísech*', *Eriu* 40 (1989): 1–40

Brubaker, L. and Haldon, J., *Byzantium in the Iconoclast Era (ca. 680–850): the sources* (Birmingham Byzantine and Ottoman Monographs 7), Aldershot (2001)

Bruno of Querfurt, *Vita Adalberti*, ed. G. H. Pertz, *MGH SS* IV, Hanover (1841), pp. 596–612

Caesar, *The Gallic War*, ed. and trans. H. J. Edwards (Loeb Classical Library), Cambridge, MA (1917)

Caesarius of Arles, *Life, Testament, Letters*, trans. W. E. Klingshirn (Translated Texts for Historians 19), Liverpool (1994) (see also Cyprianus)

Cáin Adamnáin, ed. and trans. K. Meyer, Oxford (1905)

Canu Aneirin, ed. I. Williams, Cardiff (1938)

Canu Taliesin, trans. in M. Pennar, *Taliesin Poems*, Lampeter (1988)

Capitularia Merowingica, ed. A. Boretius, *MGH Cap.* I, Hanover (1883), pp. 1–23

Capitulatio de Partibus Saxoniae, ed. A. Boretius, *MGH Cap.* I, Hanover, (1883), pp. 68–70

Carmen de Synodo Ticinensi, ed. L. Bethmann and G. Waitz, *MGH SRG* XLVIII, Hanover (1878), pp. 189–91

Cassiodorus, *Institutiones*, trans. R. A. B. Mynors, Oxford (1937)

Cassiodorus, *Variae*, ed. Å. J. Fridh (CCSL 96), Turnhout (1973), pp. 1–499

English trans. S. J. B. Barnish, *Cassiodorus: Variae* (Translated Texts for Historians 12), Liverpool (1992)

Cassius Dio, *Roman History*, ed. and trans. E. Cary (Loeb Classical Library), Cambridge, MA (1914–27)

Catalogue général d'antiquités égyptiennes du Musée du Caire: papyrus grecs d'époque byzantine, ed. J. Maspero, 2 vols., Cairo (1911, 1916)

Celtic Inscribed Stones Project on-line database, http//www.ucl.ac.uk/archaeology/cisp/database

Chartae Latinae Antiquiores, XIII–XIX, ed. H. Atsma and J. Vezin, Dietikon and Zurich (1981–87)

Chronica Gallica a. CCCCLII ad DXI, ed. T. Mommsen, *MGH AA* IX, *Chronica Minora*, I, Berlin (1892), pp. 615–66

Chronica Regum Visigothorum, ed. K. Zeumer, *MGH Legum* Sectio I, *Leges Nationum Germanicarum*, I, *Leges Visigothorum*, Hanover and Leipzig (1902), pp. 457–61

Chronicon Dictum Monemvasiae, ed. I. Dujev (Istituto siciliano di studi bizantini eneoellenici 12), Palermo (1976)

Chronicon Paschale, ed. L. Dindorf, 2 vols., Bonn (1832)

English trans. Ma. and Mi. Whitby, *Chronicon Paschale 284–628 AD* (Translated Texts for Historians 7), Liverpool (1989)

Chronicorum Caesaraugustanorum Reliquiae a. CCCCL–DLXVIII, ed. T. Mommsen, *MGH AA* XI, *Chronica Minora*, II, Berlin (1894), pp. 221–3

Cicero, Marcus Tullius, *De Officiis, Libri ad Marcum Filium*, ed. O. Heine, Berlin (1866)

Cicero, Marcus Tullius, *Tusculanae Disputationes*, ed. and trans. A. E. Douglas, Warminster (1990)

Claudian, *De Bello Gothico*, ed. and trans. M. Platnauer, *Claudian*, 2 vols., London (1922)

Claudian, *Panegyricus de Sexto Consulatu Honorii Augusti*, ed. and trans. M. Dewar, Oxford (1996)

Clotharii II Edictum, ed. A. Boretius, *MGH Cap.* I, Hanover (1883), pp. 20–3

Codex Euricianus, ed. K. Zeumer, *MGH, Leges Nationum Germanicarum*, I: *Leges Visigothorum*, Hanover (1902), pp. 3–32

Codex Theodosianus: *Theodosiani Libri xvi cum Constitutionibus Sirmondianis*, ed. T. Mommsen and P. Meyer, 2 vols., Berlin (1905, repr. 1971)

Eng. trans. C. Pharr, *The Theodosian Code and Novels and the Sirmondian Constitutions*, Princeton, NJ (1952)

Codice Diplomatico Longobardo III (l), ed. C.-R. Brühl (Fonti per la Storia d'Italia), Rome (1973)

Cogitosus, *Vita Sanctae Brigitae*, ed. R. Sharpe, *The Earliest Lives of St Brigit*, Dublin (forthcoming)

Cogitosus, *Vita Sanctae Brigitae*, ed. J. Bolland and G. Henschen, *AA SS*, Feb. I, pp. 129–41, Antwerp (1658)

Cohen, G. D., 'The Story of the Four Captives', *Proceedings of the American Academy of Jewish Research* 29 (1960/1): 55–131

Colección Canónica Hispana, ed. G. Martínez Díez, *Monumenta Hispaniae Sacra* (Serie Canónica), Madrid (1976)

Collectio Canonum Hibernensis, ed. H. Wasserschleben, *Die irische Kanonensammlung*, 2nd edn, Leipzig (1885)

Columbanus, *Epistulae*, ed. and trans. G. S. M. Walker, *Sancti Columbani Opera*, Dublin (1957)

Concilia Galliae A.314–A.695, ed. C. Munier and C. de Clercq, 2 vols. (CCSL 148 and 148A), Turnhout (1963); ed. and French trans. J. Gaudemet and B. Basdevant, *Les Canons des conciles mérovingiens* (*VIe–VIIe siècles*), 2 vols. (Sources Chrétiennes 353–4), Paris (1989)

Concilios Visigóticos e Hispano-Romanos, ed. J. Vives (España Cristiana Textos I), Barcelona and Madrid (1963)

Constantin VII Porphyrogénète, *Le Livre des Cérémonies*, ed. A. Vogt, Paris (1935–40)

Constantine Porphyrogenitus, *De Administrando Imperio*, ed. G. Moravcsik, and English trans. R. J. H. Jenkins (Dumbarton Oaks Texts I), Washington, DC (1967)

Conversio Bagoariorum et Carantanorum, ed. F. Losek, *MGH Studien und Texte* XV, Hanover (1997)

Corpus Inscriptionum Latinarum, consilio et auctoritate Academiae Litterarum Regiae Borussicae editum etc., Berlin (1862–)

Councils and Ecclesiastical Documents relating to Great Britain and Ireland, ed. A. W. Haddan and W. Stubbs, Oxford (1869, 1964)

Críth Gablach, ed. D. A. Binchy, Dublin (1941)

Críth Gablach, trans. E. MacNeill, 'Ancient Irish Law. The law of status or franchise', *PRIA* 36C (1921–4): 265–316

Crónica mozárabe = *Continuatio Hispana a. DCCLIV*, ed. T. Mommsen, *MGH AA* XI, *Chronica Minora* II (1894), pp. 334–68

Ed. and Spanish trans., J. E. López Pereira, *Crónica mozárabe de 754*, Saragossa (1980)

Crónicas asturianas, ed. J. Gil, Oviedo (1985)

Cummian, *Cummian's Letter* 'De Controversia paschali' *and the* 'De Ratione Conputandi', ed. and trans. M. Walsh and D. Ó Cróinín (Studies and Texts 86), Toronto (1988)

Cyprianus, *Life, Testament, Letters of Caesarius of Arles*, trans. W. E. Klingshirn (Translated Texts for Historians 19), Liverpool (1994)

Cyril of Scythopolis, ed. E. Schwartz, *Kyrillos von Skythopolis* (Texte und Untersuchungen 49.2,) Leipzig (1939)

English trans. R. M. Price, *Lives of the Monks of Palestine* (Cistercian Studies Series 114), Kalamazoo (1991)

De Duodecim Abusivis Saeculi, ed. S. Hellmann (Texte und Untersuchungen zur Geschichte der altchristlichen Literatur 34, series 3, vol. 4), part 1, Leipzig (1909–10), pp. 32–60

De Lange, N., *Greek Jewish Texts from the Cairo Genizah*, Tübingen (1996)

Decretio Childeberti, see Lex Salica (65-tit.)

Dekkers, E. (ed.), *Clavis Patrum Latinorum*, 3rd rev. edn, Turnhout (1995)

Descombes, F. (ed.), *Recueil des Inscriptions chrétiennes de la Gaule antérieures à la Renaissance carolingienne* xv Paris (1985)

Dhuoda, *Liber Manualis*, *PL* 106

Die von Guidi herausgegebene syrische Chronik, trans. T. Nöldeke, Vienna (1893)

Die Gesetze der Angelsachsen, ed. F. Liebermann, Halle (1903–16)

al-Dinawari, *Akhbar al-tiwal*, ed. V. Guirgass and I. I. Krachkovskii, Leiden (1912)

Diplomata, Chartae, Epistolae. Leges, aliaque Instrumenta ad Res Gallo-Francicas Spectantia, ed. J. Pardessus, 2 vols., Paris (1843–9)

Diplomata Regum Francorum e Stirpe Merovingica, ed. D. T. Kölzer, *Die Urkunden der Merowinger*, 2 vols., Hanover (2001)

Diplomata Regum Francorum e Stirpe Merowingica, ed. K. Pertz, *MGH Dipl. in fol.*, Hanover (1872)

Discipline générale antique (IIe–IXe siècles), ed. (both Greek and Latin texts) and French trans. P.-P. Joannou (Pontificia Commissione per la Redazione del Codice di Diritto Canonico Orientale, Fonti, Fascicolo IX), 2 vols. in 3 parts, Rome, 1962–3; *Decrees of the Ecumenical Councils* (text with Eng. trans. of canons of Ecumenical Councils recognised by the Roman Catholic Church, both doctrinal and disciplinary), ed. N. P. Tanner, 2 vols., London and Washington, DC (1990)

Doctrina Jacobi Nuper Baptizati, in G. Dagron and V. Déroche, 'Juifs et Chrétiens dans l'Orient du VIIe siècle', *Travaux et Mémoires du Centre de Recherche d'Histoire et Civilisation de Byzance* 11 (1991): 70–219

Donatus, *Artes*, ed. H. Keil, *Grammatici Latini*, IV, Leipzig (1857), pp. 355–402

The Dream of the Rood, ed. M. Swanton, Manchester (1970).

Dumville, D. N. (ed.), *The Historia Brittonum*, III: *the 'Vatican' Recension*, Cambridge (1985)

The Earliest Life of Gregory the Great, ed. and trans. B. Colgrave, Kansas (1968)

The Ecloga, trans. E. Freshfield, Cambridge (1926)

Ecloga. Das Gesetzbuch Leons III und Konstantins V, ed. L. Burgmann (Forschungen zur byzantinischen Rechtsgeschichte 10), Frankfurt (1983)

Eddius Stephanus, *Vita Wilfridi*, ed. and trans. B. Colgrave, *The Life of Bishop Wilfrid by Eddius Stephanus*, Cambridge (1927)

Edictum Rothari, ed. F. Bluhme, *Leges Langobardorum*, *MGH Leges in fol.* IV, Hanover (1868)

Edictus Chilperici, ed. A. Boretius, *MGH Cap.* I, Hanover (1883), pp. 8–10

Einhard, *Vita Karoli Magni*, ed. G. Waitz, *MGH SRG* XXV, Hanover and Leipzig (1911)

English trans. in P. Dutton, *Charlemagne's Courtier: The Complete Einhard*, Ontario (1999), pp. 15–39

Elias bar Shinaya, *Opus chronologicum*, ed. E. W. Brooks and J. B. Chabot, 2 vols., Paris (1910); repr. Louvain (1954)

French trans. L. J. Delaporte, *La Chronographie d'Élie bar-Shinaya*, Paris (1910)

Eligius, *Praedicatio Sancti Eligii*, ed. B. Krusch, *MGH SRM* IV, Hanover (1902), pp. 749–61

English Historical Documents, I, ed. D. Whitelock, 2nd edn, London and New York (1979)

Ennodius, *Opera*, ed. E. Vogel, *MGH AA* VII, Berlin (1885)

Epistolae Aevi Merowingici Collectae, ed. W. Gundlach, *MGH Epp.* III, Hanover (1892), pp. 434–68

Epistolae Austrasicae, ed. W. Gundlach, *MGH Epp.* III, Hanover (1892), pp. 111–53; repr. in CCSL 117, Turnhout (1957), pp. 405–70

Epistolae S. Desiderii Cadurcensis, ed. D. Norberg, *Studia Latina Stockholmiensia* VI, Uppsala (1961)

Erchanberti Breviarium, ed. G. Pertz *MGH SS* II, Hanover (1829), p. 328

Ermoldus Nigellus, *Poème sur Louis le Pieux et Epîtres au roi Pépin*, ed. E. Faral, Paris (1964)

Eugenius Toletanus, *Carmina*, ed. F. Vollmer, *MGH AA* XIV, pp. 229–82, Berlin (1905)

Eugippius, *Vita Severini*, ed. P. Régerat (Sources Chrétiennes 374), Paris (1991)

Eutychius, *Chronicle*, ed. L. Cheikho, Beirut (1906–9)

Evagrius, *Ecclesiastical History*, ed. J. Bidez and L. Parmentier, London (1898); repr. Amsterdam (1964)

French trans. A.-J. Festugière, *Byzantion* 45 (1975): 187–488

English trans. M. Whitby, *Ecclesiastical History*, Liverpool (2000)

Farmer's Law, ed. I. Medvedev, E. Piotrovskaja and E. Lipsic, *Vizantijskij zemledel'eskij zakon*, Leningrad (1984); English trans. W. Ashburner, 'The Farmer's Law', *JHS* 32 (1912): 68–95

Felix, *Life of Guthlac*, ed. and trans. B. Colgrave, Cambridge (1956)

Fiebiger, O. and Schmidt, L. (eds.), *Inschriftensammlung zur Geschichte der Ostgermaner*, Vienna (1917)

Finnian, *Penitentialis*, ed. and trans. L. Bieler, *The Irish Penitentials*, Dublin (1963), pp. 74–95

First Synod of St Patrick, ed. and trans. L. Bieler, *The Irish Penitentials*, Dublin (1963), pp. 54–9

Fontes Hispaniae Antiquae, IX: *Las fuentes de época visigoda y bizantina*, ed. R. Grosse, Barcelona (1947)

Fontes Iuris Romani Antejustiniani, 3 vols., ed. S. Riccobono, J. Baviera, C. Ferrini, J. Furlani and V. Arangio-Ruiz, Florence (1940–3).

Formulae Visigothicae, ed. I. Gil, *Miscellanea Wisigothica*, Seville (1972), pp. 69–111

Fredegar, *Chronicorum quae Dicuntur Fredegarii Scolastica Libri IV, cum continuationibus*, ed. B. Krusch, *MGH SRM* II, Hanover (1888), pp. 18–168

English trans. of Book IV and the *Continuations*, J. M. Wallace-Hadrill, *The Fourth Book of the Chronicle of Fredegar with Its Continuations*, London (1960)

Gaudemet, J. and Basdevant, B., ed. and French trans., *Les Canons des conciles mérovingiens (VIe–VIIe siècles)*, 2 vols. (Sources Chrétiennes 353–4) Paris (1989)

Gauthier, N., *Recueil des inscriptions chrétiennes de la Gaule antérieures à la Renaissance carolingienne*, I, Paris (1975)

George of Cyprus, *Descriptio Orbis Romani*, ed. H. Gelzer, Leipzig (1890)

George of Pisidia, *Poemi*, ed. A. Pertusi, Ettal (1959)

Georgii Syncelli Ecloga Chronographica, ed. A. Mosshammer, Leipzig (1984)

Gerstinger, H., *Dioscorides, Codex Vindobonensis med. gr.1 der Österreichischen Nationalbibliothek*, Graz (1970)

Gesta Archiepiscoporum Salispurgensium, ed. W. Wattenbach, *MGH SS* XI, Hanover (1854), pp. 1–103

Gil, M., *In the Kingdom of Ishmael*, 4 vols. (Hebrew), Tel Aviv (1997)

Gildas, *De Excidio et Conquestu Britanniae*, ed. T. Mommsen, *MGH AA* XIII, *Chronica Minora* III, Berlin (1898), pp. 1–85

Gildas, *De Excidio et Conquestu Britanniae and Fragmenta*, ed. and trans. M. Winterbottom, *Gildas: The Ruin of Britain and Other Documents*, Chichester (1978)

Giorgio di Pisidia, *Poemi e Panegirici epici*, ed. A. Pertusi, Ettal (1960)

Gregory of Nazianzus, *Orations*, ed. and French trans. J. Bernardi, C. Moreschini and P. Gallay (Sources Chrétiennes 247, 358, 384), Paris (1978–92)

Gregory of Rome (Gregorius Magnus), *Dialogues*, ed. A. de Vogüé and P. Antin, 3 vols. (Sources Chrétiennes 251, 260, 265), Paris (1978–80)

Gregory of Rome, *Homiliae in Hezechielem Prophetam*, ed. and French trans. C. Morel, *Homélies sur Ézéchiel*, Paris (1990)

Gregory of Rome, *Liber Regulae Pastoralis*, ed. B. Judic, F. Rommel and E. Dekkers, with French trans. by C. Morel, *Règle pastorale* (Sources Chrétiennes 381), 2 vols., Paris (1992)

Gregory of Rome, *In Librum Primum Regum*, ed. P. Verbraken (CCSL 144), Turnhout (1963)

Gregory of Rome, *Registrum Epistolarum*, ed. P. Ewald and L. M. Hartmann, *MGH Epp.* I, pt II, Berlin (1887–99)

Gregory of Tours, *De Passione et Virtutibus Sancti Iuliani Martyris*, ed. B. Krusch, *MGH SRM* I, Hanover (1885), pp. 562–84; repr. *MGH SRM* I, Hanover (1969), pp. 112–33

English trans. R. Van Dam, *Saints and Their Miracles in Late Antique Gaul*, Princeton, NJ (1993), pp. 163–95

Gregory of Tours, *De Virtutibus Sancti Martini Episcopi*, ed. B. Krusch, *MGH SRM* I, Hanover (1885), pp. 584–661; repr. *MGH SRM* I, Hanover (1969), pp. 134–210

English trans. R. Van Dam, *Saints and Their Miracles in Late Antique Gaul*, Princeton, NJ (1993), pp. 200–303

Gregory of Tours, *Decem Libri Historiarum*, ed. W. Arndt, *MGH SRM* I, Hanover (1885), pp. 31–450; new edn, B. Krusch and W. Levison, *MGH SRM* I.1, Hanover (1951)

English trans. O. M. Dalton, *The History of the Franks by Gregory of Tours*, 2 vols., Oxford (1927); L. Thorpe, *Gregory of Tours: The History of the Franks*, Harmondsworth (1974)

Gregory of Tours, *Historiarum Libri Decem*, ed. R. Buchner, 2 vols., Darmstadt (1955)

Gregory of Tours, *Liber in Gloria Confessorum*, ed. B. Krusch, *MGH SRM* I, Hanover (1885), pp. 744–820; repr. *MGH SRM* I, Hanover (1969), pp. 284–370

English trans. R. Van Dam, *Gregory of Tours, Glory of the Confessors* (Translated Texts for Historians 5), rev. edn., Liverpool (1988)

Gregory of Tours, *Liber in Gloria Martyrum*, ed. B. Krusch, *MGH, SRM* I, Hanover (1885), pp. 384–561; repr. *MGH SRM* I, Hanover (1969), pp. 34–111

English trans. R. Van Dam, *Gregory of Tours, Glory of the Martyrs* (Translated Texts for Historians 4), Liverpool (1988)

Gregory of Tours, *Vita Patrum*, ed. B. Krusch, *MGH SRM* I, Hanover (1885), pp. 661–744; repr. *MGH SRM* I.2, Hanover (1969), pp. 211–94

English trans. E. James, *Gregory of Tours, The Life of the Fathers* (Translated Texts for Historians 1), rev. edn, Liverpool (1991)

Habermann, A., *Book of Persecutions of Germany and France*, Jerusalem (Hebrew) (1945)

Hamza al-Isfahani, *Kitab ta'rikh sini muluk al-ard wa'l anbiya'*, Berlin (1922).

Hildefonsus Toletanus, *De Viris Illustribus*, ed. C. Codoñer, *El 'De viris illustribus' de Ildefonso de Toledo, estudio y edición crítica*, Salamanca (1972)

Hippocrates, *Airs, Waters, Places*, I, ed. and trans. W. H. S. Jones, London (1923)

Hisperica Famina, ed. M. W. Herren, 2 vols., Toronto (1974–87)

Historia Augusta, ed. D. Magie (Loeb Classical Library), 3 vols., Cambridge, MA and London (1921–32)

Hugeberc, *Vita Willibaldi*, ed. O. Holder-Egger, *MGH SS* xv.i, pp. 80–117, Hanover (1887)

Hydatius, *Chronicle*, ed. and trans. R. W. Burgess, *The Chronicle of Hydatius and the Consularia Constantinopolitana, Two Contemporary Accounts of the Final Years of the Roman Empire*, Oxford (1993)

Hydatius, *Continuatio Chronicorum Hyeronimianorum ad a. CCCCLXVIIII*, ed. T. Mommsen, *MGH AA* XI, *Chronica Minora* II, Berlin (1894), pp. 1–36

Ed. and French trans. A. Tranoy, *Hydace: Chronique*, I: *Introduction, texte critique, traduction*; II: *Commentaire et index*, 2 vols., Paris (1974)

Ibn 'Abd al-Hakam, *Futuh Misr*, ed. C. Torrey, New Haven, CT (1922)

Ibn A'tham, *Kitab al-futuh*, ed. M. A. Khan *et al.*, 8 vols, Hyderabad (1968–75)

Ibn Hisham, *Sirat al-nabi*, ed. F. Wüstenfeld, 2 vols., Göttingen (1858–60)

French trans. A. Guillaume, Karachi (1955)

Ibn Khaldun, *The Muqaddimah*, trans. F. Rosenthal, abridged and ed. N. J. Dawood, London (1969)

Ibn Khayyat, *Ta'rikh*, ed. A. D. al-'Umari, Najaf (1967)

Ibn Sa'd, *Kitab al-tabaqat al-kabir*, 9 vols., ed. E. Sachau, Berlin (1904–40)

Indiculus Superstitionum et Paganiarum, ed. A. Boretius, *MGH Cap.* I, Hanover (1893), pp. 361–401

Indiculus Superstitionum et Paganiarum, ed. A. Dierkens, 'Superstitions, christianisme et paganisme à la fin de l'époque mérovingienne', in H. Hasquin (ed.), *Magie, sorcellerie, parapsychologie*, Brussels (1985), pp. 9–26

Inscriptiones Latinae Selectae, ed. H. Dessau, repr. Zurich (1974)

The Instructions of King Cormac mac Airt, ed. K. Meyer (Royal Irish Academy Todd Lectures 15), Dublin (1909)

Iohannes Biclarensis (John of Biclaro), *Chronicon*, ed. T. Mommsen, *MGH AA* XI, *Chronica Minora* II, Berlin (1894), pp. 207–20

Ed. and Spanish trans. J. Campos, *Juan de Bíclaro, obispo de Gerona: su vida y su obra*, Madrid (1960)

English trans., *John of Biclaro, Chronicle*, K. Baxter Wolf, *Conquerors and Chroniclers of Early Medieval Spain*, Liverpool (1990), pp. 61–80

al-Isfahani, *Kitab al-aghani*, 24 vols., Beirut (1955)

Isidore of Seville, *Etymologiae*, ed. W. M. Lindsay, *Isidori Hispalensis Episcopi Etymologiarum sive Originum Libri XX* (Scriptorum Classicorum Bibliotheca Oxoniensis), 2 vols., Oxford (1911)

Ed. and Spanish trans. J. Oroz Reta, *Etimologías*, 2 vols., Madrid (1982)

Isidore of Seville, *De Viris Illustribus*, ed. C. Codoñer Merino, *El 'De viris illustribus' de Isidoro, estudio y edición crítica*, Salamanca (1964)

Isidore of Seville, *Historia Gothorum, Vandalorum et Suevorum*, ed. T. Mommsen, *MGH AA* XI, *Chronica Minora* II, Berlin (1894), pp. 241–303

Ed. and Spanish trans. C. Rodriguez Alonso, *La historia de los godos, vándalos y suevos de Isidoro de Sevilla, estudio, edición crítica y traducción*, León (1975)

English trans. K. Baxter Wolf, *Conquerors and Chroniclers of Early Medieval Spain*, Liverpool (1990), pp. 81–110

Isidore of Seville, *Regula Monachorum*, ed. and Spanish trans. J. Campos Ruiz and I. Roca Melia, *Reglas Monasticas de la España visigoda* (Biblioteca de autores cristianos 321), Madrid (1971), pp. 79–125

Ius Greco-Romanum, ed. J. and P. Zepos, repr. Aalen (1962)

John Lydos, *De Magistratibus Populi Romani Libri Tres*, ed. R. Wünsch, Leipzig (1903)

English trans. T. F. Carney, *Bureaucracy in Traditional Society: Romano-Byzantine Bureaucracies Viewed from Within*, Laurence, Kansas (1971)

John Lydos, *De Mensibus*, ed. R. Wünsch, Leipzig (1898)

John Lydos, *Liber de Ostentis*, ed. C. Wachsmuth, Leipzig (1897)

John Lydos, *On Powers*, ed. and trans. A. C. Bandy, Philadelphia (1983)

John Moschus, *Pratum Spirituale*, *PG* 87, cols 2852–3116

English trans. J. Wortley, *The Spiritual Meadow of John Moschos* (Cistercian Studies Series 139), Kalamazoo (1992)

John of Ephesus, *Historiae Ecclesiasticae Pars Tertia*, ed. with Latin trans. E. W. Brooks, 2 vols., Paris (1936); repr. Louvain (1952)

John of Ephesus, *Lives of the Eastern Saints*, ed. and trans. E. W. Brooks, *Patrologia Orientalis* 17 (1923), pp. 1–307; 18 (1924), pp. 513–698; 20 (1926), pp. 153–285

John of Nikiu, *Chronique de Jean, évêque de Nikiou, texte éthiopien*, ed. and French trans. H. Zotenburg, Paris (1883)

English trans. R. H. Charles, *The Chronicle of John, Bishop of Nikiu*, London and Oxford (1916)

Jonas of Bobbio, *Vita Columbani*, ed. B. Krusch, *MGH SRM* IV, Hanover (1902), pp. 64–108

English trans. D. C. Munro, in E. Peters (ed.), *Monks, Bishops and Pagans: Christian Culture in Gaul and Italy, 500–700*, Philadelphia (1975), pp. 75–113

Jordanes, *De Origine Actibusque Getarum*, ed. F. Giunta and A. Grillone (Fonti per la Storia d'Italia 117), Rome (1991)

Jordanes, *De Origine Actibusque Getarum*, ed. W. Martens, Leipzig (1913)

Jordanes, *Getica*, ed. T. Mommsen, *MGH AA* V.1, Berlin (1882), pp. 53–188

Jordanes, *The Gothic History*, English trans. C. C. Mierow, Princeton, NJ (1915)

Julian of Toledo, *Historia Wambae*, ed. W. Levison, *MGH SRM* V, Hanover (1910), pp. 486–535

Justinian, *Corpus Iuris Civilis*, ed. T. Mommsen and P. Kreuger, 3 vols.: I, *Institutiones, Digesta*; II, *Codex Justinianus*; III, *Novellae*, Berlin (1872–95), 14th edn (1967)

Digest, trans. C. H. Munro, *The Digest of Justinian* , 2 vols., Cambridge (1904 and 1909)

Justinian, *Drei dogmatische Schriften Justinians*, ed. T. Mommsen, P. Krueger et al. (Abhandlungen der Bayerischen Akademie der Wissenschaften, Phil.-hist. Klasse, Neue folge 18), Munich (1939); repr. Milan (1973)

English trans. K. P. Wesche, *On the Person of Christ: The Christology of Emperor Justinian*, Crestwood, NY (1991)

al-Kindi, *The Governors and Judges of Egypt*, ed. R. Guest, London (1912)

Klar, B., *Megillat Ahimaaz: The Chronicle of Ahimaaz, with a Collection of Poems from Byzantine Southern Italy and Additions*, Jerusalem (1944/1974) (Hebrew)

Das Konzil von Chalkedon, ed. A. Grillmeier and H. Bacht, Würzburg (1951–64)

Krauss, S. (ed.), *Das Leben Jesu nach jüdischen Quellen*, Berlin (1902)

Laws of Aethelberht, ed. and trans. D. Whitelock, *English Historical Documents* I, 2nd edn, London (1979), pp. 3357–9

The Laws of the Earliest English Kings, ed. F. L. Attenborough, Cambridge (1922)

Laws of Hlothere, ed. and trans. D. Whitelock, *English Historical Documents* I, 2nd edn, London (1979), pp. 360–1

Laws of Ine, ed. D. Whitelock, *English Historical Documents*, I, 2nd edn, London (1979), pp. 398–407

Laws of Whitred, ed. and trans. D. Whitelock, *English Historical Documents* I, 2nd edn, London (1979), pp. 361–4.

Le Blant, E. (ed.) *Inscriptions chrétiennes de la Gaule antérieures du VIIe siècle*, 2 vols. Paris (1856–65)

Le Sacrementaire Grégorien, ed. J. Deshusses, Fribourg (1971–82)

Leander of Seville, *De Institutione Virginum et Contemptu Mundi*, ed. J. Velázquez, Madrid (1979)

Lebor na Cert, The Book of Rights, ed. M. Dillon (Irish Texts Society 45), Dublin (1962)

Leges Alamannorum, ed. K. Lehmann, revised K. A. Eckhardt, *MGH Legum sectio* I.v(i), Hanover (1888, 1966)

Leontius of Naples, *Vie de Jean de Chypre* (Life of St John the Almsgiver), ed. and French trans. A. J. Festugière, *Vie de Syméon le Fou et vie de Jean de Chypre*, Paris (1974), pp. 339–637

Leontius, *Life of John the Almsgiver*, ed. H. Delehaye, 'Une vie inédite de Saint Jean l'Aumônier', *An. Boll.* 45 (1927): 5–74

Lex Baiwariorum, ed. E. de Schwind, *MGH Legum sectio* I.v (ii), Hanover (1926)

Lex Frisionum, ed. K. von Richthofen, *MGH Leges in folio* III, Hanover (1863)

Lex Salica (65-tit.), Lex Salica (100-tit.), ed. K. A. Eckhardt, *MGH Legum sectio* I.iv (ii), Hanover (1962–9)

Lex Visigothorum (Liber Iudiciorum), ed. K. Zeumer, *MGH Legum sectio* I.i, Hanover and Leipzig (1902), pp. 35–456

Liber Angeli, ed. and trans. L. Bieler, *The Patrician Texts in the Book of Armagh*, Dublin (1979), pp. 184–91

Liber Historiae Francorum, ed. B. Krusch *MGH SRM* II, Hanover (1888), pp. 241–328

English trans. (chs. 43–53) P. Fouracre and R. Gerberding, *Late Merovingian France*, Manchester (1996), pp. 79–96

Liber Landavensis: The Text of the Book of Llan Dâv, ed. J. G. Evans and J. Rhys, Oxford (1893)

Liber Pontificalis, ed. L. Duchesne, 2 vols. (Bibliothèque des Écoles Françaises d'Athènes et de Rome, Series 2, 3), (1886–92)

English trans. R. Davies, 3 vols. (Translated Texts for Historians 5, 13, 20), Liverpool (1989–95)

The Life of St. Wilfrid by Eddius Stephanus, ed. and trans. B. Colgrave, Cambridge (1927); repr. New York (1985)

Linder, A., *The Jews in Roman Imperial Legislation*, Detroit and Jerusalem (1987)

Linder, A., *The Jews in the Legal Sources of the Early Middle Ages*, Detroit and Jerusalem (1997)

Liudger, *Vita Gregorii Traiectensis*, ed. O. Holder-Egger, *MGH SS* xv, Hanover (1887), pp. 66–79

Macalister, R. A. S., *Corpus Inscriptionum Insularum Celticarum*, 2 vols., Dublin (1945, 1949)

Macler, F., *Histoire d'Héraclius par l'évêque Sebêos*, Paris (1904)

Macrobius, *Ambrosi Theodosii Macrobii commentarii in Somnium Scipionis*, ed. J. Willis, Leipzig (1963).

Malalas, John, *Chronographia*, ed. L. Dindorf, Bonn (1981); Books 9–12, ed. A. Schenk von Stauffenberg, *Die römische Kaisergeschichte bei Malalas*, Stuttgart (1930)

English trans. E. Jeffreys, M. Jeffreys and R. Scott, *The Chronicle of John Malalas* (Byzantina Australiensia 4), Melbourne (1986)

Mann, J., *Texts and Studies in Jewish History and Literature*, Cincinnati, 2 vols. (1931)

Mann, J., *The Jews in Egypt and in Palestine under the Fatimid Caliphs: A Contribution to their Political and Communal History Based Chiefly on Genizah Material Hitherto Unpublished*, London, 2 vols. (1920)

Mann, J., *The Responsa of the Babylonian Geonim as a Source of Jewish History*, New York (1973)

Marcellinus comes, *Chronicon*, ed. T. Mommsen, *MGH AA* XI, Berlin (1894), pp. 37–108

English trans. B. Croke, *The Chronicle of Marcellinus*, Sydney (1995)

Marculfi Formularum Libri Duo, ed. and French trans. A. Uddholm, Uppsala (1962)
Marius of Avenches, *Chronica*, ed. T. Mommsen, *MGH AA* XI, Berlin (1894), pp. 232–9
French trans. J. Favrod, *La Chronique de Marius d'Avenches (455–581): texte, traduction et commentaire* (Cahiers Lausannois d'Histoire Médiévale 4), Lausanne (1991), pp. 64–87
Martianus Capella, *De Nuptiis Mercurii et Philologiae*, ed. James Willis, Leipzig (1983)
Martianus Capella, *Martianus Capella and The Seven Liberal Arts*, trans. W. H. Stahl, New York (1971)
Martin of Braga, *De Correctione Rusticorum*, ed. C. W. Barlow, *Martini Episcopi Bracarensis Opera Omni*, New Haven, CT (1950)
al-Mas'udi, *Muruj al-dhahab*, ed. and trans. C. Barbier de Meynard and A. Pavet de Courteille, 9 vols., Paris (1861–77)
Maurice, *Das Strategikon des Maurikios*, ed. and German trans. G. T. Dennis and E. Gamillscheg (Corpus Fontium Historiae Byzantinae 17), Vienna (1981)
English trans. G. T. Dennis, *Maurice's Strategikon: Handbook of Byzantine Military Strategy*, Philadelphia (1984)
Maximos the Confessor (Syriac Life), ed. Sebastian Brock, 'An Early Syriac Life of Maximus the Confessor', *An. Boll.* 91 (1973): 299–346
Maximos the Confessor, *Opera Omnia*, *PG* 90–1
Maximos the Confessor, *Documenta ad Vitam Maximi Confessoris Spectantia*, ed. P. Allen and B. Neil, CCSG, (forthcoming)
English trans., P. Allen and B. Neil, *Maximus the Confessor and His Companions: Biographical Documents* (forthcoming)
Menander Protector, *Historia: Excerpta de Legationibus*, ed. C. de Boor, Berlin (1903)
Menander Protector, *The History of Menander the Guardsman*, ed. and trans. R. C. Blockley (ARCA Classical and Medieval Texts 17), Liverpool (1985)
Michael the Syrian, *Chronique*, ed. and French trans. J. B. Chabot, 4 vols., Paris (1899–1924); repr. Brussels (1960)
Miracula Sancti Demetrii, ed. and French trans., with commentary P. Lemerle, *Les Plus Anciens Recueils des Miracles de Saint Démétrius et la pénétration des Slaves dans les Balkans*, 2 vols, Paris (1979)
Muirchú, *Life of St Patrick*, ed. and trans. A. B. E. Hood (History from the Sources), Chichester (1978)
Muirchú, *Vita Sancti Patricii*, ed. and trans. L. Bieler, *The Patrician Texts in the Book of Armagh*, Dublin (1979), pp. 60–123
Mutius, H.-G. v., *Jüdische Urkundenformulare aus Barcelona*, Frankfurt am Main (1996)
Mutius, H.-G. v., *Jüdische Urkundenformulare aus dem muslimischen Spanien*, Frankfurt am Main (1997)
Mutius, H.-G. v., *Jüdische Urkundenformulare aus Marseille in babylonisch-aramäischer Sprache*, Frankfurt am Main (1994)
Mutius, H.-G. v., *Rechtsentscheide jüdischer Gesetzeslehrer aus dem maurischen Cordoba*, Frankfurt am Main (1990)
Mutius, H.-G. v., *Rechtsentscheide Raschis aus Troyes (1040–1105)*, Frankfurt am Main (1986)

Mutius, H.-G. v., *Rechtsentscheide rheinischer Rabbinen vor dem ersten Kreuzzug*, 2 vols., Frankfurt am Main (1984)

Nennius, *Historia Brittonum*, ed. T. Mommsen, *MGH AA* XIII, *Chronica Minora* III, Berlin (1898), pp. 143–222

Neubauer A. and Stern, M. (1892), *Hebräische Berichte über die Judenverfolgungen während der Kreuzzüge*, Berlin

Nikephoros, trans. with commentary C. Mango, *Nikephoros, Patriarch of Constantinople, Short History* (Dumbarton Oaks Texts 10), Washington, DC (1990)

Notitia Dignitatum Accedunt Notitia Urbis Constantinopolitanae et Latercula Provinciarum, ed. O. Seeck, Frankfurt am Main (1876); repr. Frankfurt (1962)

Notker Balbulus, *Gesta Karoli Magni Imperatoris*, ed. H. F. Haefele, *MGH SRG*, n.s. XII, Berlin (1959)

Noy, D., *Jewish Inscriptions of Western Europe*, I: *Italy, Spain and Gaul*, Cambridge (1993)

Noy, D., *Jewish Inscriptions of Western Europe*, II: *The City of Rome*, Cambridge (1995)

O'Brien, M. A. (ed.), *Corpus Genealogiarum Hiberniae*, Dublin (1962)

Oengus, *Félire Óengusso*, ed. and trans. W. Stokes, *Félire Óengusso Céli Dé* (Henry Bradshaw Society), London (1905)

Ó Ricain, P. (ed.), *Corpus Genealogiarum Sanctorum Hiberniae*, Dublin (1985)

Orosius, *Historiarum adversus Paganos Libri VII*, ed. C. Zangemeister, Vienna (1882)

Orosius, *Seven Books of History against the Pagans*, ed. and French trans. M. P. Arnaud-Lindet, *Orose, Histoires contre les Païens*, 3 vols., Paris (1991)

D'Ors, A. 'El Código de Eurico', *Estudios Visigóticos* 2 (1960): 20–43

Pactus pro Tenore Pacis, see Lex Salica, 65-tit.

Palladius, *The Lausiac History of Palladius*, ed. and trans. C. Butler, 2 vols, Cambridge (1989–1904)

Panegyrici Latini, ed. R. A. B. Mynors, Oxford (1964)

Panegyrici Latini, ed. V. Paladini and P. Fedeli (Scriptores Graeci et Latini), Rome (1976)

Paolina di Milano, *Vita di S. Ambrogio*, ed. M. Pellegrino, Rome (1961)

Passio Leudegari I, ed. B. Krusch, *MGH SRM* v, Hanover and Leipzig (1910), pp. 282–322

English trans. P. Fouracre and R. Gerberding, *Late Merovingian France*, Manchester (1996), pp. 193–253

Passio Sanctorum Martyrum Kiliani et Sociorum Eius, ed. W. Levison, *MGH SRM* v, Hanover (1910)

Patrick, *Confessio*, ed. L. Bieler, *Libri Epistolarum Sancti Patricii Episcopi* (2 vols. in 1), Dublin (1952, repr. 1993)

Patrick, *Epistola ad milites Corotici*, ed. L. Bieler, *Libri Epistolarum Sancti Patricii Episcopi* (2 vols. in 1), Dublin (1952, repr. 1993), I, pp. 91–102

Patrick, *Letters*, ed. and trans. D. Howlett, *The Book of Letters of Saint Patrick the Bishop*, Blackrock (1994)

Patrick, 'The Rule of Patrick', ed. and trans. J. G. O'Keeffe, *Ériu* 1 (1904): 216–24

Paul the Deacon, *Historia Langobardorum*, ed. L. Bethmann and G. Waitz, *MGH SRG* XLVIII, Hanover (1878)

English trans. W. D. Foulke, *Paul the Deacon, History of the Lombards*, Philadelphia (1907)
Paulinus of Nola, *Letters*, trans. P. Walsh (Ancient Christian Writers 35–6), Westminster (1966–67)
Paulinus of Pella, *Eucharisticos*, ed. and trans. C. Moussy, *Paulin de Pella: Poème d'action de grâces et Prière* (Sources Chrétiennes 209), Paris (1974)
Penitential of Theodore (Poenitentiale Theodori), ed. A. W. Haddan and W. Stubbs, *Councils and Ecclesiastical Documents Relating to Great Britain and Ireland*, III, Oxford (1871), pp. 173–204
Pirmin, *Dicta de Singulis Libris Canonicis* (*Scarapsus*), ed. G. Jecker, in *Die Heimat des heiligen Pirmin des Apostels der Alemannen*, Münster (1927), pp. 34–73
Plato, *Phaedo*, trans. E. Brann, P. Kalkavage and E. Salem, Newburyport, MA (1998)
Pliny the Elder, *Natural History*, ed. and trans. H. Rackham, *Pliny, Natural History*, London (1938)
Pliny the Younger, *C. Plinii Secundi Epistolarum Libri Novem, Epistolarum ad Traianum Liber, Panegyricus*, ed. F. W. Mueller, Leipzig (1903)
The Poetic Edda, trans L. M. Hollander, Austin, (1994) (1st edn 1962)
Das Polyptychon von Saint-Germain-des-Prés, ed. D. Hägermann, Cologne (1993)
Praefatio Gildae de Poenitentia, ed. and trans. L. Bieler, *The Irish Penitentials*, Dublin (1963), pp. 60–5
Prévot, F. (ed.), *Recueil des Inscriptions chrétiennes de la Gaule antérieures à la Renaissance Carolingienne*, VIII, Paris (1997)
Priscian, *De Laude Anastasii Imperatoris*, ed. and French trans. A. Chauvot, *Procope de Gaza, Priscien de Césarée, Panégyriques de l'empereur Anastase Ier*, Bonn (1986)
Priscian, *Grammatici Latini*, ed. H. Keil, 2 vols., Leipzig (1885)
Priscus, *Fragmenta*, ed. C. D. Gordon, *The Age of Attila*, Ann Arbor (1960)
Procopius of Caesarea, *Anecdota*, ed. and trans. H. B. Dewing (Loeb Classical Library), Cambridge, MA (1935)
Procopius of Caesarea, *Buildings*, ed. and trans. H. B. Dewing and G. Downey (Loeb Classical Library), Cambridge, MA (1940)
Procopius of Caesarea, *Gothic War*, German trans. D. Coste, *Prokop, Gotenkrieg*, Munich (1966)
Procopius of Caesarea, *Opera Omnia*, ed. J. Haury, revised G. Wirth, I-II: *Bella*, I–VIII; III: *Historia arcana*, Leipzig (1962–3)
Trans H. B. Dewing (Loeb Classical Library), 7 vols, London (1914–40)
Procopius of Caesarea, *Wars*, ed. and trans. H. B. Dewing (Loeb Classical Library), 5 vols., Cambridge, MA and London (1914–28)
Prosper, *Chronicle*, ed. T. Mommsen, *Chronica Minora* I, *MGH AA* IX, Berlin (1892)
Pseudo-Cyprianus, *De XII Abusivis Saeculi*, ed. S. Hellmann (Texte und Untersuchungen zur Geschichte der Altchristlichen Literatur, ed. A. Harnack and C. Schmidt, 34 (i)), Leipzig (1910), pp. 1–60
Pseudo-Dionysios of Tel-Mahre, ed. J.-B. Chabot, *Chronique de Denys de Tel-Mahré, quatrième partie*, Paris (1895)
English trans. W. Witakowski, *Pseudo-Dionysius of Tel-Mahre, Chronicle Part III* (Translated Texts for Historians 22), Liverpool (1996)

Latin trans. J.-B. Chabot (ed.), *Incerti Auctoris Chronicon Pseudo-Dionysianum vulgo dictum*, 2 vols. (Corpus Scriptorum Christianorum Orientalium 91, 104, 121), Paris (1927–33)

Ptolemy, *Claudii Ptolemaei Geographica*, ed. C. Nobbe, Hildesheim (1966; reprint of the 1843–45 edn)

The Quran, trans. R. M. Pickthall, London (1957)

Ravennatis Anonymi Cosmographia, ed. J. Schnetz (Itineraria Romana 2), Stuttgart (1940)

Recueil des actes de Lothaire et Louis V, rois de France, ed. L. Halphen and F. Lot, Paris (1908)

Rhigyfarch, *Vita Davidis*, ed. J. W. James, *Rhigyfarch's Life of St David*, Cardiff (1967)

The Rhodian Sea Law, ed. W. Ashburner, Oxford (1909); repr. Aalen (1976)

Rimbert, *Vita Anskarii*, ed. W. Trillmich, *Quellen des 9. und 11. Jahrhunderts zur Geschichte der hamburgischen Kirche und des Reiches*, Darmstadt (1961)

Rivlin, J., *Bills and Contracts from Lucena (1020–1025 C.E.)*, Ramat Gan (Hebrew) (1994)

Romanos the Melodist, *Cantica Genuina*, ed. P. Maas and C. A. Trypanis, Oxford (1963)

English trans. M. Carpenter, *Kontakia of Romanos, Byzantine Melodist*, 2 vols., Columbia (1970–3); (selection) Ephrem Lash, *St Romanos the Melodist, Kontakia on the Life of Christ*, San Francisco, London and Pymble (1996)

Rutilius Namatianus, *On His Return*, ed. and French trans. J. Vessereau and F. Préchac, *Rutilius Namatianus, Sur son Retour*, Paris (1933)

English trans. H. Ibsell, *The Last Poets of Imperial Rome*, Harmondsworth (1971), pp. 217–41

Sacrorum Conciliorum Nova et Amplissima Collectio, ed. J. D. Mansi, 31 vols., Florence (1759–98)

Salfeld, S. (ed.), *Das Martyrologium des Nürnberger Memorbuches*, Berlin (1898)

Salvian, *De Gubernatione Dei*, ed. C. Halm, *MGH AA* 1, Berlin, (1877)

English trans. J. F. Sullivan, *The Writings of Salvian the Presbyter*, Washington, DC (1962)

Salzman, M. (ed.), *The Chronicle of Ahima'az*, New York (1924)

Scriptores Historiae Augustae, ed. E. Hohl, Leipzig (1927); repr. (1965)

Sebeos, *Patmut'iwn*, ed. G. V. Abgaryan, Erevan (1979)

French trans. F. Macler, *Histoire d'Héraclius*, Paris (1904)

Severus, bishop of Malaga?, *Severi Episcopi Malacitani(?) In Evangelia Libri XII: das Triererfragment der Bücher VIII–X*, ed. R. Herzog, B. Bischoff and W. Schetter with O. Zwierlein, Munich (1994)

Sidonius Apollinaris, *Carmina*, ed. and French trans. A. Loyen, *Sidoine Apollinaire*, Paris (1960)

Sidonius Apollinaris, *Epistolae*, ed. and French trans. A. Loyen, *Sidoine Apollinaire*, Paris (1960)

Sidonius Apollinaris, *Poems and Letters*, ed. and trans. W. B. Anderson (Loeb Classical Library), 2 vols., Cambridge, MA and London (1936–65)

Simonsohn, S., *The Jews in Sicily*, Leiden (1997)

Sinodus Aquilonalis Britanniae, ed. and trans. L. Bieler, *The Irish Penitentials*, Dublin (1963), pp. 66–7

Sisebut, *Vita Desiderii*, ed. B. Krusch, *MGH SRM* III, Hanover (1896), pp. 630–7

Sisebut rex, *Epistolae*, ed. I. Gil, *Miscelanea wisigothica*, Seville (1972), pp. 3–27

Sisebut rex, *Vita sancti Desiderii*, ed. I. Gil, *Miscelanea wisigothica*, Seville (1972), pp. 50–68

Sophronios of Jerusalem, *Omnia Opera*, *PG* 87, cols. 3148–4004

English trans. P. Allen, *Sophronius of Jerusalem: Synodical Letter and a Monoenergist Dossier* (forthcoming)

Stuiber, A., *Libelli Sacramentorum Romani* (Theophaneia 6), Bonn (1950)

Sturluson, Snorri, *Nordiska Kungasagor*, trans. with introduction K. Johansson, Stockholm

Sulpicius Severus, *Chronica*, ed. and French trans. G. de Senneville-Grave (Sources Chrétiennes 441), Paris (1999)

Sulpicius Severus, *Vita Martini*, ed. J. Fontaine, *Vie de saint Martin*, I, (Sources Chrétiennes 133), Paris (1967)

Symeon of Durham, *Libellus de Exordio atque Procursu Istius, Hoc Est Dunhelmensis Ecclesiae*, ed. and trans. D. Rollason, Oxford (2000)

Syriac Chronicles, trans. and annotated A. Palmer, *The Seventh Century in the West-Syrian Chronicles*, including two seventh-century Syriac apocalyptic texts, trans. and annotated by S. Brock, with added annotation and an historical introduction by Robert Hoyland (Translated Texts for Historians 15), Liverpool (1993)

al-Tabari, *Ta'rikh al-rusul wa'l muluk*, ed. M. J. de Goeje *et al.*, Leiden (1879–1901)

Tablettes Albertini, ed. C. Courtois, L. Leschi and C. Saumagne, Paris (1952)

Tacitus, *Germania*, ed. M. Winterbottom, *Cornelii Taciti Opera Minora*, Oxford (1975)

Tacitus, *The Annals*, ed. and trans. J. Jackson (Loeb Classical Library), Cambridge, MA (1931–7)

The Táin Bó Cúalnge from the Book of Leinster, ed. C. O'Rahilly (Irish Texts Society 49), Dublin (1967) includes translation of this version; earlier version trans. T. Kinsella as *The Táin*, Dublin (1969)

The Text of the Book of Llan Dâv, ed. J. G. Evans with J. Rhys, Oxford (1893)

Tertullianus, *De Pallio*, ed. and Dutch trans. A. Gerlo, Kritische Uitgave met Vertaling en Commentar, Wetteren (1940)

Testimonia najdawniejszych dziejów Slowian, ed. A. Brzóstkowska and W. Swoboda (Polish critical edition of excerpts on the earliest history of the Slavs), Warsaw (1989)

al-Tha'alibi, *Histoire des rois des Perses*, ed. and trans. H. Zotenberg, Paris (1900)

Theodore's Penitential, ed A. Haddan and W. Stubbs (Councils and Ecclesiastical Documents 3), Oxford (1871)

Theophanes, *Chronographia*, ed. C. de Boor, 2 vols., Leipzig (1883–5); repr. Hildesheim (1963)

English trans. H. Turtledove, *The Chronicle of Theophanes*, Philadelphia (1982), and also trans. with introduction and commentary C. Mango and R. Scott with the assistance of G. Greatrex, *The Chronicle of Theophanes Confessor: Byzantine and Near Eastern History AD 284–813*, Oxford (1997)

Theophylact Simocatta, *Historiae*, ed. E. Bekker, Bonn (1834)
Theophylact Simocatta, *Historiae*, ed. C. de Boor, revised P. Wirth, Stuttgart (1972)
Trans. Mi. and Ma. Whitby, *The History of Theophylact Simocatta*, Oxford (1986)
Thietmar of Merseburg, *Chronicon*, ed. R. Holtzmann, *MGH SRG* n.s. IX, Berlin (1936)
Tírechán, *Collectanea de Sancto Patricio*, ed. and trans. L. Bieler, *The Patrician Texts in the Book of Armagh*, Dublin (1979), pp. 124–63
Tjäder, J. O., *Die nichtliterarischen lateinischen Papyri Italiens aus der zeit 445–700*, Lund and Stockholm (1954–82)
Trypanis, C. (ed.), *Penguin Book of Greek Verse*, Harmondsworth (1971)
Two Lives of St Cuthbert, ed. and trans. B. Colgrave, Cambridge (1940)
Uraicecht Becc, trans. E. MacNeill, 'Ancient Irish Law. The law of status or franchise', *PRIA* 36C (1921–4): 265–316
Vegetius, *Epitoma de Rei Militari*, trans. N. P. Milner, *Epitome of Military Science*, Liverpool (1993)
Velázquez, Soriano I. (ed.), *Las pizarras Visigodas: edición crítica y estudio* (Antigüedad y Cristianismo 6), Murcia (1989)
Venantius Fortunatus, *Ad Chilpericum Regem*, ed. and trans. J. George, *Venantius Fortunatus: A Poet in Merovingian Gaul*, Oxford (1992), pp. 198–207
Venantius Fortunatus, *Carmina*, ed. F. Leo, *MGH AA* IV.1, Berlin (1881)
English trans. J. George, *Venantius Fortunatus: Personal and Political Poems* (Translated Texts for Historians 23), Liverpool (1995)
Venantius Fortunatus, *Vita Germani Episcopi Parisiaci*, ed. B. Krusch, *MGH SRM* VII, Hanover (1920), pp. 372–418
Venantius Fortunatus, *Vita Radegundis*, ed. B. Krusch, *MGH SRM* II, Hanover (1888), pp. 364–77
English trans. in J. A. McNamara, J. E. Halborg and E. G. Whatley, *Sainted Women of the Dark Ages*, Durham, NC and London (1992)
Venantius Fortunatus, *Vitae*, ed. B. Krusch, *MGH AA* IV.2, Berlin (1885)
Victor of Tunnuna, *Chronica*, ed. T. Mommsen, *MGH AA* XI, *Chronica Minora* II, Berlin (1884), pp. 184–206
Vita (Altera) Bonifatii, ed. W. Levison, *Vitae Sancti Bonifatii*, *MGH SRG* LVII, Hanover (1905), pp. 62–78
Vita Amandi, ed. B. Krusch, *MGH SRM* V, Hanover (1910), pp. 428–49
Vita Annonis Archiepiscopi Coloniensis, ed. R. Koepke, *MGH SS* XI, Hanover (1853), pp. 465–514
Vita Balthildis, ed. B. Krusch, *MGH SRM* II, Hanover (1888), pp. 482–508
English trans. P. Fouracre and R. Gerberding, *Late Merovingian France*, Manchester (1996), pp. 97–132
Vita Beati Ferreoli Episcopi et Confessoris Christi, Lect. II (Catalogus Codicum Hagiographicorum Latinorum Antiquiorum qui Asserv. in Biblioth. Nat. Parisiensi, II), Brussels (1890), pp. 101–2
Vita Boniti, ed. B. Krusch, *MGH SRM* VI, Hanover (1913), pp. 110–39
Vita Brigitae I, ed. J. Colgan, *Triadis Thaumaturgae . . . Acta*, Louvain (1647), pp. 527–45
Vita Brigitae II, ed. J. Bollandus and G. Henschenius, *AASS* Feb. 1st, Antwerp (1658), pp. 129–41

Vita Cadoci: *Vitae Sanctorum Britanniae et Genealogiae*, ed. A. W. Wode-Evans, Cardiff (1944), pp. 24–141
Vita Ceolfridi, ed. C. Plummer, *Baedae Opera Historica*, Oxford (1896)
Vita Desiderii Cadurcae Urbis Episcopi, ed. B. Krusch, *MGH SRM* IV, Hanover (1902), pp. 563–602; repr. in CCSL 117, Turnhout (1957), pp. 345–401
Vita Eligii, ed. B. Krusch, *MGH SRM* IV, Hanover (1902), pp. 663–741
Vita Fulgentii, ed. J. Migne, *PL* 67 (1844)
Vita Genovefae, ed. B. Krusch, *MGH SRM* II, Hanover (1896), pp. 215–38
English trans. J. A. McNamara, J. E. Halborg and E. G. Whatley, *Sainted Women of the Dark Ages*, Durham, NC and London (1992), pp. 19–37
Vita Hrodberti, ed. W. Levison, *MGH SRG* IV, Hanover (1913), pp. 140–62
Vita Lebuini Antiqua, ed. A. Hofmeister, *MGH SS* XXX, Leipzig (1934), pp. 791–5
Vita Liutbirgae, ed. O. Menzel, *Das Leben der Liutbirg* (Deutsches Mittelalter, Kritische Studientexte des Reichsinstituts für Altere Deutsche Geschichtskunde 3), Leipzig (1937)
Vita Patrum Emeretensium, ed. and trans. J. N. Garvin, *The 'vita sanctorum patrum emeretensium': Text and Translation with an Introduction and Commentary*, Washington, DC (1946)
Vita Pauli, ed. C. Cuissard, 'Vie de S. Paul de Léon en Bretagne', *Revue Celtique* 5 (1881–3): 413–60
Vita Samsonis, ed. R. Fawtier, *La Vie de S. Samson*, Paris (1912)
Vita Sancti Samsonis Episcopi, ed. with French trans. P. Flobert, *La Vie ancienne de Saint Samson de Dol*, Paris (1997)
Vita Sancti Coemgeni, ed. C. Plummer, *Vitae Sanctorum Hiberniae*, 2 vols., Oxford (1910), I, pp. 234–57
Vita Sancti Endei, ed. C. Plummer, *Vitae Sanctorum Hiberniae*, 2 vols., Oxford (1910), II, pp. 60–75
Vita Sancti Fructuosi, ed. and Spanish trans. M. C. Díaz y Díaz, *La vida de San Fructuoso de Braga*, Braga (1974)
Vita Vulframni, ed. W. Levison, *MGH SRG* V, Hanover (1910), pp. 657–73
Vita Willehadi, ed. A. Poncelet, *AASS*, Nov. III, Brussels (1910), pp. 842–6
Vitruvius, *De Architectura*, ed. and trans. F. Granger, *Vitruvius: De Architectura*, London (1934)
Vives, J. (ed.), *Inscripciones cristianas de la España romana y visigoda*, Barcelona (1969)
al-Waqidi, *Kitab al-maghazi*, ed. J. B. Marsden Jones, Oxford (1966)
Weitzmann, K. and Kessler, H. L., *The Cotton Genesis: British Library, Codex Cotton Otho B VI*, Illustrations in the manuscripts of the Septuagint I, Princeton, NJ (1986)
Willibald, *Vita Bonifatii*, ed. W. Levison, *Vitae Sancti Bonifatii*, *MGH SRG* LVII, Hanover (1905), pp. 1–58
Wrdisten, *Vita S. Winwaloei*, ed. C. D[e] S[medt], *An. Boll.* 7 (1888): 167–249
Ya'qubi -al, *Ta'rikh*, ed. M. T. Houtsma, 2 vols., Leiden (1883)
Zosimus, *New History*, trans. R. T. Ridley (Australian Association for Byzantine Studies, Byzantina Australiensia), Canberra (1982)

BIBLIOGRAPHY OF SECONDARY WORKS ARRANGED BY CHAPTER

1 THE LATER ROMAN EMPIRE

Bowersock, G. W. (1978), *Julian the Apostate*, London

Brown, P. (1971), *The World of Late Antiquity*, London

Brown, P. (1972), *Religion and Society in the Age of Saint Augustine*, London

Bury, J. B. (1923), *History of the Later Roman Empire*, London

Cameron, Av. (1993), *The Later Roman Empire, AD 284–430*, Cambridge

Cameron, Av. (1993), *The Mediterranean World in Late Antiquity AD 395–600*, New York

Carcopino, J. (1940), *Daily Life in Ancient Rome*, New Haven

Collins, R. (1983), *Early Medieval Spain*, London

Dill, S. (1898, reprint 1958), *Roman Society in the Last Century of the Western Empire*, London

Fantham, E., Peet Foley, H., Boymel Kampen, N., Pomeroy, S. B. and Shapiro, H. A. (1994), *Women in the Classical World: Image and Text*, New York

Finley, M. (1985), *The Ancient Economy*, 2nd edn, Berkeley

Gibbon, E. (1909–14), *Decline and Fall of the Roman Empire*, 7 vols., ed. J. B. Bury, London

Goffart, W. (1972), 'From Roman taxation to medieval seigneurie', *Speculum* 47: 165–87 and 373–94

Goffart, W. (1974), *Caput and Colonate: Towards a History of Late Roman Taxation*, Toronto

Honoré, T. (1987), 'The making of the Theodosian Code', *ZRG RA* 104: 133–222

Jones, A. H. M. (1948), *Constantine and the Conversion of Europe*, London

Jones, A. H. M. (1964), *The Later Roman Empire 284–602*, 3 vols., Oxford

Jones, A. H. M. (1975), *The Decline of the Ancient World*, London

Levy, E. (1951), *West Roman Vulgar Law: The Law of Property* (Memoirs of the American Philological Society 29), Philadelphia

Marrou, H. (1956), *History of Education in the Ancient World*, London

Matthews, J. (1989), *The Roman Empire of Ammianus*, London

Mommsen, T. (1887, reprint 1969), *Römisches Staatsrecht*, 2nd edn, 3 vols., Graz

Mommsen, T. (1899), *Römisches Strafrecht*, Leipzig

Mommsen, T. (1909), *The Provinces of the Roman Empire from Caesar to Diocletian*, 2 vols., London

Mommsen, T. (1996), *The History of Rome*, reprint, London
Percival, J. (1969), 'Seigneurial aspects of late Roman estate management', *EHR* 85: 449–73
Percival, J. (1976), *The Roman Villa: An Historical Introduction*, London
Rostovtzeff, M. (1957), *The Social and Economic History of the Roman Empire*, 2nd edn, 2 vols., Oxford
Syme, R. (1968), *Ammianus and the Historia Augusta*, Oxford
Turpin, W. (1985), 'The Law Codes and late Roman law', *Revue Internationale des Droits de l'Antiquité*, 3rd series 32: 339–53
Ward-Perkins, B. (1984), *From Classical Antiquity to the Middle Ages*, Oxford
Wickham, C. (1984), 'The other transition: from the ancient world to feudalism', *Past and Present* 103: 3–36
Wood, I. (1986), 'Disputes in late fifth- and sixth-century Gaul: some problems', in W. Davies and P. Fouracre (eds.), *The Settlement of Disputes in Early Medieval Europe*, Cambridge, pp. 7–22
Wood, I. (1993), 'The [Theodosian] Code in Merovingian Gaul', in J. Harries and I. Wood (eds.), *The Theodosian Code*, London, pp. 161–77
Wood, I. (1994), *The Merovingian Kingdoms 450–751*, London

2 THE BARBARIAN INVASIONS

Alcock, L. (1971), *Arthur's Britain: History and Archaeology 367–654*, Harmondsworth
Alcock, L. (1988), 'The activities of potentates in Celtic Britain, AD 500–800: a positivist approach', in S. T. Driscoll and M. R. Nieke (eds.), *Power and Politics in Early Medieval Britain and Ireland*, Edinburgh, pp. 22–46
Alcock, L. (1992), 'Message from the dark side of the moon: western and northern Britain in the age of Sutton Hoo', in M. O. H. Carver (ed.), *The Age of Sutton Hoo: The Seventh Century in North-Western Europe*, Woodbridge, pp. 205–15
Amory, P. (1993), 'The meaning and purpose of ethnic terminology in the Burgundian laws', *EME* 2: 1–28
Amory, P. (1997), *People and Identity in Ostrogothic Italy, 489–554*, Cambridge
Balsdon, J. P. V. D. (1979), *Romans and Aliens*, London
Barnwell, P. S. (1992), *Emperor, Prefects and Kings: The Roman West, 395–565*, London
Barnwell, P. S. (1997), *Kings, Courtiers and Imperium: The Barbarian West, 565–725*, London
Bassett, S. (1989), 'In search of the origins of Anglo-Saxon kingdoms', in S. Bassett (ed.), *The Origins of Anglo-Saxon Kingdoms*, London, pp. 3–27
Böhme, H. W. (1974), *Germanische Grabfunde des 4 bis 5 Jahrhunderts zwischen untere Elbe und Loire* (Studien zur Chronologie und Bevölkerungsgeschichte), Munich
Böhme, H. W. (1986), 'Das Ende der Römerherrschaft in Britannien und die angelsächsische Besiedlung Englands im 5. Jahrhundert', *Jahrbuch der Römisch-Germanischen Zentralmuseums Mainz* 33: 469–574
Boissonade, P. (1927), *Life and Work in Medieval Europe: The Evolution of Medieval Economy from the Fifth to the Fifteenth Century*, London; extract reprinted as 'The destructiveness of the invasions', in K. Fischer Drew (ed.), *The Barbarian Invasions*, New York (1970), pp. 9–14

Burns, T. S. (1994), *Barbarians within the Gates of Rome: A Study of Roman Military Policy and the Barbarians, ca.375–425*, Bloomington

Bury, J. B. (1926), *The Invasions of Europe by the Barbarians*, London

Cameron, Av. (1993a), *The Later Roman Empire, AD 284–430*, London

Cameron, Av. (1993b), *The Mediterranean World in Late Antiquity AD 395–600*, London

Chadwick-Hawkes, S. (1989), 'The south-east after the Romans: the Saxon settlement', in V. A. Maxfield (ed.), *The Saxon Shore: A Handbook*, Exeter, pp. 78–95

Christie, N. (1994), *The Lombards*, Oxford

Collins, R. (1980), 'Merida and Toledo, 550–585', in E. James (ed.), *Visigothic Spain: New Approaches*, Oxford, pp. 189–219

Collins, R. (1983), *Early Medieval Spain*, London

Collins, R. (1984), 'The Basques in Aquitaine and Navarre', in J. Gillingham and J. M. Holt (eds.), *War and Government in the Middle Ages*, Cambridge, pp. 3–17

Collins, R. (1986), *The Basques*, Oxford

Courcelle, P. (1964), *Histoire littéraire des grandes invasions germaniques*, Paris

Delbrück, H. (1980), *History of the Art of War within the Framework of Political History*, trans. W. T. Renfroe, vol. II: *The Germans*, Westport, CT and London

Dench, E. (1995), *From Barbarians to New Men: Greek, Roman and Modern Perceptions of Peoples from the Central Apennines*, Oxford

Dixon, P. (1982), 'How Saxon is a Saxon house?', in J. Dury (ed.), *Structural Reconstruction* (BAR British Series 110), Oxford, pp. 275–88

Drew, K. F. (1987), 'Another look at the origins of the middle ages: a reassessment of the role of the Germanic kingdoms', *Speculum* 62: 803–12

Drinkwater, J. F. (1983), *Roman Gaul*, London

Drinkwater, J. F. (1996), '"The Germanic threat on the Rhine frontier": a Romano-Gallic artefact?', in R. W. Mathisen and H. S. Sivan (eds.), *Shifting Frontiers in Late Antiquity*, Aldershot, pp. 20–30

Elton, H. (1996), *Warfare in Roman Europe, 350–425*, Oxford

Eriksen, T. H. (1993), *Ethnicity and Nationalism: Anthropological Perspectives*, London

Esmonde Cleary, A. S. (1989), *The Ending of Roman Britain*, London

Feachem, R. W. (1955–56), 'The fortifications on Traprain Law', *Proceedings of the Society of Antiquaries for Scotland* 89: 284–9

Geary, P. (1999), 'Barbarianism and ethnicity', in G. Bowerstock, P. Brown and O. Graber (eds.), *Late Antiquity: A Guide to the Postclassical World*, Cambridge, MA and London, pp. 107–29

Gerberding, R. (1987), *The Rise of the Carolingians and the* 'Liber Historiae Francorum', Oxford

Goffart, W. (1980), *Romans and Barbarians: Techniques of Accommodation*, Princeton

Goffart, W. (1982), 'Old and new in Merovingian taxation', *Past and Present* 96: 3–21

Goffart, W. (1989), 'The theme of the barbarian invasions in later antique and modern historiography', in E. Chrysos and A. Schwarcz (eds.), *Das Reich und die Barbaren*, Vienna, pp. 87–107; reprinted in W. Goffart, *Rome's Fall and After*, London (1989), pp. 111–32

Goffart, W. (1995), 'Two notes on Germanic antiquity today', *Traditio* 50: 9–30

Groenewoudt, B. J. and van Nie, M. (1995), 'Assessing the scale and organisation of Germanic iron production in Heeten, the Netherlands', *Journal of Archaeologists* 3.2: 187–215

Hall, E. (1989), *Inventing the Barbarian*, Oxford
Halsall, G. (1995a), *Early Medieval Cemeteries: An Introduction to Burial Archaeology in the Post-Roman West*, Glasgow
Halsall, G. (1995b), *Settlement and Social Organisation: The Merovingian Region of Metz*, Cambridge
Halsall, G. (2003), *Warfare and Society in the Barbarian West 450–900*, London
Hansen, H. J. (1989), 'Dankirke: affluence in late Iron Age Denmark', in K. Randsborg (ed.), *The Birth of Europe: Archaeology and Social Development in the First Millennium* AD, Rome, pp. 123–8
Heather, P. (1994a), 'State formation in Europe in the first millennium AD', in B. E. Crawford (ed.), *Scotland in Dark Age Europe*, St Andrews, pp. 47–70
Heather, P. (1994b), 'Literacy and power in the migration period', in A. K. Bowman and G. Woolf (eds.), *Literacy and Power in the Ancient World*, Cambridge, pp. 177–97
Heather, P. (1995), 'The Huns and the end of the Roman Empire in western Europe', *EHR* 110: 4–41
Heather, P. (1996), *The Goths*, Oxford
Heather, P. (1999), 'The barbarian in late antiquity: image, reality and transformation', in R. Miles (ed.), *Construction of Identities in Late Antiquity*, London, pp. 234–68
Heidinga, H. A. (1994), 'Frankish settlement at Gennep: a migration period settlement in the Dutch Meuse area', in P. O. Nielsen, K. Randsborg and H. Thrane (eds.), *The Archaeology of Gudme and Lundeborg*, Copenhagen, pp. 202–8
Higham, N. (1992), *Rome, Britain and the Anglo-Saxons*, London
James, E. (1977), *The Merovingian Archaeology of South-West Gaul* (BAR Supplementary Series 25), 2 vols., Oxford
James, E. (1988a), *The Franks*, Oxford
James, E. (1988b), 'Childéric, Syagrius et la disparition du royaume de Soissons', *Revue Archéologique de Picardie* 3–4: 9–12
James, E. (1989), 'The origins of barbarian kingdoms. The continental evidence', in S. Bassett (ed.), *The Origins of Anglo-Saxon Kingdoms*, London, pp. 40–52
Jones, A. H. M. (1964), *The Later Roman Empire, 284–602*, Oxford
Jones, M. E. (1996), *The End of Roman Britain*, Ithaca
Keay, S. (1988), *Roman Spain*, London
Knowles, D. (1962), *Great Historical Enterprises: Problems in Monastic History*, London
Lepelley, C. (1979), *Les Cités de l'Afrique romaine au Bas-Empire*, I, Paris
Levick, B. (1985), *The Government of the Roman Empire: A Sourcebook*, London
Lintott, A. W. (1993), *Imperium Romanum: Politics and Administration*, London
Loseby, S. T. (1997), 'Arles in late antiquity: Gallula Roma Arelas and Urbs Genesii', in N. Christie and S. T. Loseby (eds.), *Towns in Transition: Urban Evolution in Late Antiquity and the Early Middle Ages*, Aldershot, pp. 45–70
McCormick, M. (1986), *Eternal Victory: Triumphal Rulership in Late Antiquity, Byzantium and the Early Medieval West*, Cambridge
Mathisen, R. W. (1993), *Roman Aristocrats in Barbarian Gaul: Strategies for Survival in an Age of Transition*, Austin, TX
Matthews, J. (1989), *The Roman Empire of Ammianus*, London
Millar, F. (ed.) (1981), *The Roman Empire and Its Neighbours*, rev. edn, London
Moorhead, J. (1992), *Theoderic in Italy*, Oxford

Moorhead, J. (1994), *Justinian*, London

Musset, L. (1975), *The Germanic Invasions*, trans. E. and C. James, London

Nielsen, P. O. (1994), 'The Gudme–Lundeborg project – interdisciplinary research 1988–91', in P. O. Nielsen, K. Randsborg and H. Thrane (eds.), *The Archaeology of Gudme and Lundeborg*, Copenhagen, pp. 16–22

Nuber, H. U. (1993), 'Der Verlust der obergermanisch-raetischen Limesgebiete und die Grenzsicherung bis zum Ende des 3. Jahrhunderts', in F. Vallet and M. Kazanski (eds.), *L'Armée romaine et les barbares du IIIe au VIIe siècle*, Paris, pp. 101–8

Pirenne, H. (1925), *Medieval Cities*, New York

Pohl, W. (ed.) (1997), *Kingdoms of the Empire: The Integration of Barbarians in Late Antiquity*, London

Pohl, W. and Reimitz, H. (eds.) (1998), *Strategies of Distinction: The Construction of Ethnic Communities 300–800*, Leiden

Pohl, W., Reimitz, H. and Wood, I. (eds.) (2001), *The Transformation of Frontiers: From Late Antiquity to the Carolingians*, Leiden

Potter, T. W. (1987), *Roman Italy*, London

Rahtz, P. A. (1982–83), 'Celtic society in Somerset, AD 400–700', *BBCS* 30: 176–200

Rouche, M. (1979), *L'Aquitaine des Wisigoths aux Arabes, 418–781: naissance d'une région*, Paris

Steuer, H. (1994), 'Handwerk auf spätantiken Höhensiedlungen des 4/5. Jahrhunderts in Südwestdeutschland', in P. O. Nielsen, K. Randsborg and H. Thrane (eds.), *The Archaeology of Gudme and Lundeborg*, Copenhagen, pp. 128–44

Steuer, H. (1997), 'Herrschaft von der Höhe. Von mobilen Soldatentruppe zur Residenz auf repräsentativen Bergkuppen', in K. Fuchs, M. Kempa, R. Redies, B. Theune-Großkopf and A. Wais (eds.), *Die Alamannen*, Stuttgart, pp. 149–62

Stroheker, K. F. (1948), *Die senatorische Adel im spätantiken Gallien*, Tübingen

Thompson, E. A. (1956), 'The settlement of the barbarians in southern Gaul', *JRS* 46: 65–75; reprinted in E. A. Thompson (1982), *Romans and Barbarians: The Decline of the Western Empire*, Madison, Wisconsin, ch. 2

Thompson, E. A. (1976), 'The end of Roman Spain (Part I)', *NMS* 20: 3–28

Thompson, E. A. (1977), 'The end of Roman Spain (Part II)', *NMS* 21: 3–31

Wallace-Hadrill, J. M. (1971), *Early Germanic Kingship in England and on the Continent*, Oxford

Wells, C. (1992), *The Roman Empire*, 2nd edn, London

Wightman, E. M. (1985), *Gallia Belgica*, London

Wolfram, H. (1975), 'Athanaric the Visigoth: monarchy or judgeship?', *JMH* 1: 259–78

Wolfram, H. (1988), *History of the Goths*, trans. T. J. Dunlap, Berkeley, CA

Wolfram, H. (1997), *The Roman Empire and Its Germanic Peoples*, Berkeley, CA

Wood, I. N. (1977), 'Kings, kingdoms and consent', in I. N. Wood and P. H. Sawyer (eds.), *Early Medieval Kingship*, Leeds, pp. 6–29

Wood, I. N. (1990), 'Ethnicity and ethnogenesis of the Burgundians', in H. Wolfram and W. Pohl (eds.), *Typen der Ethnogenese unter besondere Berücksichtigung der Bayern*, Vienna, pp. 53–69

Wood, I. N. (1998), 'The barbarian invasions and first settlements', in A. Cameron and P. Garnsey (eds.), *Cambridge Ancient History*, XIII: *The Late Empire*, AD *337–425*, Cambridge, pp. 516–37

3 SOURCES AND INTERPRETATION

Amory, P. (1997), *People and Identity in Ostrogothic Italy, 489–554*, Cambridge

Arce, J. (1988), *España entre el mundo antiguo y el mundo medieval*, Madrid

Barker, P. A. (1993), *The Techniques of Archaeological Excavation*, 3rd edn, London

Barley, M. W. (ed.) (1977), *European Towns: Their Archaeology and Early History*, London

Bentley, M. (ed.) (1997), *The Routledge Companion to Historiography*, London

Berlioz, J. *et al.* (1994), *Identifier sources et citations* (L'Atelier du Médiéviste 1), Turnhout

Bierbrauer, V. (1992), 'La diffusione dei reperti longobardi in Italia', in G. C. Menis (ed.), *I Longobardi*, 2nd edn, Milan, pp. 97–127

Binford, L. (1962), 'Archaeology as anthropology', *American Anthropology* 28: 217–25

Bintliff, J. (ed.) (1991), *The Annales School and Archaeology*, Leicester

Bischoff, B. (1990), *Latin Palaeography: Antiquity and the Middle Ages*, trans. D. O'Croinin and D. Ganz, Cambridge

Bourdieu, P. (1977), *Outline of a Theory of Practice*, trans. R. Nice, Cambridge

Bowman, A. (1994), *Life and Letters on the Roman Frontier: Vindolanda and Its People*, London

Bowman, A. and Thomas, J. D. (1984), *Vindolanda: The Latin Writing Tablets*, Gloucester

Braudel, F. (1972), *The Mediterranean and the Mediterranean World in the Age of Philip II*, 2nd edn, London

Breukelaar, A. (1994), *Historiography and Episcopal Authority in Sixth-Century Gaul: The Histories of Gregory of Tours Interpreted in Their Historical Context*, Göttingen

Brogiolo, G. P., Gauthier, N. and Christie, N. (eds.) (2000), *Towns and Their Territories between Late Antiquity and the Early Middle Ages*, Leiden

Brogiolo, G. P. and Ward Perkins, B. (eds.) (1999), *The Idea and the Ideal of the Town between Late Antiquity and the Early Middle Ages*, Leiden

Brown, P. R. L. (1971), 'The rise and function of the holy man in late antiquity', *JRS* 61: 80–101; repr. in Brown (1982a), pp. 103–52

Brown, P. R. L. (1977), 'Relics and social status in the age of Gregory of Tours', *The Stenton Lecture, University of Reading, 1977*; repr. in Brown (1982a), pp. 222–50

Brown, P. R. L. (1978), *The Making of Late Antiquity*, Cambridge, MA

Brown, P. R. L. (1981), *The Cult of the Saints: Its Rise and Function in Latin Christianity*, Chicago

Brown, P. R. L. (1982a), *Society and the Holy in Late Antiquity*, London

Brown, P. R. L. (1982b), 'Town, village and holy man: the case of Syria', in Brown (1982a), pp. 153–165

Brown, P. R. L. (2000), 'Enjoying the saints in late antiquity', *EME* 9: 1–24

Brown, P. R. L. (2002), *Authority and the Sacred: Aspects of the Christianization of the Roman World*, 2nd edn, Cambridge

Brulet, R. (1990), *Les Fouilles du quartier Saint-Brice à Tournai: l'environnement funéraire de la sépulture de Childéric*, I, Louvain-la-Neuve

Brulet, R. (1991), *Les Fouilles du quartier Saint-Brice à Tournai: l'environnement funéraire de la sépulture de Childéric*, II, Louvain-la-Neuve

Brulet, R. (1997), 'La tombe de Childéric et la topographie funéraire de Tournai à la fin du Ve siècle', in Rouche (1997), pp. 59–78

Buchner, R. (1953), *Wattenbach-Levison: Deutschlands Geschichtsquellen im Mittelalter: Vorzeit und Karolinger: Beiheft: Die Rechtsquellen*, Weimar

Buchwald, W., Hohlweg, A. and Prinz, O. (1991), *Dictionnaire des auteurs grecs et latins de l'antiquité et du moyen âge*, trans. D. Berger and J. Billen, Turnhout

Cameron, Av. (1970), *Agathias*, Oxford

Cameron, Av. (1985), *Procopius and the Sixth Century*, London

Carver, M. (1992), 'Ideology and allegiance in East Anglia', in R. T. Farrell and C. Neuman De Vegvar (eds.), *Sutton Hoo: Fifty Years After*, Oxford, OH, pp. 173–82

Chavarría Arnau, A. (2001), 'Villae y necrópolis en Hispania durante la antigüedad tardía', *Bulletin de l'Association Pour l'Antiquité Tardive* 10 (n.p.)

Clark, A. (1990), *Seeing Beneath the Soil*, London

Collins, R. (1977), 'Julian of Toledo and the royal succession in late seventh-century Spain', in P. H. Sawyer and I. N. Wood (eds.), *Early Medieval Kingship*, Leeds, pp. 30–49

Cruickshank, G. D. R. (2000), 'The battle of Dunnichen and the Aberlemno battle-scene', in E. J. Cowan and B. A. McDonald (eds.), *Alba: Celtic Scotland in the Medieval Era*, East Linton, pp. 69–87

Damminger, F. (1998), 'Dwellings, settlements and settlement patterns in Merovingian southwest Germany and adjacent areas', in I. N. Wood (ed.), *Franks and Alamanni in the Merovingian Period: An Ethnographic Perspective*, Woodbridge, pp. 33–89

Dark, K. R. (1995), *Theoretical Archaeology*, London

Dark, K. R. (2000), *Britain and the End of the Roman Empire*, Stroud

de Boe, G. and Verhaeghe, F. (eds.) (1997), *Rural Settlements in Medieval Europe* (Papers of the Medieval Europe Brugge 1997 Conference 6), Bruges

de Jong, M. (1999), 'Adding insult to injury: Julian of Toledo and his *Historia Wambae*', in P. Heather (ed.), *The Visigoths: From the Migration Period to the Seventh Century*, Woodbridge, pp. 373–89

Delano-Smith, C. (1992), 'The Annales for archaeology?', *Antiquity* 66: 539–41

Delestre, X. and Périn, P. (eds.) (1998), *La Datation des structures et des objets du haut moyen âge: méthodes et résultats* (Mémoires de l'Association Française d'Archéologie Mérovingienne 7), Condé-sur-Noireau

Delogu, P. (2002), *An Introduction to Medieval History*, London

Demolon, P., Galinié, H. and Verhaeghe, F. (eds.) (1994), *Archéologie des villes dans le Nord-Ouest de l'Europe (VIIe–XIIIe siècle)*, Douai

de Nie, G. (1987), *Views from a Many-Windowed Tower: Studies of Imagination in the Work of Gregory of Tours*, Amsterdam

Dennett, D. C. (1948), 'Pirenne and Muhammad', *Speculum* 23: 167–90

de Rubeis, F. (2002), 'Epigraphs', in C. La Rocca (ed.), *Italy in the Early Middle Ages*, Oxford, pp. 220–7

Dickinson, T. M. (1980), 'The present state of Anglo-Saxon cemetery studies', in P. Rahtz, T. M. Dickinson and L. Watts (eds.), *Anglo-Saxon Cemeteries 1979* (BAR British Series 82), Oxford

Dickinson, T. M. (2002), 'What's new in early medieval burial archaeology?', *EME* 11: 71–87

Dill, S. (1926), *Roman Society in Gaul in the Merovingian Age*, London

Drijvers, J. W. and Hunt, D. (eds.) (1999), *The Late Roman World and Its Historian: Interpreting Ammianus Marcellinus*, London

Dubois, J. and Lemaitre, J.-L. (1993), *Sources et méthodes de l'hagiographie médiévale*, Paris

Dumville, D. (1986), 'The historical value of the *Historia Brittonum*', *Arthurian Literature* 6: 1–26

Dyer, C. (1992), Review of Bintliff (ed.), *The Annales School and Archaeology*, *Medieval Archaeology* 36: 361

Effros, B. (2002), *Caring for Body and Soul: Burial and the Afterlife in the Merovingian World*, University Park, PA

Effros, B. (2003), *Merovingian Mortuary Archaeology and the Making of the Early Middle Ages*, Berkeley

Fasham, P. J., Schadla-Hall, R. T., Shennan, S. J. and Bates, P. J. (1980), *Fieldwalking for Archaeologists*, Andover

Foucault, M. (1994), *Power (The Essential Works 3)*, ed. J. B. Faubion, London, 1994

Fouracre, P. (1990), 'Merovingian history and Merovingian hagiography', *Past and Present* 127: 3–38

Fouracre, P. (1999), 'The origins of the Carolingian attempt to regulate the cult of saints', in Howard-Johnston and Hayward (1999), pp. 143–65

Galinié, H. (1997), 'Tours de Grégoire, Tours des archives du sol', in Gauthier and Galinié (1997), pp. 65–80

Garrison, M. D. (2000), 'The Franks as the New Israel: education for an identity from Pippin to Charlemagne', in Y. Hen and M. J. Innes (eds.), *The Uses of the Past in Early Medieval Europe*, Cambridge, pp. 114–61

Gauthier, N. and Galinié, H. (eds.) (1997), *Grégoire de Tours et l'espace gaulois: Actes du Congrès international Tours, 3–5 Novembre 1994* (13e supplément à la Revue Archéologique du Centre de la France), Tours

Gerberding, R. (1987), *The Rise of the Carolingians* and *the* 'Liber Historiae Francorum', Oxford

Giddens, A. (1984), *The Constitution of Society: Outline of the Theory of Structuration*, London

Goffart, W. (1987), 'From *Historiae* to *Historia Francorum* and back again: aspects of the textual history of Gregory of Tours', in T. F. X. Noble and J. J. Contreni (eds.), *Religion, Culture and Society in the Early Middle Ages*, Kalamazoo, pp. 55–76; repr. in Goffart (1989), no. 10

Goffart, W. (1988), *The Narrators of Barbarian History, AD 550–800: Jordanes, Gregory of Tours, Bede, Paul the Deacon*, Princeton, NJ

Goffart, W. (1989), *Rome's Fall and After*, London

Grierson, P. (1951), *Numismatics and History* (Historical Association pamphlet G19), London

Gurevich, A. (1988), *Medieval Popular Culture: Problems of Belief and Perception*, Cambridge

Haldon, J. (1999), 'The idea of the town in the Byzantine Empire', in G. P. Brogiolo and B. Ward Perkins (eds.), *The Idea and the Ideal of the Town between Late Antiquity and the Early Middle Ages*, Leiden, pp. 1–23

Halsall, G. (1992), 'The origins of the Reihengräberzivilisation: forty years on', in J. F. Drinkwater and H. Elton (eds.), *Fifth-Century Gaul: A Crisis of Identity?*, Cambridge, pp. 196–207

Halsall, G. (1995), *Early Medieval Cemeteries: An Introduction to Burial Archaeology in the Post-Roman West*, Glasgow

Halsall, G. (1997), 'Archaeology and historiography', in Bentley (1997), pp. 807–29

Halsall, G. (1998), 'Burial, ritual and Merovingian society', in J. Hill and M. Swan (eds.), *The Community, the Family and the Saint: Patterns of Power in Early Medieval Europe*, Turnhout, pp. 325–38

Halsall, G. (2000a), 'La Christianisation de la région de Metz à travers les sources archéologiques (5ème–7ème siècle): problèmes et possibilités', in M. Polfer (ed.), *L'Evangélisation des régions entre Meuse et Moselle et la fondation de l'abbaye d'Echternach (Ve–IXe siècle)*, Luxemburg, pp. 123–46

Halsall, G. (2000b), 'Archaeology and the late Roman frontier in northern Gaul: the so-called Föderatengräber reconsidered', in W. Pohl and H. Reimitz (eds.), *Grenze und Differenz im früheren Mittelalter*, Vienna, pp. 167–80

Halsall, G. (ed.) (2002), *Humour, History and Politics in Late Antiquity and the Early Middle Ages*, Cambridge

Hamerow, H. (1994), 'Review article: the archaeology of rural settlement in early medieval Europe', *EME* 3.2: 167–79

Handley, M. (1999), 'Tiempo y identidad. La datación por la Era en las inscripciones de la España tardoromana y visigoda', *Iberia: Revista de la Antigüedad* 2: 191–201

Handley, M. (2000), 'Inscribing time and identity in the kingdom of Burgundy', in S. Mitchell and G. Greatrex (eds.), *Ethnicity and Culture in Late Antiquity*, London, pp. 83–102

Hansen, I. and Wickham, C. J. (eds.) (2000), *The Long Eighth Century*, Leiden

Härke, H. (1989), 'Early Saxon weapon burials: frequencies, distributions and weapon combinations', in S. Chadwick-Hawkes (ed.), *Weapons and Warfare in Anglo-Saxon England*, Oxford, pp. 49–61

Härke, H. (1990), '"Weapon graves"? The background of the Anglo-Saxon weapon burial rite', *Past and Present* 126: 22–43

Härke, H. (1992a), *Angelsächsische Waffengräber des 5. bis 7. Jahrhunderts* (Zeitschrift für Archäologie des Mittelalters, Beiheft 6), Cologne

Härke, H. (1992b), 'Changing symbols in a changing society: the Anglo-Saxon weapon rite', in M. Carver (ed.), *The Age of Sutton Hoo: The Seventh Century in North-Western Europe*, Woodbridge, pp. 149–65

Heather, P. (1991), *Goths and Romans, 332–489*, Oxford

Heinzelmann, M. (2001), *Gregory of Tours*, trans. C. Carroll, Cambridge

Hendy, M. F. (1988), 'From public to private: the western barbarian coinages as a mirror of the disintegration of Late Roman state structures', *Viator* 19: 29–78

Hillgarth, J. N. (1966), 'Coins and chronicles: propaganda in sixth-century Spain and the Byzantine background', *Historia* 15: 483–508

Hodder, I. (ed.) (1987), *Archaeology as Long-Term History*, Cambridge

Hodder, I. (ed.) (1991), *Archaeological Theory in Europe: The Last Three Decades*, London

Hodges, R. (1982a), 'Method and theory in medieval archaeology', *Archeologia Medievale* 9: 7–38

Hodges, R. (1982b), *Dark Age Economics: The Origins of Towns and Trade, AD 600–1000*, London
Hodges, R. and Bowden, W. (eds.) (1998), *The Sixth Century: Production, Distribution and Demand*, Leiden
Hodges, R. and Hobley, B. (eds.) (1988), *The Rebirth of Towns in the West, 700–1050*, London
Hooper, N. (1993), 'The Aberlemno stone and cavalry in Anglo-Saxon England', *Northern History* 29: 188–96
Howard-Johnston, J. and Hayward, P. A. (eds.) (1999), *The Cult of the Saints in Late Antiquity and the Middle Ages: Essays on the Contribution of Peter Brown*, Oxford
James, E. (1977), *The Merovingian Archaeology of South-West Gaul* (BAR Supplementary Series 25), 2 vols., Oxford
James, E. (1989), 'Burial and status in the early medieval west', *TRHS*, 5th series, 39: 23–40
Johnson, M. (1999), *Archaeological Theory*, Oxford
Kazanski, M. (1991), *Les Goths (Ier–VIIe siècles après J.-C.)*, Paris
Knowles, D. (1963), *Great Historical Enterprises: Problems in Monastic History*, London
Lamm, J. P. and Nordstrom, H. A. (eds.) (1983), *Statens Historiska Museum Studies 2: Vendel Period*, Stockholm
Levison, W. (1952), *Wattenbach-Levison: Deutschlands Geschichtsquellen im Mittelalter: Vorzeit und Karolinger: 1 Heft: Die Vorzeit von den Anfänge bis zur Herrschaft der Karolinger*, Weimar
Lifshitz, F. (1994), 'Beyond positivism and genre: "hagiographical" texts as historical narrative', *Viator* 25: 95–113
Linehan, P. (1982), 'The making of the *Cambridge Medieval History*', *Speculum* 57: 463–94
Lorren, C. and Périn, P. (eds.) (1995), *L'Habitat rural du haut moyen âge (France, Pays-Bas, Danemark et Grand-Bretagne)*, Paris
Lorren, C. and Périn, P. (1997), 'Images de la Gaule rurale au VIe siècle', in Gauthier and Galinié (1997), pp. 90–109
Lucy, S. (1997), 'Housewives, warriors and slaves? Sex and gender in Anglo-Saxon burials', in J. Moore and E. Scott (eds.), *Invisible People and Processes: Writing Gender and Childhood into European Archaeology*, London, pp. 150–68
McKitterick, R. (1999), 'Paul the Deacon and the Franks', *EME* 8: 319–39
Mann, M. (1986), *The Sources of Social Power, 1: A History of Power from the Beginning to AD 1760*, Cambridge
Matthews, J. F. (1989), *The Roman Empire of Ammianus Marcellinus*, London
Mitchell, K. and Wood, I. N. (eds.) (2002), *The World of Gregory of Tours*, Leiden
Momigliano, A. (1955), 'Cassiodorus and the Italian culture of his time', *Proceedings of the British Academy* 41: 207–45
Mordek, H. (ed.) (1984), *Überlieferung und Geltung normativer Texte des frühen und hohen Mittelalters* (Quellen und Forschungen zum Recht im Mittelalter 4), Sigmaringen
Murray Callander, A. (1983), *Germanic Kinship Structure: Studies in Law and Society in Antiquity and the Early Middle Ages*, Toronto
Myres, J. N. L. (1986), *The English Settlements*, Oxford

O'Donnell, J. J. (1982), 'The aims of Jordanes', *Historia* 31: 223–40

Périn, P. (1980), *La Datation des tombes mérovingiennes: historique – méthodes – applications*, Paris and Geneva

Périn, P. (1998a), 'La progression des Francs en Gaule du nord au Ve siècle: histoire et archéologie', in D. Geuenich (ed.), *Die Franken und die Alemannen bis zur 'Schlacht bei Zülpich'*, Berlin, pp. 59–81

Périn, P. (1998b), 'Possibilités et limites de l'interprétation sociale des cimetières mérovingiens', *Antiquités Nationales* 30: 169–83

Périn, P. (2002), 'Cemeteries and settlements in Merovingian Gaul', in Mitchell and Wood (2002), pp. 67–99

Pohl, W. (2001), 'History in fragments: Montecassino's politics of memory', *EME* 10: 343–74

Porte, P. (1980), *Un Exemple de site fortifié au haut moyen-âge: l'habitat mérovingien de Larina*, Grenoble

Preucel, R. W. and Hodder, I. (eds.) (1996), *Contemporary Archaeology in Theory: A Reader*, Oxford

Rahtz, P. A. (1983), 'New approaches to medieval archaeology Part 1', in D. A. Hinton (ed.), *25 Years of Medieval Archaeology*, Sheffield

Ripoll, G. (1994), 'Archaeologia Visigota in Hispania', in V. Bierbrauer, O. Von Hessen and E. A. Arslan (eds.), *I Goti*, Milan, pp. 301–27

Roskams, S. P. (2001), *Excavation*, Cambridge

Rouche, M. (ed.) (1997), *Clovis: histoire et mémoire*, I: *Clovis, son temps, l'événement*, Paris

Runciman, W. G. (1989), *A Treatise on Social Theory*, II: *Substantive Social Theory*, Cambridge

Samson, R. (1987), 'Social structures from Reihengräber: mirror or mirage', *Scottish Archaeological Review* 4.2: 116–26

Scharer, A. and Scheibelreiter, G. (eds.) (1994), *Historiographie im frühen Mittelalter*, Vienna

Sims-Williams, P. (1983), 'The settlement of England in Bede and the Chronicle', *ASE* 12: 1–42

Smith, J. M. H. (1997), 'Introduction. Regarding medievalists: contexts and approaches', in Bentley (1997), pp. 105–16

Southworth, E. (ed.) (1990), *Anglo-Saxon Cemeteries: A Reappraisal*, Stroud

Steuer, H. (1982), *Frühgeschichtliche Sozialstrukturen in Europa: Eine Analyse der Auswertungsmethoden des archäologischen Quellenmaterials*, Göttingen

Stoodley, N. (1999), *The Spindle and the Spear: A Critical Enquiry into the Construction and Meaning of Gender in the Early Anglo-Saxon Burial Rite* (BAR British Series 288), Oxford

Theuws, F. (1991), 'Landed property and manorial organisation in northern Austrasia: some considerations and a case study', in N. Roymans and F. Theuws (eds.), *Images of the Past: Studies on Ancient Societies in Northwestern Europe*, Amsterdam, pp. 299–407

Thurlemann, F. (1974), *Der historische Diskurs bei Gregor von Tours: Topoi; Wirklichkeit*, Berne

Trigger, B. G. (1989), *A History of Archaeological Thought*, Cambridge

Van Caenegem, R. (1997), *Introduction aux sources de l'histoire médiévale*, new edn, Turnhout
Van Dam, R. (1985), *Leadership and Community in Late Antique Gaul*, Berkeley, CA
Van Dam, R. (1993), *Saints and Their Miracles in Late Antique Gaul*, Princeton
Van Ossel, P. (1997), 'La part du Bas Empire dans la formation de l'habitat rural du VIe siècle', in Gauthier and Galinié (1997), pp. 81–9
Van Regteren Altena, H. H. (1990), 'On the growth of young medieval archaeology: a recollection', in J. C. Besteman, J. M. Bos and H. A. Heidinga (eds.), *Medieval Archaeology in the Netherlands*, Assen and Maastricht, pp. 1–7
Welch, M. (1992), *English Heritage Book of Anglo-Saxon England*, London
Wharton, A. (1995), *Refiguring the Post-Classical City: Dura Europos, Jerash, Jerusalem and Ravenna*, Cambridge
Whitby, M. (1988), *The Emperor Maurice and His Historian: Theophylact Simocatta on Persian and Balkan Warfare*, Oxford
Williams, H. (1997), 'Ancient landscapes and the dead: the reuse of prehistoric and Roman monuments as early Anglo-Saxon burial sites', *Medieval Archaeology* 41: 1–32
Williams, H. (1998), 'Monuments and the past in early Anglo-Saxon England', *World Archaeology* 30.1: 90–108
Wood, I. N. (1987), 'The fall of the western empire and the end of Roman Britain', *Britannia* 18: 251–62
Wood, I. N. (2002), 'The individuality of Gregory of Tours', in K. Mitchell and I. N. Wood (eds.), *The World of Gregory of Tours*, Leiden, pp. 29–46
Yorke, B. A. E. (1989), 'The Jutes of Hampshire and Wight and the origins of Wessex', in S. Bassett (ed.), *The Origins of Anglo-Saxon Kingdoms*, London, pp. 84–96
Young, B. K. (1975), 'Merovingian funeral rites and the evolution of Christianity: a study in the historical interpretation of archaeological material', PhD thesis, University of Pennsylvania: Ann Arbor
Young, B. K. (1977), 'Paganisme, christianisme et rites funéraires mérovingiens', *Archéologie Médiévale* 7: 5–81
Young, B. K. (1997), 'Pratiques funéraires et mentalités païennes', in Rouche (1997), pp. 15–42

4 THE EASTERN EMPIRE IN THE SIXTH CENTURY

Allen, P. and Jeffreys, E. (eds.) (1996), *The Sixth Century: End or Beginning?* (Byzantina Australiensia 10), Brisbane
Blockley, R. C. (1981, 1983), *The Fragmentary Classicising Historians of the Later Roman Empire*, 2 vols., Liverpool
Brock, S. (1980), 'The Orthodox–Oriental Orthodox Conversations of 532', *Apostolos Varnavas* 41: 219–27; repr. in Brock (1984), XI
Brock, S. (1984), *Syriac Perspectives on Late Antiquity*, London
Brown, P. (1973), 'A Dark Age crisis: aspects of the Iconoclastic controversy', *EHR* 88: 1–34; repr. in Brown (1982), pp. 251–301
Brown, P. (1982), *Society and the Holy in Late Antiquity*, London
Bury, J. B. (1923), *History of the Later Roman Empire from the Death of Theodosius I to the Death of Justinian (AD 395 to AD 565)*, 2 vols., London

Cameron, A. (1969), 'The last days of the Academy at Athens', *Proceedings of the Cambridge Philological Society*, ns 15: 7–29; repr. in Cameron (1985a), XIII
Cameron, A. (1985a), *Literature and Society in the Early Byzantine World*, London
Cameron, Av. (1975), 'The empress Sophia', *Byzantion* 45: 5–21; repr. in Cameron (1981), XI
Cameron, Av. (1976), 'The early religious policies of Justin II', in D. Baker (ed.), *The Orthodox Churches and the West* (Studies in Church History 13), Cambridge, pp. 51–67; repr. in Cameron (1981)
Cameron, Av. (1979), 'Images of authority: elites and icons in late sixth-century Byzantium', *Past and Present* 84: 3–35; repr. in Cameron (1981), XVIII
Cameron, Av. (1981), *Continuity and Change in Sixth Century Byzantium*, London
Cameron, Av. (1985b), *Procopius and the Sixth Century*, London
Cameron, Av. (1993), *The Mediterranean World in Late Antiquity AD 395–600*, London
Farquharson, P. (1996), 'Byzantium, planet earth and the solar system', in Allen and Jeffreys (1996), pp. 263–9
Fowden, G. (1993), *Empire to Commonwealth: The Consequences of Monotheism in Late Antiquity*, Princeton, NJ
Grillmeier, A. (1995), *Christ in Christian Tradition*, II, part 2: *The Church of Constantinople in the Sixth Century*, London
Guillaumont, A. (1962), *Les 'Kephalaia Gnostica' d'Evagre le Pontique et l'histoire de l'origénisme chez les Grecs et chez les Syriens* (Patristica Sorbonensia 5), Paris
Haldon, J. F. (1997), *Byzantium in the Seventh Century: The Transformation of a Culture*, rev. edn, Cambridge
Harrison, M. (1989), *A Temple for Byzantium: The Discovery and Excavation of Anicia Juliana's Palace Church in Istanbul*, London
Honoré, T. (1978), *Tribonian*, London
Jones, A. H. M. (1964), *The Later Roman Empire 284–602: A Social, Economic and Administrative Survey*, 3 vols. and maps, Oxford
Koder, J. (1996), 'Climatic change in the fifth and sixth centuries?', in Allen and Jeffreys (1996), pp. 270–85
Lemerle, P. (1979, 1981), *Les Plus Anciens Recueils des miracles de Saint Démétrius*, 2 vols., Paris
Liebeschuetz, W. (1992), 'The end of the ancient city', in Rich (1992), pp. 1–49
Maas, M. (1992), *John Lydus and the Roman Past*, London
Mango, C. (1980), *Byzantium: The Empire of New Rome*, London
Meyendorff, J. (1989), *Imperial Unity and Christian Divisions: The Church 450–680 AD*, Crestwood, NY
Moorhead, J. (1994), *Justinian*, London
Patlagean, E. (1977), *Pauvreté économique et pauvreté sociale à Byzance, 4e–7e siècles*, Paris
Poulter, A. G. (1983), 'Town and country in Moesia Inferior', in A. G. Poulter (ed.), *Ancient Bulgaria*, 2 vols., Nottingham, II, pp. 74–118
Rich, J. (ed.) (1992), *The City in Late Antiquity*, London
Rousseau, P. (1996), 'Inheriting the fifth century: who bequeathed what?', in Allen and Jeffreys (1996), pp. 1–19
Scott, R. (1996), 'Writing the reign of Justinian: Malalas *versus* Theophanes', in Allen and Jeffreys (1996), pp. 20–34

Sharf, A. (1971), *Byzantine Jewry: From Justinian to the Fourth Crusade*, London
Whitby, M. (1988), *The Emperor Maurice and His Historian: Theophylact Simocatta on Persian and Balkan Warfare*, Oxford
Whittow, M. (1996), *The Making of Orthodox Byzantium, 600–1025*, London

5 THE BYZANTINES IN THE WEST

Amory, P. (1997), *People and Identity in Ostrogothic Italy 489–554*, Cambridge
Barnwell, P. S. (1992), *Emperors, Prefects and Kings: The Roman West, 395–565*, London
Brown, P. (1976), 'Eastern and Western Christendom in late antiquity: a parting of the ways', in *The Orthodox Churches and the West* (Studies in Church History 13), pp. 1–24
Brown, T. S. (1984), *Gentlemen and Officers: Imperial Administration and Aristocratic Power in Byzantine Italy 554–800*, London
Bury, J. B. (1923), *History of the Later Roman Empire from the Death of Theodosius I to the Death of Justinian*, 2 vols., London
Cameron, Av. (1985), *Procopius and the Sixth Century*, London
Chrysos, E. and Schwarcz, A. (eds.) (1989), *Das Reich und die Barbaren*, Vienna
Clover, F. and Humphreys, R. (eds.) (1989), *Tradition and Innovation in Late Antiquity*, Madison, WI
Courtois, C. (1955), *Les Vandales et l'Afrique*, Paris
Durliat, J. (1982), 'Les attributions civiles des évêques byzantins: l'exemple du diocèse d'Afrique 553–709', *Jahrbuch der Österreichischen Byzantinistik* 32.2: 73–84
Février, P. A. (1983), 'Approches récents de l'Afrique byzantine', *Revue de l'Occident Musulman et de la Méditerranée* 35: 25–53
Goffart, W. (1957), 'Byzantine policy in the West under Tiberius II and Maurice: the pretenders Hermengild and Gundovald', *Traditio* 13: 73–118
Goffart, W. (1981), 'Rome, Constantinople and the Barbarians', *American Historical Review* 76: 275–306
Haldon, J. F. (1984), *Byzantine Praetorians*, Bonn
Hannestad, K. (1961), 'Les forces militaires d'après la guerre gothique de Procope', *Classica et Medievalia* 21: 136–83
Heather, P. (1991), *Goths and Romans 332–489*, Oxford
Kaegi, W. (1968), *Byzantium and the Decline of Rome*, Princeton, NJ
Krieger, R. (1991), *Untersuchungen und Hypothesen zur Ansiedlung der Westgoten, Burgunder und Ostgoten*, Berlin
MacCormack, S. (1981), *Art and Ceremony in Late Antiquity*, Berkeley, CA
Markey, T. (1989), 'Germanic in the Mediterranean: Lombards, Vandals and Visigoths', in Clover and Humphreys (1989), pp. 51–71
Martindale, J. (ed.) (1992), *The Prosopography of the Later Roman Empire 527–641*, III, Cambridge
Momigliano, A. (1995), 'Cassiodorus and the Italian culture of his time', *Proceedings of the British Academy* 41: 207–45
Moorhead, J. (1981), 'The last years of Theoderic', *Historia* 32: 106–20
Moorhead, J. (1983), 'Italian loyalties during Justinian's Gothic War', *Byzantion* 53: 575–96
Moorhead, J. (1994), *Justinian*, London

Pringle, D. (1981), *The Defence of Byzantine Africa from Justinian to the Arab Conquest: An Account of the Military History and Archaeology of the African Provinces in the Sixth and Seventh Centuries* (BAR International Series 99), Oxford

Richards, J. (1980), *Consul of God*, London

Roisl, H. (1981), 'Tofila und die Schlacht bei den Busten Gallorum, Ende Juni/Anfang Juli 552', *Jahrbuch der Österreichischen Byzantinistik* 30: 25–41

Ruprechtsberger, E. M. (1989), 'Byzantinische Befestigungen in Algerien und Tunisien', *Antike Welt* 20: 3–21

Stein, E. (1949), *Histoire du Bas-Empire*, II, Paris and Bruges

Teall, J. (1985), 'The barbarians in Justinian's armies', *Speculum* 40: 294–322

Treadgold, W. (1995), *Byzantium and Its Army 284–1081*, Stanford, CA

Wickham, C. (1981), *Early Medieval Italy: Central Power and Local Society 400–1000*, London

Wolfram, H. (1988), *History of the Goths*, trans. T. J. Dunlap, Berkeley, CA

6 OSTROGOTHIC ITALY AND THE LOMBARD INVASIONS

Amory, P. (1997), *People and Identity in Ostrogothic Italy 489–554*, Cambridge

Archi, G. (ed.) (1978), *L'Imperatore Giustiniano: storia e mito: giornate di studio a Ravenna, 14–16 Ottobre 1976*, Milan

Barnish, S. (1990), 'Maximian, Cassiodorus, Boethius, Theodehad: literature, philosophy and politics in Ostrogothic Italy', *NMS* 34: 16–32

Barnwell, P. (1992), *Emperor, Prefects and Kings: The Roman West, 392–565*, London

Bognetti, G. (1966–68), *L'età Longobarda*, 4 vols., Milan

Brown, T. S. (1984), *Gentlemen and Officers: Imperial Administration and Autocratic Power in Byzantine Italy* AD *554–800*, London

Burns, T. (1984), *A History of the Ostrogoths*, Bloomington, IN

Cameron, Av. (1985), *Procopius and the Sixth Century*, London

Chastagnol, A. (1966), *Le Sénat romain sous le règne d'Odoacre: recherches sur l'épigraphie du Colisée au Ve siècle*, Bonn

Christie, N. (1995), *The Lombards*, Oxford

Chrysos, E. and Schwarcz, A. (eds.) (1989), *Das Reich und die Barbaren*, Vienna

Croke, B. (1983), 'The context and date of Priscus fragment 6', *Classical Philology* 78: 296–308

Delogu, P., Guillou, A. and Ortalli, G. (1980), *Longobardi e bizantini* (Storia d'Italia I), Venice

Durliat, J. (1981), *Les Dédicaces d'ouvrages de défense dans l'Afrique byzantine*, Paris

Ensslin, W. (1947), *Theoderich der Grosse*, Munich

Gïardina, A. (ed.) (1986), *Società Romana e imperio tardoantico*, 4 vols.: I: *Istitutioni, ceti, economie*; II: *Roma: politica, economia, paesaggio urbano*; III: *Le Merci, gli insediamenti*; IV: *Tradizione dei classici, trasformazioni della cultura*, Rome and Bari

Goffart, W. (1980), *Barbarians and Romans* AD *418–584: The Techniques of Accommodation*, Princeton, NJ

Harrison, D. (1993), *The Early State and the Towns: Forms of Integration in Lombard Italy 568–774*, Lund

Hartmann, L. M. (1897), *Geschichte Italiens im Mittelalter*, Leipzig

Hessen, O. von (1983), *Il materiale altomedievale nelle collezioni Stibbert di Firenze*, Florence
Hodgkin, T. (1896), *Italy and Her Invaders*, IV and V, Oxford
Hudson, P. and La Rocca Hudson, M. C. (1985), 'Lombard immigration and its effects on north Italian rural and urban settlement', in C. Malone and S. Studdart (eds.), *Papers in Italian Archaeology*, IV. 4: *Classical and Medieval Archaeology*, Oxford
Menis, G. C. (ed.) (1990), *I Longobardi*, Milan
Menis, G. C. (ed.) (1991), *Italia Longobarda*, Venice
Meyer-Flugel, B. (1992), *Das Bild der ostgotisch-römischen Gesellschaft bei Cassiodor*, Berne
Moorhead, J. (1992), *Theoderic in Italy*, Oxford
Stein, E. (1949), *Histoire du Bas-Empire*, II, Paris and Bruges
Stroheker, K. F. (1965), *Germanentum und Spätantike*, Zurich and Stuttgart
Sundwall, J. (1919), *Abhandlungen zur Geschichte des ausgehenden Römertums*, Helsinki, Lund and Stockholm
Tonnies, B. (1989), *Die Amalertradition in den Quellen zur Geschichte der ostgoten Untersuchungen zu Cassiodor, Jordanes, Ennodius und den Excerpta Valesiana*, Hildesheim
Ward-Perkins, B. (1984), *From Classical Antiquity to the Middle Ages: Urban Public Building in Northern and Central Italy AD 300–850*, Oxford
Wenskus, R. (1961), *Stammesbildung und Verfassung: Das Werden der frümittelalterlichen Gentes*, Cologne
Wes, M. A. (1967), *Das Ende des Kaisertums im Westen des römischen Reichs*, The Hague
Wickham, C. (1981), *Early Medieval Italy: Central Power and Local Society 400–1000*, London
Wolfram, H. (1988), *History of the Goths*, trans. T. J. Dunlap, Berkeley, CA
Wolfram, H. and Schwarcz, A. (eds.) (1988), *Anerkennung und Integration: Zu den wirtschaftlichen Grundlagen der Völkerwanderungzeit (400–600)* (Denkschriften der Österreichischen Akademie der Wissenschaften, phil.-hist. Kl. 193, 201), Vienna

7 THE SUEVE AND VISIGOTHIC KINGDOMS AND 13 THE CATHOLIC VISIGOTHIC KINGDOM

Abadal y de Vinyals, R. de (1960), *Del reino de Tolosa al reino de Toledo*, Madrid; repr. in Abadal y de Vinyals (1969), pp. 27–56
Abadal y de Vinyals, R. de (1962–63), 'Els concilis de Toledo', in *Homenaje a Johannes Vincke para el 11 de mayo de 1962*, Madrid, I, pp. 21–45; repr. in Abadal y de Vinyals (1969), pp. 69–93
Abadal y de Vinyals, R. de (1969), *Dels Visigots als Catalans*, I: *La Hispània visigòtica i la Catalunya carolíngia*, Barcelona
Arce, J. (1982), *El último siglo de la España romana: 284–409*, Madrid
Arce, J. (1988), *España entre el mundo antiguo y el medieval*, Madrid
Barbero de Aguilera, A. (1970), 'El pensamiento político visigodo y las primeras unciones regias en la Europa medieval', *Hispania* 30: 245–326; repr. in Barbero de Aguilera (1992), pp. 1–77
Barbero de Aguilera, A. (1987), 'El conflicto de los Tres Capítulos y las iglesias hispánicas', *Studia Historica, Historia Medieval* 5: 123–44; repr. in Barbero de Aguilera (1992), pp. 136–67

Barbero de Aguilera, A. (1989), 'Las divisiones eclesiásticas y las relaciones entre iglesia y estado en la España de los siglos VI y VII', in M. J. Hidalgo de la Vega (ed.), *Homenaje a Marcelo Vigil Pascual*, Salamanca, pp. 169–89; repr. in Barbero de Aguilera (1992), pp. 168–98

Barbero de Aguilera, A. (1992), *La sociedad visigoda y su entorno histórico*, Madrid

Barbero de Aguilera, A. and Loring Garcia, M. I. (1988), 'El reino visigodo y la transición al mundo medieval', in Planeta (ed.), *Historia de España*, I: *La España romana y visigoda (siglos III a.C.–VII d.C.)*, Barcelona, pp. 410–583

Barbero, A. and Vigil, M. (1965), 'Sobre los orígenes sociales de la Reconquista: Cántabros y Vascones desde fines del imperio romano hasta la invasión musulmana', *Boletín de la Real Academia de la Historia* 156.2: 271–329; repr. in Barbero and Vigil (1974), pp. 11–98

Barbero, A. and Vigil, M. (1970), 'Algunos aspectos de la feudalización del reino visigodo en relación con su organización financiera y militar', *Moneda y Crédito* 112: 71–91; repr. in Barbero and Vigil (1974), pp. 107–37

Barbero, A. and Vigil, M. (1974), *Sobre los orígenes sociales de la Reconquista*, Barcelona

Barbero, A. and Vigil, M. (1978), *La formación del feudalismo en la Península ibérica*, Barcelona

Barnish, S. J. B. (1986), 'Taxation, land and barbarian settlement in the Western Empire', *PBSR* 54: 170–94

Campos, J. (1960), *Juan de Bíclaro, obispo de Gerona: su vida y su obra*, Madrid

Castellanos, Santiago (1998), *Poder social, aristocracias y 'hombre santo' en la Hispania visigoda*, Logroño

Codoñér Merino, C. (1991), 'La literatura', in J. M. Jover Zamora (ed.), *Historia de España de Don Ramón Menéndez Pidal*, III, 2: *España visigoda*, Madrid, pp. 209–67

Collins, R. (1980), 'Merida and Toledo: 550–585', in James (1980), pp. 189–219

Collins, R. (1983), *Early Medieval Spain: Unity in Diversity, 400–1000*, London

David, P. (1947), *Etudes historiques sur la Galice et le Portugal du VIe au XIIe siècle*, Lisbon and Paris

Delmaire, R. (1989), *Largesses sacrées et res privata: l'aerarium impérial et son administration du IVe au VIe siècle*, Rome

Demougeot, E. (1979), *La Formation de l'Europe et les invasions barbares*, II: *De l'Avènement de Dioclétien au début du VIe siècle*, Paris

Díaz Martínez, P. C. (1986–87), 'La monarquía sueva en el s. V. Aspectos políticos y prosopográficos', *Studia Historica, Historia Antigua* 4–5. I: 205–26

Díaz Martínez, P. C. (1987), *Formas económicas y sociales en el monacato visigodo*, Salamanca

D'Ors, A. (1956), 'La territorialidad del derecho de los Visigodos', in *Estudios visigóticos*, I, Rome and Madrid, pp. 91–124

D'Ors, A. (1960), 'El Código de Eurico. Edición, palingenesia, indices', in *Estudios visigóticos*, II, Rome and Madrid

Ferreiro, A. (ed.) (1998), *The Visigoths: Studies in Culture and Society*, Leiden

Fontaine, J. (1959), *Isidore de Séville et la culture classique dans l'Espagne wisigothique*, 3 vols., Paris

Fontaine, J. (1980), 'King Sisebut's *Vita Desiderii* and the political function of Visigothic hagiography', in James (1980), pp. 93–129
Fontaine, J. and Pellistrandi, C. (eds.) (1992), *L'Europe héritière de l'Espagne wisigothique*, Madrid
Fuentes Hinojo, P. (1996), 'La obra política de Teudis y sus aportaciones a la construccion del reino visigodo de Toledo', *En la España Medieval* 19: 9–36
García Gallo, A. (1942–43), 'La territorialidad de la legislación visigoda', *Anuario de Historia del Derecho Español* 14: 593–609
García Gallo, A. (1974), 'Consideración crítica de los estudios sobre la legislación y la costumbre visigodas', *Anuario de Historia del Derecho Español* 4: 343–464
García Iglesias, L. (1975), 'El intermedio ostrogodo en Hispania (507–549 d.C.)', *Hispania Antiqua* 5: 89–120
García Iglesias, L. (1978), *Los Judíos en la España antigua*, Madrid
García Moreno, L. A. (1974a), 'Estudios sobre la organización administrativa del reino visigodo de Toledo', *Anuario de Historia del Derecho Español* 44: 5–155
García Moreno, L. A. (1974b), *Prosopografía del reino visigodo de Toledo*, Salamanca
García Moreno, L. A. (1975), *El fin del reino visigodo de Toledo*, Madrid
García Moreno, L. A. (1989), *Historia de España visigoda*, Madrid
García Moreno, L. A. (1991a), 'La economía y las vidas rurales. La ciudad y la vida urbana', in J. M. Jover Zamora (ed.), *Historia de España de Don Ramón Menéndez Pidal*, III, 1: *España visigoda*, Madrid, pp. 281–404
García Moreno, L. A. (1991b), 'Las invasiones, la ocupación de la Península y las etapas hacia la unificación territorial', in J. M. Jover Zamora (ed.), *Historia de España de Don Ramón Menéndez Pidal*, III, 1: *España visigoda*, Madrid, pp. 61–268
García Moreno, L. A. and Sayas Abengochea, J. J. (1981), *Romanismo y Germanismo: el despertar de los pueblos hispánicos (siglos IV–X)* (*Historia de España*, dir. M. Tuñón de Lara, II) Barcelona
Goffart, W. (1980), *Barbarians and Romans, AD 418–584: The Techniques of Accommodation*, Princeton, NJ
Grierson, P. (1979), 'Visigothic metrology', *Dark Age Numismatics* 12: 74–87
Heather, P. (1991), *Goths and Romans 332–489*, Oxford
Heather, P. (1996), *The Goths*, Oxford
Hillgarth, J. N. (1970), 'Historiography in Visigothic Spain', *Settimane* 17: 261–313
Isla Frez, A. (1990), 'Las relaciones entre el reino visigodo y los reyes merovingios a finales del siglo VI', *En la España Medieval* 13: 11–32
James, E. (ed.) (1980), *Visigothic Spain: New Approaches*, Oxford
Jover Zamora, J. M. (ed.) (1991), *Historia de España de Don Ramón Menéndez Pidal*, III, 1: *España visigoda*, I, *Las invasiones, las sociedades, la iglesia*, II, *La monarquía, la cultura y las artes*, Madrid
King, P. D. (1972), *Law and Society in the Visigothic Kingdom*, Cambridge
King, P. D. (1980), 'King Chindasvint and the first territorial law-code of the Visigothic kingdom', in James (1980), pp. 131–57
Linehan, P. (1993), *History and the Historians of Medieval Spain*, Oxford
Loring García, M. I. and Fuentes Hinojo, P. (1998), 'Esclavitud y servidumbre en el tránsito del mundo antiguo al medieval', in *Romanización y Reconquista en la Península ibérica: Nuevas perspectivas*, Salamanca, pp. 247–56

Martindale, J. R. (1980, 1992), *The Prosopography of the Later Roman Empire*, II *(AD 395–527)*; III *(AD 527–640)*, Cambridge

Mateu y Llopis, F. (1949), 'La ceca visigoda de Córdoba, notas sobre acuñaciones', *Boletín de la Real Academia de Bellas Artes, Ciencias y Artes Nobles de Córdoba* 20: 45–64

Miles, G. C. (1952), *The Coinage of Visigothic Spain: Leowigild to Achila II*, New York

Olmo Enciso, L. (1992), 'El reino visigodo de Toledo y los territorios bizantinos. Datos sobre la heterogeneidad de la Península ibérica' (Coloquio Hispano-Italiano de Arqueología Medieval), Granada, pp. 185–98

Orlandis, J. (1962), 'La sucesión al trono en la monarquía visigoda', in *Estudios Visigóticos*, III, Rome and Madrid, pp. 57–102

Orlandis, J. (1976), *La iglesia en la España visigótica y medieval*, Pamplona

Orlandis, J. (1977), *Historia de España: España visigoda (407–711)*, Madrid

Orlandis, J. (1991), 'El cristianismo y la iglesia en la España visigoda' in J. M. Jover Zamora (ed.), *Historia de España de Don Ramón Menéndez Pidal*, III, 1: *España visigoda*, Madrid, pp. 433–511

Orlandis, J. (1992), *Semblanzas visigodas*, Madrid

Orlandis, J. and Ramos Lissón, D. (1986), *Historia de los concilios de la España romana y visigoda*, Pamplona

Palol Salellas, P. de (1991), 'Arte y arqueología', in J. M. Jover Zamora (ed.), *Historia de España de Don Ramón Menéndez Pidal*, III, 2: *España visigoda*, Madrid, pp. 271–443

Pérez Prendes (1991), 'La monarquía. El poder político, el estado, el derecho', in J. M. Jover Zamora (ed.), *Historia de España de Don Ramón Menéndez Pidal*, III, 2: *España visigoda*, Madrid, pp. 61–268

Pérez Sánchez, D. (1989), *El ejército en la sociedad visigoda*, Salamanca

Pérez Sánchez, D. (1998), 'Legislación y dependencia en la España visigoda', in *Romanización y Reconquista en la Península Ibérica: nuevas perspectivas*, Salamanca, pp. 227–45

Reinhart, W. (1945), 'Sobre el asentamiento de los Visigodos en la Península', *Archivo Español de Arqueología* 18: 124–35

Reinhart, W. (1952), *Historia general del reino hispánico de los Suevos*, Madrid

Rouche, M. (1979), *L'Aquitaine des Wisigoths aux Arabes (418–781): naissance d'une région*, Paris

Sánchez Albornoz, C. (1974), *En torno a los orígenes del feudalismo*, I, 1: *Fideles y gardingos en la monarquía visigoda: raices del vasallaje y del beneficio hispanos*, Buenos Aires

Stein, E. (1949, 1959), *Histoire du Bas-Empire*, I: *De l'état romain à l'état byzantin, 284–476*; II: *De la disparition de l'Empire d'Occident à la mort de Justinien 476–565*, both volumes ed. J.-R. Palanque, Paris, Brussels and Amsterdam

Stroheker, K. F. (1965), *Germanentum und Spätantike*, Zurich

Thompson, E. A. (1956), 'The settlement of the barbarians in southern Gaul', *JRS* 46: 65–75; repr. in Thompson (1982), pp. 23–37

Thompson, E. A. (1963), 'The Visigoths from Fritigern to Euric', *Historia*, 12: 105–26; repr. in Thompson (1982), pp. 38–57

Thompson, E. A. (1969), *The Goths in Spain*, Oxford

Thompson, E. A. (1976–79), 'The end of Roman Spain', *NMS* 20: 3–28; 21: 3–31; 22: 3–22, 23: 1–22

Thompson, E. A. (1980), 'The conversion of the Spanish Suevi to Catholicism', in James (1980), pp. 77–92
Thompson, E. A. (1982), *Romans and Barbarians: The Decline of the Western Empire*, Madison, WI
Vallejo Girvés, M. (1993), *Bizancio y la España tardoantigua (ss. V–VIII): un capítulo de historia mediterránea*, Alcalá de Henares
Werner, K. F. (1984), *Histoire de France sous la direction de J. Favier*, I: *Les origines*, Paris
Wolfram, H. (1990), *Histoire des Goths*, Paris
Zeumer, K. (1944), *Historia de la legislación visigoda*, Barcelona

8 MEROVINGIAN GAUL AND THE FRANKISH CONQUESTS

Bachrach, B. S. (1972), *Merovingian Military Organization 481–751*, Minneapolis
Barnes, T. D. (1994), 'The Franci before Diocletian', in G. Bonamente and F. Paschoud (eds.), *Historiae Augustae Colloquium Genevense* (Historiae Augustae Colloquia, n.s. 2), Bari, pp. 11–18
Brennan, B. (1984), 'The image of the Frankish kings in the poetry of Venantius Fortunatus', *JMH* 10: 1–11
Brennan, B. (1985), 'St Radegund and the early development of her cult at Poitiers', *JRH* 13: 340–54
Buchner, R. (1933), *Die Provence in merowingischer Zeit: Verfassung, Wirtschaft, Kultur*, Stuttgart
Cameron, Av. (1968), 'Agathias on the early Merovingians', *Annali della Scuola Normale Superiore di Pisa*, 2nd series 37: 95–140
Cameron, Av. (1985), *Procopius and the Sixth Century*, Berkeley and Los Angeles
Claude, D. (1964), 'Untersuchungen zum frühfränkischen Comitat', *ZRG, GA* 81: 1–79
Collins, R. (1983), 'Theodebert I, "Rex magnus Francorum"', in P. Wormald, D. Bullough and R. Collins (eds.), *Ideal and Reality in Frankish and Anglo-Saxon Society: Studies Presented to J. M. Wallace-Hadrill*, Oxford, pp. 7–33
Collins, R. (1986), *The Basques*, Oxford
Daly, W. M. (1994), 'Clovis: how barbaric, how pagan?', *Speculum* 69: 619–64
Dannheimer, H. and Dopsch, H. (eds.) (1998), *Die Bajuwaren von Severin bis Tassilo 488–788: Gemeinsame Landesausstellung des Freistaates Bayern und des Landes Salzburg, Rosenheim/Bayern, Mattsee/Salzburg, 19. Mai bis 6. November 1988*, Munich and Salzburg
Durliat, J. (1979), 'Les attributions civiles des évêques mérovingiens: l'exemple de Didier, évêque de Cahors (630–655)', *Annales du Midi* 91: 237–54
Durliat, J. (1990), *Les Finances publiques de Dioclétien aux Carolingiens (284–889)* (Beihefte der Francia 21), Sigmaringen
Ebling, H. (1974), *Prosopographie der Amtsträger des Merowingerreiches von Chlothar II, (613) bis Karl Martell (741)* (Beihefte der Francia 2), Munich
Ewig, E. (1953), 'Die fränkischen Teilungen und Teilreiche (511–613)', *Akademie der Wissenschaften und der Literatur [in Mainz]. Abhandlungen der geistes- und sozialwissenschaftlichen Klasse*, Jahrgang 1952, 9: 651–715; repr. in Ewig (1976–79), I, pp. 114–71
Ewig, E. (1963), 'Résidence et capitale pendant le haut moyen âge', *Revue Historique* 230: 25–72; repr. in Ewig (1976–79), I, pp. 362–408

Ewig, E. (1965), 'Descriptio Franciae', in H. Beumann (ed.), *Karl der Grosse*, 1: *Persönlichkeit und Geschichte*, Düsseldorf, pp. 143–77; repr. in Ewig (1976–79), 1, pp. 274–322

Ewig, E. (1974), 'Studien zur merowingischen Dynastie', *FrSt* 8: 15–59

Ewig, E. (1976–79), *Spätantikes und fränkisches Gallien: Gesammelte Schriften (1952–1973)*, ed. H. Atsma, 2 vols. (Beihefte der Francia 3/1–2), Munich

Fontaine, J. (1980), 'King Sisebut's *Vita Desiderii* and the political function of Visigothic hagiography', in E. James (ed.), *Visigothic Spain: New Approaches*, Oxford, pp. 93–129

Fouracre, P. (1995), 'Eternal light and earthly needs: practical aspects of the development of Frankish immunities', in W. Davies and P. Fouracre (eds.), *Property and Power in the Early Middle Ages*, Cambridge, pp. 53–81

Gäbe, S. (1989), 'Radegundis: sancta, regina, ancilla. Zum Heiligkeitsideal der Radegundisviten von Fortunat und Baudonivia', *Francia* 16.1: 1–30

Galliou, P. and Jones, M. (1991), *The Bretons*, Oxford

Geary, P. J. (1985), *Aristocracy in Provence: The Rhône Basin at the Dawn of the Carolingian Age*, Philadelphia

George, J. W. (1992), *Venantius Fortunatus: A Latin Poet in Merovingian Gaul*, Oxford

Gerberding, R. A. (1987), *The Rise of the Carolingians and the* 'Liber Historiae Francorum', Oxford

Goffart, W. (1957), 'Byzantine policy in the West under Tiberius II and Maurice: the pretenders Hermenegild and Gundovald (579–585)', *Traditio* 13: 73–118

Goffart, W. (1982), 'Old and new in Merovingian taxation', *Past and Present* 96: 3–21; repr. in W. Goffart, *Rome's Fall and After*, London and Ronceverte (1989), pp. 213–31

Goffart, W. (1988), *The Narrators of Barbarian History (AD 550–800): Jordanes, Gregory of Tours, Bede, and Paul the Deacon*, Princeton, NJ

Gradowicz-Pancer, N. (2002), 'De-gendering female violence. Merovingian female honour as an exchange of violence', *EME* 11: 1–18

Grahn-Hoek, H. (1976), *Die fränkische Oberschicht im 6. Jahrhundert: Studien zu ihrer rechtlichen und politischen Stellung* (Vorträge und Forschungen, Sonderband 21), Sigmaringen

Grierson, P. and Blackburn, M. (1986), *Medieval European Coinage. With a Catalogue of the Coins in the Fitzwilliam Museum, Cambridge*, 1: *The Early Middle Ages (5th–10th Centuries)*, Cambridge

Halsall, G. (1995), *Settlement and Social Organization: The Merovingian Region of Metz*, Cambridge

Heinzelmann, M. (1975), 'L'aristocratie et les évêchés entre Loire et Rhin jusqu'à la fin du VIIe siècle', *RHEF* 62: 75–90

Heinzelmann, M. (1976), *Bischofsherrschaft in Gallien: Zur Kontinuität römischer Führungsschichten vom 4. bis zum 7. Jahrhundert, soziale, prosopographische und bildungsgeschichtliche Aspekte* (Beihefte der Francia 5), Munich

Heinzelmann, M. (1982), 'Gallische Prosopographie 260–527', *Francia* 10: 531–718

Heinzelmann, M. (1994), 'Die Franken und die fränkische Geschichte in der Perspektive der Historiographie Gregors von Tours', in A. Scharer and G. Scheibelreiter (eds.), *Historiographie im frühen Mittelalter* (Veröffentlichungen des Instituts für Österreichische Geschichtsforschung 32), Vienna and Munich, pp. 326–44

Heinzelmann, M. and Poulin, J. C. (1986), *Les Vies anciennes de Sainte Geneviève de Paris: études critiques* (Bibliothèque de l'Ecole des Hautes Etudes, IVe section, Sciences Historiques et Philologiques 329), Paris

Hendy, M. F. (1988), 'From public to private: the western barbarian coinages as a mirror of the disintegration of late Roman state structures', *Viator* 19: 29–78

Irsigler, F. (1969), *Untersuchungen zur Geschichte des frühfränkischen Adels* (Rheinisches Archiv 70), Bonn

James, E. (1979), 'Cemeteries and the problem of Frankish settlement in Gaul', in P. H. Sawyer (ed.), *Names, Words and Graves: Early Medieval Settlement*, Leeds, pp. 55–89

James, E. (1980), 'Septimania and its frontier: an archaeological approach', in E. James (ed.), *Visigothic Spain: New Approaches*, Oxford, pp. 223–41

James, E. (1988), *The Franks*, Oxford

James, E. (1989), 'The origins of barbarian kingdoms: the continental evidence', in S. Bassett (ed.), *The Origins of Anglo-Saxon Kingdoms*, London and New York, pp. 40–52, 249–50

Jarnut, J. (1986), *Agilolfingerstudien: Untersuchungen zur Geschichte einer adligen Familie im 6. und 7. Jahrhundert* (Monographien zur Geschichte des Mittelalters 32), Stuttgart

Jarnut, J. (1994), 'Gregor von Tours, Frankengeschichte II, 12: Franci Egidium sibi regem adsciscunt. Faktum oder Sage?', in K. Brunner and B. Merta (eds.), *Ethnogenese und Überlieferung: Angewandte Methoden der Frühmittelalterforschung* (Veröffentlichungen des Instituts für Österreichische Geschichtsforschung 31), Vienna and Munich, pp. 129–34

Jussen, B. (1991), *Patenschaft und Adoption im frühen Mittelalter: Künstliche Verwandtschaft als soziale Praxis* (Veröffentlichungen des Max-Planck-Instituts für Geschichte 98), Göttingen

Kaiser, R. (1973), *Untersuchungen zur Geschichte der Civatas und Diözese Soissons in römischer und merowingischer Zeit* (Rheinisches Archiv 8–9), Bonn

Keller, H. (1976), 'Fränkische Herrschaft und alemannisches Herzogtum im 6. und 7. Jahrhundert', *Zeitschrift für die Geschichte des Oberrheins* 124 (n.s. 85): 1–30

Klingshirn, W. E. (1985), 'Charity and power: Caesarius of Arles and the ransoming of captives in sub-Roman Gaul', *JRS* 75: 183–203

Klingshirn, W. E. (1994), *Caesarius of Arles: The Making of a Christian Community in Late Antique Gaul*, Cambridge

Lewis, A. R. (1976), 'The dukes in the *Regnum Francorum*, AD 550–751', *Speculum* 51: 381–410

Longnon, A. (1878), *Géographie de la Gaule au VIe siècle*, Paris

McCormick, M. (1986), *Eternal Victory: Triumphal Rulership in Late Antiquity. Byzantium, and the Early Medieval West*, Cambridge and Paris

McCormick, M. (1989), 'Clovis at Tours, Byzantine public ritual and the origins of medieval ruler symbolism', in E. K. Chrysos and A. Schwarcz (eds.), *Das Reich und die Barbaren* (Veröffentlichungen des Instituts für Österreichische Geschichtsforschung 29), Vienna and Cologne, pp. 155–80

Moorhead, J. (1992), *Theoderic in Italy*, Oxford

Murray, A. C. (1986), 'The position of the *grafio* in the constitutional history of Merovingian Gaul', *Speculum* 61: 787–805

Murray, A. C. (1988), 'From Roman to Frankish Gaul: "centenarii" and "centenae" in the administration of the Merovingian kingdom', *Traditio* 44: 59–100

Murray, A. C. (1994), 'Immunity, nobility, and the *Edict of Paris*', *Speculum* 69: 18–39

Nelson, J. L. (1978), 'Queens as Jezebels: the careers of Brunhild and Balthild in Merovingian history', in D. Baker (ed.), *Medieval Women* (Studies in Church History, Subsidia 1), Oxford, pp. 31–77; repr. in J. L. Nelson, *Politics and Ritual in Early Medieval Europe*, London and Ronceverte (1986), pp. 1–48

de Nie, G. (1987), *Views from a Many-Windowed Tower: Studies of Imagination in the Works of Gregory of Tours* (Studies in Classical Antiquity 7), Amsterdam

Nonn, U. (1975), 'Eine fränkische Adelssippe um 600. Zur Familie des Bischofs Berthram von Le Mans', *FrSt* 9: 186–201

Pietri, L. (1983), *La Ville de Tours du IVe au VIe siècle: naissance d'une cité chrétienne* (Collection de l'Ecole Française de Rome 69), Rome

Prinz, F. (1965), *Frühes Mönchtum im Frankenreich: Kultur und Gesellschaft in Gallien, den Rheinlanden und Bayern am Beispiel der monastischen Entwicklung (4, bis 8. Jahrhundert)*, Munich and Vienna

Prinz, F. (1981), 'Columbanus, the Frankish nobility and the territories east of the Rhine', in H. B. Clarke and M. Brennan (eds.), *Columbanus and Merovingian Monasticism* (BAR International Series 113), Oxford, pp. 73–87

Reydellet, M. (1981), *La Royauté dans la littérature latine de Sidoine Apollinaire à Isidore de Séville*, Rome

Riché, P. (1962), *Education et culture dans l'Occident barbare VIe–VIIIe siècles*, Paris; trans. J. J. Contreni, *Education and Culture in the Barbarian West, Sixth through Eighth Centuries*, Columbia (1976)

Riché, P. (1981), 'Columbanus, his followers and the Merovingian church', in H. B. Clarke and M. Brennan (eds.), *Columbanus and Merovingian Monasticism* (BAR International Series 113), Oxford, pp. 59–72

Rouche, M. (1979), *L'Aquitaine des Wisigoths aux Arabes: naissance d'une région*, Paris

Scheibelreiter, G. (1983), *Der Bischof in merowingischer Zeit* (Veröffentlichungen des Instituts für Österreichische Geschichtsforschung 27), Vienna

Selle-Hosbach, K. (1974), *Prosopographie merowingischer Amtsträger in der Zeit von 511 bis 613*, Bonn

Semmler, J. (1989), 'Saint-Denis: von der bischöflichen Coemeterialbasilika zur königlichen Benediktinerabtei', in H. Atsma (ed.), *La Neustrie: les pays au nord de la Loire de 650 à 850. Colloque historique international*, vol. II (Beihefte der Francia 16.2), Sigmaringen, pp. 5–123

Spencer, M. (1994), 'Dating the baptism of Clovis, 1886–1993', *EME* 3: 97–116

Stroheker, K. F. (1948), *Der senatorische Adel im spätantiken Gallien*, Tübingen

Stroheker, K. F. (1955), 'Zur Rolle der Heermeister fränkischer Abstammung im späten vierten Jahrhundert', *Historia* 4: 314–30; repr. in K. F. Stroheker, *Germanentum und Spätantike*, Zurich and Stuttgart (1965), pp. 9–29

Thiele, A. (1969), 'Studien zur Vermögensbildung und Vermögensverwertung der Kirche im Merowingerreich (6. Jh.)', *Studien und Mitteilungen zur Geschichte des Benediktiner-Ordens* 80: 7–143

Van Dam, R. (1985), *Leadership and Community in Late Antique Gaul*, Berkeley and Los Angeles

Van Dam, R. (1992), 'The Pirenne Thesis and fifth-century Gaul', in J. Drinkwater and H. Elton (eds.), *Fifth-Century Gaul: A Crisis of Identity?*, Cambridge, pp. 321–33
Van Dam, R. (1993), *Saints and Their Miracles in Late Antique Gaul*, Princeton, NJ
Wallace-Hadrill, J. M. (1962), *The Long-Haired Kings*, London
Wallace-Hadrill, J. M. (1968), 'Gregory of Tours and Bede: their views on the personal qualities of kings', *FrSt* 2: 31–44; repr. in J. M. Wallace-Hadrill, *Early Medieval History*, Oxford (1975), pp. 96–114
Weidemann, M. (1982), *Kulturgeschichte der Merowingerzeit nach den Werken Gregors von Tours*, 2 vols. (Römisch-Germanisches Zentralmuseum, Forschungsinstitut für Vor- und Frühgeschichte, Monographien 3.1–2), Mainz
Weidemann, M. (1986), *Das Testament des Bischofs Berthramn von Le Mans vom 27. März 616: Untersuchungen zu Besitz und Geschichte einer fränkischen Familie im 6. und 7. Jahrhundert* (Römisch-Germanisches Zentralmuseum, Forschungsinstitut für Vor- und Frühgeschichte, Monographien 9), Mainz
Wemple, S. F. (1981), *Women in Frankish Society: Marriage and the Cloister 500 to 900*, Philadelphia
Whittaker, C. R. (1994), *Frontiers of the Roman Empire: A Social and Economic Study*, Baltimore and London
Wolfram, H. (1988), *History of the Goths*, trans. T. J. Dunlap, Berkeley, CA
Wood, I. N. (1977), 'Kings, kingdoms and consent', in P. H. Sawyer and I. N. Wood (eds.), *Early Medieval Kingship*, Leeds, pp. 6–29
Wood, I. N. (1983), *The Merovingian North Sea* (Viktoria Bokforlag, Occasional Papers on Medieval Topics 1), Alingsås
Wood, I. N. (1985), 'Gregory of Tours and Clovis', *Revue Belge de Philologie et d'Histoire* 63: 249–72
Wood, I. N. (1994), *The Merovingian Kingdoms 450–751*, London and New York
Wormald, P. (1977), '*Lex scripta* and *Verbum regis:* legislation and Germanic kingship, from Euric to Cnut', in P. H. Sawyer and I. N. Wood (eds.), *Early Medieval Kingship*, Leeds, pp. 105–38
Zöllner, E. (1970), *Geschichte der Franken bis zum Mitte des sechsten Jahrhunderts*, Munich

9 THE CELTIC KINGDOMS

Anderson, M. O. (1973), *Kings and Kingship in Early Scotland*, Edinburgh
Astill, G. and Davies, W. (1997), *A Breton Landscape*, London
Baillie, M. G. L. (1995), 'Patrick, comets and Christianity', *Emania* 13: 69–78
Barrow, G. W. S. (1973), *The Kingdom of the Scots*, London
Bartrum, P. C. (ed.) (1966), *Early Welsh Genealogical Tracts*, Cardiff
Bernier, G. (1982), *Les Chrétientés bretonnes continentales depuis les origines jusqu'au IXème siècle* (Dossiers du Centre Régional Archéologique d'Alet E), Rennes
Byrne, F. J. (1973), *Irish Kings and High-Kings*, London
Campbell, E. (1984), 'E ware and Aquitaine – a reconsideration of the petrological evidence', *Scottish Archaeological Review* 3: 35–41
Campbell, E. and Lane, A. (1992), 'Celtic and Germanic interaction in Dalriada: the seventh-century metalworking site at Dunadd', in J. Higgitt and M. Spearman (eds.), *The Age of Migrating Ideas: Early Medieval Art in Britain and Ireland*, Edinburgh

Carney, J. (1955), *Studies in Irish Literature and History*, Dublin
Dark, K. (1993), *Civitas to Kingdom: British Political Continuity 300–800*, Leicester
Davies, W. (1978), *An Early Welsh Microcosm*, London
Davies, W. (1979a), *The Llandaff Charters*, Aberystwyth
Davies, W. (1979b), 'Roman settlements and post-Roman estates in south-east Wales', in P. J. Casey (ed.), *The End of Roman Britain* (BAR British Series 71), Oxford, pp. 153–73
Davies, W. (1982a), *Wales in the Early Middle Ages*, Leicester
Davies, W. (1982b), 'The Latin charter-tradition in western Britain, Brittany and Ireland in the early mediaeval period', in D. Whitelock, R. McKitterick and D. Dumville (eds.), *Ireland in Early Mediaeval Europe*, Cambridge, pp. 258–80
Davies, W. (1993), 'Celtic kingships in the early middle ages', in A. J. Duggan (ed.), *Kings and Kingship in Medieval Europe*, London, pp. 101–24
Dumville, D. N. (1972–74), 'Some aspects of chronology of the *Historia Brittonum*', *Bulletin of the Board of Celtic Studies* 25: 439–45
Dumville, D. N. (1975–76), '"Nennius" and the *Historia Brittonum*', *Studia Celtica* 10–11: 78–95
Dumville, D. N. (1985), see Primary Sources
Falc'hun, F. (1963), *Histoire de la langue bretonne d'après la géographie linguistique*, 2 vols., Rennes
Falc'hun, F. (1970), *Les noms de lieux celtiques*, Rennes
Fleuriot, L. (1980), *Les origines de la Bretagne*, Paris
Forsyth, K. (1997), 'Pictish symbols as a formal writing system', in D. Henry (ed.), *The Worm, the Germ and the Thorn*, Balgavies
Galliou, P. and Jones, M. (1991), *The Bretons*, Oxford
Goodburn, R., Hassall, M. W. C. and Tomlin, R. S. O. (1978), 'Roman Britain in 1977', *Britannia* 9: 404–85
Grabowski, K. and Dumville, D. (1984), *Chronicles and Annals of Mediaeval Ireland and Wales*, Woodbridge
Henderson, I. (1967), *The Picts*, London
Henderson, I. (1975), 'Pictish territorial divisions', in P. McNeill and R. Nicholson (eds.), *A Historical Atlas of Scotland c. 400–1600*, St Andrews, pp. 8–9
Herren, M. W. (1974–87), *The Hisperica Famina*, 2 vols., Toronto
Hill, P. (1997), *Whithorn and Saint Ninian: The Excavation of a Monastic Town 1984–91*, Whithorn
Hughes, K. (1972), *Early Christian Ireland: Introduction to the Sources*, London
Irwin, P. (1998), 'Aspects of dynastic kingship in early Ireland', DPhil thesis, University of Oxford
Jackson, K. H. (1953), *Language and History in Early Britain*, Edinburgh
Jackson, K. H. (1963), 'On the northern British section in Nennius', in N. K. Chadwick *et al.*, *Celt and Saxon*, Cambridge, pp. 20–62
Jackson, K. H. (1967), *A Historical Phonology of Breton*, Dublin
Jackson, K. H. (1980), 'The Pictish language', in F. T. Wainwright (ed.), *The Problem of the Picts*, Perth, pp. 129–66, 173–76 (revision of Wainwright 1955)
Koch, J. T. (1995), 'The conversion and the transition from Primitive to Old Irish, *c.*367–*c.*637', *Emania* 13: 39–50
Koch, J. T. (1997), *The Aneirin of Gododdin*, Cardiff

La Borderie, A. Le Moyne de (1896–1904), *Histoire de Bretagne*, 6 vols., Rennes and Paris
Lane, A. (1984), 'Some Pictish problems at Dunadd', in J. G. P. Friell and W. G. Watson (eds.), *Pictish Studies: Settlement, Burial and Art in Dark Age Northern Britain* (BAR British Series 125), Oxford, pp. 43–62
Lane, A. and Campbell, E. (1993), *Excavations at Dunadd*, Edinburgh
McCone, K. (1982), 'Brigit in the seventh century', *Peritia* 1: 107–45
McManus, D. (1991), *A Guide to Ogam*, Dublin
Meckler, M. (1997), 'The Annals of Ulster and the date of the meeting at Druim Cett', *Peritia* 11: 44–52
Murphy, G. (1952), 'On the dates of two sources used in Thurneysen's Heldensage 1: *Baile Chuind* and the date of *Cín Dromma Snechtaí*', *Ériu* 16: 145–51
Nash-Williams, V. E. (1950), *The Early Christian Monuments of Wales*, Cardiff
Ní Dhonnchadha, M. (1982), 'The guarantor list of *Cáin Adomnáin*, 697', *Peritia* 1: 178–215
Ó Cróinín, D. (1995), *Early Medieval Ireland, 400–1200*, London
Okasha, E. (1993), *Corpus of Early Inscribed Stones of South-West Britain*, Leicester
Padel, O. J. (1972), 'The inscriptions of Pictland', MLitt thesis, University of Edinburgh
Padel, O. J. (1981), 'The Cornish background of the Tristan stories', *Cambridge Medieval Celtic Studies* 1: 53–81
Pearce, S. M. (1978), *The Kingdom of Dumnonia*, Padstow
Radford, C. A. R. (1951), 'Report on the excavations at Castle Dore', *Journal of the Royal Institution of Cornwall* n.s. 1, Appendix: 1–119
Rowland, J. (1990), *Early Welsh Saga Poetry*, Cambridge
Small, A. (ed.) (1987), *The Picts: A New Look at Old Problems*, Dundee
Smyth, A. P. (1972), 'The earliest Irish annals: their first contemporary entries, and the earliest centres of recording', *Proceedings of the Royal Irish Academy* 72C: 1–48
Thomas, C. (1990), '"Gallici Nautae de Galliarum Provinciis" – a sixth/seventh century trade with Gaul, reconsidered', *Medieval Archaeology* 34: 1–26
Thomas, C. (1994), *And Shall These Mute Stones Speak? Post-Roman Inscriptions in Western Britain*, Cardiff
Tonnerre, N.-Y. (1994), *Naissance de la Bretagne*, Angers
Wainwright, F. T. (ed.) (1955), *The Problem of the Picts*, Edinburgh and London (repr. with revisions, 1980)
Weir, D. A. (1993), 'Dark ages and the pollen record', *Emania* 11: 21–30
Wood, I. (1988), 'Forgery in Merovingian hagiography', in *Fälschungen im Mittelalter*, 6 vols., Hanover (1988–90), v, pp. 369–84
Wooding, J. M. (1996), *Communication and Commerce along the Western Sealanes AD 400–800* (BAR International Series 654), Oxford

10 THE EARLIEST ANGLO-SAXON KINGDOMS

Addyman, P. (1972), 'The Anglo-Saxon house: a new review', *ASE* 1: 273–308
Arnold, C. (1984), *Roman Britain to Anglo-Saxon England: An Archaeological Study*, London

Ausenda, G. (ed.) (1995), *After Empire: Towards an Ethnology of Europe's Barbarians*, San Marino, CA

Axboe, M. (1995), 'Danish kings and dendrochronology: archaeological insights into the early history of the Danish state', in Ausenda (1995), pp. 217–38

Balkwill, C. (1993), 'Old English *wic* and the origins of the hundred', *Landscape History* 15: 5–12

Barnwell, P. (1996), '*Hlafaeta, ceorl, hid* and *scir*: Celtic, Roman or Germanic?', *Anglo-Saxon Studies in Archaeology and History* 9: 53–61

Bassett, S. (1989a), 'In search of the origins of Anglo-Saxon kingdoms', in Bassett (1989c), pp. 3–27

Bassett, S. (1989b), 'Churches in Worcester before and after the conversion of the Anglo-Saxons', *Antiquity* 69: 225–56

Bassett, S. (ed.) (1989c), *The Origins of Anglo-Saxon Kingdoms*, London and New York

Beck, F. (1911), 'The Teutonic conquest of Britain', in H. Gwatlein and J. Whitney (eds.), *The Cambridge Medieval History*, I, pp. 382–91

Biddle, M. (1989), 'London: a city in transition: AD 400–800', in M. Lobel (ed.), *The City of London: The British Atlas of Historic Towns*, III, Oxford

Blair, W. J. (1994), *Anglo-Saxon Oxfordshire*, Stroud

Boddington, A. (1990), 'Models of burial, settlement and worship: the final phase reviewed', in E. Southworth (ed.), *Anglo-Saxon Cemeteries: A Reappraisal*, Stroud, pp. 177–99

Boyle, A., Dodd, A., Miles, D. and Mudd, A. (1995), *Two Oxfordshire Anglo-Saxon Cemeteries: Berinsfield and Didcot*, Oxford

Boyle, A., Jennings, D., Miles, D. and Palmer, S. (1998), *The Anglo-Saxon Cemetery at Butler's Field, Lechlade, Gloc.*, I, Oxford

Bradley, R. (1987), 'Time regained: the creation of continuity', *Journal of the British Archaeological Association* 140: 1–17

Carver, M. (ed.) (1992), *The Age of Sutton Hoo*, Woodbridge

Chambers, R. (1988), 'The late- and sub-Roman cemetery at Queenford Farm, Dorchester-on-Thames, Oxon., *Oxoniensia* 52: 35–70

Chapman, J. and Hamerow, H. (eds.) (1997), *Migrations and Invasions in Archaeological Explanation*, Oxford

Chapman, R. (1992), *The Celts*, London

Charles-Edwards, T. (1972), 'Kinship, status and the origins of the hide', *Past and Present* 56: 3–33

Charles-Edwards, T. (1995), 'Language and society among the insular Celts, AD 400–1000', in M. Green (ed.), *The Celtic World*, London and New York, pp. 703–36

Charles-Edwards, T. (1997), 'Anglo-Saxon kinship revisited', in Hines (1977), pp. 171–203

Cox, P. (1989), 'A seventh-century inhumation cemetery at Shepherd's Farm, Ulwell, near Wantage, Dorset', *Proceedings of the Dorset Nature, History and Archaeological Society* 110: 37–48

Crawford, S. (1999), *Anglo-Saxon Childhood*, Stroud

Davies, W. and Vierck, H. (1974), 'The contexts of Tribal Hidage: social aggregates and settlement patterns', *FrSt* 8: 223–93

Dickinson, T. (1993), 'Early Saxon saucer brooches: a preliminary overview', *Anglo-Saxon Studies in Archaeology and History* 6: 11–44
Dickinson, T. and Speake, G. (1992), 'The seventh-century cremation burial in Asthall Barrow, Oxfordshire: a reassessment', in Carver (1992), pp. 95–130
Dodgson, J. McN. (1966), 'The significance of the distribution of the English place-name in *-ingas*, *-inga*, in south-east England', *Medieval Archaeology* 10: 1–29
Dölling, H. (1958), *Haus und Hof in westgermanischen Volksrechten*, Münster
Down, A. and Welch, M. (1990), *Chichester Excavations 7: Apple Down and the Mardens*, Chichester
Dumville, D. (1989), 'The Tribal Hidage: an introduction to its texts and their history', in Bassett (1989), pp. 225–30
Esmonde Cleary, S. (1989), *The Ending of Roman Britain*, London
Faull, M. (1977), 'British survival in Anglo-Saxon Northumbria', in L. Laing (ed.), *Studies in Celtic Survival* (BAR British Series 37), Oxford, pp. 1–56
Filmer-Sankey, W. (1992), 'Snape Anglo-Saxon cemetery: the current state of knowledge', in Carver (1992), pp. 39–52
Geake, H. (1997), *The Use of Grave-Goods in Conversion-Period England, c600–c850AD* (BAR British Series 261), Oxford
Green, B., Rogerson, A. and White, S. (1987), *Morningthorpe Anglo-Saxon Cemetery*, 2 vols. (East Anglian Archaeology 36), Gressenhall
Halsall, G. (1995), 'The Merovingian period in north-east Gaul: transition or change?', in J. Bintliff and H. Hamerow (eds.), *Europe between Late Antiquity and the Middle Ages*, Oxford, pp. 38–52
Halsall, G. (1996), 'Female status and power in early Merovingian central Austrasia: the burial evidence', *EME* 5.1: 1–24
Halsall, G. (1997), 'The origins of Anglo-Saxon kingdoms: a Merovingianist speaks out', unpublished paper delivered to the Institute for Historical Research
Hamerow, H. (1991), 'Settlement mobility and the "Middle Saxon Shift": rural settlements and settlement patterns in Anglo-Saxon England', *ASE* 20: 1–17
Hamerow, H. (1992), 'Settlement on the gravels in the Anglo-Saxon period', in M. Fulford and L. Nichols (eds.), *Developing Landscapes of Lowland Britain: The Archaeology of the British Gravels*, London, pp. 39–46
Hamerow, H. (1993), *Excavations at Mucking*, II: *The Anglo-Saxon Settlement*, London
Hamerow, H. (1999), 'Anglo-Saxon timber buildings: the continental connection', in H. Sarfatij, W. Verwers and P. Woltering (eds.), *In Discussion with the Past: Archaeological Studies Presented to W. A. van Es*, Zwolle, pp. 119–28
Härke, H. (1992a), 'Changing symbols in a changing society: the Anglo-Saxon burial rite in the seventh century', in Carver (1992), pp. 149–66
Härke, H. (1992b), *Angelsächsische Waffengräber des 5. bis 7. Jahrhunderts*, Cologne
Härke, H. (1997), 'Early Anglo-Saxon social structure', in Hines (1997), pp. 125–70
Härke, H. (1998), 'Briten und Angelsachsen im nachrömischen England: Zum Nachweis der einheimischen Bevölkerung in den angelsächsischen Landnahmegebieten', in H.-J. Häßler (ed.), *Studien zur Sachsenforschung* XI, pp. 87–120
Hawkes, S. C. (1982), 'Finglesham: a cemetery in East Kent', in J. Campbell (ed.), *The Anglo-Saxons*, Oxford, pp. 24–5

Hawkes, S. C. and Meaney, A. (1970), *Two Anglo-Saxon Cemeteries at Winnall, Winchester, Hants.*, London
Higham, N. (1992), *Rome, Britain and the Anglo-Saxons*, London
Hills, C. (1998), 'Did the people from Spong Hill come from Schleswig-Holstein?', in H.-J. Häßler (ed.), *Studien zur Sachsenforschung* XI, pp. 145–54
Hills, C. (1999), 'Spong Hill and the Adventus Saxonum', in C. Karkov, K. Wickham Crowley and B. Young (eds.), *Spaces of the Living and the Dead*, Oxford, pp. 15–25
Hills, C., Penn, K. and Rickett, R. (1984), *Spong Hill*, III: *Catalogue of Inhumations* (East Anglian Archaeology 21), Gressenhall
Hines, J. (1984), *The Scandinavian Character of Anglian England in the Pre Viking Period* (BAR British Series 124), Oxford
Hines, J. (1995), 'Cultural change and social organisation in early Anglo-Saxon England', in Ausenda (1995), pp. 75–87
Hines, J. (ed.) (1997), *The Anglo-Saxons from the Migration Period to the Eighth Century*, Woodbridge
Hines, J. (1998), *A New Corpus of Anglo-Saxon Great Square-Headed Brooches*, Woodbridge
Hodges, R. (1989), *The Anglo-Saxon Achievement*, London
Høilund Nielsen, K. (1997), 'Animal art and the weapon-burial rite: a political badge?', in C. Kjeld Jensen and K. Høilund Nielsen (eds.), *Burial and Society: The Chronological and Social Analysis of Archaeological Burial Data*, Århus
Høilund Nielsen, K. (1999), 'Style II and the Anglo-Saxon elite', in T. Dickinson and D. Griffiths (eds.), *The Origins of Kingdoms* (Anglo-Saxon Studies in Archaeology and History 10), pp. 185–202
Hope-Taylor, B. (1977), *Yeavering: An Anglo-British Centre of Early Northumbria*, London
Huggett, J. (1988), 'Imported grave goods and the early Anglo-Saxon economy', *Medieval Archaeology* 32: 63–96
Keynes, S. (1995), 'England, 700–900', in *The New Cambridge Medieval History*, Cambridge, II, pp. 18–42
Kinsley, G. (2002), *Catholme: An Anglo-Saxon Settlement on the Trent Gravels in Staffordshire*, Nottingham
Leech, R. (1986), 'The excavation of a Romano-Celtic temple and a later cemetery on Lamyett Beacon, Somerset', *Britannia* 17: 259–328
Leeds, E. T. (1912), 'The distribution of the Anglo-Saxon saucer brooch in relation to the battle of Bedford AD. 571', *Archaeologica*, series 2, 13: 159–202
Losco-Bradley, S. and Wheeler, H. (1984), 'Anglo-Saxon settlement in the Trent Valley: some aspects', in M. Faull (ed.), *Studies in Late Anglo-Saxon Settlement*, Oxford, pp. 101–14
Loseby, S. (2000), 'Power and towns in late Roman Britain and early Anglo-Saxon England', in J. Gurt and G. Ripoll (eds.), *Sedes regiae (Ann. 400–800)*, Barcelona, pp. 319–70
Loveluck, C. (1994), 'Exchange and society in early medieval England 400 –700 AD', PhD thesis, University of Durham
McKinley, J. (1994), *The Anglo-Saxon Cemetery at Spong Hill, N. Elmham*, VIII: *The Cremations* (East Anglian Archaeology 69), Gressenhall

MacKreth, D. (1996), *Orton Hall Farm: A Roman and Early Anglo-Saxon Farmstead*, Manchester
Marshall, A. and Marshall, G. (1994), 'Differentiation, change and continuity in Anglo-Saxon buildings', *The Archaeological Journal* 150: 366–402
Meaney, A. (1964), *A Gazetteer of Early Anglo-Saxon Burial Sites*, London
Miles, D. (1986), *Archaeology at Barton Court Farm, Abingdon, Oxon.*, Oxford
Millett, M. (1990), *The Romanization of Britain*, Cambridge
Millett, M. with James, S. (1984), 'Excavations at Cowdery's Down, Basingstoke, Hants. 1978–81', *The Archaeological Journal* 140: 151–279
Müller-Wille, M., Meier, D., Kroll D. and Kroll, H. (1988), 'The transformation of rural society, economy and landscape during the first millennium AD: archaeological and palaeobotanical contributions from northern Germany and southern Scandinavia', *Geografiska Annaler* 70.B.1
Murphy, P. (1994), 'The Anglo-Saxon landscape and rural economy: some results from sites in East Anglia and Essex', in J. Rackham (ed.), *Environment and Economy in Anglo-Saxon England* (CBA Research Report 89), York, pp. 23–39
Myres, J. N. L. (1954), 'Two Saxon urns from Ickwell Bury, Beds. and the Saxon penetration of the East Midlands', *Antiquaries Journal* 34: 201–8
Myres, J. N. L. (1977), *A Corpus of Anglo-Saxon Pottery*, 2 vols., Cambridge
Myres, J. N. L. and Green, B. (1973), *The Anglo-Saxon Cemeteries of Caistor-by-Norwich and Markshall*, London
O'Brien, C. and Miket, R. (1991), 'The early medieval settlements of Thirlings, Northumberland', *Durham Archaeological Journal* 7: 57–91
Pader, E.-J. (1982), *Symbolism, Social Relations and the Interpretation of Mortuary Remains* (BAR International Series 130), Oxford
Pohl, W. (1997), 'Ethnic names and identities in the British Isles: a comparative perspective', in Hines (1997), pp. 7–31
Powlesland, D. (1997), 'Early Anglo-Saxon settlements, structures, form and layout', in Hines (1997), pp. 101–24
Powlesland, D., Haughton, C. and Hanson, J. (1986), 'Excavations at Heslerton, North Yorkshire, 1978–1982', *The Archaeological Journal* 143: 53–173
Pretty, K. (1989), 'Defining the Magonsaete', in Bassett (1989), pp. 171–83
Richards, J. (1987), *The Significance of Form and Decoration of Anglo-Saxon Cremation Urns* (BAR International Series 166), Oxford
Richards, J. (1992), 'Anglo-Saxon symbolism', in Carver (1992), pp. 131–48
Richards, J. (1995), 'An archaeology of Anglo-Saxon England', in Ausenda (1995), pp. 51–65
Rodwell, W. and Rodwell, K. (1985), *Rivenhall: Investigations of a Villa, Church and Village 1950–1977* (CBA Research Report 55), London
Russel, A. D. (1984), 'Early Anglo-Saxon ceramics from East Anglia: a microprovenience study', PhD thesis, University of Southampton
Scull, C. (1990), 'Scales and weights in early Anglo-Saxon England', *The Archaeological Journal* 147: 183–215
Scull, C. (1992), 'Before Sutton Hoo: structures of power and society in early East Anglia', in Carver (1992), pp. 3–24
Scull, C. (1993), 'Archaeology, early Anglo-Saxon society and the origins of Anglo-Saxon kingdoms', *Anglo-Saxon Studies in Archaeology and History* 6: 65–82

Scull, C. (1997), 'Urban centres in Pre-Viking England?', in Hines (1997), pp. 269–98
Shepherd, J. (1979), 'The social identity of the individual in isolated barrows and barrow cemeteries in Anglo-Saxon England', in B. Burnham and J. Kingsbury (eds.), *Space, Hierarchy and Society* (BAR International Series 59), Oxford, pp. 47–79
Sherlock, S. and Welch, M. (1992), *An Anglo-Saxon Cemetery at Norton, Cleveland* (CBA Research Report 82), London
Speake, G. (1980), *Anglo-Saxon Animal Art and Its Germanic Background*, Oxford
Speake, G. (1989), *A Saxon Bed Burial on Swallowcliffe Down*, London
Steedman, K. (1995), 'Excavation of a Saxon site at Riby Cross Roads, Lincolnshire', *Archaeological Journal* 151: 212–306
Stoodley, N. (1998), 'Post-migration age structures and age related grave goods in Anglo-Saxon cemeteries in England', in H.-J. Häßler (ed.), *Studien zur Sachsenforschung* XI, pp. 187–98
Stoodley, N. (1999), *The Spindle and the Spear: A Critical Enquiry into the Construction of Gender in the Early Anglo-Saxon Burial Rite* (BAR British Series 288), Oxford
Struth, P. and Eagles, B. (1999), 'An Anglo-Saxon barrow cemetery in Greenwich Park', in P. Pattison, D. Field and S. Ainsworth (eds.), *Patterns of the Past: Essays in Landscape Archaeology for Christopher Taylor*, Oxford, pp. 37–52
Timby, J. (1994), 'Sancton I Anglo-Saxon cemetery: excavations carried out between 1976 and 1980', *The Archaeological Journal* 150: 243–365
Tummuscheit, A. (1995), 'Ländliche Siedlungen des 5.–7. Jh. in England und ihre kontinentalen Vorgänger', MA thesis, Christian-Albrechts University, Kiel
Tyers, I., Hillam, J. and Groves, C. (1994), 'Trees and woodland in the Saxon period: the dendrochronological evidence', in J. Rackham (ed.), *Environment and Economy in Anglo-Saxon England* (CBA Research Report 89), York, pp. 12–22
Van de Noort, R. (1993), 'The context of early medieval barrows in western Europe', *Antiquity* 67: 66–73
Ward-Perkins, B. (2000), 'Why did the Anglo-Saxons not become British?', *HER* 115: 513–33
Watts, L. and Leech, P. (1996), *Henley Wood, Temples and Cemetery*, London
Welch, M. (1992), *Anglo-Saxon England*, London
West, S. (1986), *West Stow: The Anglo-Saxon Village*, 2 vols. (East Anglian Archaeology 14), Gressenhall
Williams, D. and Vince, A. (1998), 'The characterization and interpretation of Early to Middle Saxon granite-tempered pottery in England', *Medieval Archaeology* 4, 1: 214–19
Williams, R. J. (1993), *Pennyland and Hartigans: Two Iron Age and Saxon Sites in Milton Keynes* (Buckinghamshire Archaeological Society Monograph 4), Aylesbury
Wise, P. (1991), 'Wasperton', *Current Archaeology* 126: 256–9
Wood, I. (1997), 'Before and after the migration to Britain', in Hines (1997), pp. 41–54
Wormald, P. (1990), Review of Bassett (ed.) 1989, *Oxoniensia* 54: 420–2
Yorke, B. (1990), *Kings and Kingdoms of Anglo-Saxon England*, Guildford
Yorke, B. (1993), 'Fact or fiction? The written evidence for the fifth and sixth centuries AD', *Anglo-Saxon Studies in Archaeology and History* 6: 45–50
Zimmermann, W. H. (1988), 'Regelhafte Innengliederung prähistorischer Langhäuser in den Nordseeanrainerstatten: Ein Zeugnis enger, langandauender kultureller Kontakte', *Germania* 66.2: 465–89

11 THE BYZANTINE EMPIRE IN THE SEVENTH CENTURY

Alexander, P. J. (1985), *The Byzantine Apocalyptic Tradition*, Berkeley, Los Angeles and London

Angold, M. (1995), *Church and Society in Byzantium under the Comneni, 1081–1261*, Cambridge

Brock, S. (1984), *Syriac Perspectives on Late Antiquity*, London

Brown, P. (1976), 'Eastern and Western Christendom in late antiquity: a parting of the ways', in D. Baker (ed.), *The Orthodox Churches and the West* (Studies in Church History 13), Oxford, pp. 1–24; repr. in Brown (1982), pp. 166–95

Brown, P. (1982), *Society and the Holy in Late Antiquity*, London

Cameron, A. (1991), 'The eastern provinces in the seventh century: Hellenism and the emergence of Islam', in S. Said (ed.), *Hellenismes: quelques jalons pour une histoire de l'identité grecque, Actes du Colloque de Strasbourg, 25–27 octobre 1989*, Leiden, pp. 287–313

Cameron, A. (1992), 'Byzantium and the past in the seventh century: the search for redefinition', in Fontaine and Hillgarth (1992), pp. 250–76; repr. in Cameron (1996b), v

Cameron, A. (1996a), 'Byzantines and Jews: some recent work on early Byzantium', *Byzantine and Modern Greek Studies* 20: 249–74

Cameron, A. (1996b), *Changing Cultures in Early Byzantium*, London

Cameron, A. and Conrad, L. I. (eds.) (1992), *The Byzantine and Early Islamic Near East*, 1: *Problems in the Literary Source Materials* (Studies in Late Antiquity and Early Islam 1), Princeton

Conrad, L. I. (1992), 'The conquest of Arwad: a source-critical study in the historiography of the early medieval Near East', in Cameron and Conrad (1992), pp. 317–401

Cook, M. and Crone, P. (1977), *Hagarism: The Making of the Islamic World*, Cambridge

Crone, P. (1980), *Slaves on Horses: The Evolution of the Islamic Polity*, London and New York

Crone, P. (1987), *Meccan Trade and the Rise of Islam*, Princeton, NJ

Déroche, V. (1991), 'La polémique anti-judaïque au VIe et VIIe siècle, une mémoire inédite: Les Kephalaia', *Travaux et Mémoires* 11: 275–311

Devreese, R. (1937), 'La fin inédite d'une lettre de saint Maxime: un baptême forcé de Juifs et de Samaritains à Carthage en 632', *Revue des Sciences Religieuses* 17: 25–35

Ditten, H. (1993), *Ethnische Verschiebungen zwischen des Balkanhalbinsel und Kleinasien vom Ende des 6. bis zur zweiten Hälfte des 9. Jahrhunderts* (Berliner Byzantinische Arbeiten 59), Berlin

Donner, F. M. (1981), *The Early Islamic Conquests*, Princeton, NJ

Flusin, B. (1992), *Saint Athanase le Perse et l'histoire de la Palestine au début du VIIe siècle*, 2 vols., Paris

Fontaine, J. and Hillgarth, J. N. (eds.) (1992), *The Seventh Century: Change and Continuity, Proceedings of a Joint French and British Colloquium at the Warburg Institute, 8–9 July 1988*, London

Foss, C. (1975), 'The Persians in Asia Minor and the end of antiquity', *EHR* 90: 721–47; repr. in Foss (1990), I

Foss, C. (1977), 'Archaeology and the "Twenty Cities" of Byzantine Asia', *American Journal of Archaeology* 81: 469–86; repr. in Foss (1990), II

Foss, C. (1990), *History and Archaeology of Byzantine Asia Minor*, London
Haldon, J. (1992), 'The works of Anastasius of Sinai: a key source for the history of seventh-century east Mediterranean society and belief', in Cameron and Conrad (1992), pp. 107–47
Haldon, J. F. (1997), *Byzantium in the Seventh Century: The Transformation of a Culture*, rev. edn, Cambridge
Howard-Johnston, J. (1994), 'The official history of Heraclius' campaigns', in E. Daçbrowa (ed.), *The Roman and Byzantine Army in the East*, Cracow, 1994, pp. 57–87
Humphries, R. S. (1991), *Islamic History: A Framework for Inquiry*, rev. edn, London and New York
Kaegi, W. E. (1992), *Byzantium and the Early Islamic Conquests*, Cambridge
Köpstein, H. and Winkelmann, F. (eds.) (1976), *Studien zum 7. Jahrhundert in Byzanz: Probleme der Herausbildung des Feudalismus*, Berlin
Leder, S. (1992), 'The literary use of the *Khabar*: a basic form of historical writing', in Cameron and Conrad (1992), pp. 277–315
Louth, A. (1996a), *Maximus the Confessor*, London
Louth, A. (1996b), 'A Christian theologian at the court of the caliph: some cross-cultural reflections', *Dialogos, Hellenic Studies Review* 3: 4–19
Louth, A. (2000), 'Arab Palestine 650–750: the crucible of Byzantine Orthodoxy', in R. Swanson (ed.), *The Holy Land, Holy Lands and Christian History* (Studies in Church History 36), Oxford, pp. 67–77
Mango, C. (1985), *Le Développement urbain de Constantinople (VIe–VIIe siècles)*, Paris
Mango, C. (1989), 'Greek culture in Palestine after the Arab Conquest', in G. Cavallo, G. de Gregorio and M. Maniaci (eds.), *Scritture, libri e testi nelle aree provinciali di Bisanzio, Atti del seminario di Erice, 18–25 settembre 1988*, Spoleto, pp. 149–60
Meyendorff, J. (1989), *Imperial Unity and Christian Divisions: The Church 450–680* AD (The Church in History 2), Crestwood, NY
Ostrogorsky, G. (1958), 'Die Entstehung der Themeverfassung', Korreferat zu A. Pertusi, 'La formation des thèmes byzantins', *Akten des XI. Internationalen Byzantinisten-Kongresses*, Munich, pp. 1–8; repr. in Ostrogorsky (1973), pp. 72–9
Ostrogorsky, G. (1962), 'La commune rurale byzantine', *Byzantion* 32: 139–66; repr. in Ostrogorsky (1973), pp. 44–71
Ostrogorsky, G. (1969), *History of the Byzantine State*, trans. and rev. Joan Hussey, New Brunswick
Ostrogorsky, G. (1973), *Zur byzantinischen Geschichte: Ausgewählte kleine Schriften*, Darmstadt
Riedinger, R. (1982), 'Die Lateransynode von 649 und Maximos der Bekenner', in F. Heinzer and C. von Schönborn (eds.), *Maximus Confessor, Actes du Symposium sur Maxime le Confesseur, Fribourg, 2–5 septembre 1980* (Paradosis 27), Fribourg, Suisse
Treadgold, W. (1990), 'The break in Byzantium and the gap in Byzantine studies', *Byzantinische Forschungen* 14: 289–316
Treadgold, W. (1997), *A History of the Byzantine State and Society*, Stanford, CA
Whitby, M. (1992), 'Greek historical writing after Procopius', in Cameron and Conrad (1992), pp. 25–80
Young, F., Ayres, L. and Louth, A. (2004), *The Cambridge History of Early Christian Literature*, Cambridge

12 MUHAMMAD AND THE RISE OF ISLAM

Abbott, N. (1957–72), *Studies in Arabic Literary Papyri*, Chicago

Altheim, F. and Stiehl, R. (1964–9), *Die Araben in der alten Welt*, Berlin

Andrae, T. (1960), *Mohammed: The Man and His Faith*, New York

Arnold, T. (1913), *The Preaching of Islam*, London

Bakhit, M. A. and Asfour, M. (eds.) (1986), *Proceedings of the Symposium on Bilad al-Sham during the Byzantine Period*, Amman

Bakhit, M. A. and Asfour, M. (eds.) (1989), *The Fourth International Conference in the History of Bilad al-Sham during the Umayyad Period*, Amman

Bates, M. (1982), *Islamic Coins*, New York

Becker, C. H. (1924), *Islamstudien*, I, Leipzig

Beeston, A. F. L. (1972), 'Kingship in ancient Arabia', *JESHO* 15: 256–68

Bell, H. I. (1928), 'The administration of Egypt under the Umayyad khalifs', *BZ* 28: 278–86

Bell, H. W. (1956), *Egypt from Alexander the Great to the Arab Conquest*, Oxford

Bell, R. (1926), *The Origin of Islam in Its Christian Environment*, London

Belyaev, E. A. (1969), *Arabs, Islam and the Arab Caliphate in the Early Middle Ages*, London

Blacherè, R. (1952), *Le Problème de Mahomet*, Paris

Bosworth, C. E. (1983), 'Iran and the Arabs before Islam', in E. Yarshater (ed.), *Cambridge History of Iran*, III, pt I, Cambridge, pp. 593–612

Boyce, M. (1979), *Zoroastrians: Their Religious Beliefs and Practices*, London

Brock, S. P. (1976), 'Syriac sources for seventh-century history', *BMGS* 2: 17–36

Brock, S. P. (1982), 'Syriac views of emergent Islam', in G. H. A. Juynboll (ed.), *Studies on the First Century of Islamic Society*, Carbondale and Edwardsville, pp. 9–22

Brown, P. (1983), *The World of Late Antiquity*, London

Brunner, V. (1982–3), *Die Erforschung der antiken Oase von Marib mit Hilfe geomorphologischer Untersuchungsmethoden* (Archäologische Bericht aus dem Yemen I and II), Mainz

Buhl, F. (1930), *Das Leben Muhammads*, Leipzig

Butler, A. J. (1978), *The Arab Conquest of Egypt*, Oxford

Cahen, C. (1964), 'Note sur l'accueil des chrétiens d'Orient à l'Islam', *Revue de l'Histoire des Religions* 166: 51–8

Cameron, A. (1991), 'The eastern provinces in the seventh century AD: Hellenism and the emergence of Islam', in S. Said (ed.), *Hellenismes: quelques jalons pour une histoire de l'identité grecque*, Strasbourg, pp. 287–313

Cameron, A. and Conrad, L. I. (eds.) (1991), *The Byzantine and Early Islamic Near East*, Princeton, NJ

Christensen, A. (1944), *L'Iran sous les Sassanides*, Copenhagen

Combe, E., Sauvaget, J. and Wiet, G. (eds.) (1931), *Répertoire chronologique d'épigraphie arabe*, Cairo

Conrad, L. I. (1990), 'Theophanes and the Arabic historical tradition: some indications of intercultural transmission', *BF* 15: 1–44

Constantelos, D. J. (1973), 'The Muslim conquests of the Near East as revealed in the Greek sources of the 7th and 8th centuries', *Byz.* 42, I: 325–57

Cook, M. (1983), *Muhammad*, Oxford

Creswell, K. A. C. (1932–40), *Early Muslim Architecture*, 2 vols., Oxford
Crone, P. (1987), *Meccan Trade and the Rise of Islam*, Princeton
Crone, P. and Cook, M. (1977), *Hagarism: The Making of the Islamic World*, Cambridge
Crone, P. and Hinds, M. (1986), *God's Caliph: Religious Authority in the First Centuries of Islam*, Cambridge
de Goeje, M. J. (1900), *Mémoire sur la conquête de la Syrie*, Leiden
Dennett, D. C. (1950), *Conversion and the Poll Tax in Early Islam*, Cambridge, MA
Dixon, A. A. A. (1971), *The Umayyad Caliphate*, London
Doe, B. (1971), *Southern Arabia*, London
Donner, F. M. (1981), *The Early Islamic Conquests*, Princeton, NJ
Duchesne-Guillemin, J. (1964), *La Religion de l'Iran ancien*, Paris
Duri, A. A. (1960), *Muqaddima fi tarikh sadr al-Islam*, Beirut
Duri, A. A. (1983), *The Rise of Historical Writing among the Arabs*, ed. and trans. L. I. Conrad, Princeton, NJ
Dussaud, R. (1955), *Les Arabes en Syrie avant l'Islam*, Paris
Eikhoff, E. (1966), *Seekrieg und Seepolitik zwischen Islam und Abendland*, Berlin
Ende, W. (1977), *Arabische Nation und islamische Geschichte: Die Umayyaden im Urteil arabischer Autoren des 20 Jahrhunderts*, Beirut
Erdmann, K. (1943), *Die Kunst Irans zur Zeit der Sasaniden*, Berlin
Ettinghausen, R. (1972), *From Byzantium to Sasanian Iran and the Islamic World*, Leiden
Ezzati, A. (1978), *An Introduction to the Spread of Islam*, London
Fattal, A. (1959), *Le Statut légal des non-musulmans en pays d'Islam*, Beirut
Fowden, G. (2004), *Art and the Umayyad Elite in Late Antique Syria*, Berkeley, Los Angeles and London
Foye, R. N. (1983), 'The political history of Iran under the Sasanians', in E. Yarshater (ed.), *The Cambridge History of Iran*, III, pt 1, Cambridge, pp. 116–80
Frye, R. (1962), *The Heritage of Persia*, London
Frye, R. (1975), *The Golden Age of Persia*, London
Frye, R. N. (1984), *The History of Ancient Iran*, Munich
Gabrieli, F. (ed.) (1959), *L'antica società Beduina*, Rome
Gabrieli, F. (1968), *Muhammad and the Conquests of Islam*, New York and Toronto
Gaube, H. (1973), *Arabo-sassanidische Numismatik*, Braunschweig
Ghirshman, R. (1962), *Iran, Parthians and Sassanians*, London
Gibb, H. A. R. (1923), *The Arab Conquests in Central Asia*, London
Gibb, H. A. R. (1962), *Studies on the Civilisation of Islam*, London
Gibb, H. A. R. *et al.* (eds.) (1960), *The Encyclopaedia of Islam*, Leiden and London
Gil, M. (1992), *A History of Palestine*, Cambridge
Glaser, E. (1895), *Die Abessinier in Arabien und Afrika*, Munich
Glaser, E. (1913), *Eduard Glaser's Reise nach Marib*, Vienna
Göbl, R. (1971), *Sassanian Numismatics*, Brunswick
Goldziher, I. (1967, 1971), *Muslim Studies*, I and II, London
Grierson, P. (1960), 'The monetary reforms of 'Abd al-Malik', *JESHO* 3: 241–64
Grohmann, A. (1952), *From the World of Arabic Papyri*, Cairo
Grohmann, A. (1955), *Einführung und Chrestomathie zur arabischen Papyruskunde*, Prague
Grohmann, A. (1963), *Arabic Papyri from Hirbet el-Mird*, Louvain

Hawting, G. R. (1986), *The First Dynasty of Islam: The Umayyad Caliphate, AD 661–750*, London
Herrmann, G. (1977), *The Iranian Revival*, Oxford
Herzfeld, E. (1941), *Iran in the Ancient East*, London
Hill, D. R. (1971), *The Termination of Hostilities in the Early Arab Conquests*, London
Hill, D. R. (1975), 'The role of the camel and horse in the early Arab conquests', in V. J. Parry and M. R. Yapp (eds.), *War, Technology and Society in the Middle East*, London, pp. 32–43
Hinds, M. (1996), *Studies in Early Islamic History*, ed. J. Bacharach, L. J. Conrad and P. Crone, Princeton, NJ
Hitti, P. K. (1904), *History of the Arabs*, London and New York
Hitti, P. (1951), *History of Syria*, London
Hodgson, M. G. S. (1974), *The Venture of Islam*, 1, Chicago and London
Hofkunst van de Sassanieden (1993), Brussels
Holt, P. M., Lamberton, A. and Lewis, B. (eds.) (1970), *The Cambridge History of Islam*, I, Cambridge
Hoyland, R. (1997), *Seeing Islam as Others Saw it: A Survey and Evaluation of Christian, Jewish and Zoroastrian Writings on Early Islam*, Princeton, NJ
Humphreys, R. (1991), *Islamic History: A Framework for Inquiry*, Princeton
Kaegi, W. E. (1992), *Byzantium and the Early Islamic Conquests*, Cambridge
Katsh, A. I. (1954), *Judaism in Islam*, New York
Kennedy, H. (1986), *The Prophet and the Age of the Caliphates: The Islamic Near East from the Sixth to the Eleventh Century*, London
Kessler, C. (1970), 'Abd al-Malik's inscription in the Dome of the Rock: a reconsideration', *JRAS* (unnumbered): 2–14
Khoury, R.-G. (1987), 'Pour une nouvelle compréhension de la transmission des textes dans les trois premiers siècles islamiques', *Arabica* 34: 181–96
Kister, M. J. (1965), 'Mecca and Tamim', *JESHO* 8.2: 113–14
Kister, M. J. (1968), 'al-Hira. Some notes on its relations with Arabia', *Arabica* 15: 143–69
Kister, M. J. (1980), *Studies in Jahiliyya and Early Islam*, London
Lammens, H. (1914), *Le Berceau de l'Islam*, Rome
Lammens, H. (1928), *L'Arabie occidentale avant l'Héjire*, Beirut
Lammens, H. (1930), *Etudes sur le siècle des Omayyades*, Beirut
Lancaster, W. and Lancaster, F. (1992), 'Tribal formations in the Arabian peninsula', *Arabian Archaeology and Epigraphy* 3: 145–72
Miles, G. (1959), 'The iconography of Umayyad coinage', *Ars Orientalis* 3: 207–13
Morimoto, K. (1981), *The Fiscal Administration of Egypt in the Early Islamic Period*, Kyoto
Morony, M. G. (1984), *Iraq after the Muslim Conquest*, Princeton, NJ
Muir, W. (1923), *The Life of Muhammad*, Edinburgh
Musil, A. (1927), *Arabia Deserta*, New York
Nöldeke, T. (1887), *Die ghassanischen Fürsten aus dem Hause Gafnas*, Berlin
Noth, A. (1994), *The Early Arabic Historical Tradition: A Source-Critical Study*, Princeton, NJ
Obermann, J. (1955), *Early Islam*, New Haven, CT

Olinder, G. (1927), *The Kings of Kinda*, Lund
Ostrogorsky, G. (1989), *History of the Byzantine State*, Oxford
Paret, R. (1961), 'Der Koran als Geschichtsquelle', *Der Islam* 37: 24–42
Paret, R. (1975), *Der Koran*, Darmstadt
Patkanian, K. (1866), 'Essai d'une histoire de la dynastie des Sassanides', *Journal Asiatique*: 101–244
Puin, G. (1970), *Der Diwan von 'Umar b. al-Hattab*, Bonn
Raby, J. (ed.), *Jerusalem in the First Century A. H.*, Oxford
Rippin, A. (1990), *Muslims: Their Religious Beliefs and Practices*, 1: *The Formative Period*, London
Rodinson, M. (1971), *Mohammed*, London
Rothstein, G. (1899), *Die Dynastie der Lahmiden in al-Hira*, Berlin
Rotter, G. (1982), *Die Umayyaden und der zweite Bürgerkrieg (680–692)*, Wiesbaden
Ryckmans, J. (1951), *L'Institution monarchique en Arabie méridionale avant l'Islam*, Louvain
Saunders, J. J. (1965), 'The nomad as empire builder: a comparison of the Arab and Mongol conquests', *Diogenes* 52: 79–103
Schick, R. (1992), *The Christian Communities of Palestine from Byzantine to Islamic Rule: An Historical and Archaeological Study*, Princeton, NJ
Schippmann, K. (1990), *Grundzüge der Geschichte des sasanidischen Reiches*, Darmstadt
Serjeant, R. B. (1964a), 'Some irrigation systems in Hadramawt', *BSOAS* 27: 33–76
Serjeant, R. B. (1964b), 'The Constitution of Medina', *Islamic Quarterly* 8: 3–16
Serjeant, R. B. (1967), 'Société et gouvernement en Arabie du Sud', *Arabica* 14: 284–97
Serjeant, R. B. (1981), 'Haram and hawtah, the sacred enclave in Arabia', in *Studies in Arabian History and Civilisation*, London, pp. 41–8
Sezgin, F. (1967), *Geschichte des arabischen Schrifttums*, 1, Leiden
Sezgin, U. (1971), *Abu Mihnaf*, Leiden
Shaban, M. (1971), *Islamic History*, Cambridge
Shahid, I. (1970), 'Pre-Islamic Arabia', in Holt, Lambton and Lewis (1970), pp. 2–29
Shahid, I. (1971), *The Martyrs of Najran: New Documents*, Brussels
Shahid, I. (1989), *Byzantium and the Arabs in the Fifth Century*, Washington, DC
Shoufany, E. (1972), *Al-Riddah and the Muslim Conquest of Arabia*, Toronto
Simon, R. (1989), *Meccan Trade and Islam*, Budapest
Smith, S. (1954), 'Events in Arabia in the 6th century AD', *BSOAS* 16: 425–68
Spuler, B. (1952), *Iran in früh-islamischer Zeit*, Wiesbaden
Trimingham, J. S. (1979), *Christianity among the Arabs in Pre-Islamic Times*, London
Vasiliev, A. A. (1961), *History of the Byzantine Empire*, Madison, WI
von Botmer, H.-K. (1987), 'Architekturbilder im Koran. Eine Prachthandschrift der Umayyadenzeit aus dem Yemen', *Pantheon* 45: 4–20
von Oppenheim, M. (1967), *Die Beduinen*, Wiesbaden
Walker, J. (1941a), *A Catalogue of the Arab-Byzantine and Post-reform Umayyad Coins*, London
Walker, J. (1941b), *A Catalogue of the Arab-Sassanian Coins*, London
Wansborough, J. (1977), *Qur'anic Studies: Sources and Methods of Scriptural Interpretation*, Oxford
Wansborough, J. (1978), *The Sectarian Milieu: Content and Composition of Islamic Salvation History*, Oxford

Watt, W. M. (1953), *Muhammad at Mecca*, London
Watt, W. M. (1956), *Muhammad at Medina*, Oxford
Wellhausen, J. (1887), *Reste des arabischen Heidentums*, Berlin
Wellhausen, J. (1899), *Skizzen und Vorarbeiten*, Berlin
Wellhausen, J. (1927), *The Arab Kingdom and Its Fall*, trans. M. G. Weir, Calcutta
Widengren, G. (1965), *Die Religionen Irans*, Stuttgart
Wissman, H. and Hofner, M. (1953), *Beiträge zur historischen Geographie des vorislamischen Sudarabien*, Wiesbaden
Yarshater, E. (ed.) (1983), *The Cambridge History of Iran*, III, 1–2, *The Seleucid, Parthian and Sasanian periods*, Cambridge

14 FRANCIA IN THE SEVENTH CENTURY

Atsma, H. (ed.) (1989), *La Neustrie: les pays au nord de la Loire de 650 à 850*, 2 vols. (Beihefte der Francia 16), Sigmaringen
Becher, M. (1994), 'Die Sogennante Staatsstreich Grimoalds. Versuch einer Neubewertung', in J. Jarnut, U. Nonn and M. Richter (eds.), *Karl Martell in Seiner Zeit* (Beihefte der Francia 37), Sigmaringen, pp. 119–47
Bleiber, W. (1981), *Naturalwirtschaft und Ware-Geld-Beziehungen zwischen Somme und Loire während des 7 Jahrhunderts*, Berlin
Collins, R. (1996), *Fredegar* (Authors of the Middle Ages 13), Aldershot
Dierkens, A. (1985), *Abbayes et chapitres entre Sambre et Meuse (VII–XI siècles)* (Beihefte der Francia 14), Sigmaringen
Durliat, J. (1979), 'Les attributions civiles des évêques mérovingiens: l'exemple de Didier évêque de Cahors, 630–655', *Annales du Midi* 91: 237–53
Durliat, J. (1990), *Les Finances publiques de Diocletien aux Carolingiens (284–889)* (Beihefte der Francia 21), Sigmaringen
Ebling, H. (1974), *Prosopographie der Amtsträger des Merowingerreiches* (Beihefte der Francia 2), Sigmaringen
Ewig, E. (1952), 'Die fränkischen Teilreiche im 7 Jahrhundert (613–714)', *Trierer Zeitschrift* 22: 85–144; repr. in Ewig, *Gallien* I, pp. 172–230
Ewig, E. (1965), 'Noch einmal zum "Staatsstreich" Grimoalds', in C. Bauer, L. Böhm and M. Miller (eds.), *Speculum historiale: Geschichte im Spiegel von Geschichtsschreibung und Geschichtsdeutung*, Freiburg and Munich, pp. 454–7; repr. in Ewig, *Gallien* I, pp. 573–7
Ewig, E. (1976, 1979), *Spätantikes und Fränkisches Gallien: Gesammelten Schriften (1952–1973)*, 2 vols. (Beihefte der Francia 3), Zurich and Munich
Fouracre, P. (1984), 'Observations on the outgrowth of Pippinid influence in the "Regnum Francorum" after the Battle of Tertry (687–715)', *Medieval Prosopography* 5: 1–31
Fouracre, P. (1986), '"Placita" and the settlement of disputes in later Merovingian Francia', in W. Davies and P. Fouracre (eds.), *The Settlement of Disputes in Early Medieval Europe*, Cambridge, pp. 23–43
Fouracre, P. (1990), 'Merovingian history and Merovingian hagiography', *Past and Present* 127: 3–38
Fouracre, P. (2000), *The Age of Charles Martel*, London

Fouracre, P. and Gerberding, R. (1996), *Late Merovingian France: History and Hagiography 640–720*, Manchester

Fritze, W. (1971), 'Zur Entstehungsgeschichte des Bistums Utrecht. Franken und Friesen 690–734', *Rheinische Vierteljahrsblätter* 35: 107–51

Geary, P. (1985), *Aristocracy in Provence: The Rhône Basin at the Dawn of the Carolingian Age*, Stuttgart

Geary, P. (1988), *Before France and Germany*, Oxford

Gerberding, R. (1987), *The Rise of the Carolingians and the* 'Liber Historiae Francorum', Oxford

Goffart, W. (1988), *The Narrators of Barbarian History*, Princeton, NJ

Graus, F. (1965), *Volk, Herrscher und Heiliger im Reich der Merowinger*, Prague

Halsall, G. (1995), *Settlement and Social Organization: The Merovingian Region of Metz*, Cambridge

Heinzelmann, M. (1994), *Gregor von Tours (538–594): 'Zehn Bücher Geschichte' Historiographie und Gesellschaftskonzept im 6 Jahrhundert*, Sigmaringen

Jahn, J. (1991), *Ducatus Bawariorum: Das bairische Herzogtum des Agilolfinger* (Monographien zur Geschichte des Mittelalters 35), Stuttgart

James, E. (1982), *The Origins of France: From Clovis to the Capetians 500–1000*, London

Kaiser, R. (1989), 'Royauté et pouvoir épiscopal au nord de la Gaule (VIIe–IXe siècles)', in Atsma (1989), I, pp. 143–60

Kent, J. (1972), 'Merovingian gold coinage 580–700', in R. Hall and D. Metcalf (eds.), *Methods of Chemical and Metallurgical Investigation of Ancient Coinage*, London, pp. 69–74

Krusch, B. (1910), 'Der Staatsstreich des fränkischen Hausmeier, Grimoald I', in *Festgabe für Karl Zeumer*, Weimar, pp. 411–38

Levillain, L. (1913), 'La succession d'Austrasie au VIIe siècle', *Revue Historique* 112: 62–93

Levillain, L. (1945/6), 'Encore la succession d'Austrasie', *BEC* 106: 296–306

Nelson, J. L. (1978), 'Queens as Jezabels: the careers of Brunhild and Balthild in Merovingian History' (Studies in Church History, Subsidia 1), pp. 31–77; reprinted in J. L. Nelson, *Politics and Ritual in Early Medieval Europe*, London (1986), pp. 1–48

Prinz, F. (1965), *Frühes Mönchtum im Frankenreich*, Munich

Prinz. F. (1974), 'Die bischöfliche Stadtherrschaft im Frankenreich von 5 bis 7 Jahrhundert', *HZ* 217: 1–35

Sato, M. (2000), 'The Merovingian accounting documents of Tours', *EME* 9: 143–61

Theuws, F. (1991), 'Landed property and manorial organization in northern Austrasia: some considerations and a case study', in N. Roymans and F. Theuws (eds.), *Images of the Past: Studies on Ancient Societies in Northwestern Europe*, Amsterdam, pp. 299–407

Wallace-Hadrill, J. M. (1962), *The Long Haired Kings and Other Studies in Frankish History*, London

Werner, K.-F. (1972), 'Les principautés périphériques dans le monde franc du VIIIe siècle', *Settimane* 20: 483–514

Werner, M. (1982), *Adelsfamilien im Umkreis der frühen Karolinger: Die Verwandtschaft Irminas von Oeren und Adelas von Pfalzel* (VuF 28), Sigmaringen

Wood, I. (1981), 'A prelude to Columbanus: the monastic achievement in the Burgundian territories', in H. B. Clarke and M. Brennan (eds.), *Columbanus and Merovingian Monasticism* (BAR International Series 113), Oxford, pp. 3–32
Wood, I. (1994), *The Merovingian Kingdoms 450–751*, London

15 RELIGION AND SOCIETY IN IRELAND AND 16 BRITONS, DALRIADAN IRISH AND PICTS

Alcock, E. (1992), 'Burials and cemeteries in Scotland', in N. Edwards and A. Lane (eds.), *The Early Church in Wales and the West*, Oxford, pp. 125–9
Anderson, M. O. (1965), 'Columba and other Irish saints in Scotland', *Historical Studies* 5: 26–36
Anderson, M. O. (1973), *Kings and Kingship in Early Scotland*, Edinburgh and London
Bannerman, J. (1974), *Studies in the History of Dalriada*, Edinburgh and London
Barrow, G. W. S. (1973), *The Kingdom of the Scots*, London
Barrow, G. W. S. (1983), 'The childhood of Scottish Christianity: a note on some place-name evidence', *Scottish Studies* 27: 1–15
Bassett, S. (1992), 'Church and diocese in the West Midlands: the transition from British to Anglo-Saxon control', in Blair and Sharpe (1992), pp. 13–40
Beckensall, S. (no date), *Northumberland Field Names*, Newcastle-upon-Tyne
Binchy, D. (1958), 'The fair of Tailtiu and the feast of Tara', *Ériu* 18: 113–38
Binchy, D. (1962), 'Patrick and his biographers: ancient and modern', *Studia Hibernica* 2: 7–173
Bischoff, B. (1954), 'Wendepunkte in der Geschichte der lateinischen Exegese im Frühmittelalter', *Sacris Erudiri* 6: 189–281
Bischoff, B. (1957), 'Il monachesimo irlandese nei suoi rapporti col continente', in *Il monachesimo nell'alto medioevo e la formazione della civiltà occidentale, Settimane* 4
Bittermann, H. R. (1938), 'The council of Chalcedon and episcopal jurisdiction', *Speculum* 13: 198–203
Blair, J. and Sharpe, R. (eds.) (1992), *Pastoral Care before the Parish*, Leicester
Bowen, E. G. (1969), *Saints, Seaways and Settlements in the Celtic Lands*, Cardiff
Breatnach, L. (1986), 'The ecclesiastical element in the Old-Irish legal tract *Cáin Fhuithirbe*', *Peritia* 5: 36–52
Breatnach, L. (ed.) (1987), *Uraicecht na Ríar*, Dublin
Brown, P. D. C. (1971), 'The church at Richborough', *Britannia* 2: 225–31
Bullock, J. D. (1956), 'Early Christian memorial formulae', *Archaeologia Cambrensis* 105: 133–41
Bullough, D. A. (1982), 'The missions to the English and Picts and their heritage (to c.800)', in H. Löwe (ed.), *Die Iren und Europa im früheren Mittelalter*, 1, Stuttgart, pp. 80–97
Burt, J. R. F. (1997), 'Long cist cemeteries in Fife', in D. Henry (ed.), *The Worm, the Germ, and the Thorn: Pictish and Related Studies Presented to Isabel Henderson*, Balgavies, Angus, pp. 64–6
Byrne, F. J. (1973), *Irish Kings and High-Kings*, London
Byrne, F. J. (1984), 'A note on Trim and Sletty', *Peritia* 3: 316–19
Cameron, K. (1968), 'Eccles in English place-names', in M. W. Barley and R. P. C. Hanson (eds.), *Christianity in Britain, 300–700*, Leicester, pp. 87–92

Campbell, E. (1996), 'The archaeological evidence for external contacts: imports, trade and economy in Celtic Britain AD 400–800', in K. R. Dark (ed.), *External Contacts and the Economy of Late Roman and Post-Roman Britain*, Woodbridge, pp. 83–96
Campbell, J. (1986), *Essays in Anglo-Saxon History*, London and Ronceverte
Carver, M. O. H. (1999), *Bulletin of the Tarbat Discovery Programme*, http://www.york.ac.uk/depts/arch/staff/sites/tarbat
Chadwick, N. K. (1964), 'The conversion of Northumbria: a comparison of sources', in N. K. Chadwick (ed.), *Celt and Saxon*, Cambridge, pp. 138–66
Chadwick, N. K. (1969), *Early Brittany*, Cardiff
Charles-Edwards, T. M. (1970–72), 'The seven bishop-houses of Dyfed', *BBCS* 24: 247–62
Charles-Edwards, T. M. (1976), 'The social background to Irish *peregrinatio*', *Celtica* 11: 43–59
Charles-Edwards, T. M. (1984), 'The church and settlement', in Ní Chatháin and Richter (1984), pp. 167–75
Charles-Edwards, T. M. (1989), 'Early medieval kingships in the British Isles', in S. Bassett (ed.), *The Origins of Anglo-Saxon Kingdoms*, London and New York, pp. 28–39
Charles-Edwards, T. M. (1992), 'The pastoral role of the church in the early Irish laws', in Blair and Sharpe (1992), pp. 63–80
Charles-Edwards, T. M. (1993a), 'Palladius, Prosper, and Leo the Great: mission and primatial authority', in D. N. Dumville *et al.* (eds.), *Saint Patrick, AD 493–1993*, Woodbridge, pp. 1–12
Charles-Edwards, T. M. (1993b), *Early Irish and Welsh Kinship*, Oxford
Charles-Edwards, T. M. (1998), 'The context and uses of literacy in early Christian Ireland', in H. Price (ed.), *Literacy in Medieval Celtic Societies*, Cambridge, pp. 62–82
Charles-Edwards, T. M. (2000), *Early Christian Ireland*, Cambridge
Chédeville, A. and Guillotel, H. (1984), *La Bretagne des saints et des rois Ve–Xe siècle*, Rennes
Clancy, T. O. and Márkus, G. (1995), *Iona: The Earliest Poetry of a Celtic Monastery*, Edinburgh
Craig, D. (1997), 'The provenance of the early Christian inscriptions of Galloway', in P. Hill (ed.), *Whithorn and St Ninian*, Stroud, pp. 614–19
Crawford, B. E. (1987), *Scandinavian Scotland*, Leicester
Dalland, M. (1992), 'Long cist burials at Four Winds, Longniddry, East Lothian', *Proceedings of the Society of Antiquaries of Scotland* 122: 197–206
Danaher, K. (1972), *The Year in Ireland*, Cork and Minneapolis
Daniélou, J. (1961), *The Ministry of Women in the Early Church*, English translation G. Simon, London
Dark, K. R. (1994), *Civitas to Kingdom: British Political Continuity 300–800*, Leicester, London and New York
Davies, W. H. (1968), 'The church in Wales', in M. W. Barley and R. P. C. Hanson (eds.), *Christianity in Britain, 300–700*, Leicester, pp. 131–50
Davies, Wendy (1978), *An Early Welsh Microcosm: Studies in the Llandaff Charters*, London
Davies, Wendy (1982), *Wales in the Early Middle Ages*, Leicester

Davies, Wendy (1983), 'Priests and rural communities in east Brittany in the ninth century', *EC* 20: 177–97
Davies, Wendy (1992), 'The myth of the Celtic church', in N. Edwards and A. Lane (eds.), *The Early Church in Wales and the West*, Oxford, pp. 12–21
Davies, Wendy *et al.* (2000), *The Inscriptions of Early Medieval Brittany*, Oakville, CT and Aberystwyth
Doherty, C. (1982), 'Some aspects of hagiography as a source for Irish economic history', *Peritia* 1: 300–28
Doherty, C. (1985), 'The monastic town in early medieval Ireland', in H. B. Clarke and A. Simms (eds.), *The Comparative History of Urban Origins in Non-Roman Europe*, I (BAR International Series 255. i), Oxford, pp. 45–75
Doherty, C. (1991), 'The cult of St Patrick and the politics of Armagh in the seventh century', in J.-M. Picard (ed.), *Ireland and Northern France AD 600–850*, Blackrock, Dublin, pp. 53–94
Duchesne, L. (1910), *Fastes épiscopaux de l'ancienne Gaule*, II, 2nd edn, Paris
Duine, F. (1912–13, 1914–15), 'La vie de saint Samson', *Annales de Bretagne* 28: 332–56; 30: 123–64
Dumville, D. N. (1984a), 'Gildas and Maelgwn: problems of dating', in Lapidge and Dumville (1984), pp. 51–9
Dumville, D. N. (1984b), 'The chronology of *De Excidio Britanniae*, Book I', in Lapidge and Dumville (1984), pp. 61–84
Dumville, D. N. (1984c), 'Some British aspects of the earliest Irish Christianity', in Ní Chatháin and Richter (1984), pp. 16–24
Dumville, D. N. *et al.* (eds.) (1993), *Saint Patrick, AD 493–1993*, Woodbridge
Duncan, A. A. M. (1981), 'Bede, Iona, and the Picts', in R. H. C. Davis and J. M. Wallace-Hadrill (eds.), *The Writing of History in the Middle Ages: Essays Presented to R. W. Southern*, Oxford, pp. 1–42
Edwards, N. (1990), *The Archaeology of Early Medieval Ireland*, London
Ellis Davidson, H. R. (1988), *Myths and Symbols in Pagan Europe*, Manchester
Etchingham, C. (1994), 'Bishops in the early Irish church: a reassessment', *Studia Hibernica* 28: 35–62
Etchingham, C. (1999), *Church Organisation in Ireland AD 650 to 1000*, Maynooth
Farwell, D. H. and Molleson, T. I. (1993), *Excavations at Poundbury 966–80*, II: *The Cemeteries*, Dorchester
Flanagan, D. (1984), 'The Christian impact on early Ireland: place-names evidence', in Ní Chatháin and Richter (1984), pp. 25–51
Fleuriot, L. (1980), *Les Origines de la Bretagne*, Paris
Flobert, P. (1997), *La Vie ancienne de saint Samson de Dol*, Paris
Forsyth, K. (1998), 'Literacy in Pictland', in H. Price (ed.), *Literacy in Medieval Celtic Societies*, Cambridge, pp. 39–61
Foster, S. M. (1996), *Picts, Gaels and Scots*, London
Frantzen, A. J. (1983), *The Literature of Penance in Anglo-Saxon England*, New Brunswick, NJ
Frend, W. H. C. (1979), '*Ecclesia Britannica*: prelude or dead end?', *JEH* 30: 129–44
Frend, W. H. C. (1992), 'Pagans, Christians, and the "Barbarian Conspiracy" of AD 367 in Roman Britain', *Britannica* 23: 121–31

Frere, S. S. (1976), 'The Silchester church: the excavation by Sir Ian Richmond in 1961', *Archaeologia* 105: 277–302

Gelling, M. (1978), *Signposts to the Past*, London, Melbourne and Toronto

Giot, P.-R. (1982), 'Saint Budoc on the Isle of Lavret, Brittany', in S. M. Pearce (ed.), *The Early Church in Western Britain and Ireland* (BAR British Series 102), Oxford, pp. 197–210

Greene, D. (1968), 'Some linguistic evidence relating to the British church', in M. W. Barley and R. P. C. Hanson (eds.), *Christianity in Britain, 300–700*, Leicester, pp. 75–86

Greene, D. and O'Connor, F. (1967), *A Golden Treasury of Irish Poetry AD 600 to 1200*, London, Melbourne and Toronto

Gruffydd, G. and Owen, H. P. (1956–58), 'The earliest mention of St David?', *BBCS* 17: 185–93

Hamlin, A. and Lynn, C. (1988), *Pieces of the Past: Archaeological Excavations by the Department of the Environment for Northern Ireland 1970–1986*, Belfast

Handley, M. (1998), 'The early medieval inscriptions of western Britain: function and sociology', in J. Hill and M. Swan (eds.), *The Community, the Family and the Saint*, Turnhout, pp. 339–61

Handley, M. (2001), 'The origins of Christian commemoration in late antique Britain', *EME* 10: 177–99

Harden, J. (1995), 'A potential archaeological context for the Early Christian sculptured stones from Tarbat, Easter Ross', in C. Bourke (ed.), *From the Isles of the North*, Belfast, pp. 221–7

Henderson, I. (1967), *The Picts*, London

Henderson, I. (1987), 'Early Christian monuments of Scotland displaying crosses but no other ornament', in A. Small (ed.), *The Picts: A New Look at Old Problems*, Dundee, pp. 45–58

Henry, F. (1964), *L'Art irlandais*, II, La Pierre-qui-Vire, Yonne

Herbert, M. (1988), *Iona, Kells and Derry: The History and Hagiography of the Monastic Familia of Columba*, Oxford

Herity, M. (1984), 'The layout of Irish early Christian monasteries', in Ní Chatháin and Richter (1984), pp. 105–16

Herity, M. (1989), 'Early Irish hermitages in the light of the *Lives* of Cuthbert', in G. Bonner, D. Rollason and C. Stancliffe (eds.), *St Cuthbert, His Cult and His Community to AD 1200*, Woodbridge, pp. 45–63

Herren, M. W. (1989), 'Mission and monasticism in the *Confessio* of Patrick', in D. Ó Corráin, L. Breatnach and K. McCone (eds.), *Sages, Saints and Storytellers: Celtic Studies in Honour of Professor James Carney*, Maynooth, pp. 76–85

Herren, M. W. (1990), 'Gildas and early British monasticism', in A. Bammesberger and A. Wollmann (eds.), *Britain 400–600: Language and History*, pp. 65–78

Higgitt, J. (1982), 'The Pictish Latin inscription at Tarbat in Ross-shire', *Proceedings of the Society of Antiquaries of Scotland* 112: 300–21

Hill, P. (1997), *Whithorn and St Ninian*, Stroud

Holtz, L. (1981), 'Irish grammarians and the Continent in the seventh century', in H. B. Clarke and M. Brennan (eds.), *Columbanus and Merovingian Monasticism* (BAR International Series 113), Oxford, pp. 135–52

Hope-Taylor, B. (1977), *Yeavering: An Anglo-British Centre of Early Northumbria*, London

Horn, W., Marshall, J. W. and Rourke, G. D. (1990), *The Forgotten Hermitage of Skellig Michael*, Berkeley and Los Angeles

Hughes, K. (1966), *The Church in Early Irish Society*, London

Hughes, K. (1970), *Early Christianity in Pictland*, Jarrow

Hughes, K. (1980), *Celtic Britain in the Early Middle Ages: Studies in Scottish and Welsh Sources*, Woodbridge

Hughes, K. (1981), 'The Celtic church: is this a valid concept?', *Cambridge Medieval Celtic Studies* 1: 1–20

Hughes, K. (1987), *Church and Society in Ireland AD 400–1200*, ed. D. Dumville, London

Hurley, V. (1982), 'The early church in the south-west of Ireland: settlement and organisation', in S. M. Pearce (ed.), *The Early Church in Western Britain and Ireland: Studies Presented to C. A. Ralegh Radford* (BAR British Series 102), Oxford, pp. 297–320

Jackson, K. H. (1953), *Language and History in Early Britain*, Edinburgh

Jackson, K. H. (1964), 'On the Northern British Section in Nennius', in N. K. Chadwick (ed.), *Celt and Saxon: Studies in the Early British Border*, Cambridge, pp. 20–62

Jones, B. and Mattingly, D. (1990), *An Atlas of Roman Britain*, Oxford

Jones, M. J. (1994), 'St Paul in the Bail, Lincoln: Britain in Europe?', in K. Painter (ed.), *'Churches Built in Ancient Times': Recent Studies in Early Christian Archaeology* (Society of Antiquaries of London), London, pp. 325–47

Jülicher, A. (1896), 'Ein gallisches Bischofsschreiben des 6. Jahrhunderts als Zeuge für die Verfassung der Montanistenkirche', *Zeitschrift für Kirchengeschichte* 16: 664–71

Kelly, F. (1988), *A Guide to Early Irish Law*, Dublin

Kenney, J. F. (1929), *The Sources for the Early History of Ireland: An Introduction and Guide*, 1: *Ecclesiastical*, New York

Kerlouégan, F. (1987), *Le De Excidio de Gildas: les destinées de la culture latine dans l'Ile de Bretagne au VIe siècle*, Paris

Keys, D. (1999), *Catastrophe: An Investigation into the Origins of the Modern World*, London

King, A. (1983), 'The Roman church at Silchester reconsidered', *Oxford Journal of Archaeology* 2: 255–37

Kirby, D. P. (1973), 'Bede and the Pictish Church', *The Innes Review* 24: 6–25

Kirby, D. P. (1976), '. . . per universas Pictorum provincias', in G. Bonner (ed.), *Famulus Christi: Essays in Commemoration of the Thirteenth Centenary of the Birth of the Venerable Bede*, London, pp. 286–324

Kirby, D. P. (1995), 'The genesis of a cult: Cuthbert of Farne and ecclesiastical politics in Northumbria in the late seventh and early eighth centuries', *JEH* 46: 383–97

Knight, J. K. (1981), '*In tempore Iustini consulis*: contacts between the British and Gaulish churches before Augustine', in A. Detsicas (ed.), *Collectanea Historica: Essays in Memory of Stuart Rigold*, Maidstone, pp. 54–62

Knight, J. K. (1984), 'Glamorgan AD 400–1100: archaeology and history', in H. N. Savory (ed.), *Glamorgan County History*, II: *Early Glamorgan: Pre-history and Early History*, Cardiff, pp. 315–64

Knight, J. K. (1999), *The End of Antiquity: Archaeology, Society and Religion AD 235–700*, Stroud

Lamb, R. G. (1974), 'Coastal settlements of the North', *Scottish Archaeological Forum* 5: 76–98

Lamb, R. G. (1975–76), 'The Burri stacks of Culswick, Shetland, and other paired stack-settlements', *Proceedings of the Society of Antiquaries of Scotland* 107: 144–54

Lapidge, M. (1984), 'Gildas's education and the Latin culture of sub-Roman Britain', in Lapidge and Dumville (1984), pp. 27–50

Lapidge, M. and Dumville, D. (eds.) (1984), *Gildas: New Approaches*, Woodbridge

Lapidge, M. and Sharpe, R. (1985), *A Bibliography of Celtic–Latin Literature 400–1200*, Dublin

Logan, P. (1980), *The Holy Wells of Ireland*, Gerrards Cross

Low, M. (1996), *Celtic Christianity and Nature*, Edinburgh

Loyn, H. (1984), 'The conversion of the English to Christianity: some comments on the Celtic Contribution', in R. R. Davies, R. A. Griffiths, I. G. Jones and K. O. Morgan (eds.), *Welsh Society and Nationhood: Historical Essays Presented to Glanmor Williams*, Cardiff, pp. 5–18

Mac Cana, P. (1981, for 1979), '*Regnum* and *Sacerdotium*: notes on Irish tradition', *Proceedings of the British Academy* 65: 443–79

Mac Cana, P. (1986), 'Christianisme et paganisme dans l'Irlande ancienne', in P. Mac Cana and M. Meslin (eds.), *Rencontres de religions: Actes du Colloque du Collège des Irlandais tenu sous les auspices de l'Académie Royale Irlandaise (juin 1981)*, Paris, pp. 57–74

McCarthy, D. (1994), 'The origin of the *Latercus* Paschal cycle of the Insular Celtic churches', *Cambrian Medieval Celtic Studies* 28: 25–49

McCone, K. (1990), *Pagan Past and Christian Present in Early Irish Literature*, Maynooth

MacDonald, A. D. S. (1974), 'Two major early monasteries of Scottish Dalriata: Lismore and Eigg', *Scottish Archaeological Forum* 5: 47–70

MacDonald, A. D. S. (1977), 'Old Norse "Papar" names in N. and W. Scotland: summary', in L. Laing (ed.), *Studies in Celtic Survival* (BAR British Series 37), Oxford, pp. 107–11

MacDonald, A. D. S. (1982), 'Notes on terminology in the Annals of Ulster, 650–1050', *Peritia* 1: 329–33

MacDonald, A. D. S. (1984), 'Aspects of the monastery and monastic life in Adomnán's Life of Columba', *Peritia* 3: 271–302

MacDonald, A. D. S. (1985), 'Iona's style of government among the Picts and Scots: the toponymic evidence of Adomnán's Life of Columba', *Peritia* 4: 174–86

MacLean, D. (1997), 'Maelrubai, Applecross and the late Pictish contribution west of Druimalban', in D. Henry (ed.), *The Worm, the Germ, and the Thorn: Pictish and Related Studies Presented to Isabel Henderson*, Balgavies, Angus, pp. 173–87

McManus, D. (1984), 'The so-called *Cothrige* and *Pátraic* strata of Latin loan words in early Irish', in Ní Chatháin and Richter (1984), pp. 179–96

MacNeill, E. (1921, new edn 1981), *Celtic Ireland*, Dublin

MacNeill, M. (1982), *The Festival of Lughnasa: A Study of the Survival of the Celtic Festival of the Beginning of Harvest*, second edn, Dublin

Mac Niocaill, G. (1984), 'Christian influences in early Irish law', in Ní Chatháin and Richter (1984), pp. 151–6

Macquarrie, A. (1992), 'Early Christian religious houses in Scotland: foundation and function', in Blair and Sharpe (1992), pp. 110–33

Mac Shamhráin, A. (1996), *Church and Polity in Pre-Norman Ireland: The Case of Glendalough*, Maynooth

Mann, J. C. (1961), 'The administration of Roman Britain', *Antiquity* 35: 316–20

Markus, R. A. (1990), *The End of Ancient Christianity*, Cambridge

Mawer, C. F. (1995), *Evidence for Christianity in Roman Britain: The Small Finds* (BAR British Series 243), Oxford

Meates, G. W. (1979), *The Roman Villa at Lullingstone, Kent*, 1 (Monographs of the Kent Archaeological Society 1), Chichester

Merdrignac, B. (1991), 'Bretons et Irlandais en France du Nord – VIe–VIIIe siècles', in J.-M. Picard (ed.), *Ireland and Northern France AD 600–850*, Dublin, pp. 119–42

Merdrignac, B. (1993), *Les Vies de saints bretons durant le haut moyen âge*, Rennes

Miller, M. (1977–78), 'Date-guessing and Dyfed', *Studia Celtica* 12–13: 33–61

Miller, M. (1978), 'Eanfrith's Pictish son', *Northern History* 14: 47–66

Moisl, H. (1983), 'The Bernician Royal Dynasty and the Irish in the seventh century', *Peritia* 11

Moisl, H. (1987), 'The Church and the native tradition of learning in early medieval Ireland', in Ní Chatháin and Richter (1987), pp. 258–71

Morris, R. (1983), *The Church in British Archaeology* (CBA Research Report 47), London

Morris, R. (1989), *Churches in the Landscape*, London

Mytum, H. (1992), *The Origins of Early Christian Ireland*, London and New York

Nash-Williams, V. E. (1950), *The Early Christian Monuments of Wales*, Cardiff

Ní Chatháin, P. and Richter, M. (eds.) (1984), *Irland und Europa: Die Kirche im Frühmittelalter*, Stuttgart

Ní Chatháin, P. and Richter, M. (eds.) (1987), *Irland und die Christenheit: Bibelstudien und Mission*, Stuttgart

Ní Dhonnchadha, M. (1982), 'The guarantor list of *Cáin Adomnáin*', *Peritia* 1: 178–215

Ní Dhonnchadha, M. (1995), 'The *Lex Innocentium*: Adomnán's Law for women, clerics and youths, 697 AD', in M. O'Dowd and S. Wichert (eds.), *Chattel, Servant or Citizen: Women's Status in Church, State and Society* (Historical Studies 19), Belfast, pp. 58–69

Nisbet, H. C. and Gailey, R. A. (1960 [1962]), 'A survey of the antiquities of North Rona', *The Archaeological Journal* 117: 88–115

Ó Catháin, S. (1999), 'The festival of Brigit the Holy Woman', *Celtica* 23: 231–60

Ó Corráin, D. (1981), 'The early Irish churches: some aspects of organisation', in D. Ó Corráin (ed.), *Irish Antiquity: Essays and Studies Presented to Professor M. J. O'Kelly*, Cork (reprinted Blackrock, Dublin, 1994), pp. 327–41

Ó Corráin, D. (1984), 'Irish law and canon law', in Ní Chatháin and Richter (1984), pp. 157–66

Ó Corráin, D. (1987), 'Irish vernacular law and the Old Testament', in Ní Chatháin and Richter (1987), pp. 284–307

Ó Corráin, D., Breatnach, L. and Breen, A. (1984), 'The laws of the Irish', *Peritia* 3: 382–438

Ó Cróinín, D. (1982), 'Mo-Sinnu moccu Min and the computus of Bangor', *Peritia* 1: 281–95

Ó Cróinín, D. (1995), *Early Medieval Ireland, 400–1200*, London and New York

Okasha, E. (1993), *Corpus of Early Christian Inscribed Stones of South-West Britain*, London and New York
O'Kelly, M. J. (1958), 'Church Island near Valencia, Co. Kerry', *PRIA* 59C: 57–136
O'Loughlin, T. (1994), 'The library of Iona in the late seventh century', *Ériu* 45: 34–52
O'Loughlin, T. (2000), *Celtic Theology*, London and New York
Olson, B. L. (1989), *Early Monasteries in Cornwall*, Woodbridge
Ó Néill, P. (1984), '*Romani* influences on seventh-century Hiberno-Latin literature', in Ní Chatháin and Richter (1984), pp. 280–90
Ó Néill, P. (1987), 'The date and authorship of *Apgitir Chrábaid*: some internal evidence', in Ní Chatháin and Richter (1987), pp. 203–15
O'Rahilly, T. F. (1964), *Early Irish History and Mythology*, Dublin
Ó Riain, P. (1989), 'Conservation in the vocabulary of the early Irish church', in D. Ó Corráin, L. Breatnach and K. McCone (eds.), *Sages, Saints and Storytellers: Celtic Studies in Honour of Professor James Carney*, Maynooth, pp. 358–66
Orlandi, G. (1984), '*Clausulae* in Gildas's *De Excidio Britanniae*', in Lapidge and Dumville (1984), pp. 129–49
O'Sullivan, A. and Sheehan, J. (1996), *The Iveragh Peninsula: An Archaeological Survey of South Kerry*, Cork
Padel, O. J. (1985), *Cornish Place-Name Elements*, Nottingham
Picard, J.-M. (1984), 'Bede, Adomnán, and the writing of history', *Peritia* 3: 50–70
Picard, J.-M. (2000), '*Princeps* and *principatus* in the early Irish church: a reassessment', in A. P. Smyth (ed.), *Seanchas: Studies in Early and Medieval Irish Archaeology, History and Literature in Honour of Francis J. Byrne*, Dublin, pp. 146–60
Pietri, L. and Biarne, J. (1987), *Topographie chrétienne des cités de la Gaule des origines au milieu du VIIIe siècle*, v: *Province ecclésiastique de Tours (Lugdunensis Tertia)*, Paris
Pontal, O. (1989), *Histoire des conciles mérovingiens*, Paris
Pringle, D. (ed.) (1994), *The Ancient Monuments of the Western Isles*, Edinburgh
Proudfoot, E. (1996), 'Excavations at the long cist cemetery on the Hallow Hill, St Andrews, Fife, 1975–7', *Proceedings of the Society of Antiquaries of Scotland* 126: 387–454
Proudfoot, E. (1997), 'Abernethy and Mugdrum: towards reassessment', in D. Henry (ed.), *The Worm, the Germ, and the Thorn: Pictish and Related Studies Presented to Isabel Henderson*, Balgavies, Angus, pp. 47–63
Pryce, H. (1992), 'Pastoral care in early medieval Wales', in Blair and Sharpe (1992), pp. 41–62
Radford, C. A. R. (1967), 'The early church in Strathclyde and Galloway', *Medieval Archaeology* 11: 105–26
Radford, C. A. R. (1971), 'Christian origins in Britain', *Medieval Archaeology* 15: 1–12
Radford, C. A. R. (1983), 'Birsay and the spread of Christianity to the North', in W. P. L. Thomson (ed.), *Orkney Heritage*, II (Orkney Heritage Society), Kirkwall
Rahtz, P. (1977), 'Late Roman cemeteries and beyond', in R. Reece (ed.), *Burial in the Roman World* (CBA Research Report 22), London, pp. 53–64
Richter, M. (1999), *Ireland and Her Neighbours in the Seventh Century*, Dublin
Ritchie, A. (1989), *Picts*, Edinburgh
Roberts, R. (1992), 'Welsh ecclesiastical place-names and archaeology', in N. Edwards and A. Lane (eds.), *The Early Church in Wales and the West*, Oxford, pp. 41–4

Salway, P. (1981, paperback edn 1984), *Roman Britain*, Oxford
Scull, C. (1991), 'Post-Roman Phase 1 at Yeavering: a reconsideration', *Medieval Archaeology* 35: 51–63
Sharpe, R. (1979), 'Hiberno-Latin *laicus*, Irish *láech* and the devil's men', *Ériu* 30: 75–92
Sharpe, R. (1982), 'St Patrick and the see of Armagh', *Cambridge Medieval Celtic Studies* 4: 33–59
Sharpe, R. (1984a), 'Gildas as a Father of the church', in Lapidge and Dumville (1984), pp. 193–205
Sharpe, R. (1984b), 'Some problems concerning the organization of the church in early medieval Ireland', *Peritia* 3: 230–70
Sharpe, R. (1984c), 'Armagh and Rome in the seventh century', in Ní Chatháin and Richter (1984), pp. 58–72
Sharpe, R. (1990), 'Saint Mauchteus, *discipulus Patricii*', in A. Bammesberger and A. Wollmann (eds.), *Britain 400–600: Language and History*, Heidelberg, pp. 85–93
Sharpe, R. (1992a), 'Churches and communities in early medieval Ireland: towards a pastoral model', in Blair and Sharpe (1992), pp. 81–109
Sharpe, R. (1992b), 'An Irish textual critic and the *Carmen paschale* of Sedulius: Colmán's letter to Feradach', *Journal of Medieval Latin* 2: 44–54
Sharpe, R. (1995), *Adomnán of Iona, Life of St Columba*, London
Sheehy, M. P. (1987), 'The Bible and the *Collectio Canonum Hibernensis*', in Ní Chatháin and Richter (1987), pp. 277–83
Sims-Williams, P. (1990), *Religion and Literature in Western England, 600–800*, Cambridge
Sims-Williams, P. (1998), 'The uses of writing in early medieval Wales', in H. Pryce (ed.), *Literacy in Medieval Celtic Societies*, Cambridge, pp. 15–38
Smith, I. (1996), 'The origins and development of Christianity in north Britain and southern Pictland', in J. Blair and C. Pyrah (eds.), *Church Archaeology: Research Directions for the Future* (CBA Research Report 104), York, pp. 19–37
Smith, J. M. H. (1992), *Province and Empire: Brittany and the Carolingians*, Cambridge
Smyth, A. P. (1972), 'The earliest Irish annals: their first contemporary entries, and the earliest centres of recording', *PRIA* 72C: 1–48
Smyth, A. P. (1984), *Warlords and Holy Men: Scotland AD 80–1000*, London
Stancliffe, C. E. (1980), 'Kings and conversion: some comparisons between the Roman mission to England and Patrick's to Ireland', *FrSt* 14: 59–94
Stancliffe, C. (1983), *St Martin and his Hagiographer: History and Miracle in Sulpicius Severus*, Oxford
Stancliffe, C. (1989), 'Cuthbert and the polarity between pastor and solitary', in G. Bonner, D. Rollason and C. Stancliffe (eds.), *St Cuthbert, His Cult and His Community to AD 1200*, Woodbridge, pp. 21–44
Stancliffe, C. (1995), 'Oswald, "Most Holy and Most Victorious King of the Northumbrians"', in C. Stancliffe and E. Cambridge (eds.), *Oswald: Northumbrian King to European Saint*, Stamford
Stancliffe, C. (1997), 'The thirteen sermons attributed to Columbanus and the question of their authorship', in M. Lapidge (ed.), *Columbanus: Studies on the Latin Writings*, Woodbridge, pp. 93–202

Stancliffe, C. (1999), 'The British Church and the mission of Augustine', in R. Gameson (ed.), *St Augustine and the Conversion of England*, Stroud, pp. 107–51
Stancliffe, C. (2001), 'Jonas's *Life of Columbanus and His Disciples*', in J. Carey, M. Herbert and P. Ó Riain (eds.), *Studies in Irish Hagiography: Saints and Scholars*, Dublin, pp. 189–220
Stancliffe, C. (2004), 'Patrick', in H. C. G. Matthew and B. Harrison (eds.), *Oxford Dictionary of National Biography*, 60 vols., vol. 43, Oxford, pp. 69–80
Stevenson, J. (1989), 'The beginnings of literacy in Ireland', *PRIA* 89C: 127–65
Stevenson, J. (1990), 'Literacy in Ireland: the evidence of the Patrick dossier in the Book of Armagh', in R. McKitterick (ed.), *The Uses of Literacy in Early Mediaeval Europe*, Cambridge, pp. 11–35
Stokes, W. (1899), 'The Bodleian Amra Coluimb Chille', *Revue Celtique* 20: 30–55, 132–83, 248–89 and 400–37
Swan, L. (1985), 'Monastic proto-towns in early medieval Ireland: the evidence of aerial photography, plan analysis and survey', in H. B. Clarke and A. Simms (eds.), *The Comparative History of Urban Origins in Non-Roman Europe*, I (BAR, International Series 255.I), Oxford, pp. 77–102
Tanguy, B. (1984), 'Des cités et diocèses chez les Coriosolites et les Osismes', *Bulletin de la Société Archéologique du Finistère* 113: 93–116
Thacker, A. (1992), 'Monks, preaching and pastoral care in early Anglo-Saxon England', in Blair and Sharpe (1992), pp. 137–70
Thomas, C. (1968), 'The evidence from north Britain', in M. W. Barley and R. P. C. Hanson (eds.), *Christianity in Britain, 300–700*, Leicester, pp. 93–121
Thomas, C. (1981), *Christianity in Roman Britain to AD 500*, London
Thomas, C. (1991–92), 'The early inscriptions of southern Scotland', *Glasgow Archaeological Journal* 17: 1–10
Thomas, C. (1992), *Whithorn's Christian Beginnings*, Whithorn
Thompson, E. A. (1963), 'Christianity and the northern barbarians', in A. Momigliano (ed.), *The Conflict between Paganism and Christianity in the Fourth Century*, Oxford, pp. 56–78
Thompson, E. A. (1968), 'Britonia', in M. W. Barley and R. P. C. Hanson (eds.), *Christianity in Britain, 300–700*, Leicester, pp. 201–5
Thompson, E. A. (1985), *Who Was Saint Patrick?*, Woodbridge
Toynbee, J. M. C. (1953), 'Christianity in Roman Britain', *Journal of the British Archaeological Association*, 3rd series, 16: 1–25
Veitch, K. (1997), 'The Columban Church in northern Britain, 664–717: a reassessment', *Proceedings of the Society of Antiquaries of Scotland* 127: 627–47
Victory, S. (1977), *The Celtic Church in Wales*, London
Wallace-Hadrill, J. M. (1988), *Bede's Ecclesiastical History of the English People: A Historical Commentary*, Oxford
Watts, D. (1991), *Christians and Pagans in Roman Britain*, London and New York
West. S. E. (1976), 'The Romano-British site at Icklingham', *East Anglian Archaeology* 3: 63–125
Wilson, P. A. (1966), 'Romano-British and Welsh Christianity: continuity or discontinuity?', *Welsh History Review* 3: 5–21, and 103–20
Winterbottom, M. (1976), 'Columbanus and Gildas', *Vigiliae Christianae* 30: 310–17

Wood, I. (1988), 'Forgery in Merovingian hagiography', in *Fälschungen im Mittelalter. Internationaler Kongress der Monumenta Germaniae Historica, München, 16–17 September 1986* (MGH Schriften 33, pt 5, *Fingierte Briefe, Frömmigkeit und Fälschungen, Realienfälschungen*), Hanover, pp. 369–84
Wright, N. (1984), 'Gildas's prose style and its origins', in Lapidge and Dumville (1984), pp. 107–28
Wright, N. (1997), 'Columbanus's *Epistulae*', in M. Lapidge (ed.), *Columbanus: Studies on the Latin Writings*, Woodbridge, pp. 29–92
Yeoman, P. A. (1998), 'Pilgrims to St Ethernan: the archaeology of an early saint of the Picts and Scots', in B. E. Crawford (ed.), *Conversion and Christianity in the North Sea World*, St Andrews, pp. 75–91
Yorke, B. (1995), *Wessex in the Early Middle Ages*, London

17 ENGLAND IN THE SEVENTH CENTURY

Alexander, J. J. G. (1978) *Insular Manuscripts: Sixth to Ninth Centuries*, London
Bassett, S. (1989a), 'In search of the origins of Anglo-Saxon kingdoms', in Bassett (1989b), pp. 1–27
Bassett, S. (ed.) (1989b), *The Origins of Anglo-Saxon Kingdoms*, Leicester
Behr, C. (2000), 'The origins of kingship in early medieval Kent', *EME* 9.1: 25–52
Bischoff, B. and Lapidge, M. (1994), *Biblical Commentaries from the Canterbury School of Theodore and Hadrian* (Cambridge Studies in Anglo-Saxon England 10), Cambridge
Blair, J. (1989), 'Frithuwold's kingdom and the origins of Survey', in Bassett (1989b): 77–107
Blair, J. (1991), *Early Medieval Surrey*, Stroud
Blair, J. (1995a), 'Debate: ecclesiastical organization and pastoral care in Anglo-Saxon England', *EME* 4.1: 193–212
Blair, J. (1995b), 'Anglo-Saxon pagan shrines and their prototypes', *Anglo-Saxon Studies in Archaeology and History* 8: 1–28
Blair, J. (2002), 'A saint for every minster?', in Thacker and Sharpe (2002), pp. 455–94
Blair, J. and Sharpe, R. (eds.) (1992), *Pastoral Care before the Parish*, Leicester
Bonner, G., Rollason, D. W. and Stancliffe, C. (eds.) (1989), *St Cuthbert: His Cult and His Community*, Woodbridge
Brooks, N. (1971), 'The development of military obligations in eighth- and ninth-century England', in Clemoes and Hughes (1971), pp. 69–84
Brooks, N. (1984), *The Early History of the Church of Canterbury*, London
Brooks, N. (1989), 'The creation and early structure of The Kingdom of Kent', in Bassett (1989b): 55–83
Brooks, N. (1999), *Bede and the English*, Jarrow Lecture, Newcastle
Brown, M. and Farr, C. (2001), *Mercia: An Anglo-Saxon Kingdom in Europe*, Leicester
Bruce-Mitford, R. (1975–83), *The Sutton Hoo Ship Burial*, 4 vols., London
Bullough, D. (1983), 'Burial, community and belief in the early medieval West', in Wormald, Bullough and Collins (1983), pp. 177–201
Cambridge, E. and Rollason, D. W. (1995), 'Debate: the pastoral organization of the Anglo-Saxon church: a review of the "Minster Hypothesis"', *EME* 4.2: 87–104
Campbell, J. (1979), *Bede's* Reges *and* Principes, Jarrow Lecture, Newcastle
Campbell, J. (ed.) (1982), *The Anglo-Saxons*, London

Campbell, J. (1986), *Essays in Anglo-Saxon History*, London
Campbell, J. (2003), 'Production and distribution in early and middle Anglo-Saxon England', in T. Pestell and K. Ulmschneider (eds.), *Markets in Early Medieval Europe* (Macclesfield), pp. 12–19
Carver, M. (ed.) (1992), *The Age of Sutton Hoo*, Woodbridge
Carver, M. (1998), *Sutton Hoo: Burial Ground of Kings?*, London
Chadwick, H. (1905), *Studies on Anglo-Saxon Institutions*, Cambridge
Charles-Edwards, T. M. (1972), 'Kinship, status and the origin of the hide', *Past and Present* 56: 3–33
Charles-Edwards, T. M. (1976), 'The distinction between land and moveable wealth in Anglo-Saxon England', in Sawyer (1976), pp. 180–7
Charles-Edwards, T. M. (1983), 'Bede, the Irish and the Britons', *Celtica* 15
Clemoes, P. and Hughes, K. (eds.) (1971), *England before the Conquest: Studies in Primary Sources Presented to Dorothy Whitelock*, Cambridge
Cubitt, C. (1992), 'Pastoral care and conciliar canons: the provisions of the 747 Council of *Clofeshoh*', in Blair and Sharpe (1992), pp. 193–211
Cubitt, C. (1995), *Anglo-Saxon Church Councils,* c. *650–850*, Leicester
Cubitt, C. (2000), 'Sites and sanctity: revisiting the cult of murdered and martyred Anglo-Saxon royal saints', *EME* 9.1
Cunliffe, B. (1993), *Wessex to 1000*, Harlow
Davies, W. (1982), *Wales in the Early Middle Ages*, Leicester
Davies, W. and Vierck, H. (1974), 'The contexts of Tribal Hidage: social aggregates and settlement patterns', *FrSt* 8: 223–93
Dornier, A. (ed.) (1977), *Mercian Studies*, Leicester
Dumville, D. (1976), 'The Anglian collection of royal genealogies and regnal lists', *Anglo-Saxon England* 5: 23–50
Dumville, D. (1989), 'Essex, Middle Anglia and the expansion of Mercia in the south-east Midlands', in Bassett (1989), pp. 123–40
Eagles, B. (1989), 'Lindsey', in Bassett (1989), pp. 202–12
Everitt, A. (1986), *Continuity and Colonization*, Leicester
Faith, R. (1997), *The English Peasantry and the Growth of Lordship*, Leicester
Fanning, S. (1991), 'Bede, *Imperium* and the Bretwaldas', *Speculum* 66: 1–26
Filmer-Sankey, W. (1996), 'The "Roman Emperor" in the Sutton Hoo Ship Burial', *Journal of the British Archaeological Association* 149: 1–9
Finberg, H. (1972), *Early Charters of the West Midlands*, 2nd edn, Leicester
Foot, S. (1992), 'Anglo-Saxon minsters: a review of terminology', in Blair and Sharpe (1992), pp. 212–25
Foot, S. (2000), *Veiled Women*, 2 vols., London
Fouracre, P. and Gerberding, R. A. (1996), *Late Merovingian France: History and Hagiography*, Manchester
Frazer, W. O. and Tyrell, A. (eds.) (2000), *Social Identity in Early Medieval Britain*, Leicester
Gameson, R. (ed.) (1999), *St Augustine and the Conversion of England*, Stroud
Gannon, A. (2003), *The Iconography of Early Anglo-Saxon Coinage*, Oxford
Gould, J. (1973), 'Letocetum, Christianity and Lichfield', *Transactions of the South Staffordshire Archaeological and Historical Society* 14: 30–1

Halsall, G. (1995), *Early Medieval Cemeteries*, Skelmorlie
Hamerow, H. (2002), *Early Medieval Settlements: The Archaeology of Rural Communities in North-West Europe 400–900*, Oxford
Hawkes, J. and Mills, S. (eds.) (1999), *Northumbria's Golden Age*, Stroud
Higham, N. J. (1995), *An English Empire: Bede and the Early Anglo-Saxon Kings*, Manchester
Hill, D. and Cowie, R. (2001), *Wics: The Early Medieval Trading Centres of Northern Europe*, Sheffield
Hope-Taylor, B. (1977), *Yeavering*, London
James, E. (1989), 'The origins of the barbarian kingdoms: the continental evidence', in Bassett (1989b), pp. 40–52
John, E. (1964), *Land Tenure in Early England*, Leicester
John, E. (1966), *Orbis Britanniae and Other Studies*, Leicester
Jones, G. R. J. (1976), 'Multiple estates and early settlement', in Sawyer (1976), pp. 15–40
Kirby, D. (1991), *The Earliest English Kings*, London
Lapidge, M. (ed.) (1995), *Archbishop Theodore: Comparative Studies on His Life and Influence* (Cambridge Studies in Anglo-Saxon England 11), Cambridge
McCormick, M. (2002), *The Origins of the European Economy: Communications and Commerce, 300–900*, Cambridge
McKinnon, J. (2000), *The Advent Project: The Later Seventh-Century Creation of the Roman Mass Proper*, Berkeley and Los Angeles
Mayr-Harting, H. M. (1972, 3rd edn 1991), *The Coming of Christianity to Anglo-Saxon England*, London
Moreland, J. (2000), 'Ethnicity, power and the English', in Frazer and Tyrell (2000), pp. 23–51
Nelson, J. L. (1986), *Politics and Ritual in Early Medieval Europe*, London
North, R. (1997), *Heathen Gods in Old English Literature* (Cambridge Studies in Anglo-Saxon England 22), Cambridge
Orchard, A. (1994), *The Poetic Art of Aldhelm* (Cambridge Studies in Anglo-Saxon England 8), Cambridge
Pelteret, D. A. E. (1995), *Slavery in Early Medieval England*, Woodbridge
Pretty, K. (1989), 'Defining the Magonsaete', in Bassett (1989b), pp. 171–83
Rollason, D. W. (1989), *Saints and Relics in Early England*, Oxford
Rollason, D. W. (2003), *Northumbria 500–1100: The Making and Destruction of an Early Medieval Kingdom*, Cambridge
Sawyer, P. H. (ed.) (1976), *Medieval Settlement: Continuity and Change*, London
Sawyer, P. H. and Wood, I. N. (eds.) (1977), *Early Medieval Kingship*, Leeds
Sharpe, R. (2002), 'Martyrs and saints in late antique Britain', in Thacker and Sharpe (2002), pp. 75–154
Sims-Williams, P. (1990), *Religion and Literature in Western England* (Cambridge Studies in Anglo-Saxon England 3), Cambridge
Sisam, K. (1953), 'Anglo-Saxon royal genealogies', *Proceedings of the British Academy* 39: 287–346
Smith, J. (ed.) (2000), *Early Medieval Rome and the Christian West: Essays in Honour of Donald Bullough*, Leiden

Stancliffe, C. (1983), 'Kings who opted out', in Wormald, Bullough and Collins (1983), pp. 154–76

Stancliffe, C. (1995a), 'Oswald, "Most holy and most victorious king of the Northumbrians"', in Stancliffe and Cambridge (1995), pp. 33–83

Stancliffe, C. (1995b), 'Where was Oswald killed?', in Stancliffe and Cambridge (1995), pp. 84–96

Stancliffe, C. (1997), 'The thirteen sermons attributed to Colombanus and the question of their authorship', in M. Lapidge (ed.), *Columbanus: Studies on the Latin Writings*, Woodbridge, pp. 32–202

Stancliffe, C. (1999), 'The British church and the mission of Augustine', in Gameson (1999), pp. 107–51

Stancliffe, C. and Cambridge, E. (eds.) (1995), *Oswald: Northumbrian King to European Saint*, Stamford

Stenton, F. M. (1970), *Preparatory to Anglo-Saxon England*, Oxford

Stenton, F. (1971), *Anglo-Saxon England*, 3rd edn, Oxford

Stevenson, J. (1995), *The 'Laterculus Malalianus' and the School of Archbishop Theodore* (Cambridge Studies in Anglo-Saxon England 14), Cambridge

Taylor, C. C. (1984), *Village and Farmstead*, London

Thacker, A. T. (1981) 'Some terms for noblemen in Anglo-Saxon England, *c.* 650–90', in *Anglo-Saxon Studies in Archaeology and History*, II (BAR British Series 92), Oxford, pp. 201–36

Thacker, A. T. (1983), 'Bede's ideal of reform', in Wormald, Bullough and Collins (1983), pp. 130–53

Thacker, A. T. (1992), 'Monks, preaching and pastoral care in early Anglo-Saxon England', in Blair and Sharpe (1992), pp. 137–70

Thacker, A. T. (1995), '*Membra disjecta*: the division of the body and the diffusion of the cult', in Stancliffe and Cambridge (1995), pp. 97–127

Thacker, A. T. (1996), 'Bede and the Irish', in L. A. J. R. Houwen and A. A. MacDonald (eds.), *Beda Venerabilis*, Groningen

Thacker, A. T. (1998), 'Memorializing Gregory the Great: the origin and transmission of a papal cult in the seventh and early eighth centuries', *EME* 7.1: 59–84

Thacker, A. T. (2000), 'In search of saints: the English Church and the cult of Roman apostles and martyrs in the seventh and eighth centuries', in Smith (2000), pp. 247–77

Thacker, A. T. (2002), 'The making of a local saint', in Thacker and Sharpe (eds.) (2002), pp. 45–73

Thacker, A. T. and Sharpe, R. (eds.) (2002), *Local Saints and Local Churches in the Early Medieval West*, Oxford

Vince, A. (ed.) (1993), *Pre-Viking Lindsey*, Lincoln

Wallace-Hadrill, J. M. (1971), *Early Germanic Kingship in England and on the Continent*, Oxford

Wood, I. N. (1977), 'Kings, kingdoms and consent', in P. Sawyer and I. Wood (eds.), *Early Medieval Kingship*, Leeds, pp. 6–29

Wood, I. N. (1994), *The Merovingian Kingdoms*, London

Wood, I. N. (1999), 'Augustine and Gaul', in Gameson (1999), pp. 68–82

Wormald, P. (1983), 'Bede, the *Bretwaldas*, and the origins of the *Gens Anglorum*', in Wormald, Bullough and Collins (1983), pp. 99–129
Wormald, P. (1984), *Bede and the Conversion of England: The Charter Evidence*, Jarrow Lecture, Newcastle
Wormald, P. (1999), *The Making of English Law*, 1: *Legislation and Its Limits*, Oxford
Wormald, P., Bullough, D. and Collins, R. (eds.) (1983), *Ideal and Reality in Frankish and Anglo-Saxon Society: Studies Presented to J. M. Wallace-Hadrill*, London
Yorke, B. (1981), 'The vocabulary of Anglo-Saxon overlordship', in *Anglo-Saxon Studies in Archaeology and History*, II (BAR British Series 92), Oxford, pp. 171–200
Yorke, B. (1989), 'The Jutes of Hampshire and Wight and the origins of Wessex', in Bassett (1989), pp. 84–96.
Yorke, B. (1990), *Kings and Kingdoms of Early Anglo-Saxon England*, London
Yorke, B. (1995), *Wessex in the Early Middle Ages*, Leicester
Yorke, B. (2000), 'Political and ethnic identity: a case study of Anglo-Saxon practice', in Frazer and Tyrell (2000), pp. 69–89
Yorke, B. (2003), 'The adaptation of the Anglo-Saxon royal courts to Christianity', in *The Cross Goes North: Processes of Conversion in Northern Europe, 300–1300*, York, pp. 243–57

18 SCANDINAVIA

Andersen, H. (1998), 'Vier og lunde', *Skalk*, 1: 15–27
Andréasson, A. (1995), 'Skandinaviens Guldgubbar', C-Uppsats in archaeolog, University of Gothenburg
Andrén, A. (1991), 'Guld och makt-en tolkning av de skandinaviska guldbrakteatemas funktion', in Fabech and Ringtved (1991), pp. 245–58
Andrén, A. (2000), 'Re-reading embodied texts – an interpretation of rune stones', *Current Swedish Archaeology* 8: 7–32
Arrhenius, B. (1983), 'The chronology of the Vendel graves', in J. P. Lamm and H.-Å. Nordström (eds.), *Vendel Period Studies*, Stockholm, pp. 39–70
Ausenda, G. (1995), 'The segmentary lineage in contemporary anthropology and among the Langobards', in G. Ausenda (ed.), *After Empire: Towards an Ethnology of Europe's Barbarians*, Woodbridge, pp. 15–50
Axboe, M. (1991), 'Guld og guder i folkevandringstiden', in Fabech and Ringtved (1991), pp. 187–202
Barrett, J. C., Bradley, R. and Green, M. (eds.) (1999), *Landscape, Monuments and Society: The Prehistory of Cranborne Chase*, Cambridge
Bazelmans, J. (1992), 'The gift in the Old English epic Beowulf', lecture given at a seminar on *Theory and Method in the Study of Material Culture*, Leiden 31 August/2 September 1992
Bazelmans, J. (1999), *By Weapons Made Worthy: Lords, Retainers and Their Relationship in Beowulf*, Amsterdam

Bazelmans, J. (2000), 'Beyond power. Ceremonial exchanges in Beowulf', in F. Theuws and J. L. Nelson (eds.), *Rituals of Power: From Late Antiquity to the Early Middle Ages*, Leiden, pp. 311–76

Bierbrauer, V. (1994), 'Archäologie und Geschichte der Goten vom 1.–7. Jahrhundert', *FrSt* 28: 51–171

Brink, S. (1996), 'Political and social structures in early Scandinavia', *TOR* 28: 235–81

Brøgger, N. C. (1951), 'Frøya-dyrkelse og seid', *Viking* 15: 39–63

Bruce-Mitford, R. (1979), *The Sutton Hoo Ship Burial*, London.

Buchholz, P. (1971), 'Shamanism – the testimony of Old Icelandic literary tradition', *Mediaeval Scandinavia* 4: 7–20

Busch, R. (1988), *Die Langobarden: Von der Unterelbe nach Italien*, Neumünster

Callmer, J. (1991), 'Territory and dominion in the Late Iron Age in southern Scandinavia', in K. Jennbert *et al.* (eds.), *Regions and Reflections: In Honour of Märta Strömberg*, Stockholm, pp. 257–73

Callmer, J. (1997), 'Aristokratisk präglade residens från yngre järnålderen I forskningshistorien och deres problematic', in J. Callmer and E. Rosengren (eds.), '*. . . gick Grendel att söka det höga huset . . .': arkeologiska källor till aristokratiska miljöer i Skandinavien under yngre järnålder. Rapport från ett seminarium i Falkenberg 16.–17. November 1995* (Halland Länsmuseers Skriftserie/GOTARC C. Arkeologiska Skrifter 17), Halmstad, pp. 11–18

Christensen, T. (1991), *Lejre – syn og sagn*, Roskilde

Christie, N. (1995), *The Lombards* (The Peoples of Europe), Oxford

Clunies Ross, M. (1994), *Prolonged Echoes: Old Norse Myths in Medieval Northern Society*, 1: *The Myths*, Odense

De Marrais, E. L., Castillo, J. and Earle, T. (1996), 'Ideology, materialization, and power strategies', *Current Anthropology* 37.1: 15–31

De Vries, J. (1956/1970), *Altgermanische Religionsgeschichte*, 1: Berlin

Duczko, W. (ed.) (1993), *Arkeologi och miljögeografi I Gamla Uppsala: Studier och rapport* (Opia 7), Uppsala

Dumézil, G. (1959), *Les Dieux des Germains: essai sur la formation de la religion scandinave*, Paris. Danish trans. (1969), *De nordiske Guder*, Copenhagen

Düwel, K. (1978), 'Runeninschriften', in C. Ahrens (ed.), *Sachsen und Angelsachsen* (Veröffentlichungen des Helms-Museums 32), Hamburg, pp. 219–30

Earle, T. (1990), 'Style and iconography as legitimation in complex chiefdoms', in M. Conkey and C. Hastorf (eds.), *The Use of Style in Archaeology*, Cambridge, pp. 61–72

Eliade, M. (1989), *Shamanism: Archaic Techniques of Ecstasy*, Harmondsworth

Ellis Davidson, H. R. (1978), 'Shape-changing in Old Norse sagas', in J. R. Porter and W. M. S. Russell (eds.), *Animals in Folklore*, Cambridge, pp. 126–42

Ellis Davidson, H. R. (1988), *Myths and Symbols in Pagan Europe*, Manchester

Ellmers, D. (1970), 'Zur Ikonographie nordischer Goldbrakteaten', *Jahrbuch des Römisch-Germanischen Zentralmuseums Mainz* 17: 201–84

Enright, M. J. (1996), *Lady with a Mead Cup*, Dublin

Fabech, C. (1994a), 'Reading society from the cultural landscape. South Scandinavia between sacral and political power', in P. O. Nielsen, K. Randsborg and H. Thrane (eds.), *The Archaeology of Gudme and Lundeborg*, Copenhagen, pp. 169–83

Fabech, C. (1994b), 'Society and landscape. From collective manifestations to ceremonies of a new ruling class', in H. Keller and N. Staubach (eds.), *Iconologia Sacra: Festschrift für Karl Hauck*, Berlin and New York, pp. 132–43.

Fabech, C. (1997), 'Slöinge i perspektiv', in J. Callmer and E. Rosengren (eds.), '*. . . gick Grendel att söka det höga huset . . .': arkeologiska källor till aristokratiska miljöer i Skandinavien under yngre järnålder. Rapport från ett seminarium i Falkenberg 16.–17. November 1995* (Hallands Länsmuseer Skriftserie 9/GOTARC C. Arkeologiska Skrifter 17), Halmstad, pp. 145–60

Fabech, C. (1998), 'Kult og samfund i yngre jernalder – Ravlunda som eksempel', in L. Larsson and B. Hårdh (eds.), *Centrala Platser – Centrala Frågor: En vänbok til Berta Stjernquist* (Acta Archaeologica Lundensia 28), Lund, pp. 147–64

Fabech, C. (1999), 'Centrality on sites and landscapes', in C. Fabech and J. Ringtved (eds.), *Settlement and Landscape*, Århus, pp. 455–73

Fabech, C. and Ringtved, J. (eds.) (1991), *Samfundsorganisation og Regional Variation* (Jysk Arkæologisk Selskabs Skrifter 27), Århus

Fonnesbech-Sandberg, E. (1985), 'Hoard finds from the Early Germanic Iron Age', in K. Kristiansen (ed.), *Archaeological Formation Processes*, Copenhagen, pp. 175–90

Gaimster, M. (1998), *Vendel Period Bracteates on Gotland: On the Significance of Germanic Art*, Stockholm

Gasparri, S. (1983), *La cultura tradizionale dei Longobardi*, Spoleto

Gasparri, S. (2000), 'Kingship rituals and ideology in Lombard Italy', in F. Theuws and J. Nelson (eds.), *Rituals of Power: From Late Antiquity to the Early Middle Ages*, Leiden, pp. 95–114

Geary, P. J. (2003), *The Myth of Nations: The Medieval Origins of Europe*, Princeton, NJ

Geisslinger, H. (1967), *Horte als Geschichtsquelle* (Offa-Bücher Neue Folge 19), Neumünster

Glosecki, S. O. (1989), *Shamanism and Old English Poetry*, New York and London

Godlowski, K. (1992), 'Germanische Wanderungen im 3. Jh. v. Chr. – 6. Jh. n. Chr. und ihre Widerspiegelung in den historischen und archäologischen Quellen', in E. Straume and E. Skar (eds.), *Peregrinatio Gothica*, III (Universitetets Oldsaksamlings Skrifter 14), Oslo, pp. 53–75

Goffart, W. (1980), *Barbarians and Romans:. Techniques of Accommodation*, Princeton, NJ

Goffart, W. (1988), *The Narrators of Barbarian History*, Princeton, NJ

Hachmann, R. (1970), *Die Goten und Skandinavien*, Berlin

Hårdh, B. (ed.) (2003), *Fler fynd i centrum* (Uppåkrastudier 9), Stockholm

Hårdh, B. and Larsson, L. (eds.) (2002), *Central Places in the Migration and Merovingian Periods: Papers from the 52nd Sachsensymposium Lund, August 2001* (Uppåkrastudier 6), Stockholm

Härke, H. (1992a), 'Changing symbols in a changing society: the Anglo-Saxon weapon burial rite in the seventh century', in M. Carver (ed.), *The Age of Sutton Hoo*, Woodbridge, pp. 149–66

Härke, H. (1992b), *Early Anglo-Saxon Shields*, London

Haseloff, G. (1981), *Die germanische Tierornamentik der Völkerwanderungszeit*, 3 vols., Berlin and New York

Haseloff, G. (1984), 'Stand der Forschung: Stilgeschichte Völkerwanderungs- und Merowingerzeit', in M. Høgestøl, J. H. Larsen, E. Straume and B. Weber (eds.), *Festskrift til Thorleif Sjøvold på 70-årsdagen* (Universitetets Oldsaksamlings Skrifter 5), Oslo, pp. 109–2

Haseloff, G. (1986), 'Bild und Motiv im Nydam-Stil und Stil 1', in H. Roth (ed.), *Zum Problem der Deutung frühmittelalterlicher Bildinhalte* (Akten des 1. Internationalen Kolloquiums in Marburg a.d. Lahn, 15.–19. Februar 1983), Sigmaringen, pp. 67–110

Hastrup, K. (1990), 'Iceland: sorcerers and paganism', in Ankarloo, B. and G. Henningsen (eds.), *Early Modern Witchcraft: Centres and Peripheries*, Oxford, pp. 383–401

Hauck, K. (1974), 'Ein neues Drei-Götter-Amulett von der Insel von Fünen', in *Geschichte in der Gesellschaft: Festschrift für Karl Bosl*, Stuttgart, pp. 92–159

Hauck, K. (1978), 'Gotterglaube im Spiegel der goldenen Brakteaten', in C. Ahrens (ed.), *Sachsen und Angelsachsen* (Veröffentlichungen des Helms-Museums 32), Hamburg, pp. 189–218

Hauck, K. (1985–89), *Die Goldbrakteaten der Völkerwanderungszeit*, Mit Beiträge von M. Axboe, C. Düwel, L. von Padberg, U. S. Myra and C. Wypior (Münstersche Mittelalterschriften 24), Munich

Hauck, K. (1986), 'Methodenfragen der Brakteatendeutung. Erprobung eines Interpretationsmusters für die Bildzeugnisse aus einer oralen Kultur', in H. Roth (ed.), *Zum Problem der Deutung frühmittelalterlicher Bildinhalte* (Akten des 1. Internationalen Kolloquiums in Marburg a. d. Lahn, 15.–19. Februar 1983), Sigmaringen, pp. 273–96

Hauck, K. (1994), 'Gudme als Kultort und seine Rolle beim Austausch von Bildformularen der Goldbrakteaten', in Nielsen, Randsborg and Thrane (1994), pp. 78–88

Heather, P. (1989), 'Cassiodorus and the rise of the Amals: genealogy and the Goths under Hun domination', *JRS* 89: pp. 103–28

Heather, P. (1993), 'The historical culture of Ostrogothic Italy', in *Teoderico il Grande e i Goti d'Italia* (Atti del XIII Congresso internazionale di studi sull' alto medioevo), Spoleto, pp. 317–53

Heather, P. (1994), *Goths and Romans 332–489*, Oxford

Heather, P. (1995), 'Theoderic, king of the Goths', *Early Medieval Europe* 4: 145–73

Heather, P. (1998), 'Disappearing and reappearing of tribes', in W. Pohl and H. Reimitz (eds.), *Strategies of Distinction: The Construction of Ethnic Communities, 300–800*, Leiden, pp. 92–111

Heather, P. and Matthews, J. (1991), *The Goths in the Fourth Century*, Liverpool

Hedeager, L. (1991), 'Die dänischen Golddepots der Völkerwanderungszeit', *Frühmittelalterliche Studien* 25: 73–88

Hedeager, L. (1992a), *Iron-Age Societies: From Tribe to State in Northern Europe, 500 BC to AD 700*, Oxford

Hedeager, L. (1992b), 'Kingdoms, ethnicity and material culture: Denmark in a European perspective', in M. Carver (ed.), *The Age of Sutton Hoo*, Woodbridge, pp. 279–300

Hedeager, L. (1993), 'The creation of Germanic identity. A European origin myth', in P. Brun, S. van der Leeuw and C. Whittaker (eds.), *Frontières d'Empire: nature et signification des frontières romaines* (Mémoires du Musée de Préhistoire d'Ile-de-France 5), Nemours, pp. 121–32

Hedeager, L. (1997), *Skygger af en anden virkelighed: studien i oldnordiske og tildig europaeiste myter*, Copenhagen

Hedeager, L. (1998), 'Cosmological endurance: pagan identities in Early Christian Europe', *Journal of European Archaeology* 3: 383–97

Hedeager, L. (1999a), 'Skandinavisk dyreornamentik. Symbolsk repræsentation af en førkristen kosmologi', in I. Fuglestvedt, T. Gansum and A. Opedal (eds.), *Et hus med mange rom: vennebok til Bjørn Myhre på 60-årsdagen* (AmS – Rapport 11A), Stavanger, pp. 219–37

Hedeager, L. (1999b), 'Sacred topography. Depositions of wealth in the cultural landscape', in A. Gustafsson and H. Karlsson (eds.), *Glyfer och Arkeologiska Rum: in honorem Jarl Nordbladh* (Gotarc Series A, 3), Gothenburg, pp. 229–52

Hedeager, L. (2000), 'Europe in the Migration Period. The formation of a political mentality', in F. Theuws and J. L. Nelson (eds.), *Rituals of Power: From Late Antiquity to the Early Middle Ages*, Leiden, pp. 15–57

Hedeager, L. (2001), 'Asgard reconstructed? Gudme – a "central place" in the North', in M. de Jong and F. Theuws (eds.), *Topographies of Power in the Early Middle Ages*, Leiden, pp. 467–508

Hedeager, L. (2003), 'Beyond mortality. Scandinavian animal style AD 400–1200', in J. Downes and A. Ritchie (eds.), *Sea Change: Orkney and Northern Europe in the later Iron Age AD 300–800*, Angus, pp. 127–36

Hedeager, L. (2004), 'Dyr og andre mennesker – mennesker og andre dyr. Dyreornamentikkens transcendentale realitet', in A. Andrén, K. Jennbert and C. Raudvere (eds.), *Ordning mot kaos: studier av nordisk förkristen kosmologi* (Vägar till Midgård 4), Lund, pp. 223–56

Helms, M. W. (1988), *Ulysses' Sail: An Ethnographic Odyssey of Power, Knowledge, and Geographical Distance*, Princeton, NJ

Helms, M. W. (1993), *Craft and the Kingly Ideal: Art, Trade and Power*, Austin, TX

Herschend, F. (1978–79), 'Två studier i öländska guldfynd. I: Det myntade guldet, II: Det omyntade guldet', *TOR* 18: pp. 33–294

Herschend, F. (1993), 'The origin of the hall in south Scandinavia', *TOR* 25: 175–99

Herschend, F. (1994), 'Models of petty rulership: two early settlements in Iceland', *TOR* 26: 163–92

Herschend, F. (1995), 'Hus på Helgö', *Fornvännen* 90: 222–8

Herschend, F. (1996), 'A note on Late Iron Age kingship mythology', *TOR* 28: 283–303

Herschend, F. (1997a), *Livet i Hallen* (Occasional Papers in Archaeology 14), Uppsala

Herschend, F. (1997b), 'Striden om Finnsborg', *TOR* 29

Herschend, F. (1998), *The Idea of the Good in Late Iron Age Society* (Occasional Papers in Archaeology 15), Uppsala

Herschend, F. (1999), 'Halle', *Reallexicon der germanischen Altertumskunde*, XIII Berlin

Hill, C. (2003), *Origins of the English*, London

Hines, J. (1984), *The Scandinavian Character of Anglian England in the Pre-Viking Period* (BAR British Series 124), Oxford

Hines, J. (1989), 'Ritual hoarding in Migration-Period Scandinavia: a review of recent interpretations', *Proceedings of the Prehistoric Society* 55: 193–205

Hines, J. (1992), 'The Scandinavian character of Anglian England: an update', in M. Carver (ed.), *The Age of Sutton Hoo*, Woodbridge, pp. 315–30

Hines, J. (1993), *Clasps, Hektespenner, Agraffen: Anglo-Scandinavian Clasps of Classes A–C of the 3rd to the 6th Centuries A.D.: Typology, Diffusion and Function*, Stockholm

Hines, J. (1994), 'The becoming of English: identity, material culture and language in Early Anglo-Saxon England', in W. Filmer-Sankey and D. Griffith (eds.), *Anglo-Saxon Studies in Archaeology and History*, VII, Oxford

Hines, J. (1995), 'Cultural change and social organisation in early Anglo-Saxon England', in G. Ausenda (ed.), *After Empire: Towards an Ethnology of Europe's Barbarians*, Woodbridge, pp. 75–87

Høilund Nielsen, K. (1997), 'Retainers of the Scandinavian kings: an alternative interpretation of Salin's Style II (sixth–seventh centuries AD)', *European Journal of Archaeology* 5.1: 151–69

Høilund Nielsen, K. (1999), 'Ulvekrigeren. Dyresymbolik på våbenudstyret fra 6.–7. århundrede', in O. Højris *et al.* (eds.), *Menneskelivets Mangfoldighed*, Århus, pp. 327–34

Holtsmark, A. (1964), *Studier i Snorres Mytologi*, Oslo

Hultgård, A. (1999), 'Fornskandinavisk hinsidestro i Snorre Sturlusons spegling', in U. Drobin (ed.), *Religion och Samhälle i det förkristna Norden*, Odense, pp. 109–24

Ingold, T. (2000), *The Perception of the Environment*, London and New York

Jakobsson, A. H. (2003), *Smältdeglars Härskare och Jerusalems Tillskyndare*, Stockholm

Jakobsson, M. (1997), 'Burial layout, society and sacred geography', *Current Swedish Archaeology* 5: 79–98

Johansen, B. (1996), 'The transformative dragon. The construction of social identity and the use of metaphors during the Nordic Iron Age', *Current Swedish Archaeology* 4: 83–102

Johansen, B. (1997), *Ormalur: aspekter av tillvaro och landskap* (Stockholm Studies in Archaeology 14), Stockholm

Jørgensen, L. (1990), *Bækkegård and Glasergård: Two Cemeteries from the Late Iron Age on Bornholm*, Copenhagen

Jørgensen, L. (1995), 'Stormandssreder og skattefund i 3.–12. Århundrede', *Fortid og Nutid* 2: 83–110

Jørgensen, L. (2003), 'Manor and market at Lake Tissø in the sixth to the eleventh centuries: the Danish "productive" sites', in T. Pestell and K. Ulmschneider (eds.), *Markets in Early Medieval Europe: Trading and 'Productive' Sites, 650–850*, Bollington, pp. 175–207

Jørgensen, L. and Nørgård Jørgensen, A. (1997), *Nørre Sandegård Vest: A Cemetery from the 6th–8th Centuries on Bornholm*, Copenhagen

Karlsson, L. (1983), *Nordisk Form: Om djurornamentik*, Stockholm

Kazanski, M. (1991), *Les Goths*, Paris

Kristoffersen, S. (1995), 'Transformation in Migration Period animal art', *Norwegian Archaeological Review* 28: 1–17

Kristoffersen, S. (2000a), *Sverd og Spenne: Dyreornamentikk og sosial kontekst*, Kristiansand

Kristoffersen, S. (2000b), 'Expressive objects', in D. Olausson and H. Vandkilde (eds.), *Form, Function and Context*, Stockholm, pp. 265–74

Lamm, J. P. and Nordström, H. A. (eds.) (1983), *Vendel Period Studies*, Stockholm

Larsson, L. and Hårdh, B. (eds.) (1998), *Centrala Platser, Centrala Frågor* (Acta Archaeologica Lundensia, Ser. in 8, 28), Lund

Lidén, R.–E. (1969), 'From pagan sanctuary to Christian church. The excavation of Mære Church in Trøndelag', *Norwegian Archaeological Review* 2: 3e–21

Lindstrøm, T. C. and Kristoffersen, S. (2001), 'Figure it out! Psychological perspectives on perception of Migration Period animal art', *Norwegian Archaeological Report* 34.2: 65–84

Lund Hansen, U. (1992), 'Die Rortproblematik im Licht der neuen Diskussion zur Chronologie und zur Deutung der Goldschätze in der Völkerwanderungszeit', in K. Hauck (ed.), *Der historische Horizont der Götterbild-Amulette aus der Übergangsepoche von der Spätantike zum Frühmittelalter*, Göttingen, pp. 183–94

Lundqvist, L., Lindeblad, K., Nielsen, A.-L. and Ersgard, L. (1996), *Slöinge och Borg* (Riksantikvarieämbetet; Arkeologiska Undersökningar, Skrifter 18), Linköping

Mackeprang, M. (1952), *De Nordiske Guldbrakteater* (Jysk Arkæologisk Selskabs Skrifter 2), Århus

Magnus, B. (2001), 'The enigmatic brooches', in B. Magnus (ed.), *Roman Gold and the Development of the Early Germanic Kingdoms*, Stockholm, pp. 279–95

Menghin, W. (1985), *Die Langobarden: Archäologie und Geschichte*, Stuttgart

Meulengracht Sørensen, P. (1991), 'Om eddadigtenes alder', in G. Steinsland, U. Drobin, J. Pentikäinen and P. Meulengracht Sørensen (eds.), *Nordisk Hedendom. Et symposia*, Odense, pp. 217–28

Morphy, H. (1989), 'Introduction', in H. Morphy (ed.), *Animals into Art*, London, pp. 1–17

Mortensen, P. and Rasmussen, B. (eds.) (1988), *Jernalderens Stammesamfund* (Fra Stamme til Stat i Danmark 1. Jysk Arkæologisk Selskabs Skrifter 22.1), Århus

Mortensen, P. and Rasmussen, B. (eds.) (1991), *Høvdingesamfund og Kongemagt* (Fra Stamme til Stat i Danmark 2. Jysk Arkreologisk Selskabs Skrifter 22.2), Århus

Munch, G. S., Johansen, O. S. and Roesdahl, E. (eds.) (2003), *Borg in Lofoten: A Chieftain's Farm in North Norway* (Arkeologisk Skriftserie 1), Vikingsmuseet på Borg

Munch, G. S., Roland, I. and Johansen, O. S. (1988), 'Borg in Lofoten', *Norwegian Archaeological Review* 21: 119–26

Myhre, B. (1992), 'The royal cemetery at Borre, Vestfold. A Norwegian centre in a European periphery', in M. Carver (ed.), *The Age of Sutton Hoo*, Woodbridge, pp. 301–13

Myhre, B. (2003), 'The Iron Age', in K. Helle (ed.), *The Cambridge History of Scandinavia*, Cambridge, pp. 60–93

Näsman, U. (1984), *Glas och Handel i Senromersk tid och Folkvandringstid* (AUN 5) Uppsala

Näsman, U. (1988), 'Analogislutning i nordisk jernalderarkæologi. Et bidrag til udviklingen af an nordisk historisk etnografi', in Mortensen and Rasmussen (1988), pp. 123–40

Näsman, U. (1991), 'Sea trade during the Scandinavian Iron Age. Its character, commodities and routes', in O. Crumlin-Pedersen (ed.), *Aspects of Maritime Scandinavia AD 200–1200*, Roskilde, pp. 23–40

Näsman, U. (1999), 'The ethnogenesis of the Danes and the making of a Danish kingdom', *Anglo-Saxon Studies in Archaeology and History*, 10: 1–10

Newton, S. (1993), *The Origins of Beowulf and the Pre-Viking Kingdom of East Anglia*, Woodbridge

Nielsen, P. O., Randsborg, K. and Thrane, R. (eds.) (1994), *The Archaeology of Gudme and Lundeborg*, Copenhagen

Nordén, A. (1938), 'Le problème des "Bonhommes en or"', *Acta Archaeologica* 9: 151–63

North, R. (1997), *Heathen Gods in Old English Literature*, Cambridge

Ohlmarks, Å. (1939), 'Arktischer Shamanismus und altnordischer *Seiðr*', *Archiv für Religionswissenschaft* 36: 171–80

Orchard, A. (2002), *Cassell's Dictionary of Norse Myth and Legend*, London

Oxenstierna, E. (1956), *Die Goldhörner von Gallehus*, Lidingö

Parry, J. and Bloch, M. (1993), 'Introduction: money and the morality of exchange', in J. Parry and M. Bloch (eds.), *Money and the Morality of Exchange*, Cambridge, pp. 1–32

Pohl, W. (1994), 'Tradition, Ethnogenese und literarische Gestaltung: eine Zwischenbilanz', in K. Brunner and B. Merta (eds.), *Ethnogenese und Überlieferung*, Vienna and Munich, pp. 9–26

Polomé, E. C. (1992), 'Schamanismus in der germanischen Religion?', in K. Hauck (ed.), *Der historische Horizont der Götterbild-Amulette aus der Übergangsepoche von der Spätantike zum Frühmittelalter*, Göttingen, pp. 403–20

Price, N. S. (2002), *The Viking Way: Religion and War in Late Iron Age Scandinavia* (AUN 31), Uppsala

Raudvere, C. (2001), 'Trolldom in early medieval Scandinavia', in K. Jolly, C. Raudvere and E. Peters, *Witchcraft and Magic in Europe: The Middle Ages*, Philadelphia, pp. 73–171

Raudvere, C. (2003), *Kunskap och Insikt i Norrön Tradition*, Lund

Roe, P. G. (1995), 'Style, society, myth, and structure', in C. Carr and J. E. Neitzel (eds.), *Style, Society, and Person*, New York and London, pp. 27–76

Roth, H. (1979), *Kunst der Völkerwanderungszeit*, Frankfurt a.M.

Salin, B. (1904), *Die altgermanische Thierornamentik*, Stockholm and Berlin

Simek, R. (1996), *Dictionary of Northern Mythology*, Woodbridge

Skre, D. (1998), *Herredømmet: bosetning og besittelse på Romerike 200–1350 e.Kr.* (Acta Humaniora 32), Oslo

Skre, D. (2004), *Kaupangen i Skiringssal: Vikingenes by*, Oslo

Solli, B. (2002), *Seid: myter, sjamanisme og kjønn i vikingenes tid*, Oslo

Speake, G. (1980), *Anglo-Saxon Animal Art and Its Germanic Background*, Oxford

Steinsland, G. (1991), *Det hellige Bryllup og norrøn kongeideologi*, Oslo

Steinsland, G. (1994), 'Eros og død – de to hovedkomponenter i norrøn kongeideologi', in H. Uecker (ed.), *Studien zum altgermanischen: Festschrift für Heinrich Beck*, Berlin and New York, pp. 626–41

Storms, G. (1970), 'The significance of Hygelac's raid', *NMS* 14: 3–26

Strömbäck, D. (1935), *Sejd*, Stockholm

Strömbäck, D. (1970), 'Sejd', in A. Karker (ed.), *Kulturhistorisk leksikon for nordisk middelalder* xv, Copenhagen

Svennung, J. (1967), *Jordanes und Scandia*, Stockholm

Svennung, J. (1972), 'Jordanes und die gotische Stammsage', in U. E. Hagberg (ed.), *Studia Gotica* (Antikvariska Serien 25), Stockholm, pp. 20–56

Turville-Petre, E. O. G. (1975), *Myth and Religion of the North*, Westport, CT
Wagner, N. (1967), *Getica: Untersuchungen zum Leben des Jordanes und zur frühen Geschichte der Goten* (Quellen und Forschungen zur Sprach- und Kulturgeschichte der germanischen Völke, NF 22), Berlin
Watt, M. (1992), 'Die Goldblechfiguren (goldgubber) aus Sorte Muld', in K. Hauck (ed.), *Der historische Horizont der Götterbildamulette aus der Übergangsepoche von Spätantike zum Frühmittelalter*, Göttingen, pp. 195–227
Weibull, C. (1958), *Die Auswanderung der Goten aus Schweden*, Göteborg
Weiner, J. (1999), 'Myth and metaphor', in T. Ingold (ed.), *Companion Encyclopedia of Anthropology*, London, pp. 591–612
Wiker, G. (1999), *Gullbrakteatene – i dialog med naturkreftene: ideologi og endring sett i lys av de skandinaviske brakteatnedleggelsene*, Olso
Wolfram, H. (1990), *The History of the Goths*, trans. J. T. Dunlap, Berkeley, CA
Wolfram, H. (1994), 'Origo et religio. Ethnic traditions and literature in early medieval texts', *EME* 3: 19–38
Wood, I. (1983), *The Merovingian North Sea* (Occasional Papers on Medieval Topics 1), Alingsås

19 THE SLAVS

Angelova, S. (1980), 'Po váprosa za rannoslavjanskata kultura na jug i na sever ot Dunav prez VI–VII v.', *Archeologija* 22: 1–12
Baran, V. D. (1972), *Ranni slovyani mizh Dnistrom i Pripyattyu*, Kiev
Baran, V. D. (1988), *Prazhskaya kultura Podnestrovya*, Kiev
Baran, V. D. (ed.) (1990), *Slavyane yugo-vostochnoy Evropy v predgosudarstvennyy period*, Kiev
Beranová, M. (1988), *Slované*, Prague
Birnbaum, H. (1979), *Common Slavic: Progress and Problems in Its Reconstruction*, Columbus, OH
Birnbaum, H. (1987), *Praslavyanskiy jazyk*, Moscow
Bóna, I. (1968), 'Über einen archäologischen Beweis des langobardisch-slawisch-awarischen Zusammenlebens', *Študijné Zvesti Archeologického Ústavu Slovenskej Akadémie Vied* 16: 34–44
Brachmann, H. (1978), *Slawische Stämme an Elbe und Saale*, Berlin
Charanis, P. (1949), 'On the question of the Slavonic settlements in Greece during the Middle Ages', *BSl* 10: 254–8
Charanis, P. (1950), 'The Chronicle of Monemvasia and the question of the Slavonic settlement in Greece', *DOP* 5: 141–66
Charanis, P. (1953), 'On the Slavic settlement in the Peloponnesus', *BZ* 46: 91–103
Charanis, P. (1959), 'Ethnic changes in the Byzantine Empire in the seventh century', *DOP* 13: 25–44
Chernysh, A. P. (ed.) (1990), *Archeologiya Prikarpatya, Volyni i Zakarpatya (ranneslovyanskiy i drevnerusskiy periody)*, Kiev
Chropovský, B. (ed.) (1984), *Interaktionen der mitteleuropäischen Slawen und anderen Ethnika im 6–10. Jahrhundert*, Nitra

Chrysos, E. (1987), 'Die Nordgrenze des byzantinischen Reiches im 6. bis 8. Jahrhundert', in B. Hänsel (ed.), *Die Völker Südosteuropas im 6. bis 8. Jahrhundert* (Südosteuropa Jahrbuch 17), Munich, pp. 27–40

Comşa, M. (1973), 'Die Slawen im karpatisch-donauländischen Raum im 6.–7. Jahrhundert', *Zeitschrift für Archäologie* 7: 197–228

Comşa, M. (1987), 'Einige Betrachtungen fiber den Kontakt zwischen den slawischen und den bodenständigen romanischen Gemeinschaften im Donau-Karpaten-Raum (6. und 7. Jahrhundert)', in G. Labuda and S. Tabaczyński (eds.), *Studia nad etnogeneza Słowian i kultura Europy wczesnośredniowiecznej*, Warsaw, pp. 65–70

Conte, F. (1986), *Les Slaves: aux origines des civilisations d'Europe centrale et orientale (VI–XIII siècles)*, Paris

Daim, F. (1993), 'Vorbild und Konfrontation – Slawen und Awaren im Ostalpen- und Donauraum. Bemerkungen zur Forschungssituation', in T. Winkelbauer (ed.), *Kontakte und Konflikte. Böhmen, Mähren und Österreich: Aspekte eines Jahrtausends gemeinsamer Geschichte* (*Schriftenreihe des Waldviertel Heimatbundes* 36), pp. 27–41

Daim, F. (ed.) (1996), *Reitervölker aus dem Osten*, Eisenstadt

Ditten, H. (1978a), 'Zur Bedeutung der Einwanderung der Slawen', in F. Winkelmann *et al.* (eds.), *Byzanz im 7. Jahrhundert: Untersuchungen zur Herausbildung des Feudalismus*, Berlin, pp. 73–160

Ditten, H. (1978b), 'Bemerkungen zu den ersten Ansatzen zur Staatsbildung bei Kroaten und Serben im 7. Jahrhundert', in V. Vavřinek (ed.), *Beiträge zur byzantinischen Geschichte im 9.-11. Jahrhundert*, Prague, pp. 441–62

Ditten, H. (1981), 'Die Veränderungen auf dem Balkan in der Zeit vom 6. bis zum 10. Jh. im Spiegel der veränderterten Bedeutung der Provinzen der thrakischen Diözese', *Byzantinobulgarica* 7: 157–79

Ditten, H. (1983a), 'Zum Verhältnis zwischen Protobulgaren und Slawen vom Ende des 7. bis zum Anfang des 9. Jahrhunderts', in H. Köpstein (ed.), *Besonderheiten der byzantinischen Feudalentwicklung*, Berlin, pp. 85–95

Ditten, H. (1983b), 'Prominente Slawen und Bulgaren im byzantinischen Diensten (Ende des 7. bis Anfang des 10. Jahrhunderts)', in H. Köpstein and F. Winkelmann (eds.), *Studien zum 8. und 9. Jahrhunderts im Byzanz*, Berlin, pp. 95–119

Dolinescu-Ferche, S. (1984), 'La culture "Ipoteşti-Ciurel-Cindeşti" (Ve–VIIe siècles). La situation en Valachie', *Dacia* 28: 117–47

Donat, P. (1980), *Haus, Hof und Dorf in Mitteleuropa von 7.–12. Jahrhundert*, Berlin

Donat, P. and Fischer, R. E. (1994), 'Die Anfänge slawischer Siedlung westlich der Oder', *Jahrbuch für Brandenburgische Landesgeschichte* 45: 7–30

Dralle, L. (1981), *Slaven an Havel und Spree: Studien zur Geschichte des hevellisch-wilzischen Fürstentums (6.–10. Jahrhundert)*, Berlin

Dvornik, F. (1962), *The Slavs in European History and Civilization*, New Brunswick, NJ

Eisner, J. (1966), *Rukovět' slovanské archeologie*, Prague

Erhart, A. (1985), 'U kolébky slovanských jazyků', *Slavia* 54: 337–45

Ernst, R. (1976), *Die Nordwestslaven und das fränkische Reich: Beobachtungen zur Geschichte ihrer Nachbarschaft und zur Elbe als nordöstlicher Reichsgrenze bis in die Zeit Karl des Großen*, Berlin

Friesinger, H. (ed.) (1971–76), *Studien zur Archäologie der Slawen in Niederösterreich*, 2 vols., Vienna
Friesinger, H. (1976), *Die Slawen in Niederösterreich*, St Pölten
Fritze, W. H. (ed.) (1982), *Frühzeit zwischen Ostsee und Donau: Ausgewählte Beiträge zum geschichtlichen Werden im östlichen Mitteleuropa vom 6. bis zum 13. Jahrhundert*, Berlin
Fusek, G. (1994), *Slovensko vo včasnoslovanskom obdobi*, Nitra
Gavrituchin, I. O. and Oblomskiy, A. M. (1996), *Gaponovskiy klad i ego kulturno-istoricheskiy kontekst*, Moscow
Godowski, K. (1979), *Z badań nad zagadnieniem rozprzestrzenienia Slowian w V–VII w. n.e.*, Cracow
Godowski, K. (1983), 'Zur Frage der Slawensitze vor der grossen Slawenwanderung im 6. Jahrhundert', *Settimane* 30: 257–302
Goehrke, C. (1992), *Frühzeit des Ostslaventums*, Darmstadt
Gojda, M. (1991), *The Ancient Slavs: Settlement and Society*, Edinburgh
Gołąb, Z. (1987), 'Etnogeneza Slowian w świetle językoznawstwa', in G. Labuda and S. Tabaczyński (eds), *Studia nad etnogenezą Slowian i kulturą Europy wczesnośredniowiecznej*, Wrocław, pp. 71–80
Gołąb, Z. (1992), *The Origins of the Slavs: A Linguist's View*, Columbus, OH
Goryunov, E. A. (1981), *Rannie etapy istorii slavyan Dneprovskogo Levoberezhya*, Leningrad
Graebner, M. (1978), 'The Slavs in Byzantine Empire – absorption, semi-autonomy and the limits of Byzantinization', *Byzantinobulgarica* 5: 41–55
Grafenauer, B. (1966), *Die ethnische Gliederung und geschichtliche Rolle der westlichen Südslawen im Mittelalter*, Ljubljana
Grebe, K. (1976), 'Zur frühslawischen Besiedlung des Havelgebietes', *Veröffentlichungen des Museums für Ur- und Frühgeschichte*, Potsdam, 10: 167–204
Hannick, C. (ed.) (1987), *Sprachen und Nationen im Balkanraum: Die historischen Bedingungen der Entstehung der heutigen Nationalsprachen*, Cologne
Henning, J. (1987), *Südosteuropa zwischen Antike und Mittelalter: Archäologische Beiträge zur Landwirtschaft des 1. Jahrtausends u. Z.*, Berlin
Hensel, W. (1965), *Die Slawen im frühen Mittelalter*, Berlin
Hensel, W. (1984), *Skąd przyszli Slowianie?*, Wrocław
Herrmann, J. (1965), *Kultur und Kunst der Slawen in Deutschland vom 7. bis 13. Jh.*, Berlin
Herrmann, J. (1968), *Siedlung, Wirtschaft und gesellschaftliche Verhältnisse der slawischen Stämme zwischen Oder/Neiße und Elbe: Studien auf der Grundlage archäologischen Materials*, Berlin
Herrmann, J. (ed.) (1985), *Die Slawen in Deutschland*, Berlin
Herrmann, J. (ed.) (1986), *Welt der Slawen*, Leipzig
Herrmann, J. (1987), 'Die Verterritorialisierung – ein methodisches und historische Problem slawischer Wanderung, Landnahme und Ethnogenese', in G. Labuda and S. Tabaczyński (eds), *Studia nad etnogenezą Slowian i kultura Europy wczesnośredniowiecznej*, Wrocław, pp. 81–90
Horedt, K. (1987), 'Die Völker Südosteuropas im 6.–8. Jahrhundert. Probleme und Ergebnisse', *Südosteuropa*, pp. 11–26

Justová, J. (1990), *Dolnorakouské Podunaji v raném středověku: Slovanská archeologie k jeho osidleni v 6.–11. stoleti*, Prague

Karayannopoulos, J. (1971), 'Zur Frage der Slawenansiedlungen auf dem Peloponnes', *Revue des Etudes Sud-Est Européennes* 9: 443–60

Karayannopoulos, J. (1989), *Les Slaves en Macédoine: la prétendue interruption des communications entre Constantinople et Thessalonique du 7e au 9e siècles*, Athens

Klanica, Z. (1986), *Počatky slovanského osidleni našich zemi*, Prague

Kobyliński, Z. (1988), *Struktury osadnicze na ziemiach polskich u schyłku starożytności i w początkach wczesnego średniowiecza*, Wrocław

Kobyliński, Z. (1989), 'An ethnic change or a socio-economic one? The 5th and 6th centuries AD in the Polish lands', in S. J. Shennan (ed.), *Archaeological Approaches to Cultural Identity*, London, pp. 303–12

Kobyliński, Z. (1994), 'Early Slavs: are they archaeologically visible?', *META-Medeltidsarkeologisk Tidskrift* 3–4: 13–27

Kobyliński, Z. (1997), 'Settlement structures in Central Europe at the beginning of the Middle Ages', in P. Urbańczyk (ed.), *Origins of Central Europe*, Warsaw, pp. 97–116

Koder, J. (1978), 'Zur Frage der slawischen Siedlungsgebiete im mittelalterlichen Griechenland', *BZ* 71: 315–31

Köhler, R. (1980), 'Frühe slawische Siedlungen in Pommern unter besonderer Berücksichtung der neuen Grabungen in Dziedzice/Deetz', *Offa-Bücher* 37: 177–83

Kolendo, J. (1984), 'Wenetowie w Europie środkowej i wschodniej. Lokalizacja i rzeczywistość historyczna', *Przegląd Historyczny* 75: 637–53

Korošec, P. (1987), 'Die Ethnogenese der Alpslawen durch das Prisma der materiellen Kultur', in G. Labuda and S. Tabaczyńiski (eds.), *Studia nad etnogenezą Słowian i kulturą Europy wczesnośredniowiecznej*, Wrocław, pp. 97–103

Kurnatowska, Z. (1977), *Slowianszczyzna południawa*, Wrocław

Kwilecka, I. (ed.) (1980), *Etnogeneza i topogeneza Slowian*, Warsaw

Labuda, G. (1949), *Pierwsze państwo słowiańskie: Państwo Samona*, Poznań

Labuda, G. (1977), 'Aktualny stan dyskusji nad etnogenezą Slowian w historiografii', *Slavia Antiqua* 24: 1–16

Leciejewicz, L. (1976), *Słowiańszczyzna zachodnia*, Wrocław

Leciejewicz, L. (1989), *Slowianie Zachodni: Z dziejów tworzenia się średniowiecznej Europy*, Wrocław

Lemerłe, P. (1979–81), *Les Plus Anciens Recueils des miracles de Saint Démétrius et la pénétration des Slaves dans les Balkans*, 2 vols., Paris

Lodowski, J. (1980), *Dolny Śląsk na początku wczesnego średniowiecza (VI–X w)*, Wrocław

Losert, H. (1993), 'Die slawische Besiedlung Nordostbayerns aus archäologischer Sicht', in *Vorträge 11: Niederbayerischer Archäologentag*, Deggendorf, pp. 207–70

Lowmiafiski, H. (1963–73), *Początki Polski: Z dziejów Słowian w I tysiącleciu n.e.*, 5 vols., Warsaw

Malingoudis, P. (1981), *Studien zu den slawischen Ortsnamen Griechenlands*, Wiesbaden

Malingoudis, P. (1987), 'Frühe slawische Elemente im Namensgut Griechenland', in B. Hänsel (ed.), *Die Völker Südosteuropas im 6. bis 8. Jahrhundert* (Südosteuropa Jahrbuch 17), Munich, pp. 53–68

Malingoudis, P. (1988), *Slaboi stén mesaioniké Ellada*, Thessalonica

Mańczak, W. (1981), *Praojczyzna Słowian*, Wrocław

Miodowicz, K. (1984), 'Współczesne koncepcje lokalizacji pierwotnych siedzib Słowian. Dane językoznawcze', *Zeszyty Naukowe Uniwersytetu Jagiellońskiego. Prace Etnograficzne* 19: 7–49

Obolensky, D. (1971), *Byzantium and the Slavs*, London

Okulicz, J. (1986), 'Einige Aspekte der Ethnogenese der Balten und Slawen im Lichte archäologischer und sprachwissenschaftlicher Forschungen', *Quaestiones Medii Aevi* 3: 7–34

Ostrogorsky, G. (1974), *Byzanz und die Welt der Slawen*, Darmstadt

Parczewski, M. (1988a), *Najstarsza faza kultury wczesnosłowiańskiej w Polsce*, Cracow

Parczewski, M. (1988b), *Początki kultury wczesnosłowiańskiej w Polsce: Krytyka i datowanie źródeł archeologicznych*, Wrocław

Parczewski, M. (1993), *Die Anfänge der frühslawischen Kultur in Polen*, Vienna

Parczewski, M. (1997), 'Beginnings of the Slavs' culture', in P. Urbańczyk (ed.), *Origins of Central Europe*, Warsaw, pp. 79–90

Penyak, S. I. (1980), *Rannoslovyanske i davnoruske naselennya Zakarpattya VI–XIII st.*, Kiev

Pleinerová, I. (1975), *Březno: vesnice prvních Slovanů v severozapadních Čechách*, Prague

Pleinerová, I. (1986), 'Březno. Experiments with building old Slavic houses and living in them', *Památky Archeologické* 77: 104–76

Pleterski, A. (1990), *Etnogeneza Slovanov*, Ljubljana

Pleterski, A. (1996), 'Modell der Ethnogenese der Slawen auf der Grundlage einiger neuerer Forschungen', in Z. Kurnatowska (ed.), *Słowiańszczyzna w Europie średniowiecznej*, Wrocław, 1, pp. 19–37

Popowska-Taborska, H. (1991), *Wczesne dzieje Słowian w świetle ich języka*, Wrocław

Popowska-Taborska, H. (1997), 'The Slavs in the Early Middle Ages from the viewpoint of contemporary linguistics', in P. Urbańczyk (ed.), *Origins of Central Europe*, Warsaw, pp. 91–6

Pritsak, O. (1983), 'The Slavs and the Avars', *Settimane* 30.1: 353–432

Rafalovich, I. A. (1972), *Slavyane VI–IX vekov v Moldavii*, Kishinev

Rusanova, I. P. (1976), *Slavyanskie drevnosti VI–VII vv.*, Moscow

Rusanova, I. P. and Timoshchuk, B. A. (1984), *Kodyn – slavyanskie poseleniya V–VIII vv. na r. Prut*, Moscow

Rusu, M. (1971), 'Zu den Kulturbeziehungen zwischen den Slawen und der romanischen Bevölkerung Siebenbürgens (6.–10. Jh.)', *Apulum* 9: 713–30

Schuster-Šewc, H. (1987), 'Zu den ethnischen und linguistischen Grundlagen der westslawischen Stammesgruppe der Sorben/Serben', in G. Labuda and S. Tabaczyński (eds.), *Studia nad etnogenezą Słowian i kulturą Europy wczesnośredniowiecznej*, Wrocław, pp. 153–9

Sedov, V. V. (1982), *Vostochnye slavyane v VI–XIII vv.*, Moscow

Sedov, V. V. (1987), 'Origine de la branche du nord des Slaves orientaux', in G. Labuda and S. Tabaczyński (eds.), *Studia nad etnogenezą Słowian i kulturą Europy wczesnośredniowiecznej*, Wrocław, pp. 161–5

Sedov, V. V. (1994), *Slavyane v drevnosti*, Moscow

Sedov, V. V. (1995), *Slavyane v rannem srednevekove*, Moscow

Shevelov, G. Y. (1964), *A Prehistory of Slavic: The Historical Phonology of Common Slavic*, Heidelberg

Slupecki, L. (1994), *Slavonic Pagan Sanctuaries*, Warsaw

Strzelczyk, J. (1976), *Słowianie i Germanie w Niemczech środkowych we wczesnym średniowieczu*, Poznań

Strzelczyk, J. (ed.) (1981), *Słowiańszczyzna Połabska między Niemcami a Polską*, Poznań

Strzelczyk, J. (1988), 'Slavic and Germanic peoples in Antiquity and the Early Middle Ages', *Polish Western Affairs* 2: 163–82

Swoboda, W. (1962), 'Powstanie państwa bułgarskiego w Dolnej Mezji – Słowianie federaci czy trybutariusze Protobułgarów', *Slavia Occidentalis* 22: 49–66

Swoboda, W. (1971), 'O charakterze państwa bulgarskiego do połowy IX w. w świetle jego stosunków z sąsiednimi plemionami słowiańskimi', *Slavia Antiqua* 18: 83–103

Szekély, Z. (1970), 'Die frühesten slawischen Siedlungen in Siebenbürgen', *Slavia Antiqua* 17: 125–36

Szymański, W. (1973), *Słowiańszczyzna wschodnia*, Wrocław

Szymański, W. (1985), 'Ziemie na północ od Karpat a kaganat awarski', *Prace i Materiały Muzeum Archeologicznego i Etnograficznego w Łodzi, Seria Archeologiczna* 29: 239–60

Terpilovskiy, R. V. (1984), *Rannie slavyane Podesenya III–V vv.*, Kiev

Terpilovskiy, R. V. and Abashina, N. S. (1992), *Pamyatniki kievskoy kultury*, Kiev

Timoshchuk, B. A. (1990), *Vostochnoslavyanskaya obshchina VI–X vv. n. e.*, Moscow

Tolochko, P. P. (ed.) (1990), *Slavyane i Rus*, Kiev

Udolph, J. (1987), 'Kammen die Slawen aus Pannonien?', in G. Labuda and S. Tabaczyński (eds.), *Studia nad etnogenezą Słowian i kulturą Europy wczesnośredniowiecznej*, Wrocław, pp. 167–73

Váňa, Z. (1980), 'Poznámky k etnogenezi a diferenciaci Slovanů z hledsika poznatků archeologie a jazykovědi', *Památky Archeologické* 71: 225–37

Váňa, Z. (1983), *The World of the Ancient Slavs*, London

Vasmer, M. (1941), *Die Slawen in Griechenland*, Berlin

Vlasto, A. P. (1970), *The Entry of the Slavs into Christendom*, Cambridge

Vyzharova, Z. N. (1965), *Slavianski i slavianob uł garski selishta v b uł lgarskite zemi ot kraia na VI–XI vek*, Sofia

Vyzharova, Z. N. (1976), *Slaviani i Prabułlgari po danni na nekropolite ot VI–XI v. na teritoriiata na Bułlgariia*, Sofia

Waldmüller, L. (1976), *Die ersten Begegnungen der Slawen mit dem Christentum und den christlichen Völkern vom 6. bis 8. Jahrhundert: Die Slawen zwischen Byzanz und Abendland*, Amsterdam

Weithmann, M. W. (1978), *Die slawische Bevölkerung auf der griechischen Halbinsel: Ein Beitrag zur historischen Ethnographie Südosteuropas*, Munich

Wenskus, R. (1967), 'Die slawischen Stämme in Böhmen als ethnische Einheiten' in F. Graus and H. Ludat (eds.), *Siedlung und Verfassung Böhmens in der Frühzeit*, Wiesbaden, pp. 32–41

Wolfram, H. and Daim, F. (eds.) (1980), *Die Völker an der mittleren und unteren Donau im 5. und 6. Jahrhundert*, Vienna

Zeman, J. (1976), 'Nejstarši slovanské osídleni Čech', *Památky Archeologické* 67: 115–235

Zeman, J. (1979), 'K problematice časně slavanské kultury ve střední Evropě, *Památky Archeologické* 70: 113–30

20 THE JEWS IN EUROPE

Adler, M. N. (1907), *The Itinerary of Benjamin of Tudela*, London

Agus, I. (1965), *Urban Civilization in Pre-Crusade Europe*, 2 vols., New York

Agus, I. (1966), 'Rabbinic scholarship in northern Europe', in Roth (1966b), pp. 189–209

Agus, I. (1969), *The Heroic Age of Franco-German Jewry: The Jews of Germany and France of the 10th and 11th Centuries, the Pioneers and Builders of Town-Life, Town-Government and Institutions*, New York

Albert, B. S. (1990), 'Isidore of Seville; his attitude towards Judaism and his impact on early medieval canon law', *Jewish Quarterly Review* 80: 207–20

Albert, B. S. (1996), '*Adversus Iudaeos* in the Carolingian Empire', in O. Limor and G. Stroumsa (eds.), *Contra Iudaeos: Ancient and Medieval Polemics between Christians and Jews*, Tübingen, pp. 119–42

Ankori, Z. (1959), *Karaites in Byzantium: The Formative Years, 970–1100*, New York and Jerusalem

Argenti, P. (1966), 'The Jewish community in Chios during the 11th century', in P. Wirth (ed.), *Polychronion: Festschrift Franz Dölger zum 75 Geburtstag*, Heidelberg, pp. 39–68

Aronius, J. (ed.) (1902), *Regesten zur Geschichte der Juden im fränkischen und deutschen Reich bis zum Jahre 1273*, Berlin

Ashtor, E. (1964), 'Documentos españoles de la Genizah', *Sefarad* 24: 41–80

Ashtor, E. (1973), *The Jews of Moslem Spain*, 1, Philadelphia

Assis, Y. T. (1995), 'The Judeo-Arabic tradition in Christian Spain', in D. Frank (ed.), *The Jews of Medieval Islam: Community, Society, and Identity*, Leiden, pp. 111–24

Bachrach, B. (1977), *Early Medieval Jewish Policy in Western Europe*, Minneapolis

Baer, F. (1929), *Die Juden im christlichen Spanien. Erster Teil. Urkunden und Regesten*, Berlin

Bar-Ilan University (2002), *The Responsa Project.* Version 10+, CD-Rom, Ramat Gan

Bautier, R. H. (1991), 'L'origine des populations juives de la France médiévale, constatations et hypothèse de recherche', in Xavier Barrai i Altet *et al.* (eds.), *La Catalogne et la France méridionale autour de l'an mil*, Barcelona, pp. 306–16

Beinart, H. (1992), 'The Jews in Castile', in Beinart (ed.), *Moreshet Sepharad: The Sephardi Legacy*, Jerusalem, 1, pp. 11–43

Ben-Sasson, M. (1991), *The Jews of Sicily 825-1068: Documents and Sources*, Jerusalem (Hebrew)

Blumenkranz, B. (1949), 'Die Juden als Zeugen der Kirche', *Theologische Zeitschrift* 5: 396–8

Blumenkranz, B. (1960), *Juifs et Chrétiens dans le monde occidental 430–1096*, Paris

Blumenkranz, B. (1961), 'Die christlich-jüdische Missionskonkurrenz (3.–6. Jh.)', *Klio* 39: 227–33

Blumenkranz, B. (1963), *Les Auteurs chrétiens latins du moyen âge sur les Juifs et le Judaïsme*, Paris

Blumenkranz, B. (1965), '*Iudaeorum convivia* à propos du concile de Vannes (465, c. 12)', in *Etudes d'histoire du droit canonique dédiées à Gabriel Le Bras*, II, Paris, pp. 1055–8

Blumenkranz, B. (1969), 'Les premiers implantations des Juifs en France', *Académie des Inscriptions et Belles-Lettres, Comptes Rendus des Séances*, pp. 162–74

Blumenkranz, B. (1974), 'Premiers témoignages épigraphiques sur les Juifs en France', in *Salo Wittmayer Baron Jubilee Volume*, 1, Jerusalem, pp. 229–35

Blumenkranz, B. (1989), 'Cultivateurs et vignerons juifs en Bourgogne du IXe au XIe siècles', in Blumenkranz, *Juifs en France: écrits dispersés*, Paris, pp. 89–99

Bonfil, R. (1983), 'Tra due mondi: prospettive di ricerca sulla storia culturale degli ebrei nell'Italia meridionale nell'alto medioevo', in *Italia Judaica*, 1: *Atti del I Convegno Internazionale*, Rome, pp. 135–58

Bonfil, R. (1994a), 'Can medieval storytelling help understanding Midrash?', in M. Fishbane (ed.), *The Midrashic Imagination: Jewish Exegesis, Thought, and History*, Albany, NY, pp. 228–54

Bonfil, R. (1994b), 'Cultural and religious traditions in ninth-century French Jewry', *Binah* 3: 1–17

Bonfil, R. (1996), *Tra due mondi: cultura ebraica e cultura cristiana nel medioevo*, Naples

Bowman, S. (1993), 'Sefer Yosippon: history and Midrash', in M. Fishbane (ed.), *The Midrashic Imagination: Jewish Exegesis, Thought, and History*, Albany, NY, pp. 280–94

Bresc, H. (1998), 'L'artisanat juif sicilien; culture et technique', in N. Bucaria (ed.), *Gli Ebrei in Sicilia dal tardoantico al medioevo*, Palermo, pp. 65–87

Brody, R. (1998), *The Geonim of Babylonia and the Shaping of Medieval Jewish Culture*, New Haven, CT

Cantera Burgos, F. (1966), 'Christian Spain', in Roth (1966b), pp. 357–81

Chazan, R. (1970), 'The Persecution of 992', *Revue des Etudes Juives* 129: 217–21

Chazan, R. (1970/1), '1007–1012: initial crisis for northern European Jewry', *Proceedings of the American Academy for Jewish Research* 38–9: 101–17

Citarella, A. (1971), 'A puzzling question concerning the relations between the Jewish communities of Christian Europe and those represented in the Geniza documents', *Journal of the American Oriental Society* 91: 390–7

Cohen, G. D. (1960/61), 'The story of the four captives', *Proceedings of the American Academy of Jewish Research* 29: 55–131

Cohen, J. (1999), *Living Letters of the Law: Ideas of the Jew in Medieval Christianity*, Berkeley, CA

Cohen, M. (1994), *Under Crescent and Cross: The Jews in the Middle Ages*, Princeton, NJ

Colafemmina, C. (1980), 'Insediamenti e condizioni degli Ebrei nell'Italia meridionale e insulare', *Settimane* 26: 197–227

Colorni, V. (1980), 'Gli Ebrei nei territori Italiani a nord di Roma dal 568 agli inizi del secolo XIII', *Settimane* 26: 241–307

Dagron, G. and Déroche, V. (1998), 'Juifs et Chrétiens dans l'Orient du VIIe siècle', *Travaux et Mémoires du Centre de Recherche d'Histoire et Civilisation de Byzance* 11: 17–273

De Lange, N. (1996), *Greek Jewish Texts from the Cairo Genizah*, Tübingen

Devroey, J.-P. (2000), 'La participation des Juifs au commerce dans le monde franc (VIe–Xe siècles)', in A. Dierkens and J. M. Sansterre (eds.), *Voyages et voyageurs à Byzance et en Occident du VIe au XIe siècle*, Geneva, pp. 339–74

Dunlop, D. M. (1966), 'The Khazars', in Roth (1966b), pp. 325–56

Eidelberg, S. (1953), '*Maarufia* in Rabbenu Gershom's Responsa', *Historia Judaica* 15: 59–66

Ettinger, S. (1966), 'Kievan Russia', in Roth (1966b), pp. 319–24

Gil, M. (1974), 'The Radhanite merchants and the land of Radhan', *JESHO* 17: 299–328

Gil, M. (1993), 'Between two worlds. The relations between Babylonia and the communities of Europe in the Gaonic Period', in *Festschrift S. Simonsohn*, Tel Aviv, Hebrew pagination (Hebrew)

Goffart, W. (1985), 'The conversions of Bishop Avitus and similar passages in Gregory of Tours', in J. Neusner and E. R. Frerichs (eds.), *'To See Ourselves as Others See Us': Christians, Jews, 'Others' in Late Antiquity*, Chico, CA, pp. 473–97

Goitein, S. (1967), *A Mediterranean Society: The Jewish Communities of the Arab World as Portrayed in the Documents of the Cairo Geniza*, I, Berkeley, CA

Golb, N. (1987), *Jewish Proselytism – A Phenomenon in the Religious History of Early Medieval Europe*, Cincinatti

Golb, N. (1998), *The Jews in Medieval Normandy*, Cambridge

González-Salinero, R. (1999), 'Catholic anti-Judaism in Visigothic Spain', in A. Ferreiro (ed.), *The Visigoths: Studies in Culture and Society*, Leiden, pp. 123–50

Goodman, M. (1994), *Mission and Conversion: Proselytising in the Religious History of the Roman Empire*, Oxford and New York

Grabois, A. (1987/1993), *Les Sources hébraïques médiévales*, I: *Chroniques, lettres et Responsa*; II, *Les Commentaires exégétiques*, Turnhout

Grabois, A. (1997), 'Le "roi juif" de Narbonne', *Annales du Midi* 218: 165–88

Gross, H. (1897/1969), *Gallia Judaica: dictionnaire géographique de la France d'après les sources rabbiniques; avec un supplément bibliographique, additions et corrections par S. Schwarzfuchs*, Paris and Amsterdam

Grossman, A. (1975), 'The migration of the Kalonymos family from Italy to Germany', *Zion* 40: 154–85 (Hebrew)

Grossman, A. (1980), 'Family lineage and its place in early Ashkenazic Jewish society', in E. Etkes and Y. Salmon (eds.), *Studies in the History of Jewish Society in the Middle Ages and in the Modern Period: Presented to Prof. Jacob Katz*, Jerusalem, Hebrew pagination (Hebrew)

Grossman, A. (1982), 'The migration of Jews to and settlement in Germany in the 9th–11th century', in A. Shinan (ed.), *Emigration and Settlement in Jewish and General History*, Jerusalem, pp. 109–28 (Hebrew)

Grossman, A. (1988a), *The Early Sages of Ashkenaz: Their Lives, Leadership and Works (900–1096)*, Jerusalem, 2nd edn (Hebrew)

Grossman, A. (1988b), 'The historical background to the ordinances on family affairs attributed to Rabbenu Gershom Me'or ha-Golah ("The Light of the Exile")', in A. Rapoport-Albert and S. J. Zipperstein (eds.), *Jewish History: Essays in Honour of Chaim Abramsky*, London, pp. 3–23

Grossman, A. (1995), *The Early Sages of France: Their Lives, Leadership and Works*, Jerusalem (Hebrew)

Heil, J. (1998a), *Kompilation oder Konstruktion? Die Juden in den Pauluskommentaren des 9. Jahrhunderts*, Hanover

Heil, J. (1998b), 'Agobard, Amolo, das Kirchengut und die Juden von Lyon', *Francia* 25: 39–76

Jacoby, D. (1993), 'Les Juifs de Byzance, une communauté marginalisée', in C. A. Maltezou (ed.), *Hai Perithoriakoi sto Byzantio. Marginality in Byzantium*, Athens, pp. 103–54; repr. in Jacoby, *Byzantium, Latin Romania and the Mediterranean*, Aldershot, 2001, no. III

Jacoby, D. (1995), 'The Jews of Constantinople and their demographic hinterland', in C. Mango and G. Dagron (eds.), *Constantinople and Its Hinterland*, Aldershot, pp. 221–32; repr. in Jacoby, *Byzantium, Latin Romania and the Mediterranean*, Aldershot, 2001, no. IV

Jacoby, D. (2001), 'The Jews and the silk industry of Constantinople', in Jacoby, *Byzantium, Latin Romania and the Mediterranean*, Aldershot, no. IX

Katz, J. (1958), 'Even though he sinned he remains an Israelite', *Tarbiz* 27: 203–17 (Hebrew)

Katz, S. (1937), *The Jews in the Visigothic and Frankish Kingdoms of Spain and Gaul*, Cambridge, MA

Klar, B. (1944/74), *Megillat Ahimaaz: The Chronicle of Ahimaaz, with a Collection of Poems from Byzantine Southern Italy and Additions*, Jerusalem (Hebrew)

Lapp, E. C. (1993), 'Jewish archaeological evidence from the Roman Rhineland', *Journal of Jewish Studies* 44: 70–82

Latouche, R. (1966), 'Le Bourg des Juifs (Hebraeorum Burgus) de Vienne (Isère) au Xe siècle', in Latouche, *Etudes médiévales: Le haut moyen âge, la France de l'Ouest, des Pyrénées aux Alpes*, Paris, pp. 194–6

Leon, H. J. (1953/4), 'The Jews of Venusia', *Jewish Quarterly Review* 44: 267–84

Linder, A. (1978), 'Christlich-jüdische Konfrontation im kirchlichen Frühmittelalter', in K. Schäferdiek (ed.), *Kirchengeschichte als Missionsgeschichte*, II: *Die Kirche des frühen Mittelalters*, Munich, pp. 397–441

Linder, A. (1987), *The Jews in Roman Imperial Legislation*, Detroit and Jerusalem

Linder, A. (1997), *The Jews in the Legal Sources of the Early Middle Ages*, Detroit and Jerusalem

Lotter, F. (1999), 'Die Juden und die städtische Kontinuität von der Spätantike zum Mittelalter im lateinischen Westen', in F. Mayrhofer and F. Oppl (eds.), *Juden in der Stadt*, Linz, pp. 21–79

Lotter, F. (2001), 'Totale Finsternis über "Dunklen Jahrhunderten". Zum Methodenverständnis von Michael Toch und seinen Folgen', *Aschkenas* 11: 215–32

McCormick, M. (2002), *Origins of the European Economy: Communications and Commerce AD 300–900*, Cambridge

Máillo Salgado, F. (1993), 'The city of Lucena in Arab sources', *Mediterranean Historical Review* 8: 149–65

Mann, J. (1920), *The Jews in Egypt and in Palestine under the Fatimid Caliphs: A Contribution to Their Political and Communal History Based Chiefly on Genizah Material Hitherto Unpublished*, 2 vols., London

Mann, J. (1931), *Texts and Studies in Jewish History and Literature*, 2 vols., Cincinnati

Mann, J. (1973), *The Responsa of the Babylonian Geonim as a Source of Jewish History*, New York

Marcus, I. (1993), 'History, story and collective memory: narrativity in early Ashkenazic culture', in M. Fishbane (ed.), *The Midrashic Imagination: Jewish Exegesis, Thought, and History*, Albany, pp. 255–79

Marcus, I. (1996), *Rituals of Childhood: Jewish Acculturation in Medieval Europe*, New Haven, CT

Milano, A. (1954), 'Vicende economiche degli ebrei nell'Italia meridionale ed insulare durante il Medioevo', *La Rassegna Mensile di Israel* 20: 76–89, 110–22, 155–74, 217–22, 276–81, 322–31, 372–84

Mutius, H.-G. von (1984), *Rechtsentscheide rheinischer Rabbinen vor dem ersten Kreuzzug*, 2 vols., Frankfurt am Main

Mutius, H.-G. von (1986), *Rechtsentscheide Raschis aus Troyes (1040–1105)*, Frankfurt am Main

Mutius, H.-G. von (1990), *Rechtsentscheide jüdischer Gesetzeslehrer aus dem maurischen Cordoba*, Frankfurt am Main

Mutius, H.-G. von (1994), *Jüdische Urkundenformulare aus Marseille in babylonisch-aramäischer Sprache*, Frankfurt am Main

Mutius, H.-G. von (1996), *Jüdische Urkundenformulare aus Barcelona*, Frankfurt am Main

Mutius, H.-G. von (1997), *Jüdische Urkundenformulare aus dem muslimischen Spanien*, Frankfurt am Main

Nelson, B. and Starr, J. (1939–44), 'The legend of the divine surety and the Jewish moneylender', *Annuaire de l'Institut de Philologie et d'Histoire Orientales et Slaves* 7: 289–338

Neubauer A. and Stern, M. (eds.) (1982), *Hebräische Berichte über die Judenverfolgungen während der Kreuzzüge*, Berlin

Noy, D. (1993), *Jewish Inscriptions of Western Europe*, I: *Italy, Spain and Gaul*, Cambridge

Noy, D. (1995), *Jewish Inscriptions of Western Europe*, II: *The City of Rome*, Cambridge

Patschovsky, A. (1993), 'Das Rechtsverhältnis der Juden zum deutschen König (9.–14. Jahrhundert). Ein europäischer Vergleich', *ZRG GA* 110: 331–71

Pellat, C. (1993), 'al-Radhaniya', in *Encyclopedia of Islam*, new edn, VIII, Leiden, cols. 363–7

Rabinowitz, L. (1945), *The Herem Hayyishub: A Contribution to the Medieval Economic History of the Jews*, London

Régné, J. (1912/81), *Etude sur la condition des juifs de Narbonne du Ve au XIVe siècle*, Narbonne and Marseilles

Rivlin, J. (1994), *Bills and Contracts from Lucena (1020–1025 C.E.)*, Ramat Gan (Hebrew)

Romano, D. (1991), 'Les Juifs de Catalogne aux alentours de l'an mil', in Xavier Barrai i Altet *et al.* (eds.), *La Catalogne et la France méridionale autour de l'an mil*, Barcelona, pp. 317–31

Roth, C. (1966a), 'Italy', in Roth (1966b), pp. 100–21

Roth, C. (ed.) (1966b), *The World History of the Jewish People*, 2nd series, II: *The Dark Ages*, Tel Aviv

Roth, N. (1976), 'The Jews and the Muslim conquest of Spain', *Jewish Social Studies* 38: 145–58

Roth, N. (1994), *Jews, Visigoths and Muslims in Medieval Spain: Cooperation and Conflict*, Leiden
Rutgers, L. V. (1995a), *The Jews in Late Ancient Rome: Evidence of Cultural Interaction in the Roman Diaspora*, Leiden
Rutgers, L. V. (1995b), 'Attitudes to Judaism in the Greco-Roman period; reflections on Feldman's "Jew and Gentile in the Ancient World"', *Jewish Quarterly Review* 85: 361–95
Salfeld, S. (ed.) (1898), *Das Martyrologium des nürnberger Memorbuches*, Berlin
Salzman, M. (1924), *The Chronicle of Ahimaíaz*, New York
Sapir Abulafia, A. (1985), 'Invectives against Christianity in the Hebrew Chronicles of the First Crusade', in P. Edbury (ed.), *Crusade and Settlement*, Cardiff, pp. 66–72
Scheiber, A. (1966), 'Hungary', in Roth (1966b), pp. 313–18
Schirmann, J. (1966), 'The beginning of Hebrew poetry in Italy and northern Europe. 1. Italy', in Roth (1966b), pp. 249–66
Schreckenberg, H. (1995), *Die christlichen Adversus-Judaeos-Texte und ihr literarisches und historisches Umfeld (1.–11. Jh.)*, 3rd edn, Frankfurt am Main
Schwarzfuchs, S. (1980), 'L'opposition *Tsarfat*–Provence: la formation du Judaïsme du Nord de la France', in G. Nahon and C. Touati (eds.), *Hommage à Georges Vajda*, Louvain, pp. 135–50
Sharf, A. (1976), *The Universe of Shabbetai Donnolo*, New York
Simonsohn, S. (1974), 'The Hebrew revival among early medieval European Jews', in *Salo Wittmayer Baron Jubilee Volume*, II, Jerusalem, pp. 831–58
Simonsohn, S. (1997), *The Jews in Sicily*, Leiden
Solin, H. (1983), 'Juden und Syrer in der römischen Welt', in W. Haase (ed.), *Aufstieg und Niedergang der römischen Welt*, II/29, Berlin and New York, pp. 587–789
Starr, J. (1939), *The Jews in the Byzantine Empire, 641–1204*, Athens
Stemberger, G. (1993), 'Zwangstaufen von Juden im 4. bis 7. Jahrhundert; Mythos oder Wirklichkeit?', in C. Thoma *et al.* (eds.), *Judentum – Ausblicke und Einsichten: Festgabe für Kurt Schubert*, Frankfurt am Main, pp. 81–114
Stow, K. R. (1984), *The '1007 Anonymous' and Papal Sovereignty*, Cincinnati
Ta-Shma, I. M. (2001), *Rabbi Moses Hadarshan and the Apocryphal Literature* (Studies in Jewish History and Literature, Touro Graduate School of Jewish Studies), Jerusalem
Toaff, A. (1996), 'Gli Ebrei a Roma', in C. Vivanti (ed.), *Storia d'Italia: Gli Ebrei in Italia* (Annali 11), Turin, pp. 121–52
Toch, M. (1998a), *Die Juden im mittelalterlichen Reich*, Munich
Toch, M. (1998b), 'Wirtschaft und Verfolgung, die Bedeutung der Ökonomie für die Kreuzzugspogrome des 11. und 12. Jahrhunderts. Mit einem Anhang zum Sklavenhandel der Juden', in A. Haverkamp (ed.), *Juden und Christen zur Zeit der Kreuzzüge*, Sigmaringen, pp. 253–85
Toch, M. (1999), 'The European Jews of the early Middle Ages, slave-traders?', *Zion* 64: 39–63, v–vii (Hebrew, English summary)
Toch, M. (2000a), 'Jews and commerce: modern fancies and medieval realities', in S. Cavaciocchi (ed.), *Il ruolo economico delle minoranze in Europa. Secc. XIII–XVIII* (Atti della XXXI Settimana di Studi, Istituto Francesco Datini, Prato), Florence, pp. 43–58
Toch, M. (2000b), 'The economic activity of German Jews in the 10th–12th centuries: between historiography and history', in Y. T. Assis, O. Limor, J. Cohen and M.

Toch (eds.), *Facing the Cross: The Persecutions of 1096 in History and Historiography*, Jerusalem, pp. 32–54 (Hebrew)

Toch, M. (2001a), *'Dunkle Jahrhunderte': Gab es ein jüdisches Frühmittelalter?* (Kleine Schriften des Arye-Maimon Instituts 4), Trier

Toch, M. (2001b), 'Mehr Licht: Eine Entgegnung zu Friedrich Lotter', *Aschkenas* 11: 465–87

Toch, M. (2001c), 'Kultur des Mittelalters, jüdische Kulturen des Mittelalters. Das Problem aus der Sicht der Wirtschaftsgeschichte', in M. Borgolte (ed.), *Unaufhebbare Pluralität der Kulturen? Zur Dekonstruktion und Konstruktion des mittelalterlichen Europa*, Munich, pp. 7–17

Verhulst, A. (1970), 'Der Handel im Merowingerreich: Gesamtdarstellung nach schriftlichen Quellen', *Antikvariskt Arkiv* 39: 2–54

Verhulst, A. (1995), 'Economic organisation', in R. McKitterick (ed.), *The New Cambridge Medieval History*, II, Cambridge, pp. 481–509

Yuval, I. J. (1999), 'Passover in the Middle Ages', in P. F. Bradshaw and L. A. Hoffman (eds.), *Passover and Easter: Origin and History to Modern Times*, Notre Dame, IN, pp. 127–60

Yuval, I. J. (2000), *'Two Nations in Your Womb': Perceptions of Jews and Christians*, Tel Aviv (Hebrew, English trans. in preparation)

Zimmels, H. J. (1966), 'Scholars and scholarship in Byzantium and Italy', in Roth (1966b), pp. 175–88

Zuckerman, A. J. (1972), *A Jewish Princedom in Feudal France, 768–900*, London and New York

21 KINGS AND KINGSHIP

Alcock, L. (1988), 'Pictish studies, present and future', in A. Small (ed.), *The Picts: A New Look at Old Problems*, Dundee, pp. 80–92

Almagro, M. *et al.* (1975), *Ou'sayr 'Amra: Residencia y Baños Omeyas en el Desierto de Jordania*, Madrid

Anderson, M. O. (1973), *Kings and Kingship in Early Scotland*, Edinburgh

Barnwell, P. S. (1992), *Emperors, Prefects and Kings: The Roman West, 395–565*, London

Bassett, S. (ed.) (1989), *The Origins of Anglo-Saxon Kingdoms* (Studies in the Early History of Britain), Leicester

Binchy, D. A. (1970), *Celtic and Anglo-Saxon Kingship*, Oxford

Binchy, D. A. (1971), 'An archaic legal poem', *Celtica* 9: 152–68

Bognetti, G. P. (1939), 'Longobardi e Romani', repr. in his *L'Età Longobardi*, Milan, pp. 83–141

Bowman, A. and Woolf, G. (eds.) (1994), *Literacy and Power in the Ancient World*, Cambridge

Breckenridge, J. D. (1959), *The Numismatic Iconography of Justinian* II (Numismatic Notes and Monographs 144), New York

Bréhier, L. (1906), 'L'origine des titres impériaux à Byzance', *BZ* 15: 161–78

Brooks, N. (1984), *The Early History of the Church of Canterbury* (Studies in the Early History of Britain), Leicester

Brown, P. R. L. (1993), *Power and Persuasion in Late Antiquity: Towards a Christian Empire*, Madison, WI

Browning, R. (1975), *Byzantium and Bulgaria: A Comparative Study across the Early Medieval Frontier*, London

Bruce Mitford, R. *et al.* (eds.) (1975–83), *The Sutton Hoo Ship Burial*, London

Brühl, C.-R. (1968), *Fodrum, Gistum, Servitium Regis: Studien zu den wirtschaftlichen Grundlagen des Königtums im Frankenreich und in den frankischen Nachfolgestaaten Deutschland, Frankreich und Italien, vom 6. bis zur Mitte des 14. Jahrhunderts* (Kölner Historische Abhandlungen 14), Cologne

Byrne, F. J. (1973), *Irish Kings and High Kings*, London

Byrne, F. J. (1974), '"Senchas": the nature of the Gaelic historical tradition', in J. G. Barry (ed.), *Papers Read before the Irish Conference of Historians (Cork, 1971)* (Historical Studies 9), Belfast, pp. 137–59

Campbell, J. (ed.) (1982), *The Anglo-Saxons*, London

Campbell, J. (1992), 'The impact of the Sutton Hoo discovery on Anglo-Saxon history', in C. B. Kendall and P. S. Wells (eds.), *Voyage to the Other World* (Medieval Studies at Minnesota), Minneapolis, pp. 79–101

Campbell, J. B. (1984), *The Emperor and the Roman Army 31 BC–AD 235*, Oxford

Cameron, A. (1976), *Circus Factions: Blues and Greens at Rome and Byzantium*, Oxford

Cameron, Av. (1976), *In laudem Iustini Augusti Minoris*, London

Cameron, Av. (1979), 'The Virgin's robe: an episode in the history of early seventh-century Constantinople', *Byzantion* 49: 42–56

Cameron, Av. (1985), *Procopius and the Sixth Century*, London

Carver, M. O. H. (ed.) (1992), *The Age of Sutton Hoo: The Seventh Century in North-Western Europe*, Woodbridge

Charles-Edwards, T. M. (1986), '*Crith Gablach* and the law of status', *Peritia* 5: 53–73

Charles-Edwards, T. M. (1989), 'Early medieval kingships in the British Isles', in Bassett (1989), pp. 28–39

Charles-Edwards, T. M. (forthcoming), 'A contract between king and people in early medieval Ireland? *Crith Gablach* on kingship'

Chrysos, E. (1978), 'The title *basileus* in early Byzantine international relations', *DOP* 32: 29–75

Chrysos, E. (1979), 'Konzilspräsident und Konzilsvorstand. Zur Frage des Vorsitzes in den Konzilien der byzantinischen Reichskirche', *Annuarium Historiae Conciliorum* 11(i): 1–17

Claude, D. (1971), *Adel, Kirche und Königtum im Westgotenreich* (VuF Sonderband 8), Constance

Clover, F. M. (1986), 'Felix Karthago', *DOP* 40: 1–16

Collinet, E. (1925), *Histoire de l' École de Droit de Beyrouth* (Études historiques sur le droit de Justinien 2), Paris

Collins, R. (1983a), *Early Medieval Spain: Unity in Diversity 400–1000*, London

Collins, R. (1983b), 'Theodebert I, Rex Magnus Francorum' in Wormald *et al.* (1983), pp. 7–33

Collins, R. (1985), '"*Sicut lex Gothorum continet*" in law and charters in ninth- and tenth-century León and Catalonia', *EHR* 100: 489–512

Crone, P. and Hinds, M. (1986), *God's Caliph: Religious Authority in the First Centuries of Islam*, Cambridge

Davies, W. (1978), *An Early Welsh Microcosm: Studies in the Llandaff Charters* (Royal Historical Society), London
Davies, W. (1993), 'Celtic kingships in the early Middle Ages', in A. J. Duggan (ed.), *Kings and Kingship in Medieval Europe* (King's College London Medieval Studies 10), pp. 101–24
Davies, W. and Fouracre, P. (eds.) (1986), *The Settlement of Disputes in Early Medieval Europe*, Cambridge
De Vries, J. (1956), 'Das Königtum bei den Germanen', *Saeculum* 7: 289–309
Dillon, M. (1946), *The Cycles of the Kings*, Oxford
Dumville, D. N. (1976), 'The Anglian collection of royal genealogies and regnal lists', *Anglo-Saxon England* 5: 23–50
Dumville, D. N. (1977), 'Kingship, genealogies and regnal lists', in Sawyer and Wood (1977), pp. 72–104
Ebling, H. (1974), *Prosopographie der Amtsträger des Merowingerreiches: von Chlothar II (613) bis Karl Martell (714)* (Beihefte der Francia 2), Munich
Ellis Davidson, H. (1988), *Myths and Symbols in Pagan Europe: Early Scandinavian and Celtic Religions*, Manchester
Engel, J. (ed.) (1970), *Großer historischer Weltatlas*, Munich
Ensslin, W. (1967), 'The government and administration of the Byzantine Empire', in J. M. Hussey (ed.), *The Cambridge Medieval History*, IV, ii: *The Byzantine Empire*, Cambridge, pp. 1–54
Eogan, G. and Byrne, F. J. (1968), 'Excavations at Knowth, Co. Meath 1962–5', *PRIA* 66, Section C: 299–400
Erdmann, C. (1935), *The Origin of the Idea of Crusade*, trans. M. W. Baldwin and W. Goffart (1977), Princeton, NJ
Ewig, E. (1956), 'Zum christlichen Königsgedanken im Frühmittelalter', in Mayer (1956), pp. 7–73
Ewig, E. (1963), 'Residence et capitale pendant le haut moyen âge', *Revue Historique* 230: 25–72
Filmer-Sankey, W. (1996), 'The "Roman Emperor" in the Sutton Hoo ship burial', *Journal of the British Archaeological Association* 149: 1–9
Finsen, H. (1962), *Domus Flavia sur le Palatin: Aula Regia Basilica* (Analecta Romana Instituti Danici 2nd supplement), Copenhagen
Förstemann, E. (1900), *Altdeutsches Namenbuch*, I: *Personennamen*, 2nd edn, Bonn
Fouracre, P. (1986), '"Placita" and the settlement of disputes in later Merovingian Francia', in Davies and Fouracre (1986), pp. 23–43
Ganz, D. (1983), 'Bureaucratic shorthand and Merovingian learning', in Wormald *et al.* (1983), pp. 58–75
García Moreno, L. (1974), *Prosografía del reino visigodo de Toledo* (Acta Salamanticensia, Filosofía y Letras 77), Salamanca
Gerberding, R. (1987), *The Rise of the Carolingians and the* 'Liber Historiae Francorum', Oxford
Gerriets, M. (1988), 'The king as judge in early Ireland', *Celtica* 20: 29–52
Gibb, H. A. R. (1955), 'The fiscal rescript of Umar II', *Arabica* 2: 1–16
Gibb, H. A. R. (1958), 'Arab–Byzantine relations under the Umayyad Caliphate', *DOP* 12: 219–33

Goffart, W. (1980), *Barbarians and Romans, A.D. 418–584: The Techniques of Accommodation*, Princeton, NJ

Mordek, H. (1994), 'Die Hedenen als politische Kraft im Austrasischen Frankenreich', in J. Jarnut *et al.* (eds.), *Karl Martell in seiner Zeit* (Beihefte der Francia 37), Sigmaringen, pp. 345–66

Murray, A. C. (1986), 'The position of the *Grafio* in the constitutional history of Merovingian Gaul', *Speculum* 61: 787–805

Murray, A. C. (1988), 'From Roman to Frankish Gaul: "centenarii" and "centenae" in the administration of the Merovingian kingdom', *Traditio* 44: 59–100

Murray, O. (1990), 'The idea of the Shepherd king from Cyrus to Charlemagne', in P. Godman and O. Murray (eds.), *Latin Poetry and the Classical Tradition*, Oxford, pp. 1–14

Nasrullah, P. J. (1950), *Saint Jean de Damas: son époque, sa vie, son œuvre*, Paris

Nehlsen, H. (1977), 'Zur Aktualität und Effektivität germanischer Rechtsaufzeichnungen', in P. Classen (ed.), *Recht und Schrift im Mittelalter* (VuF 23), Constance

Ní Dhonnchadha, M. (1982), 'The guarantor list of *Cáin Adomnáin*, 697', *Peritia* 1: 178–215

O'Cathasaigh, T. (1977), *The Heroic Biography of Cormac mac Airt*, Dublin

O'Corráin, D. (1971), 'Irish regnal succession: a reappraisal', *Studia Hibernica* 11: 7–39

O'Corráin, D. (1978), 'Nationality and kingship in pre-Norman Ireland', in T. W. Moody (ed.), *Nationality and the Pursuit of National Independence* (Historical Studies 11), Belfast, pp. 1–35

O'Corráin, D., Breatnach, L. and Breen, A. (1984), 'The laws of the Irish', *Peritia* 3: 382–438

Périn, P. (1992), 'The undiscovered grave of King Clovis (+511)', in Carver (1992), pp. 255–64

Pohl, W. (1988), *Die Awaren: Ein Steppenvolk in Mitteleuropa, 567–822 n. Chr.*, Munich

Reydellet, M. (1981), *La Royauté dans la littérature latine de Sidoine Apollinaire à Isidore de Séville* (Bibliothèque des écoles françaises d'Athènes et de Rome 243), Rome

Rösch, G. (1978), *Onoma Basileias: Studien zum offiziellen Gebrauch der Kaisertitel in spätantiker und frühbyzantinischer Zeit* (Byzantina Vindobonensia 10), Vienna

Sansterre, J. (1972), 'Eusèbe de Césarée et la naissance de la théorie césaropapiste', *Byzantion* 42: 131–95, 532–94

Sawyer, P. H. and Woods, I. N. (eds.) (1977), *Early Medieval Kingship*, Leeds

Schlesinger, W. (1956), 'Obergermanisches Heerkönigtum', in Mayer (1956), pp. 105–41

Sharf, A. (1971), *Byzantine Jewry from Justinian to the Fourth Crusade*, New York

Sirks, B. (1993), 'The sources of the Code', in Harries and Wood (1993), pp. 45–67

Sisam, K. (1953), 'Anglo-Saxon royal genealogies', *PBA* 39: 287–348

Smyth, A. P. (1972), 'The earliest Irish Annals: their first contemporary entries and the earliest centres of recording', *PRIA* 72, Section C: 1–48

Stancliffe, C. (1983), 'Kings who opted out', in Wormald *et al.* (1983), pp. 154–76

Stepanov, T. (2001), 'The Bulgar Title ΚΑΝΑΥΒΙΓΙ: reconstructing the notions of divine kingship in Bulgaria. AD 822–836', *EME* 10: 1–19

Talbot Rice, D. (1966), *The Dark Ages*, London

Thacker, A. T. (1983), 'Bede's ideal of reform', in Wormald *et al.* (1983), pp. 130–53

Thompson, E. A. (1965), *The Early Germans*, Oxford
Thompson, E. A. (1966), *The Visigoths in the Time of Ulfila*, Oxford
Todd, M. (1992), *The Early Germans* (The Peoples of Europe), Oxford
Voss, W. E. (1982), *Recht und Retorik in den Kaisergesetzen der Spätantike: Eine Untersuchung zum nachklassischen Kauf und Übereignungsrecht* (Forschungen zur byzantinischen Rechtsgeschichte 9), Frankfurt
Wailes, B. (1982), 'The Irish "royal sites" in history and archaeology', *Cambridge Medieval Celtic Studies* 3: 1–29
Wallace-Hadrill, J. M. (1960), 'The graves of kings: an historical note on some archaeological evidence', *Studi Medievali* series 1: 177–94: repr. with postscript in his essays, *Early Medieval History*, Oxford (1975), pp. 39–59
Wallace-Hadrill, J. M. (1962), *The Long-Haired Kings and Other Studies in Frankish History*, London
Wallace-Hadrill, J. M. (1971), *Early Germanic Kingship in England and on the Continent*, Oxford
Wallace-Hadrill, J. M. (1975), *Early Medieval History*, Oxford
Ward-Perkins, B. (1984), *From Classical Antiquity to the Middle Ages: Urban Public Building in Northern and Central Italy AD 300–850*, Oxford
Werner, K.-F. (1972), 'Les principautés périphériques dans le monde franc du VIIIe siècle', *Settimane* 20: 484–514
Whitby, Ma. (1994), 'A new image for a new age: George of Pisidia on the Emperor Heraclius', in E. Dabrowa (ed.), *The Roman and Byzantine Army in the East* (Proceedings of a colloquium held at the Jagiellonian University, Kraków, September 1992), Cracow, pp. 197–225
Whitby, Ma. (1995), 'The devil in disguise: the end of George of Pisidia's *Hexaemeron* reconsidered', *Journal of Hellenic Studies* 115: 115–29
Whitby, Mi. (1982), 'Theophylact's knowledge of languages', *Byzantion* 52: 425–8
Whitby, Mi. (1988), *The Emperor Maurice and His Historian: Theophylact Simocatta on Persian and Balkan Warfare*, Oxford
Whitby, Mi. (1994), 'The Persian king at war' in E. Dabrowa (ed.), *The Roman and Byzantine Army in the East* (Proceedings of a colloquium held at the Jagiellonian University, Kraków, September 1992), Cracow, pp. 227–63
Whitting, P. (1973), *Byzantine Coins*, London
Wickham, C. (1981), *Early Medieval Italy: Central Power and Local Society 400–1000*, London
Wickham, C. (1984), 'The other transition: from the ancient world to feudalism', *Past and Present* 103: 3–36
Wickham, C. (1993), 'La Chute de Rome n'aura pas lieu', *Le Moyen Age* 99: 107–26
Wieacker, F. (1963), *Allgemeine Zustände und Rechtszustände gegen Ende des weströmischen Reichs* (Ius Romanum Medii Aevi 1, 2, a), Milan
Wolfram, H. (1967), *Intitulatio I. Lateinische Königs- und Fürstentitel bis zum Ende des 8. Jahrhunderts* (MIÖG, supplement 21), Vienna
Wolfram, H. (1970), 'The shaping of the early medieval kingdom', *Viator* 1: 1–20
Wolfram, H. (1975), 'Athanaric the Visigoth: monarchy or judgeship. A study in comparative history', *JMH* 1: 259–78
Wolfram, H. (1988), *History of the Goths*, trans. T. J. Dunlap, Berkeley, CA

Wood, I. (1989), 'The Irish and social subversion in the early middle ages', in D. Siegmund-Schulze (ed.), *Irland, Gesellschaft und Kultur*, VI (Martin-Luther-Universität Halle-Wittenberg Wissenschaftliche Beiträge 44), Halle, pp. 263–70

Wood, I. (1994), *The Merovingian Kingdoms*, London

Wormald, P. (1977), '*Lex scripta* and *verbum regis*: legislation and Germanic kingship, from Euric to Cnut', in Sawyer and Wood (1977), pp. 105–38

Wormald, P. (1982), 'Viking studies: whence and whither?', in R. T. Farrell (ed.), *The Vikings*, Chichester, pp. 128–53

Wormald, P. (1986a), 'Celtic and Anglo-Saxon kingship: some further thoughts', in P. Szarmach and V. Oggins (eds.), *Sources of Anglo-Saxon Culture* (Studies in Medieval Culture 20), Kalamazoo, pp. 151–83

Wormald, P. (1986b), 'Charters, law and the settlement of disputes in Anglo-Saxon England', in Davies and Fouracre (1986), pp. 149–68

Wormald, P. (1995), '*Inter Cetera Bona Genti Suae*: law-making and peace-keeping in the earliest English kingdoms', *Settimane* 42: 963–96

Wormald, P. (1996), 'The emergence of the *Regnum Scottorum*: a Carolingian hegemony?', in B. Crawford (ed.), *Scotland in Dark Age Britain* (St John's House Papers 6), St Andrews, pp. 131–60

Wormald, P. (1998), *The Making of English Law: King Alfred to the Twelfth Century*, I: *Legislation and Its Limits*, Oxford

Wormald, P. (1999), 'Law and dispute settlement', in P. Heather and B. Ward-Perkins (eds.), *Romans and Barbarians: The Oxford Illustrated History of the End of Antiquity, 300–700*, Oxford

Wormald, P., Bullough, D. A. and Collins, R. (eds.) (1983), *Ideal and Reality in Frankish and Anglo-Saxon Society: Studies presented to J. M. Wallace-Hadrill*, Oxford

22 THE MEDITERRANEAN ECONOMY

Abadie-Reynal, C. (1989), 'Céramique et commerce dans le bassin égéen du IVe au VIIe siècle', in *Hommes et richesses dans l'empire byzantin*, I: *IVe–VIIe siècle*, Paris, pp. 143–59

Arnaldi, G. (1986), 'L'approvvigionamento di Roma e l'amministrazione de "patrimonii di S. Pietro" al tempo di Gregorio Magno', *Roczniki Humanistyczne* 34: 63–74

Arthur, P. (1986), 'Amphorae and the Byzantine world', in J.-Y. Empereur and Y. Garlan (eds.), *Recherches sur les amphores grecques* (*BCH*, suppl. 13), Paris, pp. 655–60

Arthur, P. (1989), 'Some observations on the economy of Bruttium under the later Roman Empire', *JRA* 2: 133–42

Arthur, P. (1993), 'Early medieval amphorae, the duchy of Naples and the food supply of Rome', *PBSR* 61: 231–44

Arthur, P. (1998), 'Eastern Mediterranean amphorae between 500 and 700: a view from Italy', in Saguì (1998b), pp. 157–83

Arthur, P. and Oren, E. D. (1998), 'The North Sinai survey and the evidence of transport amphorae for Roman and Byzantine trading patterns', *JRA* 11: 193–212

Arthur, P. and Patterson, H. (1994), 'Ceramics and early medieval central and southern Italy: "a potted history"', in Francovich and Noyé (1994), pp. 409–41

Bacchelli, B. and Pasqualucci, R. (1998), 'Lucerne dal contesto di VII secolo della Crypta Balbi', in Saguì (1998b), pp. 343–50

Bailey, D. M. (1998), *Excavations at El-Ashmunein*, v: *Pottery, Lamps and Glass of the Late Roman and Early Arab Periods,* London

Ballet, P. and Picon, M. (1987), 'Recherches préliminaires sur les origines de la céramique des Kellia (Egypte)', *CCE* 1: 17–48

Balzaretti, R. (1996), 'Cities, emporia and monasteries: local economies in the Po Valley, c. AD 700–875', in N. Christie and S. T. Loseby (eds.), *Towns in Transition: Urban Evolution in Late Antiquity and the Early Middle Ages*, Aldershot, pp. 213–34

Ben Abed, A., Bonifay, M., Fixot, M. *et al.* (1997), 'Note préliminaire sur la céramique de la basilique orientale de Sidi Jdidi (Tunisie) (Ve–VIIe s.)', in *La Céramique médiévale en Méditerranée. Actes du 6e Congrès*, Aix-en-Provence, pp. 13–25

Bonifay, M., Carré, M.-B., Rigoir, Y. *et al.* (1998), *Fouilles à Marseille: les mobiliers (Ire–VIIe siècles ap. J.-C.)* (Etudes Massaliètes 5), Paris

Bonifay, M. and Pieri, D. (1995), 'Amphores du Ve au VIIe siècle à Marseille: nouvelles données sur la typologie et le contenu', *JRA* 8: 94–120

Bonifay, M. and Villedieu, F. (1989), 'Importations d'amphores orientales en Gaule (Ve–VIIe siècle)', in V. Déroche and J.-M. Spieser (eds.), *Recherches sur la céramique byzantine* (*BCH*, suppl. 18), Paris, pp. 17–46

Braudel, F. (1972), *The Mediterranean and the Mediterranean World in the Age of Philip II,* 2nd edn, trans. S. Reynolds, 2 vols., London

Cameron, A., Ward-Perkins, B. and Whitby, M. (eds.) (2000), *The Cambridge Ancient History*, xiv: *Late Antiquity: Empire and Successors, A.D. 425–600*, Cambridge

Canivet, P. and Rey-Coquais, J.-P. (eds.) (1992), *La Syrie de Byzance à l'Islam, VIIe–VIIIe siècles*, Damascus

Carandini, A. (1981), 'Sviluppo e crisi delle manifatture rurali e urbane', in A. Giardina and A. Schiavone (eds.), *Società romana e produzione schiavistica*, 3 vols., Rome and Bari, ii, pp. 249–60

Carandini, A. (1986), 'Il mondo della tarda antichità visto attraverso le merci', in A. Giardina (ed.), *Società romana e impero tardoantico*, 3 vols., Rome and Bari, iii, pp. 3–19

Carrié, J.-M. (1975), 'Les distributions alimentaires dans les cités de l'empire romain tardif', *MEFRA* 87: 995–1010

CATHMA (1993), 'Céramiques languedociennes du haut moyen âge (VIe–XIe s.). Etudes micro-régionales et essai de synthèse', *Archéologie du Midi Médiéval* 11: 111–228

Claude, D. (1985), *Untersuchungen zu Handel und Verkehr der vor- und frühgeschichtlichen Zeit in Mittel- und Nordeuropa*, ii: *Der Handel im westlichen Mittelmeer während des Frühmittelalters*, Göttingen

Dagron, G. (1985), 'Un tarif des sportules à payer aux *curiosi* du port de Séleucie de Piérie', *Travaux et Mémoires* 9: 435–55

Dagron, G. and Déroche, V. (1991), 'Juifs et Chrétiens dans l'Orient du VIIe siècle', *Travaux et Mémoires* 11: 17–273

Dagron, G. and Feissel, D. (1987), *Inscriptions de Cilicie* (Travaux et Mémoires du Centre de Recherche Historique et Civilisation de Byzance 4), Paris

Dark, K. R. (ed.) (1995), *External Contacts and the Economy of Late Roman and Post-Roman Britain*, Woodbridge

Decker, M. (2001), 'Food for an empire: wine and oil production in North Syria', in Kingsley and Decker (2001), pp. 69–86

Démians d'Archimbaud, G. *et al.* (1994), *L'Oppidum de Saint-Blaise du Ve au VIIe s.* (Documents d'Archéologie Française 45), Paris

Dentzer, J.-M. (ed.) (1985), *Hauran I: recherches archéologiques sur la Syrie du Sud à l'époque hellénistique et romaine*, Paris

Devroey, J.-P. (1995), 'Juifs et Syriens. A propos de la géographie économique de la Gaule au haut moyen âge', in J.-M. Duvosquel and E. Thoen (eds.), *Peasants and Townsmen in Medieval Europe: Studia in honorem Adriaan Verhulst*, Ghent, pp. 51–72

Durliat, J. (1982), 'Taxes sur l'entrée des marchandises dans la cité de *Carales*-Cagliari à l'époque byzantine (582–602)', *DOP* 36: 1–14

Durliat, J. (1990), *De la Ville antique à la ville byzantine: le problème des subsistences* (Collection de l'Ecole Française de Rome 136), Rome

Durliat, J. (1998), 'Les conditions du commerce au VIe siècle', in Hodges (1998), pp. 89–117

Durliat, J. and Guillou, A. (1984), 'Le tarif d'Abydos (vers 492)', *BCH* 10: 581–98

Egloff, M. (1977), *Kellia: la poterie copte. Quatre siècles d'artisanat et d'échanges en Basse-Egypte* (Recherches Suisses d'Archéologie Copte 3), Geneva

Empereur, J.-Y. and Picon, M. (1989), 'Les régions de production d'amphores impériales en Méditerranée orientale', in *Amphores romaines et histoire économique: dix ans de recherche* (Collection de l'Ecole Française de Rome 114), Rome, pp. 223–48

Eyice, S. (1988), 'Ricerche e scoperte nella regione di Silifke nella Turchia meridionale', in C. Barsanti, A. G. Guidobaldi and A. Iacobini (eds.), *Milion: studi e ricerche d'arte bizantina*, 1, Rome, pp. 15–57

Fentress, E. and Perkins, P. (1987), 'Counting African Red Slip Ware', *L'Africa Romana* 5: 205–14

Finley, M. I. (1985), *The Ancient Economy*, 2nd edn, London

Fontana, S. (1998), 'Le "imitazioni" della sigillata africana e le ceramiche da mensa italiche tardo-antiche', in Saguì (1998b), pp. 83–100

Foss, C. (1994), 'The Lycian coast in the Byzantine age', *DOP* 48: 1–52

Foss, C. (1995), 'The near eastern countryside in late antiquity: a review article', in J. Humphrey (ed.), *The Roman and Byzantine Near East: Some Recent Archaeological Research* (*JRA* suppl. ser. 14), Ann Arbor, pp. 213–34

Foss, C. (1997), 'Syria in transition, A.D. 550–750; an archaeological approach', *DOP* 51: 189–269

Fouracre, P. (1995), 'Eternal light and earthly needs: practical aspects of the development of Frankish immunities', in W. Davies and P. Fouracre (eds.), *Property and Power in the Early Middle Ages*, Cambridge, pp. 53–81

Francovich, R. and Noyé, G. (eds.) (1994), *La storia dell'alto medioevo italiano (VI–X secolo) alla luce dell'archaeologia*, Florence

Fulford, M. G. (1980), 'Carthage. Overseas trade and the political economy, c. A.D. 400–700', *Reading Medieval Studies* 6: 68–80

Fulford, M. G. (1983), 'Pottery and the economy of Carthage and its hinterland', *Opus* 2: 5–14

Gatier, P.-L. (1988), 'Le commerce maritime de Gaza au VIe siècle', in *Navires et commerces de la Méditerranée antique: hommage à J. Rougé* (Cahiers d'Histoire 33), Lyons, pp. 361–70

Gutiérrez-Lloret, S. (1998a), 'Eastern Spain in the sixth century in the light of archaeology', in Hodges (1998), pp. 161–84

Gutiérrez-Lloret, S. (1998b), 'Il confronto con la Hispania orientale: la ceramica nei secoli VI–VII', in Saguì (1998b), pp. 549–67

Haldon, J. (1990), *Byzantium in the Seventh Century: The Transformation of a Culture*, Cambridge

Haldon, J. (2000), 'Production, distribution and demand in the Byzantine world, c. 660–840', in Wickham and Hansen (2000), pp. 225–64

Hartmann, L. M. (1904), *Zur Wirtschaftsgeschichte Italiens im frühen Mittelalter*, Gotha

Hayes, J. W. (1972), *Late Roman Pottery*, London

Hayes, J. W. (1980), *A Supplement to Late Roman Pottery*, London

Hayes, J. W. (1992), *Excavations at Saraçhane in Istanbul*, II: *The pottery*, Princeton, NJ

Hendy, M. F. (1985), *Studies in the Byzantine Monetary Economy, c. 300–1450*, Cambridge

Hendy, M. F. (1988), 'From public to private: the western barbarian coinages as a mirror of the disintegration of late Roman state structures', *Viator* 19: 29–78

Hendy, M. F. (1993), 'From antiquity to the Middle Ages: economic and monetary aspects of the transition', in *De la antigüedad al medioevo, siglos IV–VIII*, León, pp. 325–60

Hodges, R. (ed.) (1998), *The Sixth Century: Production, Distribution and Demand*, Leiden

Hodges, R. and Whitehouse, D. (1983), *Mohammed, Charlemagne and the Origins of Europe: Archaeology and the Pirenne Thesis*, London; revised French trans. C. Morrisson (1996), Paris

Hollerich, M. J. (1982), 'The Alexandrian bishops and the grain trade: ecclesiastical commerce in Late Roman Egypt', *JESHO* 25: 187–207

Hopkins, K. (1980), 'Taxes and trade in the Roman empire (200 B.C.–A. D. 400)', *JRS* 70: 101–25

Hopkins, K. (1983), 'Introduction', in P. Garnsey, K. Hopkins and C. R. Whittaker (eds.), *Trade in the Ancient Economy*, Berkeley and Los Angeles, pp. ix–xxv

Horden, P. and Purcell, N. (2000), *The Corrupting Sea: A Study of Mediterranean History*, Oxford

Johnson, A. C. and West, L. C. (1949), *Byzantine Egypt: Economic Studies* (Princeton University Studies in Papyrology 6), Princeton, NJ

Jones, A. H. M. (1964), *The Later Roman Empire, 284–602: A Social, Economic, and Administrative Survey*, 3 vols., Oxford

Jones, A. H. M. (1974), *The Roman Economy: Studies in Ancient Economic and Administrative History*, ed. P. A. Brunt, Oxford

Keay, S. J. (1984), *Late Roman Amphorae in the Western Mediterranean: A Typology and Economic Study: the Catalan Evidence* (BAR International Series 196), Oxford

Keay, S. J. (1998), 'African amphorae', in Saguì (1998b), pp. 141–55

Keenan, J. G. (1984), 'The Aphrodito papyri and village life in Byzantine Egypt', *BSAC* 26: 1–63

Kennedy, H. (1995), 'The financing of the military in the early Islamic state', in A. Cameron (ed.), *The Byzantine and Early Islamic Near East*, III: *States, Resources and Armies*, Princeton, NJ, pp. 361–78

Kennedy, H. (2000), 'Syria, Palestine and Mesopotamia', in Cameron *et al.* (2000), pp. 588–611
Kieslinger, E. (1999), 'Zum Weinhandel in frühbyzantinischer Zeit', *Tyche* 14: 141–56
Kingsley, S. and Decker, M. (eds.) (2001), *Economy and Exchange in the East Mediterranean during Late Antiquity*, Oxford
Lebecq, S. (2000), 'The role of the monasteries in the systems of production and exchange of the Frankish world between the seventh and the beginning of the ninth centuries', in Wickham and Hansen (2000), pp. 121–48
Levillain, L. (1902), *Examen critique des chartes mérovingiennes et carolingiennes de l'abbaye de Corbie*, Paris
Loseby, S. T. (1992), 'Marseille: a late antique success story?', *JRS* 82: 165–85
Loseby, S. T. (1998), 'Marseille and the Pirenne thesis, I: Gregory of Tours, the Merovingian kings, and "un grand port"', in Hodges (1998), pp. 203–29
Loseby, S. T. (2000), 'Marseille and the Pirenne thesis, II: "ville morte"', in Wickham and Hansen (2000), pp. 167–93
McCormick, M. (1998), 'Bateaux de vie, bateaux de mort. Maladie, commerce, transports annonaires et le passage économique du bas-empire au moyen âge', in *Morfologie sociali e culturali in Europa fra tarda antichità e alto medioevo, Settimane* 45: 35–118
McCormick, M. (2002), *Origins of the European Economy: Communications and Commerce, AD 300–900*, Cambridge
Mackensen, M. (1993), *Die spätantiken Sigillata- und Lampentöpfereien von El Mahrine (Nordtunisien): Studien zur nordafrikanischen Feinkeramik des 4. bis 7. Jahrhunderts*, Munich
Mackensen, M. (1998), 'Centres of African Red Slip Ware production in Tunisia from the late 5th to the 7th century', in Saguì (1998b), pp. 23–39
Mannoni, T., Murialdo, G. *et al.* (2001), *S. Antonino: un insediamento fortificato nella Liguria bizantina*, 2 vols., Bordighera
Marazzi, F. (1998a), *I 'Patrimonio Sanctae Romanae Ecclesiae' nel Lazio, secoli IV–X: strutture amministrative e prassi gestionale*, Rome
Marazzi, F. (1998b), 'The destinies of the late antique Italies: politico-economic developments of the sixth century', in Hodges (1998), pp. 119–59
Martin, A. (1998), 'La sigillata focese (Phocaean Red-Slip/Late Roman C ware)', in Saguì (1998b), pp. 109–22
Mattingly, D. J. (1988), 'Oil for export? A comparison of Libyan, Spanish and Tunisian olive oil production in the Roman empire', *JRA* 1: 33–56
Mattingly, D. J. and Hitchner, R. B. (1995), 'Roman Africa: an archaeological review', *JRS* 85: 165–213
Mayerson, P. (1985), 'The wine and vineyards of Gaza in the Byzantine period', *BASOR* 257: 75–80
Miller, J. I. (1969), *The Spice Trade of the Roman Empire, 29 B.C. to A.D. 641*, Oxford
Mundell Mango, M. (1996), 'Byzantine maritime trade with the East (4th–7th centuries)', *ARAM* 8: 139–63
Orssaud, D. (1992), 'De la céramique Byzantine à la céramique islamique', in Canivet and Rey-Coquais (1992), pp. 219–28

Pacetti, F. (1998), 'La questione delle Keay LII nell'ambito della produzione anforica in Italia', in Saguì (1998b), pp. 185–208

Panella, C. (1993), 'Merci e scambi nel Mediterraneo tardoantico', in *Storia di Roma*, III: *L'età tardoantica, ii, I luoghi e le culture*, Turin, pp. 613–97

Parker, A. J. (1992), *Ancient Shipwrecks of the Mediterranean and the Roman Provinces* (BAR International Series 580), Oxford

Peacock, D. P. S. (1982), *Pottery in the Roman World: An Ethnoarchaeological Approach*, London

Peacock, D. P. S. and Williams, D. F. (1986), *Amphorae and the Roman Economy*, London

Pelletier, J.-P. (1997), 'Les Céramiques communes grises en Provence de l'antiquité tardive au XIIIe siècle', in *La céramique médiévale en Méditerranée. Actes du 6e Congrès*, Aix-en-Provence, pp. 111–24

Pirenne, H. (1939), *Mohammed and Charlemagne*, trans. B. Miall, London

Reynolds, P. (1995), *Trade in the Western Mediterranean A.D. 400–700: The Ceramic Evidence* (BAR International Series 604), Oxford

Ricci, M. (1998), 'La ceramica comune dal contesto di VII secolo della Crypta Balbi', in Saguì (1998b), pp. 351–82

Rigoir, Y. (1998), 'Les dérivées-des-sigillées paléochrétiennes', in Saguì (1998b), pp. 101–7

Riising, A. (1952), 'The fate of Henri Pirenne's thesis on the consequences of Islamic expansion', *Classica et Medievalia* 13: 87–130

Riley, J. A. (1979), 'The coarse pottery', in J. A. Lloyd (ed.), *Excavations at Sidi Khrebish Benghazi (Berenice)*, II (suppl. to *Libya Antiqua* 5.2), Tripoli, pp. 91–467

Rougé, J. (1966), *Recherches sur l'organisation du commerce maritime en Méditerranée sous l'empire romain*, Paris

Ruggini, L. (1959), 'Ebrei e orientali nell'Italia settentrionale fra il IV e il VI secolo d. Cr.', *Studia e Documenta Historiae et Iuris* 25: 187–308

Ruggini, L. (1961), *Economia e società nell' 'Italia annonaria': rapporti fra agricoltura e commercio del IV secolo al VI secolo d. C.*, Milan

Saguì, L. (1998a), 'Il deposito della Crypta Balbi: una testimonianza imprevedibile sulla Roma del VII secolo?', in Saguì (1998b), pp. 305–33

Saguì, L. (ed.) (1998b), *Ceramica in Italia: VI–VII secolo: atti del convegno in onore di John Hayes*, Florence

Saguì, L., Ricci, M. and Romei, D. (1997), 'Nuovi dati ceramologici per la storia economica di Roma tra VII e VIII secolo', in *La Céramique médiévale en Méditerranée. Actes du 6e Congrès*, Aix-en-Provence, pp. 35–48

Sartre, M. (1985), *Bostra: des origines à l'Islam*, Paris

Schick, R. (1998), 'Palestine in the early Islamic period: luxuriant legacy', *Near Eastern Archaeology* 61: 74–108

Shereshevski, J. (1991), *Byzantine Urban Settlements in the Negev Desert*, Beer-Sheva

Sodini, J.-P. (1989), 'Le commerce des marbres à l'époque protobyzantine', in *Hommes et richesses dans l'empire byzantin*, I: *IVe–VIIe siècle*, Paris, pp. 163–86

Sodini, J.-P. (1993), 'La contribution de l'archéologie à la connaissance du monde byzantin (IVe–VII siècles)', *DOP* 47: 139–84

Sodini, J.-P. and Villeneuve, E. (1992), 'Le passage de la céramique byzantine à la céramique omeyyade en Syrie du Nord, en Palestine et en Transjordanie', in Canivet and Rey-Coquais (1992), pp. 195–218

Sodini, J.-P. *et al.* (1980), 'Déhès (Syrie du Nord): campagnes I–III (1976–1978). Recherches sur l'habitat rural', *Syria* 57: 1–304

Tate, G. (1992), *Les Campagnes de la Syrie du Nord du IIe au VIIe siècle: un exemple d'expansion démographique et économique à la fin de l'antiquité*, I, Paris

Tchalenko, G. (1953–58), *Villages antiques de la Syrie du Nord: le massif du Bélus à l'époque romaine*, 3 vols., Paris

Thomas, C. (1981), *A Provisional List of Imported Pottery in Post-Roman Western Britain and Ireland*, Redruth

Tortorella, S. (1986), 'La ceramica fine da mensa africana dal IV al VII secolo d. C.', in A Giardina (ed.), *Società romana e impero tardoantico*, III, Rome and Bari, pp. 211–25

Tortorella, S. (1998), 'La sigillata africana in Italia nel VI e nel VII secolo d. C.: problemi di cronologia e distribuzione', in Saguì (1998b), pp. 41–69

van Alfen, P. G. (1996), 'New light on the 7th-c. Yassi Ada shipwreck: capacities and standard sizes of LRA 1 amphoras', *JRA* 9: 189–213

van Minnen, P. (1986), 'The volume of the Oxyrhynchite textile trade', *Münsterische Beiträge zur Antiken Handelsgeschichte* 5: 88–95

Vera, D. (1983), 'Strutture agrarie e strutture patrimoniali nella tarda antichità: l'aristocrazia romana tra agricoltura e commercio', *Opus* 2: 489–533

Walmsley, A. (1996), 'Byzantine Palestine and Arabia: urban prosperity in Late Antiquity', in Christie and Loseby (1996), pp. 126–58

Walmsley, A. (2000), 'Production, exchange and regional trade in the Islamic east Mediterranean: old structures, new systems?', in Wickham and Hansen (2000), pp. 265–343

Ward-Perkins, B. (2000a), 'Land, labour and settlement', in Cameron *et al.* (2000), pp. 315–45

Ward-Perkins, B. (2000b), 'Specialised production and exchange', in Cameron *et al.* (2000), pp. 346–91

Watson, P. (1992), 'Change in foreign and regional economic links with Pella in the seventh century AD: the ceramic evidence', in Canivet and Rey-Coquais (1992), pp. 233–47

Whittaker, C. R. (1983), 'Late Roman trade and traders', in P. Garnsey, K. Hopkins and C. R. Whittaker (eds.), *Trade in the Ancient Economy*, Berkeley and Los Angeles, pp. 163–80

Wickham, C. (1988), 'Marx, Sherlock Holmes, and late Roman commerce', *JRS* 78: 183–93

Wickham, C. (1994), 'Considerazioni conclusive', in Francovich and Noyé (1994), pp. 741–59

Wickham, C. (1998), 'Overview: production, distribution and demand', in Hodges (1998), pp. 279–92

Wickham, C. (2000a), 'Overview: production, distribution and demand, II', in Wickham and Hansen (2000), pp. 345–7

Wickham, C. (2000b), 'Italy at the end of the Mediterranean world-system', *JRA* 13: 818–24
Wickham, C. and Hansen, I. L. (eds.) (2000), *The Long Eighth Century: Production, Distribution and Demand*, Leiden
Wipszycka, E. (1965), *L'Industrie textile dans l'Egypte romaine*, Wrocław, Warsaw and Cracow
Wipszycka, E. (1972), *Les Ressources et les activités économiques des églises en Egypte du IVe au VIIIe siècle*, Brussels
Woolf, G. (1990), 'World systems analysis and the Roman empire', *JRA* 3: 44–58
Zanini, E. (1996), 'Ricontando la terra sigillata africana', *Archeologia Medievale* 23: 677–88

23 THE NORTHERN SEAS

Bencard, M. (ed.) (1981), *Ribe Excavations 1970–1976*, I, Esbjerg
Besteman, J. C., Bos, J. M., Gerrets, D. A. and Heidinga, H. A. (forthcoming), *The Excavation near Wijnaldum*, Rotterdam
Carver, M. (1998), *Sutton Hoo, Burial Ground of Kings?*, London
Cassard, J. C. (1998), *Les Bretons et la mer au Moyen Age*, Rennes
Clarke, H. and Ambrosiani, B. (1995), *Towns in the Viking Age*, 2nd edn, Leicester, London and New York
Claude, D. (1985), 'Aspekte des Binnenhandels im Merowingerreich auf Grund der Schriftquellen', in K. Düwel *et al.* (1985), pp. 9–99
Devroey, J. P. (1984), 'Un monastère dans l'économie d'échanges: les services de transport de l'abbaye de Saint-Germain-des-Prés au IXe siècle', *Annales ESC* 39: 570–89
Düwel, K., Jankuhn, H., Siems, H. and Dimpe, D. K. (eds.) (1985, 1987), *Untersuchungen zu Handel und Verkehr der vor- und frühgeschichtlichen Zeit in Mittel und Nordeuropa*, III: *Der Handel des frühen Mittelalters*; IV: *Der Handel der Karolinger- und Wikingerzeit*, Göttingen
Edwards, N. (1990), *The Archaeology of Early Medieval Ireland*, London
Ellmers, D. (1972), *Frühmittelalterliche Handelsschiffahrt in Mittel- und Nordeuropa*, Neumünster
Evans, A. C. (1986), *The Sutton Hoo Ship Burial*, London
Fleuriot, L. (1980), *Les Origines de la Bretagne*, Paris
Fulford, M. (1989), 'Byzantium and Britain. A Mediterranean perspective on post-Roman Mediterranean imports in western Britain and Ireland', *Medieval Archaeology* 8: 1–6
Grierson, P. (1959), 'Commerce in the Dark Ages: a critique of the evidence', *TRHS*, 5th series, 9: 123–40
Grierson, P. (1961), 'La fonction sociale de la monnaie en Angleterre aux VIIe–VIIIe siècles', *Settimane* 8: 341–62
Grierson, P. (1970), 'The purpose of the Sutton Hoo coins', *Antiquity* 44: 14–18
Grierson, P. (1979), *Dark Age Numismatics: Selected Studies*, London
Grierson, P. and Blackburn, M. (1986), *Medieval European Coinage*, I: *The Early Middle Ages (5th–10th Centuries)*, Cambridge
Hall, R. (ed.) (1978), *Viking Age York and the North* (CBA Research Report 27), London

Hall, R. (1988), 'York 700–1050', in Hodges and Hobley (1988), pp. 125–32
Haywood, J. (1991), *Dark Age Naval Power: A Reassessment of Frankish and Anglo-Saxon Seafaring*, London and New York
Heidinga, H. A. (1997), *Frisia in the First Millennium, An Outline*, Utrecht
Higham, N. (1992), *Rome, Britain and the Anglo-Saxons*, London
Hill, D. and Metcalf, D. M. (eds.) (1984), *Sceattas in England and on the Continent* (BAR British Series 128), Oxford
Hodges, R. (1980), *The Hamwih Pottery: The Local and Imported Wares from Thirty Years' Excavations and Their European Context*, London
Hodges, R. (1982), *Dark Age Economics: The Origins of Towns and Trade A.D. 600–1000*, London
Hodges, R. (1989), *The Anglo-Saxon Achievement*, London
Hodges, R. (1991), 'The eighth-century pottery industry at La Londe near Rouen, and its implications for cross-Channel trade with Hamwic, Anglo-Saxon Southampton', *Antiquity* 65: 882–7
Hodges, R. (2000), *Towns and Trade in the Age of Charlemagne*, London
Hodges, R. and Hobley, B. (eds.) (1988), *The Rebirth of Towns in the West, AD 700–1050* (CBA Research Report 68), London
Hodges, R. and Whitehouse, D. (1983), *Mohammed, Charlemagne and the Origins of Europe: Archaeology and the Pirenne Thesis*, London
James, E. (1982), 'Ireland and western Gaul in the Merovingian period', in D. Whitelock (ed.), *Ireland in Early Medieval Europe*, Cambridge, pp. 362–86
James, E. (2001), *Britain in the First Millennium*, London
Jankuhn, H. (1986), *Haithabu: Ein Handelsplatz der Wikingerzeit*, 8th edn, Neumünster
Jankuhn, H., Schietzel, K. and Reichstein, H. (eds.) (1984), *Archäologische und naturwissenschaftliche Untersuchungen an Siedlungen im deutschen Küstengebiet*, 1: *Handelsplätze des frühen und hohen Mittelalters*, Weinheim
Jensen, S. (1991), *The Vikings of Ribe*, Ribe
Johanek, P. (1985), 'Der Aussenhandel des Frankenreiches der Merowingerzeit nach Norden und Osten im Spiegel der Schriftquellen', in Düwel *et al.* (1985), pp. 214–54
Johanek P. (1987), 'Der fränkische Handel der Karolingerzeit im Spiegel der Schriftquellen', in Düwel *et al.* (1987), pp. 7–68
Johnson, S. (1976), *The Roman Forts of the Saxon Shore*, London
Johnston, D. E. (ed.) (1977), *The Saxon Shore* (CBA Research Report 18), London
Jones, M. E. (1996), *The End of Roman Britain*, Ithaca, New York and London
Lebecq, S. (1983), *Marchands et navigateurs frisons du haut Moyen Âge*, 2 vols., Lille
Lebecq, S. (1986), 'Dans l'Europe du Nord aux VIIe–IXe siècles: commerce frison ou commerce franco-frison?', *Annales ESC* 41: 361–77
Lebecq, S. (1989), 'La Neustrie et la mer', in H. Atsma (ed.), *La Neustrie: les pays au nord de la Loire de 650 à 850*, Sigmaringen, 1, pp. 405–40
Lebecq, S. (1991), 'Pour une histoire parallèle de Quentovic et Dorestad', in J. M. Duvosquel and A. Dierkens (eds.), *Villes et campagnes au Moyen Âge: mélanges Georges Despy*, Liège, pp. 415–28
Lebecq, S. (1993), 'Quentovic: un état de la question', *Studien zur Sachsenforschung* 8: 73–82

Lebecq, S. (1995), 'L'emporium proto-médiéval de Walcheren-Domburg: une mise en perspective', in J. M. Duvosquel and E. Thoen (eds.), *Peasants and Townsmen in Medieval Europe: Studia in honorem Adriaan Verhulst*, Ghent, pp. 73–89

Lebecq, S. (1997), 'Le premier Moyen Age', in P. Contamine *et al.* (eds.), *L'Economie médiévale*, 2nd edn, Paris, pp. 9–102

Lebecq, S. (1999), 'England and the Continent in the sixth and seventh centuries: the question of logistics', in R. Gameson (ed.), *St Augustine and the Conversion of England*, Stroud, pp. 50–67

Lebecq, S. (2000), 'The role of the monasteries in the systems of production and exchange of the Frankish world, between the seventh and the beginning of the ninth centuries', in I. L. Hansen and C. Wickham (eds.), *The Long Eighth Century: Production, Distribution and Demand*, Leiden, pp. 121–48

McGrail, S. (1987), *Ancient Boats in N. W. Europe: The Archaeology of Water Transport to AD 1500*, London and New York

McGrail, S. (ed.) (1990), *Maritime Celts, Frisians and Saxons* (CBA Research Report 71), London

Myres, J. N. L. (1989), *The English Settlements*, 2nd edn, Oxford

Pirenne, H. (1939), *Mohammed and Charlemagne*, trans. B. Miall, London

Sawyer, P. (1977), 'Kings and merchants', in P. Sawyer and I. Wood (eds.), *Early Medieval Kingship*, Leeds, pp. 139–58

Stenton, F. (1971), *Anglo-Saxon England*, 3rd edn, Oxford

Steuer, H. (1987), 'Gewichtsgeldwirtschaften im frühgeschichtlichen Europa – Feinwaagen und Gewichte als Quellen zur Währungsgeschichte', in K. Düwel *et al.* (1987), pp. 405–527

Thomas, C. (1986), *Celtic Britain*, London

Thomas, C. (1988), 'The context of Tintagel. A new model for the diffusion of post-Roman Mediterranean imports', *Cornish Archaeology* 33: 7–25

Thomas, C. (1990), 'Gallici Nautae de Galliarum Provinciis – A sixth–seventh century trade with Gaul, reconsidered', *Medieval Archaeology* 34: 1–26

Thomas, C. (1993), *Tintagel, Arthur and Archaeology*, London

Thrane, H. (1987), 'Das Gudme-Problem und die Gudme-Untersuchung', *FrSt* 21: 1–48

Van Es, W. A. and Hessing, W. A. M. (eds.) (1994), *Romeinen, Friezen en Franken in het hart van Nederland: Van Traiectum tot Dorestad (50 v.C.–900 n.C.)*, Amersfoort

Van Es, W. A. and Verwers, W. J. H. (eds.) (1980), *Excavations at Dorestad*, 1: *The Harbour: Hoogstraat I*, 2 vols., Amersfoort

Verhulst, A. (1999), *The Rise of Cities in North-West Europe*, Cambridge

Vince, A. (1990), *Anglo-Saxon London*, London

Wade, K. (1988), 'Ipswich', in Hodges and Hobley (1988), pp. 93–100

Welch, M. (1991), 'Contacts across the Channel between the fifth and seventh centuries: a review of the archaeological evidence', *Studien zur Sachsenforschung* 7: 261–70

Wood, I. (1983), *The Merovingian North Sea*, Alingsas

Zedelius, V. (1991), 'Zur Münzpragung von Quentovic', *Studien zur Sachsenforschung* 7: 367–77

24 MONEY AND COINAGE

Alföldi, M. R. (1978), 'Il medaglione d'oro di Teoderico', *Rivista Italiana di Numismatica* 80: 133–41

Alföldi, M. R. (1988), 'Das Goldmultiplum Theoderichs des Grossen – Neue Überlegungen', *Rivista Italiana di Numismatica* 90: 367–72

Arslan, E. A. (1986), 'Una riforma monetaria di Cuniperto re dei Longobardi (688–700)', *Numismatica e Antichità Classiche* 15: 249–75

Arslan, E. A. (1989), 'La monetazione dei Goti', *XXXVI Corso di cultura sull'arte Ravennate e Bizantina*, Ravenna, pp. 17–72

Arslan, E. A. (1993), 'La struttura delle emissioni monetarie dei Goti in Italia', in *Teoderico il Grande e i Goti d'Italia': Atti del XIII Congresso internazionale di studi sull'alto medioevo*, Spoleto, pp. 517–55

Arslan, E. A. (1998), 'Mutamenti di funzione e di struttura degli stock monetari in Europa tra V e VII secolo', in *Morfologie sociali e culturali in Europa fra tarda antichità e alto medioevo*, Spoleto, pp. 379–460

Blackburn, M. (1995), 'Money and coinage', in R. McKitterick (ed.), *The New Cambridge Medieval History* II, Cambridge, pp. 538–59.

Brown, D. (1981), 'The dating of the Sutton Hoo coins', in *Anglo-Saxon Studies in Archaeology and History,* II (BAR British Series 92), Oxford, pp. 71–86

Clover, F. M. (1991), 'Relations between North Africa and Italy AD 476–500: some numismatic evidence', *Revue Numismatique*, 6th series, 33: 112–33

Crusafont i Sabater, M. (1994), *El sistema monetario visigodo: cobre y oro*, Barcelona and Madrid

Gomes, M., Peixoto, J. M. and Rodrigues, J. (1985), *Ensaios sobre história monetária da monarquia visigoda*, Oporto

Grierson, P. (1982), *Byzantine Coins*, London

Grierson, P. (1985), 'The date of Theoderic's gold medallion', *Hikuin* 11: 19–26

Grierson, P. and Blackburn, M. (1986), *Medieval European Coinage*, I: *The Early Middle Ages (5th to 10th Centuries)*, Cambridge

Grierson, P. and Mays, M. (1992), *Catalogue of Late Roman Coins in the Dumbarton Oaks Collection and in the Whittemore Collection: From Arcadius and Honorius to the Accession of Anastasius*, Washington, DC

Hahn, W., with Metlich, M. A. (2000), *Money of the Incipient Byzantine Empire (Anastasius I to Justinian I, 491–565)*, Vienna

Hendy, M. F. (1985), *Studies in the Byzantine Monetary Economy, c. 300–1450*, Cambridge

Hendy, M. F. (1988), 'From public to private: the western barbarian coinages as a mirror of the disintegration of Late Roman state structures', *Viator* 1988: 29–88

Kent, J. P. C. (1975), 'The date of the Sutton Hoo hoard', in R. L. S. Bruce-Mitford (ed.), *The Sutton Hoo Ship Burial*, I, London, pp. 588–647

Kent, J. P. C. (1994), *The Roman Imperial Coinage*, X: *The Divided Empire and the Fall of the Western Parts 395–491*, London

Lafaurie, J. (1987), 'Les dernières émissions impériales d'argent à Trèves au 5e siècle', in H. Huvelin, M. Christol and G. Gautier (eds.), *Mélanges de numismatique offerts à Pierre Bastien*, Wetteren, pp. 297–323

Metcalf, D. M. (1986), 'Some geographical aspects of early medieval monetary circulation in the Iberian Peninsula', in M. Gomes Marques and M. Crusafont i Sabater (eds.), *Problems of Medieval Coinage in the Iberian Area*, II, Aviles, pp. 307–24

Metcalf, D. M. (1992), 'The coinage of the first and second Suevic kingdoms: from Romanitas to Latinization', in *Galicia: da romanidade á xermanización: problemas históricos e culturais*, Santiago de Compostela, pp. 355–65

Metcalf, D. M. (1993–94), *Thrymsas and Sceattas in the Ashmolean Museum Oxford*, 3 vols. (Royal Numismatic Society Special Publication 27), London

Metcalf, D. M. (1995), 'Viking-Age numismatics: 1. Late Roman and Byzantine gold in the Northern Lands', *Numismatic Chronicle* 155: 413–41

Metlich, M. A. (2004), *The Coinage of Ostrogothic Italy*, London

Miles, C. C. (1952), *The Coinage of the Visigoths of Spain, Leovigild to Achila* II, New York

Morrisson, C. (1983), 'The re-use of obsolete coins: the case of Roman Imperial bronzes revived in the late fifth century', in C. N. L. Brooke, B. H. I. H. Stewart, J. G. Pollard and T. R. Volk (eds.), *Studies in Numismatic Method presented to Philip Grierson*, Cambridge, pp. 95–111

Morrisson, C. (1988), 'Carthage: the "moneta auri" under Justinian I and Justin II', in W. R. O. Hahn and W. E. Metcalf (eds.), *Studies in Early Byzantine Gold Coinage* (American Numismatic Society's Numismatic Studies 17), New York, pp. 41–64

Oddy, W. A. (1988), 'The debasement of the provincial Byzantine gold coinage from the seventh to ninth centuries', in W. R. O. Hahn and W. E. Metcalf (eds.), *Studies in Early Byzantine Gold Coinage* (American Numismatic Society's Numismatic Studies 17), New York, pp. 135–42

Peixoto Cabral, J. M. and Metcalf, D. M. (1997), *A moeda sueva. Suevic Coinage*, Oporto

Rigold, S. E. (1954), 'An imperial coinage in southern Gaul in the sixth and seventh centuries?', *Numismatic Chronicle*, 6th series, 14: 93–133

Spufford, P. (1988), *Money and Its Use in Medieval Europe*, Cambridge

Stahl, A. M. (1992), 'The nature of the Sutton Hoo coin parcel', in C. B. Kendall and P. S. Wells (eds.), *Voyage to the Other World: The Legacy of Sutton Hoo* (Medieval Studies at Minnesota 5), Minneapolis

Stahl, A. M. and Oddy, W. A. (1992), 'The date of the Sutton Hoo coins', in *Sutton Hoo: Fifty Years After* (American Early Medieval Studies 2), Oxford, MA, pp. 129–47

25 CHURCH STRUCTURE AND ORGANISATION

Andrieu, M. (1925), *Les Ordres mineurs*, Paris

Andrieu, M. (1947), 'La carrière ecclésiastique des papes', *Revue des Sciences Religieuses* 21: 90–120

Angenendt, A. (1990), *Das Frühmittelalter: Die abendländische Christenheit von 400 bis 900*, Stuttgart

Anton, H. H. (1975), *Studien zu den Klosterprivilegien der Päpste im frühen Mittelalter unter besonderer Berücksichtigung der Privilegierung von St. Maurice d'Agaune* (Beiträge zur Geschichte und Quellenkunde des Mittelalters 4), Berlin

Beck, H. G. (1950), *The Pastoral Care of Souls in South-East France during the Sixth Century* (Analecta Gregoriana 51), Rome

Biarne, J. (1997), 'Etat du monachisme en Gaule à la fin du Ve siècle. Clovis – histoire et mémoire', in M. Rouche (ed.), *Clovis – Histoire et mémoire*, I: *Le baptême de Clovis, l'événement*, Paris, pp. 115–26

Bidagor, R. (1933), *La 'iglesia propria' en España* (Analecta Gregoriana 4), Rome

Bieler, L. (1966), 'The Irish penitentials. Their religious and social background', *Studia Patristica* 4: 329–39

Blair, J. (1995), 'Debate: ecclesiastical organization and pastoral care in Anglo-Saxon England' *EME* 4: 193–212

Blair, J. and Sharpe, R. (eds.) (1992), *Pastoral Care before the Parish*, Leicester

Blair, P. H. (1970), *The World of Bede*, London

Blazovich, F. A. (1954), *Soziologie des Mönchtums und die Benediktinerregal*, Vienna

Blockscha, J. (1931), 'Altersvorschriften für die höheren Weihen im ersten Jahrtausend', *Archiv für Katholisches Kirchenrecht* 111: 31–83, Mainz

Bulloch, J. (1963), *The Life of the Celtic Church*, Edinburgh

Cambridge, E. and Rollason, D. (1995), 'Debate. The pastoral organization of the Anglo-Saxon church: a review of the minster hypothesis', *EME* 4: 87–104

Caspar, E. (1933), *Geschichte des Papsttums*, II, Tübingen

Chadwick, N. (1963), 'The conversion of Northumbria. A comparison of sources', in N. Chadwick (ed.), *Celt and Saxon*, Cambridge, pp. 138–66

Chaney, W. A. (1963), 'Anglo Saxon church dues: a study in historical continuity', *Church History* 32: 268–77

Chavasse, A. (1958), *Le Sacramentaire Gélasien* (Vaticanus Reginensis 316; Bibliothèque de Théologie 4, Histoire de la Théologie 1), Paris

Clarke, H. B. and Brennan, M. (eds.) (1981), *Columbanus and Merovingian Monasticism* (BAR International Series 113), Oxford

Claude, D. (1963), 'Die Bestellung der Bischöfe im merowingischen Reiche', *ZRG KA* 49: 1–75

Coebergh, C. (1961), 'Le sacramentaire Gélasien ancien, un compilation de clercs romanisants du VIIIe siècle', *Archiv für Liturgiewissenschaft* 7: 45–88

Comyns, J. J. (1942), *Papal and Episcopal Administration of Church Property*, Washington, DC

Conte, P. (1971), *Chiesa e Primato nelle lettere dei Papi del secolo VII*, Milan

Croce, W. (1948), 'Die niederen Weihen und ihre hierarchische Wertung', *ZKTh* 70: 257–315

Cross, F. L. (1965), 'Early Western liturgical manuscripts', *JTS* 116: 61–67

Deanesley, M. (1961), *The Pre-Conquest Church in England*, London

de Jong, M. (1986), *Kind en klooster in de vroege middeleeuwen. Aspecten van de schenking van kinderen aan klooster in het frankishe rijk 500–900* (Amsterdamse Historische Reeks 8), Amsterdam

Desalle, L. R. (1961), 'Comparaison, datation, localisation relative des Règles monastiques de S. Césaire d'Arles, S. Ferréol d'Uzès et de la Regula Tarnatensis monasterii', *Augustiniana* 11: 5–26

Deshusses, J. (1982), 'Les sacramentaires. Etat actuel de la recherche', *Archiv für Liturgiewissenschaft* 28: 19–46

Díaz y Díaz, M. C. (1970), 'La vida eremítica en el reino visigodo', in *España Eremítica. Actas de la VI Semana de Estudios Monásticos. Abadia de San Salvador de Leyre, 15–20 Septiembre 1963*, Pamplona, pp. 49–62

Diesner, J. (1964), 'Das Mönchtum der Vandalenzeit in Africa', in *Kirche und Staat im spätrömischen Reich*, Berlin, pp. 140–8
Dijk, S. J. P. van (1961), 'The urban and papal rites in seventh and eighth century Rome', *Sacris Erudiri* 12: 411–87
Ewig, E. (1970), 'Beobachtungen zu den Bischofslisten der merowingischen Konzilien und Bischofsprivilegien', in *Festschrift Franz Petri* (Landschaft und Geschichte), Bonn, pp. 171–92
Feine, E. (1972), *Kirchliche Rechtsgeschichte*, I: *Die Katholische Kirche*, Cologne
Feine, H. E. (1950), 'Ursprung, Wesen und Bedeutung des Eigenkirchentums', *MIÖG* 58: 195–208
Fernandez Alonso, J. (1955), *La cura pastoral en la España romano-visigoda*, Rome
Findlay, S. W. (1941), *Canonical Norms Governing the Deposition and Degradation of Clerics*, Washington, DC
Fliche, A. and Martin, V. (eds.) (1948), *Histoire de l'église depuis les origines jusqu'à nos jours*, IV, Paris
Foot, S. (1989), 'Parochial ministry in early Anglo-Saxon England: the role of monastic communities', *Studies in Church History* 21: 43–54
Foot, S. (1992a), '"By water in the spirit": the administration of baptism in early Anglo-Saxon England', in Blair and Sharpe (1992), pp. 171–92
Foot, S. (1992b), 'Anglo-Saxon minsters: a review of terminology', in Blair and Sharpe (1992), pp. 212–25
Frank, K. S. (1975), *Frühes Mönchtum im Abendland*, I: *Lebensnomen*, Munich
Gamber, K. (1958), *Sakramentartypen* (Texte und Arbeiten 49/50), Beuron
Gamber, K. (1968), *Codices Liturgici Latini Antiquiores* (Spicilegii Friburgensis Subsidia 1/2), Fribourg
Ganz, D. (1995), 'The ideology of sharing apostolic community and ecclesiastical property in the early middle ages', in W. Davies and P. Fouracre (eds.), *Property and Power in the Early Middle Ages*, Cambridge, pp. 17–30
Griffe, É. (1951), 'Aux origines de la liturgie gallicane', *Bulletin de Littérature Ecclésiastique* 52: 17–43
Griffe, É. (1953), 'Les paroisses rurales de la Gaule', *Maison-Dieu* 36: 33–62
Griffe, É. (1975), 'A travers les paroisses rurales de la Gaule au VIe siècle', *Bulletin de Littérature Ecclésiastique* 76: 3–26
Grillmeir, A. and Bacht, H. (eds.) (1951–64), *Das Konzil von Chalkedon*, Würzburg
Gryson, R. (1970), *Les Origines du célibat ecclésiastique du premier au septième siècle: recherches et synthèses* (Histoire 2), Gembloux
Gryson, R. (1972), *Le Ministère des femmes dans l'église ancienne*, Gembloux
Hartmann, W. (1982), 'Der rechtliche Zustand der Kirche auf dem Lande. Die Eigenkirche in der fränkischen Gesetzgebung des 7.–9. Jahrhunderts', *Settimane* 28: 397–441
Hastings, A. (1950), 'St. Benedict and the eremitical life', *DR* 68: 191–211
Heinzelmann, M. (1976), *Bischofsherrschaft in Gallien* (Beihefte der Francia 5), Munich
Heuclin, J. (1998), *Hommes de Dieu et fonctionnaires du roi en Gaule du nord du Ve au IXe siècle*, Villeneurve-d'Ascq
Hilpisch, S. (1928), *Die Doppelklöster: Entstehung und Organisation* (Beiträge zur Geschichte des alten Mönchtums 15), Münster

Hughes, K. (1966), *The Church in Early Irish Society*, London
Jaspert, B. (1971), 'Regula Magistri – Regular Benedicti', *Studia Monastica* 13: 129–71
Jedin, H. (ed.) (1975), *Handbuch der Kirchengeschichte* II/2, Freiburg
Jenal, G. (1995), *Italia ascetica et monastica. Das Asketen- und Mönchtum*, I: *Italien von den Anfängen bis zur Zeit der Langobarden (ca. 150/250–604)* (Monographien zur Geschichte des Mittelalters 39/1–2), Stuttgart
Jungmann, J. A. (1932), *Die lateinischen Bußriten in ihrer geschichtlichen Entwicklung*, Innsbruck
Kaiser, R. (1981), *Bischofherrschaft zwischen Königtum und Fürstenmacht* (Pariser Historische Studien 7), Sigmaringen
Kellner, H. (1863), *Das Buß- und Strafverfahren gegen Kleriker in den ersten sechs Jahrhunderten*, Trier
Kempf, F. (1978), 'Primatiale und episkopal-synodale Struktur der Kirche vor der gregorienischen Reform', *AHP* 16: 22–66
Kottje, R. (1987), 'Bußpraxis und Bußritus', *Settimane* 33: 369–96
Lacarra, J. M. (1960), 'La iglesia visigoda en el siglo VII y sus relaciones con Roma', *Settimane* 7: 353–84
Langgärtner, G. (1964), *Die Gallienpolitik der Päpste im 5. und 6. Jahrhundert: Eine Studie über den apostolischen Vikariat von Arles* (Theophaneia 16), Bonn
Laporte, J. (1958), *Le Pénitentiel de s. Colomban*, Tournai
Le Bras, G. (1960), 'Sociologie de l'Église dans le Haut Moyen Age', *Settimane* 7: 595–611
Lesne, G. (1910), *Histoire de la propriété ecclésiastique en France*, I, Paris
Linage Conde, A. (1973), *Los orígenes del monacato benedictino en la peninsular ibérica*, I: *El monacato hispano pre-benedictino*, León
Lorcin, A. (1945), 'La vie scolaire dans les monastères d'Irlande aux 5e–7e siècles', *Moyen Age Latin* I: 221–36
Lorlandis, J. and Ramos-Lisson, D. (1981), *Die Synoden auf der iberischen Halbinsel bis zum Einbruch des Islam* (Konziliengeschichte A), Paderborn
Löwe, H. (ed.) (1982), *Die Iren und Europa*, Stuttgart
Lumpe, A. (1970), 'Zur Geschichte der Wörter 'concilium' und 'synodus' in der antiken Latinität', *AHP* 8: 1–21
Maccarrone, M. (1960), 'La dottrina del primato papale dal IV all' VIII secolo nelle relazioni con le chiese occidentali', *Settimane* 7: 633–742
MacManus, F. (1962), *Saint Columban*, New York
Mansilla, D. (1959), 'Orígenes de la organización metropolitana en la iglesia española', *HS* 12: 1–36
Markus, R. A. (1983), *From Augustine to Gregory the Great: History and Christianity in Late Antiquity*, London
Markus, R. A. (1997), *Gregory the Great and His World*, Cambridge
Marot, H. (1965), 'La collégialité et le vocabulaire épiscopal du Ve au VIIe siècle', in *La Collégialité épiscopale*, Paris, pp. 61–98
Matthiae, G. (1963), *Le chiese di Roma dal IV all' IX secolo*, Bologna
Mayr-Harting, H. (1972), *The Coming of Christianity to Anglo-Saxon England*, London
Mochi-Onory, S. (1933), *Vescovi e città*, Bologna
Moriarty, F. E. (1938), *The Extraordinary Absolution from Censures*, Washington, DC

Mortari, L. (1969), *Consacrazione episcopale e collegialità*, Florence
Müller, K. (1933), 'Parochie und Diözese', *Zeitschrift für die Neutestamentliche Wissenschaft und die Kunde die Älteren Kirche* 32: 149–85, Berlin
Mundó, A. (1967), 'Las reglas monásticas del siglo VI y la "lectio divina"', *Studia Monastica* 9: 229–55
Parisse, M. (1983), *Les Nonnes au Moyen Age*, Le Puy
Penco, G. (1959), 'Il concetto di monaco e di vita monástica in occidente nel secolo VI', *Studia Monastica* I: 7–50
Penco, G. (1961), *Storia del monachesimo in Italia* (*Collana universale storica. Tempi e figure* II, 31), Rome
Plöchl, W. M. (1953), *Geschichte des Kirchenrechts*, I, Vienna
Pontal, O. (1986), *Die Synoden im Merowingerreich* (Konziliengeschichte, Reihe A), Paderborn
Poschmann, B. (1930), *Die abendländische Kirchenbuße im frühen Mittelalter*, Breslau
Prinz, F. (1974), 'Die bischöfliche Stadtherrschaft im Frankenreich vom 5. bis zum 7. Jahrhundert', *HZ* 217: 1–35
Prinz, F. (1988), *Frühes Mönchtum im Frankenreich*, Munich
Quacquarelli, A. (1959), 'Alle origini del lector', in *Convivium Dominicum* (Studi sull'Eucaristia nei padri della chiesa antica), University of Catania, pp. 381–406
Richards, J. (1979), *The Popes and the Papacy in the Early Middle Ages*, London
Richards, J. (1980), *Consul of God: The Life and Times of Gregory the Great*, London
Riché, P. (1962), *Éducation et culture dans l'occident barbare, VIe–VIIIe siècle*, Paris
Ryan, J. (1931), *Irish Monasticism*, Dublin
Sägmüller, J. B. (1898), *Die Entwicklung des Archipresbyterats und Dekanats bis zum Ende der Karolingerzeit*, Tübingen
Schäferdiek, K. (1967), *Die Kirche in den Reichen der Westgoten und Suewen bis zur Errichtung der westgotischen katholischen Staatskirche*, Berlin
Scheibelreiter, G. (1979), 'Königstöchter im Kloster. Radegund (+587) und der Nonnenaufstand in Poitiers (589)', *MIÖG* 87: 1–38
Scheibelreiter, G. (1983), *Der Bischof in merowingischer Zeit* (Veröffentlichungen der Instituts für Österreichische Geschichtsforschung 27), Vienna
Scheuermann, A. (1957), 'Diözese', in *RAC* III, pp. 1053–62
Schmidinger, H. (1950), 'Die Besetzung des Patriarchatstuhls von Aquileja bis zur Mitte des 13. Jahrhunderts', *MIÖG* 60: 335–54
Schmidt, H. A. P. (1952), 'De lectionibus variantibus in formulis, identicis Sacramentariorum Leoniani, Gelasiani et Gregoriani', *Sacris Erudiri* 4: 103–73
Schneider, D. B. (1985), *Anglo-Saxon Women in the Religious Life: A Study of the Status and Position of Women in Early Medieval Society*, Cambridge
Schubert, H. von (1975), *Geschichte der Kirche im Frühmittelalter*, Tübingen
Schwöbel, H. (1973), *Synode und König im Westgotenreich*, Marburg
Semmler, J. (1982), 'Mission und Pfarrorganisation in den rheinischen, mosel- und maasländischen Bistümern (5.–10. Jahrhundert)', *Settimane* 28: 813–88
Seppelt, F. X. (1954–55), *Geschichte der Päpste von den Anfängen bis zur Mitte des 20. Jahrhunderts*, 2 vols., Munich
Seston, W. (1935), 'Note sur les origines religieuses des paroisses rurales', *RHPhR* 35: 241–54

Stutz, U. (1895), *Geschichte des kirchlichen Benefizialwesens*, 1, Berlin
Thacker, A. (1992), 'Monks, preaching and pastoral care in early Anglo-Saxon England', in Blair and Sharpe (1992), pp. 137–70
Ueding, L. (1935), *Geschichte der Klostergründungen der frühen Merowingerzeit*, Berlin
Ullmann, W. (1981), *Gelasius I. (492–496): Das Papsttum an der Wende der Spätantike zum Mittelalter*, Stuttgart
van de Vyver, A. (1941), 'Les institutions de Cassiodore et sa fondation à Vivarium', *RB* 53: 59–88
Vinayo Gonzalez, A. (1966), *San Fructuoso de Braga*, León
Vogel, C. (1952), *La Discipline pénitentielle en Gaule des origines à la fin du VIIe siècle*, Paris
Vogel, C. (1960), 'Les échanges liturgiques entre Rome et les pays francs jusqu'à l'époque de Charlemagne', *Settimane* 7: 185–295
Vogel, C. (1986), *Medieval Liturgy: An Introduction to the Sources*, Washington, DC
Voigt, K. (1936), *Staat und Kirche von Konstantin dem Großen bis zum Ende der Karolingerzeit*, Stuttgart
Vollrath, H. (1985), *Die Synoden Englands bis 1066* (Konziliengeschichte A), Paderborn
Vos, M. (1974), 'A la recherche de normes pour les textes liturgiques de la messe (Ve–VIIe siècles)', *RHE* 69: 5–37
Wallace-Hadrill, J. M. (1960), 'Rome and the early English church, some questions of transmission', *Settimane* 7: 519–48
Wallace-Hadrill, J. M. (1983), *The Frankish Church*, Oxford
Weißengruber, F. (1964/67), 'Weltliche Bildung der Mönche (5./6. Jahrhundert)', *RHM* 8/9: 13–28; 10: 12–42

26 CHRISTIANISATION AND CHRISTIAN TEACHING

Angenendt, A. (1972), *Monachi Peregrini: Studien zu Pirmin und den monastischen Vorstellungen des frühen Mittelalters*, Munich
Angenendt, A. (1986), 'The conversion of the Anglo-Saxons considered against the background of the early medieval mission', *Settimane* 32: 747–81
Axboe, M. (1995), 'Danish kings and dendrochronology: archaeological insights into the early history of the Danish state', in G. Ausenda (ed.), *After Empire: Towards an Ethnology of Europe's Barbarians*, Woodbridge, pp. 217–51
Boudriot, W. (1928), *Die altgermanische Religion*, Bonn
Brown, P. (1996), *The Rise of Western Christendom*, Oxford
Büttner, H. (1965), 'Mission und Kirchenorganisation des Frankenreiches bis zum Tode Karls des Großen', in H. Beumann (ed.), *Karl der Große*, 1: *Persönlichkeit und Geschichte*, Düsseldorf, pp. 454–87
Campbell J. (1986), 'The first century of Christianity in England', in Campbell, *Essays in Anglo-Saxon History*, London, pp. 49–67
Charles-Edwards, T. M. (1993), 'Palladius, Prosper, and Leo the Great: mission and primatial authority', in Dumville (1993), pp. 1–12
Christie, N. (1995), *The Lombards*, Oxford
Collins, R. (1983), *Early Medieval Spain: Unity in Diversity*, London
Courtois, C. (1955), *Les Vandales et l'Afrique*, Paris
Dumville, D. N. (1993), *Saint Patrick A.D. 493–1993*, Woodbridge

Fletcher, R. (1997), *The Conversion of Europe from Paganism to Christianity 371–1386 AD*, London
Flint, V. (1991), *The Rise of Magic in Early Medieval Europe*, Oxford
Fritze, W. H. (1969), '*Universalis gentium confessio*. Formeln, Träger und Wege universalmissionarischen Denkens im 7. Jahrhundert', *FrSt* 3: 78–130
Goody, J. (1983), *The Development of the Family and Marriage in Europe*, Cambridge
Green, D. (1998a), *Language and History in the Early Germanic World*, Cambridge
Green, D. (1998b), 'The influence of the Christian Franks on the Christian vocabulary of Germany', in I. N. Wood (ed.), *Franks and Alamanni in the Merovingian Period*, Woodbridge, pp. 343–61
Hauck, K. (1957), 'Brakteatenikonologie', in *RAC* III, pp. 361–401
Heather, P. (1986), 'The crossing of the Danube and the Gothic conversion', *GRBS* 27: 289–318
Heather, P. and Matthews, J. (1991), *The Goths in the Fourth Century*, Liverpool
Hen, Y. (1995), *Culture and Religion in Merovingian Gaul, A.D. 481–751*, Leiden
Lebecq, S. (1994), 'Le baptême manqué du roi Radbod', in O. Redon and B. Rosenberger (eds.), *Les Assises du Pouvoir: temps médiévaux, territoires africains*, St-Denis, pp. 141–50
Markus, R. A. (1970), 'Gregory the Great and a papal missionary strategy', *Studies in Church History* 6: 29–38; repr. in Markus, *From Augustine to Gregory the Great* (1983), London
Markus, R. (1997), *Gregory the Great and His World*, Cambridge
Mayr-Harting, H. (1972), *The Coming of Christianity to Anglo-Saxon England*, London
Meens, R. (1994), 'A background to Augustine's mission to Anglo-Saxon England', *ASE* 23: 5–17
Salin, E. (1959), *La Civilisation mérovingienne*, IV, Paris
Shanzer, D. (1998), 'Dating the baptism of Clovis: the bishop of Vienne vs the bishop of Tours', *EME* 7: 28–57
Sims-Williams, P. (1990), *Religion and Literature in Western England, 600–800*, Cambridge
Stancliffe, C. (1979), 'From town to country: the Christianisation of the Touraine 370–600', *Studies in Church History* 16: 43–59
Thompson, E. A. (1982), *Romans and Barbarians: The Decline of the Western Empire*, Madison, WI
Wallace-Hadrill, J. M. (1962), *The Long-Haired Kings*, London
Wallace-Hadrill, J. M. (1983), *The Frankish Church*, Oxford
Wampach, C. (1930), *Geschichte der Grundherrschaft Echternach im Frühmittelalter*, I.2, Luxembourg
Wolfram, H. (1987), *Die Geburt Mitteleuropas*, Vienna
Wood, I. N. (1987), 'Pagans and holy men, 600–800', in P. Ní Chatáin and M. Richter (eds.), *Irland und die Christenheit*, Stuttgart, pp. 347–61
Wood, I. N. (1990), 'Ethnicity and the ethnogenesis of the Burgundians', in H. Wolfram and W. Pohl (eds.), *Typen der Ethnogenese unter besonderer Berücksichtigung der Bayern*, Vienna, pp. 53–69
Wood, I. N. (1991a), 'The Franks and Sutton Hoo', in I. N. Wood and N. Lund (eds.), *People and Places in Northern Europe, 500–1600*, Woodbridge, pp. 1–14

Wood, I. N. (1991b), 'Saint Wandrille and its hagiography', in I. N. Wood and G. A. Loud (eds.), *Church and Chronicle in the Middle Ages*, London, pp. 1–14

Wood, I. N. (1994a), *The Merovingian Kingdoms, 450–751*, London

Wood, I. N. (1994b), 'The mission of Augustine of Canterbury to the English', *Speculum* 69: 1–17

Wood, I. N. (1995), 'Paganism and superstition east of the Rhine from the fifth to the ninth century', in G. Ausenda, (ed.), *After Empire: Towards an Ethnology of Europe's Barbarians*, Woodbridge, pp. 253–79

Wood, I. N. (1998), 'Jonas, the Merovingians, and Pope Honorius: *Diplomata* and the *Vita Columbani*', in A. C. Murray (ed.), *After Rome's Fall*, Toronto, pp. 99–120

Wood, I. N. (1999a), 'The missionary *Life*', in J. Howard-Johnston and P. A. Hayward (eds.), *The Cult of the Saints in Late Antiquity and the Early Middle Ages*, Oxford, pp. 167–83

Wood, I. N. (1999b), 'The use and abuse of Latin hagiography', in E. Chrysos and I. N. Wood (eds.), *East and West: Modes of Communication*, Leiden, pp. 93–109

Wood, I. N. (2000), 'Augustine and Aidan: bureaucrat and charismatic?', in C. de Dreuille (ed.), *L'Église et la mission au VIe siècle*, Paris, pp. 160–74

27 EDUCATION AND LEARNING

Auerbach, E. (1958), *Literatursprache und Publikum in der lateinischen Spätantike*, Berne

Banniard, M. (1980), *Le Haut Moyen Age Occidental*, Paris

Banniard, M. (1989), *Genèse culturelle de l'Europe (Ve–VIIIe siècle)*, Paris and Munich

Banniard, M. (1992a), 'Latin et communication orale en Gaule franque: le témoignage de *Vita Eligii*', in Fontaine and Hillgarth (1992), pp. 58–86 and 259–63

Banniard, M. (1992b), *'Viva voce': communication écrite et communication orale du IVe au IXe siècle en Occident latin*, Paris

Bauer, J. and Felber, A. (1988), *Herz*, in *RAC* XIV, pp. 1093–1131

Berschin, W. (1968), 'Abendland und Byzanz, III Literatur und Sprache . . . Epochen des Griechischen im lateinischen Mittelalter', in *Reallexikon der Byzantinistik*, I, cc. 238–70

Berschin, W. (1980), *Griechisch-lateinisches Mittelalter: Von Hieronymus bis Nikolaus von Kues*, Berne and Munich

Bischoff, B. (1960), 'Die europäische Verbreitung der Werke Isidors von Sevilla', in *Isidoriana*, León, pp. 317–44

Bischoff, B. and Lapidge, M. (eds.) (1995), *Biblical Commentaries from the Canterbury School of Theodore and Hadrian*, Cambridge

Bonner, G. (ed.) (1976), *Famulus Christi: Essays in Commemoration of the Thirteenth Century of the Birth of the Venerable Bede*, London

Brown, P. (1971), *The World of Late Antiquity*, London

Cameron, Av. (1992), 'Byzantium and the past in the seventh century: the search for redefinition', in Fontaine and Hillgarth (1992), pp. 250–76

Cazier, P. (1986), 'Les Sentences d'Isidore de Séville et le IVe Concile de Tolède, réflexions sur les rapports entre l'Eglise et le pouvoir politique en Espagne', in *Los Visigodos: historia y civilización* (Antigüedad y Cristianismo 3), Murcia

Cazier, P. (1994), *Isidore de Séville et la naissance de l'Espagne catholique*, Paris
Clarke, H. B. and Brennan, M. (eds.) (1981), *Columbanus and the Merovingian Monasticism* (BAR International Series 113), Oxford
Courcelle, P. (1948), *Les Lettres grecques en Occident de Macrobe à Cassiodore*, Paris
Courcelle, P. (1967), *La Consolation de Philosophie dans la tradition littéraire*, Paris
Curtius, E. (1938), 'Zur Literarästhetik des Mittelalters', *Zeitschrift für Romanische Philologie* 58
Dagens, C. (1977), *Saint Grégoire le Grand: culture et expérience chrétienne*, Paris
Delage, M.-J. (1971), *Césaire d'Arles: sermons au peuple*, 1 (Sources Chrétiennes 175), Paris
Díaz y Díaz, M. C. (1982), 'Introductión general' in J. Oroz Reta *et al.* (eds.), *Isidoro de Sevilla, Etimologías*, 1, Madrid, pp. 1–257
Díaz y Díaz, M. C. (1992), 'El latín de España en el siglo VII: lengua y escritura según los textos documentales', in Fontaine and Hillgarth (1992), pp. 25–40
Diesner, H. J. (1981), 'Das christliche Bildungsprogramm des Beda Venerabilis (672/73–735)', *Theologische Literaturzeitung* 106, 12:. 865–872
Duane, W. H. and Bright, P. (eds.) (1995), *De doctrina Christiana, A Classic of Western Culture*, Notre-Dame and London
Durliat, J. (1990), *Les finances publiques dans le monde latin, de Dioclétien aux Carolingiens, 284–888* (Beihefte der Francia 21), Sigmaringen.
Fontaine, J. (1962), 'La diffusion de l'oeuvre d'Isidore de Séville dans les scriptoria helvétiques du haut Moyen Age', *Revue suisse d'histoire* 12: 305–327
Fontaine, J. (1972), 'Valeurs antiques et valeurs chrétiennes dans la spiritualité des grands propriétaires terriens à la fin du IVe siècle Occidental', in Fontaine J. and Kannengiesser Ch. (eds.), *Epektasis, Mélanges patristiques offerts au Cardinal Jean Daniélou*, Paris
Fontaine, J. (1982), 'La culture carolingienne dans les abbayes normandes: l'exemple de Saint-Wandrille', in L. Musset (ed.), *Aspects du monachisme en Normandie (Ve–XVIIIe siècles)*, Paris, pp. 38ff
Fontaine, J. (1983a), *Isidore de Séville et la culture classique dans l'Espagne wisigothique*, 3 vols., Paris
Fontaine, J. (1983b), 'L'apport du Christianisme à la prise de conscience de la "patrie gauloise", sous la dynastie théodosienne', in *La Patrie gauloise d'Agrippa au VIe siècle* (Centre d'études romaines et gallo-romaines), Lyons, pp. 183–201
Fontaine, J. (1992a), *De l'éducation antique à l'éducation chrétienne* (Connaissance des Pères de l'Eglise 48), Paris
Fontaine, J. (1992b), 'La figure d'Isidore de Séville à l'époque carolingienne', in J. Fontaine and C. Pellistrandi (eds.), *L'Europe héritière de l'Espagne wisigothique,* Madrid, pp. 195–212
Fontaine, J. (1994), 'Sulpice Sévère témoin de la communication orale en latin à la fin du IVe siècle gallo-romain', in *Transitions latines et émergences langagières en Europe, Ve–Xe siècles* (*Médiévales*, special issue 25)
Fontaine, J. (1996), *Isidor von Sevilla*, in *RAC* XVIII, cols. 1002–27 (Bonn)
Fontaine, J. (1997), *Handbuch der lateinischen Literatur*, VII, pp. 774ff.
Fontaine, J. (2000), *Isidore de Séville: genèse et originalité de la culture hispanique au temps des Wisigoths*, Turnhout

Fontaine, J. (2002), *Isidore de Séville, Traité de la nature* (Bibliothèque de l'Ecole des Hautes Etudes Hispaniques 28), Paris
Fontaine, J. and Hillgarth, J. N. (eds.) (1992), *The Seventh Century: Change and Continuity* (Studies of the Warburg Institute 42), London
Gaudemet, J. and Basdevant, B. (1989), *Les Canons des conciles mérovingiens (VIe–VIIe siècles)*, 2 vols. (Sources Chrétiennes 353–4), Paris
Gibbon, E. (1839), *The History of the Decline and Fall of the Roman Empire*, London
Gibson, M. (ed.) (1981), *Boethius: His Life, Thought and Influence*, Oxford
Hadot, I. (1984), *Arts libéraux et philosophie dans la pensée antique*, Paris
Heinzelmann, M. (1990), 'Studia sanctorum: éducation, milieux d'instruction et valeurs éducatives dans l'hagiographie en Gaule jusqu'à la fin de l'époque mérovingienne', in Sot (1990), pp. 105–38
Heinzelmann, M. (1994), *Gregorius von Tours, 'Zehn Bücher Geschichte': Historiographie und Gesellschaftskonzept im 6. Jahrhundert*, Darmstadt
Herren, M. (1974), *The Hisperica Famina*, I: *The A-Text*, Toronto
Herren, M. (1987), *The Hisperica Famina.* II: *Related Poems*, Toronto
Herren, M. (ed.) (1988), *The Sacred Nectar of the Greeks: The Study of Greek in the West in the Early Middle Ages*, London
Hunter Blair, P. (1970), *The World of Bede*, London
Illmer, D. (1971), *Formen der Erziehung und Wissensvermittlung im frühen Mittelalter: Quellenstudien zur Frage der Kontinuität des abendländischen Erziehungswesens* (Münchener Beiträge zur Mediävistik und Renaissance-Forschung 7), Munich
Kazhdan, A. P. (1983), *La produzione intellettuale a Bisanzio: libri e scrittura in una società colta*, Moscow
Kerlouégan, F. (1993), *Le monde celte et la Bretagne* (Connaissance des Pères de l'Eglise 49), Paris
King, M. H. and Stevens, W. M. (eds.) (1979), *Studies in Medieval Culture in Honour of Ch. W. Jones*, St John's
La cultura in Italia fra tardoantico e alto medioevo (1981), Convegno tenuto a Roma in 1979, Rome
La scuola nell'Occidente latino dell'alto medioevo (1972), *Settimane* 19, 2 vols., Spoleto
Laistner, M. L. W. (1957), *Thought and Letters in Western Europe*, London
Leanza, L. (ed.) (1986), *Flavio Magno Aurelio Cassiodoro*, Catanzaro
Lehmann, P. (1957), 'Panorama der literarischen Kultur des Abendlandes im VII. Jahrhundert', *Settimane* 5: 845–71
Lemerle, P. (1971), *Le Premier Humanisme byzantin: notes et remarques sur enseignement et culture à Byzance des origines au Xe siècle*, Paris
Levison, W. (1946), *England and the Continent in the Eighth Century*, Oxford
Lourdaux, W. and Verheist, D. (1979), *The Bible and Mediaeval Culture*, Louvain
Löwe, H. (1982), *Die Iren und Europa im früheren Mittelalter*, 2 vols., Stuttgart
Marrou, H. I. (1937), *MOYCIKOC ANHP: étude sur les scènes de la vie intellectuelle figurant sur les monuments funéraires romains*, Grenoble
Marrou, H. I. (1950), *Histoire de l'éducation dans l'antiquité*, Paris
Marrou, H. I. (1958), *Saint Augustin et la fin de la culture antique*, Paris
Marrou, H. I. (1977), *Décadence romaine ou antiquité tardive, IIIe–VIe siècles* (Editions du Seuil, coll. Histoire 29), Paris

Martin, R. (1976), 'Qu'est-ce que l'antiquité "tardive"? Réflexions sur un problème de périodisation', *Caesarodunum* 10: 261–304

Maxsein, A. (1954), '*Philosophia cordis* bei Augustinus', in *Augustinus Magister: Congrès International Augustinien, Paris, 21–25 September 1954*, 1, Paris

O'Daly, G. (1991), *The Poetry of Boethius*, London

O'Donnell, J. J. (1979), *Cassiodorus*, Berkeley

Opelt, I. (1974), 'Materialien zur Nachwirkung von Augustinus', Schrift De doctrina Christiana', *Jahrbuch für Antike und Christentum* 17: 64–73

Orlandis, J. and Ramos Lissón, D. (1986), *Historia de los concilios de la España romana y visigoda*, Pamplona

Petrucci, A. (1995), *Writers and Readers in Mediaeval Italy*, ed. and trans. C. M. Radding, New Haven and London

Picard, J.-M. (ed.) (1991), *Ireland and Northern France, 600–850*, Dublin

Polara, G. (1987), *Letteratura latina tardoantica e altomedievale*, Rome

Pontal, O. (1989), *Histoire des conciles mérovingiens*, Paris

Rand, E. K. (1928), *Founders of the Middle Ages*, Cambridge, MA

Riché, P. (1962), *Education et culture dans l'Occident barbare*, Paris; 2nd edn, Paris (1972)

Richter, M. (1994), *The Formation of the Medieval West: Studies in the Oral Culture of the Barbarians*, Dublin

San Benedetto nel suo tempo (1982) (Atti del 70 Congresso internazionale di Studi sull'alto medioevo), 2 vols., Spoleto

Sot, M. (ed.) (1990), *Haut Moyen Age, culture, éducation et société: études offertes à P. Riché*, Paris

Stancliffe, C. (1992), 'The Miracle Stories in seventh-century Irish Saints' Lives', in Fontaine and Hillgarth (1992), pp. 87–115

Teillet, S. (1986), *Des Goths à la nation gothique*, Paris

Van Uytfanghe, M. (1974), 'La Bible et l'instruction des laïcs en Gaule mérovingienne: des témoignages textuels à une approche langagière de la question', *SEJG* 34: 67–123

Velázquez Soriano, 1. (1989), *El latín de las pizarras visigodaas (edición y comentario)*, 2 vols., Madrid; 2nd edn (1991), *Las pizarras visigodas, edición y comentario*, Murcia

Vives, J. (1969), *Inscripciones cristianas de la España romana y visigoda*, 2nd edn, Barcelona

Von der Nahmer, D. (1983), 'Dominici scola servitutis, Über Schultermini in Klosterregeln', *Regula Benedicti Studia* 12: 143–85

Werner, K. F. (1989), *Die Ursprünge Frankreichs bis zum Jahr 1000*, Stuttgart

Werner, K. F. (1992), 'La place du VIIe siècle dans l'évolution politique et institutionnelle de la Gaule franque', in Fontaine and Hillgarth (1992), pp. 173–211

Wilson, N. G. (1983), *Scholars of Byzantium*, London

28A ART AND ARCHITECTURE OF WESTERN EUROPE

Bailey, R. (1991), 'Saint Wilfrid, Ripon and Hexham', in C. Karkov and R. Farrell (eds.), *Studies in Insular Art and Archaeology* (American Medieval Studies 1), pp. 3–25

Bailey, R. (1996), *England's Earliest Sculptors*, Toronto

Beckwith, J. (1979), *Early Christian and Byzantine Art*, 2nd edn, Harmondsworth
Brown, P. (1999), 'Images as a substitute for writing', in E. Chrysos and I. N. Wood (eds.), *East and West: Modes of Communication*, Leiden, pp. 15–34
Bruce-Mitford, R. (1967), *The Art of the Codex Amiatinus* (Jarrow Lecture), Newcastle
Bruce-Mitford, R. (1975–83), *The Sutton Hoo Ship Burial*, 3 vols., London
Cabanot, J. (1993), 'Sarcophages et chapiteaux de marbre en Gaule', *Antiquité Tardive* 1: 111–19
Caillet, J.-P. (1993), *L'Evergétisme monumental chrétien en Italie et à ses marges*, Rome
Chazelle, C. (1990), 'Pictures, books, and the illiterate: Pope Gregory I's letters to Serenus of Marseilles', *Word and Image* 6: 138–53
Chazelle, C. (1995), 'Memory, instruction, worship: "Gregory's" influence on early medieval doctrines of the artistic image', in J. C. Cavadini (ed.), *Gregory the Great, A Symposium*, Notre Dame, pp. 181–215
Christie, N. (1995), *The Lombards*, Oxford
Cramp, R. (1984), *Corpus of Anglo-Saxon Sculpture*, 1, pt 1: *County Durham and Northumberland*, Oxford
Davis-Weyer, C. (1971), *Early Medieval Art 300–1150*, New York
de Hamel, C. (1986), *A History of Illuminated Manuscripts*, Oxford
de Maillé, M. (1971), *Les Cryptes de Jouarre*, Paris
Deichmann, F. W. (1958), *Frühchristliche Bauten und Mosaiken von Ravenna*, Baden-Baden
Deichmann, F. W. (1974), *Ravenna, Hauptstadt des spätantiken Abendlandes*, II, 1, Wiesbaden
Deichmann, F. W. (1976), *Ravenna, Hauptstadt des spätantiken Abendlandes*, II, 2, Wiesbaden
Delbrück, R. (1929), *Die Consulardiptychen und verwandte Denkmäler*, Berlin
Delmaire, R. (1989), *Largesses sacrées et res privata: l'aerarium impérial et son administration du IVe au VIe siècle*, Rome
Duval, N. (ed.) (1996), *Les Premiers Monuments chrétiens de la France*, II, Paris
Duval, N. (ed.) (1998), *Les Premiers Monuments chrétiens de la France*, III, Paris.
Elsner, J. (1995), *Art and the Roman Viewer: The Transformation of Art from the Pagan World to Christianity*, Cambridge
Fontaine, J. (1973), *L'Art préroman hispanique*, La-Pierre-qui-Vire, Yonne
Gaillard, M. (1996), 'Die Frauenklöster in Austrasien', in *Die Franken, Wegbereiter Europas*, 1, Mainz, pp. 452–8
Galey, J. (1980), *Sinai and the Monastery of St Catherine*, London
Harbison, P. (1998), *L'Art médiéval en Irlande*, La-Pierre-qui-Vire, Yonne
Hawkes, J. (1999), 'Anglo-Saxon sculpture: questions of context', in J. Hawkes and S. Mills (eds.), *Northumbria's Golden Age*, Stroud, pp. 204–15
Heather, P. (1996), *The Goths*, Oxford
Henderson, G. (1987), *From Durrow to Kells: The Insular Gospel Books 650–800*, London
Kitzinger, E. (1977), *Byzantine Art in the Making*, London
Kitzinger, E. (1993), 'Interlace and icons: form and function in early Insular art', in R. M. Spearman, and J. Higgitt (eds.), *The Age of Migrating Ideas: Early Medieval Art in Northern Britain and Ireland*, Stroud, pp. 3–15

Knögel-Anrich, E. (1936), *Schriftquellen zur Kunstgeschichte der Merowingerzeit*, Darmstadt
Krautheimer, R. (1942), 'Introduction to an "iconography" of medieval architecture', *Journal of the Warburg and Courtauld Institutes* 5: 1–38
Krautheimer, R. (1980), *Rome: Profile of a City, 312–1308*, Princeton, NJ
MacCormack, S. (1981), *Art and Ceremony in Late Antiquity*, Berkeley, CA
MacMullen, R. (1962), 'The Emperor's largesses', *Latomus* 21: 159–66
Magnus, B. (1997), 'The Firebed of the Serpent: myth and religion in the Migration period mirrored through some golden objects', in L. Webster and M. Brown (eds.), *The Transformation of the Roman World AD 400–900*, London, pp. 194–202
Markus, R. A. (1978), 'The cult of icons in sixth-century Gaul', *Journal of Theological Studies*, n.s. 19: 151–7; repr. in Markus (1983), *From Augustine to Gregory the Great*, London
Markus, R. A. (1979), 'Carthage – Prima Justiniana – Ravenna: an aspect of Justinian's Kirchenpolitik', *Byzantion* 49: 277–306; repr. in Markus (1983), *From Augustine to Gregory the Great*, London
Markus, R. A. (1981), 'Ravenna and Rome, 554–604', *Byzantion* 51: 566–78; repr. in Markus (1983), *From Augustine to Gregory the Great*, London
Mertens, J. (1979), *Le Sous-sol archéologique de la collégiale de Nivelles*, Nivelles
Meyvaert, P. (1996), 'Bede, Cassiodorus and the Codex Amiatinus', *Speculum* 71: 827–83
Mostert, M. (1995), 'Celtic, Anglo-Saxon or Insular? Some considerations on "Irish" manuscript production and their implications for Insular Latin culture, c. AD 500–800', in D. Edel (ed.), *Cultural Identity and Cultural Integration: Ireland and Europe in the Early Middle Ages*, Blackrock, pp. 92–115
Naissance des arts chrétiens (1991), Paris
Nees, L. (1997), 'Introduction', *Speculum* 72: 959–69
Netzer, N. (1994), *Cultural Interplay in the Eighth Century: The Trier Gospels and the Making of a Scriptorium at Echternach*, Cambridge
Nordhagen, P. J. (1990), *Studies in Byzantine and Early Medieval Painting*, London
Oakeshott, W. (1967), *The Mosaics of Rome*, London
Onians, J. (1988), *Bearers of Meaning*, Princeton, NJ
Orton, L. F. (1998), 'Rethinking the Ruthwell monument: fragments and critique; tradition and history; tongues and sockets', *Art History* 21: 65–106
Pizarro, J. M. (1995), *Writing Ravenna: The* Liber Pontificalis *of Andreas Agnellus*, Ann Arbor
Prelog, M. (1994), *The Basilica of Euphrasius in Porec*, Zagreb
Schmauder, M. (1998), 'Imperial representation or barbaric imitation? The imperial brooches (Kaiserfibeln)', in W. Pohl and H. Reimitz (eds.), *Strategies of Distinction: The Construction of Ethnic Communities, 300–800*, Leiden, pp. 281–97
Stevenson, R. B. K. (1993), 'Further thoughts on some well known problems', in R. M. Spearman and J. Higgitt (eds.), *The Age of Migrating Ideas: Early Medieval Art in Northern Britain and Ireland*, Stroud, pp. 16–26
Taylor, H. M. and Taylor, J. (1965), *Anglo-Saxon Architecture*, Cambridge
Van Dam, R. (1985), *Leadership and Community in Late Antique Gaul*, Berkeley, CA

Van Dam, R. (1993), *Saints and Their Miracles in Late Antique Gaul*, Princeton, NJ
von Simson O. (1948), *Sacred Fortress: Byzantine Art and Statecraft in Ravenna*, Chicago
Webster, L. and Backhouse, J. (eds.) (1991), *The Making of England: Anglo-Saxon Art and Culture A.D. 600–900*, London
Weitzmann, K. (1977), *Late Antique and Early Christian Book Illumination*, New York
Wilson, D. (1984), *Anglo-Saxon Art*, London
Wood, I. N. (1986), 'The audience of architecture in post-Roman Gaul', in L. A. S. Butler and R. K. Morris (eds.), *The Anglo-Saxon Church*, London, pp. 74–9
Wood, I. N. (1987), 'Anglo-Saxon Otley: an archiepiscopal estate and its crosses', *Northern History* 23: 20–38
Wood, I. N. (1994), *The Merovingian Kingdoms 450–751*, London
Wood, I. N. (1996), *The Most Holy Abbot Ceolfrid* (Jarrow Lecture), Newcastle
Wood, I. N. (1997), 'The transmission of ideas', in L. Webster and M. Brown (eds.), *The Transformation of the Roman World AD 400–900*, London, pp. 111–27
Wood, I. N. (1999), 'Images as a substitute for writing: a reply', in E. Chrysos and I. N. Wood (eds.), *East and West: Modes of Communication*, Leiden, pp. 35–46

28B ART AND ARCHITECTURE: THE EAST

Auzépy, M.-F. (1987), 'L'iconodoulie: défense de l'image ou de la dévotion à l'images?', in F. Boespflug and N. Lossky (eds.), *Nicée II, 787–1987: douze siècles d'images religieuses*, Paris, pp. 157–65
Auzépy, M.-F. (1995), 'L'évolution de l'attitude face au miracle à Byzance (VIIe–IXe siècle)', in *Miracles, prodiges et merveilles au moyen âge*, Paris, pp. 31–46
Bauer, A. and Strzygowski, J. (1906), *Eine alexandrinische Weltchronik: Text und Miniaturen eines griechischen Papyrus der Sammlung W. Goleniscev* (Denkschriften der kaiserlichen Akademie der Wissenschaften in Wien, phil.-hist. Klasse 51), Vienna
Bell, G. and Mundell Mango, M. (1982), *The Churches and Monasteries of Tur 'Abdin*, London
Boyd, S. A. and Mundell Mango, M. (eds.) (1992), *Ecclesiastical Silver Plate in Sixth-Century Byzantium*, Washington, DC
Brett, G. (1947), *The Great Palace of the Byzantine Emperors: Being a First Report on Excavations Carried Out in Istanbul on Behalf of the Walker Trust (The University of St Andrews) 1935–1938*, Oxford
Brogiolo, M. and Ward-Perkins, B. (eds.) (1999), *The Idea and Ideal of the Town between Late Antiquity and the Early Middle Ages*, London
Brubaker, L. (1998), *Icons before Iconoclasm?*, *Settimane* 45, Spoleto
Brubaker, L. (2002), 'The Vienna Dioskourides and Anicia Juliana', in A. Littlewood, H. Maguire and J. Wolschke-Bulmahn (eds.), *Byzantine Garden Culture*, Washington, DC, pp. 189–214
Buckton, D. (ed.) (1994), *Byzantium: Treasures of Byzantine Art and Culture*, London
Cameron, A. (1979), 'Images of authority: elites and icons in late sixth-century Byzantium', *Past and Present* 84: 3–35

Cameron, A. (1983), 'The history of the image of Edessa: the telling of a story', in C. Mango and O. Pritsak (eds.), *Okeanos: Essays Presented to Ihor Ševčenko on his Sixtieth Birthday by His Colleagues and Students* (Harvard Ukrainian Studies 7), Cambridge, MA, pp. 80–94; repr. in Cameron (1996), XI

Cameron, A. (1996), *Changing Cultures in Early Byzantium*, Aldershot

Cavallo, G., Gribomont, J. and Loerke, W. C. (1987), *Il evangeli di Rossano: le miniature; The Rossano Gospels: the miniatures. Codex purpureus rossanensis: Museo dell'Arcivescovado, Rossano Calabrio: commentarium*, Rome

Cecchelli, C., Furlani G. and Salmi, M. (1959), *The Rabbula Gospels*, Olten and Lausanne

Christie, N. and Loseby, S. (eds.) (1996), *Towns in Transition: Urban Evolution in Late Antiquity and the Early Middle Ages*, Aldershot

Coleman, S. and Elsner, J. (1994), 'The pilgrim's progress: art, architecture and ritual movement at Sinai', *World Archaeology* 26. 1: 73–89

Cormack, R. (1969), 'The mosaic decoration of S. Demetrios, Thessaloniki: a re-examination in the light of the drawings of W. S. George', *Annual of the British School of Archaeology at Athens* 64: 27–52; repr. in Cormack, *The Byzantine Eye: Studies in Art and Patronage*, I, London

Cutler, A. (1985), *The Craft of Ivory: Sources, Techniques, and Uses in the Mediterranean World: A.D. 200–1400*, Washington, DC

Cutler, A. (1994), *The Hand of the Master: Craftsmanship, Ivory, and Society in Byzantium (9th–11th Centuries)*, Princeton, NJ

Dauterman Maguire, E., Maguire H. and Duncan-Flowers, M. (1989), *Art and Holy Powers in the Early Christian House* (Illinois Byzantine Studies 2), Urbana

Delbrück, R. (1978), *Die Consulardiptychen und verwandte Denkmäler*, Berlin

Der Nersessian, S. (1978), *Armenian Art*, London

Dodd, E. C. (1961), *Byzantine Silver Stamps* (Dumbarton Oaks Studies 7), Washington, DC

Dodd, E. C. (1992), 'The location of silver stamping: evidence from newly discovered stamps', in Boyd and Mundell Mango (1992), pp. 217–23

Dunn, A. (1994), 'The transition from *polis* to *kastron* in the Balkans (3rd–8th/9th century): general and regional perspectives', *BMGS* 18: 60–80

Forsyth, G. and Weitzmann, K. (1973), *The Monastery of Saint Catherine at Mount Sinai: The Church and Fortress of Justinian*, Ann Arbor, MI

George, W. S. (1912), *The Church of Saint Eirene at Constantinople*, Oxford

Gerstinger, H. (1931), *Die Wiener Genesis*, Vienna

Grabar, A. (1948), *Les Peintures de l'évangélaire de Sinope*, Paris

Grabar, A. (1958), *Ampoules de Terre-Sainte (Monza-Bobbio)*, Paris

Grierson, P. (1992), 'The role of silver in the early Byzantine economy', in Boyd and Mundell Mango (1992), pp. 137–46

Haldon, J. F. (1997), *Byzantium in the Seventh Century: The Transformation of a Culture*, rev. edn, Cambridge

Harrison, R. M. (1986), *Excavations at Saraçhane in Istanbul*, I, Princeton, NJ

Harrison, R. M. (1989), *A Temple for Byzantium: The Discovery and Excavation of Anicia Juliana's Palace Church in Istanbul*, London

Hendy, M. (1989), 'The administration of mints and treasuries, 4th to 7th centuries, with an appendix on the production of silver plate', in M. Hendy, *The Economy, Fiscal Administration and Coinage of Byzantium*, VI, Northampton

Jobst, W., Erdal, B. and Gurtner, C. (1997), *Istanbul, Bayak Saray Mozayiği; Istanbul, Das grosse byzantinische Palastmosaik; Istanbul the Great Palace Mosaic*, Istanbul

Kent, J. and Painter, K. (1977), *Wealth of the Roman World AD 300–700*, London

Kitzinger, E. (1954), 'The cult of images in the age before Iconoclasm', *DOP* 8: 83–150; repr. in Kitzinger (1976), *The Art of Byzantium and the Medieval West, Selected Studies*, ed. E. Kleinbauer, Bloomington

Krautheimer, R. with Curcic, S. (1986), *Early Christian and Byzantine Architecture*, 4th edn, Harmondsworth

Kurz, O. (1972), 'The date of the Alexandrian World Chronicle', in A. Rosenauer and G. Weber (eds.), *Kunsthistorische Forschungen: Otto Pacht zu seinem 70. Geburtstag*, Salzburg, pp. 17–22

Lavan, L. (2001), *Recent Research in Late-Antique Urbanism* (*JRA* Supplementary Series 42), Portsmouth, RI

Lemerle, P. (1945), *Philippes et la Macédoine orientale*, Paris

Leroy, J. (1964), *Les Manuscrits syriaques à peintures*, Paris.

Liebeschuetz, J. H. W. G. (2000), *The Decline and Fall of the Roman City*, Oxford

Lowden, J. (1992), 'Concerning the Cotton Genesis and other illustrated manuscripts of Genesis', *Gesta* 31.1: 40–53

Maguire, H. (1995), 'Magic and the Christian image', in H. Maguire (ed.), *Byzantine Magic*, Washington, DC, pp. 51–71

Maguire, H. (1996), *The Icons of Their Bodies: Saints and Their Images in Byzantium*, Princeton, NJ

Mainstone, R. (1988), *Hagia Sophia: Architecture, Structure and Liturgy of Justinian's Great Church*, London

Mango, C. (1972a), *The Art of the Byzantine Empire, 312–1453*, Englewood Cliffs, NJ

Mango, C. (1972b), 'The Church of Sts Sergius and Bacchus at Constantinople and the alleged tradition of octagonal palace churches', *Jahrbuch der Österreichischen Byzantinistik* 21: 189–93; repr. in C. Mango (1993), XIII

Mango, C. (1974), *Byzantine Architecture*, New York

Mango, C. (1975), 'The Church of Sts Sergius and Bacchus once again', *BZ* 68: 385–92; repr. in C. Mango (1993), XIV

Mango, C. (1993), *Studies on Constantinople*, Aldershot

Mark, R. and Çakmak, A. (1992), *Hagia Sophia from the Age of Justinian to the Present*, Cambridge

Mundell Mango, M. (1983), 'Where was Beth Zagba?', in C. Mango and O. Pritsak (eds.), *Okeanos: Essays Presented to Ihor Ševčenko on His Sixtieth Birthday by His Colleagues and Students* (Harvard Ukrainian Studies 7), Cambridge, MA, pp. 405–30

Mundell Mango, M. (1986), *Silver from Early Byzantium: The Kaper Koraon and Related Treasures*, Baltimore

Mundell Mango, M. (1992a), 'The monetary value of silver revetments and objects belonging to churches, A.D. 300–700', in Boyd and Mundell Mango (1992), pp. 123–36

Mundell Mango, M. (1992b), 'The purpose and places of Byzantine silver stamping', in Boyd and Mundell Mango (1992), pp. 203–15
Muthesius, A. (1997), *Byzantine Silk Weaving AD 400 to AD 1200*, Vienna
Omont, H. (1909), 'Peintures de l'Ancien Testament dans un manuscrit syriaque du VIIe au VIIIe siècle', *Monuments Piot* 17: 85–98
Ousterhout, R. (ed.) (1990), *The Blessings of Pilgrimage* (Illinois Byzantine Studies 1), Urbana
Pentcheva, B. (2002), 'The supernatural protector of Constantinople: the Virgin and her icons in the tradition of the Avar siege', *BMGS* 26: 2–41
Peschlow, U. (1977), *Die Irenenkirche in Istanbul: Untersuchungen zur Architektur* (Istanbuler Mitteilungen 18), Tübingen
Peschlow, U. (1996), 'Die Baugeschichte der Irenenkirche in Istanbul neu betrachtet', in C. L. Striker (ed.), *Architectural Studies in Memory of Richard Krautheimer*, Mainz, pp. 133–6
Poulter, A. (1995), *Nicopolis ad Istrum: A Roman, Late Roman and Early Byzantine City* (*JRS* Monograph 8), London
Ruggieri, V. (1991), *Byzantine Religious Architecture (582–867): Its History and Structural Elements* (Orientalia Christiana Analecta 237), Rome
Sansterre, J.-M. (1994), 'La parole, le texte et l'image selon les auteurs byzantins des époques iconoclastes et posticonoclaste', *Settimane* 41: 197–240
Ševčenko, N. P. (1991), 'Icons in the Liturgy', *DOP* 45: 45–57
Striker, C. L. and Dogan Kuban, Y. (eds.) (1997), *Kalenderhane in Istanbul: The Buildings, Their History, Architecture, and Decoration*, Mainz
Talbot Rice, D. (ed.) (1958), *The Great Palace of the Byzantine Emperors: Second Report*, Edinburgh
Tate, G. (1992), *Les Campagnes de la Syrie du Nord du IIe au VIIe siècle*, Paris
Tchalenko, G. (1953–58), *Villages antiques de la Syrie du Nord*, 3 vols., Paris
Trilling, J. (1989), 'The soul of empire: style and meaning in the mosaic pavement of the Byzantine Imperial Palace in Constantinople', *DOP* 43: 27–72
Vikan, G. (1982), *Byzantine Pilgrimage Art*, Washington, DC
Vikan, G. (1984), 'Art, medicine, and magic in early Byzantium', *DOP* 38: 65–86
Volbach, W. F. (1976), *Elfenbeinarbeiten der Spätantike und des frühen Mittelalters*, Mainz am Rhein; 3rd edn 1982, Mainz am Rhein
Weitzmann, K. (1976), *The Monastery of Saint Catherine at Mount Sinai, the Icons: From the Sixth to the Tenth Century*, Princeton, NJ
Weitzmann, K. (1977), *Late Antique and Early Christian Book Illumination*, New York
Weitzmann, K. (1978), *The Icon*, New York
Weitzmann, K. (ed.) (1997), *The Age of Spirituality: Late Antique and Early Christian Art, Third to Seventh Century*, New York
Weitzmann, K. and Kessler, H. (1986), *The Cotton Genesis: British Library, Codex Otho* B IV, Princeton, NJ
Wright, D. (1973), 'The date and arrangement of the illustrations in the Rabbula Gospels', *DOP* 27: 197–208

INDEX